THE MODERN ENGLISH
LEGAL SYSTEM

AUSTRALIA AND NEW ZEALAND
The Law Book Company Ltd.
Sydney : Melbourne : Perth

CANADA AND U.S.A.
The Carswell Company Ltd.
Agincourt, Ontario

INDIA
N. M. Tripathi Private Ltd.
Bombay
and
Eastern Law House Private Ltd.
Calcutta and Delhi
M.P.P. House
Bangalore

ISRAEL
Steimatzky's Agency Ltd.
Jerusalem : Tel Aviv : Haifa

MALAYSIA : SINGAPORE : BRUNEI
Malayan Law Journal (Pte.) Ltd.
Singapore and Kuala Lumpur

PAKISTAN
Pakistan Law House
Karachi

THE MODERN ENGLISH

LEGAL SYSTEM

by

P. F. SMITH, LL.B.,

*Senior Lecturer in Law at the
University of Nottingham*

and

S. H. BAILEY, LL.B.,

*Senior Lecturer in Law at the
University of Nottingham*

London
Sweet & Maxwell
1984

Published in 1984 by
Sweet & Maxwell Limited of
11, New Fetter Lane, London
Computerset by Promenade Graphics Limited, Cheltenham
Printed and bound in Great Britain by
Hazell Watson and Viney Limited

Reprinted 1986
Reprinted 1987

British Library Cataloguing in Publication Data
Smith, P.F.
The modern English legal system.
1. Law—England   2. Justice, Administration
of—England
I. Title   II. Bailey, S.H.
344.207   KD660

ISBN 0–421–27180–9
ISBN 0–421–27190–6–Pbk

PREFACE

Courses which bear the title "English Legal System" frequently reflect the particular interests and idiosyncracies of their teachers: the subject is sufficiently wide-ranging to allow the content of any particular course to be individual. Our selection of material in this book is equally individual yet, we hope, sufficiently comprehensive to satisfy the needs of undergraduate students and others who may need to inform themselves about the legal system. One of our especial objectives has been the provision of a substantial number of bibliographical references so that the book may serve to stimulate interest and encourage further reading, as well as providing a source of information and reference.

We are particularly indebted to two colleagues at Nottingham who have each written a chapter to extend the range of the book into areas not always regarded as a natural part of English Legal System studies but which we consider to be of interest and significance in this context. Professor Alan Prichard has contributed the chapter on Remedies, and Diane Birch has contributed the chapter on Sentencing. We are grateful for their collaboration and scholarship.

In the course of producing this book we have received assistance from many people but we wish to record our particular thanks to Rod Edmunds, Nigel Gravells, Michael Gunn, Louisa Hardman, Philippa Hayes, Gavin Love, Alan Prichard, Mark Sterling and Louise Woodhead. They have variously undertaken research, read and commented upon manuscripts, scrutinised proofs and collectively provided correction, support and inspiration. In addition we are grateful to Christine Mason, Jan Goodman and Margaret Marchant for producing typescript from manuscript, often under considerable temporal pressure.

It is customary for authors to acknowledge support and assistance from their publishers. In our case it is no token gesture. All authors need publishers like ours, but not all publishers need authors like us! The patience and forebearance of our publishers has been a vital factor in the appearance of this book.

We have tried to state the law as at May 1, 1984, although there has been some opportunity to incorporate later developments in page proof.

NOTTINGHAM

September 1, 1984.

P. F. SMITH

S. H. BAILEY

v

CONTENTS

ACKNOWLEDGMENTS

The Green Form, Key Card and accompanying notes reproduced in Chapter 9 at pp. 344–347 are included by kind permission of the Law Society.

The County Court forms reproduced in Chapter 11 at pp. 400–401, 403–404, 406–407 and 411 are reproduced by kind permission of the Lord Chancellor's Department.

The High Court forms included in Chapter 11 at pp. 417–420, 422–427 and 436–438 are reproduced by kind permission of the Solicitors' Law Stationery Society plc.

The forms reproduced in Chapter 12 at pp. 450–468 and 471–473 are reproduced by kind permission of Her Majesty's Stationery Office.

TABLE OF CASES

xiii

TABLE OF STATUTES

xxvii

CHAPTER 1

INTRODUCTION

A. THE ENGLISH LEGAL SYSTEM

THE study of the English legal system is a vital part of any law student's course. Not only are the legal institutions and processes integral to every other legal course he will study, they are also the subject of necessary scrutiny for assessing how well the law provides solutions to the problems it is intended to meet.

Law students are not always aware of the social context in which the rules of law they learn about will actually operate. Some of their teachers are more enthusiastic than others about ensuring that their study is not directed solely to the rules of law contained in statutes or gleaned from the decisions of the superior courts. In respect of the institutions, processes and people of the English legal system in particular, some students affect impatience at the study of matters which they think are better left to social scientists. Some even have the misguided belief that the study of the institutions and processes of our law does not carry the intellectual challenge of other legal subjects. Yet a failure to understand the English legal system will make much of what the student learns of those other subjects either incomprehensible or misleading.

For example, those studying the law of negligence need to know the basic elements of the tort and their respective functions. They will discover that until comparatively recently its scope has been confined to cases of physical damage to person or property and that the great majority of cases actually brought arise out of accidents on the road or at work. Liability in tort will be compared with other sources of accident compensation, such as social security, and related to the insurance position. As regards a tort claim, however, the student should not only be aware of the rules which prescribe who has a right to bring a claim for damages, but also of the processes whereby legal rights are actually vindicated, and indeed the enormous practical difficulties that face potential claimants. These processes form an important part of the subject matter of this book.

Almost every aspect of life in the modern state is regulated or affected in some way by law. There are laws which provide for the remedying of defined grievances (*e.g.* by the payment of damages in respect of accidentally inflicted injuries), laws which prohibit anti-social activities and provide for the imposition of penal sanctions for breach (*e.g.* the criminal law of murder or theft), laws which regulate potentially harmful activities by, for example, systems for licensing, registration or inspection, usually in conjunction with the prescription of standards (*e.g.* liquor licensing, the protection of health and safety at work), laws which confer state benefits upon individuals (*e.g.* education, highways, social security, national health service) and laws which facilitate private arrangements (*e.g.* marriages.

1

contracts, wills).[1] In a sense, the whole body of English law could be said to constitute the English legal system. However, we use the term in a narrower sense to cover the distinctive legal institutions and processes that come into operation when for some reason there is doubt or disagreement as to how the law applies in a given situation: there may be recourse to a lawyer or some other agency for legal advice, or, usually as a last resort, involvement in litigation before a court or tribunal.

The label "English legal system" is convenient, but has to be treated with a little care. For one thing, it extends to both England and Wales (Scotland, Northern Ireland, the Isle of Man and the Channel Islands have separate systems). For another, it is not systematically organised as a "system" perhaps should be.

B. SOME BASIC CONCEPTS

There is not room here for an introduction to the theoretical background of the role of law in society.[2] There are, however, certain concepts that will appear at various points in this book and require some explanation here.

1. "Common Law" and "Civil Law"

The "common law" was the term that came to be used for the laws and customs applied by the royal courts which emerged after the Norman Conquest, and which progressively replaced local laws and customs applied in sundry local courts.[3] As the decisions of these courts came to be recorded and published, so the practice developed whereby past decisions would be cited in argument before the courts, and would be regarded as being of persuasive or even binding authority.[4] The point that decisions of the superior courts are a source of law in their own right is a distinctive feature of "common law systems," the term here being used to distinguish such systems from continental, "civil law,"[4a] systems based in origin upon Roman law but now upon a series of codes established in the nineteenth and twentieth centuries. The basic elements of English law have become established in a number of Commonwealth countries (most notably Australia, New Zealand and Canada, excluding Quebec) and the United States (except Louisiana).

2. "Common Law" and Statute

Apart from its use as a convenient label for one kind of legal system, the term "common law" is used, in a narrower sense, for one of a number of

---

[1] These five legal techniques were distinguished by R. Summers, "The Technique Element in Law," 59 Calif. L.R. 733 (1971). See also J. Farrar and A.M. Dugdale, *Introduction to Legal Method* (2nd ed., 1984), Chap. 2, who distinguish two further techniques: the "constitutive" technique whereby the law recognises a group of people as constituting a legal person (*e.g.* a company), and the "fiscal" technique whereby the government raises money by taxation.

[2] See B. Roshier and H. Teff, *Law and Society in England* (1980); P.S. Atiyah, *Law and Modern Society* (1983).

[3] See below, pp. 28–29 on the growth of the royal courts.

[4] See Chap. 7.

[4a] This usage of the term "civil" should be distinguished from its uses "as opposed to (i) ecclesiastical; (ii) criminal; (iii) military": *Osborn's Concise Law Dictionary* (7th ed., 1983).

distinct sources of law that exist within such a system. Laws enacted by the Queen in Parliament ("Acts of Parliament" or "statutes"), or made under delegated powers conferred by statute, have come to be of arguably greater significance than the decisions of the courts.[5] The common law has always been particularly associated with the protection of such matters as personal freedom, rights of property and contract, and individual interests in reputation and bodily security. However, the nineteenth and twentieth centuries have seen a substantial expansion of the accepted role of government to include the pursuit of such collective purposes as the protection of public health and welfare and the direction of the economy. The National Health Service, state education and social security are all examples of services established and regulated by legislation. It has also come to be felt that important changes in areas still dominated by the common law are more legitimately made by statute than by judges, although the vein of judicial creativity is by no means exhausted.[6]

The term "common law" is thus used to denote rules derived from decisions of the superior courts in contrast to those derived from statute. There is, however, one usage that is narrower still. Only some judge-made rules are rules of the common law in this narrower sense—the others are rules of "equity" which are of distinct historical origin.

3. "COMMON LAW" AND "EQUITY"

By the thirteenth century, the Crown had, in effect, delegated its inherent power to dispense justice to the judges of three royal courts: the Exchequer, the Common Bench—or as it came to be known in Tudor times, the Common Pleas—and the King's Bench.[7] At this time, the Common Bench was by far the busiest court as regards civil cases, with jurisdiction over matters between subject and subject such as disputes over rights to land and actions for debt.[8] Proceedings were commenced by the plaintiff's purchase of a writ from the Chancery.[9] The Chancery was originally the royal secretariat, the place where all kinds of royal documents were prepared and authenticated by the Great Seal. Its head was the Chancellor,[10] whose office came to be one of the great offices of state. In medieval times, most Chancellors were bishops and graduates in civil or canon law. Some holders of the office were in effect the King's chief minister.

---

[5] See Chaps. 5 and 6.

[6] See pp. 175–183.

[7] See further below, pp. 28–29 on the development of these courts.

[8] The King's Bench shared with the Common Bench cases of "trespass" (the term then simply meaning "wrong" as in the Lord's Prayer) and heard proceedings to correct errors in the Common Bench and local courts. Its main function was to deal with what are now called criminal cases—pleas of the Crown. By the end of the sixteenth century it had by a series of procedural devices obtained a civil jurisdiction comparable with the Common Pleas.

[9] Proceedings in the King's Bench were commenced by a petition known as a "bill" addressed directly to the court by the plaintiff, a simpler and cheaper procedure.

[10] Where a Chancellor was not appointed, the Great Seal could be entrusted to temporary "Keepers of the Seal." Occasionally, a permanent appointment was made to the office of "Lord Keeper of the Great Seal" where it was wished not to make an appointment to the more dignified office of Lord Chancellor; the powers of the two offices were the same.

The plaintiff was obliged to obtain a writ in a form appropriate to his claim. At first, if there was no precedent the Chancery would be prepared to draft a new one, but by the end of the thirteenth century this could no longer be done. Once the writ was obtained this governed the detailed form the action would take: if the wrong one had been chosen, the plaintiff was required to recommence proceedings.

Among the duties of the Chancellor were those of determining questions relating to Crown property, hearing common law actions concerning his clerks, servants and officials, and entertaining "petitions of right" (*i.e.* claims against the Crown). In addition, the Chancellor came to deal exclusively with petitions addressed to the King or the Council in respect of grievances which for some reason were not redressed or redressible by proceedings in the common law courts. This might be because of corruption or undue influence affecting proceedings (*e.g.* the bribery of jurors), or because in a particular case strict common law requirements for proof appeared to lead to injustice, or because the matter did not fall within the scope of writs recognised by the common law. The Chancellor would give relief in particular cases by an order directed to the parties, his intervention being based on the dictates of their consciences judged in accordance with his own view of what was just. Proceedings before the Chancellor were simpler, and were in other respects advantageous when compared with the procedures of the common law courts. Moreover, the Chancellor developed several remedies which were not available in other courts, most notably specific performance and the injunction—an order requiring the person to whom it is addressed to perform or to refrain from performing a stated act. When performing these judicial functions, the Chancellor came to be regarded as constituting a court: the Court of Chancery.

The standard illustration of how the Chancellor operated was provided by the person who borrowed money, acknowledged the debt by entering into a bond under seal, subsequently paid the debt, but failed to have the bond cancelled. For a common law court, the sealed bond provided incontrovertible proof of the existence of the debt: the court would enforce a second payment if proceedings were instituted by the creditor. However, the Chancellor could restrain such unconscionable action on the part of the creditor by an injunction directed to him, and order that the bond be cancelled.

At first it was not thought that there were separate systems of "law" and "equity." The Chancellor was frequently advised by the common law judges, and there were suggestions that the common law courts could take account of matters of conscience. However, tensions developed. The arguments on each side indeed reflected what is an inevitable dilemma in any system of law, the problem of reconciling the competing demands of justice and certainty. The more general a rule, the less likely it is to do justice in all the particular cases to which it applies; moreover, an attempt to construct in advance the qualifications to the rule necessary to do justice in all cases would lead to a system of rules of enormous complexity, even if all the problems could be foreseen. Hence, the need for some means whereby particular cases could be dealt with justly. Ad hoc decision-making can however be unjust if like cases are treated differently and, in any event, tends to be unpredictable.[11] The Chancellors reacted to criticisms from common lawyers and to the need to introduce regularity into the processing of an increasing caseload by developing principles of "equity" or justice from their ad hoc interventions. At times, however, the tensions also reflected personal difficulties between the Chancellor and common lawyers. In the sixteenth century Cardinal Wolsey caused much discontent among common lawyers by his preference for his own robust "common sense" over legal learning, and in the early seventeenth century a dispute between Lord Chancellor Ellesmere and Sir Edward Coke, the Chief Justice of the King's Bench, was settled by King James I in favour of the former. The Chancellor's power to issue injunctions preventing a litigant from suing at common law or enforcing a judgment obtained at law was confirmed.[12] By the end of the century the common lawyers had given up the struggle. By this time it was also the established practice for lawyers rather than ecclesiastics to be appointed to the office of Lord Chancellor,[13] and, indeed, men trained in English common law and equity rather than civil law.

The principles of equity were progressively refined and developed, most notably during the course of the seventeenth and eighteenth centuries. Of fundamental significance was the development of the concept of the "trust," whereby property could be legally owned by one person, but held by that person for the benefit of another, the latter's rights being recognised and enforced by the Court of Chancery. By the nineteenth century the organisation of the Court of Chancery was totally incapable of dealing with the business, and a series of reforms increased the number of judges sharing the work of the court with the Lord Chancellor. It was also obvious that the presence of two systems with separate courts was highly inconvenient for litigants. Further reforms in the middle of the century made some of the procedural devices of the Court of Chancery (discovery of documents, injunctions) available in the common law courts, allowed those courts to consider equitable defences, and empowered the Chancery to decide questions of common law, receive oral evidence, to determine issues of fact by jury trial and to award damages. One aspect of the general reorganisation of the superior courts by the Supreme Court of Judicature Acts 1873 and 1875[14] was the *procedural* fusion of law and equity. Matters of both law and equity can now be determined in the course of one set of proceedings: if there is any conflict between rules of law and rules of equity, the latter are to prevail.[15] In most instances there are differences between the operation of law and equity rather than conflict. For example, different remedies may be available in respect of what both systems

---

[11] This point was made in the 17th century by John Selden (*Table Talk*, edited by F. Pollock, 1927)—"Equity is a roguish thing, for law we have a measure, knowing what to trust to. Equity is according to the conscience of him that is Chancellor, and as it is larger or narrower so is equity. It is all one as if they should make the standard for the measure we call a foot to be the Chancellor's foot; what an uncertain measure would this be; one Chancellor has a long foot, another a short foot, a third an indifferent foot; it is the same thing in the Chancellor's conscience." These matters are considered further, below, at pp. 11–13.

[12] See J.H. Baker, "The Common Lawyers and the Chancery: 1616" (1969) 4 Ir. Jur. (N.S.) 368.

[13] It became customary for the Chancellor to be ennobled.

[14] See below p. 29.

[15] 1873 Act, s.25(11). See now the Supreme Court Act 1981, s.49.

acknowledge to be a wrong (*e.g.* damages (common law) and an injunction (equity) in respect of a nuisance). Equity may impose additional obligations on a person while recognising his rights at common law (*e.g.* by accepting that a trustee is the legal owner of property while requiring him to hold it for the benefit of another).

4. "LAW" AND "FACT"

(i) *Historical background*

Today, English law is expounded to law students as a system of substantive rules, derived from the common law and statute, which confer rights, impose obligations, create immunities, confer legal powers and so on. This is, however, a comparatively modern way of looking at the law.[16]

The earliest methods of conducting a law suit, adopted by royal courts from the practice of local courts, involved the intervention of the Almighty. The plaintiff was required to state his claim in the appropriate form. The defendant would make a formal denial of the claim. One of them, usually the defendant, would then be required to swear on oath that his cause was just, and the oath would be tested, or put to proof. This might be done by "compurgation," whereby a fixed number of persons (eventually 12) swore oaths in his support; by "battle" where a party or a person swearing an oath in his support could be compelled to prove his veracity by successfully defending himself in a fight, it being presumed that God would aid the righteous, or by "ordeal"—

> "we find that the person who can carry red-hot iron, who can plunge his hand or his arm into boiling water, who will sink when thrown into the water, is deemed to have right on his side."[17]

By the thirteenth century all these methods were regarded with disfavour although compurgation lingered on as the method of proof in actions of debt and detinue (*i.e.* actions to recover money owed or property) for several centuries beyond. In such systems there was comparatively little scope for legal learning outside the forms of writs and the correct formulation of claim and defence.

These modes of proof were replaced in both civil and criminal cases by trial by jury, whereby the sheriff (a local officer appointed by the Crown) was required to bring 12 men before the court to enquire into the disputed matter and state the truth of it. At first the "jurors" might be aware of this themselves or might be informed before they came to court, but it came to be the rule that they should only act upon evidence given in open court, and that their verdict should be unanimous. The development of the jury caused an elaboration of legal technique in disputes as to what was the material question to be put to the jury.

In civil cases, the material question would be an issue of fact, alleged in pleadings on behalf of the plaintiff and denied by the defendant, which would decide the case one way or another. The lawyers appearing on

---

[16] On the historical background see J.H. Baker, *An Introduction to English Legal History* (2nd ed., 1979), Chaps. 4, 5; S.F.C. Milsom, *Historical Foundations of the Common Law* (2nd ed., 1981), Chaps. 2, 3.

[17] Sir William Holdsworth, *A History of English Law* (7th ed., 1956), Vol. 1, p. 310. The person who sunk in water was of course rescued—this was not a medieval "Catch-22" situation.

behalf of each party could debate with the judges in court the appropriate wording of their pleas before they were formally enrolled in the court records. Furthermore, a party was entitled to admit all the facts alleged by his opponent but claim that they did not give rise to a good claim: this process of "demurrer" raised an issue of law for the judges to decide. Again, it was possible for tentative demurrers to be debated in court. These debates provided the opportunity for an increasing level of sophistication in legal argument. The judges were, however, reluctant to commit themselves to formal legal exceptions to general rules. Where possible, parties were encouraged to "plead the general issue," *i.e.* simply to deny all the allegations put forward by the opponent. This form of plea remains the standard form of plea in a criminal trial ("not guilty") but originally it was the norm in civil trials as well. This meant that many matters that today would be reflected in detailed rules of law were left to the jury for it to do justice on the facts of the particular case. The best example was the issue of whether a defendant was liable in trespass if he was not at fault. For a long time it was thought that the absence of any legal rule on the point meant that liability was strict—the better view held today is that the jury was entitled to acquit the defendant if he was not at fault, but that that was never recorded as it was not then a matter for the lawyers. By contrast "special" pleas were only permitted where there was a serious chance that the jury was likely to go wrong if the "general issue" was left to it. Much of the lawyers' debate in court would, in practice, turn on whether a special plea was permitted in the given situation rather than the substantive question of which of the parties in that situation ought to "win."

In the sixteenth century, the judges evinced a much greater willingness to refine and determine questions of law. Pleadings became written rather than oral, and were entered before the appearance in court rather than at it. Informal, tentative discussions of pleas before formal enrolment were replaced by procedures that enabled matters of law to be raised at Westminster after the jury trial.[18] These procedures[19] enabled the lawyers to argue and the judges to determine the legal implications of facts that had already been found: there could be, for example, an objection to the opponent's plea or to the direction on the law given by the judge for the guidance of the jury. The court at Westminster could order that the plaintiff or defendant should succeed notwithstanding the jury verdict against him. A later development was the power to order a new trial.[20] In the same period demurrers became much more common and the judges permitted greater use to be made of the "special verdict" whereby the jury would answer specific questions of fact put to them rather than return a general verdict for one or other of the parties, and the court would enter judgment in the light of these findings. Formal errors could be corrected by a "writ of error."[21]

The development of procedures such as these enabled attention to be

[18] The jury trial would normally be conducted from Westminster see below, p. 29.
[19] The defendant could enter a "motion in arrest of judgment" and the plaintiff a motion *non obstante veredicto*.
[20] This was of wider significance in that the court could quash a verdict that was against the weight of evidence or where there was a misdirection on a point of law.
[21] See below, pp. 30, 700–701.

switched from matters of form to matters of the substance of the law. The distinction between matters for the judge and matters for the jury now corresponded much more closely to the present day distinction between matters of "law" and matters of "fact."

In the nineteenth century the various procedures whereby decisions could be challenged on procedural or substantive legal grounds were replaced by appeals on points of law (and in some circumstances points of fact) to the High Court, the Court of Appeal and the House of Lords,[22] and as the decisions of these courts constitute precedents for the future,[23] it is in the course of such appeals that common law and equity can be developed.

In criminal cases, special pleading was virtually never permitted, and the general plea of "not guilty" has remained the standard form of pleading for the defendant. Questions of law concerning the indictment or the evidence could be raised informally at the trial, an indictment could be removed on a writ of certiorari into the Queen's Bench where the defendant could challenge it for insufficiency in form and the trial judge could adjourn a difficult case for discussion in Serjeants' Inn or the Exchequer Chamber. This last procedure was only regularised in the nineteenth century. In 1908 it was replaced by a proper appeal to a Court of Criminal Appeal.[24] The scope for the systematic development of criminal law has thus, until comparatively recent times, been limited.

(ii) *The distinction today*

A distinction between matters of "law" and matters of "fact" is drawn for a number of different purposes: one of the consequent difficulties is that it is possible for the line between "law" and "fact" to be drawn in slightly different places for each of these purposes. Three areas[25] where the distinction is of importance for the operation of the English legal system are (1) the division of function between judge and jury; (2) the rule that only a decision on a point of law can constitute a precedent that can be cited in future cases; and (3) the question whether a particular point may be raised on an appeal limited to matters of law.

The first of these situations has declined in significance with the dramatic decline over the last hundred years of the use of the jury in civil cases.[26] In all but a tiny proportion of cases the judge determines the facts in issue, states and applies the law and decides what remedy or remedies should be given. The discursive statement of reasons delivered by the judge may well contain a mixture of factual and legal determinations, and will be arranged for convenience of exposition rather than in clearly separated sections. The components of the mixture will normally, however, be appropriately "labelled," and the precedent status and the scope of any further appeal will of course vary according to the true nature of the particular determination. The judge/jury distinction remains of significance in

[22] See below, pp. 30, 80–84.
[23] See Chap. 7.
[24] See further below, p. 79.
[25] There are others, *e.g.* the effect of a misrepresentation in contract, estoppel and judicial review of administrative action under the *ultra vires* doctrine.
[26] See below p. 534.

criminal cases where the mode of trial for the numerically small proportion of contested serious cases is still trial by jury.[27]

Rights of appeal can only be created by statute, and the grounds on which an appeal may be taken are almost invariably expressed in the statute. The commonest pattern is for a person aggrieved by the decision of a court, or, in numerous but certainly not all situations, a public authority, to be given one chance to appeal on a matter of fact but several chances to raise a matter of law.[28] Appeals from tribunals are normally limited to points of law.[29]

Some aspects of the law/fact distinction are fairly clear. An issue is one of fact where its resolution depends on the reliability or credibility of direct evidence such as a witness's testimony.[30] An issue whose resolution depends on probabilities, for example by way of inference from circumstantial evidence, is also one of fact.[31] These issues normally constitute answers to the question "what happened?" By contrast, if there is a dispute as to the existence or exact scope of a rule of the common law or a dispute over the meaning of the words of a statute, it is a dispute concerning a matter of law. This leaves one kind of issue that is difficult to classify: whether facts found fall within a common law rule or statutory description. This kind of question, one of "application,"[32] has been variously characterised as "law," "fact," "mixed law and fact," "fact and degree," "degree" or *sui generis*. As a matter of theory it is difficult to resist the conclusion that this is really a question of law.[33] However, there have been many cases in which it has not been so categorised.

A number of arguments have been advanced to support the classification of a question of application as one of fact.

(1) The matter can as well be determined by a layman as by a trained lawyer.[34]

(2) The words to be applied are "ordinary words of the English language." This argument was used by the House of Lords in *Cozens* v. *Brutus*.[35] Here, the application of "insulting" in section 5 of the Public Order Act 1936, which makes it an offence to use threatening, abusive or insulting words or behaviour where that is conducive to a breach of the peace, was held to be a matter of fact for the magistrates. Lord Reid stressed the undesirability of courts providing definitions of "ordinary" statutory words, whether from dictionaries or otherwise:

---

[27] See below, p. 606. A few factual matters are determined by the judge, *e.g.* those relating to admissibility of evidence (such as whether a confession was voluntary) and those relating to mitigation.

[28] See generally Chap. 19.

[29] See below, p. 740.

[30] These are sometimes termed "primary facts." Such facts may be admitted, or "judicial" notice of them may be taken (*i.e.* the facts are of general knowledge or can easily be ascertained from standard reference works).

[31] These are sometimes termed "secondary facts." An example would be inferring the speed of a vehicle from tyre marks left on the road.

[32] The term used by E. Mureinik, "The Application of Rules: Law or Fact?" (1982) 98 L.Q.R. 587.

[33] *Ibid.*

[34] Denning L.J. in *British Launderers' Association* v. *Borough of Hendon* [1949] 1 K.B. 462.

[35] [1973] A.C. 854.

"we have been warned time and again not to substitute other words for the words of a statute. And there is very good reason for that. Few words have exact synonyms. The overtones are almost always different."[36]

Similarly, it has been held that whether an appropriation is "dishonest" for the purpose of the law of theft is, within certain limits, a question of fact for the jury.[37]

(3) The rule in question sets a standard, such as one of "reasonableness."[38] The best example here is whether a defendant's conduct has been "unreasonable" and accordingly in breach of a duty to take care imposed by the law of negligence. This is clearly regarded as a question of fact.[39]

(4) The question is one of "degree." In *Edwards* v. *Bairstow*[40] the question was whether a particular transaction was an "adventure in the nature of trade." If it was, the profit was subject to tax. Lord Radcliffe stated that this matter was one "in which the facts warrant a determination either way" and "in which it could not be said to be wrong to arrive at a conclusion either way."[41] It was a question of degree and therefore a question of fact.

Running through all these points is the wish to avoid the multiplication of decisions that can be cited as a precedent, and an increase in the number of decisions that can be taken further on appeal.[42]

The view that some questions of application are to be classified as ones of fact is a classic illustration of the competing requirements of principle and pragmatism. On the one hand it is, for example, difficult to see that there is any clear distinction between matters requiring the attention of a "trained lawyer" and those that do not, or between English words that are "ordinary" and those that are not. The "ordinary English word" argument in particular has occasioned much academic criticism.[43] On the other hand it is equally possible to appreciate the dangers of excessive complexity. It would, for example, cause chaos, even in an age of computerised legal data bases, if every decision on whether a defendant had behaved "unreasonably" for the purposes of the law of negligence could potentially be cited as an authority.

Finally, there are two factors which further blur the distinction between law and fact. First, there may sometimes be a tendency for an appellate court, if it is satisfied that the decision on a point is wrong, to classify the point as one of law precisely to enable it to intervene. Secondly, if a

---

[36] *Ibid.* p. 861.

[37] *R.* v. *Feely* [1973] Q.B. 530; *R.* v. *Ghosh* [1982] Q.B. 1053.

[38] This is described by Glanville Williams as raising a question of "evaluative fact": [1976] Crim. L.R. 472.

[39] See *Qualcast (Wolverhampton) Ltd.* v. *Haynes* [1959] A.C. 743, below, p. 280.

[40] [1956] A.C. 14.

[41] *Ibid.* p. 33.

[42] See, *e.g.* the statements in *Qualcast (Wolverhampton) Ltd.* v. *Haynes* below, p. 280, n.11.

[43] See Glanville Williams, *Textbook of Criminal Law* (2nd ed., 1983), pp. 59–67 and [1976] Crim. L.R. 472, 532; J.C. Smith and B. Hogan, *Criminal Law* (5th ed., 1983) pp. 109, 461, 494–496). These authors point out that many apparently ordinary words have been the subject of judicial definition for the guidance of juries.

decision on an undoubted question of fact is unsupported by any evidence, or is a decision which no reasonable person could have reached, it is regarded as erroneous in point of law.[44] This convenient fiction enables an appellate court to retain control over factual determinations that are palpably wrong.

5. "Rules" and "Discretion"

As has already been touched upon, it is inherent in any decision-making process that is required to handle more than a small number of cases (1) that consistency and certainty are likely to be regarded as important objectives (albeit not the only ones) but (2) that their achievement is likely to be at the expense of an individualised consideration of and reaction to the merits of each case. This is as true of the handling of cases by courts and tribunals as it is of programmes established by government for the administration of, for example, state welfare benefits. In each of these situations it can loosely be said that the basic rules are made by Parliament (statute) or under the authority of Parliament (delegated legislation) or by certain senior judges (common law), and then put into effect by others (judges, magistrates, tribunal members, administrators in government offices and so on).[45]

It will be difficult, and usually impossible, for the "rulemaker" to draft a set of rules that covers all the possible cases that may arise and indicate with precision the outcome desired in each of them. The consequence will be that a measure of "discretion" will be conferred on the "implementer": the word "discretion" being used here to mean an ability to choose among alternative courses of action or inaction. The inevitable imprecisions of language will be such that the persons charged with the task of implementation will have to interpret some of the words used and decide whether the words apply to the circumstances before them. Indeed, a measure of flexibility or uncertainty may be created deliberately to enable the rules to be applied to situations not anticipated by the rulemaker. This can be done by the use of words of general rather than particular meaning, or by the incorporation in the rules of a standard such as "reasonable," "fair" or "just." The element of choice that may be present here is limited.[46] The rulemaker may go further and *expressly* confer a discretion upon the implementer. This express discretion may to a greater or lesser extent be hedged around by restrictions or limits set by the rulemaker. It must be emphasised that it is not possible to draw a clear line between rule-based and discretion-based decision-making processes: the implementation of rules tends to involve the exercise of a measure of discretion, and discretions tend to be hedged around by rules. All that can be said is that the element of discretion may be weaker or stronger as the case may be.

These points may be illustrated by some examples, both real and hypothetical. Parliament, at the instigation of the government, has enacted

---

[44] See below, p. 729.

[45] The two groups overlap in the person of a High Court judge who can propound a rule of the common law and apply it in successive breaths.

[46] It is also less usual, although not incorrect, to use the term "discretion" here than in the situations about to be described.

that a person who is injured in an "accident arising out of and in the course of his employment" is entitled to certain welfare benefits.[47] This phrase, which first appeared in the Workmen's Compensation Act 1897, has to be applied by the DHSS officer who decides in the first instance whether a particular claim for benefit is made out. The issue then may be taken on appeal to a Social Security Appeal Tribunal, then to a Social Security Commissioner and then to the courts.[48] The application of the phrase has indeed given rise to a vast number of cases.[49] It would clearly be absurd to expect any person to construct a set of rules which would cover in advance all the possible circumstances that might arise where there could be doubts as to the applicability of the phrase: even assuming a perfect set of rules *could* be constructed, it would be equally absurd to expect any mere mortal to find his way around them, as the rules would be of great complexity. Moreover, an attempt to spell out in detail what would count as an "accident" and the "course of employment" might prevent the extension of the right to benefit to persons injured in novel ways or when employed in novel kinds of employment, where the extension would have been desired by the rulemaker. Accordingly, a certain measure of judgment has to be exercised by those determining the applicability of the statutory phrase, and in the sense that their task is not simple and mechanical they can be said to exercise a discretion.

It would, however, have been possible for an Act of Parliament to have provided that a sum of money should be allocated to a board, and that the board could "pay such sum as it thinks fit to any person who in the opinion of the board has suffered an accident at work." This would have entailed the delegation of a considerably greater measure of discretion than is inherent in the present statutory scheme. Moreover, the wording of the board's powers could have been varied so as to increase or decrease the area of choice open to it. The area of choice could be increased by, for example, deleting the words "at work." Conversely, it could be decreased by, for example, replacing "may" by "shall," by setting a limit to the sum payable in any one case, by deleting the words "in the opinion of the board" or by listing a number of factors that the board would be required to take into account. The wider the area of choice, the better able the board would be to reach the "right" or "most appropriate" decision in each individual case (according to its own concept of "rightness" or "propriety"). On the other hand, its greater freedom of action would enable it more easily to diverge from the rulemaker's conception of justice. Even if the board were comparatively free of fetters imposed by the rulemaker it might still have wished to develop policies for its own guidance to ensure a reasonable measure of flexibility.

A good example of a discretion-based decision making process concerned the "exceptional circumstances additions" and the "exceptional needs payments" which were formerly part of the supplementary benefits scheme. These provided, respectively, for an increase in the weekly payment, or a lump sum, in "exceptional cases" at the discretion of the

---

[47] See Social Security Act 1975, s.50. The range of benefits specially linked to this concept has been reduced by the Social Security and Housing Benefits Act 1982.

[48] See below, pp. 55–58.

[49] See A.I. Ogus and E.M. Barendt, *The Law of Social Security* (2nd ed., 1982), pp. 267–287.

Supplementary Benefits Commission. In practice, the Commission produced detailed codes for the guidance of the local officials who determined the claims on a day-to-day basis, although the codes were not published.[50] These arrangements contrasted with the rule-based system of national insurance including those for industrial injuries. Following what was the classic "rules" v. "discretion" debate, these discretions were replaced by a rule-based structure.[51]

Accordingly, among the advantages[52] of predetermined rules over discretions are that like cases will be treated alike (consistency), that persons will not in effect be punished by rules applied *ex post facto* (predictability), that the rulemaker is more likely than a person exercising a discretion to be accountable to an electorate, that the implementer will have a more limited scope to deviate from the rulemaker's objective by arbitrary decision-making, that such divergent decisions can more easily be challenged, that the rules will normally be open to public criticism and that decision-making processes can more easily be planned and routinised. Conversely, rules can be inflexible, and can "permit unreasoned official behaviour."[53]

The "rules" v. "discretion" issue crops up at a number of points in the English legal system. The original development of equity was a discretionary case-by-case response to the generality or inadequacy of common law rules or procedures.[54] The subsequent development of rules of equity was a response to the arbitrariness of a system which could vary as the length of the Chancellor's foot.[55] The issue also arises in debates as to the extent to which courts and tribunals should be bound by precedent,[56] the comparative merits of different styles of statutory drafting,[56a] whether it is proper for a jury to acquit a defendant who would by a strict application of the rules of criminal law be liable to be convicted, and the extent to which the discretion of a criminal court as to sentence should be limited or "structured" by the provision of guidelines.[57] As the widest discretionary powers are allocated to administrative bodies such as ministers, officials and local authorities, the extent to which the courts should control or review exercises or non-exercises of power is an important feature of administrative law[58]; however, analogous principles apply to the control by appellate courts of exercises of discretion by judges.[59] The "rules" v. "discretion" issue does not admit of easy or general solutions: the appropriate balance has to be sought depending upon the precise context in which the issue arises.

[50] See generally, J.A. Farmer, *Tribunals and Government* (1974), pp. 89–99; M. Adler and A. Bradley, *Justice, Discretion and Poverty* (1975).

[51] See Ogus and Barendt (1982), pp. 453–455. For a spirited defence of discretion see R. Titmuss, "Welfare 'Rights,' Law and Discretion" (1971) 42 *The Political Quarterly*, p. 113; answered by R. White in P. Morris *et al*, *Social Needs and Legal Action* (1973), pp. 23–32; *cf.* M. Adler and S. Asquith (eds.), *Discretion and Welfare* (1981) especially Chaps. 1, 7, 11.

[52] See generally J. Jowell, "The Legal Control of Administrative Discretion" [1973] P.L. 178, 184–194; the pioneering work in the field is K.C. Davis, *Discretionary Justice, A Preliminary Inquiry* (1969) (see P.P. Craig, *Administrative Law* (1983) pp. 380–383).

[53] [1973] P.L. 178 at p. 193.

[54] See above pp. 3–4.

[55] See above pp. 4–5.

[56] See below, pp. 175–183.

[56a] See below, pp. 194–195.

[57] See below, p. 664.

[58] See below, p. 738.

[59] See below, p. 731.

C. THE BASIC INSTITUTIONS OF THE ENGLISH LEGAL SYSTEM

A number of institutions are of central importance to the creation of law. Statute law is enacted by Parliament; a vast quantity of delegated legislation is made under powers conferred by Act of Parliament.[60] Both processes are heavily dominated by the government of the day; indeed, most of the delegated powers are exerciseable by government departments.[61] Legislative authority has also been accorded to the institutions of the European Communities: the Council of Ministers and the Commission.[62] Decisions of the superior courts may also constitute sources of law.[63]

The administration of the legal system, in the sense of the mechanisms for the provision of legal services, the courts and tribunals established for the resolution of legal disputes and the processes for effecting law reform, is almost entirely a matter for central government. In many countries, responsibility for legal affairs is exercised by a "Minister of Justice." However, in the United Kingdom, responsibility for different aspects of the legal system is divided among separate ministries or departments of state, the main ones being the Lord Chancellor's Department, the Home Office, the Law Officers' Department, the office of the Director of Public Prosecutions and the Treasury.

1. THE LORD CHANCELLOR'S DEPARTMENT

As is mentioned elsewhere,[64] the Lord Chancellor exercises a wide range of disparate functions, including those of judge, Speaker of the House of Lords, cabinet minister and government legal adviser. He also has extensive responsibilities concerning the administration of justice, including making or advising on judicial appointments,[65] arranging business in the House of Lords and Privy Council and acting as chairman of the committees that make procedural rules for the Supreme Court and Crown Court.[66] He controls the unified court service, which provides administrative support for the Court of Appeal, High Court, Crown Court and county courts,[67] and supervises the legal aid and advice schemes.[68] He is also

---

[60] See Chaps. 5 and 6.

[61] A detailed consideration of Parliament and government may be found in such works as S.A. de Smith, *Constitutional and Administrative Law* (4th ed., 1981).

[62] See generally T.C. Hartley, *Foundations of the Law of the European Communities* (1981). The Council comprises one minister from each Member State; the appropriate ministers attend according to the nature of the business (*e.g.* agriculture ministers for questions of agricultural policy). The Commission comprises 14 persons appointed by governments of the Member States, in practice two each from W. Germany, France, Italy and the U.K. and one each from the rest. The Commission is designed to represent the Community interest and is designed to counteract the Council, which tends to reflect national interests.

[63] See Chaps. 2, 7.

[64] See below, pp. 155–156.

[65] See below, pp. 159–165.

[66] See below, pp. 75–76.

[67] See below, p. 68.

[68] See below pp. 339–351, 387–397. The Lord Chancellor has been responsible for civil legal aid since its introduction and responsibility for criminal legal aid was transferred from the Home Secretary in July 1980.

generally responsible for law reform in civil matters, although other government departments have their own specialised areas of concern. For example, company law is within the province of the Department of Trade and Industry and employment law within that of the Department of Employment.

Since the Second World War the Lord Chancellor's Department has grown from a small office of personal assistants and advisers to the Lord Chancellor into a medium-sized government department employing a staff of about 10,000. It has its headquarters in the House of Lords and at Neville House, Page Street, London. The most senior official holds the offices of Permanent Secretary to the Lord Chancellor and Clerk of the Crown in Chancery. There are several Divisions dealing, respectively, with Legal Administration, Appointments (including the Commissions Branch which deals with magistrates), Legislation, and Establishment and Finance. For the purposes of courts administration the country is divided into six areas or "Circuits," each controlled by a Circuit Administrator.[69]

There is no departmental minister in the House of Commons[70]: instead, the Attorney-General acts as spokesman for the Lord Chancellor. This seems unsatisfactory, given the many other calls on the Attorney-General's time and the fact that he is not actually responsible for any aspect of the work of the Lord Chancellor's Department.

2. THE HOME OFFICE

The Home Secretary is responsible for the maintenance of law and order, and as a result performs various functions that might be regarded as those of a Minister of Justice. These include overall responsibility for prisons and other aspects of the penal system, the working of magistrates' courts[71] and the reform of the criminal law, on which he is advised by the Criminal Law Revision Committee. The Home Secretary advises the Queen on the exercise of the royal prerogative of mercy to grant a free pardon in respect of a conviction or to remit all or part of a penalty.

3. THE LAW OFFICERS[72]

The Attorney-General and the Solicitor-General are the Law Officers of the Crown for England and Wales.[73] They are members of and the chief legal advisers to the government, and are normally members of the House

---

[69] See below, p. 68.

[70] The nearest has been Sir Eric Fletcher, a solicitor, who was Minister without Portfolio between 1964 and 1966. His main responsibility was the passage of the Law Commission Bill through the Commons, and he otherwise assisted the law officers and government departments: see J.H. Farrar, *Law Reform and the Law Commission* (1974), pp. 23–24.

[71] The Lord Chancellor appoints magistrates and makes procedural rules for magistrates' courts; certain administrative functions are performed by magistrates' courts committees: see below p. 51. The division of responsibility between Lord Chancellor and Home Secretary can cause problems: see Sir Thomas Skyrme, *The Changing Image of the Magistracy* (2nd ed., 1983) pp. 32–35.

[72] See J.Ll. J. Edwards, *The Law Officers of the Crown* (1964) and *The Attorney-General, Politics and the Public Interest* (1984); Sir Elwyn Jones, [1969] C.L.J. 43; S.C. Silkin, (1980) 4 Trent L.J. 21.

[73] There are separate Law Officers for Scotland: the Lord Advocate and the Solicitor-General for Scotland.

of Commons. Occasionally the Attorney-General has been appointed to the cabinet. The Law Officers may appear on behalf of the Crown at the International Court in the Hague and the European Court of Human Rights in Strasbourg. In this country they may appear in civil litigation or conduct prosecutions. They may not, however, undertake private work.

In civil matters the Attorney may institute proceedings in the High Court for the enforcement of public rights[74] or on behalf of the interests of charity. His consent is required for the institution of criminal proceedings for a large number of criminal offences,[75] and he may stop trials or indictments by entering a *nolle prosequi*.[76] He superintends the work of the Queen's Proctor, who has certain duties in matrimonial cases, and the Director of Public Prosecutions.[77] The law officers are assisted by a small staff of civil servants, based in the Attorney-General's chambers in the Royal Courts of Justice, and generally divide the duties between them according to their own preferences.[78] The Attorney is also the head of the Bar.

4. THE DIRECTOR OF PUBLIC PROSECUTIONS

In 1879 pressure for the introduction of a system of public prosecution led to the establishment of the office of Director of Public Prosecutions.[79] It was originally contemplated that he would be provided with a number of locally-based assistants, but this development never took place. The Director and his staff have thus always been based in London. The first Director took a narrow view of the scope of his functions, and between 1884 and 1908 the office was combined with that of Treasury Solicitor.

The Director's responsibilities are now set out in the Prosecution of Offences Act 1979 (a consolidation measure), and the Prosecution of Offences Regulations 1978.[80] He is appointed by the Home Secretary and must be a barrister or solicitor of not less than 10 years' standing. Assistant Directors may also be appointed from barristers or solicitors of not less than seven years standing.[81] It is the duty of the Director, under the superintendence of the Attorney-General:

"(a) to institute, undertake or carry on such criminal proceedings . . . ; and
(b) to give such advice and assistance to chief officers of police, justices' clerks and other persons (whether officers or not) concerned in any

---

[74] *e.g.* to seek an injunction to restrain a public nuisance or to restrain repeated or threatened breaches of the criminal law.

[75] See below, p. 481.

[76] See below, p. 481.

[77] See below.

[78] Technically, the Solicitor-General is the Attorney-General's deputy. He may act in the Attorney's place if that office is vacant, if the Attorney is away ill, or if the Attorney authorises him to act: Law Officers Act 1944.

[79] Prosecution of Offences Act 1879, J.Ll.J. Edwards, *The Law Officers of the Crown* (1964), Chaps. 16, 17.

[80] S.I. 1978 No. 1357, as amended by S.I. 1978 No. 1846.

[81] 1979 Act, s.1. There are currently one Deputy Director, two principal Assistant Directors and nine Assistant Directors. There are 56 other legally qualified members of the staff: *Bar List* (1983), pp. 63–64.

criminal proceedings respecting the conduct of those proceedings, as may be prescribed [in regulations] or as may be directed, in a special case, by the Attorney-General."[82]

The Regulations require the Director to act "in any case which appears to him to be of importance or difficulty or which for any other reason requires his intervention."[83] Chief officers of police must report to the Director whenever there is a prima facie case for instituting a prosecution in respect of one of a list of serious offences specified either by the regulations[84] or by the Director.[85] The Director may be directed by the Divisional Court to appear for the prosecution on any criminal appeal to the House of Lords, and by the Court of Appeal (Criminal Division) to appear in appeals to that court from the Crown Court or from it to the House of Lords.[86] He also has the power to intervene in prosecutions. The 1979 Act[87] provides that:

"Nothing in this Act shall preclude any person from instituting or carrying on any criminal proceedings; but the Director may undertake, at any stage, the conduct of those proceedings, if he thinks fit."

This power is used rarely, for example where private prosecutions are instituted maliciously. It includes the right to discontinue proceedings.[88] Finally, the Director's consent to prosecution is required by statute in certain classes of case.[89]

The Director will be the head of the proposed national prosecution service.[90]

5. THE TREASURY AND OTHER GOVERNMENT DEPARTMENTS

The Treasury is involved in the administration of justice at a number of points. It has overall responsibilities for government expenditure and the organisation of the civil service. The Parliamentary draftsmen are technically Parliamentary Counsel to the Treasury. The Treasury Solicitor heads a large legal department which does legal work for the treasury and for other government departments which do not have their own legal sections. He also presides over inter-departmental management machinery for civil service lawyers and for most purposes is the *de facto* head of the civil service Civil Legal Group in England and Wales.[91]

---

[82] 1979 Act, s.2.

[83] S.I. 1978 No. 1357, reg. 3.

[84] *Ibid.* reg. 6(1). Examples include homicide (except causing death by reckless driving), treason, sedition and abortion.

[85] Reg. 6(2). The present list was published in March 1979 (see Archbold, *Criminal Pleading Evidence and Practice* (41st ed., 1982), para. 1–124), and includes perjury, large scale drugs conspiracies, kidnapping, large scale robbery and arson involving grave damage to public property.

[86] Prosecution of Offences Act 1979, s.3.

[87] s.4.

[88] *Raymond* v. *Att.-Gen.* [1982] Q.B. 839.

[89] See below, p. 480.

[90] See below, p. 522.

[91] See G. Drewry, "The Office of Treasury Solicitor" (1980) 130 N.L.J. 753 and "Lawyers in the U.K. Civil Service" (1981) 59 *Public Administration* 15.

D. LAW REFORM

It is inevitable that any legal system cannot be static: there will always be aspects both of the substantive law and the institutional and procedural features of the system that require change. Many aspects of the common law are developed by the decisions of the superior courts. However, the judges seem generally to hold the view that this power should be exercised with caution, although this caution is from time to time thrown to the winds.[92] Commonly, a distinction is drawn between the application of an existing principle to new circumstances, which is regarded as a legitimate exercise for the judges, and the creation of a new principle, which is regarded as a matter for government and Parliament.[93]

Reform by the judges is further handicapped by the fact that the accidents of litigation may not throw up the right cases, that the precise issues in dispute are formulated by the parties (the opinions of the judges on other matters amounting to *obiter dicta* which are not binding in future cases),[94] and that the judges must normally confine themselves to the arguments and information presented by the parties. The judges cannot in any event commission empirical research and even the information derived from existing research is not admissible in evidence. Judicial reforms tend also to be retrospective in nature and hence potentially unfair.[95] Accordingly, most significant law reforms must be achieved by statute.

There are several mechanisms which exist to further the cause of law reform by statute, including one permanent body, the Law Commission, several part-time bodies such as the Law Reform Committee and the Criminal Law Revision Committee, and any number of ad hoc Royal Commissions and departmental committees.

1. THE LAW COMMISSION[96]

Calls for a permanent law reform institution were answered in 1965 by the establishment of two Law Commissions, one for England and Wales and one for Scotland.[97] This move was associated particularly with Lord Gardiner L.C.[98] The Law Commission for England and Wales comprises five "persons appearing . . . to be suitably qualified by the holding of judicial office or by experience as a barrister or solicitor or as a teacher of law in a university."[99] In practice, the chairman has been a High Court judge, who works full-time for the Commission and normally receives promotion to the Court of Appeal. The pattern for the other appointments

---

[92] See below, pp. 175–183.

[93] See, *e.g.* Lord Pearson and Lord Salmon in *Launchbury* v. *Morgans* [1973] A.C. 127, 142, 151.

[94] See below, pp. 280–284.

[95] *Cf.* below, pp. 299–300.

[96] See generally on the work of the Law Commission, J.H. Farrar, *Law Reform and the Law Commission* (1974); N. Marsh, (1971) 13 William and Mary L.R. 263; L.C.B. Gower, (1973) 23 Univ. of Toronto L.J. 257; A.L. Diamond, (1976) 10 The Law Teacher 11, and (1977) 51 A.L.J. 396; Kerr J., (1980) 96 L.Q.R. 515.

[97] Law Commissions Act 1965; Lord Chorley and G. Dworkin, (1965) 28 M.L.R. 675.

[98] He had argued the case for such a body in Chap. 1 of G. Gardiner and A. Martin (eds.) *Law Reform NOW* (1963) and *cf.* (1953) 69 L.Q.R. 46.

[99] 1965 Act, s.1(2).

has become settled with one common law Q.C. experienced in criminal law, a solicitor with experience of land law and equity and two academics. There is a legal secretary of under-secretary rank, a staff of barristers and solicitors from the legal Civil Service and several parliamentary draftsmen.[1]

The Commission's task is:

> "to take and keep under review all the law with which [it is] concerned with a view to its systematic development and reform, including in particular the codification of such law, the elimination of anomalies, the repeal of obsolete and unnecessary enactments, the reduction of the number of separate enactments and generally the simplification and modernisation of the law."[2]

The topics investigated are either referred to it by the Lord Chancellor or are aspects of one of the programmes for examination of different branches of the law with a view to reform that have been approved by the Lord Chancellor and laid before Parliament.[3] The Commission is also required to provide advice and information to government and other bodies concerned with law reform.

In the course of its existence the Law Commission has dealt with a large number of substantive legal topics and projects for the consolidation of statutes and the repeal of obsolete provisions ("Statute Law Reform").[4] It has also worked on the codification of the law of contract and of the law of landlord and tenant, although these tasks have proved too onerous and the work has been suspended indefinitely.[5] The prospects for codification of the criminal law are brighter.[5a]

A notable feature of the Law Commission's working methods in connection with the reform of a substantive legal topic is the circulation of a "working paper." This consists of a detailed statement of the present law on the topic, an account of the criticisms and supposed defects of the law and a statement of the options for change. The Commission normally states a provisional view as to the option that should be preferred. The paper, in both full and summarised forms, is circulated widely and the views of interested parties sought.[6] Following consultation a final report is produced, which includes a draft bill prepared by the parliamentary draftsmen seconded to the Commission. The chances of implementation are reasonably high, although they are less where the matter falls within the purview of a government department other than the Lord Chancellor's

---

[1] Kerr J., "Law Reform in Changing Times" (1980) 96 L.Q.R. 515, 523. Four of the five senior Civil Service legal posts are, however, to be abolished: (1984) 134 N.L.J. 467.

[2] 1965 Act s.3(1).

[3] Ibid. ss.3(1)(a)(b), (2). There are general programmes covering Family Law and Criminal Law. The Commission may also consider reform proposals from any other quarter.

[4] See below, pp. 189–190.

[5] See A.L. Diamond, (1968) 31 M.L.R. 361; Kerr J., (1980) 96 L.Q.R. 515, 527–530.

[5a] See J.C. Smith (1984) Stat.L.R. 17.

[6] See P.M. North, "Law Reform: the Consultation Process" (1982) 6 Trent L.J. 19. The Commission has not followed the example of the Australian Law Reform Commission and organised public meetings or hearings: see the paper by the A.L.R.C. Chairman, Mr. Justice M.D. Kirby, "Reforming Law Reform: New Methods of Law Reform in Australia," to the 1979 Colloquium of the U.K. National Committee on Comparative Law, summarised in M. Zander, *The Law-Making Process* (1980), pp. 301–304.

Department, and have generally become lower with the passage of time. The main problems concern the pressures on Parliamentary time.[7]

2. The Law Reform Committee[8]

A part-time Law Revision Committee was appointed by Lord Sankey in 1934 and produced eight reports between then and 1939, most of which were implemented. It was reconstituted by Lord Simonds in 1952 under the present title of Law Reform Committee, and comprises judges, practising lawyers and academics. Its permanent secretariat is provided by the Lord Chancellor's Department, but it lacks research facilities and suffers from the inevitable problems of any part-time body. By 1982 it had produced 23 reports.

3. The Criminal Law Revision Committee

This committee, the counterpart to the Law Reform Committee, but responsible to the Home Secretary rather than the Lord Chancellor, was established in 1959, and includes judges, academics and the D.P.P.[9] Its reports have led to important reforming legislation, most notably the Theft Acts 1968 and 1978. Perhaps the best known report was its 11th Report on Evidence, which aroused a storm of opposition, in part at least, according to its defenders, based on the misrepresentation of some of its recommendations.[10] For the purposes of its review of sexual offences, the Committee was advised by a Policy Advisory Committee comprising 5 members of the C.L.R.C. and 10 members from other disciplines, including probation officers, a consultant psychiatrist, a social worker and a sociologist. There was here a greater potentional for fundamental disagreement about what it is that the law should be attempting to achieve than there had been on earlier references to the C.L.R.C.[10a]

4. Other Bodies

Other bodies which require mention include the rule committees which make procedural rules for the courts[11] and the newly established committee to consider reforms in the Supreme Court.[12]

---

[7] See Lord Hailsham, "Obstacles to Law Reform" (1981) 34 C.L.P. 279; P.M. North, "The Law Commission: Methods and Stresses" (1981) III (I) *Liverpool Law Review* 5; Lord Hooson Q.C., "Reform of the Legislative Process in the Light of the Law Commission's Work" (1983) 17 *The Law Teacher* 67.

[8] See E.C.S. Wade, (1961) 24 M.L.R. 3; J.H. Farrar, *Law Reform and the Law Commission* (1974), pp. 9–14, 133–137; M.C. Blair, (1982) 1 C.J.Q. 64.

[9] See generally, Glanville Williams, "The Work of Criminal Law Reform" (1975) 13 J.S.P.T.L. 183; J.C. Smith, "An academic lawyer and law reform" (1981) 1 L.S. 119.

[10] See the articles cited in the previous footnote and M. Zander in P. Glazebrook (ed.), *Reshaping the Criminal Law* (1978).

[10a] Criminal Law Revision Committee, 15th Report on Sexual Offences (Cmnd. 9213, 1984) pp. 1, 100.

[11] See below, pp. 64, 75–76.

[12] See below, p. 76.

5. Ad Hoc Committees

Investigations by Royal Commissions and departmental committees have long been a familiar feature of the law reform scene. They have the advantage over part-time advisory committees of a much greater commitment of resources, both of the time of their members and in money for research. They have the disadvantage when compared with permanent bodies that, having accumulated a large amount of information and expertise, their members disperse once the body has done its work. Other points of contrast with the law reform bodies discussed above are that ad hoc committees usually have a majority, or at least a large contingent of non-lawyers, and are more likely than those others to be employed in connection with institutional reforms. In recent times there have been four Royal Commissions of particular importance for the English legal system. The Royal Commission on Assizes and Quarter Sessions,[13] chaired by Lord Beeching, made proposals for the reorganisation of the criminal courts (other than magistrates courts) which were speedily implemented.[14] The Royal Commission on Civil Liability and Compensation for Personal Injury reported in 1978.[15] It found the private law system for claiming damages in tort to be too dependent on chance, unduly slow and expensive to operate, but felt unable because of its terms of reference to recommend a comprehensive state scheme for the compensation of all accident victims. Such a scheme would have had serious implications for the large number of lawyers, particularly barristers, who specialise in tort work. In the event, the Commission made a large number of piecemeal proposals for reform, only some of which have been implemented.

The Royal Commission on Legal Services, chaired by an accountant, Sir Henry Benson, reported in 1979.[16] Its terms of reference were:

> "to inquire into the law and practice relating to the provision of legal services in England, Wales and Northern Ireland, and to consider whether any, and if so what, changes are desirable in the public interest in the structure, organisation, training, regulation of and entry to the legal profession, including the arrangements for determining its remuneration, whether from private sources or public funds, and in the rules which prevent persons who are neither barristers nor solicitors from undertaking coveyancing and other legal business on behalf of other persons."

The report was widely regarded as a disappointment.[17] It was criticised for its pedestrian style, its paucity of reasoning, the fact that only a limited amount of research[18] was commissioned and its apparent over-dependence on the information and arguments presented by the legal profession. The *Legal Action Group Bulletin* was tempted to ignore the report: it would

---

[13] Cmnd. 4153, 1969.

[14] See below, pp. 64–66, 68.

[15] Cmnd. 7054, Chairman: Lord Pearson.   [16] Cmnd. 7648.

[17] See C. Glasser, *L.A.G. Bull*, September 1979, p. 201; (1979) 129 N.L.J. 1116–1122, 1131–1135, 1140–1146, 1223–1224; M. Elliott, (1980) J.S.W.L.1; O. Hanson and J. Levin (1979) *Yearbook of Social Policy*, Chap. 12; (1980) 43 M.L.R. 543–566; (1981) *Windsor Yearbook of Access to Justice* 121 (T.A. Downes, P.R. Hopkins and W.M. Rees) and 179 (P.A. Thomas); P.A. Thomas (ed.) *Law in the Balance* (1982).

[18] See C. Glasser, *op. cit.*

certainly be kinder so shaky were its foundations.[19] Professor Zander, who had played a significant role in securing the establishment of the Commission and who had submitted a considerable body of evidence, was more welcoming: he counted well over a hundred recommendations that he thought would amount to valuable changes.[20] The only real enthusiasts were the two branches of the legal profession, which is unsurprising given that on many issues their position was endorsed by the Commission. Aspects of the report will be considered at various points in the book. Many of the recommendations directed at the profession have been the subject of action; those directed at the government have had little impact, except that responsibility for criminal legal aid has been transferred from Home Secretary to Lord Chancellor.[20a] Indeed, the government has decided, contrary to the recommendation of a majority of members of the Royal Commission, to end the solicitors' conveyancing "monopoly."

The Royal Commission on Criminal Procedure[21] provides an interesting contrast. It was established in 1978 to consider the powers and duties of the police in respect of the investigation of criminal offences and the rights and duties of suspects and accused persons, the process of and responsibility for the prosecution of criminal offences and related matters. Three features of the report are especially noteworthy. First, the Commission was much more active than the Royal Commission on Legal Services in sponsoring research. Second, there was a clear intention to identify basic points of principle to which the specific recommendations were to be related.[22] Third, the report indicated the lines that reform should take leaving the details to be worked out. In consequence, the Police and Criminal Evidence Bill was presented to Parliament in 1983, together with proposals for the establishment of a national prosecution service.

E. POSSIBLE INSTITUTIONAL REFORMS

Proposals have regularly been made for the establishment of a Ministry of Justice, performing all the functions concerning justice at present divided among separate ministries.[23] The calls have commonly been associated with demands for a more systematic approach to law reform,[24] and have equally commonly been resisted on the highly dubious ground that the establishment of such a ministry might pose a threat to the administration of justice. In 1918, the Machinery of Government Committee chaired by

[19] November 1979, p. 246.

[20] (1980) 33 C.L.P. 33, 50.

[20a] See *The Government Response to the Report of the Royal Commission on Legal Services* (Cmnd. 9077, 1983). The Law Society and the Bar have also published their responses: see *L.A.G. Bulletin*, December 1983, pp. 3, 6.

[21] Cmnd. 8092, 1981.

[22] The Commission applied three standards for judging both the existing system and its own recommendations: are the arrangements, actual or proposed, fair and clear?; are they open, that is, not secret, and is there accountability?; are they workable and efficient?

[23] See JUSTICE Conference, *Do we Need a Ministry of Justice?* (1970); G. Drewry, "Ministry of Justice—a Matter of Meaning" (1982) 132 N.L.J. 602–603; G. Drewry, "Lord Haldane's Ministry of Justice—Stillborn or Strangled at Birth?" (1983) 61 *Public Administration*, 396.

[24] See, *e.g.* Glanville Williams (ed.) *The Reform of the Law* (1951); *cf.* G. Gardiner and A. Martin (eds.) *Law Reform NOW* (1963); P. Archer and A. Martin (eds.) *More Law Reform NOW* (1983) pp. 15–20.

Lord Haldane[25] proposed a redistribution of functions between Lord Chancellor and Home Secretary. The former would cease to be Speaker of the House of Lords and to sit judicially, but would be responsible for all judicial appointments, would continue as chief constitutional adviser to the Crown and would "watch and master all questions relating to legislation." Other matters concerning the administration of justice would pass to the Home Secretary, who would be redesignated as Minister of Justice, and would probably sit in the Commons. These proposals were supported by The Law Society but opposed by the Bar. Four years later, the case against a Ministry of Justice (albeit a ministry on the continental pattern including responsibility for the judiciary) was powerfully made by Lord Birkenhead.[26] Some of the steam was taken out of the case for a Ministry by the establishment of the Law Commissions in 1965. However, the large increases in the amount of money spent on courts' administration and the provision of legal services, and the general argument in favour of greater political accountability have led both the Labour and Liberal parties to favour the appointment of a minister answerable to the House of Commons to take charge of these matters.[27] It would also seem desirable for the Home Affairs Committee of the House of Commons to extend its remit to include matters concerning the administration of justice other than judicial appointments.[28]

Other anticipated or possible developments include the establishment of a national prosecution system and the creation of a Legal Services Council of laymen and lawyers to review and carry out research on the provision of legal services, to advise the Lord Chancellor and possibly to carry out some executive functions. These were recommended, respectively, by the Royal Commissions on Criminal Procedure and Legal Services.[29] More generally, there is a good case for a permanent body analogous to the Law Commission to concern itself with the reform of civil and criminal procedure and the operation of the legal system.[30]

[25] Cd. 9230.

[26] *Points of View* (1922), Vol. I, p. 112. This was apparently prepared by Sir Claud Schuster, Permanent Secretary to the Lord Chancellor 1915–1944: Drewry (1983) *op. cit.*

[27] See respectively, A. Davidson Q.C., M.P., and T. Clement-Jones, *L.A.G. Bulletin*, May 1983, pp. 12, 13; A. Lester, (1984) 134 N.L.J. 138; S.C. Silkin, [1984] P.L. 179.

[28] See G. Drewry "The Administration of Justice and Parliamentary Scrutiny" (1983) 133 N.L.J. 959–960. The Select Committee on Procedure, 1977–78 H.C. 588, recommended that the L.C.D. and Law Officers' Department should be subject to scrutiny by the H.A.C., but this was not accepted by the government: N. St. John Stevas: "the new Committees should not be allowed to threaten either the independence of the judiciary or the judicial process." "Civil Law administration" was regarded as a "minor part of the work of those departments." H.C. Deb., Vol. 969, col. 38, June 25, 1979). In 1983 the Liaison Committee proposed that the original recommendation should be implemented: 1982—83 H.C. 92, para. 24.

[29] R.C.C.P. Report, pp. 125–170; R.C.L.S., Vol. 1, pp. 62–65. See below, pp. 517 and 352–353, 357–358. The Government has rejected the proposal for a Legal Services Council: *Government Response* (above, p. 22, n. 20a) p. 6.

[30] See M. Zander, "Promoting Change in the Legal System" (1979) 42 L.Q.R. 489, 502–505. The suggested model is the Vera Institute of Justice of New York, which has assisted in various reform projects in the U.K. The Law Commission is to hold a Seminar on civil procedure in 1984: 18th Annual Report, 1982–83 (1983–84 H.C. 266) pp. 5–6. This is an early part of the "complete and systematic review of civil procedure" that has been instituted by the Lord Chancellor: see the *Government Response* (above, p. 22, n. 20a) pp. 31–32.

F. INFORMATION ABOUT THE LEGAL SYSTEM

Statistical and factual information about the operation of the English legal system can be gleaned from various official sources. Official publications are grouped into a number of classes.[31] "Command papers" are "Presented to Parliament by Command of Her Majesty"[32] and include reports of Royal Commissions, departmental committees and the Law Commission. "House of Commons" and "House of Lords Papers" are published on behalf of the respective Houses of Parliament.[33] Other documents are published as "Non-Parliamentary Publications" by Her Majesty's Stationery Office[34] or by the department concerned.[35]

Statistical information may be found in the series of *Judicial Statistics* (1856–1922) published by the Home Office and covering both civil and criminal matters; and *Criminal Statistics* (1922 to date) also published by the Home Office. The Lord Chancellor's Department has published various series: *Civil Judicial Statistics* (1922–1974); *Statistics on Judicial Administration* (1972–1974) and *Judicial Statistics: England and Wales* (1975 to date). Information on legal services is given in the Annual Report of the Law Society and the Lord Chancellor's Advisory Committee, first issued in 1951 and since 1974–1975 termed the *Legal Aid Annual Reports*.

---

[31] See generally J.E. Pemberton, *British Official Publications* (2nd ed., 1973).
[32] These papers are numbered in series and since 1870 have been prefixed by an abbreviation for "Command": 1st series [1]–[4222] 1833–1869; 2nd series [C.1]–[C.9550] 1870–1899; 3rd series [Cd.1]–[Cd.9239] 1900–1918; 4th series [Cmd.1]–Cmd.9889, 1919–1956; 5th series Cmnd.1–, 1956–.
[33] These are numbered in the session of publication (*e.g.* 1983–84 H.C. or H.L.1).
[34] H.M.S.O. also publish Command Papers and Parliamentary Papers: see the annual H.M.S.O. lists.
[35] See the *Catalogue of British Official Publications Not Published by H.M.S.O.* (1980–).

PART I

COURTS, PERSONNEL AND SOURCES OF LAW

CHAPTER 2

COURTS AND TRIBUNALS

A. INTRODUCTION

THERE are several ways in which a legal dispute (which the parties also characterise as "legal") may be resolved. It may be settled by force or by agreement. The dispute may be referred informally or formally to a third party for him to arbitrate. Exceptionally, the dispute may be referred to one of the institutions established by the state expressly for the purpose of resolving such matters. Some of these institutions are termed "courts," others "tribunals." These terms cannot be defined with precision, and, for the most part, little turns on whether a particular institution is labelled a court or a tribunal, or whether an institution, however labelled, falls within the legal definition of a "court."

The term "tribunal" can be used very generally to mean any "judicial assembly,"[1] including a court; in the present context it is commonly used for "judicial assemblies" other than courts. If established by the state they are generally described as "administrative tribunals" to distinguish them from "domestic tribunals" established by non-state institutions such as professional and sporting associations and trade unions as part of their disciplinary procedures. The label "administrative" reflects the fact that most such tribunals are established to perform judicial functions as part of the administration of some government scheme or programme.

Finally, it should be remembered that while the settlement of disputes is the main function of almost all courts and most tribunals, it is not the only one: a number of administrative functions have also been allocated to them.[2]

B. COURTS

1. SIGNIFICANCE

Apart from the police, the courts of law are perhaps the most visible feature of the English legal system. Only the courts have power to impose punishment in criminal cases; reports of these, and important civil cases decided by the superior courts commonly appear in the national and local press, and they may be covered by radio and television. Lawyers, and to an even greater extent, law students and lecturers place great emphasis on the decisions of the superior courts. It is, however, difficult to estimate the significance of the courts in the legal system as a whole. The number of cases determined by the courts is small, and by the superior courts[3] minute, in comparison with the number of disputes settled by other means.

[1] O.E.D.

[2] *e.g.* the licensing functions of magistrates and the discretionary powers of the High Court in relation to the administration of estates or the supervision of the affairs of infants and mental patients; *cf.* below, pp. 34–35.

[3] See below, p. 37.

Moreover, in a high proportion of the cases dealt with by the magistrates' courts and county courts the proceedings are merely mechanical processes for, respectively, the fining of minor traffic offenders and the collection of debts, with no live issue to be determined.

On the other hand, the courts do have a much wider indirect impact, given, first, that the chances of success in legal proceedings will influence the settlement of disputes,[4] and, secondly, that the decisions of superior courts are a source of law.[5]

2. HISTORICAL BACKGROUND[6]

(a) Courts of common law and equity

As we have said, the main function of almost all courts today is the adjudication of disputes. They can, however, trace their origins to local and central institutions in which no distinctions were drawn between the functions of administration, legislation and adjudication. At the local level in the Dark Ages there were community assemblies or "moots" which, *inter alia*, dealt with disputes according to local custom. These assemblies, apart from the smallest, village, assemblies, came to be based on administrative units established by the Crown: the shires, and their subdivisions, the hundreds and the boroughs. At the centre was the *Curia Regis* (King's Court).

Three related themes in early legal development can be discerned. First, the administration of justice came to be regarded as an adjunct of feudal lordship rather than a matter for the community as a whole. Then there was a further shift whereby it came in particular to be one of the prerogatives of the Crown. Thirdly, the administration of justice came to be differentiated from other functions of government. The strengthening of royal justice at the expense of local, communal, justice was a gradual process, and was neither intended nor planned, but it took place at all levels. This process involved the establishment of distinct royal courts, the placing of royal officials in the localities, whether temporarily or permanently, and the development of the supervisory jurisdiction of the royal courts over local courts.

At the centre, three common law courts evolved at different times out of the *Curia Regis*: the Exchequer,[7] the Common Pleas and the King's (or Queen's) Bench. They sat at Westminster Hall. The jurisdictional lines between these courts were complex. In theory, the Exchequer dealt with matters concerning the revenues of the Crown, the Common Pleas suits between subject and subject in which the Crown had no interest, and the King's Bench "pleas of the Crown" (*i.e.* criminal matters and civil cases involving a breach of the King's peace or some other royal interest). By the eighteenth century a variety of fictions had enabled each court to exercise a jurisdiction that was similar in substance although different in form to the others.

Parallel to the development of the common law courts at the centre was

---

[4] See below, pp. 379–386.

[5] See below, Chap. 7.

[6] See generally J.H. Baker, *An Introduction to Legal History* (2nd ed., 1979) Chaps. 1–7.

[7] As well as a common law jurisdiction, this court had an established equity jurisdiction, which was transferred to the Court of Chancery as late as 1842.

that of the Court of Chancery, and in particular its function of dealing with petitions.[8] For a time in the sixteenth and seventeenth centuries a number of "conciliar courts" also assumed importance, being courts established under the prerogative to handle judicial matters that came before the Privy Council but were not dealt with by the Chancellor. These included the Court of Star Chamber, which became notorious towards the end of its life for its handling of political crimes, the Court of Requests and several regional offshoots. They were looked on with suspicion by the common law courts and were abolished in the 1640s. The pattern of superior courts otherwise remained substantially unchanged until the nineteenth century, when some new courts were created, and there was subsequently a general reorganisation under the Supreme Court of Judicature Acts 1873–75.[9] In this re-organisation the various superior courts[10] were replaced by one Supreme Court of Judicature comprising the High Court (in five divisions) and the Court of Appeal. The intention initially was for the appellate jurisdiction of the House of Lords to be abolished, but a successful rearguard action was fought for its retention.[11]

Royal justices from the common law courts were also sent out to travel the country. Originally, they conducted all manner of governmental affairs, but they came to concentrate on judicial proceedings. There were two bases for their jurisdiction. In criminal and some civil cases they were given ad hoc commissions from the Crown. In other civil cases they sat with a jury to try issues that arose in litigation in the superior courts at Westminster: the juries technically were summoned to Westminster "unless before then (*nisi prius*) the King's justices have come" into the country. It was obviously more convenient to try the issues locally and transmit the result to London. The system came to be known as the "assize system" and continued until the 1970s,[12] and even the present arrangements have maintained the concept of High Court judges hearing cases in the provinces, albeit now reinforced by local judges.

The significant development in the handling of criminal cases less serious than those dealt with at the assizes was the appointment by the Crown of justices of the peace and the progressive widening of their criminal jurisdiction from the thirteenth century onwards.[13] Civil cases were heard by the successors of the old community assemblies, a variegated pattern of county, hundred, manorial and borough courts. These courts were subject to the supervisory jurisdiction of the superior royal courts and came to apply the common law. They declined for different reasons and at different times, although many were only formally abolished in the 1970s.[14] The

---

[8] See above, pp. 4–5.

[9] This followed the recommendations of the First Report of the Judicature Commission (H.M.S.O., 1869).

[10] *i.e.* the Courts of Chancery, Queen's Bench, Common Pleas, Exchequer, Admiralty (see below, p. 30), Probate (below, p. 31), and Divorce and Matrimonial Causes (*ibid.*). The London Court of Bankruptcy, originally established by an Act of 1831 to relieve the Court of Chancery of some of its business, was incorporated in 1884.

[11] See below, p. 82.

[12] See below, pp. 65–66.

[13] See below, pp. 132–134. The justices also had many administrative responsibilities.

[14] Courts Act 1971, ss.42, 43; Administration of Justice Act 1977, s.23, Sched. 4.

important step in the establishment of a regular system of local civil courts was the creation of new, statutory, county courts in 1846.[15]

(b) Appeals[16]

Provision for appeals was complex. The record of a court's proceedings could be reviewed for error[17] by another common law court[18] or a special court, a number of which were established by statute at various times to sit in a room at Westminster Hall known as the Exchequer Chamber.[19] Error lay from the Courts of Exchequer Chamber to Parliament, this jurisdiction being exercised by the House of Lords. Another, informal, method of review was the practice of judges to reserve cases for the opinion of their brethren, expressed at meetings held in Serjeants' Inn or the Exchequer Chamber.[20] In Chancery proceedings, a case argued before the Master of the Rolls or a Vice-Chancellor[20a] could be re-argued before the Chancellor, and the Chancellor could review his own previous decisions and those of his predecessors. In the seventeenth century it was established that proceedings in error lay from the Court of Chancery to the House of Lords. A Court of Appeal in Chancery with appellate judges (Lords Justices) specially appointed to it was created in 1851 to hear appeals from the Master of the Rolls and the Vice-Chancellors. This became the model for the Court of Appeal established by the Judicature Acts 1873–1875. The nineteenth century also saw the replacement of proceedings in error by statutory appeals in the modern form.

(c) Other courts

Apart from the courts of common law and equity there were courts that followed civil law procedure: the High Court of Admiralty,[21] which dealt with maritime matters and the High Court of Chivalry,[22] a court of honour. Canon law was administered by archdeacons' courts, the bishops' consistory courts, each presided over by the chancellor of the diocese, and

---

[15] See below, pp. 59–64. These must not be confused with the old shire or county courts presided over by the sheriff.

[16] See Baker (1979), Chap. 9.

[17] This process was more akin to the modern application for judicial review than statutory appeal: see Chap. 19.

[18] Proceedings in error lay from the Common Pleas to the King's Bench until 1830.

[19] (1) One was established in 1357 to hear error from the Exchequer. This comprised the Chancellor and the Treasurer with judges as assistants. (2) A second was established in 1585 to hear error from the Queen's Bench, this court comprising the justices of the Common Pleas and the barons of the Exchequer. (3) In 1830 a new Court of Exchequer Chamber was established to hear error from each of the common law courts. This comprised all the judges of the superior courts, error from one court being heard by the judges of the other two.

[20] In criminal cases such meetings became formalised with the creation of the Court for Crown Cases Reserved in 1848.

[20a] See below pp. 156, 157.

[21] This court became part of the Supreme Court of Judicature in the 1873–75 reorganisation. See F. Wiswall, *The Development of Admiralty Jurisdiction and Practice since 1800* (1971).

[22] This court has sat once since 1737: *Manchester Corporation* v. *Manchester Palace of Varieties Ltd.* [1955] P. 133. See G.D. Squibb, *The High Court of Chivalry* (1959). It has jurisdiction over such questions as the right to arms, precedence and descent. In the 1955 case the corporation claimed successfully that the company should be prevented from using the former's arms in their seal and displayed above the main curtain at the Palace Theatre, Manchester.

the archbishops' provincial courts, the Chancery Court of York and the Court of Arches.[23] Further appeals lay to the Pope or to Papal Delegates. Following the Reformation this jurisdiction passed to the Court of High Commission, which lapsed in the 1640s, and the Court of Delegates. The latter court was replaced by the Privy Council in 1832. The relationship between the ecclesiastical courts and the royal courts was stormy and complicated.[24] The jurisdiction of ecclesiastical courts over marriage, divorce and probate ended in 1857 with the creation of the Court of Divorce and Matrimonial Causes and the Court of Probate.[25] Since then, their jurisdiction has been confined to church matters. The present court structure was introduced by the Ecclesiastical Jurisdiction Measure 1963, which retained the consistory courts, but created an appellate system of gothic complexity, largely replacing the appellate jurisdiction of the Privy Council.[26]

C. TRIBUNALS

1. INTRODUCTION

The significant role played by administrative tribunals in the adjudication of legal disputes is a development of the present century, although it is possible to find examples of similar institutions in earlier centuries.[27] For example, the General and Special Commissioners of Income Tax were established in 1799 and 1805 respectively, with both assessment and appellate functions. The Railway and Canal Commission was established in 1873, *inter alia*, to settle disputes between railway companies and between companies and their customers, and subsequently evolved into the Transport Tribunal.

The most important factors behind the expansion of the number of tribunals and the range of their work have been the advent of the welfare state and the development of state economic controls. The National Insurance Act 1911 set up the unemployment benefit scheme. All questions concerning claims to benefit were to be determined initially by an insurance officer. A workman dissatisfied with a determination could have it referred to a "court of referees" consisting of a chairman appointed by the Board of Trade, one member from an "employers' panel" and one from a "workmens' panel." A further right of appeal lay to an "umpire"—a national appellate authority appointed by the Crown. This arrangement proved superior to alternative methods of adjudication used in legislation of the period,[28] and was adopted as the general model for many of the new tribunals established in the following decades:

[23] So called because it usually sat in the arched crypt of the church of St. Mary le Bow in London. Its judge became known as the Dean of Arches.

[24] See Baker (1979) Chap. 8.

[25] These courts became part of the Supreme Court of Judicature in the 1873–75 reorganisation.

[26] See E. Garth Moore, *An Introduction to Canon Law* (1967) Chap. XIV.

[27] See R.E. Wraith and P.G. Hutchesson, *Administrative Tribunals* (1973) Chap. 1.

[28] *i.e.* Workmen's Compensation Act 1897: disputes concerning compensation for industrial injuries were supposed to be settled by arbitration but in practice went to county court judges and beyond on appeal; Old Age Pensions Act 1908: pensions were administered by pensions committees of local authorities, which also adjudicated disputes, with an appeal to the Local Government Board; National Insurance Act 1911, Part I: national health insurance was administered by friendly societies with an appeal to one of four Insurance Commissioners.

"The extension of governmental responsibility for welfare provision, regulation of the economy, employment policy and resource development has created new statutory rights, obligations and restraints. Consequently, new areas of potential dispute have opened up, the boundaries of which have been progressively extended, and which require legislative provision for adjudication. The tendency, for a variety of reasons, has been to use tribunals rather than ordinary courts for settling disputes of this kind."[29]

This is not to say that there have been clear principles governing either the decision to allocate a particular decision to a tribunal or the details of the machinery established:

"Parliament's selection of subjects to be referred to tribunals and inquiries does not form a regular pattern. Certain basic guidelines can be detected, but the choice is influenced by the interplay of various factors—the nature of the decisions, accidents of history, departmental preferences and political considerations—rather than by the application of a set of coherent principles."[29a]

These tribunals commonly determine disputes between the citizen and the state arising out of the administration of a statutory scheme.[30] In addition, some determine disputes between citizens, normally arising out of protective legislation enacted for the benefit of one of the parties.[31]

2. THE FRANKS REPORT

A significant landmark in the development of tribunals was the 1957 report of the Committee on Administrative Tribunals and Enquiries chaired by Sir Oliver Franks.[32] Part of the terms of reference required the Committee to review the constitution of and working of tribunals other than the ordinary courts of law, constituted by a minister or for the purposes of a minister's functions.[33] Among the general points made by the Committee were, first, that the special procedures within their terms of reference should be marked by the characteristics of "openness, fairness and impartiality"[34]:

"In the field of tribunals openness appears to us to require the publicity of proceedings and knowledge of the essential reasoning underlying the decisions; fairness to require the adoption of a clear procedure which enables parties to know their rights, to present their case fully and to know the case which they have to meet; and impartiality to require the freedom of tribunals from the influence,

---

[29] *The Functions of the Council on Tribunals*: Special Report by the Council (Cmnd. 7805, 1980) p. 1.

[29a] *Ibid.* pp. 1–2.

[30] *e.g.* disputes concerning claims to welfare benefits.

[31] *e.g.* disputes between landlord and tenant arising out of rent controls, and between employer and employee concerning allegedly unfair dismissals.

[32] Cmnd. 218.

[33] The other part of the terms of reference concerned public inquiry procedures.

[34] Cmnd. 218, p. 5.

real or apparent, of Departments concerned with the subject matter of their decisions."[35]

Secondly, the Committee noted that tribunals as a system for adjudication had come to stay, and indeed that the tendency to refer issues arising from legislative schemes to special tribunals was likely to grow rather than to diminish.[36]

Thirdly, the Committee recommended the establishment of two permanent Councils on Tribunals, one for England and Wales and one for Scotland, to supervise tribunal and inquiry procedures.

In addition, the report made a whole series of detailed recommendations concerning both the constitution and procedures of tribunals generally and particular tribunals. Most of the proposals were implemented in the Tribunals and Inquiries Act 1958, subsequently consolidated in the Tribunals and Inquiries Act 1971, and in changes of regulation and departmental practice.

3. THE COUNCIL ON TRIBUNALS[37]

The 1958 Act established one Council on Tribunals, with a Scottish Committee. Its functions in respect of tribunals are:

"(a) to keep under review the construction and working of the tribunals specified in Schedule 1 to the [1971] Act;
(b) to consider and report on particular matters referred to the Council by the Lord Chancellor and the Lord Advocate with respect to any tribunal other than a court of law whether or not specified in Schedule 1; . . . ."[38]

Thus, its powers are consultative and advisory. It was not given the executive powers recommended by the Franks Report as to the appointment of tribunal members, the review of remuneration and the formulation of procedural codes.[39] Certainly it has no power to reverse or require reconsideration or specific tribunal decisions. The Council has 15 members appointed by the Lord Chancellor and the Lord Advocate, and the Parliamentary Commissioner for Administration is a member *ex officio*. The membership comprises a mixture of lawyers, both practising and academic, and non-lawyers, with the latter predominating. The Council's requests for additional powers, put forward in its Special Report of 1980, were generally not accepted, although a code for consultation with government departments has been introduced.[40] The Council has done much useful work in minor matters, securing, for example, many

---

[35] *Ibid.* p. 10.

[36] *Ibid.* p. 8.

[37] See *The Functions of the Council on Tribunals*: Special Report by the Council (Cmnd. 7805, 1980); the Council's Annual Reports; H.W.R. Wade [1960] P.L. 351; J.F. Garner [1965] P.L. 321.

[38] Special Report, p. 3. It has similar, although not identical functions in respect of procedures involving inquiries held on behalf of a minister.

[39] It must be consulted before procedural rules are made for Schedule 1 tribunals, but does not make the rules itself: 1971 Act, s.10.

[40] See the Council's Annual Reports for 1980–81 (1981–82 H.C. 89) pp. 6–7 and 1981–82 (1982–83 H.C. 64) p. 8 and Appendix C.

amendments to draft bills, rules and regulations, and some changes in tribunal practice. However, its political position is weak and it "remains an inconspicuous advisory committee."[41]

4. ADJUDICATION OR ADMINISTRATION

There has been some debate on whether tribunals are to be regarded as part of the machinery of justice or part of the machinery of administration. The Franks Committee stated[42]:

> "Tribunals are not ordinary courts, but neither are they appendages of Government Departments. Much of the official evidence, including that of the Joint Permanent Secretary to the Treasury, appeared to reflect the view that tribunals should properly be regarded as part of the machinery of administration, for which the Government must retain a close and continuing responsibility. Thus, for example, tribunals in the social service field would be regarded as adjuncts to the administration of the services themselves. We do not accept this view. We consider that tribunals should properly be regarded as machinery provided by Parliament for adjudication rather than as part of the machinery of administration. The essential point is that in all these cases Parliament has deliberately provided for a decision outside and independent of the Department concerned, either at first instance (for example in the case of Rent Tribunals and the Licensing Authorities for Public Service and Goods Vehicles) or on appeal from a decision of a Minister or of an official in a special statutory position (for example a valuation officer or an insurance officer). Although the relevant statutes do not in all cases expressly enact that tribunals are to consist entirely of persons outside the Government service, the use of the term "tribunal" in legislation undoubtedly bears this connotation, and the intention of Parliament to provide for the independence of tribunals is clear and unmistakable."

The supposed characteristic of independence cannot, however, be taken too far. Clearly it is desirable that the expression of the "departmental view" in an individual case should be confined to the representations made at the hearing itself. However, in many respects the departments retain a general influence over tribunal decision-making. They are responsible for the formulation of the relevant primary legislation and procedural rules, albeit in consultation with the Council on Tribunals, and indeed for the "detailed arrangements" for the working of tribunals.[43]

The Franks view on this point has been criticised in two respects. First, it has been pointed out that some tribunals are "policy-oriented" rather than "court-substitute":

> "For instance, where there is a dispute about social security entitlement, tribunals are basically used in place of the ordinary courts

---

[41] H.W.R. Wade, *Administrative Law* (5th ed., 1982) p. 801.

[42] Cmnd. 218; p. 9.

[43] Annual Report of the Council on Tribunals for 1975–76 (1976–77 H.C. 236) p. 3. The Council recognises that it is not always practicable for a tribunal to use non-departmental staff and premises: Annual Report for 1981–82 (1982–83 H.C. 64) pp. 26–27.

because the latter have become too expensive, formal and technical in their procedure. On the other hand, many matters of planning, whether in transport, land use, or industrial expertise, are given to tribunals because of the lack of expertise and doctrinal flexibility, or policy consciousness, on the part of the courts. Thus different weaknesses in the courts give rise to different types of tribunals."[44]

Examples of policy-oriented tribunals include the Transport Tribunal[45] and the Civil Aviation Authority.[46]

Secondly, it has been argued that even court-substitute tribunals should be seen as hybrid in nature; not only machinery for adjudication but, as well, "vital components of administration."[47]

5. SUPPOSED ADVANTAGES OF TRIBUNALS AS COURT-SUBSTITUTES

The Franks Committee noted that tribunals have certain characteristics which often give them advantages over the courts: "cheapness, accessibility, freedom from technicality, expedition and expert knowledge of their particular subject."[48] Generally, tribunal proceedings are cheaper, speedier,[49] and more expert than courts of law. However, accessibility is hindered by the great complexity of the system of tribunals and the lack of publicity given to their work. Moreover, the Council on Tribunals has stated that:

"Significant changes have . . . taken place in the general constitutional and administrative climate. There is, for example, a movement towards greater formalism in procedures for settling disputes. The process started with reforms following the Franks Report which, in general, made tribunals more like courts . . . . Since then the trend towards judicialisation has gathered momentum with the result that tribunals are becoming more formal, expensive and procedurally complex. Consequently they tend to become more difficult for an ordinary citizen to comprehend and cope with on his own."[50]

Associated with this movement are the Council's arguments in favour of the extension of legal aid to tribunals, the appointment of lawyer chairmen

[44] B. Abel-Smith and R. Stevens, *In Search of Justice* (1968) p. 220; see J.A. Farmer, *Tribunals and Government* (1974) Chap. 8 for an argument in favour of the establishment of more policy-oriented tribunals as an alternative to ministerial decision-making.

[45] Goods vehicle licensing appeals: Transport Act 1968, s.70.

[46] Air transport licensing: Civil Aviation Acts 1971, 1980, 1982. Other possible candidates were the Patents Appeal Tribunal (now the Patents Court), the Lands Tribunal and the Industrial Court (renamed the Industrial Arbitration Board in 1971 and the Central Arbitration Committee in 1976): Abel-Smith and Stevens (1968) p. 225.

[47] K. Hendry, "The Tasks of Tribunals: Some Thoughts" (1982) 1 C.J.Q. 253, 259; *cf.* J.A.G. Griffith, "Tribunals and Inquiries" (1959) 22 M.L.R. 125, 129.

[48] Cmnd. 218, p. 9.

[49] The Council on Tribunals has, however, noted delays in the hearing of appeals by Immigration Adjudicators: see Annual Reports for 1979–80 (1980–81 H.C. 246) p. 20 and 1980–81 (1981–82 H.C. 89) p. 6. The delays have been reduced partly by transferring cases to other parts of the country: *i.e.* at the expense of accessibility. There have also been delays before the Social Security Commissioners: see Annual Reports for 1980–81, p. 6 and 1981–82, p. 28. See further, Annual Report for 1982–83 (1983–84 H.C. 129) pp. 12–13, 20.

[50] *The Functions of the Council on Tribunals*: Special Report by the Council (Cmnd. 7805, 1980) p. 21.

and the extension of rights of appeal to the courts. It has also been pointed out that, despite declarations by tribunals that they are not bound by precedent, the requirements of consistency and predictability of decision lead to the development of general principles and an informal *de facto* system of precedent,[51] especially as the decisions of certain tribunals are systematically reported.

Accordingly, it is perhaps more true today than ever that "such differences as there are between [courts and tribunals] are not in any sense fundamental but at most differences in degree. . . . "[52] In particular, it is not possible to argue that courts administer rules of law while tribunals administer both law and policy:

> "[N]o such clear line can or should be drawn. Indeed it was the evolution of this myth which helped establish the tribunal system by convincing the judges of the ordinary courts that they were concerned with legal but not with policy questions. . . . Properly understood, tribunals are a more modern form of court. In some cases they may have more discretion than the courts, and this is particularly true of the policy oriented tribunals. But certainly they have no more discretion than the Chancery Division has in handling trusts, wards or companies."[53]

Other, more pragmatic, reasons for establishing tribunals rather than entrusting matters to courts include the need not to overburden the judiciary,[54] the avoidance of Ministerial responsibility for sensitive decisions and the easing of the workload of government departments.[55]

6. THE TRIBUNALS AND INQUIRIES ACT 1971

Apart from establishing the Council on Tribunals, the 1971 Act makes provision for the selection of chairmen of certain tribunals,[56] requires reasons to be given by Schedule 1 tribunals,[57] provides in many cases for an appeal on a point of law to the High Court[58] and renders inoperative most clauses in statutes passed before August 1, 1958 purporting to exclude judicial review.[59]

[51] J.A. Farmer, *Tribunals and Government* (1974) pp. 174–180 and Chap. 3; below, p. 301.

[52] B. Abel-Smith and R. Stevens, *In Search of Justice* (1968) pp. 224, 228. This is perhaps not true of the policy-oriented tribunals: see Farmer (1974) p. 189.

[53] Abel-Smith and Stevens (1968) pp. 227–228.

[54] Franks Report, Cmnd. 218, p. 9. In evidence the Permanent Secretary to the Lord Chancellor had stated that the wholesale transfer of tribunal work to the courts would necessitate the creation of a large number of additional judges, particularly in the county courts. Much of the work did not need the services of a highly remunerated judge. Moreover, a dilution of the bench was undesirable. Since then, there has been a large increase in the number of such judges, but they have been directed towards criminal and not tribunal work: see below, pp. 64–69, 153–154.

[55] See Hendry (1982) 1 C.J.Q. 253, 257–58, giving the immigration appeals system as an example. See also Griffith (1959) 22 M.L.R. 125, 129 in relation to national insurance and rent tribunals: "the truth was that the Department did not wish to be bothered with these decisions. And this for the most obvious of reasons: that the Department did not mind what the decisions were, for no questions of policy were involved."

[56] s.7. See below, p. 150.

[57] s.12.

[58] s.13.

[59] s.14. Such clauses are not to prevent applications for certiorari or mandamus: see below, p. 747.

D. THE SYSTEM IN OUTLINE

1. COURTS

The courts structure is shown on pp. 38–39 in diagrammatic form, with a table below showing the current workload. The main courts are considered in detail in section E.

Workload of the courts: Proceedings commenced
Comparative Tables[60]

	1938	1963	1977	1979	1982
1. Appellate Courts					
Judicial Committee of the					
Privy Council	107	46	48	46	62
House of Lords:					
From courts in England &					
Wales	32	21	58	70	65
From elsewhere	11	18	6	6	6
Court of Appeal					
Civil Division	574	711	1,359	1,419	1,627
Criminal Division	—	2,065	6,399	5,594	6,674
High Court	263	484	1,029	916	1,482
2. Crown Court (disposals)					
Committals for trial	—	—	53,118	49,466	66,186
Committals for sentence	—	—	12,846	13,961	14,544
Appeals	—	—	15,497	16,274	20,775
3. High Court					
Chancery Division	9,826	16,137	14,615	13,848	17,119
Queen's Bench	83,641	123,998	176,128	157,143	164,396
Family Division (excluding					
probate grants)	—	—	1,285	997	1,019
4. County Courts					
Plaints entered	1,262,402	1,543,324	1,673,966	1,462,650	2,048,568
Judgments on hearing	30,821	34,746	141,950	136,587	168,682
5. Magistrates' Courts					
Indictable offences	—	—	470,000	460,000	539,000
Summary offences					
(excluding motoring)	—	—	458,000	441,000	469,000
Motoring offences	—	—	1,165,000	1,147,000	1,214,000
6. Other courts and tribunals					
Restrictive Practices Court	—	33	4	7	—
Employment Appeal					
Tribunal	—	—	748	595	829

[60] Based on *Judicial Statistics, 1981* (Cmnd. 8770) Section J; *Judicial Statistics, 1982* (Cmnd. 9065) and (for magistrates' courts) *Criminal Statistics, 1982* (Cmnd. 9048) p. 131.

THE COURTS EXERCISING CRIMINAL JURISDICTION

HOUSE of LORDS

Appeal from the Divisional Court subject to the same conditions attached to appeal from the Court of Appeal.

Appeal from the Court of Appeal, subject to the grant of a certificate by that court that a point of law of general public importance is involved, and to the granting of leave by that court or the House of Lords.

COURT of APPEAL
CRIMINAL DIVISION

Appeal from the Crown Court against conviction on indictment on a question of fact or law or against sentence. (Leave is needed for an appeal on any ground which involves a question of fact alone or mixed law and fact or an appeal against sentence.)

QUEEN'S BENCH DIVISION
DIVISIONAL COURT

Appeal by way of Case Stated by prosecution or defence on a matter of law.

Appeal by way of Case Stated, on a question of law only, arising on appeal from the Magistrates' Court.

CROWN COURT

Appeal from the Magistrates' Court against conviction or sentence on a question of law or fact, or committal for sentence.

Committal for trial on indictment after committal proceedings. Jury trial in the Crown Court.

MAGISTRATES' COURTS

SUMMARY JURISDICTION

Trial of summary offences and other offences triable summarily with the consent of the accused.

EXAMINING JUSTICES

The conduct of committal proceedings to establish the existence of a prima facie case against an accused on a charge on indictment.

THE PRINCIPAL COURTS EXERCISING CIVIL JURISDICTION

HOUSE of LORDS

'Leapfrog' appeal direct from the High Court provided:- (i) all parties consent, and (ii) a point of law of general public importance is involved relating to the construction of an enactment or on a point on which the trial judge was bound by precedent. Certificate of trial judge and leave of House of Lords required.

Appeal from the Court of Appeal only by leave of that court or the House of Lords.

COURT of APPEAL
CIVIL DIVISION

Appeal from the High Court as of right, save in exceptional cases.

Appeal from the County Court as of right except in certain cases where leave is necessary (e.g. where the claim is for an amount not exceeding half the relevant County Court limit) and a few cases where the appeal is excluded altogether.

HIGH COURT

Any division of the High Court *may* sit at any place in England or Wales, but sittings of the Queen's Bench and Family Divisions are regularly held at the Crown Court first-tier centres.

QUEEN'S BENCH DIVISION

Trial of civil actions relating to:- contract and tort and other matters not within the scope of the Family and Chancery Divisions. Two separate courts within the Division exercise jurisdiction over commercial matters and Admiralty matters. The Division supervises the operation of inferior courts and tribunals on applications for judicial review.

FAMILY DIVISION

Trial of all defended matrimonial proceedings, and actions relating to legitimacy, validity of marriage, the guardianship of minors, the Married Woman's Property Act 1882 and other matters relating to matrimonial disputes and children.

Divisional Court hears appeals from Magistrates' and County Courts on family matters (e.g. affiliation, guardianship, adoption).

CHANCERY DIVISION

Trials of actions relating to:- Mortgages, deeds, specific performance of contracts for the sale of land, partnerships, companies, bankruptcy, revenue matters and contentious probate business.

Divisional Court has certain limited jurisdiction consisting of appeals from the County Court in bankruptcy and land registration matters.

COUNTY COURT

JURISDICTION INCLUDES

(i) Actions in contract or tort where the claim does not exceed £5,000 (except defamation);

(ii) Equity matters (trusts, mortgages, partnership etc.) where the value of the fund does not exceed £30,000;

(iii) Actions for recovering land where the rateable value does not exceed £1,000;

(iv) Undefended matrimonial cases;

(v) Bankruptcy.

2. TRIBUNALS

There are now over 50 types of tribunal within the jurisdiction of the Council on Tribunals,[61] and several others outside it. They may be roughly grouped according to subject matter.[62] The table on pp. 41–45 does not, however, purport to be a comprehensive list. Some tribunals are considered in detail in the next section.

Other tribunals of note that have not been included within the jurisdiction of the Council on Tribunals include the Criminal Injuries Compensation Board, set up under the royal prerogative to consider claims for *ex gratia* compensation from the victims of crimes of violence,[63] the Foreign Compensation Commission, which considers claims by British subjects as a result of nationalisation or sequestration in foreign countries and the Attendance Allowance Board, which determines whether the medical conditions are satisfied for the payment of attendance allowance.

E. PARTICULAR COURTS AND TRIBUNALS

In this section we consider the courts and tribunals that feature most prominently in the English legal system, by virtue either of their status in the hierarchy or their caseload. For reasons of space it is not possible to cover all tribunals in detail. We have not divided this section into "courts" and "tribunals" but have incorporated coverage of certain tribunals approximately in accordance with their position in the overall hierarchy.

1. MAGISTRATES' COURTS

(a) Introduction

Magistrates' courts are the inferior criminal courts. In addition they exercise certain family law, administrative law and minor civil functions. England and Wales is divided into "commission areas" (each county, the City of London, and five London commission areas).[64] Each non-metropolitan county, metropolitan district and London commission area constitutes a "petty sessions area" unless it is divided into "petty sessional divisions" in which case each division constitutes a petty sessions area.[65] Each petty sessions area has its own "bench" of magistrates with an elected chairman and one or more deputy chairmen.

(b) Criminal jurisdiction

Magistrates' courts are involved in some way in virtually all criminal prosecutions. Proceedings may be commenced by a summons or an arrest

---

[61] An alphabetical list is published as an appendix to each Annual Report.

[62] See R.E. Wraith and P.G. Hutchesson, *Administrative Tribunals* (1973) Chap. 2. See also the table in H.W.R. Wade, *Administrative Law* (5th ed., 1982) pp. 824–828, and J.F. Garner, *Administrative Law* (5th ed., 1979) Chap. VIII and D. Price, *Appeals* (1982).

[63] See the White Paper on Compensation for Victims of Crimes of Violence (Cmnd. 2323, 1964); Annual Reports of the Board; Review of the Criminal Injuries Compensation Scheme: Report of an Interdepartmental Working Party (H.M.S.O., 1978).

[64] Justices of the Peace Act 1979, ss.1, 2.

[65] *Ibid.* s.4. See the Local Government (Petty Sessional Divisions etc.) Order 1973 (S.I. 1973 No. 1593) as amended and, for London, S.I. 1964 Nos. 854 and 1529.

Table of Tribunals

General Subject Matter	Tribunal	Jurisdiction	Cases in 1982—England and Wales[66]	Number of Tribunals as at 31.12.82. England and Wales[66]
(a) *Social Administration* (1) Personal Welfare	Supplementary Benefit Appeal Tribunals	See pp. 56–57	57,650	112
	National Insurance Local Tribunals	See pp. 55–56	29,510	155
	Social Security Commissioners	See p. 58	4,029	13 Commissioners
	Medical Appeal Tribunals	Appeals concerning disablement questions arising in claims for disablement benefit	13,300	12
	Mental Health Review Tribunals	Review of the compulsory admission to hospital of mental patients	858	15
	Vaccine Damage Payment Tribunals	Medical Appeal Tribunals specially constituted to review refusals of vaccine damage payments	77	6
(2) Pensions	Pensions Appeal Tribunals	Appeals from decisions of the Secretary of State for Social Services concerning war pensions	2,477	Ad hoc

Table of Tribunals—cont.

General Subject Matter	Tribunal	Jurisdiction	Cases in 1982—England and Wales[66]	Number of Tribunals as at 31.12.82. England and Wales[66]
(3) Education	Education Appeal Committees	Appeals against allocation of school places	8,887[67]	Not available
(4) Employment	Industrial Tribunals	See pp. 52–54	37,597[67a]	51 centres
(5) National Health Service	Family Practitioner Committees and Service Committees	Complaints by patients of practitioner's failure to comply with terms of service	1,454	90 (FPC) 360 (SC)
	National Health Service Tribunal	Appeals against a decision that a practitioner should be removed from the N.H.S.	1	Nil
(6) Immigration	Immigration Adjudicators	Appeals against decisions of Immigration Officers	11,069	1 Chief 15 full time 56 part time
	Immigration Appeal Tribunal	Appeals from Immigration Officers and Adjudicators	476	1 sitting in 4 divs.
(b) *Economic matters* (7) Agriculture	Agricultural Land Tribunals	Disputes between landlord and tenant in respect of notice to quit, bad husbandry and drainage	506	8
	Arbitrators under the Agricultural Holdings Act 1948	Certain disputes over agricultural tenancies	168	N/A

				Commissioners
(8) Commerce	Commons Commissioners	Determination of claims in respect of common land	1,101	4
	Plant Variety Right Tribunal	Disputes between citizens concerning plant variety rights	Nil	3
	Comptroller of Patents	Adjudication in respect of patents, registered designs and trade marks	6,605	3
	Director-General of Fair Trading	Licensing decisions concerning consumer credit and estate agent activities	73	4
	Performing Rights Tribunal	Disputes between citizens concerning the performance of broadcasting of copyright works	Nil	1
	Tribunal of Inquiry under Prevention of Fraud (Investment) Act 1958	Refusal of licences to deal in securities	Nil	1
(9) Transport	Traffic Commissioners	Licensing of public service passenger vehicles	11,964[68]	10
	Licensing Authority for Goods Vehicles	Licensing of goods vehicles	2,369[68]	10
	Transport Tribunal	Appeals from Licensing Authority for Goods Vehicles	21	1
	Civil Aviation Authority	Air transport and travel organisers' licensing	1,230	1
(10) Housing	Rent assessment committees	Appeals against fair rents fixed by rent officers	14,210	Appointed ad hoc from 14 panels

Table of Tribunals—cont.

General Subject Matter	Tribunal	Jurisdiction	Cases in 1982—England and Wales[66]	Number of Tribunals as at 31.12.82. England and Wales[66]
	Rent Tribunals[69]	Disputes between landlord and tenant relating to the rent or security of tenure of certain dwellings	1,975	Appointed ad hoc from 14 panels
	Leasehold Valuation Tribunals[70]	Valuation of leaseholds for purposes of the Leasehold Reform Act 1967	95	..
(c) *Revenue* (11) Taxation	Special and General Commissioners of Income Tax	Tax appeals	Not available	1 (special) 429 (general)
	Value Added Tax Tribunals	V.A.T. appeals	626	3
	Tribunal for Part XVII of the Income and Corporation Taxes Act 1970	Nullification of tax advantages from certain transactions in securities, *e.g.* dividend-stripping	Not available	Not available
(12) Statutory Levies	Levy Exemption Referees	Disputes concerning refusal of industrial training boards to grant certificates of exemption from industrial training level	3[68]	1
	Betting Levy Appeal Tribunals	Appeals in respect of levy on bookmakers by the Horserace Betting Levy Board	56	1

				Courts drawn from 64 panels
(13) Property, Valuation and Rating	Local Valuation Courts	Rating appeals	36,598[71]	
	Lands Tribunal	See pp. 76–77	1,369[72]	1
	Aircraft and Shipbuilding Industries Arbitration Tribunal	Disputes arising out of nationalisation	Nil	1
	London Building Act Tribunal of Appeal	Appeals under the Acts	Nil	Nil

[66] Figures from Annual Report of the Council on Tribunals for 1982–83, Appendix C.
[67] These first apply to school placements for autumn 1982. The figures for Wales and non L.E.A. schools were not available.
[67a] 14,595 were disposed of after a hearing.
[68] These figures include Scotland.
[69] Under the Housing Act 1980 the functions of rent tribunals are to be performed by rent assessment committees, although when so acting the committees are to be known as "rent tribunals."
[70] Under the Housing Act 1980 rent assessment committees are established as leasehold valuation tribunals.
[71] A further 109,856 cases were settled or withdrawn.
[72] Includes withdrawal consent orders.

warrant issued by a justice of the peace.[73] Magistrates' courts try those offences triable only summarily, and act as examining justices to determine whether persons charged with offences triable only on indictment should be committed for trial in the Crown Court. Where proceedings are brought in respect of the intermediate category of offences "triable either way," the court must decide whether the offence appears more suitable for summary trial or for trial on indictment. Once this is decided, and subject to the right of the accused to insist on trial by a jury, the court proceeds either to summary trial or committal proceedings.[74]

A magistrates' court must be composed of at least two justices of the peace[75] unless there is express provision for a single justice to act,[76] as there is, for example, in the case of committal proceedings. Stipendiary magistrates[77] normally sit alone.

(c) Proceedings concerning juveniles[78]

(i) Background

The first steps towards treating children separately from adults in criminal proceedings were taken in the nineteenth century, and involved the extension of the scope of magistrates' summary jurisdiction. The Children Act 1908 established separate juvenile courts with power to deal both with children who had committed criminal offences and with those who were in need of care.[79] These were, however, simply special sittings of the ordinary magistrates' courts, and it was not until the 1930s that legislation required that special justices be selected to sit in juvenile courts, introduced reporting restrictions and stated expressly that regard was to be had to the welfare of the children.[80]

A perennial, but possibly inevitable problem of the juvenile justice system has been that it has attempted to balance two competing approaches.[81] The "criminal justice" approach assumes that behaviour is within the control of the individual and involves a procedure for the establishment of guilt and the imposition of a sentence related to the seriousness of the crime. Related considerations are the protection on the one hand of society and on the other of the procedural rights of the individual. This approach conforms to the position in respect of adult offenders and is particularly associated with lawyers, magistrates and the

---

[73] Magistrates' Courts Act 1980, s.1. The other methods of commencing proceedings are by an arrest without warrants and by a voluntary bill of indictment: see below, p. 507. Only this last method by-passes the magistrates' court. As to the geographical limits of the jurisdiction of magistrates' courts see the 1980 Act, s.2.

[74] These proceedings are explained more fully in the chapter on criminal procedure: see pp. 500–506, 524–527.

[75] The office of justice of the peace is considered below, pp. 132–149.

[76] Magistrates' Courts Act 1980, s.121(1). Normally, three justices sit.

[77] See below, pp. 148–149.

[78] See H.K. Bevan, *The Law Relating to Children* (1973) Chaps. 1–4; M. Berlins and G. Wansell, *Caught in the Act* (1974); K.W. Pain, *Practice and Procedure in Juvenile Courts* (1982). For research into the "consumer's" view of the juvenile justice system see H. Parker *et al.*, *Receiving Juvenile Justice* (1981).

[79] See P. Parsloe, *Juvenile Justice in Britain and the United States* (1978) Chap. 5.

[80] Children and Young Persons Act 1933.

[81] See Parsloe (1978) Chap. 1.

police. The "welfare" approach looks upon specific acts as indicators of the individual's problems, and involves the provision of help and treatment related to his needs rather than to his actions. As "punishment" is not imposed there is no need to protect procedural rights. This approach is most strongly associated with psychiatrists and social workers.[82] Politically, the former approach has tended to be favoured by the Conservatives and the latter by Labour. It cannot be said that any of these groups favours one approach to the exclusion of the other, but there are significant differences in emphasis. The present arrangements are based on the Children and Young Persons Acts 1933 and 1969. The latter Act was promoted by the Labour government,[83] and provided for, *inter alia*, the replacement of criminal proceedings by care proceedings in the case of children between 10 and 14, the restriction of prosecutions for children between 14 and 17 to exceptional cases, and the transfer of much of the discretion in relation to the disposition of offenders from magistrates to social workers. In the event, the Conservative government did not implement either of the first two points; and the Act had little impact on the system. Since then, magistrates have pressed for the strengthening of their powers.[84] Others have argued for the enhanced protection of the legal rights of the children concerned.[85] Some steps have been taken in response.[86]

(ii) *Juvenile courts*

A juvenile court must be composed of not more than three justices, and must normally include a man and a woman.[87] The justices must be drawn from the juvenile court panel appointed by the justices for each petty sessions area at their annual meeting.[88] They must be under 65 and should be "specially qualified for dealing with juvenile cases."[89] Each panel elects

---

[82] A third approach, the "community" approach, regards the person who breaks the law as a victim of society, and that the function of the juvenile court is to label and stigmatise selected children, particularly from poorer and disadvantaged backgrounds. The aim should be to divert children from the courts and refer them to "non-stigmatising agencies." This approach has yet to be significantly reflected in practice in England.

[83] The Act was based on the White Paper, *Children in Trouble* (Cmnd. 3601, 1968), which was itself a watered-down version of a report of a Labour party committee chaired by Lord Longford (*Crime—A Challenge to Us All* (1964) and another White Paper, *The Child, The Family and The Young Offender* (Cmnd. 2742, 1965).

[84] See the 11th Report of the Expenditure Committee, 1974–75 H.C. 534.

[85] See, *e.g.* L. Taylor *et al.*, *In Whose Best Interests* (1979); A. Morris *et al.*, *Justice for Children* (1980); M.D.A. Freeman, *The Rights and Wrongs of Children* (1983); H. Geach and E. Szwed (eds.) *Providing Civil Justice for Children* (1983); A. Morris and H. Giller (eds.) *Providing Criminal Justice for Children* (1983).

[86] See J. McEwan, "In Search of Juvenile Justice—The Criminal Justice Act 1982" [1983] J.S.W.L. 112.

[87] The Juvenile Courts (Constitution) Rules 1954 (S.I. 1954 No. 1711), r. 12.

[88] Children and Young Persons Act 1963, Sched. 2. In London, the panels are appointed by the Lord Chancellor. Outside London there has been little progress towards the amalgamation of panels in areas where juvenile courts do not sit often enough for the justices to gain adequate experience of the work: See C. Ball (1983) 147 J.P.N. 148.

[89] 1954 Rules, r. 1. The rules do not specify any qualifications. The Home Secretary has suggested that they "should include some direct practical experience of dealing with young persons (*e.g.* through working with youth organisations, teaching or similar work) and a real appreciation of the surroundings and way of life of the children who are likely to come before courts." The most suitable age for first appointment would be between 30 and 40 and no one should normally be first appointed when over 50: Home Office Circular No. 138/79 printed in *Clarke Hall and Morrison on Children* (2nd cum.suppt. to 9th ed., 1981) pp. B568–9.

a chairman and deputy chairman, one of whom must normally preside over each juvenile court. Stipendiary magistrates are members of the panel *ex officio* although one may only sit alone if he thinks it inexpedient in the interests of justice for there to be an adjournment.[90] A court may be held in buildings set apart for the purpose, or, as is more usually the case, in a courtroom normally used for an adult magistrates' court.[91] However, a juvenile court may not sit in a room that has been or will be used within an hour by another court.[92]

(iii) *Jurisdiction*

Criminal proceedings may not be instituted against children who are under 10: it is conclusively presumed that they cannot be guilty of any offence.[93] Where a child between 10 and 14 is prosecuted it must be proved that he was of a "mischievous discretion," *i.e.* that he knew that what he was doing was legally or morally wrong. Young persons of 14 and over are regarded as fully responsible for their acts.

There are two main branches to the juvenile court's jurisdiction. First, all criminal proceedings against juveniles[94] must normally take place in a juvenile court. The main exceptions are that an adult magistrates' court *must* deal with a juvenile where he is charged jointly with an adult and *may* do so where different charges are made against an adult arising out of the same or connected circumstances or where either an adult or a juvenile is charged with aiding, abetting, causing, procuring, allowing or permitting the other's alleged offence.[95] The juvenile court will try the case summarily except (1) where the charge is murder or manslaughter in which case the juvenile *must* be committed for trial in the Crown Court and (2) where the offence is one which carries a penalty for an adult of 14 years' imprisonment or more and the defendant is over 14, in which event the court *may* commit for trial.[96]

---

[90] 1954 Rules, rr. 2, 12(2).

[91] Guidance on the design of juvenile courts was given in Home Office Circular No. 39/1971 (*Clarke Hall and Morrison* (9th ed., 1979) pp. 1154–6). For a description of some courtrooms see L. Hilgendorf, *Social Workers and Solicitors in Child Care Cases* (H.M.S.O., 1981) pp. 89–98, criticising the poor conditions provided in many courts for waiting areas, the scheduling of care and criminal proceedings for the same day, and the continued use of old-fashioned magistrates' courts for care cases.

[92] Children and Young Persons Act 1933, s.47 as amended by the 1963 Act, s.17.

[93] Children and Young Persons Act 1933, s.50, as amended by the 1963 Act, s.16(1). At common law the relevant age was seven. Section 4 of the Children and Young Persons Act 1969 provides for the age to be raised to 14, but this has not been, and is unlikely to be, implemented.

[94] This term applies to children and young persons under 17. For most purposes under the 1933 Act "child" is defined as a person under 14 and "young person" as a person of 14 or over but under 17: s.107(1). The term "child" is differently defined for other purposes: see *Halsbury's Laws of England* (4th ed.) Vol. 24, para. 403.

[95] Children and Young Persons Act 1933, s.46 as extended by the 1963 Act, s.18. Applications for bail or for a remand may be heard by any justice or justices (1933 Act, s.46(2)). The adult magistrates' court will normally try the juvenile summarily but may commit him for trial in the Crown Court (Magistrates' Courts Act 1980, s.24) or remit for trial (*ibid.* s.29) or sentence (Children and Young Persons Act 1969, s.7(8)) in the juvenile court.

[96] Magistrates' Courts Act 1980, s.24. This enables the Crown Court to invoke the power under section 53(2) of the Children and Young Persons Act 1933 to impose a long sentence of detention.

Any person may institute criminal proceedings against a juvenile,[97] but he must notify the appropriate local authority.[98]

Secondly, a juvenile court may entertain civil "care proceedings" in relation to a juvenile. An order may only be made in such proceedings if one or more of a number of conditions are satisfied in respect of him:

"(a) his proper development is being avoidably prevented or neglected or his health is being avoidably impaired or neglected or he is being ill-treated; or

(b) it is probable that the condition set out in the preceding paragraph will be satisfied in his case, having regard to the fact that the court or another court has found that the condition is or was satisfied in the case of another child or young person who is or was a member of the household to which he belongs; or

(bb) it is probable that the condition set out in paragraph (a) of this subsection will be satisfied in his case, having regard to the fact that a person who has been convicted of an offence mentioned in Schedule 1 to the Act of 1933, including a person convicted of such an offence on whose conviction for the offence an order was made under Part I of the Powers of Criminal Courts Act 1973 placing him on probation or discharging him absolutely or conditionally is, or may become, a member of the same household as the child;

(c) he is exposed to moral danger; or

(d) he is beyond the control of his parent or guardian; or

(e) he is of compulsory school age within the meaning of the Education Act 1944 and is not receiving efficient full-time education suitable to his age, ability and aptitude and to any special educational needs he may have; or

(f) he is guilty of an offence, excluding homicide,
and also that he is in need of care or control which he is unlikely to receive unless the court makes an order under this section in respect of him . . . ."[99]

A variety of orders may be made in care proceedings, including the payment of compensation, the binding-over of parent, guardian or juvenile, a supervision order, a care order (committal to the care of a local authority), or a hospital order or guardianship order under the Mental Health Act 1983.[1] Where the "offence condition" is relied upon the usual requirements for establishing criminal liability must be observed,[2] and the normal course has been for criminal rather than care proceedings to be instituted. Care proceedings can only be started by a local authority, a

---

[97] The provisions of section 5 of the Children and Young Persons Act 1969 which restrict private prosecutions have not been implemented.

[98] 1969 Act, s.5(8) (9).

[99] Children and Young Persons Act 1969, s.1(2), as amended by the Children Act 1975, Sched. 3, para. 67, the Education Act 1981, Sched. 3, para. 9 and the Health and Social Services and Social Security Adjudications Act 1983, Sched. 2, para. 10.

[1] *Ibid.* s.1(3), see below, pp. 674–698. Guardianship orders may no longer be made in respect of persons under 16: see Mental Health Act 1983, s.37(2)(a)(ii).

[2] *Ibid.* s.3.

constable or authorised person[3] who reasonably believes that there are grounds for making an order.[4]

In addition, a juvenile court has jurisdiction to determine whether a local authority may permanently assume parental rights in respect of a child already voluntarily in its care where the parent or parents object,[5] and to entertain an application by a parent for such an assumption of parental rights to be ended.[6] It also has certain powers relating to foster children.[7]

(iv) *Procedure*

The procedure of juvenile courts is less formal than for adult magistrates' courts. Only members and officers of the court, the parties, their lawyers, witnesses and other persons directly concerned, press representatives, and other persons specially authorised may be present.[8] There are strict limits as to what may be reported.[9] In the case of juveniles dealt with summarily the expression "finding of guilt" must be used instead of "conviction" and the expression "order made upon a finding of guilt" instead of "sentence."[10]

(d) Domestic proceedings

Magistrates have an extensive jurisdiction in family law matters.[11] The list includes powers to make orders for financial provision for, or the protection of, parties to a marriage and children of the family, for the custody or supervision of children and committing children to the care of a local authority, affiliation orders, guardianship orders and adoption orders. Proceedings concerning these matters are termed "domestic proceedings" and the courts when hearing them "domestic courts."[12] The justices must be appointed from a domestic court panel constituted on a similar basis to the juvenile court panel.[13]

(e) Civil jurisdiction

Apart from domestic proceedings, magistrates' courts have powers in relation to certain other civil matters, including enforcement of the payment of rates, income tax and charges for supplies of gas, electricity and water. They also have an important jurisdiction in respect of the granting of liquor licences to public houses and clubs, and licences for bookmakers, betting offices, and premises for gaming and bingo. Finally,

---

[3] *e.g.* the N.S.P.C.C.

[4] 1969 Act, s.1(1). Only a local authority or constable may rely on the offence condition: *ibid.* s.3(2).

[5] Child Care Act 1980, s.3.

[6] *Ibid.* s.5(4).

[7] Foster Children Act 1980, ss.11, 12.

[8] Children and Young Persons Act 1933, s.47 as amended by the Children and Young Persons Act 1963, s.17(2).

[9] 1933 Act, s.49, as amended by the Children and Young Persons Acts 1963, s.57 and 1969, s.10.

[10] *Ibid.* s.59.

[11] Magistrates' Courts Act 1980, s.65.

[12] *Ibid.* s.67(1).

[13] *Ibid.* s.66(1); Domestic Courts (Constitution) Rules 1979 (S.I. 1979 No. 757), as amended by S.I. 1983 No. 676.

there is a vast number[14] of statutory provisions enabling appeals to be brought against administrative decisions of various kinds.

(f) Appeals[15]

Appeals lie from a magistrates' court either as of right to the Crown Court,[16] where proceedings take the form of a complete rehearing, or to the High Court by a procedure whereby the magistrates state a case for the opinion of the High Court on a point of law. In family matters the appeal is heard by the Family Division, otherwise the appeal will lie to the Queen's Bench Division. Any further appeal from the High Court lies to the House of Lords in criminal cases and to the Court of Appeal and House of Lords in civil cases.

(g) Administration

There is a "magistrates' courts committee" for each non-metropolitan county, metropolitan district and outer London commission area and for the City of London.[17] The committee consists of magistrates appointed by the magistrates for each petty sessions area at their annual meeting.[18] Each committee may co-opt a High Court judge, Circuit judge or recorder,[19] and must appoint a chairman and a clerk. The clerk is usually either the local clerk to the justices or the clerk to the local authority.[20] The functions of the committee include making proposals as to the division of their area into petty sessional divisions,[21] the appointment or removal of justices' clerks and other staff,[22] the indemnification of justices and clerks[23] and the provision of courses of instruction.[24] It is also responsible for determining what accommodation, books and equipment should be provided, although the actual provision is made by the local non-metropolitan county or metropolitan district council.[25] The council also pays the committee's expenses, including staff salaries. A council may appeal to the Secretary of State against a determination by the committee. This division of function can cause problems, although there seems to be a general desire to avoid confrontation.[26]

---

[14] D. Price, *Appeals* (1982) pp. 53–96, including appeals against refusal of a petshop licence, of a driving licence or a knacker's yard licence, a notice requiring a fire certificate and a notice requiring that an earth closet be replaced by a water closet.

[15] See generally, Chap. 19, below.

[16] See below, pp. 64–69, 702–703.

[17] Justices of the Peace Act 1979, ss.19–22. In Inner London there is a "committee of magistrates" under ss.35–38.

[18] See the Magistrates' Courts Committees (Constitution) Regulations 1973 (S.I. 1973 No. 1522), which determine the number appointed for each division.

[19] 1979 Act, s.20(2).

[20] If the area of the committee coincides with a petty sessions area it must be the clerk to the justices: *ibid.* s.22(2).

[21] *Ibid.* ss.23, 24.

[22] *Ibid.* ss.25–27.   [23] *Ibid.* s.53.   [24] *Ibid.* s.63. See below, pp. 140–141.

[25] *Ibid.* ss.55, 56. In 1971–72 the Justices' Clerks' Society and the Magistrates' Association pressed unsuccessfully for the link with local authorities to be broken and the administration of magistrates' courts to be merged with the new unified court service: see (1971) *The Magistrate*, pp. 52–56, 93, 109, 124–125, 142–43; (1972) *The Magistrate*, p. 49.

[26] See generally the *Report of the Working Group on Magistrates' Courts* (Home Office, 1982) Chap. 2; comments by C. Moiser (1983) 133 N.L.J. 149–150, 517–519. Procedural rules are made by the Lord Chancellor after consultation with a rule committee: Magistrates' Courts Act 1980, s.144.

The organisation of magistrates' courts varies according to the workload:

"In the dignified Victorian courthouse of one Midlands city 15 adult and two juvenile courts are held each morning, and up to 10 adult courts in the afternoon. Over 300 magistrates are on the rota, the staff numbers 150, fines collected annually amount to £1½ million, and the turnover in the maintenance department is £3 million.

At the opposite end of the scale you find a country district with eight different courts, each several miles from the next, but all served by one Justices' Clerk. . . .

The majority of courts, however, lie between these two extremes, with perhaps two to five courts a day."[27]

In a small court the list may be a mixture of all kinds of case; in a large court there may be specialised courts to hear traffic offences or applications, or to deal with debtors.

The administration is headed by the justices' clerk.[28] In a large court there may be separate sections for documentation concerning court proceedings, fines and fees, maintenance and licensing. In smaller courts the functional divisions are more blurred.[29]

Justices comprise at least two-thirds of the membership of the 56 "probation and after care committees" that are responsible, under the overall supervision of the Home Office, for the Probation and After-Care Service.[30] Probation officers have responsibilities in connection with probation orders, supervision orders for young offenders, suspended sentence supervision orders, community service orders,[31] the after-care of persons released from custody and the preparation of social inquiry reports and reports concerning the custody of children and the selection of prisoners for parole. They also provide a welfare service in domestic and matrimonial cases, and work in prison establishments.

2. INDUSTRIAL TRIBUNALS[32]

Industrial tribunals were first established by the Industrial Training Act 1964 to hear appeals by employers assessed for levy payable to an industrial training board. They were then given jurisdiction over disputes about redundancy pay. The Royal Commission on Trade Unions and Employers' Associations[33] recommended that the tribunal's jurisdiction should be enlarged to comprise, subject to certain limitations, all disputes between the individual worker and his employer, the primary aim being to make available "a procedure which is easily accessible, informal, speedy and inexpensive, and which gives them the best possible opportunities of

[27] *A Career in the Magistrates Courts* (H.M.S.O., 1979) p. 7.

[28] See below, pp. 143–147.

[29] Procedures for the scheduling of cases and fine enforcement were examined in the Report, *op. cit.* n. 25 above.

[30] See *The Probation and After-Care Service in England and Wales* (H.M.S.O., 5th ed., 1973); F.V. Jarvis, *Probation Officers' Manual* (3rd ed., 1980).

[31] See below, pp. 680–684.

[32] See K. Whitesides and G. Hawker, *Industrial Tribunals* (1975); D.J. Walker and D.B. Williams, *Industrial Tribunals—Practice and Procedure* (1979).

[33] Cmnd. 3623, 1968: Chairman: Lord Donovan.

arriving at an amicable settlement of their differences."[34] To a large extent this recommendation has been fulfilled. In addition to the points already mentioned industrial tribunals have jurisdiction in respect of complaints of unfair dismissal,[35] questions as to terms required to be included in a contract of employment,[36] claims to equal pay,[37] appeals against improvement notices or prohibition notices served by a health and safety inspector[38] and certain complaints relating to sex[39] and race[40] discrimination. This list is not exhaustive.

The tribunals sit at over 50 centres, grouped under 16 Regional Offices of Industrial Tribunals and the Central Office of Industrial Tribunals in London. There is a President of Industrial Tribunals (England and Wales) who both sits as a chairman and has important administrative responsibilities in relation to the system.[41] Each tribunal has a legally qualified chairman and two "wingmen."[42]

A common criticism of industrial tribunals has been that they have become increasingly "legalistic":

> "First, it is observed that the immense quantity of case law reported and cited in the courts is complicating the work of tribunals. Secondly, statutes, which were intended to be straightforward enactments, are increasingly being subjected to subtle lawyers' reasoning."[43]

Lord Denning has suggested that some limit be placed on the reporting of cases:

> "If we are not careful, we shall find the Industrial Tribunals bent down under the weight of the law books or, what is worse, asleep under them. Let principles be reported, but not particular instances."[44]

On the other hand, it has been suggested that growing "legalism" is inevitable given that the legislation is in fact complex and interpretative difficulties unavoidable, that there is a legally qualified chairman, that legal representation is increasingly common, that in practice litigants require consistency in decision-making, and that there must be a reliable yardstick for the conciliatory procedures incorporated in the legislation to work:

> "Naturally, tribunals will continue to dispense with the flummery and much of the procedural and evidential paraphernalia of the law courts—in this sense they are informal and comparatively free. But in most important respects, tribunals do closely resemble courts. Thus, if

---

[34] *Ibid.*, para. 572.
[35] Employment Protection (Consolidation) Act 1978, s.67.
[36] *Ibid.* s.11.
[37] Equal Pay Act 1970, as amended.
[38] Health and Safety at Work etc. Act 1974, ss.21–24.
[39] Sex Discrimination Act 1975, ss.63, 72, 73.
[40] Race Relations Act 1976, s.54.
[41] See the Industrial Tribunals (England and Wales) Regulations 1965 (S.I. 1965 No. 1101) as amended.
[42] See below, pp. 149–152.
[43] R. Munday, "Tribunal Lore: Legalism and the Industrial Tribunals" (1981) 10 I.L.J. 146, 147.
[44] *Walls Meat Co. Ltd.* v. *Khan* [1979] I.C.R. 52, 57, *cf.* Lawton L.J. in *Clay Cross (Quarry Services) Ltd.* v. *Fletcher* [1979] 1 All E.R. 474, 479.

charges of legalism mean that they interpret the law in legal fashion, one would expect to find these charges fully proven for it is quite impossible to see how else tribunals could be expected to behave."[45]

Industrial tribunals do not have jurisdiction over common law claims arising out of breaches of contracts of employment.[46] In accordance with the recommendation of the Donovan Commission they have not been given jurisdiction over tort actions arising out of accidents at work.

Appeals lie on a point of law[47] in most cases to the Employment Appeal Tribunal,[48] and in the others[49] to the Queen's Bench Division.

3. THE EMPLOYMENT APPEAL TRIBUNAL

The Employment Appeal Tribunal[50] was established by the Employment Protection Act 1975[51] as the successor of the politically controversial National Industrial Relations Court, inheriting the latter's appellate functions. Its membership comprises judges of the High Court or Court of Appeal[52] nominated by the Lord Chancellor, at least one judge of the Court of Session nominated by the Lord President of that court, and lay members appointed by the Queen on the recommendation of the Lord Chancellor and the Secretary of State, being persons who "appear . . . to have special knowledge or experience of industrial relations, either as representatives of employers or as representatives of workers."[53] One of the judges is appointed President. Each appeal is normally heard by a judge sitting with two or four lay members. Decisions can be by a majority, and the judge can be outvoted, even on a point of law, by the lay members. The E.A.T. hears appeals from industrial tribunals and from the Certification Officer, who performs various functions in respect of trade unions, mostly on points of law. The Court of Appeal has expressed the view that the E.A.T. has taken too wide a view of what constitutes an error of law and has thus interfered too readily with the decisions of industrial tribunals.[54] It suggested that the E.A.T. should be less ready to lay down

---

[45] Munday, *op. cit.* p. 159. On the procedure of industrial tribunals see below, pp. 470–475.

[46] Where there is a termination of employment these are termed claims for wrongful dismissal, to distinguish them from the statutory claims in respect of unfair dismissal arising out of the Employment Protection (Consolidation) Act 1978. There is a power, as yet unused, for industrial tribunals to be given jurisdiction over certain wrongful dismissal claims: 1978 Act, s.131.

[47] Fact or law where the question is whether a person has been unreasonably excluded or expelled from membership of a trade union in a closed shop situation.

[48] See below.

[49] *e.g.* industrial training levy assessments, appeals against an improvement or prohibition notice.

[50] A superior court of record. See Phillips J., "Some notes on the Employment Appeal Tribunal" (1978) 7 I.L.J. 137 and Brown-Wilkinson J., "The role of the EAT in the 1980s" (1982) 11 I.L.J. 69.

[51] See now the Employment Protection (Consolidation) Act 1978, ss.135, 136, Sched. 11.

[52] Only the former have so far been nominated. In 1983 there were eight High Court judges (including the President) and one judge of the Court of Session nominated to the E.A.T.

[53] The lay members do not in practice act in a partisan manner.

[54] See *Retarded Children's Aid Society* v. *Day* [1978] I.C.R 437; *Methven* v. *Cow Industrial Polymers Ltd.* [1980] I.C.R. 463; *Pedersen* v. *Camden London B.C.* [1981] I.C.R. 674; *Woods* v. *W.M. Car Services (Peterborough) Ltd.* [1982] I.C.R. 693; and the articles cited in n. 50 above. See also *O'Kelly* v. *Trusthouse Forte plc* [1983] I.C.R. 728.

"guidelines" for industrial tribunals. For example, whether a dismissal is "fair" should essentially be regarded as a question of fact. The consequent advantage of greater flexibility for industrial tribunals has to be balanced against the consequent inconsistency amongst them.[55]

Appeals lie on a point of law from the E.A.T. to the Court of Appeal,[56] with the leave of either court.

4. SOCIAL SECURITY TRIBUNALS[57]

A variety of cash benefits are available under the Social Security Act 1975 (*e.g.* unemployment benefit, invalidity and sickness benefit, retirement pension, widow's benefit, child's special allowance, death grant, maternity allowance, and non-contributory attendance, invalid care and mobility allowances), the Child Benefit Act 1975, the Family Income Supplements Act 1970 and the Supplementary Benefits Act 1976. Several tribunals have been established to determine questions arising in the administration of these benefits.

Two discernible trends in the development of the structure of social security tribunals have been, first, the amalgamation of different tribunal jurisdictions and, secondly, the integration of tribunals within the court system. In sections (a) and (b) we describe the position before amalgamation of National Insurance Local Tribunals and Supplementary Benefit Appeal Tribunals. Section (c) covers the position after amalgamation and section (d) the Social Security Commissioners.

(a) Social Security Act 1975; Child Benefit Act 1975

Claims and questions arising under these Acts[58] were determined initially by an insurance officer, a civil servant appointed by the Secretary of State for Social Services or, in relation to unemployment benefit, the Secretary of State for Employment. An appeal lay to a National Insurance Local Tribunal[59] comprising a legally-qualified chairman,[60] one member from a panel representing employers and self-employed earners and one from a panel representing employed earners.[61] A medical practitioner might sit with a tribunal as an assessor. The administrative arrangements were made by the clerk, a civil servant of the DHSS. Tribunals might meet in their own premises, in Town Halls or in rooms in DHSS offices set apart for the purpose. Research into the work of N.I.L.T.s showed that

[55] See Browne-Wilkinson J., *op. cit.* n. 50, p. 72: " . . . there are signs that . . . Industrial Tribunals are beginning to demonstrate a lack of uniformity in their approach to what constitutes fair industrial practice." His Lordship suggested that it would be desirable to aim for a middle way between the early practice of the E.A.T. and the restrictive approach of the Court of Appeal.

[56] In Scotland, appeals lie to the Court of Session.

[57] See generally A.I. Ogus and E.M. Barendt, *The Law of Social Security* (2nd ed., 1982) Chap. 15.

[58] Family allowances (the forerunner of Child Benefit) were brought into this system in 1959: previously, decisions were made by the Minister of Pensions and National Insurance with an appeal to a Referee (a barrister or advocate). The industrial injuries scheme was merged with the national insurance scheme in 1966.

[59] This term did not appear in the legislation, but was the title commonly used. Another label sometimes found was "Social Security Local Tribunal."

[60] This was not a legal requirement but was the almost invariable practice: see below, p. 151.

[61] Social Security Act 1975, s.97(2): see below, p. 151.

claimants were generally satisfied with the chairman and rather less so with the lay members. It was common for there to be criticism of the members' lack of participation in proceedings. Decisions could be by a majority but were usually unanimous.[62]

Certain questions, including whether a person is an "earner," whether he is "employed" or "self-employed" and whether he complies with "contribution conditions" necessary for receipt of contributory benefits, are still determined by the Secretary of State: in practice by a member of the DHSS Solicitors' Office.[63] The Secretary of State may refer a point of law, and a dissatisfied claimant may appeal on such a point, to the High Court.

Certain questions concerning disablement benefit are determined by "Medical Boards" of two medical practitioners, which also hear certain appeals on medical questions from the decisions of insurance officers. There is a right of appeal to a Medical Appeal Tribunal, comprising a legally qualified chairman and two doctors of consultant status.[64]

The Attendance Allowance Board,[65] most members of which are medical practitioners, determine whether the medical conditions for attendance allowance are satisfied. In practice the Board delegates the decision to a medical practitioner.

(b) Supplementary Benefits Act 1976; Family Income Supplements Act 1970

The administration of the supplementary benefit scheme has until recently rested on a significantly different basis than those mentioned in the previous section. A distinction was drawn between insurance schemes and the provision of means-tested benefits involving the exercise of discretion. Supplementary benefit, and its predecessors, unemployment assistance and then national assistance, fell into the latter category. In the 1930s, a right of appeal to an unemployment assistance tribunal was only established after some resistance, in order to make "an inherently unpopular reform more acceptable" and to protect the Ministry of Labour from the impact of parliamentary and public criticism.[66] The tribunals were heavily influenced by the Unemployment Assistance Board.[67] There were some changes in the structure of their successors, the national assistance tribunals, but the Franks Report endorsed the view that they were to be distinguished from N.I.L.T.s:

> "Although in form these Tribunals hear and determine appeals against decisions of local officers of the National Assistance Board and therefore exercise adjudicating functions, in practice their task much resembles that of an assessment or case committee, taking a further look at the facts and in some cases arriving at a fresh decision on the extent of need."[68]

---

[62] See generally K. Bell *et al.*, "National Insurance Local Tribunals: A Research Study" (1974) 3 *Journal of Social Policy* 289 and (1975) 4 *ibid*. 1.

[63] Social Security Act 1975, ss.93–95.

[64] *Ibid*. s.108.

[65] *Ibid*. Sched. 11.

[66] T. Lynes in M. Adler and A.W. Bradley (eds.) *Justice, Discretion and Poverty* (1976) pp. 5–8.

[67] *Ibid*. Chap. 2; G. Lach in R. Pollard (ed.) *Administrative Tribunals at Work* (1950).

[68] Cmnd. 218, 1957, p. 42.

The Report accepted that these tribunals should sit in private, as their hearings would involve the disclosure of the applicant's financial position, and recommended that there should be no further right of appeal either on the merits or on a point of law. They were renamed Supplementary Benefit Appeal Tribunals in 1966, without any change in structure. In the 1970s considerable attention was focused on S.B.A.T.s by researchers, and much of their comment was critical. The decision-making of S.B.A.T.s was described as "grossly inadequate." They "cannot distinguish policy from law, they allow presenting officers to introduce entirely irrelevant prejudicial matter, and they have little concept of how to weigh up evidence."[69] The comparison with N.I.L.T.s was unfavourable. A number of steps were taken to improve matters. A greater number of lawyer chairmen were appointed,[70] provision was made for the appointment of senior chairmen, the DHSS issued instructions emphasising the subordinate role of clerks, advice was given by the Council on Tribunals on the giving of reasons and a right of appeal was created. However, the most significant event was the replacement in 1980[71] of much of the discretion inherent in the system by detailed rules, in "about a dozen sets of regulations, some of which are difficult for lawyers to understand and almost all of which are wholly incomprehensible to laymen."[72] The "case committee" analysis of the Franks Report, which was always dubious, was clearly doomed.

S.B.A.T.s[73] comprised a chairman appointed by the Secretary of State from a panel drawn up by the Lord Chancellor, one "ordinary member" from a panel appointed by the Secretary of State from people "appearing to have knowledge or experience of conditions in the area to which the panel relates and of the problems of people living on low incomes" and one from a panel "appearing to the Secretary of State to represent workpeople."[74] The latter in practice were nominated by local County Assocations of Trades Councils. DHSS officers acted as clerks. Each S.B.A.T. sat for a district assigned by the Secretary of State. In addition to hearing appeals against decisions of benefit and supplement officers in relation to supplementary benefits, they were in 1970 given jurisdiction in respect of family income supplement, notwithstanding that little discretion was involved.

(c) Amalgamation

One of the consequences of the recent bout of "quango-hunting" has been the merger of N.I.L.T.s and S.B.A.T.s.[75] This is also the logical result of the reforms in the supplementary benefit scheme that have

---

[69] N. Lewis, "Supplementary Benefit Appeal Tribunals" [1973] P.L. 257, 258; *cf.* R. Lister, *Justice for the Claimant* (1974); K. Bell, *Research Study on S.B.A.T.s*; *Review of Main Findings, Conclusions and Recommendations* (H.M.S.O., 1975); A.W. Bradley, (1976) 27 N.I.L.Q. 96.

[70] See below, p. 151.

[71] Social Security Act 1980, Sched. 2.

[72] Ogus and Barendt (2nd ed., 1982), p. 454.

[73] See *Supplementary Benefit Appeal Tribunals: A Guide to Procedure* (H.M.S.O.).

[74] Supplementary Benefits Act 1976, Sched. 4.

[75] *Report on Non-Departmental Public Bodies* (Cmnd. 7797, 1980) p. 81.

brought it closer to the national insurance scheme. The Health and Social Services and Social Security Adjudications Act 1983[76] replaces insurance, benefit and supplement officers by "adjudication officers." Appeals will lie to "Social Security Appeal Tribunals." Each tribunal will comprise a chairman and two members. The chairman will be nominated by the "President of social security appeal tribunals and medical appeal tribunals," and can either be the President himself, a member of the panel appointed by the Lord Chancellor under section 7 of the Tribunals and Inquiries Act 1971, or a member of a panel appointed under a new provision inserted in the Social Security Act 1975.[77] The latter panel includes regional and other full-time chairmen of S.S.A.T.s. A barrister, advocate or solicitor of 10 years' standing may be appointed President and of seven years' standing to be a regional or full-time chairman. The President will also be responsible for assigning clerks and for arranging meetings of and training for tribunal chairmen and members. There are two members' panels, one composed of persons who appear to represent employed earners and the other of (1) persons who appear to represent employers and self-employed earners and (2) persons who appear to have knowledge or experience of conditions in the area and to represent persons living or working in it. Appointments to the panels will be made by the President rather than the Secretary of State.

(d) Social Security Commissioners[78]

The National Insurance Commissioners heard appeals from N.I.L.T.s, and appeals on a point of law from Medical Appeal Tribunals and the Attendance Allowance Board. In 1980, a right of appeal on a point of law was created from S.B.A.T.s to the Commissioners, who were renamed Social Security Commissioners.[79] From April 23, 1984 they will hear appeals from S.S.A.T.s.[79a] At present there is a Chief Social Security Commissioner and 13 Commissioners. In practice two sit in Edinburgh, one in Cardiff and the others in London. The Chief Commissioner may convene a Tribunal of these Commissioners to hear an appeal involving a point of law of special difficulty. He is also responsible for selecting the decisions that are to be reported. Until 1980, the only further possibility of review was an application for judicial review. There is now a right of appeal on a point of law to the Court of Appeal, with the leave of the Commissioner or the court.[80]

[76] Sched. 8: in force from April 23, 1984. See J. Mesher, (1983) 10 *Journal of Law and Society* 135.

[77] Sched. 10, para. 1A. These persons are also eligible to act as chairmen of Medical Appeal Tribunals.

[78] See R. Micklethwait, *The National Insurance Commissioners* (1976): below, p. 150. Under the 1946 legislation there was a National Insurance Commissioner and an Industrial Injuries Commissioner, each with several deputies. The same man commonly held appointments under both schemes. In 1966, these posts were merged, the National Insurance Commissioner was retitled the Chief National Insurance Commissioner, and the deputies became full Commissioners.

[79] Supplementary Benefits Act 1976, s.15A, inserted by the Social Security Act 1979, s.6. This replaced an appeal from S.B.A.T.s to the High Court that had been created in 1978.

[79a] Appeals concerning supplementary benefit or family income supplement will continue to be restricted to points of law (Social Security (Adjudication) Regulations 1984 (S.I. 1984 No. 451) Sched. 4), as will appeals from M.A.T.s and the A.A.B.

[80] Social Security Act 1980, s.14.

5. County Courts

(a) Establishment

The present county courts were originally established by the County Courts Act 1846. This Act followed a lengthy campaign, which aroused hostility in several quarters, including the Bar and certain large London solicitors' firms.[81] The hostility was based essentially on fears of loss of business to provincial attornies and solicitors. In the case of the Bar there was also resistance to the development of provincial Bars, which were seen to be the only effective way of competing for county court business.[82] The aim of the Act was to set up an effective local court for minor cases, and, in particular, the recovery of small debts: proceedings in the superior courts were prohibitively expensive and civil proceedings at the assizes were prone to delay. It is ironic that similar criticisms of ordinary county court proceedings in recent times have led to the development of new, more informal, procedures for small claims, and arguments that a further tier of small claims courts should be established.[83] Indeed, right from the outset the new courts were much more heavily used by shopkeepers, tradesmen, and other creditors than by ordinary people, their establishment leading to "an infinite expansion of credit."[84]

(b) Organisation

England and Wales is divided into districts and at least one court is held in each district.[85] The districts and locations are specified by the Lord Chancellor.[86]

(c) Judges

Under the original arrangements the districts were grouped into 60 county court circuits, each with its own judge appointed by the Lord Chancellor from barristers of at least seven years' standing. On the re-organisation of the criminal courts under the Courts Act 1971[87] the existing county court judges became Circuit judges.[88] Every Circuit judge is by virtue of his office capable of sitting as a judge for any county court district and at least one is assigned to each district by the Lord Chancellor.[89] The regular sittings are normally taken by the assigned judges. In addition, a registrar is appointed for each county court district by the Lord Chancellor, and assistant and deputy registrars may also be appointed, from solicitors of at least seven years' standing.[90] A registrar or

[81] See B. Abel-Smith and R. Stevens, *Lawyers and the Courts* (1967) pp. 32–37.
[82] See R. Cocks, *Foundations of the Modern Bar* (1983) pp. 25–26, 56–57.
[83] See below, pp. 409–414.
[84] Lord Westbury L.C., quoted by Abel-Smith and Stevens (1967) p. 35.
[85] County Courts Act 1984, s.1; Civil Courts Order 1983 (S.I. 1983 No. 713). The county court for the City of London is known as the Mayor's and City of London Court: the name is that of a court of similar jurisdiction abolished by the Courts Act 1971. The court is maintained by the City of London rather than the Department of the Environment.
[86] County Courts Act 1984, s.2.
[87] See below, pp. 64–66.
[88] See below, pp. 153–154.
[89] County Courts Act 1984, s.5. A judge of the Court of Appeal or the High Court or a recorder may also sit as a county court judge: *ibid.*
[90] County Courts Act 1984, ss.6–9. A deputy registrar is appointed as a temporary measure.

assistant registrar may not practise as a solicitor unless authorised to do so by the Lord Chancellor.[91] The main functions of the registrar are now judicial: he is responsible for procedural steps in court proceedings, this responsibility being analogous to those of Masters and Registrars of the High Court, and he tries or arbitrates most small claims. His administrative functions have now largely been transferred to the chief clerk or some other administrative officer, in accordance with the Lord Chancellor's directions.[92] County courts are administered by the unified court service.[93] There are substantial staffs of clerks and bailiffs.

(d) Jurisdiction

A county court has jurisdiction in almost the whole range of civil proceedings. In some matters the jurisdiction is exclusive, in others it is exercised concurrently with the High Court. In the latter event there is normally a monetary limit to the county court's jurisdiction, the "county court limit," specified by Order in Council.[94]

A county court may hear and determine the following matters—

(i) Contract and tort

An action founded on contract or tort where the amount claimed is not more than £5,000, whether the full original claim or the balance left after an arrangement or set off between the parties.[95] A plaintiff may abandon the excess of a claim over the limit to give the county court jurisdiction.[96] This head of jurisdiction covers the bulk of cases brought in the county court.

(ii) Actions in respect of land

An action for the recovery of land or in respect of title to any hereditament, or for an injunction or declaration relating to any land, where the net rateable value does not exceed £1,000.[97]

(iii) Equity proceedings

A variety of equity proceedings where the amount involved is not more than £30,000[98]: these include proceedings for the administration of the estate of a deceased person, for foreclosure or redemption of a mortgage, for the specific performance of an agreement for the sale of property, for the maintenance or advancement of an infant and for the dissolution of a

---

[91] County Courts Act 1984, s.10.

[92] County Court Rules 1981, Ord. 1, r.3.

[93] See below, p. 68.

[94] Made under section 145 of the County Courts Act 1984. The current limits are set by the County Court Jurisdiction Order 1981 (S.I. 1981 No. 1123) and s.147 of the 1984 Act.

[95] County Courts Act 1984, s.15. This head does not apply to actions for the recovery of land, any action where title to any hereditament is in question or any action for libel or slander: *ibid*. There is a similar jurisdiction in respect of money recoverable under a statute: *ibid*. s.16.

[96] *Ibid*. s.17.

[97] *Ibid*. ss.21, 22.

[98] *Ibid*. s.23. In addition, many specific powers under the Trustee Act 1925 and the Law of Property Act 1925 are conferred by the 1984 Act, Sched. 2.

partnership. These correspond to matters that would be dealt with in the Chancery Division of the High Court.

(iv) *Admiralty proceedings*

A variety of Admiralty matters,[99] such as claims for damage done by or to a ship, for loss or damage to goods carried in a ship, or for salvage, towage or pilotage. The jurisdictional limit is £5,000, except for salvage claims, where it is £15,000.[1] Only some county courts are appointed by the Lord Chancellor to take Admiralty proceedings, most of which are on or near the coast.

(v) *Probate proceedings*

Contentious matters arising in respect of the grant or revocation of probate or administration of estates where the value of the estate is less than £30,000.[2]

(vi) *Jurisdiction by agreement*

Matters outside the monetary limits where the parties confer jurisdiction on a county court by agreement.[3]

(vii) *Family matters*

Every matrimonial cause[4] must be commenced in a county court designated by the Lord Chancellor as a "divorce county court."[5] If a petition is defended it is transferred to the High Court.[6] If it is undefended it is dealt with by the divorce court provided that it has also been designated as a "court of trial," or transferred to such a court.[7] Other family matters may be dealt with by divorce county courts, or, in some cases, any county court. There is a concurrent jurisdiction with magistrates' courts and the High Court in adoption and guardianship matters.

(viii) *Other proceedings*

Jurisdiction in a large number of other matters is conferred by specific statutory provisions,[8] including hire-purchase, consumer credit, the Rent Acts, landlord and tenant, housing and sex discrimination. Designated county courts have jurisdiction in bankruptcy matters[9] and race relations.[10]

---

[99] County Courts Act 1984, ss.26, 27.

[1] Civil Courts Order 1983 (S.I. 1983 No. 713).

[2] County Courts Act 1984, s.32.

[3] *Ibid*. ss.18 (Queen's Bench Division matters), 24 (many equity proceedings), 27(6) (most Admiralty proceedings).

[4] *i.e.* an action for divorce, nullity of marriage, judicial separation or jactitation of marriage, or an application under section 3 of the Matrimonial Causes Act 1973 for leave to petition for divorce within three years of marriage: Matrimonial Causes Act 1967 s.10, as substituted by the Supreme Court Act 1981, Sched. 5.

[5] Matrimonial Causes Act 1967, s.1. Civil Courts Order 1983 (S.I. 1983 No. 713). In London, the Divorce Registry of the Family Division is deemed to be a county court for this purpose.

[6] See below, p. 73.

[7] Proceedings commenced in the Divorce Registry are dealt with by Circuit judges sitting as such in the Royal Courts of Justice.

[8] See the annual *County Court Practice* (the "Green Book").

[9] Civil Courts Order 1983 (S.I. 1983 No. 713).

[10] *Ibid.*

Appeals also lie to the county court in a number of administrative matters.[11]

(ix) *Jurisdiction of the registrar*

The registrar has jurisdiction:
  (1) to determine interlocutory applications;
  (2) to conduct pre-trial reviews;
  (3) to hear any action or matter
    —where the defendant fails to appear at the hearing or admits the claim;
    —where the amount involved does not exceed £500;
    —where jurisdiction is expressly conferred; or
    —with the leave of the judge and the consent of the parties.[12]

His determinations may be reviewed by the judge. The role of the registrar is particularly significant in family matters,[13] where (*inter alia*) he determines interlocutory applications and applications for ancillary relief,[14] and, in undefended divorces under the special procedure, where he examines the evidence and issues a certificate which enables the judge to pronounce the decree.

Where the amount involved is £500 or less, defended claims are referred for arbitration by the registrar unless he otherwise orders.[14a]

(e) The boundary between High Court and County Court

As regards those matters where there is concurrent jurisdiction with the High Court the usual arrangement is for there to be a maximum monetary limit for the county court, but no minimum limit for the High Court. There is, however, provision for the transfer of cases from High Court to county court, and vice versa, and for costs sanctions for those who use the High Court where there is no reason not to use the county court.

(i) *Transfer*[15]

(1) *High Court to county court.* Any proceedings in the High Court which a county court would have jurisdiction to hear,[16] apart from any monetary limit, may be transferred by the High Court to a county court either on its own motion or on the application of a party. One of the four conditions must be established—
  1. the parties consent to the transfer; or
  2. the High Court is satisfied that the subject matter in dispute is or is likely to be within the relevant county court jurisdictional limit; or
  3. where only a counterclaim remains in dispute, the High Court considers that the amount recoverable is likely to be within the relevant limit; or

---

[11] D. Price, *Appeals* (1982) pp. 46–49 lists 29 situations.
[12] County Court Rules 1981, Ord. 21, r. 5.
[13] See W. Barrington-Baker *et al.*, *The Matrimonial Jurisdiction of Registrars* (S.S.R.C., 1977).
[14] *e.g.* financial provision and adjustment of property rights on divorce.
[14a] See below, pp. 409–414, on small claims in the county court.
[15] County Courts Act 1984, ss.40–45. By comparison with the provisions replaced, the powers to transfer proceedings to or retain them in the county court have been strengthened.
[16] Excluding certain family law matters.

4. the High Court considers that the proceedings are not likely to raise any important question of law or fact and are suitable for determination by a county court.

The proceedings are transferred to such county court as the High Court considers convenient to the parties, and the county court may award any relief, including any amount of damages, which could have been awarded by the High Court.

(2) *County court to High Court by order of the High Court.* The High Court may order the transfer of the whole or any part of proceedings in a county court if it "thinks it desirable."

(3) *County court to High Court by order of the county court.* The whole or any part of the proceedings in a county court which the High Court would have jurisdiction to hear and determine may be transferred by the county court to the High Court either on its own motion or on the application of any party. The same family law matters are excluded as in respect of transfers the other way. One of three conditions must be established:

1. the court considers that some important question of law or fact is likely to arise; or

2. the court considers that one or other of the parties is likely to be entitled to an amount exceeding the amount recoverable in the county court; or

3. any counterclaim or set off and counterclaim of a defendant involves matters beyond the county court's jurisdiction.

(ii) *The costs sanction*

Given that there is no minimum limit for High Court jurisdiction it has been thought necessary to encourage litigants to use the county court by the imposition of a "costs sanction."[17] Thus, if an action in contract or tort is commenced in the High Court which could have been commenced in the county court,

—if a plaintiff recovers less than £3,000 he may only be awarded costs on the county court scale.

—if he recovers less than £600 he is not entitled to any costs.

This is so unless it appears either that there was reasonable ground for supposing the amount recoverable to be in excess of the county court limit or that there was sufficient reason for bringing the action in the High Court or that the defendant objected to transfer to the county court.

(f) Reform

(i) *Integration with the High Court*

From time to time it has been proposed that the county court should be integrated with the High Court.[18] The main advantage would be the ending of the existing differences in practice and procedure between two courts which to a significant extent exercise jurisdiction in respect of the same subject-matter. On the other hand, improvements can be and have been achieved by procedural reforms, without raising problems that integration

---

[17] County Courts Act 1984, ss.19, 20.

[18] See, *e.g.* Sir Jack Jacob, *The Reform of Civil Procedural Law* (1982) pp. 7–13.

would create such as the extension of rights of audience for solicitors. This last consideration has impelled the Bar to oppose increases in the monetary limits of county court jurisdiction,[19] although not always with success. Proposals for integration were considered and rejected by the Gorell Committee on County Court Procedure,[20] mainly on the ground that the county courts should not take larger cases which would affect prejudicially the handling of small claims, and by the Beeching Commission on Assizes and Quarter Sessions,[21] more on the ground that full consideration of the question would have seriously delayed their report. The current trend seems to be for the greater assimilation of the standard county court and High Court procedures, with a greater contrast between both of these and the small claims procedures.

(ii) *Monetary limits*

The limits are raised periodically. Other possible arrangements would include making the jurisdiction of the county court exclusive within its limit, unless leave is obtained for a hearing in the High Court.[22]

(g) Procedural Rules

The County Court Rules are made by a rule committee consisting of eleven persons appointed by the Lord Chancellor (five judges of county courts, two barristers, two registrars and two solicitors). They are subject to the approval of the Lord Chancellor, either as submitted or after amendment by him.[23] The rules were substantially revised in 1981 and are to be found in the current edition of the *County Court Practice* (the "Green Book").[24]

(h) Appeals[25]

Appeals lie to the Court of Appeal (Civil Division)[26] on questions of fact, law or evidence. The leave of either court is in general necessary if the claim is for an amount not exceeding half the relevant county court limit, or the matter came to the county court on appeal. In a few cases appeals lie to the High Court.[27]

6. THE CROWN COURT[28]

(a) The Beeching Royal Commission

In 1966 the Royal Commission on Assizes and Quarter Sessions was appointed, under the chairmanship of Lord Beeching, to inquire into the

---

[19] See B. Abel-Smith and R. Stevens, *Lawyers and the Courts* (1967) pp. 92–93, 249–250.
[20] 1908–09 H.C. 71.
[21] Cmnd. 4153, 1969, p. 73.
[22] This was recommended by the Payne Committee on the *Enforcement of Judgment Debts* in respect of debt recovery (Cmnd. 3909, 1969), paras. 119–120, but was not accepted.
[23] County Courts Act 1959, s.102.
[24] County Court Rules 1981, (S.I. 1981 No. 1687). See R.C.L. Gregory Q.C., "The Genesis of the County Court Rules" (1983) 2 C.J.Q. 1; F. Arnold L.A.G. Bull., November 1982, p. 121 and December 1982, p. 133.
[25] See generally, Chap. 19.
[26] See below, pp. 80–81, 721–722.
[27] *e.g.* bankruptcy matters are heard by the Divisional Court of the Chancery Division.
[28] See I.R. Scott, *The Crown Court* (1971).

arrangements for the administration of justice at assizes and quarter sessions outside London, and to report what reforms should be made for the more convenient, economic and efficient disposal of the civil and criminal business dealt with by those courts. The *assize courts* were presided over by High Court judges sent out "on circuit," a system that could be traced back to the twelfth century and which had changed comparatively little since medieval times.[29] There were seven circuits of assize towns. Assizes had jurisdiction over all indictable criminal offences and exclusive jurisdiction over some, including homicide, serious crimes of violence and rape. In addition, assize courts had the same civil jurisdiction as the High Court sitting in London, although priority was given to criminal cases. There were *courts of quarter sessions* for each of the 58 counties and for 93 boroughs; there were five such courts in Greater London and one for the City of London. The borough quarter sessions were presided over by a part-time Recorder, sitting alone. The county quarter sessions comprised a bench of magistrates normally with a legally qualified Chairman or Deputy Chairman, some of whom were whole-time appointments. These courts had jurisdiction to try many indictable offences with a jury, and to hear appeals from magistrates' courts and from a variety of administrative orders. In London, the *Central Criminal Court* at the Old Bailey was in effect the Assize court for criminal cases. It had a number of full time judges, including the Recorder of London and the Common Serjeant; in addition some cases would be taken by High Court judges. In 1956, new courts known as *Crown Courts* were established for Liverpool and Manchester to deal with both quarter sessions and assize work. A full time Recorder was appointed for each court. Responsibility for providing judges, court staff and court buildings was "as fragmented as the system itself."[30]

The Beeching Report identified many defects of assizes and quarter sessions and recommended a fundamental reorganisation. A number of features which a good court system should provide were identified[31]:

Convenience	(a) Ease of physical access.
	(b) An early hearing.
	(c) The assurance of trial on a date of which reasonable notice has been given.
	(d) Suitable accommodation.
Quality	(e) Judicial expertise.
	(f) Adequate and dependable legal representation.
Economy	(g) Efficient use of all manpower.
	(h) Optimum use of buildings.

The restricting factors were cost and the capacity of the Bar. The report's proposals were designed to[32]:

"(a) simplify the structure of the courts;

(b) deploy judge power as flexibly as possible;

[29] See above, p. 29. Additional "Commissioners of Assize," usually senior Q.C.s, could be appointed ad hoc.

[30] Beeching Report, p. 31.

[31] *Ibid.* p. 48.

[32] *Ibid.* p. 64.

(c) relate court locations to travelling facilities for the public;
(d) secure the efficient administration of all court services;
(e) ensure that courts are built and maintained as economically and efficiently as possible."

The proposals, which involved the creation of a new superior court of criminal jurisdiction, to be called the Crown Court, were largely accepted. They were enacted in the Courts Act 1971, substantial parts of which were re-enacted in the Supreme Court Act 1981.

(b) The constitution of the Crown Court

The Crown Court is part of the Supreme Court of England and Wales.[33] It is a single court, but sittings may be conducted at any place in England and Wales, in accordance with directions given by the Lord Chancellor.[34] There are at present over 90 centres and over 130 separate court houses.[35] The name "Central Criminal Court" has been retained for the Crown Court sitting in the City of London. There are three kinds of Crown Court centre: "first-tier" centres are visited by High Court judges, Circuit judges and recorders for the complete range of Crown Court business, and by High Court judges for High Court civil work; "second-tier" centres are the same as first-tier except that no civil business is done; "third-tier" centres are visited only by Circuit judges and recorders. The centres are grouped into six circuits: Midland and Oxford, North Eastern, Northern, South Eastern, Wales and Chester and Western.[36]

The jurisdiction of the Crown Court is exerciseable by any judge of the High Court, Circuit judge or recorder.[37] In some cases one of these may sit with not more than four justices of the peace[38]: a court must normally be so comprised when hearing an appeal or proceedings on committal for sentence,[39] and may be so comprised for trying certain offences.[40]

(c) Jurisdiction

The Crown Court has exclusive jurisdiction with respect to criminal trials on indictment.[41] It also has an extensive appellate jurisdiction inherited from quarter sessions, including appeals from magistrates' courts in criminal cases and appeals in a wide variety of administrative matters, such as betting, gaming and liquor licensing. Magistrates' courts may also commit convicted persons to the Crown Court for sentence.

(d) Distribution of business

The classes of cases in the Crown Court suitable for allocation respectively to a High Court judge, Circuit judge or recorder, and to a court including justices, are prescribed in directions given by the Lord

---

[33] Supreme Court Act 1981, s.1. Procedural rules can be prescribed by the Crown Court Rule Committee: *ibid.* s.86.

[34] *Ibid.* s.78.

[35] See *Shaw's Directory of Courts in the United Kingdom.*

[36] See H.L. Deb. Vol. 314, col. 948, January 26, 1971; H.L. Deb. Vol. 321, col. 572, July 1, 1971; H.L. Deb. Vol. 343, col. 968, June 14, 1973.

[37] Supreme Court Act 1981, s.8. See below pp. 153–154.

[38] *Ibid.* and see below, pp. 147–148.

[39] Supreme Court Act 1981, s.74; Crown Court Rules 1982 (S.I. 1982 No. 1109).

[40] See below, p. 67.

[41] Supreme Court Act 1981, s.46.

Chief Justice, with the concurrence of the Lord Chancellor.[42] For the purposes of trial in the Crown Court, offences are grouped in four classes.

Class 1

These offences are to be tried by a High Court judge and include any offence carrying the death penalty, murder, genocide and offences under section 1 of the Official Secrets Act 1911.

Class 2

These offences are to be tried by a High Court judge unless a particular case is released by or on the authority of a presiding judge, and include manslaughter, infanticide, abortion, rape, sexual intercourse with a girl under 13 and sedition.

Class 3

These offences may be listed for trial by a High Court judge, or a Circuit judge, or a recorder, and comprise all offences triable only on indictment other than those in classes, 1, 2 and 4.

Class 4

These may be tried by a High Court judge, Circuit judge or recorder, but are normally listed for trial by a Circuit judge or recorder, and include (1) all offences triable either way; (2) any Class 3 offences included in directions given by a presiding judge; and (3) a number of specific offences including wounding, causing grievous bodily harm and robbery.

The allocation decision in a class 2 case is taken by the presiding judge, and in a class 3 or 4 case by the listing officer after consultation with the presiding judge, or a judge acting for him, or in accordance with directions given by a presiding judge. A number of considerations are set out as favouring trial of a case in classes 3 or 4 by a High Court judge: the case involves (i) death or serious risk to life (other than reckless driving cases with no aggravating features); (ii) widespread public concern; (iii) serious violence; or (iv) dishonesty in respect of a substantial sum of money; (v) the accused holds a public position or is a professional or other person owing a duty to the public; (vi) the circumstances are otherwise of unusual gravity; (vii) a novel or difficult issue of law is likely to be involved, or a prosecution for the offence is rare or novel.[43] In a class 4 case the officer must bear in mind any views expressed by the justices who committed the defendant for trial.

Most other Crown Court proceedings are normally listed for hearing by a court presided over by a Circuit judge or a recorder. Any proceedings listed for hearing by a Circuit judge or recorder are stated to be suitable for allocation to a court including justices of the peace.

The same Practice Direction prescribes the general principles for the distribution of business among the different court centres geographically. Generally, the magistrates committing for trial should select the "most convenient location" of the appropriate tier of Crown Court centre, having regard to the convenience of defence, prosecution and witnesses and the

---

[42] Supreme Court Act 1981, s.75; *Practice Direction (Crime: Crown Court Business)* [1971] 1 W.L.R. 1535, as amended by [1978] 1 W.L.R. 926. Other amendments of this Direction, dealing with matters other than the classification of offences, are to be found at [1971] 1 W.L.R. 1763; [1973] 1 W.L.R. 73; [1974] 1 W.L.R. 441; [1981] 1 W.L.R. 1324.

[43] *Ibid.* para. 2.

expediting of the trial,[44] and to the location or locations designated by the presiding judge as the normal ones for committals from their petty sessions area. It is possible for the location to be changed.[45] In addition, the "catchment areas" are varied if the work-load at a particular Crown Court centre requires cases to be directed to a less busy centre.

(e) Administration

Another important feature of the Beeching Report and the Courts Act 1971 was the establishment of a "unified court service" under the direction of the Lord Chancellor, providing administrative support to the Supreme Court, including the Crown Court and county courts.[46] The service is organised on a circuit basis. The administration in each circuit is headed by a Circuit Administrator, a civil servant of Under Secretary rank responsible to the Lord Chancellor. Each of these has a small headquarters staff and three or four Courts Administrators working under him, each responsible for a particular area.[47] Each court has a chief clerk responsible to one of the Courts Administrators. The Circuit Administrators work closely with the presiding judges and deal with such matters as personnel management, finance and accommodation. The Courts Administrator has responsibility for planning the courts' sittings and ensuring the smooth disposal of business between courts, and is a point of contact for the various parties concerned with the running of the courts.

Two[48] High Court judges are assigned to each circuit by the Lord Chief Justice to act as presiding judges: at least one should be present in the circuit at any given time. Presiding judges have certain functions in relation to the allocation of cases.[49]

Their position has been summarised as follows[50]:

> "The presiding judges are the judicial authority for the circuit paralleling the administrative authority of the Circuit Administrators. . . . Where they perform properly (and there is some unevenness) the presiding judges make a substantial effort to control judicial performance on their circuits. They know the capabilities of the Circuit judges and in consultation with the Circuit Administrators they see that these judges are properly assigned and utilised according to skill and expertise."

However, it has also been noted that the presiding judges frequently lack confidence when dealing with their more senior colleagues, that some do not capture the respect of Circuit judges in their circuit, that there is too much doubt as to their proper role, that uncertainty is created by the fact that so much depends on the respective personalities of presiding judge and Circuit Administrator and that the judge's position is weakened by the

---

[44] Magistrates' Courts Act 1980, s.7.

[45] Supreme Court Act 1981, s.76.

[46] Courts Act 1971, s.27. See I.R. Scott, *The Crown Court* (1971) Chap. IV; E.C. Friesen and I.R. Scott, *English Criminal Justice* (1977) pp. 121–5 and I.R. Scott, *Court Administration: The Case for a Judicial Council* (1979).

[47] There is a Courts Administrator responsible for the Central Criminal Court.

[48] There are three for the South Eastern circuit, including the Lord Chief Justice.

[49] See above, p. 67.

[50] Friesen and Scott (1977) p. 124.

fact that appointments are only for short periods.[51] A Lord Justice of Appeal has been appointed as a senior presiding judge who will be available for consultation by the presiding judges and who will relieve the Lord Chief Justice of certain administrative responsibilities.[52]

(f) Workload

The workload of the Crown Court has increased significantly since it was established:

> "It is undoubtedly true to say that in the light of the inexorable increase in caseloads chaos would have ensued but for the implementation of the Beeching Reforms. The number of persons working in the court service is now about 10,000 and the range of quasi-judicial and administrative tasks undertaken by this bureaucracy is far greater and much more sophisticated than those attempted under the pre-1971 arrangements."[53]

Other important factors have been the establishment of the circuit bench and the increase in the number of High Court judges, and the court-building programme. Nevertheless, the increase in workload has meant that waiting times have increased dramatically.[54]

(g) Appeals[55]

Appeals in relation to trials on indictment and in cases where a defendant has been committed for sentence to the Crown Court lie to the Court of Appeal (Criminal Division).[56] Appeals from an exercise of the Crown Court's appellate jurisdiction lie to the High Court on the same basis as appeals there from the magistrates' court.

7. THE HIGH COURT

(a) Constitution

The High Court of Justice is a court of unlimited civil jurisdiction and also has an important appellate jurisdiction in both civil and criminal matters. It is part of the Supreme Court of England and Wales,[57] and was created as part of the reorganisation of the superior courts under the Supreme Court of Judicature Acts 1873–75. It sits at the Royal Courts of Justice in the Strand[58] and at 24 first-tier Crown Court centres outside

---

[51] Scott (1979) p. 16.

[52] (1983) 133 N.L.J. 732.

[53] Scott (1979) p. 5.

[54] In 1973, of the 13,925 defendants disposed of on indictment and who had awaited trial in custody, 74 per cent. were dealt with within 8 weeks of committal and 96 per cent. within 20 weeks. In 1980 the figures were 16,088, 54 per cent. and 87 per cent. respectively, improving in 1981 to 17,917, 59 per cent. and 91 per cent. respectively. See generally, I.R. Scott, "Crown Court Productivity" [1980] Crim.L.R. 193, noting the growing proportion of not guilty pleas and the lengthening of hearing times in contested cases.

[55] See generally, Chap. 19, below.

[56] See below, pp. 78–79, 705–715.

[57] The Supreme Court was thus re-titled by the Supreme Court Act 1981.

[58] The Supreme Court moved here from Westminster Hall in 1883. See F.W. Maitland (1942) 8 C.L.J. 2; J. Kinnard in P. Ferriday (ed.) *Victorian Architecture* (1963); M.H. Port, "The New Law Courts Competition, 1866–67" (1968) *Architectural History* 75–93.

London.[59] There are three divisions: the Chancery Division, Queen's Bench Division and Family Division,[60] headed, respectively, by the Vice-Chancellor,[61] the Lord Chief Justice and the President of the Family Division.[62] Each High Court judge[63] is attached to one of the divisions, but he may be transferred to one of the others with his consent, and he may act as an additional judge of one of them at the request of the Lord Chancellor.[64] Different classes of business are allocated for administrative convenience to each division by rules of court,[65] although technically all the jurisdiction of the High Court belongs to all the divisions alike.[66] There have been two major reorganisations. In 1881 the Exchequer and Common Pleas Divisions were merged into the Queen's Bench Division,[67] and in 1971 the Probate, Divorce and Admiralty Division was re-named the Family Division, with Admiralty business assigned to the Queen's Bench Division, probate business other than non-contentious or common form matters assigned to the Chancery Division, and wardship, guardianship and adoption jurisdiction transferred from Chancery Division to Family Division.[68]

Most High Court work is taken by a single judge sitting alone.[69] This should be in open court, except where under rules of court or in accordance with the practice of the court it is dealt with in chambers.[70] A proportion of the appellate and supervisory work of the High Court is dealt with by "divisional courts," which comprise two or more judges.[71]

The business is mainly conducted by the heads of division and the puisne judges of the High Court. In addition, High Court work may be taken by a deputy High Court judge, a Circuit judge, a recorder, a judge of the Court of Appeal or a former judge of the High Court or the Court of Appeal.[72]

(b) The Chancery Division

The division deals with property, trusts, the administration of estates, bankruptcy, partnership, companies, revenue cases, probate business other than non-contentious common form business, and other matters

---

[59] See above, p. 66.

[60] Supreme Court Act 1981, s.5(1). The number of divisions can be altered by order in Council: *ibid*. s.7.

[61] Technically, the Lord Chancellor is the president and the Vice-Chancellor the vice-president of the Chancery Division, but the latter is the effective head.

[62] See below, pp. 156, 157.

[63] See below, p. 154.

[64] Supreme Court Act 1981, s.5(2) (3).

[65] Supreme Court Act 1981, s.61.

[66] *Ibid*. s.5(5). Any Division to which a cause or matter is assigned has jurisdiction to grant any remedy or relief sought notwithstanding that proceedings for such remedy or relief are assigned to another Division: *Practice Direction (High Court: Divisions)* [1973] 1 W.L.R. 627.

[67] This was done by an Order in Council which was made on December 16, 1880 and which came into force on February 26, 1881.

[68] Administration of Justice Act 1970, with effect from August 2, 1971.

[69] There is provision for a judge to sit with assessors who are specially qualified in relation to the proceedings in question: 1981 Act, s.70. They are mainly used in Admiralty proceedings. See below, p. 540.

[70] Supreme Court Act 1981, s.67.

[71] *Ibid*. s.66.

[72] *Ibid*. s.9.

specifically assigned.[73] The Patents Court established in 1977[74] is part of this division. In addition the judges of the division have been assigned to deal with the management of the property and affairs of mental patients under the Mental Health Act 1983. This work is the responsibility of the "Court of Protection" which is in fact an office of the Supreme Court rather than a court.

The business is at present handled by the Vice-Chancellor and 12 puisne judges, two of whom are nominated to the Patents Court although they are available to help with the other work of the Division. The judges are assisted by six Chancery masters and four registrars in bankruptcy.[75] The work is done in London and at eight centres in the provinces.[76] In the latter the work is done by Circuit judges who specialise in Chancery work and who sit for this purpose as judges of the High Court.[77]

The administrative arrangements for the Chancery Division were substantially revised in 1982[78] following the Report of the Review Body on the Chancery Division of the High Court.[79] Amongst other matters the changes were designed to produce greater flexibility in the deployment of judges and a new approach to the drafting of orders "which should eliminate their present sesquipedalian pedantry."[80] As from October 1, 1982, orders have been simpler in form and drawn by clerks (known as associates) rather than professionally qualified officers, thus bringing practice more into line with the other divisions.

(c) The Queen's Bench Division

This Division deals mainly with claims in contract and tort, and also exercises supervisory and appellate jurisdiction over inferior courts and tribunals. The supervisory jurisdiction includes most applications for habeas corpus and all applications for judicial review.[81] The appellate jurisdiction includes appeals by case stated on a point of law from Magistrates' courts and the Crown Court. Also part of this division are the Admiralty Court and the Commercial Court.[82] The work is at present

---

[73] *Ibid.* Sched. 1. The judges who deal with bankruptcy are referred to as the "High Court of Justice in Bankruptcy" and those who deal with company matters as the "Companies Court," but these are not formally constituted as courts under the 1981 Act.

[74] Patents Act 1977. The judge may sit with scientific advisers: Supreme Court Act 1981, s.70.

[75] See R.E. Ball, "The Chancery Master" (1961) 77 L.Q.R. 331.

[76] Leeds, Liverpool, Manchester, Newcastle-upon-Tyne, Preston, and, as from October 10, 1982. Birmingham, Bristol and Cardiff. See *Practice Direction (Proceedings outside London)* [1972] 1 W.L.R. 1 and *(No. 2)* [1973] 1 W.L.R. 657; *Practice Direction (Chancery Chambers)* [1982] 1 W.L.R. 1189; *Practice Direction (Chancery: Proceedings Outside London)* [1984] 1 W.L.R. 417.

[77] See below, p. 153. They may also take equity work in county courts.

[78] See R.S.C. (Amendment No. 2) 1982 (S.I. 1982 No. 1111); *Practice Direction (Chancery Chambers)*. n. 76 above.

[79] Cmnd. 8205, 1981: report by Oliver L.J. and J.M. Woolf Esq.: see R. Blackford, (1981) 78 L.S.Gaz. 590.

[80] Blackford (1981) p. 590.

[81] Supreme Court Act 1981, s.61 and Sched. 1. See below, pp. 742–749.

[82] Supreme Court Act 1981, s.6.

handled by the Lord Chief Justice[83] and 49 puisne judges. The business is done in London and at the 24 first-tier Crown Court centres in the provinces.

In London, the judges are assisted by 11[84] masters of the Queen's Bench Division. A master can perform all the functions of the High Court or a judge in chambers, with certain exceptions, and, with the parties' consent, may try actions.[85] Much of the work involves the determination of interlocutory applications.[86] One master sits each day as the Practice Master, to deal with procedural and practice problems arising in the Central Office and generally to supervise the work of the office. The right of audience before a master is not limited to barristers; solicitors and their clerks may appear, including unadmitted clerks. The work is normally done in chambers, which lead off from an ante-chamber generally known as "the Bear Garden."

(i) The Admiralty Court

This court has jurisdiction in a wide variety of matters concerning ships and aircraft, including claims arising out of collisions, claims for damage to cargo, for goods supplied and for repairs.[87] When necessary, it also exercises the jurisdiction of the High Court as a prize court.[88]

(ii) The Commercial Court

There were a number of attempts in the nineteenth century to establish some form of specialised commercial court.[89] A Commercial List was established in the Queen's Bench Division in 1895, partly as the result of dissatisfaction with the handling of a commercial case by Lawrance J.[90] This did not, however, end the drift to arbitration.[91] The list was transformed into a court in 1970.[92] The interlocutory stages are handled by the judge rather than a master and pleadings must be "as brief as possible."[93] A judge of the Commercial Court may be appointed as an arbitrator, provided the Lord Chief Justice informs him that he can be made available.[94]

---

[83] The Lord Chief Justice's time is mainly spent on appellate criminal work in the Divisional Court of the Queen's Bench Division or the Court of Appeal (Criminal Division). He no longer takes applications for judicial review at first instance, but sits in administrative law matters in the Court of Appeal (Civil Division).

[84] This figure includes the Master of the Crown Office, who is also Registrar of the Criminal Appeal Office.

[85] See A.S. Diamond, "The Queen's Bench Master" (1960) 76 L.Q.R. 504; Sir Jack Jacob, "The Masters of the Queen's Bench Division" (1971) reprinted in The Reform of Civil Procedural Law (1982); R.S.C. Ords. 36, 63.

[86] e.g. in relation to the extension of time, pleadings, striking out, discovery, summons for directions, summary judgment under R.S.C., Ord. 14: see pp. 415–438.

[87] Supreme Court Act 1981, ss.20–24.

[88] Ibid. s.62.

[89] A.D. Colman, The Practice and Procedure of the Commercial Court (1983) Chap. 1.

[90] See below, p. 161; (1895–96) 1 Com.Cas. pp. i–x; MacKinnon L.J. (1944) 60 L.Q.R. 324–325; Lord Parker C.J., History and Development of Commercial Arbitration (1959).

[91] See G. Wilson, Cases and Materials on the English Legal System (1973) pp. 31–43; R.B. Ferguson, "The Adjudication of commercial disputes and the legal system in modern England" (1980) 7 B.J.L.S. 141.

[92] Administration of Justice Act 1970, s.3(1).

[93] R.S.C., Ord. 72, rr. 2, 7; Practice Statement (1979) 123 S.J. 132.

[94] Administration of Justice Act 1970, s.4.

A Commercial Court Committee was established in 1977 to consider and keep under review the working of the Court and the appeal procedures in arbitration proceedings, and to report to the Lord Chancellor.[95] A report of this committee[96] led to the enactment of the Arbitration Act 1979, which was designed to limit rights of appeal to the courts from the decisions of arbitrators, and thereby to halt a decline in the standing of London as a leading centre of international commercial arbitration.[97]

In recent years the caseload of the Commercial Court has increased significantly,[98] although it is still small in relation to the number of arbitrations. Three features of its work are that in many cases either one or both litigants are foreigners, that a significant part of the court's work comes from London arbitrations, and that it is commonplace for cases to involve millions of pounds.[99]

(d) The Family Division

This division exercises the matrimonial and domestic jurisdiction of the High Court, which includes defended divorce cases[1] and matters relating to the wardship, guardianship, custody, maintenance or adoption of children, and deals with non-contentious or common form probate business. It also hears appeals from magistrates' courts in domestic proceedings.[2] The work is at present handled by the President, 16 puisne judges, and 14 registrars of the Family Division. It is done in London and at first-tier Crown Court centres.[3]

Many important aspects of High Court family work are dealt with by the registrars of the Family Division and district registrars, including decisions on ancillary matters (*e.g.* maintenance, adjustment of property rights and the arrangements for access to children).

A number of proposals have been made for the establishment of "family courts."[4] Under the present system, there is jurisdictional confusion as between magistrates' courts, county courts and the High Court, and there are also discrepancies in the substantive law applied and doubt as to whether a system of accusatorial hearings is appropriate for family matters. The Finer Committee on One Parent Families[5] recommended the establishment of family courts to take over all family matters dealt with in

---

[95] See its Annual Report for 1980 (1981) 78 L.S.Gaz. 100; Colman (1983), Chap. 2.

[96] Commercial Court Committee, *Report on Arbitration* (Cmnd. 7284, 1978).

[97] See Ferguson (1980) pp. 151–154, Kerr J., "The Arbitration Act 1979" (1980) 43 M.L.R. 45.

[98] The number of cases heard and disposed of increased from an average of 20 a year between 1946 and 1959 (*Report of the Commercial Court Users' Conference* (Cmnd. 1616, 1962) Appendix G) to figures of 110 (1978), 118 (1979) and 125 (1980): (1981) 78 L.S.Gaz. 100). The figures for 1981 and 1982 were 157 and 153: Colman (1983) p. 17.

[99] Goff. J., "The Commercial Court—How it Works" (1980) 77 L.S.Gaz. 1035. See generally on the working of the court, Colman, *op. cit.*

[1] See above, p. 61.

[2] Supreme Court Act 1981, Sched. 1. See above, p. 50.

[3] Most of these have been designated as "divorce towns" for the purpose of hearing defended matrimonial causes and ancillary applications: see *Practice Direction* (*Divorce Towns: Defended Causes*) [1971] 1 W.L.R. 1762; Matrimonial Causes Rules 1977 (S.I. 1977 No. 344) rr. 2, 43, 44. The cases here may be dealt with by High Court judges or Circuit judges sitting as High Court judges.

[4] See S. Cretney, *Principles of Family Law* (3rd ed., 1979), Chap. 27.

[5] Cmnd. 5629, 1974.

magistrates' courts, county courts and the High Court. The family courts would be organised in tiers, on the analogy of the Crown Court. The lowest tier would comprise Circuit judges and magistrates and sit in county courts: magistrates' court buildings would not be used. There would be facilities for conciliation and support by a professional welfare service. The government has, however, been unwilling to provide extra court buildings or add to the workload of the circuit bench. Moreover, many of the significant differences between the law applicable by the High Court and county court on the one hand and by magistrates' courts on the other, have been removed,[6] and moves have been made to keep the domestic jurisdiction of magistrates' courts separate from criminal proceedings.[7] The number of cases dealt with by magistrates has not declined to the extent at one time thought.[8] Accordingly, the only changes likely appear to involve the rationalisation of the allocation of family business between the High Court and county courts, possibly involving the merger of the family jurisdiction of each court into a new single court which would be part of the Supreme Court.[9]

(e) Official Referees' business

There are four Circuit judges nominated by the Lord Chancellor to deal with "Official Referees' business."[10] This is business appropriate to be dealt with by an official referee (as these judges are still commonly known) because (a) it involves a prolonged examination of documents or accounts or a technical, scientific or local investigation, or (b) because that is in the interests of one or more of the parties on grounds of expedition, economy or convenience or otherwise.[11] A matter for trial may either be commenced as official referees' business or transferred to a referee.[12] A matter may also be referred for inquiry and report concerning any issue of fact.[12a]

In practice, official referees' business:

"covers a surprisingly wide range of subject matter, but much of it involves very substantial building and civil engineering claims with allied disputes about the provision of materials and services, often

[6] Domestic Proceedings and Magistrates' Courts Act 1978.

[7] See the Justices' Clerks' Society, *Resolving Family Conflict in the 1980s* (1982); "Making the Domestic Proceedings Act Work: A joint declaration by the Magistrates' Association and the Justices' Clerks' Society" (1982) 146 J.P.N. 756–758; C. Latham, "Magistrates' courts and the family jurisdiction: A re-assessment of the Finer Concept of Family Court" (1983) 147 J.P.N. 233–236, 246–247.

[8] "The Domestic Court: A declining jurisdiction" (1982) 146 J.P.N. 754–755; (1984) 148 J.P.N. 179–180.

[9] Lord Chancellor's Department, *Family Jurisdiction of the High Court and County Courts, A Consultative Paper* (1983). See J. Levin, L.A.G. Bull., March 1983, pp. 5–6. For other proposals see G.G. Brown, "A Two-Tier Family Court" (1983) 133 N.L.J. 310; "The Family Court—A New and Practical Proposal" (1983) 13 *Family Law* 63 G. Roberts (1984) 14 Br. J. Social Work 285.

[10] Supreme Court Act 1981, s.68. See E. Fay, *Official Referees' Business* (1983); F. Meisel, (1984) 3 C.J.Q. 97. The office of Official Referee, first established by the Supreme Court of Judicature Act 1873, was abolished by the Courts Act 1971. Existing holders became Circuit judges: 1971 Act, Sched. 2. On each circuit other than the South Eastern two Circuit judges are appointed to conduct this business, although most is taken in London. The Lord Chancellor has authorised an increase in the establishment of official referees to six: H.C. Deb. Vol. 57, col. 628 March 30, 1984.

[11] R.S.C., Ord. 36, rr., 1, as substituted by S.I. 1982 No. 1111, para. 100.

[12] *Ibid.* rr. 2, 3.   [12a] *Ibid.* r. 8.

including a technical or design element, together with the associated liabilities of architects, engineers, surveyors and other professional men."[13]

An Official Referees' Users Committee and an Official Referees' Bar Association have recently been established.[14]

(f) Administration

Administrative support for the High Court is provided by officials who are technically part of the unified court service.[15] Apart from the masters and registrars appointed under the Supreme Court Act 1981 the officials are civil servants who are members of the Lord Chancellor's department.[16] In London, the principal offices are the Central Office of the Supreme Court, Chancery Chambers, the Principal Registry of the Family Division,[17] the Admiralty Registry and the Accounting Department.

Outside London there are district registries of the High Court in about 130 locations.[18] A county court registrar[19] is appointed by the Lord Chancellor as district registrar for each registry,[20] and there is provision for the appointment of deputy and assistant district registrars.[21] Writs and originating summonses in the Queen's Bench Division may be issued in any district registry; writs and originating summonses in most Chancery actions may be issued out of eight Chancery district registries[22] and in certain specified cases out of any district registry.[22a] The other interlocutory steps are also taken here. Matrimonial causes and most other proceedings in the Family Division may be dealt with at those district registries that have a divorce county court within its district,[23] although they can only be tried at the Royal Courts or one of the divorce towns.[24] There are district probate registries in 11 places and sub-registries in 18 others.[25] District probate registrars are appointed by the Lord Chancellor.[26]

(g) Procedural rules

Rules for the purpose of regulating and prescribing the practice and procedure to be followed in the High Court and Court of Appeal may be

[13] "Referens", "Official Referee's Business—A New Dawn?" (1983) 80 L.S.Gaz. 478, 479. The author noted a trend away from arbitration to official referees in professional negligence cases.

[14] *Ibid.*

[15] The Review Body on the Chancery Division found that the establishment of the service had had little impact on the Division, and were highly critical of the Division's administrative arrangements.

[16] Appointed under the Courts Act 1971, s.27.

[17] Referred to as Principal Probate Registry or the Divorce Registry depending on which branch of the Division's work is concerned.

[18] Supreme Court Act 1981, s.99; Civil Courts Order 1983 (S.I. 1983 No. 713).

[19] See above, pp. 59–60.

[20] Supreme Court Act 1981, s.100.   [21] *Ibid.* ss.102, 103.

[22] *i.e.* the district registries for the eight centres mentioned above, p. 71, n. 76.

[22a] See R. Blackford and C. Jacque, *Chancery Practice Handbook* (1983) pp. 78–80, 100–101.

[23] See the Matrimonial Causes Rules 1977 (S.I. 1977 No. 344), r. 2 (definition of "district registry" for the purpose of the rules), r. 43; R.S.C., Ord. 9, rr. 3, 5, 17.

[24] Above, p. 73, n. 3.

[25] Supreme Court Act 1981, s.104; District Probate Registries Order 1982 (S.I. 1982 No. 379).

[26] Supreme Court Act 1981, s.89, Sched. 2.

made by the Supreme Court Rule Committee.[27] Most cases[28] are regulated
by the Rules of the Supreme Court.[29] These first appeared in 1885 and the
most recent major revision was in 1965. They are regularly amended, and
are printed, with extensive annotations, in the current edition of *The
Supreme Court Practice* (known as the "White Book"). The rules may not
alter any matter of substantive law.[30] In 1982, a Supreme Court Procedure
Committee was established by the Lord Chief Justice and the other heads
of the divisions, in conjunction with the Presidents of the Senate and The
Law Society, to consider and recommend reforms in practice and
procedure for saving time and costs. Their recommendations will be placed
before the Rule Committee.[31]

(h) Appeals[32]

Appeals lie either to the Court of Appeal (Civil Division)[33] or direct to
the House of Lords.[34] The appeal lies direct to the House of Lords where
the case has reached the High Court on appeal from a magistrates' court or
the Crown Court in a criminal matter, or, otherwise, under the "leap frog"
procedure.

8. THE LANDS TRIBUNAL

The Lands Tribunal was set up in 1949[35] to take over the jurisdiction of
official arbitrators to determine disputes concerning the assessment of
compensation for the compulsory acquisition of land. It consists of a
President,[36] who must be a person who has held judicial office or a
barrister of at least seven years' standing, a number of members who are
barristers or solicitors of seven years' standing, and a number who are
persons with experience in land valuation (*i.e.* qualified surveyors). All are
appointed by the Lord Chancellor, the valuation experts after consultation
with the president of the Royal Institute of Chartered Surveyors. The
Tribunal's jurisdiction may be exercised by any one or more of its
members, as selected by the President, and the selection depends on the

[27] Supreme Court Act 1981, ss.84, 85. The Committee comprises the heads of division,
three High Court judges, two practising barristers and two solicitors. See Sir Jack Jacob, "The
Machinery of the Rule Committee of the Supreme Court" (1971) reprinted in *The Reform of
Civil Procedural Law* (1982).

[28] There are separate sets of rules for bankruptcy, the winding up of companies,
non-contentious or common form probate proceedings, prize matters, certain proceedings
under the Mental Health Act 1983 and matrimonial proceedings.

[29] The Rules are divided into Orders, rules and paragraphs, and are referred to in
abbreviated form as (*e.g.*) R.S.C., Ord 1, r. 1.

[30] *e.g.* doubts as to whether certain aspects of the "New Order 53," which introduced the
"application for judicial review," were *ultra vires* were settled by the enactment of section 31
of the Supreme Court Act 1981 (see below, p. 746).

[31] (1982) 79 L.S.Gaz. 711. The first chairman appointed was Kerr L.J., and the
membership includes judges, masters, barristers, and solicitors. There is a sub-committee for
each division of the High Court.

[32] See generally Chap. 19.

[33] See below, pp. 80–81.

[34] See below, pp. 81–84.

[35] Lands Tribunal Act 1949. For its rules of procedure see the Lands Tribunal Rules 1975
(S.I. 1975 No. 299).

[36] Recently, the President has combined this role with frequent sittings in the High Court as
a Deputy High Court judge.

nature of the matters at issue. The Tribunal's permanent office and secretariat are in London, although it may sit in the provinces if appropriate, for example to facilitate the inspection of the relevant land and buildings. In addition to the jurisdiction in respect of compensation, it has the power to determine disputes as to the valuation of land for taxation, it hears appeals from local valuation courts, in matters concerning disputed assessments of land and buildings for rating and from leasehold valuation tribunals, and it has a discretionary power to vary, modify or discharge restrictive covenants under section 84 of the Law of Property Act 1925. An appeal lies to the Court of Appeal by case stated on a point of law. The Lands Tribunal is regarded as having a high status in the court structure, notwithstanding that, unlike the Transport Tribunal and the Employment Appeal Tribunal, it is not constituted under the 1949 Act as a court of record.[37] Its proceedings are conducted fairly formally.

9. THE RESTRICTIVE PRACTICES COURT

An institution of some analytical interest is the Restrictive Practices Court, which started its operations in 1958 and is now constituted under the Restrictive Practices Court Act 1976. It consists of three puisne judges of the High Court nominated by the Lord Chancellor, one judge of the Court of Session nominated by the Lord President of that Court, one judge of the Supreme Court of Northern Ireland nominated by the Lord Chief Justice of Northern Ireland and up to 10 non-judicial members appointed by the Crown on the recommendation of the Lord Chancellor. One of the High Court judges is selected by the Lord Chancellor to be the president. The "appointed members" must be persons appearing to the Lord Chancellor to be qualified by their knowledge of or experience in industry, commerce or public affairs, and the appointments are for periods of at least three years. The Court, which is a superior court of record, has its central office in London, and although it may sit anywhere in the United Kingdom it normally sits in the Royal Courts of Justice. For the hearing of a case the court consists of a judge and at least two other members, although the opinion of the judge or judges must prevail in any question of law. The rights of audience before the court when sitting in England and Wales are limited to those who would have such a right before the High Court.

The main functions of the court are derived from the Restrictive Trade Practices Act 1976.[38] It must determine whether restrictive agreements[39] as to goods or services are contrary to the public interest. The agreements have to be registered with the Director-General of Fair Trading, and it is for him to refer an agreement to the court. A number of professional

---

[37] See *Att.-Gen.* v. *British Broadcasting Corporation* [1981] A.C. 303, 338, (Viscount Dilhorne). *Cf.* the Annual Report of the Council on Tribunals, 1980–81 (1981–82 H.C. 89), p. 8: "The Lands Tribunal is generally regarded as of High Court standing . . . ."

[38] This consolidated the original powers included in the Restrictive Trade Practices Act 1956, and the extra powers granted by the Restrictive Trade Practices Act 1968. See generally, R.B. Stevens and B.S. Yamey, *The Restrictive Practices Court* (1965); D. Swann *et al.*, *Competition in British Industry* (1974); V. Korah, *Competition Law of Britain and the Common Market* (3rd ed., 1982).

[39] *e.g.* price-fixing agreements, quota agreements, market sharing agreements and collective boycotts. The controls may be extended to agreements to exchange information about prices, quantities produced, etc.

services, including legal services, were expressly exempted from the scope of the legislation.[40] There is a presumption that a restriction is contrary to the public interest unless the court is satisfied that one (or more) of eight specified conditions (known as "gateways") both exists and outweighs the detriment caused by the restriction.[41] Much of the debate concerning the justiciability of the issues before the court centred on whether these conditions were sufficiently precisely drawn to enable the court to operate in a judicial manner. Stevens and Yamey[42] concluded that they were not. The early decision-making of the courts showed that it would be difficult for firms to justify restrictive agreements, and a large number were ended without recourse to proceedings under the Act:

> "The cases require considerable preparation and the hearing of some of the more recent ones has lasted over 40 days. The trade witnesses, often pillars of the establishment, frequently find that being cross-examined for several consecutive days is a considerable strain and the costs, both in lawyers' fees and in time that might otherwise might be spent managing the business, are high. Consequently, apart from three lengthy hearings under the Resale Prices Act 1964, there have been only two contested hearings since 1965 as to whether an agreement is contrary to the public interest."[43]

Moreover:

> "Most of the judgments that have upheld agreements have been subjected to devastating criticism showing logical inconsistencies or complex and unlikely assumptions that are not expressly mentioned in the judgments."[44]

The Court also has jurisdiction in respect of the exemption of resale price maintenance agreements from prohibition[45] and applications by the Director-General of Fair Trading for an order directing the respondent to refrain from conduct detrimental to the interests of consumers.[46]

10. THE COURT OF APPEAL (CRIMINAL DIVISION)

The Court of Appeal (Criminal Division) hears appeals from trials on indictment or sentences passed by the Crown Court,[47] and references by

---

[40] See the Restrictive Trade Practices Act 1976, s.13, Sched. 1.

[41] *Ibid.* ss.10(1), 19(1). For example, the restriction is reasonably necessary to protect the public against injury (gateway (a)); or provides "specific and substantial benefits" to the public (gateway (b)); removal of the restriction "would be likely to have a serious and persistent adverse effect on the general level of unemployment" (gateway (e)); or to cause a substantial reduction in export earnings (gateway (f)).

[42] *Op. cit.* n. 38, above, Chap. 6. Particularly problematic has been the necessity for the court "to decide which of two or more economic hypotheses is the appropriate one on which to base specific economic predictions." *Ibid.* p. 49.

[43] Korah (1982) p. 95.

[44] *Ibid.* p. 179.

[45] Resale Prices Act 1976, ss.14–21.

[46] Fair Trading Act 1973, ss.35–39.

[47] Criminal Appeal Act 1968, Parts I and II. See below, pp. 705–715.

the Attorney-General under the Criminal Justice Act 1972.[48] It replaced the Court of Criminal Appeal[49] with effect from October 1, 1966.[50] The Lord Chief Justice is the president of the division, and the Lord Chancellor may appoint a vice-president.[51] The work is done by the Lord Chief Justice, Lords Justices and High Court judges.[51a] For the following purposes, a court of the division must comprise an uneven number of judges not less than three[52]:

(i) determining appeals against conviction;
(ii) determining appeals against a verdict of not guilty by reason of insanity;
(iii) determining appeals against a finding of unfitness to be tried because of a disability;
(iv) determining applications for leave to appeal to the House of Lords;
(v) refusing leave to appeal in situations (i) (ii), (iii) above except where the application has already been refused by a single judge.

Otherwise, matters may be determined by a court comprising two judges.[53] A single judge may grant leave to appeal, grant bail and perform certain other functions.[54] Any number of courts may sit at the same time. The court gives a single judgment unless the judge presiding states that in his opinion the question is one of law on which it is convenient that separate judgments should be pronounced by the members of the court.[55] Procedural rules may be made by the Crown Court Rule Committee.[56] The administration of criminal appeals is handled by the Criminal Appeal Office, headed by the Registrar of Criminal Appeals.[57]

Appeals lie to the House of Lords, with the leave of the House or the Court of Appeal, where the Court of Appeal has certified that a point of law of general public importance is involved.[58]

---

[48] s.36. See below, pp. 717–718.

[49] Established by the Criminal Appeal Act 1907. This Act for the first time established a right of appeal for the *accused*, as distinct from the discretion of the *judge* to refer a point to his fellow judges (see above, p. 30).

[50] Criminal Appeal Act 1966. This followed the Report of the Committee on the Court of Criminal Appeal (Chairman: Lord Donovan; Cmnd. 2755, 1965).

[51] Supreme Court Act 1981, s.3.

[51a] On occasion, one or more of the Law Lords (see below, p. 155) may sit: *e.g. R. v. Husseyn* (Note) (1977) 67 Cr.App.R. 131, "explained" in *Attorney-General's References (Nos. 1 and 2 of 1979)* [1980] Q.B. 180, see below p. 718.

[52] Supreme Court Act 1981, s.55.

[53] *Ibid., e.g.* appeals against sentence. If the court is equally divided the case must be re-argued before an uneven number of judges not less than three: *ibid.* s.55(5).

[54] Criminal Appeal Act 1968, s.31.

[55] Supreme Court Act 1981, s.59. See *R. v. Head* [1958] 1 Q.B. 132, 137; *R. v. Harz* [1967] 1 A.C. 760, 765.

[56] *Ibid.* s.86. This comprises the Lord Chancellor and any four of: the Lord Chief Justice, two other judges of the Supreme Court, two Circuit judges, the Registrar of Criminal Appeals, a J.P., two practising barristers and two practising solicitors. See the Criminal Appeal Rules 1968 (S.I. 1968 No. 1262 as amended); *A Guide to Proceedings in the Court of Appeal Criminal Division* [1983] Crim.L.R. 415; D. Thompson and H.W. Wollaston, *Court of Appeal—Criminal Division* (1969); M. Knight, *Criminal Appeals* (1970) and I. McLean, *Criminal Appeals* (1980).

[57] This office is held in combination with that of Master of the Crown Office.

[58] See below, pp. 81–84 and 719–721.

11. THE COURT OF APPEAL (CIVIL DIVISION)[59]

The Court of Appeal was established as part of the Supreme Court by the Supreme Court of Judicature Acts 1873 and 1875. It was reconstituted with Civil and Criminal Divisions in 1966.[60] The jurisdiction of the Civil Division includes appeals from the High Court and county courts in civil matters, and from certain other courts and tribunals.[61] The Master of the Rolls[62] is president of the division, and the Lord Chancellor may appoint a vice-president.[63] The work is mainly done by the Master of the Rolls and the Lords Justices,[64] with occasional assistance from Law Lords, High Court judges and former judges of the Court of Appeal or High Court.

A court of two judges may hear appeals in interlocutory matters, any other appeal with the consent of the parties, and, as a recent development, certain other appeals, including appeals from county courts.[65] Otherwise the court must comprise an uneven number of judges of three or more. A single judge may determine an application for leave to appeal and deal with other matters arising incidentally.[66] The work of the division is administered by the Registrar of Civil Appeals. This office was created by the Supreme Court Act 1981,[67] following the report of a Working Party headed by Lord Scarman.[68] The Scarman Committee had identified four main sources of wasted time in the Court of Appeal: (1) failure of parties to an appeal to provide the necessary documentation in a suitable form; (2) the requirement that at least two Lords Justices hear procedural applications; (3) the absence of a flexible and co-ordinated listing system; (4) the length of oral hearings. The Registrar's functions include ensuring that the proper documentation is prepared, advising those unfamiliar with the procedure and practice of the court and the establishment of a co-ordinated listing system. The Scarman Committee considered and rejected a change to the system of written briefs and limitations on the time allowed for oral argument which is the practice, for example, in the Supreme Court of the United States. This system was regarded as alien to the British tradition of oral presentation and argument, and not necessarily less expensive because of the time devoted to preparing highly complex briefs. Instead, arrangements will be made for the pre-reading of documents before the oral hearing begins, and for the submission of "skeleton arguments" (*i.e.* an abbreviated note of arguments and other

[59] For accounts of the working of the Court of Appeal see Lord Asquith, (1947–51) 1 J.S.P.T.L. (N.S.) 350, reproduced in L.Blom-Cooper, *The Language of the Law* (1965); Sir R. Evershed, *The Court of Appeal in England* (1950); D. Karlen, *Appellate Courts in the United States and England* (1963) Chap. 6.

[60] Criminal Appeal Act 1966.

[61] See below, pp. 721–734.

[62] See below, p. 156.

[63] Supreme Court Act 1981, s.3.

[64] See below, p. 155.

[65] Supreme Court Act 1981, s.54; Court of Appeal (Civil Division) Order 1982 (S.I. 1982 No. 543). If a court is evenly divided the case is re-argued before an uneven number of judges not less than three: s.54(5).

[66] *Ibid.* ss.54(6), 58.

[67] s.89 and Sched. 2.

[68] *Practice Note* (*Court of Appeal: New Procedure*) [1982] 1 W.L.R. 1312 (Sir John Donaldson M.R.).

matters which would otherwise be dictated to the court at the oral hearing).[69]

Appeals lie to the House of Lords, with the leave of the court or the House, on questions of law or fact.[70]

12. THE HOUSE OF LORDS[71]

The House of Lords hears appeals (1) from the Court of Appeal; (2) in certain circumstances, direct from the High Court; (3) from the Court of Session (the highest civil court in Scotland); (4) from the Court of Appeal in Northern Ireland; and (5) in certain circumstances, direct from the High Court of Justice in Northern Ireland.[72]

An appeal may not be heard or determined unless at least three of the following are present (1) the Lord Chancellor[73]; (2) the Lords of Appeals in Ordinary[74]; (3) any peer who has held one of the high judicial offices of Lord Chancellor, member of the Judicial Committee of the Privy Council, Lord of Appeal in Ordinary, judge of the Supreme Court of England and Wales or Northern Ireland or judge of the Court of Session.[75] Technically, it seems that all members of the House of Lords have the right to vote on appeals, but the practice has fallen into disuse. In the early nineteenth century lay peers were used to make up the necessary quorum but by the 1830s there were sufficient Law Lords[76] for a "professional" court to be possible.[77] In 1844 the convention that lay peers' did not vote was established in *O'Connell* v. *R.*[78] Daniel O'Connell appealed against a conviction for conspiracy. Three Law Lords were in favour of allowing the appeal, two were against it. Several lay peers purported to vote with the minority, but were persuaded to withdraw on the ground that in reality the "Court of Law" in the House was constituted by the Law Lords and interference by lay peers would greatly lessen the authority of the House. The last occasion when a lay peer attempted to vote was in *Bradlaugh* v. *Clarke*[79] when Lord Denman[80] attended throughout the proceedings and purported to vote with Lord Blackburn against the majority of the Law

---

[69] *Practice Note (Court of Appeal: skeleton arguments)* [1983] 2 All E.R. 34.

[70] See below, and pp. 735–737.

[71] See L. Blom-Cooper and Gavin Drewry, *Final Appeal* (1972); R. Stevens, *Law and Politics* (1978); A. Paterson, *The Law Lords* (1982).

[72] Appeals in English cases are considered in detail below, pp. 735–737.

[73] Above, pp. 14–15; below, pp. 155–156.

[74] Below, p. 155.

[75] Appellate Jurisdiction Act 1876, ss.5, 25; Appellate Jurisdiction Act 1887, s.5. The current list includes eleven retired Lords of Appeal, two former Lord Chancellors (Gardiner and Elwyn-Jones) and two Scottish judges (Emslie and Wheatley): *Bar List* 1983.

[76] The term then covered the Lord Chancellor, the Lord Chancellor of Ireland, former Lord Chancellors, ennobled judges, and occasionally a peer who had held a minor judicial office.

[77] Stevens (1978) p. 29.

[78] (1844) 11 Cl. & F. 155, 421–426.

[79] (1883) 8 App. Cas 354. See R.E. Megarry, (1949) 65 L.Q.R. 22–24.

[80] This was the second Lord Denman, son of the Lord Chief Justice and brother of Denman J., a High Court judge, 1872–1892. "Lord Denman was aged seventy-eight at the time of his fling, and he had been a peer for nearly thirty years and a barrister for fifty, so that his was no mere indiscretion of youth and inexperience" (Megarry (1949) p. 24). He "won notoriety rather from his eccentricities than any eminent qualifications" (D.N.B.).

Lords. His attempt was ignored by the Lord Chancellor and the Law Reports, but was noted by *The Times*.[81] In response to a question in the House of Commons, the Home Secretary stated that as the Appellate Jurisdiction Act 1876 had not excluded lay peers, it had been competent for Lord Denman to sit: had his opinion affected the result, he would have been asked to withdraw his vote on the precedent of *O'Connell's* case.[82]

Under the original arrangements for reorganisation incorporated in the Supreme Court of Judicature Act 1873 the appellate role of the House of Lords was to be abolished. The Court of Appeal was to be the final appeal court for England, and ultimately for Scotland, Ireland and the colonies. However, before the arrangements came into effect opposition developed in several quarters, the appeal to the House was retained and provision was made for the appointment of salaried Law Lords.[83]

Up to 1948, appeals to the House of Lords were heard in the chamber of the House. In that year, the process of repairing the Palace of Westminister caused the House to commit the hearing of appeals to an Appellate Committee meeting in a committee room and this practice has been maintained ever since. The committee hears appeals and reports its conclusions to the House, where judgment is delivered at a judicial sitting.[84] The House, or the Appellate Committee, as the case may be, is presided over by the Lord Chancellor or, as is more usually the case, the senior Lord of Appeal in Ordinary present.[85] The Appellate Committee must be distinguished from the "Appeal Committee" which sits to consider and report on petitions for leave to appeal and other incidental matters and which normally comprises three Law Lords.

Selection of Law Lords to sit on Appeal Committees is done by the Principal Clerk to the Judicial Office: selection of Appellate Committees, although theoretically in the hands of the Lord Chancellor, is delegated to his Permanent Secretary who consults the Lord Chancellor in cases of difficulty.[86] Normally, the most convenient panel available is chosen; occasionally, special considerations may apply, such as the exclusion of judges with a political background from adjudicating in a case with party-political implications,[87] the strong desirability of one or both of the Scottish Law Lords sitting on an appeal from Scotland and the desirability of the presence of a Chancery judge in a Chancery appeal. The room for manoeuvre is in practice limited.

Procedure on appeals to the House of Lords is regulated by Directions

[81] April 10, 1883, p. 4.

[82] Sir William Harcourt, H.C. Deb. Vol. 278, col. 68, April 12, 1883.

[83] See Stevens (1979) Chap. 2 and R. Stevens, "The Final Appeal: Reform of the House of Lords and Privy Council, 1867–1876" (1964) 80 L.Q.R. 343.

[84] A morning sitting in the Chamber of the House. Some appeals may be heard in the Chamber, *e.g.* during Parliamentary recesses.

[85] Seniority formerly depended on the date of first appointment to the office: Blom-Cooper and Drewry (1972), p. 179. From 1984, the first and second senior Law Lords have been specifically appointed as such by the Queen: H.L. Deb. Vol. 453, cols. 914–919, June 27, 1984. The presiding judge may exert significant influence over the course of proceedings: Paterson (1982) pp. 66–72. The most recent senior Lords of Appeal have been Lord Simonds (1954–1962); Lord Reid (1962–1975); Lord Wilberforce (1975–1982); Lord Diplock (1982–1984) Lord Fraser (1984–).

[86] See Paterson (1982) pp. 87–89. The selections have to be co-ordinated with those for the Judicial Committee of the Privy Council.

[87] This was done for *Heaton's Transport Co.* v. *T.G.W.U.* [1973] A.C. 15. See A. Paterson, (1979) 1 B.J.L.S. 118, 126.

and Standing Orders of the House.[88] Each side must submit a "printed case," drawn up by counsel, which is a "succinct statement of their argument in the Appeal,"[89] although in practice the oral submissions of counsel and the interchange between them and the Law Lords are of greater significance.[90] The Law Lords are generally expected to confine their propositions of law to matters covered by the argument of counsel, although this view is held today less strongly than formerly.[91] Moreover, they will not normally consider a point not raised in the courts below,[92]

> "But if [the Law Lords] think it is something that really goes to the root of the thing, if they think the whole thing would be rather a mess if they did not allow it to be argued, then they would probably allow it on terms as to costs."[93]

Informal discussions among the Law Lords take place during the hearing of an appeal.[94] Judgment is invariably reserved. At the conclusion of the hearing there is a conference at which provisional opinions are expressed, and a general discussion follows. If there appears to be general agreement, it may also be agreed that a particular Law Lord should write the major opinion. Occasionally, a second conference may be convened.

Each Law Lord is entitled to write his own opinion,[95] although they attempt to avoid the unnecessary multiplication of opinions. Views differ on the desirability of multiple opinions.[96] Paterson found that of those studied:

> "although in non-criminal common law cases only two active Law Lords generally favoured a single judgment in criminal appeals on a point of statutory construction, probably a majority of the active Law Lords favoured that approach."[97]

The main problem with multiple assenting judgments is that the differences in language may make it difficult to discern the *ratio decidendi*[98]; conversely, the same feature may leave subsequent judges greater scope for developing the law. The main problem with single opinions is that they may reflect an uneasy compromise. Recently, the proportion of cases with a single opinion seems to have increased.[99]

The House of Lords has a limited original, as distinct from appellate,

---

[88] See "Directions as to Petitions for Leave to Appeal," *Supreme Court Practice 1985*, Vol. 2, Part 16.

[89] *Ibid*.

[90] See A. Paterson, *The Law Lords* (1982) Chaps. 3 and 4.

[91] *Ibid*. pp. 38–45.

[92] *Ibid*. pp. 45–49.

[93] Lord Cross, cited by Paterson, *op. cit.* (1982) p. 47.

[94] The interaction among the Law Lords is discussed by Paterson, *op. cit.* (1982) Chap. 5.

[95] Occasionally the presiding judge may press for a single opinion: see *D.P.P.* v. *Smith* [1961] A.C. 290 and *Heaton's Transport Ltd.* v. *T.G.W.U.* [1973] A.C. 15: *cf.* the position in the Judicial Committee of the Privy Council, below, p. 85.

[96] See Blom-Cooper and Drewry, *op. cit.* (1979) Chap. V; R. Cross, (1977) 93 L.Q.R. 378; Paterson, *op. cit.* (1982) pp. 96–109 and 183–187.

[97] *Op. cit.* p. 185.

[98] See, *e.g. Boys* v. *Chaplin* [1971] A.C. 356; *British Railways Board* v. *Herrington* [1972] A.C. 877: below, pp. 283–284.

[99] See P.V. Baker, (1983) 99 L.Q.R. 371; Lord Diplock in *In re Prestige Group plc* [1984] 1 W.L.R. 335, 338, referring to this as "a frequent practice in this House when dealing with questions of statutory construction."

jurisdiction, which includes the power to determine peerage claims and the power to conduct impeachment proceedings.[1] The right of a peer to be tried by his peers in cases of treason, felony or misprision of felony was abolished in 1948.[2]

13. The Judicial Committee of the Privy Council

The Judicial Committee of the Privy Council was established in 1833,[3] largely as the result of the efforts of Lord Brougham.[4] Previously, appeals to the Crown from the colonies, which arose out of the prerogative right of the Sovereign as the fountainhead of all justice, were dealt with by a committee of the Privy Council which did not have a regular judicial composition. The 1833 Act limited the membership almost exclusively to senior judges. The present position is that the Committee comprises the Lord President of the Council, the Lord Chancellor, the Lords of Appeal in Ordinary and other members of the Privy Council who hold "high judicial office,"[5] and former holders of these offices.[6] In addition, privy councillors who hold or have held one of a number of judicial offices in Australia, Canada, New Zealand and other Commonwealth countries are also members.[7]

The Judicial Committee hears appeals from certain Commonwealth countries, from the Channel Islands, in certain admiralty and ecclesiastical matters and from the General Medical Council[8] and other professional bodies.[9] The Commonwealth appellate jurisdiction was formerly regarded as an important unifying influence: it has now dwindled significantly as an increasing number of Commonwealth countries have abandoned the appeal.[10] For example, Canada and India abolished appeals in 1949 and Sri Lanka did so in 1971. Australia has virtually completed the process of abandonment. At present appeals lie from over 25 Commonwealth countries. The Committee's decision takes the form of advice to the

[1] The last such cases were those of Warren Hastings (1788–1795: see P.J. Marshall, *The Impeachment of Warren Hastings* (1965)) and Viscount Melville (1806); *cf.* below, p. 166.
[2] Criminal Justice Act 1948, s.30. The last trial was that of Lord de Clifford 1936. See generally P. Marsden, *In Peril Before Parliament* (1965).
[3] Judicial Committee Act 1833.
[4] See P.A. Howell, *The Judicial Committee of the Privy Council 1833–1876* (1979) Chap. 12, and D.B. Swinfen, "Henry Brougham and the Judicial Committee of the Privy Council" (1975) 90 L.Q.R. 396; L.P. Beth, [1975] P.L. 219.
[5] As defined by the Appellate Jurisdiction Acts 1876, ss.5, 25 and 1877, s.5. This extends the membership of the Committee to the Lords Justices of Appeal, although they rarely sit in practice.
[6] Judicial Committee Act 1833, s.1; Appellate Jurisdiction Act 1876, s.6; Appellate Jurisdiction Act 1887, s.3.
[7] Judicial Committee Amendment Act 1895, s.1, Sched.; Appellate Jurisdiction Act 1908, s.3. The list in 1983 included one judge from Australia, six from New Zealand and one from Barbados (*The Bar List* 1983, p. 4).
[8] Medical Act 1983.
[9] *e.g.* dentists, vets, chiropodists and remedial gymnasts: Dentists Act 1957, ss.22, 25; Veterinary Surgeons Act 1966, s.17; Professions Supplementary to Medicine Act 1960, ss.1, 9. See, *e.g. Libman* v. *General Medical Council* [1972] A.C. 217; *McEniff* v. *General Dental Council* [1980] 1 W.L.R. 328 (Dentist struck off for allowing an assistant and a receptionist to fill teeth after he had completed the drilling); *Le Scroog* v. *General Optical Council* [1982] 1 W.L.R. 1238 (optician struck off for advertising).
[10] Dominions were given the power to do this by the Statute of Westminster 1931, ss.2, 3.

Queen, to which effect is given by an Order in Council.[11] It is binding on the relevant Commonwealth courts.[12]

The Committee sits in London. The recording of dissenting opinions has only been permitted since 1966.[13] There is either one unanimous opinion, or one for the majority and one for the minority. Lord Reid thought that the single opinion rule had led to Privy Council judgments being much inferior to speeches in the House of Lords:

> "They are perfectly adequate to decide the particular case but not often of wider importance. Yet the same Law Lords have sat and they have taken just as much trouble. The reason is that a single judgment must get the agreement of at least all in the majority so it tends to be no more than the highest common factor of all the views."[14]

Apart from the appellate jurisdiction the Judicial Committee may entertain an application for a declaration that a person purporting to be a member of the House of Commons is disqualified by the House of Commons Disqualification Act 1975.[15] Finally, Her Majesty may refer any matter to the Judicial Committee for hearing or consideration.[16]

14. THE COURT OF JUSTICE OF THE EUROPEAN COMMUNITIES[17]

(a) Establishment

This Court is one of the four major institutions created by the Treaties establishing the European Communities. There was originally a Court of Justice for the European Coal and Steel Community, but when the treaties establishing the European Economic Community and Euratom were concluded it was agreed that there should be one court for the three communities.

(b) Composition

The Court consists of eleven judges,[18] assisted by five advocates general.[19] It may sit either in "plenary session" (*i.e.* with all the judges entitled to be present) or, where permitted by the Rules of Procedure, in "chambers" of three or five judges. It must sit in plenary session—

(1) to hear cases brought by a Member State or Community institution, or

---

[11] For Malaysia, an independent monarchy, the advice is tendered to the Head of Malaysia (Yang di-pertuan Agong); for the republics (The Gambia, Singapore, Trinidad and Tobago) the Committee itself is the decision-making authority.

[12] At least while that country retains the appeal to the Privy Council. For example, in *Viro* v. *R.* (1978) 18 A.L.R. 257, the High Court of Australia held that it was no longer bound by decisions of the Privy Council: see R.S. Geddis, (1978) 9 Fed. L.R. 427.

[13] Judicial Committee (Dissenting Opinion) Order 1966. See D.B. Swinfen, "Single Judgment in the Privy Council 1833–1966" 1975 20 J.R. 153.

[14] "The Judge as Law Maker" (1972) XII J.S.P.T.L. (N.S.) 22, 29.

[15] See s.7.

[16] Judicial Committee Act 1833, s.4. See D.B. Swinfen, "Politics and the Privy Council: Special Reference to the Judicial Committee" 1978 23 J.R. 126.

[17] T.C. Hartley, *The Foundations of European Community Law* (1981); L. Neville Brown and F.G. Jacobs, *The Court of Justice of the European Communities* (2nd ed., 1983).

[18] Art. 165/EEC (*i.e.* Article 165 of the EEC Treaty), as amended.

[19] Art. 166/EEC, as amended.

(2) to give preliminary rulings under Article 177/EEC, unless the case may be dealt with by a chamber under the Rules of Procedure.

Otherwise, matters may be dealt with by a chamber, as, for example, may cases brought by an official against an institution, matters concerning costs and legal aid, and references for a preliminary ruling or direct actions where the difficulty or importance of the case or the circumstances are not such as to require a decision of the court in plenary session. Only one judgment is delivered by the Chamber or Court and it is not revealed whether the decision was unanimous or reached by a majority.

The function of the advocate general is:

> "acting with complete impartiality, and independence, to make, in open court, reasoned submissions on cases brought before the Court of Justice, in order to assist the Court . . . ."[20]

This office has no exact equivalent in any national legal system although it is loosely based on that of *commissaire du gouvernement* in proceedings before French administrative courts, especially the Conseil d'Etat. One advocate general is assigned to each case. He sits on the bench, next to the judges, and may put questions to the parties. His opinion on the case is normally expressed about three weeks after the submissions of counsel have been heard, and, unlike such submissions on behalf of a client, "the Advocate General speaks for no-one but himself."[21] The opinion sets out the facts and relevant legal provisions, analyses the issues in the light of the case law of the court and suggests the appropriate decision for the court to adopt. It tends to be longer, more informative and less bland in style than the judgments of the court. The advocate general does not attend the deliberations of the judges. It is thought that his opinion is followed in about 70 per cent. of cases, but this may be an overestimate.[22]

The judges and advocates general are chosen by agreement among the governments of the Member States. They have to be:

> "chosen from persons whose independence is beyond doubt and who possess the qualifications required for appointment to the highest judicial offices in their respective countries or who are jurisconsults of recognised competence,"[23]

and are appointed for a term of six years. A proportion[24] of the judges and advocates general are replaced every three years. The incumbents are eligible for re-appointment. The judges elect one of their number to be President for a (renewable) three year term. His functions are to direct the judicial business and the administration of the court and to preside at hearings. One of the advocates general is designated as first advocate general, and performs certain administrative functions, including the distribution of cases among his colleagues.

There is one judge of each of the 10 nationalities: the eleventh judge will serve a single term and will be drawn in rotation from France, Germany,

---

[20] Art. 166/EEC. See A.A. Dashwood, "The Advocate General in the Court of Justice of the European Communities" (1982) 2 L.S. 202.

[21] Dashwood, *op. cit.* p. 207.

[22] *Ibid.* p. 212.

[23] Art. 167/EEC. See also the Protocols on the Statute of the Court of Justice.

[24] Six or five judges; two or three advocates general.

Italy and the United Kingdom.[25] There is one advocate general from each of the four large states[26] and one from one of the smaller states.

(c) Jurisdiction

The jurisdiction of the Court of Justice under the EEC Treaty[27] can be classified under four main heads: (i) Applications for preliminary rulings under Article 177/EEC in the course of proceedings in a national court or tribunal; (ii) Direct actions against Member States or Community institutions; (iii) Staff cases; (iv) Opinions.

(i) *Applications for Preliminary rulings*

These are considered in Chapter 19.

(ii) *Direct actions*

(1) *Actions against Member States.* Under Article 169/EEC, if the Commission considers that a Member State has failed to fulfil an obligation imposed by the Treaty or secondary Community legislation, it must deliver a reasoned opinion on the matter, after giving the State concerned the opportunity to submit its observations. If the State does not comply with the opinion within the period laid down by the Commission, the Commission may bring the matter before the Court of Justice. Under Article 170/EEC a Member State may bring similar proceedings against another Member State, after bringing the matter to the Commission's attention. If a breach is established the Court will make a declaratory order to that effect. The Member State is required by Article 170/EEC to take the necessary measures to comply, but the sanctions are political rather than legal.[28] A majority of cases are settled before they reach the Court.

(2) *Actions against community institutions.* These include (1) actions under Article 173/EEC for the annulment of acts of the Council and Commission[29]; (2) actions under Article 175/EEC against the Council or the Commission where either has, contrary to the requirements of the Treaty, failed to act[30]; (3) actions under Article 172/EEC to review penalties or fines imposed by the Commission; (4) actions under Article 178/EEC for damages based on the non-contractual (including tortious) liability of the Communities.[31]

---

[25] These are not legal requirements but are the consequence in practice of the need for the agreement of all the member states. The U.K. judge has been Lord Mackenzie Stuart, formerly a judge of the Court of Session, since 1973.

[26] France, Germany, Italy, the United Kingdom. Those from the U.K. have been J.-P. Warner (1973–1981) and Sir Gordon Slynn (1981—).

[27] There are analogous procedures under the other Treaties, with some differences in point of detail between the E.C.S.C. and the others.

[28] See, *e.g.* Case 232/78 *Commission* v. *France* [1979] E.C.R. 2729: French ban on the import of mutton and lamb from the U.K. held to be an infringement of the Treaty; the dispute was eventually compromised. Only one case under Art. 170 has proceeded to judgment: Case 141/78 *France* v. *United Kingdom* [1979] E.C.R. 2923. *Cf.* the procedure under Art. 93/EEC. whereby the Commission may require a state to abolish or alter a state aid that distorts or threatens to distort competition: if the state does not comply the matter may be referred to the court.

[29] See below, pp. 231–233. Community legislation is considered below at pp. 217–234, and its interpretation at pp. 270–277.

[30] See below, p. 234.

[31] Art. 215/EEC provides that "the Community shall, in accordance with the general provisions common to the laws of the Member States, make good any damage caused by its institutions or by its servants in the performance of their duties."

(iii) *Staff cases*

The court has jurisdiction under Article 179/EEC in any dispute between the Community and its servants within the limits and under the conditions laid down in the Staff Regulations or the Conditions of Employment.

(iv) *Opinions*

The court may under Article 228/EEC give an opinion as to whether an international agreement that the Community proposes to enter is compatible with the Treaty.

(d) Some aspects of procedure

Proceedings before the court are governed by the Rules of Procedure[32] drawn up by the court with the approval of the Council. There are four stages—

(1) Written proceedings. Proceedings are commenced by filing an application specifying the subject matter of the dispute, the grounds, the form of order sought and certain other matters. A defence must be filed within one month, and a reply and rejoinder may follow.

(2) Investigation or preliminary inquiry. The case will have been assigned by the President to one of the five chambers. He will also nominate one of the judges in that chamber to act as rapporteur. After the close of pleadings the judge-rapporteur makes a preliminary report which enables the court to decide whether the submission of any evidence is required, such as the oral testimony of witnesses, an expert's report or the personal appearance of the parties. These matters are dealt with at this stage. The judge-rapporteur then prepares a report summarising facts and arguments.

(3) Oral proceedings. At this stage the parties' lawyers address the court.[33] Interchange between court and advocate is a comparatively recent development. The final step of this stage is the delivery of the advocate general's opinion, which takes place in open court, normally a few weeks later.

(4) Judgment. Proceedings may be conducted in Danish, Dutch, English, French, German, Greek, Irish or Italian. The language is chosen by the applicant except where an application is made against a Member State, where the state's language is used, and in applications for preliminary rulings, which are conducted in the language of the referring court or tribunal. In practice, the working language is normally French.

There are no court fees. Costs are normally awarded to the successful party against his opponent. The court may grant legal aid: aid for an application for a preliminary ruling is, however, regarded as an aspect of the national proceedings, and aid will only be granted by the court if it is not available in those proceedings.

---

[32] A codified version of the 1974 rules as amended was published in the Official Journal 1982, C.39/1. See *Encyclopedia of European Community Law*, B8–142 *et seq.*

[33] Any lawyer entitled to practice before a court of a Member State may appear. Thus, either a barrister or solicitor from the U.K. may appear. A litigant may not normally appear in person. *cf.* below, p. 131.

(e) Administration

This is the responsibility of the Registrar and his staff. There is a Registry, translation, library and documentation and interpretation services and an information office. In addition, two legal secretaries are attached to each judge and advocate general.

15. THE EUROPEAN COURT OF HUMAN RIGHTS[34]

Decisions of the European Court of Human Rights have become of increasing significance for the English legal system in recent years. The Convention for the Protection of Human Rights and Fundamental Freedoms of November 4, 1950, generally known as the European Convention on Human Rights, was one of the first achievements of the Council of Europe, an association of 21 states. It came into force in 1953 and by 1982 all these states were parties to the Convention.[35] Article 1 provides that these parties "shall secure to everyone within their jurisdiction" the rights and freedoms defined in Articles 2 to 18. These are mostly civil and political rights,[36] including the right to life (Art. 2), the right not to be subjected to torture or to inhuman or degrading treatment or punishment (Art. 3), the right to liberty and security of person (Art. 5), the right to a fair trial in both civil and criminal cases (Art. 6), the right to respect for private and family life, home and correspondence (Art. 8), the right to freedom of thought, conscience and religion (Art. 9), the right to freedom of expression (Art. 10) and the right to freedom of peaceful assembly and to freedom of association with others (Art. 11). Further rights are specified in the First Protocol to the Convention.[37] Article 13 requires that persons whose guaranteed rights are isolated "have an effective remedy before a national authority."

For the purposes of enforcement the Convention established the European Commission of Human Rights and the European Court of Human Rights, each with one member in respect of each party. Each member is elected by the Consultative Assembly of the Council of Europe and sits in his individual capacity and not as a representative of his country.

Alleged breaches of the Convention may be raised either by a state party[38] or, if the state against which the complaint is made has accepted the right of individual petition, by an individual.[39] All applications are made first to the Commission. They must normally be made after all effective domestic remedies have been exhausted and within 6 months from the date

---

[34] See F.G. Jacobs, *The European Convention on Human Rights* (1975); R. Beddard, *Human Rights in Europe* (2nd ed., 1980); D.J. Harris, *Cases and Materials on International Law* (3rd ed., 1983) pp. 471–532.

[35] The United Kingdom was the first state to ratify the Convention in 1951.

[36] Economic, social and cultural rights are protected under the European Charter 1961.

[37] In force 1954; all member states except Spain and Switzerland are parties to the protocol. Eleven states, not including the U.K., are parties to the Fourth Protocol.

[38] Art. 24. Few such applications have been made. One example is *Ireland* v. *United Kingdom*. Eur. Court H.R. No. 25 Series A, Judgment of January 18, 1978.

[39] Art. 25. On October 31, 1982, 17 states had made the necessary declarations. (See Harris, *op. cit.* (1983) p. 480). The U.K. first made a declaration on January 14, 1966, and this was renewed for five years from January 14, 1981.

when the final decision was taken.[40] They are investigated by the
Commission, which may seek to secure a friendly settlement.[41] If a
solution is not reached the Commission draws up a Report on the facts,
and also states in the Report its opinion[42] as to whether a breach of the
Convention has been established. The Report is sent to the Committee of
Ministers of the Council of Europe and the states concerned. If the
question is not referred to the Court within three months, the matter is
dealt with by the Committee.

A matter may only be referred to the Court if the state against which the
complaint is made has accepted the compulsory jurisdiction of the Court,[43]
or otherwise consents and may only be referred by (1) the Commission; (2)
a state party to the Convention whose national is alleged to be a victim; (3)
a state party which referred the case to the Commission; and (4) a state
party against which the complaint has been lodged.[44] The individual
concerned has no right to insist on a reference to the Court.[45]

Each case is heard either by a Chamber of the Court composed of seven
judges,[46] or by the full or "plenary" Court.[47]

As from January 1, 1983, an individual applicant may be represented by
an advocate authorised to practise in any of the party states or any other
person approved by the President of the Court, or he may be given leave to
present his own case.[48]

Legal aid may be awarded in respect of proceedings before the
Commission and the Court. The official languages are English and
French.[49] There is provision for the submission of written documents and
an oral hearing.[50] The Court deliberates and votes on its decision in
private. A judgment of the Court is prepared: each judge is entitled to
annex a separate opinion, whether concurring or dissenting, or a bare
statement of dissent.[51] In most cases a declaratory judgment is given. If the
Court finds that a decision or measure taken by an authority of a state party
is in conflict with the obligations imposed by the Convention, it must "if
necessary afford just satisfaction to the injured party."[52] In a number of

[40] Art. 216. There are other grounds on which an application may be considered
inadmissible: Art. 27.

[41] Art. 28.

[42] This may be reached by a majority: Art. 34.

[43] Art. 46. On October 31, 1982 all Members except Malta and Turkey had done so.

[44] Art. 48.

[45] 59 cases had been referred to the Court by March 21, 1983. Breaches of the Convention
had been found in 30 of the 43 cases decided on the merits by then: Information Document B
(83) 4, 21.3.83.

[46] Art. 43. The seven must include the President or Vice-President, and the judge who is a
national of any state party concerned. If the national judge is unable to sit or withdraws, the
relevant state may appoint another member of the court or an ad hoc judge.

[47] See the Revised Rules of Court (adopted on November 24, 1982): Cour. (82) 107 of
December 2, 1982, r. 50.

[48] Ibid. r. 30: see P.J. Duffy [1983] P.L. 32–33. Previously, the applicant technically had no
independent right to appear although in practice his lawyer was permitted to address the
Court as part of the Commission's case.

[49] Revised Rules of Court, r. 27. Another language may be used at the oral stage, with the
leave of the President.

[50] Revised Rules of Court, rr. 37, 39, 41–46.

[51] Ibid. r. 52.

[52] Art. 50.

cases monetary compensation has been awarded as "just satisfaction" covering costs and expenses, pecuniary losses and non-pecuniary loss.

As of March 1983, the Court has determined ten cases[53] involving the United Kingdom. In all but one the Court found there to be violations of one or more articles. Either as a consequence, or in anticipation of these findings,[54] English law has been changed in a number of significant respects.[55] For example, the law of contempt of court has been amended following the *Sunday Times* case[56]; the law relating to the correspondence of persons in prisons has been radically altered[57]; the law in Northern Ireland concerning homosexual acts has been brought into line with the rest of the United Kingdom[58]; and Isle of Man courts have been advised that birching is contrary to the European Convention.[59] The Convention has also had some influence in statutory interpretation,[60] although judges have emphasised on a number of occasions that it is not part of English law.[61]

[53] Excluding separate applications under Art. 50 where the merits have already been determined.

[54] There are also some changes that can be traced to friendly settlements or Commission decisions.

[55] See P.J. Duffy (1980) I.C.L.Q. 585–618; A. Drzemczewski, *European Human Rights Convention in Domestic Law* (1983) pp. 314–322; M.P. Furmston, *et al.*, (eds.) *The Effect on English Domestic Law of Membership of the European Communities and of Ratifications of the European Convention on Human Rights* (1983).

[56] See *Sunday Times Case*, Series A No. 30, Judgment of April 26, 1979: violation of Art. 10; Contempt of Court Act 1981; S.H. Bailey, (1982) 45 M.L.R. 301. It is not certain that the Act goes far enough.

[57] See the *Golder Case*, Series A No. 18, Judgment of February 21, 1975; *Case of Silver and Others*: Series A No. 61, Judgment of March 25, 1983: violations of Arts. 6 §1 and 3; S.H. Bailey, D.J. Harris and B. Jones, *Civil Liberties: Cases and Materials* (1980) pp. 418–421; G.J. Zellick [1981] P.L. 435–438, [1983] P.L. 167–169.

[58] *Dudgeon Case* Series A No. 45 Judgment of October 22, 1981: violation of Art. 8; Homosexual Offences (Northern Ireland) Order 1982.

[59] *Tyrer Case* Series A No. 26, Judgment of April 25, 1978; G.J. Zellick [1982] P.L. 4–5. The United Kingdom does not now accept the rights of individual petition in respect of the Isle of Man. The Convention has also influenced the law affecting mental patients, children in secure accommodation, immigration, and the right of parents to forbid the imposition by a school of corporal punishment on their children.

[60] See below, p. 262; A. Drzemczewski, *European Human Rights Convention in Domestic Law* (1983) pp. 166–187.

[61] *Ibid.* pp. 314–322. See, *e.g. Malone* v. *Metropolitan Police Commissioner* [1979] Ch. 344; *Att.-Gen.* v. *B.B.C.* [1981] A.C. 303 (Lord Scarman).

CHAPTER 3

LAWYERS

A. INTRODUCTION: THE "LEGAL PROFESSION"

THE title "lawyer" is reserved to those who have achieved the special status of membership of the "legal profession."[1] It is not a straightforward job description: many non-lawyers perform legal tasks, some of them full-time. For example, accountants may specialise in revenue law, trade union officials may appear regularly before industrial tribunals on behalf of their members,[2] and solicitors may delegate work to legal executives.[3] Conversely, many of the tasks performed by lawyers are not strictly "legal."[4] Membership of the legal profession in England and Wales involves qualification as either a solicitor or a barrister; it is usual to speak of two branches of the profession although historically it would be more accurate to refer to two professions.[5]

It is significant that lawyers are accepted to be members of a "profession." Much has been written about the supposedly distinctive attributes of professions, and how and why occupational groups seek professional status.[6] Medicine and law have been regarded as classic models, although important differences between them have been perceived.[7] The self-conception of the legal profession was articulated by The Law Society in evidence to the Monopolies Commission in 1968[8]:

> "When a profession is fully developed it may be described as a body of men and women (a) identifiable by reference to some register or record; (b) recognised as having a special skill and learning in some field of activity in which the public needs protection against incompetence, the standards of skill and learning being prescribed by the profession itself; (c) hold themselves out as being willing to serve the public; (d) voluntarily submitting themselves to standards of ethical conduct beyond those required of the ordinary citizen by law; (e) undertaking to accept personal responsibility to those whom they

---

[1] "Barrack-room" lawyers don't count. Law lecturers commonly refer to themselves as "academic lawyers" even if they are not qualified.

[2] See below, p. 330.

[3] See below, pp. 129–130.

[4] See below, p. 101.

[5] M. Birks, *Gentlemen of the Law* (1960) p. 3. See further, below pp. 94–97.

[6] See T.J. Johnson, *Professions and Power* (1972) pp. 21–38. For an argument that the concept of "profession . . . obscures more than it reveals about the work people do" see M. Cain, (1979) 7 *International Journal of the Sociology of Law* 331. See generally R. Dingwall and P. Lewis, *The Sociology of the Professions* (1983), in which Cain's paper is reprinted.

[7] D. Rueschemeyer, "Lawyers and Doctors: a Comparison of Two Professions" in V. Aubert (ed.) *Sociology of Law* (1969) pp. 267–277, abridged from (1964) 1 *Canadian Review of Sociology and Anthropology*, 17–30.

[8] Quoted in the Report of the Royal Commission on Legal Services (Cmnd. 7648, 1969) Vol. 1, p. 30.

serve for their actions and to their profession for maintaining public confidence."

This approach was accepted uncritically by the Royal Commission on Legal Services.[9] They emphasised five main features of a profession: (a) central organisation: a governing body with powers of control and discipline; (b) the primary function of giving advice or service in a specialised field of knowledge; (c) the restriction of admission to those with the required standard of education and training; (d) a measure of self-regulation by the profession; and (e) the paramountcy of the duty owed to the client, subject only to responsibility to the court. A rule of conduct or restriction on practice should "stand or fall on its capacity to protect the interests of, or to enhance the level of service to the public." Thus, in theory at least, "altruistic service" is offered subject to self-regulation, in return for considerable autonomy from external control.[10] The Royal Commission, having noted that these features existed, found that they promoted the public interest, subject to points of detail, and proposed no fundamental changes. There was no exploration of other features that have been associated with the "rise of professionalism." For example, Larson has described professionalisation as:

> "the process by which producers of special services sought to constitute *and control* a market for their expertise . . . a collective assertion of special social status (and) a collective process of upward social mobility."[11]

Arguments for maintaining standards tend to coincide with arguments for monopolies, restrictions on practice and high rewards.[12] There was also no proper analysis of the ways in which professionalism may impede the expansion of legal services.[13] Thus, problems may be defined in the professional's terms and alternative definitions regarded as irrelevant; outsiders, whether lay people or members of other disciplines, may be ignored on the grounds that they are not competent either to assist or to criticise; "specialised knowledge" may be guarded by such means as "the creation of special forms of jargonised discourse and the fostering of an air of impenetrable mystery"[14]; the emphasis on the individual lawyer-client relationship may inhibit the development of group representation and test-case strategies[15]; the proper advertisement of legal services may be prevented.

[9] R.C.L.S. Vol. 1, pp. 28, 30. Johnson has mentioned the error made by many sociologists in accepting the professions' own definitions of themselves: Johnson (1972) p. 25. The Commission did not discuss the literature on the sociology of the professions.

[10] Johnson sees professionalism as a form of occupational control rather than an expression of the inherent nature of particular occupations: Johnson (1972) p. 45.

[11] M.S. Larson, *The Rise of Professionalism* (1977) p. xvi.

[12] See below, pp. 106–110, 112–115. The case for increased rewards is set out in "The Law Society's Memorandum No. 5 to the Royal Commission on Legal Services" (1978) 75 L.S.Gaz. 422, 427.

[13] R. Cotterell, "Legal Services and Professional Ideology" (1980) (Paper presented at the Conference on Legal Services in the Eighties, University College, Cardiff). P. Fennell, "Solicitors, their markets and their 'ignorant public': the crisis of the professional ideal" in Z. Bankowski and G. Mungham (eds.) *Essays in Law and Society* (1980) p. 1.

[14] Cotterell, *op. cit.*, p. 10.

[15] See below, p. 322.

In the following sections, we deal briefly with the historical development of the legal profession, and then with the main features of the profession today.

B. FROM "OCCUPATION" TO "PROFESSION"

1. MEDIEVAL LAWYERS

In medieval times, legal life in London outside the courts was centred on the four inns of court (Lincoln's Inn, Gray's Inn, the Inner Temple and the Middle Temple) and the nine or so inns of chancery. Together they constituted a "great legal university situated in the western suburbs of London."[16] Membership of an inn was the clearest indicator of professional status, but not a sufficient one as most of the members attended only for general social and educational purposes and took no part in the legal learning exercises. Each inn had a chapel and a library, and a hall which was used both for meals and for moots, readings and debates. A moot was a form of mock trial consisting of the submission of legal argument relating to a given set of facts. The hypothetical pleadings were recited by "inner barristers" and the arguments conducted by "utter barristers," so called because they spoke from outside the bar of the inn. The moots were judged by senior members of the inn: the "benchers." The inns of chancery were lower in status than the inns of court; a man might spend a couple of years in an inn of chancery before moving to an inn of court, or he might remain a member of an inn of chancery all his life.

Baker[17] has distinguished six classes of common lawyer in late medieval times. Of the legal practitioners other than judges and court clerks, the most senior were the *serjeants-at-law*. The serjeants were appointed by the judges of the Court of Common Pleas, the main common-law court in London. They had the exclusive right of audience in that court, and the exclusive right to be appointed judges of the Common Pleas and King's Bench. On appointment, a serjeant would move from his inn of court to one of the two serjeants' inns, joining his fellow serjeants and the judges. *Apprentices-at-law* were, notwithstanding the name, "fully-fledged advocates below the degree of serjeant,"[18] who appeared in the King's Bench and other courts. They were senior members of the inns of court. The *utter barristers* did not at this stage appear as advocates in the superior courts. The largest group were the *attorneys*. Litigants were originally required to act personally in the course of litigation, meeting their adversaries face to face. This rule was progessively relaxed.[19] A litigant could then appoint an attorney to act in his name for specific or general purposes. He could appoint a friend, a relation or a stranger as he wished; court clerks and sheriff's officers were often selected. The appointments were supervised by the judges, and the names of the attorneys entitled to practise in a

---

[16] J.H. Baker, "The English Legal Profession, 1450–1550" in W. Prest, *Lawyers in Early Modern Europe and America* (1981) p. 17.

[17] *Ibid.* See also J.H. Baker, *Introduction to Legal History* (2nd ed., 1979) Chap. 10; Birks (1960); H. Kirk, *Portrait of a Profession* (1976) Chap. 1.

[18] Baker (1981) p. 27.

[19] Birks (1960) Chap. 1; Kirk (1976) pp. 1–4.

particular court would be endorsed in that court's records. By the fifteenth century a number of people earned a living as "common attorneys" prepared to act for any client wishing to employ them. Most were members of inns of chancery; the more affluent and those intending to become barristers joined one of the inns of court. Attorneys also came to be permitted in local courts, although they would not necessarily be members of an inn.[20] They took formal steps in litigation, which bound their clients, and "also acted as general practitioners, retaining counsel and giving it."[21] *Solicitors* performed a variety of miscellaneous clerical tasks for employers such as land owners and attorneys. Their name was derived from their function of "soliciting" or prosecuting actions in courts of which they were not officers or attorneys. Thus the nomenclature of early common lawyers was confusing. Some titles indicated a public position or status (*e.g.* serjeants); others a position within one of the inns, which might not be of significance outside (*e.g.* utter barrister, bencher); yet others were descriptive of a type of legal work (*e.g.* attorney, solicitor). Strict lines of demarcation were few. For example, serjeants, apprentices and attorneys might all give legal advice and an apprentice or utter barrister might act as an attorney.

A separate set of lawyers practised in the ecclesiastical courts, the Admiralty and the Court of Chivalry. The *doctors of law* acted as advocates; the *proctors* as attorneys.[22] Other quasi-legal functionaries included *scriveners*, who drew up legal and other documents and enjoyed a monopoly over the drawing of deeds in London and York, and *notaries*, who authenticated documents to be used abroad.[23]

2. SPECIALISATION AND DEMARCATION

A dramatic increase of legal business in the late fifteenth and early sixteenth centuries was accompanied by a rise in the number of barristers and attorneys in the common law courts and a reduction in the number of attorneys attached to local courts.[24] Much more work came to be available in the King's Bench and this came to be done by utter barristers as well as apprentices. The slow decline of the order of serjeants which set in was closely related to the decline in the importance of the Common Pleas compared to the other superior courts, and to the fact that holders of the new office of "King's Counsel" which became established in the seventeenth century took precedence. By 1600, practice at the Bar was limited by royal proclamation and judicial decision to utter barristers of the inns of court and their seniors.[25] Barristers concentrated more on advocacy and less on counselling. At the same time, the judges began to object to men acting as "solicitors." Intermeddling in another person's law suit

[20] C.W. Brooks, "The Common Lawyers in England, c.1558–1642" in Prest (1981) pp. 46–50.
[21] Baker (1981) p. 24.
[22] Baker (1979) p. 147; G.D. Squibb, *Doctors' Commons* (1977); B.P. Levack, "The English Civilians, 1500–1750" in Prest (1981) p. 108.
[23] Birks (1960) Chap. 4; Baker (1981) p. 27.
[24] Brooks (1981) pp. 51–54.
[25] See J.H. Baker, "Solicitors and the Law of Maintenance" 1590–1640 [1973] C.L.J. 56, 59–66.

constituted "maintenance," which was both a crime and a tort.[26] Serjeants and barristers obviously had a good defence, as did an attorney acting in his own court. A servant could act as solicitor for his master. However, "common solicitors" prepared to act for any client were regarded by many judges as "maintainers." They were described by Lord Keeper Egerton as "caterpillars of the common weal" and by one Hudson as:

> "a new sort of people . . . who, like grasshoppers of Egypt, devour the whole land . . . ; these are the retainers of causes, and devourers of men's estates by contention, and prolonging suits to make them without end."[27]

Some judges thought that solicitors' work should be done by young barristers rather than "ignorant and vagrant" solicitors. Nevertheless, the attempt to abolish solicitors failed. A statute of 1605[28] instead subjected both attorneys and solicitors to a measure of control to prevent overcharging and to cut their numbers; only "skilful" and "honest" men were to be allowed to practise. Solicitors became particularly associated with the Court of Chancery where there was a rule that only court clerks could be appointed as attorneys; there was, however, too much work for the clerks to handle.

At the same time, the judges and benchers began the process of excluding attorneys from the inns of court and prohibiting such persons from being called to the bar while in practice, thereby asserting the bar's intellectual and social superiority.[29] The Judges' Order of 1614 described attorneys and solicitors as "but ministerial persons *and* of an inferior nature. . . . " In the seventeenth century, the superior status of barristers was further consolidated by their growing unwillingness to accept instructions directly from a lay client without the intervention of an attorney or solicitor,[30] by rules which prohibited social contact between barristers and solicitors, and by the development of the presumption that fees paid to barristers were *honoraria* which if unpaid could not be recovered by an action.[31] In the long term, attorneys and solicitors benefitted financially from the Bar's pursuit of a separate elite status and continued reluctance to perform "mechanic" legal work even when it fell on harder times. Moreover, barristers came to be dependent upon the patronage of attorneys and solicitors.

By the eighteenth century[32] the judges and the government had ceased to attempt to exercise any control over the Bar. The government of the inns of court had long since passed from the membership as a whole into the hands of the benchers.[33] The inns' educational functions disappeared;

---

[26] *Ibid.* pp. 66–80.

[27] *Ibid.* pp. 72, 73–4.

[28] 3 Jac. 1, c.7.

[29] J.H. Baker, "Counsellors and Barristers" [1969] C.L.J. 205, 222–224; H.H.L. Bellot, "The Exclusion of Attorneys from the Inns of Court" (1910) 26 L.Q.R. 137.

[30] This was a clear rule of etiquette by the second half of the eighteenth century: it was not, however, a rule of law: *Doe d. Bennett* v. *Hale* (1850) 15 Q.B. 171.

[31] Baker (1969) pp. 222–9. Fees were then usually paid in advance and so the *honorarium* concept reinforced the barrister's status without seriously affecting his pocket.

[32] See D. Duman, "The English Bar in the Georgian Era" in Prest (1981) pp. 86–107.

[33] A.W.B. Simpson, "The Early Constitution of the Inns of Court" [1970] C.L.J. 241; "The Early Constitution of Gray's Inn" [1975] C.L.J. 131.

the only requirements for call to the Bar were enrolment as a student for a number of years and the eating of dinners for twelve terms in one of the inns. The lines of demarcation between barristers and solicitors were strengthened during the century. Common practice became firm rules of etiquette. The expulsion of attorneys from the inns was completed.[34]

3. THE RISE OF THE SOLICITORS' PROFESSION

The eighteenth century saw the establishment of a professional organisation for attorneys and solicitors,[35] the development of statutory controls and subsequently the expansion of work associated with the Industrial Revolution. The inns of chancery were dominated by the attorneys and their links with the bar were severed. However, the inns did not develop as a professional organisation as they had no control over admission to practice or discipline. Attorneys were still admitted to the rolls by the judges,[36] and, albeit only in serious cases of a misbehaviour, struck off by them.[37] Solicitors were not subject to any formal control until the 1728 Act "for the better regulation of Attornies and Solicitors."[38] A roll of solicitors was then established in the Court of Chancery.[39] An applicant for admission as an attorney or solicitor had to have been articled to a practitioner and the judges had to be satisfied of his fitness. This Act established the mechanisms of control but the judges did not examine applicants for admission and some of its provisions were easily evaded.

In the early 1730s some London lawyers formed the Society of Gentlemen Practisers in the Courts of Law and Equity, for the purpose of "supporting the honour and independence of the profession, promoting fair and liberal practice, and preventing unnecessary expense and delay to suitors."[40] It did not claim to be representative of the profession, or even of London practitioners, but it did attempt, with limited success, to ensure compliance with the legislation and to promote the profession's interests. In 1831[41] a new society received its Royal Charter: "The Society of Attorneys Solicitors Proctors and others not being barristers practising in the Courts of Law and Equity in the United Kingdom." Its original object had been the establishment of a central "Law Institution" where lawyers could meet. The idea was popular, and a Hall was erected in Chancery Lane. The society's objects widened. It never actually amalgamated with the Society of Gentlemen Practisers but began to undertake disciplinary proceedings in the courts against attorneys and solicitors and to lobby on behalf of the profession's interests. In 1833 it decided to use the name "The

---

[34] Duman (1981) pp. 100–104.

[35] Kirk (1976) Chap. 2.

[36] By the late eighteenth century this was a formality: Birks (1960) pp. 171–172.

[37] An attorney struck off was physically pitched over the bar, presumably not by the judges personally.

[38] 2 Geo. 2, c.23. The Act was renewed in 1739 and 1749, made perpetual in 1757, and amended on these and other occasions.

[39] "Accordingly they became entitled to call themselves 'gentlemen'. This is the origin of the jibe that solicitors are gentlemen by Act of Parliament": Birks (1960) p. 136.

[40] Kirk (1976) Chap. 2.

[41] Its inaugural meeting was in 1825.

Incorporated Law Society of the United Kingdom."[42] The Solicitors Act 1843 provided that it was to be the Registrar of Attorneys and Solicitors.

Another nineteenth century preoccupation of attorneys and solicitors[43] was the improvement of their status in society. Improvements in the general educational standards of entrants and in their subsequent legal education were regarded as prerequisites.[44] In 1836 the common law judges were persuaded to revive a rule of 1654 enabling them to appoint persons to examine those wishing to be admitted as attorneys. The examiners nominated included 12 members of the Council of The Incorporated Law Society. Similar steps were taken by the Court of Chancery and examinations were duly held.[45] Nevertheless, a Select Committee of the House of Commons reported in 1846 that the state of legal education was still extremely unsatisfactory.[46] For solicitors and attorneys they recommended the introduction of a preliminary examination to ensure a sound general education, the provision of lectures for articled clerks, higher standards in the final examination, and, eventually, a college of law. These recommendations were progressively adopted. In 1860, a preliminary and an intermediate examination were introduced, the latter intended to be taken midway through articles. In 1877 The Incorporated Law Society acquired control of the education and qualifying arrangements for admission. Tuition by private coaches such as Messrs. Gibson and Weldon proved more attractive than Law Society lectures, although the Society did establish a law school in 1903.[47] Failure rates in the final examination increased, particularly at times when there was concern that there were too many solicitors.[47a]

University legal education also developed from slender origins in the second half of the century.[48] Graduates were exempted from the preliminary examination in 1877 and law graduates from the intermediate as late as 1922. It has indeed been a notable feature of legal education in this country that the universities and polytechnics have played a much more minor role in the education of intending practitioners than in other systems, including, for example, those in Scotland and the United States. The profession has fought hard to retain ultimate control.[49]

Parliament confirmed the authority of The Law Society in 1888 and 1919 when disciplinary functions in respect of all solicitors, including those not members of the Society, were transferred from the courts to a disciplinary committee appointed by the Master of the Rolls from past and present

---

[42] By a charter of 1903 it became "The Law Society."

[43] By now solicitors were regarded as more respectable than attorneys. Most practitioners were qualified as both. The offices of attorney and proctor were abolished in 1875 as one of the consequences of the reorganisation of the superior courts. See above, p. 29.

[44] See Kirk (1976) Chap. 3.

[45] Birks (1960) pp. 176–180. All the entrants passed the first attorneys' examination.

[46] *Report from the Select Committee on Legal Education*, August 25, 1846, H.C. 686.

[47] The Society's school and Gibson and Weldon's were amalgamated to form the College of Law in 1961, perhaps on the "if you can't beat 'em join 'em" principle.

[47a] *Cf.* S. Hughes, *Legal Action*, July 1984, p. 10.

[48] *Report of the Committee on Legal Education* (1971, Cmnd. 4595) pp. 5–9; J.H. Baker, "University College and Legal Education 1826–1976" (1977) 30 C.L.P.1. Until the eighteenth century the universities taught only Roman-based Civil law.

[49] See further, pp. 124–129 below.

members of the Council of The Law Society.[50] According to Abel-Smith and Stevens:

> "it is almost certain that it was in the fifty years after 1860 that the solicitors' branch of the profession built its financial prosperity and social respectability."[51]

The nineteenth century development of an active professional organisation with educational and disciplinary responsibilities was no doubt associated with this transformation. Two factors of particular significance were the right of solicitors to appear as advocates in the new county courts created in 1846 and an increase in income from conveyancing following the introduction of scale fees in 1883.[51a]

In the twentieth century, further steps were taken to deal with dishonest solicitors, and those who indulged in the supposedly objectionable practices of touting and of undercutting on conveyancing. The Solicitors Act 1933 enabled the Council of The Law Society to make rules about the keeping of clients' accounts and for regulating any other matter of professional practice. Solicitors' Account Rules came into effect in 1935, and Practice Rules in 1936. The Solicitors Act 1941 established a compensation fund to which all practising solicitors had to contribute, and required that solicitors' accounts be audited each year. Solicitors also lost their struggle to resist the entry of women to the profession.[52]

4. The Bar in the Nineteenth and Twentieth Centuries

The main concerns of the Bar in the mid-nineteenth century were the problems created by a lack of work[53] and the improvement of legal education in response to sustained public criticism.[54] The 1846 Select Committee reported that the inns of court provided no legal education worthy of the name, and recommended the introduction of lectures and examinations and the establishment of a college of law. A Council of Legal Education was set up by the inns in 1852. Lectures were organised, but not compulsory examinations. A Royal Commission recommended in 1855 that there should be an entrance examination for non-graduates, compulsory lectures and pupillage and a final examination before call to the bar.[55] These proposals were vetoed by Lincoln's Inn and Gray's Inn. Attempts in the second half of the nineteenth century to establish a "Law University"

---

[50] Solicitors Acts 1888 and 1919. Between these dates the committee could investigate and dismiss complaints but only the High Court could punish offenders.

[51] *Lawyers and the Courts* (1967) p. 187.

[51a] A. Offer, *Property and Politics 1870–1914* (1981) pp. 39–40. Part I of this work considers the relationship of solicitors to the land market and to land law reform.

[52] Sex Disqualification (Removal) Act 1919. In *Bebb* v. *Law Society* [1914] 1 Ch. 286 the Court of Appeal had held that women were not "persons" within the meaning of the Solicitors Act 1843, one of many similar cases in various fields: A. Sachs and J.H. Wilson, *Sexism and the Law* (1978) Chap. 1.

[53] Abel-Smith and Stevens (1967) pp. 53–57.

[54] *Ibid.* pp. 63–74; A.H. Manchester, *Modern Legal History* (1980) pp. 54–63. See generally, on the bar in the nineteenth century, D. Duman, *The English and Colonial Bars in the Nineteenth Century* (1983) and R. Cocks, *Foundations of the Modern Bar* (1983).

[55] *Report of the Commissioners appointed to inquire into arrangements in the Inns of Court and Inns of Chancery for promoting the study of Law and Jurisprudence*, 1855.

based on the inns were also successfully resisted, at the "cost" of the introduction of compulsory examinations in 1872.

Further problems were caused by the need of the Bar to adjust to the reforms introduced by the Supreme Court of Judicature Acts 1873–75. A Bar Committee was formed in 1883 to protest against new Rules of the Supreme Court which were thought likely to deprive younger barristers of work. It was felt that the benchers, who were mostly judges[56] and Q.C.s, could not adequately protect the interests of barristers. The Committee, and its replacement, the Bar Council, began to make representations on other matters and to make rulings on matters of etiquette.[56a] Disciplinary powers remained with the inns, subject to an appeal to the judges.[57]

Significant improvements in the education and training of barristers did not take place until the 1960s when the Inns of Court School of Law was established with a full-time Dean, new premises, remodelled syllabuses and improved teaching. Pupillage became compulsory. Further structural changes did not take place until 1966 when a "Senate of the Four Inns of Court" was established. In 1974 this was replaced by the "Senate of the Inns of Court and the Bar." This is in theory the governing body of the barristers' branch of the profession although the inns have retained significant financial autonomy, and the Bar Council has also retained its separate identity.[58]

C. THE LEGAL PROFESSION TODAY

1. ORGANISATION

As we have seen, the government of the Bar is somewhat fragmented between the Senate and the inns of court and is not regulated by statute. The powers and duties of The Law Society are derived from the Solicitors Act 1974. Membership of the Society is not compulsory, although it is the governing body for the profession as a whole. Thus the Master of the Rolls may only admit as a solicitor a person certified by the Society to have complied with its training regulations and to be suitable for admission.[59] The Society also issues the "practising certificate" which each solicitor wishing to practise must obtain.[60] Many of its statutory functions relate to the maintenance of standards for the protection of the public. However, it is also the main professional association for solicitors. The feeling that these two roles were inconsistent and that the Society was not sufficiently active in pursuing the interests of solicitors led to the founding of the British Legal Association in 1974. By 1977 it had only about 2,100

---

[56] After the abolition of the order of serjeants in 1875 and the closure of Serjeants' Inn, the judges remained as benchers of the inns of court and began to take part in their management.

[56a] The Judicature Act reforms, in conjunction with the development of the railways, significantly weakened the role of circuit messes (clubs formed by barristers travelling on circuit) as mechanisms for influencing or controlling the conduct of barristers: see Cocks (1983) and Duman (1983) Chap. 2.

[57] Abel-Smith and Stevens (1967) pp. 214–220.

[58] The Royal Commission recommended that the Senate should assume the central responsibility for all matters affecting barristers: R.C.L.S. Vol. 1, pp. 425–443.

[59] Solicitors Act 1974, s.3.

[60] *Ibid.* ss.1, 9–18.

members by comparison with the Society's membership of 27,257,[61] and the Royal Commission rejected its offer to take over from the Society the function of representing the profession's interests. In any event, the Society could then point to its success in defending solicitors' interests during the deliberations of the Royal Commission, although there have also been a number of matters on which it has fallen out with sections of the rank-and-file[62] and its success in defending the solicitors' "conveyancing monopoly" has proved short lived.

2. LAWYERS AND THEIR WORK

(a) Introduction

In their study of the legal profession in the United States and England, Johnstone and Hopson identified nineteen different "work tasks" performed by lawyers in the United States: giving advice, both legal and non legal; negotiations; drafting letters and legal documents; litigation, including the preparation of cases and advocacy; investigation of facts; legal research and analysis; lobbying legislators and administrators; acting as broker; public relations; filing submissions to government and other organisations; adjudication; financing; property management; referral of clients to other sources of assistance; supervision of others; emotional support to clients; immoral and unpleasant tasks (taking care of disagreeable matters for clients which the clients could do themselves but prefer to have someone else do); acting as scapegoat; and getting business.[63] Any one lawyer might never perform all these tasks, and some, such as advising and negotiation, were generally more significant than others. The variety of combinations in which these tasks were performed by individual lawyers was "almost endless."[64] Laymen could be found performing any of them. English lawyers may be less likely than their American counterparts to act in some of these areas, but it is difficult to think of any of them that no English lawyer would touch. It has been noted that the expertise of many lawyers may be founded not so much on their mastery of legal technique as on their possession of "worldly knowledge" in "giving economic advice or providing organisational 'know-how' and in their interpersonal skills."[65]

(b) Fusion[66]

The English pattern of work is complicated by the division of the legal profession into barristers and solicitors. It is not possible for anyone to be qualified in both branches at the same time. Barristers have an exclusive right of audience in the superior courts, and may not normally be

---

[61] 1979 figures: R.C.L.S., Vol. 1, p. 384.

[62] e.g. education and training, the problems of sole practitioners, advertising, compulsory insurance: D. Podmore, "Bucher and Strauss Revisited—the Case of the Solicitors' Profession" (1980) 7 B.J.L.S. 1, 4–11.

[63] Q. Johnstone and D. Hopson, Lawyers and their Work (1967) Chap. 3.

[64] Ibid. p.77.

[65] Rueschemeyer, op cit., p. 92, n. 7, at p. 271.

[66] R.C.L.S., Vol. 1, pp. 187–202; G. Gardiner, "Two Lawyers or One" (1970) 23 C.L.P.1; M. Zander, Lawyers and the Public Interest (1968) pp. 271–332, (1976) 73 L.S.Gaz. 882, Legal Services for the Community (1978) pp. 170–174; F.A. Mann, "Fusion of the Legal Professions?" (1977) 93 L.Q.R. 367.

instructed by a lay client direct without the intervention of a solicitor. There is not, however, any *kind* of work done by barristers which is not also done by solicitors. In the lower courts the advocacy work is shared between the two branches; in tribunals it is also shared with non-lawyers. Both barristers and solicitors do drafting work. Both may give legal advice, the solicitor direct to the client, the barrister only if he is approached for his oral or written opinion by a solicitor. This would be done where the solicitor lacks the time or resources to do the work himself, to satisfy a "difficult" client or simply because "counsel's opinion" is often regarded as especially authoritative.

The different emphases in the functions of solicitors and barristers have led to marked differences in their geographical distribution: solicitors' offices may be found throughout the country[67]; over 70 per cent. of barristers work from chambers in central London, where the superior courts sit, the rest being spread through 28 provincial centres.[68] A further difference which affects the way that practices are organised is that each barrister must act on his own account, whereas solicitors may form partnerships.[69] Many solicitors' firms have several partners and a large employed staff, including fee-earners. Barristers are generally grouped in chambers, which provide administrative support, but a barrister may not share his fees or employ fee-earners.

Over the years, there have been many advocates of fusion of the two branches. The profession was not always divided as it is today.[70] The legal professions of other countries are not normally divided. It was argued in submissions to the Royal Commission that the necessity of employing a solicitor as well as a barrister, where the latter's services are required, causes inefficiency (failures in communication, delay and the return of briefs by barristers who are double-booked), harms the confidence of clients (barristers being regarded by some clients as too remote or insufficiently prepared) and is more expensive for clients obliged to pay for two lawyers rather than one. Most of the professional bodies who gave evidence, including the Senate and The Law Society, opposed fusion. It was feared that fusion would lead to a serious fall in the quality of advocacy. The leading barristers might join the larger firms of solicitors and so be less accessible. Smaller practices might generate insufficient business to justify partnership with a barrister and find it increasingly difficult to brief a barrister of equal standing to the one retained by an opponent. The drift from smaller to larger firms might increase, with a corresponding reduction in the number of offices in smaller towns and rural areas. Smaller firms might be reluctant to refer a client to a large firm for fear of losing him permanently. A reduction in the number of specialist advocates might also contribute to the lowering of standards, and make it more difficult for the Lord Chancellor to make "suitable" appointments to the bench: the numbers for consideration would be increased but the candidates would not be as well known to the Lord Chancellor and his senior advisers.

[67] See below, p. 104.
[68] See below, p. 110.
[69] See below, pp. 113–114 and 104.
[70] See above, pp. 94–97.

Other arguments against fusion have centred on the English form of court procedure.[71] First, there is heavy reliance on the oral rather than written presentation of evidence and argument. Secondly, hearings are single and continuous, this being designed to make best use of judicial time at the cost of inconvenience to practitioners and clients. Barristers are more easily and more economically organised to meet such inconvenience than solicitors could be. Thirdly, there is the "principle of judicial unpreparedness." The judge relies upon the parties to present the case; he has no research or investigative staff, and limited time to do his own research. The requirement that the judges have confidence in the advocates appearing before them is particularly acute under such a system.[71a]

It is not surprising that the Royal Commission unanimously recommended against fusion, notwithstanding the speculative nature of some of the arguments. They saw that the present system had its advantages; fusion might lead to some saving, but only in small cases and in larger cases the expense might be greater. Employing two lawyers did not necessarily mean that work was duplicated. Some of the adverse criticisms of the present system could be met by other changes.

Nevertheless, it has been argued that the Bar may cease to be viable as a separate branch in the relatively near future in view of constraints on public expenditure, the possible establishment of a public prosecution service with rights of audience, the introduction of computerised legal information retrieval systems within solicitors' offices, and the facts that the Bar has become progressively less "specialist," and that entry is not professionally more rigorous than qualification as a solicitor.[72]

(c) Solicitors' practices and their work

(i) Numbers

In 1982 there were 41,738 solicitors with practising certificates. Most were in private practice, on their own account (3,398) or as a partner (19,065), consultant (1,773) or assistant solicitor (10,860) or otherwise (727). There were 1,799 in commerce or industry, 66 in the government service, 2,899 in local government and 102 were abroad.[73] The numbers have consistently increased, apart from periods of decline in the 1840s and between the wars, and have risen dramatically in the last decade.[74] The number per head of the population declined to the point that there was a period of acute shortage after the second world war; this trend was reversed in the late 1960s and 1970s. Thus in 1967 there were 22,233 solicitors (1:2164 of the population) and in 1977 32,812 (1:1497).[75] Fears have been expressed that there are too many in and seeking entry to the

---

[71] See Mann, op. cit. n.66.

[71a] The advocate's "duty to the court" rests on rules of professional conduct: see below, pp. 116–123.

[72] P. Wallington, Lawyers in the 1990's (1981) III (2) Liverpool Law Review 5, 6–13.

[73] Annual Report of The Law Society, 1982–83, p. 21. Johnstone and Hopson estimated that in 1963 there was about one qualified solicitor engaged in legal work who did not hold a practising certificate for every ten who did: see D. Podmore, Solicitors in the Wider Community (1980) pp. 18, 159, 178.

[74] Podmore (1980) pp. 13–19.

[75] Ibid.

solicitors' branch.[76] The number of law graduates doubled between 1967 and 1977.[77] Other trends in recent years have been a steady increase in the proportion of employed assistant solicitors in private practice, a decline in the proportion of sole practitioners,[78] and a slight increase in the proportion of solicitors outside private practice.

(ii) Solicitors firms: private practice

In 1979 there were 6,667 firms of which 34.3 per cent. were run by sole practitioners.[79] According to The Law Society the "typical firm" has three principals, five other fee earners (one assistant solicitor, two legal executives, one articled clerk, one junior clerk) ten other full time and three part-time staff (accounts clerks, an outdoor clerk, secretaries, a telephonist and a receptionist).[80] There are, however, many kinds of solicitors' practice, ranging from large, highly specialised firms in the City of London to small provincial practices specialising in legal aid work.[81] Geographically, the spread is uneven.[82] Foster's survey based on the 1971 Law List showed an irregular dispersal within towns, between urban and rural areas, and nationally. A majority of solicitors practised in the centre of urban areas, near each other, the courts and commercial and financial institutions. Solicitors' offices were, however, more widely dispersed than solicitors. For example, in Greater London 77 per cent. of solicitors were found to work in central London, but only 44 per cent. of solicitors' offices were found there. Nearly two-thirds of all solicitors practised in towns with over 100,000 people. The proportion of offices to population varied between 1:1896 (Guildford) and 1:66,629 (Huyton). The Royal Commission thought the most likely reason for the lack of solicitors in areas of social deprivation to be the low level of remuneration for legally-aided contentious work rather than simply the "preference" of solicitors to practise elsewhere. Unless "mass production" methods were employed, legal aid work had to be subsidised by other more profitable work of a kind not generally available in the areas in question. They recommended that legal aid should be adequately remunerated, that law centres should be supported and that private solicitors should be encouraged to open in areas of need by the provision of interest-free loans.[83]

(iii) Solicitors' work

The remuneration survey commissioned by The Law Society showed that in 1975–76 75·8 per cent. of the gross fees of solicitors in private practice came from non-contentious, and 24·2 per cent. from contentious work. The breakdown according to the category of work was: conveyanc-

[76] e.g. P.A. Leach, (1980) 77 L.S.Gaz. 29; J. Clarke (President of The Law Society) (1980) 77 L.S.Gaz. 981–2.

[77] R.C.L.S., Vol. 2, p. 47.

[78] D. Podmore, "The Sole Practitioner—a Declining Species" (1979) 129 N.L.J. 356–7; Podmore (1980) pp. 21–2.

[79] R.C.L.S., Vol. 1, p. 187.

[80] Memorandum No. 5 to the Royal Commission, (1978) 75 L.S.Gaz. 422, 426. 66 per cent. of all firms were of this size or smaller.

[81] Podmore suggests a classification of 14 groups, based on Abel-Smith and Stevens (1967) pp. 144–8: Podmore (1980) pp. 22–4.

[82] Ibid. pp. 27–9; K. Foster, "The Location of Solicitors" (1973) 36 M.L.R. 153; L. Bridges et al., Legal Services in Birmingham (1975).

[83] R.C.L.S., Vol. 1, pp. 46–48, 181–2.

ing 47·4 per cent., probate 13·5 per cent., company 12·5 percent., other non-contentious 4·3 per cent., matrimonial 5·4 per cent., crime 4·5 per cent., personal injury 3·3 per cent. and other contentious 9·1 per cent.[84] Unfortunately, there was no clear indication of the profitability of the different categories of work.[85] In 1968 the Prices and Incomes Board estimated that conveyancing accounted for 55·6 per cent. of solicitors' income, 40·8 per cent. of expenses and 41·4 per cent. of productive time.[86] The "overall impression" from the 1975–76 survey was that conveyancing was more profitable than the other classes of work apart from company and commercial.[87] Solicitors are generally much less dependent on legal aid than barristers.[88] Overall, the Commission concluded that the earnings of private practice solicitors were not out of line with comparable occupations: middle management in industry and the legal and adminsitrative class of the civil service.[89] However, no useful information was obtained for accountants, engineers, surveyors and members of other professions, and the general quality of the research has been adversely criticised.[90]

A survey of 103 solicitors in private practice in the West Midlands showed that most of them typically worked under some pressure, often found it necessary to take work home and did not often appear in court.[91] Individual solicitors were more likely to specialise than their firms, to enable the latter to offer a wide range of services.[92]

A substantial number of solicitors are employed outside private practice, mainly in central[93] and local government, industry and commerce.[94] Their work is obviously geared to the needs of their employers, lawyers in industry being particularly concerned with employment law, property and commercial work, lawyers in local government with prosecutions, property, rating and so on. The Royal Commission thought that the rules against "touting" should be relaxed to enable employed solicitors to undertake conveyancing for and give free legal advice on any matter to fellow employees.[95]

---

[84] R.C.L.S., Vol. 2, pp. 488–9.

[85] The response rate to the relevant question in the survey was 14 per cent.: R.C.L.S. Vol. 2, p. 487.

[86] Cmnd. 3529, Tables 14 and 15. The other work categories were also analysed.

[87] R.C.L.S., Vol. 2, p. 496.

[88] R.C.L.S., Vol. 2, p. 491. 65·7 per cent. of firms earned less than 10 per cent. from this source and a further 20·9 per cent. less than 20 per cent. Cf. p. 111 below.

[89] In private practice in 1976 the average profit of principals (before tax, pensions and interest on capital invested) was £13,581. The median salary of salaried solicitors was £4,346, for articled clerks £1,635 and for legal executives, £3,692: R.C.L.S., Vol. 2, pp. 478, 505. See generally Vol. 1, pp. 507–542, Vol. 2, pp. 447–578 (earnings surveys) and 627–698 (comparisons). Comparisons with other professional groups based on figures for 1976–77 are given in Chap.11 of *Report No. 8 of the Royal Commission on the Distribution of Income & Wealth* (Cmnd. 7679, 1979). The Report concluded that *self-employed* solicitors occupied a prominent position among the professional groups, being the group whose members were most highly concentrated in the upper groups of self-employment income (see Tables 11.2 and 11.7).

[90] C. Glasser, *L.A.G. Bull.*, September 1979, p. 201.

[91] Podmore (1980) pp. 37, 96, 97.

[92] D. Podmore, (1977) 74 L.S.Gaz. 636.

[93] See Civil Service Commission: *Lawyers: Civil Service Careers* (4th ed. 1980); G. Drewry, "Lawyers in the UK Civil Service (1981) 59 *Public Administration* 15.

[94] See above, p. 103.

[95] R.C.L.S., Vol. 1, pp. 234–6. See below, p. 356.

(iv) *"Monopolies"*

Solicitors enjoy certain statutory monopolies.[96] Section 20 of the Solicitors Act 1974 makes it an offence for an unqualified person to act as a solicitor and as such commence or conduct litigation on behalf of another. An unqualified person may not pretend to be a solicitor,[97] and a solicitor may not act as an agent for an unqualified person or do any other act enabling such a person to act as a solicitor.[98]

It is also an offence for an unqualified person[99] to prepare (directly or indirectly) any instrument "relating to real or personal estate, or any legal proceeding,"[1] to take instructions for a grant of probate or letters of administration, or to prepare papers on which to found or oppose such a grant,[2] unless he proves that this was not done for or in expectation of any fee, gain or reward. An offence is committed even where the unqualified person does not personally receive the fee.[3] No person may bring proceedings to recover costs in respect of anything done by an unqualified person acting as a solicitor.[4] The Royal Commission found these restrictions to be in the public interest.[5] In litigation heavy reliance was placed on the knowledge and integrity of solicitors, acting as they did as officers of the court. Solicitors had the responsibility of disclosing documents even where it would be contrary to his client's interests. A person "not subject to the same direct duty to the court and to professional disciplines"[6] could not be expected to exercise such responsibility. The Commission proposed a relaxation of the probate restrictions in non-contentious cases in favour of trust corporations, and resisted Law Society suggestions for new restictions on unqualified persons preparing for reward wills or powers of attorney.

The economic dependence of many solicitors upon conveyancing, when put alongside criticisms of the low quality of service provided[7] and the level of charges, naturally made the "conveyancing monopoly" one of the most controversial areas before the Commission.[8] This monopoly had been sought by the Society of Gentlemen Practisers in the eighteenth century, and was finally granted by William Pitt in 1804 as a *quid pro quo* for an increase in the tax on practising certificates and articles.[9] The restriction was possibly designed to facilitate the collection of revenue rather than to

[96] A non-lawyer may always act in person in matters affecting himself. Some of the "monopolies" are shared with other relatively small groups.

[97] Solicitors Act 1974, s.21. See, *e.g. Carter* v. *Butcher* [1966] 1 Q.B. 526.

[98] Solicitors Act 1974, s.39.

[99] Here the term covers a person who is not a solicitor, barrister or notary public, and there are some other exclusions: *ibid.* ss.22(2), 23(2).

[1] *Ibid.* s.22. "Instrument" does not include a will, an agreement not under seal, a letter of power of attorney, or a "transfer of stock containing no trust or limitation thereof:" s.22(3). Thus a contract for the sale of land is not within the restriction whereas the deed which effects the conveyance is.

[2] *Ibid.* s.23(1).

[3] *Reynolds* v. *Hoyle* [1976] 1 W.L.R. 207; *cf. Green* v. *Hoyle* [1976] 1 W.L.R. 575.

[4] 1974 Act, s.25.

[5] R.C.L.S., Vol. 1, pp. 225–31.

[6] *Ibid.* p.227.

[7] M. Joseph, *The Conveyancing Fraud* (1976): a book by a practising solicitor.

[8] R.C.L.S. Vol. 1, pp. 243–282. The Commission preferred the expression "closed shop."

[9] Stamp Act 1804. See Abel-Smith and Stevens (1967) pp. 22–3, Kirk (1976) Chap. 7. It was moved from fiscal legislation to a Solicitors Act in 1932.

protect the public interest. A majority[10] of the Commission accepted The Law Society's case that the restrictions were in the public interest in view of the complexity of the law relating to the ownership of land, the complexity of the conveyancing process and the need to protect clients from dishonesty, incompetence and overcharging. The Commission were unanimous that a "free-for-all" would not be in the public interest. By a majority they rejected proposals for a system of licensed conveyancers. Such a "new profession" would have to be subjected to requirements as to examinations and conditions of practice similar to those affecting the solicitors; they would have similar overhead expenses and it was unlikely that charges would be held down. Indeed they suggested that the restrictions should be extended to cover the preparation of the contract of sale as well as the final document and to apply to provincial notaries who may qualify in the future, that the maximum penalty should be raised for the first time since 1894 from £50 to £500 and that prosecutions should be brought by the police rather than The Law Society. They did not find that charges were excessive. In order to reintroduce more certainty to charging, they suggested there whould be a scale of "standard" charges covering the general run of domestic conveyancing. Matters have not, however, remained there. In December 1983, a second reading was given to a Private Member's Bill, the House Buyer's Bill, which proposed the introduction of a system whereby licensed conveyancers would be permitted to undertake the conveyancing of "houses" with registered title. In response, the government indicated its intention to promote legislation to enable solicitors employed by building societies, banks and other organisations to undertake conveyancing for their employers' clients, whether or not the land was registered. Either way, the private profession is poised to lose a significant section of its business. As a result there have been calls for the establishment of a Solicitors' Building Society, and for solicitors to be permitted to act as estate agents, mortgage and insurance brokers.[11]

An analogous area is that of rights of audience.[12] These are limited by the practice of the court and tribunals concerned rather than by rules of law. Litigants in person have a right of audience throughout the legal system.[13] Barristers enjoy a virtual monopoly of advocacy before the House of Lords, Court of Appeal and High Court.[14] They also have exclusive rights of audience in all Crown Court cases, except that a solicitor may appear (a) in appeals to the Crown Court from a magistrates' court in civil or criminal proceedings or on committal for sentence, if the solicitor or anyone in his firm appeared in the court below[15]; and (b) in a wider

---

[10] A third of the members were unconvinced: R.C.L.S. Vol. 1, pp. 808, 809–812, 813–816.

[11] (1984) 81 L.S.Gaz. 2–5, 337–341, 1010–1.

[12] R.C.L.S. Vol. 1, pp. 203–221. For a summary, see *ibid.* p. 221.

[13] Prosecutions in the Crown Court must be conducted by a barrister.

[14] Solicitors may appear before the single judge of the Court of Appeal (Criminal Division) sitting in chambers, in certain High Court bankruptcy applications and in any High Court proceedings heard in chambers (before a judge, official referee, master or registrar). Rights of audience before the Judicial Committee of the Privy Council are limited to English and Northern Ireland barristers, Scottish advocates and all advocates duly qualified in countries from which appeals lie to the Privy Council.

[15] *Practice Direction* [1972] 1 W.L.R. 307.

class of cases in certain remote areas.[16] Barristers and solicitors have rights of audience in the county courts and magistrates' courts; laymen may be permitted to appear. For example, by custom magistrates allow police officers, local government officials and civil servants employed by the D.P.P. to appear. In most tribunals there are no restrictions. Any person may attend a trial as a friend of a party to take notes and give advice but he will not be accorded a right of audience.[17] The Royal Commission came down resoundingly in favour of the *status quo*. They rejected suggestions that the rights of audience of laymen should be extended, stressing, paticularly for the higher courts, the importance of proceedings for the individual concerned, the "special skill and expertise" called for, and their other proposals for the extension of financial support for legal services. Guidelines should be issued to county courts to achieve greater consistency in the exercise of their discretion to allow laymen rights of audience.

The existing position of litigants in person and laymen should not, however, be restricted. In the case of the former this was not because the Commission thought they were any good at advocacy, but because their right of audience was "long-established" and no-one had actually proposed its removal. In evidence, there had been some jockeying for position among lawyers. The Bar and the judges resisted solicitors' claims[18] for wider rights of audience, particularly in the Crown Court; The Law Society resisted the claims of legal executives.[19] By and large, the resisters won, apart from minor changes to enable a solicitor to appear in any court to deal with formal or unopposed matters.[20] The Commission thought that any significant changes would lead to a lowering of standards. Crown Court advocacy required different skills (*e.g.* addressing a jury) or greater expertise (*e.g.* knowledge of the laws of evidence and experience in cross-examination) than advocacy in the magistrates' courts. The Commission's enthusiasm for solicitor-advocates was markedly lukewarm:

> "Many solicitors make competent advocates in magistrates' courts and some are very good. Some could achieve the same standard in the Crown Court if they could so arrange their professional lives as to enable them to concentrate on the work there."[21]

They thought it unlikely that many solicitors, except in large firms, would be able to have the constant practice in Crown Court advocacy which competence and progressive improvement required. However, they feared that enough solicitors would move into this area to have a "serious and

---

[16] *Practice Direction* [1972] 1 W.L.R. 5. The areas are Caernarvon, Barnstaple, Bodmin, Doncaster and Lincoln.

[17] *McKenzie* v. *McKenzie* [1971] P. 33; *Merry* v. *Persons Unknown* [1974] C.L.Y. 3003. A superior court may exceptionally hear persons who technically have no right of audience: *Engineers' and Managers' Association* v. *A.C.A.S.* [1979] 1 W.L.R. 113 (trade union official).

[18] The solicitors were refighting a battle lost when the criminal courts were reorganised in 1971: see the *Royal Commission on Assizes and Quarter Sessions* 1966–69, Cmnd. 4153 Written Evidence Nos. 32 and 47.

[19] See R.C.L.S., Vol. 1, pp. 413–5. The Law Society raised the matter again in 1984: Annual Statement, 1983–84, pp. 48–49; (1984) 81 L.S.Gaz. 1507.

[20] Seven members of the Commission favoured some extension of the right of audience of solicitors in the Crown Court, particularly to make pleas in mitigation: Vol. 1, pp. 807, 816–823, 828–9.

[21] R.C.L.S., Vol. 1, p. 212. The competence of barristers was not discussed in the chapter on rights of audience. Their increasing prolixity was discussed in Vol. 1, pp. 307–8.

disproportionate impact on the income and capacity of barristers to continue in practice."[22] The fear of fusion was thus in the background.

(v) *Restrictions on practice*

A solicitor may employ, but may not form a partnership with a member of another profession.[23] This prevents the development of "group practices" of lawyers and members of other professions. The Royal Commission was not in favour of any change. Some of the candidates for patnership, such as doctors, engineers, architects, patent agents and actuaries would most often be needed to give expert evidence in litigation; it would be inappropriate for them to be in partnership with the lawyers who were preparing the case for trial. If partnerships with estate agents were allowed, there was a danger that sole practitioners and small firms would be absorbed into large estate agents' firms, to the detriment of general practice in small towns and rural areas. The Commission thought that in general it was in the client's interest to be able to choose his adviser without restriction; with inter-disciplinary partnerships there would be a tendency to keep a client within the firm. There would also be difficulties in drawing up common codes of conduct. The Commission did, however, accept that solicitors' firms should be allowed to incorporate, with unlimited liability only, under the Companies Acts.[24]

Another important area of restriction concerns advertising by individual solicitors or firms.[25] "Touting" is regarded as unprofessional and associated with "trade."[26] Collective advertising by the profession and detailed referral lists[27] are, by contrast, officially acceptable. The Law Society has been responsible for various national advertising campaigns,[28] financed by levies on practising certificates. They have proved controversial.[29] The introduction of individual advertising, subject to restrictions preventing claims of superiority, inaccurate or misleading statements and publicity likely to bring the profession into disrepute, was recommended by both the Monopolies Commission[30] and the Royal Commission.[31] Providing information to the public would thus be

[22] R.C.L.S., Vol. 1, p. 216.

[23] Solicitors' Practice Rules 1936–72, r.3.

[24] R.C.L.S., Vol. 1, pp. 401–4.

[25] It used to be prohibited: Solicitors' Practice Rules, 1936–72, r.1. See below, p. 116; Zander (1978) pp. 46–54; P. Fennell in P.A. Thomas (ed.) *Law in the Balance* (1982) Chap. 6.

[26] Fennell notes that in fact "professional ideology is not exclusively anti-entrepreneurial, but . . . incorporates elements of the value systems of both the 'pre-industrial gentleman' and the tradesman." (*Law in the Balance* (1982) p. 144).

[27] See below, p. 356.

[28] The "Mr. Whatsisname" campaign in 1977 (see R. Neill, (1977) 74 L.S.Gaz. 883; G. Sanctuary (1978) 75 L.S.Gaz. 267), a second in 1979 and a third in 1980, the latter two produced by Saatchi and Saatchi. The 1980 theme was that people should "consult a solicitor before problems got out of hand;" one of the advertisements illustrated an action for damages in respect of an injured thumb: (1980) 77 L.S.Gaz. 501.

[29] D. Podmore, (1980) 7 B.J.L.S. 1, 8.

[30] *Report on the supply of services of Solicitors in England and Wales in relation to restrictions on advertising*, 1976 (1975–76 H.C. 557).

[31] Vol. 1, pp. 367–373. Similar guidelines have been promulgated by the Consultative Committee of the Bars and Law Societies of the European Community (C.C.B.E.) governing advertising of lawyers' services in the Community: (1980) 77 L.S.Gaz. 662. In *Bates* v. *State Bar of Arizona*, 53 L.Ed. 2d 810 (1977) the United States Supreme Court held that it was unconstitutional to prevent lawyers advertising the availability and cost of routine legal services.

permitted; drumming up business would still be prohibited. The Royal Commission also suggested that The Law Society should introduce a scheme for the designation of "specialists."[32]

The relaxation of the restrictions on advertising was regarded by the Royal Commission not simply as helping to improve access to legal services but also as the "necessary concomitant" to their conclusion that the solicitors' conveyancing monopoly should be retained. Individual advertising should help the public to "shop around."[33] The Law Society has responded by introducing a new national Solicitors' Directory, including information as to the categories of work undertaken (published as part of the *Solicitors' and Barristers' Directory and Diary*) and 28 regional directories (replacing the *Legal Aid Solicitors' List*). It has also agreed that individual advertising should be permitted, subject to the recommended restrictions. Charges may be advertised.[34]

(d) Barristers and their work

(i) *Numbers*

In October 1983 there were 5,032 barristers (including 512 Q.C.s) practising in 330 sets of chambers. 3,629 were in 215 sets in central London, and the rest were spread through 30 provincial centres.[35] As was the case with solicitors, the numbers of practising barristers increased significantly in the late 1960s and 1970s following a period of shortage. They more than doubled between 1963 and 1979.[36] The net annual increase declined between 1975 and 1979, with increasing numbers ceasing practice.[37] The proportion of the profession of 10 years' call and under has also shown a marked increase: in 1966 there were 769 (34 per cent. of the practising Bar) and in 1983, 2,367 (47 per cent.).[38]

(ii) *Work*

A barrister may have a general or specialist common law practice (contract, crime, tort—especially personal injury cases, landlord and tenant, family matters), or may specialise in Chancery work (trusts, land law, conveyancing, wills, company law, revenue matters) or in one of a number of narrower fields (tax, patents, commercial matters, planning, admiralty, libel). Most of the recent increase in the size of this branch of the profession has been in the generalist common law area. In London, common law chambers are concentrated in the Temple; Chancery

---

[32] Vol. 1, pp. 365–6.

[33] Sir Henry Benson, (1979) 76 L.S.Gaz. 1029, 1030.

[34] (1983) 80 L.S.Gaz. 1797, 3222 and 3223; (1984) 81 L.S.Gaz. 1802–3.

[35] Annual Statement of the Senate 1983–84, pp. 68–9; R.C.L.S., Vol. 1, pp. 188, 447–457. Barristers in London may also join their provincial colleagues on one of the six Circuits: Northern, North Eastern, Midland and Oxford, Western, South Eastern and Wales and Chester. The circuits now are important as the units of regional court administration. Each Circuit elects a Leader and Committee.

[36] R.C.L.S., Vol. 2, p. 54.

[37] Annual Statement, 1983–84, p. 68. The figure since then has fluctuated. In 1978–79 153 barristers ceased practice, including 82 of under 10 years' call; in 1979–80 the corresponding figures were 132 and 82, in 1980–81, 174 and 72, in 1981–82, 103 and 52, and in 1982–83, 155 and 60.

[38] *Ibid.* p. 19. The figures for 1979, 1980 and 1982 were 57, 47 and 50 per cent. respectively.

barristers are concentrated in Lincoln's Inn. There is no rule requiring chambers to be in one of the inns of court. Concentration there is preferred as the inns charge barristers only a proportion of the market rent, for the convenience of access to the courts and because of long tradition.[39]

There is little information available on the importance of various kinds of barristers' work. Zander[40] suggests that the Bar devotes most of its collective time to crime and personal injury work, with a substantial proportion to divorce. As we have seen, their rights of audience were firmly upheld by the Royal Commission, although a state prosecution service is now to be introduced.[41] For the moment, crime rates continue to rise. It is unlikely that civil actions for negligence will in the near future be replaced by a comprehensive state scheme for compensating accident victims.[42] Apart from difficulties caused by the dramatic increase in numbers, prospects for barristers in private practice do not seem as bleak as was feared before the recent spate of Royal Commissions.

As to remuneration, the Royal Commission concluded that the earnings of barristers were not out of line with those in comparable occupations, except that the earnings of barristers in the early years of practice were low.[43] Their figures confirmed that barristers are increasingly dependent on fees from public funds.[44] The late payment of fees by solicitors has been a serious cause for complaint among barristers. The Law Society and the Senate have responded by tightening up the procedures for enforcing payments, and the Bar has clarified the terms of work on which barristers are prepared to act. These developments have not satisfied all the critics.[44a]

There are almost as many barristers employed in commerce, industry and central and local government as there are in private practice.[45] Their work compares much more closely with that done by employed solicitors in the same fields than with that done by barristers in private practice. Indeed, in 1976 the Chairman of the Solicitors' Commerce and Industry Group said that:

"Fusion is a word that we in commerce and industry never use in

---

[39] R.C.L.S., Vol. 1, pp. 449–50. There is a set in Wellington St., Covent Garden.

[40] *State of Knowledge about the Legal Profession* (1980) p. 17.

[41] See below, p. 522.

[42] Even the modest, piecemeal proposals of the Royal Commission on Civil Liability and Compensation (Cmnd. 7054, 1979) have not found favour with the Conservative government, apart from some changes to the law of damages (Administration of Justice Act, 1982).

[43] See R.C.L.S., Vol. 1, pp. 507–542 and Vol. 2, pp. 579–626 (surveys of barristers' earnings). The 1976/77 average for all barristers (before tax and pensions but net of expenses) was £8,715 (£13,270 gross). The figures for Q.C.s were £21,087 (£30,656), for all juniors, £7,319 (£11,309) and for juniors of three years standing or less £2,769 (£4,856): R.C.L.S., Vol. 2, p. 590. Figures for senior barristers are given in the Reports of the Top Salaries Review Board: see, *e.g.* Cmnd. 8243 pp. 41–52. A survey of all practising barristers for 1981–82 (26 per cent. response rate) produced average figures of £46,100 (net of expenses and pension premium) (£72,700 gross) for Q.C.s and £13,700 (£22,100 gross) for juniors. Earnings, except for criminal practitioners, had roughly kept pace with inflation since 1974–75: (1983) 80 L.S.Gaz. 3227.

[44] In 1976/77 £23 millions out of £48 millions total gross fees were from public funds: R.C.L.S., Vol. 2, pp. 595–7.

[44a] Annual Statement, 1982–83, pp. 23–41; (1983) 80 L.S.Gaz. 1912–13; (1984) L.S.Gaz. 915–16; J. Ferris, (1982) 132 N.L.J. 745; S. Best (1982) 132 N.L.J. 803.

[45] R.C.L.S., Vol. 1, p. 232.

practice, because it is an accomplished fact with us. Barristers and solicitors are almost completely interchangeable. . . . "[46]

The Law Society has expressed the view that people who wish to practise as a solicitor should become a solicitor. It has also been suggested that one reason why such barristers do not change is snobbery.[47] However, the Bar Association for Commerce, Finance and Industry persuaded the Royal Commission that the rules preventing employed barristers from undertaking conveyancing and briefing other barristers in non-contentious matters should be relaxed.[48] The Bar Council acted on this recommendation,[49] much to the displeasure of The Law Society.[50]

(iii) *Restrictions on practice*

One of the main restrictions is the general rule that they may only take instructions from a solicior.[51] There are several particular exceptions,[52] covering such matters as foreign work, the examination of material to be published to check for libel and contempt, and briefing by a patent agent or parliamentary agent. There are also special rules covering barristers employed in law centres.[53] The general rule is of comparatively recent origin, being settled as regards contentious work in 1888 and non-contentious work in 1955. Perhaps the most significant exceptions are those enabling barristers to compete more effectively for foreign work. The Overseas Practice Rules were introduced in 1973[54] and relaxed many of the basic rules of conduct for barristers: apart from being able to receive instructions direct, barristers may negotiate fees direct, accept an annual retainer, a fixed fee or a contingent fee, and enter into partnership with any lawyer other than a solicitor for the purpose of sharing an office or services abroad. A barrister may also be employed in an office of a firm of English solicitors situated abroad provided that the consent of the Bar Council is obtained, that he does not enter into partnership with a solicitor and that he does not hold himself out as a barrister.[55]

There have from time to time been rumblings from the Bar that their "self-denying ordinance" might be withdrawn,[56] but the Senate suggested to the Royal Commission that barristers were not at present equipped to deal with the office work necessary if they were to deal directly with clients. Having decided that fusion would not be in the public interest[57] it was

[46] (1976) 73 L.S.Gaz. 369.

[47] R.C.L.S., Vol. 1, p. 237; "Enobarbus" (1980) 77 L.S.Gaz. 766.

[48] R.C.L.S., Vol. 1, pp. 237–241.

[49] Annual Statement, 1979–80, pp. 52–55; Code of Conduct, Annex 17.

[50] Anon., "A Road to Fusion?" (1980) 77 L.S.Gaz. 637–8. This issue had previously been a bone of contention between the two branches: Abel-Smith and Stevens (1967) pp. 439–443.

[51] R.C.L.S., Vol. 1, pp. 222–5; In Re T. (A Barrister) [1982] Q.B. 430 the visitors to Lincoln's Inn upheld an order that a barrister be suspended for four months for breach of this rule and another act of professional misconduct.

[52] Code of Conduct, para. 50 and Annex 14: Sir William Boulton, Conduct and Etiquette at the Bar (6th ed., 1975) pp. 8–14.

[53] See below, pp. 332–336.

[54] Annual Statement of the Bar Council, 1973–4, pp. 33–4. They were subsequently relaxed even further: see Code of Conduct, Annex 14.

[55] (1982) 79 L.S.Gaz. 1024; Annual Statement, 1982–83, p. 63.

[56] R. Hazell, The Bar on Trial (1978) pp. 172–3.

[57] See above, pp. 101–103.

inevitable that the Royal Commission would not favour the wholesale removal of restrictions on direct access.[58]

A pactising barrister may not enter a partnership with another practising barrister.[59] "The Bar is a profession for the individualist."[60] The Royal Commission recognised that partnerships might often be advantageous for barristers. An income could more easily be provided for a beginner, work could be distributed more evenly and provision for sickness and retirement would be easier. They concluded, however, that a change would not be in the public interest as it would restrict choice, on the assumption that partners would not be permitted to appear on opposite sides. Problems might be acute at the specialist and provincial bars.[61] Individualism is tempered by the requirement that practising barristers join a set of chambers[62] and have the services of the clerk to the chambers.[63] It is possible for a set of chambers to contain only one member, but in 1979 the average number of barristers per set in London was 15 and only six of 199 sets had fewer than six members.[64]

In evidence to the Royal Commission the Senate saw dangers in barristers practising alone, particularly in the criminal courts. They would be exposed to pressure to ignore the rules against touting and improper association with clients and witnesses; the younger the barrister, the greater the risk. Practice in chambers provided the "mutual support in respect of expenses and the allocation of work, professional association, informal advice and guidance, devilling and assistance to newcomers."[65] The Senate also prefers to see "balanced" sets with barristers of all grades of seniority.[66] In addition to the provision of mutual aid and comfort, the chambers rule was seen by the Royal Commission as aiding the Senate in its task of "controlling backsliders" and maintaining standards.[67] In many respects chambers operate as *de facto* partnerships, with the sharing of expenses, the common fund of goodwill and the fact that briefs may be sent to a set of chambers rather than an individual barrister. Furthermore, a barrister may obtain the assistance of a fellow barrister in the preparation of his paperwork, and, with the consent of the instructing solicitor, at a hearing. Such arrangements are known as "devilling." The barrister briefed retains his personal responsibility but must pay the "devil"

---

[58] They suggested minor relaxations in favour of patent agents and London notaries. The latter change was effected in 1980: (1980) 77 L.S.Gaz. 1277. Otherwise, the matter has been dropped for lack of demand.

[59] Code of Conduct, para. 28.

[60] Senate of the Inns of Court and the Bar, *A Career at the Bar* (1980) p. 5.

[61] R.C.L.S., Vol. 1, pp. 462–5, Vol. 2, pp. 375–392. The case for allowing partnerships is argued in M. Zander, *Lawyers and the Public Interest* (1968) pp. 252–269 and Hazell (1978) pp. 123–9.

[62] Code of Conduct, para. 25.

[63] *Ibid.* para. 26c. See below, pp. 130–131 as to clerks.

[64] R.C.L.S., Vol. 1, p. 447. The average in the provinces was 12 and there were 20 sets with fewer than six members.

[65] R.C.L.S., Vol. 1, p. 455. The internal management of chambers has been made the subject of "Chambers Guidelines" issued by the Senate in 1977 (R.C.L.S., Vol. 1, pp. 475–8). A barrister who wishes to open a set of chambers (or a branch of or an annexe to an existing set) outside the inns must now obtain the consent of the Circuit or (in Greater London) the Bar Committee. Appeals against refusals lie to the Bar Council: Code of Conduct, para. 74 and Annex 18; (1983) 80 L.S.Gaz. 2379.

[66] R.C.L.S., Vol. 1, p. 452.

[67] R.C.L.S., Vol. 1, pp. 454, 455.

adequate and reasonable remuneration, normally half the fee. So, while barristers are supposed to "stand on their own two feet," there are many ways in which their colleagues can help them remain upright.

As a result of the recent growth in numbers, coupled with the lack of space, young barristers have found it increasingly difficult to obtain a permanent place ("seat" or "tenancy") in chambers, although a number have been allowed to remain after pupillage as "squatters" or "floaters." Insofar as the problem was caused by shortage of work, the Royal Commission felt there were no real remedies, although potential entrants should be informed of the difficulties.[68] However, the Senate "should adopt a vigorous policy to secure the provision of more accommodation."[69] The Senate's Accommodation Committee subsequently expressed the opinion that it was doing just that.[70]

Another distinctive feature of practice at the bar is the division into two ranks: Queen's Counsel[71] and "junior" barristers.[72] Appointment as a Q.C. is made by the Queen on the advice of the Lord Chancellor, and is today a mark of eminence in the profession rather than a retainer for Crown work. It is for the juniors who wish to "take silk" (Q.C.s wear silk gowns) to apply; between 20 per cent. and 30 per cent. of the applications are successful,[73] and re-applications are permissible. The main difference as regards work done is that Q.C.s do not normally do paperwork, except in those cases where they are briefed to appear alone: their role is that of the skilled and experienced advocate or specialist adviser, and they are in a position to concentrate on heavy cases. After his elevation a Q.C. would expect, or at least hope, to take work that is more remunerative, and to reduce his work load. The change can be something of a gamble,[74] but it may be that the risks are not as great as they used to be.[75] Most High Court judges are appointed from among the Q.C.s and there are many other judicial appointments available.

Formerly, there were rules of etiquette which prevented a Q.C. from appearing in court without a junior (the two-counsel rule) and which entitled the junior to a fee of two-thirds that of his leader. In 1966 the

[68] R.C.L.S., Vol. 1, pp. 459–60.

[69] *Ibid.* pp.460–2. Specific rules of conduct might also have to be waived.

[70] Annual Statement, 1979–80, p. 27. The amount available for interest-free loans was doubled to £120,000 in 1980–81. The inns are also moving towards a common rent policy: (1981) 78 L.S.Gaz. 326; Annual Statement, 1981–82, pp. 26–46. Although the Senate's proposal that market rents should be charged with no more than a 10 per cent. discount was thrown out at a Special General Meeting of Senate Subscribers: (1982) 79 L.S.Gaz. 981, 986; Annual Statement, 1982–83, pp. 8–12, the Accommodation Committee decided that the alternative (accepted) proposal, that sufficient rent should be charged to finance the prudent and economical administration of the inns' activities, would enable market rents to be charged (*ibid.* p.13).

[71] "One of Our Counsel learned in the Law." Q.C.s become K.C.s when there are Kings.

[72] R.C.L.S., Vol. 1, pp. 465–471. All barristers who are not Q.C.s are "juniors." There can be very senior "juniors."

[73] R.C.L.S., Vol. 1, p. 479. There were 52 appointments in 1981, 57 in 1982, 43 in 1983 and 43 in 1984.

[74] R.E. Megarry, *Lawyer and Litigant in England* (1962) pp. 90–92: "a great adventure with much to gain and much to lose."

[75] Hazell (1978) pp. 23–34. Q.C.s reliant on public funds may be at risk when there are pressures on public expenditure. The remuneration survey showed that the net earnings of Q.C.s were substantially higher than senior juniors, although the response rate of juniors of over 15 years standing was low: R.C.L.S., Vol. 1, pp. 591, 601.

two-thirds rule was abolished[76]; the junior is now simply entitled to a "proper fee."[77] Ten years later the Monopolies Commission reported that the two-counsel rule was contrary to the public interest.[78] The rule was accordingly abrogated as from October 1, 1977 and the Bar Council issued revised rules.[79] A Q.C. may appear alone but must decline to do so if he would be unable properly to conduct the case, or fulfil other professional commitments. The change seems to have made little practical difference.[80] A majority of the Commission favoured continuance of the two-tier system, with minor changes.[81]

3. QUALITY OF SERVICE AND COMPLAINTS AGAINST LAWYERS

(a) Introduction

The Royal Commission reported that most legal work was transacted well and efficiently,[82] an opinion based on evidence from users of legal services, informed observers such as CABx and the Lay Observer, and members of the profession. The Users' Survey conducted on their behalf showed that 67 per cent. of the 2,064 people interviewed who had consulted solicitors were completely satisfied, 17 per cent. fairly satisfied and 13 per cent. to some extent dissatisfied.[83] The main causes of complaint were inefficiency, incompetence, failure of communication, delay and cost. As regards barristers, the general opinion among judges and practising lawyers appeared to be that standards fell in the 1960s and 1970s but were rising again.[84] Such dissatisfaction as there was could not be ignored, and substantial improvements were needed in several areas, affecting aspects both of the way in which lawyers went about their work and of the legal system in which they operated.[85]

A broad distinction may be drawn between factors that are designed to maintain standards by preventing problems arising, and the procedures available whereby a client may obtain redress when things go wrong. As regards the former, the Royal Commission emphasised the features of "professions" mentioned earlier in the chapter,[86] such as education and training and rules of conduct, and other points such as supervision by the

---

[76] See Zander (1968) pp. 146–152.

[77] Annual Statement of the Bar Council, 1971–72, p. 20.

[78] *Barristers Services: A report on the supply by Her Majesty's Counsel alone of their services*, 1976 (1975–76 H.C. 512).

[79] Annual Statement, 1977–78, pp. 42–5; R.C.L.S., Vol. 1, pp. 480–1; Code of Conduct, Annex 6.

[80] R.C.L.S., Vol. 1, pp. 468–470.

[81] *Ibid.* Four members thought that the title should be conferred as a mark of honour only: R.C.L.S., Vol. 1, pp. 823, 829. See A. Samuels, (1984) 134 N.L.J. 503.

[82] R.C.L.S., Vol. 1, p. 292. This point is of course separate from the question whether there is work which lawyers should be doing but are not: see Chap. 8.

[83] R.C.L.S., Vol. 2, pp. 223–233. Other surveys are summarised in Zander, *S.K.L.P.* (1980) pp. 55–57. Convicted prisoners seem generally less enthusiastic about lawyers: M. Zander [1972] Crim.L.R. 155. *Cf.* J. Bottoms and J. McLean, *Defendants in the Criminal Process* (1976) pp. 154–160. The role of solicitors in divorce proceedings is discussed in M. Murch, *Justice and Welfare in Divorce* (1980) Chap. 1.

[84] R.C.L.S., Vol. 1, p. 292.

[85] R.C.L.S., Vol. 1, pp. 293–308. Problems discussed including delay, returned briefs, relations with clients, listing cases, etc.

[86] Above, pp. 92–93.

courts and fellow practitioners, control of fees by certification and taxation and control by the legal aid authorities.[87] They thought that the introduction of Written Professional Standards as an indication of good practice would be helpful. These would, for example, cover areas where weaknesses could be discerned at present, such as the steps taken to keep clients fully informed and the preparation and handling of briefs.[88] Guidance should also be given on modern methods of office administration.

When things go wrong, there are a number of avenues open to the client affected although there may be considerable practical difficulties in following them. He may, for example, raise the matter with the firm to which his lawyer belongs. He may complain to the appropriate professional body, and this may lead to disciplinary action. He may bring legal proceedings. He may refuse to pay the lawyer's bill, and defend any proceedings for payment brought by the lawyer. A criminal offence such as theft may have been committed.

(b) Professional misconduct: solicitors

The Law Society may make rules, with the concurrence of the Master of the Rolls, for regulating the professional practice, conduct and discipline of solicitors.[89] The current practice rules cover a limited number of matters. A solicitor must not:

    (a) attempt to gain business by inviting instructions, advertising or touting[90];

    (b) act for both parties in a transfer or lease of land[91];

    (c) share or agree to share professional fees except with another solicitor or a lawyer practising abroad[92];

    (d) act in association with a claims assessor, or for a client introduced by a claims assessor[93];

    (e) agree to receive a contingency fee[94];

    (f) permit to appear on his name plate or professional stationery the name of any person other than a solicitor who holds a current practising certificate[95];

and must ensure that every office where he or his firm practise is properly supervised in accordance with prescribed minimum standards.[96] The Council of The Law Society may waive these rules in any particular case or cases.[97] If a solicitor fails to comply, any person may make a

---

[87] R.C.L.S., Vol. 1, pp. 288–290.

[88] R.C.L.S., Vol. 1, pp. 296, 303–305. Draft standards have been produced dealing with communication with the client, information on costs and responsibility for the client's case or matter: (1984) 81 L.S.Gaz. 1182.

[89] Solicitors Act 1974, s.31(1). See *Cordery on Solicitors* (7th ed., 1981) Chap. 10.

[90] The Solicitors' Practice Rules 1936–1972, r.1. See above, pp. 109–110.

[91] *Ibid.* r.2: this rule applies to firms as well as individual solicitors and there are detailed exceptions.

[92] *Ibid.* r.3.

[93] *Ibid.* r.4(1)(2).

[94] *Ibid.* r.4(3). See below, pp. 371–372.

[95] The Solicitors' Practice Rules 1967: the name of the practice may include the name of a predecessor or former partner, and the firm may continue to use its 1967 name.

[96] The Solicitors' Practice Rules 1975.

[97] For waivers affecting law centres see below p. 334.

complaint to the Disciplinary Tribunal constituted under the 1974 Act,[98] or to The Law Society.

The rules are amplified in *A Guide to the Professional Conduct of Solicitors* issued by the Council in 1974. The *Guide* also covers many other matters in what is described as "an extensive unwritten or 'common law' code of conduct."[99] Solicitors must comply with detailed rules made by The Law Society as to the holding of clients' money: a separate clients' account must be maintained, records kept and so on.[1] An accountants' report must be made annually.[2] The Law Society may inspect a solicitor's books to ascertain whether the rules have been observed. Clients are further protected by the compensation fund first set up in 1942.[3] The Council has a discretion to make a grant where it is satisfied that a person has suffered *loss* through the dishonesty of a solicitor or his employee, or *hardship* through a solicitor's failure to account for money. A grant may also be made to a solicitor who has suffered loss or hardship by reason of his liability to a client following misappropriation by a partner or employee. This scheme is complementary to the requirement that solicitors be insured in respect of their civil liability as insurance is not available to cover deliberate misconduct.[4]

The Law Society is prepared to deal with cases of "professional misconduct," acting either of its own motion or on a complaint made to it. "Professional misconduct" or "conduct unbefitting a solicitor" is widely and in some respects vaguely defined. It includes offences under the Solicitors Act 1974, offences of dishonesty or moral turpitude[5] or other blatant inpropriety in the absence of a criminal conviction.[6] Indeed "any conduct which brings the name of the profession into disrepute is *prima facie* cause for disciplinary action."[7]

"Unbefitting conduct" must be distinguished from "professional negligence." At present The Law Society will not take action against a solicitor in respect of negligence unless it is "of such a degree as to amount to unbefitting conduct" or conduct "dishonourable in his profession, or such as to be regarded as deplorable by his fellows in the profession."[8] The reason advanced for this limitation is that "The Society cannot act as a court or supplant the normal machinery of justice by dealing with complaints of negligence and awarding damages."[9] The Royal Commission thought that this policy should change, and that the Society should

---

[98] s.31(2). See below.

[99] *Guide*, p. 5.

[1] The Solicitors' Accounts Rules 1975 and the Solicitors' Trust Accounts Rules 1975, made under the Solicitors' Act 1974, s.32. Such rules were first made in 1935 following a period when the number of frauds by solicitors was causing public concern: Abel-Smith and Stevens (1967) pp. 190–192.

[2] Solicitors Act 1974, s.34; The Accountants' Report Rules 1975.

[3] Now regulated by the Solicitors Act 1974, s.36 and the Solicitors' Compensation Fund Rules 1975. See R.C.L.S., Vol. 1, pp. 321–324.

[4] See below, p. 122.

[5] *i.e.* an act that is "personally disgraceful because it involves an act of baseness, vileness or depravity . . . or more simply, actions which involve a wicked intent": *Guide*, p. 120.

[6] *e.g.* intoxication in court: *Guide*, p. 122.

[7] *Guide*, p. 118. *Cp.* the similarly imprecise charge used by the Football Association to deal with footballers who say the wrong things as distinct from kicking the wrong things.

[8] *Guide*, p. 28.

[9] *Guide*, p. 138.

investigate all complaints unless clearly misconceived or frivolous, including cases of "bad professional work." Even if formal disciplinary proceedings were not instituted, the solicitor could be given appropriate advice or prevailed upon to supply a satisfactory explanation or apology.[10] This procedure would not, however, lead to the award of compensation.[11]

At present, a complaint is examined first by The Law Society's Professional Purposes Department to see if it involves an allegation of professional misconduct. If it does, and the complainant agrees, the solicitor concerned is asked for his comments.[12] If the matter remains unresolved it is referred to the Society's Professional Purposes Committee. After further enquiry,[13] the Committee may decide to take no action, reject the complaint, or impose one or more of a range of sanctions. They may issue a reprimand, require the solicitor to submit monthly progress reports, or withhold or attach conditions to[14] the solicitor's next practising certificate. In serious cases they may institute proceedings before the Solicitors' Disciplinary Tribunal,[15] constituted under the Solicitors Act 1974.[16] The name was changed from the "Solicitors' Disciplinary Committee" by the 1974 Act to make it clear that it was independent of The Law Society. Its proceedings are protected by absolute privilege in the law of defamation.[17] The members are appointed by the Master of the Rolls and include both practising solicitors of not less than ten years' standing and lay members.[18] It sits in divisions of three, comprising two solicitors and one lay member. Applications are heard in private, but the findings are made public. If a complaint is proved the Tribunal may impose any one or more of a number of sanctions: that the solicitor concerned be struck off the roll,[19] suspended from practice (usually for a period not exceeding five years), fined (not more than £3,000) or reprimanded. An appeal lies to the

---

[10] R.C.L.S., Vol. 1, pp. 341–343. The Society's Professional Purposes Committee has proposed that it should seek further statutory powers to deal with bad professional work, including power to order a solicitor to remit or forgo his costs in whole or in part and power to order a solicitor to rectify mistakes at his own expense: (1983) 80 L.S.Gaz. 2354.

[11] The Lay Observer (see below, p. 119) has suggested that The Law Society should arbitrate on small claims: Sixth Annual Report, 1980–81 H.C. 291, p. 3. The Society's Professional Development Committee has recommended the introduction of an arbitration scheme based on the pattern of trade schemes approved by the Office of Fair Trading: (1984) 81 L.S.Gaz. 948–9. See also R. Egerton, (1983) 80 L.S.Gaz. 1048 and J.F. Phillips, *ibid.* p. 2125–6.

[12] Complaints are protected by qualified privilege in the law of defamation: *Beach* v. *Freeson* [1972] 1 Q.B. 14. The Law Society discourages solicitors from taking proceedings for defamation in respect of complaints: *Guide*, p. 140.

[13] There is no oral inquiry, but the complainant may be interviewed.

[14] *e.g.* preventing the solicitor practising as a principal or without a partner.

[15] Only about 1 per cent. of complaints investigated reached the Tribunal. Most of the Trinunal's cases follow this route although a member of the public may apply directly to the Tribunal: *Guide*, pp. 131–2. The Tribunal also hears applications for restoration to the roll from solicitors who have been struck off and various other applications: 1974 Act, ss.43(3), 47(1)(*b*).

[16] s.46; the Solicitors (Disciplinary Proceedings) Rules 1975. See generally R.C L.S., Vol. 1, pp. 348–350; (1980) 77 L.S.Gaz. 1006–7.

[17] *Addis v. Crocker* [1961] 1 Q.B. 11.

[18] See (1980) 77 L.S.Gaz. 54. Under the 1974 Act the solicitor members need no longer be either past or present members of the Council of The Law Society.

[19] This is obligatory in some cases *e.g.* where a solicitor acts as agent for an unqualified person: 1974 Act s.39; *cf.* s.41(4).

High Court[20] and then on a point of law to the Court of Appeal and House of Lords. The High Court, the Crown Court and the Court of Appeal may also exercise disciplinary jurisdiction directly over solicitors as officers of the court.[21]

The Royal Commission proposed a number of changes in the procedure, including the organisational separation of the department responsible for investigation (a proposed "Investigation Committee") from that responsible for adjudication (the Professional Purposes Committee); the introduction of a lay element on both committees; the widening of the sanctions available; and the introduction of a right of appeal from the Committee to the Tribunal.

Apart from lay membership of the Tribunal, the only lay element in the existing structure is provided by the "Lay Observer," whose office was introduced by the Solicitors Act 1974,[22] and whose function is to examine:

> "any written allegation made by or on behalf of a member of the public concerning the Society's treatment of a complaint. . . . "

He cannot examine the merits of a complaint. The Observers' reports have noted a significant improvement in the handling of complaints by the Society, particularly in avoiding unreasonable delay and explaining matters to the complainant more helpfully.[23] They have also included general comments and recommendations about common causes of complaint, while recognising that they see but a tiny proportion of all the cases dealt with by solicitors.[24]

(c) Professional misconduct: barristers[25]

The professional conduct of barristers is regulated by the profession itself rather than by legislation. It is the duty of every barrister (1) to comply with the *Code of Conduct for the Bar of England and Wales*; (2) not

---

[20] Solicitors Act 1974, s.49. In some cases the appeal lies to the Master of the Rolls (ss.43(3), 47(1)(*b*)) and his decision is final. Examples of appeals include *Re a Solicitor* [1956] 1 W.L.R. 1312; *Re a Solicitor* [1960] 2 Q.B. 212 and *Re a Solicitor* [1975] Q.B. 475.

[21] Solicitors Act 1974, ss.50–53. The jurisdiction to strike off is rarely exercised. In 1983 a former member of the council of The Law Society, Glanville Davies, was struck off by Vinelott J. following a finding in earlier proceedings before McCowan J. that he had been guilty of gross and persistent misconduct in the presentation and maintenance of a bill of costs which had been reduced on taxation from some £197,000 to £67,000. (*Parsons* v. *Davies*, October 24, 1983). A Committee of Enquiry found that The Law Society's handling of complaints against Davies had been a "disgrace": Ely Report (Supplement to (1984) 81 L.S.Gaz., February 22); see the response of The Society's Professional Purposes Committee: (1984) 81 L.S.Gaz. 938–948. See generally on the Davies affair (1984) 134 N.L.J. 42, 48–9, 189–90; *L.A.G. Bull.*, December 1983, pp. 11–14, *Legal Action*, Jan. 1984 pp. 3–4, Feb. 1984 pp. 4–6, Mar. 1984 pp. 4–5. Orders to pay costs incurred through neglect or misconduct or without authority are more common; see the *Supreme Court Practice 1985*, Vol. 2, Part 11, *R.* v. *Smith* (*Martin*) [1975] Q.B. 531 and *R. & T. Thew Ltd.* v. *Reeves* (No. 2) [1982] Q.B. 1283.

[22] s.45. The first Lay Observer was Rear Admiral B.C.G. Place, V.C., C.B., D.S.C.; the second, Major-General J.G.R. Allen, C.B. His office is at the Royal Courts of Justice. He is appointed by the Lord Chancellor, remunerated out of public funds and is independent of The Law Society.

[23] Fifth Report, 1979–80 H.C. 507; p. 1; Sixth Report, 1980–81 H.C. 291, p. 2.

[24] The numbers of complaints received and found to be within the Observer's jurisdiction did not exceed the figures of 437 and 162 recorded in the first year of operation until 1981 and 1982, when the latter figure was 171 and 187, respectively: Annual Reports, appendices.

[25] R.C.L.S., Vol. 1, pp. 352–359; (1980) 77 L.S.Gaz. 420.

to engage in conduct "which is dishonest or which may otherwise bring the profession of barrister into disrepute, or which is prejudicial to the administration of justice;" (3) to observe the ethics and etiquette of the profession; and (4), if a practising or employed barrister, to be competent in all professional activities.[26] The new *Code* took effect from January 1, 1981. It embodies the main rulings on professional conduct made from time to time by the Bar Council, on the recommendation of the Council's Professional Conduct Committee[27] and published in the Annual Statements of the Senate.[28] These rules do not require the approval of the judges as a condition of their validity, although a particular rule could be held by the judges to be contrary to public policy or liable to undermine the proper administration of justice; such a rule would be ineffective.[29] A wide variety of matters are covered, including acceptance of instructions, the administration of a barrister's practice, delegation of work, relations with solicitors, advertising and touting, duties to client and court[29a] and fees. There are detailed notes for guidance on dress in court.[30] One distinctive rule affecting barristers is the so-called "cab-rank principle:"

"A practising barrister is bound to accept any brief to appear before a Court in the field in which he professes to practise at a proper professional fee having regard to the length and difficulty of the case. Special circumstances such as a conflict of interest or the possession of relevant and confidential information may justify his refusal to accept a particular brief."[31]

The Senate told the Royal Commission that "it secures for the public a right of representation in the court which is a pillar of British liberty."[32] Its real significance lies in serious criminal cases, where it would obviously be undesirable for barristers to avoid unpopular causes, but the Senate has also looked with disfavour on barristers who accept instructions in civil cases only from a "selected section of the community" (*i.e.* the working class and immigrant communities).[33] Lord Diplock has doubted whether in civil litigation counsel often has to accept work which he would not otherwise be willing to undertake.[34]

---

[26] Code of Conduct, para. 6. By bringing questions of competence within the disciplinary structure in April 1977 (Annual Statement, 1977–78, pp. 25–6) the Bar anticipated the thinking of the Royal Commission. *Cf.* pp. 117–118 above.

[27] This comprising 15 members of Senate and two laymen, of whom one is present at each meeting.

[28] Formerly the Annual Statements of the Bar Council. Rulings not incorporated remain in force unless inconsistent with the new Code. The authoritative but unofficial *Guide to Conduct and Etiquette at the Bar* by Sir William Boulton (6th ed., 1975) is not to be republished. A second edition of the Code was published in January 1983.

[29] *Re T. (A Barrister)* [1982] Q.B. 430.

[29a] For an argument that the advocate's duty to justice ought to be enshrined in law and not just rules of professional conduct, see D.L. Carey Miller, (1981) 97 L.Q.R. 127.

[30] Code of Conduct, Annex 11. Dress should be "unobtrusive." Suits and dresses should be dark; dresses and blouses should be long-sleeved and high to the neck; shirts and blouses should be predominantly white "or of other unemphatic appearance."

[31] *Ibid.* para. 21.

[32] R.C.L.S., Vol. 1, p. 31.

[33] Note the critical response of the members of chambers at 35, Wellington Street, London: "Barristers and the Cab Rank Rule: Some people can't afford taxis . . . " *L.A.G. Bull.*, December 1978, pp. 279–281.

[34] *Saif Ali* v. *Sydney Mitchell & Co.* [1980] A.C. 198, 221.

A serious failure to comply with any of the four duties mentioned above, including that of competence, constitutes "professional misconduct." Any other failure amounts to a "breach of proper professional standards." Complaints[35] against barristers are dealt with first by the Professional Conduct Committee. Where possible, complainants are interviewed by an investigation officer employed by the Senate. The Committee may dismiss the complaint,[36] decide that no action is necessary, order that the barrister be admonished or given appropriate advice, require the barrister concerned to attend the Senate's Oral English Panel, or, in cases of professional misconduct, prefer charges before a Disciplinary Tribunal of the Senate.[37] The Tribunal consists of five members: a judge, who acts as chairman,[38] a lay representative[39] from a panel appointed by the Lord Chancellor and three practising barristers.[40] If misconduct is proved, the Tribunal may decide to take no action, reprimand the barrister, order him to repay or forgo fees, order that he be suspended, removed from the register of employed barristers or disbarred. Thus, minor cases are dealt with by the committee; only the most serious go to a Tribunal.[41] An appeal lies to the judges of the High Court as visitors to the inns of court.[42] Formerly, disciplinary functions were exercised by each of the inns in relation to its own members, but they were passed to the Senate in 1966, and then the reformed Senate in 1974. The inns and circuits retain responsibility in respect of matters within their respective domestic jurisdictions.

(d) Legal proceedings against lawyers

A lawyer's misconduct or incompetence may give rise to a cause of action against him. For example, a client may be able to sue for breach of contract, breach of trust[43] or the tort of negligence.[44] Recent decisions have widened the scope of liability. The House of Lords in *Hedley, Byrne & Co. Ltd.* v. *Heller & Partners Ltd.*[45] established that a special relationship could give rise to a duty of care in the giving of information or advice, and that there would be liability in damages in such cases in respect of losses that were purely economic. In *Midland Bank Trust Co. Ltd.* v. *Hett, Stubbs & Kemp*[46] Oliver J. stated that the case of a layman consulting a solicitor seemed:

[35] Conviction for a serious offence is treated as a complaint.

[36] In practice no complaint is rejected unless the lay member agrees.

[37] Code of Conduct, Annex 1.

[38] Tribunals are appointed for each case, but there is a permanent chairman.

[39] It is not clear whom they "represent."

[40] One may be a non-practising barrister if the barrister charged is not in practice.

[41] In 1983, 161 complaints were dealt with of which 76 were rejected, 7 referred to a Tribunal and 15 dealt with informally or by advice or admonition; 27 were withdrawn or no action was taken and 36 were still under investigation: Annual Statement, 1983–84, p. 46.

[42] See the Hearings before the Visitors Rules, 1980 (Code of Conduct, Annex No. 2); *Re S. (A Barrister)* [1970] 1 Q.B. 160; *Re S. (A Barrister)* [1981] Q.B. 683.

[43] *e.g. Re Bell's Indenture* [1980] 1 W.L.R. 1217.

[44] See R.M. Jackson and J.L. Powell, *Professional Negligence* (1982) Chaps. 4, 5 and A.M. Dugdale and K.M. Stanton, *Professional Negligence* (1982) and (1983) 17 *The Law Teacher* 166–180.

[45] [1964] A.C. 465.

[46] [1979] Ch. 384. Solicitors acting for both grantor and grantee of an option (to purchase the freehold reversion of a farm) carelessly failed to register the option. The grantor subsequently sold the reversion to a third party, and thereby achieved the desired result of defeating the option. The executors of the grantee recovered damages from the solicitors.

"to be as typical a case as one could find of the sort of relationship in which the duty of care described in the *Hedley Byrne* case exists."[47]

His Lordship held that authorities that indicated that the existence of a contract between solicitor and client precluded any action in tort[48] were inconsistent with *Hedley Byrne* and should not be followed. The six year limitation period in tort ran from the time when the damage occurred: *i.e.* the date of the sale which defeated the option.[49] In *Ross* v. *Caunters*[50] Sir Robert Megarry V.-C. took matters a step further. Solicitors failed to warn a client that his will should not be witnessed by a spouse of a beneficiary, and failed to notice that this had happened. They were held liable to the disappointed beneficiary whose bequest failed.

The position of the victims of incompetence is further secured by the requirement that solicitors carry indemnity insurance under the terms of a Master Policy taken out by The Law Society,[51] and the fact that all barristers must carry such insurance.[52] The Law Society's scheme has been unpopular with many solicitors, not because of any objection to the principle of compulsory insurance, but because of the Society's insistence on a single centrally controlled scheme,[53] and the high premiums charged.[54]

Even assuming the client has perceived that his lawyer has done his work incompetently, which is itself problematic, there are a number of problems facing those who wish to sue lawyers. First, legal assistance is advisable, but someone whose dealings with a lawyer have been unsatisfactory, and probably protracted and a source of frustration and annoyance, is unlikely to relish the prospect of inolvement with yet more lawyers in a kind of "double-or-quits" routine. Moreover, there may be difficulties in finding solicitors prepared to bring negligence proceedings against fellow practitioners, although The Law Society with the co-operation of local law societies, has established a panel of solicitors prepared to act in such cases (the "Negligence Panel").[55]

[47] [1979] Ch. 384, 417.

[48] *Groom* v. *Crocker* [1939] 1 K.B. 194 (Court of Appeal); *Clark* v. *Kirby-Smith* [1964] Ch. 506 (Plowman J.).

[49] Oliver J. held that the claim in contract succeeded as well as the claim in tort. The duty to register was a continuing one which lasted to the same date. (A barrister in private practice is not employed under a contract and can only be sued in tort. See below.).

[50] [1980] Ch. 297.

[51] Solicitors Act 1974, s.37; The Solicitors' Indemnity Rules 1975–83; R.C.L.S., Vol. 1, pp. 326–328. The rules were held to be *intra vires*: *Swain* v. *The Law Society* [1982] 1 W.L.R. 52, C.A.

[52] Code of Conduct, paras. 34, 71(c) (d), 75; Annual Statement, 1982–83, p. 75. Proposals for a compulsory single scheme were defeated: Annual Statement, 1981–82, pp. 12–18, 65–75. Barristers may make their own arrangements provided that they comply with certain minimum terms (*e.g.* minimum cover of £250,000, cover for pupils, "squatters," clerks and employees). Failure to be insured after October 1, 1983 will constitute professional misconduct.

[53] D. Podmore, (1980) 7 B.J.L.S. 1, 5–6. The Law Society is not liable to account to solicitors for the commission received from the insurance brokers: *Swain* v. *The Law Society* [1983] 1 A.C. 598, H.L.

[54] For 1983–84 they were £1,565 for a principal in private practice in Inner London and £1,204 elsewhere with reduced rates for low earning sole practitioners. From 1984, premiums will be calculated on the basis of gross fees, subject to tapering and claims loading: (1983) 80 L.S.Gaz. 3217–3222, (1984) 81 L.S.Gaz. 322, 1170, 1571–4, 1804.

[55] R.C.L.S., Vol. 1, pp. 343–4; Sixth Annual Report of the Lay Observer, 1980 (1980–81 H.C. 291) pp. 3,4.

Secondly, there is a special immunity from an action for negligence which attaches to acts or omissions in the conduct of litigation. The House of Lords in *Rondel* v. *Worsley*[56] held that a barrister was immune from action in respect of his conduct of a trial. The immunity was justified by public policy:

> "mainly upon the ground that a barrister owes a duty to the court as well as to his client and should not be inhibited, through fear of an action by his client, from performing it; partly on the undesirability of relitigation as between barrister and client of what was litigated between the client and his opponent."[57]

In *Saif Ali* v. *Sydney Mitchell & Co.*[58] the House of Lords held that the immunity extended only to pre-trial work which was:

> "so intimately connected with the conduct of the cause in Court that it can fairly be said to be a preliminary decision affecting the way that cause is to be conducted when it comes to a hearing."[59]

It was alleged that a barrister negligently gave advice which led to the wrong person being joined as defendant. The House of Lords held that he was not immune as the alleged negligence had prevented the plaintiff's cause coming to court. A solicitor acting as advocate enjoys the same immunity.[60] The Royal Commission did not favour any change in this area.[61]

Thirdly, it must be remembered that liability in negligence does not attach simply because a lawyer turns out to be wrong or makes an error of judgment. He is only liable if the error is "such as no reasonably well informed and competent member of that profession could have made."[62]

Fourthly, a solicitor who has done work for a client and remains unpaid has the right to retain the papers concerning the client's affairs (the right of "lien").[63] This may cause both difficulty and resentment. If the solicitor declines to act further, the client of his new solicitor may obtain a court order for delivery of the papers on an undertaking to hold them without prejudice to the lien and to return them on completion of the matter.[64] If

---

[56] [1969] 1 A.C. 191. Until *Hedley Byrne* and *Rondel* v. *Worsley* were decided it was thought that a barrister could not be sued as he could not enter a contractual relationship with either the instructing solicitor or the lay client.

[57] *Per* Lord Wilberforce in *Saif Ali* v. *Sydney Mitchell & Co.* [1980] A.C. 198, 212. Zander has argued that it is not probable that barristers would be influenced by possible negligence actions and that the fear of relitigation has been greatly exaggerated: Zander (1978) pp. 134–6.

[58] *Ibid.*

[59] *Per* McCarthy P. in *Rees* v. *Sinclair* [1974] 1 N.Z.L.R. 180, 187, endorsed by Lords Wilberforce, Diplock and Salmon. Lord Russell and Lord Keith favoured a wider test under which immunity would extend to all work in connection with litigation.

[60] *Saif Ali* v. *Sydney Mitchell & Co.* [1980] A.C. 198, 215, 224, 227.

[61] R.C.L.S., Vol. 1, pp. 332–3, criticised by C.G. Veljanovski and C.J. Whelan (1983) 46 M.L.R. 700, 711–718.

[62] *Per* Lord Diplock in *Saif Ali* v. *Sydney Mitchell & Co.* [1980] A.C. 198, 220. For an example of a "reasonable mistake" see *Jones* v. *Jones* [1970] 2 Q.B. 576.

[63] R.C.L.S., Vol. 1, pp. 328–330. There is also a "lien" over any property, except real property, or any judgment obtained for the client by the solicitor in litigation; this only covers the costs related to that work.

[64] The Royal Commission recommended that this should be normal practice without a court order where a solicitor is replaced for any reason.

the client justifiably discharges the solicitor, The Law Society may gain possession of the documents.[65]

4. SOCIAL BACKGROUND, ENTRY AND TRAINING

Lawyers predominantly come from middle class homes.[66] The College of Law reported to the Royal Commission that the parental occupation of 60·9 per cent. of its solicitor students and 67·3 per cent. of its bar students were professional or managerial, compared with 8 per cent. that were manual.[67] A similar imbalance was shown in statistics on the backgrounds of university students reading law and entering the profession prepared by the Commission. The present and probable future arrangements for entry are unlikely to alter the position. The Royal Commission stated that it was for the educational system rather than for the profession to redress the social imbalance in the numbers of those reaching the required standard of admission to a university or profession.[68] There are, however, as the Commission recognised, other hurdles which entrants must overcome, particularly financial ones.

Women are seriously under-represented in both branches of the profession.[69] In 1976–77 6·5 per cent. of solicitors holding practising certificates and 8·2 per cent. of barristers were women, although the proportions of new entrants who were women were significantly higher. By 1981 these figures had risen to 17 per cent. and 10 per cent. respectively. There are very few women in the higher echelons of the profession (judges, benchers, Q.C.s, tribunal chairmen, members of the Council of The Law Society, etc.). The Royal Commission felt that sex discrimination based on prejudice had diminished in recent years although its effects were still strongly felt. There was also an effect "similar to that of discrimination" arising from hesitancy to accept women as members of chambers or partners in case they were lost to the "demands of the family or for fear (not always unjustified) that they may be less acceptable to clients than men."[70] Guidance should be issued on the obligation to maintain equality of opportunity; more flexible work arrangements should be encouraged; and arrangements should be made to assist mothers to return to work after childbirth; courses should be provided for women returning to practice.

As regards racial discrimination the Commission concluded that the

---

[65] Solicitors Act 1974, s.35, Sched. 1. This power is rarely exercised. The Royal Commission recommended that it should be exercised wherever the client would otherwise suffer.

[66] See R.C.L.S., Vol. 2, pp. 57–61; D. Podmore, (1977) 74 L.S.Gaz. 611; Podmore (1980) pp. 30–32, 90–93.

[67] Zander S.K.L.P. (1980) pp. 22–3. The dominance of "professional or managerial" backgrounds was confirmed by a study undertaken at University College, Cardiff: P. McDonald, (1982) 9 *Journal of Law and Society* 267–276.

[68] R.C.L.S., Vol. 1, p. 629.

[69] R.C.L.S., Vol. 1, pp. 495–501; Vol. 2, pp. 435–446. H. Kennedy, "Women at the Bar" in Hazell (1978); A. Sachs and J. Hoff Wilson, *Sexism and the Law* (1978) pp. 169–186; A. Sachs and R. Pearson, "Barristers and Gentlemen" (1980) 43 M.L.R. 400; D. Podmore and A. Spencer, "Women Lawyers in England" (1982) *Work and Occupations* Vol. 9, No. 3, pp. 337–361 and "The Law as a Sex-Typed Profession" (1982) 9 *Journal of Law and Society*, 21–36.

[70] R.C.L.S., Vol. 1, p. 499. In its response to the Report in November 1983, the Senate claimed that sex discrimination has "ceased to be a serious problem."

situation was not satisfactory and that the trends were unfavourable.[71] A "major effort by the Bar" was called for. The difficulty of finding seats in chambers was leading to the development of sets drawn exclusively from ethnic minorities which felt themselves to be "outside the normal run of professional practice." Urgent steps should be taken by The Law Society to prevent a similar situation arising. There should be a clear voluntary commitment by the profession to ensure that all racial groups enter and practise on equal terms, accompanied by strong guidance from the governing bodies.

Entry to the Bar has since 1975 been restricted to granduates and mature students.[72] An entrant must join one of the inns of court and complete two educational stages. The "academic stage" is satisfied by obtaining either a "qualifying law degree" recognised by the Council of Legal Education[73] or the Diploma in Law taught and examined by the City University and the Polytechnic of North London.[74] The "vocational stage" comprises courses at the Inns of Court School of Law[75]; practical exercises conducted by practitioners covering such matters as advocacy, drafting, court visits, film work and professional ethics; and the Bar Examination. Students wishing to practise must attend the courses and exercises as well as passing the Examination. Students who complete the two stages, and who have dined in the hall of their inn three times a term for eight terms,[76] are then "called to the Bar." They are not, however, entitled to practise unless they complete twelve months pupillage in the chambers of a barrister of at least five years' standing, and may not accept instructions until the second six months of pupillage.[77] The Royal Commission were satisfied that pupillages were found for those that wanted them.[78] There are special provisions for barristers from Ireland, Scottish advocates, Commonwealth lawyers and former solicitors.[79] The costs of entry in 1983 were estimated

---

[71] R.C.L.S., Vol. 1, pp. 501–504. See the Senate's Annual Statement, 1983–84, pp. 32–36.

[72] See the Consolidated Regulations of the Inns of Court published by the Council of Legal Education; R.C.L.S., Vol. 1, pp. 619–621; B. Hogan, *A Career in Law* (1981). E. Usher, *Careers in the Law in England and Wales* (1982).

[73] Essentially an English or Welsh university or C.N.A.A. degree in law or the licence in law of the University College at Buckingham, which includes the six "core" subjects: Contract, Tort, Criminal Law, Land Law, Constitutional and Administrative Law, Equity and Trusts, passed to a satisfactory standard. Partial exemption may be given on a subject by subject basis. From October 1981, at least 2(2) Honours standard has been required.

[74] The course for non-law graduates lasts one year; for mature students, two years. Students may be permitted to prepare by private study or by attendance at certain provincial polytechnics.

[75] For 1982–83 the school was limited to 1,000 places, priority being given to those who could validly declare an intention to practise at the Bar of England and Wales. 1,034 were accepted. Numbers for 1983–84 were to be limited to 950: Annual Statement, 1982–83, pp. 57, 58. Courses for those wishing to take the Bar Examination but not intending to practise have been started by the City University (M.A./Diploma in Law and Practice) and Ealing College of Further Education.

[76] See the Consolidated Regulations, regs. 10–13. There are four "dining terms" of 23 days duration in each year. A pupil may keep up to four terms by dining in a Circuit Mess at least three times per term. The dining requirements have long been a matter of contention. The Royal Commission recommended their abolition unless improvements to ensure that benchers and barristers mix with the students are made and found to work satisfactorily: R.C.L.S., Vol. 1, pp. 641–2.

[77] Consolidated Regulations, regs. 39, 40.

[78] R.C.L.S., Vol. 1, p. 643.

[79] Consolidated Regulations, regs. 34–38.

at £1,343 for law graduates intending to practise (£85 for joining an inn; £860 tuition fees; £48 for the Bar Examination; £75 for eating dinners; £75 for call to the bar; £200 for a new wig, gown and suitable clothing).[80] In addition, students have to provide for their own maintenance and for the necessary books, and will not earn enough to live on for some years. One small consolation is that pupillage fees may not now be charged.[81] Discretionary grants may be available from local education authorities and various scholarships, grants, prizes and loans are available from the inns, some of the latter covering the early years of practice.

The Senate has agreed in principle that the obligation of the C.L.E. is to provide a vocational course for sufficient qualified applicants to supply the public need for practising barristers. It is currently estimated that this need is about 300 per annum. A working party is to consider the problem of selection of students for the inns and for the course.[81a]

The position as regards entry to the solicitors' branch is more complex.[82] The academic stage consists of either (1) an approved law degree; or (2) the "Common Professional Examination" for non-law graduates and mature students[83]; or (3) the "Solicitors' First Examination" for school leavers (non-graduates under 25).[84] The Law Society's policy of introducing "all-graduate" entry announced in 1974 was abandoned following the spirited defence by certain sections of the solicitors' branch of entry by school leavers.[85] There are special arrangements for fellows of the Institute of Legal Executives and holders of the Diploma for Justices' Clerks' Assistants. After the academic stage, all candidates must attend the new vocational course leading to the Final Examination.[86] The course lasts about 36 weeks and is held at the College of Law in London, Guildford and Chester and at eight polytechnics. It has been welcomed as being of much more practical use than the previous Part II Examination, at least for students about to enter a private practice solicitors' office.[87] Two years must then be spent articled to a solicitor.[88] The basic costs of entry for 1984/85 were £1,587 for law graduates and £2,881 for non-law graduates,

[80] A.G.C.A.S. Careers Information Booklet, *Legal Profession*, October 1983.

[81] Code of Conduct, para. 30.

[81a] (1983) 80 L.S.Gaz. 743–4.

[82] R.C.L.S., Vol. 1, pp. 613–618. Revised arrangements came into force in 1979. See the Qualifying Regulations 1979 (as amended in 1980 and 1982).

[83] Non-law graduates cover the core subjects in a one year course; mature students take a two year course. Courses are run by the College of Law and eight polytechnics.

[84] The first part of the S.F.E. is taken after a year at a polytechnic. The student then enters into five-year articles, taking further subjects during the first two years with part-time study.

[85] See G. Sammons and K. Pickthorn, (1977) 74 L.S.Gaz. 635 and (1978) 75 L.S.Gaz. 121–2; cf. (1977) 74 L.S.Gaz. 1087, 1101 and (1978) 75 L.S.Gaz. 1250. In 1982 97·8 per cent. of those applying for enrolment as a student with The Law Society and 89·5 per cent. of those admitted as solicitors were graduates: Annual Report, 1982–83, p. 20.

[86] Fellows of the Institute of Legal Executives may serve two years' articles instead of attending the course but must pass the Final Examination; if they attend the course, in certain circumstances they need not serve in articles.

[87] e.g. T. Guise, (1980) 77 L.S.Gaz. 1145; R. Bloom, (1981) 78 L.S.Gaz. 8; P.H. Kenny, (1982) 79 L.S.Gaz. 601.

[88] Non-law graduates may be permitted to serve the two years as an articled clerk before taking the Final Examination. From 1982 a further accounts course will have to be taken during articles, and continuing education during the first three years after qualification will be mandatory for solicitors admitted after August 1, 1985: (1983) 80 L.S.Gaz. 2987–8; M. Zander, (1984) 81 L.S.Gaz. 1502–3.

assuming the more expensive College of Law courses were attended.[89] As with barristers there are many additional expenses. Local authority discretionary grants may be available but much less assistance (for many more students) is available from The Law Society than from the inns.

Legal education was the subject of detailed examination by a committee chaired by Ormrod J. that reported in 1971.[90] Many of their recommendations are reflected in the current arrangements, but some of great significance are not. There have undoubtedly been improvements in the 1970s but it is difficult to see that academic and vocational legal education have been "integrated into a coherent whole."[91] School leaver entry has been retained for solicitors: the Ormrod Committee recommended all-graduate entry. The relationship between the two stages is not as envisaged. The Ormrod Committee proposed that vocational courses should be provided within the university and college of higher education (now polytechnic) structure, and possibly be common to both branches of the profession.[92] The courses should not be "primarily regarded as a means of preparing for qualifying examinations" and the amount of substantive law studied and of conventional law lectures should be kept to a minimum. They should be followed by a period of in-training: pupillage for barristers and three years limited practice after qualification rather than articles for solicitors. In the event finance was not forthcoming for the vocational courses from either central government or the profession. The proposal to abolish articles, originally favoured by The Law Society, was successfully resisted by the solicitors; even an experimental vocational course as an alternative to articles for 250 students did not materialise.[93] The vocational courses that did emerge are controlled by the respective branches of the profession. Eight polytechnics teach the solicitors' course but the universities have remained aloof. The courses are also more of an academic slog than envisaged by Ormrod, although they are superior to their forerunners.

The Royal Commission did not propose any significant alteration to the present structure.[94] They rejected the idea of a quota system notwithstanding the fears that have been expressed that there may be too many law places.[95] Precise estimates of future needs were "notoriously difficult to

[89] The elements for law graduates are: Enrolment with The Law Society (£40); acceptance of Qualifying Law Degree (£12); Course fee for Final Examination (£1,420); Examination fee (£100); Admission fee (£15). Maintenance expenses are extra.

[90] Report of the Committee on Legal Education (Cmnd. 4595, 1971). See the commentary by P.A. Thomas and G. Mungham, (1972) 7 Valparaiso L.R. 87 and the discussion at the 1971 meeting of the Society of Public Teachers of Law (university and College of Law law teachers): (1972) 12 J.S.P.T.L. (N.S.) 39.

[91] Ormrod, para. 85.

[92] See Ormrod, Chap. 5.

[93] R.C.L.S., Vol. 1, pp. 612–3.

[94] See C.G. Blake in M. Slade (ed.) *Law in Higher Education: Into the 1980s* p.13; R. Goode (1979) 129 N.L.J. 1117; W. Twining in P.A. Thomas (ed.) *Law in the Balance* (1982) Chap. 8.

[95] See, *e.g.* G.A. Seabrooke, (1978) 14 J.S.P.T.L. (N.S.) 161. A much publicised speech by the President of The Law Society in October 1980 expressing concern at the numbers ((1980) 77 L.S.Gaz. 982–3) was followed by a fall in the number of applicants for university law places although a causal connection cannot be proved. The Law Society has decided that it would be wrong to limit numbers: (1981) 78 L.S.Gaz. 1018.

achieve." Some areas of concern in legal education were largely ignored. For example, there have been difficulties in the relationships between the profession and the universities and polytechnics. These have not been solved by the establishment of the Advisory Committee on Legal Education, recommended by Ormrod, which comprises representatives of these interest groups.[96] In particular, there have been arguments over the curriculum of degree courses (*e.g.* the extent to which administrative law should be covered in Constitutional and Administrative law courses[97]) and teaching methods (the profession is suspicious of methods of continuous assessment). Academics and practitioners have long shown a mutual lack of esteem.[98] The Royal Commission accepted without analysis that the existing core subjects were "essential topics." As academics were free to develop the non-core part of the degree "no cause for complaint need arise."[99] They suggested that the Advisory Committee should be renamed and have a non-lawyer chairman, although they did not explain why they thought this would achieve anything.[1] There was no discussion by the Commission of the development of contextual approaches to law teaching[2] and of clinical legal education,[3] or of the problems posed in providing a degree course suitable both for those who wish to qualify and those that do not.

The new vocational courses had been introduced too recently for the Commission to offer any appraisal. They had rather more to say about in-training.[4] They endorsed the Senate's recent guidelines on the obligations and functions of pupil-masters[5] and recommended that a training record should be kept and monitored, that call to the Bar should be deferred until after the first six months of pupillage, and that the inns should establish a joint pupillage committee to check the suitability of pupil-masters and to maintain a joint register of prospective pupil-masters and pupils. Complaints about articles have been common, particularly that the instruction given has been inadequate and the wages low. In 1980 the Council of The Law Society issued guidelines on articles, consisting partly of mandatory requirements and partly of recommendations.[6] For example, articled clerks must be given experience in at least three of the main legal topics, training records must be kept and a salary at least equivalent to the

[96] The Committee was not provided with the secretarial and financial assistance from public funds recommended by Ormrod. It is dependent on the professions rather than the Lord Chancellor's Office.

[97] The universities have had greater success than the polytechnics in deflecting scrutiny of the content of their courses. The latter have the additional hurdle of validation of their courses by the Council for National Academic Awards.

[98] A recent example was the furore over *Negotiated Justice* by J. Baldwin and M. McConville: see M. Zander, (1977) 74 L.S.Gaz. 1121–2, 1134.

[99] R.C.L.S., Vol. 1, p. 632–3.

[1] *Ibid.* pp.659–60. These suggestions have not been adopted.

[2] See, *e.g.* R. Folsom and N. Roberts, "The Warwick Story" (1979) 30 J. of Legal Education 166.

[3] See W.M. Rees (1975) 9 *The Law Teacher* 125; R.J. Spjut (1977) 11 *The Law Teacher* 89. *Cf.* Z. Bankowski and G. Mungham, *Images of Law* (1976) pp. 1–6, who argue that such developments merely train "better technicians for capitalist society."

[4] R.C.L.S., Vol. 1, pp. 634–651.

[5] Code of Conduct, Annex 5. See generally on pupillage Hazell (1980) Chap. 4.

[6] (1980) 77 L.S.Gaz. 824; A. Sherr, "Lip Service Under Articles or Chances Missed" (1982) 132 N.L.J. 395.

grossed up university maintenance grant should normally be paid. The new rules may make solicitors less willing to employ articled clerks.[7] Even before the recent changes students were finding it increasingly difficult to obtain articles, although steps have been taken by the Association of Graduate Careers Advisory Service to place the search for articles on a more organised footing.[8] Family connections may well become more significant. The Royal Commission made it clear that if changes such as those now in operaion were not put into effect and shown to be adequate "it will be clear that a satisfactory system of articles is unlikely even to be established."[9] Articles should then be replaced by a system based on two year vocational courses followed by two years of restricted practice. They suggested that a training levy might be imposed on firms that failed to assist in placement, although there was no attempt to analyse the economics of the alternative system. An attractive model is in fact provided by the one-year vocational course for intending barristers and solicitors in Northern Ireland held at the Institute of Professional Legal Studies within Queen's University, Belfast.[10]

The Commission had little hope to offer on the question of grants for the vocational stage, and for non-law graduates at the academic stage. At present, the local authority grants, which cover fees and maintenance, are discretionary, and the way in which the discretion is exercised varies from authority to authority.[11] Some refuse to award any grants, some offer only part of the maintenance element and some only offer grants for the cheaper polytechnic courses. The position has deteriorated in recent years. The geographical variations make no sense and a cloud of uncertainty hangs over the final year of many students. More are forced to rely on family resources and vacation earnings; the social background of entrants is further constricted. The Royal Commission thought that grants for the vocational stage should be mandatory but did not believe that a change was likely.[12] No such change has taken place.

5. UNADMITTED PERSONNEL

Most solicitors' firms employ "legal executives," formerly known as "managing clerks," who are not admitted as solicitors but who do undertake professional work under their employers' supervision. The

[7] See, e.g. (1980) 77 L.S.Gaz. 384 and 1125, but cf. (1980) 77 L.S.Gaz. 542 and 1220 and (1981) 78 L.S.Gaz. 8, the latter pointing out that clerks who have taken the new vocational course should be capable of earning much more for their firm than their remuneration. The Law Society may refuse to register articles if the salary is not acceptable. Local guides should be prepared by local law societies, based on figures of £3,900 for clerks living in Inner London, £3,650 for those in the remainder of Greater London and £3,150 for those outside (year beginning August 1, 1983).
[8] B. Read, (1979) 76 L.S.Gaz. 891 and (1980) L.S.Gaz. 536. See also the reports issued regularly by A.G.C.A.S. on "Becoming a Solicitor."
[9] R.C.L.S., Vol. 1, p. 650.
[10] R.C.L.S., Vol. 1, pp. 621–2, 709–714. A close working relationship has developed between the Institute, the University and the profession of a kind that is lacking in England and Wales. This has, however, been marred by the decision of the profession to require students to take two extra "core subjects" (Evidence and Company law), which was reached with minimal consultation with law schools.
[11] R.C.L.S., Vol. 2, pp. 609–704 (surveys).
[12] R.C.L.S., Vol. 1, p. 656.

Institute of Legal Executives in evidence to the Royal Commission estimated their numbers at over 20,000, although the numbers of solicitors, particularly assistant solicitors, have been expanding more rapidly.[13] There are no requirements as to their qualification and training, although they may voluntarily take examinations in order to qualify as Associates or Fellows of the Institute of Legal Executives (ILEX). They tend to specialise in a particular class of work, and the amount of supervision exercised over an experienced executive may in practice be minimal. The Institute made various proposals to the Royal Commision for improving the professional status of legal executives. Having resisted suggestions that the two branches of the legal profession be fused, the Commission was unwilling to contemplate a third branch. The Institute's proposals for profit-sharing, enhanced pay for executives with ILEX qualifications or compulsory qualifications, compulsory arrangements for day release and payment for courses and extended right of audience all fell on stony ground, if not an impenetrable slab of concrete.[14]

Barristers' clerks have the rather different role in chambers of acting as office administrator and accountant for chambers as a whole, and as business manager and agent for each individual member. The employment of a clerk is a requirement of practice.[15] The Royal Commission recommended that this rule should be relaxed provided a practice is administered efficiently, but recognised that a clerk would almost invariably be employed.[16] The clerk manipulates the flow of work in chambers by virtue of his functions of negotiating fees and arranging each barrister's timetable, and his relationships, built up over many years, with solicitors' firms. A minority are employed under a formal contract, although the Senate has suggested that this should become the normal practice.[17] Most senior clerks are paid a percentage of gross fees, and their earnings are significantly higher than those of junior barristers.[18] The Royal Commission did not regard this disparity as justified by any difference in the nature and intensity of the work done. They suggested that clerks should be paid a fair remuneration for the work done, with a bonus of not more than one per cent. of gross fees to reward a high pressure of work (the present arrangements provide for a minimum of 5 per cent.[19]). The present system has the advantage for the barrister that the clerk has a "direct incentive to promote [his] practice,"[20] although the distinction between promoting the practice and simply "promoting" the level of fees is a fine one.[21] The Commission "deplored" cases where the

[13] R.C.L.S., Vol. 1, p. 408.

[14] R.C.L.S., Vol. 1, pp. 406–417.

[15] See above, p. 113. On barristers' clerks generally see R. Hazell, *The Bar on Trial* (1978) Chap. 5; J. Flood, "Barristers' Clerks," Warwick Law Working Paper No. 2, July 1977, and *Barristers' Clerks* (1983).

[16] R.C.L.S., Vol. 1, p. 484.

[17] Chambers guidelines (1977): R.C.L.S., Vol. 1, p. 477. Forms of contracts have been recommended: Annual Statement, 1982–83, pp. 69–74.

[18] R.C.L.S., Vol. 1, p. 487; see also Vol. 2, pp. 395–433.

[19] Annual Statement, 1969–70, pp. 33–36. The Bar has responded to the effect that payment by commission is not wrong in principle, although steps should be taken to stop excessive earnings: *Comments of the Senate* on R.C.L.S. (November 1983) pp. 9–13.

[20] "Lincoln", (1980) 77 L.S.Gaz. 1275.

[21] "Lincoln" argues that it is the responsibility of the solicitor to protect *his* client when negotiating the fee.

clerk exercised too much authority, although all they could suggest was that barristers should not allow it to happen and that the head of chambers should exercise control in cases where a clerk restricted the flow of work to a particular barrister on grounds of supposed incompetence or inexperience, or simply personal dislike. The possibility of barristers arranging their own timetable and negotiating fees, leaving other administrative tasks to clerks, which system is operated by advocates in Ireland, Australia and South Africa,[22] was not seriously explored.

6. Lawyers and the European Community

A lawyer from another Community country may provide any service in connection with legal proceedings in the United Kingdom, provided that he acts in conjunction with a British lawyer entitled to provide that service.[23] The restrictions on conveyancing and probate work are not affected. The C.C.B.E.[24] has produced a draft directive on the right of establishment of lawyers, which was submitted to the Commission of the European Communities in December 1980.[25] To date, however, no directive has been made.

---

[22] Hazell (1978) pp. 122–3.

[23] Council Directive 77/249/EEC of March 22, 1977; D.B. Walters (1978) 3 Eur.L.R. 265; European Communities (Services of Lawyers) Order 1978, (S.I. 1978, No. 1901). See also above, p. 112. The 1977 Directive does not provide for any right of establishment or mutual recognition of diplomas.

[24] See above, p. 109, n. 31.

[25] (1981) 78 L.S.Gaz. 215–7. See also D. Lasok and J.W. Bridge, *An Introduction to the Law and Institutions of the European Communities* (3rd ed., 1982) pp. 58–62 and D. Edward, "The Legal Profession in the Community" in St. J. Bates, *et al.*, (eds.) *In Memoriam J.D.B. Mitchell* (1983).

CHAPTER 4

JUDGES

IN this chapter we consider the men and women who are appointed to adjudicate upon such disputes that are referred to a court or tribunal for determination. The term "judge" is used in the title of this chapter in its wide sense to cover all such persons. More commonly, however, the term is used in a narrower sense to cover those who are appointed to adjudicate in the House of Lords, the Supreme Court of England and Wales (*i.e.* the Court of Appeal, the High Court and the Crown Court) and county courts. In addition, some judicial functions are performed by officers below the rank of judge known as "masters" and "registrars." "Magistrates" or "justices of the peace" sit in the magistrates' courts (and in some cases in the Crown Court).[1] Those persons who sit on tribunals are normally simply referred to as tribunal "chairmen" or "members," although there are some with special designations, such as the Social Security Commissioners,[2] the Special and General Commissioners of Income Tax, Immigration Adjudicators and the Commons Commissioners.

A. MAGISTRATES[3]

1. NUMBERS AND FUNCTIONS

In January 1984 there were 25,778 active part-time lay magistrates or "justices of the peace."[4] There was provision for the appointment of up to 60 full-time, paid, "stipendiary magistrates" in London and up to 40 in the provinces.[5] In the City of London the Lord Mayor and Aldermen are justices *ex officio.*[6] Magistrates sit in the magistrates' courts[7] and in the Crown Court,[8] perform certain administrative tasks such as the granting of liquor licences, issue arrest and search warrants and sign various forms for members of the public.

2. HISTORICAL ORIGINS OF JUSTICES OF THE PEACE[9]

The history of the justice of the peace as a judicial officer can be traced to the Justices of the Peace Act 1361, which provided:

[1] When they are known as "judges of the Crown Court": Supreme Court Act 1981, s.8(1).
[2] Social Security Act 1980, ss.12, 13. They were formerly known as National Insurance Commissioners: Social Security Act 1975, s.97(3)(4) and Sched. 10. See above, p. 58.
[3] Two recent studies are Sir Thomas Skyrme, *The Changing Image of the Magistracy* (2nd ed., 1983) and E. Burney, *J.P: Magistrate, Court and Community* (1979).
[4] (1984) 40 *The Magistrate* 71–72.
[5] Justice of the Peace Act 1979, ss.13, 31. See below, pp. 148–149.
[6] 1979 Act, s.39.
[7] Above, pp. 40, 46–52.
[8] Above, pp. 64–69; below, pp. 147–148.
[9] On the historical development of the office see E. Moir, *The Justice of the Peace* (1969).

"First, That in every County of *England* shall be assigned for the keeping of the Peace, one Lord, and with him three of four of the most worthy in the County, with some learned in the Law, and they shall have Power to restrain the Offenders, Rioters, and all other Barators, and to pursue, arrest, take, and chastise them according to their Trespass or Offence; and to cause them to be imprisoned and duly punished according to the Law and Customs of the Realm, and according to that which to them shall seem best to do by their Discretions and good Advisement; and also to inform them, and to enquire of all those that have been Pillors and Robbers in the Parts beyond the Sea, and be now come again, and go wandering, and will not labour as they were wont in Times past, and to take and arrest all those that they may find by Indictment, or by Suspicion, and to put them in Prison; and to take of all them that be not of good Fame, where they shall be found, sufficient Surety and Mainprise of their good behaviour towards the King and his People, and the other duly to punish, to the Intent that the People be not by such Rioters or Rebels troubled nor endamaged, nor the Peace blemished, nor Merchants nor other passing by the Highways of the Realm disturbed, nor put in the Peril which may happen of such Offenders . . . ."[10]

The Crown had previously appointed keepers or conservators of the peace (*Custodes Pacis*) with powers to arrest suspects and initiate criminal proceedings: the Act of 1361 gave in addition the power to determine proceedings. In 1362 the justices were required to hold formal meetings four times a year: these became known as quarter sessions. Over the ensuing centuries, more and more administrative duties were imposed by statute on the justices, including such matters as the construction and maintenance of fortifications, highways, bridges and gaols, the fixing of prices and the recruitment of soldiers. The list of provisions to be implemented or enforced became lengthy and burdensome.[11] Indeed, until the nineteenth century, the business of local government was largely entrusted to the justices. Different functions were committed to one, two or three justices or to quarter sessions. The informal meetings of two or more justices out of quarter sessions came to be known as "petty sessions," the forerunner of magistrates' courts.

The persons appointed in the counties were generally from the "gentry." In the eighteenth century, the justices came into growing disrepute. The corruption of the Middlesex Justices, described by Edmund Burke as "generally the scum of the earth," was such that they were replaced for most purposes by metropolitan stipendiary magistrates. Elsewhere, their administration of the Poor Law and the Game Laws attracted much criticism. In the nineteenth century they lost most of their administrative functions to central government departments and the new, elected, local authorities, the process of transfer culminating in the Local Government

---

[10] This is still in force, apart from the words "and also to inform . . . in Times past."

[11] In 1485 Lambard asked, "How many Justices, think you, may now suffice, without breaking their backs, to bear so many, not loads, but stacks of statutes?": 1 *Eirenarchia* (1581) Chap. 7. F. Milton (*The English Magistracy* (1967)) gives many examples of statutory provisions, including one forbidding a man who was not a Lord to wear a cloak that did not "cover his privy member and Buttocks (he being upright)" (p. 9).

Act 1888. At the same time, their judicial functions were extended, with more offences becoming triable at petty sessions, and with the establishment and development of their matrimonial jurisdiction.[12]

3. APPOINTMENT

The Commission of the Peace is a document issued by the Crown setting out in very general terms the functions of the justices.[13] There is one Commission for each county, each of five London commission areas and the City of London.[14] Justices of the peace for any commission area are appointed in the name of the Queen by the Lord Chancellor,[15] or, in Greater Manchester, Merseyside and Lancashire, by the Chancellor of the Duchy of Lancaster.[16]

The only qualification for appointment laid down by statute is that the person resides in or within 15 miles of the commission area for which he is appointed.[17] However, the booklet on "The appointment and duties of Justices of the Peace in England and Wales" published on behalf of the Lord Chancellor, makes it clear that the following will not be appointed:

"(a) a person over 60 years of age;
 (b) a person convicted of certain offences, or subject to certain court orders[18];
 (c) an undischarged bankrupt[19];
 (d) a person whose sight or hearing is impaired, or who by reason of infirmity cannot carry out all the duties of a Justice;
 (e) a serving member of Her Majesty's Forces; a member of the Police;
 (f) a close relative of a person who is already a Justice on the same Bench."

The notes on the application/recommendation form state that certain other classes of person will not be appointed:

(g) a traffic warden;
 (h) a close relative of a member of the local police force;
 (i) an officer or servant of a magistrates' court in his own Petty Sessional Division;
 (j) an M.P., adopted candidate or full-time political agent for the local constituency;
 (k) "a person, the nature of whose work is such that it would conflict, or clearly be incompatible with, the duties of a magistrate."

---

[12] From the Matrimonial Causes Act 1878 onwards.

[13] Justices of the Peace Act 1979, s.5; The Crown Office (Commissions of the Peace) Rules 1973 (S.I. 1973 No. 2099).

[14] 1979 Act, s.1.

[15] *Ibid.* s.6. The work of the Lord Chancellor's Office concerning magistrates is dealt with by the Secretary of Commissions and his staff: see Skyrme (1983), Chap. 3.

[16] *Ibid.* s.68. The policy of the two offices is almost invariably identical: Skyrme (1983), p. 240. The Chancellor of the Duchy has concurrent powers with the Lord Chancellor on the appointment, removal and residence of justices, entry on or removal from the Supplemental List and records. On other matters the Lord Chancellor has exclusive powers.

[17] *Ibid.* s.7. The Lord Chancellor can direct that this restriction shall not apply: s.7(2).

[18] The notes on the application/recommendation form say "a serious offence or a series of minor offences."

[19] Bankruptcy Act 1883, s.32(1)(c).

The person must also be a British subject.[20] There is no property qualification[21] and women became eligible in 1919.[22]

The Lord Chancellor's booklet states that justices:

> "should be personally suitable in character, integrity and under-standing . . . and . . . should be generally recognised as such by those among whom they live and work."

They are appointed on the advice of Advisory Committees. These were first established following recommendations of the Royal Commission on the Selection of Justices of the Peace of 1910[23] in response to complaints that the Benches were dominated by Conservatives.

There are about 100 committees, generally one for each non-metropolitan county and metropolitan district, the City of London, some of the larger urban areas and each London commission area. Most of the county committees have sub-committees or area panels. County committees are normally chaired by the Lord Lieutenant, the London Committees by Circuit judges. Most committees have eight to ten members, and sub-committees about six to eight. The term of office is normally six years. Appointments to a committee are made by the Lord Chancellor, usually after consulting the chairman.[24] Members are almost invariably existing magistrates. Each committee has at least one Conservative and one Labour member; most have a Liberal, and some in Wales a member of Plaid Cymru. It is the practice to check with the party headquarters that they are known supporters. The names of the committee members are normally kept secret in order to keep them free from pressure and lobbying,[25] although the name and address of the secretary is published. A candidate can be recommended to a committee by any person or organisation, or can put himself or herself forward. In turn, the recommendations of the committee can be rejected by the Lord Chancellor.

The main areas of difficulty have been those of politics and social background. The problems here are linked. The official position as to politics is stated in the Lord Chancellor's booklet:

> "Political views are neither a qualification nor a disqualification for appointment as a Justice of the Peace. The Lord Chancellor, when making appointments, has regard to political affiliations only in order that he may ensure that no Bench becomes unduly overweighted in favour of any one political party."

As regards politics, there have been a number of separate strands of thought. First, some people have been recommended for appointment as a reward for political services rather than because of their fitness for the

---

[20] This is a policy not a rule of law: Skyrme (1983), p. 50.

[21] This was abolished by the Liberal government in 1906: Justices of the Peace Act, 1906, s.1.

[22] Sex Disqualification (Removal) Act 1919. Appointments do not, however, appear to fall within the scope of the Sex Discrimination Act 1975: see Skyrme (1983) p. 51. The proportion of women to men has increased steadily—from 1:3·5 in 1947 to 1:1·4 in 1984.

[23] Cd. 5250.

[24] Skyrme (1983), pp. 44–46. See also B. Cooke, (1984) 40 *The Magistrate* 69.

[25] The Inner London Advisory Committee is an exception; membership of the Nottingham Committee was revealed in 1966.

office. This was condemned by the Royal Commissions of both 1910 and 1946–48.[26] The latter noted that there were still "political appointments" in this sense, although their extent could not be stated with precision.[27]

Secondly, the 1910 Royal Commission stated unequivocally that "it is not in the public interest that there should be an undue preponderance of Justices drawn from one political party."[28] It is not clear whether this was intended to refer to the position nationally or the composition of particular benches, but the latter view seems to be emphasised today. It was certainly the contemporary preponderance of Conservatives on the bench that led to the appointment of both the Royal Commissions of 1910 and 1946–48, by, respectively, a Liberal and a Labour government. However, overall statistics kept of political affiliation are largely based on the declared position of each justice at the time of appointment and are thus of limited reliability. There is no policy to maintain "proportional representation" on the benches.[29] Conversely, it is not at all unusual for the Lord Chancellor to refuse to accept recommendations because a certain party is under-represented.[30]

Thirdly, the attention may be focused on the political affiliation of *new appointees*. This was emphasised by the 1946–48 Royal Commission, which stated that if after preliminary selection on merit:

> "it is found that a considerable majority of the proposed new justices are of one political faith, the list should be revised with a view to seeing whether equally good, or better, nominations can be made from among members of political parties. If the answer is that they cannot, then the original list should stand."[31] .

Fourthly, some have argued that political opinions should be ignored entirely.[32] This has, however, been regarded as impractical by successive Lord Chancellors.

Both Royal Commissions recommended that justices be drawn from different social backgrounds. The 1946–48 Report stated that:

> "Care must be taken to see that there are persons in the commission representative of various sections of the community. It is an advantage that a justice should have knowledge of the way of life of other classes than the class to which he belongs, and it is essential that there should be many among the justices who know enough of the lives of the poorest people to understand their outlook and their difficulties."[33]

[26] Note 23, above; *Royal Commission on Justices of the Peace* (Cmd. 7463, 1948).

[27] *Ibid.* para. 20.

[28] Cd. 5250, Summary of Conclusions: quoted in the 1946–48 Report (Cmd. 7463, p. 4).

[29] Skyrme (1983), p. 58. In 1983 the percentages, based on statements at the time of appointment, were Conservative 41, Labour 28, Liberal 11, S.D.P. 1, Plaid Cymru 0.3 and "Independent and not known" 18.7: Skyrme (1983) p. 58.

[30] *Ibid.* p. 59. It can prove difficult to find suitable candidates with a Labour background. A survey by the Labour Campaign for Criminal Justice showed that in one in three of 140 constituencies studied, people were unwilling to put their names forward because two in three Labour party nominees were not appointed. Of 1,500 J.P.s appointed a year there were 100 Labour party nominees, although that did not take account of Labour voters who were not members: *The Observer*, February 2, 1983.

[31] Cmd. 7463, para. 84.

[32] See the dissent by Lord Merthyr and two other members of the 1946–48 Royal Commission: Cmd. 7463 pp. 92–95.

[33] Para. 84.

The Royal Commission's survey distinguished six classes[34]:

		% Male		% Female	
Class O	Persons without gainful occupation	3.5		16.7	
Class P	Professional	21.3 ⎫	51.3	29.6 ⎫	43.00
Class E	Employers of 10 or more, directors, higher managerial posts in business or industry	30.0 ⎭		13.4 ⎭	
Class OA	Persons in business on their own account or employing less than 10	16.5		11.2	
Class S	Persons paid salaries	13.7 ⎫	28.7	10.5 ⎫	18.2
Class W	Persons paid wages	15.0 ⎭		7.7 ⎭	
	Not classifiable			10.9	

Subsequent studies have shown that there has been little change.[35]

	Hood % Male		Baldwin % Male		% Female	
O	0.8		0.6		3.5	
P	30.8 ⎫	[52.6][36]	34.5 ⎫	53.0	44.8 ⎫	55.1
E	21.8 ⎭		18.5 ⎭		10.3 ⎭	
OA	14.6		12.5		13.8	
S	11.4 ⎫		17.2 ⎫		19.5	
		27.3		30.3		
W	15.9 ⎭		13.1 ⎭		3.5	
Not Classifiable	4.3		3.6		4.6	

Arranged according to the Registrar-General's Classification, the surveys of both Hood and Baldwin show the predominance of the professional and intermediate occupations, with figures of 76·9 per cent. and 83·9 per cent. respectively.[36a]

Efforts have been made to increase the proportion of wage earners. In 1968, loss-of-earnings allowances were introduced.[37] The Employment Protection (Consolidation) Act 1978[38] provides that an employer must give

[34] Minutes of Evidence, Appendix 4. Postal survey of all justices; 87 per cent. response rate.

[35] R. Hood, *Sentencing the Motoring Offender* (1972), Chap. 3. Sample of 650 justices from 32 benches in 1966–67 with an 83 per cent. response rate. Chairmen and deputy chairmen and small benches were overrepresented.

J. Baldwin, (1976) 16 B.J. Criminology 171. Sample of 339 (one in five of all magistrates newly appointed between July 1971 and June 1972, from 128 benches) with a 75.2 per cent. response rate.

In 1977, 8·2 per cent of magistrates were manual workers: Skyrme (1983), p. 64, based on the Lord Chancellor's records.

[36] Hood (1972), p. 51 gives this figure as 51·8 and attaches the wrong label to the column.

[36a] Baldwin (1976) p. 172: the classes are I: Professional; II: Intermediate; III: Skilled; IV: Partly skilled; and V: Unskilled.

[37] Justices of the Peace Act 1968. See now the 1979 Act, s.12.

[38] s.29. A refusal to pay the person for the time off may constitute a failure to comply with the duty: see *Corner* v. *Buckinghamshire County Council* [1978] I.R.L.R. 320.

an employee magistrate reasonable time off.[39] However, as Lord Hailsham has pointed out,[40] the 1978 Act does not oblige an employer to give a magistrate a job, or to promote him if he has one. It provides no immunity from redundancy. These have been proper developments, but they seem to have had little effect, and the current economic climate has added to the pressures.

That a political and social balance is desirable has generally been assumed or asserted rather than explained. It is possible to detect three considerations: the interests of potential appointees; the need to maintain general public confidence in magistrates' courts; and the interests of defendants. The first factor lay behind the appointment of the Royal Commissions of 1910 and 1946–48, although the Reports played down what was clearly not a respectable consideration and placed more emphasis on the second factor. For example, Lord Loreburn L.C. said in evidence to the 1910 Royal Commission:

> "I regard it as an indignity and an injustice that any section of opinion should be, in practice, excluded from a legitimate ambition, and I think that it is contrary to the public interest that the authority of the bench of justices should be weakened by any widespread suspicion that the members of it are not fairly selected."[41]

The subsequent Report[42] simply took up the second strand of this reasoning. The interests of actual defendants came a poor third. It will of course be a matter of "pot luck" whether a working class defendant enjoys the supposed benefit of a court with one or more justices thought to be better able than the others to understand his outlook and difficulties. The respective social backgrounds of juries and justices do not seem to figure significantly among the considerations that affect the defendant's choice between summary trial and trial on indictment.[43]

A study[44] of 160 newly appointed magistrates in three English counties suggested that there were no significant differences according to social class in attitudes concerning penal philosophy, sentencing practice, the causes of crime, court procedure, and the role of the magistrate. It was noted, however, that there may have been a tendency to appoint magistrates with particular views, whatever the social class. There were differences in attitude related to different political background, with Conservatives tending particularly to be more punitive in their penal philosophy. The authors concluded that "although the relationship between attitudes and

---

[39] Magistrates who are public employees and employees of nationalised industries are customarily given 18 days' extra paid leave to enable them to sit. Many large private firms have made similar arrangements.

[40] (1981) 37 *The Magistrate* 166.

[41] Minutes of Evidence. Lord Loreburn was caught between the pressure imposed by Liberal politicians and his own feelings that appointments should be made on merit without reference to politics: R.F.V. Heuston, *Lives of the Lord Chancellors* (1964), pp. 153–158.

[42] Report, p. 8.

[43] A. E. Bottoms and J. D. McClean, *Defendants in the Criminal Process* (1976), Chap. 4. The research did show that defendants in general had a higher opinion of the Crown Court than the magistrates, for a variety of reasons.

[44] R. A. Bond and N. F. Lemon, "Changes in Magistrates' Attitudes During the First Year on the Bench" in D.P. Farrington *et al.* (eds.) *Psychology, Law and Legal Processes* (1979), Chap. 8.

behaviour is a problematic one, there is nevertheless a good prima facie case for arguing that differences in viewpoint expressed here are also likely to be expressed in some way in procedural and sentencing policies."[45] An earlier English study had not, however, found there to be such a correlation.[46] Indeed, the most significant factor seemed to be the general attitudes of the bench to which a particular magistrate belonged. Accordingly, it may well be that social and political background may neither be perceived to be of significance by defendants, nor actually of significance in affecting the way they are dealt with, although the evidence on the latter point is not entirely clear.

The authorities seem to take strong exception to charges that the processes of selection are shrouded in secrecy.[47] It is certainly true that the *formal* procedure is clearly stated in the booklet published by the Lord Chancellor's Department. It is also true that the detailed deliberations of the committees are kept confidential: rightly so, given that the debate will concern the personal qualities of individuals. What is noticeable, however, is the lack of general research on how the advisory committees operate in practice. One exception has been the work of Elizabeth Burney.[48] In her study of six advisory committees or sub-committees she found that only 16 per cent. of the committee members were "non-aligned" politically, almost all of them were members of the benches concerned and few were under 40. The selection of members of the committees was in practice normally left to the committee chairman. The local chairman of the bench commonly played a lead role. Some, but not all committees used interviews, which might be conducted by several magistrates, or by the chairman either alone or with the clerk. The two dominant routes to the bench seemed to be through personal recommendation from an existing magistrate or through some form of "voluntary work" background (churches, chambers of commerce, youth organisations, sports associations, political parties, etc.). The selectors would seek to weed out people of "extreme" views by pointed questions about the "Shrewsbury pickets." People who would be likely to "fit in" would be favoured. Burney's overall description was that selection "remains a largely personal and intimate affair, almost entirely dominated by existing magistrates who can too easily turn into self-perpetuating oligarchies."[49]

---

[45] *Ibid.* p. 141. *Cf.* J. Hogarth, *Sentencing as a Human Process* (1971) (survey of magistrates in Ontario); A. K. Bottomley, *Decisions in the Penal Process* (1973), Chap. 4. By contrast, a study based upon simulated sentencing exercises found that differences of sentence could not be explained by the group composition of "benches" in terms of age, political affiliation, education, sex or length of experience: A. Kapardis, (1981) 145 J.P.N. 289–291.

[46] R. Hood, *Sentencing the Motoring Offender* (1972); *Cf.* Hood, *Sentencing in Magistrates' Courts* (1962), where the author's findings suggested that the social composition of a bench, in combination with particular community conditions, might affect the prison rate (pp. 76–78, 119–120).

[47] Sir Thomas Skyrme, a former Secretary of Commissions, refers to the "myth of secrecy" and the "old chestnut of the clandestine routes to the magistracy" (Skyrme (1983), pp. 48, 49).

[48] Burney (1979), Chaps. 4 and 5. See also R. Pearson in Z. Bankowski and G. Mungham (eds.) *Essays in Law and Society* (1980), Chap. 5.

[49] Burney (1979), p. 73.

4. UNDERTAKINGS ON APPOINTMENT

A person selected to be a justice must give certain undertakings before being appointed. These are to complete the required training, to carry out a fair share of magisterial duties (normally to sit for at least 26 times a year), to resign if he or she fails to honour these undertakings or becomes unable to perform the duties of a justice through change of residence, infirmity or any other cause, to inform the justices' clerk if he or she is summoned for or charged with a criminal offence or becomes a party to civil proceedings, and to inform the Secretary of Commissions of any conviction or court order against him or her.

5. TRAINING

Since 1953 it has been the duty of every magistrates' courts committee to provide courses of instruction for justices in their area, in accordance with arrangements approved by the Lord Chancellor.[50] All justices appointed since January 1, 1966[51] have been required to attend a course of basic training designed to enable them to understand the nature of their duties so that they "act judicially," to obtain sufficient knowledge of the law to follow normal cases and a working knowledge of the law of evidence, to understand the nature and purpose of the sentences they impose and other methods of treatment, and to understand the relationship which should exist between justices and the others taking part in the operation of magistrates' courts.[52] The First Stage of training has to be completed before a magistrate first sits, and comprises attendance at court as an observer, some instruction by the clerk to the justices and/or the chairman of the bench or a senior magistrate and some reading. The Second Stage should not normally commence until the justice has been adjudicating for six months and must be completed within 12 months of the date of appointment. It comprises further sessions of instruction or practical exercises, visits to a prison and other penal institutions and attendance as an observer at a domestic proceedings court and a different magistrates' court.

Justices appointed after January 1, 1980 have also been required to undertake refresher training.[53] The commitment is for 12 hours training every three years, beginning in October 1983. There is no complete prescribed syllabus, but there must be training in chairmanship and training for the Crown Court. Otherwise "the aim should be to provide a broadly based programme to widen experience and knowledge, to increase understanding and thus to increase confidence." In addition there are

[50] See now the Justice of the Peace Act 1979, s.63.

[51] See *The Training of Justices of the Peace in England and Wales* (Cmnd. 2856, 1967) (White Paper). The Lord Chancellor has been assisted since 1974 by an Advisory Committee on Training, chaired by Boreham J. This replaced a National Advisory Council which had been set up to consider the introduction of compulsory training. It is expected that the Committee will be absorbed into the Judicial Studies Board (see below, p. 169): Skyrme (1983) p. 73.

[52] See the booklet published by the Lord Chancellor's Department on *The Training of Magistrates* (1978).

[53] See the Lord Chancellor's Department booklet on *Further Training For Magistrates*.

courses for justices appointed to juvenile court or domestic court panels.[54]

The organisation of the courses is in the hands of Training Officers who are responsible to the Training Committee of the magistrates' courts committees. Most are justices' clerks, although the net is spread more widely for tutors.

Within the limits laid down by the Lord Chancellor there is in fact considerable scope for local variation.[55] Moreover, a survey conducted in 1974 showed that while magistrates in the sample were well-satisfied with their basic training, many had not actually fulfilled the training requirements.[56] For example, one-fifth of the magistrates had adjudicated on the bench before completing the first stage, and one-quarter had not visited the required number and type of penal institutions. Sir Thomas Skyrme[57] notes that in spite of the Lord Chancellor's power to act in default if the required courses are not provided[58] the system "still falls short of what is needed to ensure that justices are trained in the most efficaceous and economic manner." Expenditure on training has always been "negligible." One problem seems to be that training is organised by magistrates' courts committees but paid for by local councils.

The training programmes are not designed to turn magistrates into "experts": the best form of training is regarded as experience on the bench. The work of Bond and Lemon[59] suggests that experience is more likely than training to modify the attitudes of newly-appointed magistrates, although neither has much effect in changing previous attitudes on penal policy.

6. CONDUCT AND REMOVAL

A justice of the peace may be removed by the Lord Chancellor.[60] No grounds are specified in the Act. The Lord Chancellor also has power to direct that a justice be transferred to the "supplemental list" if he is satisfied either:

> "(a) that by reason of the justice's age or infirmity or other like cause it is expedient that he should cease to exercise judicial functions as a justice for that area, or
> (b) that the justice declines or neglects to take a proper part in the exercise of those functions."[61]

Justices are also automatically transferred to the supplemental list on reaching the age of 70, or in the case of a justice who holds or who has held high judicial office, 75.[62] A justice who is on the list may not act as a justice except to authenticate a signature or written declaration, or to give a

---

[54] See the Lord Chancellor's Department booklets on *Basic Training for Juvenile Court Magistrates* (1976) and *Basic Training for Domestic Court Panels* (1979).
[55] See Burney (1979), Chap. 12.
[56] J. Baldwin, "The Compulsory Training of the Magistracy" [1975] Crim.L.R. 634.
[57] Skyrme (1983), p. 80.
[58] Administration of Justice Act 1973, s.3; now the Justices of the Peace Act 1979, s.63(4).
[59] *Op. cit.* n. 44 above.
[60] Justices of the Peace Act 1979, s.6.
[61] *Ibid.* s.8(4).
[62] *Ibid.* s.8(2).

certificate of facts within his knowledge or of his opinion as to any matter.[63] He or she may, however, be authorised by the Lord Chancellor to sit in the Crown Court up to the age of 72.

In practice, a justice would only be removed for good cause. Most have to leave office because they are unable to fulfil their share of the work or because they move outside the area.[64] In relation to misbehaviour, the "overriding consideration" is that "public confidence in the administration of justice may be preserved."[65] Justices have been removed if they or a spouse have been convicted of an offence, although a conviction for a minor motoring offence will lead to a reprimand rather than suspension or removal. Convictions for drunken driving have in recent years led to suspension during the period of disqualification rather than removal. Justices have also been removed for refusing to apply a law he or she has found distasteful.[66] Allegations of incapacity or misbehaviour are normally referred to the Local Advisory Committee for investigation: if they conclude that the justice should be removed, that is reported to the Lord Chancellor. If the justice does not accept the committee's finding there is then a further inquiry by the Secretary of Commissions. The justice may be interviewed. A recent case shows, however, that the Committee may not permit the justice to appear before them in person and may act on allegations of which he or she is not fully informed.[66a] On three occasions in the 1940s the improper conduct of particular court proceedings led to an inquiry, and on one occasion Lord Dilhorne conducted a private inquiry into a lenient sentence imposed by three magistrates.[67]

7. DISQUALIFICATION

Justices are subject to the same common law rules as to disqualification for interest or bias as other judicial officers.[68] In addition, they are expressly disqualified from acting in a case involving a local authority if they are a member of that authority.[69] A celebrated case where a magistrate was sufficiently incautious as to admit actual bias was *R.* v. *Bingham JJ., ex p.*

---

[63] *Ibid.* s.10.

[64] Each year, about 1 per cent. of all justices on the active list are required to resign for the first reason, and 1 per cent. for the second: Skyrme (1983), p. 153.

[65] *Ibid.* p. 154.

[66] Colonel Delmer Davies-Evans, who disapproved of certain regulations governing the use of petrol, was removed in 1947 (see Skyrme (1983), pp. 156–7). A Welsh justice who stated that she was not prepared to impose penalties on people who, non-violently, broke laws which she considered unjust to the Welsh language, resigned in 1972: R. Pearson (*op. cit.* n. 48) pp. 89–90; see also Lord Hailsham, (1972) 28 *The Magistrate* 132–134: in a similar case, Lord Gardiner required a Welsh magistrate to resign.

[66a] *L.A.G. Bull.*, April 1983, pp. 9–12 (two magistrates removed on account of an "adulterous association," "conducted indiscreetly in a manner likely to give rise to scandal").

[67] Skyrme (1983), pp. 168–169.

[68] Below, pp. 744–745. See, generally, R.D.S. Stevens, *Bias and Impartiality in Magistrates' Courts* (1982). For cases concerning justices see *R.* v. *Altrincham JJ., ex p. Pennington* [1975] Q.B. 549; *R.* v. *Smethwick JJ., ex p. Hands, The Times*, December 4, 1980 (decision on allegation of statutory nuisance against local authority quashed because one of the justices was the wife of the former chairman of the housing committee); *R.* v. *Liverpool City JJ., ex. p. Topping* [1983] 1 W.L.R. 119.

[69] Justices of the Peace Act 1979, s.64. For the rules relating to disqualification of licensing justices see the Licensing Act 1964, s.193 and *R.* v. *Barnsley Justices* [1960] 2 Q.B. 167.

Jowitt.[70] The chairman of a bench hearing a speeding case, where the only evidence was that of the motorist and a police constable, said:

> "Quite the most unpleasant cases that we have to decide are those where the evidence is a direct conflict between a police officer and a member of the public. My principle in such cases has always been to believe the evidence of the police officer, and therefore we find the case proved."

The conviction was quashed.

8. LEGAL LIABILITY

A justice enjoys a statutory immunity from an action for damages in respect of an act within jurisdiction unless the act is done maliciously and without reasonable and probable cause.[71] Malice and lack of cause do not have to be established if the act is done outside jurisdiction.[72] These provisions have been overtaken by the restatement in wider terms of the scope of a justice's common law immunity from suit in *Sirros* v. *Moore.*[73] No action may be brought in respect of the manner in which a discretionary power is exercised.[74] A justice or justices' clerk may be indemnified out of local funds for the expenses of defending proceedings, including any damages awarded against him. If he has acted reasonably and in good faith he is entitled to an indemnity.[75]

9. JUSTICES' CLERKS[76]

The justices' clerk is in charge of the administration of the magistrates' court and is also its chief legal advisor. Originally the clerks were the personal clerks to individual justices or benches. They are now appointed by the magistrates' courts committees subject to the approval of the Lord Chancellor.[77] They hold office "during the pleasure of the committee" although the approval of the Lord Chancellor is necessary for their removal where the magistrates for their division do not consent.[78] A candidate for appointment has to be either a barrister or solicitor of five years' standing, an existing justices' clerk, a barrister or solicitor who has served as a justices' clerk's assistant[79] and, in special circumstances, a justices' clerk's assistant with 10 years' experience prior to 1960.[80] Remuneration is fixed by national negotiating machinery, and varies according to the size of the area served. In 1983 there were 333 clerkships in England and Wales: 309

---

[70] *The Times,* July 3, 1974.

[71] Justices of the Peace Act 1979, s.44.

[72] *Ibid.* s.45. See L.A. Sheridan, (1951) 14 M.L.R. 267; D. Thompson, (1958) 21 M.L.R. 517.

[73] Below, p. 174.

[74] 1979 Act, s.47.

[75] 1979 Act, s.53.

[76] K.C. Clarke, [1964] Crim. L.R. 620, 697; P. Darbyshire, (1980) 144 J.P.N., 186, 201, 219, 233.

[77] Justices of the Peace Act 1979, s.25.

[78] *Ibid.*

[79] Or service in certain other clerkships before February 1, 1969.

[80] Justices of the Peace Act 1979, s.26.

wholetime and 24 part-time. Of the 312 members of the Justices' Clerks' Society, 147 were solicitors, 105 barristers and 24 qualified by experience.[81] The trend is for the number of clerkships to be reduced by amalgamation of areas served by one clerk.[82]

The justices' clerk is the head of what may be a large staff.[83] There will be a deputy and a number of assistants. There are normally four categories of staff: court clerks, general administrative and clerical staff, staff employed on accounts and financial matters and ushers. There is also a trainee grade. Those who act as court clerks are senior assistants. As from October 1, 1980, a person may not act as a court clerk unless he or she possesses one of a series of prescribed qualifications.[84] These include being qualified for appointment as a justices' clerk, being a barrister or solicitor possessing a certificate of competence or a training certificate granted by a magistrates' courts committee, or holding a "Diploma in Magisterial Law."[85]

In large offices the justices' clerk will rarely have time to act as a court clerk personally[86] although his advice on the law or procedure may be sought by a court clerk or bench of justices. He may act as clerk to the magistrates' courts committee,[87] to licensing committees, to the juvenile court panel and the Lord Chancellor's Advisory Committee. He may grant but not refuse legal aid. He will supervise the listing of cases and organise the sittings of magistrates. He will also normally arrange and participate in the training of magistrates. Under the Justices' Clerks Rules 1970[88] a justices' clerk may perform a number of functions otherwise exercisable by a single justice, such as the issuing of a summons and adjourning a hearing with the consent of prosecutor and accused. Similarly, an information may be laid before either a justice or a justice's clerk. Judicial functions such as issuing a summons may not be delegated by the justices' clerk to his assistant[89]; the ministerial functions of receiving an information may, however, be performed by the court staff.[90]

One of the issues that has caused problems since the 1940s has been the role of the court clerk in magistrates' court proceedings.[91] The clerk's function is to advise on law and procedure, but not to participate in the decision on the facts. In *R. v. East Kerrier JJ., ex p. Mundy*[92] Lord

[81] (1984) 40 *The Magistrate* 49.

[82] (1980) 36 *The Magistrate* 44.

[83] See *A Career in the Magistrates' Courts* (1979).

[84] The Justices' Clerks (Qualifications of Assistants) Rules 1979, S.I. 1979 No. 570 as amended by S.I. 1980 No. 1897.

[85] Courses for such a diploma are run by three polytechnics.

[86] "In 1947 the justices' clerk himself was present in about 9 courts in 10; by 1977 the average was not more than 1 in 10": Skyrme (1983), p. 179.

[87] Until the reorganisation of the areas of magistrates' courts committees as part of local government reorganisation in 1974 this clerkship was commonly held by the clerk to the local authority.

[88] S.I. 1970 No. 231, as amended.

[89] *R. v. Gateshead JJ., ex p. Tesco Stores Ltd.* [1981] Q.B. 470. This case caused consternation in magistrates' courts as it had been common practice to delegate such matters in line with the recommendations of the Justices' Clerks' Society.

[90] *R. v. Manchester Stipendiary Magistrate, ex p. Hill* [1983] 1 A.C. 328.

[91] The court clerk has been described as the "key worker in setting the tone of the courtroom atmosphere": H. Parker, M. Casburn and D. Turnbull, *Receiving Juvenile Justice* (1981), p. 48.

[92] [1952] 2 Q.B. 719.

Goddard C.J. stated that the clerk should not retire with the justices as a matter of course but should wait to be sent for should his advice on a point of law be needed. Otherwise, observers might conclude that the clerk was influencing the justices on questions of fact, and this would constitute a breach of the principle that justice must be seen to be done. This apparently caused "alarm and despondency" in some quarters,[93] somewhat to Lord Goddard's surprise, and this led to some further "clarification,"[94] or back-pedalling (depending on one's point of view). At the same time Lord Goddard C.J. threatened that justices who knowingly disobeyed the Divisional Court's directions would be reported to the Lord Chancellor.[95] Since then the trend has been for emphasis to be placed increasingly on the point that lay justices must be given proper professional advice, and less on the need to avoid the appearance that the clerk might have given his opinion on the facts.[96] Recently, a new Practice Direction has been issued by Lord Lane C.J., with the concurrence of the President of the Family Division[97]:

"1. A justices' clerk is responsible to the justices for the performance of any of the functions set out below by any member of his staff acting as court clerk[98] and may be called in to advise the justices even when he is not personally sitting with the justices as clerk to the court.

2. It shall be the responsibility of the justices' clerk to advise the justices, as follows: (a) on question of law or of mixed law and fact[99]; (b) as to matters of practice and procedure.

3. If it appears to him necessary to do so, or he is so requested by the justices, the justices' clerk has the responsibility to (a) refresh the justices' memory as to any matter of evidence and to draw attention to any issues involved in the matters before the court, (b) advise the justices generally on the range of penalties which the law allows them to impose and on any guidance relevant to the choice of penalty provided by the law, the decisions of the superior courts or other authorities.[1] If no request for advice has been made by the justices, the justices' clerk shall discharge his responsibility in court in the presence of the parties.

4. The way in which the justices' clerk should perform his functions should be stated as follows. (a) The justices are entitled to the advice of their clerk when they retire in order that the clerk may fulfil his

---

[93] (1953) 10 *The Magistrate* 65.

[94] *R.* v. *Welshpool JJ., ex p. Holley* [1953] 2 Q.B. 403 (justices can invite the clerk to join them as they retire to advise on a point of law; the fact that he remains while the facts are discussed not sufficient to invalidate their decision); *Practice Note (Justices' Clerks)* [1953] 1 W.L.R. 1416.

[95] *R.* v. *Barry JJ., ex p. Nagi Kasim* [1953] 1 W.L.R. 1320, 1322.

[96] N. Crampton, (1979) 129 N.L.J. 208. See also the joint statement by the Magistrates' Association and the Justices' Clerks' Society: (1975) 31 *The Magistrate* 4.

[97] *Practice Direction (Justices: Clerk to Court)* [1981] 1 W.L.R. 1163. See B. Harris, (1981) 145 J.P.N. 403. Some of these points as to the functions of a justices' clerk are also made in the Justices of the Peace Act 1979, s.28(3); it is stated that this subsection is not exhaustive (subs. (4)).

[98] The implication is that these rules apply to all court clerks.

[99] See, *e.g. R.* v. *Consett JJ., ex p. Postal Bingo Ltd.* [1967] 2 Q.B. 9.

[1] See (1976) 140 J.P.N. 496.

responsibility outlined above. (b) Some justices may prefer to take their own notes of evidence. There is, however, no obligation on them to do so. Whether they do so or not, there is nothing to prevent them from enlisting the aid of their clerk and his notes if they are in any doubt as to the evidence which has been given.[2] (c) If the justices wish to consult their clerk solely about the evidence or his notes of it, this should ordinarily, and certainly in simple cases, be done in open court. The object is to avoid any suspicion that the clerk has been involved in deciding issues of fact.

5. For the reasons stated in the practice direction of January 15, 1954, *Practice Note (Justices' Clerks)* [1954] 1 W.L.R. 213, which remains in full force and effect, in domestic proceedings it is more likely than not that the justices will wish to consult their clerk. In particular, where rules of court require the reasons for their decision to be drawn up in consultation with the clerk, they will need to receive his advice for this purpose."

If justices summon the clerk when only issues of fact are involved and the clerk has made no note of evidence, a conviction may well be quashed.[3]

It has been held that the clerk may ask questions in court in order to clear up ambiguities, so long as it is at the express or implied request of the bench,[4] and that it is proper for the clerk, in the absence of the justices and in conjunction with the prosecutor, to explain to an unrepresented defendant that if he attacks a prosecution witness his previous convictions can be revealed to the court.[5]

In some areas, clerks rule on questions of the admissibility of evidence in the absence of the justices. This is generally accepted to be irregular as the clerk has no legal authority to rule on such matters. On the other hand it is also accepted that it is undesirable for the justices who are to determine guilt to determine disputed questions of admissibility, which may well involve hearing evidence which subsequently has to be disregarded as inadmissible. There is in fact no reason why the parties should not by agreement submit the issue to the clerk and, once his ruling is made, voluntarily abide by it: the real limitation is that his ruling will not technically be binding. It is likely to be in the defendant's interests for this to be done in the absence of the justices: it is unlikely that the justices could be persuaded to differ from the clerk's view on such a question.

It is also a well established practice for lawyers to refer doubtful points of law to the clerk in advance of the hearing in order to obtain what in practice, although again not in theory, amounts to a ruling.[6]

---

[2] This impliedly overrules the statements of Donaldson L.J. in *R.* v. *Guildford JJ., ex p. Harding* (1981) 145 J.P. 174.

[3] *R.* v. *Worley JJ., ex p. Nash* [1982] C.L. 1932. See the comment at (1983) 147 J.P.N. 209, where the case is referred to as *R.* v. *Warley JJ.*

[4] *R.* v. *Consett JJ., ex p. Postal Bingo Ltd.* [1967] 2 Q.B. 9. In general, clerks should not otherwise take an active part in proceedings, except where an unrepresented party is not competent to examine witnesses properly: Lord Parker C.J. in *Simms* v. *Moore* [1970] 2 Q.B. 327, 332–333.

[5] *R.* v. *Weston-super-Mare JJ., ex p. Townsend* [1968] 3 All E.R. 225. Magistrates may delegate to the clerk the function of telling a defendant his rights at a committal: *R.* v. *Horseferry Road JJ., ex p. Farooki, The Times,* October 29, 1982.

[6] See P. Darbyshire, 144 J.P.N. 201.

From time to time, suggestions are made for changing the status of the justices' clerk.[7] One possibility would be to appoint him to the bench, so that he would become, in those courts where he presided, a legally qualified chairman. Another possibility would be to give him the formal power to rule on points of law, while leaving the determination of the facts, as at present, to the lay justices. This is virtually the present position. There is a persistent minority of cases in which lay justices exert their power to determine a point of law contrary to the clerk's advice. Lord Widgery C.J., however, warned that if justices fly in the face of their clerk's advice and are subsequently reversed on appeal, costs may be awarded against them.[8]

10. MAGISTRATES IN THE CROWN COURT

The Beeching Committee[9] recommended that magistrates should sit as assessors with Circuit judges in the Crown Court. Before reorganization, justices had participated in quarter sessions in the counties, but not in the assizes or borough quarter sessions. The Courts Act 1971[10] provided that justices may sit with a Circuit judge or recorder when conducting a trial on indictment and must do so when the Crown Court is hearing an appeal or dealing with a person committed there for sentence. Moreover, it provided that the justices would act as judges of the Crown Court and not merely as assessors. Lord Gardiner L.C. and Lord Hailsham L.C. were advised to adopt this course by Sir Thomas Skyrme,[11] who argued that the experience would be of benefit to the justices; that justices could play a valuable part in sentencing, especially where the judge had no local knowledge; that they could exercise a useful restriction on any idiosyncrasy of a judge or recorder; that this would avoid the friction which had previously occurred between borough benches and their recorder; that the association of laymen with the higher courts was in line with current thinking; and that previous experience with county quarter sessions suggested that this would be advantageous. However, Skyrme has acknowledged that the differences between the Crown Court and quarter sessions turned out to be greater than expected. Long trials that formerly would have been dealt with at assizes were now conducted by a court including justices at the Crown Court. The Crown Court was in continuous session. Trials might be conducted by judges with no experience of sitting with lay justices. The facilities provided for justices often fell short of those that had been provided at quarter sessions. Cases commonly ran over a day and this would cause problems for many lay justices. In some areas only those who could sit for several days were summoned: courts were accordingly composed disproportionately of women and the elderly. On the other hand, Circuit judges have been appointed as "liaison judges," and in some areas they have been able to improve relationships.

---

[7] Here the suggestions are usually confined to the justices' clerk himself and do not extend to his assistants.

[8] *Jones* v. *Nicks* [1977] R.T.R. 72, 76. The advice concerned what might constitute a "special reason" for not imposing an endorsement following a speeding conviction.

[9] *Royal Commission on Assizes and Quarter Sessions* (Cmnd. 4153, 1979).

[10] See now the Supreme Court Act 1981, ss.8, 74, 75; The Crown Court Rules 1982, rr. 3–5.

[11] Skyrme (1983), pp. 125–130.

Dissatisfaction with the role of justices in the Crown Court has continued in many places.[12] Nevertheless, the suggestion of Lord Elwyn-Jones L.C. that justices should no longer sit in trials was resisted by a majority of justices, and there was no desire to restrict their role contrary to their wishes.[12a]

The Lord Chancellor has asked that no justice should sit in the Crown Court unless he had completed his basic training and had two years' experience. The justices may outvote the judge, although in the case of a tie the latter has a second and casting vote.[13] This is most likely to happen on a question of sentence, but may occur on other matters, such as the discretion to exclude evidence.[14]

11. STIPENDIARY MAGISTRATES

The Queen may appoint up to 60 "metropolitan stipendiary magistrates" for the inner London area,[15] and up to 40 "stipendiary magistrates" elsewhere.[16] The former can trace their existence back to 1792, when they took over criminal jurisdiction from the largely corrupt lay justices.[17] The Metropolitan Police Courts Act 1839 provided that only barristers were to be eligible for appointment. From 1964, they have shared their duties with lay justices, who, with the passage of time, have been restored to respectability.

In the provinces, stipendiaries were appointed in places where there were not enough justices to cope with the work, and where, at the same time, there was a resistance to the appointment of men who had acquired wealth through industry or trade. Boroughs might petition the Home Secretary to appoint a stipendiary; alternatively, a local Act of Parliament might provide for an appointment. The role of provincial stipendiaries was to supplement rather than to replace the lay justices. The 1948 Royal Commission noted that the determining factor behind whether a particular area had a stipendiary was "not a rational assessment of the present need but the course of past history."[18] The rationalisation of commission areas, which was a by-product of local government reorganisation, provided the opportunity for the right to take the initiative in the making of new appointments to be transferred from local authorities to the Lord Chancellor.[19] The requirements of each area were assessed by the Lord Chancellor's office.[20] The area of jurisdiction of some stipendiaries was

---

[12] *Ibid.* see also G. Hawker, *Magistrates in the Crown Court* (1974): Survey by the Institute of Judicial Administration, University of Birmingham.

[12a] Skyrme (1983) pp. 129–130; (1975) 31 *The Magistrate* 185, (1976) 32 *The Magistrate* 13–14, (1977) *The Magistrate* 83.

[13] Supreme Court Act 1981, s.73.

[14] *R. v. Smith (Benjamin Walker)* [1978] Crim.L.R. 296.

[15] Justices of the Peace Act 1979, s.31. In 1983 there were 46.

[16] 1979 Act, s.13. In 1983 there were 12.

[17] See generally F. Milton, *The English Magistracy* (1967), Chap. 2. Some of the existing justices managed to secure stipendiary appointments, but ministers in the early nineteenth century took greater care over appointments.

[18] Cmd. 7463, p. 57.

[19] Administration of Justice Act 1973, s.2.

[20] Skyrme (1983), Chap. 13.

increased to enable the post to be retained. One additional stipendiary was appointed in Sheffield.

Appointments are made on the recommendation of the Lord Chancellor.[21] An appointee must be a barrister or solicitor[22] of seven years' standing. Metropolitan stipendiaries may be removed by the Lord Chancellor for inability or misbehaviour[23]; provincial stipendiaries hold office "during pleasure" but may only be removed on the Lord Chancellor's recommendation.[24] The retiring age is 70, although the Lord Chancellor may authorise a stipendiary to continue in office up to the age of 72.[25] The Lord Chancellor may appoint acting stipendiary magistrates.[26] The current salary is £28,500,[27] stipendiaries being grouped with, *inter alia*, masters and registrars of the Supreme Court and chairmen of Industrial Tribunals.

Traditionally, appointment to judicial office has been on the understanding that the appointee will remain in that office. Today there is a growing trend for judicial officers to be "promoted," although it is still very much the exception rather than the rule. Stipendiaries may be invited to sit as recorders. Some have been appointed to the Circuit Bench.

Proposals have been made on a number of occasions for extending the role of stipendiaries outside Inner London. One possibility would be to replace all lay justices by stipendiaries. Another would be to require that each bench of magistrates should comprise one stipendiary sitting with lay justices. A third would be to increase the numbers so that there is at least one in each area, operating on a peripatetic basis. The 1948 Royal Commission reported against any radical change in the system.[28] There would not be sufficient candidates for appointment. The cost of the salaries would be large. Legal training was not in fact necessary provided legal advice was available. The present system gave the citizen a part to play in the administration of the law. The third proposal was advanced by the Bar to the 1948 Royal Commission. The stipendiary would visit the various benches and sit as chairman and would be available to take difficult cases. However, the Royal Commission noted that it was difficult to predict those cases where guidance from a professional magistrate would be useful, and that it would be undesirable to dilute the responsibility and authority of lay justices.

B. TRIBUNAL CHAIRMEN AND MEMBERS

There are several patterns on which the composition of a tribunal may be organised.[29] The variations reflect partly the differences in the kind of

[21] This requirement is express as regards provincial stipendiaries: 1979 Act, s.14(3).

[22] This first became possible under the Justices of the Peace Act 1949. The first was appointed in 1957. By 1983 20 solicitors had been appointed, 15 in London and five elsewhere: Skyrme (1983) p. 187.

[23] 1979 Act, s.31(4)(c).

[24] 1979 Act, s.13(1).

[25] 1979 Act, s.14. The ages for persons appointed before October 25, 1968 are 72 and 75 respectively.

[26] 1979 Act, ss.15, 34.

[27] As from November 1, 1984.

[28] Cmd. 7463, Chap. VIII.

[29] See above, pp. 31–32, 41–45, 52–54, 56–58, 76–77.

work undertaken by different tribunals and partly their diverse historical origins. Full-time appointments are commonly of similar status to one or other of the ranks of the judiciary. The Presidents of the Lands Tribunal, of the Transport Tribunal and of Industrial Tribunals and the Chief Social Security Commissioner receive a higher salary than a Circuit judge[30]; members of the Lands Tribunal and Social Security Commissioners receive the same as a Circuit judge; chairmen of Industrial Tribunals receive the same as a stipendiary magistrate.[31] Most appointments are part-time.

It is not possible to consider here the details of appointment and tenure for all tribunals.[32] Some general observations can, however, be made.

1. WHO APPOINTS?

The Franks Committee on Administrative Tribunals and Enquiries[33] reported that appointments to tribunals were usually made by the minister responsible for legislation under which they operated. They had received no significant evidence that any influence was in fact exerted on tribunal members by government departments, but recommended, nevertheless, that chairmen, whether legally qualified or not, should be appointed by the Lord Chancellor and members by the Council on Tribunals.[34] The position today is that the Lord Chancellor is involved in the appointment of a majority of chairmen. He either appoints the chairman directly[35] or appoints a panel from which a selection is made by the relevant department or President of tribunals.[36] The appointment of members has, however, not been transferred to the Council on Tribunals, and it is not seriously argued that it should be. Most tribunal members are appointed by the relevant government department: some are appointed by the Crown or the Lord Chancellor.

2. QUALIFICATIONS FOR APPOINTMENT

The Franks Committee recommended that *chairmen* of tribunals:

"should ordinarily have legal qualifications but that the appointment of persons without legal qualifications should not be ruled out when they are particularly suitable."[37]

---

[30] £36,000, as from November 1, 1984. The first two may in practice carry out other judicial work in addition to their tribunal duties.

[31] Regional chairmen receive a little more.

[32] See J.F. Garner, *Administrative Law* (5th ed., 1979), Chap. 8; R.E. Wraith and P.G. Hutchesson, *Administrative Tribunals* (1973), Chap. 4.

[33] Cmnd. 218, 1957.

[34] Cmnd. 218 pp. 11–12.

[35] *e.g.* the President (and members) of the Lands Tribunal: Lands Tribunal Act 1949, s.2); chairman (and members) of Mental Health Review Tribunals: Mental Health Act 1983, s.65(2), Sched. 2. Some are Crown appointments: for example, the provisions governing the appointment and tenure of Social Security Commissioners (Social Security Act 1975, s.97(3), as amended; Social Security Act 1980, ss.12, 13) are very similar to those governing Circuit judges (see below, pp. 153–154), except that a solicitor is eligible for direct appointment as a Commissioner but only via a recordership as a Circuit judge.

[36] See the Tribunals and Inquiries Act 1971, s.7: examples include the chairmen of industrial tribunals, N.I.L.T.s and S.B.A.T.s and, from 1984, S.S.A.T.s (see above, pp. 57–58).

[37] Cmnd. 218, p. 12.

There should be no such requirement for members. The possession of a legal qualification is thought to be desirable not so much for the expertise in handling legal rules as for the qualities necessary for good chairmanship. "Objectivity in the treatment of cases and the proper sifting of facts are most often best secured by having a legally qualified chairman . . . ."[38] Many criticisms of Supplementary Benefit Appeal Tribunals were related to the general lack of legally qualified chairmen. They were regularly contrasted unfavourably with National Insurance Local Tribunals where a legal qualification was in practice required.[39] Not all commentators favoured a change to lawyer-chairmen, but the government indicated in 1977 that there would be a "gradual, but significant move to appoint more legally-qualified chairmen of S.B.A.T.s."[40] Between 1977 and 1980 the overall proportion of lawyer chairmen increased from 12 per cent. to 26·4 per cent.[41]

In some cases, a legal qualification or legal experience is required by statute[42]: in others it is normally required as a matter of practice.[43] It has also been noted that it has become more common for people to hold part-time appointments to more than one tribunal.[44]

The background of *members* will obviously be related to the nature of the tribunal's work. For example, doctors sit on Medical Appeal Tribunals. A pattern commonly adopted is that of the "representative panel." For example, in National Insurance Local Tribunals, one "wingman" was taken from a panel representing employers and self-employed persons and the other from a panel representing employed persons.[45] A similar arrangement applies to Industrial Tribunals.[46] In Supplementary Benefit Appeal Tribunals one panel was directly appointed by the Secretary of State and the other was appointed by him "from among persons appearing to the Secretary of State to represent workpeople."[47] On the employees' side the practice is for nominations from the local Trades Council to be accepted relatively automatically. On the other side nominations are received from a wide

---

[38] *Ibid.*

[39] See, *e.g.* Kathleen Bell *et al*, "National Insurance Local Tribunals: A Research Study" (1974) 3 *Journal of Social Policy* 289 and (1975) 4 *Journal of Social Policy* 1; Kathleen Bell, *Research Study on Supplementary Benefit Appeal Tribunals—Review of Main Findings: Conclusions: Recommendations* (1975); J. Fulbrook, *Administrative Justice and the Unemployed* (1978), pp. 209–220.

[40] Annual Report of the Council on Tribunals, 1976–77 (1977–78 H.C. 108), p. 26.

[41] N. Harris, "The Appointment of Legally Qualified Chairmen for S.B.A.T.s" (1982) 132 N.L.J. 495. There have been some reports of consequential improvements in the conduct of proceedings.

[42] *e.g.* Social Security Commissioners, (barrister, solicitor or advocate of 10 years' standing), Lands Tribunal members (either lawyer or qualified surveyor), chairmen of Industrial Tribunals (barristers or solicitors of seven years' standing), chairmen of Mental Health Review Tribunals (persons of suitable legal experience).

[43] *e.g.* N.I.L.T.s, Medical Appeal Tribunals, Immigration Appeal Adjudicators.

[44] Wraith and Hutchesson (1973), pp. 114–115; Fulbrook (1978), p. 212.

[45] Social Security Act 1975, s.97.

[46] Industrial Tribunals (England and Wales) Regulations 1965 (S.I. 1965 No. 1101), reg. 5. One panel is appointed by the Secretary of State after consultation with the T.U.C., the other after consultation with the C.B.I.

[47] Supplementary Benefits Act 1976, Sched. 2, as substituted by the Social Security Act 1979, Sched. 4. For the position in relation to the new Social Security Appeal Tribunals, see above, p. 58.

variety of organisations.[48] Part-time appointments are commonly for three years with the possibility of renewal, but there are variations.[49]

3. Dismissal

No power of a minister to terminate a person's membership of a tribunal is exercisable except with the consent of the Lord Chancellor.[50]

4. Training

The Council on Tribunals has noted the benefits derived from regular meetings of tribunal chairmen, at which difficulties can be discussed and opinions ventilated.[51] There have also been developments in the training of tribunal chairmen, although these have lagged behind developments in the training of magistrates.[52] There is little provision of training for tribunal members.

5. Clerks to Tribunals[53]

The Franks Committee noted that the practice:

"whereby the majority of clerks of tribunals are provided by the Government Departments concerned from their local and regional staffs seems partly to be responsible for the feeling in the minds of some people that tribunals are dependent upon and influenced by those Departments."[54]

They considered the possibility of establishing under the Lord Chancellor's Department a central corps of clerks for all tribunals, but rejected it on the grounds that it was difficult to see how reasonable career prospects could be held out, that it would be difficult to arrange sittings to ensure that the clerks were fully occupied and that it was in any event desirable for the civil servants in social service departments to spend a period as tribunal clerk.[55] To ensure that clerks did not exert a departmental influence, the Committee stated that their duties and conduct should be regulated on the advice of the Council on Tribunals. The duties of a clerk should generally be confined to secretarial work, taking notes of evidence and tendering advice, when requested, on points connected with the tribunal's functions.

---

[48] See Fulbrook (1978), pp. 222–224. Little has been written about the social and political background of tribunal members: see W.E. Cavanagh and G.N. Hawker, "Laymen on Administrative Tribunals" (1974) 52 *Public Administration* 215 (Rent Assessment Panels and S.B.A.T.s) and the study of N.I.L.T.s by Kathleen Bell and others: *op. cit.* n. 39, pp. 310–315.

[49] Wraith and Hutchesson (1973) p. 109.

[50] Tribunals and Inquiries Act 1971, s.8. The tribunals to which this applies are specified in Sched. 1.

[51] Annual Report for 1976–77, pp. 19–20.

[52] For example, there was a system for training S.B.A.T. chairmen (see Annual Report of the Council on Tribunals 1977–78 (1978–79 H.C. 74), pp. 16–17), and some training courses have been held for chairmen of Local Valuation Courts (Report for 1978–79 (1979–80 H.C. 359), p. 18).

[53] See Wraith and Hutchesson (1973) Chap. 5, and pp. 300–306.

[54] Cmnd. 218, p. 13.

[55] *Ibid.* pp. 13–14.

He should not retire with the tribunal unless sent for to advise on a specific point.

The role of the clerk has proved problematic most notably in relation to hearings of Supplementary Benefit Appeal Tribunals.[56] In 1971, the D.H.S.S., following consultation with the Council on Tribunals, issued revised official instructions which curtailed the clerk's previous role. They were subsequently made a little less restrictive,[57] and are similar to those applicable to justices' clerks.[58] Kathleen Bell's study found that for the most part the clerk played a minor role in the hearing.[59]

C. THE CIRCUIT BENCH

The Circuit Bench was created by the Courts Act 1971 as part of the reorganisation of the criminal courts following the Beeching Commission.[60] The Queen may appoint Circuit judges and recorders on the recommendation of the Lord Chancellor.[61] Circuit judges are appointed to serve full-time in the Crown Court and county courts, recorders to serve as part-time judges in the Crown Court.[62] Only a barrister or solicitor of 10 years' standing may be appointed as a recorder. A barrister of 10 years' standing or a recorder who has held office for at least five years may be appointed as a Circuit judge. A solicitor may accordingly reach the position of Circuit judge after time as a recorder.

On reorganisation, a number of middle-rank judges automatically become Circuit judges, including the Vice-Chancellor of the County Palatine of Lancaster, the Recorder of London, the Common Serjeant, the Recorders of Liverpool and Manchester, Official Referees, the Additional Judges of the Central Criminal Court, county court judges and the whole-time chairmen or deputy chairmen of quarter sessions.[63] Most of these offices were abolished, but some were retained. The Vice-Chancellor of the County Palatine of Lancaster conducts High Court Chancery business in the North.[64] The Common Serjeant and the Recorder of London[65] sit at the Central Criminal Court. Those appointed to these offices become Circuit judges ex officio. In addition, the senior Circuit

---

[56] See Fulbrook (1978), pp. 229–236.

[57] Supplementary Benefit Appeal Tribunals: A guide to procedure (1977) Appendix 1; Annual Report of the Council on Tribunals, 1973–74 (1974–75 H.C. 289), pp. 22–23.

[58] See above, pp. 143–147.

[59] Op. cit. n. 39 above, p. 9.

[60] Royal Commission on Assizes and Quarter Sessions (Cmnd. 4153, 1969).

[61] Courts Act 1971, s.16. In 1984 there were 348 Circuit judges (including 11 women) and 471 recorders (including 20 women).

[62] And to carry out such other judicial functions as may be conferred on them by statute. A Circuit judge or recorder may be requested to act as a judge of the High Court: Supreme Court Act 1981, s.9 as amended by the Administration of Justice Act 1982, s.58. They are addressed as "Your Honour," unless sitting as a judge of the High Court or at the Central Criminal Court when they are addressed as "My Lord" or "My Lady." Circuit judges are referred to as His (or Her) Honour Judge X and recorders as Mr. (or Mrs. but not Miss) recorder B: Practice Direction (Judges: Mode of Address) [1982] 1 W.L.R. 101.

[63] Courts Act 1971, Sched. 2, Part I.

[64] He is appointed by the Chancellor of the Duchy of Lancaster.

[65] The Recorder is elected by the City, but appointed by the Crown to exercise judicial functions. The Common Serjeant is appointed by the Crown. They are paid by the City of London authorities.

judges at certain large court complexes (the Recorders of Liverpool and Manchester[66] and the Senior Circuit judge at Newington Causeway) and the Circuit judges who conduct Official Referees' business in London are regarded as holding appointments more burdensome than that of the ordinary Circuit judge, and are paid higher salaries.[67]

The Lord Chancellor may, if he thinks fit, remove a Circuit judge from office on the ground of incapacity or misbehaviour.[68] In 1983, Judge Bruce Campbell was removed from office following his conviction for smuggling whisky and cigarettes.[68a] The retiring age is 72, although the Lord Chancellor may authorise a judge to continue in office up to the age of 75.

The appointment of a person as a recorder specifies the term for which he is appointed and the frequency and duration of the occasions when he will be required to sit. The term may not last beyond the year in which he attains 72. The Lord Chancellor may terminate the appointment on the grounds of incapacity, misbehaviour or a failure to comply with the conditions of the appointment.[69] The general terms and conditions for appointment were set out in a statement by the Lord Chancellor's Office.[70] Those seeking appointment are invited to write to the Permanent Secretary to the Lord Chancellor. Initial appointments are likely to be for three years. Recorders are expected to sit for not less than four working weeks (20 days) a year. A daily fee, travelling expenses and subsistence allowances are payable.

The Lord Chancellor may also appoint deputy Circuit judges and assistant recorders.[71] Any barrister or solicitor of 10 years' standing may be appointed an assistant recorder; only a former judge of the Court of Appeal or the High Court or former Circuit judge may be appointed as a deputy Circuit judge.

D. JUDGES OF THE SUPERIOR COURTS

1. THE CLASSES OF JUDICIAL OFFICE

Appointments to the High Court Bench are to the office of *puisne*[72] *judge* or *Justice of the High Court*.[73] A High Court judge is almost invariably knighted (or made a Dame Commander of the British Empire) upon appointment, but is referred to as, for example, "Mr.[74] Justice Swallow."[75]

[66] These are honorary recorderships under the Courts Act 1971, s.54. The holders are addressed as "My Lord."

[67] £35,000 as compared with £33,000, as from November 1, 1984. Four judges are assigned to Official Referees' business: see the Supreme Court Act 1981, s.68 above, pp. 74–75.

[68] Courts Act 1971, s.17(4).

[68a] *The Times*, December 6, 1983.

[69] *Ibid*. s.21.

[70] (1971) 68 L.S.Gaz. 303.

[71] *Ibid*. s.24, as substituted by the Supreme Court Act 1981, s.146. Under section 24 as originally enacted there was no separate appointment of assistant recorder and the qualifications for a deputy Circuit judge were wider.

[72] Pronounced as if it were "puny." The two words are related, a puisne judge being a "junior" judge in the superior courts of common law.

[73] See the Supreme Court Act 1981, s.4(2).

[74] Or Mrs. There has not yet been a Miss and may never be a Ms. It has been suggested that an unmarried lady would be referred to as "Mrs. Justice": A. Samuels, (1982) 79 L.S.Gaz. 509.

[75] Written as Swallow J. If there are two Swallows on the bench, Christian names are also used.

Promotion to the Court of Appeal involves elevation to the position of *Lord Justice of Appeal*, which is normally associated with an appointment to membership of the Privy Council. "Swallow J." becomes "Lord Justice Swallow."[76] The next step is membership of the House of Lords as a *Lord of Appeal in Ordinary*,[77] one of the "Law Lords." Although he will have been addressed in court as "My Lord" from the time of his appointment as a High Court judge, it is only at this stage (in the normal course of events) that he actually acquires a life peerage, as, say, "Lord Swallow of Somerset."[78]

In addition, there are several specific judicial offices. The *Lord Chancellor*[79] has long been regarded as the head of the judiciary, and has now received formal recognition as "president of the Supreme Court."[80] He is an *ex officio* member of the Court of Appeal,[81] and is the president of the Chancery Division[82] although the effective head of that Division is the Vice-Chancellor. If he sits as a judge at all it is in the House of Lords or the Privy Council, and only Lord Hailsham of St. Marylebone of the recent Lord Chancellors has sat at all regularly.[83] The Lord Chancellor has many administrative functions to perform as head of the judiciary. For example, he has the effective say in most judicial appointments and assignments, and various powers to give directions affecting the business of the courts. He also has general responsibility for the unified court service,[84] the Law Commissions, the legal advice and assistance and legal aid schemes,[85] the Land Registry and the Public Records Office. He is normally a Cabinet minister, and is the Speaker of the House of Lords.[86] Lord Gardiner has stated that his paperwork was about half political and half judicial administration.[87] He is appointed by the Queen on the advice of the Prime Minister, and, as a political appointment, holds office "during pleasure." He goes out of office with the government of which he is a member, and is,

---

[76] Written as Swallow L.J.

[77] "The word 'Ordinary' is a technical term used in law to describe a judge who has jurisdiction to hear cases by virtue of his office. In contrast to other persons who have jurisdiction only by being peers": Lord Denning, *The Family Story* (1981), p. 184.

[78] Lord Jenkins of Ashley Gardens apparently had wished to be styled Lord Jenkins of 24 Ashley Gardens, but was thwarted by the College of Arms.

[79] *i.e.* the Lord High Chancellor of Great Britain. Written as Lord Hailsham of St. Marylebone L.C.

[80] Supreme Court Act 1981, s.1.

[81] *Ibid.* s.2.

[82] *Ibid.* s.5(1)(*a*).

[83] See G. Drewry, "Lord Chancellor as Judge" (1972) 122 N.L.J. 855. Until the Second World War the legislative sittings of the House of Lords commenced at 4.15 p.m., enabling the Lord Chancellor to sit regularly on appeals during the standard hours of 10.30 a.m. to 4.00 p.m. However, wartime difficulties caused the start of legislative sittings to be advanced to 2.30 p.m. and the Lord Chancellor was compelled to choose between two kinds of work: R.F.V. Heuston, *Lives of the Lord Chancellors* 1885–1940 (1964) p. xviii.

[84] Courts Act 1971, s.27(1).

[85] See below, pp. 339–351, 387–397.

[86] See generally on the functions of the Lord Chancellor: *Halsbury's Laws of England* (4th ed.) Vol. 8, paras. 1171–1191; the accounts cited in Heuston (1964) p. xv, n. 1; the addresses by Lord Gardiner (1968) and Lord Hailsham (1972) to the Holdsworth Club (published in B.W. Harvey (ed.) *The Lawyer and Justice* (1978)); and Lord Hailsham, *The Door Wherein I Went* (1975), pp. 244–258.

[87] Harvey (ed.) (1978), p. 216.

indeed, as subject to dismissal by the Prime Minister as any other minister.[88]

The *Lord Chief Justice of England*[89] takes precedence over all judges other than the Lord Chancellor. He is the president of the Court of Appeal (Criminal Division) and the Queen's Bench Division of the High Court. The office was created as part of the reorganisation of the superior courts under the Supreme Court of Judicature Acts 1873–75. Before then each of the superior common law courts had its own chief: the Chief Justices of the Queen's Bench and the Common Pleas, and the Chief Baron of the Exchequer. The first Lord Chief Justice of England appointed as such was, accordingly, Lord Coleridge,[90] Chief Justice of the Common Pleas from 1873, who took the office in 1880 following the deaths of Sir Alexander Cockburn C.J. of the Queen's Bench Division and Chief Baron Kelly.[91] From that date new incumbents have been ennobled if not already peers. The holder is referred to as Lord Lane, Chief Justice or Lord Lane, Lord Chief Justice.[92]

The office of *Master of the Rolls*[93] dates from at least the thirteenth century. He was originally the keeper of the rolls or records of the Chancery, but with the passage of time he became recognised as a judge in the Court of Chancery: until 1813 he was the only judge in that court other than the Chancellor. After the reorganisation of the courts under the Judicature Acts 1873–75 he continued as a judge of first instance, but the man appointed in 1873, Sir George Jessel, was such an able lawyer that it was thought appropriate for the Master of the Rolls to become a judge of the Court of Appeal.[94] He is now the president of the Court of Appeal (Civil Division).[95] In view of the large number of important civil cases determined in that court and the power of the Master of the Rolls over the allocation of cases, the holder of that office may exert considerable influence over the development of the civil law. It was for this reason that Lord Denning, then a Lord of Appeal in Ordinary, welcomed the appointment as Master of the Rolls.[96] The holder is referred to as Sir John Donaldson, Master of the Rolls.[97]

---

[88] Viscount Kilmuir was dismissed by Harold Macmillan on the "night of the long knives" in July 1962.

[89] See F. Bresler, *Lord Goddard* (1977), Chap. 9.

[90] Lord Parker, (1961) 35 A.L.J. 97. Some Chief Justices of the King's Bench had styled themselves, or had been referred to informally as Lord Chief Justice of England, although this was technically incorrect. A notable example of the former was Sir Edward Coke, whose action was said to have displeased the King and to have been one of the causes of his dismissal.

[91] The opportunity was also taken to amalgamate the three common law divisions. The following have held the office: Lord Coleridge 1880–94; Lord Russell of Killowen 1894–1900; Lord Alverstone 1900–1914; Lord Reading 1914–1921; Lord Trevethin 1921–1922; Lord Hewart 1922–1940; Viscount Caldecote 1940–1946; Lord Goddard 1946–1958; Lord Parker 1958–1971; Lord Widgery 1971–1980; Lord Lane 1980– .

[92] Written as Lord Lane C.J. or Lord Lane L.C.J.

[93] See Lord Denning, *The Family Story* (1981) pp. 201–204; Sir John Donaldson, M.R., (1984) 17 Bracton L.J. 19.

[94] Sir Robert Megarry, (1982) 98 L.Q.R. 370, 395.   [95] Supreme Court Act 1981, s.3(2).

[96] Lord Denning, *The Family Story* (1981) pp. 172, 197; "the Master of the Rolls is still one of the most coveted posts in the land": *ibid.* p. 204. Lord Denning also found himself "too often in a minority" in the House of Lords: *The Discipline of Law* (1979), p. 287.

[97] Written as Sir John Donaldson M.R. It is common for the holder of the office to be ennobled, although not necessarily on appointment. Recent holders have been Lord Wright 1935–1949; Lord Evershed 1949–1962; Lord Denning 1962–1982; Sir John Donaldson 1982– .

The *President of the Family Division* and the *Vice-Chancellor* head, respectively, the Family and Chancery Divisions of the High Court, and are *ex officio* members of the Court of Appeal. The former office was created in 1970, with the transition from the Probate, Divorce and Admiralty Division.[98] The holder is referred to as Sir John Arnold, President.[99] The latter office was created in 1970, the holder to be nominated by the Lord Chancellor.[1] It was made a royal appointment analogous to the other heads of division in 1982.[2] The holder is technically the vice-president of the Chancery Division,[3] but is effectively the head. He is referred to as Sir Robert Megarry, Vice-Chancellor.[4] The title "Vice Chancellor of England" was used in the nineteenth century for the judges appointed to assist the Lord Chancellor in the Court of Chancery.[5]

2. MASTERS AND REGISTRARS

There are a number of officers of the Supreme Court below the ranks of the judges, who perform both administrative and judicial tasks, the latter in particular in interlocutory matters arising in the course of litigation. There are, for example,[6] a number of Masters of the Queen's Bench and Chancery Divisions, Registrars of the Family Division, Taxing Masters and Registrars in Bankruptcy. One of each of these groups is appointed as a "senior" or "chief."[7] Particularly important offices held by individuals are those of Master of the Crown Office and Registrar of Criminal Appeals,[8] and the newly created office of Registrar of Civil Appeals.[9]

3. ELIGIBILITY FOR APPOINTMENT AND NUMBERS

Appointments as a judge of the Supreme Court are confined to members of the bar[10]:

[98] See above, p. 70. The old division was also headed by a President. The incumbents have been Sir Jocelyn Simon 1962–1971; Sir George Baker 1971–1979; and Sir John Arnold 1979– .

[99] Written as Sir John Arnold P.

[1] Administration of Justice Act 1970, s.5.

[2] Supreme Court Act 1981, s.10(1). See generally Sir Robert Megarry, (1982) 98 L.Q.R. 370.

[3] 1981 Act, s.5(1)(*a*).

[4] Written as Sir Robert Megarry V.-C. Sir Robert is the third of the modern Vice-Chancellors. The others were Sir John Pennycuick 1970–1974 and Sir John Plowman 1974–1976.

[5] 53 Geo III c. 24, 1813. In 1841 two additional Vice-Chancellors were appointed. With the death of the last Vice Chancellor of England (Sir Lancelot Shadwell) in 1850 the words "of England" were dropped. The Vice-Chancellors were transferred to the Chancery Division under the Judicature Act 1873. On their death or retirement their successors were syled as High Court justices. See A.B. Schofield, (1966) L.S.Gaz. 298; Megarry, *op. cit.*

[6] Schedule 2 to the Supreme Court Act 1981 lists 18 offices. See also s.89. On the work of the Queen's Bench Masters see A.S. Diamond, (1960) 76 L.Q.R. 504 and Sir Jack Jacob, *The Reform of Civil Procedural Law* (1982) p. 349; on Chancery Masters see R.E. Ball, (1961) 77 L.Q.R. 331.

[7] Supreme Court Act 1981, s.89(3).

[8] Currently held by one man. The first post carries responsibility for civil work and appeals in the Queen's Bench Division, the second for appeals to the Court of Appeal (Criminal Division).

[9] Supreme Court Act 1981, Sched. 2. This post carries responsibility for appeals to the Court of Appeal (Civil Division).

[10] Supreme Court Act 1981, s.10(3).

Position	Max. Number	Qualification
Puisne judges	80[11]	Barrister of at least 10 years' standing
Lord Justices of Appeal	23[12]	Barrister of at least 15 years' standing or High Court judge.
Lord Chief Justice		Barrister of at least 15 years' standing or High Court judge or Judge of the Court of Appeal
Master of the Rolls		
President of the Family Division		
Vice-Chancellor		

In order to be qualified for appointment as a Lord of Appeal in Ordinary a person must have (1) practised for 15 years as a barrister in England or Northern Ireland or as an advocate in Scotland; or (2) have held for two years one or more of the "high judicial offices" of Lord Chancellor, or judge of the High Court, Court of Appeal, Court of Session or Supreme Court of Judicature of Northern Ireland.[13] There is a maximum number of 11.[14] Most of the offices below the rank of judge may be held by barristers or solicitors, usually with a minimum of 10 years' standing.[15] These are very much in the way of minimum requirements: a barrister would expect to wait much longer than 10 years before becoming a serious candidate for appointment.

The most controversial issue relating to the list of qualifications for appointment is whether it is right that a solicitor may not become a judge of the Supreme Court or a Lord of Appeal in Ordinary.[16] Solicitors have become eligible for appointment as stipendiary magistrates, recorders and Circuit judges. The next logical step would seem to be to allow service as a Circuit judge to render the holder eligible for appointment to the Supreme Court irrespective of whether his career as a lawyer was as a solicitor or barrister. This was supported by the JUSTICE Sub-Committee in its Report on the Judiciary,[17] and strongly urged in Parliament during the passage of the Supreme Court Act 1981. However, it was successfully resisted by the government, mainly on the basis that experience as an advocate in the Supreme Court was necessary for appointment to the bench there.[18] The JUSTICE Sub-Committee argued that the Bar had become numerically inadequate to provide the exclusive source for

[11] *Ibid*. s.2(1).

[12] *Ibid*. s.4(1)(e). The number of puisne judges and Lords Justices may be increased by Order in Council: ss.2(4) and 4(4). The maximum number of Lords Justices was increased from 18 to 23 by the Maximum Number of Judges Order 1983 (S.I. 1983 No. 1705).

[13] Appellate Jurisdiction Act 1876, ss.6, 25.

[14] Administration of Justice Act 1968, s.1. This number may be increased by Order in Council: *ibid*.

[15] Supreme Court Act 1981, Sched. 2.

[16] A solicitor, or indeed a bus driver could theoretically be appointed Lord Chancellor, but neither is even a remote possibility.

[17] (1972) pp. 9–20. See also S. Shetreet, *Judges on Trial* (1976) pp. 55–58.

[18] See (1981) 131 N.L.J. 273; (1981) L.S.Gaz. 193.

appointment, unless the quality of possibly both the Bench and the Bar was to be jeopardised; it could not be said that *no* solicitor would make a competent judge; the larger the pool of candidates, the better the chance of a good appointment; and eligibility would enhance the dignity, self-respect and pride of the solicitors' branch of the legal profession. The committee doubted whether any particular experience or qualification was indispensible, but noted that many solicitors had experience of advocacy in the lower courts. The distinction between the two branches of the profession might become blurred, but if it were thought undesirable for other reasons to have a fused profession, extending the eligibility of solicitors for judicial appointment would not do anything significant to promote it. As few solicitors would probably seek or receive appointment the attractions of the Bar as a profession would not significantly be reduced. A successful period as a Circuit judge would seem, as a matter of common sense, to be a rather better demonstration of one's qualities for *judicial* appointment than experience as an advocate.

The current defence of the *status quo* seems close to a straightforward defence of the privileges of the Bar. Conversely, it must be acknowledged that an extension of eligibility would have little if any effect on the background or outlook of the judiciary.

Academic lawyers are not appointed to the Bench in the United Kingdom, even if they are barristers of the requisite standing.[19] Moreover, it seems to have become progressively less common for academic lawyers to be a member of either branch of the profession. It is generally agreed that it would not be appropriate to appoint academic lawyers as trial judges, in view of their lack of experience with the process of ascertaining the facts of cases. It is, however, arguable that academics should be eligible for appointment to the Court of Appeal or the House of Lords.[20] The salary and prestige would be particularly attractive to professors of law, who are commonly required to retire at 65, and may currently be encouraged to retire earlier. It could not be disputed that there would be candidates with the appropriate qualities of intellect and scholarship; it would also be one method of widening the background, political and otherwise, of members of the judiciary, should that be thought to be desirable.

4. METHOD OF APPOINTMENT[21]

Appointment to the positions of Lord Chief Justice, Master of the Rolls, President of the Family Division, Vice-Chancellor, Lord of Appeal in Ordinary and Lord Justice of Appeal are made by the Queen,[22] acting by

---

[19] The only reference to "practising" barristers relates to eligibility for appointment as a Law Lord, above p. 158.

[20] The JUSTICE Sub-Committee on The Judiciary favoured this proposal: Report (1972) pp. 21–24.

[21] See Shetreet (1976) pp. 46–84; Lord Hailsham, *The Door Wherein I Went* (1975), pp. 254–258. A. Paterson, "Becoming a Judge" in R. Dingwall and P.Lewis (eds.) *The Sociology of the Professions* (1983) Chap. 12; A. Samuels, "Appointing the Judges" (1984) 134 N.L.J. 85, 107.

[22] Supreme Court Act 1981, s.10(1)(2).

convention on the advice of the Prime Minister, who, in turn, will have consulted the Lord Chancellor. The effective voice in all appointments is normally that of the Lord Chancellor, following consultations with members of the judiciary[23] and leading members of the Bar. Occasionally, the Prime Minister may override the Lord Chancellor's view in relation to senior appointments.[24] Records on potential candidates are maintained by the staff of the Lord Chancellor's Office, and candidates are interviewed.

Appointments to the High Court Bench are normally made from the ranks of Queen's Counsel. Junior barristers may be appointed direct but the only persons normally so appointed are the Junior Counsel to the Treasury, who indeed, are normally elevated to the Bench after their period in that position. From time to time there have been promotions from the positions of Official Referee,[25] county court judge,[26] Recorder of Liverpool or Manchester, Circuit judge[27] and Registrar of the Family Division,[28] but these constitute a fairly small minority.[29] One person has been appointed to the High Court Bench after being an advocate general of the Court of Justice of the European Communities.[30]

Put shortly, the qualities looked for would seem to be good character, success as an advocate and, if appropriate, in a lower judicial office, the rather mystical quality known as "common sense," and good health. Those appointed are normally in their fifties, although some are appointed in their forties.[31] Brilliance as a technical lawyer is not regarded as a necessary precondition, although greater weight is placed on legal ability when appointments to the Chancery Division or to the appellate courts are considered. It is normal for those appointed to have served previously as a recorder. Unlike the position in relation to appointments as recorder or Circuit judge, it is not the normal practice for barristers to apply for appointment to the High Court Bench: it is expected that they wait to be invited.

Several observers have noted an improvement in the quality of judges.[32] "On the whole, I have no doubt that judges are much better educated, more polite and more patient than they used to be."[33]

---

[23] There is a meeting between the Lord Chancellor and the Heads of Division at which "a consensus is usually arrived at": Lord Hailsham (1975) p. 254; *Cf.* Sir Robert Megarry, (1982) 98 L.Q.R. 370, 397. Lord Halsbury was exceptional in not consulting the Lord Chief Justice: R.F.V. Heuston, *Lives of the Lord Chancellors* 1885–1940 (1964), pp. 47–48.

[24] *e.g.* the appointment of Sir Ernest Pollock rather than Bankes L.J. as Master of the Rolls in 1923: Heuston, *Lives*, p. 428. *Cf.* Samuels (1984) 134 N.L.J. 85, 86.

[25] Sir Edward Ridley (1897). The fact that he held office was regarded as counting against him rather than for him. He was the brother of the Home Secretary, and was subsequently thought to be a poor judge: See Heuston, *Lives*, pp. 49–52.

[26] The first was Sir Edward Acton (1920), the Nottingham county court judge. Ten more were elevated between 1945 and 1971.

[27] Eight were elevated between 1973 and 1983.

[28] Butler Sloss J. (1979).

[29] Twelve out of 98 appointments between 1970 and 1983.

[30] Warner J. (1981).

[31] The youngest in the last 50 years were Lords Hodson and Devlin who were 42 when appointed High Court judges in 1937 and 1948 respectively.

[32] C.P. Harvey Q.C., *The Advocate's Devil* (1958), pp. 33–4, comparing the fifties with the twenties; Lord Devlin, *The Judge* (1979), p. 24.

[33] Lord Hailsham, *The Door Wherein I Went* (1975), p. 257.

Political service was formerly a significant factor in many judicial appointments.[34] Of the 139 judges appointed between 1832 and 1906, 80 were M.P.s at the time of their nomination; 11 others had been candidates for Parliament. Of those 80, 63 were appointed by their own party while in office.[35] Lord Halsbury, Unionist Lord Chancellor for three periods,[36] was criticised for making bad appointments of Tory M.P.s.[37] Lord Salisbury, the Prime Minister for most of Halsbury's time as Lord Chancellor, "would never apologise for the practice of making [legal promotions] a reward for political 'right thinking,' "[38] although he expressed the need for caution following public criticism of some of the early appointments.[39] There was contemporary criticism of the appointments of Grantham, J.C. Lawrance, Bruce, Darling, Ridley and Kekewich, all of whom turned out to be poor judges,[40] although each had his defenders. The first four were Conservative M.P.s at the time of their appointment. Ridley had briefly been a Conservative M.P. nearly 20 years before, although that did not seem to have influenced the choice, and Kekewich had been a Conservative candidate. Heuston argues that the last two appointments were unlucky and that "four dubious appointments out of thirty during a tenure of the woolsack lasting seventeen years should not weigh too heavily in the scales when making a final judgment."[41]

Lord Haldane, when Lord Chancellor between 1912 and 1915, introduced a policy of appointing "only on the footing of high legal and professional qualifications,"[42] and this position, as regards puisne judgeships, has more or less been maintained since. The only political tradition that took significantly longer to die was the idea that the Attorney-General and Solicitor-General had a special claim should one of the higher judicial offices fall vacant.[43] The Attorney's claim on the position of Lord Chief Justice was supposed to be particularly strong.[44]

Between 1873 and 1945 only four of the 23 holders of the office of

---

[34] See A. Paterson, (1974) 1 B.J.L.S. 118. Party politics continues to play a larger role in the appointment of judges in Scotland. This has given rise to adverse criticism: I.D. Willock, 1969 J.R. 193; C.M. Campbell, 1973 J.R. 254.

[35] H. Laski, (1926) 24 Michigan L.R. 529.

[36] 1885–86; 1886–92; 1895–1905.

[37] See Heuston, Lives, pp. 36–66.

[38] G. Cecil (Lord Salisbury's daughter and biographer) cited by Heuston, Lives p. 36.

[39] Ibid. p. 57.

[40] Grantham J. attracted severe criticism in Parliament for his partisan trial of two election petitions in 1906: see H. Cecil, Tipping the Scales (1965), pp. 194–208; Darling J. was described by C.P. Harvey as a "real shocker" (The Advocate's Devil (1958) pp. 32–33) and renowned for his "jokes;" MacKinnon L.J. wrote that J.C. Lawrance J. was "a stupid man, a very ill-equipped lawyer and a bad judge. He was not the worst judge I have appeared before: that distinction I would assign to Mr. Justice Ridley. Ridley had much better brains than Lawrance, but he had a perverse instinct for unfairness that Lawrance could never approach." ((1944) 60 L.Q.R. 324).

[41] Lives, p. 66.

[42] R.B. Haldane, An Autobiography (1929), p. 253.

[43] J.Ll.J. Edwards, The Law Officers of the Crown (1964), pp. 309–334.

[44] Eighteen of the 42 Chief Justices of the Common Pleas between 1600 and 1873 were ex-Attorneys, 16 appointed directly. Between 1725 and 1873 all but two of the Chief Justices of the King's Bench were ex-Attorneys, four appointed directly: Edwards (1964), p. 320–21.

Attorney-General did not go on to hold one of the higher judicial offices.[45] All those appointed Lord Chief Justice, with one exception,[46] were former Attorneys. Nine of the 17 men who were Solicitor-General without becoming Attorney-General also progressed to one of the higher judicial offices.[47]

However, much controversy surrounded the appointment of Sir Gordon Hewart as Lord Chief Justice.[48] In 1921 it was arranged that Lord Reading C.J. was to become Viceroy of India. Hewart, as Attorney-General, pressed his claim to the position of Lord Chief Justice but could not be spared from the Commons. Lloyd George appointed a 77 year-old Queen's Bench judge, A.T. Lawrence J., on the understanding that he would retire when called upon, although neither Lord Birkenhead L.C. nor Hewart approved of the plan. Nevertheless, in 1922 Lord Trevethin (as Lawrence became) read of his own resignation in *The Times*, and Hewart duly succeeded him. To add injury to insult, Hewart proved to be "perhaps the worst Lord Chief Justice of England since the seventeenth century. Although no imputation of corruption or dishonesty could be brought against him, as against Scroggs and Jeffreys, on the bench he rivalled them in arbitrary and unjudicial behaviour."[49] Since 1945 the position seems to have changed significantly. In 1946, Viscount Caldecote C.J. was succeeded by a Lord of Appeal, Lord Goddard, after the post had been declined by Sir Hartley Shawcross, the Attorney-General.[50] Lord Goddard and his successors have not had political careers.[51] Lord Goddard was followed by Lord Parker,[52] who subsequently commented that the non-political nature of the appointment, made clear by the appointments of Lord Goddard, himself and Lord Widgery, was of "vital importance for the administration of justice in this country."[53] The only Law Officers subsequently appointed to the bench have been Lynn Ungoed-Thomas[54]

---

[45] Lord Chancellor (8), L.C.J. (5), M.R. (2), Lord of Appeal (4), L.J. (4): four held two of these offices. The exceptions were Karslake (1874) who suffered a complete physical breakdown in 1875, Walton (1905–8) who died in office and Patrick Hastings (1924), Attorney-General in the first Labour Government, who apparently "had no wish to be made a judge" (Lord Birkett, *Six Great Advocates* (1961), p. 37). Sir Henry James (1880–85) was given a peerage and often sat in the House of Lords.

[46] Lord Trevethin (1921).

[47] Lord Chancellor (4); L.J. (3); President of the P.D.A. (2); Lord of Appeal (1: Lord Davey, promoted from Lord Justice). Of the other eight, four held other ministerial offices (Harcourt (1873–74), Gorst (1885–86), Cripps (1930–31) and Monckton (1945)), three died in office or shortly after leaving it (Lockwood (1894–95), Melville (1929–30) and O'Connor (1936–40)), and the other, Clarke (1886–92), refused the position of Master of the Rolls in 1897.

[48] See R. Jackson, *The Chief* (1959), Chap. 9; J. Campbell, *F. E. Smith, First Earl of Birkenhead* (1983) pp. 479–481.

[49] Heuston, *Lives*, pp. 603–604; *Cf*. C.P. Harvey, *The Advocate's Devil* (1958), p. 32.

[50] See F. Bresler, *Lord Goddard* (1977), pp. 112–115. Shawcross had opposed the idea that there was a "right" of succession, and preferred a political career.

[51] Goddard had stood unsuccessfully as an Independent Conservative in the 1929 General Election, a brief and "ill-starred political venture": Bresler (1977), pp. 60–62.

[52] The then Attorney-General, Sir Reginald Manningham-Buller, did not actively seek the post, but would apparently have liked to have been asked: Bresler (1977), pp. 295–298.

[53] Bresler (1977), p. 297.

[54] Labour M.P. 1945–62; Solicitor General 1951; High Court judge 1962–72.

and Sir Jocelyn Simon,[55] and only two of the others have become Lord Chancellor.[56] The appointment of Lord Chief Justices from amongst the ranks of the judiciary has been generally welcomed.

It has become progressively more difficult to combine membership of the Commons with a successful practice at the Bar. Lord Hailsham has regretted that he was unable to appoint a single High Court judge from among M.P.s.[57] There is something of a vicious circle in that the lack of a reasonable prospect of elevation to the Bench may discourage the ablest lawyers from seeking a political career. Political experience has been regarded by some as an asset for an appointee. Lord Simon has argued that:

> "although no one would wish to see a predominantly political Bench, a seasoning of judges with experience of politics and administration is far from disadvantageous; constituency duties, for example, are calculated to develop a social awareness which ordinary forensic work is not apt to inculcate."[58]

The social and educational background of the judges has been examined in a number of surveys.[59] These show that the judges are overwhelmingly upper or upper middle class in origin, with over three-quarters having attended public school, and a similar proportion either Oxford or Cambridge University.

The process of socialisation at the Bar tends to mean that those from other backgrounds do not seem markedly different, if different at all, from the majority.[60] The extent to which judicial attitudes can be related to the social background of the judges is a large and debatable question.[61] Given the continuance for the foreseeable future of the policy of appointing judges largely from the Bar, it is unlikely that there will be any significant change in the background of the people appointed. What is more plausible is that the attitudes of successive generations may gradually change.[62]

Other countries have adopted different methods of appointment. In civil law systems there is normally a career judiciary, which is part of the general civil service and separate from the legal profession. In the United States there are two basic methods of selection, *appointment* and *election*,

[55] Conservative M.P. 1951–62; Solicitor-General 1959–62; President of the Probate, Divorce and Admiralty Division 1962–71; Lord of Appeal 1971–77. Two previous Presidents had formerly been Solicitor-General: Sir Samuel Evans (1910–1919) and Sir Frank (later Lord) Merriman (1934–1962).
[56] Viscount Dilhorne and Lord Elwyn-Jones. Between 1945 and 1982 there have been 17 holders of one or both of the Law Offices.
[57] *The Door Wherein I Went* (1975), p. 256.
[58] (1965) 81 L.Q.R. 289, 295.
[59] *The Economist*, December 15, 1956, pp. 946–947; K. Goldstein-Jackson, *New Society*, May 14, 1970; H. Cecil, *The English Judge* (Revised ed., 1972) Chap. 1; J. Brock (M.Phil. dissertation, quoted in the JUSTICE Sub-Committee Report on the Judiciary (1972); F.L. Morrison, *Courts and the Political Process in England* (1973), Chap. 3. The background of the Lords of Appeal appointed betwen 1876 and 1969 is examined in L.Blom-Cooper and G. Drewry, *Final Appeal* (1972), pp. 158–169. The results of these surveys are summarised by J.A.G. Griffith, *The Politics of the Judiciary* (2nd ed., 1981) pp. 27–32.
[60] As to the social background of barristers, see above, p. 124.
[61] See below, pp. 175–183.
[62] See P. McAuslan, (1983) 46 M.L.R. 1, 19.

although a compromise between the two methods is commonly applied.[63] All federal judges are appointed by the President, subject to confirmation by the Senate. An appointment can in practice be vetoed by one of the candidate's home state Senators and candidates are also evaluated by the American Bar Association's influential Committee on Federal Judiciary, which makes its views known to the President and the Senate. In 1970, 82 per cent. of state and local judges were elected, although real contests are rare.[64] In a number of states elections are used to confirm in office judges who have been in office for a limited period following appointment by the governor, a separate Commission, or the two together.[65] It is highly unlikely that any of these methods will be introduced here,[66] although some have favoured the formal establishment of a Judicial Commission to evaluate and advise on appointments.[67]

5. Promotion

It is less easy to adhere today to the traditional view that there is no system of "promotion" of judges. The fear is that holders of judicial office might allow their promotion prospects to affect their decision-making; care might be taken to avoid offending the senior judges or the politicians responsible for making or influencing judicial appointments. Nevertheless, the trend seems to be for judges to be elevated from the Circuit Bench more regularly, and for appointments to the House of Lords and Court of Appeal to be made from the court below. It is uncommon for appointments to be made direct from the Bar to the Court of Appeal[68] or the House of Lords,[69] or direct from the High Court to the House of Lords.[70] Three Lord Chancellors, Maugham, Simonds and Dilhorne, have been appointed Lords of Appeal, but the first two of these were simply reverting to an office previously held. At first, elevation to the Court of Appeal from the High Court carried no increase in salary, although membership of the Privy Council was always conferred. The salary of a Lord Justice is now

[63] See H. Abraham, *The Judicial Process* (4th ed., 1980), pp. 23–99 and *Justices and Presidents* (1974).

[64] Abraham (1980), p. 35.

[65] The "Missouri plan" is favoured by the A.B.A. A non-partisan Commission selects three candidates, one of whom the governor must then appoint. After one year in office he must be approved by the electorate, running unopposed in a separate, non-partisan judicial ballot: Abraham (1980), p. 39.

[66] An argument that the Law Lords, the Lord Chief Justice and the Master of the Rolls, but not the other judges, should be elected, under a plan similar to the "Missouri Plan" is presented by D. Pannick, (1981) 131 N.L.J. 1064.

[67] Report of JUSTICE Sub-Committee on *The Judiciary* (1972), pp. 30–31, 61. This Commission would also act as a complaints tribunal and be involved in the processes of removing judges.

[68] The only examples have been Slesser L.J. (1929), Scott L.J. (1935) and Somervell L.J. (1946) (all Law Officers), Duke L.J. (1918; Chief Secretary for Ireland 1916–18) and Greene L.J. (1935: leader of the Chancery bar, and subsequently Master of the Rolls). Lord Denning has written that experience as a trial judge is valuable for an appeal judge: *The Family Story* (1981), pp. 169–170.

[69] Eleven examples: five Scots, two English, two Irish. The only two since 1930 have been Lord Reid (1948) and Lord Radcliffe (1949) each of whom was an outstanding judge.

[70] Seven examples: Lords Parker (1913), Tomlin (1929), Wright (1932), Porter (1938), Simonds (1944), Uthwatt (1946) and Wilberforce (1964).

roughly halfway between that of a High Court judge and a Lord of Appeal, although the differentials are small.[71] Apart from the prestige of a higher judicial office, promotion means that there is no longer the disadvantage of having to spend time away from home on circuit. There is, however, no evidence that judges are affected by "promotion sickness."

6. TENURE[72]

Every judge of the Supreme Court, other than the Lord Chancellor, who holds office "during the pleasure" of (in effect) the Prime Minister:

> "shall hold that office during good behaviour, subject to a power of removal by Her Majesty on an address presented to Her by both Houses of Parliament."[73]

Similarly:

> "Every Lord of Appeal in Ordinary shall hold his office during good behaviour but he may be removed from such office on the address of both Houses of Parliament."[74]

These arrangements date from the Act of Settlement 1700.[75] Before then judicial tenure was not regulated by statute. The King appointed on his own terms, which were usually, although not invariably, "during pleasure."[76]

The Stuarts removed or suspended a number of judges who did not conform to their expectations, James II being particularly enthusiastic in this regard.[77] From 1688, William III's appointments were made during good behaviour: the Act of Settlement took away the monarch's right to choose otherwise, although it seems that William was reluctant to see the legal position changed.[78]

It is generally accepted that under these provisions a judge may be removed from office either (1) for breach of the requirement of good behaviour or (2) by Crown on an address by both Houses of Parliament, irrespective of whether he has been of good behaviour. The "address" procedure is, theoretically, neither the exclusive procedure for removal, nor restricted to cases of misbehaviour. In cases of misbehaviour, there are indeed a number of alternative procedures for removing a judge, which do not seem to be excluded by the Supreme Court Act 1981 or any of its antecedents:

---

[71] See below, p. 170. The introduction of a differential was recommended by the Top Salaries Review Body, "in recognition of the promotion which is involved in appointment to the Court of Appeal from the High Court Bench:" Report No. 6, Cmnd. 5846, 1974, p. 31.

[72] See Shetreet (1976), pp. 1–12, 85–159; Sir Kenneth Roberts-Wray, *Commonwealth and Colonial Law* (1966), pp. 484–491.

[73] Supreme Court Act 1981, s.11(3).

[74] Appellate Jurisdiction Act 1876, s.6, as amended.

[75] Section 3. This section was to take effect should the arrangements for ensuring the Protestant succession become operative: accordingly, the section came into operation in 1714 with the accession of George I.

[76] See C.H. McIlwain, *Constitutionalism and the Changing World* (1939), pp. 294–307.

[77] See J.H. Baker, *Introduction to Legal History* (2nd ed., 1979) pp. 144–146; A. Havighurst, (1950) 66 L.Q.R. 62, 229; (1953) 69 L.Q.R. 522.

[78] D. Rubini, (1967) 83 L.Q.R. 343.

(1) Proceedings in the Queen's Bench Division commenced by the writ of *scire facias* for the repeal of the letters patent by which the office was granted.

(2) Proceedings in the Queen's Bench Division for an injunction to restrain the judge from continuing to act in an office to which he is no longer entitled.[79]

(3) Conviction for a criminal offence.

In these cases the "misbehaviour" must either be connected with the performance or non-performance of official duties, or, if not so connected, must involve the commission of a criminal offence of moral turpitude. Furthermore, a judge can be removed on any ground by an Act of Parliament, or for "high crimes and misdemeanours" by impeachment.[80] Neither would be used in preference to an address: the latter, in addition, is regarded as obsolete in the United Kingdom.[81]

Today, it is likely that the address procedure would be used in any case where a judge was to be removed, and, further, that this would only be done in a case of misbehaviour,[82] although a rather wider view might be taken of "misbehaviour" for this purpose, in particular to include private immoral conduct.[83] There have been many statements to the effect that this would be the "proper" way to proceed, notwithstanding the other possibilities.[84]

Conviction for a criminal offence does not inevitably lead to resignation or removal from office. Three judges[85] have been convicted of driving with excess alcohol, but have continued in office.

The other methods by which a judge may leave office are:

(1) resignation[86];
(2) reaching the retiring age of 75[87];
(3) under the procedure whereby the Lord Chancellor may remove a judge who is disabled by permanent infirmity from the performance of his duties and is incapacitated from resigning his office.[88]

---

[79] S.A. de Smith, *Constitutional and Administrative Law* (4th ed., 1981), p. 376.

[80] A trial by the House of Lords at the instigation of the Commons. This procedure has not been used since the trials of Warren Hastings (1788) and Lord Melville (1805). Among judges who were impeached were two Lord Chancellors, Bacon (1620) and Macclesfield (1725): see H. Cecil, *Tipping the Scales* (1964), pp. 99–126.

[81] The procedure is not obsolete in the U.S.A.: President Nixon resigned rather than face impeachment.

[82] It seems that the address procedure can be used in cases of incapacity: see Shetreet (1976), p. 274. However, resignation would be secured by informal pressure or a judge would be removed by the Lord Chancellor: see below, n. 88.

[83] *Kenrick's case* (1826): Cecil (1964), pp. 165–170.

[84] See Shetreet (1976), pp. 96–103.

[85] A Lord Justice in 1969, a Circuit judge in 1973 and a High Court judge in 1975.

[86] Supreme Court Act 1981, s.11(7); Appellate Jurisdiction Act 1876, s.6.

[87] Supreme Court Act 1981, s.11(2). This limitation did not apply to persons who held office on December 17, 1959 (when a retiring age was introduced by the Judicial Pensions Act 1959): s.11(1). The last to escape was Lord Denning M.R., who retired in 1982 aged 83. A judge may retire on full pension (half his last annual salary, index-linked) (1) after 15 years service; or (2) after attaining the age of 70; or (3) if he is disabled by permanent infirmity: Judicial Pensions Act 1981, s.2.

[88] Supreme Court Act 1981, s.11(8) (9). See A. Paterson, "The Infirm Judge" (1974) 1 B.J.L.S. 83.

If a judge were, for example, to bury a meat cleaver in someone's head the address procedure for removal from office would work swiftly and surely. Judges, however, do not indulge in acts of misbehaviour that are clearly inconsistent with their remaining in office. Where matters are not clear cut, the address procedure is complex, and uncertain in some matters of detail. Charges have been presented on a number of occasions, but only one judge has been removed as a consequence. Sir Jonah Barrington, a judge of the High Court of Admiralty in Ireland, was removed in 1830 for the embezzlement of sums of money paid into court.

7. DISCIPLINE AND CRITICISM

The mechanisms for disciplining judges who misbehave are more significant in practice than the procedures for removal. Judges may be criticised in Parliament. An extreme case is that of Lord Westbury L.C., who resigned in 1865 following votes of censure passed in both Houses concerning certain appointments he had made.

Judges are often criticised in the press. "Scurrilous abuse" of a judge may, however, be punished as contempt for "scandalising the court."[89] This head of contempt must be distinguished from that concerned with publications likely to interfere with the administration of justice in particular proceedings, by, for example, influencing juries. The former head was thought to be obsolete in 1899.[90] However, proceedings were taken against the editor of the *Birmingham Daily Argus* for a spirited attack on Darling J. (an "impudent little man in horsehair, a microcosm of conceit and empty headedness").[91] He apologised, and was fined £100, with £25 costs. According to Abel-Smith and Stevens[92] "within a decade the criticism of judicial behaviour which had been so outspoken was replaced in the press by almost unbroken sycophantic praise for the judges." Similar proceedings were taken on a number of occasions in the 1920s and 1930s. Since then, press criticism of the judiciary has become more commonplace, without matching the personal insults expressed by Mr. Gray. Proceedings against Quintin Hogg (as he then was), arising out of criticisms of the Court of Appeal published in *Punch*, were dismissed.[93] Salmon L.J. said[94]:

> "The authority and reputation of our courts are not so frail that their judgments need to be shielded from criticism, even from the criticism of Mr. Quintin Hogg . . . .[N]o criticism of a judgment, however vigorous, can amount to contempt of court, provided it keeps within the limits of reasonable courtesy and good faith."

[89] See S.H. Bailey, D.J. Harris and B.L. Jones, *Civil Liberties: Cases and Materials* (1980), pp. 262–267; A. Arlidge and D. Eady, *The Law of Contempt* (1982), pp. 156–165; Borrie and Lowe's *Law of Contempt*, (2nd ed., 1983) pp. 226–247.

[90] *McLeod* v. *St. Aubyn* [1899] A.C. 549, 561 (a colonial judge was accused of "reducing the judicial character to the level of a clown," and "being narrow, bigoted, vain, vindictive and unscrupulous." The Privy Council held that this did not require committal for contempt).

[91] *R.* v. *Gray* [1900] 2 Q.B. 36. The full passage is printed in 82 L.T. 534. *Cf.* above, p. 161 n. 40. Darling was apparently "rather amused by the vigour of its expression": D Walker-Smith, *The Life of Lord Darling* (1938), p. 122.

[92] *Lawyers and the Courts* (1967), pp. 126–7.

[93] *R.* v. *Metropolitan Police Commissioner, ex p. Blackburn* (No. 2) [1968] 2 Q.B. 150.

[94] *Ibid.* p. 155. Mr. Hogg subsequently became Lord Chancellor as Lord Hailsham of St Marylebone.

Judges are from time to time rebuked in appellate courts. Censure may be coupled with the setting aside of a conviction or the reversal of a judgment. Thus, judges have been censured for excessive interruptions,[95] threatening a jury,[96] improper behaviour on the Bench,[97] falling asleep,[98] incompetence,[99] and disloyalty to the decisions of superior courts.[1] Lord Hailsham has written that there are judges who become subject to "judge's disease, that is to say a condition of which the symptoms may be pomposity, irritability, talkativeness, proneness to *obiter dicta*, a tendency to take short cuts."[2]

There may be complaints from barristers, solicitors or litigants either expressed in court or in private to the judge personally, or made in some other quarter. Complaints may be made to the Lord Chief Justice or the Lord Chancellor. They may be channelled through a head of chambers, the Chairman of the Senate of the Inns of Court, the Attorney-General, The Law Society,[3] an M.P., or some other intermediary. There is generally a preference for taking action privately. Confrontations in court between counsel and judge may be to the client's disadvantage; it is impossible to assess the extent to which they may also be, or be feared to be, to the barrister's future disadvantage. The upshot may be an interview between the Lord Chancellor and the judge, or even, on occasion, a public rebuke.

It has been doubted whether the informal pressures on judges are sufficient. Over the years there have been a few judges whose conduct has often been criticised, but who have nevertheless remained on the Bench. On the other hand, this small minority seems to have dwindled. The JUSTICE Sub-Committee[4] argued that some form of complaints machinery should be established, probably in the form of a complaints tribunal or judicial commission. Such a reform is unlikely to occur in the foreseeable future, and, on the present evidence, the case for it is not made out. Finally, it must be remembered that criticisms of judges in the popular press are commonly marred by such weaknesses as a failure to report accurately the full facts, a failure to understand basic principles of the conduct of trials and a failure to distinguish defects of the law from the defects of the judge.

[95] *e.g. Yuill* v. *Yuill* [1945] P. 15; *Jones* v. *N.C.B.* [1957] 2 Q.B. 55. The judge in the latter case was Hallett J., who was seen by the Lord Chancellor and resigned shortly afterwards: Lord Denning, *The Due Process of Law* (1980), pp. 58–62 ("The judge who talked too much"). See generally, A. Samuels, "Judicial Misconduct in the Criminal Trial" [1982] Crim.L.R. 221.

[96] *R.* v. *McKenna* [1960] 1 Q.B. 411 (Stable J. at Nottingham Assizes threatened a jury that if they did not return a verdict within 10 minutes they would be locked up all night. They returned in six minutes with verdicts of guilty, which were quashed on appeal).

[97] *R.* v. *Hircock* [1970] 1 Q.B. 67. The judge in a criminal trial made gestures of impatience, sighed, and several times "observed in a loud voice, 'Oh God,' and then laid his head across his arm and made groaning noises" (p. 71). The court did not condone this conduct but declined to quash the conviction as being unsafe and unsatisfactory.

[98] If the judge thereby misses something of importance: *R.* v. *Edworthy* [1961] Crim.L.R. 325; *R.* v. *Langham* [1972] Crim.L.R. 457.

[99] *Taylor* v. *Taylor* [1970] 2 All E.R. 609.

[1] *Cassell & Co. Ltd.* v. *Broome* [1972] A.C. 1027, below, pp. 286–287.

[2] *The Door Wherein I Went* (1975), p. 255.

[3] It seems that the Bar and The Law Society will only act in cases of misconduct towards barristers and solicitors, respectively: JUSTICE, Sub-Committee Report on *The Judiciary*, pp. 49–50.

[4] *Op. cit.* pp. 45–61.

8. Training[4a]

In the late 1970s certain tentative steps were taken to introduce a measure of compulsory training for newly appointed judges. From 1963 onwards a series of conferences and judicial seminars on sentencing were organised by the Lord Chief Justice and the Lord Chancellor's Office. Attendance at these was voluntary. However, a Judicial Studies Board was established in 1979 following the report of a Working Party chaired by Bridge L.J.[4b] Since 1981 it has been essential for a recorder or assistant recorder, before first sitting, to have attended a three and a half-day residential course organised by the Board. They are lectured by experienced judges and experts from other disciplines about their duties, the main focus being on sentencing, and they take part in sentencing exercises. Also before sitting on their own they must sit for up to 10 days in court with an experienced Circuit judge and must visit various penal institutions. Voluntary refresher seminars are held for experienced judges, and it is intended that each recorder and Circuit judge will be invited to one such seminar every five years. A recent development has been the circulation by the Board to all new assistant recorders of a suggested summing-up structure and to all Circuit judges, recorders and assistant recorders a comprehensive set of specimen directions.[4c] The Board has also commenced publication of a Bulletin to be distributed to judges, with three issues a year.[4d]

9. Independence[5]

Much importance is attached to the independence of the judiciary. By that is meant independence from improper pressure by the executive, by litigants or by particular pressure groups. Reasons given in support of judicial independence are "(1) that independence is a condition of impartiality and therefore also of fair trials, and (2) that it makes for a separation of powers which enables the courts to check the activities of the other branches of government."[6] As to the first, it has been emphasised that judges must not only be impartial but appear to be impartial. Public confidence is only bolstered by "ostentatious impartiality."[7]

[4a] See M. Berlins and C. Dyer, *The Law Machine* (1982) pp. 68–71; (1983) 147 J.P.N. 466–467; A. Ashworth, *Sentencing and Penal Policy* (1983), pp. 65–67; Judicial Studies Board: report for 1979–82 (H.M.S.O., 1983).

[4b] *Judicial Studies and Information* (H.M.S.O. 1978). The Working Party had received "widely felt and strongly voiced objection" to the use in their working paper of the term "judicial training," on the grounds that "training" might represent a threat to judicial independence, that appointees might resent the implication that they need to be "trained" and that the "public image of the judge" would be impaired. The Working Party accordingly adopted the term "judicial studies" and emphasised that their proposals would not involve "indoctrination" or "conditioning" (*ibid.* pp. 2 and 3). Lord Devlin was caustic in his condemnation of the working paper: *The Judge* (1979), pp. 18–53; *cf.* book review by E.J. Griew, [1980] Crim.L.R. 812.

[4c] *The Observer*, January 30, 1983 ("Secret guide to stop judges blundering"); L.A.G. Bull., February 1983, p.7. Copies are sent to Circuit judges for information.

[4d] (1983) 133 N.L.J. 244.

[5] See W. Lederman (1956) 36 Can.Bar Rev. 769; G. Borrie (1970) 18 Am.J. Comp. Law 697.

[6] See T. Eckhoff, (1965) 9 *Scandinavian Studies in Law*, pp. 11–48.

[7] *Ibid.* p. 12. It has been argued that this feature has been lacking in the appointment of Scottish judges: see C.M. Campbell, 1973 J.R. 254.

The appointment and the tenure of judges have already been considered. Party political considerations seem to have been eliminated, although this does not mean that the decisions of judges are not "political" in a wider sense[8]:

"Judges are part of the machinery of authority within the State and as such cannot avoid the making of political decisions."[9]

We consider here some other factors relevant to the independence of the judiciary.

(a) Remuneration

Judges are paid large salaries, which are a charge on the Consolidated Fund and so not subject to an annual vote in Parliament. The current salaries are as follows: Lord Chief Justice: £64,000; Master of the Rolls, Lord of Appeal: £58,500; President of the Family Division: £57,000; Vice-Chancellor, Lord Justice: £55,500; High Court judge: £51,250.[10] They can be increased, but not reduced, by the Lord Chancellor, with the consent of the Prime Minister as Minister for the Civil Service.[11] From the time salaries became a charge on the Consolidated Fund,[12] they could only be changed by statute, or, between 1965 and 1973, by ministerial order.[13] Under the National Economy Act 1931, the salaries of "persons in His Majesty's service," which term was taken to include the judges, were reduced by 20 per cent. The need to secure the independence of the judiciary was placed at the forefront of their arguments both that the Act did not apply to them as a matter of interpretation, and that it should not apply in principle.[14] The government restored the cuts. This argument has, however, not figured so prominently in the recent reports of the Top Salaries Review Board on judicial salaries, in which more important considerations seem to have been the need to attract barristers with the right qualities and experience and the need to maintain the judges' status in the community. Thus the Board has taken into account both barristers' earnings and the salaries payable to Permanent Secretaries as "cross-checks," although there are no formal links with either. The written answer announcing the 1982 increases stated simply that it is "in the national interest to ensure an adequate supply of candidates of sufficient

---

[8] A. Paterson, "Judges: A Political Élite" (1974) 1 B.J.L.S. 118. "Whoever can persuade the members of a society that law is inevitable or to take 'law as a given,' and that the legal interpretation of a particular social situation is the only possible one, controls an important if not vital source of power in that society. In my contention British Judges are in precisely this position and that is why it is legitimate to characterize them as involved in the realm of politics": *ibid.* p. 129. See also R.J. Wilson, "British Judges as Political Actors" (1973) 1 Int. Journal of Criminology and Penology 197.

[9] J.A.G. Griffith, *The Politics of the Judiciary* (2nd ed., 1981), p. 212.

[10] H.C. Deb. Vol. 61, cols. 221–222, written answer, (June 7, 1984); (1984) 128 S.J. 419. In effect from November 1, 1984. These figures implement the recommendations of the Top Salaries Review Body: Report No. 21, Cmnd. 9254. As to pensions, see above, p. 166, n. 87.

[11] Supreme Court Act 1981, s.12.

[12] Judges appointed after 1786. There was no change between 1851 and 1954 (Judges' Remuneration Act 1954).

[13] Judges' Remuneration Act 1965.

[14] See Heuston, *Lives*, pp. 513–519; W. Holdsworth, (1932) 48 L.Q.R. 25 and 173 L.T. 336; E.C.S. Wade, (1932) 173 L.T. 246, 267. The judges were "in a mutinous mood": Lord Sankey L.C., quoted by Heuston, *op. cit.* p. 514.

calibre for appointment to judicial office."[15] Indeed, there have been no allegations of corruption against English judges for some centuries, and it is not plausible that it is the level of salary alone that is responsible. Even attempts to bribe judges are rare.

It is an accepted convention that judges may not hold paid appointments such as directorships, or carry on any profession or business. Even the few cases of judges taking business appointments on leaving the Bench have attracted criticism.[16]

(b) Judges and the legislature

Judges of the Supreme Court and Circuit judges are disqualified from membership of the House of Commons.[17] The judges that are members of the House of Lords may contribute to its debates, but by a convention established comparatively recently do not take part in political controversy.[18] They tend to confine their contributions to technical questions of a legal nature. The position in the twenties was not so clear cut. In 1922 Lord Carson attacked the proposals for the establishment of the Irish Free State. He was rebuked for doing so by his former supporter, Lord Birkenhead L.C., but was defended by others.[19]

(c) Judges and the executive

It is generally accepted that judges other than the Lord Chancellor should not hold ministerial office or sit in the Cabinet. Both Lord Mansfield and Lord Ellenborough served in the Cabinet while Chief Justice of the King's Bench, but both cases attracted much criticism. Lord Reading C.J. performed various executive tasks for the government during the First World War, but that can be regarded as an anomalous exception to a well-established principle, which has indeed been strengthened by the recent practice of making non-political appointments to the position of Lord Chief Justice.

The one matter that has caused some controversy is the common practice of using judges as chairmen or members of Royal Commissions, Departmental Committees and Tribunals of Inquiry.[20] Indeed, judges are

---

[15] H.C. Deb. Vol. 23, cols. 257–261, written answer, May 12, 1982.

[16] In 1970, Fisher J. resigned at the age of 52 after 2½ years on the Bench in order to join a merchant bank. This provoked some criticism: see (1970) 114 S.J. 593. On the other hand, it was pointed out that a reluctant judge was unlikely to be a good one. The position of Lord Chancellor is arguably different, given the precariousness of office. Both Lord Birkenhead and Lord Kilmuir were criticised for taking business appointments, although the latter declined to draw the pension to which he was entitled. Lord Birkenhead defended his rights to take the pension, but assigned it to the benefit of certain hospitals (see Heuston, *Lives*, pp. 396–8; J. Campbell, *F.E. Smith, First Earl of Birkenhead* (1983), pp. 812–814).

[17] House of Commons Disqualification Act 1975, s.1 and Sched. 1. There is no disqualification applicable to recorders. In 1984 there were 11 recorder/M.P.s.

[18] See generally L. Blom-Cooper and G. Drewry, *Final Appeal* (1972), pp. 196–215.

[19] H.L. Debs. Vol. 49, cols. 686–698, March 21, 1922; 715–727, March 22, 1922 and cols. 931–974 March 29, 1922.

[20] See D.G.T. Williams, *Not in the Public Interest* (1965), pp. 188–191; P. Hillyard, (1971) 6 I.J. (N.S.) 93; G. Zellick, [1972] P.L. 1; T.J. Cartwright, *Royal Commissions and Departmental Committees in Britain* (1975); G. Rhodes, *Committees of Inquiry* (1975); Griffith (1981), Chap. 2.

prominent in the ranks of "the Good and the Great."[21] This is both expected and unexceptionable where "lawyers' law" is concerned. However, the subject matter of an inquiry may well be politically controversial. The judge concerned may be called upon to explain or justify the report, and indeed to argue in public the case for or against reform. The topics covered include public disorders (Red Lion Square,[22] Brixton[23]); security matters (security procedures in the public service,[24] the Vassall case,[25] the Profumo affair,[26] the D Notice affair[27]); mismanagement in the public service (the collapse of the Vehicle and General Insurance Company,[28] the Crown Agents[29]); events in Northern Ireland (disturbances in 1969,[30] interrogation methods,[31] legal procedures for dealing with terrorists,[32] the "Bloody Sunday" deaths in Londonderry,[33] the working of anti-terrorist legislation,[34] and police interrogation procedures[35]); the interception of communications[36]; and industrial disputes (electricity supply,[37] miners,[38] and Grunwick[39]). The appointment of a committee is often thought to be a political delaying tactic or a mechanism for shuffling off responsibility for a controversial decision: whether or not either of these criticisms is in fact true, in a particular case it may be unfortunate for a judge to be associated with them. Moreover, the judge may find himself in the midst of political controversy. He may be criticised for producing what is perceived by certain sections of the community, rightly or wrongly, to be a "whitewashing report,"[40] or by the government for not producing such a report.[41] It is arguable that a judge is

[21] Judges chaired 118 of the 358 committees between 1945 and 1969: Cartwright (1975), p. 72. There is a list of some 4,500 names of people used for these purposes, which "these days . . . is a very swish affair, all floppy discs and visual display terminals, run by a staff of nine and lubricated by a budget of £250,000 a year" (*The Times*, January 22, 1983, p. 9).

[22] Cmnd. 5919, 1975: Lord Scarman.

[23] Cmnd. 8427, 1981: Lord Scarman (Inquiry under the Police Act 1964).

[24] Cmnd. 1681, 1962: Lord Radcliffe (Departmental Committee). The Security Commission is also headed by a judge; the function of this standing commission, first set up in 1964, is to investigate at the Prime Minister's request, breaches of security in the public service, and to report and advise generally on security arrangements.

[25] Cmnd. 2009, 1963: Lord Radcliffe (Tribunal of Inquiry).

[26] Cmnd. 2152, 1963: Lord Denning. See Lord Denning, *The Due Process of Law* (1980), pp. 67–73; "It was a best-seller": *ibid*. p. 68.

[27] Cmnd. 3309, 1967: Lord Radcliffe (Committee of Privy Counsellors).

[28] 1971–72 H.C. 133: James J. (Tribunal of Inquiry).

[29] 1981–82 H.C. 364: Croom-Johnson J. (Tribunal of Inquiry).

[30] Cmnd. 566 (N.I.), 1972: Scarman J. (Tribunal of Inquiry).

[31] Cmnd. 4801, 1972: Lord Parker (Committee of Privy Counsellors).

[32] Cmnd. 5185, 1972: Lord Diplock (Departmental Committee).

[33] 1971–72 H.C. 220: Lord Widgery C.J. (Tribunal of Inquiry).

[34] Cmnd. 5847, 1975: Lord Gardiner (Departmental Committee).

[35] Cmnd. 7497, 1979: Judge Bennett (Departmental Committee).

[36] Cmnd. 283, 1957: Birkett L.J. (Committee of Privy Counsellors).

[37] Cmnd. 4594, 1971: Lord Wilberforce (Court of Inquiry under the Industrial Courts Act 1919).

[38] Cmnd. 4903, 1972: Lord Wilberforce (Court of Inquiry).

[39] Cmnd. 6922, 1977: Scarman L.J. (Court of Inquiry).

[40] *e.g.* the adverse reaction to Lord Widgery's report on the Londonderry shootings K.Boyle, T. Hadden and P. Hillyard, *Law and State* (1975), pp. 126–129.

[41] *e.g.* the report of the Nyasaland Commission of Enquiry led by Devlin J. (H. Macmillan, *Riding the Storm* (1971), pp. 736–8); and the refusal of Harold Wilson to accept the Radcliffe Report on the D Notice Affair: see the White Paper on the D Notice System (Cmnd. 3312, 1967).

a suitable person to preside over a process for ascertaining the facts of particular incidents such as the Aberfan disaster and the Summerland fire disaster on the Isle of Man, where there are no political overtones. Even here, however, there can be problems.[42]

It is accepted that a judge should not become associated with party political research committees.[43]

A stricter view of the permissible range of extra-judicial activities is taken in the United States of America, where the separation of powers is formally entrenched as a constitutional principle. Even the exceptional cases such as the appointment of Justice Murphy as prosecutor at the Nuremberg trials and Chief Justice Warren to investigate the assassination of President Kennedy were controversial.[44]

Analogous problems have arisen in respect of the appointment of judges as members of the Restrictive Practices Court and the short-lived National Industrial Relations Court (N.I.R.C.). The former court determines whether restrictive agreements are contrary to the public interest.[45] Such determinations involve considerations that are political and economic rather than legal. The functions of the N.I.R.C. were more obviously judicial, but the context was that of industrial relations, where it was, and is, highly controversial whether orthodox legal mechanisms are appropriate in principle and workable. Its successor, the Employment Appeal Tribunal, has inherited its less controversial functions.

(d) Public statements by and about judges

Judges are expected to refrain from making party political statements; it is sometimes said that they should refrain from criticising the policy of Acts of Parliament, but that seems too restrictive. Reasoned, responsible criticism is acceptable: disparaging remarks are not. Thus, in 1978, Melford Stevenson J. was reprimanded by the Lord Chancellor, Lord Elwyn-Jones, for referring to the Sexual Offences Act 1967 as a "buggers' charter."[46] Members of the executive are similarly expected to refrain from attacking judges, unless provoked. It is a rule of parliamentary practice that reflections must not be cast upon a judge's character or motives except on a substantive motion specifically criticising him or leading to an address for his removal, although reasoned arguments that a

---

[42] In New Zealand, Mahon J. was appointed as sole member of a Royal Commission to inquire into the Mt. Erebus aircraft disaster. Certain statements in the report were held by the Supreme Court to have been made in excess of jurisdiction, and an order for costs against the airline was quashed: *Re Erebus Royal Commission* (No. 2) [1981] 1 N.Z.L.R. 618. Mahon J. resigned: see [1982] N.Z.L.J. 37. An appeal to the Privy Council was dismissed: *Mahon* v. *Air New Zealand Ltd.*, *The Times*, October 21, 1983.

[43] Lord Avonside, a judge of the Court of Session, resigned from a Conservative Committee on the constitutional position in Scotland following public criticism, *e.g.* by the Lord Advocate: see *The Times*, July 30, 1968, August 8, 1968; R.J. Wilson, "British Judges as Political Actors" (1973) 1 Int. Journal of Criminology and Penology, 197, 199–20.

[44] See A.T. Mason, (1953) 67 Harv. L.R. 193; (1970) 35 *Law and Contemporary Problems* (Symposium).

[45] See above, pp. 77–78.

[46] *The Times*, July 6, 1978.

judge has made a mistake or was wrong are acceptable.[47] Matters that are *sub judice* cannot be discussed, unless they relate to a ministerial decision or concern issues of national importance, and discussion would not prejudice the proceedings.[48]

(e) Judicial immunity from suit[49]

At common law, every judge of a superior or inferior court is immune from liability in damages for any act that is either (1) within his jurisdiction or (2) honestly believed to be within his jurisdiction.[50] He is also protected by absolute privilege in the law of defamation. Every judge:

> "should be able to do his work in complete independence and free from fear. He should not have to turn the pages of his books with trembling fingers, asking himself: 'If I do this, shall I be liable in damages?' "[51]

The rules also prevent the relitigation of the issues determined by the court.[52]

Deliberate misconduct such as corruption could lead to prosecution for a criminal offence[53] and removal from office.

(f) Disqualification for interest or bias

A judge is disqualified from hearing a case in which he has a direct pecuniary or proprietary interest, or in circumstances where there is a reasonable suspicion or a real likelihood that he would be biased.[54] This rule applies to judges of the superior courts as much as it does to magistrates and tribunal members. Indeed, the leading case on disqualifying interests[55] concerned decrees made by Lord Cottenham L.C. in favour of a canal company in which he held shares. The House of Lords set aside these decrees. Lord Campbell emphasised that:

> "No one can suppose that Lord Cottenham could be in the remotest degree influenced by the interest . . . but . . . it is of the last importance that the maxim that no man is to be a judge in his own cause should be held sacred."[56]

---

[47] *Erskine May's Parliamentary Practice* (20th ed., 1983), pp. 430–1; H.C. Deb. Vol. 865, cols. 1092, 1144, 1200, December 4, 1973 (criticisms of Sir John Donaldson as President of the National Industrial Relations Court; H.C. Deb. Vol. 935, cols. 1381–4, July 19, 1977; H.C. Deb. Vol 34, cols. 123–6, 285–6, December 14, 15, 1982 (description by Mrs. Thatcher of a 12 month sentence for the rape of a 6 year old girl as "incomprehensible" ruled to be in order).

[48] *Erskine May*, pp. 429–30. H.C. Deb. Vol. 681 cols. 1416–17, July 23, 1963; H.C. Deb. Vol. 839 col. 1627, June 28, 1972; H.C. Deb. Vol. 916 cols. 882–4, July 29, 1976.

[49] See M. Brazier, [1976] P.L. 397.

[50] *Sirros* v. *Moore* [1975] Q.B. 118, Lord Denning M.R. and Ormrod L.J. Buckley L.J. held that if an act were outside jurisdiction a judge would only be immune if he had so acted as a result of a reasonable mistake of fact.

[51] *Per* Lord Denning M.R., *ibid.* p. 136.

[52] *Cf.* the immunity of advocates, above, p. 123.

[53] *Cf. R.* v. *Llewellyn-Jones* [1967] 3 All E.R. 225 (misbehaviour in a public office: misuse of funds by a county court registrar).

[54] See J.M. Evans, *de Smith's Judicial Review of Administrative Action* (4th ed., 1980), Chap. 5; P. Jackson, *Natural Justice* (2nd ed., 1979), Chap. 2; R. Cranston, [1979] P.L. 237.

[55] *Dimes* v. *Grand Junction Canal Proprietors* (1852) 3 H.L. Cas. 759.

[56] *Ibid.* p. 793. Dimes was a "crazy attorney" who had "embarked upon interminable litigation" against the Canal company. Cottenham died before judgment was given in the House of Lords: "it was a common belief that Dimes had killed Lord Cottenham": J.B. Atlay, *The Victorian Chancellors* (1906) Vol. 1, p. 415.

The matters that may give rise to a suspicion or likelihood of bias include personal hostility, friendship, family relationship or acquaintance with a party or with a witness. The parties may waive the objection. Where a judge is not technically disqualified, he may well refuse to act in a case where one of the parties raises an objection. Objections, however, are not commonly made. Lord Denning M.R. withdrew from a case concerning the Church of Scientology of California as the Church felt that "there was an unconscious influence operating adversely to it" in Lord Denning's previous judgments.[57] The Church had been before Lord Denning's Court on eight previous occasions, and noted that his Lordship had doubted whether it was right to call scientology a "religion" and whether the Church was entitled to call itself a church. Shaw L.J. said that it was almost impossible to resist the application for the appeal to be transferred "even though the grounds were not merely slight but non-existent." Conversely, no objection was taken to Lord Denning's acting in a case concerning the Church Commissioners, he being one of the Commissioners,[58] or to the fact that all the members of the Court of Appeal hearing the appeal in the London Transport "fares" case were both users of public transport in London and London ratepayers.[59]

10. THE JUDICIAL FUNCTION

In the course of legal proceedings, judges may be called upon to perform one or more of the following tasks: presiding over a trial (*e.g.* controlling the course of proceedings; keeping order; ruling on questions of the admissibility of evidence; deciding when to adjourn for lunch); presiding over an appeal,[60] determining a disputed question of fact; determining a disputed question of law; directing a jury on the evidence and the law; deciding what remedy to award or punishment to impose; and giving reasons for such decisions as are his. With the marked decline in the use of the jury in civil cases over the last 60 years, the judicial task of determining disputed questions of fact has correspondingly grown in significance. When considering the "nature of the judicial function," however, it is usual to concentrate on the ways in which judges approach the determination of disputed questions of law. Furthermore, attention is directed in particular to the appeal courts,[61] as a higher proportion of time is spent on such questions, as the arguments are more likely to be evenly balanced, and because the decisions of courts at the top of the hierarchy carry most weight. In Chapters 6 and 7 we consider the principles that are applicable to the interpretation of statutes and the handling of precedent cases. We

[57] *Ex p. Church of Scientology of California, The Times,* February 21, 1978.

[58] *Hanson* v. *Church Commissioners* [1978] Q.B. 823, 831. The actual management of the estate of the Church Commissioners was vested in a separate board of governors. Various "dignitaries," including the Lord Chief Justice, the Master of the Rolls and the Lord Mayor of London were "merely titular commissioners."

[59] *Bromley London Borough Council* v. *Greater London Council* [1983] 1 A.C. 768, 771–2.

[60] The president of an appellate court can have a significant influence on the course of proceedings, although his role is more muted than that of a trial judge sitting alone: see above, p. 82, n. 85.

[61] There have been three studies of the House of Lords: L. Blom-Cooper and G. Drewry, *Final Appeal* (1972); R. Stevens, *Law and Politics* (1979); A. Paterson, *The Law Lords* (1982). The nature of the judicial function is analysed in R. Bell, *Policy Arguments in Judicial Decisions* (1983).

shall see that there is considerable room for flexibility. Moreover, even where there is no directly relevant precedent and no applicable legislation the judge must still give an answer to any legal questions that arise.

The extent to which a judge is prepared to innovate depends upon the respective weight attached to a number of factors[62]: the need for stability and certainty in law (which suggests consistency with established principles and precedents); the wish to do justice as between the parties; the need not to usurp the role of Parliament; the need to justify a decision by reasoned argument and not merely compromise between the parties; and the need to base a decision on at least one of the issues raised by the parties. Differences in approach reflect different weight attached to these factors—in particular the first two.

Debates as to the nature of the judicial function have taken place in two different, but related, fields: legal theory and socio-legal studies. Important contributions to the theoretical debate have come from some of our leading judges, speaking both extra-judicially and in decided cases. The judges' own perceptions of the proper judicial role are equally of importance as one of the important influences on judicial decision-making identified in empirical studies.

Historically, the theory that held sway for the longest time was the "declaratory theory" expounded by William Blackstone and others. Blackstone wrote[63] that:

> "it is an established rule to abide by former precedents, where the same points come again in litigation . . . [the judge] being sworn to determine, not according to his private sentiments: he being sworn to determine, not according to his own private judgment, but according to the known laws and customs of the land: not delegated to pronounce a new law, but to maintain and expound the old one. Yet this rule admits of exception, where the former determination is most evidently contrary to reason; much more if it be clearly contrary to divine law. But even in such cases the subsequent judges do not pretend to make a new law, but to vindicate the old one from misrepresentation. For if it be found that the former decision is manifestly absurd or unjust, it is declared not that such a sentence was *bad law*, but that it was *not law*, that is, not the established custom of the realm, as has been erroneously determined."

Thus the role of the judge is to declare what the law is, not to make it. This theory was not easy to square with the unconcealed law-making activities of particular judges such as Lord Mansfield,[64] and was abused by writers such as Bentham.[64a] Nevertheless, judges in the nineteenth and early twentieth centuries generally maintained (with increasing enthusiasm) the

---

[62] See Paterson (1982), pp. 122–127.

[63] *Commentaries*, Vol. 1, pp. 69–70.

[64] Chief Justice the King's Bench, 1756–1788. See C.H.S. Fifoot, *Lord Mansfield* (1936).

[64a] *A Comment on the Commentaries* (eds. J.H. Burns and H.L.A. Hart, 1977) pp. 192–206. Bentham's objections were based in part on his opposition to theories of "natural law." Moreover, he disapproved of law-making judges, taking the view that this was a matter for Parliament.

position that their function was not to make law and, indeed, that they were not concerned with the policy implications of their rulings.[65] However, this view was held less strongly in the House of Lords than in the lower courts, some of the Law Lords, with equity or Scottish backgrounds, being more concerned with principles than precedent and more likely to advert to the likely consequences of their decisions.

After 1912, the Law Lords, who tended now to be chosen from the professional judiciary, with less regard for political affiliation:

> "exhibited an increasing tendency to articulate a declaratory theory of law and to insist that the judicial function, even in the final appeal court, was primarily the formalistic or mechanical one of restating existing doctrines."[66]

At the same time there were still some judges, such as Lord Atkin and Lord Wright, who were prepared to develop private law doctrines significantly while maintaining the facade of the declaratory theory. However, there followed what Stevens terms the "era of substantive formalism" in the House of Lords:

> "For the 1940s and for much of the 1950s there were no obvious signs that the Law Lords had developed rules out of broader principles of the common law or the liberal state. Indeed, there was virtually no acceptance of an element of discretion, let alone a utilitarian balancing of interests. The process, at best fell into Karl Llewellyn's category of judicial formalism, with opinions written 'in deductive form with an air of expression of single-line inevitability.'[67] At worst, the process was a restatement of the declaratory theory in such extreme form that it denied any purpose for a second appeal court. Legal rationality became an end in itself. The literal meaning of words was to be the only criterion of statutory interpretation."[68]

Deference to the executive in public law cases was to be expected in wartime: strong judicial challenges to the Labour government elected in 1945 with a large majority would obviously have been unwise. This approach was associated particularly with Lord Jowitt, the Labour Lord Chancellor, and Lord Simonds, a Law Lord between 1944 and 1962, apart from his period as Lord Chancellor from 1951 and 1954. A few judges stood out against this approach, notably Lord Denning,[69] but to little avail. The only developments could come with the application of established principles to novel factual situations.

---

[65] See, *e.g.* Parke B. in *Egerton* v. *Brownlow* (1853) 4 H.L.C. 1, 124: "It is the province of the statesman, and not the lawyer, to discuss, and of the legislature to determine, what is the best for the public good, and to provide for it by proper enactments. It is the province of the judge to expound the law only; the written from the statutes: the unwritten or common law from the decisions of our predecessors and of our existing courts, from text-writers of acknowledged authority, and upon the principles to be clearly deduced from them by sound reason and just inference; not to speculate upon what is the best, in his opinion, for the advantage of the community."

[66] Stevens (1979), p. 196.

[67] Karl Llewellyn, *The Common Law Tradition* (1960), p. 38.

[68] Stevens (1979), pp. 319–320.

[69] See below, p. 179.

Since the mid-1950s the position has changed. It has become generally accepted by the Law Lords that they may properly exercise a limited law-making function.[70] Lord Radcliffe argued that it was best if judges went about this task "on the quiet."[71]

> "Would anyone now deny that judicial decisions are a creative, not merely an expository, contribution to the law? There are no means by which they can be otherwise, so rare is the occasion upon which a decision does not involve choice between two admissible alternatives . . . . We cannot run the risk of finding the archetypal image of the judge confused in men's minds with the very different image of the legislator . . . . [T]he image of the judge, objective, impartial, erudite and experienced declarer of the law that is, lies deeper in the consciousness of civilisation than the image of the lawmaker, propounding what are avowedly new rules of human conduct . . . . Personally, I think that judges will serve the public interest better if they keep quiet about their legislative function. No doubt they will discreetly contribute to changes in the law, because . . . they cannot do otherwise, even if they would. The judge who shows his hand, who advertises what he is about, may indeed show that he is a strong spirit, unfettered by the past; but I doubt very much whether he is not doing more harm to general confidence in the law as a constant, safe in the hands of the judges than he is doing to the law's credit as a set of rules nicely attuned to the sentiments of the day."[72]

The dominant influence in the House of Lords in this period was Lord Reid. In his well-known address entitled "The Judge as Law Maker" he swiftly disposed of the declaratory theory:

> "We do not believe in fairy tales any more. So we must accept the fact that for better or worse judges do make law, and tackle the question how do they approach their task and how they should approach it."[73]

Where public opinion was sharply divided, whether or not on party lines, no judge should lean to one side or the other if it can be avoided; if it cannot:

> " . . . we must play safe [and] decide the case on the preponderance of existing authority. Parliament is the right place to settle issues which the ordinary man regards as controversial."[74]

It was also improper for judges to disregard or innovate on settled law in areas where people rely on the certainty of the law in settling their affairs,

---

[70] See generally A. Paterson, *The Law Lords* (1982).

[71] See Lord Radcliffe, *Not in Feather Beds* (1968), pp. 265–277. Professor Atiyah has argued that most of the judges "would prefer to shelter behind the declaratory theory in public, and to confine discussion of the nature and use of the creative judicial function amongst the *cognoscenti*" (1980) 15 Israel L.R. 346, 360.

[72] Radcliffe (1968), pp. 271–272, 273.

[73] (1972) 12 J.S.P.T.L. 22. For other important contributions to the debate see Diplock L.J., "The Courts as Legislators," in B.W. Harvey (ed.) *The Lawyer and Justice* (1978), p. 263; Lord Edmund-Davies, "Judicial Activism" (1975) 28 C.L.P. 1; Lord Devlin, *The Judge* (1981), Chap. 1.

[74] (1972) 12 J.S.P.T.L. 22, 23.

in particular in making contracts or settlements. A problem might be too complex for it to be appropriate for the judges to change some aspect of it: the only proper way forward would be for there to be legislation following a wide survey of the whole field.[75] Nevertheless, there was considerable scope for judges to mould the development of the common law, which should be done having regard to "common sense, legal principle and public policy in that order."[76] The judges did not have so free a hand when interpreting statutes as when dealing with the common law.

In the late 1950s and early 1960s there were some indications that the House of Lords was taking a freer attitude to precedents. These led to the Practice Statement in 1966 in which the Law Lords announced that they would no longer regard themselves as bound by their own previous decisions.[77] Since then, the criteria for exercising the power to overrule have been analysed in some detail. Lord Reid's views have been especially influential,[78] as they have on the wider issues concerning judicial law-making. Similarly, in the field of statutory interpretation the judges have shown a greater inclination to look at the context of the words in a statute, rather than to adopt a narrow literal approach.

Paterson shows that of the 19 Law Lords who were active between 1967 and 1973 at least 12 considered that the Law Lords had an obligation to develop the common law to meet changing social conditions. An even greater proportion of the sample of barristers interviewed by him shared this view, as did at least three of the six Law Lords appointed between 1973 and 1979.[79] Ten of 11 Law Lords interviewed accepted that they ought to be concerned with the possible social and legal consequences of their decisions, at least within the acknowledged limitations of the information available to them.[80] A majority of the Law Lords considered that there were cases coming to the Lords to which there was no single correct solution on the basis of existing legal rules and principles, and in which they had a measure of choice.[81]

In the same period, the Court of Appeal was dominated by Lord Denning M.R., who showed a greater preference for innovation than the Law Lords, albeit coupled with varying success in persuading colleagues in the Court of Appeal to agree with him.[82]

---

[75] See *Myers* v. *D.P.P.* [1965] A.C. 1001, 1022.

[76] (1972) 12 J.S.P.T.L. 22, 25.

[77] See A. Paterson, *The Law Lords* (1982), pp. 143–153, and below, pp. 296–300.

[78] See Paterson (1982), pp. 153–169, and below, p. 299.

[79] Paterson (1982), pp. 173–4. But note the view expressed by Lord Scarman in *McLoughlin* v. *O'Brian* [1983] 1 A.C. 410, that where "principle" requires a decision which entails a degree of "policy risk", the court's function is to adjudicate according to "principle," leaving "policy curtailment" to Parliament. The policy issue as to where to draw the line in "nervous shock" cases is "not justiciable. The problem is one of social, economic and financial policy. The considerations relevant to a decision are not such as to be capable of being handled within the limits of the forensic process": pp. 430–431. See, *contra*, Lord Edmund-Davies pp. 427–428.

[80] Paterson (1982) pp. 177–8.

[81] *Ibid*. pp. 192–5. This runs counter to the theory developed by R.M. Dworkin that there is a right answer in all hard cases and that the judges have no discretion to make law: *Taking Rights Seriously* (1977); "No Right Answer" in P. Hacker and J. Raz (eds.) *Law, Morality and Society* (1977); J.W. Harris, *Legal Philosophies* (1980), Chap. 14; Bell (1983) Chap. VIII.

[82] See Stevens (1979), pp. 488–505; Lord Denning *The Discipline of Law* (1979), Parts 1 and 7.

The approach of appellate judges varies according to the context. For example, continued importance has been attached by the House of Lords to the "certainty" factor in commercial and property cases, and, to a lesser extent, in criminal law cases. By contrast, there has been a marked extension of liability in such aspects of the tort of negligence as negligent misstatement,[83] omissions,[84] nervous shock,[85] economic loss,[86] and injury to trespassers.[87] In public law, there has been a whole series of cases in which the courts have analysed, refined and sometimes extended the grounds upon which administrative and judicial decisions of government institutions can be challenged under the *ultra vires* doctrine. In some of these, the challenges have been successful.[88] In others, the judges have shown restraint in circumstances where it was not obvious why restraint was any more appropriate.[89]

It is also interesting to contrast the willingness of Sir Robert Megarry V.-C. to extend the field of liability in negligence for economic loss[90] with his unwillingness to create an "altogether new right" in a case where it was claimed that there was a right to hold a telephone conversation in the privacy of one's home without molestation[91]:

> "No new right in the law, fully-fledged with all the appropriate safeguards, can spring from the head of a judge deciding a particular case: only Parliament can create such a right . . . . The wider and more indefinite the right claimed, the greater the undesirability of holding that such a right exists."[92]

There are some apparently formidable arguments in favour of judicial restraint in law-making. The making of new law through the legislative process[93] rather than judicially is often said to be more in accordance with democratic theory[94] and is more likely to be based on a proper examination of all the relevant information. English civil procedure

---

[83] *Hedley Byrne & Co.* v. *Heller & Partners* [1964] A.C. 465.

[84] *Home Office* v. *Dorset Yacht Co.* [1970] A.C. 1004; *Anns* v. *London Borough of Merton* [1978] A.C. 728.

[85] *McLoughlin* v. *O'Brian* [1983] 1 A.C. 410.

[86] *Junior Books Ltd.* v. *Veitchi Co. Ltd.* [1983] 1 A.C. 520.

[87] *British Railways Board* v. *Herrington* [1972] A.C. 877.

[88] *e.g. Ridge* v. *Baldwin* [1964] A.C. 40 (dismissal of a chief constable held void for breach of natural justice); *Anisminic Ltd.* v. *Foreign Compensation Commission* [1969] 2 A.C. 147 (decision of the Commission struck down for misinterpretation of the relevant legislation notwithstanding a statutory clause purporting to exclude judicial review); *Padfield* v. *Minister of Agriculture* [1968] A.C. 997 and *Laker Airways* v. *Department of Trade* [1977] Q.B. 643 (ministerial decisions held to be abuses of discretion); *Bromley London Borough Council* v. *Greater London Council* [1983] 1 A.C. 768 (substantial cuts in fares held to be *ultra vires*).

[89] *R.* v. *Secretary of State for the Home Department, ex p. Zamir* [1980] A.C. 930 (but *cf. R.* v. *Secretary of State for the Home Department, ex p. Khawaja* [1984] A.C. 74); *Bushell* v. *Secretary of State for the Environment* [1981] A.C. 75.

[90] *Ross* v. *Caunters* [1980] Ch. 297.

[91] *Malone* v. *Metropolitan Police Commissioner (No. 2)* [1979] Ch. 344.

[92] *Ibid.* pp. 372, 373. Compare also the extension of police powers of *seizure* by the Court of Appeal in *Chic Fashions Ltd.* v. *Jones* [1968] 2 Q.B. 299 and *Ghani* v. *Jones* [1970] 1 Q.B. 693 with the refusal of the court to create a new common law power of *search*: *McLorie* v. *Oxford* [1982] Q.B. 1290.

[93] See Chap. 5.

[94] But see Atiyah, (1980) 15 Israel L.R. 362–365.

generally prevents anyone but the parties to litigation giving evidence[95] and enables the parties to choose what evidence to present. Moreover, there are difficulties in presenting *evidence* as distinct from *argument* about the possible social and economic implications of decisions. Conspicuous creativity in judicial law making is difficult to square with the "ostentatious impartiality" that is also regarded as desirable.[96] The judges have no written constitution to look to as a source of power.[97]

A more pragmatic reason sometimes advanced in favour of restraint is that:

> "if people and Parliament come to think that the judicial power is to be confined by nothing other than the judge's sense of what is right (or, as Selden put it, by the length of the Chancellor's foot), confidence in the judicial system will be replaced by fear of it becoming uncertain and arbitrary in its application. Society will then be ready for Parliament to cut the power of the judges. Their power to do justice will become more restricted by law than it need be, or is today."[98]

Nevertheless, restraint is not the same as complete withdrawal from the field. "Law reform" does not rank high in the list of priorities in the struggle for a place in the legislative timetable: if one always waited for Parliament, one would often wait in vain.

In his book, *The Politics of the Judiciary*[99] Professor Griffith argues that the discussion about how creative judges should be:

> "has been and is a somewhat unreal discussion . . . . What is lacking . . . is any clear and consistent relationship between the general pronouncements of judges on this matter of creativity and the way they conduct themselves in court."[1]

Moreover, the appellate judges:

> "have by their education and training and the pursuit of their profession as barristers, acquired a strikingly homogenous collection of attitudes, beliefs and principles, which to them represents the public interest. The judicial conception of the public interest . . . is threefold. It concerns first, the interests of the State (including its

---

[95] The rules could, of course, be changed. By contrast, in the United States interest groups are much more able to institute litigation, or to present arguments in cases involving other parties.

[96] See above, p. 169.

[97] Although here it should be noted that the power of judicial review exercised by the Supreme Court in the United States is not expressly created by the Constitution, but is itself judge-made: see *Marbury* v. *Madison* (1803) 1 Cranch 137.

[98] *Per* Lord Scarman in *Duport Steels Ltd.* v. *Sirs* [1980] 1 All E.R. 529, 551. When Roger Parker Q.C. made a similar prediction in his submissions to the Court of Appeal in *Congreve* v. *Home Office* [1976] Q.B. 629, Lord Denning M.R. stated "We trust that this was not said seriously, but only as a piece of advocate's licence." Mr. Parker subsequently apologized if anything he said had sounded like a threat. (See *The Times*, December 6 and 9, 1975).

[99] (2nd. ed., 1981.) For similar studies of particular areas see J.I. Reynolds, "Statutory Covenant of Fitness and Repair" (1974) 37 M.L.R. 377 (and the rejoinder by M.J. Robinson, (1976) 39 M.L.R. 43); J. Hackney, "The Politics of the Chancery" (1981) 34 C.L.P. 113.

[1] p. 200. Paterson, *The Law Lords* (1982), pp. 187–189, argues that the Law Lords have been more consistent than Griffith suggests.

moral welfare) and the preservation of law and order broadly interpreted; secondly, the protection of property rights; and thirdly, the promotion of certain political views normally associated with the Conservative Party."[2]

They are thus concerned to preserve and protect the existing order, to serve the prevailing political and economic forces, this being generally true of all societies today, whether capitalistic or communist. This is not regarded by Griffith as a matter for recrimination: his main concern is simply to dispel the myth that the judges are "neutral."

In relation to Griffith's view that the appellate judges have acquired a homogenous collection of attitudes, Lord Devlin commented[3]:

"Since he is writing of men in their sixties and seventies whose working life has given them a common outlook on many questions, by no means all political, I have very little doubt that he is right. I have very little doubt either that the same might be written of most English institutions, certainly of all those which like the law are not of a nature to attract the crusading or rebellious spirit."

However, he suggested that whether one agrees that the application of the law has been distorted depended on whether one:

"looks at them from right or from the left . . . . To my mind none of the evidence, general or specific adds much to the inherent probability that men and women of a certain age will be inclined to favour the *status quo*."[4]

He, and others, have, for instance, pointed out that in many of the cases discussed by Griffith there has been a division of opinion both between the Court of Appeal and the House of Lords, and within each court.[5]

Griffith does not suggest that anything can be done to change judicial attitudes. Lord Devlin notes that for a known bias allowance can be made:

"[W]here novel measures are imposed by a minister or by Parliament, they must be expressed in language which is emphatic enough and clear enough to penetrate the bias against them of those who are set in their ways: it is no use praying for the rejuvenation of the elderly."[6]

What these contributions to the debate do seem to suggest is that caution should be used in contemplating any dramatic extension of the powers of the judiciary, such as by the creation of a Bill of Rights on the American pattern with entrenched guarantees of civil liberties, expressed in general language, which override both legislation and administative action. Moreover, one can be a little sceptical about claims such as those of Lord Denning[7]:

---

[2] *Ibid.* pp. 215, 217.
[3] (1978) 41 M.L.R. 501, 505–506.
[4] *Ibid.* pp. 507, 509.
[5] B. Roshier and H. Teff, *Law in Society* (1980) p. 67.
[6] (1978) 41 M.L.R. 501, 511.
[7] *Misuse of Power* (*The Richard Dimbleby Lecture 1980*), pp. 18–19. Reprinted in *What Next in the Law?* (1982).

"May not the Judges themselves sometimes abuse or misuse their power? It is their duty to administer and apply the law of the land. If they should divert it or depart from it—and do so knowingly—they themselves would be guilty of a misuse of power. So we come up against Juvenal's question, *Sed quis custodiet ipsos custodes*?' (But who is to guard the guards themselves?) . . . . Suppose a future Prime Minister should seek to pack the Bench with judges of his own extreme political colour. Would they be tools in his hand? To that I answer 'No.' Every judge on his appointment discards all politics and all prejudices. You need have no fear. The Judges of England have always in the past—and always will—be vigilant in guarding our freedoms. Someone must be trusted. Let it be the Judges."

CHAPTER 5

LEGISLATION

A. INTRODUCTION[1]

IN medieval England there was no clear distinction between legislation and other forms of governmental action, and there was no settled procedure for enactment that had to be followed. The terminology was confusing: well-known early statutes include the "Constitutions" of Clarendon 1164, the "Great Charter" 1215, the "Statute" of Merton 1235 and the "Provisions" of Oxford 1258:

"A statute in the region of Edward I simply means something established by royal authority; whether it is established by the King in Council, or in a Parliament of nobles, or in a Parliament of nobles and commons as well is completely immaterial."[2]

By the fifteenth century the consent of the Commons to a statute was regarded as necessary and in early Tudor times the procedure for enactment took on something like its modern form:

"Legislation . . . was no longer the Government's vague reply to vaguely worded complaints, but rather the deliberate adoption of specific proposals embodied in specific texts emanating from the Crown or its officers."[3]

In the seventeenth century, Coke wrote that "There is no Act of Parliament but must have the consent of the Lords, the Commons and the Royall assent of the King."[4] The constitutional struggles of that century saw the end of serious attempts by the Crown to assert a legislative competence rivalling that of Parliament.[5] In the *Case of Proclamations*[6] the judges resolved that "the King by his proclamation cannot create any offence which was not an offence before" and "that the King hath no prerogative, but that which the law of the land allows him." However, the courts subsequently upheld the Crown's claim to a power to impose taxation incidentally to the exercise of prerogative powers such as those to conduct foreign affairs, regulate trade and take emergency measures for the defence of the realm,[7] and a power to "dispense" with the

---

[1] See generally on legislation, D.R. Miers and A.C. Page, *Legislation* (1982) and F.A.R. Bennion, *Statute Law* (2nd ed., 1983). On the history of legislation see J.H. Baker, *Introduction to Legal History* (2nd ed., 1979) pp. 177–183; C.K. Allen, *Law in the Making* (7th ed., 1964) pp. 435–469.

[2] T.F.T. Plucknett, *Concise History of the Common Law* (5th ed., 1956) p. 322.

[3] Plucknett, (1944) 60 L.Q.R. 242, 248.

[4] 4 Cokes's *Institutes of the Laws of England*, p. 25.

[5] See S.A. de Smith, *Constitutional and Administrative Law* (4th ed., 1981) pp. 79–82, 135–137.

[6] (1611) 12 Co.Rep. 74.

[7] *Case of Impositions: Bate's Case* (1606) 2 St.Tr. 371; *Case of Ship Money: R.* v. *Hampden* (1637) 3 St.Tr. 825.

operation of a statue for the benefit of an individual.[8] James II also claimed the power to "suspend" the general operation of statutes, his target being statutes that discriminated against Dissenters and Roman Catholics. The reassertion of such claims to prerogative power after the Civil War and the Restoration led to the "Glorious Revolution" of 1688 and the Bill of Rights. The latter measure, declared to be a statute by the Crown and Parliament Recognition Act 1689, provided (*inter alia*)

"That the pretended power of suspending of laws or the execution of laws by regall authority without consent of Parlyament is illegall . . . .

That the pretended power of dispensing with laws or the execution of laws by regall authoritie as it hath been assumed and exercised of late is illegall . . . .

That levying money for or to the use of the Crowne by pretence of prerogative without grant of Parlyament for longer time or in other manner than the same is or shall be granted is illegal."

The prerogative powers of the Crown were in general restricted, and not abolished, but it was now clear that they could be modified or extinguished according to Parliament's wishes. Other possible rivals have also been unable to maintain any challenge to the dominance of Parliament. The Reformation Parliament established legislative supremacy over the Church.[9] In more recent times, the courts have refused to accept that a resolution of the House of Commons may alter the law of the land.[10]

Certain periods of our history have been noted for increases in legislative activity, and complaints of the difficulty of keeping abreast of the changes. Parliament passed 677 statutes in the reign of Henry VIII and these occupied almost as much space as the whole statute book had done in 1509.[11] Between 1711 and 1811 the annual number of Acts passed increased from 74 to 423. The bulk of the increase was in the number of local and private Acts. The 1811 figures included one for change of name, two for divorce, six for the settlement of private estates, 33 for inclosure and about 150 concerning local matters such as turnpike roads, canals and bridges.[12] The most dramatic increase in legislative activity has, however, been the product of the vast expansion of the activities of the state during the nineteenth and twentieth centuries, and associated factors such as the extensive reforms in the civil service and the administrative machinery, the increasingly representative nature of Parliament, the development of political parties and the strengthening of the role of the Cabinet. The balance as regards Acts of Parliament has also shifted from private legislation to public general legislation.[13]

Having established its legislative supremacy, Parliament was reluctant to delegate its powers.[14] In the eighteenth century, public general Acts

[8] *Thomas* v. *Sorell* (1674) Vaughan 330; *Godden* v. *Hales* (1686) 11 St.Tr. 1165.
[9] J.H. Baker, *The Reports of Sir John Spelman Vol. II*, Introduction (1978), pp. 64–70.
[10] See *Stockdale* v. *Hansard* (1839) 9 A. & E. 1 where the Court of Queen's Bench held that the scope of Parliamentary privilege could not be extended by a resolution; *Bowles* v. *Bank of England* [1913] 1 Ch. 57.
[11] See Baker, *op. cit.* note 9, at pp. 43–46.
[12] S. Lambert, *Bills and Acts* (1971) p. 52.
[13] See below, pp. 187–188.
[14] C.K. Allen, *Law and Orders* (3rd ed., 1965) Chap. 2.

tended "to be either overloaded with detail or to be directed to specific instances rather than to general rules."[15] However, some law-making powers had from the time of Henry VIII been entrusted to institutions such as the Commissioners of Sewers and the Justices of the Peace, and new powers were from time to time delegated by Parliament. In the eighteenth century, for example, extensive powers were granted to the Commissioners of Customs and Excise, and the Crown was given almost exclusive disciplinary powers over the Army. The following century saw a significant increase of social legislation, and a related extension of powers delegated to local and central government, but the real explosion of delegated legislation has been in the twentieth century.[16] In addition the accession of the United Kingdom to the European Communities has meant that a large body of Community legislation has become applicable in this country. We consider in turn the various forms of legislation: Acts of Parliament, subordinate or delegated legislation and European legislation.

B. ACTS OF PARLIAMENT

1. PARLIAMENTARY SOVEREIGNTY

One of the distinctive features of the constitution of the United Kingdom is the doctrine of Parliamentary sovereignty.[17] A measure which has received the assent of the Queen, Lords and Commons, that assent being given separately and in the two Houses of Parliament by simple majorities, is accepted to have the force of law as an Act of Parliament. Its validity cannot be questioned in the courts and any earlier inconsistent legislation is repealed. Parliament (strictly the "Queen in Parliament") may pass any kind of law without restriction, except that an attempt to bind its successors either as to the content of legislation or the manner and form of its enactment cannot succeed. Acts of Parliament, thus defined, are the supreme form of law; the rule of judicial obedience to them is the "ultimate *political* fact upon which the whole system of legislation hangs."[18] The definition of "Parliament" can be altered, but the process by which that can be achieved is political rather than legal. For example, there is no reason why the British people should not be able to adopt a written constitution, perhaps incorporating a Bill of Rights, which limits the powers of both government and legislature. What is unclear is how this would be done. The people of the United States did so in 1787–88 by means of a Constitutional Convention whose proposals were ratified by specially elected state conventions; the American "Bill of Rights" was added subsequently as a series of constitutional amendments. The judges would have to be satisfied that such a change was generally accepted; a constituent assembly might provide sufficient evidence. They would look to the realities of the situation, as they did at the commencement and

[15] *Ibid.* p.28.
[16] In 1982 there were 57 Public General Statutes (2072 pages); 29 local and personal Acts; and 1827 statutory instruments (5533 pages of those printed).
[17] See S.A. de Smith, *Constitutional and Administrative Law* (4th ed., 1981) Chap. 4; E.C.S. Wade and G.G. Phillips, *Constitutional and Administrative Law* (9th ed., 1977) Chap. 5; H.W.R. Wade, *Constitutional Fundamentals* (1980) Chap. 3.
[18] H.W.R. Wade, [1955] C.L.J. 172, 188.

conclusion of the Interregnum in the seventeenth century when they adjusted first to the absence and then to the restoration of the monarchy. It seems unlikely, however, that the "ultimate political fact" will be altered in the near future.

The foregoing represents the orthodox view of Parliamentary sovereignty. It has of course been argued that the definition of "Parliament" is a matter of law rather than politics, and that as such it can be altered by the existing legislative process. Parliament as at present defined could then bind its successors as to the manner and form of legislation by redefining itself either generally or for specific purposes.[19] This view, however, has had more academic support than judicial. The constitutional adviser to the House of Lords Select Committee on a Bill of Rights clearly preferred the orthodox view,[20] and this seemed to be accepted by the Committee. Moreover, the "new view" suffers from the weakness that it would enable a redefinition of "Parliament" to be effected too easily; in effect by a small partisan majority in the House of Commons.[21] For the present, Coke's definition of an Act of Parliament holds good.

It should be noted that while the concept of "Parliamentary sovereignty" is a doctrine of great technical legal significance it should not be taken as a guide to the reality of the legislative process. First, there have always been external influences which have imposed practical restraints on the kinds of legislation which can be passed. Second, the legislative process is today dominated by the government and not by members of Parliament acting independently. Legislation is initiated and formulated outside Parliament, the functions of Parliament are limited to those of scrutiny and legitimisation, and governments normally enjoy a secure party majority. Third, within "Parliament" the House of Commons is the dominant element.[22] Finally it must not be thought that legislation is the only method by which the government can secure its aims; much is achieved by, for example, exhortation, bargaining and the exercise of its economic power.[23]

2. PUBLIC AND PRIVATE ACTS

A distinction is drawn between public and private Acts. The former are those measures that are intended to alter the general law or deal with the public revenue or the administration of justice.[24] The latter are of local[25] or

[19] See R.F.V. Heuston, *Essays in Constitutional Law* (2nd ed., 1964) Chap. 1.

[20] Evidence, 1977–78 H.L. 276, pp. 1–10 (D. Rippengal); Report: 1977–78 H.L. 176, of May 24, 1978.

[21] Given that the House of Lords can be by-passed and that the royal assent by convention cannot be withheld (see below pp. 196–197).

[22] See below, pp. 195–197.

[23] See J.J. Richardson and A.G. Jordan, *Governing under Pressure* (1979) Chap. 6.

[24] *Halsbury's Laws of England* (4th ed.) Vol. 34, para. 1223. For a useful analysis of the kinds of public Bills according to their content see I Burton and G. Drewry, *Legislation and Public Policy* (1981) pp. 32–45. The authors draw a broad distinction between innovatory "policy" Bills and non-innovatory "administration" Bills to remedy anomalies, with further sub-categories of "minor policy" Bills dealing with restricted issues within an area of public policy not otherwise intended to be changed, and "administrative reform" Bills which reorganise administrative support for an existing policy.

[25] Bills dealing with the constitution or election of local governing bodies must be introduced as public Bills: *Halsbury, ibid.*; below note 2 on p. 199. See *e.g.* the London Government Act 1963; the Charlwood and Horley Act 1974.

personal concern. The procedure for enactment differs in some respects[26]; a person who wishes to rely on a private Act in court must produce a Queen's Printer's copy or an examined or certified copy of the original whereas judicial notice is taken of public Acts[27]; and a private Act may be construed strictly against the interest of the promoter, although this approach is not always followed today.[28] An important class of private legislation is that promoted by local authorities. Under section 262 of the Local Government Act 1972 all existing local legislation is to cease to have effect.[29] The new local authorities established by the Act are in the course of presenting Bills to Parliament which incorporate the provisions that they wish to preserve and any new provisions that they wish to see enacted in respect of their areas.[30] Proposals to introduce requirements that notice be given in advance of street processions have been particularly controversial.

Public Bills which are found to affect private interests in a manner different from the way in which it affects other private interests in the same category are known as "hybrid" Bills and are subject to an amalgam of the procedural rules applicable to public and private Bills.[31]

3. GOVERNMENT BILLS AND PRIVATE MEMBERS' BILLS

A separate distinction, within the class of public general statutes, is drawn between government and "Private Members' " Bills.[32] Most of the Bills that are successful are introduced by the government of the day,[33] but Bills may also be introduced by individual M.P.s or "Private Peers." In the House of Commons certain days are set aside for Private Members' Bills and a ballot is held each session to determine which M.P.s may take priority on these days. A list of 20 names is drawn up; those near the top have some chance of success, although in practice a Bill will not get through without the support, or at least the benevolent neutrality, of the government. There are other methods by which a private member may

---

[26] See below, pp. 195–198 and 198–200.

[27] The line between "public" and "private" Acts is drawn rather differently in this context: see *Halsbury's Laws of England* (4th ed.) Vol. 17, para. 150. For this purpose an Act passed after 1850 is deemed to be a public Act and "to be judicially noticed as such unless the contrary is expressly provided by the Act": Interpretation Act 1978, s.3 and Sched. 2, para. 2. For the definition of "judicial notice" see above p. 30, n.9.

[28] *Maxwell on Interpretation of Statutes* (12th ed., 1969) pp. 262–3. See, *e.g. Allen* v. *Gulf Oil Refining Ltd.* [1981] A.C. 1001, H.L.

[29] By the end of 1980 in metropolitan counties and by the end of 1984 elsewhere (1972 Act, s.262(9) as amended by S.I. 1979 No. 969).

[30] C.A. Cross, *Encyclopedia of Local Government Law*, paras. 1–30 to 1–35; D. Foulkes [1976] P.L. 272; E.D. Graham (1979) XLVII *The Table* 109.

[31] P. Norton, *The Commons in Perspective* (1981) p. 104. In 1976 problems were caused for the government when the Speaker ruled that the Aircraft and Shipbuilding Industries Bill, which had completed its Committee stage, was *prima facie* hybrid: I. Burton and G. Drewry, (1978) 31 *Parliamentary Affairs* pp. 151–6.

[32] On Private Members' Bills see P.G. Richards in S.A. Walkland (ed.) *The House of Commons in the Twentieth Century* (1979) Chap. VI; P. Norton, *The Commons in Perspective* (1981) pp. 99–102; P.G. Richards, *Parliament and Conscience* (1970); J. Gray [1978] P.L. 242 (case study of the Unsolicited Goods and Services Acts 1971 and 1975).

[33] The number per session is generally between 45 and 80; in the average session fewer than 20 will be of major political importance, the rest amending earlier legislation to take account of administrative difficulties, revising "technical law" or consolidating earlier measures: T.C. Hartley and J.A.G. Griffith, *Government and Law* (2nd ed., 1981) p. 210.

introduce a Bill,[34] but such Bills rarely proceed because of lack of time.[35] Some important measures have commenced life as Private Members' Bills, including the Public Bodies (Admission to Meetings) Act 1960 (sponsored by Margaret Thatcher M.P.), the Abortion Act 1967 (David Steel M.P.) and the Indecent Displays (Control) Act 1981 (Timothy Sainsbury M.P.). Governments tend to prefer to leave matters of conscience to Private Members' legislation: the risks generally outweigh any possible political advantages. The special features of "private Acts" mentioned above do not apply to those "public general statutes" that happen to start their life as Private Members' Bills.

4. CONSOLIDATION ACTS AND STATUTE LAW REVISION ACTS[36]

On occasion, the law in a particular area is *codified*; the relevant rules as derived from both case-law and existing statutory provisions are set out afresh in one statute. The leading examples are the Bills of Exchange Act 1882, the Sale of Goods Act 1893 (now the Sale of Goods Act 1979) and the Theft Act 1968. The Law Commission's objects include that of the codification of areas of English law, but it has found that this kind of work can pose great problems and can require the allocation of resources on a scale which is at present impossible.[37]

The *consolidation* of statutory provisions on a particular topic is a process that is more modest in aim, and much more commonly achieved.[38] Here, the relevant provisions are re-enacted in one or more consolidating statutes. There are four kinds of consolidation Bill. First, there are straight consolidation Bills that simply re-enact the existing texts. Second, Bills presented under the Consolidation of Enactments (Procedure) Act 1949 may include "corrections and minor improvements,"[39] which must be approved by a Joint Committee of both Houses on Consolidation Bills. Third, improvements designed to facilitate the satisfactory consolidation, but beyond the scope of the 1949 Act may be proposed by the Law

---

[34] (1) After Question Time, on notice given, or (2) under the "ten minute rule" which allows time for brief speeches for and against a Bill.

[35] For example, in 1977–78 there were 20 Bills introduced through the ballot procedure (6 enacted) 80 by other Commons procedures (2 enacted) and 8 Private Peers' Bills (3 enacted). In the same session only two government Bills failed, both consolidation measures enacted the following session: I. Burton and G. Drewry, (1980) 33 *Parliamentary Affairs* 173, 196. The statistics for the 1960–80 period are given in [1981] P.L. 273.

[36] See Lord Simon of Glaisdale and J.V.D. Webb, [1975] P.L. 285; I. Burton and G. Drewry, *Legislation and Public Policy* (1981) pp.205–213. On the interpretation of consolidation legislation see below, pp. 259–260.

[37] Law Commissions Act 1965, s.3(1); Law Commission's 13th Annual Report 1977–78 (Law Com.92) para. 2.34 (codification of the law of landlord and tenant); *cf.* 15th Annual Report 1979–80 (Law Com. 107) para. 1.4 (codification of general principles of liability in criminal law). See above, p. 19.

[38] *Report of a Committee appointed by the Lord President of the Council on the Preparation of Legislation* (The Renton Report: Cmnd. 6053, 1975) pp. 17–18 and Chap. XIV; F.A.R. Bennion, *Statute Law* (2nd ed., 1983) Chap. 7.

[39] *i.e.* "amendments of which the effect is confined to resolving ambiguities, removing doubts, bringing obsolete provisions into conformity with modern practice, or removing unnecessary provisions or anomalies which are not of substantial importance, and amendments designed to facilitate improvements in the form or manner in which the law is stated . . . .": 1949 Act, s.2.

Commission; these are also considered by the Joint Committee.[40] Fourth, consolidation with substantial amendments may be prepared by an *ad hoc* expert committee, or as an ordinary departmental Bill.[41] Where the consolidation process requires some amendments of substance these may be included in an ordinary Bill (normally in a Schedule); once these "pre-consolidation amendments" have been passed one of the first three kinds of consolidation measure can be brought forward.[42]

Various Statute Law Revision Acts have been passed at intervals from 1856 for the repeal of statutory provisions that are "obsolete, spent, unnecessary or superseded." Since 1969 the Law Commissions have prepared Statute Law (Repeals) Bills for the repeal of enactments that in their opinion are "no longer of practical utility." These are wider in scope. One was passed each year between 1973 and 1978 (inclusive) and a further one in 1981. Statute Law Revision Acts are no longer promoted except in relation to Northern Ireland legislation. Both kinds of Bills are considered by the Joint Committee, and make an important contribution to the tidying up of the statute book.

The main advantage of the kinds of measures considered in this section, other than Bills for consolidation with substantial amendments, is that the Parliamentary stages, apart from consideration by the Joint Committee, are taken without debate on matters of substance.

5. PROVISIONAL ORDERS AND SPECIAL PROCEDURE ORDERS[43]

In the nineteenth century, the Provisional Order procedure was introduced as a short cut to local legislation. Many statutes provided that a Minister could make a Provisional Order granting certain powers to a local authority or statutory body, following the completion of certain prescribed formalities. Where there were objections there would normally be a local inquiry. One or more such Orders would then be placed before Parliament to be ratified by a Confirmation Act. Petitions against a Confirmation Bill could be submitted and they would be dealt with in the same manner as objections to a private Bill.[44] There are still some examples of Provisional Order powers on the statute book,[45] but the device has largely been superseded by the use of Orders subject to "special parliamentary procedure" under the Statutory Orders (Special Procedure) Act 1945.[46]

---

[40] The Law Commission report will also cover any necessary "corrections and minor improvements." Law Commission consolidations are separate from their general law reform proposals. The Commission has noted that many of its recent reports have not been implemented for lack of Parliamentary and departmental time: 15th Annual Report, 1979–80 (Law Com. No. 107, 1980–81 H.C. 161), pp. 5–8.

[41] For an example of the former see the *Report of the Committee on Consolidation of Highway Law* (Cmnd. 630) which led to the Highways Act 1959; (the Highways Act 1980 followed the Law Commission procedure.) For an example of the latter, see the Local Government Act 1972.

[42] See, *e.g.* the Limitation Amendment Act 1980 and the subsequent consolidation measure, the Limitation Act 1980, and the Mental Health (Amendment) Act 1982 and the Mental Health Act 1983.

[43] C.K. Allen, *Law and Orders* (3rd ed., 1965) pp. 76–81.

[44] See below, pp. 198–200.

[45] See, *e.g.* Local Government Act 1972, ss.240, 254(8), 262(10).

[46] See S.I. 1949 No. 2393; S.I. 1962 Nos. 409 and 2791.

This procedure also involves an opportunity for objections to be the subject of a local inquiry and for petitions either against an Order generally or for amendment to be submitted to Parliament. However, an Order against which no petitions are received comes into effect without a Confirmation Act; an Act is only required when a joint committee of both Houses amends the Order in a way unacceptable to the Minister or reports against the Order as a whole.

6. GENERAL SYNOD MEASURES

The General Synod of the Church of England may pass legislative proposals ("Measures") concerning the Church. These are then laid before Parliament. A Measure approved by each House is then submitted for royal assent, and when this is signified the Measure has the force and effect of an Act of Parliament.[47]

7. DRAFTING

The process by which proposals for legislation are converted into a form suitable for enactment is complex.[48] A government Bill originates from the relevant ministry or department, although the ideas may be put forward from many sources including party election manifestos, civil servants, reports of official committees and outside interest groups, whether established to defend some sectional interest or promote some cause. Occasionally, a pre-legislative Select Committee may be appointed by one or both of the Houses to examine a subject with a view to legislation. These are, however, uncommon and not particularly successful.[49] There is normally a considerable measure of consultation. The government may issue a "Green Paper"[50] which sets out tentative proposals, and may suggest alternatives.

Once the Future Legislation Committee of the Cabinet has approved proposals in principle,[51] and provisionally allotted a place in the legislative programme, "Instructions" to draft are prepared by the departmental lawyers[52] and sent to the Parliamentary draftsmen: the "Parliamentary Counsel to the Treasury." The Parliamentary Counsel's office was established in 1869; there are at present 19 counsel, with chambers in

---

[47] Church of England Assembly (Powers) Act 1919; Synodical Government Measure 1969. See *Halsbury's Laws of England* (4th ed.) Vol. 14, paras. 399–411.

[48] See S.A. Walkland, *The Legislative Process in Great Britain* (1968); M. Zander, *The Law Making Process* (1980) pp. 1–18; D. Johnstone [1980] Stat.L.R. 67 and *A Tax Shall Be Charged* (H.M.S.O., 1975) (preparation of VAT legislation); Miers and Page (1982) Chaps. 2–4; E.A. Dreidger, *The Composition of Legislation* (2nd ed., 1976); G.C. Thornton, *Legislative Drafting* (2nd ed., 1979).

[49] See P. Norton, *The Commons in Perspective* (1981) p. 85; *First Report of the Select Committee on Procedure*, 1977–78 H.C. 588 Vol. 1, p.xiii; Miers and Page (1982) pp. 72–77.

[50] On white paper with green covers.

[51] This work may be done by the Legislation Committee (see below, p. 195) rather than by a separate Future Legislation Committee: Sir Harold Wilson, *The Governance of Britain* (1976) p. 129n.

[52] Instructions for legislation concerning the Inland Revenue are drafted by an Assistant Secretary.

Whitehall.[53] Parliamentary counsel are either barristers or solicitors. They normally work in pairs, each Bill being allocated to one of the Senior Counsel working with a Junior Counsel. As well as the drafts of a Bill, the counsel prepare government amendments and relevant motions, give advice on Parliamentary procedure, and attend conferences with ministers as well as sittings of both Houses and their committees. They may also assist with the drafting of Private Members' Bills supported by the government or otherwise likely to become law.[54] "The hours are unpredictable and the work arduous, but correspondingly rewarding."[55] A Bill may well go through a whole series of drafts before it is presented to Parliament, clauses being revised in the light of consultation between the draftsmen and the department. Other departments including the Treasury and outside groups may also be consulted at this stage. Firm proposals may be incorporated in a government "White Paper," and this may be debated in Parliament. The actual drafts of legislation are not, however, normally circulated outside the Whitehall machine before they have been presented to Parliament.

F.A.R. Bennion, formerly one of the Parliamentary counsel, has identified a number of "drafting parameters" which the draftsman must bear in mind, and which affect the form of Bills.[56] Some of these considerations relate to the process of enactment; others to the operation of the law once it has been enacted. The "preparational" parameters include compliance with the pre-Parliamentary and Parliamentary requirements as to the form of Bills and the stages through which they must pass (*procedural legitimacy*); strict conformity with the government's timetable for legislation and other time pressures such as those imposed by emergency legislation (*timeliness*); *comprehensibility* to members of Parliament; the need to structure a Bill in such a way that the main points of policy can be debated in a rational order (*debatability*)[57]; the choice of language that will minimise objections from those involved in the legislative process (*acceptability*)[58]; and *brevity*. The "operational parameters" include the need for the text of the Bill to carry out the government's intentions (*legal effectiveness*); the desirability that the text be open to one construction only (*certainty*)[59]; *comprehensibility* to the users of the statute, who will normally be practising lawyers (judge,

---

[53] Eight more work with the Law Commission. Some appointments are part-time. On drafting in the nineteenth century see F. Bowers, "Victorian Reforms in Legislative Drafting" (1980) 48 *Revue D'Histoire Du Droit* 329–348. The working of the office in the 1930s and 1940s is described in Sir Harold Kent, *In on the Act* (1979).

[54] Private Bills are generally drafted by Parliamentary Agents. Statutory instruments are drafted by lawyers in the relevant department or the office of the Treasury Solicitor, and only exceptionally by Parliamentary counsel. This "division of labour" in respect of the parent Act and its statutory instruments has been described as a "basic weakness in the system": Bennion (1983) p. 62. Scottish Bills are drafted by members of the Lord Advocate's Department: see Lord Mackay of Clashfern [1983] Stat.L.R. 68.

[55] Civil Service Commission, *Lawyers: Civil Service Careers* (1980) p. 27.

[56] *Statute Law* (2nd ed., 1983) Chap. 3. See also G. Engle, [1983] Stat.L.R. 7.

[57] The government may, however, wish a Bill to be drawn in such a way as to restrict opportunities for debate or amendment, for example by drawing the long title narrowly.

[58] "The red-blooded terms of political controversy are toned down. The prose style is flat." (Bennion (1983) p. 37).

[59] The government may, however, intend a provision to be ambiguous.

barrister or solicitor), public officials or non-legal professional advisers[60]; and *legal compatibility* with the rest of the statute book, so that inconsistent provisions are specifically repealed and that the same words mean the same thing even though they appear in different statutes.[61] These parameters frequently conflict. The most important are procedural legitimacy, timeliness and legal effectiveness, and these may well take priority over comprehensibility and legal compatibility. "The task of making legislative proposals understood by non-lawyer politicians while securing their legal effectiveness is one of the most formidable faced by the Parliamentary draftsmen."[62]

The report of the Renton Committee on the Preparation of Legislation[63] recognised that draftsmen had to work under pressures and constraints that made it very difficult to produce simple and clear legislation. Many statutes were well drafted, but there was cause for concern that difficulty was being encountered by statute-users. They had received complaints about the use of obscure and complex language, over-elaboration of detail in the quest for "certainty," the illogical structure of some statutes and problems created by the arrangement of the statute book in a chronological series of separate Acts. There was also criticism of the use of the "non-textual" method of amendment, whereby the amending Act set out the substance of the change proposed to be made without altering the text of the Act being amended. The Renton Committee endorsed the recent change in practice whereby statutes were amended "textually" by adding words to or deleting words from the original provision whenever convenience permitted.[64] The "non-textual" method eases the task of members of Parliament when examining an amending Bill, by enabling them to comprehend its meaning without having to "look beyond the four corners of the Bill."[65] Nevertheless, the Renton Committee thought that the needs of the user should be given priority over those of the legislator, particularly now that there was an official "loose-booklet" publication in which statutes are printed as amended (*Statutes in Force*). It seems that it is now settled practice to make the maximum possible use of textual amendment.[66]

The Renton Committee made a number of other proposals for reform. For example, all available methods should be used to recruit and train more draftsmen as a matter of high priority; the use of statements of principle should be encouraged, with additional guidance given where necessary in Schedules; more use could be made of examples showing how a Bill is intended to work in particular situations; statements of purpose should be used where they are the most convenient method of clarifying the scope and effect of legislation; long un-paragraphed sentences should be avoided; a statute should be arranged to suit the convenience of its ultimate users; the typographical production should be improved, and

---

[60] Bennion (1983) pp. 111–112.

[61] "Contrary to most people's belief, however, there are no books of precedents in the Parliamentary Counsel's Office." (*ibid.* p. 42).

[62] *Ibid.* p. 36.

[63] Cmnd. 6053, 1975.

[64] *Ibid.* Chap. XIII; Statute Law Society, *Statute Law: the Key to Clarity* (1972) pp. 7–18 and *Renton and the Need for Reform* (1979) pp. 27–40.

[65] Lord Thring, *Practical Legislation* (2nd ed., 1902) p. 8 cited in Bennion (1983) p. 35.

[66] D. Johnstone [1980] Stat.L.R. 112.

there should be more consolidation. They rejected suggestions that there should be a "crash" programme of consolidation and that it should be on a "one Act, one subject basis."[67] Under the latter proposal, each subject would have a principal Act and future legislation on the subject would be effected by textual amendment to that Act. In 1978, Sir David Renton, in an address to the Statute Law Society entitled "Failure to implement the Renton Report",[68] noted that there had been a small increase in the number of draftsmen and increased momentum in the consolidation process, but that Parliament had continued to pass enormous quantities of legislation, with no diminution in the amount of detail and scarcely any use of statements of purpose. The government's response to the Report had been guarded.[69] The Lord President of the Council (Michael Foot) stated in 1977 that the government regarded the recommendations concerning drafting practice:

> "as a comprehensive and valuable summary of the best drafting practice, and they are being taken into account in the drafting of all current Government legislation. It is considered essential, however, that parliamentary draftsmen should retain discretion to apply the recommendations in accordance with the requirements of particular legislation."[70]

There is a recurrent debate on the issue whether there should be a move from the British style of "common-law" drafting to the "continental" or "civil law" method of drafting. The latter is said to be more lucid and succinct, with more emphasis on basic principles and purposes and less on detail. Proponents of such a move include Sir William Dale[71] and J.A. Clarence Smith[72]; opponents include F.A.R. Bennion[73] and Geoffrey Kolts.[74] It is claimed that civilian texts are shorter, better arranged and more easily understood by laymen; common law drafting may by contrast be "a writhing torrent of convoluted indigestion."[75] Others have argued that "civilian" texts produce a considerable degree of uncertainty, which then has to be resolved by the judges; in effect legislative power is delegated to non-elected judges and officials. "Civilian" texts can be as lengthy and complex as British statutes, and can be badly drafted.[76] Of course, the ability of each side to point to examples where the other's preferred method has gone astray proves little; generalisations as to virtues and vices are easy to make but difficult to support. It is, however, unlikely in the present climate of opinion that many English judges would wish to deal with legislative provisions that were significantly more open-textured

---

[67] Renton Report, Chap. XIV.

[68] Statute Law Society, *Renton and the Need for Reform* (1979) pp. 2–8.

[69] *Ibid.* pp. 97–98.

[70] H.C. Deb. Vol. 941, col. 329 written answer, December 15, 1977.

[71] *Legislative Drafting: A New Approach* (1977); (1981) 30 I.C.L.Q. 141.

[72] Proceedings of the Ninth International Symposium on Comparative Law (1972) pp. 155–178; [1980] Stat.L.R. 14.

[73] *Statute Law* (1983) pp. 25–28; [1980] Stat.L.R. 61.

[74] Second Parliamentary Counsel, Canberra, Australia, [1980] Stat.L.R. 144.

[75] J.A.C. Smith, *op. cit.* note 72, at pp. 158–9.

[76] See, *e.g.* the criticisms of a proposed directive of the European Commission on commercial agents expressed by the Law Commission in 1977 (Law Com. No. 84). The text was described as badly drafted, unclear, ambiguous and internally inconsistent.

than at present, and equally unlikely that they would be regarded by many in the community as well suited to undertake that role.[77]

8. PARLIAMENTARY PROCEDURE[78]

(a) Public Bills

The legislative timetable of Parliament is managed by the government. Detailed government Bills are examined and placed in the timetable by the Cabinet's Legislation Committee, and may be considered by the full Cabinet or the appropriate policy committee. A Bill may generally be introduced in either the House of Commons or the House of Lords, although money Bills must be introduced in the Commons, and politically controversial Bills are normally introduced there.

A government Bill introduced in the Commons is presented by a minister. It receives a formal *first reading*, when only the title is actually read out, and is ordered to be printed. A day is fixed for the *second reading*. A Bill as printed is accompanied by an "Explanatory Memorandum" which explains in non-technical language the content and object of the Bill. If expenditure is involved a "Financial Memorandum" is also attached. At the second reading stage the principles of the Bill are debated on the floor of the House.[79] If the Bill entails public expenditure or taxation this must be authorised by a *financial resolution* moved by a minister.[80] After receiving a second reading[81] the Bill proceeds to the *committee stage*, either at a Standing Committee of between 15 and 60 M.P.s that reflects the party composition of the House, or in Committee of the Whole House. The latter step is taken for Bills that are either straightforward or urgent, or, at the other extreme, politically contentious or of major constitutional significance. The committee examines the Bill clause by clause, first considering amendments and then the motion that the clause, as amended, "stand part of the Bill." Amendments may be proposed by the minister in charge, backbenchers or the opposition; those to be taken are selected by the chairman. Proposed new clauses are then taken, followed by the Schedules, proposed new Schedules, the preamble (if any) and the long title.[82] A recent innovation has been to send some Bills to a "Special Standing Committee" with the power to question

[77] See above, pp. 175–183.

[78] S.A. de Smith, *Constitutional and Administrative Law* (4th ed., 1981) pp. 274–284; S.A. Walkland (ed.) *The House of Commons in the Twentieth Century* (1979) Chap. V; P. Norton, *The Commons in Perspective* (1981) Chap. 5; I. Burton and G. Drewry, *Legislation and Public Policy* (1981); *Second Report from the Select Committee on Procedure*, 1970–71 H.C. 538; *First Report from the Select Committee on Procedure*, 1977–78 H.C. 588; G. Drewry (1972) 35 M.L.R. 289 and (1979) 42 M.L.R. 80.

[79] Non-controversial Bills may be referred to a Second Reading Committee of between 16 and 50 M.P.s and Scottish Bills to the Scottish Grand Committee (members for Scottish constituencies plus between 10 and 15 others). Subsequent stages may also be taken by standing committees.

[80] In the case of some Bills, such as Finance Bills, Ways and Means resolutions are passed before the Bill is introduced. Private Members' Bills rarely include provisions involving public expenditure.

[81] Only two government Bills have failed at second reading since 1905, although it is more than a mere formality and ministers do not always approach debates with closed minds: Norton (1981) p. 86–87.

[82] See below, pp. 200–202.

witnesses and request the submission of evidence.[83] Next, the House considers the Bill again at the *report stage*.[84] Any aspect of the Bill can be raised and new clauses and further amendments can be proposed. Debate is, however, confined to the contents of the Bill. Normally, the *third reading* immediately follows the conclusion of the report stage. There is no debate unless six members table a motion in advance, and only minor verbal amendments can be made; if material amendments are necessary the Bill has to be considered again in committee.

The Bill then proceeds to the House of Lords where the stages are repeated, with some minor procedural differences. Any amendment proposed may be moved; there is no selection. The committee stage, if not dispensed with, is normally taken by a Committee of the Whole House, although a Public Bills Committee is sometimes used. If amendments are made, the Bill is returned to the Commons for them to be agreed. The Commons respond with a message to the Lords which either signifies their agreement, gives reasons for disagreement or proposes other amendments. Further messages may be exchanged until either final agreement is reached, the Bill lapses at the end of a session or the Commons resorts to the Parliament Acts procedure.[85]

A Bill passed in its entirety by both Houses is presented for the *royal assent*.[85a] The monarch is expected by convention to give that assent; the last occasion on which it was refused was in 1707 when Queen Anne refused her assent to a Militia Bill. Assent may be signified (1) by the monarch in person (this was last done in 1854); (2) by Lords Commissioners in the presence of both Houses[86]; or (3) as is normally the case today, by separate notification to each House in accordance with the Royal Assent Act 1967. The third method, unlike the others, does not involve the interruption of proceedings in the Commons. The second method is only used where royal assent coincides with prorogation.

The Parliament Acts 1911–1949 lay down special procedures whereby a Bill may be presented for royal assent when it has been passed only by the Commons.[87] A money Bill may be so presented where the Lords have failed to pass it without amendment after it has been before them for one month; a non-money Bill may be presented where it has been passed by the Commons in two consecutive sessions and the Lords have failed to pass it

---

[83] *First Report from the Select Committee on Procedure*, 1977–78 H.C. 588, pp. xviii–xix; H.C. Deb. Vol. 991, cols. 716–834, October 30, 1980; proceedings in the 1980–81 session on the Criminal Attempts Bill, the Education Bill and the Deep Sea Mining (Temporary Provisions) Bill. See H.J. Beynon [1982] P.L. 193. The procedure was also used for the Mental Health (Amendment) Bill 1982.

[84] There is no report stage if a public Bill considered in Committee of the Whole House is unamended.

[85] See below.

[85a] See F.A.R. Bennion [1981] Stat. L.R. 133.

[86] Under the Royal Assent by Commission Act 1541; this was originally part of the Bill of Attainder against Catherine Howard, which did not receive the King's assent in person to spare his hearing once more the "wicked facts of the case." The Bill actually received the assent on February 11, 1542. The Reading Clerk reads out the title of the Bill; the Commissioners raise their hats; and the Clerk of the Parliaments pronounces "La Reyne le Veult." In the case of money Bills the expression is "La Reyne remercie ses bons sujets, accepte leur benevolence, et ainsi le veult"; for personal private Acts, "Soit fait comme il est désiré." If assent were refused the expression would be "La Reyne s'avisera."

[87] S.A. de Smith, *Constitutional and Administrative Law* (4th ed., 1981) pp. 306–310.

in each of those sessions; one year has elapsed between the Commons second reading in the first session and third reading in the second session; the Bill has been sent to the Lords at least one month before the end of each session and the Speaker certifies that the requirements of the Parliament Acts have been complied with. The certificate is conclusive for all purposes and may not be questioned in a court of law. These procedures may not be employed in respect of Bills to prolong the maximum duration of a Parliament beyond five years, to Provisional Order Confirmation Bills or private Bills. Objections by the House of Lords are normally dropped without the necessity of recourse to the Parliament Acts; the procedure has only been used three times.[88]

For the draftsman, the first publication of the Bill after first reading is an important deadline as changes thereafter have to be made by formal amendments. Indeed most of the amendments that are made are government amendments, and these tend to reflect second thoughts by the civil servants rather than the persuasive arguments of members. Amendments of substance proposed by backbenchers or opposition and actually agreed are few in number, and are more likely to be accepted in the Lords.[89] More amendments than usual were carried against the government during the passage of the Scotland and Wales Bills in 1977/78. These were controversial constitutional measures, and the Labour government was then in a minority in the Commons.[90] "Parliament's exposure of the successive Bills' inherent defects and illogicalities was impressive."[91] However, "the debates were poorly attended and the debating was done by a few stalwarts, with most M.P.s (though a smaller proportion than usual) content to live up to their image as lobby fodder."

The pressure on the Parliamentary timetable is such that where legislation is particularly contentious governments may secure the placing of limits on the time available for debate (timetable or "guillotine" motions); this may mean that, as in the case of the Scotland and Wales Bills, important clauses are not scrutinised by the Commons, although they will normally be considered by the Lords. The House of Commons Select Committee on Procedure reported in 1978 that:

"the balance of advantage between Parliament and Government in the day to day working of the Constitution is now weighted in favour of the Government to a degree which arouses widespread anxiety and is inimical to the proper working of our parliamentary democracy."[92]

The apparent limitations on the effectiveness of Parliamentary scrutiny have led to suggestions for the scrutiny of legislation by other bodies,

---

[88] Welsh Church Act 1914 (disestablishment); Government of Ireland Act 1914 (Home Rule: the Act was not implemented); Parliament Act 1949.

[89] See J.A.G. Griffith, *Parliamentary Scrutiny of Government Bills* (1974); P. Norton, (1976) 57 *The Parliamentarian* 17.

[90] I. Burton and G. Drewry, "Public Legislation: A Survey of the Sessions 1977/8 and 1978/9" (1980) 33 *Parliamentary Affairs* 173, 174–186. These sessions provided "significant evidence for the power that still belongs to backbenchers in the House of Commons," although "only in a minority Parliament may the fate of Government Bills be in serious doubt. Even then, most legislation, being inevitable whatever the Government in power, is secure, protected by the close rapport between the two front benches" (p. 199).

[91] *Ibid.* p. 186.

[92] First Report, 1977–78 H.C. 588, Vol. 1, p. viii.

particularly from the technical standpoint. Sir William Dale has proposed[93] the establishment of a "Law Council" to advise the government on draft Bills. "Its duty would be to examine them from the point of view of coherent and orderly presentation, clarity, conciseness, soundness of legal principle, and suitability for attaining the Government's objective," a function performed in France by the Conseil d'Etat. It would not concern itself with matters of policy, and its advice could be rejected by the government. Its membership would include judges, lawyers (practising and academic) and laymen. The Renton Committee, however, rejected proposals for formal machinery for the scrutiny of the drafting of Bills, either before or after their formal introduction in Parliament.[94] Before introduction, it was for government departments to decide what advice they should obtain as to the drafting of their Bills; after introduction, a new scrutiny stage would "impose undue strain on a Parliamentary machine which is already under great pressure, and . . . add to the labour of the draftsmen who have more than enough to do as it is to keep pace with the legislative programme." They did recommend new Parliamentary procedures (1) for incorporating improvements (including the correction of obvious inaccuracies) certified by the Speaker and the Lord Chancellor to be of a drafting nature, after the passage of a Bill by both houses and before royal assent[95]; and (2) for the re-enactment of statutes, in whole or in part, with drafting improvements.[96] In addition they suggested that the Statute Law Committee[97] should keep the structure and language of statutes under continuous review, monitor the implementation of the Renton Committee's recommendations and publish reports. None of these proposals has been accepted, the third being rejected by the Cabinet apparently on the grounds that the Committee was not an "appropriate body" to discharge these functions and that the proposal to keep the statute book under continuous review was not "likely to lead to any worthwhile improvements in the drafting of legislation."[98]

(b) Private Bills[99]

Standing Orders of each House lay down a complicated series of procedural requirements that must be observed before a private Bill is

[93] *Legislative Drafting: A New Approach* (1977), pp. 336–337.

[94] Cmnd. 6053, pp. 129–133.

[95] This was endorsed in principle by the House of Commons Select Committee on Procedure, 1977–78 H.C. 588, Vol. 1, p. xxvii. A proposed procedure for the correction of errors *after* royal assent did not find favour with the House of Lords (Acts of Parliament (Correction of Mistakes) Bill [Lords], session 1976–77, withdrawn) and was not supported by the Select Committee (*ibid.*). See A. Samuels, "Errors in Bills and Acts" [1982] Stat.L.R. 94.

[96] This would be modelled on the present procedure for consolidation Bills.

[97] A committee appointed by the Lord Chancellor and first established in 1868. Its membership includes M.P.s, draftsmen, judges, Permanent Secretaries, the Treasury Solicitor and the Chairmen of the Law Commissions. It meets once a year and supervises the Statutory Publications Office, the form of Acts and the production of *Statutes in Force*. Most of its functions in the field of consolidation and statute law revision passed to the Law Commissions in 1965.

[98] *Renton and the Need for Reform*, pp. 7–8; H.L. Deb. col. 776., March 7, 1978. The Select Committee supported the third proposal, and urged the government to reconsider its attitude: 1977–78 H.C. 588 Vol. 1, pp.xxvii–xxviii.

[99] See The Study of Parliament Group, "Private Bill Procedure; A Case for Reform" [1981] P.L. 206.

introduced, including the giving of public notice. Petitions for private Bills must normally be deposited by November 27 each session.[1] A local authority that wishes to promote a Bill must resolve to do so by a majority of the whole number of council members at a meeting of which 30 days' notice has been given in the local press; a second meeting must confirm the decision after the deposit of the Bill in Parliament.[2] The promoters must prove to the two "examiners," one appointed by each of the Houses, that the formalities have been observed, and this may be challenged by opponents of the Bill.

Private Bills normally proceed first in the House of Lords. The first reading is a formality; the second reading is normally so, but may be opposed. A Bill that passes the second reading is regarded as having received the conditional approval of the House. If the Bill passes the second reading opposed clauses are then referred to a Select Committee of five Lords. The House may agree to an Instruction to the Committee to the effect that the Committee should have regard to or be satisfied of certain matters before passing a particular provision. Procedure here is largely modelled on judicial proceedings: the case for and against the clause is put by counsel for the promoters and for the objectors; witnesses may be called and examined on oath; government departments may make representations and previous decisions of the Committee may be cited. Unopposed clauses are normally considered by the "Committee on Unopposed Bills," an informal meeting conducted by the Lord Chairman of Committees or his Counsel. The promoters, usually represented here by a Parliamentary Agent rather than counsel, must prove a need for the clauses. Unopposed clauses in local Bills promoted as a consequence of the Local Government Act 1972[3] have been referred instead to more formal Select Committees. These have applied the principles (1) that the promoters have to prove a current need in their area that can only be met by legislation; (2) that the legislation will deal effectively with the problem; and (3) that provisions to meet a need common to all or a great number of authorities should not be included in a private Bill where the government has given a firm undertaking to introduce general legislation to meet that need.[4] Model clauses have been prepared.[5] The House of Lords Select Committee on Practice and Procedure[6] has recommended *inter alia* that further Local Government (Miscellaneous Provisions) Bills should be introduced as public legislation to cover matters currently being included in local Acts, and that consideration should be given to the possibility of making such Bills subject to a special procedure for non-controversial Bills. After the committee stage, the report stage is usually a formality although the Bill may be amended. The Bill is given a third reading and sent to the other

---

[1] Personal Bills can be deposited at any time, are customarily presented first to the House of Lords and are considered by the Personal Bills Committee of the Lords before first reading. The other stages are similar to those for other private Bills.

[2] Local Government Act 1972, s.239. A Bill may not be promoted to change a local government area, its status or electoral arrangements: *ibid.* s.70.

[3] See above, p. 188.

[4] See C.A. Cross, *Encyclopedia of Local Government Law*, para. 1–31.

[5] *Ibid.* para. 1–32.

[6] First Report, 1977–78 H.L. 155.

House where the various stages are repeated, with some differences in detail.[7]

These procedures have been described as "cumbersome and expensive"; proceedings of private Bill committees "can be casual and their decisions unpredictable" and opposed Bill committees "tend to be legalistic and time-consuming."[8] Generally, private members take little interest in private legislation; when they do take an interest, however, their influence may be greater than in relation to public legislation as the whips are rarely applied and normally the government simply offers advice.[9]

9. ARRANGEMENT OF ACTS OF PARLIAMENT[10]

The elements of a public general statute are normally arranged in the following order.

(a) Short title

This is the title by which the statute is generally known (*e.g.* the "Interpretation Act 1978"). The practice of including a section providing for the citation of an Act by a short title developed in the nineteenth century; the Short Titles Act 1896[11] conferred short titles on many statutes passed before this practice became established.

(b) Year and chapter number

A statute passed today is cited by reference either to its short title or to the calendar year in which it is passed and its "chapter number" within that year. Statutes are numbered in the order in which royal assent is given. Until 1963[12] statutes were regarded as chapters of the legislation passed in the relevant *session* rather than *calendar year*, and were numbered accordingly. Thus the Interpretation Act 1889 can be cited as "52 & 53 Vict. c.63" (chapter 63 of the session that fell in the fifty-second and fifth-third years of the reign of Queen Victoria) and its replacement, the Interpretation Act 1978 as "1978 c.30" (Chapter 30 of 1978).

(c) Long title

This describes the scope of the Act; if a Bill is amended so as to go beyond the long title as printed in the Bill the long title must be amended as well.

(d) Date

The date, given in square brackets, is that on which royal assent was signified.

---

[7] There are, for example, separate committees for opposed and unopposed *Bills* rather than *clauses*.

[8] The Study of Parliament Group [1981] P.L. 206, 221. For reform proposals see *ibid.* pp. 218–227.

[9] P. Norton, (1977) 30 *Parliamentary Affairs* 356.

[10] See Bennion, *Statute Law* (1983) Chap. 4.

[11] Replacing the Short Titles Act 1892. See also the Statute Law Revision Act 1948, Sched. 2.

[12] The practice was changed by the Acts of Parliament Numbering and Citation Act 1962.

(e) Preamble

Public Acts formerly[13] included a preamble, which could be lengthy, explaining why the Act was passed. They are still necessary for private Acts, and begin with the word "Whereas." For example the Parliament Act 1911 includes the following:

> "Whereas it is expedient that provision should be made for regulating the relations between the two Houses of Parliament:
>
> And whereas it is intended to substitute for the House of Lords as it at present exists a Second Chamber constituted on a popular instead of hereditary basis, but such substitution cannot be immediately brought into operation:
>
> And whereas provision will require hereafter to be made by Parliament in a measure effecting such substitution for limiting and defining the powers of the new Second Chamber, but it is expedient to make such provision as in this Act appears for restricting the existing powers of the House of Lords:"

(f) Enacting formula

This normally runs:

> "Be it enacted by the Queen's most Excellent Majesty, by and with the advice and consent of the Lords Spiritual and Temporal, and Commons, in this present Parliament assembled, and by the authority of the same, as follows:—"

The formula is slightly different for money Bills and Bills passed under the Parliament Acts procedures.

(g) Sections and Schedules

The body of an Act is divided into *sections* (equivalent to the *clauses* of the Bill) and *subsections*, a practice introduced by Lord Brougham's Act of 1850.[14] Each section is printed with a *marginal note* indicating its content. Occasionally, errors may creep in. For example in the Married Women (Maintenance in Case of Desertion) Act 1886, a subsection (section 1(2)), which provided that a wife who had committed adultery could not claim alimony where her husband had deserted her, was printed with the marginal note "custody of children." A long Act may be divided into *Parts*. Sections dealing with related subject matter may be grouped under *headings*. Matters of detail are commonly included in *Schedules* at the end of the Act. Each schedule is linked to one of the preceding sections and may be divided into *Parts*, *paragraphs* and *sub-paragraphs*. There may also be *marginal notes* and *cross-headings*. A *Schedule* may be used to set out the provisions of an earlier Act as amended.[15]

---

[13] Preambles are occasionally found in modern public Acts, particularly those which implement international conventions (*e.g.* the Oil in Navigable Waters Act 1963), public Acts of a local nature (*e.g.* the Towyn Trewan Common Act 1963) or legislation of a formal or ceremonial character (*e.g.* the John F. Kennedy Memorial Act 1964). Another example is the Canada Act 1982.

[14] Interpretation of Acts Act 1850, 13 & 14 Vict. c.21, s.2.

[15] Known as a "Keeling schedule." Examples include the Cinematograph Films Act 1948, Sched. 2; *cf.* Education Act 1980, Sched. 5.

The body of the Act may include the following kinds of provision: "definitions, principal provisions, administrative provisions, miscellaneous clauses, penal clauses, clauses dealing with the making of rules or byelaws, saving clauses, temporary and transitory clauses, repeals and savings, date of coming into operation (if specified)" and the duration of the Act if it is limited.[16] "Common-form" clauses, those dealing with geographical extent, commencement, short title, citation and interpretation, are normally found at the end of the statute.

(h) Extent

There is a presumption that an Act applies throughout the United Kingdom[17] and not beyond.[18] "Extent clauses" are used to negative that presumption.[19] Acts which apply only to Scotland or Northern Ireland usually include the country in brackets in the short title.[20] Statutes may expressly be made to apply to transactions abroad. For example, the English courts may exercise jurisdiction in respect of murders committed by British subjects abroad[21] and some Acts extend to the territorial waters adjacent to the United Kingdom.[22]

(i) Commencement

Until 1793 each Act of Parliament was deemed to come into operation from the first day of the session in which it was passed, unless a commencement date was specified. The element of retrospectivity was seen to be unjust and the rule was changed[23]; an Act now comes into effect at the beginning of the day on which royal assent is given unless some other commencement date is specified.[24] Today, it is commonly provided that the Act shall come into effect on a specified date, or on a day to be appointed, and, in the latter event, that different days may be appointed for different provisions, different purposes or different areas. The advantages of delayed commencement are that it gives those affected time to prepare, and gives ministers and departments time to draw up the necessary regulations and orders after due consultation with interested parties. The main disadvantage is that it may be difficult for users to

---

[16] Statute Law Society, *Statute Law Deficiencies* (1972) p.6. (based on Sir Alison Russell's analysis of the general frame of a Bill.).

[17] *i.e.* England, Scotland, Wales and Northern Ireland but not the Channel Islands or the Isle of Man.

[18] See *R.* v. *Jameson* [1896] 2 Q.B. 425, 430; *Draper & Son Ltd.* v. *Edward Turner & Son Ltd.* [1965] 1 Q.B. 424; *Air-India* v. *Wiggins* [1980] 1 W.L.R. 815.

[19] Extent clauses normally indicate expressly that an Act applies to Northern Ireland even though this is not strictly necessary.

[20] The Renton Committee recommended that where an Act affects only England and Wales this too should be indicated in the short title: Cmnd. 6053, p.124. This has not been implemented.

[21] Offences against the Person Act 1861, s.9.

[22] *e.g.* Wireless Telegraphy Act 1949, ss. 1, 6; Marine, etc., Broadcasting (Offences) Act 1967, s.1; *Post Office* v. *Estuary Radio Ltd.* [1968] 2 Q.B. 740. See generally the Law Commission's *Report on the Territorial and Extraterritorial Extent of the Criminal Law* (Law Com. No. 91, 1978).

[23] Acts of Parliament (Commencement) Act 1793.

[24] Interpretation Act 1978, s.4.

establish whether a particular provision is in force.[25] There may be many commencement orders in respect of one statute,[26] and some provisions may never be implemented, for reasons such as a lack of resources[27] and governmental second thoughts about the desirability of particular provisions.[28] Complaints have been voiced about the present position and various improvements proposed.[29] Governments have been exhorted to refrain from promoting legislation unless its implementation within a reasonable time can be foreseen.

In 1982 the Management and Personnel Office (the successor to the Civil Service Department) issued new guidance on the commencement of legislation.[30] Acts which do not provide for a commencement date to be appointed by order should provide for commencement not less than two months after Royal Assent (three months for consolidation Acts). Commencement provisions should be grouped at the end of any Bill in which that is practicable, if appropriate in a separate clause or Schedule; alternatively, a full list of commencement provisions should be published with the Act or in a press notice. Commencement dates should be specified in the Act where possible and appropriate; otherwise, every effort should be made to minimise the number of commencement orders and to rationalise their issue and the dates of commencement.

In interpreting statutes there is a presumption that statutes do not operate retrospectively so as to affect an existing right or obligation, except as regards matters of procedure.[31] Parliament may, however, use words in a statute which clearly show an intention that it should so operate.[32]

(j) Definitions

Modern statutes commonly include "definition sections" in which the meaning of words and phrases found in the statute are explained, either comprehensively (X "means" ABC) or partially (X "includes" ABC). The qualification "unless the contrary intention appears" is usually added. The Interpretation Act 1978 gives definitions of a large number of words and expressions. These are applicable where the words are found "in any Act, unless the contrary intention appears."[33] For example, "Secretary of

---

[25] A useful table is printed in the Current Service Volume of *Halsbury's Laws of England* (4th ed.).

[26] See, *e.g.* the Consumer Credit Act 1974 and the Control of Pollution Act 1974.

[27] Examples include various provisions concerning legal advice and law centres (see below, p. 332).

[28] Examples include provisions of the Children and Young Persons Act 1969. See above p. 47, p. 48, n. 93 and p. 49, n. 97.

[29] A. Samuels, (1979) *The Magistrate* pp. 173–4; Statute Law Society Working Party on the Commencement of Acts of Parliament [1980] Stat.L.R. 40.

[30] (1982) 79 L.S.Gaz. 968.

[31] *Re Athlumney* [1898] 2 Q.B. 547, 551–2 *per* R.S. Wright J.; *Att.-Gen.* v. *Vernazza* [1960] A.C. 965. See below, pp. 267–268.

[32] *e.g.* the War Damage Act 1965, which reversed the decision of the House of Lords in *Burmah Oil Co.* v. *Lord Advocate* [1965] A.C. 75; the Northern Ireland Act 1972, which retrospectively removed limitations on the power of the Parliament of Northern Ireland to legislate for the armed forces: see S.H. Bailey, D.J. Harris and B. Jones, *Civil Liberties: Cases and Materials* (1980) p. 189.

[33] Interpretation Act 1978, s.5 and Sched. 1. They may also apply to subordinate legislation: see *ibid.* s.23.

State" means "one of Her Majesty's Principal Secretaries of State."[34] The 1978 Act also provides generally that:

"In any Act, unless the contrary intention appears—
    (a) words importing the masculine gender include the feminine;
    (b) words importing the feminine gender include the masculine;
    (c) words in the singular include the plural and words in the plural include the singular."[35]

There are also general provisions covering such matters as references to service by post, distance, time of day and the Sovereign, and the construction of subordinate legislation.[36]

(k) Amendments and repeals

Statutes commonly amend or repeal earlier enactments. Repeals are normally set out in a Schedule, although important changes may be included in the body of the Act. A power may be conferred to repeal or modify Acts of Parliament by statutory instrument. An earlier statute may also be amended or repealed by implication where the provisions of a later Act are so inconsistent that the two cannot stand together, although the courts seek to reconcile apparently inconsistent provisions where possible. At common law a repealed Act was treated as if it had never existed, except in relation to transactions past and closed, but this rule was changed in 1889.[37] For example, where an offence is committed against an existing statutory provision, criminal proceedings may now be instituted even after that provision is repealed, unless the repealing enactment provides otherwise.[38] There was also a common law rule that where statute A was repealed by statute B and statute B was subsequently repealed by statute C, statute A was regarded as reviving unless the contrary intention appeared. This rule was abolished in 1850: repealed statutes stay repealed unless expressly revived.[39] Unlike the Scots, the English have never had a

---

[34] Many statutory functions are entrusted to "the Secretary of State." This device enables these functions to be switched between departments without the need for the statute to be amended. Where amendment is necessary, as where a function is given to a particular minister, it is usually effected by a statutory instrument under the Ministers of the Crown (Transfer of Functions) Act 1946. The "Secretary of State" device makes it more difficult to discover where responsibility for a particular function commonly lies.

[35] Section 6. See, *e.g. Annicola Investments* v. *Minister of Housing and Local Government* [1968] 1 Q.B. 631, where the word "houses" was held to include a single house. Examples of cases where the "contrary intention" has appeared are those where the terms "every man" or "any person" have been held not to include women: *e.g. Chorlton* v. *Lings* (1868) L.R. 4 C.P. 374; *Bebb* v. *The Law Society* [1914] 1 Ch. 286, above, p. 99, n. 52.

[36] 1978 Act, ss.7–11.

[37] Interpretation Act 1889, s.38(2); see now the Interpretation Act 1978, s.16.

[38] See *Bennett* v. *Tatton* (1918) 88 L.J.K.B. 313; *Postlethwaite* v. *Katz* (1943) 59 T.L.R. 248; *R.* v. *West London Stipendiary Magistrate, ex p. Simeon* [1983] 1 A.C. 234 (repeal of the 'sus' law held not to affect a prosecution for an offence committed before the repeal came into effect).

[39] See now the Interpretation Act 1978, s.15. Similarly, the repeal of an Act does not revive anything not in force or existing at the time of the repeal: *ibid.* s.16(1)(*a*). Hence, if statute B modifies statute A by partial repeal or substitution of words, statute A continues in effect subject to the modification notwithstanding the repeal of statute B.

rule that a statute can be disregarded on the ground that it is obsolete[40]; such provisions have to be repealed by a subsequent statute.[41]

10. ENROLLMENT AND PUBLICATION

In medieval times a systematic official record of parliamentary statutes was not kept. An incomplete statute roll was started in the Chancery for internal purposes in 1299 and continued to the middle of the 15th century. *Rotuli Parliamentorum* ("Rolls of Parliament") were kept between 1290 and 1503; they contained a general record of parliamentary proceedings, but only included some of the Acts. From 1483 "Inrollments of Acts" (records of each Act "engrossed" on parchment) were certified by the Clerk of the Parliaments and delivered to the Chancery; the officers of the Chancery commonly termed them the "Parliament Rolls" although they are distinct from the *Rotuli Parliamentorum*. From the middle of the nineteenth century two copies of each Act have been printed on vellum; one copy is kept in the House of Lords, the other in the Public Records Office.[42]

Lawyers at first relied on private manuscript collections of statutes. These formed the basis of unofficial printed collections that began to appear from 1481 onwards. From 1483 *Sessional Volumes of Statutes* were printed and published; these came to be issued by the King's or Queen's Printer but were not technically an official series published by royal or parliamentary authority. Useful collections of *Statutes at Large* appeared in the late eighteenth century, with various editors (*e.g.* Pickering (1762), Ruffhead and Runnington (1786) and Tomlins and Raithby (1811)). These covered statutes from Magna Carta to date; continuation volumes, sometimes covering several sessions, and based on the King's Printer's copies, were produced in the eighteenth and nineteenth centuries under the titles of *Statutes of the United Kingdom* or *Public General Statutes*. The Controller of Her Majesty's Stationery Office was appointed as the Queen's Printer in 1886. From 1940 the King's or Queen's Printer's copies of statutes have been published on an annual rather than a sessional basis, with *Public General Acts and Measures*[43] issued separately from *Local and Personal Acts*; each Act is also published individually by H.M.S.O.

The first official collection of statutes was the edition of *Statutes of the Realm* prepared by the Record Commissioners and published in nine volumes between 1810 and 1828. This gave texts and translations of statutes between 1235 and 1713, excluding the Commonwealth period,[44] and while a considerable improvement on what was otherwise available,

---

[40] Under the doctrine of desuetude, Acts of the Scottish Parliament may become obsolete and repealed by a long period of contrary practice by the community: *M'Ara* v. *Magistrates of Edinburgh* 1931 S.C. 1059; *Brown* v. *Magistrates of Edinburgh* 1913 S.L.T. 456, 458; *Earl of Antrim's Petition* [1967] A.C. 691.

[41] See above, p. 190.

[42] See S.A. de Smith, *Constitutional and Administrative Law* (4th ed., 1981) p. 94. A third print is made of Measures of the General Synod.

[43] These also appear in the *Law Reports Statutes* series.

[44] As to which see C.H. Firth and R.S. Rait, *Acts and Ordinances of the Interregnum* (1911).

was in various respects incomplete and inaccurate.[45] Later in the century, the Statute Law Committee[46] supervised the publication of the first edition of *Statutes Revised*, which comprised the public Acts in force at the end of 1878, as amended, given in chronological order. Two further editions were produced between 1888 and 1929 and in 1950. This series has been superseded by *Statutes in Force*, which is published in loose booklet form rather than in bound volumes to facilitate the substitution of revised copies of statutes that are heavily amended; there are also regular supplements. The volumes are arranged in 131 groups according to subject-matter and are printed by computer-assisted typesetting. These official collections are supplemented by the *Index to the Statutes* and the *Chronological Table of the Statutes*.[47] As a matter of citation, references to another Act in a statute passed after 1889 are, unless the contrary intention appears, to be read as referring to (a) any revised edition of the statutes printed by authority, (b) if it is not printed there, to the *Statutes of the Realm*; or (c) in other cases, to the Queen's Printer's copy.[48] Occasionally it may be necessary to go behind the published version and check its authenticity against the original source.[49]

There are various departmental compilations of statutes and regulations published by H.M.S.O. and regularly revised, such as *The Taxes Act* (for the Inland Revenue) and several works on the law of social security (for the Department of Health and Social Security). The most important current commercial collections are *Halsbury's Statutes of England* (3rd ed.: a revised edition arranged by subject matter) and *Current Law Statutes Annotated* (arranged in chronological order). There are also many collections on particular topics published in loose-leaf encyclopedias. An important advantage of these commercial publications is that the statutes are given in annotated form. Statutes and statutory instruments are included in the *Lexis* and *Eurolex* computer databases.

11. VALIDITY

The validity of an Act of Parliament may not be questioned in an English court; there is no Bill of Rights or other constitutional limitation to which legislation must conform as there is, for example, in the United States of America.[50] This point has arisen in cases where it has been claimed that a private Act is invalid on the ground that parliamentary standing orders

[45] See T.F.T. Plucknett, *Statutes and their Interpretation in the Fourteenth Century* (1922) Chap. II.

[46] See above, p. 198.

[47] This covers public and general legislation; editions since 1974 have also recorded the effect of local and personal legislation enacted since then. A Chronological Table of the present effect of all local legislation enacted between 1925 and 1973 is due for publication in the near future: 18th Annual Report of the Law Commission, 1982–83 (1983–84 H.C. 266, pp. 31–33).

[48] Interpretation Act 1978, s.19.

[49] See, *e.g. R.* v. *Casement* [1917] 1 K.B. 98, 134, in relation to the Treason Act 1351, where the *Rotuli Parliamentorum* and the Statute Rolls were consulted.

[50] See above, pp. 186–187. The question of possible conflict with European legislation is considered below, pp. 224–230. As to whether a court may exercise a jurisdiction to determine whether an *ostensibly* authentic Act of Parliament is *in fact* authentic see S.A. de Smith, *Constitutional and Administrative Law* (4th ed., 1981) pp. 94–97.

have not been observed,[51] or that Parliament has been misled by fraudulent misrepresentations[52]: such claims have failed. In 1982, a taxpayer argued that the change in the status of M.P.s from self-employed meant that they had become employees of the Crown and so disqualified from membership. As a result, the Social Security Act 1975, which imposed on him certain obligations to pay national insurance contributions, was invalid. His argument was emphatically and summarily rejected by Nourse J.: "the court can only look at the Parliamentary roll."[53] Of much more importance was the claim of a group of Canadian Indian Chiefs that the Canada Act 1982 was *ultra vires* on the ground that the consent of the "Dominion" of Canada had not been obtained as required by section 4 of the Statute of Westminster 1931, merely the consent of the Senate and House of Commons of Canada. Sir Robert Megarry V.-C. held[54] that he owed "full and dutiful obedience" to every Act of Parliament, and that the Canada Act 1982 was such an Act. The Court of Appeal held[55] that even on the assumption that Parliament could bind its successors by a provision such as section 4, the application failed as there had been compliance with that section. Attempts to impugn statutes on the ground that they are contrary to international law have also failed.[56]

There were in the seventeenth century dicta that Acts of Parliament "against common right and reason, or repugnant, or impossible to be performed,"[57] or contrary to natural justice by making a man judge in his own cause[58] could be held by the judges to be void. However, these dicta were controversial even at that time, were not acted upon, and are not accepted today: "since the supremacy of Parliament was finally demonstrated by the Revolution of 1688 any such idea has become obsolete."[59] This position was reaffirmed by Lord Scarman in *Duport Steels Ltd.* v. *Sirs*[60]:

> " . . . [I]n the field of statute law the judge must be obedient to the will of Parliament as expressed in its enactments. In this field Parliament makes and unmakes the law: the judge's duty is to interpret and to apply the law, not to change it to meet the judge's idea of what justice requires. Interpretation does, of course, imply in the interpreter a power of choice where differing constructions are possible. But our law requires the judge to choose the construction which in his best judgement meets the legislative purposes of the enactment. If the result be unjust but inevitable, the judge may say so and invite Parliament to reconsider its provision. But he must not

---

[51] *Edinburgh and Dalkeith Rly.* v. *Wauchope* (1842) 7 Cl. & F. 710.

[52] *Lee* v. *Bude and Torrington Junction Railway* (1871) L.R. 6 C.P. 576; *Pickin* v. *British Railways Board* [1974] A.C. 765.

[53] *Martin* v. *O'Sullivan* [1982] S.T.C. 416, 419, affirmed [1984] S.T.C. 258.

[54] [1983] Ch. 77.

[55] *Ibid.*

[56] *Mortensen* v. *Peters* 1906 S.L.T. 227; *Cheney* v. *Conn* [1968] 1 W.L.R. 242.

[57] *Dr. Bonham's Case* (1610) 8 Co.Rep. 114, 118, *per* Coke C.J.; Coke subsequently expressed a different view extrajudicially: 4 *Coke's Institutes* 37, 41.

[58] *Day* v. *Savadge* (1614) Hob. 85, 87 *per* Hobart C.J.; *cf.* Holt C.J. in *City of London* v. *Wood* (1701) 12 Mod. 669, 686–8.

[59] *Pickin* v. *British Railways Board* [1974] A.C. 765, 782 *per* Lord Reid.

[60] [1980] I.C.R. 161, 189–190.

deny the statute. . . . Only if a just result can be achieved without violating the legislative purpose of the statute may the judge select the construction which best suits his idea of what justice requires."

C. SUBORDINATE LEGISLATION [61]

1. DELEGATION

Each year the output of subordinate[62] legislation vastly exceeds that of Acts of Parliament. Law-making powers have been delegated by Parliament to a wide variety of public authorities, including the Crown, ministers, local authorities and public corporations. Procedural rules may be made for the courts by Rule Committees consisting of judges and lawyers.[63] In addition, the Crown retains certain powers to legislate by virtue of the royal prerogative. There have been examples of the delegation of rule-making powers by Parliament for as long as Parliament has been acknowledged as the supreme law-making body. However, the nineteenth and twentieth centuries have seen an enormous increase, albeit "wayward and unsystematic,"[64] in the extent of delegation, matching the extension of the powers and functions of government. Each of the world wars saw the creation of a complex system of statutory powers, mostly contained in delegated legislation made, respectively, under the Defence of the Realm Acts 1914–15 and the Emergency Powers (Defence) Acts 1939–40; every aspect of national life was closely regulated.

The developments were at first welcomed on the ground that Parliament was thereby able to deal with the issues of importance while the details could be settled departmentally. Certain judges and academic commentators were less enthusiastic. The most extreme of the criticism was expressed by the then Lord Chief Justice, Lord Hewart, in a book entitled "The New Despotism" (1929). The main objections articulated were that wide powers were given to the executive, and that the safeguards against abuse, particularly Parliamentary safeguards, were inadequate. Some people held the view that the delegation of legislative power was unwise and might be dispensed with altogether. However, it was difficult to disentangle general objections to the extension of state power from objections to the particular form that the extension took. Delegated legislation was one of the issues considered by the Committee on Ministers' Powers, which reported in 1932.[65] The Committee expressed the view that "whether good or bad" the practice of delegation was inevitable[66]:

---

[60] [1980] I.C.R. 161, 189–190.

[61] See C.K. Allen, *Law and Orders* (3rd ed., 1965); H.W.R. Wade, *Administrative Law* (5th ed., 1982) Chap. 22, J.F. Garner, *Administrative Law* (5th ed., 1979) Chap. IV; S.A. de Smith, *Constitutional and Administrative Law* (4th ed., 1981) Chap. 17.

[62] Strictly, the term "subordinate" legislation covers "all legislation, permitted as well as authorised, that is inferior to statute law"; "delegated" legislation is that "authorised by Act of Parliament": H.M.S.O., *Access to Subordinate Legislation* (House of Commons Library Document No. 5).

[63] Rules of the Supreme Court; County Court Rules; Crown Court Rules.

[64] Allen (1965) p. 32.

[65] Cmnd. 4060. The first chairman was the Earl of Donoughmore; he was succeeded as chairman by Sir Leslie Scott.

[66] *Ibid.* p. 5.

> "the system of delegated legislation is both legitimate and constitutionally desirable for certain purposes, within certain limits, and under certain safeguards."[67]

It pointed to the pressure on parliamentary time, the technicality of the subject matter of modern legislation, the difficulty of working out administrative machinery in time to insert all the required provisions in the Bill, the flexibility of a system which allowed for adaptation to unknown future conditions without the necessity of an amending Act, and for the opportunity for experiment, and the need on occasion for emergency action. The Committee made a number of suggestions for improving the terminology, publication and scrutiny of delegated legislation. One of the members of the Committee, Ellen Wilkinson M.P., thought that certain passages gave:

> "the impression that the delegating of legislation is a necessary evil, inevitable in the present state of pressure on parliamentary time, but nevertheless a tendency to be watched with misgiving and carefully safeguarded."[68]

Nevertheless, since then the constitutional propriety of delegation has not seriously been questioned.

2. The Forms of Subordinate Legislation

The nomenclature of nineteenth century subordinate legislation was varied and confusing. Different procedures were followed for making and issuing the different kinds of rules. Some kind of regularity was created by the Rules Publication Act 1893, and the position was further improved by its replacement, the Statutory Instruments Act 1946.[69] Today, most subordinate legislation takes the form of *statutory instruments* made under the procedure laid down by the 1946 Act or *byelaws* made under the Local Government Act 1972, although other forms are possible. Different names are still used for different kinds of statutory instruments; these names merely indicate the general nature of the instrument and no longer reflect any difference as to the procedure whereby they are made and promulgated. The selection of a particular title is a matter of departmental practice.

The following are the main kinds of subordinate legislation. *Orders in Council* are made by the Queen with the advice of the Privy Council (the "Queen in Council"). They may be made under the royal prerogative[70]; more commonly they are made under a statutory power, in which case they are normally statutory instruments. *Proclamations* are notices given by the Queen to her subjects; again, they may be made under the royal

---

[67] *Ibid.* p. 51.

[68] *Ibid.* p. 137. She felt that in the conditions of the modern state the practice "instead of being grudgingly conceded ought to be widely extended, and new ways devised to facilitate the process."

[69] See below, pp. 210–214.

[70] *e.g.* an Order altering the constitution of a colony. An Order in Council under the prerogative may not alter the common law or statute law: *The Zamora* [1916] 2 A.C. 77, 90.

prerogative[71] or statute[72] and are published in the *London Gazette*. *Royal Warrants* are made under the royal prerogative and normally concern the pay and pensions of members of the armed forces. *Regulations, Rules, Orders, Schemes* and *Warrants* are usually statutory instruments. The usage of these terms is imprecise although "Rules" are usually[73] the procedural rules of a court or tribunal, and the term "Warrant" is used to describe some Treasury instruments which confer an authority or an entitlement to money. *Directions* may occasionally have to be promulgated as statutory instruments.

3. PREPARATION OF SUBORDINATE LEGISLATION

Subordinate legislation is generally drafted by lawyers in the government department concerned, in the Treasury Solicitor's office where the department has no legal branch, or, in cases of exceptional importance or difficulty, by one of the Parliamentary draftsmen. The "division of labour" between the Parliamentary counsel responsible for statutory drafting and departmental lawyers has been described as "a basic weakness of the system,"[74] although any significant change would obviously require a large increase in the number of counsel. The "preparational parameters" mentioned above[75] in relation to statutes are not applicable to nearly the same extent, although the draftsman has to take care to ensure that the instrument is *intra vires*[76]; the "operational parameters" are, however, equally important.[77] Prior consultation between the department and advisory bodies and interest groups is a well established practice[78]; consultation requirements may be imposed in the parent Act.[79] Local authority byelaws are prepared by the authority concerned but must normally conform to the models issued by government departments to stand much chance of being confirmed. Important statutory instruments may be examined by the Cabinet's Legislation Committee.

4. PROCEDURES FOR MAKING SUBORDINATE LEGISLATION

(a) Statutory instruments

The "statutory instrument" procedure applies to delegated legislation (1) made, confirmed or approved under a power conferred on the Crown after 1947 by statute[80] and expressed to be exercisable "by Order in Council"[81]; (2) made, confirmed or approved under a power conferred on

---

[71] *e.g.* coinage proclamations.

[72] *e.g.* proclamations of a state of emergency under the Emergency Powers Act 1920.

[73] Not invariably: see the Immigration Rules.

[74] F.A.R. Bennion, *Statute Law* (2nd ed., 1983) p. 62.

[75] At pp. 192–194.

[76] See below, pp. 215–217.

[77] Bennion (1983) p. 63.

[78] See J.F. Garner [1964] P.L. 105; A.D. Jergesen [1978] P.L. 290.

[79] A statutory duty to consult is regarded as mandatory (see below p. 215). However, a court will not imply an obligation to consult if there is no express provision: *Bates* v. *Lord Hailsham* [1972] 1 W.L.R. 1373.

[80] Sub-delegated legislation made under a power conferred by statutory instrument is thus not normally within the scope of the 1946 Act.

[81] Statutory Instruments Act 1946, s.1(1).

a minister after 1947 by statute[82] and expressed to be exercisable "by statutory instrument"[83]; (3) made under a power contained in a statute passed before 1948 to make "statutory rules"[84] within the meaning of the Rules Publication Act 1893,[85] or (4) confirmed or approved under certain powers contained in pre-1948 statutes.[86]

The procedural requirements for statutory instruments are prescribed partly by the parent Acts and partly by the 1946 Act. The parent Act may require that the instrument be laid[87] before Parliament. If it does it has to be laid "before it comes into operation," unless it is essential that it comes into operation sooner, in which case the Lord Chancellor and the Speaker must be informed of the reason.[88] This process merely brings the instrument to the attention of Parliament. An instrument may have to be laid in draft[89] or after it has been made. In addition, the instrument may be made subject to the "affirmative resolution" or the "negative resolution" procedure. Under the former, the instrument can only come into effect if a resolution approving it is passed, within the period (if any) specified in the parent Act. Under the latter, which is a much more common requirement,[90] but which is less efficacious in ensuring Parliamentary scrutiny, either House may within 40 days of its being laid resolve that the instrument should be annulled.[91] Since 1973 it has been possible for proceedings on statutory instruments to be taken in Commons Standing Committees rather than on the floor of the House. Nevertheless, Parliamentary scrutiny of the merits of instruments under these procedures is not particularly effective in either forum.[92]

An instrument may also be scrutinised by the Joint Committee on Statutory Instruments. This committee was first appointed in 1973, and replaced the separate committees of each House that had formerly

[82] See note 80 above.

[83] Statutory Instruments Act 1946, s.1(1).

[84] Provided, in most cases, that the rule is of a "legislative" and not an "executive" character: Statutory Instruments Regulations 1947 (S.I. 1948 No. 1), reg. 2(1).

[85] Statutory Instruments Act 1946, s.1(2). There are certain exceptions: see S.I. 1948 No. 1, reg. 2(3) and Schedule.

[86] Statutory Instruments Act 1946, s.9(1); S.I. 1948 No. 1, reg. 2(2); Statutory Instruments (Confirmatory Powers) Order 1947 (S.I. 1948 No. 2). The rule has to be legislative rather than executive in character and subject to the requirement that it be laid before Parliament.

[87] As to the meaning of "laying", see the Laying of Documents before Parliament (Interpretation) Act 1948. It normally involves delivery of copies to the Votes and Proceedings Office of the Commons and the Office of the Clerk of the Parliaments. Subordinate legislation other than statutory instruments may also have to be laid before Parliament, e.g. under the Immigration Act 1971: see R. v. Immigration Appeals Tribunal, ex p. Joyles [1972] 1 W.L.R. 1390.

[88] Statutory Instruments Act 1946, s.4(1).

[89] See ibid. s.6(1). The instrument may not be made within 40 days, and either House may resolve that it shall not be made.

[90] In 1976–77 there were 127 instruments subject to affirmative procedure, 669 subject to negative procedure, 37 general instruments only required to be laid, and 197 general instruments not so required: First Report from the Select Committee on Procedure, 1977–78 H.C. 588 Vol. 1, p. xxxi; an increasing proportion of instruments have been made subject to the first two procedures.

[91] Statutory Instruments Act, 1946 s.5(1). This takes the form of an address to Her Majesty praying that the instrument be annulled, and is commonly termed a "prayer."

[92] See First Report from the Select Committee on Procedure, 1977–78 H.C. 588 Vol. 1, pp. xxix–xxxix; P. Norton, The Commons in Perspective (1981) pp. 95–99; P. Byrne (1976) 29 Parliamentary Affairs 366; A. Beith M.P. (1981) 34 Parliamentary Affairs, 165.

undertaken this work.[93] The Chairman is an Opposition M.P. The Committee examines instruments laid before either House and subject to either form of resolution procedure, other instruments of a general character and special procedure orders. It may draw the attention of Parliament to a particular instrument on any of a number of specified grounds, or on any other grounds not impinging on the merits of or policy behind the instrument. The specified grounds are that:

(i) it imposes a charge on the public revenues;
(ii) it is made under an enactment excluding it from challenge in the courts;
(iii) it purports to have retrospective effect where the parent Act does not so provide;
(iv) it has been unjustifiably delayed in publication or being laid before Parliament;
(v) it has not been notified in proper time to the Lord Chancellor and the Speaker where it comes into effect before being presented to Parliament;
(vi) it may be *ultra vires*;
(vii) it appears to make an unusual or unexpected use of the powers conferred by the parent Act;
(viii) it requires elucidation as to its form or purport; or
(ix) it is defective in drafting.

Instruments subject to House of Commons proceedings only are examined by the Commons members of the Joint Committee acting as a Commons Select Committee on Statutory Instruments. No formal steps have to be taken in either House following an adverse report by one of these committees, although such reports may be referred to in other Parliamentary proceedings concerning the instruments, and the work of these committees and their predecessors seem to have played a part in reducing delays and improving drafting.[94]

Once a statutory instrument is made it must be sent to the Queen's Printer and copies must as soon as possible be printed and sold.[95] The requirements as to printing and sale do not apply to instruments classified as "local"; to general instruments otherwise regularly printed and published; to temporary instruments; to schedules whose printing and sale "is unnecessary or undesirable having regard to the nature or bulk of the document" and to any other steps taken to publicize them; and to confidential instruments not yet in operation.[96] The requirements may, however, be imposed by the Statutory Instruments Reference Committee appointed by the Lord Chancellor and the Speaker.[97] The Queen's Printer

---

[93] See the *Report from the Joint Committee on Delegated Legislation*, 1971–72 H.C. 45, H.L. 184.

[94] See S.A. de Smith, *Constitutional and Administrative Law* (4th ed., 1981) p.348.

[95] Statutory Instruments Act 1946, s.2.

[96] Statutory Instruments Regulations 1947 (S.I. 1948 No. 1) regs. 3–8. These matters have to be "certified" by the responsible authority (*i.e.* minister) in each case. This must be done in proper form: *Simmonds* v. *Newell* [1953] 1 W.L.R. 826.

[97] S.I. 1948 No. 1, reg. 11. The Committee has power to determine certain other questions which may arise as to numbering, publication, classication, etc. It consists of the Lord Chairman of Committees (Lords), the Chairman of Ways and Means (Commons) and six senior officers of both Houses: *Erskine May's Parliamentary Practice* (20th ed., 1983) p.612.

allocates statutory instruments received to the series for the calendar year in which they are made, and numbers them consecutively as near as may be in the order in which they are received.[98] They are cited by their number and year.[99]

H.M.S.O. also publishes (1) periodical lists of the titles of instruments issued; (2) an Annual Edition with full texts of instruments issued, an appendix of prerogative legislation and relevant lists, tables and indices; (3) the annual *Table of Government Orders*, a chronological list showing which instruments are still in force, amended or revoked; and (4) the *Index to Government Orders*, issued every two years, which lists existing powers to make delegated legislation and current exercises of those powers according to subject matter. Butterworth & Co. publishes *Halsbury's Statutory Instruments*, which lists and summarises delegated legislation in force according to subject matter, gives the annotated text of some rules and regulations "chosen from the point of view of the practising lawyer," and includes a regular updating service. Regulations are also normally included in encyclopedias on particular topics.

Rules and Orders made before 1949 are included in the series *Statutory Rules and Orders and Statutory Instruments Revised to Dec. 31st 1948*, which is arranged according to subject matter.[1]

The position as to the commencement of subordinate legislation is unclear. The subordinate legislation in question may expressly provide for its own commencement.[2] If it does not, there is some authority that an order can only come into effect when it is *made known*.[3] In a later case,[4] however, Streatfeild J. directed a jury as follows:

> "I do not think that it can be said that to make a valid statutory instrument it is required that all of these stages should be gone through; namely, the making, the laying before Parliament, the printing and the certification of that part of it which it might be unnecessary to have printed. In my judgment the making of an instrument is complete when it is first of all made by the Minister concerned and after it has been laid before Parliament."[5]

The defendant was prosecuted for breach of a schedule to a statutory instrument that had not been printed as required by the Act. Streatfeild J. held that it was not invalid for lack of publication.

Section 3(1) of the Statutory Instruments Act 1946 provides that regulations should be made for the publication by H.M.S.O. of lists showing the dates of issue of instruments printed and sold by the Queen's

---

[98] S.I. 1948 No. 1, reg. 3.

[99] Statutory Instruments Act 1946, s.2(2).

[1] Earlier editions were published in 1896 and 1904. Up to and including 1960 the Annual Editions were also arranged by subject-matter rather than chronologically.

[2] From 1947 all statutory instruments required to be laid before Parliament after being made must show the dates on which they come into operation; this does not, however, cover the whole field as not all instruments must be laid. Where a day is specified, the instrument comes into effect at the beginning of that day: Interpretation Act 1978, ss.4(a), 23.

[3] Bailhache J. in *Johnson* v. *Sargant* [1918] 1 K.B. 101. *Cf. Jones* v. *Robson* [1901] 1 Q.B. 673 where a requirement to give *notice* of certain orders was held to be directory (but in this case the order had been published, and the defendant knew of it).

[4] *R.* v. *Sheer Metalcraft Ltd.* [1954] 1 Q.B. 586.

[5] *Ibid.* p. 590. (There may of course be no "laying" requirement).

Printer; in any legal proceedings, "an entry therein shall be conclusive evidence of the date on which any statutory instrument was first issued" by H.M.S.O.

Section 3(2) provides that in criminal proceedings for a contravention of "any such statutory instrument" it is:

> "a defence to prove that the instrument had not been issued by Her Majesty's Stationery Office at the date of the alleged contravention unless it is proved that at that date reasonable steps had been taken for the purpose of bringing the purport of the instrument to the notice of the public, or of persons likely to be affected by it, or of the person charged."[6]

It is not, however, clear whether this defence is available (1) in respect of any instrument which has not been issued, including those exempted from publication requirements; or (2) in respect of an instrument which has not been issued in breach of a publication requirement; or (3) in respect only of the period between the making of an instrument and its issue in circumstances where such issue does subsequently take place.[7] Moreover, the statutory defence does not apply to subordinate legislation other than statutory instruments. There is much to be said for the principle of *Johnson* v. *Sargant*:[8] "To bind a citizen by a law, the terms of which he has no means of knowing,[9] is the very essence of tyranny."[10]

(b) Local authority byelaws[11]

District and London borough councils have a general power to make byelaws for the "good rule and government" of the area "and for the prevention and suppression of nuisances" therein[12]; in addition there are numerous specific byelaw making powers.[13] The procedure for making byelaws, to be followed in all cases unless specific provision is otherwise made, is laid down by section 236 of the Local Government Act 1972. Byelaws cannot take effect until they are confirmed by the appropriate minister. Public notice must be given at least one month before application is made for confirmation, and a copy must be available for inspection. The confirming authority may fix the date on which a byelaw is to come into

[6] It has been suggested that a similar defence should be created in respect of Acts of Parliament: Statute Law Society Working Party on Commencement of Acts of Parliament, [1980] Stat.L.R. 40, 51–52. The defence failed on the facts in *R.* v. *Sheer Metalcraft Ltd.*, *supra*.

[7] The difficulty is created by the word "such": see D. Lanham, (1974) 37 M.L.R. 510, 521–523. The *Sheer Metalcraft* case (1) is not inconsistent with the first interpretation, but the point as to whether the defence can apply in respect of *exempted* instruments did not arise as the minister had not certified that the instrument should be exempt; (2) is inconsistent with the second interpretation; and (3) is inconsistent with the third, as there was no suggestion that the schedule was ever published.

[8] [1918] 1 K.B. 101. Lanham (*ibid.*) argues that even where a date of commencement is specified, an instrument can only come into effect when published.; *contra*: A.I.L. Campbell [1982] P.L. 569; response by Lanham [1983] P.L. 395.

[9] Ignorance of a published instrument would probably not be regarded as a defence: ignorance of the law is no excuse.

[10] *Per* Barwick C.J. in *Watson* v. *Lee* (1980) 54 A.L.J.R. 1, 3.

[11] Sometimes spelt "by-laws".

[12] Local Government Act 1972, s.235(1).

[13] See C.A. Cross, *Encyclopedia of Local Government Law*, Appendix 6.

effect; if no date is so fixed, it comes into effect one month after it is confirmed. When confirmed, a copy must be printed and deposited at the authority's offices; it must be open to public inspection without payment at all reasonable hours, and copies supplied on payment of such sum, not exceeding 20p per copy, as the authority may determine.[14]

5. ARRANGEMENT OF STATUTORY INSTRUMENTS

A statutory instrument is normally arranged in the following order[15]:

  (i) Year and number of the instrument.
 (ii) An indication of the subject matter; this corresponds to the categories in the lists published periodically by H.M.S.O.
(iii) Title.
 (iv) The dates when the instrument was made, laid before Parliament and is due to come into operation.
  (v) A recital naming the person making the instrument and the relevant enabling powers.
 (vi) The main provisions of the instrument. These are termed *articles* (in an Order), *regulations* or *rules* as the case may be. Subdivisions are called *paragraphs*. The instrument may be divided into *Parts* and may include a *Schedule*. Common form provisions as to title, definitions and commencement are placed at the beginning.
 (vii) An indication of the minister by whom the instrument was signed.
(viii) An "Explanatory Note" stated to be "not part of" the instrument.

6. VALIDITY OF SUBORDINATE LEGISLATION[16]

All delegated legislation must conform to the limits laid down expressly or impliedly in the enabling Act; if those limits are exceeded the validity of the instrument[17] may be challenged in the courts.[18] Challenges may be made directly, for example by an action in the High Court for a declaration that the legislation is *ultra vires*; or indirectly, for example by raising the argument that an instrument is *ultra vires* as a defence to enforcement proceedings, such as a prosecution for contravening the instrument. An instrument may be *ultra vires* if there has been a failure to comply with a "mandatory" procedural requirement. Some requirements are merely "directory"; the authorities are "directed" to comply with them, but compliance is not a pre-condition to the validity of the instrument. It is not easy to predict whether a court will hold a particular requirement to be mandatory or directory. In this context the duty to consult affected parties has been held to be mandatory,[19] but requirements as to publication[20] and

---

[14] Local authorities do not always seem to be aware of these obligations.
[15] See Bennion (1983) pp. 60–62.
[16] See generally H.W.R. Wade, *Administrative Law* (5th ed., 1982) pp. 747–761.
[17] Or other form of delegated legislation.
[18] The courts may also ensure that prerogative legislation falls within the scope of an existing prerogative power.
[19] *Agricultural etc. Training Board* v. *Aylesbury Mushrooms Ltd.* [1972] 1 W.L.R. 190.
[20] *R.* v. *Sheer Metalcraft Ltd.* [1954] 1 Q.B. 586; see above, pp. 212–214.

laying[21] have been held to be directory. An instrument may be *ultra vires* if its subject matter lies beyond the scope of the enabling power. For example, in *Hotel and Catering Industry Training Board* v. *Automobile Proprietary Ltd.*[22] the House of Lords held that a power to make an order establishing a Training Board for persons employed "in any activities of industry or commerce" did not enable an order to be made in respect of members' clubs.

The established grounds upon which byelaws may be struck down are usually said to be those of *ultra vires*, uncertainty, unreasonableness and repugnancy to the general law,[23] although the last three grounds may also be regarded as facets of the *ultra vires* doctrine. For example, in *Staden* v. *Tarjanyi*[24] a district council made a byelaw in respect of a pleasure ground which provided:

> "A person shall not in the pleasure ground . . . take off, fly or land any glider, manned or unmanned, weighing in total more than four kilogrammes . . . ."

The respondent flew a hang glider over the pleasure ground and was prosecuted under the byelaw. It was conceded that "in" meant "in or over." The Divisional Court held that the byelaw was invalid for uncertainty:

> " . . . anyone engaged upon the otherwise lawful pursuit of hang gliding must know with reasonable certainty when he is breaking the law and when he is not breaking the law. . . . [T]o be valid the byelaw must set some lower level below which the glider must not fly."[25]

The leading authority on the meaning of "unreasonableness" in the context of byelaws is *Kruse* v. *Johnson*[26] where Lord Russell of Killowen C.J. stated[27] that local authority byelaws ought to be supported if possible and "benevolently" interpreted, but might be struck down if unreasonable:

> "But unreasonable in what sense? If, for instance, they were found to be partial and unequal in their operation as between different classes; if they were manifestly unjust; if they disclosed bad faith; if they involved such oppressive or gratuitous interference with the

---

[21] See *Bailey* v. *Williamson* (1873) L.R. 8 Q.B. 118; *Starey* v. *Graham* [1899] 1 Q.B. 406, 412; *Springer* v. *Doorly* (1950) L.R.B.G. 10 (W. Indian Court of Appeal); A.I.L. Campbell [1983] P.L. 43; but see J.M. Evans, *de Smith's Judicial Review of Administrative Action* (4th ed., 1980) p. 148 for the argument that laying requirements should be regarded as mandatory; *cf. Bain* v. *Thorne* (1916) 12 Tas.L.R. 57 (Sup.Ct. of Tasmania). In 1981 Ronald Biggs escaped extradition from Barbados to the U.K. because the Barbados High Court held that regulations designating the U.K. as a country to which a fugitive could be extradited should have been laid before the Barbados Parliament: *The Times*, April 24, 1981: *Biggs* v. *Commissioner of Police* [1982 May] W.I.L.J. 121. Note, however, that the decision turned on a provision of the Interpretation Act of Barbados to the effect that the term "shall" [*i.e.* in "shall . . . be laid] was "to be construed as imperative" (*ibid.*).

[22] [1969] 1 W.L.R. 697.

[23] See C.A. Cross, *Encyclopedia of Local Government Law*, paras. 1–249—1–254.

[24] (1980) 78 L.G.R. 614.

[25] *Ibid.* p. 623.

[26] [1898] 2 Q.B. 91.

[27] At pp. 99–100.

rights of those subject to them as could find no justification in the minds of reasonable men, the Court might well say, 'Parliament never intended to give authority to make such rules; they are unreasonable and ultra vires'. . . . A by-law is not unreasonable merely because particular judges may think that it goes further than is prudent or necessary or convenient, or because it is not accompanied by a qualification or an exception which some judges may think ought to be there."

Successful challenges on this ground are rare. It is not clear whether a statutory instrument, as distinct from a byelaw, can be challenged for unreasonableness. In *Maynard* v. *Osmond*[28] regulations which did not allow police officers to be legally represented in disciplinary proceedings were challenged on this ground[29]; the members of the Court of Appeal did not express any doubt as to the court's jurisdiction to entertain such a challenge, but dismissed the application on the merits.

D. COMMUNITY LEGISLATION[30]

1. INTRODUCTION

The accession of the United Kingdom to membership of the European Economic Communities (the European Economic Community, the European Coal and Steel Community and the European Atomic Energy Community) has meant that the vast and ever-increasing body of Community law has become applicable in this country. The system of Community law is founded on the provisions of the various Treaties whereby the Member States agreed to establish the Communities, new members joined, and aspects of the original Treaties were changed. The Treaty provisions are sometimes termed the *primary* legislation of the Communities. The Treaties give various powers to the Council of Ministers and the Commission to make laws by *regulation, directive* or *decision*, the resulting body of law being termed *secondary* legislation. Secondary legislation must conform to the express or implied limits set by the relevant treaty provisions. Under Community law, a further distinction is drawn between laws (both primary and secondary) that have *direct application* or *effect* without any act of implementation by Member States and laws that require such implementation.

Under United Kingdom law, rules of international law such as treaty provisions, can only take effect within our domestic legal system if expressly implemented by Act of Parliament. Accordingly, the government secured the passage of the European Communities Act 1972 to enable Community law to take effect within the United Kingdom.

In this section we consider, first, the different kinds of Community

---

[28] [1977] Q.B. 240.

[29] The Police (Discipline) Regulations 1965 (S.I. 1965 No. 543); the regulations applicable to Deputy Chief Constables, Assistant Chief Constables and Chief Constables did permit legal representation (S.I. 1965 No. 544). The court did not accept that this constituted "unfair discrimination".

[30] See L. Collins, *European Community Law in the United Kingdom* (2nd ed., 1980), Chaps. 1 and 2; J. Usher, *European Community Law and National Law, The Irreversible Transfer?* (1981); T.C. Hartley, *The Foundations of European Community Law* (1981).

legislation and the extent to which it may be directly applicable or effective, second, the question of the supremacy of Community law, and third, the methods by which the validity of Community legislation may be challenged.

2. The Kinds of Community Legislation

(a) Treaty provisions concerning Community legislation

The different kinds of Community acts are described in Article 189 of the EEC Treaty[31]:

> "In order to carry out their task the Council and the Commission shall, in accordance with the provisions of this Treaty, make regulations, issue directives, take decisions, make recommendations or deliver opinions.
>
> A regulation shall have general application. It shall be binding in its entirety and directly applicable in all Member States.
>
> A directive shall be binding, as to the result to be achieved, upon each Member State to which it is addressed, but shall leave to the national authorities choice of form and methods.
>
> A decision shall be binding in its entirety upon those to whom it is addressed.
>
> Recommendations and opinions shall have no binding force."

Recommendations and opinions cannot be regarded as legislative as they do not have binding effect; it has also been suggested that decisions directed to individuals, as distinct from Member States, are administrative rather than legislative in character.[32]

The Treaties require that regulations, directives and decisions state the reasons on which they are based and refer to any proposals or opinions that were required to be obtained pursuant to other Treaty provisions.[33] Regulations must be published in the Official Journal.[34] They enter into force on the date specified in them, or, if no date is specified, on the twentieth day following their publication.[35] Directives and decisions must

---

[31] See also Art. 14/ECSC and Art. 161/Euratom. The terminology of ECSC acts is different:

EEC Euratom	ECSC
Regulations ⎫ Decisions ⎭	Decisions
Directives	Recommendations
Recommendations ⎫ Opinions ⎭	Opinions

The following discussion is generally confined to EEC legislation.

[32] Case 19/77 *Miller* v. *Commission* [1978] E.C.R. 131, 161 *per* A.G. Warner.
[33] Art. 190/EEC.
[34] Other secondary legislation is in practice also published there: see below, pp. 223–224.
[35] Art. 191/EEC.

be notified to those to whom they are addressed and take effect upon such notification.[36]

(b) Direct applicability and direct effect

A distinction is sometimes drawn between the terms *direct applicability* and *direct effect*.[37] Article 189 of the EEC Treaty provides that regulations are "directly applicable" in all Member States; they come into force without any act of implementation by Member States. No other form of Community law is expressly stated in the treaties to be directly *applicable*, and it was at first thought that those other forms of law could only take *effect* within member states if there was an act of implementation. However, the European Court developed the view that treaty provisions could in principle confer rights and impose obligations directly upon individuals irrespective of any act of implementation. In the *Van Gend en Loos* case[38] the plaintiff claimed before a Dutch tribunal that there had been an increase in import duties which was rendered illegal by Article 12[39] of the EEC Treaty. The European Court, on a reference from the tribunal, held that Article 12 was indeed directly effective, and could be relied upon by the plaintiff in this case. The court stated[40]:

"To ascertain whether the provisions of an international treaty extend so far in their effects it is necessary to consider the spirit, the general scheme and the wording of those provisions.

The objective of the EEC Treaty, which is to establish a Common Market, the functioning of which is of direct concern to interested parties in the Community, implies that this Treaty is more than an agreement which merely creates mutual obligations between the contracting states. This view is confirmed by the preamble to the Treaty which refers not only to governments but to peoples. It is also confirmed more specifically by the establishment of institutions endowed with sovereign rights, the exercise of which affects Member States and also their citizens. Furthermore, it must be noted that the nationals of the states brought together in the Community are called upon to co-operate in the functioning of this Community through the intermediary of the European Parliament and the Economic and Social Committee.

In addition the task assigned to the Court of Justice under Article 177, the object of which is to secure uniform interpretation of the Treaty by national courts and tribunals, confirms that the states have acknowledged that Community law has an authority which can be invoked by their nationals before those courts and tribunals.

The conclusion to be drawn from this is that the Community constitutes a new legal order of international law for the benefit of which the states have limited their sovereign rights, albeit within

[36] Art. 192/EEC.

[37] See J.A. Winter, (1972) 9 C.M.L.R. 425; J.-P. Warner, (1977) 93 L.Q.R. 349; A. Dashwood, (1977–78) 16 J. of Common Market Studies 229.

[38] Case 26/62 *Van Gend en Loos* v. *Nederlandse Administratie Der Belastingen* [1963] E.C.R. 1.

[39] "Member States shall refrain from introducing between themselves any new customs duties on imports or exports or any charges having equivalent effect, and from increasing those which they already apply in their trade with each other."

[40] pp.12–13.

limited fields, and the subjects of which comprise not only Member States but also their nationals. Independently of the legislation of Member States, Community law therefore not only imposes obligations on individuals but is also intended to confer upon them rights which become part of their legal heritage. These rights arise not only where they are expressly granted by the Treaty, but also by reason of obligations which the Treaty imposes in a clearly defined way upon individuals as well as upon the Member States and upon the institutions of the Community."

Article 12 imposed a clear and unconditional negative prohibition, "ideally adapted to produce direct effects in the legal relationship between Member States and their subjects."

In this and subsequent cases the European Court has elaborated the criteria by which those *treaty provisions* that are regarded as directly effective are to be distinguished from those that are not. As more provisions have come before the court for consideration, the overall picture has become clearer.[41] The criteria[42] are:

"– the provision must impose a clear and precise obligation on Member States;
– it must be unconditional, in other words subject to no limitation; if, however, a provision is subject to certain limitations, their nature and extent must be exactly defined;
– finally, the implementation of a Community rule must not be subject to the adoption of àny subsequent rules or regulations on the part either of the Community institutions or of the Member States, so that, in particular, Member States must not be left any real discretion with regard to the application of the rule in question."

A provision may, exceptionally, be held to have direct effect prospectively only.[43]

The European Court has subsequently invoked these criteria to hold that *decisions* addressed to Member States[44] and *directives*[45] can be directly

---

[41] A useful table is given in Collins (1980) pp. 73–76.

[42] As formulated by A.G. Mayras in Case 41/74 *Van Duyn* v. *Home Office* [1974] E.C.R. 1337, 1354. See *e.g. Application des Gaz* v. *Falks Veritas* [1974] Ch. 381 (Articles 85 and 86/EEC); *Rio Tinto Zinc Corporation* v. *Westinghouse Electric Corporation* [1978] A.C. 547 (Article 85).

[43] Case 43/75 *Defrenne* v. *Sabena (No. 2)* [1976] E.C.R. 455. This case concerned the direct effect of Art. 119/EEC (equal pay for men and women). The court stated: "As the general level at which pay would have been fixed cannot be known, important considerations of legal certainty affecting all the interests involved, both public and private, make it impossible in principle to reopen the question as regards the past" (p. 481). See T. Koopmans, [1980] C.L.J. 287; M. Waelbroeck, (1982) Y.B. European Law, 115.

[44] See Case 9/70 *Grad* v. *Finanzamt Traunstein* [1970] E.C.R. 325: this concerned a decision which prohibited member states from applying specific taxes concurrently with the common turnover tax (VAT) system due to be implemented by directive.

[45] See Case 41/74 *Van Duyn* v. *Home Office* [1974] E.C.R. 1337; Case 148/78 *Pubblico Ministero* v. *Ratti* [1979] E.C.R. 162; Case 102/79 *Commission* v. *Belgium* [1980] E.C.R. 1473; Case 8/81 *Becker* v. *Finanzamt Münster-Innenstadt* [1982] 1 C.M.L.R. 499. In Case 131/79 *R.* v. *Secretary of State for the Home Department, ex p. Santillo* [1980] E.C.R. 1585, 1610–11, A.G. Warner argued that the conditions for the direct effectiveness of Treaty provisions were subject to some qualification when applied to directives. In particular, there will nearly always be some element of discretion which will not, however, prevent a directive being held to be directly effective.

effective. *Van Duyn* v. *Home Office* concerned Article 48 of the EEC Treaty, which provided for the "freedom of movement" of workers, including the right to enter and stay in any Member State "subject to limitations justified on grounds of public policy, public security or public health." The scope of these limitations was further regulated by Council Directive 64/221 which provided in art. 3(1) that, "Measures taken on grounds of public policy or of public security shall be based exclusively on the personal conduct of the individual concerned." Miss Yvonne Van Duyn, a Dutch national, was refused leave to enter the United Kingdom on the ground that she was intending to work for the Church of Scientology. The government regarded scientology as socially harmful, and although it had no power to prohibit its practice it had decided to take steps, within its powers, to curb its growth. Accordingly it decided that foreign nationals such as Miss Van Duyn should be refused entry. She claimed that the refusal was not based on her "personal conduct" and challenged its validity in the High Court. Several questions were referred to the European Court, which held (1) that Article 48 was directly effective; (2) that the relevant provision of directive 64/221 was also directly effective; but (3) that a Member State was entitled to take into account as a matter of personal conduct that the individual was associated with an organisation whose activities were considered by the state to be socially harmful. One limitation to the direct effectiveness of directives appears to be that they only give rise to such effects as between individuals and Member States; regulations in addition can affect legal relations between individuals.[46]

Overall, Member States have tended to present arguments to the European Court against direct effectiveness; Community institutions have tended, not surprisingly, to argue in favour, given that it strengthens their position at the expense of individual Member States, and helps ensure that Community law applies uniformly throughout the Member States. It enables individuals to take action to enforce the requirements of Community law without having to rely on Community institutions to act. It has also been stressed that it is inappropriate for a Member State that has failed to implement a directive or decision addressed to it to rely, in proceedings between itself and an individual, on its own failure to comply with that directive or decision on the basis that it is not directly effective.[47]

Although a regulation is "directly applicable" by virtue of Article 189, it will not necessarily create rights and obligations which may be enforced in national courts. This depends on the wording of the regulation in question[48]: it has been argued that regulations only have "direct effect" if the criteria applicable to treaty provisions and other kinds of Community secondary legislation are fulfilled.[49]

Finally, it should be noted that in these and other cases in this area the European Court has not been consistent in its use of the *terms* "directly

---

[46] Case 148/78 *Pubblico Ministero* v. *Ratti* [1979] E.C.R. 1624, 1642; but see D. Wyatt, (1982) Eur.L.R. 147, 154–157.

[47] *Ibid.* p. 1650: A.G. Reischl.

[48] Usher (1981) *op. cit.* p. 217, n. 30, pp. 18–19.

[49] A.G. Warner in Case 31/74 *Galli* [1975] E.C.R. 47 and Case 74/76 *Iannelli* v. *Meronia; Steinike and Weinlig* v. *Germany* [1977] E.C.R. 557, 583.

applicable" and "direct effect," but has tended to use them interchangeably.[50]

(c) Treaty provisions

The main treaties concerning the Communities are:

(1) the Treaty establishing the European Coal and Steel Community (Paris, 1951);

(2) the Treaties establishing the European Economic Community and the European Atomic Energy Community (Rome, 1957);

(3) the Treaty establishing a Single Council and a Single Commission of the European Communities (Brussels 1965; the "Merger Treaty");

(4) the Treaty amending certain Budgetary Provisions of the Treaties (Luxembourg, 1970); and

(5) the Accession Treaties (Brussels, 1972: Denmark, Ireland, Norway,[51] and the United Kingdom; Athens, 1979: Greece).

Several of the treaties have extensive Annexes and Protocols. The treaties are published by HMSO[52] and in various unofficial collections. There is also a series of treaties entered by the Community with non-Member States.

(d) Regulations, Directives and Decisions

Regulations are the most important form of Community secondary legislation. Under Article 189 of the EEC Treaty they are directly applicable without any act of implementation by Member States. Indeed, such acts of implementation are prohibited, in case they have the effect of altering the scope of the regulation in question. Member States may not, for example, enact measures which purport to interpret provisions contained in a regulation[53]; such interpretations might vary from state to state, and the regulation would no longer be uniform in application. This prohibition also ensures that provision of a regulation can clearly be perceived to be of Community origin and so subject to the judicial remedies available under Community law, and avoids any ambiguity as to the date of entry into force.[54] Domestic legislation may, however, make supplementary provision, for example by imposing a sanction for breach of a regulation[55] or by prescribing a limitation period for claims based on Community law.[56]

Directives are used where the approximation or harmonisation of national laws is sought rather than strict uniformity. They may only be

[50] But see A.G. Warner in *Iannelli* v. *Merioni* [1977] E.C.R. 557 at 583 and A.G. Slynn in Case 8/81 *Becker* [1982] 1 C.M.L.R. 499, 504–5; in *Ratti, supra,* A.G. Reischl argued that the term "direct applicability" should only be used in respect of *regulations.*

[51] Norway subsequently did not ratify the Treaty.

[52] Cmnd. 5189; 5179–I; 5179–II.

[53] Case 40/69 *Hauptzollamt Hamburg* v. *Bollman* [1970] E.C.R. 69; classification of products (turkey rumps) under an agricultural regulation; Case 34/73 *Variola* v. *Italian Minister of Finance* [1973] E.C.R. 981.

[54] Usher (1981) p. 17. Member States may not adopt "any measure which would conceal the Community nature and effects of any legal provision from the persons to whom it applies": Case 50/76 *Amsterdam Bulb* v. *Produktschap Voor Siergewassen* [1977] E.C.R. 137, 151.

[55] *Amsterdam Bulb* case, *supra.*

[56] Case 33/76 *Rewe* v. *Landwirtschaftkammer Saarland* [1976] E.C.R. 1989. The periods must be reasonable and non-discriminatory.

addressed to Member States. Choice of method is left to the Member States, although a time limit for implementation is commonly set.

Decisions may be addressed to member states, to corporations or to individuals. The European Court has held that:

> "a decision must appear as an act originating from the competent organisation intended to produce judicial effects, constituting the ultimate end of the internal procedure of this organisation and according to which such organisation makes its final ruling in a form allowing its nature to be identified."[57]

(e) Preparation of Community secondary legislation[58]

The treaties do not lay down a uniform legislative process to be adopted in all cases. Usually, the Commission first formulates a proposal after consulting national officials, experts and representatives of interest groups (the *avant-projet* stage). The draft proposal is then sent to the Council of Ministers; Member States may at this stage refer it to their national parliaments. A copy is sent to the European Parliament so that a preliminary unofficial study can be commenced in committee. The Council may, and in some cases must[59] consult the European Parliament and the European Economic and Social Committee (a consultative body representing the various categories of economic and social activity, including industry, workers and consumers). The European Parliament debates the report of its committee in plenary session. The opinions of the Parliament and the E.S.C. are transmitted to the Council. The Council may consider the proposal in three stages: (1) in a Working Group of national experts convened by the Council secretariat; (2) in the Committee of Permanent Representatives (COREPER); and (3) in the Council of Ministers itself.

(f) Publication of Community secondary legislation

Regulations, directives and decisions are published in the *Official Journal of the European Communities* ("L Series").[60] An English edition has been published from January 1973; English texts of pre-1972 secondary legislation were published in Special Editions of the *Official Journal* covering the pre-accession period, and by H.M.S.O. in a 42-volume work entitled *Secondary Legislation of the European Communities: Subject Edition* (1973). H.M.S.O. supplemented this series with an annual Subject List and Table of Effects up to the end of 1979. Users must now rely on the monthly and annual indices and lists published as supplements to the

---

[57] Case 54/65 *Compagnie des Forges de Châtillon Commentry et Neuves Maison* v. *High Authority* [1966] C.M.L.R. 525, 538.

[58] L.S. Adler in D.M. Palmer (ed.) *Sources of Information on the European Communities* (1979) pp. 20–28. T.St.J.N. Bates, "The Drafting of European Community Legislation" [1983] Stat.L.R. 24.

[59] A requirement to consult will be regarded as an essential procedural requirement: Case 138/79 *Roquette* v. *Council* [1980] E.C.R. 3333; Case 139/79 *Maizena* v. *Council* [1980] E.C.R. 3393: see T.C. Hartley (1981) Eur.L.R. 181. It is not sufficient that the opinion of the European Parliament is sought; an opinion must be received.

[60] Since 1968 the *Official Journal* has appeared in two series, one publishing secondary legislation (the "L Series") and the other giving general information, including drafts of proposed legislation (the "C series").

Official Journal. The European Communities also publish periodically a *Register of Current Community Legal Instruments.*[61]

(g) Arrangement and citation of Community secondary legislation

The heading of a regulation indicates the authority by which it is made, the Treaty under which it is made and its number.[62] The date on which it is made is given, followed by an indication of the subject matter. (*e.g.* "Council Regulation (EEC) No. 2194/81 of 27 July 1981 laying down the general rules for the system of production aid for dried figs and dried grapes.").

A *preamble* including an explanation of the purposes of the regulation precedes its main provisions. These comprise numbered *articles*, which may be subdivided into *paragraphs*, and grouped under *Titles*. An *annex* may be attached. Directives and decisions are similar to regulations in form.[63]

The correct forms of citation have changed several times.[64] At present they are as follows: Reg. (EEC) 1629/70; Dec. 70/381/EEC; Dir. 72/182/Euratom.

3. SUPREMACY OF COMMUNITY LAW

It is well established in terms of Community law that on a matter regulated by binding Community law, that law takes precedence over the municipal law of a Member State.[65] It is immaterial whether the municipal law is enacted before or after 'the relevant Community law,[66] and whether it forms part of that state's fundamental or constitutional law.[67] Thus in the *Van Gend en Loos* case[68] the European Court spoke of the creation of a "new legal order . . . for the benefit of which the states have limited their sovereign rights."

Costa v. *ENEL*[69] concerned the nationalization of Italian electricity undertakings. Costa, a shareholder in one of the undertakings (Edison Volta) refused to pay an invoice for electricity sent by ENEL, and claimed that the nationalisation was contrary to prior Community law (various articles of the EEC Treaty). The European Court, on a reference from the

[61] Volume I: Analytical Register; Volume II: Chronological Index; Alphabetical Index. See also *Halsbury's Statutes of England* Vol. 42A and Sweet & Maxwell's *Encyclopedia of European Community Law.*

[62] From 1958 to 1967 there were separate series of regulations for the EEC and Euratom; from 1968 there has been a single series. Regulations were numbered in a continuous sequence until 1963; from that time a new sequence has been started each calendar year.

[63] From 1968 they have been numbered in a single series with recommendations, opinions and financial regulations.

[64] *Secondary legislation of the European Communities: Subject Edition* (H.M.S.O., 1973) Vol. 42 pp. vii–viii.

[65] Case 26/62 *Van Gend en Loos* v. *Nederlandse Administratie der Belastingen* [1963] E.C.R. 1.

[66] Case 6/64 *Costa* v. *ENEL* [1964] E.C.R. 585.

[67] Case 11/70 *Internationale Handelsgesellschaft* v. *Einfuhr-und Vorratsstelle für Getreide* [1970] E.C.R. 1125; Case 106/77 *Amministrazione delle Finanze dello Stato* v. *Simmenthal* [1978] E.C.R. 629.

[68] Above, pp. 219–220.

[69] Ente Nazionale Energia Elettrica (National Electricity Board), formerly the Edison Volta undertaking.

Italian magistrate (the Guidice Conciliatore of Milan), dealt firmly with the submission of the Italian government that a national court was obliged to apply the domestic law in preference to Community law[70]:

> "By creating a Community of unlimited duration, having its own institutions, its own personality, its own legal capacity and capacity of representation on the international plane and, more particularly, real powers stemming from a limitation of sovereignty or a transfer of powers from the States to the Community, the Member States have limited their sovereign rights, albeit within limited fields, and have thus created a body of law which binds both their nationals and themselves.
>
> The integration into the laws of each Member State of provisions which derive from the Community, and more generally, the terms and the spirit of the Treaty, make it impossible for the States, as a corollary, to accord precedence to a unilateral and subsequent measure over a legal system accepted by them on a basis of reciprocity. Such a measure cannot therefore be inconsistent with that legal system. The executive force of Community law cannot vary from one State to another in deference to subsequent domestic laws, without jeopardizing the attainment of the objectives of the Treaty set out in Article 5(2) and giving rise to the discrimination prohibited by Article 7. . . .
>
> The precedence of Community law is confirmed by Article 189, whereby a regulation 'shall be binding' and 'directly applicable in all Member States'. This provision, which is subject to no reservation, would be quite meaning'ess if a State could unilaterally nullify its effects by means of a legislative measure which could prevail over Community law.
>
> It follows from all these observations that the law stemming from the Treaty, an independent source of law, could not, because of its special and original nature, be overridden by domestic legal provisions, however framed, without being deprived of its character as Community law and without the legal basis of the Community itself being called into question.
>
> The transfer by the States from their domestic legal system to the Community legal system of the rights and obligations arising under the Treaty carries with it a permanent limitation of their sovereign rights, against which a subsequent unilateral act incompatible with the concept of the Community cannot prevail. Consequently Article 177 is to be applied regardless of any domestic law, whenever questions relating to the interpretation of the Treaty arise."

In the *Simmenthal* case[71] an Italian judge was faced with a conflict between a Council regulation and Italian laws, some of which were enacted after the regulation. Under Italian law domestic legislation contrary to Community law was unconstitutional. However, only the Constitutional Court had jurisdiction to make such a ruling; the ordinary courts could not. The European Court, on a reference by the judge, held that:

[70] pp.593–594.
[71] [1978] E.C.R. 629.

"every national court must in a case within its jurisdiction apply Community law in its entirety and protect rights which the latter confers on individuals and must accordingly set aside any provision of national law which may conflict with it, whether prior or subsequent to the Community rule. . . . [I]t is not necessary for the court to request for or await the prior setting aside of such provisions by legislative or other constitutional means."[72]

The position from the point of view of Community law is thus clear; we now consider it from the standpoint of United Kingdom law. The key provisions of the European Communities Act 1972 are contained in sections 2 and 3:

"2.—(1) All such rights, powers, liabilities, obligations and restrictions from time to time created or arising by or under the Treaties, and all such remedies and procedures from time to time provided for by or under the Treaties, as in accordance with the Treaties are without further enactment to be given legal effect or used in the United Kingdom shall be recognised and available in law, and be enforced, allowed and followed accordingly; and the expression 'enforceable Community right' and similar expressions shall be read as referring to one to which this subsection applies.

(2) Subject to Schedule 2 to this Act, at any time after its passing Her Majesty may by Order in Council, and any designated Minister or department may by regulations, make provision—

(a) for the purpose of implementing any Community obligation of the United Kingdon, or enabling any such obligation to be implemented, or of enabling any rights enjoyed or to be enjoyed by the United Kingdom under or by virtue of the Treaties to be exercised; or

(b) for the purpose of dealing with matters arising out of or related to any such obligation or rights or the coming into force, or the operation from time to time, of subection (1) above;

and in the exercise of any statutory power or duty, including any power to give directions or to legislate by means of orders, rules, regulations or other subordinate instrument, the person entrusted with the power or duty may have regard to the objects of the Communities and to any such obligation or rights as aforesaid.

In this subsection 'designated Minister or department' means such Minister of the Crown or government department as may from time to time be designated by Order in Council in relation to any matter or for any purpose, but subject to such restrictions or conditions (if any) as may be specified by the Order in Council. . . .

(4) The provision that may be made under subsection (2) above includes, subject to Schedule 2 to this Act, any such provision (of any such extent) as might be made by Act of Parliament, and any enactment passed or to be passed, other than one contained in this Part of this Act, shall be construed and have effect subject to the foregoing provisions of this section; but, except as may be provided by

---

[72] *Ibid.* pp.644, 645–6.

any Act passed after this Act, Schedule 2 shall have effect in connection with the powers conferred by this and the following sections of this Act to make Orders in Council and regulations.

3.—(1) For the purposes of all legal proceedings any question as to the meaning or effect of any of the Treaties, or as to the validity, meaning or effect of any Community instrument, shall be treated as a question of law (and, if not referred to the European Court, be for determination as such in accordance with the principles laid down by and any relevant decision of the European Court).

(2) Judicial notice shall be taken of the Treaties, of the Official Journal of the Communities and of any decision of, or expression of opinion by, the European Court on any such question as aforesaid; and the Official Journal shall be admissible as evidence of any instrument or other act thereby communicated of any of the Communities or of any Community institution."[73]

Thus, directly applicable and directly effective Community laws are given effect in the United Kingdom under section 2(1); other matters are to be dealt with by statute, or by statutory instruments under section 2(2); any question as to the meaning or effect of the treaties is to be determined in accordance with Community law of which judicial notice is to be taken (section 3). There is, however, no attempt to entrench the European Communities Act itself against repeal. It is unlikely that a court would accept that the "ultimate political fact"[74] has been redefined so as to deny effect to a statute deliberately enacted by Parliament as at present constituted which conflicts with existing Community law. It is even more unlikely that the courts would decline to recognise the express repeal of the 1972 Act.[75] Where a provision of a United Kingdom statute is followed by an inconsistent provision of Community law that is directly applicable or effective, the latter is given precedence by section 2 of the European Communities Act 1972. The position is less clear where the chronology is reversed and the U.K. statute is enacted after the inconsistent provision of Community law. If both laws were made before the 1972 Act, Community law is again given precedence by section 2. If the United Kingdom law is more recent, there are a number of possible situations and the position appears to be as follows:

(1) The United Kingdom legislation may be unclear, in which case an English court will endeavour to interpret it so as to comply with Community law, given the established presumption that Parliament does not intend the United Kingdom to be in breach of its international obligations (the "interpretation" issue).[76]

---

[73] Section 2(3) authorises the necessary expenditure; section 2(5) concerns Northern Ireland; section 2(6) concerns the Channel Islands, the Isle of Man and Gibraltar. Section 3(3)–(5) makes further provision for proof of community instruments.

[74] See above, pp. 186–187.

[75] For the contrary argument that there has been a binding transfer of powers see Usher (1981) pp. 30–38; J.D.B. Mitchell, (1967–68) 5 C.M.L.R. 112, (1971) *Europarecht* 97, (1979) 56 *International Affairs* 33. A withdrawal from the Communities would, however, be negotiated; the arrangements would be enshrined in a treaty which could be construed as a transfer back from the Communities of those powers: Usher (1981) p. 38.

[76] See below, pp. 261–262, 277; *Garland* v. *British Rail Engineeering Ltd.* [1983] 2 A.C. 751, 771 (*per* Lord Diplock).

(2) If the United Kingdom legislation is clear and unambiguously conflicts with prior Community law, an English court will then determine whether that conflict was intended by Parliament. In the case of inadvertent conflict, the Community legislation will be given priority. Where conflict is intentional, the courts will give effect to the United Kingdom legislation, and the United Kingdom would be in breach of its Treaty obligations (the "sovereignty" issue).

There have been several judicial statements which support the primacy of subsequent inconsistent Acts of Parliament, without drawing a distinction between inadvertent and intentional conflicts. Some preceded accession.[77] In *Felixstowe Dock and Railway Co.* v. *British Transport Docks Board*[78] it was argued that the proposed promotion by the Board of a private Bill to take over the plaintiff company would be an abuse of a dominant position by the Board contrary to Article 86 of the EEC Treaty. Lord Denning M.R. said that there was no evidence of such an abuse and added, *obiter*[79]:

> "It seems to me that once the Bill is passed by Parliament and becomes a Statute, that will dispose of all this discussion about the Treaty. These courts will then have to abide by the Statute without regard to the Treaty at all."

Both the "interpretation" and "sovereignty" issues were subsequently raised in *Macarthys Ltd.* v. *Smith*.[80] A man was paid £60 a week for managing a stockroom. Four and a half months after he left a woman was appointed in his place at £50 a week. She claimed that she was entitled to equal pay under provisions of the Equal Pay Act 1970 that had been inserted by the Sex Discrimination Act 1975. The Court of Appeal majority[81] held that Equal Pay Act provisions were confined to cases where a man and a woman were in the same employment at the same time. The words had to be given their natural and ordinary meaning and were clear; the terms of Article 119 of the EEC Treaty[82] could therefore not be used as an aid to construction. The question whether Article 119 was so confined was referred to the European Court.

Lord Denning took a different view of the proper approach to construction of the English statute and then considered the sovereignty issue[83]:

> "Under section 2(1) and (4) of the European Communities Act 1972 the principles laid down in the Treaty are 'without further enactment' to be given legal effect in the United Kingdom: and have priority over

---

[77] *e.g.* Salmon L.J. in *Blackburn* v. *Attorney-General* [1971] 1 W.L.R. 1037, 1041. Lord Denning M.R. left the point open.

[78] [1976] 2 C.M.L.R. 655.

[79] At pp. 664–5.

[80] [1979] I.C.R. 785, [1981] Q.B. 180; P. Schofield, (1980) 9 I.L.J. 173; T.R.S. Allan, (1983) 3 O.J.L.S. 22. See also *Shields* v. *E. Coomes (Holdings) Ltd.* [1978] 1 W.L.R. 1408.

[81] Lawton and Cumming-Bruce L.JJ., Lord Denning M.R. dissenting on this point.

[82] "Each Member State shall during the first stage ensure and subsequently maintain the application of the principle that men and women should receive equal pay for equal work . . . " This was amplified by article 1 of a Council directive (Dir. 75/117/EEC).

[83] At p. 789.

'any enactment passed or to be passed' by our Parliament. So we are entitled—and think bound—to look at article 119 of the Treaty because it is directly applicable here: and also any directive which is directly applicable here: see *Van Duyn* v. *Home Office* [1975] Ch. 358. We should, I think, look to see what those provisions require about equal pay for men and women. Then we should look at our own legislation on the point—giving it, of course, full faith and credit—assuming that it does fully comply with the obligations under the Treaty. In construing our statute, we are entitled to look to the Treaty as an aid to its construction: and even more, not only as an aid but as an overriding force. If on close investigation it should appear that our legislation is deficient—or is inconsistent with Community law—by some oversight of our draftsmen—then it is our bounden duty to give priority to Community law. Such is the result of section 2(1) and (4) of the European Communities Act 1972.

I pause here, however, to make one observation on a constitutional point. Thus far I have assumed that our Parliament, whenever it passes legislation, intends to fulfil its obligations under the Treaty. If the time should come when our Parliament deliberately passes an Act—with the intention of repudiating the Treaty or any provision in it—or intentionally of acting inconsistently with it—and says so in express terms—then I should have thought that it would be the duty of our courts to follow the statute of our Parliament. I do not however envisage any such situation. As I said in *Blackburn* v. *Attorney-General* [1971] 1 W.L.R. 1037, 1040: 'But, if Parliament should do so, then I say we will consider that event when it happens.' Unless there is such an intentional and express repudiation of the Treaty, it is our duty to give priority to the Treaty."

On the sovereignty issue Lawton L.J. said[84]:

"I can see nothing in this case which infringes the sovereignty of Parliament. If I thought there were, I should not presume to take any judicial step which it would be more appropriate for the House of Lords, as part of Parliament, to take. Parliament by its own Act in the exercise of its sovereign powers has enacted that European Community law shall 'be enforced, allowed and followed' in the United Kingdom of Great Britain and Northern Ireland: see section 2(1) of the European Communities Act 1972, and that 'any enactment passed or to be passed . . . shall be construed and have effect subject to' section 2: see section 2(4) of that Act. Parliament's recognition of European Community law and of the jurisdiction of the European Court of Justice by one enactment can be withdrawn by another. There is nothing in the Equal Pay Act 1970, as amended, to indicate that Parliament intended to amend the European Communities Act 1972, or to limit its application."

Cumming-Bruce L.J. indicated that if

"the terms of the Treaty are adjudged in Luxembourg to be inconsistent with the provisions of the Equal Pay Act 1970, European law

[84] At p.796.

will prevail over that municipal legislation. But such a judgment in Luxembourg cannot affect the meaning of the English statute."[85]

The European Court subsequently held that Article 119 was not restricted to cases of contemporaneous employment,[86] and the plaintiff's claim was duly conceded in the English proceedings. The matter came before the Court of Appeal again on the question of costs.[87] Lord Denning M.R. said[88]:

"the provisions of article 119 of the EEC Treaty take priority over anything in our English statute on equal pay which is inconsistent with article 119. That priority is given by our own law. It is given by the European Communities Act 1972 itself. Community law is now part of our law; and, whenever there is any inconsistency, Community law has priority. It is not supplanting English law. It is part of our law which overrides any other part which is inconsistent with it."

The other members of the court agreed that the Community legislation prevailed.[89]

Accordingly, it appears that both Lord Denning M.R. and Lawton L.J. distinguish between cases of inadvertent and intentional conflict: it would seem that there is no room in the case of inadvertent conflict for the application of an "implied repeal rule" as there is between two inconsistent statutes, and in the case of intentional conflicts the English statute will prevail.

4. IMPLEMENTATION OF COMMUNITY LAW IN THE UNITED KINGDOM

As has been seen, Community law that is directly applicable or effective takes effect in the United Kingdom under section 2(1) of the European Communities Act 1972.[90] Section 2(2)[91] authorises the making of subordinate legislation (1) to implement other Community laws that are not directly applicable or effective; or (2) to deal with matters related to Community laws that take effect under section 2(1).[92] Subordinate legislation may not, however, (1) provide for the imposition or increase of taxation; (2) be retrospective; (3) confer the power to enact sub-delegated

---

[85] At p. 798.

[86] [1981] Q.B. 180 (C.J.E.C.).

[87] [1981] Q.B. 199 (C.A.). *Cf. Re an Absence in Ireland* [1977] 1 C.M.L.R. 5, where a national insurance commissioner allowed a claimant's appeal on two grounds, one of which involved the application of Council Regulation (EEC) No. 1408/71 in preference to the provisions of the Social Security Act 1975. See also *Re Medical Expenses Incurred in France* [1977] 2 C.M.L.R. 317.

[88] At p. 200.

[89] Professor Hood Phillips has suggested that even in cases of inadvertent conflict, an English court should give effect to a subsequent, unambiguous United Kingdom Act of Parliament: (1980) 96 L.Q.R. 31; *cf.* O. Hood Phillips and P. Jackson, *Constitutional and Administrative Law* (6th ed., 1978) pp. 98–99.

[90] Above, pp. 226–227.

[91] *Ibid.* Sections 5 and 6 of the 1972 Act confer powers to make subordinate legislation concerning customs matters and the common agricultural policy. Statutory instruments implementing Community obligations have been made under other statutes.

[92] Note, however, the limits on such legislation in respect of Community regulations: above, p. 222.

legislation; or (4) create any new criminal offence punishable with more than two years imprisonment, or three months on summary conviction, or a fine of more than £1,000, or £100 a day.[93] it is subject to the negative resolution procedure.[94]

Arrangements have been made for the scrutiny of Community legislation by the Select Committee of the House of Lords on the European Communities and the Select Committee of the House of Commons on European Legislation.[95] These committees consider draft Community legislation and other documents prepared by the Commission for submission to the Council of Ministers. Detailed explanatory memoranda are prepared by the government. The Commons committee concentrates on political implications, although the merits cannot be considered; the Lords deal more with technical legal and administrative implications.[96] The Lords committee has a number of sub-committees including one customarily chaired by one of the Law Lords on legal aspects, and each of the rest considering Community proposals within a particular subject area. The committees decide, *inter alia*, whether a particular proposal should be considered further by the respective Houses. In the Commons, a debate may be held on the floor of the House or in a standing committee.[97] The government has undertaken that it will normally[98] provide time for such consideration where recommended by the Select Committee prior to a proposal being discussed by the Council of Ministers. However, the scrutiny of European secondary legislation is indirect in effect, given that Parliament can at best influence only one of the ten members of the Council of Ministers. Moreover, it can be difficult to keep abreast of changes in draft proposals as they progress through the Community legislative process.

5. VALIDITY OF EUROPEAN SECONDARY LEGISLATION

(a) Article 173; the action for annulment

The validity of acts of Community institutions that are binding in law, and whether legislative or not, may be challenged directly by an *action for*

[93] European Communities Act 1972, Sched. 2, as amended by the Criminal Law Act 1977, s.32 and the Criminal Justice Act 1982, ss.37, 40, 46.

[94] *Ibid.* See above p. 211.

[95] Established in 1974. See 1972–73 H.C. 143 and 463–I ("Foster Committee": Commons); 1972–73 H.L. 194 ("Maybray-King Committee": Lords). See also the *First Report from the Select Committee on Procedure*, 1977–78 H.C. 588 Vol. I, pp. xl–xlvi; House of Lords Factsheet No. 2: *The House of Lords and the European Communities* (3rd ed., 1978); P. Norton, *The Commons in Perspective* (1981) pp. 160–164; Lord Fraser of Tullybelton in St. John Bates, *et al.*, (eds.) *In Memoriam J.D.B. Mitchell* (1983) pp. 29–37.

[96] Joint meetings are occasionally held.

[97] From 1981 the Standing Committee on European Community Documents has been able to consider a substantive, amendable motion rather than a neutral motion to the effect that the document has been "considered".

[98] The strength of the undertaking has varied from time to time. In 1980, the Commons resolved that no minister should agree to a proposal for Community legislation recommended by the Select Committee for consideration by the House before the House had given it tha consieration unless (a) the Committee has indicated that agreement need not be withheld o (b) the Minister decides there are special reasons; in the latter case the reasons should b explained to the House at the first opportunity: H.C. Deb. Vol. 991, col. 844, October 30 1980.

annulment brought in the European Court of Justice[99] under Article 173 of the EEC Treaty:[1]

"(1) The Court of Justice shall review the legality of acts of the Council and the Commission other than recommendations or opinions.[2] It shall for this purpose have jurisdiction in actions brought by a Member State, the Council or the Commission on the grounds of lack of competence, infringement of an essential procedural requirement, infringement of this Treaty or of any rule of law relating to its application, or misuse of powers.

(2) Any natural or legal person[3] may, under the same conditions, institute proceedings against a decision addressed to that person or against a decision which, although in the form of a regulation or a decision addressed to another person, is of direct and individual concern to the former.

(3) The proceedings provided for in this Article shall be instituted within two months of the publication of the measure, or of its notification to the plaintiff, or, in the absence thereof, of the day on which it came to the knowledge of the latter, as the case may be."

Thus the range of acts that can be challenged by an individual is narrower than those that can be reviewed under Article 173(1). First, the act must be a "decision" in that it must have legal effect[4] and must not be a regulation, in the sense of an act which applies to objectively determined situations and has legal effects on classes of persons defined in a general and abstract manner.[5] Second, the act must be of "direct and individual concern" to the applicant.[6] If the action is successful, the act challenged is declared by the Court to be void,[7] and the matter is remitted to the institution concerned.

The grounds for challenge are set out in Article 173(1). Although they are based upon the grounds for review in continental, particularly French, administrative law, arguments may be based on principles of administrative law derived from the legal systems of any Member State. The grounds may overlap in the sense that a particular set of facts may involve infringements under more than one heading.

Lack of competence corresponds to the English concept of substantive

---

[99] See above pp. 85–89. The approach adopted by the European Court to the interpretation of Community Law is considered below pp. 270–277

[1] See also Art. 33(2)/ECSC; Art.146(2)/Euratom.

[2] This covers any act intended to have legal effect, and not merely regulations, directives and decisions: Case 22/70 *Commission* v. *Council* [1971] E.C.R. 263.

[3] This term includes a Member State: Case 25/62 *Plaumann* v. *Commission* [1963] E.C.R. 95.

[4] Cases 8–11/66 *Cimenteries* v. *Commission* (the *Noordwijks Cement Accoord case*) [1967] E.C.R. 75: a notification by the Commission that certain agreements were prohibited under Article 85/EEC, which had the effect of removing a temporary immunity from fines, was held to be reviewable even though such fines could only be imposed if further steps were taken by the Commission.

[5] Collins (1980) *op. cit.* p. 217, n. 30, pp. 170–172. The Court looks to the substance and not the form; the fact that the act has been promulgated as a regulation is not conclusive. See, *e.g.* Cases 113, 118–121/77 *Japanese Ball Bearings Cases* [1979] 2 C.M.L.R. 257 where four Japanese ball-bearing manufacturers were held to be entitled to challenge a regulation imposing an import duty in general terms, but which on the facts was aimed at them.

[6] There are a number of cases on this point, which are not always easy to reconcile: Collins (1980) pp. 174–177.

[7] Article 174/EEC.

ultra vires[7a] and the French concept of *excès de pouvoir or incompétence*. It may not be easily distinguishable from an allegation of *infringement of the Treaties or any rules of law relating to their application*. An example is *Meroni* v. *High Authority*[8] where certain decisions under the Coal and Steel Treaty were held to be improperly delegated to certain subordinate bodies.

Infringement of an essential procedural requirement corresponds to the English doctrine of procedural *ultra vires* and the French concept of *vice de forme*. Only requirements of substantial importance are mandatory: for example, requirements to hold a hearing,[9] to consult the European Parliament,[10] and to give reasons.[11] Minor irregularities are ignored; for example, notification of a decision to a subsidiary rather than to the applicants where the latter had full knowledge of the decision in time to institute proceedings,[12] and the reporting of a decision in the *Official Journal* under an inaccurate title.[13]

Misuse of powers broadly corresponds to the abuse of discretion aspect of the *ultra vires* doctrine and the French concept of *détournement de pouvoir*. It covers, for example, the use of a power for an improper purpose.

(b) Article 184: the plea of illegality

Article 184 of the EEC Treaty provides that:

> "Notwithstanding the expiry of the period laid down in the third paragraph of Article 173, any party[14] may, in proceedings in which a regulation[15] of the Council or of the Commission is in issue, plead the grounds specified in the first paragraph of Article 173, in order to invoke before the Court of Justice the inapplicability of that regulation."

An individual may not challenge a *regulation* under Article 173 (*supra*); if, however, he happens to be a party to proceedings before the European Court he (and any other party) may do so under Article 184. Article 184 may be invoked where proceedings are brought under some other provision of the Treaty which concern the party making the

---

[7a] On the English *ultra vires* doctrine see below, pp. 743–745.

[8] Case 9/56 [1957–8] E.C.R. 133; see also Case 48/69; *I.C.I.* v. *Commission* (the *Dyestuffs* case) [1972] E.C.R. 619.

[9] Case 41/69 *ACF Chemiefarma* v. *Commission* [1970] E.C.R. 661; the challenge failed on the merits: see also the *Dyestuffs* case *supra*. A hearing may be necessary even though it is not expressly required by Community legislation: Case 17/74 *Transocean Marine Paint Association* v. *Commission* [1974] E.C.R. 1063.

[10] See above, p. 223.

[11] See Art. 190 above, p. 218. Case 24/62 *Germany* v. *Commission* [1963] E.C.R. 63. The reasons must be adequate: the act must "set out, in a concise, but clear and relevant manner, the principal issues of law and of fact upon which it is based and which are necessary in order that the reasoning which has led the Commission to its Decision may be understood" (*ibid.* p. 69). See also Case 166/78 *Italy* v. *Council* [1979] E.C.R. 2575.

[12] *Dyestuffs* case, *supra*.

[13] Case 6/72 *Europemballage & Continental Can* v. *Commission* [1973] E.C.R. 215.

[14] This includes Member States: Case 32/65 *Italy* v. *Council and Commission* [1966] E.C.R. 389.

[15] But not a *decision*: Case 156/77 *Commission* v. *Belgium* [1978] E.C.R. 1881. The court again looks to substance rather than form: Case 92/78 *Simmenthal* v. *Commission* [1979] E.C.R. 777.

plea of illegality; it does not give that party an independent cause of action.[16]

(c) Article 175: remedy against inaction

Article 175 of the EEC Treaty provides that:

"(1) Should the Council or the Commission, in infringement of this Treaty, fail to act, the Member States and the other institutions of the Community may bring an action before the Court of Justice to have the infringement established.

(2) The action shall be admissible only if the institution concerned has first been called upon to act. If, within two months of being so called upon, the institution concerned has not defined its position, the action may be brought within a further period of two months.

(3) Any natural or legal person may, under the conditions laid down in the preceding paragraphs, complain to the Court of Justice that an institution of the Community has failed to address to that person any act other than a recommendation or an opinion."

The European Court has built in some limitations to actions under this article. An action can only be brought where the institution in question has failed to define its position within two months. In *Lütticke* v. *Commission*[17] the Commission had declined to take action against France on the ground that it had in fact complied with the Treaty, and stated as much within the two months period; the court held that an action could therefore not be brought. An individual may not use Article 175 to circumvent the restrictions that prevent him bringing an action directly against a Member State for breach of a Treaty provision,[18] or an action outside the limits of Article 173,[19] by attempting to bring an action against the Commission (respectively) (1) for failing to take action against the Member State or (2) failing to revoke a decision not in fact open to challenge under Article 173.

(d) Articles 177 and 215

The validity of Community legislation may also be considered by the European Court on a reference under Article 177 of the EEC Treaty,[20] or on an action for damages under Article 215 of the EEC Treaty.[21] In such cases the restrictions built in to Article 173 do not necessarily apply.

---

[16] Case 31/62 *Wohrmann* v. *Commission* [1962] E.C.R. 501.

[17] Case 48/65 [1966] E.C.R. 19.

[18] Under Articles 169 and 170/EEC such actions can only be brought by a Member State or the Commission: See the *Lütticke* case, *supra*.

[19] See above, pp. 231–233; Cases 10 and 18/68, *Eridania* v. *Commission* [1969] E.C.R. 459.

[20] See below, pp. 749–750.

[21] See above, p. 87.

CHAPTER 6

STATUTORY INTERPRETATION

A. INTRODUCTION

While the enactment of a statute is the culmination of Parliament's legislative process, it is merely the starting point for what may be many years of existence, in some cases posing problems for generations of users. If it is to have its proper effect it must be read and understood, although there are many other factors which govern the extent to which a particular measure is successful. There are various kinds of statute-user and many matters which may cause them difficulty.[1] It cannot realistically be assumed that all statutes are directed at the general public and are therefore designed to be understood by them. It is argued that statutes are complicated:

> " . . . because life is complicated. The bulk of the legislation enacted nowadays is social, economic or financial; the laws they [i.e. statutes] must express and the life situations they must regulate are in themselves complicated, and these laws cannot in any language or in any style be reduced to kindergarten level, any more than can the theory of relativity."[2]

The user tends to be the public official charged with the duty of implementation, the lawyer or the non-legal professional adviser, and statutes tend to be drafted accordingly: by experts for experts. Laymen[3] who wish to use statutes thus have to become acquainted with statute-handling techniques, or rely on explanatory material, such as textbooks or government leaflets, written by experts, or consult an expert personally. This is seen by some as a vicious circle: they doubt whether statutes need to be as complicated as experts who earn a living by explaining them to the rest of us would have us believe.

Some of the problems of the user, even the professional user, relate to the discovery of the relevant provisions and the establishment of an authentic, up-to-date text. The provisions may be spread among a number of statutes and statutory instruments which have to be read together. The uninstructed layman may well not accomplish even this stage. Once established, the text also has to be understood or "interpreted."[4] The task of interpretation may vary in difficulty. Some provisions can be understood automatically, without the conscious perception of any "problem" of interpretation: some problems may be easy to solve after a moment's thought. At the other extreme, a problem may be highly complex, enough

---

[1] See F.A.R. Bennion, *Statute Law* (2nd ed., 1983), Part II (pp. 111–207); *cf.* W. Twining and D. Miers, *How To Do Things With Rules* (2nd ed., 1982), Chaps. 4–6.

[2] E.A. Dreidger, cited in *Bennion* (1983), p. 112.

[3] Or, indeed, lawyers and other professionals in matters outside their expertise.

[4] The O.E.D. definitions of this term include both "to expound the meaning of" and "to make out the meaning of, explain to oneself."

to make strong men weep. Printing or drafting errors can turn a provision into gibberish.

F.A.R. Bennion[5] has identified a number of factors that may cause doubt. Some of these doubt-factors are inevitable and even desirable: others are avoidable. First, there is what he terms the technique of *ellipsis*. Here, the draftsman refrains from using certain words that he regards as necessarily implied: the problem is that the users may not realise that this is the case. The unexpressed words may normally be implied in statutes of a particular kind unless Parliament expressly provides to the contrary: many of the principles of judicial review of administrative action rest on this basis,[6] as do certain principles of criminal liability.[7] Alternatively the implication may arise from the words that actually are used. The judges on occasion exercise a limited power (in practice but not in theory) to rewrite statutes, although it can be difficult to predict in any particular case whether a judge will be prepared to act in that way.[8]

Second, the draftsman may use a *broad term* ("a word or phrase of wide meaning") and leave it to the user to judge what situations fall within it. Most words can be said to have a core of certain meaning surrounded by a penumbra of uncertainty. A standard example is the term "vehicle." This clearly covers motor cars, buses and motor cycles, but it is less clear whether it covers an invalid carriage, a child's tricycle, a donkey-cart or a pair of roller-skates.[9] Examples from decided cases include whether the routine oiling and maintenance of points apparatus on the railway fell within the term "relaying or repairing" the permanent way[10]; whether an accident arises "out of and in the course of [the victim's] . . . employment"[11]; and whether a car from which the engine had been stolen and a car which could not move under its own power as parts were missing or rusted were "mechanically propelled vehicles" for which a licence was required.[12] Sir Rupert Cross described this sort of case as "part of the daily bread of judges and practitioners."[13] One difficulty here may be that the

---

[5] *Op. cit.* n.1 above.

[6] e.g. breach of natural justice, abuse of discretionary powers: see below, p. 744.

[7] e.g. general defences of mistake and insanity. A major defect of the drafting of many statutes creating offences is that they do not make it clear whether *mens rea* is a necessary ingredient: see, e.g. R. v. *Warner* [1969] 2 A.C. 256. Another common defect is that statutes imposing duties do not indicate whether breach of a duty can give rise to a civil action: see, e.g., *Lonhro Ltd.* v. *Shell Petroleum Co. Ltd.* (No. 2) [1982] A.C. 173.

[8] See below, pp. 248–250.

[9] Twining and Miers (1982), pp. 205–206; cf. H.L.A. Hart, (1958) 4 J.S.P.T.L. (N.S.) 144–145.

[10] *London and North-Eastern Railway* v. *Berriman* [1946] A.C. 278.

[11] See, e.g. R. v. *Industrial Injuries Commissioner, ex p. A.E.U.* (No. 2) [1966] 2 Q.B. 31. (accident befalling an employee overstaying a tea-break). There have been many cases on this expression: see A.I. Ogus and E. Barendt, *The Law of Social Security* (2nd ed., 1982), pp. 271–287, P.F. Smith, *Industrial Injuries Benefit* (1978), pp. 24–45.

[12] *Newberry* v. *Simmonds* [1961] 2 Q.B. 345; *Smart* v. *Allan* [1963] 1 Q.B. 291: the answers were, respectively, yes and no, the main difference being that in the latter case there was no reasonable prospect of the vehicle ever being made mobile again.

[13] *Statutory Interpretation* (1976), p. 68. Another good illustration is provided by the refusal of Parliament to define "disposal" and "disposition" for the purposes of respectively, capital gains tax and capital transfer tax: see J. Tiley, *Revenue Law* (3rd ed., 1981), paras. 20–01 and 42–02.

meaning of a statutory expression may change with the passage of time.[14] A further technical point that may arise when it has to be decided whether a set of facts conforms to a statutory description is whether that decision is one of fact or one of law. This governs whether it should be decided by the jury (if there is one) or the judge, and the extent to which the decision can be upset by an appellate court.[15]

Third, there may be *politic uncertainty:* ambiguous words may be used deliberately, for example where a provision is politically contentious, or where departments wish to minimise the risk of legal challenge.[15a]

Fourth, there may be *unforeseeable developments.* These the draftsman cannot be expected to cover, although he may use language that is capable of extension. A well-known example of such extension is *Attorney-General* v. *Edison Telephone Co.*[16] where the Telegraph Act 1869, passed before the telephone was invented, was held to confer on the Postmaster General certain powers concerning telephone messages. However, extension may not be possible, and fresh legislation may be necessary. For example, new provisions of revenue law are regularly passed to meet novel tax avoidance schemes developed by smart lawyers and accountants precisely to exploit unforeseen loopholes.

Fifth, there are many ways in which the wording may be inadequate. There may be a printing error.[17] There may be a drafting error such as the use of a word with two or more distinct meanings without a sufficient indication from the context or by a definition of which is meant, or grammatical or syntactic ambiguity. Examples of the latter include "ambiguous modification," where it is unclear which words are limited, restricted or described by a "modifier,"[18] and the faulty reference of pronouns.[19] There may be an erroneous reference to another statute.[20]

---

[14] See, for example, the "public good" defence in section 4 of the Obscene Publications Act 1959: *R.* v. *Jordan* [1977] A.C. 699, 718, *per* Lord Wilberforce: "[the phrase 'other objects of general concern'] is no doubt a mobile phrase; it may, and should, change in content as society changes." *Cf. Dyson Holdings Ltd.* v. *Fox* [1976] Q.B. 503 on whether the term "family" includes a "common law" spouse, criticised by D.J. Hurst, (1983) 3 L.S. 21.

[15] See above, pp. 8–11 and below, pp. 729–730.

[15a] Bennion (1983) Chap. 14; A.S. Miller, "Statutory language and the purposive use of ambiguity" 42 Va.L.Rev. 23 (1956); V. Sacks, "Towards Discovering Parliamentary Intent" [1982] Stat.L.R. 143, 157 (research on the background to a number of cases of interpretative difficulty showed that "unintelligible legislation was being added to the statute book because the Government either lacked clear objectives, or, had deliberately intended to obfuscate in order to avoid controversy").

[16] (1880) 6 Q.B.D. 244.

[17] *e.g.* the presence of the word "upon" at the end of section 6 of the Statute of Frauds Amendment Act 1828: *Lyde* v. *Barnard* (1836) 1 M. & W. 101; Local Government Act 1972, s.262(12) (reference to subsection (10) rather than subsection (9) in the Queen's Printer's copy, corrected in *Statutes in Force*); the presence of the word "convenient" in the Prescription Act 1832, s.8, apparently a misprint for "easement": R.E. Megarry and H.W.R. Wade, *The Law of Real Property* (4th ed., 1975), p. 857.

[18] G.C. Thornton, *Legislative Drafting* (2nd ed., 1979), pp. 25–31. *e.g.* "public hospital or school" (does "public" modify "school" as well as "hospital"?). A statute of Charles II disqualified those who lacked certain property qualifications "other than the son and heir apparent of an esquire, or other person of higher degree." In *Jones* v. *Smart* (1784) 1 Term Rep. 44 the court held that the words "son and heir apparent of" governed "person of higher degree" as well as "esquire."

[19] Thornton, pp. 31–33. *e.g.* "and when they arose early in the morning, behold, they were all corpses": 2 Kings XIX 35.

[20] *e.g.* War Damage Act 1943, s.66(2)(*b*) corrected by the Universities and College Estates Act 1964, s.4(1) Sched. 3.

The draftsman may be mistaken about the law that is being altered[21] or the factual situation with which he is dealing. The statutory provision may be narrower[22] or wider[23] than the object of the legislation. The provision may fail to indicate an important element, such as the time at which conditions of eligibility for some benefit are to be judged.[24] There may be the type of error described as "defective deeming, or asifism gone wrong."[25] There may be conflict within a statute or between different statutes. Overall, Bennion states that "it is extremely common for draftsman to produce a text which raises doubt unnecessarily."[26]

As mentioned already, various people may have to interpret statutes for their own purposes. Some may take action based on their own view of a statutory provision. For example, in *R. v. Adams*[27] police officers decided that they could rely on a search warrant in respect of certain premises which had already been used once. The statute did not deal expressly with the question whether a warrant could be used more than once: the court held that it could not. Tax assessments may well be based on the Inland Revenue's interpretation of a doubtful provision of tax law: it will be for the Commissioners of Taxes or the courts to rule on the matter if the Revenue view is challenged. The courts stand in a rather different position from other statute users in that they have the power to resolve authoritatively disputes concerning the meaning of statutory provisions: their decisions are binding on the parties and may constitute binding precedents for the future.

It is notable that the general methods of statutory interpretation are not themselves regulated by Parliament, but have been developed by the judges. The Interpretation Act 1978, which from its title might seem to fulfil such a function, has the comparatively unambitious aim of providing certain standard definitions of common provisions,[28] and thereby enables statutes to be drafted more briefly than otherwise would be the case. Where Parliament or, more realistically, the executive has been dissatisfied with judicial interpretation of particular provisions the response has been to pay close attention to the future drafting of specific provisions in that area rather than to attempt to introduce legislation giving general directions to the judiciary. In the remainder of this chapter we consider the general approaches taken by judges to the interpretation of statutes,

---

[21] *e.g. Inland Revenue Commissioners* v. *Ayrshire Employers' Mutual Insurance Association.* [1946] 1 All E.R. 537.

[22] *e.g. Adler* v. *George* [1964] 2 Q.B. 7: the Official Secrets Act 1920, s.3 prohibited obstruction "in the vicinity of" a prohibited place; the Divisional Court held that this was to be read as "in or in the vicinity of."

[23] *e.g.* The Criminal Law Act 1977, ss.1 and 5, which on a literal interpretation preserved a much wider range of common law conspiracies than was obviously intended; in *R. v. Duncalf* [1979] 1 W.L.R. 918 the Court of Appeal declined to give a literal reading "when the effect of so doing would be so largely to destroy the obvious purpose of this Act" (*per* Roskill L.J. at p. 923). *R. v. Duncalf* was approved by the House of Lords in *R. v. Ayres* [1984] 2 W.L.R. 257.

[24] *Jackson* v. *Hall* [1980] A.C. 854, concerning the Agriculture (Miscellaneous Provisions) Act 1976.

[25] Bennion (1983), pp. 200–201; R.E. Megarry, *Miscellany-at-law* (1955) pp. 361–362 ("there is too much of this damned deeming": *per* (A.P. Herbert's) Lord Mildew).

[26] *Ibid.* p. 206.

[27] [1980] Q.B. 575.

[28] See above, pp. 203–204.

various internal and external aids to interpretation, the main presumptions which may be invoked and proposals for reform.

B. GENERAL APPROACHES TO STATUTORY INTERPRETATION

Judicial attitudes to legislation have changed with the passage of time. One of the important factors has been the part played by statutes in the general scheme of the law: a related factor has been the conception held by judges as to the proper scope of the judicial function. Three "rules" of statutory interpretation have been identified: the "mischief rule," the "golden rule" and the "literal rule," each originating at different stages of legal history. To call them "rules" is somewhat misleading: it is better to think of them as general approaches. They were analysed by Professor John Willis in his influential article "Statute Interpretation in a Nutshell."[29] He suggested that:

> "a court invokes whichever of the rules produces a result that satisfies its sense of justice in the case before it. Although the literal rule is the one most frequently referred to in express terms, the courts treat all three as valid and refer to them as occasion demands, but, naturally enough, do not assign any reasons for choosing one rather than another."[30]

Thus, on some occasions the "literal rule" would be preferred to the "mischief rule": on others the reverse would be the case. It was impossible to predict with certainty which approach would be adopted in a particular case.[31] More recently, Sir Rupert Cross has suggested that the English approach involves not so much a choice between alternative "rules" as a progressive analysis in which the judge first considers the ordinary meaning of the words in the general context of the statute, a broad view being taken of what constitutes the "context," and then moves on to consider other possibilities where the ordinary meaning leads to an absurd result. This unified "contextual" approach is supported by dicta in recent decisions of the House of Lords where general principles of statutory interpretation have been discussed. However, generalisations as to what judges actually do are difficult to substantiate: Sir Rupert Cross made it clear that his propositions were stated "with all the diffidence, hesitancy and reservation the subject demands."[32]

In cases of doubt or difficulty, judges often say that it is necessary to discover the "intention of Parliament" as to either the meaning or the scope of a particular word or phrase, or the general purpose that was to be achieved by the statute.[33] This concept causes difficulty for a number of reasons.[34] It cannot mean the intention of "all the members of both

[29] (1938) 16 Can. Bar Rev. 1.

[30] *Ibid.* p. 16.

[31] This situation can be unkindly described as the "today's a day for the golden rule" approach. The tone of Professor Willis' article was one of scepticism.

[32] *Statutory Interpretation* (1976), p. 42.

[33] Termed respectively "particular legislative intent" and "general legislative intent" by G.C. MacCallum Jr. (1966) 75 Yale L.J. 754.

[34] See Cross (1976) pp. 34–40; M. Radin, (1930) 43 Harv. L.R. 863, 869–872; J.M. Landis, *ibid.* pp. 886–893; D. Payne, (1956) 9 C.L.P. 96; R. Dworkin, "How to read the Civil Rights Act," *New York Review of Books*, December 20, 1979, pp. 37–43.

Houses" as some may not have been aware of the measure, and others may have opposed it. If it is taken to mean "all the members of both Houses who voted for it" there may be problems in that the majority "will almost certainly have been constituted by different persons at the different stages of the passage of the Bill,"[35] and might have had different views as to its meaning or purpose. A vote in favour of a Bill may reflect loyalty to the party whip rather than an understanding or even half-hearted approval of the measure. Even assuming that there is a "collective intention" it is difficult to see how it could be ascertained. Would it be by reference to the debates or by canvassing the opinions of the legislators individually, possibly years after the event? The former would limit the "sample" to the minority who happened to speak: the latter would be a research task which might just produce usable results in respect of a provision requiring interpretation soon after enactment, but with the passage of time it would rapidly become hopeless. In any event it is questionable whether even if it is possible it would be appropriate for the meaning of a particular provision to be determined by an opinion poll of the original legislators. In fact, the courts are not allowed to consider reports of Parliamentary proceedings, or the opinions of the legislators expressed elsewhere,[36] and so references to the "intention of Parliament" may simply involve speculation as to what view might have been taken by the average member of Parliament. The judge's guess is presumably as good as anyone else's and the exercise may at least discourage him from simply deciding the issue according to his own preferences. In the case of government Bills the people who devote most thought to the purpose and wording of the statutory provisions are the ministers who steer them through Parliament, the civil servants who advise them and the draftsmen who have converted their instructions into a draft Bill. However, it would be incorrect to regard them as "Parliament" and a fiction to regard them as the agents of Parliament. As a result the judges tend to affirm that the best if not the only evidence of the "intention of Parliament" is the wording of the statute:

> "We often say that we are looking for the intention of Parliament, but that is not quite accurate. We are seeking the meaning of the words which Parliament used. We are seeking not what Parliament meant but the true meaning of what they said."[37]

If Lord Reid is right, judicial references to seeking the intention of Parliament are not so much indications of a method of solving a problem of interpretation as restatements of the problem. Such references do serve to emphasise the orthodox position to the separation of powers whereby Parliament legislates and the judges interpret. They may also conceal the fact that judges on occasion legislate when they exercise their limited power to treat statutes as if their wording were modified.

Variants of references to the "intention of Parliament" are judicial references to the purpose or object of a statute. As we shall see, the words of a statute are to be considered in the light of the object which it is

---

[35] Cross (1976) p. 34.
[36] See below, pp. 260–261.
[37] Per Lord Reid in Black-Clawson International Ltd. v. Papierwerke Waldhof-Aschaffenburg A.G. [1975] A.C. 591, 613.

intended to achieve, and interpretations that facilitate the achievement of the object are to be preferred.[38] The "intention" used in this sense approximates most closely to the intentions of the Bill's promoters.

1. The "Mischief Rule"

The classic statement of the "mischief rule" is contained in the resolutions of the Barons of the Exchequer in *Heydon's Case*[39]:

> "that for the sure and true interpretation of all statutes in general (be they penal or beneficial, restrictive or enlarging of the common law,) four things are to be discerned and considered:—
>
> 1st. What was the common law before the making of the Act.
>
> 2nd. What was the mischief and defect for which the common law did not provide.
>
> 3rd. What remedy the Parliament hath resolved and appointed to cure the disease of the commonwealth.
>
> And, 4th. The true reason of the remedy; and then the office of all the Judges is always to make such construction as shall suppress the mischief, and advance the remedy, and to suppress subtle inventions and evasions for continuance of the mischief, and *pro privato commodo,* and to add force and life to the cure and remedy, according to the true intent of the makers of the Act, *pro bono publico.*"

These resolutions were the product of a time when statutes were a comparatively minor source of law by comparison with the common law, when drafting was by no means as exact a process as it is today[40] and before the supremacy of Parliament was firmly established. The "mischief" could often be discerned from the lengthy preamble normally included.[41]

The "mischief rule" was regarded by the Law Commissions, which reported on statutory interpretation in 1969,[42] as a "rather more satisfactory approach" than the other two established "rules." This was so even though the formulation in *Heydon's Case* was archaic in language, reflected a very different constitutional balance between the executive, Parliament and the people than would now be acceptable, failed to make clear the extent to which the judge should consider the actual language of the statute, assumed that statutes were subsidiary or supplemental to the common law and predated rules which prevented judges considering certain material which might throw light on the "mischief" and the "true reason of the remedy."[43] Seemingly, therefore, it was the best of a bad lot.

It came to be accepted that the "mischief rule" should only be applied where the words were ambiguous[44]; one of the improvements of the "contextual approach" discussed below is that the purpose of the statute should be considered as part of the context of the statutory words, and not merely as a last resort where the words are ambiguous.

---

[38] See below.

[39] (1584) 3 Co.Rep. 7a, 7b.

[40] Some statutes were well drafted, such as the Statute of Uses 1535.

[41] *Black-Clawson International Ltd.* v. *Papierwerke Waldhof-Aschaffenburg A.G.* [1975] A.C. 591 *per* Lord Diplock at p. 637–638. See below, p. 252.

[42] Law Com. No. 21; Scot. Law Com. No. 11.

[43] *Ibid.* pp. 19–20. See below, pp. 260–264.

[44] See the *Sussex Peerage Case,* below, p. 242.

2. The "Literal Rule"

The eighteenth and nineteenth centuries saw a trend towards a more literal approach. Courts took an increasingly strict view of the words of a statute: if the case before them was not precisely covered they were not prepared to countenance any alteration of the statutory language. For example, in *R.* v. *Harris*[45] a statute[46] which made it an offence for someone "unlawfully and maliciously" to "stab, cut, or wound any person" was held not to apply where the defendant bit off the end of the victim's nose; the words indicated that for an offence to be committed some form of instrument had to be used.[47]

One of the leading statements of the "literal rule" was made by Tindal C.J. in advising the House of Lords in the *Sussex Peerage* case[48]:

> "My Lords, the only rule for the construction of Acts of Parliament is, that they should be construed according to the intent of the Parliament which passed the Act. If the words of the statute are in themselves precise and unambiguous, then no more can be necessary than to expound those words in their natural and ordinary sense. The words themselves alone do, in such case, best declare the intention of the lawgiver. But if any doubt arises from the terms employed by the Legislature, it has always been held a safe mean of collecting the intention, to call in aid the ground and cause of making the statute, and to have recourse to the preamble, which, according to Chief Justice Dyer (*Stowel* v. *Lord Zouch,* Plowden, 369) is 'a key to open the minds of the makers of the Act, and the mischiefs which they intended to redress.' "

This was taken to mean that the "mischief rule" was only applicable where the words were ambiguous.

The literal rule was favoured on a variety of grounds. It encouraged precision in drafting. Should any alternative approach be adopted, an alteration of the statutory language could be seen as a usurpation by non-elected judges of the legislative function of Parliament,[49] and other statute users would have the difficult task of predicting how doubtful provisions might be "rewritten" by the judges. On the other hand judges were criticised on the ground that:

> "they have tended excessively to emphasise the literal meaning of statutory provisions without giving due weight to their meaning in wider contexts. . . . "[50]

> "To place undue emphasis on the literal meaning of the words of a provision is to assume an unattainable perfection in drafts-manship; . . . [and] ignores the limitations of language, which is not

---

[45] (1836) 7 C. & P. 446.

[46] 9 Geo. IV c. 31 s.12.

[47] The judge indicated that the defendant would be indicted for aggravated assault and thus "would not escape punishment if she was guilty." *Cf. Jones* v. *Smart, above,* p. 237, n. 18.

[48] (1844) 11 Cl. & Fin. 85, 143.

[49] Conversely, it might be argued that a judge could conceal that his role was not as impersonal and objective as he would like it to appear by paying lip-service to the literal rule.

[50] Law Com. No. 21; Scot. Law Com. No. 11, p. 5.

infrequently demonstrated even at the level of the House of Lords when Law Lords differ as to the so-called 'plain meaning' of words."[51]

Moreover, the literal approach is not helpful where the court is resolving a doubt as to the applicability of a "broad term."

Much has been made of a few post-war cases where literalism has perhaps been taken too far. For example, in *Bourne* v. *Norwich Crematorium*[52] the question was whether a capital allowance could be claimed in respect of expenditure on a new furnace chamber and chimney tower of a crematorium, as expenditure on "buildings and structures" in use "for the purpose of a trade which consists of the manufacture of goods or materials or the subjection of goods or materials to any process." Stamp J. held that it could not: it would be "a distortion of the English language to describe the living or the dead as goods or materials."[53] However, it is unlikely that either the draftsman or Parliament thought specifically of cremation in connection with capital allowances and the policy of the provisions on capital allowances would seem to cover the "trade" of cremation.[54]

The "contextual approach" discussed below is based on the literal approach, but requires greater attention to be paid to the context in which the words appear.

3. THE "GOLDEN RULE"

Some judges have suggested that a court may depart from the ordinary meaning where that would lead to absurdity. In *Grey* v. *Pearson*[55] Lord Wensleydale said:

"I have been long and deeply impressed with the wisdom of the rule, now, I believe, universally adopted, at least in the Courts of Law in Westminster Hall, that in construing wills and indeed statutes, and all written instruments, the grammatical and ordinary sense of the words is to be adhered to, unless that would lead to some absurdity, or some repugnance or inconsistency with the rest of the instrument, in which case the grammatical and ordinary sense of the words may be modified, so as to avoid that absurdity and inconsistency, but no farther."

This became known as "Lord Wensleydale's golden rule" following a dictum of Lord Blackburn in *River Wear Commissioners* v. *Adamson*[56]:

"I believe that it is not disputed that what Lord Wensleydale used to call the golden rule is right, viz., that we are to take the whole statute

---

[51] *Ibid.* p. 17. For example, in *London and North Eastern Railway* v. *Berriman* [1946] A.C. 278 (below p. 247) members of the House of Lords who came to opposite conclusions on the meaning of "repairing" nevertheless each claimed to be applying the "fair and ordinary" (Lord Macmillan at p. 295) or the "natural and ordinary" meaning (Lord Wright at p. 301).

[52] [1967] 1 W.L.R. 691. See also *L.N.E.R.* v. *Berriman*, below, p. 247.

[53] *Ibid.* p. 695.

[54] See Law Com. No. 21, pp. 5–6; Cross (1976), p. 64. The decision has not, however, been reversed by statute.

[55] (1857) 6 H.L.Cas. 61, 106 (a case concerning the construction of a will). *Cf.* the same judge when he was Parke B. in *Becke* v. *Smith* (1836) 2 M. & W. 191, 195.

[56] (1877) 2 App.Cas. 743, 764–5.

> together and construe it all together, giving the words their ordinary signification, unless when so applied they produce an inconsistency, or an absurdity or inconvenience so great as to convince the Court that the intention could not have been to use them in their ordinary signification, and to justify the Court in putting on them some other signification, which, though less proper, is one which the Court thinks the words will bear."

One controversial aspect of this "rule" was whether it could only apply where the words were ambiguous, or whether it could also be used where the ordinary meaning was clear but "absurd." In so far as it was confined to the former situation it was a statement of the blindingly obvious: that where statutory words are ambiguous an interpretation that is not absurd is to be preferred to one that is. In so far as the "rule" could be applied in the latter situation it was clear that it should be used sparingly.[57] Some judges argued it could not be used in such a case at all. Lord Esher said[58]:

> "If the words of an Act are clear, you must follow them, even though they lead to a manifest absurdity. The Court has nothing to do with the question whether the legislature has committed an absurdity."

Another point of doubt was whether the concept of "absurdity" was confined to cases where a provision was "absurd" because it was "repugnant" to or "inconsistent" with other provisions of the statute, or whether it extended to "absurdity" for any reason. The Law Commissions noted that the "rule" provided no clear means to test the existence of the characteristics of absurdity, inconsistency or inconvenience, or to measure their quality or extent.[59] As it seemed that "absurdity" was in practice judged by reference to whether a particular interpretation was irreconcilable with the general policy of the legislature "the golden rule turns out to be a less explicit form of the mischief rule."[60] The ideas behind the "golden rule" are reflected in the second and third aspects of the contextual approach discussed below.

4. THE UNIFIED "CONTEXTUAL" APPROACH

Sir Rupert Cross set out a unified approach to statutory interpretation as follows[61]:

> "1. The judge must give effect to the ordinary or, where appropriate, the technical meaning of words in the general context of the statute;

---

[57] Lord Mersey in *Thompson* v. *Goold & Co.* [1910] A.C. 409, 420; Lord Loreburn in *Vickers, Sons, and Maxim Ltd.* v. *Evans* [1910] A.C. 444, 445.

[58] *R.* v. *Judge of the City of London Court* [1892] 1 Q.B. 273, 290. *Cf.* Lord Atkinson in *Vacher & Sons Ltd.* v. *London Society of Compositors* [1913] A.C. 107, 121–122.

[59] Law Com. No. 21; Scot. Law Com. No. 11, p. 19.

[60] *Ibid.* Sir Rupert Cross regarded the "golden rule" as a "gloss upon the literal rule": Cross (1976) p. 170. *Cf.* E.A. Dreidger, (1981) 59 Can. Bar Rev. 781.

[61] Cross, *Statutory Interpretation* (1976), p. 43. The label "contextual" was not attached by Cross, but is used here for convenience of reference. Rules 1 and 2 were expounded by Lord Simon in *Maunsell* v. *Olins* [1975] A.C. 373, 391; rule 3 by Lord Reid in *Federal Steam Navigation Co. Ltd.* v. *Department of Trade and Industry* [1974] 1 W.L.R. 505, 508–509. The "aids" and "presumptions" are discussed in Chapters V to VII of Cross's book.

he must also determine the extent of general words with reference to that context.

2. If the judge considers that the application of the words in their ordinary sense would produce an absurd result which cannot reasonably be supposed to have been the intention of the legislature, he may apply them in any secondary meaning which they are capable of bearing.

3. The judge may read in words which he considers to be necessarily implied by words which are already in the statute and he has a limited power to add to, alter or ignore statutory words in order to prevent a provision from being unintelligible or absurd or totally unreasonable, unworkable or totally irreconcilable with the rest of the statute.

4. In applying the above rules the judge may resort to [certain] aids to construction and presumptions. . . . "

(a) Rule 1

Under this approach a broader view is taken of the context than under previous approaches. The importance of context was discussed in *Attorney-General* v. *Prince Ernest Augustus of Hanover.*[62] A statute of Queen Anne's reign[63] provided that Princess Sophia of Hanover "and the Issue of Her Body and all Persons lineally descending from Her born or hereafter to be born be and shall be . . . deemed . . . natural born Subjects of this Kingdom." The preamble recited that in order that they might be encouraged to become acquainted with the laws and constitutions of this realm "it is just and highly reasonable that they in Your Majesties Lifetime" be naturalised.[64] The respondent, who was born in 1914 and was a lineal descendant of Sophia, was granted a declaration that he was a British subject. The enacting words were clear and could not be restricted by the words in the preamble. Viscount Simonds said[65]:

"[W]ords, and particularly general words, cannot be read in isolation; their colour and content are derived from their context. So it is that I conceive it to be my right and duty to examine every word of a statute in its context, and I use context in its widest sense which I have already indicated as including not only other enacting provisions of the same statute, but its preamble, the existing state of the law, other statutes *in pari materia,* and the mischief which I can, by those and other legitimate means, discern the statute was intended to remedy. . . .

"[N]o one should profess to understand any part of a statute or of any other document before he has read the whole of it. Until he has done so, he is not entitled to say that it, or any part of it, is clear and unambiguous."

[62] [1957] A.C. 436.

[63] 4 & 5 Anne c. 16.

[64] On the death of Queen Anne without issue the Crown of England would descend on Sophia and her heirs; Sophia's son became King George I.

[65] At pp. 461, 463. Lord Tucker expressed his "complete agreement" with Viscount Simonds' opinion (p. 472).

Lord Normand said[66]:

> "In order to discover the intention of Parliament it is proper that the court should read the whole Act, inform itself of the legal context of the Act, including Acts so related to it that they may throw light on its meaning, and of the factual context, such as the mischief to be remedied. . . . It is the merest commonplace to say that words abstracted from context may be meaningless or misleading."

Even after the context had been considered it could not be said that the enacting words were unclear; the preamble itself was ambiguous; three of their Lordships also held that there was no inherent absurdity, judged at the time when the statute was passed, in the fact that all lineal descendants would be naturalised.[67]

That the object of the statute is to be considered as part of the context was emphasised in *Maunsell* v. *Olins.*[68] The plaintiff owned the freehold of a farm. The farm's tenant had sublet a cottage to the Olins. If the cottage formed "part of premises which had been let as a whole on a superior letting" the Olins were entitled to the continued protection of the Rent Acts after the tenant's death. The House held by 3 to 2[69] that the word "premises" was to be limited to dwelling-houses[70] and as the Olins were not the subtenants of part of premises in that limited sense they were not protected. Lord Wilberforce expressly endorsed Viscount Simonds' dictum in the *Hanover* case.[71] Lord Simon, with whom Lord Diplock entirely agreed, held that the term "premises" was to be construed more widely as in ordinary legal parlance as "the subject-matter of a letting" or, more technically, as "the subject-matter of the habendum clause of the relevant lease." He did, however, make certain general observations as to interpretation, which were not controverted in the speeches of the majority[72]:

> "The rule in *Heydon's Case,* 3, Co.Rep. 7a itself is sometimes stated as a primary canon of construction, sometimes as secondary (*i.e.* available in the case of an ambiguity): *cf. Maxwell on the Interpretation of Statutes* (12th ed., 1969), pp. 40, 96, with *Craies on Statute Law,* 7th ed. (1971) pp. 94, 96. We think that the explanation of this is that the rule is available at two stages. The first task of a court of construction is to put itself in the shoes of the draftsman—to consider what knowledge he had and, importantly, what statutory objective he had—if only as a guide to the linguistic register. Here is the first consideration of the 'mischief.' Being thus placed in the shoes of the

---

[66] At p. 465. See also Lord Somervell at pp. 473–474.

[67] Most of the royal heads of Europe in the early twentieth century, including the Kaiser, were lineal descendants of Sophia.

[68] [1975] A.C. 373. See also *Stock* v. *Frank Jones (Tipton) Ltd.* [1978] 1 W.L.R. 231, 236.

[69] Lord Reid, Lord Wilberforce and Viscount Dilhorne; Lord Simon and Lord Diplock dissented.

[70] Viscount Dilhorne thought the term might mean "buildings."

[71] Above.

[72] p. 395. Other recent examples of interpretation in the light of the mischief include *Marshall* v. *British Broadcasting Corporation* [1979] 1 W.L.R. 1071, *Maidstone B.C.* v. *Mortimer* [1980] 3 All E.R. 552 and *Royal College of Nursing of the United Kingdom* v. *DHSS* [1981] A.C. 800.

draftsman, the court proceeds to ascertain the meaning of the statutory language. In this task 'the first and most elementary rule of construction' is to consider the plain and primary meaning, in their appropriate register, of the words used. If there is no such plain meaning (*i.e.*, if there is an ambiguity), a number of secondary canons are available to resolve it. Of these one of the most important is the rule in *Heydon's Case*. Here, then, may be a second consideration of the 'mischief.' "

In 1980, Lord Scarman said in a lecture in Australia that, "In London, no one would now dare to choose the literal rather than a purposive construction of a statute: and 'legalism' is currently a term of abuse."[73] This should not, however, be taken too far. In a number of cases a "purposive" approach to construction (*i.e.* one that will "promote the general legislative purpose underlying the provision"[73a]) has been adopted alongside a literal approach, each being regarded as leading to the same result.[73b] A purposive approach has been adopted where a literal approach would have led to absurdity or would have clearly defeated the purposes of the Act.[73c] However, a purposive interpretation may only be adopted if judges "can find in the statute read as a whole or in material to which they are permitted by law to refer as aids to interpretation an expression of Parliament's purpose or policy,"[73d] and the power to read in words is limited.[73e]

Examples of cases where a court has had to choose between different "ordinary meanings" include *London and North Eastern Railway Co.* v. *Berriman*,[74] where the issue was whether a railwayman was "relaying or repairing" the permanent way while oiling and cleaning points apparatus. He had been knocked down and killed by a train. If he had been so engaged, his widow was entitled to damages and the company's failure to provide an adequate warning system would be a criminal offence. By 3 to 2 the House of Lords held that "relaying or repairing" involved putting right something that was wrong and not merely maintenance work of the kind the railwayman had been doing. The object of the statute seemed to cover workmen in this situation, but there was also a presumption that penal statutes should be strictly construed.[75] It should be noted that it has

---

[73] (1981) 55 A.L.J. 175. *Cf.* Glanville Williams, "The Meaning of Literal Interpretation" (1981) 131 N.L.J. 1128, 1149, who argues that the primary question should be "What was the statute trying to do?" followed by "Will a particular proposed interpretation effectuate that object" and lastly, "Is the interpretation ruled out by the language?"

[73a] *Per* Lord Denning M.R. in *Nothman* v. *London Borough of Barnet* [1978] 1 W.L.R. 220, 228, based on the Law Commissions' Report: see below, p. 269.

[73b] *Suffolk County Council* v. *Mason* [1979] A.C. 705 (by both majority and minority judges); *Gardner* v. *Moore* [1984] 2 W.L.R. 714.

[73c] *R.* v. *Ayres* [1984] 2 W.L.R. 257; *cf.* Lord Diplock in *Jones* v. *Wrotham Park Settled Estates* [1980] A.C. 74, 105: *cf*, "rule 2" below.

[73d] *Per* Lord Scarman in *R.* v. *Barnet London Borough Council, ex p. Nilish Shah* [1983] 2 A.C. 309, 348 (the test was not satisfied here).

[73e] *Per* Lord Diplock in *Jones* v. *Wrotham Park Settled Estates, supra; cf.* "rule 3" below.

[74] [1946] A.C. 278.

[75] See further, below, p. 267. *Cf. Ealing London Borough* v. *Race Relations Board* [1972] A.C. 342, where the House of Lords held by 4 to 1 that discrimination on the ground of *nationality* was not prohibited as being discrimination on the ground of "national origins."

become increasingly common for judges to duck interpretative difficulties by classifying words as "ordinary English words."[75a]

Examples of words used in a statute in a technical rather than an ordinary sense include "fettling" (trimming up of metal castings as they come from the foundry rather than "to put into good fettle" generally[76]); "crawling boards" (special boards with battens rather than simply boards for crawling on[77]); and "offer for sale" (held not to cover the placing of a flick-knife in a shop window as this was in the law of contract merely an invitation to treat[78]). Conversely, the majority in *Maunsell* v. *Olins*[79] preferred what they regarded to be the popular meaning of "premises" to the technical legal meaning.

(b) Rule 2

A court may choose a "secondary meaning" where the primary meaning is productive of injustice, absurdity, anomaly or contradiction.[80] Thus, provisions giving a power of arrest in respect of an "offender" or "a person found committing an offence" have been held to cover *apparent* offenders[81]: police officers had to act on the facts as they appeared at the time and were not to be exposed to the risk of actions for damages merely because the suspect was subsequently acquitted. A provision of the Factories Act 1937 requiring the fencing of dangerous parts of a machine while the parts were "in motion" was held not to apply where a workman turned the machine by hand in order to repair it. The machine could not have been repaired while it was fenced.[82] The notion of "absurdity" here seems not to be confined to cases where a provision is repugnant to or inconsistent with the rest of the statute.[83]

(c) Rule 3

A judge may read in words necessarily implied by the words actually used.[84] The line between cases of "necessary implication" and cases where the statutory language is modified to prevent an anomaly arising is, however, a fine one. It is clear that such modification should be a rare event. In *Stock* v. *Frank Jones (Tipton) Ltd.*[85] Lord Scarman said[86]:

[75a] See above, pp. 9–10.
[76] *Prophet* v. *Platt Brothers & Co. Ltd.* [1961] 1 W.L.R. 1130: See Harman L.J. at p. 1133. The word "fettle" has other meanings, as in "Tom offered to . . . fettle him over the head with a brick" quoted in O.E.D.
[77] *Jenner* v. *Allen West and Co. Ltd.* [1959] 1 W.L.R. 554.
[78] *Fisher* v. *Bell* [1961] 1 Q.B. 394; *cf. Partridge* v. *Crittenden* [1968] 1 W.L.R. 1204, *British Car Auctions* v. *Wright* [1972] 1 W.L.R. 1519.
[79] See above, p. 246.
[80] *Cf.* the "golden rule," above, pp. 243–244; *Stock* v. *Frank Jones (Tipton) Ltd.* [1978] 1 W.L.R. 231; *R.* v. *Pigg* [1983] 1 W.L.R. 6, below p. 616.
[81] *Barnard* v. *Gorman* [1941] A.C. 378; *Wiltshire* v. *Barrett* [1966] 1 Q.B. 312; *Wills* v. *Bowley* [1983] 1 A.C. 57 (but note the strong dissenting speeches of Lord Elwyn-Jones and Lord Lowry, who took the view that it was not proper to depart from the literal interpretation of a statute where that would prejudice the liberty of the subject).
[82] *Richard Thomas and Baldwin's Ltd.* v. *Cummings* [1955] A.C. 321.
[83] See Cross (1976) pp. 81–83. *Cf.* above, p. 244.
[84] *Federal Steam Navigation Co.* v. *Department of Trade and Industry* [1974] 1 W.L.R. 505, 508–9. *Cf.* the concept of "ellipsis": above, p. 236; *Adler* v. *George,* above, p. 238, n. 22; *Wiltshire* v. *Barrett, Barnard* v. *Gorman,* and *Wills* v. *Bowley,* above.
[85] [1978] 1 W.L.R. 231.
[86] At p. 239.

"If the words used by Parliament are plain, there is no room for the 'anomalies' test, unless the consequences are so absurd that, without going outside the statute, one can see that Parliament must have made a drafting mistake. If words 'have been inadvertently used,' it is legitimate for the court to substitute what is apt to avoid the intention of the legislature being defeated: *per* MacKinnon L.J. in *Sutherland Publishing Co. Ltd.* v. *Caxton Publishing Co. Ltd.*[86a] This is an acceptable exception to the general rule that plain language excludes a consideration of anomalies, *i.e.* mischievous or absurd consequences. If a study of the statute as a whole leads inexorably to the conclusion that Parliament had erred in its choice of words, *e.g.* used 'and' when 'or' was clearly intended, the courts can, and must, eliminate the error by interpretation. But mere 'manifest absurdity' is not enough; it must be an error (of commission or omission) which in its context defeats the intention of the Act."

In the same case Lord Simon said that:

"a court would only be justified in departing from the plain words of the statute were it satisfied that: (1) there is clear and gross balance of anomaly; (2) Parliament, the legislative promoters and the draftsman could not have envisaged such anomaly, could not have been prepared to accept it in the interest of a supervening legislative objective; (3) the anomaly can be obviated without detriment to such legislative objective; (4) the language of the statute is susceptible of the modification required to obviate the anomaly."[87]

There are a number of cases where the word "and" has been substituted for "or," and (? or) "or" for "and." *Federal Steam Navigation Co. Ltd.* v. *Department of Trade and Industry*[88] concerned section 1(1) of the Oil in Navigable Waters Act 1955, which provided that where oil was discharged from a British ship in a prohibited sea area "the owner or master of the ship shall be guilty of an offence." The House of Lords held that where the owner and the master were separate persons both could be convicted, the provision being treated as if it read "the owner and/or the master." In *R.* v. *Oakes*[89] the Divisional Court treated section 7 of the Official Secrets Act 1920, which made it an offence where a person "aids or abets and does any act preparatory to the commission of an offence" under the Official Secrets Act as if it read "aids or abets *or* does any act preparatory." If read literally the result would have been "unintelligible."[90]

[86a] [1938] Ch. 174, 201.
[87] [1978] 1 W.L.R. 231, p. 237. See also the similar remarks of Lord Diplock in *Jones* v. *Wrotham Park Settled Estates* [1980] A.C. 74, 105, applied in *I.R.C.* v. *Trustees of Sir John Aird's Settlement* [1984] 2 W.L.R. 178, and note the cautious remarks of Sir John Donaldson M.R. in *Carrington* v. *Therm-A-Stor Ltd.* [1983] 1 W.L.R. 138.
[88] [1974] 1 W.L.R. 505. *Cf. R.F. Brown & Co. Ltd.* v. *T. & J. Harrison* (1927) 43 T.L.R. 394, 633, where the Court of Appeal suggested that "or" could sometimes be construed conjunctively; *cf.* MacKinnon L.J. at first instance and in *Sutherland Publishing Co. Ltd.* v. *Caxton Publishing Co. Ltd.* [1938] Ch. 174, 201: "That is a cowardly evasion. In truth one word is substituted for another. For 'or' can never mean 'and.' "
[89] [1959] 2 Q.B. 350.
[90] *Per* Lord Parker C.J. at p. 354.

In *Re Lockwood*[91] Harman J. ignored certain words of a provision[92] which would have had the effect on an intestacy of preferring more distant relations to nephews and nieces. In some cases, however, defective statutory provisions are regarded as beyond judicial redemption. For example, in *Inland Revenue Commissioners* v. *Hinchy*[93] section 55(3) of the Income Tax Act 1952 provided that a person who failed to submit an accurate tax return should forfeit £20 plus "treble the tax which he ought to be charged under this Act." Hinchy failed to declare some interest upon which the tax due would have been £14 5s. The Commissioners claimed £438 14s. 6d. (three times Hinchy's total tax bill for the year plus £20). The House of Lords upheld their claim; their Lordships recognised that the result was absurd, but the words actually used were not capable of a more limited interpretation.

C. THE CONTEXT: INTERNAL AIDS TO INTERPRETATION

There is a wide range of material that may be considered by a judge both (1) in determining the primary meaning of the statutory words and (2) where there is ambiguity, in pointing the way to the interpretation that is to be preferred. Some of these aids may be found within the statute in question, or in certain "rules of language" commonly applied to statutory texts: others are external to the statute. We deal first with "internal aids."

It is commonly observed that statutes must be read as a whole.[94] It may perhaps be doubted whether every word of a long and complicated statute will be examined with care, but a judge may well be presented with arguments based on (1) a comparison with enacting words elsewhere in the statute or (2) one of the non-enacting parts of the statute listed in the previous chapter.[95] There is an important distinction between these two kinds of aid. Non-enacting words of a statute may be consulted as a guide to the meaning of the provision in question; however, if the words of the provision, considered in their context, are regarded as clear, any conflict between them and any of the non-enacting parts must be disregarded. Where a conflict between enacting words cannot be resolved by interpretation, the later provision takes precedence.

1. OTHER ENACTING WORDS

An examination of the whole of a statute, or at least those Parts which deal with the subject matter of the provision to be interpreted, should give some indication of the overall purpose of the legislation. It may show that a particular interpretation of that provision will lead to absurdity when taken with another section.[96] Moreover, there is at least a weak presumption that

---

[91] [1958] Ch. 231.

[92] Administration of Estates Act 1925, s.47(5) as amended.

[93] [1960] A.C. 748. See also *Inland Revenue Commissioners* v. *Ayrshire Employers' Mutual Insurance Association Ltd.* [1946] 1 All E.R. 637.

[94] See, *e.g.* pp. 245–246 above.

[95] See above, pp. 200–201.

[96] See, *e.g. R.* v. *Prince* (1875) L.R. 2 C.C.R. 154 and cases establishing that a court may not order the forfeiture of real property used in relation to the commission of criminal offences: *R.* v. *Beard* (*Graham*) [1974] 1 W.L.R. 1549 and *R.* v. *Khan* (*Sultan Ashraf*) [1982] 1 W.L.R. 1405.

a word or phrase is to be accorded the same meaning wherever it appears in the statute. For example, in *Gibson* v. *Ryan*[97] the court had to decide whether an inflatable rubber dinghy and a fish basket came within the term "instrument" in section 7(1) of the Salmon and Freshwater Fisheries (Protection) (Scotland) Act 1951. It held that they did not in the light of section 10, which drew a distinction "between instruments on the one hand, boats on the other hand and baskets on, if there is such a thing, the third hand."[98] A court may, however, be satisfied that different meanings are intended.[99] There may, of course, be a definition section.[1]

2. LONG TITLE

It became established in the nineteenth century that the long title could be considered as an aid to interpretation,[2] once it was accepted that it could be amended as a Bill passed through Parliament. The long title should be read, as part of the context, "as the plainest of all the guides to the general objectives of a statute" although "it will not always help as to particular provisions."[3] In *Fisher* v. *Raven*[4] the House of Lords held that the term "obtained credit" in section 13 of the Debtors Act 1869 (which made it an offence to obtain credit under false pretences) was limited to the obtaining of credit in respect of the payment or repayment of money only and did not extend to cover the receipt of money on a promise to render services or deliver goods in the future. The Act's long title:

> "An Act for the Abolition of Imprisonment for Debt, for the Punishment of Fraudulent Debtors, and for other purposes"

was regarded as supporting the view that the Act concerned debtors in the ordinary sense of the word. However, in *Ward* v. *Holman*[5] the Divisional Court held that section 5 of the Public Order Act 1936, which made it an offence to use in any public place or meeting (*inter alia*) insulting behaviour likely to cause a breach of the peace, was not restricted to conduct at public meetings, processions and the like, notwithstanding the Act's long title. The relevant part of the long title read:

> "An Act to . . . make . . . provision for the preservation of public order on the occasion of public processions and meetings and in public places"

but the court regarded the enacted words as wide and "completely unambiguous"[6] and, accordingly, applicable to disputes between neighbours.

---

[97] [1968] 1 Q.B. 250.

[98] Diplock L.J. at p. 255.

[99] *e.g.* "whosoever being married, shall marry" in section 57 of the Offences Against the Person Act 1861, considered in *R.* v. *Allen* (1872) L.R. 1 C.C.R. 367: "being married" meant "being validly married" whereas "shall marry" meant "go through a marriage ceremony."

[1] Above, p. 203.

[2] *Fielding* v. *Morley Corporation* [1899] 1 Ch. 1, 34.

[3] *Per* Lord Simon in *Black-Clawson International Ltd.* v. *Papierwerke Waldhof Aschaffenburg A.G.* [1975] A.C. 591, 647.

[4] [1964] A.C. 210. See also *R.* v. *Bates* [1952] 2 All E.R. 842, 844.

[5] [1964] 2 Q.B. 580.

[6] *Per* Lord Parker C.J. at p. 587.

3. PREAMBLE

The use of preambles[7] was considered in *Attorney-General* v. *Prince Ernest Augustus of Hanover.*[8] The position was summarised by Lord Normand[9]:

> "When there is a preamble it is generally in its recitals that the mischief to be remedied and the scope of the Act are described. It is therefore clearly permissible to have recourse to it as an aid to construing the enacting provisions. The preamble is not, however, of the same weight as an aid to construction of a section of the Act as are other relevant enacting words to be found elsewhere in the Act or even in related Acts. There may be no exact correspondence between preamble and enactment, and the enactment may go beyond, or it may fall short of the indications that may be gathered from the preamble. Again, the preamble cannot be of much or any assistance in construing provisions which embody qualifications or exceptions from the operation of the general purpose of the Act. It is only when it conveys a clear and definite meaning in comparison with relatively obscure or indefinite enacting words that the preamble may legitimately prevail."

The preamble cannot prevail over clear enacting words.

4. SHORT TITLE

It seems that the short title should not be used to resolve a doubt as it is given "solely for the purpose of facility of reference" or as a "statutory nickname."[10] Some judges, however, have questioned whether it should always be ignored.[11]

5. HEADINGS

Unlike the previous three parts of a statute, headings, side-notes and punctuation are not voted on in Parliament. They may nevertheless be considered as part of the context. In *Director of Public Prosecutions* v. *Schildkamp*[12] Lord Reid said:

> "The question which has arisen in this case is whether and to what extent it is permissible to give weight to punctuation, cross-headings and side-notes to sections in the Act. Taking a strict view, one can say that these should be disregarded because they are not the product of anything done in Parliament. . . .
> But it may be more realistic to accept the Act as printed as being the product of the whole legislative process, and to give due weight to

---

[7] The long title is on occasion referred to erroneously as the preamble.

[8] [1957] A.C. 436, see above pp. 245–246.

[9] At p. 467. See also Viscount Simonds at pp. 462–464, and see *The Norwhale* [1975] Q.B. 589.

[10] Lord Moulton in *Vacher & Sons Ltd.* v. *London Society of Compositors* [1913] A.C. 107, 128. Section 4(1) of the Trade Disputes Act 1906 was held to confer upon trade unions immunity from tort actions generally and not just in trade dispute cases.

[11] Scrutton L.J. in *Re Boaler* [1915] 1 K.B. 21, 40; but *cf.* Buckley L.J. at p. 27.

[12] [1971] A.C. 1, 10.

everything found in the printed Act. I say more realistic because in very many cases the provision before the court was never even mentioned in debate in either House, and it may be that its wording was never closely scrutinised by any member of either House. In such a case it is not very meaningful to say that the words of the Act represent the intention of Parliament but that punctuation, cross-headings and side-notes do not.

So, if the authorities are equivocal and one is free to deal with the whole matter, I would not object to taking all these matters into account, provided that we realise that they cannot have equal weight with the words of the Act. Punctuation can be of some assistance in construction. A cross-heading ought to indicate the scope of the sections which follow it but there is always a possibility that the scope of one of these sections may have been widened by amendment. But a side-note is a poor guide to the scope of a section, for it can do no more than indicate the main subject with which the section deals."

This case concerned section 332(3) of the Companies' Act 1948, which makes it an offence knowingly to be a party to the carrying on of a business with intent to defraud creditors or for a fraudulent purpose. However, it appears among a group of sections grouped under the cross-heading "Offences Antecedent to and in course of Winding-Up," and section 332(1), a parallel provision making the officers of a company personally responsible for its debts in similar circumstances, includes the words "in the course of the winding-up." The House of Lords held by a majority that an offence under section 332(3) could only be committed after a winding-up order had been made.

It also seems that reference may be made to a heading to resolve a doubt where the enacted words are ambiguous. However, it may not be used to change the meaning of enacted words where they are regarded as clear. Thus, a woman was convicted of an indecent assault upon a boy notwithstanding that the relevant section appeared under the heading of "Unnatural Offences."[13] The words "any indecent assault" were not regarded as ambiguous so as to justify consideration of the heading.

6. SIDE-NOTES

There is no sensible reason why side-notes should be ignored, as Lord Reid noted in *Director of Public Prosecutions* v. *Schildkamp*.[14] However, the same judge had stated in an earlier case, *Chandler* v. *Director of Public Prosecutions*,[15] that "side-notes cannot be used as an aid to construction" as they were inserted by the draftsman, altered if necessary during the passage of a Bill by an officer of the House, and were not considered by Parliament.[16] In *Chandler* the defendants were charged under section 1(1) of the Official Secrets Act 1911, which makes it an offence to approach a

---

[13] Offences Against the Person Act 1861, s.62; *R.* v. *Hare* [1934] 1 K.B. 354. See also *R.* v. *Surrey (North-Eastern Area) Assessment Committee* [1948] 1 K.B. 28, 32–33.

[14] Above.

[15] [1964] A.C. 763.

[16] *Ibid.* p. 789.

prohibited place for a purpose prejudicial to the safety of the state, in respect of a demonstration at a military airfield in favour of nuclear disarmament. The marginal note read "Penalties for spying" and it was accepted that the defendants had not engaged in "spying." Nevertheless, the House of Lords held that the defendants were rightly convicted. In so far as this case indicates that a side-note cannot change the meaning of clear enacted words it is consistent with other cases; in so far as it would prohibit any consideration of a side-note it is inconsistent.

7. PUNCTUATION

Punctuation in statutes was considered by Lord Reid in *Inland Revenue Commissioners* v. *Hinchy*[17]:

> "[B]efore 1850 there was no punctuation in the manuscript copy of an Act which received the Royal Assent, and it does not appear that the printers had any statutory authority to insert punctuation thereafter. So even if punctuation in more modern Acts can be looked at (which is very doubtful), I do not think that one can have any regard to punctuation in older Acts."

In modern statutes, it does now seem that punctuation will be considered to the same extent as non-enacting words, although it may be altered or ignored where necessary to give effect to the purpose of the statute.[18] In *Hanlon* v. *The Law Society*[19] Lord Lowry said:

> "I consider that not to take account of punctuation disregards the reality that literate people, such as Parliamentary draftsmen, punctuate what they write, if not identically, at least in accordance with grammatical principles. Why should not literate people, such as judges, look at the punctuation in order to interpret the meaning of the legislation as accepted by Parliament."

D. THE CONTEXT: RULES OF LANGUAGE

There are a number of so-called "rules of language" commonly referred to in the context of statutory interpretation by Latin tags. They are not legal rules, but "simply refer to the way in which people speak in certain contexts."[20] Moreover, they are not as precise in their operation as would be expected from their label as "rules."

1. EJUSDEM GENERIS

General words following particular ones normally apply only to such persons or things as are *ejusdem generis* (of the same *genus* or class) as the

---

[17] [1960] A.C. 748, 765.
[18] *Alexander* v. *Mackenzie* 1947 J.C. 155, 166; *R.* v. *Brixton Prison Governor, ex p. Naranjansingh* [1962] 1 Q.B. 211; *Luby* v. *Newcastle upon Tyne Corporation* [1965] 1 Q.B. 214.
[19] [1981] A.C. 124, 198. *Cf.* Lord Reid in *D.P.P.* v. *Schildkamp* above, pp. 252–253.
[20] Cross (1976), p. 115.

particular ones. For example, the Sunday Observance Act 1677 provided that "no tradesman, artificer, workman, labourer or other person whatsoever, shall do or exercise any worldly labour, business, or work of their ordinary callings upon the Lord's Day." In a series of cases the prohibition was held to be restricted to "other persons" following callings of a similar kind to those specified.[21] There must normally, and perhaps invariably, be more than one species mentioned to constitute a "genus,"[22] and it must be possible to construct a "genus" out of the list of specific words. In *Allen* v. *Emmerson*[23] it was held that the phrase "theatres and other places of entertainment" in section 33 of the Barrow-in-Furness Corporation Act 1872 did not constitute a genus. Accordingly, a fun fair required a licence under the section even though no charge was made for admission.

The *ejusdem generis* rule may be displaced where the general words should be interpreted widely to accord with the object of the statute. *Skinner* v. *Shew*[24] concerned a provision which enabled a person to obtain an injunction against someone claiming to be the patentee of an invention who threatened him with any legal proceedings or liability "by circular advertisement or otherwise," unless he instituted those proceedings promptly. The Court of Appeal held that the desire of Parliament was "that threats of patent actions shall not hang over a man's head" and that it would be wrong to read the section as not applying to threats sent by private letter.

2. Noscitur a Sociis

This tag refers to the fact that words "derive colour from those which surround them."[25] For example, the word "floors" in the expression "floors, steps, stairs, passages and gangways," which were required to be kept free from obstruction, was held not to apply to part of a factory floor used for storage rather than passage.[26] The wider context may, however, negative any such "colouration." The "*ejusdem generis* rule" can be regarded as an application of this wider principle.

3. Expressio Unius est Exclusio Alterius

"Mention of one or more things of a particular class may be regarded as silently excluding all other members of the class. . . . Further, where a statute uses two words or expressions, one of which generally includes the other, the more general term is taken in a sense

---

[21] Not, therefore, a coach proprietor (*Sandeman* v. *Beach* (1827) 5 L.J. (o.s.) K.B. 298) farmer (*R.* v. *Cleworth* (1864) 4 B. & S. 927) or barber (*Palmer* v. *Snow* [1900] 1 Q.B. 725).

[22] *Alexander* v. *Tredegar Iron and Coal Co. Ltd.* [1944] K.B. 390; *Quazi* v. *Quazi* [1980] A.C. 744, 807–808 (*per* Lord Diplock): the term "other" in the expression "judicial or other proceedings" was held not to be confined to quasi-judicial proceedings.

[23] [1944] K.B. 362.

[24] [1893] 1 Ch. 413. *Cf.* Lord Scarman in *Quazi* v. *Quazi, supra*, at p. 824.

[25] *Per* Stamp J. in *Bourne* v. *Norwich Crematorium Ltd.* [1967] 1 W.L.R. 691.

[26] Factories Act 1961, s.28(1): *Pengelley* v. *Bell Punch Co. Ltd.* [1964] 1 W.L.R. 1055.

excluding the less general one: otherwise there would have been little point in using the latter as well as the former."[27]

For example, a provision that imposed a poor rate on the occupiers of "lands," houses, tithes and "coal mines" was held not to apply to mines other than coal mines, although the word "lands" would normally cover all kinds of mine.[28] However, a court may be satisfied that the "exclusio" was accidental, particularly where an application of the maxim would lead to absurdity.[29]

E. THE CONTEXT: EXTERNAL AIDS TO INTERPRETATION

1. HISTORICAL SETTING

A judge may consider the historical setting of the provision that is being interpreted. In *Chandler* v. *Director of Public Prosecutions*[30] the defendants sought to argue that disarmament would be beneficial to the State, and that their purpose was thus not "prejudicial to the safety or interests of the State." Lord Reid said[31]:

> "Even in recent times there have been occasions when quite large numbers of people have been bitterly opposed to the use made of the armed forces in peace or in war. The 1911 Act was passed at a time of grave misgiving about the German menace, and it would be surprising and hardly credible that the Parliament of that date intended that a person who deliberately interfered with vital dispositions of the armed forces should be entitled to submit to a jury that Government policy was wrong and that what he did was really in the best interests of the country, and then perhaps to escape conviction because a unanimous verdict on that question could not be obtained."

The Victorian attitude of sympathy towards insurgents against continental governments has been considered as part of the background of the Extradition Act 1870.[32]

2. DICTIONARIES AND OTHER LITERARY SOURCES

Dictionaries are commonly consulted as a guide to the meaning of statutory words.[33] As words are to be read in their context, as already discussed, this should only be a starting point:

> "Sentences are not mere collections of words to be taken out of the sentence, defined separately by reference to the dictionary or decided cases, and then put back into the sentence with the meaning which one

---

[27] *Maxwell on Interpretation of Statutes* (12th ed., 1969), p. 293.

[28] Poor Relief Act 1601, s.1: *R.* v. *Inhabitants of Sedgley* (1831) 2 B. & Ad. 65.

[29] *Colquhoun* v. *Brooks* (1888) 21 Q.B.D. 52, 65; *Dean* v. *Wiesengrund* [1955] 2 Q.B. 120.

[30] [1964] A.C. 763: see above pp. 253–254.

[31] At p. 791.

[32] *Schtraks* v. *Government of Israel* [1964] A.C. 556, 582, 583; *R.* v. *Governor of Pentonville Prison, ex p. Cheng* [1973] A.C. 931.

[33] See, *e.g. R.* v. *Peters* (1886) 16 Q.B.D. 636 (definitions of "credit" in Dr. Johnson's and Webster's dictionaries); *Re Ripon* (*Highfield*) *Confirmation Order* 1938, *White and Collins* v. *Minister of Health* [1939] 2 K.B. 838 (definition of "park" in O.E.D.).

has assigned to them as separate words so as to give the sentence or phrase a meaning which as a sentence or phrase it cannot bear without distortion of the English language."[34]

Textbooks may also be consulted.[35]

3. PRACTICE

The practice followed in the past may be a guide to interpretation. For example, the "uniform opinion and practice of eminent conveyancers has always had great regard paid to it by all courts of justice."[36] This is the case where the technical meaning of a word or phrase used in conveyancing is in issue.[37] Commercial usage may also be considered. In *United Dominions Trust Ltd.* v. *Kirkwood*[38] the Court of Appeal had to apply the phrase "any person bona fide carrying on the business of banking."[39] Lord Denning M.R. said[40]:

> "In such a matter as this, when Parliament has given no guidance, we cannot do better than look at the reputation of the concern amongst intelligent men of commerce."

In these cases the usage or practice precedes the enactment of related technical legislation. The *subsequent* practice of those who are involved in the implementation of a statute is not generally regarded as a permissible aid.[41] A different view may be taken in respect of old statutes:

> "It is said that the best exposition of a statute . . . is that which it has received from contemporary authority. . . . *Contemporanea expositio est fortissima in lege.* Where this has been given by enactment or judicial decision, it is of course to be accepted as conclusive. But, further, the meaning publicly given by contemporary or long professional usage is presumed to be the true one, even where the language has etymologically or popularly a different meaning."[42]

This principle cannot be applied to modern statutes.[43]

---

[34] *Per* Stamp J. in *Bourne* v. *Norwich Crematorium Ltd.* [1967] 1 W.L.R. 691, 696.

[35] *e.g. Re Castioni* [1891] 1 Q.B. 149 where Stephen J. referred to his own *History of the Criminal Law* on the meaning of "political crime"; a work by John Stuart Mill was also consulted.

[36] *Per* Lord Hardwicke L.C. in *Bassett* v. *Bassett* (1744) 3 Atk. 203, 208.

[37] See *Jenkins* v. *Inland Revenue Commissioners* [1944] 2 All E.R. 491; *cf. Pilkington* v. *Inland Revenue Commissioners* [1964] A.C. 612, 634.

[38] [1966] 2 Q.B. 431.

[39] Moneylenders Act 1900, s.6(*d*).

[40] At pp. 454, 455.

[41] *e.g.* practice notes provided by the Central Land Board for the guidance of its staff in the administration of the Town and Country Planning Act 1947: *London County Council* v. *Central Land Board* [1958] 1 W.L.R. 1296.

[42] *Maxwell on Interpretation of Statutes* (12th ed., 1969), p. 264 cited in *R.* v. *Casement* [1917] 1 K.B. 98, where the court declined to take the Statute of Treasons 1351 "and read it as though we had seen it for the first time." See D.J. Hurst, "The problem of the elderly statute" (1983) 3 L.S. 21, 23–30, who notes that the term *contemporanea expositio* should (1) be confined to exposition by commentators at or near the time of enactment, and (2) be distinguished from continuous usage and custom.

[43] *Campbell College, Belfast (Governors)* v. *Commissioners of Valuation for Northern Ireland* [1964] 1 W.L.R. 912 (strictly, a case concerning usage rather than *contemporanea expositio*: Hurst, *op. cit.*).

4. Other Statutes In Pari Materia

Related statutes dealing with the same subject matter as the provision in question may be considered both as part of the context and to resolve ambiguities.[44] A statute may indeed provide expressly that it should be read as one with an earlier statute or series of statutes. *Later* statutes *in pari materia* cannot be regarded as part of the context of the enactment but may be considered where a provision is ambiguous, "to see the meaning which Parliament puts on the self-same phrase in a similar context, in case it throws any light on the matter."[45]

Occasionally an argument may be based on a comparison with a statute not *in pari materia*, although such a statute will not be considered as part of the context.[46]

Where a later Act amends an earlier Act the position as to interpretation is not clear. In *Lewisham London Borough Council* v. *Lewisham Juvenile Court JJ.*[47] Viscount Dilhorne stated[48] that it was wrong to construe an *unamended* section of the earlier Act in the light of amendments made by the later Act, unless there was an ambiguity. Lord Salmon, however, said[49] that:

> "the whole Act as amended should be taken into consideration when construing any section in the Act. A section of an Act, whether or not it is amended, must in my view be construed in the context of the whole Act as it stands."

The other judges did not express their views unequivocally on this point, although Lord Keith seemed to incline to Viscount Dilhorne's position and Lord Scarman to Lord Salmon's.[50] Lord Salmon's view may create difficulties for the draftsman of subsequent amendments if he is to be required to judge the effect of the amendments on the interpretation of unamended provisions.

Where a later Act inserts a new provision in an earlier Act, it may be held that this provision is to be interpreted by reference to the later Act.[50a]

5. Legislative Antecedents

A slightly different situation from those considered in the previous section arises when the provision in question has been re-enacted in the same or similar form in a succession of statutes. For example, the origins of section

---

[44] See Viscount Simonds in the *Hanover* case, above, p. 245.

[45] *Per* Lord Denning M.R. in *Payne* v. *Bradley* [1962] A.C. 343, 357; *cf. Re MacManaway* [1951] A.C. 161; *Lewisham London Borough Council* v. *Lewisham Juvenile Court JJ.* [1980] A.C. 273, 281–2, 291.

[46] See, *e.g. R.* v. *Westminster Betting Licensing Committee, ex p. Peabody Donation Fund* [1963] 2 Q.B. 750.

[47] [1980] A.C. 273.

[48] At pp. 281–2.

[49] At p. 291.

[50] See pp. 302 and 310.

[50a] *R.* v. *Secretary of State for the Home Department, ex p. Margueritte* [1983] Q.B. 180; see A. Samuels, [1983] Stat.L.R. 111.

56 of the Law of Property Act 1925[51] were considered in *Beswick* v. *Beswick*,[52] where the House of Lords held that the term "other property" did not apply to personalty. However, the legislative antecedents should not be considered as part of the context of a consolidation measure, and reference to them should only be made if the words are unclear.[53] In interpreting consolidation Acts there is a presumption that Parliament does not intend to alter the existing law.[54] As with all presumptions it may be rebutted by clear language.[55]

Where other statutes are considered arguments may be based on similarities or dissimilarities in the statutory language itself, or on judicial decisions concerning provisions subsequently re-enacted. It is sometimes suggested that Parliament, or more realistically, the draftsman, must have had such decisions in mind during the preparation of consolidation legislation,[56] that there is at least a rebuttable presumption that re-enactment without alteration amounts to the Parliamentary endorsement of the decisions and that, for example, a decision of a High Court judge thus "endorsed" would have to be applied by the Court of Appeal and the House of Lords.[57] The theory of "Parliamentary endorsement" has been doubted by Lord Wilberforce and Lord Simon in *Farrell* v. *Alexander*.[58] Moreover, in *R.* v. *Chard*[58a] the House of Lords held that there might be such a presumption where the judicial interpretation is well settled and well recognised, but that it would yield to the fundamental rule that the ordinary sense of statutory words should be adhered to unless it led to some absurdity. The re-enactment of words in a consolidation Act subject to one of the special parliamentary procedures precluding debate on the merits would not have an effect on the construction of those words.

In the case of *codifying* statutes,[59] "the proper course is in the first

---

[51] "A person may take an immediate or other interest in land or other property, or the benefit of any condition, right of entry, covenant or agreement over or respecting land or other property, although he may not be named as a party to the conveyance or other instrument."

[52] [1968] A.C. 58.

[53] *Farrell* v. *Alexander* [1977] A.C. 59: Lord Wilberforce at pp. 72–73, Lord Simon at pp. 82–85 and Lord Edmund-Davies at p. 97; *R.* v. *West Yorkshire Coroner, ex p. Smith* [1983] Q.B. 335; *R.* v. *Heron* [1982] 1 W.L.R. 451; *Champion* v. *Maughan* [1984] 1 W.L.R. 469. Indeed, "it is particularly useful to have recourse to the legislative history if a real difficulty arises," whatever the form of the consolidation measure (see above, pp. 189–190) (*per* Lord Scarman in *R.* v. *Heron* [1982] 1 W.L.R. 451, 459, 460); *cf.* Lord Simon at p. 455 who stressed the point that the statute in issue here was not (unlike that in *Farrell* v. *Alexander*), a "modern consolidation Act," but was a "pure" consolidation, with verbatim reproduction of existing enactment "with all its blemishes and imperfections;" accordingly, it was more likely to be necessary to look at the legislative history. See generally, A.F. Newhouse, "Constructing and Consolidating" [1980] B.T.R. 102.

[54] *R.* v. *Governor of Brixton Prison, ex p. De Demko* [1959] 1 Q.B. 268, affirmed [1959] A.C. 654.

[55] *e.g. Re A Solicitor* [1961] Ch. 491.

[56] See Lord Evershed in *Ex p. De Demko* [1959] 1 Q.B. 268, 281.

[57] *Re Cathcart, ex p. Campbell* (1869) 5 Ch. App. 603, 706 (James L.J.); *Barras* v. *Aberdeen Fishing and Steam Trawling Co. Ltd.* [1933] A.C. 402, 411–412 (Lord Buckmaster).

[58] [1977] A.C. 59, 74, 90–91. See also Denning L.J. in *Royal Crown Derby Porcelain Ltd.* v. *Raymond Russell* [1949] 2 K.B. 417, 429; *R.* v. *Bow Road JJ.* (*Domestic Proceedings Court*) *ex p. Adedigba* [1968] 2 Q.B. 572, 583; E.A. Marshall, (1974) 90 L.Q.R. 170; C.J.F. Kidd, (1977) 51 A.L.J. 256.

[58a] [1984] A.C. 279.

[59] See above, p. 189.

instance to examine the language of the statute and to ask what is its natural meaning, uninfluenced by any considerations derived from the previous state of law."[60] The application of any presumption that the law is unaltered would destroy the utility of codification. However, the previous state of the law may be considered where a technical expression is used or a provision of the code is ambiguous.

6. STATUTORY INSTRUMENTS

The extent to which a regulation may be used in interpreting a provision in the Act under which it was made was considered in *Hanlon* v. *The Law Society*,[61] where Lord Lowry formulated the following propositions[62]:

> "(1) Subordinate legislation may be used in order to construe the parent Act, but only where power is given to amend the Act by regulations or where the meaning of the Act is ambiguous.
>
> (2) Regulations made under the Act provide a Parliamentary or administrative *contemporanea expositio* of the Act but do not decide or control its meaning: to allow this would be to substitute the rule-making authority for the judges as interpreter and would disregard the possibility that the regulation relied on was misconceived or *ultra vires*.
>
> (3) Regulations which are consistent with a certain interpretation of the Act tend to confirm that interpretation.
>
> (4) Where the Act provides a framework built on by contemporaneously prepared regulations, the latter may be a reliable guide to the meaning of the former.
>
> (5) The regulations are a clear guide, and may be decisive, where they are made in pursuance of a power to modify the Act, particularly if they come into operation on the same day as the Act which they modify.
>
> (6) Clear guidance may also be obtained from regulations which are to have effect as if enacted in the parent Act."

7. GOVERNMENT PUBLICATIONS

Legislation is commonly preceded by a report of a Royal Commission, the Law Commissions or some other official advisory committee. This kind of material may be considered as evidence of the pre-existing state of the law and the "mischief" with which the legislation was intended to deal. However, the recommendations contained therein may not be regarded as evidence of Parliamentary intention as Parliament may not have accepted the recommendations and acted upon them.[63] The first of these propositions is generally accepted: the second proposition only survived in the

---

[60] *Bank of England* v. *Vagliano Brothers* [1891] A.C. 107, 144, 145 (Lord Herschell).
[61] [1981] A.C. 124.
[62] At pp. 193–4.
[63] *Eastman Photographic Materials Co. Ltd.* v. *Comptroller General of Patents* [1898] A.C. 571; *Assam Railways and Trading Co. Ltd.* v. *Inland Revenue Commissioners* [1935] A.C. 445; *Black-Clawson International Ltd.* v. *Papierwerke Waldhof-Aschaffenburg A.G.* [1975] A.C. 591.

Black-Clawson case by 3 to 2. The question was whether a judgment in a German court dismissing the plaintiff's claim for money due, on the ground that it was brought out of time, barred such a claim in an English court. It did not have this effect at common law,[64] and the House of Lords held by 4 to 1 that this had not been altered by section 8 of the Foreign Judgments (Reciprocal Enforcement) Act 1933. Section 8 had been enacted in a form identical to clause 8 of a draft Bill attached to the report of a departmental committee of "eminent lawyers," and the report indicated that the draft Bill was not thought to change the common law. Of the majority, Lords Reid and Wilberforce held that the report could not be considered as a guide to Parliament's intention. Lord Reid thought that the rule against the citation of expressions of intention in Parliament excluded *a fortiori* such expressions in pre-Parliamentary reports. Lord Wilberforce stated that if reports were admissible as evidence of the meaning of the enacted words there would simply be two documents to construe instead of one, that it was the function of the courts to declare the meaning of enacted words, and that "it would be a degradation of that process if the courts were to be merely a reflecting mirror of what some other interpretation agency might say."[65] Viscount Dilhorne and Lord Simon of Glaisdale thought, however, that reports should be admissible as a guide to Parliament's intention; at least in a case such as this where a draft Bill had been enacted without material alteration.[66] To forbid this "would be to draw a very artificial line which serves no useful purpose."[67] "Why read the crystal when you can read the book? Here the book is already open; it is merely a matter of reading on."[68] Lord Diplock dissented as to the meaning of section 8 but agreed with Lords Reid and Wilberforce on the use of official reports.

8. TREATIES AND INTERNATIONAL CONVENTIONS

Problems of statutory interpretation relating to treaties (or international conventions) may arise in four main ways. In the background are two principles: first, that a treaty cannot have effect in English law unless incorporated by statute; and second, that there is a presumption that Parliament does not legislate in such a way that the United Kingdom would be in breach of its international obligations.

(1) An Act of Parliament may implement a treaty and expressly enact that it shall be part of English law. The text will normally be given in a schedule. Here, a broad purposive construction should be adopted rather than a literal one.[69] Textbooks, dictionaries, expert opinion and the judgments of foreign courts may be consulted; *travaux préparatoires*, such

---

[64] *Harris* v. *Quine* (1869) L.R. 4 Q.B. 653.

[65] p. 629.

[66] pp. 621–623 and 651–652 respectively.

[67] Viscount Dilhorne at p. 622.

[68] Lord Simon at p. 652.

[69] *Stag Line Ltd.* v. *Foscolo Mango & Co. Ltd.* [1932] A.C. 328, 350; *James Buchanan & Co. Ltd.* v. *Babco Forwarding and Shipping (U.K.) Ltd.* [1978] A.C. 141 *cf.* below, p. 277, n. 75 and R.J.C. Munday, (1978) 27 I.C.L.Q. 450; *Fothergill* v. *Monarch Airlines Ltd.* [1980] A.C. 251; *Rothmans Ltd.* v. *Saudi Airlines* [1981] Q.B. 368; *The Hollandia* [1983] 1 A.C. 565: see F.A. Mann, "Uniform Statutes in English Law" (1983) 99 L.Q.R. 376, who argues that the purposive approach has been carried too far.

as the proceedings of the conferences at which the treaty was prepared, may also be used, albeit with caution.[70]

(2) An Act of Parliament may implement a treaty by enacting substantive provisions of English law but without expressly incorporating the text of the treaty. The intention to implement the treaty may, however, be mentioned in the preamble or long title. The House of Lords held in *Ellerman Lines* v. *Murray*[71] that where these substantive provisions are unambiguous, the text of the treaty cannot be considered in order to give the provisions other than their "natural meaning." This decision has been criticised, and on occasion ignored.[72] The courts have not been astute to hold that the enacted provisions in such a case are clear and unambiguous,[73] and a treaty has been considered in a case where it was not mentioned in the Act but the connection between treaty and Act could be established by extrinsic evidence.[74]

(3) It may be argued that a statute should be interpreted in the light of an international convention such as the European Convention on Human Rights. In *Birdi* v. *Secretary of State for Home Affairs*[75] Lord Denning M.R. said that if an Act of Parliament contradicted the Convention "I might be inclined to hold it invalid." However, he retracted this in *Ex p. Bhajan Singh*.[76] In *R.* v. *Chief Immigration Officer, ex p. Salamat Bibi*[77] it was said that a court could look to the Convention "if there is any ambiguity in our statutes, or uncertainty in our law."[78] It cannot prevail over clear words in a statute.[79]

(4) The special case of the interpretation of Community legislation is considered below.[80]

9. PARLIAMENTARY MATERIALS

It has been reaffirmed recently by the House of Lords that a court may not refer to Parliamentary materials for any purpose whatsoever connected with the interpretation of statutes. The prohibition covers such materials as reports of debates in the House and in committee, the explanatory memoranda attached to Bills and successive drafts of Bills. Lord Denning M.R. expressed his disagreement with this rule in the Court of Appeal in *Davis* v. *Johnson*[81]:

[70] See the *Fothergill* case, *supra*.

[71] [1931] A.C. 126.

[72] *The Mecca* [1968] P. 665; *The Abadesa* (No. 2) [1968] P. 656; but *cf. Warwick Film Productions* v. *Eisinger* [1969] 1 Ch. 508, 521–523.

[73] See *Salomon* v. *Commissioners of Customs and Excise* [1967] 2 Q.B. 116; *Post Office* v. *Estuary Radio Ltd.* [1968] 2 Q.B. 740.

[74] The *Salomon* case, *supra*.

[75] Unreported, referred to in *R.* v. *Secretary of State for the Home Department, ex p. Bhajan Singh* [1976] Q.B. 198.

[76] *Ibid.*

[77] [1976] 1 W.L.R. 979.

[78] *Ibid.* p. 984 *per* Lord Denning M.R. See *Waddington* v. *Miah* [1974] 1 W.L.R. 683 and *R.* v. *Deery* [1977] Crim.L.R. 550, where the presumption against retrospective legislation was reinforced by prohibitions aginst the retrospective application of criminal penalties contained in the European Convention and the U.N. Covenant on Civil and Political Rights; S.H. Bailey, D.J. Harris and B. Jones, *Civil Liberties: Cases and Materials* (1980), pp. 5–6.

[79] *R.* v. *Greater London Council, ex p. Burgess* [1978] I.C.R. 991.

[80] pp. 270–277.

[81] [1979] A.C. 264, 276–7.

"In some cases Parliament is assured in the most explicit terms what the effect of a statute will be. . . . In such cases I think the court should be able to look at the proceedings. . . . And it is obvious that there is nothing to prevent a judge looking at these debates himself privately and getting some guidance from them. Although it may shock the purists, I may as well confess that I have sometimes done it. I have done it in this very case. It has thrown a flood of light on the position."

In earlier cases, Lord Denning had himself cited extracts from *Hansard*,[82] and passages from textbooks that happen to have contained such extracts.[83] Lord Upjohn referred to the proceedings of the Joint Committee on Consolidation Bills in *Beswick* v. *Beswick*.[84] Nevertheless, the prohibition was unanimously reaffirmed by the House of Lords in *Davis* v. *Johnson*.[85] Various reasons have been given in support of this position:

"For purely practical reasons we do not permit debates in either House to be cited: it would add greatly to the time and expense involved in preparing cases involving the construction of a statute if counsel were expected to read all the debates in Hansard, and it would often be impracticable for Counsel to get access to at least the older reports of debates in select committees of the House of Commons; moreover, in a very large proportion of cases such a search, even if practicable would throw no light on the question before the court. . . ."[86]

What is said in Parliament:

"is an unreliable guide to the meaning of what is enacted. . . . The cut and thrust of debate and the pressures of executive responsibility are not always conducive to a clear and unbiased explanation of the meaning of statutory language."[87]

---

[82] *e.g. Sagnata Investments Ltd.* v. *Norwich Corporation* [1971] 2 Q.B. 614.

[83] *R.* v. *Local Commissioner for Administration, ex p. Bradford Metropolitan City Council* [1979] Q.B. 287, 311: reference to the "Crossman catalogue" of examples of maladministration.

[84] [1968] A.C. 58, 105. In *Re C., An Infant* [1937] 3 All E.R. 783, Luxmoore J. referred to a passage in *Hansard*, although this reference did not appear in [1938] Ch. 121.

[85] [1979] A.C. 264. Lord Denning M.R. took no notice, and was reproved unanimously by the House of Lords in *Hadmor Productions* v. *Hamilton* [1983] 1 A.C. 191, 232–233. Lord Diplock pointed out that counsel were under a duty not to cite *Hansard* and a judge who cited a passage on his own initiative was acting in breach of natural justice, here, the right of each party to be informed of any point adverse to him and to be given the opportunity to comment (*ibid.*). Lord Denning's citations from *Hansard* here have been criticised as selective: V. Sacks [1982] Stat.L.R. 143, 155–156. See generally, D. Miers [1983] Stat.L.R. 98, M. Rawlinson [1983] B.T.R. 274, S.J. Gibbs [1984] Stat.L.R. 29 and Vincent J.G. Power [1984] Stat.L.R. 38.

[86] *Per* Lord Reid in *Beswick* v. *Beswick* [1968] A.C. 58, 73–74. The last point has been supported by an analysis of a series of cases where problems of interpretation arose but reference to *Hansard* would not have assisted: V. Sacks, *op. cit.*; but *cf.* H.W. Wiggin, (1983) 80 L.S.Gaz. 461, on *Leedale* v. *Lewis* [1982] 1 W.L.R. 1319, and I.B. McKenna, (1983) 46 M.L.R. 759, 763–764, on *Mandla* v. *Dowell-Lee* [1983] 2 A.C. 548.

[87] *Per* Lord Scarman in *Davis* v. *Johnson* [1979] A.C. 264, 350.

The Law Commissions reported in favour of the prohibition, after rehearsing the doubts about the reliability and availability of legislative material.[88] They did suggest that in the case of some Bills a detailed explanatory statement should be specially prepared by the promoters for use in Parliament, amended to take account of changes in the Bill during its passage, and made available for statute users after enactment.[89] This would be fuller than a preamble, or the brief explanatory memoranda used at present. (The detailed "Notes of Clauses" prepared for ministers by their civil servants could not be used: they might contain confidential information and were not intended for publication). No action has been taken upon the Law Commissions' recommendation.

Legislative materials are used in many foreign jurisdictions, including the United States of America and many European countries, where they tend to be more accessible and concise. There have, however, been criticisms that the practice of referring to legislative history has been abused.[90]

F. PRESUMPTIONS

1. PRESUMPTIONS OF GENERAL APPLICATION

There are various presumptions that may be applied in doubtful cases. These are to be distinguished from the "presumptions of general application" whereby certain basic legal principles are presumed to apply unless excluded by express words or necessary implication.[91] These principles modify even unambiguous provisions. Examples include aspects of the *ultra vires* doctrine, such as natural justice and abuse of discretion, general principles of criminal liability, and the principle that no-one shall be allowed to gain an advantage from his own wrong. Striking illustrations of this last principle include *Re Sigsworth*,[92] where Clawson J. held that apparently unambiguous provisions as to the distribution of the residuary estate on an intestacy were not to be applied so as to enable a murderer to benefit from the victim's estate, and *R. v. Secretary of State for the Home Department, ex p. Puttick*,[93] where Astrid Proll, who had achieved a marriage with a citizen of the United Kingdom and Colonies by the crimes of fraud, forgery and perjury, was held not to be entitled to registration as a United Kingdom citizen, notwithstanding the absolute terms of section 6(2) of the British Nationality Act 1948. She had entered the country under a false identity, and she had committed these crimes in satisfying the Registrar General that in her assumed identity she had been divorced and there was no impediment to the marriage, and in obtaining a marriage licence.

---

[88] Law Com. No. 21, Scot.Law Com. No. 11 (1969) pp. 31–37.
[89] *Ibid.* pp. 38–43.
[90] *Ibid.* pp. 32–34.
[91] See above, p. 236.
[92] [1935] Ch. 89.
[93] [1981] Q.B. 767. See also *R. v. Chief National Insurance Commissioner, ex p. Connor* [1981] Q.B. 758 and the Forfeiture Act 1982.

2. PRESUMPTIONS FOR USE IN DOUBTFUL CASES

These have been termed "policies of clear statement"[94]; or "in effect announcements by the courts to the legislature that certain meanings will not be assumed unless stated with special clarity."[95] The courts have created a measure of protection for certain values by establishing a requirement that Parliament use clear words if they are to be compromised or overridden. There are many difficulties. The Law Commissions pointed out that there was no established order or precedence in the case of conflict between different presumptions; that the individual presumptions were often of doubtful status or imprecise in scope; that reference to a presumption was unnecessary where a court decided that the words are clear; and that there was no accepted test for resolving a conflict between a presumption, such as the presumption that penal statutes should be construed restrictively, and giving effect to the purpose of a statute, for example the purpose of factory legislation to secure safe working conditions.[96]

It is impossible to produce a definitive list of presumptions which may be applied. As the Law Commissions noted, particular presumptions may be "modified or even abandoned with the passage of time, and with the modification of the social values which they embody."[97] Some of the principles of interpretation that have already been mentioned are sometimes put in the form of a presumption, for example presumptions against "intending what is inconvenient or unreasonable" or "intending injustice or absurdity."[98]

(a) Presumptions against changes in the common law

This is one of the more controversial presumptions, given that modern legislation may often be intended to change the common law or may deal with matters with which the common law was unconcerned, such as the "welfare state." Lord Reid formulated the presumption as follows in *Black-Clawson International Ltd.* v. *Papierwerke Waldhof-Aschaffenburg A.G.*[99]:

> "In addition to reading the Act you look at the facts presumed to be known to Parliament when the Bill which became the Act in question was before it, and you consider whether there is disclosed some unsatisfactory state of affairs which Parliament can properly be supposed to have intended to remedy by the Act. There is a presumption which can be stated in various ways. One is that in the absence of any clear indication to the contrary, Parliament can be presumed not to have altered the common law further than was necessary to remedy the 'mischief.' Of course it may and quite often does go further. But the principle is that if the enactment is ambiguous, that meaning which relates the scope of the Act to the

[94] H.M. Hart and A.M. Sacks, cited in Law Com. No. 21, p. 21.
[95] Law Com. No. 21, p. 21.
[96] *Ibid.* p. 22.
[97] *Ibid.* p. 21.
[98] See *Maxwell on Interpretation of Statutes* (12th ed., 1969), pp. 199–212.
[99] [1975] A.C. 591, 614.

mischief should be taken rather than a different or wider meaning which the contemporary situation did not call for."

In *Leach* v. *R.*[1] a provision that a spouse of a defendant "may" be called as a witness was held not to overturn the common law rule that a wife was not *compellable*; it merely made her a *competent* witness. In *Beswick* v. *Beswick*[2] the House of Lords refused to interpret section 56 of the Law of Property Act 1925 in such a way as to overturn the doctrine of privity of contract. A more doubtful use of the presumption was made in *Chertsey Urban District Council* v. *Mixnam's Properties Ltd.*[3] where the House held that a power for a local authority to attach "such conditions as . . . [it] may think it necessary or desirable to impose" to a caravan site licence could only be used to impose conditions relating to the use of the land: conditions by which the authority sought to protect the interests of tenants were held to be *ultra vires*.

(b) Presumption against ousting the jurisdiction of the courts

The courts have generally looked with disfavour upon Parliament's attempts to oust their jurisdiction. Such attempts have been particularly common in the administrative law context,[4] where "exclusion clauses" have been construed narrowly[5] or evaded.[6] It is notable that where the courts have given effect to an "exclusion clause" the clause has only purported to oust their jurisdiction after a six-week period.[7]

(c) Presumption against interference with vested rights

If there is any ambiguity it is presumed that, "the legislature does not intend to limit vested rights further than clearly appears from the enactment."[8] There is an associated presumption that proprietary rights are not to be taken away without compensation.[9] It has been suggested that where the words are ambiguous, they should be construed in such a way as will cause less interference with existing rights notwithstanding that it appears that Parliament intended a more "stringent" meaning.[10]

---

[1] [1912] A.C. 305; Criminal Evidence Act 1898, s.4(1).

[2] [1968] A.C. 58, See above, p. 259.

[3] [1965] A.C. 745.

[4] See J.M. Evans, *de Smith's Judicial Review of Administrative Action* (4th ed., 1980), pp. 364–376.

[5] *e.g.* where a statute provides that a decision shall be "final," that is read as meaning only that there is no right of *appeal*: the remedy of certiorari is not excluded: *R.* v. *Medical Appeal Tribunal, ex p. Gilmore* [1957] 1 Q.B. 574.

[6] *e.g.* a provision that a "determination by the Commission . . . shall not be called in question in any court of law" was held not to exclude proceedings for judicial review where the "determination" was *ultra vires* and a nullity, and thus not a "determination" at all: *Anisminic Ltd.* v. *Foreign Compensation Commission* [1969] 2 A.C. 147 (Foreign Compensation Act 1950, s.4(4)).

[7] *Smith* v. *East Elloe Rural District Council* [1956] A.C. 585; *R.* v. *Secretary of State for the Environment, ex p. Ostler* [1977] Q.B. 122.

[8] *Per* Ungoed-Thomas J. in *Re Metropolitan Film Studios Application* [1962] 1 W.L.R. 1315, 1323.

[9] *Belfast Corporation* v. *O.D. Cars Ltd.* [1960] A.C. 490; *cf. Westminster Bank Ltd.* v. *Beverley Borough Council* [1971] A.C. 509.

[10] *Per* Winn L.J. *obiter* in *Allen* v. *Thorn Electrical Industries Ltd.* [1968] 1 Q.B. 487.

(d) Strict construction of penal laws in favour of the citizen

Laws which impose criminal or other penalties are strictly construed, so that if the words are ambiguous and there are two reasonable interpretations, the more lenient one will be given.[11] Thus, the provision that "all lotteries are unlawful" was not interpreted as creating a criminal offence.[12] A provision penalising the personation at an election of "any person entitled to vote" was held not to apply to a person who personated a deceased voter.[13] Other examples are *R.* v. *Harris*[14] and *London and North Eastern Railway Co.* v. *Berriman.*[15] It has, however, been suggested that while the courts still pay lip service to this principle, it is rarely applied in practice if there are social reasons for convicting.[16]

Statutes giving the police a power of arrest are not regarded as "penal laws" for this purpose[17]:

"no one doubts that a prime factor in the process of construction [of statutes conferring arrest powers] is a strong presumption in favour of the liberty of the innocent subject. But it is clear from the authorities at least that a statute may be held to have rebutted the presumption by something falling short of clear express language."[18]

(e) Presumption against retrospective operation

"Perhaps no rule of construction is more firmly established than this—that a retrospective operation is not to be given to a statute so as to impair an existing right or obligation, otherwise than as regards matter of procedure, unless that effect cannot be avoided without doing violence to the language of the enactment. If the enactment is expressed in language which is fairly capable of either interpretation, it ought to be construed as prospective only."[19]

In *Yew Bon Tew* v. *Kenderaan Bas Maria*[19a] the Privy Council emphasised that the expression "procedural" in this context could be misleading. An apparently "procedural" alteration, such as a change in a limitation period, could in some circumstances affect existing rights or obligations. Here, a statute extending a limitation period came into operation, (1) after the plaintiff's claim was statute-barred under the existing law, but (2) so that the claim would not be barred according to the

---

[11] *Per* Lord Esher in *Tuck & Sons* v. *Priester* (1887) 19 Q.B.D. 629, 638; but *cf. R.* v. *Caldwell* [1982] A.C. 341 where the House of Lords majority held that the word "reckless" was to be construed as an "ordinary English word" notwithstanding that this was contrary to: (1) the interests of the defendant; (2) the views of the Law Commission and (3) established decisions of lower courts, and that it would cause great complexity in the law: see J.C. Smith, [1981] Crim.L.R. 393.

[12] Betting and Lotteries Act 1934: *Sales-Matic Ltd.* v. *Hinchcliffe* [1959] 1 W.L.R. 1005.

[13] Poor Law Amendment Act 1851, s.3: *Whiteley* v. *Chappell* (1868) L.R. 4 Q.B. 147.

[14] Above, p. 242.

[15] Above, p. 247.

[16] Glanville Williams, *Textbook of Criminal Law* (2nd ed., 1983) pp. 12–18; *cf. Fisher* v. *Bell* (p. 248, above); *R.* v. *Bloxham* [1983] 1 A.C. 198, 114.

[17] See above, p. 248, n. 81.

[18] *Per* Lord Bridge in *Wills* v. *Bowley* [1983] 1 A.C. 57, 101. It is difficult to see how such a presumption can be regarded as either "strong" or even much of a "presumption."

[19] R.S. Wright J. in *Re Athlumney* [1898] 2 Q.B. 547, 551–2. See above, p. 203.

[19a] [1983] 1 A.C. 553.

new law: it was held not to operate retrospectively so as to affect the
defendant's accrued right to plead a time bar.

In *Waddington* v. *Miah*[20] the House of Lords held that certain offences
created by the Immigration Act 1971 were not intended to operate
retrospectively. Lord Reid stated[21] that in view of the prohibitions
contained in the Universal Declaration of Human Rights and the
European Convention on Human Rights, "it is hardly credible that any
government department would promote or that Parliament would pass
retrospective criminal legislation."

(f) Presumption that statutes do not affect the Crown

It is presumed that the Crown is not bound by a statute unless reference
is made to it expressly or by necessary implication:

> "Since laws are made by rulers for subjects a general expression in a
> statute such as 'any person,' descriptive of those upon whom the
> statute imposes obligations or restraints is not to be read as including
> the ruler himself."[22]

Questions may arise as to whether a particular institution is a servant or
agent of the Crown and so within the "shield of the Crown."[23]

(g) Others

Other presumptions that may be invoked include the presumption that
Parliament does not intend to violate international law,[24] and that a statute
does not apply to acts committed abroad.[25]

G. REFORM

As mentioned above,[26] Parliament has refrained from intervening to give
general directions to the judges as to methods of statutory interpretation.
The Law Commissions saw their report on *The Interpretation of Statutes*[27]
as a contribution to the process of educating judges and practitioners, and
only proposed a limited degree of statutory intervention. They appended
draft clauses of which these were the first two[28]:

> "1.—(1) In ascertaining the meaning of any provision of an Act, the
> matters which may be considered shall, in addition to those which may
> be considered for that purpose apart from this section, include the
> following, that is to say—

---

[20] [1974] 1 W.L.R. 683.

[21] At p. 694.

[22] *Per* Diplock L.J. in *B.B.C.* v. *Johns* [1965] Ch. 32, 78; *cf.* Wrottesley J. in *Att.-Gen.* v.
Hancock [1940] 1 All E.R. 32, 34. The Crown may rely on any statutory defence that would
be available to a private party: Crown Proceedings Act 1947, s. 31(1). See generally, P.W.
Hogg, *Liability of the Crown* (1971) Chap. 7.

[23] See, *e.g. Tamlin* v. *Hannaford* [1950] 1 K.B. 18.

[24] See above, pp. 261–262.

[25] See above, p. 202.

[26] p. 238.

[27] Law Com. No. 21; Scot. Law Com. No. 11 (1969).

[28] Clause 3 provided for the application of the first two clauses to subordinate legislation;
Clause 4 provided for a presumption that breach of a statutory duty should be actionable at
the suit of any person who sustains damage.

    (a) all indications provided by the Act as printed by authority, including punctuation and side-notes, and the short title of the Act;

    (b) any relevant report of a Royal Commission, Committee or other body which had been presented or made to or laid before Parliament or either House before the time when the Act was passed;

    (c) any relevant treaty or other international agreement which is referred to in the Act or of which copies had been presented to Parliament by command of Her Majesty before that time, whether or not the United Kingdom were bound by it at that time;

    (d) any other document bearing upon the subject-matter of the legislation which had been presented to Parliament by command of Her Majesty before that time;

    (e) any document (whether falling within the foregoing paragraphs or not) which is declared by the Act to be a relevant document for the purposes of this section.

    (2) The weight to be given for the purposes of this section to any such matter as is mentioned in subsection (1) shall be no more than is appropriate in the circumstances.

    (3) Nothing in this section shall be construed as authorising the consideration of reports of proceedings in Parliament for any purpose for which they could not be considered apart from this section.

    2.—The following shall be included among the principles to be applied in the interpretation of Acts, namely—

    (a) that a construction which would promote the general legislative purpose underlying the provision in question is to be preferred to a construction which would not; and

    (b) that a construction which is consistent with the international obligations of Her Majesty's Government in the United Kingdom is to be preferred to a construction which is not."

Clause 1 would clarify, and in some respects relax the strictness of the rules which excluded altogether, or excluded when the meaning was otherwise unambiguous, certain internal and external aids from consideration by a court. Clause 1(1)(e) would also encourage the preparation in selected cases of explanatory material for use by the courts, which might "elucidate the contextual assumptions on which legislation has been passed."[29] Clause 2 emphasised the importance in interpretation of a provision of the general legislative purpose underlying it (clause (2)(a)) and the fulfilment of international obligations (clause 2(b)).[30]

    The Renton Committee[31] approved the whole of clauses 1 and 2 except paragraphs (b) and (d) of clause 1: unrestricted admission of such materials would place too great a burden on litigants, their advisers and the courts, would do nothing to make statutes more immediately intelligible to the lay

[29] See above. p. 264.
[30] Law Com. No. 21; Scot. Law Com. No. 11, pp. 49–50.
[31] Cmnd. 6053, 1975 pp. 139–148. See above, p. 193.

public and might greatly lengthen court proceedings. They doubted the value of clause 1(e) as it was already open to Parliament to do this.[32] Clause 2 was regarded as reflecting current practice. No opinion was expressed on the other two clauses. The Committee proposed in addition the enactment of a provision that "In the absence of any express indication to the contrary, a construction that would exclude retrospective effect is to be preferred to one that would not." it should also be made clear that a court in interpreting legislation intended to give effect to a provision of a Community treaty or instrument should take the relevant provisions of Community law into account.

Lord Scarman, who had been chairman of the Law Commission at the time of the 1969 report, introduced the Commissions' proposals as a draft Bill in 1980. The following year he introduced a Bill based on those proposals modified largely to take account of the Renton Committee's suggestions. The first Bill failed on second reading in the Lords; the second passed the Lords but was the subject of objections on the motion for second reading in the Commons, and as a Private Peer's Bill without government support did not proceed further.[33]

In so far as the proposed provisions reflect current practice they seem superfluous; the few that go beyond it, such as the use of official reports and White Papers, are highly controversial.[34] Clause 1(c)[35] would have the effect of reversing the decision in *Ellerman Lines* v. *Murray*,[36] and as such would be useful, but that decision has been largely outflanked, and might well be reconsidered by the House of Lords if the occasion were to arise. Overall, the enactment of these proposals would probably make little difference in practice.

The Renton Committee's recommendation that the preparation of a new Interpretation Act should be put in hand eventually led to the Interpretation Act 1978, a consolidation measure with minor changes incorporating Law Commission proposals. This is an aid to drafting rather than interpretation.[37] "At the more exalted level of general principles the subject does not lend itself to legislation."[38]

H. THE INTERPRETATION OF COMMUNITY LEGISLATION

1. METHODS OF INTERPRETATION

Close attention has been paid to the methods of interpretation of Community legislation adopted by the Court of Justice of the European

---

[32] Clauses in the Matrimonial Proceedings and Properties Bill 1970 and the Animals Bill 1970, which provided that regard could be had to relevant, specified Law Commission reports, were successfully opposed in the House of Commons.

[33] Interpretation of Legislation Bill (1979–80 H.L. Bill 141); Interpretation of Legislation Bill (1980–81 H.C. Bill 120); F.A.R. Bennion, (1981) 131 N.L.J. 840; Miers and Page (1982) pp. 198–206.

[34] See above, pp. 260–261.

[35] Clause 1(b) of the 1980–81 Bill.

[36] [1931] A.C. 126; above, p. 262.

[37] Above, pp. 203–204.

[38] Cross (1976) p. 164. Courts of Commonwealth countries where declarations of general principles of interpretation have been enacted seem rarely to refer to them in practice: W.A. Leitch [1980] Stat.L.R. 5, 8.

Communities.[39] A number of different techniques have been identified, to which commentators have attached a variety of labels. The Court has consistently shown that it is more likely to be influenced by the *context*[40] and *purposes*[41] of a legislative provision than its exact *wording*[42] or the subjective intentions of those who promulgated the legislation.[43] The extent to which the Court's overall approach differs from the so-called "common law" approach of English judges is debatable. It has also probably been exaggerated.[44] Certainly the ideas underlying the various techniques of interpretation adopted by the Court are more familiar than some of the labels. It should also be noted that the techniques tend to be employed cumulatively rather than as alternatives.[45]

The process of interpretation must obviously commence with an analysis of the text. However, literal interpretation, in so far as that implies an exclusive or predominant concern with wording and grammar, is not favoured. The Court has shown little inclination to hold that words carry one "plain," "ordinary" or "clear" meaning so that considerations of context and purpose are rendered irrelevant. There are several reasons for this.

(a) The method of drafting

Many of the key provisions of the EEC and Euratom Treaties are drafted in general terms, and with no "definition sections." For example, Article 9/EEC refers to the prohibition between Member States of customs duties and "all charges having equivalent effect." Article 86/EEC prohibits the "abuse by one or more undertakings of a dominant position within the common market or in a substantial part of it." It gives four examples of an "abuse" but no indication of what is meant by "dominant position." These concepts are left to be developed by the Community institutions, including the Court. The ECSC Treaty and Community secondary legislation are in general more tightly drafted, but they still, inevitably, employ broad terms.

(b) Languages

The texts of the EEC and Euratom Treaties and all Community secondary legislation are published in several languages, each of which is equally authentic.[46] Arguments based on the exact wording of any one version are accordingly less compelling; it can never have been intended that Community law applies differently in different Member States. In

---

[39] See the *Reports of the Judicial and Academic Conference,* Court of Justice of the European Communities, September 27–28, 1976; A. Bredimas, *Methods of Interpretation and Community Law* (1978); L.N. Brown and F.G. Jacobs, *The Court of Justice of the European Communities* (2nd ed. 1983) Chap. 12; R. Plender, "The Interpretation of Community Acts by Reference to the Intentions of the Authors" (1982) 2 Y.B. European Law 57.

[40] "Contextual" or "schematic" interpretation.

[41] "Purposive" or "teleological" interpretation.

[42] "Literal" interpretation.

[43] "Historical" or "subjective" interpretation.

[44] P. Dagtoglou, "The English Judges and European Community Law" [1978] C.L.J. 76.

[45] There is, for example, no place for a "today's the day for the teleological rule" approach.

[46] The only authentic text of the ECSC Treaty is French. The other two basic Treaties are authentic in Danish, Dutch, English, French, German, Greek, Irish and Italian, and the secondary legislation in all these except Irish. Spanish and Portuguese will be added when Spain and Portugal join the Community.

cases of doubt it may be necessary to consider all the versions, in the light, as ever, of context and purposes. For example, in *Stauder* v. *City of Ulm*[47] the Court considered a decision of the Commission on the sale of butter at reduced prices to persons in receipt of welfare benefits. The German and Dutch versions provided that the butter had to be exchanged for a "coupon indicating [the recipients'] names." A German citizen argued that this was an infringement of fundamental rights. The Court found that the French and Italian versions referred to a "coupon referring to the person concerned," and preferred this more liberal wording. The objective of the decision could be achieved by methods of identification other than names.

(c) The status of the Court

The Court is in a stronger position in relation to the other Community institutions than a national court in relation to its national parliament. Legislation is not promulgated by an elected body, but by the nominated Commission and Council of Ministers. The European Parliament is now directly elected, but its role in law making is merely consultative. The Court is expressly enjoined to "ensure that in the interpetation and application of this Treaty the law is observed"[48] and is expressly empowered to review the legality of acts of the Council and Commission.[48a] It is placed on an equal footing with the other institutions in Article 4 of the EEC Treaty. Moreover, it has proved more difficult than expected for the Council to agree upon legislative proposals placed before it by the Commission. The resultant "legislative short-fall" has compelled the Court to determine questions of interpretation, and to fill gaps, in the light of the general aims of the Community and general principles of law. To an extent it has been forced to adopt a legislative role, and has not felt the need to disguise it.[49]

The Court's position in relation to the Member States is more problematic. There is an inevitable tension between the Community's harmonisation aims and the interests of individual Member States. The Court could have adopted a position of neutrality; instead it has chosen to take a "partisan" line in favour of the achievement of the aims of the Community, as a kind of counterweight to the Council of Ministers, which has tended more to reflect state interests. Member States are indeed expressly required by Article 5/EEC to take all appropriate measures to fulfil obligations arising out of the Treaty or acts of Community institutions, to facilitate the achievement of the Community's tasks and to abstain from any measure that could jeopardise the attainment of the objectives of the Treaty.

(d) Community purposes

The freedom of the Court to adopt a purposive approach is naturally facilitated by the express statement of the Community's aims and objectives included in the Treaties (including their preambles). Articles 2 and 3/EEC provide:

[47] Case 29/69 [1969] E.C.R. 419.
[48] Article 164/EEC.
[48a] Article 173/EEC. Above, pp. 231–233.
[49] Note, for example, the enunciation of a rule with *prospective* effect only in the second *Defrenne* case: Case 43/75 [1976] E.C.R. 455.

"ARTICLE 2

The Community shall have as its task, by establishing a common market and progressively approximating the economic policies of Member States, to promote throughout the Community a harmonious development of economic activities, a continuous and balanced expansion, an increase in stability, an accelerated raising of the standard of living and closer relations between the States belonging to it.

ARTICLE 3

For the purposes set out in Article 2, the activities of the Community shall include, as provided in this Treaty and in accordance with the timetable set out therein:

(a) the elimination, as between Member States, of customs duties and of quantitative restrictions on the import and export of goods, and of all other measures having equivalent effect;

(b) the establishment of a common customs tariff and of a common commercial policy towards third countries;

(c) the abolition, as between Member States, of obstacles to freedom of movement for persons, services and capital;

(d) the adoption of a common policy in the sphere of agriculture;

(e) the adoption of a common policy in the sphere of transport;

(f) the institution of a system ensuring that competition in the common market is not distorted;

(g) the application of procedures by which the economic policies of Member States can be co-ordinated and disequilibria in their balances of payments remedied;

(h) the approximation of the laws of Member States to the extent required for the proper functioning of the common market;

(i) the creation of a European Social Fund in order to improve employment opportunities for workers and to contribute to the raising of their standard of living;

(j) the establishment of a European Investment Bank to facilitate the economic expansion of the Community by opening up fresh resources;

(k) the association of the overseas countries and territories in order to increase trade and to promote jointly economic and social development."

Moreover, the reasons on which regulations, directives and decisions are based are stated in a preamble. The Court has attached much more importance to these express statements of purpose than to attempts to discern from other sources the subjective intentions of the authors of Community legislation.[50] Indeed, the details of the negotiations leading up

---

[50] In Case 136/79 *National Panasonic (U.K.) Ltd.* v. *Commission* [1980] E.C.R. 2033 A.G. Warner argued that statements by individual members of the Council, the European Parliament, the Commission or the Commission's staff could not be relied upon for guidance as to the meaning of a Council Regulation (pp. 2066–7). See generally Plender (1982), *op. cit.* n. 39 above.

to the Treaties and of debates within the Council and Commission concerning secondary legislation have not been published. There have been occasional references by Advocates General to a statement made by the government of a Member State to the national parliament in the course of a ratification debate, but not to the exclusion of other considerations.[51]

In relation to purposive interpretation reference has been made to the so-called "rule of effectiveness" (*règle de l'effet utile*), a concept borrowed from international law. This means that, "preference should be given to the construction which gives the rule its fullest effect and maximum practical value."[52] This concept has been used as a justification for holding that the Community or one of its institutions has certain "implied powers," such as the power to require the repayment of a state aid granted in breach of the Treaty.[53] Similarly, in the *E.R.T.A.* Case[54] it was held that the Community had the implied power to establish treaty relations with non-Member States. The Court argued that it was the "necessary effect" or "consequence" of the making of a regulation on the harmonisation of provisions in the road transport field that the Community assume the exclusive right to conclude international agreements relating to the same subject matter.

(e) Context

References by the Court to the purposes of the Community are commonly closely associated with arguments that seek to place the provision to be interpreted in the context of relevant rules of Community law. The Court may refer to the "general scheme of the Treaty," or to other treaty provisions in the relevant Part or to general principles of Community law. In the case of secondary legislation reference will be made to the enabling provisions in the Treaty.

(f) Examples

Striking examples of the Court's dynamic approach to interpretation are provided by its decisions already discussed on the direct effectiveness of treaty provisions and secondary legislation, and the supremacy of Community law.[55] Another good example is the *Continental Can* case.[56] A New York company (Continental Can) held, through a German subsidiary (SLW), what the Commission determined to be a dominant position over a substantial part of the common market in meat tins, fish tins and metal closures for glass jars. Subsequently, acting through a Belgian subsidiary (Europemballage), Continental Can acquired a Dutch firm (TDV) which specialised in similar products. The Commission decided that the merger amounted to an abuse of the dominant position mentioned above, as the effect was practically to eliminate competition in the relevant products. The ECSC treaty expressly provided for merger control (Article 66); the EEC Treaty did not. Nevertheless, the Court held that a merger could in principle amount to an abuse of a dominant position contrary to Article

---

[51] See, *e.g.*, Case 6/60 *Humblet* v. *Belgium* [1960] E.C.R. 559.

[52] H. Kutscher, *Conference Reports* (see p. 271, n. 39, above), I–41.

[53] *e.g.* Case 70/72 *Commission* v. *Germany* [1973] E.C.R. 829.

[54] Case 22/70 *Commission* v. *Council* (*E.R.T.A.*) [1971] E.C.R. 263.

[55] The *Van Gend en Loos* case, above, pp. 219–220; *Costa* v. *E.N.E.L.*, above, pp. 224–225.

[56] Case 6/72 *Europemballage Corporation and Continental Can Co. Inc.* v. *Commission* [1973] E.C.R. 215.

86/EEC, although it did not do so on the facts of the case. In so deciding the Court stated that it was necessary "to go back to the spirit, general scheme and wording of Article 86, as well as to the system and objectives of the Treaty."[57] It referred to Article 2 and 3(f),[58] and to Article 85, which prohibited:

> "all agreements between undertakings, decisions by associations of undertakings and concerted practices which may affect trade between Member States and which have as their object or effect the prevention, restriction or distortion of competition within the common market . . . "

The Court observed[59]:

> "[I]f Article 3(f) provides for the institution of a system ensuring that competition in the common market is not distorted, then it requires *a fortiori* that a competition must not be eliminated. This requirement is so essential that without it numerous provisions of the Treaty would be pointless. Moreover, it corresponds to the precept of Article 2 of the Treaty. . . .
>
> . . . Articles 85 and 86 seek to achieve the same aim on different levels, that is, the maintenance of effective competition within the common market. The restraint of competition which is prohibited if it is the result of behaviour falling under Article 85, cannot become permissible by the fact that such behaviour, succeeds under the influence of a dominant undertaking and results in the merger of the undertaking concerned."

In other words, the prohibition of certain acts when done in concert by separate undertakings was not to be evaded by merger of those undertakings.

(g) Restrictive interpretation

Interpretation in the light of purposes and context does not necessarily mean that such interpretation is "broad" or "liberal." Exceptions to general Community rules and derogations to Treaty obligations are restrictively interpreted. For example, the principle of the free movement of workers is subject to "limitations justified on grounds of public policy, public security or public health."[60] These limitations are strictly construed.[61] Restrictions may not be imposed unless the person's presence or conduct "constitutes a genuine and sufficiently serious threat to public policy,"[62] and the requirements of public policy must affect "one of the fundamental interests of society,"[63] although it is for the national authorities to determine whether the facts of a particular case fall within these principles.

---

[57] *Ibid.* p. 243.

[58] Above, p. 273.

[59] p. 244.

[60] Article 48(3)/EEC; Directive 64/221/EEC.

[61] Case 41/74 *Van Duyn* v. *Home Office* [1974] E.C.R. 1337, above, p. 221; Case 67/74 *Bonsignore* v. *Oberstadtdirektor Cologne* [1975] E.C.R. 297; Case 36/75 *Rutili* v. *French Minister of the Interior* [1975] E.C.R. 1219; Case 30/77 *R.* v. *Bouchereau* [1977] E.C.R. 1999.

[62] *Rutili* [1975] E.C.R. 1219, 1231.

[63] *Bouchereau* [1977] E.C.R. 1999, 2014.

2. GENERAL PRINCIPLES OF LAW[64]

The Court often refers to "general principles of law" derived from the national laws of Member States.[65] These are regarded as part of "the law" of which the Court is to ensure observance.[66] They can be employed in the interpretation of Treaty provisions but cannot override them. In relation to secondary legislation and other acts of the institutions they are not so confined: a challenge to the legality of a measure may be based on breach of one of these principles.[67]

Examples include:

—the principle of *proportionality*, which requires that:
   "the individual should not have his freedom of action limited beyond the degree necessary for the public interest;"[68]
—the *audi alteram partem* principle of natural justice, which requires that persons affected by an adverse decision be given an opportunity to make representations[69];
—the principle of *equality*:
   "whereby differentiation between comparable situations must be based on objective factors;"[70]
—the principle of *legal certainty*, which
   "requires, essentially, that reasonable persons acting on the basis of the law as it is at the time . . . must not be frustrated in their expectations."[71]

These "general principles" include respect for "fundamental rights,"[72] derived from national constitutions or from international conventions concerning human rights, such as the European Convention on Human Rights.[73]. This does not mean that the Convention is part of Community law and so directly enforceable under the European Communities Act

[64] L.N. Brown and F.G. Jacobs, *The Court of Justice of the European Communities* (2nd ed., 1983), Chap. 13; D. Wyatt and A. Dashwood, *The Substantive Law of the E.E.C.* (1980), Chap. 5; T.C. Hartley, *The Foundations of European Community Law* (1981), Chap. 5.

[65] They may also be derived from Treaty provisions.

[66] Article 164/EEC, above, p. 272. See also Article 173/EEC, above, p. 232 which provides expressly that a community act may be annulled for infringement of "any rule of law relating to its application." *Cf.* Article 215(2).

[67] See above, pp. 231–234.

[68] A.G. de Lamothe in Case 11/70 *Internationale Handelsgesellschaft* v. *EVSt.* [1970] E.C.R. 1125, 1147; *cf. R.* v. *Barnsley Metropolitan Borough Council, ex p. Hook* [1976] 1 W.L.R. 1052 and the *Rutili* case above, p. 275 (requirement of a *genuine and sufficiently serious* threat to public policy to justify interference with freedom of movement).

[69] Case 11/74 *Transocean Marine Paint Association* v. *Commission* [1974] E.C.R. 1063; *cf.* Case 136/79 *National Panasonic Ltd.* v. *Commission* [1980] E.C.R. 2033 (no need to give prior warning of an investigation by Commission inspectors).

[70] Wyatt and Dashwood (1980), p. 51. See Case 20/71 *Sabbatini* v. *European Parliament* [1972] E.C.R. 345 (Council Regulation concerning expatriation allowances for employees of the Parliament held invalid on the ground of sex discrimination.)

[71] Wyatt and Dashwood (1980), p. 48.

[72] T.C. Hartley (1975–76) 1 Eur.L.R. 54; the *International Handels* case (n. 68, above).

[73] Case 4/73 *Nold* v. *Commission* [1974] E.C.R. 491; the *Rutili* Case (n. 61, above); Case 118/75 *Watson and Belmann* [1976] E.C.R. 1185; Case 136/79 *National Panasonic (U.K.) Ltd.* v. *Commission* [1980] E.C.R. 2033 (no infringement of the right of privacy guaranteed by article 8(1) of the European Convention: an investigation of a company's books without prior warning was held to be justified as "necessary in a democratic society in the interests of . . . the economic well-being of the country," within the one of the exceptions specified in article 8(2).)

1972: "the European Court does not deal with fundamental rights in the abstract; it only deals with them if they arise under Treaties and have a bearing on Community law questions."[74]

3. INTERPRETATION BY ENGLISH COURTS

The approach that should be taken by English judges was considered by Lord Denning M.R. in *Bulmer* v. *Bollinger*[75]:

> "Beyond doubt the English courts must follow the same principles as the European court. Otherwise there would be differences between the countries of the nine. . . . It is enjoined on the English courts by section 3 of the European Community Act 1972. . . .
>
> No longer must they examine the words in meticulous detail. No longer must they argue about the precise grammatical sense. They must look to the purpose or intent. To quote the words of the European court in the *Da Costa* case [1963] C.M.L.R. 224, 237, they must deduce "from the wording and the spirit of the Treaty the meaning of the community rules." They must not confine themselves to the English text. They must consider, if need be, all the authentic texts. . . . They must divine the spirit of the Treaty and gain inspiration from it. If they find a gap, they must fill it as best they can. They must do what the framers of the instrument would have done if they had thought about it. So we must do the same. Those are the principles, as I understand it, on which the European court acts."

The dangers of applying a strict literal interpretation to provisions of Community law are illustrated by *R.* v. *Henn.*[76] Article 30/EEC prohibits the imposition of "quantitative restrictions on imports and all measures having equivalent effect." The Court of Appeal (Criminal Division) held that the ban on the importation of indecent or obscene material imposed by section 42 of the Customs Consolidation Act 1876 did not fall within Article 30 as it imposed a total prohibition rather than a mere restriction "measured by quantity." This view was, not, however, relied upon by counsel on appeal to the House of Lords, or in argument before the European Court, as it was clearly contrary to a number of earlier decisions of the European Court, and inconsistent with the purposes of the Community. As a matter of common sense, a complete prohibition on the free movement of goods is likely to be more questionable under Community law than a partial restriction. Lord Diplock said that this showed "the danger of an English court applying English canons of statutory construction."[77] It is submitted that the Court of Appeal's interpretation was excessively "literalist" even by English standards.

[74] *Surjit Kaur* v. *Lord Advocate* [1980] 3 C.M.L.R. 79, 96 (Lord Ross, Court of Session (Outer House)).

[75] [1974] Ch. 401, 425–426. See also the similar views expressed by Lord Denning M.R. in *Buchanan & Co. Ltd.* v. *Babco Forwarding & Shippping (U.K.) Ltd.* [1977] Q.B. 208, 213–214. His Lordship's attempt to apply the "European Method" of "filling gaps" to the interpretation of an international convention on the carriage of goods by road was resisted by the House of Lords: [1978] A.C. 141, 153 (Lord Wilberforce) 156 (Viscount Dilhorne) and 160 (Lord Salmon). *Cf.* above, pp. 261–262.

[76] [1978] 1 W.L.R. 1031, C.A.; [1981] A.C. 850, E.C.J., H.L.; Case 34/79 [1979] E.C.R. 3795.

[77] [1981] A.C. at p. 904.

CHAPTER 7

JUDICIAL PRECEDENT

A. INTRODUCTION

ONE of the hallmarks of any good decision-making process is consistency: like cases should be treated alike. Consistency is not, however, always appropriate, as, for example, where a case is seen with the passage of time and changes of circumstance no longer to offer a just solution to a recurring problem. Moreover, there are always difficulties in determining whether two cases are truly "like." Nevertheless, unjustifiable inconsistency may lead to a sense of grievance on the part of those affected and to a reasonable suspicion that the people making the decisions do not know what they are about. One of the main functions of the superior courts of law is the authoritative determination of disputed questions of law. A court's decision is expected to be consistent with decisions in previous cases and to provide certainty for the future so that the parties and others may arrange their affairs in reliance on the court's opinion. These considerations are reflected in the English system of judicial precedent.

The decisions of judges must be reasoned, and the reasons will include propositions of law. A judge in a later case is bound to consider the relevant case law and will normally accept the propositions stated as correct unless there is good reason to disagree; in some circumstances he is required to accept them even if they are in his view obviously wrong. So all relevant precedents are to a greater or lesser extent "persuasive" and some of them may be "binding" under what is termed the doctrine of *stare decisis*.[1] The characteristic that an individual precedent may be binding is distinctive of common law systems. In continental systems based upon codes that are theoretically complete, judicial decisions are not, technically, sources of legal rules. They may, however, carry great persuasive weight, particularly where there is a trend of cases to the same effect, and they have been of great importance in the development of certain areas of the law.[2]

Under the English system, a proposition stated in or derived from case A is binding in case B if (1) it is a proposition of law; (2) it forms part of the *ratio decidendi* of case A (the reason or ground upon which the decision is based); (3) case A was decided in a court whose decisions are binding on the court that is deciding case B; and (4) there is no relevant difference between cases A and B which renders case A "distinguishable." A precedent which is not binding may nevertheless be persuasive. These points are developed below. As we shall see, a judge faced with a precedent that he does not like has a number of possible escape routes to explore, and there is for the litigant who can afford it the possibility of

[1] "Keep to what has been decided previously:" R. Cross, *Precedent in English Law* (3rd ed., 1977), p. 1.

[2] Ibid. pp. 12–17. R. David and J. Brierley, *Major Legal Systems in the World Today* (2nd ed., 1978) pp. 121–134; R. David, *English Law and French Law* (1980) pp. 21–26.

recourse to a higher court for a bad precedent to be overruled. The system seeks to balance the general benefits of consistency and certainty against the requirement of justice in individual cases.

On one view judges are seen as picking their way through dusty old volumes of law reports and loyally following the precedents without too much regard for the justice of the case. On another they are seen as paying lip service to the system, and "loyally" following all the precedents that they agree with; those that they do not agree with are distinguished on spurious grounds, or just ignored. These views lie at the extremes and contain elements of caricature as well as truth. It is not possible to make a useful generalisation about judicial behaviour in practice; there are variations in approach from judge to judge, and the same judge may even vary his position according to the nature of the case before him.[3]

The notion that judges ought generally to abide by relevant precedents developed over several centuries.[4] Blackstone wrote in the eighteenth century that it was "an established rule to abide by former precedents, where the same points come again in litigation . . . unless flatly absurd or unjust,"[5] and Parke J. said in 1833[6]:

> "Our common-law system consists in the applying to new combinations of circumstances those rules of law which we derive from legal principles and judicial precedent; and for the sake of attaining uniformity, consistency and certainty, we must apply those rules, where they are not plainly unreasonable and inconvenient, to all cases which arise; and we are not at liberty to reject them, and to abandon all anology to them, in those to which they have not yet been judicially applied, because we think that the rules are not as convenient and reasonable as we ourselves could have devised."

The practice of relying on precedents in equity was also established by the eighteenth century. The modern strict rules whereby a single precedent can be binding, and precedents can be binding even if "unreasonable and inconvenient," developed in the nineteenth and twentieth centuries. Important factors were the regularisation of and improvements in law reporting following the establishment of the Incorporated Council of Law Reporting[7] and the reorganisation of the courts with a clear hierarchical structure in the latter part of the nineteenth century.[8] The rule that appellate courts are normally bound by their own previous decisions was clearly established for the House of Lords in 1898[9] and for the Court of Appeal in 1944.[10]

---

[3] See further above, pp. 175–183.

[4] See C.K. Allen, *Law in the Making* (7th ed., 1964), pp. 187–235, 380–382; T. Ellis Lewis (1930) 46 L.Q.R. 207, 341, (1931) 47 L.Q.R. 411, (1932) 48 L.Q.R. 230; W.H.D. Winder (1941) 57 L.Q.R. 245 (Precedent in equity).

[5] 1 *Blackstone's Commentaries* 69, 70.

[6] *Mirehouse* v. *Rennell* (1833) 1 Cl. & F. 527, 546.

[7] See below, p. 308.

[8] See above, p. 29.

[9] See below, pp. 296–300. It was changed in 1966.

[10] See below, pp. 286–294.

B. PROPOSITION OF "LAW"

Decisions on questions of fact may not be cited as precedents.[11] The line between "law" and "fact" may, however, be difficult to draw. An issue is one of fact where it turns on the reliability or credibility of direct evidence, or on inferences from circumstantial evidence. For example, the fact that a man was driving at a high speed may be established by the testimony of a witness, or by inference from such evidence as tyre marks. More difficult are cases which raise an issue whether the facts found conform to a legal description. Such issues are sometimes classified as issues of fact. For example, whether conduct is "unreasonable," and so a breach of the duty of care for the purposes of the tort of negligence, is a question of fact. In *Baker* v. *E. Longhurst & Sons Ltd.*[12] Scrutton L.J. stated[13] that "if a person rides in the dark he must ride at such a pace that he can pull up within the limit of his vision . . . ." This was treated as a proposition of law until the Court of Appeal ruled that it was not.[14] In *Qualcast (Wolverhampton) Ltd.* v. *Haynes*[15] the House of Lords held that a county court judge could not be bound by precedent to hold that an employer who failed to give instructions to an employee as to the use of protective clothing had been negligent.

Where a legal description contained in a statute is "an ordinary word of the English language" its application to the facts found is a question of fact, and it may not be the subject of judicial definition or interpretation.[16] The judges are particularly inclined to classify questions as questions of fact where they wish to avoid the proliferation of authorities.[17] However, where words are used in an unusual sense, or a statute has to be "construed" or "interpreted" before it can be applied, a question of law is raised.[18]

C. DETERMINING THE RATIO DECIDENDI

1. RATIO AND DICTUM

A proposition of law can only be binding if it forms part of the *ratio decidendi*[19] (commonly shortened to *ratio*) of the case.

---

[11] *Qualcast (Wolverhampton) Ltd.* v. *Haynes* [1959] A.C. 743. Otherwise, "the precedent system will die from a surfeit of authorities" (*per* Lord Somervell at p. 758), or the judges might be "crushed under the weight of our own reports" (*per* Lord Denning at p. 761).

[12] [1933] 2 K.B. 461.

[13] At p. 468.

[14] *Tidy* v. *Battman* [1934] 1 K.B. 319; *Morris* v. *Luton Corporation* [1946] 1 K.B. 114; Lord Greene hoped that this "suggested principle" would "rest peacefully in the grave" (p. 116). Cf. *Worsfold* v. *Howe* [1980] 1 W.L.R. 1175.

[15] [1959] A.C. 743.

[16] See above, pp. 8–11.

[17] *e.g. R.* v. *Industrial Injuries Commissioner, ex p. A.E.U.* (*No.* 2) [1966] 2 Q.B. 31, 45, 48–49, *per* Lord Denning M.R., in relation to the expression "arising out of and in the course of his employment."

[18] Denning L.J. in *British Launderers' Association* v. *Borough of Hendon Rating Authority* [1949] 1 K.B. 462, 471–472; Lord Reid in *Cozens* v. *Brutus*, above, pp. 9–10.

[19] Usually pronounced "rayshio," although variants may be encountered in practice.

Sir Rupert Cross, in the leading English monograph on precedent, gives this description[20]:

> "The *ratio decidendi* of a case is any rule of law expressly or impliedly treated by the judge as a necessary step in reaching his conclusion, having regard to the line of reasoning adopted by him, or a necessary part of his direction to the jury."

He also points out that a judge may adopt more than one line of reasoning leading to the same result, in which case there may be more than one *ratio*. A proposition of law stated by a judge that is not necessary for his conclusion is termed an *obiter dictum* or *dictum*.[21] It may, for example, be a proposition wider than is necessary for the facts of the case, or a proposition concerning some matter not raised in the case. Statements of law on points which are fully argued by counsel and considered by the judge, but which do not technically play any part in determining the result are sometimes termed "judicial *dicta*."[22]

Conversely, where a court *assumes* a proposition of law to be correct without addressing its mind to it, the decision of that court is not binding authority for that proposition.[22a]

2. The Principle Enunciated by the Judge

The task of determining the *ratio* of a case can be complicated, and writers on the subject are not agreed as to how that task is approached by the judges in practice, or how, in theory, it should be approached.[23] It is impossible to assert with confidence that there is any one method of approach which is invariably adopted by the judges. The obvious starting point is the wording of the judgment in question. A judge in giving the reasons for his decision will indicate the proposition[24] of law upon which he regards his decision as based. He will explain why he thinks this proposition is correct, usually by referring to earlier authorities and showing that it makes good sense. These "explanations" or "justifications" must be distinguished from the proposition of law which they support, as only the latter can be part of the *ratio*.[25] The proposition as enunciated by the judge has a good claim to be regarded as the *ratio*. For example, the editor of a published law report who endeavours to state the *ratio* in the

---

[20] *Precedent in English Law* (3rd ed., 1977), p. 76.

[21] Not "an *obiter*." The plural is *obiter dicta*. See, *e.g.* *Penn-Texas Corporation* v. *Murat Anstalt* (*No.* 2) [1964] 2 Q.B. 647, 661 (Lord Denning M.R.).

[22] Megarry J. in *Brunner* v. *Greenslade* [1971] Ch. 993, 1002–3.

[22a] *Per* Warner J. in *Barrs* v. *Bethell* [1982] Ch. 294, 308, relying on Lord Diplock in *Baker* v. *The Queen* [1975] A.C. 774, 788 and Russell L.J. in *National Enterprises Ltd.* v. *Racal Communications Ltd.* [1975] Ch. 397, 406. This principle, however, is not always observed, *e.g.* in respect of the *Havana* case: see below, pp. 290–291.

[23] See, *e.g.* Cross (1977), Chap. 2; A.L. Goodhart, "Determining the *Ratio Decidendi* of a Case" in *Essays in Jurisprudence and the Common Law* (1931), pp. 1–26; the somewhat acerbic dispute between J.L. Montrose and A.W.B. Simpson: (1957) 20 M.L.R. 124, 413, 587, (1958) 21 M.L.R. 155; A.L. Goodhart (1959) 22 M.L.R. 117; Simpson, in A.G. Guest (ed.) *Oxford Essays in Jurisprudence* (1961) Chap. VI.

[24] There may be more than one relevant proposition; the singular is used here for convenience.

[25] *Cf.* Goodhart (1931), pp. 3–4: "A bad reason may often make good law."

headnote to the case, will frequently use actual sentences from the judgment. A judge in a later case will commonly summarise the effect of a case by citing a passage from the judgment. However, with the passage of time the case may be subject to critical analysis by academic commentators, by counsel and by judges, and the *ratio* restated in a wider or narrower form.

3. THE "INTERPRETATION" OF PRECEDENTS

The judge who is called upon to determine a disputed point of law himself chooses the generality of the language in which he expresses his conclusion. The proposition may be very general, it may be closely tailored to the facts of the case before him or it may be formulated at some intermediate level. Most, although not all judges are reluctant to make general statements of law, and it is anyway well established that a judgment must be read in the light of the facts of the case in which is was given. In *Quinn* v. *Leathem*,[26] the Earl of Halsbury L.C. said that:

> "every judgment must be read as applicable to the particular facts proved, or assumed to be proved, since the generality of the expressions which may be found there are not intended to be expositions of the whole law, but governed and qualified by the particular facts of the case in which such expressions are to be found."

This point is commonly made where the judge in case B wishes to hold that the *ratio* of case A is narrower than that apparently expounded by the judge or court in case A, and is accordingly not applicable. An example of this is given by the decision of the majority of the Privy Council in *Mutual Life and Citizens' Assurance Co. Ltd.* v. *Evatt*,[27] which sought to restrict the scope of liability in tort for negligent misstatement to cases where the defendant was or claimed to be in the business of giving information or advice of the relevant kind. The speeches in the leading case, *Hedley Byrne & Co. Ltd.* v. *Heller and Partners Ltd.*[28] were interpreted to support the incorporation of such a condition, notwithstanding the dissent of Lord Reid and Lord Morris of Borth-y-Gest, who had taken part in the *Hedley Byrne* decision and who said that they were "unable to construe the passages from our speeches cited in the judgment of the majority in the way in which they are there construed."[29] Conversely, a proposition stated by a judge may be regarded as too restrictive. A well known example is *Barwick* v. *The English Joint Stock Bank*,[30] where Willes J. said:

> "The general rule is, that the master is answerable for every such wrong of the servant or agent as is committed in the course of the

---

[26] [1901] A.C. 495, 506. Cf. Diplock L.J. in *Miller-Mead* v. *Minister of Housing and Local Government* [1963] 2 Q.B. 196, 235–236.

[27] [1971] A.C. 793. On the Privy Council and precedent, see below, pp. 291, 300, 303.

[28] [1964] A.C. 465.

[29] [1971] A.C. 793, 813. The minority position has been preferred by several English judges: see *Esso Petroleum Co. Ltd.* v. *Mardon* [1975] Q.B. 819, 830 (Lawson J.) and [1976] Q.B. 801, 827 (Ormrod L.J.); *Howard Marine and Dredging Co. Ltd.* v. *Ogden & Sons Ltd.* [1978] Q.B. 574, 591 (Lord Denning M.R.), 600 (Shaw L.J.).

[30] (1866) L.R. 2 Ex. 259.

service and for the master's benefit, though no express command or privity of the master be proved."[31]

It had previously been doubted whether a master was vicariously liable in respect of the fraud, as distinct from the non-deliberate wrongdoing, of a servant. On the facts of the case the master had benefitted, albeit unwittingly, from the fraud. Subsequently, in *Lloyd* v. *Grace, Smith & Co.*[32] the House of Lords held that an employer could be vicariously liable for the fraud of an employee committed in the course of employment, notwithstanding that the employer received no benefit. The reference to the "master's benefit" was not to be regarded as part of the *ratio* of *Barwick's* case in the light of Willes J.'s judgment when read as a whole and of judgments in other cases both before and after *Barwick*. These are examples of the *ratio* of a case being reformulated *by a court not bound by it*. It has been doubted whether courts "exercise any power of correcting statements of law drawn from binding decisions."[33]

4. CASES WHERE NO REASONS ARE GIVEN

The report of an old case may simply contain a statement of the facts, the arguments of counsel and an order of the court based on those facts. Here, the *ratio* has, if possible, to be inferred, but its authority is understandably very weak.[34] It would be most unusual for such a case to be decisive in modern litigation.

5. JUDGMENTS WITH MORE THAN ONE RATIO

A number of distinct points of law may be at issue in a case, each of which taken separately would be sufficient to determine the case in favour of one side (say the plaintiff). The judge may be content to take one point only, give judgment for the plaintiff, and decline to comment on the other points. Instead, he may express his opinion on these points, while making it clear that his decision is to rest on the first point and that the other remarks are *dicta*. Yet again, he may state his conclusion on each point without any distinction, resolving them all in favour of the plaintiff. In the third situation, each conclusion is a separate *ratio*, and in principle, each *ratio* is binding.[35]

6. THE RATIO DECIDENDI OF APPELLATE COURTS[36]

Determining the *ratio* of the decision of an appellate court where separate judgments are given can be a difficult task. Some principles are reasonably

---

[31] *Ibid*. p. 265.

[32] [1912] A.C. 716.

[33] See A.W.B. Simpson (1959) 22 M.L.R. 453, 455–457.

[34] Cross (1977), p. 48.

[35] *Jacobs* v. *London County Council* [1950] A.C. 361, 369 (Lord Simonds); *Behrens* v. *Bertram Mills Circus Ltd.* [1957] 2 Q.B. 1, 24–25 (Devlin J.); *Miliangos* v. *George Frank (Textiles) Ltd.* [1975] Q.B. 487, 502–503 (Lord Denning M.R.); R.E. Megarry (1958) 74 L.Q.R. 350. On other occasions Lord Denning has argued that the Court of Appeal is not necessarily bound by both or all the *rationes* of an earlier *Court of Appeal* decision: *Hanning* v. *Maitland (No. 2)* [1970] 1 Q.B. 580; *Ministry of Defence* v. *Jeremiah* [1980] 1 Q.B. 87. On this he stood alone: see Hazel Carty (1981) 1 L.S. 68, 71–72.

[36] Cross (1977) pp. 90–102; Paton and G. Sawer (1947) 63 L.Q.R. 461; A.M. Honoré (1955) 71 L.Q.R. 196.

clear. Where all the members of the court are agreed as to the result of the case, any *ratio* that commands the support of a majority is binding.[37] For example, in a three-member court where two judges support ground A and the third ground B, ground A is the *ratio*. If three judges support ground A and two ground B, there are two *rationes*. Where a judge dissents as to the result, his views must technically be disregarded for the purpose of ascertaining the *ratio* on the ground that his reasons cannot be "necessary" for a decision he opposes. Dissenting judgments may, however, carry persuasive weight. Where there is no majority in favour of any particular *ratio*, a later court may hold that the case has no discernible *ratio* which has to be followed, although it may not adopt any reasoning which would show the decision itself to be wrong.[38] In some cases there may be much time and effort spent in the search for a *ratio* which is as elusive as the holy grail.[39]

D. THE HIERARCHY OF THE COURTS AND THE RULES OF BINDING PRECEDENT

Broadly speaking, a court is only *obliged* to follow the decisions of courts at a higher or the same level in the court structure, and there are a number of exceptions even to that requirement. For the purposes of the following discussion it must be assumed that all the other factors mentioned in Section A above are present which combine to make a precedent binding in a particular case.

1. MAGISTRATES' COURTS AND COUNTY COURTS

Decisions of these courts are rarely reported outside the pages of local newspapers, but even if they were properly reported they would not constitute precedents binding on anyone. They do not bind themselves, although it is to be expected that an individual magistrate or county court judge will attempt to be consistent in his own decision-making. A magistrates' court may also be reminded by the clerk of the practice of the local bench, and other benches in the area. The matter upon which a "local view" may develop will rarely be a point of law; more commonly it will relate to a procedural requirement or the exercise of discretion, as in sentencing or the granting of bail.[40] Magistrates' courts and county courts

---

[37] *e.g. Amalagamated Society of Railway Servants* v. *Osborne* [1910] A.C. 87. A statement "I agree" may simply indicate concurrence with the order proposed in the leading judgment and not necessarily all the reasoning: Lord Russell of Killowen (then Russell L.J.), Address to the Holdsworth Club of the University of Birmingham 1968–69, reprinted in B.W. Harvey (ed.), *The Lawyer and Justice* (1978).

[38] See the analysis of the decision of the House of Lords in *Central Asbestos Ltd.* v. *Dodd* [1973] A.C. 518 by the Court of Appeal in *In re Harper* v. *National Coal Board* (*Intended Action*) [1974] Q.B. 614.

[39] See, for example, the decision of the House of Lords in *Chaplin* v. *Boys* [1971] A.C. 356. First-year law students are not recommended to read this case; it should, however, be one of the party pieces of students of Conflict of Laws.

[40] See, *e.g. R.* v. *Nottingham JJ., ex p. Davies* [1981] 1 Q.B. 38 where the practice of the City of Nottingham bench of refusing to hear full argument on a third or subsequent application for bail, unless there were "new circumstances," was endorsed by the Divisional Court.

are bound by decisions of the High Court, Court of Appeal and House of Lords.

2. THE CROWN COURT

Decisions of judges in the Crown Court are reported rather more frequently than those of magistrates' and county courts. This is partly because the judge may be a High Court judge whose pronouncements are inevitably more authoritative, and partly because reports of cases on points of criminal law, even at this level, find an outlet in the pages of publications such as the Criminal Law Review and the Criminal Appeal Reports. However, there is no regular reporting, and it has been suggested that Crown Court decisions are merely persuasive authorities whatever the status of the judge.[41] The Crown Court is bound by decisions of the Court of Appeal and the House of Lords. It has been asserted that it is not bound by decisions of the Divisional Court,[42] but this is hard to square with the rule that Divisional Courts are bound by their own previous decisions.[43]

3. THE HIGH COURT

The decision of a High Court judge is binding on inferior courts, but not technically on another High Court judge, and certainly not on a Divisional Court (*i.e.* a court of two or more judges). High Court judges are reluctant to depart from the decisions of their brethren,[44] Chancery judges being particularly loath to disagree with their colleagues for fear of upsetting transactions affecting property rights and the like.[45] There are, however, examples of judicial disagreement, one of the most notable in recent years being on the question whether failure to wear a seat-belt in a car can amount to contributory negligence. This had to be settled by the Court of Appeal.[46] However, it has been stated that where there are conflicting decisions of judges of co-ordinate jurisdiction, the later decision should thereafter be preferred, provided that it was reached after full consideration of the first decision: the only, rare, exception would be where the third judge was convinced that the second judge was wrong in not following the first, for example where some binding or persuasive authority had not been cited in either of the first two cases.[46a]

---

[41] A. Ashworth, "The Binding Effect of Crown Court Decisions" [1980] Crim. L.R. 402–403; cf. Cross (1977), pp. 7, 122. Some cases are reported in the regular law reports: see, *e.g. R.* v. *Bourne* [1939] 1 K.B. 687, where the summing up of Macnaghten J. on the pre-Abortion Act 1967 law of procuring an abortion was generally accepted as authoritative (*cf.* [1938] 3 All E.R. 615).

[42] *R.* v. *Colyer* [1974] Crim. L.R. 243 (Judge Stinson).

[43] See below, p. 286.

[44] See *Police Authority for Huddersfield* v. *Watson* [1947] K.B. 842, 848, where it is explained by Lord Goddard C.J. to be a matter of "judicial comity."

[45] There are also many fewer Chancery judges than Queen's Bench judges and so they are more likely to meet each other; whether this boosts "judicial comity" is a matter for speculation.

[46] *Froom* v. *Butcher* [1976] Q.B. 286 answered the question in the affirmative.

[46a] *Colchester Estates (Cardiff)* v. *Carlton Industries plc.*, *The Times*, April 9, 1984.

4. DIVISIONAL COURTS

The present position is that a Divisional Court is bound by decisions of the Court of Appeal and the House of Lords, and is bound by previous Divisional Court decisions to the same extent that the Court of Appeal is bound by its own previous decisions.[47] Its decisions are binding on High Court judges sitting alone[48] and inferior courts, but not the Employment Appeal Tribunal.[49]

5. THE COURT OF APPEAL (CIVIL DIVISION)

(a) The general position

Decisions of the Court of Appeal are binding on the Divisional Court, the Employment Appeal Tribunal, High Court judges[50] and inferior courts. The Court of Appeal is bound to follow decisions of the House of Lords. On occasion, the House has felt it necessary to remind the Court of Appeal of this. In 1970, Captain Jack Broome R.N. (retd.) brought a libel action against David Irving and Cassell & Co. Ltd. respectively author and publisher of a book entitled *The Destruction of Convoy P.Q.17*. The case was heard over 17 days by Lawton J. and a jury.[51] The jury awarded £15,000 "compensatory damages" and £25,000 "exemplary damages." The situations in which exemplary damages could be awarded had been listed by Lord Devlin in *Rookes* v. *Barnard*,[52] a decision of the House of Lords, and the principles subsequently applied by the Court of Appeal to the tort of defamation.[53] Not surprisingly, Lawton J. had directed the jury accordingly in the *P.Q.17* case. Both author and publisher appealed against the award of exemplary damages. The Court of Appeal, after a nine-day hearing, rejected the appeal.[54] The case fell within one of the situations in which Lord Devlin had held that exemplary damages could be awarded,[55] the judge's direction had been adequate and the jury's award was not perversely large. The Court of Appeal was not, however, content with that. The members of the court (Lord Denning M.R., Salmon and Phillimore L.JJ.) took the view that the law on exemplary damages as expounded by Lord Devlin was "unworkable." Lord Denning M.R. said that the common law on exemplary damages had been well settled before

[47] *Police Authority for Huddersfield* v. *Watson* [1947] K.B. 842; *Younghusband* v. *Luftig* [1949] 2 K.B. 356, 361. But *cf. R.* v. *Greater Manchester Coroner, ex p. Tal, The Times*, May 28, 1984. See below on precedent in the Court of Appeal.

[48] *Ibid.; Ettenfield* v. *Ettenfield* [1939] P. 377, 380; *contra: Elderton* v. *United Kingdom Totalisator Co. Ltd.* (1945) 61 T.L.R. 529 where a judge of the Chancery Division declined to follow the decision of a Divisional Court of the Queen's Bench Division.

[49] *Portec (U.K.) Ltd.* v. *Mogensen* [1976] I.C.R. 396, 400; *Breach* v. *Epsylon Industries Ltd.* [1976] I.C.R. 316, 320.

[50] In *Lane* v. *Willis* [1972] 1 W.L.R. 326, 332, Davies L.J. rebuked Lawson J. for expressing the opinion, though accepting he was bound by it, that a Court of Appeal decision was wrong.

[51] It survived an interruption by Welsh language demonstrators: *Morris* v. *Crown Office* [1970] 2 Q.B. 114.

[52] [1964] A.C. 1129. The other members of the House expressly concurred with Lord Devlin's statement on exemplary damages.

[53] *McCarey* v. *Associated Newspapers Ltd.* [1965] 2 Q.B. 86; *Broadway Approvals Ltd.* v. *Odhams Press Ltd.* [1965] 1 W.L.R. 805.

[54] *Broome* v. *Cassell & Co. Ltd.* [1971] 2 Q.B. 354.

[55] See below, pp. 654–655.

1964, that there were two House of Lords cases[56] which had approved that settled doctrine and which Lord Devlin must have "overlooked" or "misunderstood," that *Rookes* v. *Barnard* had not been followed in Commonwealth courts, and that the new doctrine was "hopelessly illogical and inconsistent." He concluded:

> "I think the difficulties presented by *Rookes* v. *Barnard* are so great that the judges should direct the juries in accordance with the law as it was understood before *Rookes* v. *Barnard*. Any attempt to follow *Rookes* v. *Barnard* is bound to lead to confusion."[57]

Surprisingly, there was no discussion of the question whether Lord Devlin's statement formed part of the *ratio decidendi* of *Rookes* v. *Barnard*.

Cassells appealed to the House of Lords; a 13-day hearing was held before seven Law Lords. The Court of Appeal's decision to uphold the jury's verdict was affirmed by a majority.[58] Lord Devlin's approach to exemplary damages was endorsed, with varying enthusiasm, by a majority. The approach of the Court of Appeal to *Rookes* v. *Barnard* was roundly condemned. Lord Hailsham L.C.:

> "[I]t is not open to the Court of Appeal to give gratuitous advice to judges of first instance to ignore decisions of the House of Lords in this way and, if it were open to the Court of Appeal to do so, it would be highly undesirable . . . .
>
> "The fact is, and I hope it will never be necessary to say so again, that, in the hierarchical system of courts which exists in this country, it is necessary for each lower tier, including the Court of Appeal, to accept loyally the decisions of the higher tiers. Where decisions manifestly conflict, the decision in *Young* v. *Bristol Aeroplane Co. Ltd.* offers guidance to each tier in matters affecting its own decisions. It does not entitle it to question considered decisions in the upper tiers with the same freedom."[59]

Other members of the House of Lords added their voices to the chorus of disapproval.[60] They pointed out that the parties had been put to much expense in litigating broad legal issues unnecessary for the disposal of their dispute. Lord Devlin had not overlooked the two House of Lords cases (*Ley* v. *Hamilton* was discussed at length in his speech) and, on proper analysis, they were not binding authorities on the award of exemplary damages.[61]

The House of Lords similarly found it necessary to assert its authority over the Court of Appeal in *Miliangos* v. *George Frank (Textiles) Ltd.*[62]

---

[56] *E. Hulton & Co.* v. *Jones* [1910] A.C. 20 and *Ley* v. *Hamilton* (1935) 153 L.T. 384.

[57] [1971] 2 Q.B. 354, 381, 384.

[58] *Cassell & Co. Ltd.* v. *Broome* [1972] A.C. 1027. It has been described as "what may well be the most hostile *affirmation* of a Court of Appeal decision in our history:" Julius Stone, "On the Liberation of Appellate Judges—How not to do it!" (1972) 35 M.L.R. 449.

[59] [1972] A.C. 1027, 1054.

[60] See Lord Reid at pp. 1084, 1091–3; Lord Wilberforce at pp. 1112–3; Lord Diplock at pp. 1131–2; Lord Kilbrandon at pp. 1132, 1135.

[61] Viscount Dilhorne dissented on this last point: [1972] A.C. at pp. 1109–11.

[62] [1976] A.C. 443, discussed below, pp. 290–291.

(b) Young v. Bristol Aeroplane Co. Ltd.

In *Young* v. *Bristol Aeroplane Co. Ltd.*[63] the Court of Appeal[64] held that it was bound by its own previous decisions, and by decisions of courts of co-ordinate jurisdiction such as the Courts of Exchequer Chamber. Three exceptions were identified. First, a decision of the Court of Appeal given *per incuriam* need not be followed. Secondly, where the court is faced by previous conflicting decisions of the Court of Appeal or a court of co-ordinate jurisdiction, it may choose which to follow. Thirdly, where a previous decision of the Court of Appeal, although not expressly overruled, cannot stand with a subsequent decision of the House of Lords, the decision of the House must be followed. Since *Young's* case further light has been thrown on the scope of these three exceptions, suggestions have been made for additional ones, and Lord Denning M.R. has fought, almost single-handed, against the notion that the Court of Appeal should be bound by its own previous decisions at all. In addition, it has been unclear whether the grounds upon which the Court of Appeal may question one of its own decisions may be employed by a court lower in the hierarchy in respect of a decision of a higher court. These matters are considered in turn.

(c) Accepted exceptions to Young v. Bristol Aeroplane Co. Ltd.

(i) *Decisions given per incuriam*

If interpreted and applied literally the *per incuriam* doctrine could be used to evade the effect of any decision thought to have been reached "through want of care." However, the term in this context is interpreted narrowly. A decision will not be regarded as *per incuriam* merely on the ground that another court thinks it wrongly decided, that it has been inadequately argued[65] or that the decision contains points which are not derived from the arguments of counsel.[66] In *Morelle* v. *Wakeling* Sir Raymond Evershed M.R. said that as a general rule the *per incuriam* doctrine could only apply to:

> "decisions given in ignorance or forgetfulness of some inconsistent statutory provision or of some authority binding on the court concerned: so that in such cases some part of the decision or some step in the reasoning on which it is based is found, on that account to be demonstrably wrong."[67]

---

[63] [1944] K.B. 718.

[64] A "full court" consisting of Lord Greene M.R., Scott, MacKinnon, Luxmoore, Goddard and du Parcq L.JJ. Note that it was held in this case a "full court" is bound by previous Court of Appeal decisions to the same extent as a court ordinarily constituted. See further below pp. 295–296.

[65] *Morelle* v. *Wakeling* [1955] 2 Q.B. 379, 406; *Miliangos* v. *George Frank (Textiles) Ltd.* [1975] Q.B. 487, 503 (Lord Denning M.R.).

[66] *Per* Lord Diplock in *Cassell & Co. Ltd.* v. *Broome* [1972] A.C. 1027, 1131.

[67] [1955] 2 Q.B. 379, 406. See generally, P. Wesley-Smith (1980) 15 J.S.P.T.L. (N.S.) 58. In *Industrial Properties Ltd.* v. *A.E.I.* [1977] Q.B. 580 *dicta* in a Court of Appeal decision were held to have been made *per incuriam* on the ground that the court had misunderstood a decision of the Court of Exchequer Chamber; they had only been referred to an inadequate report of that decision.

In *Dixon* v. *British Broadcasting Corporation*[68] a decision on the construction of a statutory provision was regarded as *per incuriam* on the ground that other relevant provisions which threw light on the words in question had not been brought to the attention of the court.

(ii) *Conflicting decisions*

Decisions in the Court of Appeal may conflict. The decision in case A may not be cited to the court in case B whereas both cases A and B are cited in case C[69]; case A may not have been reported,[70] or may simply have been overlooked. Cases A and B may be decided by different divisions of the Court of Appeal at roughly the same time. Case A may be cited in case B but, in the view of the court in case C, erroneously interpreted. The resulting confusion may be settled by the Court of Appeal choosing which case or line of cases to follow and overruling any cases that conflict.[71] It has been argued that the court should be bound by the earlier case, case A (as the court in case B was not entitled to depart from it[72]) and, alternatively, that it should follow case B (as the later case[73]) but neither argument has prevailed.

(iii) *Decisions impliedly overruled by the House of Lords*

In *Young* v. *Bristol Aeroplane Co.*[74] Lord Greene M.R. stated that the Court of Appeal was not bound by a previous decision which "although not expressly overruled, cannot stand with a subsequent decision of the House of Lords."[75] This principle was relied upon by Oliver J. in *Midland Bank Trust Co. Ltd.* v. *Hett, Stubbs & Kemp*[76] where he declined to follow the decision of the Court of Appeal in *Groom* v. *Crocker*[77] on the ground that it was inconsistent with the subsequent decision of the House of Lords in *Hedley Byrne & Co. Ltd.* v. *Heller & Partners Ltd.*[78]

(iv) *Decisions on interlocutory appeals*

In *Boys* v. *Chaplin*[79] the Court of Appeal held that it was not bound by a previous decision of the Court of Appeal where that court comprised two Lords Justices hearing an interlocutory appeal.

---

[68] [1979] Q.B. 546.

[69] See the cases discussed in *Fisher* v. *Ruislip-Northwood Urban District Council* [1945] K.B. 584. The decision in case B may be regarded as given *per incuriam*: see above.

[70] *E.g. Cathrineholm A/S* v. *Norequipment Trading Ltd.* [1972] 2 Q.B. 314.

[71] *Ibid.; Ross-Smith* v. *Ross-Smith* [1961] P. 39; *cf. Midland Bank Trust Co. Ltd.* v. *Hett, Stubbs & Kemp* [1979] Ch. 384.

[72] A.L. Goodhart (1947) 9 C.L.J. 349.

[73] R.N. Gooderson (1950) 10 C.L.J. 432.

[74] [1944] K.B. 718.

[75] *Ibid.* p. 722.

[76] [1979] Ch. 384. The case concerned the liability of a solicitor for negligence: see above pp. 121–122.

[77] [1939] 1 K.B. 194. Authorities following *Groom* v. *Crocker* and decided after *Hedley Byrne* were regarded as inconsistent with the decision of the Court of Appeal in *Esso Petroleum Co. Ltd.* v. *Mardon* [1976] Q.B. 801.

[78] [1964] A.C. 465.

[79] [1968] 2 Q.B. 1.

(d) Possible exceptions to Young v. Bristol Aeroplane Co. Ltd.

(i) *Inconsistency with an earlier House of Lords decision*

Lord Greene M.R.'s summary of conclusions in the *Young* case and the headnotes of most of the reports indicate that a Court of Appeal decision which is inconsistent with *any* House of Lords case, whether prior or subsequent, does not bind the Court of Appeal. The relevant passage from the main body of Lord Greene's judgment,[80] however, includes the word "subsequent." Moreover, in *Williams* v. *Glasbrook Bros.*[81] Lord Greene expressly asserted that the exception was so limited; if the Court of Appeal misinterprets an earlier House of Lords decision "nobody but the House of Lords can put that mistake right."[82] This position has been supported by Lord Denning M.R.[83] and Lord Simon,[84] and is to be preferred "in the interests of certainty."[85] Against these authorities, and in favour of a more widely drawn exception to *Young's* case, are the decision of the Court of Appeal in *Fitzsimons* v. *The Ford Motor Co.*[86] and the opinion of Lord Cross in *Miliangos* v. *George Frank (Textiles) Ltd.*[87]

The *Miliangos* case illustrates some of the difficulties that can arise. In 1960 the House of Lords in the *Havana* case[88] made a decision which was based on the unchallenged assumption that a judgment in an English court could only be given in sterling. The actual point in issue was the date at which a debt payable in U.S. dollars had to be converted to the equivalent in sterling for the purposes of proceedings in England to enforce payment. In *Schorsch Meier G.m.b.H.* v. *Hennin*[89] the Court of Appeal[90] held (1) that the operation of the *Havana* case had been limited by Article 106 of the EEC Treaty, which was regarded as enabling EEC nationals to obtain judgments in a foreign currency and (2) (Lawton L.J. dissenting) that in any event the *Havana* rule could be disregarded as the fact that sterling was no longer a stable currency meant that the rationale behind the rule no longer stood. On the latter point, the majority founded themselves on the maxim *cessante ratione legis cessat ipsa lex* (if the reason for a law ceases to be valid the law itself ceases). In *Miliangos* v. *George Franks (Textiles) Ltd.* a plaintiff who was not an EEC national sought to take advantage of the second *ratio* of *Schorsch Meier*. Bristow J.[91] held that he was obliged to follow the House of Lords decision in *Havana* in preference to that of the Court of Appeal in *Schorsch Meier*, notwithstanding the fact that it had been cited to the court in *Schorsch Meier*. The *Havana* rule could only be altered by statute or another decision of the House. On appeal, the Court

---

[80] Above, p. 288.

[81] [1947] 2 All E.R. 884.

[82] *Ibid.* p. 885. If the House of Lords decision had not been cited, the Court of Appeal decision would be *per incuriam*: see above.

[83] *Miliangos* v. *George Frank (Textiles) Ltd.* [1975] Q.B. 416, 502.

[84] *Ibid.* [1976] A.C. 443, 478–479.

[85] Cross (1977), p. 143.

[86] [1946] 1 All E.R. 429. This was not cited in *Williams* v. *Glasbrook Bros.*

[87] [1976] A.C. 443, 496.

[88] *In re United Railways of Havana and Regla Warehouses Ltd.* [1961] A.C. 1007.

[89] [1975] Q.B. 416.

[90] Lord Denning M.R., Lawton L.J. and Foster J.

[91] [1975] Q.B. 487, 491.

of Appeal[92] then held that *Schorsch Meier* was binding (1) on courts beneath the Court of Appeal in the hierarchy and (2) on the Court of Appeal itself, the relevant exception to *Young* v. *Bristol Aeroplane Co. Ltd.* being confined to inconsistent *subsequent* House of Lords decisions. The House of Lords held (1) that the Court of Appeal had acted incorrectly in *Schorsch Meier* in failing to follow *Havana*; but (2) (Lord Simon dissenting) that the *Havana* case should be overruled. As to the dilemma facing the trial judge and the Court of Appeal in *Miliangos*, Lord Cross[93] took the view that *Schorsch Meier* should not have been followed (endorsing Bristow J.'s approach), Lord Simon[94] thought that the Court of Appeal in *Miliangos* had acted correctly, and the other members of the House of Lords expressed no definite opinion.[95] The position taken by Bristow J. and Lord Cross assumes that:

> "the *Schorsch Meier* majority decision was not law in any proper sense, since it was reached in total disregard of the proper law as it then existed in a rule of the House of Lords, and which . . . bound the Court of Appeal to reach a decision contrary to that actually reached."[96]

However, the analogous argument is not accepted in cases of "horizontal conflict" between decisions in the same court. Thus, where Court of Appeal decisions conflict, the Court of Appeal in a subsequent case may choose which to follow.[97]

(ii) *Inconsistency with a Privy Council decision*

In *Worcester Works Finance Ltd.* v. *Cooden Engineering Co. Ltd.*[98] Lord Denning M.R. said[99]:

> "Although decisions of the Privy Council are not binding on this Court, nevertheless when the Privy Council disapproves of a previous decision of this Court or casts doubt on it, we are at liberty to depart from the previous decision."

This statement can be seen as part of Lord Denning's battle against the rule that the Court of Appeal is bound by its own previous decisions, and it is not clear whether it is still authoritative in the light of the strictures of the House of Lords in *Davis* v. *Johnson*.[1]

(iii) *Other possibilities*

In *B.* v. *B.*[2] the Court of Appeal held that section 1(1) of the Domestic Violence and Matrimonial Proceedings Act 1976 did not give a county

[92] [1975] Q.B. 487, 499.
[93] [1976] A.C. 443, 496.
[94] [1976] A.C. 443, 470.
[95] Professor Cross thought the desirability of contradictory statements on this point to be "highly questionable" and that there was "something to be said for the discreet silence" of the other three members of the House: P.M.S. Hacker and J. Raz (eds.) *Law, Morality and Society* (1977) p. 153.
[96] C.E.F. Rickett (1980) 43 M.L.R. 136, 141.
[97] See above, p. 289.
[98] [1972] 1 Q.B. 210.
[99] At p. 217.
[1] Below. On the Privy Council and precedent see further below, pp. 300 and 303.
[2] [1978] Fam. 26, decided on October 13, 1977 by Bridge, Waller and Megaw L.JJ.

court jurisdiction to grant an injunction excluding a spouse[3] from the "matrimonial home" where that spouse had a proprietary interest in the home. A few days later this decision was followed by the Court of Appeal in *Cantliff* v. *Jenkins*.[4] These cases caused some consternation as the plain words of the statute seemed to give the county court that jurisdiction. The point was raised again in *Davis* v. *Johnson*, and a five-member Court of Appeal was assembled.[5] Only Cumming-Bruce L.J. held that the earlier cases were correctly decided. Goff L.J. held that they were binding even though they were wrong. The other three members of the court held that they were wrong, and, on a variety of grounds, not binding. Lord Denning said that:

> "while the court should regard itself as normally bound by a previous decision of the court, nevertheless it should be at liberty to depart from it if it is convinced that the previous decision was wrong."[6]

Either the Court of Appeal should take for itself guidelines similar to those taken by the House of Lords,[7] or this should be regarded as an additional exception to *Young* v. *Bristol Aeroplane Co. Ltd.*[8] Lord Denning has long argued for such a change,[9] but has been unable to convince either his colleagues or the House of Lords.

Sir George Baker P. was prepared to distinguish *B.* v. *B.* on the ground that the welfare of a child was not involved as it was in *Davis* v. *Johnson*. If that distinction were not acceptable,[10] a new exception to *Young* v. *Bristol Aeroplane Co. Ltd.* should be created:

> "The Court is not bound to follow a previous decision of its own if satisfied that that decision was clearly wrong and cannot stand in the face of the will and intention of Parliament expressed in simple language in a recent statute passed to remedy a serious mischief or abuse, and further adherence to the previous decision must lead to injustice in the particular case and unduly restrict proper development of the law with injustice to others."[11]

Shaw L.J. suggested a new exception to *Young*'s case that was even narrower:

---

[3] Whether real, or for want of a better expression, "common law."

[4] [1978] Fam. 47, decided on October 20, 1977 by Stamp, Orr and Ormrod L.JJ. The couple were joint tenants.

[5] [1979] A.C. 264. Lord Denning M.R., Sir George Baker P., Goff, Shaw and Cumming-Bruce L.JJ: described by Lord Denning as "a court of all the talents" [1979] A.C. 264, 271.

[6] [1979] A.C. 264, 278–282.

[7] See below, pp. 296–300.

[8] [1944] K.B. 718.

[9] *The Discipline of Law* (1979) pp. 297–300; *Gallie* v. *Lee* [1969] 2 Ch. 17, 37; *Hanning* v. *Maitland* (*No.* 2) [1970] 1 Q.B. 580, 587; *Barrington* v. *Lee* [1972] 1 Q.B. 326, 338. He temporarily conceded defeat in *Tiverton Estates Ltd.* v. *Wearwell Ltd.* [1975] Ch. 146, 160–161, but raised the point again in *Davis* v. *Johnson* and suffered a "crushing rebuff" (*The Discipline of Law* (1979) p. 299).

[10] That this distinction was not acceptable was subsequently conceded in the House of Lords.

[11] [1979] A.C. 264, 290.

"in some such terms as that the principle of *stare decisis* should be relaxed where its application would have the effect of depriving actual and potential victims of violence of a vital protection which an Act of Parliament was plainly designed to afford to them, especially where, as in the context of domestic violence, that deprivation must inevitably give rise to an irremediable detriment to such victims and create in regard to them an injustice irreversible by a later decision of the House of Lords."[12]

The House of Lords unanimously dismissed an appeal; *B.* v. *B.* and *Cantliff* v. *Jenkins* were overruled.[13] However, the House strongly re-affirmed the rule that the Court of Appeal was bound by its own previous decisions, subject to clearly defined exceptions which did not include those advanced in the Court of Appeal. The argument in favour of *Young's* case was summarised by Lord Diplock[14]:

"In an appellate court of last resort a balance must be struck between the need on the one hand for the legal certainty resulting from the binding effect of previous decisions, and, on the other side the avoidance of undue restriction on the proper development of the law. In the case of an intermediate appellate court, however, the second desideratum can be taken care of by appeal to a superior appellate court, if reasonable means of access to it are available; while the risk to the first desideratum, legal certainty if the court is not bound by its own previous decisions grows even greater with increasing membership and the number of three-judge divisions in which it sits . . . ."

The argument against is that "the House of Lords may never have an opportunity to correct [an] error; and thus it may be perpetuated indefinitely, perhaps for ever."[15] Litigants may be unable to finance a further appeal; the case may be settled; an insurance company or big employer who wins in the Court of Appeal may "buy off an appeal to the House of Lords by paying ample compensation to the appellant."[16] Lord Diplock responded by pointing out that in view of *Cantliff* v. *Jenkins* there had been no need for anything but the briefest of hearings in the Court of Appeal, and an appeal to the House could have been heard and decided quickly. The argument of delay and expense could also be used to justify any High Court or county court judge in refusing to follow a decision of the Court of Appeal that he thought was wrong. There is also the possibility of

[12] [1979] A.C. 264, 308.

[13] Lord Diplock alone thought that *B.* v. *B.* had been correctly decided, making the overall division of appellate judicial opinion eight all: [1979] A.C. 264, 323. That case had concerned the situation where the man was sole tenant. However, his Lordship held that an injunction could be awarded where both parties were joint tenants: as the facts of *Davis* v. *Johnson* fell into that category he was in favour of dismissing the appeal.

[14] [1979] A.C. 264, 326. Viscount Dilhorne, Lord Kilbrandon, and Lord Scarman expressly agreed with Lord Diplock's views on precedent: [1979] A.C. 264, 336, 340, 349. See also Scarman L.J. in *Tiverton Estates Ltd.* v. *Wearwell Ltd.* [1975] Ch. 146, 172–173 and in *Farrell* v. *Alexander* [1976] Q.B. 345, 371.

[15] *Per* Lord Denning M.R. in *Davis* v. *Johnson* [1979] A.C. 264, 278.

[16] *Ibid.* p. 278.

using the "leap-frog" procedure under the Administration of Justice Act 1969.[17]

Lord Salmon expressed some sympathy for Lord Denning's views, but said that "until such time, if ever, as all his colleagues in the Court of Appeal agree with those views, *stare decisis* must still hold the field."[18] In view of the large number of Lord Justices, keeping to *stare decisis* might be "no bad thing." He suggested that where the Court of Appeal gave leave to appeal from a decision it felt bound to make by authority and with which it disagreed, it should have the statutory power to order that the costs of the appeal be paid from public funds. This would be a very rare occurrence, and the cost minimal.

According to the Court of Appeal *stare decisis* does not prevent an English court giving effect to a change in a rule of international law notwithstanding the existence of English precedents based on the old rule.[19] It also seems that the Court of Appeal is not bound by its own previous decisions where it is the court of last resort, with no possible appeal to the House of Lords.[20]

(e) Can lower tiers rely on the exceptions to Young v. Bristol Aeroplane Co. Ltd.?

This question was answered in the negative by Lord Hailsham L.C. in *Cassell & Co. Ltd.* v. *Broome*,[21] but there have been cases where the Divisional Court or a trial judge has declined to follow a decision of the Court of Appeal on the ground that it was inconsistent with a House of Lords decision,[22] and the point cannot be regarded as settled. It is difficult, for example, to see that a trial judge should follow a decision of a higher court given in ignorance of a binding statutory provision. According to Lord Denning M.R., where decisions of the same court conflict, lower courts should follow the later case[23]; Donaldson J. disagreed.[24]

---

[17] See below, pp. 734–735. Lord Diplock [1979] A.C. 264, 324–325.

[18] [1979] A.C. 264, 344.

[19] *Trendtex Trading Corporation* v. *Central Bank of Nigeria* [1977] Q.B. 529, 554 (Lord Denning M.R.), 579 (Shaw L.J.) (a case on the scope of the doctrine of state immunity). Stephenson L.J. dissented on this point. The Court of Appeal's decision was followed by Robert Goff J. and the Court of Appeal in *I Congreso del Partido* [1978] Q.B. 500 and [1981] 1 All E.R. 1092, and Lloyd J. in *Planmount Ltd.* v. *Republic of Zaire* [1981] 1 All E.R. 1110; but not by Donaldson J. in *Uganda Co. (Holdings) Ltd.* v. *Government of Uganda* [1979] 1 Lloyd's Rep. 481. The House of Lords in *I Congreso del Partido* endorsed the general approach of the Court of Appeal in *Trendtex* but did not advert to the "precedent" aspect [1983] 1 A.C. 244.

[20] Lord Denning M.R. in *Davis* v. *Johnson* [1979] A.C. 264, 282.

[21] [1972] A.C. 1027, 1054; above, pp. 286–287. In *Baker* v. *The Queen* [1975] A.C. 774, 788, Lord Diplock stated that a lower court could not rely on the *per incuriam* rule in relation to the decision of a higher court, but could choose between conflicting decisions.

[22] *R.* v. *Northumberland Compensation Appeal Tribunal, ex p. Shaw* [1951] 1 K.B. 711, where the Divisional Court declined to follow the decision of the Court of Appeal in *Racecourse Betting Control Board* v. *Secretary for Air* [1944] Ch. 114 on the ground that it was inconsistent with the views expressed by the House of Lords in *Walsall Overseers* v. *L.N.W. Ry. Co.* (1878) 4 App.Cas. 30 and the Privy Council in *R.* v. *Nat. Bell Liquors Ltd.* [1922] 2 A.C. 128, which cases had not been cited. The *Shaw* case was not cited in *Cassell & Co. Ltd.* v. *Broome*. See also *Midland Bank* v. *Hett, Stubbs & Kemp*, above, pp. 121–122.

[23] *Davis* v. *Johnson* [1979] A.C. 264, 279.

[24] *Uganda Co. (Holdings) Ltd.* v. *Government of Uganda* [1979] 1 Lloyd's Rep. 481, 485: a trial judge should "seek to anticipate how the Court of Appeal itself would . . . resolve the conflict."

6. THE COURT OF APPEAL (CRIMINAL DIVISION)[25]

This court is obviously bound by decisions of the House of Lords. It is also generally bound by its own previous decisions and those of its forerunners, the Court of Criminal Appeal and the Court for Crown Cases Reserved. However, as the liberty of the subject is involved, *stare decisis* is not applied with the same rigidity as in the Civil Division. A decision may not be followed if it falls within one of the established exceptions to *Young* v. *Bristol Aeroplane Co. Ltd.*[26] An example is *R.* v. *Gould*[27] where the Court of Appeal (Criminal Division) followed a decision of the Court of Crown Cases Reserved in 1889[28] in preference to a later conflicting decision of the Court of Criminal Appeal in 1921,[29] on the question whether *mens rea* was an essential ingredient of the offence of bigamy. In addition, Diplock L.J. stated in *Gould* that:

> "if upon due consideration we were to be of opinion that the law had been either misapplied or misunderstood in an earlier decision of this court or its predecessor, the Court of Criminal Appeal, we should be entitled to depart from the view as to the law expressed in the earlier decision notwithstanding that the case could not be brought within any of the exceptions laid down in *Young* v. *Bristol Aeroplane Co. Ltd.*"[30]

In *R.* v. *Newsome, R.* v. *Brown*[31] the Court of Appeal (Criminal Division) overruled two earlier decisions of the court[32] to the effect that a judge could not increase a sentence of imprisonment once passed to ensure that it would not be suspended even if this were to be done immediately. Widgery L.J. said[33] that if a court of five members is constituted:

> "to consider an issue of discretion and the principles upon which discretion should be exercised, that court ought to have the right to depart from an earlier view expressed by a court of three, especially where it was a matter in which the court did not have the opportunity of hearing argument on both sides."

The view that a "full court"[34] has greater power to overrule than an ordinarily constituted court was also held by the Court of Criminal Appeal,[35] although it has been rejected by the Divisional Court[36] and the

[25] See G. Zellick, [1974] Crim.L.R. 222.
[26] [1944] K.B. 718. See above, pp. 288–294. For an example of an application of the *per incuriam* doctrine, see *R.* v. *Ewing* [1983] Q.B. 1039, disapproving *R.* v. *Angeli* [1979] 1 W.L.R. 26 on the ground that it could not stand with the decision of the House of Lords in *Blyth* v. *Blyth* [1966] A.C. 643. See also n. 40 below.
[27] [1968] 2 Q.B. 65.
[28] *R.* v. *Tolson* (1889) 23 Q.B.D. 168.
[29] *R.* v. *Wheat* [1921] 2 K.B. 119.
[30] [1968] 2 Q.B. 65, 69.
[31] [1970] 2 Q.B. 711, decided in July 1970.
[32] *R.* v. *Corr, The Times*, January 16, 1970 and *R.* v. *Maylam* (unreported) decided on February 26, 1970.
[33] At p. 717.
[34] A term which usually denotes a court of more than the usual number of judges (*e.g.* five or seven for the Divisional Court, five for the Court of Appeal and seven in the House of Lords) and not a court of all the judges eligible to sit.
[35] *R.* v. *Taylor* [1950] 2 K.B. 368.
[36] *Younghusband* v. *Luftig* [1949] 2 K.B. 354: curiously, a criminal case.

Court of Appeal.[37] It seems in practice that a full court is not necessary
where one of the exceptions to *Young* v. *Bristol Aeroplane Co. Ltd.* is
applied, but is thought appropriate where overruling is contemplated on
wider grounds.[38] In *Newsome* Widgery L.J. stressed that the court would
be more reluctant to depart from an earlier decision where guilt or
innocence was involved as distinct from the exercise of the court's
discretion. Moreover, the court is more likely to overrule an erroneous
case on the strength of which an accused person has been sentenced and
imprisoned, rather than one which had led to an acquittal.[39] Overruling
need not, however, always be in the accused's interest.[40]

It is uncertain whether the Court of Appeal (Criminal Division) is bound
by decisions of the Court of Appeal (Civil Division), and *vice versa*. Before
reorganisation the Court of Appeal and Court of Criminal Appeal seemed
not to be bound by each other's decisions.[41]

A decision of the court is treated as a binding authority notwithstanding
that the appellant who has won the argument on the point of law has had
his appeal dismissed under the proviso to section 2 of the Criminal Appeal
Act 1968.[42]

7. THE HOUSE OF LORDS

Decisions of the House of Lords are binding on courts lower in the
hierarchy, including, if not especially, the Court of Appeal. In *London
Tramways* v. *London County Council*[43] the House of Lords held that it was
bound by its own previous decisions in the interests of finality and certainty
in the law. It was accepted that a decision could be questioned where it
conflicted with another decision of the House or was made *per incuriam*.[44]
Other exceptions were suggested. However, as the House was the final
court of appeal the correction of error was normally dependent on the
vagaries of the legislative process. In 1966 Lord Gardiner L.C. made the

---

[37] In the exercise of its civil jurisdiction: *Young* v. *Bristol Aeroplane Co. Ltd.* [1944] K.B.
718, 725.

[38] *Gould* was decided by a three-member court: see Zellick *op cit.* pp. 231–232.

[39] *Per* Lord Goddard C.J. in *R.* v. *Taylor* [1950] 2 K.B. 368, 371.

[40] E.g. *R.* v. *Newsome*; *R.* v. *Browne, supra*, where the actual sentences were suspended as
it was "the only fair thing to do" (a form of prospective overruling: see below, pp. 299–300).
Contra, per Lord Diplock, *obiter*, in *R.* v. *Merriman* [1973] A.C. 584, 605: the liberty of the
Court of Appeal (Criminal Division) "to depart from a precedent which it is convinced was
erroneous is restricted to cases where the departure is in favour of the accused." This *dictum*
was applied by the court in *R.* v. *Jenkins* [1983] 1 All E.R. 993, 1005, but the better view is
that the consideration was irrelevant as the court was choosing between conflicting decisions
and not overruling a single decision: J.C. Smith [1983] Crim.L.R. at pp. 388–389. No
authorities on precedent were cited in *Merriman*.

[41] See *Hardie & Lane* v. *Chilton* [1928] 2 K.B. 306, C.A. versus *R.* v. *Denyer* [1926] 2 K.B.
258, C.C.A. and the statement of Lord Hewart C.J. in the Court of Criminal Appeal at 20
Crim. App. Rep. 185.

[42] See below, p. 712. Here the distinction between *ratio* and *dictum* is "meaningless in
practice:" Cross (1977), p. 85; above, pp. 280–284.

[43] [1898] A.C. 375: not "London Street Tramways" see the list of errata at the start of the
[1898] A.C. volume (Cross (1977), p. 107, n. 4).

[44] See above, pp. 288–289.

following statement on behalf of himself and the Lords of Appeal in Ordinary[45]:

> "Their Lordships regard the use of precedent as an indispensable · foundation upon which to decide what is the law and its application to individual cases. It provides at least some degree of certainty upon which individuals can rely on the conduct of their affairs, as well as a basis for orderly development of legal rules.
>
> Their Lordships nevertheless recognise that too rigid adherence to precedent may lead to injustice in a particular case and also unduly restrict the proper development of the law. They propose, therefore, to modify their present practice and, while treating former decisions of this House as normally binding, to depart from a previous decision when it appears right to do so.
>
> In this connection they will bear in mind the danger of disturbing retrospectively the basis on which contracts, settlements of property and fiscal arrangements have been entered into and also the especial need for certainty as to the criminal law.
>
> This announcement is not intended to affect the use of precedent elsewhere than in this House."

A press notice issued at the same time[46] indicated that the statement was of great importance although it should not be supposed that it would frequently be applied. An example of a case where it might be used would be where an earlier decision was "influenced by the existence of conditions which no longer prevail, and that in modern conditions the law ought to be different." The change would also enable the House to pay greater attention to Commonwealth decisions critical of the House. As predicted the power has been used sparingly. Members of the House seem reluctant to state expressly that an earlier decision is "overruled" even where that appears to be the case.

The decision in *The Aello*[47] on a point of shipping law[48] was overruled in the *Johanna Oldendorff*.[49] As we have seen, the *Havana* case,[50] or at least the assumption upon which it was based, was overruled in *Miliangos* v. *George Frank (Textiles) Ltd.*[51] The decision in *Congreve* v. *Inland Revenue*

---

[45] *Practice Statement (Judicial Precedent)* [1966] 1 W.L.R. 1234. Lord Denning M.R. and Lord Parker C.J. were also present. See R.W.M. Dias [1966] C.L.J. 153; R. Stone [1968] C.L.J. 35; J. Stone (1969) 69 Columbia L.R. 1162. The circumstances surrounding the introduction of the Statement and the way in which it has been used are examined by A. Paterson in *The Law Lords* (1982), Chap. 6 and pp. 154–169 and G. Maher [1981] Stat.L.R. 85. See also below, p. 301.

[46] See M. Zander, *The Law-Making Process* (1980), pp. 104–105.

[47] [1961] A.C. 135.

[48] The test for determining when a ship has "arrived" in port. The expense of delay in discharging cargo from an "arrived" ship caused, for example, by congestion at the berths, normally falls on the charterer and not on the owners of the vessel.

[49] *E.L. Oldendorff* v. *Tradax Export* [1974] A.C. 479. This was the first occasion when the statement was clearly used. It has been argued that it had already been used in *Conway* v. *Rimmer* [1968] A.C. 910 and *British Railways Board* v. *Herrington* [1972] A.C. 879: see Paterson (1982) p. 164. On *Conway* v. *Rimmer* see J. Stone, *op. cit.* n. 45 above.

[50] [1961] A.C. 1007: see above, p. 291.

[51] [1976] A.C. 443. In the same year the Statement was used in the Scottish case of *Dick* v. *Burgh of Falkirk* 1976 S.L.T. 21.

Commissioners[52] was overruled in *Vestey* v. *Inland Revenue Commissioners (Nos. 1 and 2)*[53] on the ground that the earlier decision, on a point of construction of a Finance Act, had led to unforeseen results that were "arbitrary, potentially unjust and fundamentally unconstitutional."[54] The law as to the liability of the occupiers of land towards trespassers was restated by the House, with some differences of formulation among their Lordships, in *British Railways Board* v. *Herrington*.[55] The law as expounded, more restrictively, by the House in *Robert Addie & Sons (Collieries) Ltd.* v. *Dumbreck*[56] was, according to the headnote in the Law Reports, "reconsidered."[57] More spectacularly, the House in *R.* v. *Secretary of State for the Home Department, ex p. Khawaja*[57a] overruled the recent decision in *R* v. *Secretary of State for the Home Deparment ex p. Zamir*,[57b] holding that a person could only be removed as an "illegal immigrant" if the *court* was satisfied that the entry was illegal: it would no longer be sufficient that the *immigration officer* was satisfied and had some evidence for that belief. The issue concerned the liberty of the subject and did not fall into any of the categories in which the *Practice Statement* indicated the need for special caution.

Other invitations to the House to overrule a past decision have not been accepted. A remarkable example is *Jones* v. *Secretary of State for Social Services*[58] where four out of seven members of the House held that the earlier decision of the House in *Re Dowling*[59] on a point of national insurance law[60] was incorrect, but only three thought that *Re Dowling* should be overruled. The main "defector" was Lord Simon of Glaisdale, who stated[61] that the 1966 declaration should be used most sparingly; that

---

[52] [1948] 1 All E.R. 948.

[53] [1980] A.C. 1148.

[54] *Per* Lord Wilberforce at p. 1176.

[55] [1972] A.C. 879.

[56] [1929] A.C. 358.

[57] Lord Reid's word at p. 879. Lord Reid (p. 898) and Lord Morris did, however, say that *Addie's* case was "wrongly decided." Lord Pearson regarded the *Addie* formulation as an "anomaly" which "should be discarded" (p. 930). Lord Diplock rejected it "as amounting to an exclusive or comprehensive statement" of the duty owed to a trespasser (p. 941). Lord Wilberforce spoke of "developing" the law in *Addie's* case (p. 921). See now the Occupiers' Liability Act 1984.

[57a] [1984] A.C. 74.

[57b] [1980] A.C. 930.

[58] [1972] A.C. 944. Alternatively entitled *R.* v. *National Insurance Commissioners, ex p. Hudson.* See J. Stone (1972) 35 M.L.R. 449, 469–477.

[59] *R* v. *Deputy Industrial Injuries Commissioner, ex p. Amalgamated Engineering Union, In re Dowling* [1967] 1 A.C. 725.

[60] Whether a decision by a National Insurance Commissioner (adjudicating a claim for industrial injuries benefit) that injuries were caused by an industrial accident, was binding on a Medical Appeal Tribunal (adjudicating a subsequent claim for industrial disablement benefit).

[61] At pp. 1024–5. Lord Wilberforce would not have favoured overruling *Re Dowling* if its *ratio* had been narrowly interpreted (see pp. 995–996). Lord Diplock was in favour of overruling but recognised he was in the minority and so he reluctantly agreed that the appeal should be allowed (p. 1015). Cf. Lord Reid in *R.* v. *Knuller* [1973] A.C. 435, 455–456, where he expressed the view that the House should not overrule *Shaw* v. *D.P.P.* [1962] A.C. 220, notwithstanding that he had dissented in *Shaw* and still thought that it had been wrongly decided *cf.* Lord Hailsham and Lord Edmund-Davies in *R.* v. *Cunningham* [1982] A.C. 566, 581, 582. See R. Brazier [1973] Crim.L.R. 98.

a variation of view on a matter of statutory construction would rarely provide a suitable occasion for its use unless it could be convincingly shown that a previous, erroneous, construction was causing administrative difficulties or individual injustice; that the House should be reluctant to encourage litigants to reopen arguments once concluded; that there was much to be said for each side of this case; and that *Re Dowling* was not unworkable and could in any event be altered more appropriately by Parliament.[62] In *Fitzleet Estates Ltd.* v. *Cherry*[63] the House refused to review a 1965 majority decision on a point of tax law, in the absence of any new argument, any change of circumstances or any suggestion that it was productive of injustice. In *Hesperides Hotels Ltd.* v. *Muftizade*[64] the House declined to modify the long established rule that the High Court has no jurisdiction to entertain an action for damages for trespass to land situated abroad.[65] The rule was accepted in other jurisdictions, a change might involve conflict with foreign jurisdictions and there had been no change of circumstances.

Paterson[65a] has identified seven criteria relating to the proper use of the *Statement* which were articulated by Lord Reid, and which reflected the dominant consensus of the Law Lords in the mid-seventies both in what they said and in how they acted. The freedom to depart from a previous decision should be exercised sparingly. A decision should not normally be overruled if that would upset the legitimate expectations of people who had regulated their affairs in reliance on it; or if it concerned the construction of a statute or document; or if it was impracticable to foresee the consequences of overruling; or if there ought to be a comprehensive reform by legislation. A decision ought not to be overruled merely because it was wrong; there should be additional reasons justifying that step. Conversely, a decision should be overruled if it gave rise to great uncertainty, or was unjust or outmoded.

In *Jones* v. *Secretary of State for Social Services*,[66] Lord Simon of Glaisdale suggested that consideration should be given to the introduction, preferably by statute, of a power for the House of Lords to overrule a decision "prospectively" (*i.e.* for future cases only). Such a power is exercised by the United States Supreme Court[67] and in several states in the U.S.A. This involves the express recognition that the notion that judges do not make law is a fiction, but avoids the undesirable consequences of

---

[62] It was so altered: see A.I. Ogus and E.M. Barendt, *The Law of Social Security* (2nd ed., 1982), pp. 301–302.

[63] [1977] 1 W.L.R. 1345. Similarly, in *Paal Wilson & Co.* v. *Partenreederei Hannah Blumenthal* [1983] 1 A.C. 854 the House declined to overrule the recent decision in *Bremer Vulkan* v. *South India Shipping Corp.* [1981] A.C. 909, which had attracted "widespread disapproval, if not dismay" (E.A. Marshall, [1983] J.B.L. 234, 239). One point was "the special need for certainty, consistency and continuity in the field of commercial law" (*per* Lord Brandon at p. 913).

[64] [1979] A.C. 508.

[65] *British South African Co.* v. *Companhia de Moçambique* [1893] A.C. 602.

[65a] *The Law Lords* (1982), pp. 156–167.

[66] [1972] A.C. 944, 1026–7. See also his Lordship's statement in *Miliangos* v. *George Frank (Textiles) Ltd.* [1976] A.C. 443, 490, and Lord Diplock [1972] A.C. 944, 1015.

[67] See, *e.g. Mapp* v. *Ohio* 367 U.S. 643 (1961); *Linkletter* v. *Walker* 381 U.S. 618 (1965); *Miranda* v. *Arizona* 384 U.S. 436 (1966).

retrospectively upsetting established arrangements.[68] There are difficulties in choosing the date of transition: for example, should the litigant who has successfully argued that a case should be overruled be entitled to the retrospective effect of that decision, notwithstanding the general determination that the rule should be changed prospectively? If the answer is no, litigants will have little incentive to mount the necessary arguments. Lord Devlin has opposed the general idea of prospective overruling on the ground that it "turns judges into undisguised legislators."[69] The House of Lords changed a rule of *practice* (as distinct from a rule of *law*) prospectively in *Connelly* v. *D.P.P.*[70]

In practice a decision of the House of Lords on an appeal from Scotland or Northern Ireland will be regarded as binding on English courts lower in the hierarchy on points where the law of the two countries is the same.[71]

8. THE PRIVY COUNCIL

Decisions of the Judicial Committee of the Privy Council are not technically binding on English courts except in respect of matters where an appeal lies from such a court to the Privy Council.[72] They may, however, be highly persuasive.[73] The Privy Council will normally follow its own previous decisions, but is not bound to do so.[74] It is not bound to follow decisions of the House of Lords on common law issues, although the latter have great persuasive authority: the common law may develop differently in different parts of the Commonwealth.[75] A House of Lords decision on the interpretation of recent legislation common to England and another part of the Commonwealth will however, be treated as binding.[76]

9. THE EUROPEAN COURT OF JUSTICE

The decisions of this court on matters of Community law are binding on English courts up to and including the House of Lords.[77] It tends to follow its own previous decisions, although it is not bound to do so.[78]

---

[68] See generally W. Friedmann (1966) 29 M.L.R. 593; M.D.A. Freeman (1973) 26 C.L.P. 166; A. Nichol (1976) 39 M.L.R. 542; Cross (1977), pp. 229–233.

[69] Lord Devlin, "Judges and Lawmakers" (1976) 39 M.L.R. 11, 20: reprinted in *The Judge* (1979), p. 12.   [70] [1964] A.C. 1254.

[71] Cross (1977), p. 20; *Heyman* v. *Darwins Ltd.* [1942] A.C. 356, 401 (Lord Porter); *Glasgow Corporation* v. *Central Land Board* 1956 S.C. (H.L.) 1: where the law of "crown privilege" was held to be different in the two countries; *Re Tuck's Settlement Trusts; Public Trustee* v. *Tuck* [1978] Ch. 49, 61 (Lord Denning M.R.).

[72] *e.g.* in ecclesiastical and prize matters: *Combe* v. *Edwards* (1877) 2 P.D. 354. In *Port Line Ltd.* v. *Ben Line Steamers Ltd.* [1958] 2 Q.B. 146, Diplock J. declined to follow a Privy Council decision that was in his view wrongly decided.

[73] See, *e.g.* above, p. 282, below, p. 303.

[74] *Gideon Nkambule* v. *R.* [1950] A.C. 379; *Fatuma Binti Mohamed Bin Salim* v. *Mohamed Bin Salim* [1952] A.C. 1; *Baker* v. *The Queen* [1975] A.C. 774, 787–788.

[75] *e.g.* on the right to punitive damages in tort: the Privy Council in *Australian Consolidated Press Ltd.* v. *Uren* [1969] 1 A.C. 590 did not follow the House of Lords decision in *Rookes* v. *Barnard* [1964] A.C. 1129.

[76] *de Lasala* v. *de Lasala* [1980] A.C. 546.

[77] See above, pp. 224–230; European Communities Act 1972, s.3(1).

[78] *Da Costa en Schaake NV* v. *Nederlandse Belasting-administratie* (Cases 2, 8, 29, 30/62) [1963] E.C.R. 31; L.N. Brown and F.G. Jacobs, *The Court of Justice of the European Communities* (2nd ed., 1983) pp. 275–281; T. Koopmans in D. O'Keefe and H.G. Schermers (eds.) *Essays in European Law and Integration* (1982).

10. Tribunals

Where there is a hierarchy of tribunals, the decisions of the appellate tribunals will bind lower tribunals. For example, social security appeal tribunals must follow decisions of the social security commissioners (formerly known as the national insurance commissioners).[79] Tribunals are not permitted to lay down precedents binding on themselves,[80] the emphasis, in theory at least, being on deciding each case on its own facts. However, the case law of some tribunals is systematically reported and general principles tend to become established,[81] and the "essential differences in practice from, say, the House of Lords or the Court of Appeal . . . are not as marked as one might think."[82]

11. The Nature of Rules of Binding Precedent

Apart from the 1966 *Practice Statement*, propositions as to the binding effects of previous decisions have been contained in the judgments of decided cases. It has been pointed out that such propositions cannot form part of the *ratio* of a case as they are "necessarily irrelevant to the issues of law and fact that have to be decided by the court."[83] Professor Cross[84] has argued that this only seems applicable to statements of higher courts about the way in which lower courts should behave,[85] but that in any event statements about the rules of precedent are statements about the courts' own practice which fall outside the *ratio-obiter* distinction. The 1966 *Practice Statement* owed its validity "to the inherent power of any court to regulate its own practice."[86] The possibility that the Court of Appeal might change the rule that it is bound by its own previous decisions by a similar practice statement has been mooted.[87] However, Lord Simon of Glaisdale has asserted that any change would require legislation,[88] Cumming-Bruce L.J. has accepted loyally that the constitutional functions of the House of Lords include that of declaring with authority the extent to which the Court of Appeal is bound by its previous decisions,[89] and Lord Denning has in any event failed to pursuade his colleagues that a change would be desirable.[90]

[79] R.(I) 12/75 (Tribunal of Commissioners); A.I. Ogus and E.M. Barendt, *The Law of Social Security* (2nd ed., 1982), pp. 595–596.

[80] *Merchandise Transport Ltd.* v. *British Transport Commission* [1962] 2 Q.B. 173, C.A., in relation to the Transport Tribunal.

[81] J.A. Farmer, *Tribunals and Government* (1974), Chap. 3, pp. 171–180.

[82] *Ibid.* p. 175.

[83] Glanville Williams, (1954) 70 L.Q.R. 469, 471; *cf.* Diplock L.J. in *Boys* v. *Chaplin* [1968] 2 K.B. 1, 35.

[84] "The House of Lords and the Rules of Precedent" in P.M.S. Hacker and J. Raz (eds.), *Law, Morality and Society* (1977), pp. 144–160. For the contrary argument that pronouncements on precedent do indeed establish rules of law, see P.J. Evans [1982] C.L.J. 162, criticised by L. Goldstein [1984] C.L.J. 88, with a reply by Evans, *ibid.* p. 108; and for the argument that they establish rules of *customary* law see P. Aldridge, (1984) 47 M.L.R. 187.

[85] *Ibid.* p. 154.

[86] *Ibid.* p. 157; Salmon L.J. in *Gallie* v. *Lee* [1969] 2 Ch. 17, 49; Lord Denning M.R. in *Davis* v. *Johnson* [1979] A.C. 264, 281; Lord Salmon in *Davis* v. *Johnson* (above p. 294).

[87] *Ibid.*

[88] *Miliangos* v. *George Frank (Textiles) Ltd.* [1976] A.C. 443, 470.

[89] *Davis* v. *Johnson* [1979] A.C. 264, 311.

[90] See above, p. 292.

E. PERSUASIVE AUTHORITIES

Precedents that are not technically binding may be cited as persuasive authorities. The extent to which a precedent will be persuasive may depend on a variety of factors including the status of the court, the country in which it was located, the reputation of the judge, whether the relevant proposition formed part of the *ratio*, whether the judgment was considered or *ex tempore*[91] and whether the judge in the later case agrees with it. Thus the attention of the court may be drawn to the *ratio* of a decision of an English court lower in the hierarchy, to *obiter dicta*, to a dissenting judgment, to a decision of the Privy Council or to a court abroad.

Great weight will be attached to considered statements by the House of Lords whatever their technical standing. For example, in *Hedley Byrne & Co. Ltd.* v. *Heller and Partners Ltd.*,[92] the House of Lords held that the existence of a special relationship could give rise to a duty to take care in giving information or advice; breach of the duty could in turn lead to an action for damages in respect of purely economic losses. The Court of Appeal had held that such a duty could not arise, following its earlier decision in *Candler* v. *Crane, Christmas & Co.*[93] The House overruled the *Candler* decision and endorsed the dissenting judgment in that case by Denning L.J. Having found that a duty of care *did* arise as the plaintiffs claimed, the House nonetheless found for the *defendants* on the ground that they had effectively disclaimed responsibility for the statements in question. There was much debate on the issue whether the observations concerning the duty of care were *obiter*.[94] Cairns J. in *W.B. Anderson and Sons Ltd.* v. *Rhodes*[95] regarded such a suggestion as "unrealistic":

> "When five members of the House of Lords have all said, after close examination of the authorities, that a certain type of tort exists, I think that a judge of first instance should proceed on the basis that it does exist without pausing to embark on an investigation whether what was said was necessary to the ultimate decision."[96]

Similarly, it is now accepted that solicitors acting as advocates are entitled to the same immunity from legal action as barristers, notwithstanding that the view has been expressed in decisions of the House of Lords concerning barristers.[97]

The "neighbour principle" expounded by Lord Atkin in *Donoghue* v. *Stevenson*[98] can be regarded as part of the *ratio* of his speech, but not as part of the *ratio* of the House of Lords as a whole.[99] Nevertheless the principle has been influential in subsequent decisions which have extended

---

[91] Lord Russell of Killowen has suggested that unreserved judgments should be approached with "great caution:" *op cit.* p. 284, n. 37; *cf.* Lord Reid in *Haley* v. *London Electricity Board* [1965] A.C. 778, 792.

[92] [1964] A.C. 465.

[93] [1951] 2 K.B. 164.

[94] See W.V.H. Rogers, *Winfield and Jolowicz on Tort* (11th ed., 1979), p. 257, n. 86.

[95] [1967] 2 All E.R. 850.

[96] *Ibid.* p. 857.

[97] See above, p. 123.

[98] [1932] A.C. 562, 580.

[99] Two of the five members dissented and the other two did not expressly concur with Lord Atkin's formulation: see R.F.V. Heuston (1957) 20 M.L.R. 1, 5–9.

the scope of the tort of negligence,[1] and the House has now held that it should be applied in novel situations unless there is a valid reason for its limitation or exclusion.[2] Decisions of the Privy Council may be strongly persuasive, particularly now that membership of the Judicial Committee is mainly drawn from Lords of Appeal. The Privy Council decision in *The Wagon Mound (No. 1)*[3] is accepted to be the leading authority on remoteness of damage in the tort of negligence, and has been applied in preference to the decision of the Court of Appeal in *Re Polemis*.[4]

The desirability of uniformity between Scottish and English courts on points common to both systems has often been stressed, particularly on the construction of statutes and revenue and taxation matters.[5] The citation of overseas authorities seems to be increasingly common.[6] Lord Denning would not, however, in practice have followed a decision of the deputy magistrate of East Tonga in preference to six decisions of the House of Lords.[7] There have been complaints that counsel, particularly in busy appellate courts, cite too many authorities both English and foreign[8]; at the same time, counsel owes a duty to the court to cite all relevant authorities whether for or against him.

Textbooks may be cited as authorities although they can never be binding.[9] Some treatises have long been accepted as authoritative guides to the law in previous centuries, including the Abridgments of the Year Books[10] compiled by Fitzherbert and Brooke, the treatise known as "Glanvill" dating from the late twelfth century, Bracton's *De Legibus et Consuetudinibus Angliae* from the thirteenth, Littleton's *Tenures* from the fourteenth, Fitzherbert's *Nature Brevium*, Coke's *Institutes of the Laws of England* first published in 1628, eighteenth century works on criminal law by Hale, Hawkins and Foster[11] and Blackstone's *Commentaries on the*

---

[1] See, *e.g. Hedley Byrne & Co. Ltd.* v. *Heller and Partners Ltd.* [1964] A.C. 465.

[2] *Anns* v. *London Borough of Merton* [1978] A.C. 728, *per* Lord Wilberforce at pp. 751–752.

[3] *Overseas Tankship (U.K.) Ltd.* v. *Morts Dock Engineering Co. Ltd.* [1961] A.C. 388.

[4] *Re Polemis and Furness, Withy & Co. Ltd.* [1921] 2 K.B. 560: see *Doughty* v. *Turner Manufacturing Co. Ltd.* [1964] 1 Q.B. 518, C.A.; *Smith* v. *Leech Brain & Co. Ltd.* [1962] 2 Q.B. 405, 415, where Lord Parker C.J. indicated *obiter* that the *Wagon Mound* case enabled a trial judge to follow other decisions of the Court of Appeal prior to *Polemis*. The test for remoteness is now whether the kind of damage was reasonably foreseeable: the former test was whether the damage was the direct consequence of the defendant's conduct. Cf. Robert Goff J. in *I Congreso del Partido* [1978] Q.B. 500, 517–519.

[5] See, *e.g. Abbott* v. *Philbin (Inspector of Taxes)* [1960] Ch. 27, rvsd. [1961] A.C. 352; *Westward Television Ltd.* v. *Hart (Inspector of Taxes)* [1969] 1 Ch. 201, 212; *Secretary of State for Employment and Productivity* v. *Clarke, Chapman & Co. Ltd.* [1971] 1 W.L.R. 1094, 1102.

[6] See R.J.C. Munday (1978) 14 J.S.P.T.L. (N.S.) 201, 203–207. Even dissenting judgments in Commonwealth courts have been cited: see *Anns* v. *Merton London Borough Council* [1978] A.C. 728, 760.

[7] See the (regrettably) fictional report of *Grenouille* v. *National Union of Seamen* reproduced in Denning, *The Family Story* (1981) pp. 219–220.

[8] See, *e.g.* Lawton L.J. (1980) 14 *The Law Teacher* 163, 166.

[9] *Cordell* v. *Second Clanfield Properties Ltd.* [1969] 2 Ch. 9, 16: Megarry J. in relation to Sir Robert Megarry and H.W.R. Wade, *The Law of Real Property*.

[10] See below, p. 307.

[11] Sir Matthew Hale, *The History of the Pleas of the Crown* published posthumously in 1736 but written in the previous century; William Hawkins, *Pleas of the Crown* (1716); Sir Michael Foster, *Crown Cases* and *Crown Law* (1762).

Laws of England first published in 1765–69. These works are not cited often today, the ones on criminal law perhaps being referred to most commonly.[12] It used to be convention that living authors could not be cited as authorities, although their words could be adopted by counsel as part of his argument,[13] on the doubtful ground that while alive the author might change his mind.[14] This convention is no longer observed,[15] and books and articles by authors both living and dead are commonly cited.[16] In appropriate cases reference may also be made to principles of Roman law, and especially, in that regard, Justinian's *Digest*.[17]

F. DISTINGUISHING

A precedent, whether persuasive or binding, need not be applied or followed if it can be "distinguished:" *i.e.* there is a material distinction between the facts of the precedent case and the case in question. What counts as a "material" distinction is obviously crucial. The judge in the later case is expected to explain why the distinction is such as to justify the application of a different rule. If the distinction is spurious, the judge may be criticised or reversed or, if the case distinguished is generally regarded as a bad precedent, applauded for his boldness. There is no test or set of tests of whether a distinction is legally relevant; it all depends upon the circumstances of the case.

An example is provided by *R.* v. *Secretary of State for the Environment, ex p. Ostler*.[18] In 1956, the House of Lords in *Smith* v. *East Elloe R.D.C.*[19] ruled that a provision[20] that the validity of a compulsory purchase order should not be questioned in any legal proceedings, other than a statutory application to quash made within six weeks, meant what it said: an action to impugn an order on the ground of fraud could not be brought some six years later. However, in *Anisminic Ltd.* v. *The Foreign Compensation Commission*[21] the House held that section 4 of the Foreign Compensation Act 1950, which provided that a determination by the Commission "shall not be called in question in any court of law," was not effective to render immune from judicial review a purported determination that was in truth a

---

[12] See, *e.g. Button* v. *D.P.P.* [1966] A.C. 591; *R.* v. *Merriman* [1973] A.C. 584 (*Hale and Hawkins*).

[13] See, *e.g.* Vaughan Williams L.J. in *Greenlands Ltd.* v. *Wilmshurst* (1913) 29 T.L.R. 685, 687.

[14] Lord Reid (1972) 12 J.S.P.T.L. (N.S.) 22. This convention was the basis of somewhat leaden jokes to the effect that certain celebrated works were "fortunately" not works of authority.

[15] See *Halsbury's Laws of England* (4th ed.) Vol. 26, para. 587.

[16] For example, in criminal law cases references to books by Glanville Williams and J.C. Smith and B. Hogan are frequent; in administrative law, H.W.R. Wade, *Administrative Law*, (5th ed., 1982) and J.M. Evans, *de Smith's Judicial Review of Administrative Action* (4th ed., 1980) are similarly authoritative. See the splendid story by A. Arden [1980] Conv. 454, 458 (review of *de Smith*).

[17] See, *e.g. Coggs* v. *Bernard* (1703) 2 Ld. Raym. 909 and *Dalton* v. *Angus* (1881) 6 App.Cas. 740.

[18] [1977] Q.B. 122.

[19] [1956] A.C. 736.

[20] Acquisition of Land (Authorisation Procedure) Act 1946, Sched. 1, Part IV, paras. 15, 16.

[21] [1969] 2 A.C. 147.

nullity and thus not a "determination" at all. The decision in *Smith* v. *East Elloe R.D.C.* was adversely criticised but not overruled. In *Ostler* the Court of Appeal was faced with an ouster clause of the kind at issue in *Smith* v. *East Elloe R.D.C.*, and it followed *Smith* in preference to *Anisminic*, which was distinguished on a variety of grounds. For example, the point was taken that section 4 of the 1950 Act purported to exclude judicial review altogether whereas the provision in *Ostler* was more akin to a limitation period in that it excluded review only after a six-week period. It was said that *Anisminic* concerned a "judicial" decision and *Ostler* an "administrative" one. Their Lordships were not, however, unanimous as to their reasons, and Lord Denning M.R. subsequently indicated extra-judicially that he no longer regarded most of his own as sound.[22]

G. PRECEDENT AND STATUTORY INTERPRETATION

A decision on a question of the construction of a statute is binding to the same extent as a decision on other kinds of question.[23] Thus it is applicable in cases concerning the same words in the same Act and "in all cases which do not provide substantial relevant differences."[24] The same words appearing in a different statute may be interpreted differently, although a decision on the construction of a particular set of words may be used as a guide when other statutes dealing with the same or a similar subject-matter are considered.[25] If words which have been the subject of construction by a court are re-enacted by Parliament without alteration, a court will be very slow to overrule that decision but not always unwilling to do so.[26] Moreover Lord Wilberforce has stated[27] that:

"Self-contained statutes, whether consolidating previous law, or so doing with amendments, should be interpreted, if reasonably possible, without recourse to antecedents,[28] and that recourse should only be had when there is a real and substantial difficulty or ambiguity which classical methods of construction cannot resolve."

H. RATIO DECIDENDI AND RES JUDICATA

In its wider meaning the term "judgment" is used to cover the whole of the judge's pronouncement after the arguments of each side have been heard (*e.g.* as in "I will deliver my judgment after lunch"). In its narrower meaning it is used to cover the order of the court as distinct from the reasons for it (*e.g.* "There will be judgment for the plaintiff for £500"). Assuming the order lies within the judge's jurisdiction it is binding on the parties (*res*

---

[22] *The Discipline of Law* (1979), pp. 108–109.

[23] *Per* Lord Reid in *Goodrich* v. *Paisner* [1957] A.C. 65, 88 and *London Transport Executive* v. *Betts* [1959] A.C. 211, 232.

[24] *Goodrich* v. *Paisner, ibid.*

[25] *Ibid.*; Lord Upjohn in *Ogden Industries Pty. Ltd.* v. *Lucas* [1970] A.C. 113, 127; *R.* v. *Freeman* [1970] 1 W.L.R. 788 (meaning of "firearm" in successive Firearms Acts).

[26] *Royal Crown Derby Porcelain Ltd.* v. *Raymond Russell* [1949] 2 K.B. 417, 429, *per* Denning L.J.; cf. *R.* v. *Bow Road JJ., ex p. Adedigba* [1968] 2 Q.B. 572.

[27] *Farrell* v. *Alexander* [1977] A.C. 59, 73. Lord Simon and Lord Edmund-Davies agreed with this approach *cf.* above p. 259.

[28] *i.e.* the history of the provisions and the cases decided on them.

judicata). They may not reopen the issue that has just been determined, unless a statute has provided for an appeal.[29] Thus the court's *order* is binding on the *parties* under the *res judicata* doctrine; the *ratio decidendi* is binding on other *courts* in accordance with the principles outlined above under the doctrine of binding precedent. A startling illustration of the distinction was provided by the following series of cases. A testator, John Arkle Waring, left annuities to Mr. Howard and Mrs. Louie Burton-Butler "free of income tax." In 1942 the Court of Appeal in *In re Waring, Westminster Bank Ltd.* v. *Awdry*,[30] on an appeal in which Howard was a party, held that income tax had to be deducted. Louie was not a party as she was in an enemy occupied country. Leave to appeal to the House of Lords was refused. Four years later the House of Lords in *Berkeley* v. *Berkeley*[31] overruled the *Awdry* case. Subsequently, Jenkins J. held that the *Awdry* case was *res judicata* so far as Howard was concerned notwithstanding that its *ratio* had been overruled in *Berkeley* v. *Berkeley* and that Louie's annuity would be dealt with in accordance with the latter case.[32]

I. LAW REPORTS

(a) Introduction

Any legal system that is based on any significant extent upon judicial precedent requires an effective system whereby those precedents are reported and indexed. In theory, a case may be cited as a precedent even it if has not been reported. In practice, comparatively few cases are referred to in textbooks or cited in court unless they have been reported in one of the series of published law reports, although such references seem to be becoming more common.[33] Occasionally a judge may refer to an unreported case with which he was concerned as counsel or judge.[34] Indexed transcripts of all unreported cases in the Court of Appeal (Civil Division) are kept in the Supreme Court Library and listed in *Current Law* and copies of unreported House of Lords decisions are kept in the House of Lords Records Office. Thousands of unreported cases decided since January 1, 1980, including all decisions of the House of Lords and Court of Appeal (Civil Division), are included on *Lexis* (Butterworths' computer-assisted legal research service). Until recently, the only condition for admission of a report has been that it has been vouched for by a barrister present during the whole time when the judgment was given.[35] However,

---

[29] See Chap. 19. In the case of courts and tribunals with a jurisdiction limited by statute there is also the possibility of judicial review under the *ultra vires* doctrine where the jurisdiction has been exceeded or abused.

[30] [1942] Ch. 426.

[31] [1946] A.C. 555.

[32] *Re Waring, Westminster Bank* v. *Burton-Butler* [1948] Ch. 221.

[33] R.J.C. Munday (1978) 14 J.S.P.T.L. (N.S.) 201, 207–216.

[34] *e.g. Wilkinson* v. *Downton* [1897] 2 Q.B. 57, 61; *Harling* v. *Eddy* [1951] 2 K.B. 739, 746 (Denning L.J.).

[35] See *Parkinson* v. *Parkinson* [1939] P. 346, 348, 351–352; *Birtwistle* v. *Tweedale* [1954] 1 W.L.R. 190n: *Estates Gazette* report not admitted. *Cf. Baker* v. *Sims* [1959] 1 Q.B. 114 and *Smith* v. *Wyles* [1959] 1 Q.B. 164.

in *Roberts Petroleum Ltd.* v. *Kenney Ltd.*,[35a] the House of Lords stated that in future it would decline to allow transcripts of unreported judgments of the Court of Appeal (Civil Division) to be cited in the House without leave; such leave would only be granted on counsel giving an assurance that the transcript contained some relevant principle of law, that was binding on the Court of Appeal and of which the substance, as distinct from the mere choice of phraseology, was not to be found in any judgment of that court that had appeared in one of the generalised or specialised series of reports.

(b) A modern law report

A full law report today commonly includes the following information:

> The names of the parties[36]; the court in which the case was decided; the name of the judge or judges; the date or dates of the hearing; the headnote (a summary of the decision prepared by the reporter)[37]; lists of the cases discussed and cited; the previous history of the litigation, including a summary of the claims made and the result of proceedings in lower courts; the facts[38]; the names of counsel; the arguments of counsel[39]; an indication of whether judgment is reserved by the inclusion of the expression *Cur. adv. vult*[40]; the judgment or judgments[41]; the order of the court and an indication of whether leave to appeal is granted or refused; the names of the solicitors; the name of the barrister who reports the case.

(c) Law reporting[42]

The earliest law reports were contained in the "Year Books" compiled annually between the thirteenth and sixteenth centuries. These reports concentrated upon points of procedure and pleading rather than the final decisions of the courts, and were written first in Norman French and later in "law French" (an amalgam of English, French and Latin).[43] These are today mainly of interest to legal historians. Between the sixteenth and nineteenth centuries a large number of "private" or "nominate" reports

---

[35a] [1983] 2 A.C. 192. See R.J.C. Munday, (1983) 80 L.S.Gaz 1337, and note the critical response of F.A.R. Bennion (*ibid.* p. 1635) and N. Harrison (Managing Director of the company which markets *Lexis*), (1984) 81 L.S.Gaz. 257. It is uncertain whether the Court of Appeal will adopt a similar stance, but note the remarks of Sir John Donaldson M.R. in *Stanley* v. *International Harvester Co. of Great Britain Ltd.*, *The Times*, February 7, 1983.

[36] Appeals to the House of Lords have since 1974 carried the same title as in the court of first instance: *Procedure Direction* [1974] 1 W.L.R. 305. Previously, the name of the appellant appeared first.

[37] The headnote may be inaccurate (see, *e.g. Young* v. *Bristol Aeroplane Co. Ltd.* above, p. 290) although modern headnotes are generally reliable. It may include a summary of the facts or simply be the reporter's version of the *ratio decidendi*.

[38] The facts stated in the judgments may be left unedited or the reporter may set out the facts separately.

[39] These are only regularly printed in a few sets of reports such as The Law Reports and Lloyds' Law Reports. Interjections from the bench may also be included.

[40] *Curia advisari vult*: "the court wishes to consider the matter."

[41] In full reports these are printed verbatim, in some, such as in the Criminal Law Review and the Solicitors' Journal, only summaries are given.

[42] See J.H. Baker, *An Introduction to English Legal History* (2nd ed., 1979), pp. 151–158, 167–168; L.W. Abbott, *Law Reporting in England 1485–1585* (1973).

[43] See J.H. Baker, *Manual of Law French* (1979).

appeared. Most were named after the reporter. They varied widely in their style and content, their accuracy and their reputation.[44] Some, such as those of Coke, Plowden and Saunders were of high authority. Others were regarded as of little value. Some were in law French; most were in English. The focus of attention switched from the pleadings to the Court's decision and the best reports included the full reasons. The first to be published in more or less the form we have today, although not verbatim reports, were Burrow's reports of the eighteenth century. The first that regularly published reports of newly decided cases were Durnford and East's "Term Reports." The private reports are cited by the name, usually abbreviated, of the reporter or the reports, the volume and the page.[45] The year is not technically part of the reference but is normally included.[46] Most of the cases in the private reports were reprinted in *The English Reports* published in 176 volumes between 1900 and 1930. There was also a series entitled *The Revised Reports* edited by Sir Frederick Pollock and included such cases reported between 1785 and 1865 as were "still of practical utility."

The patchwork coverage of private enterprise law reports was seen to be unsatisfactory.[47] In 1865 a council consisting of the Attorney-General, the Solicitor-General, two barristers from each of the inns of court, two serjeants and two solicitors was formed; in 1870 it was incorporated as "The Incorporated Council of Law Reporting for England and Wales" with as its primary object:

> "the preparation and publication in a convenient form, at a moderate price, and under gratuitous professional control of Reports of Judicial Decisions of the Superior and Appellate Courts of England."

The Council is not funded by the state and is non-profit-making.[48] Its reports are semi-official in that judgments appearing in the Law Reports are revised by the judges, and that this series should be cited in preference to any alternative.[49] The corrections may make the report conform to what was actually said; on occasion a report is changed to conform to what the judge meant to say, which is rather more controversial.[50] There have been three series of the Law Reports: the first from 1865 to 1875,[51] the second

---

[44] C.K. Allen, *Law in the Making* (7th ed., 1964), pp. 221–232.

[45] *e.g. Coggs* v. *Bernard* (1703) 2 Ld. Raym. 909 (Lord Raymond).

[46] In round brackets. Where the year is part of a reference it is given in square brackets.

[47] See W.T.S. Daniel, *The History and Origin of "The Law Reports"* [1884].

[48] *Incorporated Council of Law Reporting* v. *Att.-Gen.* [1972] Ch. 73. The Court of Appeal held that the Council's purposes were charitable.

[49] *Westminster Bank Executors and Trustee Co. (Channel Islands) Ltd.* v. *National Bank of Greece S.A. (Practice Note)* [1970] 1 W.L.R. 1400.

[50] See, *e.g. Ghani* v. *Jones* [1970] 1 Q.B. 693; R.M. Jackson [1970] C.L.J. 1, 3; (1969) 119 N.L.J. 1011; (1970) 120 N.L.J. 423.

[51] *e.g. Osgood* v. *Nelson* (1872) L.R. 5 H.L. 636. A reference to this series normally includes the year of the decision (in round brackets as it is not technically part of the reference); the letters "L.R."; the volume number of the relevant series; the abbreviation for that series (there were 11 in all, running concurrently); and the page number.

from 1875 to 1890[52] and the third from 1891 to date.[53] The Incorporated Council also publishes the (unrevised) "Weekly Law Reports" and the "Industrial Cases Reports." There are a number of series of specialist official reports including the "Reports of Tax Cases" published under the direction of the Inland Revenue, the "Reports of Patent, Design and Trade Mark Cases" published by the Patent Office and the "Immigration Appeal Reports" published by H.M.S.O. There are also a number of series associated more obviously with private enterprise, of which the "All England Law Reports" is a general series rivalling the Weekly Law Reports.[54] The trend is for an increasing number of cases to be reported and for new series of reports to be started,[55] with concomitant problems of expense for law libraries and practitioners, duplication[56] and pressure on research time.

The system of law reporting was examined by a committee which reported in 1940.[57] The committee did not favour any radical change, such as giving the Incorporated Council a monopoly of reporting or the licensing of reporters. The majority rejected the proposals of A.L. Goodhart, who wrote a dissenting report, that a shorthand writer should take down the text of every judgment, that a transcript be sent to the judge for correction and that the corrected report be filed in the court records and made available to any reporter or member of the public for a small fee. The reasons put forward were the cost, the extra burden on the judges and the fact that almost every decision of importance was already reported: "What remains is less likely to be a treasure house than a rubbish heap in which a jewel will rarely, if ever, be discovered."[58]

Decisions of the Court of Justice of the European Communities are reported in the *European Court Reports*, an official series, and in the *Common Market Law Reports*, a private enterprise series, which includes in addition reports of the decisions of national courts on Community law matters.

The most significant developments in the near future may lie in the field of the computerisation of statutes, statutory instruments and law reports.[59] Butterworths offer the American *Lexis* system, which includes English and American materials[60]; the European Law Centre offers *Eurolex*, with a more limited selection of English materials and a range of European reports.

---

[52] *e.g. Huth* v. *Clarke* (1890) 25 Q.B.D. 391. A reference no longer includes the letters "L.R." and there are six series: one for Appeal Cases and one for each of the five divisions of the High Court (reduced to three in 1888).

[53] *e.g. Ridge* v. *Baldwin* [1964] A.C. 40. A reference includes the year of the *report*, not the decision, in square brackets; the series (A.C.; Q.B.; Ch.; Fam.) and the page number.

[54] See further, J. Dane and P.A. Thomas, *How to Use a Law Library* (1979), Chap. 2; Sweet & Maxwell's *Guide to Law Reports and Statutes* (4th ed., 1962).

[55] R.J.C. Munday (1978) 14 J.S.P.T.L. (N.S.) 201–203.

[56] A glance at Sweet & Maxwell's *Current Law Citator* will confirm this.

[57] Report of the Law Reporting Committee (H.M.S.O., 1940).

[58] *Ibid.* p. 20.

[59] See generally G. Bull (1980) 11 *The Law Librarian* 34–40; *Poly Law Review*, Vol. 5, No. 2, Spring 1980; C. Campbell (ed.) *Data Processing and the Law* (1984) (introduction).

[60] (1979) 130 N.L.J. 507.

PART II

SOLVING LEGAL PROBLEMS

CHAPTER 8

PROBLEMS ABOUT PROBLEMS

WE encounter a difficulty at the beginning of this part of the book by directing our attention to the solution of "legal" problems. How should such problems be defined? Are there distinctions to be drawn between legal problems and social problems? How effective are lawyers in solving legal problems? How far should lawyers be "creating" problems by identifying malpractice and abuse and making the victims aware of it? What is a problem?

These are issues which have been the subject of research and discussion in the last decade reflecting the growing awareness of the existence of an unmet need for legal assistance with problems and the development of law centres and other agencies to meet it. They are central to the debate over the provision of legal services and the response to these issues will affect the formulation of policy.

This chapter explores some of these issues and Chapter 9 then assesses the strengths and weaknesses of the major agencies currently involved in giving advice and solving problems. Throughout both chapters we shall be particularly concerned with the role of lawyers.

A great deal of emphasis is placed on the role of courts in settling disputes. The law student learns much of his law from decided cases[1]; public attention is inevitably focused upon the adversarial contest; civil and criminal procedure is lengthy and complex; books on the English legal system (including ours) devote a considerable amount of space to litigation; English procedure tends to individualise grievances and tailor them to the adversarial model.[2] Yet it remains true that only a tiny fraction of legal matters end up in court. If it were otherwise the court system would simply collapse under the strain.

This is partly explained by the ability of lawyers to advise on and negotiate settlements to the mutual satisfaction of the parties to the dispute. Such settlements are entirely acceptable.[3] Again, some legal matters are non-contentious and would not, in any event, come to court. Other matters may be resolved simply by the giving of information or advice about the law.

However, it is now clear that many legal matters never emerge even for legal assistance, let alone litigation, because they are never identified as legal problems by the sufferers, or never reach lawyers, or, having reached

---

[1] Through the doctrine of *stare decisis*, see Chap. 7 above.

[2] It is, of course, true that a successful individual action will have an effect on the rights and duties of other people through the definition of the law, but there is no general provision in the English legal system for a group or class action except in certain matters of company law. This can make things difficult in, for example, environmental matters where the residents of a whole area are disadvantaged. The potential of class actions and their use elsewhere is discussed in M. Zander, *Legal Services for the Community* (1978), pp. 227–232.

[3] The general question of settlements and the factors which may influence the parties are discussed in Chap. 10.

lawyers, are not recognised as problems within the purview of the law.[4] This situation is not acceptable and the success of any scheme to provide legal services to the public should be judged on its ability to bridge this gap by involving lawyers in the resolution of all matters that require their assistance.

A. WHAT IS A PROBLEM?

This may appear to be an odd question to pose, but it has a bearing on our approach to the provision of legal services and the involvement of lawyers. Does a situation only become a problem when the sufferer identifies it as something which he might be able to do something about? If the mood is one of resigned acceptance, that the situation represents one of life's difficulties, that there is no help to be obtained in dealing with the matter, then should we consider that such a person has a problem?

This is not confined to legal problems (although in many situations there may be an unrecognised legal solution) but has its effect in other matters as well. The failure on the part of the sufferer to appreciate that solutions may exist may be the result of a combination of factors including ignorance,[5] apathy,[6] complexity of the situation, generality of the problem and the extent of financial or physical resources required to rectify matters.[7] When the need for assistance is not even recognised, there is the utmost difficulty for any advice agency in assisting. The role of the lawyer or adviser in taking the initiative in identifying problems with which he can help then becomes important, and it is in this type of work that the law centres have been highly successful. The identification of the problem is then made by the adviser rather than the sufferer and the relationship between the *need* for legal services and the *demands* actually made by clients is exposed.[8]

If the provision of legal services is to be limited to those matters in which the sufferer realises that he is in a situation of difficulty for which the law provides a means of solution and with which a lawyer can assist him much of the pioneering work of law centres will be nullified.[9]

[4] This general difficulty has been termed "unmet legal need" and has been the subject of much study. See, for example, B. Abel-Smith, M. Zander and R. Brooke, *Legal Problems and the Citizen* (1973); P. Morris, R. White and P. Lewis, *Social Needs and Legal Action* (1973); Law Society, "Law Society's Memo No. 2—Unmet Need" (1976) 73 L.S. Gaz. 1061; A. Byles and P. Morris, *Unmet need: the case of the neighbourhood law centre* (1977).

[5] Ignorance of the criminal law does not excuse from liability for its breach—ignorance of the civil law on the part of the public seems almost to be assumed. Some improvement may be effected by the increased willingness to include legal topics on the school curriculum, see R.C.L.S., Vol. 1, p. 46. *Cf.* M.P. Furmston, "Ignorance of the Law" (1981) 1 L.S. 37.

[6] Not necessarily in a pejorative sense, more the feeling that, "It's not worth it . . . ", "Let's just forget about it . . . ", "It's just one of those things. . . . ".

[7] Technically the sufferer may recognise a problem but see no realistic opportunity of solving it.

[8] For an analysis of this particular problem, see Adamsdown Community Trust, *Community Need and Law Centre Practice* (1978), pp. 36–37. The solicitor in private practice is restricted in the way in which he might encourage people to approach him by the rules against touting and advertising, see p. 109, above.

[9] It can be extremely difficult to draw the line between intervention on behalf of those suffering in the local community and the mounting of "campaigns." This has been one of the most sensitive issues in the development of law centres and is still unresolved. See R.C.L.S., Vol. 1, pp. 83–84 and the Law Centres Federation, "A response to the Royal Commission on Legal Services" (1980). For the problems encountered in this area by N.A.C.A.B., see *Review of the National Association of Citizens Advice Bureaux* (Cmnd. 9139, 1983).

B. WHEN IS A PROBLEM "LEGAL"?

The attribution of a particular "legal" character to certain problems underlies the research which has been done into "unmet legal need" for it is by no means every problem which requires the assistance of a lawyer in its resolution. Equally, not every problem which a lawyer is asked to deal with is necessarily a legal one since many lawyers are proud of their reputation as sound advisers on general financial and property matters. In any event, it would be impossible to define as legal problems those which are *actually* dealt with by lawyers for that would exclude all those problems which never reach them.

However, would it be realistic to define legal problems as those with which the private practitioner normally deals? This definition involves the combination of two factors—the selection of appropriate problems by potential clients (for individual solicitors are not permitted to advertise or tout for business) and, on presentation, their acceptance by the solicitor as appropriate for him to handle. This combination of factors establishes a pattern of work to be regarded as normally appropriate for a solicitor and, arguably, a definition of legal problems. In fact, this definition would be highly restrictive because it depends upon the subjective views of both client and practitioner. If a client does not identify a failure on the part of a landlord to make repairs to a rented house as a problem appropriate to a solicitor, or if a solicitor considered such a matter outside his field then it would not, under such a definition, become a legal problem. This cannot be right.[10]

There have certainly been criticisms of the relatively narrow view which the private practitioner has taken of his work (a failing which results partly from the type of legal education currently provided) and it is true that the introduction of the legal advice and assistance scheme in 1973 was intended to give solicitors the opportunity to take a wider range of work. It did not succeed in this objective.[11]

An alternative approach is to attempt an objective definition of problems which have a legal component by reference to a list or catalogue of types of problem. This approach does not place the emphasis upon the problems that solicitors *do* deal with, but upon those they *could* deal with. The list is composed of a variety of types of problem including those traditionally accepted as legal by both lawyer and client, those regarded as legal by lawyers but not necessarily by clients, and those not normally viewed by either as legal. This approach was adopted by Abel-Smith, Zander and Brooke in their research into unmet legal need, published as

---

[10] If this definition were acceptable there would, presumably, be no unmet legal need except where a client could not afford to seek advice on a matter accepted as "legal." Despite the strange results of such a definition there is a good deal of evidence that the range of problems on which the public would expect to seek the advice of a solicitor is even narrower than the range of problems that solicitors recognise as theirs. See P. Morris, R. Cooper and A. Byles, "Public Attitudes to Problem Definition and Problem Solving; A Pilot Study" (1973–74) 3 Brit. J. Social Work 301, 309–310; Adamsdown Community Trust, *Community Need and Law Centre Practice* (1978), p. 44.

[11] See below, p. 349.

Legal Problems and the Citizen, and 17 specific and common situations were chosen by them as the basis of a questionnaire.[12]

This approach was adopted because of the differing perceptions of what is a legal problem and the consequent inadequacy of a questionnaire which simply sought information on legal problems. It is important to note the particular purpose of the definition before being too critical of the notion that legal problems can be objectively defined by reference to specific situations. The authors acknowledge that " . . . new needs will come to be recognised and new legal remedies will come to be developed," but assert that " . . . at any time there will be some problems which are clearly perceived by lawyers or laymen as more 'legal' than others."[13]

An objective definition of this nature is inevitably open to criticism on the grounds of particular exclusions from or inclusions in the categories on the list and as to the extent of the categories themselves. However, there is a more fundamental objection. Such a definition involves the construction of categories within the general scope of the law and, though they may be widely drawn, is open to the same objection as a definition based upon the perceptions of solicitors. It tends to be *exclusive* rather than *inclusive*, in that our thinking may be confined to those matters which fall within accepted categories rather than accepting that all situations to which the law pertains can give rise to legal problems no matter that there is no immediately available legal framework for their solution.

A definition of a legal problem as "an unresolved difficulty to which the law is relevant," may appear to be far too vague and begging too many questions. Who determines relevance? However, it may form the basis of a new approach to problems in which lawyers/advisers will not seek to establish the legal nature of the problem and then find the relevant law, but will rather seek to establish the nature of the problem and then contemplate if any part of the law might be relevant. Such a definition tries to indicate an approach, an attitude, rather than provide a litmus-paper test.

Three potential advantages of such an approach have been demonstrated by research projects and other developments in recent years. First, it diminishes the tendency to distinguish between legal problems and, for example, social problems.[14] Even in some official reports there are discussions of social need *or* legal need and the likelihood of overlapping problems is too often ignored. Any definition which helps to recognise that there may be substantial overlapping of legal and social issues, and that neither can be adequately dealt with in isolation is to be commended. Secondly, the inclusive approach may act as a positive encouragement to clients to make use of legal services. It would appear that the major stumbling-block for those who need advice is the identification of the "correct" agency to approach.[15] The legal profession has a distinct image

[12] The situations were: taking a lease; repairs undone; attempted eviction; an attempt to evict by a landlord; buying a house; defective goods; instalments arrears; unpaid debt owed; taken to court for debt; death in the family; making a will; accidents; social security benefits; employment problems; matrimonial problems; court proceedings; juvenile court proceedings.

[13] *Legal Problems and the Citizen*, p. 120.

[14] This dichotomy is considered and criticised in Morris, Cooper and Byles, *op.cit.* n. 10 above.

[15] See, for example, Adamsdown Community Trust, *op.cit.* n. 8 above, at p. 41.

and the number of matters which are identified by the public as appropriate to a solicitor is relatively narrow.[16] The adoption of a more broadly-based approach might help. Finally, the acceptance of a problem and the consequent search for any law which might be relevant may disclose a novel application of the law or a new remedy.[17] It is certainly an approach which encourages the lawyer to use a little imagination in the solution of the problem.

We have considered alternative definitions of a legal problem and indicated what we consider to be the best working definition to adopt, but this discussion will remain largely academic (save in estimating the extent of unmet legal need) unless there is some effective way of ensuring that those who have legal problems, however defined, secure legal assistance.

C. LEGAL PROBLEMS AND THE USE OF LAWYERS

Some writers would not accept the proposition that the best people to assist with legal problems are always lawyers. In an important article, Titmuss suggested that laymen are better advocates than lawyers in certain tribunals[18] and the Consumer Council doubted the wisdom of allowing lawyers to practise in the new small claims courts which it proposed.[19] These arguments are based on the disadvantages of applying established legal techniques in situations where speed, flexibility and informality are the objectives of the tribunal.[20]

However, whilst noting that view, we are primarily concerned with the passage of legal problems through to lawyers and the reasons why that passage may become obstructed.

1. WHO USES SOLICITORS?

The most recent survey of what the private profession do and for whom, was conducted on behalf of the Royal Commission on Legal Services[21] and confirmed the results of earlier, more limited surveys.[22] The range of problems on which solicitors are consulted is quite narrow, and of 27 categories adopted in the survey, seven accounted for over 80 per cent. of all matters taken to solicitors. These seven were domestic conveyancing

[16] *Ibid.* p. 55. See also Abel-Smith, Zander and Brooke, *op.cit.* pp. 156–160; and R.C.L.S., Vol. II, Part B, pp. 195–206. For an interesting survey of a particular problem area, see S. Burman, H. Genn and J. Lyons, "The Use of Legal Services by Victims of Accidents in the Home—A Pilot Survey" (1977) 40 M.L.R. 47.

[17] For example, the application of the law of trusts to give an unmarried partner an interest in a shared home, *Cooke* v. *Head* [1972] 1 W.L.R. 518; the planning of welfare benefits so as to maximise the amount received by the claimant, particularly on the breakdown of marriage, see S. Cretney, *Family Law* (3rd ed., 1979), p. 378 and "Tax and Welfare Benefit Planning", *LAG Bulletin*, August and September 1975, pp. 209, 240.

[18] "Welfare 'Rights', Law and Discretion" (1971) 42 *Political Quarterly*, 113.

[19] The Consumer Council, *Justice Out of Reach* (1970). See also p. 412 below.

[20] R. Lawrence, "Solicitors and Tribunals" [1980] J.S.W.L. 13.

[21] Survey of Users and Non–users of legal services in England and Wales, R.C.L.S., Vol. 2, Section 8, pp. 173–298.

[22] For example, M. Zander, "Who goes to solicitors" (1969) 66 L.S. Gaz. 174; Morris, Cooper and Byles, "Public Attitudes to Problem Definition and Problem Solving : A Pilot Study" (1973–74) 3 Brit.J. Social Work 301; Abel–Smith, Zander and Brooke, *Legal Problems and the Citizen* (1973); Adamsdown Community Trust, *Community Need and Law Centre Practice* (1978).

(30 per cent.); dealing with the estate of a dead person (11 per cent.); making or altering wills (10 per cent.); divorce and matrimonial (12 per cent.); motoring and other offences (7 per cent.); personal injuries compensation (7 per cent.) and domestic property matters (5 per cent.).[23] The sample was based on 2026 consultations in 1977.[24]

Is this pattern of usage of solicitors evidence of a restricted perception of the sorts of matters they deal with? Or do people consider that solicitors could help with other matters but fail to approach them? The answer is unclear. The Royal Commission survey indicated that a number of people felt that there were occasions on which the advice of a solicitor would have been useful (on matters generally different to those on which solicitors were actually consulted)[25] but no contact was made for diverse reasons. Other surveys have found a much more limited perception of the solicitor's role.[26]

Whether there is truth in either, or both, of these hypotheses it is clear that not enough use is made of solicitors for the solution of legal problems. Is there something wrong with their image?

2. THE PUBLIC IMAGE

It has been convincingly argued that the image of an advice-giving agency is crucial because it is at the stage of identification of the appropriate agency that most people are obstructed on the way to the solution of their problem.[27] A strong image will assist in this identification, although it can act negatively as well as positively. The Law Society is aware of the problems of image and is anxious to convey to the public that solicitors are skilled and competent in a wide variety of matters,[28] but it does not seem to be succeeding.[29] Whilst it appears that many people accept that they *must* seek help in really serious matters, in other situations solicitors have the image of people to be avoided rather than sought out.

It is interesting to note the different sorts of problems brought to lawyers in law centres and other advice agencies. They do not seem to be burdened with the same difficulties as the private profession, presumably partly because of the different image of the agency involved and the different expectations of the client involved.[30]

---

[23] R.C.L.S., Vol. 2, p. 197.

[24] These 2026 consultations involved 1770 people out of 7941 households interviewed. Some 15 per cent. of adults used a lawyer's services in some matter in 1977, R.C.L.S., Vol. 2, p. 183. A more rudimentary analysis is published annually in the Legal Aid Annual Reports. See, for example, *33rd Legal Aid Annual Reports* [1982–83], p. 57.

[25] The most common matter *not* taken to a solicitor was a neighbour dispute; other matters more commonly not taken than taken included defective goods and services, landlord and tenant, social security, welfare and employment problems.

[26] See the surveys cited in n. 22 above.

[27] In the report of the Adamsdown Community Trust, *Community Need and Law Centre Practice*, at pp. 41–46.

[28] Through the medium of advertising and publicity. See G. Sanctuary, "The Solicitor's Public Image" (1974) 124 N.L.J. 533, and p. 109 above.

[29] On the evidence of the user surveys and also the disappointing response to the green form scheme, see p. 349 below, and R.C.L.S., Vol. 1, pp. 33–35.

[30] This is the experience of the Adamsdown Community and Advice Centre (see n. 27 above) and has been one of the strengths of the Citizens' Advice Bureaux—they have a very strong *generalist* image. For a broad analysis of the comparative problems taken to solicitors, CABx and law centres, see *33rd Legal Aid Annual Report* [1982–83], p. 57.

3. Barriers

We have identified difficulties which may be encountered in realising that a problem has a legal dimension and in connecting that problem to the sort of work that lawyers are commonly understood to deal with. There are, however, further barriers in the way of those needing legal advice, notably its cost and its accessibility.

The Royal Commission placed especial emphasis on the deterrent effect of cost,[31] supported in some measure by the findings of the user survey.[32] However, those findings are of limited value in that they relate only to those people who had already identified a problem that a solicitor could help with, *i.e.* they had already overcome two major obstacles. The findings do show that cost is in itself a deterrent but they tell us nothing about its relative significance to the other difficulties known to exist. It is obviously vital to know the relative weight of these various factors when deploying (limited) resources to improve the situation. It is no good increasing the number of lawyers and law centres (improving the accessibility) if people still do not know when they need assistance. Public education about the nature of legal problems and the role of lawyers in solving them might be much more effective.

The proposals of the Royal Commission, outlined in the following chapter,[33] should be evaluated in the light of *all* the factors which are preventing people getting the legal advice they need.

D. UNMET LEGAL NEED

It may appear that we consider every problem with a legal component requires legal assistance, for we have not proposed any other criterion for the provision of legal services than that a legal problem exists. This may seem a profligate approach, yet just as there are difficulties in defining legal problems so there are difficulties in defining when an individual *needs* assistance. It is obvious that his circumstances, financial resources and personal competence will differ, as will the importance of the matter to him. How can a general proposition of need be formulated when there are so many personal variables? Should any such proposition even be attempted?

In conducting their pioneering survey,[34] Abel-Smith, Zander and Brooke were faced with this problem. The solution they adopted was to assess, in respect of each category of problems identified,[35] what would constitute " . . . a risk of substantial loss or disadvantage which would be important for the individual concerned."[36] This standard differed for each category and it is difficult to see how it could be translated into more general form. Zander, indeed, later acknowledged that the decisions as to what amounted to a need for advice in each category " . . . were not only conservative but also highly artificial, suitable, if at all, only for research

[31] R.C.L.S., Vol. 1, pp. 48–49.
[32] *Ibid.* Vol. 2, p. 262.
[33] Below, p. 352.
[34] *Legal Problems and the Citizen* (1973).
[35] The categories are listed at n. 12 above.
[36] *Ibid.* p. 112.

purposes," and described the test as " . . . necessarily crude and inadequate."[37]

These comments are not cited with the object of criticising the survey but rather of illustrating the exceptional difficulty of defining need. Other writers have not made the attempt.[38]

In respect of the provision of Legal Aid, the test of need (usually described as a "merit" test) is based upon whether a solicitor would advise a private client, with sufficient means to pay his own costs, to assert or dispute the claim.[39] Is it reasonable? A similar test can hardly be applied to legal advice.

The Royal Commission recommended that an initial half-hour's worth of advice should be provided free of charge to anyone who requests it, despite the possibilities of abuse by those who have adequate financial resources.[40] This would seem to accept that legal need can be defined by reference to the existence of a legal problem on which an individual wishes to be advised, albeit that part of the half-hour will be to examine the case and determine the "need" for further advice. At least the individual concerned will have got to the solicitor who may then be able to satisfy those further needs.

If it be conceded that the need for legal advice arises from the existence of a legal problem, then the difficulties in supplying that need would appear to have been exposed earlier in the chapter. However, studies demonstrate that the obstructions on the way to obtaining legal advice have different effects on different sorts of people.

The most obvious differential obstruction is cost, and it is no surprise to learn that those in the higher socio-economic groups use lawyers more often than those in the lower.[41] This evidence has been used to substantiate a theory that poverty is the primary cause of the failure to seek legal advice,[42] and to support a slightly wider hypothesis that the failure is due to a lack of "legal competence" among the less affluent who suffer not only from lack of money, but also from lack of influence, lack of energy and lack of awareness.[43]

Zander has criticised both these theories[44] and advances an alternative

---

[37] *Legal Services for the Community* (1978), p. 280.

[38] For example in the Adamsdown survey (*op. cit.* n. 22 above) the writer concluded that " . . . there are no objective yardsticks for legal need . . . the purpose of the interviews therefore was simply to assess the spread and types of problems which the respondents had subjectively felt."

[39] This is an interpretation of the statutory provision contained in the Legal Aid Act 1974, s.7(5), used in deciding elegibility. See further p. 390 below.

[40] R.C.L.S., Vol. 1, pp. 134–135.

[41] There are a number of surveys which demonstrate this, amongst them are Abel-Smith, Zander and Brooke, *Legal Problems and the Citizen* (1973) (U.K.); M. Cass and R. Sackville, *Legal Needs of the Poor* (1975) (Australian Government Commission of Inquiry into Poverty); B. Curran, *The Legal Needs of the Public: The Final Report of a National Survey* (1977) (American Bar Association—American Bar Foundation study); *Survey of Users and Non-users of Legal Services in England and Wales*, R.C.L.S., Vol. 2, Section 8.

[42] Partly, according to Zander, because the researchers concentrated on the poor, without extending the survey to whole population: *Legal Services for the Community*, p. 288.

[43] J. Carlin and J. Howard, "Legal Representation and Class Justice" (1965) 12 U.C.L.A. Law Review 381.

[44] In *Legal Services for the Community*, pp. 288–290. The whole of this chapter on the need for legal services is extremely helpful.

explanation based on contact between the individual with a problem and a knowledgeable lay person. He relies on the unpublished evidence of a survey conducted by the Oxford Centre for Socio-Legal Studies[45] and some American studies.[46] His assessment of the importance of lay intermediaries in getting individuals to seek legal advice is not based upon the work of generalist advice agencies, or referral lists, or official advertising, but more upon the influence of friends, relations, union officials, neighbours and like people. Building upon this theory he suggests a greater reliance upon lay advisers not only in the existing advice-giving agencies but also amongst counter clerks, court officials, police officers, doctors and others in official agencies.[47] By greater education and training the awareness both of the general public and those who might be able to advise/persuade them to see lawyers when necessary would be heightened.

This attractive approach to the problem of unmet need is confounded somewhat by the Royal Commission users' survey.[48] In three out of four matters on which the interviewees had consulted lawyers in 1977, those making the consultation had received no help or advice from people outside the household on the matter in question.[49] These results are out of line with those cited by Zander and must cast some doubt on the correctness of his explanation. However, they are not totally against him for in the remaining 25 per cent. of cases in which advice had been obtained before consultation, the main sources had been friends/work-mates, relatives or a citizens advice bureau and the advice given in three-quarters of those cases was to go to a lawyer.[50]

Returning to the findings of the survey in relation to those who had legal problems but did *not* go to a lawyer,[51] a higher proportion (42 per cent.) had received help from outside the household and of that group only one-quarter had received advice to go to a lawyer which they had ignored.[52]

What emerges from this particular survey is that the absence of contact with a knowledgeable lay person does not appear to have the significance ascribed to it by Zander (since 75 per cent. of the group taking advice did not have this contact), but, where a lay person *is* involved, the advice given about the need to consult a lawyer is given considerable weight. Thus, although Zander's proposals might not have the overall stimulatory effect which he anticipated, they would be very important in the cases where lay people did become involved.

It is quite possible that the extent of unmet need, like the extent of

---

[45] H.G. Genn, "Factors Influencing the Decision to Use Legal Services by Accident Victims" (unpublished paper given at L.A.G. seminar, May 1977).

[46] P. Lochner, "The No Fee and Low Fee Legal Practice of Private Attorneys" (1975) *Law and Society Review* 436; R. Hunting and G. Neuwirth, *Who sues in New York?* (1962).

[47] Social workers are obviously important in this respect and there is a growing body of literature to suggest that social workers' perceptions of law and lawyers are not as helpful as they might be. See, for example, A. Phillips, "Social Work and the Delivery of Legal Services" (1979) 42 M.L.R. 29. It is not just a British problem, see J. Fogelson, "How social workers perceive lawyers" (1970) *Social Casework* 95.

[48] R.C.L.S., Vol. 2, Section 8.

[49] *Ibid*. p. 207, para. 8.127.

[50] *Ibid*. p.207, para. 8.130.

[51] *Ibid*. pp. 256–263, and see p. 318 above.

[52] *Ibid*. p. 262, para. 8.395.

undetected crime, can never be ascertained and that which can be ascertained cannot be adequately explained. The barriers are clear enough, what remains unclear is why some people are able to surmount them when others fail miserably.

E. INTERVENTION OF LAWYERS—THE "CREATING" OF PROBLEMS

Lawyers have not usually been slow in their individual involvement with causes and with legal reform, but questions have recently arisen over the extent to which it is proper to intervene in socio-legal problems as part of a professional service. The law centre, in particular, has taken a broad view of its obligation to service the local community and some have been active in stimulating and articulating local protest. Is this proper?

The Royal Commission on Legal Services concluded that this sort of work should *not* be part of the responsibilities of the new citizens' law centres that were proposed.[53] What was identified as " . . . general community work . . . organising groups to bring pressure to bear . . . becoming a focus in the neighbourhood for campaigns,"[54] was said to be inappropriate for a legal service. The Commission took the view that the responsibility of a legal service was the provision of legal advice and assistance to individuals; that community action tends to involve only one section of the community; and that the independence of a centre is compromised if it becomes a base for campaigns. Consequently although special provision should be made for providing legal advice to groups,[55] "campaigning" should be funded from elsewhere and not undertaken by law centres.

The Report was published after a very interesting and well-argued case was made by the Adamsdown Community Trust[56] for precisely the sort of intervention which the Report proscribed.[57] Independence was not compromised, it was alleged, and although the identification of causes deserving of support and finance from the advice agency might be questionable, in practice only those problems which give real cause for community concern could be pursued successfully because of the need for public support. It was also noted that interventionist action could include leafletting in the area, talks to local groups and the preparation of kits and materials as well as the organisation of pressure groups and similar activities.

There may be difficulties in particular law centres in finding the right balance between assisting clients in individual case work and taking on group work and projects, but it seems unduly restrictive to deny that the latter was a proper role for lawyers to play.

[53] R.C.L.S., Vol. 1, pp. 83–84, and see below, p. 355.

[54] *Ibid.* p. 83, para. 8.19.

[55] *Ibid.* pp. 128–130. The Adamsdown Community and Advice Centre had managed to secure £1800 of legal advice under the green form scheme (see p. 339 below) by getting extensions to £120 in respect of 15 clients, selected from 270 with the same general problem. This useful precedent prompted consideration of the granting of legal aid and advice to groups.

[56] Adamsdown Community Trust, *Community Need and Law Centre Practice* (1978).

[57] The projects described in the survey concerned a provisional slum clearance programme and roads and pavements in disrepair in the Adamsdown area.

CHAPTER 9

INFORMATION AND ADVICE SERVICES

By discussing in the preceding chapter the ways in which the public may perceive a problem as a "legal" problem and the steps which the profession might take to assist in the identification of problems which require legal advice for their solution we have already indicated that we are concerned, in the main, with the provision of information and advice by lawyers. However, legal advice is not provided solely by lawyers and it is certainly not restricted to those operating within the professional structure described in Chapter 3.[1] In this chapter we shall deal with the major advice-giving agencies prior to a discussion of the arrangements under which the private profession and the law centres provide legal advice and assistance.

A. THE SPECIAL FEATURES OF INFORMATION AND ADVICE PROVISION

A person may seek advice for one or more purposes and it is important to distinguish those who may need help in establishing whether they have a problem, those who need help in establishing what action they can take and those who need help in pursuing a remedy. Even when the problem has been identified as having a legal perspective it is by no means certain that the client will conclude that a solicitor is the most appropriate source of advice. Different agencies may assist in different situations and lawyers still labour under the handicap of their public image.[2]

1. WHICH AGENCY?

What are the factors which influence the choice of a particular agency? Whilst there may be circumstances which influence individuals in their selection of an adviser,[3] it seems likely that the crucial factors are availability, cost and reputation.

The distribution of advice agencies around the country leaves large areas (especially the rural districts) without some of the basic agencies,[4] and even within urban areas it is unusual to find solicitors, in particular, located in the districts with the greatest density of population.[5] Advice needs to be locally available.

[1] See particularly pp. 101–115 above.
[2] R.C.L.S., Vol. 1, pp. 33–36, 45.
[3] For example, previous contact with a particular agency; personal knowledge of existing agencies; recommendations from friends.
[4] See the maps taken from various sources collected in *The Fourth Right of Citizenship*, a National Consumer Council Discussion Paper (1977), pp. 47–55. For an analysis of the especial problems of rural areas, see *Rural Advice and Information*, NACAB Occasional Paper No. 2, (1978); *33rd Legal Aid Annual Reports* [1982–83] pp. 176–8.
[5] The distribution of solicitors' offices is discussed in M. Zander, *Legal Services for the Community* (1978), pp. 28–30, where he makes use of K. Foster, "The Location of Solicitors" (1973) 36 M.L.R. 153. See above, p. 104.

. The cost of obtaining advice becomes significant when a client considers using professional agencies. Cost is obviously a factor which is balanced against the need for special skill or expertise, but it was an appreciation of the fears of the public about the financial consequences of visiting a solicitor which led the Royal Commission on Legal Services to recommend the "free initial half-hour" despite the possibilities of abuse.[6] Many of the statutory and voluntary agencies provide advice without charge.

The reputation of a particular agency will depend on the public perception of its efficiency, its impartiality, its independence and its approachability. That there is concern over the indifferent public image of the legal profession is evident—other agencies place varying degrees of emphasis upon different features of their reputation, some stressing their independence, others their approachability.

2. What Help?

Information and advice may be different and may require different communicative skills on the part of the adviser. Again, advice and assistance may be different with the latter requiring some positive action on behalf of the client. Most of the agencies that we shall be describing in the following sections would claim to offer information, advice and assistance but some are dubious as to the extent to which they *should* act on behalf of a client[7] and some will refer a matter on to specialists when they reach the limits of their competence. This raises the question of the role of the specialist agency in relation to the generalist and the development of a referral system. Co-ordination of generalist and specialist advice services is of prime importance and the National Consumer Council identified as a fundamental objective of a national advice system:

" . . . the achievement of a proper mix of specialist and voluntary services and of working links and effective referral systems for the handling of people's problems where more than one agency needs to be involved."[8]

We have already noted that lawyers can be expected to provide a whole range of help which would certainly include information, advice and assistance.[9]

3. Given by Whom?

Some agencies we shall be discussing rely solely upon one type of adviser so that there is no dispute about his suitability. In others, however, there

---

[6] R.C.L.S., Vol. 1, pp. 45, 134–135. See also pp. 355–356 below. This recommendation has not been accepted by the Government: see p. 358, below.

[7] See, for example, the Chairman's statement in the National Association of Citizens Advice Bureaux Annual Report and Accounts 1979–80, at p.5.

[8] *The Fourth Right of Citizenship*, p. 65, cited with approval in R.C.L.S., Vol. 1, p. 72. The National Consumer Council are concerned about the lack of a national policy for generalist advice provision. See their discussion paper, *A National Policy for Local Information and Advice Services* (1980).

[9] Above, p. 315.

can be tensions over the relative desirability of volunteers and professionals. Citizens' Advice Bureaux, for example, rely heavily upon volunteers with very few paid advisers and it is argued that this gives the organisation a positive strength and a particularly good claim to independence and impartiality. On the other hand, professional advisers (including lawyers) tend to lay emphasis upon the skill and expertise which are supposed to come with professional status and training.

The dispute between the volunteer and the professional is likely to continue[10] but it should not be allowed to obscure the fact that the skills of the good adviser are not necessarily professional skills, nor are they especially lawyerly skills. The client wants an adviser who can interview sympathetically, ascertain the facts, analyse the problem and suggest a course of action. The expertise of the adviser in the particular problem which emerges will doubtless influence the proposed course of action (which might include a referral) but the preliminary *advisory* skills may be possessed by a volunteer as by a professional. We shall return to these points later in the chapter but should now describe the range of information and advice agencies which will offer help with legal problems.

B. GENERALIST AGENCIES OFFERING LEGAL ADVICE

1. THE CITIZENS' ADVICE BUREAUX

It is somehow ironic that the major generalist agency owes its existence to wartime necessity. The CAB service has its origins in the combined operation set up in 1938 by the Ministry of Health, the National Council for Social Service and the Family Welfare Association to provide advice and information in an emergency. The outbreak of war was the emergency and a centrally-funded national service came into being. At the end of the war government assistance was withdrawn and local Bureaux were left to scrape along on what they could glean from local authorities and other sources. Many disappeared.

The service was revived at the beginning of the 1960s by the injection of government funding and was stimulated by honourable mention from two major enquiries. In 1962 the Molony Committee on Consumer Protection declared itself to be strongly in favour of the service and recognised its potential:

> "The aggrieved consumer needs an accessible local service to which he can take his troubles and where he will receive a realistic appraisal, a measure of help in presenting his case, or a pointer to the next step. This need cannot be better filled than by the Citizens Advice Bureaux."[11]

In 1980 the Royal Commission on Legal Services reported that it had:

> " . . . identified a particular national advice service, provided by the citizens advice bureaux, which together form the largest and, in our

[10] If only because the evidence of other areas of social work is of increased professional involvement. However, since 97 per cent. of the staff of Citizens Advice Bureaux are volunteers the dispute is likely to be spirited and prolonged.

[11] *Final Report of the Committee on Consumer Protection*, Cmnd. 1781 (1962). Recommendation 108, relating to paras. 481, 491–3.

view, the best placed organisation to provide a primary or first tier service."

The central body, the National Association of Citizens' Advice Bureaux has recently been the subject of a review[12] initiated by Dr. Gerard Vaughan, as Minister for Consumer Affairs, which described the C.A.B. service as, " . . . an invaluable national asset."

At the present time there are 936 Bureaux and extensions[13] in the United Kingdom which are registered with the National Association of Citizens' Advice Bureaux (NACAB). All these Bureaux are required to conform with national standards in their operation and to conform to the training requirements adopted by NACAB. The advantage of membership of the national association is the receipt of the NACAB monthly information service and the Citizens Advice Notes Service provided by the National Council of Voluntary Organisations.[14]

The aims of the Citizens' Advice Bureaux are:

(a) to ensure that individuals do not suffer through ignorance of their rights and responsibilities or of the services available; or through an inability to express their needs effectively;

(b) to exercise a responsible influence on the development of social policies and services, both locally and nationally;

(c) to achieve these results by providing free to all individuals a confidential, impartial and independent service of information, guidance and support, and making responsible use of the experience so gained.

There is strong evidence that greater and greater use is being made of the CAB service, especially in the current economic climate. In 1982–83 the service handled 5,034,000 enquiries, an increase of over 11 per cent. from the preceding year,[15] and social security enquiries showed a startling increase of 29 per cent. over the preceding year, totalling 768,000.[16] In the categorisation adopted by NACAB the greatest number of enquiries were concerned with consumer, trade and business (17½ per cent.); housing, property and land (15 per cent.); family and personal (12½ per cent.); and social security (15½ per cent.)[17]

In relation to those enquiries which have a legal content, a Citizens' Advice Bureau may adopt one of a number of approaches. It may train its advisers sufficiently to be able to give para-legal advice in those cases which do not require professional assistance; it may refer the client to a solicitor; it may arrange a rota scheme whereby a solicitor attends at the CAB office to see clients; it may try to appoint its own solicitor.

The Royal Commission on Legal Services considered these possibilities and favoured the first three.[18] However, the CAB service has appointed

[12] *Review of the National Association of Citizens' Advice Bureaux* (Cmnd. 9139, 1984).

[13] NACAB Annual Report and Accounts 1982–83, p. 7.

[14] Formerly the National Council of Social Service. The change of name dates from April 1980.

[15] NACAB Annual Report and Accounts 1982–83, Table 4, p. 4.

[16] *Ibid.* Table 8, p. 6. These figures exclude the enquiries for Scotland.

[17] *Ibid.* p. 3.

[18] R.C.L.S., Vol. 2., pp. 77–73.

several solicitors to work in Bureaux in London and the provinces[19] and it remains to be seen how the Royal Commission's view that the CAB service should not appoint lawyers to its staff[20] will be received.

The Royal Commission has given a firm indication of how it considers the CAB should resolve the conflict between its generalist role and the inclination to become involved in specialist areas:

" . . . the functions to be fulfilled by the CAB service [must] be defined with care. There is sometimes a tendency for a generalist service to expand into specialisms with which it is in daily contact. If this were to happen in the case of the CABx, they would have lost their primary purpose as first tier advisory agencies; there would be duplication of effort, waste of public money and, in all probability, deterioration in the quality of specialised advice provided."[21]

In 1982–1983 the financial assistance from central government amounted to £5,647,465 compared with £4,781,968 in 1981–1982.[22] This money goes to maintain the national organisation and to provide central services for Bureaux. The running expenses of the actual Bureaux are met mainly from local sources. They are minimal. Over 60 per cent. of Bureaux receive less than £5000 per year and over 80 per cent. less than £10,000.

2. NEIGHBOURHOOD ADVICE CENTRES[23]

These are informal groups operating in a wide diversity of localities and conditions, with very different structures and objectives. In general they offer assistance with all types of problem but are often to be found in the areas of urban development and rehousing which are likely to expose housing, welfare benefit and educational problems.[24] These centres may attract finance from a variety of sources, but there is some government funding which has been available to sustain them.[25]

3. THE MEDIA

It is impossible to ignore the increasing use of the media as a source of information and advice. Quite apart from the communication of information of all kinds which is the function of radio, television and the Press, more and more time is being devoted to the provision of general and specific advice usually at the request of individuals. This development is

---

[19] For an indication of the scope and nature of a Bureau solicitor's work see, *The Legal Service*, First Annual Report by the Nottingham and District CAB, 1976.

[20] R.C.L.S., Vol. 1, p. 76. It has not been well received by NACAB!

[21] *Ibid.* p. 75.

[22] NACAB Annual Report and Accounts 1982–83, p. 24.

[23] There is a dearth of material charting the activities of centres of this kind. An early appraisal is contained in Leissner, *Family Advice Centres*, National Bureau for Co-operation in Child Care (1967), and particular studies include Bond, *The Hillfields Information and Opinion Centre—the Evolution of A Social Agency Controlled by Local Residents*, CDP Occasional Paper (1972); *Report, Evaluation and Recommendations from Cumbria CDP*, Dept. of Soc. Admin., York University (1975); *Information and Advice Services in the U.K.* (1983), National Consumer Council.

[24] *The Fourth Right of Citizenship.*

[25] Notably from the Home Office Community Development Project (hence CDP in n. 23).

not unconnected with the development of local radio and the popularity of the phone-in programme.

Depending on resources, the media can respond to enquiries in much the same way as any other agency. The particular organisation can build up its own expertise[26]; it can acquire answers which are then relayed[27]; it can refer the enquirer to another agency; it can bring in specialists to answer the enquiries direct.[28] Legal advice frequently forms the basis of specific programmes or articles, no doubt because of the inherent fascination of legal problems for the layman.[29] There is also some credit to be gained by radio, television or the press where an individual's problem is solved and (as it is normally represented) the forces of darkness are vanquished.[30]

C. SPECIALIST AGENCIES OFFERING LEGAL ADVICE TO THE PUBLIC

1. CONSUMER ADVICE CENTRES

The fact that the highest percentage of enquiries to the CABx concerns consumer, trade and business affairs[31] demonstrates the particular need for specialist advice in the field. Before 1970 it was largely left to the Weights and Measures Departments of the local authorities to enforce those statutes which gave protection to the consumer of goods and they often took the view that they had no competence to deal with complaints which did not indicate a possible breach of the criminal law.

It was an irresistible combination of pressure from the Consumers' Association; the introduction of more consumer protection legislation; the injection of national government funding[32] and the reorganisation of local government in 1974 that led to the establishment of some 110 Consumer Advice Centres run by local authorities by the end of 1976. These centres provided both pre-shopping advice on quality, fitness and "value for money"[33] and a complaints service for disgruntled consumers. In most places they were very closely integrated with the (newly-named) Trading Standards Department.

They attracted criticism from a number of quarters and only 58 remain; the remainder of them fell victim to a political change in the relevant local

---

[26] As where a particular phone-in presenter gains local knowledge and experience, or where a presenter researches problems raised by listeners and makes them into a programme through his own investigation, e.g. Roger Cook in "Checkpoint," a BBC Radio 4 programme.

[27] By getting those who have the answers, for example local authority departments or welfare agencies, to take part in the programme by telephone.

[28] To answer questions on particular topics specified in advance either in print or on radio/television.

[29] So long as they are well-presented, e.g. Jimmy Young and his "legal beagle" on BBC Radio 2.

[30] e.g. "That's Life," BBC Television; "Action Desk," Nottingham Evening Post.

[31] See above p. 326.

[32] £1·4 million in December 1975 and a further £3 million in November 1976, see The Fourth Right of Citizenship (1977), National Consumer Council.

[33] By comparative testing with the justification that the consumer can often be better protected by buying wisely than by complaining vigourously.

authority coupled with a withdrawal of central government funding.[34] With a further political change we may see a reappearance. It is unfortunate that the CACs may be seen as a political football and they provide an interesting indication of what might possibly happen were all legal services to be funded from local or central government.[35] However, there is some advantage for the consumer in the close links between the centres and the enforcement mechanisms of the Trading Standards Department.[36]

2. Housing Advice Centres

These centres were coming into existence at about the time that the first law centre was being opened,[37] and it is not unrealistic to attribute their inception to the generally increased awareness of the need for advice services. However, the direct impetus came from the Seebohm Report[38] in 1968 which recommended the establishment of an official housing advice agency to give assistance with, *inter alia*, landlord and tenant problems, public health legislation and rent fixing. The obligation to provide such a service should rest, it was said, with the local authority.

In the event the first two centres demonstrated the dual approach to much advisory work in that one was set up by a local authority (in Lambeth) and one by voluntary bodies (in South Kensington).[39] That pattern has continued, and about two-thirds of the centres now in operation are run by the local authority. Financial assistance from the Urban Aid programme has acted as an inducement to many local authorities and Department of the Environment schemes fund some centres directly.

Some centres have not sufficient contact with solicitors or have not developed sufficient internal expertise to avoid referring clients with legal problems to another agency. Liaison with other independent groups is good, however, and the necessary assistance can often be found through those contacts.

3. Charities and Pressure Groups

Organisations with charitable status operating in a particular field often acquire knowledge and expertise which can prove extremely valuable to individuals who may be in need of that sort of advice. The housing charity, Shelter, was in at the beginning of the Housing Advice Centre movement and the Child Poverty Action Group has been extremely active in the field

---

[34] But that was not the only reason. The CAC in Nottingham attracted strong criticism when it embarked upon a survey of the level of professional fees. The criticism came from the professions, not the consumers.

[35] See below p. 355.

[36] These centres are considered further in R. Cranston, *Consumers and the Law* (2nd ed., 1984); B. Harvey, *The Law of Consumer Protection and Fair Trading* (2nd ed., 1982) pp. 45–6.

[37] See below p. 332.

[38] *Report of the Committee on Local Authority and Allied Personal Social Services*, Cmnd. 3703 (1968).

[39] The bodies concerned were Shelter and the Catholic Housing Aid Society.

of welfare rights.[40] DIAL (the Disablement Information Alliance) gives a great deal of assistance to the disabled and Gingerbread, the charity concerned with one-parent families, does much educative and advisory work.

The Claimants Union has been active in the field of social security and welfare benefits and, in some areas of the country, offers advice and representation at tribunals to those in need.

D. SPECIALIST AGENCIES OFFERING LEGAL ADVICE TO MEMBERS

One of the benefits of membership of some organisations is that specialist legal advice is made available, normally connected with the main business of the organisation. This may be done through the employment of lawyers within the organisation or by the engagement of lawyers in private practice at the expense of the organisation. It is not proposed to list all the groups providing this sort of service, merely to select three examples.

1. THE TRADE UNIONS[41]

Legal services provided through a trade union have been, and remain, a significant factor in the recruitment and retention of members. It appears that most, if not all, trade unions offer some form of legal advice service to members although it is likely to be restricted to those matters which touch directly on employment.[42] The unions have been heavily involved in the development of industrial injuries law; common law claims arising out of accidents at work; employment law; and health and safety standards. Additionally, they provide representation at Social Security Appeal Tribunals and at Industrial Tribunals.

This has placed trade unions in something of a dilemma. Whilst their representatives might wish to see a general extension of legal services in the public sector, they would not wish the value of their own legal services to members to diminish. The TUC evidence to the Royal Commission appeared to place greater emphasis upon the preservation of the union role in advice-giving than on a general expansion of legal services.[43]

The unions provide advice in a variety of ways, some using legal staff engaged for the purpose and others relying on the general full-time officials supported by recourse to the private practitioner.[44]

[40] Especially in publications, notably the *National Welfare Benefits Handbook*, and in the establishment of the Citizens' Rights Office handling telephone enquiries from all over the country.

[41] See generally, G. Latta and R. Lewis, "Trade Union Legal Services" (1974) XII *British Journal of Industrial Relations* 561, R. Lewis and G. Latta, "Union Legal Services" (1973) 123 N.L.J. 386; M. Zander, *Legal Services for the Community*, pp. 305–308; R. Lewis, "Legal Services in the Trade Unions," in, *Advice Services in Welfare Rights* (ed. Brooke), Fabian research series 329 (1976). Much of the work is based on the survey conducted by Lewis and Latta at the L.S.E.

[42] Taken from the results of a 1976 questionnaire sent out by the T.U.C. and forming the basis of evidence to the Royal Commission. Of 55 unions who replied, *all* provided advice on employment but only 9 provided general legal advice to members.

[43] For a critical analysis of the T.U.C. position, see G. Bindman, "Trade Unions and Legal Services," *LAG Bulletin*, March 1979, p. 56.

[44] Mr. Arthur Scargill claimed his legal expenses from the N.U.M. in a recent road traffic case which involved the use of solicitor and counsel.

The professional associations will normally offer a legal advice service in exactly the same way as trade unions and in the medical profession a specific group has been established to assist members who get into particular difficulties.[45]

2. THE MOTORING ORGANISATIONS

The Automobile Association and the Royal Automobile Club provide a variety of benefits for their members which includes legal advice. Naturally, this is confined to motoring but can include the cost of representation in summary proceedings as well as advice on claims and general motoring law.

The benefits offered by the AA are not as substantial as they may, at first sight, appear since the free legal representation scheme may be withheld altogether at the discretion of the Association; advice on claims arising out of accidents is available to all members but the AA will not negotiate in respect of defence claims made against members; the Association cannot give advice or act where the Association or a wholly-owned associate may be involved.[46] Notwithstanding these limitations, members must be reassured by such a scheme and it must be an aid to recruitment.

3. THE CONSUMERS' ASSOCIATION

The CA began in 1957 as a small group publishing a magazine with the results of the comparative testing of aspirins and kettles and has since then become a multi-million pound operation with influence over manufacturers and retailers as well as those responsible for the formulation of consumer policy.

The information function is performed through the magazine *Which?* available to subscribers but having a general impact because of its availability in libraries and the extent to which it is referred to and talked about. In addition to the basic monthly magazine there are a number of supplements on specialist subjects.[47] The value of the information lies in its comparative nature and in the reputation for thoroughness which the CA has acquired. Unfavourable mention in *Which?* is regarded as a major problem for well-known manufacturers.[48]

On the legal advice side, the CA is responsible for six advice centres[49] specialising in consumer problems and also operates a legal service for individual members on payment of a separate subscription. Legal advice, in the form of answers to readers' questions, is also contained in the magazines, and there are statements of law in other CA publications.[50]

---

[45] The Medical Defence Union.

[46] *Automobile Association Members' Handbook* 1982/83, p. 20.

[47] e.g. *Money Which?*; *Motoring Which?*

[48] As exemplified by the critical report of the B.L. Metro in the July 1981 *Motoring Which?* and the responses of the manufacturer and users, *Sunday Times*, June 28, 1981, *The Times*, June 29, 1981.

[49] The first consumer advice centre was opened by the CA in conjunction with a Citizens' Advice Bureau.

[50] *The Good Food Guide* attempts to set out the law about eating in a restaurant.

E. LAW CENTRES[51]

One of the most significant developments in the provision of legal advice and assistance over the last 15 years has been the emergence of the law centres. Drawing some inspiration from the American system of neighbourhood law firms but adapting themselves to local conditions and the rules of the legal profession in this country, the law centres now provide a local base for the dissemination of legal services outside the private profession.

1. THE BEGINNINGS

Some provision was made for the giving of legal advice by salaried solicitors outside the ambit of private practice in the Legal Aid and Advice Act 1949, but the part of the Act which would have established full-time paid solicitors located at the Legal Aid Area Headquarters and travelling to smaller places was never brought into force.[52] An alternative scheme for the provision of advice was proposed and adopted after 10 years of pressure had failed to get the original scheme implemented.[53]

The real origins of the law centre movement are usually attributed to the publication of pamphlets by the lawyers of the Conservative and Labour parties and the individual initiative of pioneers who became impatient at the slowness of the official bodies to respond to the pressure for change. *Justice for All*[54] analysed the unmet need for professional legal services and proposed the establishment of local legal centres in places of deprivation, to be staffed by salaried lawyers and to exist with and be supplemental to the private profession. It was suggested that the type of work undertaken by the centres should be restricted but that they should be free of those rules of professional etiquette (*e.g.* advertising and touting for business) which would inhibit their work.[55] It is not, perhaps, surprising that the solution of the Conservative lawyers in their pamphlet, *Rough Justice*,[56] to the same problem of unmet legal need was the introduction of subsidies for practitioners operating privately in deprived areas and an extension of the assistance given by lawyers to voluntary advice agencies. However, they were prepared to countenance the appointment of salaried lawyers as a last resort.

---

[51] For a comprehensive survey of the origins, development and current scope of the law centre movement, see M. Zander, *Legal Services for the Community*, Chaps. 2 and 3. R.C.L.S., Vol. 1, Chap. 8.

[52] s.7 contains the appropriate provisions. The significance of the failure to implement the proposals should not be underestimated. This part of the scheme was, " . . . an essential part of the total Scheme without which it would lack the necessary impact." The failure to implement it, " . . . was a fatal mistake from which the inevitable consequences are now being reaped": *Legal Aid and Advice, Report of The Law Society* 1973–74 (24th Report), Special Appendix 18, "Legal aid at the cross-roads."

[53] The "statutory" and the "voluntary" scheme introduced in 1959, see below, p. 339.

[54] A report of the Society of Labour Lawyers, Fabian research series 273 (1968). Quite apart from the well-argued and well-documented proposals the report contains references to most of the written material then available about law centres and a helpful description of the American experience.

[55] *Ibid*. pp. 61–62.

[56] Society of Conservative Lawyers, *Rough Justice* (1968).

The Law Society was striking various poses in 1968 and 1969,[57] but from apparently implacable opposition to the original scheme of salaried solicitors contemplated in the 1949 Act (to depart from the alternative system adopted in 1959 would be "a serious mistake")[58] and the proposals of *Justice for All*[59] it moved to acceptance of salaried solicitors as part of its own proposals for an Advisory Liaison Service,[60] in a memorandum published in 1969.

The Advisory Liaison Service would have the following duties:

"(a) To provide the kind of help that hitherto honorary solicitors have rendered to the Citizens' Advice Bureaux, but placing this on a basis which will enable the Bureaux to look to the Service as of right rather than on the basis of charity, and to extend a similar service to other social agencies in the district concerned;

(b) To establish a close liaison between the local profession and the Citizens' Advice Bureaux and other social services, to see that cases of need are placed in the hands of a solicitor promptly and, where appropriate, with a sufficient note of the nature of the problem to enable the solicitor to take the matter up without delay;

(c) To provide oral advice for the public in cases that can be readily disposed of and where reference to a solicitor in private practice would be unnecessarily cumbersome;

(d) To maintain, where this is found to be required, permanent advisory centres in particular districts to give advice and to perform services similar to those falling within the category of advice and assistance, such as correspondence, the preparation of application forms for legal aid, taking statements, and many other similar functions not involving proceedings or representation in court;

(e) To set up permanent local centres similar to those maintained during the early days of legal aid (which dealt with the special problem of divorce) but adapted to the general needs of the district including, if necessary, representation in magistrates' courts and county courts and the conduct of litigation so far as this cannot be absorbed by solicitors' firms."[61]

When the Legal Advice and Assistance Act 1972 was passed, Part II of the Act contained provisions which appeared to be designed to give The Law Society power to carry out the proposals contained in the 1969 memorandum. The Lord Chancellor's Legal Aid Advisory Committee had already indicated that The Law Society should be given these powers,[62] but it, and The Law Society, had been frustrated[63] by the failure of successive

---

[57] These are fully explored and possible explanations offered in M. Zander, *Legal Services for the Community*, pp. 64–76.

[58] *Legal Advice and Assistance*, Memorandum of the Council of The Law Society, February 1968, para. 21.

[59] (1968) 65 L.S. Gaz. 655: Inaugural address of Mr. H. E. Sargant.

[60] *Legal Advice and Assistance*, Memorandum of the Council of the Law Society, July 1969.

[61] *Ibid.* p. 9.

[62] *Report of the Advisory Committee on the better provision of Legal Advice and Assistance*, (Cmnd. 4249, 1970).

[63] See, *e.g.* 23rd and 24th Annual Reports on Legal Aid, 1972–73 and 1973–74.

governments to bring this part of the Act into force.[64] The Law Society has had minimal involvement in projects connected with the Advisory Liaison Service and the whole scheme must be taken to have been subsumed in the proposals of the Royal Commission.

2. DEVELOPMENT

Impatient of the slow progress made through the "official channels" local lawyers and community workers set up a law centre in North Kensington in 1970. After a lapse of three years a variety of centres emerged in 1973/74 and by October 1982 there were 38 centres around the country.[65]

The struggle for most of the centres has been for funds. There are a variety of sources ranging from the Urban Programme of the Department of the Environment[66] to charities[67] but there is much uncertainty about funding and the government has had to come to the rescue on more than one occasion. Of course, law centres earn money through taking on work financed under the statutory legal advice scheme.

The other problem which has affected some law centres has been the necessity to obtain exemption (a "waiver") from the professional rules of etiquette which are imposed by The Law Society. The particular rules in question relate to advertising and touting and became the focus for the antagonism which some of the established members of the profession displayed towards the new centres. After much acrimony[68] an agreement was reached in 1977 about the conditions under which The Law Society would grant waivers to law centres[69] and it is no longer a source of difficulty. The objective of the operation of the power to grant waivers is to produce harmonious relations between all lawyers and to ensure that the roles of the "public" and "private" sectors of the profession continue broadly to complement one another.

3. WORK

As there are many centres, so there are many different ways of operating, but in a survey conducted for the Royal Commission[70] an extract from a document prepared by the Legal Action Group was found helpful, not only

[64] It would appear that it was always the intention of the government of the day to assess the impact of the other provisions of the 1972 Act, before deciding whether to implement Part II. Indeed, the development of law centres which was then taking place outside the legal aid and advice scheme made this a wise course which was commended by the Legal Action Group, see *LAG Bulletin*, December 1972, p. 2.

[65] As at October 1982, *31st Legal Aid Annual Reports* [1980–81], pp. 128–129. The stages of development are chartered by M. Zander and P. Russell, "Law Centres Survey" (1976) 73 L.S. Gaz 208; R.C.L.S., Vol. 2, Part B, Section 3. The National Consumer Council give the number as 42 in April 1983: *Information and Advice Services in the U.K.* (1983).

[66] *e.g.* The two new projects in Lambeth and approved projected centres in Hounslow, North Manchester, Sandwell and South Islington. For a breakdown of the sources of funding see R.C.L.S., Vol. 2, Part B, Section 3.17. Table 3.4.

[67] The North Kensington Law Centre started on funds from the City Parochial Foundation and the Pilgrim Trust.

[68] M. Zander, "Waivers—the end of a long story?" (1977) 127 N.L.J. 1236, and *Legal Services for the Community*, pp. 89–93.

[69] Contained in a note, printed in full in (1977) 74 L.S. Gaz. 698.

[70] R.C.L.S., Vol. 2, Part B, Section 3.1.

for the description of law centres, but also for the distinction it drew between their function and that of *legal advice centres*.

"Legal advice centres are staffed by volunteer lawyers (solicitors, barristers and articled clerks) and have limited opening hours. The centres are essentially for advice and usually offer only a limited amount, if any, of further assistance. There is no charge for the service . . . . The telephone, where there is one, may be staffed only during advice sessions . . . .

Law centres employ full-time staff, including lawyers, and will handle a client's case from beginning to end, including representation in court or at a tribunal. The service is free unless the centre explains otherwise. Law centres vary in the services that they provide for individual clients.

(a) They are all restricted to acting for clients living (or sometimes working) within a limited geographical area round the centre.

(b) They all operate on a very broad restriction against acting for clients who can afford to pay solicitors' fees.

(c) They are restricted in the kind of work they undertake. This varies from centre to centre but most specialise in landlord/tenant, juvenile crimes and care cases, employment and welfare benefits.

(d) Some centres concentrate on group work and do little individual case work.

All centres may be prepared to give preliminary advice to clients falling outside these categories . . . ."[71]

It is important to point out the major differences between the work of law centres and that of the private profession. The subject-matter of the problems dealt with by a law centre will tend to reflect local community conditions and housing, employment, social security and consumer problems are likely to be predominant. These problems may be sought out by a law centre with a view to running "campaigns" to benefit all those in the local community who may be in similar difficulties. It is in the nature of a law centre that the test case strategy will be utilised more extensively because the perception of community need will be greater and because limited resources may best be deployed through group work.[72]

The division of work between the private profession and the law centre is not based entirely on the choice of clients in deciding which problems to bring in to the law centre. The waiver agreement requires that a law centre should not normally deal in particular matters, save in an emergency or for the provision of initial advice, or for other carefully circumscribed reasons.[73] Conveyancing, divorce, probate and criminal matters concerning adults are all in this category. Thus, the profession is protected against competition from law centres in these matters but is not required to refrain

---

[71] LAG directory of legal advice and law centres.

[72] *Community Need and Law Centre Practice*, Adamdown Community Trust (1978).

[73] (1977) 74 L.S. Gaz. 698, para. 9. The expressed object is to ensure that law centres do not duplicate the services provided by solicitors in private practice.

from dealing in those matters which "normally" go to law centres. This overlap raises difficulty about the extent to which a client should be expected to contribute to the cost of the services he is receiving.

Traditionally, the law centres have not levied any charges on those using the service. This means that there is financial discrimination operating between those clients who use a law centre and those who may go to a solicitor with the same problem and who will then have to pay his fees or a contribution towards the cost under the Legal Aid or Legal Advice schemes.[74] Should the law centres operate a means test? Or should certain classes of work be reserved exclusively for law centres? Or should we continue to accept the anomaly?[75] The Royal Commission, in recommending the establishment of Citizens' Law Centres, took the view that, "Those who obtain legal services in law centres should be expected to make the same financial contributions as they would have made had they sought similar services from a solicitor in private practice."[76]

4. THE FUTURE

The recommendations of the Royal Commission are considered fully in a later section, but since their implementation is uncertain it is clear that law centres will continue to play a significant part in the provision of legal advice in the immediate future. There are contrasting indications about the future well-being of the centres. Some have run into considerable financial and political difficulty. The long and bitter dispute in Hillingdon which culminated in the closure of the centre in April 1979[77] and the closure of the three Wandsworth law centres in January 1980[78] reflects the problems faced by law centres. Others have had to rely on the initiative of the Government in injecting funds to keep them going.

Against that there is the evidence of new law centres opening and continued expressions of support from successive Lord Chancellors and their Legal Aid Advisory Committee. Few could doubt Zander's conclusion in 1978 that, " . . . publicly funded legal services are now fully established as a proper part of the system for providing legal services."[79]

F. SOLICITORS IN PRIVATE PRACTICE

For all the varieties of advice agency that have flourished in the past decade it is still the established legal profession who are the major purveyors of legal advice. The role of the private practitioner has, however, been called

[74] Unless, on the operation of the means test, a nil contribution is calculated. See below, pp. 344–347, 389–392.

[75] For a full discussion of the various possibilities, see M. Zander, *Legal Services for the Community*, pp. 94–100.

[76] R.C.L.S., Vol. 1, p. 84.

[77] "The Lessons of Hillingdon", *LAG Bulletin*, November 1978, p. 250 and August 1979, p. 176.

[78] "Wandsworth Law Centre," *LAG Bulletin*, August 1979, p. 177 and January 1980, p. 4. It is interesting that in both Hillingdon and Wandsworth, "Legal Resource Centres" were established by those who wished to continue the provision of legal advice on a voluntary basis.

[79] *Legal Services for the Community*, p. 86. The government response to the Royal Commission Report merely indicates that the recommendations are still under consideration, Cmnd. 9077 (1983), p. 8; and see p. 358, below.

into question in respect of two of the requirements of an advice agency discussed at the beginning of this chapter, namely the cost and availability of the service.

Evidence that the cost of a solicitor's advice (together with fear about cost) and the relative inaccessibility of many offices combined to deter large sections of the community from using a solicitor led to speculation about the degree of "unmet legal need" which exists.[80] It was that speculation and accompanying doubts about the ability of the private practitioner to meet this need which led to the rapid growth of interest in alternative means of providing legal advice. Other agencies have already been described—we are now concerned with the response of the private profession to these problems of cost and access.

If a client is able to pay the bill he can get advice from a solicitor as often as he desires and on whatever topic he chooses. If he cannot pay the bill he must rely on the services provided voluntarily by solicitors and barristers; or a law centre; or bring himself within the statutory advice scheme; or use another agency; or do without.

1. VOLUNTARY SCHEMES

It is unnecessary to go too far back in history to discover the origins of some of the voluntary schemes for the provision of legal advice which now exist. Lawyers have traditionally been generous with their time and talents, more so than any other profession except, perhaps, medicine, and they are accustomed to rendering assistance to those who are genuinely unable to afford professional fees. This help took the form of the poor persons' procedure in litigation[81] but it was realised that procedures were no good unless those who might need them were aware of them. From the beginning of this century there was a growing awareness of the need for legal advice.[82]

However, in 1944 the Rushcliffe Committee[83] were still able to conclude that, "There is no organised provision for legal advice throughout the country . . . ." Amongst the disorganised provision were to be found examples of clients who would never be charged by solicitors; advice-giving by Stipendiary Magistrates, Magistrates' clerks, and County Court registrars; a Poor Man's Lawyer service in London and the provinces staffed by volunteers; trade union legal advice and Citizens' Advice Bureaux.[84]

Of these the Poor Man's Lawyer scheme involved the greatest number of solicitors and barristers, having begun at Toynbee Hall in 1893 and spread from there. Cambridge House Legal Advice Centre and Mary Ward Settlement Centre flourished on either side of the Thames. These are the direct forerunners of the legal advice centres now to be referred to and all such centres relied exclusively on volunteer professional legal personnel.

---

[80] The best examination of this problem is to be found in *Legal Problems and the Citizen*, B. Abel-Smith, M. Zander and R. Brooke (1973). See also a memorandum of The Law Society, "Unmet Need" (1976) 73 L.S. Gaz. 1061.

[81] Below, p. 388.

[82] See the description in B. Abel-Smith and R. Stevens, *Lawyers and the Courts*, pp. 148–9.

[83] *Report of the Committee on Legal Aid and Advice* (Cmd. 6641, 1945).

[84] *Ibid* pp. 17–21.

(a) Legal advice centres

These have already been compared and contrasted with law centres earlier in this chapter[85] and it was noted then that they are staffed by volunteer lawyers; have limited opening hours; offer only advice; and make no charge for the service provided. There are about 130 such centres and, although most of them are relatively new and situated in London,[86] they can attribute their origins to the individual legal and charitable initiatives of members of the profession.[87]

They operate to give advice and to act as a referral agency for the private profession. It may be that the development of rota schemes within CABx and the increasing use of law centres will diminish the significance of this form of provision of legal advice, but their ultimate role in the national provision of legal services may depend upon the acceptance of the recommendation of the Royal Commission that Citizens' Law Centres should be established.[88]

(b) Rota schemes

The CAB service has taken the initiative in setting up a system of advisory sessions in which local solicitors, operating on a rota, give free legal advice to clients who have been "booked in" to a special session by a local CAB. These sessions are particularly appropriate where the bureau worker is of the opinion that the problem can be dealt with in one interview with a solicitor, but it is permissible for the solicitor taking the session to accept the interviewee as his own client if further advice is needed.[89] More and more Bureaux are establishing this arrangement with the consent and encouragement of The Law Society and the goodwill of very many members of the profession.

The importance of the rota scheme should not be underestimated. It ensures that the solicitor only sees those clients who have been identified by a volunteer worker as being in need of professional advice; it provides a free initial interview to encourage those who may be worried about cost; and it permits the solicitor to take on those clients who may need more extensive legal assistance. The drawback, inevitably, is that everything is dependant upon the existence of a CAB in the area, its willingness to set up the scheme, and the co-operation of the local profession.

The development of the scheme ought to be assured since it was commended by the Royal Commission,[90] is greatly valued by NACAB[91] and has the support of The Law Society. There are currently some 441 schemes in operation throughout the country.[92]

---

[85] Above, p. 335.

[86] R.C.L.S., Vol. 1, p. 76; LAG Report, *Legal Advice Centres—an explosion* (1972), referred to in *LAG Bulletin*, October 1972, p. 11.

[87] The assistance and advice provided through Toynbee Hall, the Mary Ward Settlement and Cambridge House, three London charities, was the model for much of what followed.

[88] R.C.L.S. Vol. 1, pp. 83–90, and below, p. 355.

[89] This requires a waiver from The Law Society in respect of the Solicitors' Practice Rules, rule 1. This waiver has been given quite readily subject to conditions being satisfied relating to the organisation of the rota scheme—see The Law Society, *A Guide to the Professional conduct of solicitors* (1974), pp. 85–86.

[90] R.C.L.S., Vol. 1, p. 73.

[91] NACAB Annual Report 1981–82, p. 8.

[92] This figure includes both bureaux and extensions.

(c) General

There is some evidence that solicitors also provide a form of gratuitous legal advice by waiving their charges in respect of a short initial consultation which does not require action on their part or a further interview. This is partly philanthropic and partly economic—it may cost more to process the bill and collect the money than to write off the charge! Needless to say, this service is not advertised but nonetheless appreciated.

2. THE GREEN FORM SCHEME

We have already noted that the Legal Aid and Advice Act 1949 made provision for the establishment of a statutory system of legal advice, but that the appropriate part of the Act was never brought into force.[93] After 10 years of effort to get some form of advice scheme started The Law Society settled for the introduction, in 1959, of two schemes designed to alleviate the growing problem.[94] Both relied heavily upon the goodwill of the private profession because the payment involved was minimal. The Statutory Advice Scheme (the "pink form" scheme) was means-tested with the top limit for eligibility set very low, involved an initial payment of half-a-crown by the client and permitted the solicitor to claim £1 per half-hour from The Law Society up to a maximum of £3. The scheme was not greatly used and was complemented by a Voluntary Advice Scheme under which solicitors would give up to half-hour's advice for a flat fee of £1 paid by the client irrespective of means. In the statutory and voluntary schemes we see the ideas behind the modern provision of advice and, also, behind the Royal Commission's recommendation of a fixed fee for an initial short interview.[95]

The current "green form" scheme came into existence with the passing of the Legal Advice and Assistance Act 1972.[96]

(a) Administration

As the Legal Aid scheme was given to The Law Society to administer in 1949 and it had also been responsible for the voluntary and statutory schemes in 1959 it was quite logical that The Law Society should also run the new advice scheme and that it should use the local and regional structure which already existed to administer the legal aid scheme. Indeed, the basis of the new scheme had been proposed by The Law Society itself in a memorandum published in 1968.[97]

However, it is notable that the individual practitioner has far more discretion in legal advice than legal aid, and he need only refer to the Area Secretary where he requires an extension to the financial limit placed on the amount of advice which can be given.[98] He also has power to refuse for reasonable cause to accept an application or to decline to give advice.[99]

---

[93] Above, p. 332.

[94] See generally S. Pollock, *Legal Aid—the first 25 years* (1975), pp. 79–81.

[95] R.C.L.S., Vol. 1, p. 45, 134–135.

[96] Now consolidated in the Legal Aid Act 1974.

[97] *Legal Advice and Assistance* (1968).

[98] Legal Aid Act 1974, s.3(1); Legal Advice and Assistance (No. 2) Regulations 1980 (S.I. 1980 No. 1898), reg. 15.

[99] *Ibid.* reg. 12.

(b) Scope

The object of the green form scheme is to make readily available a cheap and effective source of legal advice for those who would otherwise be unable to afford it. To that end, a solicitor may give oral or written advice on the application of English law to any particular circumstances in relation to the person seeking the advice, and on any steps which he might appropriately take.[1] If necessary, the solicitor may seek the advice of counsel[2] but this may be difficult because of the financial limits imposed.

It will be observed that although the range of matters which fall within the scheme is very wide, the solicitor is limited to the giving of advice and that the provision does not appear to include representation. Since legal aid is also unavailable for representation at the vast majority of tribunals,[3] the scheme was immediately criticised for leaving out of its scope those who needed the services of an advocate at a tribunal. This was alleged to be a very serious omission, and a great handicap to the efficacy of the scheme.

In fact, various techniques and a belated statutory intervention have combined to lessen the effect of the omission. It is, of course, possible for a solicitor's written advice to include a "brief" for the client to read out at a tribunal hearing. Alternatively, the solicitor may accompany his client to the hearing and advise him orally as a McKenzie man[4] in the course of the hearing. This can be very tiresome for the tribunal with the constant interruptions and the solicitor may end up as advocate. Provided that the solicitor does not claim more than the rate for "travelling and waiting"[5] with his client and that the tribunal does not object to the "representation" of the client, the solicitor can in practice act as advocate for his client and get paid. Finally, the Legal Aid Act 1979 made special provision for "assistance by way of representation" in certain situations and this development considered further below.[6]

It is fair to say that there are two views about the desirability of representation by solicitors at tribunals and the use of the green form scheme to achieve it. The Law Society were in no doubt in 1974 that, " . . . no effective expansion into the field of administrative and welfare law can be achieved in the absence of representation in tribunals dealing with matters likely to affect those eligible for legal aid and, in particular, the very poor,"[7] and their view was supported by the Lord Chancellor's

---

[1] Legal Aid Act 1974, s.2(1).

[2] *Ibid.* This would involve seeking an extension to the financial limit, see below p. 341.

[3] Below, p. 389.

[4] A "McKenzie man" is an adviser who accompanies a party to proceedings before a court or tribunal and gives advice on the conduct of the case. He is so called as a result of *McKenzie* v. *McKenzie* [1971] Ch. 33 where an Australian barrister (not called McKenzie) was held to have been wrongly excluded from the hearing of the action. The Court of Appeal adopted the words of Lord Tenterden C.J. in *Collier* v. *Hicks* (1831) 2 B.A. 663 at p. 669: "Any person, whether he be a professional man or not, may attend as a friend of either party, may take notes, may quietly make suggestions, and give advice; but no one can demand to take part in the proceedings as an advocate, contrary to the regulations of the court as settled by the discretion of the justices."

[5] Which is lower than the rate allowed on legal advice for representation. (Representation, £32 per hour: travelling and waiting, £17 per hour: (1984) 81 L.S.Gaz. 1194).

[6] At p. 342.

[7] *24th Legal Aid Annual Reports* [1973–74], p. 7.

Advisory Committee.[8] However, it has been equally strongly argued that to allow lawyers into tribunals would ruin all those advantages which tribunals are said to have over courts. *If* representation is to be extended it seems likely to be under the green form scheme.[9]

The other limitation placed upon the scheme is the amount of advice which a solicitor is permitted to give without reference to the Area Secretary. From March 1973 (when the scheme started) until October 1980 this figure stood at £25 worth of advice.[10] The figure is remarkable for several reasons. First, it appears absurdly low. Secondly, it remained unchanged for so long. Thirdly, that despite the low figure there were relatively few applications for an extension.[11] How can these observations be reconciled?

Much attention was devoted to the number of cases in which solicitors were forced to apply for an extension and the additional (unnecessary) work thereby created for Legal Aid Area Offices. In the report for 1979–80 The Law Society observed that, " . . . it was a matter for great regret that the £25 initial limit . . . was not altered during the year . . . In many cases a solicitor had to apply for an increase in the £25 limit immediately after the first interview."[12]

In the event the initial limit was raised to £40 in October 1980 and raised again to £50 in November 1983.[13] The limit in respect of advice in relation to undefended divorce proceedings had been raised to £45 in April 1977 when legal aid ceased to be available for such proceedings and that figure was raised to £55 in August 1979. It is currently £75.[14] The Law Society has expressed the hope that the limits will be regularly adjusted for inflation in the future," . . . to avoid the administrative waste and other serious consequences of too low an initial limit."[15]

(c) Eligibility

Would-be recipients of advice under the green form scheme must demonstrate their eligibility by complying with a means test. The result of

---

[8] *Ibid.* p. 47–55 where the LCAC discuss the subject fully. Further reference was made to the desirability of representation in the *27th Report* [1976–77] at pp. 116–7 and the *30th Report* [1979–1980] at p. 97, and the topic is fully discussed in the *33rd Report* [1982–83] at pp. 194–209. See also pp. 563–575, below.

[9] Both the 27th and 30th Legal Aid Reports (above) advocate the extension of the green form scheme for this purpose. By the time of the publication of the 30th Report, "assistance by way of representation" had been introduced in respect of domestic proceedings in magistrates' courts. Since then it has been further extended: see p. 342, below.

[10] Legal Advice and Assistance Act 1972, s.3; Legal Aid Act 1974, s.3(2) Hence the alternative nomenclature, £25 scheme.

[11] In 1979–80 there were 438,519 bills paid under the scheme and 52,286 applications for authority to exceed the £25 limit. This is a high number in absolute terms, but less startling as a percentage of cases dealt with under the scheme.

[12] *30th Legal Aid Annual Reports* [1979–80] p. 5. The Law Society was influenced by the fact that applications for extensions had risen by 111 per cent. over 1978–1979, and that solicitors were irritated and inconvenienced, clients were losing goodwill, and legal aid officers were wasting effort since a high percentage of applications were granted.

[13] By the Legal Advice and Assistance (Prospective Cost) (No. 2) Regulations 1983 (S.I. 1983 No. 1785) reg. 2.

[14] This is dealt with by way of an authorised extension of the £50 limit in all such cases to £75.

[15] *30th Legal Aid Annual Reports* [1979–80] p. 6.

the application of the test will establish entitlement to advice free of charge; or entitlement subject to a contribution; or disentitlement. The test is administered by the solicitor who will require information about the *"disposable capital"* and *"disposable income"* of the applicant. Where an applicant is in receipt of supplementary benefit he is automatically entitled to advice without payment of contribution provided that his capital does not exceed the prescribed limits. The financial criteria are altered from time to time by regulations, usually in line with the changes in supplementary benefit rates in November each year.

Where a client has *disposable capital* in excess of the prescribed limit he is not entitled to assistance at all—where he has *disposable income* in excess of the lower limit he is liable to pay a contribution towards the cost of the advice. If he has disposable income in excess of the higher limit he becomes disentitled.[16]

The solicitor calculates entitlement by use of the "Key Card" and the green form itself. The Key Card and the green form are intended to be placed side by side and are reproduced on pages 344–347. The card discloses the financial limits, the range of contributions and the advice given to the solicitor on the completion of the form. One further point to note is that The Law Society may exercise a statutory charge on any money or property recovered or preserved by the client in respect of unpaid fees.[17] Even though there are both specific and general exemptions from this provision[18] it is so important to the client that the solicitor must be at pains to explain its effect very carefully to an applicant for legal advice.

(d) Assistance by way of representation

The Legal Aid Act 1979, section 1 by virtue of an amendment to section 2 of the Legal Aid Act 1974, extended the scope of legal advice and assistance so as to include within the ambit of the scheme, "assistance by way of representation" at certain designated proceedings.

Whilst the new section 2A of the 1974 Act appears to create a very wide power to use the scheme for representation in all manner of courts, tribunals or statutory inquiries,[19] the detailed implementation of the section is left to regulations to be made by the Lord Chancellor. We have seen a cautious approach at the outset. From April 18, 1980 the green form scheme became available for domestic proceedings in magistrates' courts; transferring the cost of representation from civil legal aid to legal advice. The Supplementary Benefits Commission (who carried out the means assessment in legal aid) were released from 50,000 assessments a year, but the overall effect is minimal. Indeed, there is some inconsistency in the provisions since the capital limits for legal advice and legal aid are different

[16] Legal Aid Act 1974, ss.1, 4 as amended by Legal Aid Act 1979, s.3.

[17] Legal Aid Act 1974, s.5(3)(*b*).

[18] Legal Advice and Assistance (No. 2) Regulations 1980 (S.I. 1980 No. 1898) Regs. 25 and 26, and Schedule 5.

[19] The new subsection provides:

"2A—(1) In this part of the Act 'assistance by way of representation' means any assistance given to a person by taking on his behalf any step in the institution or conduct of any proceedings before a court of tribunal, or of any proceedings in connection with a statutory inquiry, whether by representing him in those proceedings or by otherwise taking any steps on his behalf (as distinct from assisting him to take such a step on his own behalf)."

and some applicants may still be forced to apply for legal aid.[20] Since 1980, assistance by way of representation has been made available in Mental Health Review Tribunals; care proceedings in magistrates' courts; applications by parents, guardians or custodians to a magistrates' court for an access order under the Child Care Act 1980; and in prison disciplinary proceedings before a board of visitors where legal representation has been granted.[21]

The potential effect of assistance by way of representation is highly significant but only if it is used for a much wider range of proceedings, especially those for which legal aid is not available. One critic has expressed fears that it may " . . . become a new kind of legal aid on the cheap,"[22] yet others are concerned lest it be thought that the green form is appropriate for anything other than low-cost proceedings. The Law Society concedes that it might, " . . . be suitable for some tribunal proceedings or even some criminal proceedings in magistrates' courts, but remains firmly convinced of the necessity for retaining the certificate [legal aid] procedure for cases which are likely to be lengthy and costly."[23]

At least the powers are there in the statute and are being used in some cases. Assistance by way of representation may become a very useful peg on which to collect piecemeal extensions into areas which appear to be ill-served at any particular time.

A solicitor is required to obtain authority to use the green form scheme in such proceedings.[24] It will usually be granted by the Area Secretary, but where it is refused he must refer it to the general committee.[25] Counsel may be briefed with the approval of the general committee; assistance may be withdrawn in certain circumstances; costs may be awarded out of the legal aid fund to an unassisted party; the statutory charge operates subject to specified exceptions.[26] All these provisions indicate the hybrid nature of assistance by way of representation. Legal advice in form—legal aid in substance.

(e) Duty solicitor schemes[27]

The first duty solicitor scheme was initiated by the Bristol Law Society in 1972 with the objective of discovering whether there were defendants appearing before Bristol Magistrates who were in need of legal advice but not receiving it.[28] Experienced solicitors took turns in seeing defendants in custody and those referred to them by the court so that they could advise

---

[20] *30th Legal Aid Annual Reports* [1979–80] p. 12.

[21] See Legal Advice and Assistance Regulations (No. 2) 1980, (S.I. 1980 No. 1898) as amended.

[22] Lord Gifford, in the debate on the Legal Aid Act 1979 (H.L. Deb. Vol. 398, col. 919).

[23] *30th Legal Aid Annual Reports* [1979–80] p. 12.

[24] The main reason for this may be that the average bill in such cases is likely to be higher than in normal advice cases. In 1982–3 the average cost was £141: *33rd Legal Aid Annual Reports* [1982–83] p. 58.

[25] Legal Advice and Assistance (No. 2) Regulations 1980 (S.I. 1980 No. 1898) regs. 16, 17.

[26] *Ibid.* regs. 18, 21, 24–26 and Schedule 5; Legal Aid Act 1979, s.1(4).

[27] There is a good deal of periodical literature about these schemes, the majority of which is collected in D. Campbell, P. Smith and P.Thomas, *Annotated Bibliography on the Legal Profession and Legal Services*, Chap. 6.4.

[28] The pilot scheme is described in (1972) 69 L.S. Gaz 819.

LA/Rep/6A
GREEN FORM

THE LAW SOCIETY

LEGAL AID

ENGLAND and WALES

SOLICITOR'S REPORT ON LEGAL ADVICE AND ASSISTANCE GIVEN UNDER
THE LEGAL AID ACT 1974

Key Card

PLEASE USE BLOCK CAPITALS

Surname	Forenames	Male/Female	AREA REF No.
Address			

CAPITAL

TOTAL SAVINGS and OTHER CAPITAL

	CLIENT	£
	SPOUSE	£
	TOTAL	£

Ⓐ

INCOME

State whether in receipt of Supplementary Benefit or Family Income Supplement.
YES/NO If the answer is YES ignore the rest of this Section.

Ⓑ

Total weekly Gross Income

Client	£
Spouse	£
TOTAL	£

Allowances and Deductions from Income

Income tax	£
National Health Contributions, etc.	£
Spouse	£

Ⓒ
Ⓓ
Ⓔ

Dependent children and/or other dependants

	Number	
Under 5		£
5 but under 11		£
11 ,, ,, 13		£
13 ,, ,, 16		£
16 ,, ,, 18		£
18 and over		£

Ⓕ

LESS TOTAL DEDUCTIONS ➡ £

TOTAL WEEKLY DISPOSABLE INCOME £

NOTE TO SOLICITORS

With effect from 1st April 1977

Where advice and assistance are being given in respect of divorce or judicial separation proceedings and the work to be carried out includes the preparation of a petition, the solicitor will be entitled to ask for his claim for Costs and Disbursements to be assessed up to an amount referred to in a general authority given by the Area Committee to exceed the prescribed basic sum in such cases.

TO BE COMPLETED AND SIGNED BY CLIENT

I am over the compulsory school-leaving age.

I have/have not previously received help from a solicitor about this matter under the Legal Aid and Advice Schemes.

I am liable to pay a contribution not exceeding .. .. £

Ⓖ

I understand that any money or property which is recovered or preserved for me may be subject to a deduction if my contribution (if any) is less than my Solicitor's charges.

The information on this page is to the best of my knowledge correct and complete. I understand that dishonesty in providing such information may lead to a prosecution.

Date.. Signature..

THE LAW SOCIETY

Please see over for explanatory notes.

Green Form

GREEN FORM KEY CARD
(No. 14)

Effective from 21st November 1983 in respect of income allowances
and from 29th November 1983 in respect of capital allowances

CAPITAL means the amount or value of every resource of a capital nature
In computing Disposable Capital disregard
(i) the value of the main or only dwelling house in which the client resides, and
(ii) the value of household furniture and effects, articles of personal clothing and tools or implements of the client's trade, and
(iii) the subject matter of the advice and assistance.

 Maximum Disposable Capital for Financial Eligibility (effective from 29th November 1983)
£730 client with no dependants.
£930 ,, ,, 1 dependant (whether spouse, child or other relative)
£1050 ,, ,, 2 such dependants
£1110 ,, ,, 3 such dependants
(Add £60 for each additional dependant.)

INCOME means the total income from all sources which the client received or became entitled to during or in respect of the seven days up to and including the date of this application.

Note – a client in receipt of supplementary benefit or family income supplement is entitled to advice and assistance without contribution provided that his disposable capital is within the limits set out in **A** above.

> The capital and weekly income of both husband and wife must be taken into account, unless:
> *(a)* they have a contrary interest;
> *(b)* they live apart; or
> *(c)* it is inequitable or impracticable to aggregate their means.
> If a housewife living with her husband is seeking advice in connection with a matter in which he has a contrary interest, the money which she receives from him for normal household expenses should not be included as part of her own separate income.

In computing Disposable Income deduct:-
(i) Income Tax

(ii) Payments under the Social Security Acts 1975-80

These deductions also apply to the spouse's income if there is aggregation.

(iii) £30.68 in respect of either husband or wife (if living together) whether or not their means are aggregated. Where they are separated or divorced, the allowance will be the actual maintenance paid by the client in respect of the previous 7 days. (Effective from 21st November 1983)

(iv) £13.73 for each child under 11 years of age
£20.55 ,, ,, ,, of 11 but under 16 years of age
£24.75 for each dependant (or child) of 16 and 17 years of age
£32.17 ,, ,, ,, of 18 years of age or over

(Effective from 21st November 1983)

Client's Contributions

Disposable Income	Maximum Contribution	Disposable Income	Maximum Contribution
Not exceeding £49 a week	nil	Not exceeding £75 a week	£26
,, £55 ,,	£5	,, £79 ,,	£30
,, £59 ,,	£9	,, £83 ,,	£35
,, £63 ,,	£13	,, £87 ,,	£39
,, £67 ,,	£17	,, £91 ,,	£43
,, £71 ,,	£22	,, £95 ,,	£48
		,, £99 ,,	£52
		,, £103 ,,	£57

 Where the initial green form limit is £40 (or £50 as from 29th November 1983) client's contribution in excess of this amount can only be called for if a financial extension has been obtained from the general committee.

Note The green form must be signed by the client at the initial interview as soon as his eligibility has been determined except in the case of an authorised postal application.

CLAIM FOR PAYMENT TO ACCOMPANY FORM LA/ACC/8B

Name of Client

Where appropriate did the Court give approval to assistance under Section 2 (4) of the Legal Aid Act 1974 ?   Yes/No.

Has a Legal Aid Order been made ?   Yes/No.

If so, give date..

PLEASE ATTACH ANY AUTHORITIES GIVEN BY THE AREA COMMITTEE

TICK THE APPROPRIATE LETTER TO INDICATE THE NATURE OF THE PROBLEM

A. Divorce or judicial separation (see note on page 1)

B. Other family matters (Specify in Summary)

C. Crime

D. Landlord/tenant/housing

E. H.P. and Debt

F. Employment

G. Accident/injuries

H. Welfare benefits/tribunals

J. Immigration/Nationality

K. Consumer problems

L. Other matters (Specify in Summary)

Has any money or property been recovered? If so, give details.

No. of letters written

No. of telephone calls
Made
Received

Time otherwise spent:
Specify in
Summary

Has a legal aid certificate or order been granted ?
Yes/No.

If not, is one being applied for ? Yes/No.

Certificate or Order No.
if appropriate :

Summary of work done :

PARTICULARS OF COSTS

	£		£
1. Profit costs		Details of disbursements :—	
2. Disbursements (including Counsel's fees)		Counsel's fees (if any)	
3. Add VAT as appropriate		Other disbursements (listed)	
TOTAL CLAIM			
4. Deduct maximum contribution (if any)			
NET CLAIM			

Have you previously made a claim for legal advice and assistance for your client in respect of divorce or judicial separation proceedings or matters connected therewith.   YES/NO   If Yes, how much was allowed £..................

Signed .... Solicitor   Date.................... Solicitor's ref..................

Firm name (in full) ....

Address ....

Date.....................

NOTICE OF PROVISIONAL ASSESSMENT

The Area Committee have assessed your costs in this matter as set out below. In view of the fact that the sum assessed is less than that claimed, you may make written representations to the Committee in support of your claim as originally submitted or on any item in it, if you wish. These representations must be received within 14 days of the date hereof. I have deleted this matter from the consolidated claim form LA/ACC/8B with which it was sent and I should be obliged if you would do the same. If you accept the provisional assessment, please include this matter on your next consolidated claim form as assessed below AND RE-SUBMIT THIS FORM WITH IT.

Area Secretary.

£

1. Profit costs

2. Disbursements

3. Add VAT as appropriate

    TOTAL CLAIM

4. Deduct maximum contribution (if any)

    NET CLAIM

NOTE.--You are advised to keep a copy of this page because if in the same matter your client obtains a L.A. Certificate or Order, you may on taxation of your costs and disbursements be required to produce to the Taxing Officer a copy of this form indicating work done and quantum of payment. You may also require a copy of this page if after submitting your claim for payment you apply to the Area Committee for a financial extension to enable you to give further advice and assistance to your Client.

APRIL 1977

EXPLANATORY NOTES

1. General

Your attention is particularly drawn to the *Legal Advice and Assistance Regulations (No. 2) 1980* ("the regulations") *pp. 89-104 Legal Aid Handbook 1983* and the *Notes for Guidance on Advice and Assistance* issued by the Council of The Law Society which appear in the *Handbook* pp. 179-185.

2. Financial Eligibility

(a) The responsibility for determining eligibility is placed upon the solicitor (*reg. 7*).

(b) *Schedule 2* of the regulations sets out the method of assessment of resources of the client. The only deductions and allowances which can be made are those referred to in *schedule 2*. Built-in deductions have already been made for miscellaneous expenditure such as rent, mortgage repayments and hire-purchase repayments etc.

(c) When considering a client's means it may be useful to have the following points in mind –

   (i) If part of the main dwelling is let and the client lives in the remaining part, although the capital value of the main dwelling house should be left out of account in computing capital, the rent should be included in computing income.

   (ii) Capital means the amount or value of every resource of a capital nature so that capital derived from a bank loan or borrowing facilities should be taken into account.

   (iii) There is no power to disregard income in self-employed cases merely because the client may have incurred unspecified expenses at an earlier date.

3. Solicitor and Client relationship

(a) A solicitor for reasonable cause may either refuse to accept an application for legal advice and assistance or having accepted it, decline to give advice and assistance without giving reasons to the client. He may however be required to give reasons to the general committee.

(b) Once financial eligibility has been established, a client should be told of the amount of the contribution due (if any), and arrangements should be made for payment either outright or by instalments. Any contribution paid should be retained on client's account until the matter for which advice and assistance has been given has been concluded.

(c) When the contribution exceeds the costs payable and VAT, the excess should be returned to the client.

4. Remuneration

(a) No VAT is payable on the client's contribution but VAT is of course, payable upon the solicitors costs whether paid out of the legal aid fund or from the contribution paid by the client.

(b) The initial financial limit of expenditure (at present £40, but as from 29th November 1983 £50, or in the case of an undefended divorce or judicial separation petition case £75) is exclusive of VAT as is any financial extension granted.

(c) The financial limit of £75 in undefended divorce or judicial separation cases is only applicable where a petition has been drafted. It need not however have been filed.

(d) The legal aid fund is only responsible for paying to solicitor and counsel such of their costs as are not covered by the client's contribution (if any) and party and party costs awarded and the charge which arises in the solicitors favour on any property recovered or preserved. *Schedule 5* of the regulations sets out the circumstances when the charge does not apply. Application may be made to the area committee for authority not to enforce the charge where (a) it would cause grave hardship or distress to the client, or (b) it could be enforced only with unreasonable difficulty – *(reg 26.)*

5. Authorities

A solicitor may not take steps in court proceedings unless either approval is given by the general committee for assistance by way of representation in a magistrates' court or the court has made a request under *reg 19* of the regulations. It should be noted that the financial limit prescribed by *section 3(2) of the Legal Aid Act 1974* (at present £40, but as from 29th November 1983 £50) cannot be exceeded when a request has been made under *reg 19* and the solicitor has represented the client.

(a) The authority of the general committee is required before accepting an application from a child *(reg 8(1))*, a person on behalf of a child or patient, such person not falling within the categories referred to in reg 8(2)(a) (b) or (c) *(reg 8(2)(d))*, a person residing outside England and Wales *(reg 9)* and a person who has already received advice and assistance from another solicitor on the same matter *(reg 10)*.

(b) Approval of the general committee is required for assistance by way of representation *(reg 17(1))*. Even if approval is given the prior permission of the general committee is required to obtain a report, or opinion of an expert to tender expert evidence and to perform an act which is either unusual in its nature or involves unusually large expenditure *(reg 17(4).)* Thus the prior permission of the general committee would be required before obtaining a blood test in affiliation proceedings.

NOVEMBER 1983

Printed by Oakley Press Limited

(not represent) an appropriate course of action. This could involve an adjournment for legal aid application, social welfare report, referral to another solicitor, bail application or simply suggestions for a plea in mitigation. All those involved in the Bristol scheme (local Law Society, magistrates, magistrates' clerks and police) expressed themselves to be satisfied with the result and this scheme provided the model for others which have followed.

Since the development of schemes was left to local initiative and was dependent upon the co-operation of the local magistrates' court, national coverage was patchy and the services offered were variable. By mid-1975 there were 29 duty solicitor schemes operating[29] and The Law Society, in consultation with other interested parties, prepared and published a guide for the assistance of local Law Societies.[30] This helpful document lists the functions of a duty solicitor, the scope of the scheme, remuneration,[31] emergency services, waivers[32] and also contains an appendix with the instructions issued to solicitors operating the Marylebone scheme.

These schemes were well received and had extended considerably by the end of the 1970s. Limited statistical returns demonstrate that nearly 50,000 people received advice in this way in 1979–80[33] and the Royal Commission described the schemes as " . . . indispensable in a number of ways: they provide pre-trial advice to defendants who are often confused or ignorant and who have not previously obtained it, they encourage the adequate preparation of bail applications and help to reduce the number of ill-advised pleas, whether of guilt or innocence, and the number of remands required."[34]

The Legal Aid Act 1982[35] enables The Law Society, under scheme-making powers contained in the Legal Aid Act 1974,[36] to formulate a uniform scheme for the provision of duty solicitor services. The 130 schemes which are in existence[37] will be able to establish themselves on a statutory basis providing that they can come under the arrangements for

---

[29] 25th Legal Aid Annual Reports [1974–75] pp. 6–7.

[30] (1975) 72 L.S. Gaz. 577–579. This is an extremely helpful exposition of a model scheme.

[31] Although this general topic is included in the section on the green form scheme, that is not the only way of financing the advice given under the duty solicitor scheme. The establishment of the Bristol pilot scheme occurred before the Legal Advice and Assistance Act 1972 was implemented, but the Act did contain a power to use the green form for representation where it had been so requested by a court of a solicitor within the precincts (s.2(4)). This has now been removed from the legislation by section 1(1)(b) of the Legal Aid Act 1979, but included as regulation 19 of the Legal Advice and Assistance Regulations (No. 2) 1980. The other possibilities for funding are the criminal legal aid scheme or the solicitor himself giving advice free. The Law Society's Guide advises that neither the green form nor criminal legal aid is ideal, but that the former should where possible be used for advice and the latter for representation.

[32] A waiver of Rule 1 of the Solicitors' Practice Rules is required as in law centres and legal advice centres.

[33] Limited in that only 72 out of 127 schemes made returns: 30th Legal Aid Annual Reports [1979–80] p. 18.

[34] R.C.L.S. Vol. 1, p. 93.

[35] s. 1.

[36] s. 15. The duty solicitor scheme will be put on the same basis as the Legal Aid scheme and the Legal Advice scheme.

[37] They are, of course, based upon the busiest magistrates' courts: see 31st Legal Aid Annual Reports [1980–81] Appendix 27.

administration formulated by The Law Society.[38] The advantage of coming under the statutory scheme will be the better standard of remuneration available.[39] In due course, regional duty-solicitor committees will be appointed to identify the courts which require a duty-solicitor and to establish local committees which will organise the local scheme. The scope of the service[40] and selection criteria designed to ensure the competence of duty-solicitors are also contained in the scheme. Those solicitors who participate will be remunerated for the whole of the time spent at court.

(f) Green form usage

It was quite clear in 1973 that the new advice scheme was intended to bring into solicitors' offices problems of a kind which had not hitherto surfaced. The analysis of the unmet need for legal services identified types of problem which were not being dealt with as well as types of people. Since the advice scheme now permitted access to a solicitor on *any* question of English law and the advertising campaign which launched it stressed the "social welfare" problems now within the scheme, it was disappointing that the first evidence of usage showed little deviation from the traditional pattern.[41] The absence of legal aid for tribunal representation was advanced as a reason for the very low percentage of cases concerned with tribunals, as well as the expectation that cases categorised under other headings (*e.g.* "Employment," "Landlord and Tenant") might have included tribunal work.

In fact, the statistics on the type of problems on which advice is sought have remained remarkably constant since 1973/74. Despite some changes in the categorisation of problems from 1977/78 onwards which makes direct comparison slightly unreliable, matrimonial and family matters have always accounted for between 46 per cent. and 61 per cent. of all problems; criminal matters for 10 per cent. to 24 per cent.; tribunals never more than 2·2 per cent. It was inevitable that after the withdrawal of legal aid for undefended divorce in April 1977[42] the green form scheme would be used for matrimonial matters, but the statistics demonstrate that it always has been. The only significant alteration has been in the distribution between family matters and crime with the other categories remaining constant.

---

[38] Set out in S. Hillyard, "The Legal Aid (Duty Solicitor) Scheme 1983" (1983) 80 L.S.Gaz. 2649 and commented upon in *33rd Legal Aid Annual Reports* [1982–83] pp. 157–9. See also S. Hillyard, "Legal Aid (Duty Solicitor) Scheme: Progress Report" (1984) 81 L.S.Gaz. 1184.

[39] Remuneration will be on a time basis and not on a case basis. The current rate is £23.25 per hour.

[40] The scope is narrower than some schemes in existence: committal proceedings and not guilty pleas are excluded, as are defendants charged with imprisonable offences. Legal aid will be available in those cases subject to the usual criteria, see p. 512, below.

[41] *24th Legal Aid Annual Reports* [1973–74] Appendix 4, Part II, 2. The analysis, based on a sample of 10 per cent. of claims for payment under the scheme in 1973/74, showed the following results: Matrimonial, 60·2 per cent; Criminal, 10·2 per cent,; Landlord and Tenant, 4·7 per cent.; Employer (sic) 1·2 per cent.; Hire purchase and Debt, 2·6 per cent.; Wills, 2·3 per cent.; Accidents and Injuries 3·8 per cent.; Affiliation, 3·5 per cent.; Conveyancing 1 per cent.; Tribunals, 1 per cent.; Others, 9·2 per cent. The latest (1982–83) figures display a similar pattern save for a rise to 24 per cent. in criminal matters, and a reduction to 46 per cent. in matrimonial matters: *33rd Legal Aid Annual Reports* [1982–83] p. 57.

[42] Above, p. 341.

It may be that difficulty in getting people with problems to consult a solicitor is more to do with their perception of the problem and the ability of a solicitor to help than with the cost and availability of the advice service. The Law Society is left to reflect that " . . . the types of problem on which advice and assistance was sought during the past year is surprisingly, and perhaps regrettably, consistent with the experience of previous years . . . people who are eligible for advice and assistance are still accustomed to consult solicitors for a comparatively narrow range of problems."[43]

(g) Green form deficiencies

Some would argue that the major deficiency in the green form scheme is that it is administered through solicitors and must, therefore, share the same unattractiveness to some members of the public. The arguments about the location, availability, approachability and cost of the solicitors' offices emerge again in this context. The evidence to support these contentions is equivocal. On the one hand it would appear that only the traditional problems are being brought in (see above), on the other, the fact that 90 per cent. of green form assessments require no contribution from the client despite the strict financial criteria suggests that the scheme is serving the least well-off.[44] Is it that the "right" people are reaching solicitors with the "wrong" problems?

Three other major criticisms of the scheme have been advanced—that the initial limit is too low; that the financial criteria are too strict; that the scheme is not sufficiently well-known to attract those who need it.

We have seen that the initial limit remained at £25 for over seven years[45] despite fears expressed from an early stage that it was inadequate. The criticism mounted—"We believe the £25 limit . . . to be too low" (1978)[46]; "It remains a continuing source of disappointment that this limit has not been altered." (1979)[47]; " . . . it was a matter for great regret that the £25 initial limit . . . was not altered during the year" (1980)[48]. In October 1980 the initial limit was raised to £40 and now stands at £50.[49]

The statistics are interesting. In 1982–83 there were 733,410 claims for payment by solicitors under the green form scheme. There were 147,434 applications for an extension of the £40 (ordinary) or £75 (divorce and judicial separation) limit.[50] It is not possible to correlate the figures exactly since an unknown number of the applications for extension would not be claims for payment until 1983–84, but it is reasonable to assume that one case in five (in the opinion of the solicitor) required an extension. Turned round, that means that four cases out of five could be settled within the limit—is that not good evidence that the limit was adequate?

The persuasive argument is that each extension application costs, at a

---

[43] *30th Legal Aid Annual Reports* [1979–80] p.6.
[44] *33rd Legal Aid Annual Reports* [1982–83] p. 55.
[45] Above, p. 341.
[46] *28th Legal Aid Annual Reports* [1977–78] p. 83.
[47] *29th Legal Aid Annual Reports* [1978–79] p. 9.
[48] *30th Legal Aid Annual Reports* [1979–80] p. 5.
[49] Above, p. 341.
[50] *33rd Legal Aid Annual Reports* [1982–83].

conservative estimate, £10 worth of solicitor's and Area Office time.[51] This is regarded as wasted money because of the *volume* of applications. The limit was changed, then, not to accommodate the majority who could be treated adequately within it, but to save money on the minority who could not be so treated.

The financial criteria are contained on the Key Card reproduced earlier in the chapter[52] and the substantial changes in eligibility introduced in 1979 took away most of the grounds for the criticism that they were pitched too low. However, there are still some inconsistencies, in particular the fact that the capital limit is so much lower than that for legal aid. The Law Society have argued for a greater degree of consistency if not complete standardisation.[53]

The advertising of the scheme and the consequent level of public awareness has been a constant source of concern. Two targets have been identified. One, the general public can really only be reached by direct advertising in the media—the other, the "gate-keepers," those who work in the social field and in advice agencies, need to be approached much more selectively. They are the people who can refer clients on to solicitors and it is highly likely that the "Advisory Liaison Service" and the proposed liaison officers[54] could have played a significant part in making and fostering those contacts. In their absence, the information circulating about the green form scheme can be haphazard depending upon the enthusiasm of voluntary and statutory advice agencies and the activities of local Law Societies. Advertising campaigns have been sporadic and their effect is extremely difficult to assess.[55]

G. THE ROYAL COMMISSION RECOMMENDATIONS

"In the last analysis, therefore, it is for Parliament to decide the extent to which legal services are to be provided at public expense to meet the needs of the majority of the population. But, unless legal services are provided, the full benefit of our legal rights and safeguards cannot be realised."[56]

The preceding parts of the chapter have shown that the present diversity of sources for legal information and advice has resulted from piecemeal development, partly by lawyers, partly by non-lawyers, without any coherent structure or philosophy. There is legal advice from non-lawyers, from salaried lawyers and from the private profession paid for by the client, the State, local government, charities or provided gratuitously—or a combination of them. The Royal Commission had the opportunity (and the obligation) to "inquire into the law and practice relating to the provision of legal services . . . "[57] and the results of that inquiry might have been expected to point to a rationalisation of the system and the provision of a

---

[51] At 1980 costs: *30th Legal Aid Annual Reports* [1979–80] pp. 5–6.
[52] Above, p. 345.
[53] *29th Legal Aid Annual Reports* [1978–79] p.2.
[54] Above, p. 333.
[55] Some have been specific, such as that to launch the £25 scheme, in 1973 and that directed at the North-East, others more general, such as the "Don't Trust Whatsisname" campaign. See above p. 109.
[56] R.C.L.S., Vol. 1, p. 58.
[57] *Ibid.* p. iii.

guiding philosophy. It is not possible to rehearse all the arguments, all the conclusions and all the recommendations of the Commission and we deal with the different aspects of the Report elsewhere. Here we can consider the principles identified by the Commission and the particular recommendations related to the topics in this chapter.

1. Principles[58]

The Commission expounded three principles which are all related to the general principle, said to have been established with the introduction of legal aid in 1950, that " . . . legal services should be available to those who need them but cannot afford to pay for them." Despite the acceptance of this principle the Commission found that a large number of people are not obtaining adequate legal services and set out the principles that should, in future, govern the provision of legal services:

(i) Financial assistance out of public funds should be available for every individual (not corporations) who, without it, would suffer an undue financial burden in properly pursuing or defending his legal rights;

(ii) All those who receive legal services are entitled to expect the same standard of legal service irrespective of their personal circumstances;

(iii) The client, whether supported out of public funds or fee-paying, should always have a free choice among available lawyers and should not be required to retain an assigned lawyer.

The difficulty amongst those principles (which are unexceptionable as the statement of the ideal) is to assess what would amount to an undue financial burden. Naturally, there is no easy answer to this, particularly since the Commission concluded that it should favour an overall scheme in which the client made a contribution (if possible) to the legal costs rather than a completely free service. In expressing the appropriate level of contribution the Commission simply advocated the abolition of an upper limit which would render people ineligible and recommended from everyone above a generous mininum level of income and capital, a contribution which would not constitute an undue financial burden.[59]

In turning these principles into the means by which legal services were to be provided the Commission did not recommend any radical departure from the present "mixed economy" in legal advice and information. There is still a place for amateurs, for salaried professionals and for private professionals, all of them supported in varying degrees by government funds.

2. Proposals

(a) Organisation[60]

The Commission recommended the establishment of a new body, the Council for Legal Services, to take interest in and keep under review the

---

[58] The material for the majority of this section is to be found in R.C.L.S., Vol. 1, pp. 50–54.

[59] *Ibid.* p. 54.

[60] *Ibid.* Chap. 6 generally.

provision of all forms of legal services.[61] Tribute was paid to the Lord Chancellor's Legal Aid Advisory Committee and the respect it had gained in the field, but it was considered necessary to grant a wider remit to a new body. The decision as to whether this body should have executive or advisory functions was difficult and the Commission received conflicting evidence. In the event, the functions of the Council were defined in advisory terms to include review of, and research on, the provision of legal services; preparation of proposals for better provision; implementing or reviewing the implementation by others of proposals accepted by the Lord Chancellor; the doing of such other things as the Lord Chancellor might request.[62] The responsibility of the Council would be to the Lord Chancellor, who, the Commission recommended, should be responsible for all forms of legal aid and legal services.[63]

In addition to this Council, the Commission proposed the establishment of regional committees to represent the public, the professions and others engaged in the provision of legal services to assess the need for legal and para-legal services in the region and to co-ordinate the various agencies within the region.[64] The blueprint for these regional committees is provided by an organisational experiment in Manchester which greatly impressed the Commission.

The Greater Manchester Legal Services Committee was established in April 1977. It consists of various types of lawyer and representatives of voluntary and statutory organisations with the common objective of co-ordinating and improving legal services in Manchester.[65] The progress of the Committee over the past six-years has been charted in the Legal Aid Annual Reports[66] and it now has an impressive lists of achievements. It has stimulated duty solicitor schemes; monitored the grant and refusal of legal aid in magistrates' courts; provided training for volunteer workers at advice agencies; published a leaflet aimed at those who have suffered accidents; and taken on other responsibilities connected with legal services. Most importantly, it has shown what advances are possible given enthusiasm, goodwill and, thanks to the Law Society, a full-time secretary paid for out of the Legal Aid Fund.[67]

The exact constitution of the Manchester committee, the position of its members and its relationship with Lord Chancellor and the Legal Aid Area

[61] Ibid. pp. 62–65.

[62] Ibid. p. 63.

[63] Ibid. p. 110.

[64] Ibid. p. 66.

[65] The original members included members of both branches of the legal profession, the Legal Aid Area Secretary, the Director of the Local Law Centre, the clerk to the Bury Magistrates and representatives of the C.A.B., the Child Poverty Action Group, the probation service, the local Social Services Department, the local trades council and other groups.

[66] 27th Legal Aid Annual Reports [1976–77] pp.6–7, 68; 28th Legal Aid Annual Reports [1977–78] pp. 8–10, 93–4. 29th Legal Aid Annual Reports [1978–79] pp. 79–80. 30th Legal Aid Annual Reports [1979–80] pp. 19–20, 101–2. 32nd Legal Aid Annual Reports [1981–82] p. 121. 33rd Legal Aid Annual Reports [1982–83] p. 175.

[67] The full-time official has undoubtedly played a major part in the success of the experiment. This was a liaison officer appointment authorised by the Lord Chancellor and demonstrates how useful the provisions of the Legal Advice and Assistance Act 1972 (see above, p. 333) could have been if applied nationally.

Committee have not been fully worked out[68] but those problems would no doubt provide the guidance required if the Commission's proposed regional committees were to be set up.[69]

(b) The role of lay persons and professional volunteers

The Commission recognised the value of a generalist advice agency service not only to sift out those matters which required legal assistance, but also to provide a "para-legal service, based on laymen with common sense."[70] The recommendation was that the Citizens' Advice Bureaux service should provide this first-tier service, so long as they had a good knowledge of the specialist services available, used rota schemes, did not become over-specialised and secured adequate funding from government. High standards would need to be maintained and long-term development plans defining the scope of CAB work prepared.

It is inherent in the encouragement of rota schemes that private practitioners should still be asked to give time and expertise voluntarily. The schemes were commended because they gave solicitors the opportunity to become more aware of the range of problems arising in their locality and, in general, the work of lawyers acting voluntarily is a valuable expression of the profession's desire to serve the public.[71]

Legal advice centres did not find a great deal of favour with the Commission mainly because it was thought that the strengthening of CABx and the establishment of citizens' law centres (CLCs) would diminish the need for them. The voluntary work which lawyers currently put into them might be made available to rota schemes or to the CLCs.

(c) Advice and assistance from paid professionals

(i) Salaried Solicitors[72]

The work of law centres was well-established by the time that the Royal Commission was conducting its investigations and it is surprising that the Report did not give greater attention to this development in legal services. Chapter 8, which deals with law centres, has been the subject of much criticism both for its findings and its recommendations.

The continued existence of salaried solicitors within the system of advice-giving was acknowledged by the Commission, who took the view that there are classes of work which are peculiarly appropriate to a salaried service. The impact of law centres was said to be out of all proportion to their size; a great deal of valuable work had been done; the volume of work attracted had shown the depth of need; the desirability of encouraging lawyers to take up work in non-traditional areas of practice had been

---

[68] For a personal view, see "Greater Manchester Legal Services Committee . . . . Modified Rapture" *LAG Bulletin*, June 1979, p. 127.

[69] Note should also be taken of an experiment in Bristol described in "The Bristol Legal Services Agency: A Project that failed," *LAG Bulletin*, March 1980, p. 54. The Manchester committee publishes Annual Reports which are available from the Law Society, 67 King Street, Manchester.

[70] R.C.L.S. Vol. 1, p.71.

[71] *Ibid.* p. 51.

[72] The consideration of this topic is to be found in R.C.L.S., Vol. 1, Chap. 8. It does not, unfortunately, take long to read.

shown. However, in the opinion of the Commission, " . . . the time has come to move forward from a period of experiment to one of consolidation, characterised by continuity, orderly development, adequate resources and proper administrative and financial control."[73]

These were ominous words for existing law centres, which had all been established in response to particular local need and were responsive to local conditions both in the nature of the services provided and in the structure of the centre. The diversity of the centres was illustrated in the survey instituted by the Commission itself.[74]

The outcome of the Commission's deliberations was a recommendation for the establishment of a new species of law centre, "Citizens' Law Centres" (CLCs), financed out of public funds, to supplement the efforts of private practitioners in certain areas. The purposes of the new centres were so expressed as specifically to exclude involvement in general community work such as the mounting of campaigns or political or social activities. Involvement in community work goes beyond the provision of legal advice and assistance and may prejudice the independence of the centre.

The clients of the new centres should pay for legal services on the same basis as legally-aided clients of private practitioners; the centre should be financed and managed by a central agency but advised by a local advisory committee; law centres which do not come under the aegis of the central agency should not receive funds; waivers would have to be negotiated with The Law Society; guidelines for the operation of the centre should be laid down.

The objective of this proposed structure would be to "consolidate" the service whilst retaining the special qualities (dedication, imagination, commitment to local needs, upholding citizens' rights) which have been the hallmark of the established law centres. The administrative arrangements are designed to guarantee independence of both local and central government and to provide for the organised interchange of staff between centres and the private profession.

(ii) The Private Profession

The proposals in respect of the private profession are largely designed to improve the legal aid scheme so as to make it more remunerative for solicitors whilst simplifying the provisions for the benefit of the client and the profession. Even the recommendation that a standard duty solicitor scheme in all magistrates' courts should be instituted and supervised by The Law Society[75] has legal aid implications, since a complementary recommendation was that the work done should be properly remunerated out of the fund and enhanced payment made for work involving special inconvenience.[76]

The other recommendations fall mainly into two categories—financial considerations and administrative arrangements. On the financial side it

[73] R.C.L.S., Vol. 1, p. 81.
[74] *Ibid.* Vol. 2, Part B, Section 3.
[75] *Ibid.* Vol. 1, Chap. 9 generally. On duty solicitor schemes, see above p. 343.
[76] *Ibid.* Vol. 1, p. 96.

was recommended that the green form scheme should be assimilated with legal aid when the levels of eligibility and contribution can be made the same. The Commission saw no substantial reason why there should be separate (and different) financial conditions for the two schemes. In general, the Commission recommended substantial changes in the limits of disposable income and disposable capital to correct the long, downward drift which had taken place up to April 1979.[77]

Hidden under the heading of administrative arrangements are two quite fundamental proposals which would have an immediate effect on the provision of legal advice. Because of the fears of the public about solicitors' costs, it is proposed that an initial half-hour interview with a solicitor should be available to all at no cost whatever their means, provided that the subject-matter is within the scope of the legal advice and assistance scheme.[78] In addition, it is proposed that the initial limit on advice under the green form scheme should be defined in hourly terms rather than financial terms, as at present. A solicitor, it is proposed, should be able to give up to four hours of advice on his own authority without reference to the Area Secretary.[79]

The two proposals are highly significant and would undoubtedly have a stimulating effect of the green form scheme. For the past four years a large number of solicitors have operated a voluntary scheme in conjunction with CABx whereby a client may obtain an initial half-hour interview at a fee of £5. This has been partly superseded by rota schemes but is clearly the basis of the Commission's proposals. There were some fears expressed about possible abuse of such a scheme and there are doubts about how much it would cost, but it was recommended that a carefully monitored pilot scheme be set up as soon as possible to assess the effects.[80]

There are also recommendations in other parts of the Report which, if implemented, would have an effect on the provision of legal services. It is suggested that employed lawyers should be able to undertake conveyancing and give free legal advice to fellow-employees[81]; that interest-free loans should be made available to encourage private practitioners to move to areas of need as defined by the Lord Chancellor[82]; that information about legal services in general, and legal aid in particular, should be much more readily available[83]; and that the information about individual firms of solicitors, provided in referral lists,[84] should be fuller to permit clients to "shop around."[85] These proposals would all in their own way help to improve the provision of legal service—if implemented.

---

[77] *Ibid.* Vol. 1, p. 121, and Chap. 12 generally.

[78] *Ibid.* Vol. 1, pp. 134–135.

[79] *Ibid.* Vol. 1, pp. 135–136.

[80] *Ibid.* Vol. 1, p. 135.

[81] *Ibid.* Vol. 1, p. 235.

[82] *Ibid.* Vol. 1, pp. 181–82, and see above p. 332. This echoes the sentiments of Conservative lawyers expressed in 1968.

[83] *Ibid.* Vol. 1, pp. 362–363.

[84] Referral lists are lists of local solicitors with information about the firm, its members and their specialisms. They are used by CABx and other social agencies to get clients to the right solicitor. For an example, see R.C.L.S. Vol. 1, p. 377.

[85] R.C.L.S., Vol. 1 pp. 363–5.

(d) Tribunals

The Commission referred to the particular problems of advice and representation before tribunals,[86] and it is, of course, pertinent that the details of assistance by way of representation under the Legal Aid Act 1979[87] (which could be extended to cover designated tribunals) came after the Report was published. However, it is worth referring briefly to the Commission's proposals since they take a different line to that which might have been expected.

The involvement of lay agencies in advice and representation before tribunals is greatly encouraged. Resources should be provided and public funds should be made available to assist in the training of staff in approved lay agencies. This development would need to be linked to a simplification in tribunal procedure although it was recognised that there can be complex matters raised in tribunals which necessitate some legal training and skills.

To allow for those cases in which the services of a lawyer really are required the Commission recommended the extension of legal aid to certain tribunal cases. It should be noted that the recommended extension is to *cases*, not tribunals. This will involve application to the Legal Aid Area Committee in the normal way[88] but with additional criteria to be satisfied. These criteria would include the significance of any point of law arising, the complexity of the case, the possibility of deprivation of liberty or loss of occupation, or the nature of the case as a test case. Allied to this provision, the Commission recommended that the Lord Chancellor should from time to time consider advice from the proposed Council for Legal Services[89] and the Council on Tribunals about which tribunals should be designated by him for the purposes of assistance by way of representation under the Legal Aid Act 1979.

This appears to be a very mixed provision. Lay agencies always available, green form assistance for *some* tribunals, legal aid for *some* cases. Would this result in blanket coverage, or total confusion?

3. RESPONSES

The public response to the Royal Commission Report has been largely predictable. Particularly in its treatment of legal services the Report was alleged to be unduly supportive of the private profession and insufficiently imaginative in its proposals for the development of the public sector. The attitudes which had been taken in the presentation of evidence were adopted again after the appearance of the Report and certain criticisms emerge as re-statements of the preferred scheme of the critic.[90]

However, the critical response of four organisations heavily involved in the current provision of legal services cannot be ignored. The Legal Action Group attacked the Report on all fronts,[91] making particularly strong comment about the failure to recommend significant changes in the private profession and the ineffectual role assigned to the proposed Council for

---

[86] R.C.L.S., Vol. 1, chap. 15 generally.
[87] See above p. 342.
[88] See below p. 389.
[89] See above p. 352.
[90] Which does not necessarily diminish their value!
[91] "Legal Services—A new start" LAG (1980).

Legal Services. Only a Legal Service Commission with executive powers could do the necessary research and co-ordination job. The Law Centres Federation,[92] not surprisingly, were entirely hostile to the proposed Citizens' Law Centres and their response was directed mainly to that topic. The Federation was especially opposed to the means-testing of clients and the prospect of central control. Following the pattern, the Greater Manchester Legal Services Committee was also critical of the particular proposals which affect its area of concern and took the view that the regional committees proposed in the Report would not achieve what is required. Despite receiving warm commendation from the Commission, the Committee's response was cool with further criticism of the proposals on law centres and practice in deprived areas. The National Association of Citizens' Advice Bureaux responses[93] were less strident in tone but contain detailed criticisms of many aspects of the Report, again, with particular reference to its own area of operation.

There have been other individual views expressed[94] and the professions have welcomed the majority of the recommendations with more than a hint of relief.

The Government response has been belated and almost insulting.[95] The two volumes of the Commission's Report are dismissed in a very short document which gives little encouragement to reformers. In particular:

(a) the case for the creation of a Council for Legal Services is rejected;

(b) the role of generalist agencies is endorsed, but with no additional funding;

(c) the recommendations on Citizen's Law Centres are still under consideration;

(d) eligibility limits for legal aid are to be retained, and the contributions currently payable are not unreasonable;

(e) the "free half-hour" of advice will not be introduced;

(f) extension to the scheme for assistance by way of representation will be made when necessary.

The debate on the appropriate provision of legal services will continue but the climate is hardly encouraging!

---

[92] *A response to the Royal Commission on Legal Services*, Law Centres Federation (1980).
[93] Memoranda in response to the Report published by NACAB in August 1980 and March 1981.
[94] C. Glasser, "After the Report: Remuneration" *LAG Bulletin*, February 1980, p. 29.
[95] *The Government Response to the Report of the Royal Commission on Legal Services* (Cmnd. 9077, 1983).

PART III

PRE-TRIAL PROCEDURE

CHAPTER 10

THE FEATURES OF LITIGATION

In Part II we looked at advice and information. Now we begin a Part called Pre-trial Procedure and it may appear that we are progressing inexorably towards the courtroom. Yet between the recognition of a dispute which may end in a trial and its actual arrival before the judge lies a lengthy period of negotiation before or during the operation of the formal pre-trial procedure. An understanding of the significance of these negotiations and the resulting settlements is fundamental to civil litigation. We concentrate on civil matters, because there is inevitably less scope for settlement in the criminal process given the limited bargaining power of the defendant.[1] The other two topics we consider in this chapter, costs and delay, do have significance in both civil and criminal litigation.

Influencing both civil and criminal procedure before and at trial, the English *adversarial* approach permits the parties to dictate the issues to be resolved and to settle the pace of the action. In civil cases, the court has no role in directing the course of the proceedings except on the application of one or other party. It may impose penalties on parties who break the rules without permission, by the award of costs against them,[2] but it cannot enforce the rules of its own volition. This is an important consideration when we discuss delays in civil procedure and, in the next chapter, the procedure itself.

Further, the parties select the issues on which to fight and the evidence with which to support their case. Whilst it may be in the interests of the court and a "fair result" for as much as possible to be disclosed in the early stages so that the matters really in dispute can be identified and the strength of the evidence assessed, it will often be in the interests of the parties to conceal what is known. Negotiation can proceed more effectively through a process of bluff[3] and, some would argue, even at trial there are advantages to be gained by surprise. Subject to certain pre-trial procedures designed to elicit information,[4] the parties control what is disclosed, what is admitted and, ultimately, what is litigated.

It is a matter of judgment whether the problems of cost and delay in the law could be alleviated by the more active participation of the court and the diminution of the control of the parties. Further, given that the vast majority of cases end in settlement one may ask whether we ought not to direct our civil procedure primarily towards settlements with incidental

---

[1] There is some similarity between settlements and "plea-bargaining" in criminal trials, but this latter topic is considered separately at p. 625 below.

[2] See below, p. 364.

[3] The analogy is usually with card games, particularly poker. This takes into account the gamble involved and that the parties do not disclose their hands. The "game" analogy persists throughout the civil and criminal process with sides, winners and losers, prizes or penalties, results, etc.

[4] Applications for Discovery of Documents and the administering of Interrogatories, see below, p. 435.

provision for cases that go to trial. In looking at the procedures which are set out in the next chapter, you may assess the extent to which they may assist in the settlement of the action as well as in the preparation of the case for trial.

A. COSTS

The costs involved in civil litigation are of the utmost importance to the parties—they may prevent an action ever being brought, they may render a victory in court Pyrrhic when damages are swallowed up in costs, they may prevent a meritorious appeal and they will always be a factor in the risk of litigation. The costs involved in criminal litigation matter to the Lord Chancellor's Department, the Exchequer and, sometimes, the acquitted or convicted defendant. Tribunals are supposed to be cheap.

1. CIVIL CASES[5]

The costs payable by a client to his solicitor in a civil matter will depend partly upon whether the matter is classified as "contentious" since that term only applies where an action has been begun.[6] The negotiation of a settlement in a civil matter where no writ is issued would count as "non-contentious" business.

The basic rule in contentious matters is that "costs follow the event," that is to say that the successful party can expect the judge to order his opponent to pay some or all of his solicitor's bill.[7] This rule provides a forceful reason for settling in cases where the outcome is in doubt, and also provides the basis for agreeing the apportionment of costs in cases which are settled.

It is important to note that the principles we are about to discuss in relation to the taxation of costs after a trial will not prevent the parties reaching their own agreement about costs in cases where a settlement is effected before trial. Indeed, in the majority of cases costs are agreed between the parties, but the taxation rules remain significant in providing the framework within which the parties can negotiate.

After a trial, the successful party will normally expect an order for costs to be made in his favour, and the procedure is then for his solicitor to compile a bill of costs and send it to the appropriate officer of the court for "taxing."[8] In this process, the court has regard both to the basis for taxation ordered by the judge and the relevant scale of fees[9] and then determines the proportion of the bill which is to be paid by the losing party.

---

[5] This topic is dealt with more fully in J. O'Hare and R.N. Hill, *Civil Litigation* (2nd ed. 1983), Chap. 23, and D. Casson and I.H. Dennis, *Odgers' Principles of Pleading and Practice in Civil Actions in the High Court of Justice* (22nd ed., 1981), Chap. 25.

[6] The definition is contained in Solicitors Act 1974, s.87.

[7] The award of costs is always a matter of discretion for the judge, but the discretion is usually exercised along well-established lines.

[8] "Taxing" is the term given to the procedure which is conducted by a taxing master (or, in minor matters, a principal clerk of the taxing office) in the High Court in London; a district registrar in the High Court outside London; and a registrar in the county court.

[9] There is one scale of fees for the High Court, four for the county court depending on the value of the claim.

This is designed to ensure that the losing party only has to pay those expenses properly incurred and is not saddled with the cost of unnecessary or unduly expensive work.

A judge may order that costs are to be taxed on one of four bases[10]:

(a) *Party and party basis* where the loser must pay such of the winner's costs " . . . as were necessary or proper for the attainment of justice or for enforcing or defending his rights."[11] This is the least generous basis for taxation and party and party costs would hardly ever cover all the charges incurred in pursuing litigation. The Royal Commission on Legal Services, relying on the evidence of the Supreme Court taxing masters, expressed the view that this was an unsatisfactory basis for taxation and that it should be abolished,[12] in favour of . . .

(b) *Common fund basis* where " . . . a reasonable amount in respect of all costs reasonably incurred"[13] is allowed. The Chief Taxing Master told the Royal Commission that a bill taxed on this basis currently would work out between 5 and 10 per cent. higher than a bill taxed on a party and party basis.[14] However, at the moment, this is a less common basis for assessment than party and party which is the normal basis unless the judge orders otherwise.

(c) *Trustees' basis* where the loser must pay all the costs of his opponent if the opponent was acting as a trustee or personal representative.[15]

(d) *Solicitor and own client basis* where the costs allowable are those which a solicitor would be permitted to charge his own client in a contentious matter, *i.e.* all costs incurred with the express or implied approval of the client, even though they may be unreasonably incurred (*e.g.* too many consultations demanded by the client) or unreasonable in amount (*e.g.* briefing a Queen's Counsel unnecessarily). It is very unusual for a court to order the taxation of costs on this basis.[16]

The preparation of a bill of costs for a taxation hearing is a very skilled and detailed task.[17] Specialists exist who will undertake the drafting of the bill, usually for a commission calculated on the total amount of the bill. This commission is an additional cost for the solicitor (*i.e.* his client) since it is

[10] This standard view has been expanded by Sir Robert Megarry V.-C. in *E.M.I. Records Ltd.* v. *Ian Cameron Wallace Ltd.* [1983] Ch. 59. In this judgment, the Vice-Chancellor analyses the bases of taxation, indicates that there are still discretionary powers left to a judge to adopt a different basis, and suggests some improvements in R.S.C. Order 62, which deals with costs. It would appear that substantial amendments to Order 62 are "under active consideration." See n. 12, below.

[11] R.S.C. Ord. 62., r. 28 (2).

[12] R.C.L.S. Report, p. 552. A working party was established to consider simplification of taxation and it reported in 1983, but no action has yet been taken; see Outlaw, "The Simplification of Taxation of Costs" (1984) 81 L.S.Gaz. 364.

[13] R.C.S. Ord. 62, r. 28(4).

[14] R.C.L.S. Report, p. 551.

[15] R.C.S. Ord. 62, r. 31.

[16] R.C.S. Ord. 62, r. 29. For a fuller discussion of the bases of taxation, see J. O'Hare and R.N. Hill, *Civil Litigation* (2nd ed., 1983), Chapter 23, and see *E.M.I. Records Ltd.* v. *Ian Cameron Wallace Ltd.* [1983] Ch. 59.

[17] For further proof, see the specimen bills of costs reproduced in R.C.L.S. Report, pp. 581–594, and O'Hare and Hill, *op. cit.* pp. 367–372.

not allowable on taxation and so not recoverable from the losing party. The taxing officer on a hearing, will hear the parties and decide any issues in dispute, either allowing the item in the bill to stand or disallowing or reducing it. The total arrived at by this process is the total of "taxed costs" and it is that amount which the loser is required to pay.

The obligation on each client, however, will be to pay the bill presented by his own solicitor which will be calculated on the solicitor and own client basis referred to above. The winner will be assisted by the amount of taxed costs, but will almost inevitably find a discrepancy between the actual bill and the taxed costs. The size of that discrepancy will depend partly on the basis of taxation, partly on the frugality of his solicitor and partly on whether he has actually recovered any costs from the loser. An award of costs, like an award of damages, has to be enforced. If the loser is impecunious, the "winner" may end up with no damages, no costs and his own solicitor's bill still to pay. (Where the client is legally-aided, the solicitor's bill will be paid, after taxation, by The Law Society).

If a client objects to the bill submitted by his solicitor in a contentious matter he may apply to the High Court for an order for taxation of the bill[18] which will, of course, be on a solicitor and own client basis. This would be the appropriate procedure for resolving a dispute about whether work charged for had been authorised by the client, but the Royal Commission found that it was rarely used. This seemed to be partly through the ignorance and fear of disgruntled clients, and partly through a generally high level of satisfaction with the services provided.[19]

The general rule that costs follow the event is subject to some exceptions. In the various stages of pre-trial procedure the party who is ultimately successful may have caused undue delay or not followed proper procedure and been penalised at that time by the award of costs against him in respect of a particular hearing.[20] These will eventually be disallowed on taxation. However, there is one very serious cost penalty which can place a plaintiff in grave difficulties. At any stage after an action has been begun in the High Court or the County Court, the defendant may make a *payment into court* [21] in satisfaction of the plaintiff's claim against him. The plaintiff may accept the payment in settlement or may continue the action. If he fails to recover at trial a sum greater than that paid in he will be liable for the defendant's taxed costs from the time of the payment in, even though he has "won" the action. This rule has been criticised[22] and adds considerably to the "risk" element in litigation.[23]

Two other cases should be mentioned. The successful party in an action where his opponent is legally aided may be awarded costs against the Legal

---

[18] Solicitors Act 1974, s.70.

[19] R.C.L.S. Report, pp. 544–546. See also n. 31, below.

[20] For example, the failure to observe specified time limits, see below, p. 416.

[21] For the place of payment into court in pre-trial procedure, see below, p. 439; for its effect in the settlement process, see below, p. 385. The procedure is considered in some detail in O'Hare and Hill, *op. cit.* Chap. 16.

[22] P.S. Atiyah, *Accidents, Compensation and the Law* (3rd ed., 1980), pp. 308–310.

[23] It is tempting to pursue the "one-armed bandit" analogy. Some machines permit punters to "collect" prizes already won, or gamble on in the hope of doubling or trebling the payout with the attendant risk of losing everything. For "collect" substitute "accept payment in."

Aid Fund on a party and party basis where certain statutory conditions are met.[24] The person who conducts his own litigation has only recently become entitled to costs in respect of his own time and effort spent preparing and presenting his case.[25] In addition to costs incurred by such a person which would also have been incurred by a solicitor acting on his behalf, the court can allow on taxation a sum not more than two-thirds of that which a solicitor would have been allowed for profit costs. If the litigant in person has not actually suffered pecuniary loss in the preparation of his case (which this sum would compensate) then the court will only allow him up to £2 per hour for the time reasonably spent by him in preparation.[26]

In *non-contentious* civil matters a solicitor may charge his client such sum as is fair and reasonable having regard to the circumstances of the case and, inter alia, its complexity; the skill and responsibility involved; the time spent; the number and importance of the documents; the amount or value of money or property involved; the importance of the matter to the client.[27] Conveyancing is classed as non-contentious business and solicitors used to charge a fee based on the value of the property involved and fixed by reference to a specific scale of charges. Since 1972, the fee for conveyancing has been calculated on the "fair and reasonable" basis with the value of the property as only one of the factors. The Royal Commission on Legal Services recommended a standard scale of charges should be re-introduced.[28] The client who is dissatisfied with his bill may either apply to the High Court to have it taxed,[29] or require his solicitor to send it to The Law Society for certification.[30] The Law Society will then peruse the bill and documents and certify that the sum charged is fair and reasonable, or that a lower sum should be charged.

The Royal Commission commented on the limited use by the public of the opportunity of taxation or certification by The Law Society and recommended that clients be given more information about challenging a bill, that laymen be added to The Law Society committees which consider disputed bills and that an estimate of charges should be given wherever it is reasonable and possible.[31]

[24] See below, p. 393.
[25] The Litigants in Person (Costs and Expenses) Act 1975. This is one of those rare statutes which started life as a Private Member's Bill.
[26] R.S.C. Ord. 62, r. 28A. 98 Litigants in person had bills taxed in the county court in 1981, the average amount allowed was £199: *Judicial Statistics 1981*, Cmnd. 8770, Table H.1.
[27] Solicitors Remuneration Order 1972. Article 2.
[28] R.C.L.S. Rep. , pp. 269–280.
[29] Solicitors Act 1974, s.70.
[30] Solicitors Remuneration Order 1972.
[31] R.C.L.S. Report pp. 546–547. The National Association of Citizens Advice Bureaux would support similar reforms. At the Annual General Meeting in September 1982, a resolution was passed urging, " . . . The Law Society to introduce without further delay a means of settling minor complaints, and that this should include direct lay involvement." The matter has been taken a stage further by The Law Society's response to the complaints made against Mr. Glanville Davies, see above p. 119, n. 21. In that case the client never actually asked The Law Society to certify the bill, but the resulting controversy can hardly have increased the confidence of the public in the efficiency or independence of the procedure. See (1984) 81 L.S.Gaz. 474, 938 and 1091.

2. CRIMINAL CASES[32]

To what extent can the "loser pays costs" rule apply in criminal matters? Clearly it is of lesser significance because of the existence of criminal legal aid and the different system of funding for prosecutions. Further, the defendant does not have the option of minimising the cost by deciding not to go ahead with the case! Criminal courts do, however, have powers to make orders about costs in various circumstances.

Costs may be ordered in favour of an *acquitted defendant* by the Crown Court or the magistrates' court where the offence charged was indictable.[33] These costs are awarded out of central funds or against the prosecutor and the circumstances in which such an award should be made are set out in a Practice Direction.

"It should be accepted as normal practice that an order should normally be made for the payment of the costs of an acquitted defendant out of central funds under s.3 of the 1973 Act unless there are positive reasons for making a different order. Examples of such reasons are: (a) where the prosecution has acted spitefully or has instituted or continued proceedings without reasonable cause, the defendant's costs should be paid by the prosecutor under s.4 of the 1973 Act; (b) where the defendant's conduct has brought suspicion on himself and has misled the prosecution into thinking that the case against him is stronger than it is, the defendant can be left to pay his own costs; (c) where there is ample evidence to support a conviction but the defendant is acquitted on a technicality which has no merit here again the defendant can be left to pay his own costs."[34] In many cases the acquitted defendant will have been receiving legal aid and the Practice Direction will still apply, although it may be simpler for the court to achieve the same object in those cases by ordering that no contribution need be made by the defendant to his own costs.[35] Similar rules apply where the defendant has been committed on an indictable offence which is not proceeded with at the Crown Court[36]; or an information charging an indictable offence is not proceeded with at a magistrates' court[37]; or on committal proceedings.[38]

Although the rules appear quite unambiguous, doubts have been expressed about the extent to which they are being used, to the possible detriment of acquitted defendants who are not in receipt of legal aid.[39]

In respect of a summary offence, the magistrates have power to award

---

[32] The governing statute is the Costs in Criminal Cases Act 1973. For further detail see G.J. Graham Green, *Criminal Costs and Legal Aid* (3rd ed., 1973); J.P. Teasdale, *A Guide to Costs and Legal Aid in Criminal Cases* (1979).

[33] CCCA 1973, ss.3(1)(*b*), 4(1)(*b*) (Crown Court); ss.1(2), 2(1) (magistrates' court). See generally, R. Thoresby, "Costs on Acquittal" (1973) 36 M.L.R. 647.

[34] [1981] 3 All E.R. 783 (Lane L.C.J.). This is, with minor changes, the direction previously reported at [1973] 2 All E.R. 592.

[35] See below, p. 512 for the rules governing criminal legal aid.

[36] CCCA 1973, s.12(5). For the classification of offences, see below, p. 486.

[37] *Ibid.* s.12(1)(*a*).

[38] *Ibid.* s.1(2); s.2(4). In the case of committal proceedings, costs may only be awarded to the defendant against the prosecutor if the charge was not made in good faith.

[39] M. Zander, *Cases and Materials on the English Legal System* (3rd ed., 1980), at p. 357.

costs against the prosecutor in favour of an acquitted defendant[40] on the principles contained in the Practice Direction, subject to the proviso that there is no presumption in favour of an award.[41] The discretion must be properly exercised by the magistrates. It is wrong to adopt a practice of not making awards against the prosecutor.[42]

Costs may be awarded to a successful prosecutor either out of central funds or against a convicted defendant.[43] Courts adopt different policies in their treatment of defendants but regard must be had to the defendant's means. In respect of the Crown Court, the Court of Appeal has said that the judge ought to fix a specified sum where possible, only making an order where there is a likelihood that the defendant will be able to comply with it.[44] An order for substantial costs and a five-year prison sentence are not really compatible unless the defendant is known to have private means!

The award of costs to a successful prosecutor can include a person who brings a private prosecution,[45] but the private individual who wishes to prosecute will still bear the risk of failure and that the award is discretionary even if he is successful, and that costs may be awarded against him if he is unsuccessful.

3. TRIBUNALS

We shall repeat elsewhere that it is difficult to generalise about tribunals. Broadly, the parties to a dispute which is settled by a tribunal will bear their own costs, subject to any specific rules applicable to a particular tribunal. We can merely give a number of examples.

In Social Security Appeal Tribunals,[46] the claimant will receive only compensation for loss of earnings (if any) and travelling expenses. These are payable whatever the outcome of the hearing. No costs can be awarded against the claimant.

In Industrial Tribunals, the tribunal will not normally make an award of costs. There is a power to make an award only where a party has acted frivolously or vexatiously, either for a fixed sum or for taxed costs.[47]

In the Lands Tribunal, costs are within the discretion of the tribunal[48] and it is interesting to note that of the 25 Lands Tribunal bills taxed in 1981, the average amount allowed on taxation was £7,523.[49]

The last example is highly unusual. Legal aid is not generally available

[40] CCCA 1973, s.2(1)(3).
[41] This seems to be the result of the decision of the Divisional Court in *R. v. Lytham Justices, ex p. Carter* [1975] Crim. L.R. 225.
[42] *R. v. Lytham Justices* (above).
[43] CCCA 1973, ss.1(1), 2(2) (magistrates' court); 3(1)(*a*), 4(1) (Crown Court).
[44] *R. v. Hier* (1976) 62 Cr. App. R. 233; *R. v. Judd* [1971] 1 All E.R. 127
[45] For the powers of a private individual to prosecute, see below, p. 481.
[46] The same rules apply to appeals to the Social Security Commissioners.
[47] Industrial Tribunals (Labour Relations) Regulations 1974, (S.I. 1974 No. 1386), Rules of Procedure, Rule 10. Similar provisions apply to the Employment Appeal Tribunal.
[48] Lands Tribunal Rules 1963, (S.I. 1963, No. 483), r. 53(1).
[49] *Judicial Statistics 1982*, Cmnd. 9065. Table 10.1, p. 104. The figure is quite startling in comparison with the much lower figure for actions in the Queen's Bench Division, see p. 370, below.

for tribunals,[50] they are intended to be cheap and both sides are clearly expected to bear their own costs.[51]

4. CIVIL PROCEEDINGS—WHAT DO THEY ACTUALLY COST?

Despite the significance of costs it is difficult to be precise about the *actual* cost of a civil action. Of course, the cost will vary with the circumstances but critics of the high cost of the law tend to support their views with horror stories in the absence of methodical research and information. The following is an example[52]:

"WIN A CASE, LOSE A FORTUNE"

"Eighteen years ago, Christopher Ings, 56, went into business for himself with £97, a tax rebate from his last job. By 1979 he had a factory with a turnover of £100,000 a year . . . he bought on hire purchase some sheet metal machinery from P.S. Ltd. for a deposit of £6,000 plus VAT.

The machinery could not do the job for which he had bought it so, against his will, he went to law. "Either I sued for my £6,000 back because I had been sold unmerchantable goods or I would be sued for the balance of the purchase price," he said. "At that stage we were disputing £6,000 and it didn't seem a big deal. My lawyers said it would take three months and my costs wouldn't be more than £10,000 to £15,000."

In fact, the case took nearly three years and the total costs of both sides were closer to £250,000. It involved at various times, nine judges, six barristers, six court appearances, countless claims, counter-claims, awards and appeals until one judge felt moved to comment, "This little firm must be wondering when the law will be finished with it."

And—the crux of this story—although Ings eventually won his case hands down, he is left not only broke but in debt. "When I won, the judge said that he was going to put me in the position I would have been in if the machinery had been okay," Ings said last week. "Instead I've lost everything I've ever had. I sit here looking at my garden wondering whether I'm mad or the legal system's mad and no one's noticed it."

Ings' solicitors . . . issued the writ on his behalf on October 5, 1979.

In July 1980—10 months after the writ—Ings finally got a date for his hearing: March 1981! When he complained, he was told he was lucky. His hearing was in the Commercial Court which was speedy; if he had wanted to go to the Queen's Bench Division of the High Court his case would have been set down for October 1981—two years after

---

[50] See below, p. 389.

[51] There are some examples of money being made available to agencies providing a representation and advice service for those using tribunals, *e.g.* government grants are made to the United Kingdom Immigrants Advisory Service, by virtue of Immigration Act 1971, s.23. The Royal Commission on Legal Services advocated that this approach should be adopted more widely.

[52] Taken from the *Sunday Times*, August 8, 1982.

the writ. By the time the case began Ings' claim had risen to £639,000 because it related to the profits he said his business was losing, and these were escalating while waiting for the case to come to trial.

After a 15 day hearing the judge found 100 per cent. for Ings. But that was only on the question of liability—whether P.S. were at fault. Now there had to be a hearing on "quantum"—since P.S. were at fault, how much should they pay Ings? Ings' lawyers told him the quantum hearing would come on in three to four weeks and last about four hours. Because of, amongst other things, the shortage of court time, it did not come on until a year later under another judge, lasted 16 days, and ran up legal bills of more than £80,000.

[Ings claimed an interim payment of damages.]

A law vacation hearing took place (available in cases of emergency) with Ings represented at short notice by a different barrister, his original one being on holiday.

Ings asked for £50,000; the judge awarded £36,000; P.S. appealed and this was cut to £26,000 with each side to pay its own costs. Ings' costs came to £10,000.

In November 1981 Ings went back to court again to get a date for his quantum hearing. It was fixed for April 1982 . . . in February 1982, he applied for and was granted another interim payment of £42,751. Again P.S. appealed, but this time, since the full hearing was so close, the payment was allowed to stand.

On June 22, after virtually re-hearing the first case, Judge Hawser, Q.C., gave his judgment. He cut Ings' claim from £639,000 to £145,711 after a lengthy argument about likely profits. When the interim awards had been deducted, Ings received about £77,000. Or rather, *would* have received about £77,000 because his solicitors immediately handed him a rough, unitemised bill for £101,000 and slapped a lien on the £77,000 and his papers pending his payment of it.

. . . it took months to get his costs for the first trial taxed (approved by the court). They were taxed at £17,000. It actually *cost* Ings £36,000. So he owes his solicitor £19,000 (of which he has already paid £11,500). The costs of the second trial have yet to be taxed, but Ings expects to be out of pocket on that, too.

"The other side worked on the assumption that the costs of fighting a long trial would wipe me out. They were right. I won, but I still got wiped out. If I could have it over again I'd give them the £6,000 and forget about justice. The lesson is: never go to law."

The Law Reports contain some examples of costs in non-contentious business where the court has considered the interpretation of the Solicitors' Remuneration Order 1972.[53] In *Property and Reversionary Investment Corporation Ltd.* v. *Secretary of State for the Environment*,[54] Donaldson J. sitting with assessors held that £5,500 was a fair and reasonable sum to charge for acting in connection with the compulsory purchase of a block of flats worth £2,250,000. The time involved was 30 hours. The original bill submitted was for £11,250 which worked out at £375 an hour. (This was in

---

[53] See above, p. 365.
[54] [1975] 1 W.L.R. 1504.

1974.) Two later cases[55] appeared slightly less generous, but stressed the importance of taking into account all the factors specified in the Order when arriving at a fair and reasonable sum.

The only organised survey on High Court costs was published by Professor Zander in 1975.[56] In it he analysed 664 personal injury actions in the Queen's Bench Division where the costs were taxed in 1973 and 1974. This means that the actual figures are now seriously out of date, but they can be scaled up to give a rough idea of present day costs. In a contested case the average cost claimed was £1,027; in a case settled at the door of the court, £1,323; in a case settled without a hearing, £464. These are the costs claimed, *i.e.* the costs of the successful party. Zander suggests that when the costs of both sides are put together they were likely to exceed the amount in dispute in about one-third of all contested cases.

The Judicial Statistics contain a statement of the average amount at which bills are taxed in a particular year. In 1982, the average amount of bills taxed in the 4,285 actions or matters was £2,030 compared with £2,018 in 1981. Again, these are the costs of the successful party only. The Queen's Bench figures may be compared with the average county court taxed bill at £634 in 1982 and £477 in 1981.[57]

5. CIVIL PROCEEDINGS—WHO ELSE COULD PAY THE COSTS?

We have not yet described pre-trial civil procedure, so we are not at this stage concerned with procedural reforms which might reduce the cost burden. Rather, we want to examine possible ways of diverting the cost from the parties (at least initially) so that those who would otherwise find payment difficult or impossible might be enabled to bring or defend an action. *Civil legal aid* already exists to assist litigants who fall within its limits. Varying degrees of support have been given to two other proposals for a system of *contingency fees* and/or a system of financing certain cases out of *public funds* (perhaps by the establishment of a *suitors' fund*).

The system of *civil legal aid* is fully discussed at the beginning of the following chapter.[58] It alleviates the burden of costs by providing financial assistance to litigants who can satisfy a means test,[59] a merits test[60] and provide the contribution towards their own costs which may be required under the rules of eligibility.[61] This scheme does not always divert costs away from the assisted litigant to the Legal Aid Fund—far from it. More often it works as a way of postponing the cost to the successful assisted litigant until he receives damages and costs from his opponent. The costs

---

[55] *Maltby* v. *D.J. Freeman and Co.* [1978] 1 W.L.R. 431; *Treasury Solicitor* v. *Regester* [1978] 1 W.L.R. 446.

[56] "Costs of Litigation—A Study in the Queen's Bench Division" (1975) 72 L.S. Gaz. 679. Beware of printing errors, see M. Zander, *Cases and Materials, op. cit.* pp. 336–7.

[57] *Judicial Statistics 1982*, Cmnd. 9065 Table 10.1. p. 104.

[58] See below, pp. 387–397.

[59] Taking into account both the income and capital of the applicant. For the current figures, see below, p. 390.

[60] Broadly, "Would a solicitor advise a private client to bring (or defend) this action?" See below, p. 390.

[61] Above the lower limit of financial eligibility (below which no contribution is required) the contribution is ¼ of disposable income and all disposable capital. See below, p. 390.

incurred by the Fund on behalf of a successful assisted party are defrayed from costs awarded against the loser[62]; any further outstanding amount is taken from the contribution levied on the assisted party (if any); any amount still outstanding will normally be taken from any damages awarded in the action.[63] In the end, the successful assisted party probably pays exactly the same amount as a private client would have done. The benefits of the scheme are two-fold. The responsibility for payment is assumed by the fund and if the total costs of the assisted party cannot be covered by costs awarded, contribution and damages, his liability to the fund is nonetheless limited to his original assessed contribution. More importantly, liability is similarly limited in the event of the assisted party being unsuccessful.[64] The Legal Aid Fund bears the costs risk rather than the litigant.[65]

The legal aid scheme, then, permits those eligible to take the risk of litigation at the possible expense of the Fund. People who could not afford litigation (because they could not pay the difference between their costs and the taxed costs recoverable) or who could not afford the risk of litigation (because costs awarded might not be recoverable or because they might lose) might be assisted by the scheme. However, two substantial hurdles exist which protect the Fund. Each applicant for assistance must satisfy a means test with upper limits beyond which the applicant will be totally ineligible and must convince the awarding body that his case merits assistance.

The Royal Commission advocated the development of the legal aid scheme by the removal of the financial criteria. Without the constraint of fixed eligibility limits a contribution could be assessed according to the means of the applicant.[66] This would allow the benefits of the scheme to be extended to all litigants with a meritorious case, whilst limiting the burden on the Fund by assessing an appropriate contribution in each case. In the era of public spending cuts, the Government has given a predictably frosty reception to this proposal.

Under a *contingency fee* system,[67] a lawyer agrees to act for a client on the basis that he will receive an agreed proportion of any damages recovered. If no damages are recovered, he receives no fee. This is the way in which many accident cases are conducted in the United States,[68] and some evidence was given to the Royal Commission advocating its introduction in this country. It is argued that it allows litigation which would otherwise not be brought; that the lawyers involved act more

[62] *i.e.* taxed costs awarded on the normal basis (see above, p. 363). This is on the assumption that these costs can actually be recovered from the loser.

[63] The so-called "statutory charge" on the proceeds of the action. There are certain exceptions, see below, p. 393.

[64] The unsuccessful assisted party may find an order for costs made against him, but most successful unassisted litigants realise that they are not likely actually to recover very much from an opponent who was sufficiently poor to be eligible for legal aid.

[65] Since the fund is only substantially at risk where the assisted party loses, the object is, naturally, only to back winners.

[66] R.C.L.S. Report, pp. 120–121.

[67] For detailed consideration of this and other proposals, see M. Zander, *Legal Services for the Community* (1978), Chap. 7. See also, R. White, "Contingent Fees: a Supplement to Legal Aid?" (1978) 41 M.L.R. 286.

[68] For the United States position: G. McKinnon, *Contingent Fees for Legal Services* (1964).

conscientiously on behalf of their client because of the mutual financial interest; and that it is a simpler method of payment.[69]

Neither branch of the legal profession gives any support to such a scheme, alleging that the undesirable consequences of its introduction would include an open invitation to unprofessional conduct; a tendency for lawyers to refuse to take on weaker cases; an increased pressure to accept an early settlement (when actual costs will have been relatively low) rather than press on to trial and incur the heavy costs involved.[70] The Royal Commission accepted these arguments and recommended that a contingency fee arrangement should continue to be prohibited.[71] Zander is more sceptical. He refuses to believe that the legal profession could lose its standards overnight and suggests that the proportion of the damages payable to a lawyer could be statutorily regulated.[72] Although the proposal was decisively rejected by the Royal Commission, together with a related proposal from JUSTICE,[73] one suspects that its entrepreneurial, free-market aspect would commend it more highly to the present Government than the Commission's preferred alternative of an extension in the civil legal aid scheme.

A proposal for litigation financed from *public funds* irrespective of the means of the parties seeks to combine provision for various circumstances which are not the fault of parties to litigation, yet involve them in cost. In the form considered by the Royal Commission,[74] a *suitors' fund* could indemnify litigants against the additional costs resulting from a successful appeal; the death or illness of a trial judge; the determination of an unsettled point of law of public importance.

The last point may appear the strongest. It is a feature of our system of judge-made law that the resolution of points of law by judges depends almost entirely on the willingness of parties to litigate. There is very little provision for the bringing of actions by public officials,[75] and no specific financial assistance for private litigants. Not even the legal aid scheme will provide assistance, unless the case passes the merits test in addition to involving an important point of law.[76] Support for the establishment of a

---

[69] R.C.L.S. Report, p. 176.

[70] Because of the pressure to win. Among techniques mentioned by the Royal Commission were the construction of evidence, the coaching of witnesses and competitive touting for work: R.C.L.S. Report, p. 177. These views are echoed by the majority in *Wallersteiner* v. *Moir* (No. 2) [1975] Q.B. 373. Lord Denning M.R., in the minority, put in a strong plea for the contingency fee in a particular type of company law action brought by a shareholder.

[71] *Ibid.* p. 177. Until the Criminal Law Act 1967, a contingency fee arrangement would have involved the commission of the criminal offences of maintenance and champerty. Now it would merely be an unenforceable contract and contrary to professional rules of conduct.

[72] Zander, *op. cit.* p. 218. For an even more spirited defence, see R. White, "Contingent Fees: A Supplement to Legal Aid?" (1978) 41 M.L.R. 286.

[73] This advocated the establishment of a Contingency Legal Aid Fund, financed by contributions from successful litigants, which would pay lawyers on a normal basis but recoup costs on a contingency basis. The proposal emerged from their report, *Trial of Motor Accident Cases* (1966), but has been convincingly criticised by the Royal Commission (Report, pp. 177–178). Zander (*op. cit.* p. 219) sees some merit in it.

[74] R.C.L.S. Report p. 179.

[75] The Attorney General has limited powers, see Edwards, *The Law Officers of the Crown* (1964) and above, p. 15, and below, p. 747.

[76] R. v. *Legal Aid Committee No. 1 (London) Legal Aid Area, ex p. Rondel* [1967] 2 Q.B. 482.

fund to help litigants in this position goes back to the Evershed committee[77] in 1953, which recommended that such a fund should be available for actions at first instance and on appeal, certified by the Attorney General as raising a question of law of exceptional public interest which it is in the public interest to clarify. The Committee further proposed that the Attorney General should be able to act on his own initiative and apply to intervene in an action, or to pursue an appeal even where the parties had settled their differences. The Law Society put forward rather wider proposals in 1964,[78] which would have included cases in which on appeal it appears that the inferior court was precluded from reaching a just decision by virtue of the doctrine of precedent.

These proposals have not been implemented although there have been three related developments. The Administration of Justice Act 1969[79] introduced the leap-frog appeal whereby cases in which the Court of Appeal will be bound by precedent can go straight from first instance to the House of Lords, thus saving the costs in the Court of Appeal. The Criminal Justice Act 1972[80] provides for an appeal to the Court of Appeal by the Attorney General in a case tried in the Crown Court on indictment where the defendant was acquitted on an (allegedly) erroneous view of the law. Any subsequent decision on the point of law will not affect the acquittal. In a different way, the Equal Opportunities Commission and the Commission for Racial Equality are empowered by the Sex Discrimination Act 1975[81] and the Race Relations Act 1976[82] respectively to render assistance to individuals alleging discrimination. This assistance can include the provision of legal services, and similar assistance to those who might become involved with Immigration Appeal Tribunals is given by U.K.I.A.S., who receive Government money for the purpose.[83]

The Royal Commission supported the proposals of the Evershed Committee with the proviso that the judge at trial or on appeal should also be able to determine eligibility in cases where the point at issue does not emerge until later.[84]

The Commission also recommended that costs thrown away as the result of the death or illness of a judge in the course of a trial should be paid out of public funds. It is quite possible to insure against this possibility, but the Commission took the view that it was not the responsibility of the parties even to provide an insurance premium.[85] This reform had been advocated

---

[77] *Committee on Supreme Court Practice and Procedure* Cmnd. 8878 (1953). Chairman: Lord Evershed, M.R.

[78] The Law Society, "The Indemnity Rule" *Annual Report* 1963–64.

[79] ss.12, 13.

[80] s.36.

[81] s.75.

[82] s.66.

[83] See above, n. 50.

[84] This modification was suggested in a JUSTICE report, *Lawyers and the Legal System* (1977). In America, considerable attention has been given to the development of public interest litigation by individuals and groups: see M. Zander, *Legal Services for the Community* (1978), pp. 228–232. In this country there is no comparable development. Litigation is the responsibility of an individual and the possibilities for group actions are limited.

[85] R.C.L.S. Report, p. 180.

by JUSTICE in 1969, along with a more radical reform which did not find favour with the Commission.

The JUSTICE report, *A proposal for a Suitors' Fund*, suggested that public funds should be used to indemnify litigants against "faults in the system" amongst which it included appeals on fact or law. At the moment it is the ultimate loser who pays the costs even if he happens to have won at first instance and in the Court of Appeal. The report suggested that it was not the ultimate loser's fault that the judge at first instance did not get the right answers, nor the Court of Appeal, and that he should not be liable for the appellate costs. He should, of course, remain liable for the first instance costs which would have been incurred in any event. This proposal was rejected outright by the Royal Commission in a very short paragraph containing only two sentences. The second reads, "The risk that a decision may be overturned on appeal is inherent in all litigation and should be taken into account by all who embark on it."[86]

A recent innovation which defrays the cost of litigation is a scheme of *legal expenses insurance* providing cover for individuals, members of families or groups. Such insurance is common in Europe, particularly West Germany, and it has been launched in this country with the support of The Law Society. As with other insurance policies, cover varies according to the company and according to the premium paid, but the approach favoured by The Law Society and exemplified by Sun Alliance is a blanket cover subject to specified exclusions. It is to be marketed through the profession but to date there has been only a small response.

The Royal Commission favoured legal expenses insurance, whilst advocating its own solution of widening legal aid eligibility, and in the absence of any other reform designed to alleviate the costs burden, it may yet prove popular.[87]

B. DELAY

Delay causes problems in both civil and criminal matters despite the existence of time-limits which are intended to expedite cases. The reasons for delay differ in civil and criminal procedure, not least because in civil matters the conduct of the action is in the hands of the parties who may agree through their lawyers to delays in proceeding.

1. CIVIL MATTERS

The reasons for the slow progress of actions in the High Court are diverse. At the outset, the plaintiff may be slow to contact a solicitor; negotiations for a settlement may drag on; the extent of the plaintiff's injuries may not become clear until the end of a lengthy period of treatment; investigations may have to be carried out to ascertain the evidence; the advice of counsel will be taken; pleadings are often extended; the length of time spent waiting for the trial to begin can be substantial. Apart from these common reasons, there are other human and procedural delays which can prove

[86] *Ibid.* p. 180.
[87] See M. Berlins and C. Dyer, *The Law Machine* (1982) pp. 176–7; R.C.L.S. Report, p. 179; P.J. Purton, "Legal Expenses Insurance" (1982) 79 L.S.Gaz. 1341, (1984) 81 L.S.Gaz. 1196.

extremely frustrating to the parties, most particularly to the plaintiff who will feel that delay amounts to a denial of justice.[88]

The complexities of the law can add to the amount of time taken to resolve a case. *Saif Ali* v. *Sydney Mitchell and Co.*[89] provides an example of a remarkably prolonged action, complicated by the lapse of the limitation period. The timetable was as follows[90]:

March 26, 1966	Mr Saif Ali, a passenger in a van driven by his friend Mr Akram, was injured in a collision with a car driven by Mrs Sugden.
October 16, 1966	Mrs Sugden was convicted of driving without due care and attention.
1967	Mr Ali and Mr Akram consulted a solicitor with a view to making a claim. The solicitor took counsel's opinion.
October 1968	The solicitor instructed the barrister to draft the proceedings and to advise.
November 14, 1968	A writ and statement of claim was issued claiming damages against Mr Sugden only, alleging that his wife was driving as his agent at the time of the accident. Mr Sugden was the owner of the car and he had insured it.
Later	A meeting was held between Mr Ali's solicitor and the insurance company at which the company indicated that the agency question might be disputed, and that contributory negligence might be alleged against Mr Akram.
March 26, 1969	The limitation period expired[91] without any amendment to the writ, and without Mr Ali issuing proceedings against either Mr Akram or Mrs Sugden, the actual drivers in the collision.[92]
August 29, 1969	The writ was served on Mr Sugden.
October 16, 1969	Mr Sugden entered a defence denying his wife's agency.
November 1969	The barrister advised that Mr Ali should be separately represented.[93]
June 24, 1971	Mr Sugden amended his defence and admitted that his wife *was* acting as his agent.

[88] Because the onus is very largely on the plaintiff to keep the action moving, it is he who is most likely to become frustrated by delay. Various writers refer to a recognisable medical condition, "litigation neurosis," which can afflict those enmeshed in an unfinished action.

[89] [1978] Q.B. 95, C.A.; [1980] A.C. 198, H.L.

[90] The timetable is culled from the judgments in both the Court of Appeal and the House of Lords. There are, unfortunately, some discrepancies in the dates given in the two courts—naturally, the House of Lords version has been accepted!

[91] In a personal injuries action such as this, the writ must be issued within three years of the cause of action arising.

[92] There would appear to have been good cases against both the actual drivers—presumably, Mr. Ali was advised to proceed against Mr. Sugden because he was the insured person, and Mr. Akram was (at least, at the outset) his friend.

[93] It was perceived, too late, that Mr. Ali's interests and Mr. Akram's interests were not identical!

January 21, 1972	Mr Sugden applied to the court for leave to withdraw his admission of agency with consent of plaintiff's solicitors. Leave was granted.
May 9, 1972	House of Lords decision in *Launchbury* v. *Morgans*[94] led Mr Ali's advisers to believe that it was impossible to continue the action.
April 22, 1974	The action against Mr Sugden was discontinued and Mr Ali's impregnable claim had disappeared.
September 19, 1974	Freshly advised, Mr Ali issued a writ against the solicitors who had represented him until November 1969 alleging negligence.
May 29, 1975	The defendant solicitors issued a third party notice[95] against the barrister whose advice they had taken, asking that he should indemnify them on the grounds that they had acted on his advice.
July 26, 1976	The barrister successfully applied to have the third party notice struck out on the grounds that it disclosed no cause of action.
February 24, 1977	The solicitors successfully appealed to Kerr J. and the third party notice was restored. The barrister successfully appealed to the Court of Appeal and the third party notice was again struck out.[96]
November 2, 1978	The solicitors successfully appealed to the House of Lords and the third party notice was restored.[97]
	N.B. The third party action between the solicitors and the barrister did not decide that he *was* negligent—merely that *if* he was negligent he *would* be liable to the solicitors. The question of whether he *was* negligent remained for trial if disputed by the barrister.

This is clearly an unusual case, but there was still a considerable lapse of time while the normal procedures were being followed.

Two official committees have considered the incidence and causes of delay with particular reference to personal injuries litigation and have made certain recommendations to alleviate the problem. The Winn Committee,[98] which reported in 1968, paid particular attention to the

---

[94] [1973] A.C. 127. A case in which the House of Lords held that a husband who had borrowed his wife's car to go on a "pub-crawl" would not be her agent for the purpose of fixing her with liability for his negligent driving.

[95] *i.e.* joining the barrister in Mr. Ali's action.

[96] [1978] Q.B. 95. The court relied heavily on *Rondel* v. *Worsley* [1969] A.C. 191, see above, p. 123.

[97] [1980] A.C. 198.

[98] *Report of the Committee on Personal Injuries Litigation*, Cmnd. 3691 (1968). The chairman was Winn L.J.

delays experienced in consulting a solicitor through the ignorance of the plaintiff, or through the unwillingness of claims assessors or trade unions to hand over cases. In addition, the report cited the inexperience of some solicitors in the practice of litigation, delay in counsel's chambers, and the desire of defendants (especially insurance companies) to hang on to their money as long as possible. Two statutory innovations resulted from the Winn Committee Report. The Administration of Justice Act 1969 made provision for the payment of interim damages where it was reasonably clear that damages would ultimately be awarded,[99] and also provided for the payment of interest on damages.[1] Further recommendations in the Report that parties should be encouraged to adhere more closely to time-limits by the imposition of severe penalties for failure were not implemented.[2]

The Cantley Committee,[3] reporting in 1979, analysed delay in all High Court personal injury cases between 1974 and 1977. Of the 21,018 cases surveyed, only 2 per cent. were concluded within one year of the incident giving rise to the claim; 17 per cent. were concluded within two years; 36 per cent. took more than four years. The *average* period was 3½ years.[4] Against these figures, however, the Committee made several observations that are relevant to any recommended acceleration in High Court procedure. The present system of procedure achieves economy and flexibility by leaving the conduct of actions in the hands of the parties—those advantages should not be lost in any more interventionist system. Further, the present system relies heavily upon settlements and delay can often be helpful in allowing negotiations to come to fruition. Where a high number of cases eventually settle, any procedures which substantially increase the costs of the early stages of the action could be counter-productive.[5]

In the event, the Cantley Committee rejected the automatic striking-out of an action which did not follow a prescribed timetable and also the suggestion that the court should keep a file, monitoring the progress of a case and sending out reminders when necessary. The former was regarded as too draconian, the latter was too time-consuming. The only recommendation to find real support was the proposal that the plaintiff's solicitor should be required to report to the court on the state of proceedings 18 months after the issue of the writ if the action had not been set down for trial. The court could then consider giving directions for the progress of the action.[6] This proposal has not been implemented.

---

[99] s.20; see below, p. 384.

[1] The power to award interest is now contained in the Supreme Court Act 1981, s. 35A, inserted by the Administration of Justice Act 1982, s. 15. See p. 384, below.

[2] The Committee were not unanimous on this point, Master Jacob entering a Note of Reservation (Report) pp. 151–152.

[3] *Report of the Personal Injuries Litigation Working Party*, Cmnd. 7476 (1979). The chairman was Cantley J.

[4] *Ibid*. Appendix E.

[5] *Ibid*. paras. 8.9. The argument would be that additional costs should not be imposed merely to increase the pressure to settle, and that once incurred, the costs might hinder settlement. County Court procedure is far more "interventionist", and problems of delay are minimised. Perhaps the increased amount of money involved in the High Court encourages caution and delay.

[6] *Ibid*. paras. 37–42.

Other groups and commentators have put forward their own suggestions for speeding up the civil process,[7] but have also expressed reservations about the need to ensure proper preparation if the case should eventually come to trial. This is the dilemma of pre-trial civil procedure—it must ensure that a case is adequately prepared for trial whilst giving every opportunity for a settlement.

The preceding remarks have been concerned entirely with High Court procedure. The county court experiences little difficulty over delay and the great majority of its cases are dealt with expeditiously.

2. CRIMINAL MATTERS

Although the delay in criminal cases is of a different order of magnitude, it still gives rise to concern. The concern is expressed on behalf of defendants in custody because they may ultimately be acquitted or given non-custodial sentences, and on behalf of defendants on bail because of the uncertainty and unpleasantness of a pending criminal trial. In addition there are difficulties associated with trials relating to incidents which happened in times long gone by. Witnesses forget.

There is, in theory, a time limit which prescribes the amount of time which may elapse between committal and trial on indictment but it appears to be honoured more in the breach than the observance. The Crown Court Rules 1982 make provision for trial not later than eight weeks after committal,[8] but that rule may be dispensed with by the Crown Court[9] and the following figures indicate the present position. In England and Wales in 1982, of the 59,091 defendants committed for trial who pleaded guilty 51 per cent. were deal with in less than eight weeks; of the 32,506 who pleaded not guilty only 18 per cent. were dealt with in less than eight weeks. Indeed, of this latter group ("not-guilty pleas"), 42 per cent. had to wait longer than 20 weeks for trial.[10]

Delays for defendants in trials on indictment were giving cause for concern in 1975 when the James Committee reported, but at that stage over 70 per cent. of cases were disposed of within eight weeks.[11] The overall figure for 1982 would now appear to be 39 per cent.[12]

Those defendants awaiting trial in custody might seem to be the most seriously disadvantaged by delay and they do tend to take priority. In 1981, 57 per cent. of this group waited less than eight weeks for trial, and 90 per cent. less than 20 weeks. This compares well with the figures for those defendants on bail which were 34 per cent. and 72 per cent. respectively.[13]

The situation differs around the country and the *average* length of time

---

[7] See, *e.g.* the judgment of Templeman J. in *Towli* v. *Fourth River Property Co. Ltd., The Times*, November 23, 1976, where the case took nine years from writ to hearing; "Accelerating the Process of Law", in Sir J. Jacob, *The Reform of Civil Procedural Law* (1982); *Going to Law; A critique of English Civil Procedure*, a Report by JUSTICE (1974).

[8] Crown Court Rules 1982, (S.I. 1982 No. 1109), rule 24. This rule has been characterised as "directory" rather than "mandatory". *R.* v. *Urbanowski* [1976] 1 W.L.R. 455.

[9] *Ibid.* rule 26 (14).

[10] *Judicial Statistics 1982*, Cmnd. 9065. Table 5.6.

[11] *The Distribution of Criminal Business between the Crown Court and the Magistrates' Courts*, Cmnd. 6323 (1975), para. 23.

[12] *Judicial Statistics 1982*, Table 5.5.

[13] *Ibid.* Table 5.7.

between committal and trial varies from 8·8 weeks on the North-Eastern circuit to 23·6 weeks in London. The national average is 14·6 weeks.[14]

It is remarkable, in the light of these figures (which showed a slight *reduction* in delays over the 1981 position) that the Royal Commission on Criminal Procedure[15] did not pay closer attention to the problem. Its Report recorded the concern which had been expressed but said little else. The suggestion of further time limits was rejected, mainly on the ground that the one limit in existence was not very effective. The Royal Commission recognised that in the light of its proposal to abolish committal proceedings there would have to be some limit on the amount of time that could elapse between receipt of accusation and trial, and they recommended an eight week period after which an accused might challenge the accusation by way of the "application for discharge."[16]

There is little information on waiting times in magistrates' courts. The Royal Commission noted research which suggests that only 15 per cent. of contested cases were dealt with in less than six weeks, and further noted the delay that can occur between the defendant's first contact with the police and the issue of the summons.

The Royal Commission concluded that, "The speed with which cases are brought to trial is in our view determined almost entirely by the volume of business and the resources available to deal with it."[17] This distinguishes the criminal problem from the civil, but it sounds like a counsel of despair. If there were more judges, more lawyers and/or less criminals, and/or more guilty pleas then the problem would diminish. Indeed it would, but there may be more imaginative solutions to be commended. The widespread adoption of a rigorous and effective pre-trial review?[18]

C. SETTLEMENT

Cost and delay are just two of the factors which persuade the great majority of those in dispute to effect a compromise and settle their differences without trial. The Lord Chief Justice has commented that, "If it were not that a high proportion of cases are compromised long before they reach court the administration of justice would soon grind to a halt; the courts would be overwhelmed by the volume of work."[19]

1. WHO SETTLES WHEN?

The settlement of a dispute is achieved by an agreement between the parties to abandon any further claim in respect of the subject of the dispute. It takes the form of a legally binding contract and the normal rules

---

[14] *Ibid*. Table 5.4.

[15] *The Royal Commission on Criminal Procedure, Report*, Cmnd. 8092 (1981), paras. 8.29, 8.32–35.

[16] *Ibid*. para. 8.29.

[17] *Ibid*. para. 8.35. The Lord Chancellor recently announced his intention of creating more judges but only if he could find suitable candidates who were "up to snuff." (April, 1984).

[18] See below, p. 509.

[19] In the course of a Foreword to D. Foskett, *The Law and Practice of Compromise* (1980). This is a practitioner's work which gathers together the technical law on compromise.

of contract apply to establish the existence, meaning and effect of the agreement. Certain cases require the approval of the court,[20] but in general the parties are completely free to negotiate the terms of the settlement. Once agreement is reached, the settlement is just as final as a judgment and, unless the agreement has been improperly procured, the issues of fact and law raised in the original claim may not be the subject of further litigation.[21]

There is relatively little published research on settlements, so that deductions have to be made from the information available in the judicial statistics. This is, inevitably, an incomplete picture since it only begins with the issue of a writ and many disputes may have been settled by then.[22] However, the following figures are culled from the Judicial Statistics for 1982,[23] and relate to the Queen's Bench Division:

WRITS ISSUED	164,396	
JUDGMENT GIVEN WITHOUT HEARING	70,743	
CASES SET DOWN FOR TRIAL	12,716	
CASES DISPOSED OF:—	11,915	
comprising—		
Determined after trial		2,252
Settled during trial or hearing		749
Approval of prior settlement		1,052
Settlement without notice after court attendance		363
Withdrawn before hearing		7,499
		(11,915)

Clearly these figures are not entirely comparable because they relate to cases at different stages in the procedure. Most of the cases determined after a trial would have been begun by a writ issued in 1978 or 1979. However, the figures do indicate an order of magnitude.

You will see that a high proportion of cases disappear after the issue of a writ, presumably either settled or discontinued. A similarly high proportion end in a swift judgment because the defendant is in default or has no real defence.[24] About one case in 13 goes through all the pre-trial procedure and is set down for trial. Even then, a large proportion are

[20] For example, some matrimonial disputes, and matters concerning infants and mental patients. See Foskett, *op. cit.* Chaps. 16 and 17.
[21] Foskett, *op. cit.* Part I.
[22] See below, p. 382.
[23] Cmnd. 9065. Tables 3.2, 3.3, 3.4, pp. 32–34.
[24] See pp. 416 and 421 below for judgment in default and "Order 14" procedure.

withdrawn, presumably settled, before a hearing. A surprisingly high
number of cases are settled "at the door of the court" with the parties in
attendance ready for trial.[25] A number of settlements require the formal
approval of the court.[26] A high proportion of trials that begin, will end in
settlement rather than judgment. By the end, we find that for every 70
writs that were issued in 1982, one case was determined by trial. There is
no reason to believe that 1982 was an untypical year.

These statistics relate to all actions in the Queen's Bench Division. A
slightly different picture emerges if we sift out the figures relating to
personal injury negligence actions alone—the category most discussed in
relation to the efficacy of settlements. Again from the Judicial Statistics
1982,[27] the table now looks like this:

WRITS ISSUED	31,002	
JUDGMENT GIVEN WITHOUT HEARING	Not specified	
CASES SET DOWN FOR TRIAL	Not specified	
CASES DISPOSED OF:—	8,644	
comprising		
Determined after trial		1,499
Settled during trial or hearing		381
Approval of prior settlement		687
Settlement without notice after court attendance		182
Withdrawn before hearing		5,895
		(8,644)

From these figures we can see that a high proportion of the cases disposed
of in 1982 were personal injury actions (8,644 out of 11,915) hence the
attention paid to this category of cases, and that in such cases for every 10
writs issued, three cases are determined by trial.

These figures tend to confirm the conclusions of the Winn Committee
which reported in 1968.[28] That Committee found that, " . . . of all
personal injury claims asserted about 20–25 per cent. reach the stage of
proceedings being started, and only about 10 per cent. of these reach the
doors of the court, of which between one-third and one-half are then

---

[25] The prospect of immediate trial concentrates the minds of the parties and the advisers
wonderfully.

[26] See n. 20, above.

[27] Cmnd. 9065. Extracted from Tables 3.2 and 3.4, pp. 32, 34.

[28] *The Report of the Committee on Personal Injuries Litigation,* Cmnd. 3691 (1968), para.
59.

settled without trial." In the 1982 figures, 31,002 were actions started, 2,769 reached the doors of the court of which 1,270 were settled. Given the time-lag inherent in these figures, the proportions seem to have remained remarkably constant.[29] In evidence to the Winn Committee, the London Passenger Transport Board reported that of the 5,000 or so claims it was receiving each year only 100 reached the stage of proceedings. The Coal Board said that 17 per cent. of claims reached that stage, and for the Transport and General Workers Union the figure was 10 per cent. The later studies conducted for the Pearson Commission produced figures of 86 per cent. of cases settled without proceedings being started.[30] From these statistics it can be seen that the proportion of trials to *claims* must be infinitesimal.

We should by now have demonstrated to your satisfaction the enormous importance of the process of settlement. It is the normal procedure in the vast majority of cases. Is it fair?

2. NEGOTIATIONS FOR A SETTLEMENT

"The settlement process is very much a matter of bargaining, and it is bargaining of a difficult and expensive character. As economists would say, the case involves a bilateral monopoly, since the plaintiff has to "sell" his claim to only one potential buyer—the insurer—and the insurer has to "buy" the claim from only one potential seller—the plaintiff."[31]

Having taken pains in Part II to point out that there are a number of non-legal sources of advice and assistance, we do not now wish to give the impression that the negotiation of settlements is exclusively the province of lawyers. Other agencies are quite heavily involved, some in the capacity of mediator or arbitrator,[32] others representing the interests of members in a more specialised field.[33] Professor Atiyah indicates that the defendant, in a personal injury action, is likely to be an insurance company whose staff in the claims department will be skilful and experienced negotiators. Whether or not the defendant is an insurance company, whether or not the plaintiff is represented by a solicitor, or a trade union or himself, the analysis in the first paragraph holds good. The plaintiff cannot shop around for the best offer, the two parties must deal with each other and strike an acceptable bargain through their own negotiating skill.

Let us consider the position of a plaintiff in a personal injury action[34] who has found his way to a solicitor, and discuss the problems that may

---

[29] Again, the real comparison should be between writs issued in 1978 or 1979 in personal injuries cases (25,713 and 32,657 respectively) but the proportions remain fairly constant.

[30] *The Report of the Royal Commission on Civil Liability and Compensation for Personal Injury* Cmnd. 7054 (1978), Vol. 2 Table 24. The statistical evidence is more fully discussed in P.S. Atiyah, *Accidents, Compensation and the Law* (3rd ed., 1980), pp. 296–298.

[31] Atiyah, *op. cit.* p. 307.

[32] In industrial disputes the Advisory, Conciliation and Arbitration Service may be involved. The Equal Opportunities Commission and the Commission for Racial Equality both have a role in the settlement of disputes in their field of interest.

[33] Primarily the trade unions, but also the motoring organisations. Advice agencies also involve themselves on behalf of clients, from time to time taking an active part in negotiation and settlement.

[34] On this subject generally see J. Pritchard, *Personal Injury Litigation* (3rd ed., 1981).

face him in the initial stages of negotiation. Two questions arise. Is the defendant liable in law? If so, what should the damages be?

Proving liability will depend, if it is denied by the defendant, upon the information which the client has about the accident, what more might be discovered and how good the witnesses are. It may be difficult discovering whether there is enough evidence to pursue a claim. Some help is given by section 33 of the Supreme Court Act 1981 which establishes a procedure by which a plaintiff may seek an order requiring a defendant to disclose any documents relevant to issues arising out of a claim for personal injuries by the plaintiff.[35] Unfortunately, the plaintiff must specify the documents he believes to be in possession of the defendant, but the power is still useful in assisting the plaintiff to evaluate his case.

Any witnesses will need to be contacted and the quality of their evidence assessed[36] and the client will need a medical report to help with the quantification of damages. If a possible action is emerging from the evidence available, an attempt will be made to put a monetary valuation on the injuries suffered by the plaintiff. At this stage negotiations are likely to begin.

The orthodox view of civil pre-trial procedure is that the more the two parties know about the real issues between them the more likely it is that a "realistic" settlement can be reached.[37] In the early stages, however, it may not be in the plaintiff's interests to disclose too much. He is out to strike as good a bargain as he can. In setting out general guidelines for a solicitor negotiating on behalf of a plaintiff, Pritchard counsels caution. Do not provide too much detailed information; do not disclose medical reports; do not indicate the financial status of the client or his willingness and ability to litigate. This advice, along with other useful hints,[38] emphasises that negotiations are conducted in an atmosphere of pressure. The plaintiff seeks to utilise what advantages he has, but there is much pressure on him as well.

3. PRESSURES

"FIRM PAYS UP AS FAMILY MOURN"

An out of court settlement has been accepted by the daughter of a man who died five days before he was due to pursue a claim for unfair dismissal. Before a Manchester Industrial Tribunal, Mrs. B.S., accepted a settlement of £750 on behalf of her late father . . . After the hearing Mrs. S. said: "I am still bitter about his treatment. The settlement is a pittance, but getting it over quickly will save my mother further anguish."[39]

---

[35] R.S.C. Ord. 29, r. 7A.

[36] On discovery before action, see M. Zander, *Cases and Materials*, *op. cit.* pp. 43–47.

[37] This is the especial function of pleadings, see below, pp. 421–434; discovery, see below, pp. 435–438; and interrogatories, see below, p. 435. All these procedures take place well after the start of the action and, as we have already seen, a considerable time after the accident.

[38] Ask for an interim payment before proceedings commence; leave it to the insurers to put forward the settlement figure; the time to negotiate is when the other side is under pressure. Pritchard, *op. cit.* pp. 30–38.

[39] *The Advertiser*, (a free newspaper published in Tameside), September 16, 1982.

The news report indicates that the circumstances of that settlement were especially difficult, but the bitterness felt by the daughter is not uncommon amongst plaintiffs. The pressure to conclude a settlement is almost always on the plaintiff and puts him at a considerable disadvantage against the skilled defendant. Broadly, the pressures are attributable to delay, cost and the risk of litigation.

We have considered the *delay* likely to occur in a personal injury action which goes to trial in the High Court.[40] The incentive to settle and clear the matter up quickly is significant. The plaintiff may be urgently in need of the money. It is he, after all, who will be incurring additional expenses as a result of the accident and whose earning power may have been impaired. Social security payments are unlikely to be adequate compensation for loss of earnings and injuries. Interest is payable on damages from the date of the cause of action to the date of judgment in all personal injury cases (unless there are special reasons to the contrary) and the court *may* order interest on that basis in other cases,[41] but the plaintiff may still prefer to have the money in hand. An interim payment may be ordered by the court on application, but an order will only be made when it is clear that the defendant will be held liable at trial.[42]

There is some evidence that delay and the associated anxiety can cause a recognisable psychological state of "litigation neurosis,"[43] a complaint which disappears on the resolution of the dispute. It is almost inevitable that the circumstances associated with a legal dispute will cause worry and upset, but long delays weaken the spirit as well as the claim.[44]

The plaintiff has little to gain by delay. It may be that his injuries are such that their full effects will not become apparent for some time and a hasty settlement might lead to an underestimation of the damage[45] but generally delay is on the side of the defendant. Apart from the interest charges involved, the longer a defendant can spin out the negotiations the better. American evidence cited by Phillips and Hawkins demonstrates that delay can be used as a deliberate tactic either against unmeritorious or

[40] See above, p. 374.

[41] Supreme Court Act 1981, s. 35A (and County Courts Act 1984, s.69) inserted by Administration of Justice Act 1982, s.15 and Sched. 1 with effect from April 1, 1983.

[42] Supreme Court Act 1981, s.32. An order may be made after an interlocutory hearing if the master is satisfied that the defendant has admitted liability *or* the plaintiff has obtained judgment with damages to be assessed *or* the plaintiff will win on liability at trial without substantial contributory negligence AND the defendant is insured *or* a public authority *or* has the means to pay: R.S.C. Ord. 29, r. 12.

[43] See the material cited by Atiyah, *op. cit.*, p. 177 and footnotes thereto.

[44] The circumstances of the plaintiff are also important. An elderly, infirm person might want to receive money quickly in order to enjoy it while he can.

[45] This problem is alleviated by a new power given to the court to award provisional damages in an action for personal injuries in which there is proved or admitted to be a chance that in the future the injured person will develop some serious disease or suffer some serious deterioration caused by the wrongful act or omission of the defendant, Administration of Justice Act 1982, s.6, inserting new s.32A in the Supreme Court Act 1981. This power is unlikely to assist the *settlement* process, since it only applies to judgments. Indeed, it may encourage plaintiffs to go to court to take advantage of the power. It will not be possible to reopen settlements on this account so that the plaintiff will now have an additional choice to make in deciding on settlement or action. On the other hand, it may give the plaintiff greater bargaining power with the defendant, since a settlement may now be in the defendant's interests. The section is not yet in force.

unreasonable claims, or to alleviate the cash-flow problems of smaller insurance companies.[46]

Plaintiffs have cash-flow problems as well. It is cash flowing on *costs* as the case progresses which provides another incentive to settle. We need not elaborate on our earlier discussion of costs,[47] save in two respects. The rule that costs follow the event is important in negotiation because it adds another factor to the equation. The calculation of costs, which would ultimately be awarded to the successful party, complicates the estimation of the total value of the claim. Secondly, the costs pressure can be greatly increased by a judicious payment into court. The mechanics of the payment in have been explained.[48] The tactical advantages to the defendant are considerable. They accrue mainly from the uncertainty which surrounds the calculation of damages.

Solicitors and barristers experienced in personal injury litigation will have to estimate a sum for loss of amenity and pain and suffering based on awards in similar cases, their own practice and the published awards contained in specialist books.[49] A rather gruesome price list emerges which indicates the value of a leg, arm or toe—but not a precise value. The figure is almost always expressed as a range which will expand according to the seriousness of the injury.[50] When pecuniary losses are added the outcome of an assessment of the plaintiff's damage may be that it is worth somewhere between £8,000 and £10,500. If the defendant makes a payment into court of £8,250, the gamble is obvious. The effect of the payment in is to make impossible a net gain to the plaintiff of a little less than the estimated bottom of the range. Either the plaintiff will receive £8,251 plus costs (if the judge's estimate tallies with that of his advisers) or a much lower figure (if it doesn't, and he has to pay costs). No wonder that a large number of payments in are accepted, and that it is a tactic well used by defendants.[51]

Does a payment in place unfair pressure on a plaintiff? Both sides are gambling because the defendant may be paying more than a judge would award at trial. The plaintiff is playing with higher stakes because the cost penalty is likely to be bigger than the amount by which the defendant might overestimate the claim. The procedure saves costs and time and though it has been criticised and examined, no better procedure has been proposed. The Winn Committee described it as, " . . . rather a hit-and-miss affair; it is not sufficiently discriminating to achieve the object which it sets out to achieve; and it may work injustice."[52]

---

[46] J. Phillips and K. Hawkins, "Economic aspects of the settlement process" (1976) 39 M.L.R. 497, at pp. 502–3. There is also some English evidence, see *Report of the Committee on Personal Injuries Litigation*, Cmnd. 3691 (1968), paras. 46–62.

[47] Above, p. 362.

[48] Above, p. 364.

[49] Kemp and Kemp, *The Quantum of Damages* (Revised ed., 1982 (Vol. 1) and 4th ed., 1975 (Vol. 2)) and supplements. The monthly parts of *Current Law* also contain details of the latest awards categorised anatomically.

[50] The more serious the injury the more difficult the estimate. The highest damages in a personal injury action reported in Kemp and Kemp, *op. cit.* are £398,529 awarded in December 1981: Vol. 2, Personal Injury Reports, para. 1–154.

[51] M. Zander, "Payment into Court" (1975) 125 N.L.J. 638.

[52] *Winn Committee Report*, (n. 46 above) para. 512.

The third factor is the *risk* of litigation. The onus lies on the plaintiff, if the dispute goes to trial, to prove his case on a balance of probabilities.[53] Uncertainties abound. It may be unsettled as to whether the defendant is liable at law for the plaintiff's damage.[54] In the absence of a settlement the parties have to litigate to find out. Even if the law is clear, the case may be difficult because of lack of evidence.[55] Evidence depends on witnesses and, to some extent, their credibility is dependent upon their performance in the witness box.[56] Some witnesses perform very badly. Some are unavailable at the trial.[57] Assuming the case is proved, the judge's estimate of the injuries and the consequent amount of the award is uncertain. After trial, there could be *two* appeals.[58] Looming large over all these doubts is the spectre of costs.

It is also worth noting that where the plaintiff is an individual (as in all personal injury cases) he will inevitably feel the risks and pressure of litigation much more keenly than the defendant who is likely to be, or is "backed" by, a corporation or insurance company. Since settlement is a contractual matter, one wonders what can be done to achieve equality of bargaining power in the settlement process. The statutory protection afforded to the individual consumer in other areas has not yet reached litigation.

No one could be surprised that only one writ in a hundred comes to trial.

[53] This is the standard of proof in a civil action. It means, "Is it more likely than not?"

[54] The case of the unborn children injured by the drug thalidomide illustrates the difficulty. At the time it was by no means certain that there was any liability towards unborn children. The position has now been resolved by The Congenital Disabilities (Civil Liability) Act 1976.

[55] The plaintiff is aided by discovery and other pre-trial procedures, but it is still up to him to find the evidence. The alleged defective machine may have been broken up for scrap; the precise way in which a manufacturer has been negligent in making a defective product may be very hard to prove; expert evidence may also be very expensive.

[56] Any inherent difficulties will be greatly exacerbated by the problem of delay. Witnesses are often giving evidence about incidents which happened some years before the trial.

[57] Abroad; ill; dead. All things are possible.

[58] Creating further delay and further potential costs.

CHAPTER 11

CIVIL COURTS

The procedures which must be followed before a trial in the High Court or county court can be used by the parties to expose the real area of difference between them and to concentrate attention upon it. Issues which are not in dispute can be eliminated and the scope of the disagreement can be narrowed. If the procedures are operated in this way they can have the dual effect of preparing the case as precisely as possible for the trial judge and of encouraging a settlement by revealing to the parties the exact nature of their dispute. However, it is equally possible to operate the procedures in such a way as to leave all the issues open and so reveal very little to the other party about the case he will have to meet. It is important to bear in mind as we consider pre-trial procedures in the civil courts that their utility is based very much upon the spirit in which they are undertaken by the parties.

The alleged complexity of pre-trial procedure, particularly in the High Court, is said to act not only as a deterrent to all but the most determined litigant but also as a weapon for the recalcitrant defendant who may manipulate it so as to place the pressure of delay upon the plaintiff. This may be a factor in leading a plaintiff to sue in the county court rather than the High Court where his claim lies within its jurisdiction limit,[1] and has also been used as an argument in support of the establishment of special courts with simplified procedure to deal with small claims.[2]

Procedural complexities are one of the likeliest reasons for the conclusion that the services of a lawyer are necessary in the pursuit of a claim. The legal advice scheme may be invoked for initial advice and assistance,[3] but if a litigant requires the services of a lawyer in civil proceedings he must rely on the provisions of the legal aid scheme or meet the cost himself. Since many people are unable to meet the costs of litigation from their own resources, the availability of legal aid will often be the crucial factor in deciding whether the case goes on at all. Therefore, we consider first in this chapter the operation of the legal aid scheme.

A. OBTAINING LEGAL AID

1. The Development of the Scheme[4]

The modern legal aid scheme, which provides financial assistance (subject to eligibility) in connection with proceedings in most of our civil courts, has

---

[1] See below p. 397, this is very much a matter of judgment. Where the sum in dispute is substantial, the county court also has highly detailed procedural provisions.

[2] See below, p. 409.

[3] As discussed at above p. 339.

[4] For a full consideration of the origins of the legal aid scheme see Seton Pollock, *Legal Aid, the first 25 years* (1975) and the useful bibliography contained therein. See also R. Egerton, "Historical Aspects of Legal Aid," (1945) 61 L.Q.R. 87.

come a long way since 1495 when "An Act to admit such persons as are poor to sue *in forma pauperis*" was passed in the reign of Henry VII. This statute provided for poor people to sue writs without payment to the Crown, to have those writs made and written by a clerk, and to have counsel and attornies assigned to them without fee—all at the discretion of the Lord Chancellor. A more formal Poor Persons Procedure, which exhibited the hallmarks of the modern scheme, was established in 1914[5] and was put under the control of The Law Society in 1925.[6] This proved to be a highly significant decision made partly because the procedure needed a solid administrative structure and partly because it was those solicitors who participated in the scheme who provided the bulk of the finance by giving their services free. Government money was only made available to meet the cost of the administrative work involved.

The Poor Persons Procedure, dependent as it was upon the charity of the legal profession, could not cope with the increasing pressure of work in the 1930s and was supplemented in 1942 by a newly-established Services Divorce Department. This department, consisting of salaried solicitors employed by The Law Society with Government funds, dealt with the matrimonial problems occasioned by the Second World War and proved to be an important development which must have been very much in the minds of the members of the Rushcliffe Committee as they took evidence. This committee had been set up, under the chairmanship of Lord Rushcliffe, in 1944, to review the provision of professional help for those who were unable to afford it, in both civil and criminal matters. The report of the Rushcliffe Committee[7] provided the basis upon which The Law Society were invited by the Lord Chancellor to undertake the task of organising a legal aid scheme and the negotiation and discussion which ensued came to fruition in the Legal Aid and Advice Act 1949 and the regulations made thereunder. The scheme is currently governed by the Legal Aid Act 1974, as amended, and its associated regulations.[8]

2. THE SCOPE OF THE SCHEME

The scope of the legal aid scheme is restricted in four respects. It only applies in specified *courts,* for specified *proceedings,* to those who fall within the *financial conditions* and have *reasonable grounds* for taking, defending or being party to an action. If all the requirements are fulfilled then legal aid consists of representation by a solicitor and so far as necessary by counsel, including all such assistance as is usually given by a solicitor or counsel in the steps preliminary or incidental to any

---

[5] Described as, " . . . the first regular scheme for legal aid in the Supreme Court." See H. Kirk, *Portrait of a Profession* (1976), p. 164.

[6] After it had fallen into complete chaos and on the recommendation of a committee under Mr. Justice P.O. Lawrence. (The Poor Persons' Rules Committee, Cmd. 2358, 1925).

[7] *Report of the Committee on Legal Aid and Advice,* (Cmd. 6641, 1945). This report also contains a good review of the then existing facilities for legal aid and advice.

[8] The Legal Aid Act 1974 has been amended by the Legal Aid Act 1979. The principal regulations governing the Legal Aid scheme are the Legal Aid (General) Regulations 1980 (S.I. 1980 No. 1894), as amended by the Legal Aid (General) (Amendment) Regulations 1981 (S.I. 1981 No. 173).

proceedings or in arriving at or giving effect to a compromise to avoid or bring to an end any proceedings.[9] The cost of such representation is met by the Legal Aid Fund, although a contribution may be required from the assisted party in accordance with the rules discussed below.

Taking the first two restrictions, s.7 and Schedule 1 of the Legal Aid Act 1974 prescribe the courts and the proceedings to which the legal aid scheme applies. Legal aid is currently available for almost all cases in the House of Lords,[10] Court of Appeal, High Court and county courts; the Employment Appeal Tribunal; the Lands Tribunal; a Coroner's court and the Restrictive Practices Court.[11] The specified exceptions[12] are actions in defamation; undefended proceedings for divorce or judicial separation[13]; actions for the loss of services of a woman or girl in consequence of her rape or seduction; relator actions and certain other minor actions. Additionally, aid is available in certain proceedings in the magistrates' court, notably those relating to the welfare of children. The unavailability of legal aid for certain tribunals, notably industrial tribunals and mental health review tribunals, has been criticised[14] and demonstrates the significance of the legal advice scheme in this field and the new provision for "assistance by way of representation."[15]

3. MAKING APPLICATION—THE MEANS AND MERITS TESTS

The administration of the legal aid scheme rests with The Law Society and it originally established a network of Local Committees and Area Committees to take decisions on applications. A Local Committee heard all original applications except for proceedings in appellate courts, and there was a right of appeal in most cases to the Area Committee. However, The Law Society re-organised the system under the auspices of the Legal Aid Scheme 1980. The original application is now made to a general committee,[16] normally in the area in which the applicant lives, which will determine the application.[17] There is a right of appeal to an area committee against the refusal of legal aid.[18] The country is divided into 15 areas each with a Secretary appointed by The Law Society and an appropriate administrative staff. The general committee, on receiving an

---

[9] Legal Aid Act 1974, s.7(4).

[10] Save for appeals from Northern Ireland, Legal Aid Act 1979, s.13(1).

[11] Under Part III of the Fair Trading Act 1973.

[12] Contained in Legal Aid Act 1974, Sched. 1, Part II.

[13] Legal Aid (Matrimonial Proceedings) Regulations 1977. Matrimonial problems had been a major factor in getting the legal aid scheme started, and continue to account for a large proportion of the money spent on the legal advice and assistance scheme (see above p. 349), but the withdrawal of legal aid for undefended divorce has provided a substantial saving for the scheme from 1977 onward. Aid is still available for ancillary proceedings and proceedings related to children.

[14] On mental health review tribunals see *31st Legal Aid Annual Reports* [1980–81] pp. 16, 17, 89 and *30th Legal Aid Annual Reports* [1979–80] pp. 95–97.

[15] See above, p. 342. Mental health review tribunals are now covered by the ABWOR scheme.

[16] Legal Aid (General) Regulations 1980, Part II.

[17] In accordance with the rules in the same regulations, Part IV.

[18] *Ibid.* reg. 36.

application for legal aid in respect of a court and proceedings which fall within the scope of the scheme will consider the *financial conditions* and the *merits* of the applicant.

The assessment of the applicant's resources, upon which his financial eligibility is based, is undertaken by an "assessment officer" at the Department of Health and Social Security.[19] The two significant assessments are of the applicant's *disposable income* and *disposable capital*. These are calculated by reference to the regulations[20] and allowance is made for dependants, tax, national insurance, housing costs and work expenses. As from November 29, 1983, the levels of eligibility are as set out in the following table:

Disposable income

(a)   more than £4925 p.a.   :   ineligible

(b)   £2050 – £4925 p.a.   :   eligible subject to a contribution of one-quarter of the sum by which the disposable income exceeds £2050

(c)   less than £2050   :   eligible without contribution

Disposable capital

(a)   more than £4500   :   ineligible, if it appears that the applicant could afford to proceed without legal aid.

(b)   £3000 – £4500   :   eligible subject to a contribution of the sum by which the disposable capital exceeds £3000

(c)   less than £3000   :   eligible without contribution.

The applicant must be eligible both in respect of income and capital. The levels have usually been uprated annually although there was no change in these figures between November 1979 and April 1982 and there were upratings in both April and November 1983.[21]

If an applicant can establish his financial eligibility, the general committee must further be satisfied that he has reasonable grounds for taking or defending the action.[22] This test is often expressed by asking, "If this applicant were the private client of a solicitor would he be advised to take or defend the action?" The regulations give a little guidance by directing that an application may be refused where it appears that any advantage accruing would only be trivial or where the simple nature of the

---

[19] Formerly the responsibility of the Supplementary Benefits Commission. The Law Society criticised the procedure for the assessment of resources partly on the grounds of delay, partly because 74 per cent. of assisted parties in 1980/81 made no contribution and of them between one-third and one-half were on supplementary benefit. The administrative cost to the Department was almost £4,000,000 p.a.: *31st Legal Aid Annual Reports* [1980–81] p. 7. The latest report indicates an average wait of 12 weeks for a contributory certificate, and half that for a non-contributory certificate: *33rd Annual Report* [1982–83] p. 70.

[20] Legal Aid (Assessment of Resources) Regulations 1980 (S.I. 1980 No. 1630).

[21] The Legal Aid (Financial Conditions) (No. 2) Regulations 1983 (S.I. 1983 No. 1783).

[22] Legal Aid Act 1974, s.7(5).

proceedings would not normally require the assistance of a solicitor.[23] However, a good deal of discretion is left in the hands of the general committee to determine the merits of the application, having considered, " . . . all questions of fact or law arising out of the action, cause or matter to which the application relates and the circumstances in which it was made."[24]

4. The Legal Aid Certificate and the Applicant's Contribution

If the application is approved by the general committee a legal aid certificate will be issued, subject to the acceptance by the applicant of any conditions attached to it. The certificate is likely to specify the extent of the aid available and will often be limited to the taking of particular steps in the action.[25] In the first instance the certificate may be limited to the taking of counsel's opinion and another application may have to be made to the committee to amend the certificate for further action if counsel's opinion appears to warrant it. In this way, the general committee can keep an action under review at all the crucial stages.

The applicant is notified of the willingness of the general committee to issue a certificate and he then has 28 days in which to signify his acceptance of any conditions attached, and give an undertaking to pay out any contribution required.[26]

The certificate will specify a contribution in respect of those applicants whose disposable income and capital exceed the minimum figure. The contribution from income will be assessed at one-quarter of the sum by which the disposable income exceeds the minimum figure and from capital at the whole sum by which the disposable capital exceeds the minimum figure.[27] The contribution from capital is normally payable forthwith if it is readily available and the contribution from income payable by instalments so as to secure the whole sum within 12 months.[28] These are significant financial burdens for an applicant towards the top end of the financial eligibility range and probably lead to rejection of the offered certificate by a number of applicants who cannot afford the contribution. Given that the level of eligibility for free legal aid is so low, it is interesting to note that in 1982/83 78 per cent. of the certificates issued granted legal aid without any contribution. This figure may suggest that the requirement of a contribution acts as a serious deterrent. The analysis of maximum contributions determined during 1982/83 contained in the 33rd Legal Aid Annual Reports[29] contains the following figures relating to all courts:

[23] Legal Aid (General) Regulations 1980, reg. 30.
[24] *Ibid.* reg. 29.
[25] *Ibid.* reg. 47.
[26] *Ibid.* reg. 46.
[27] Legal Aid Act 1974, s.9(1), as substituted by Legal Aid Act 1979, s.4. The Royal Commission on Legal Services, as well as suggesting a substantial uplift in the bottom figure for eligibility, recommended that the maximum contribution should be reduced to one-fifth in respect of both income and capital. For the current figures, see above, p. 390.
[28] Legal Aid (General) Regulations 1980, reg. 44.
[29] p. 44.

Contribution required	Number	%
Nil	148,026	78
Under £30	4,202	2
£30–49	2,584	1
£50–74	3,211	2
£75–99	2,960	2
£100–149	5,524	3
£150–299	11,581	6
£300–499	7,868	4
£500 and over	3,818	2
Total	190,044	100

Once a certificate has been issued there are wide powers vested in the general committee to amend, discharge or revoke it upon the happening of specified events including a request from the applicant so to do.[30] In the event of the general committee refusing an application for legal aid there is an appeal to the area committee except in respect of certain specific grounds of refusal.[31]

Obviously there may be circumstances in which the normal procedure of application and issue cannot be followed because of the urgency of the matter and a procedure exists for obtaining an emergency legal aid certificate in such cases.[32]

5. The Assisted Client and his Liabilities

When the provision of legal services for those who could not afford the normal fees was dependent upon the charity of the profession, the relationship between client and lawyer must have been somewhat awkward. The object of the legal aid scheme is to ensure that the relationship between solicitor and assisted client is on exactly the same basis as that between solicitor and private client. To that end, all financial obligations of the client are to the Legal Aid Fund and the solicitor receives payment from that fund. It is true that both solicitor and barrister receive reduced fees in respect of assisted clients[33] but that does not affect in any way the professional duties owed to the client or the conduct of his case.

The financial obligations of an assisted party will, inevitably, depend upon the outcome of his case. He is under no obligation to pay any costs to his solicitor whatever the result (these costs being met from the Legal Aid Fund as we have explained), but he may be under a liability to pay costs to a successful opponent.

If the assisted party is *successful* he may expect to receive costs from his opponent in the normal way.[34] These costs are paid straight into the Legal

[30] Legal Aid (General) Regulations 1980, regs. 52, 53, 75–87.

[31] *Ibid.* reg. 36.

[32] *Ibid.* regs. 19–24.

[33] Apart from proceedings in the county court where solicitor and counsel are allowed the full amount on taxation of costs, a solicitor will receive 90 per cent. of his profit costs allowed on taxation and a barrister 90 per cent. of his fee allowed on taxation: Legal Aid Act 1974, s.10 and Sched. 2.

[34] For an explanation of costs, see above, p. 362.

Aid Fund and go to defray the actual cost of the action in the accounts rendered to the Fund by solicitors and counsel acting for the assisted party. If the costs recovered are *not* sufficient to cover the cost to the Fund the difference is recouped from the contribution made by the assisted party. Any balance remaining from the contribution is returned to him.[35] However, if the contribution is not sufficient to make up the difference (or, more likely, if there has been no contribution required) then the Legal Aid Fund has a first charge on any money or other property recovered by the assisted party in the proceedings.[36] There are certain exceptions to this charge, notably in respect of matrimonial proceedings,[37] but it does generally ensure that the Legal Aid Fund is not out of pocket. This is particularly so when it is remembered that certificates are only granted in those cases where there are reasonable grounds for taking action.[38]

If the assisted party is *unsuccessful* his liability to the Legal Aid Fund is limited to the amount of his contribution and, in that respect, the Fund bears the financial risk of litigation. However, it is possible for the court to order an assisted party to pay his opponent's costs in the action. This order will not relate to the full taxed costs of the successful opponent but to so much of those costs as are reasonable having regard to the means of the parties and their conduct in connection with the dispute.[39] This is not likely to be an especially serious problem for the assisted party, particularly where he has been assessed at a nil contribution—if he has not been assessed as sufficiently well off to make a contribution, he is not likely to be able to pay much in the way of costs to his opponent. This leaves successful unassisted parties in a rather unfortunate position.

6. THE COSTS OF SUCCESSFUL UNASSISTED PARTIES

Prior to 1964 the only costs available to the successful unassisted party in an action against an assisted opponent were those which the court might order under the provision discussed in the last paragraph. As often as not this meant he got nothing, yet he was liable to pay full costs if he lost and might justifiably feel aggrieved, if he won, that the Legal Aid Fund had used public money in support of a losing cause which had cost him money

---

[35] Legal Aid (General) Regulations 1980, reg. 93.

[36] Legal Aid Act 1974, s.9(6). The "statutory charge" came into operation in 2,811 non-matrimonial cases in 1982/83. A total of £1,258,867 was recovered for the Legal Aid Fund. In 1,673 of those cases the amount of money recovered was less than £500 from an award of less than £2,500. For a full analysis see *33rd Legal Aid Annual Reports* [1982–83] pp. 79, 80.

[37] Although the matrimonial exceptions extend to maintenance payments, and to the first £2,500 of an order made in various matrimonial proceedings, nonetheless the statutory charge operated in matrimonial proceedings realised £5,318,935 in 1982/83, from 6,893 cases. *33rd Legal Aid Annual Reports* [1982–83] pp. 79–80. For a full list of the exceptions from the operation of the charge see Legal Aid (General) Regulations 1980, reg. 96.

[38] The whole question of the operation of the charge has given rise to debate and concern has been expressed that clients have not been properly informed about the possible consequences when accepting a legal aid certificate. Recent examples of the way in which the charge can operate have been provided by *Hanlon* v. *The Law Society* [1981] A.C. 124; and *Manley* v. *Law Society* [1981] 1 W.L.R. 335. There are also some interesting observations in the latter case about the responsibility of legal advisers in the conduct of an action for an assisted party.

[39] Legal Aid Act 1974, s.8(1)(e).

to defeat. The Legal Aid Act 1964 was supposed to rectify this anomaly and provided that a court could order costs out of the Legal Aid Fund in favour of a successful unassisted party subject to certain conditions.[40] Those conditions were interpreted so restrictively by the courts that the object of the statute was frustrated.

The provisions in question permitted a court to award costs out of the Legal Aid Fund if:

  (i) the proceedings are finally decided in favour of the unassisted party;
 (ii) it is just and equitable that provision for those costs should be made out of public funds;
(iii) the proceedings in the court of first instance had been instituted by the assisted party;
(iv) the court has considered the personal liability for costs of the assisted party; and
 (v) the unassisted party would otherwise suffer severe financial hardship. [41]

After *Nowotnik* v. *Nowotnik*[42] in which the Court of Appeal placed a highly restrictive interpretation on the Act, trifling sums were awarded in costs[43] and it took a bold decision by the same court in *Hanning* v. *Maitland (No. 2)*[44] to admit the error of the earlier interpretation and relax the application of the conditions. In that case, Lord Denning, M.R., said that the "severe financial hardship" condition should not be construed so as "to exclude people of modest income or modest capital who find it hard to bear their own costs."[45] This condition only applies to costs in the court of first instance and not to costs on appeal, and the House of Lords has been generous in deciding that it is just and equitable to award costs on appeal to a building society,[46] a person indemnified by the Automobile Association,[47] or by an insurance company,[48] and the Court of Appeal permitted costs against the fund where the costs were being met out of public funds by a county police authority.[49]

This relaxation of attitude has led to a significant increase in the annual amount paid out of the fund to successful unassisted parties[50] but it still remains perilous to be sued by an assisted person. This places an additional

---

[40] Legal Aid Act 1964, s.1.

[41] The current provisions are in exactly the same form as the original, Legal Aid Act 1974, ss.13, 14. The Legal Aid (General) Regulations 1980, regs. 127–140 make additional provision.

[42] [1967] P. 83. The fact that the husband had not had to restrict his activities on account of his solicitor's bill led the court to conclude that there was no severe financial hardship.

[43] 1964–5, £74; 1965–6, £838; 1966–7, £243; 1967–8, £251; 1968–9, £239. These are the total annual payments out of the Fund for the years stated. *Hanning* v. *Maitland (No. 2)* [1970] 1 Q.B. 580, at p. 587.

[44] [1970] Q.B. 580.

[45] *Ibid.* p. 588.

[46] *Gallie* v. *Lee (No. 2)* [1971] A.C. 1039.

[47] *Lewis* v. *Averay (No. 2)* [1973] 1 W.L.R. 510.

[48] *Davies* v. *Taylor (No. 2)* [1974] A.C. 225.

[49] *Maynard* v. *Osmond (No. 2)* [1979] 1 All E.R. 483. This case also contains observations by the Court of Appeal on the procedure to be adopted by the court in the case of an application by a successful unassisted party.

[50] £65,484 in 1978/9; £81,564 in 1979/80; £129,068 in 1980/81; £137,005 in 1981/82; £271,855 in 1982/83: *Legal Aid Annual Reports* [1978–79] to [1982–83].

responsibility on a general committee in deciding whether an applicant for legal aid has reasonable grounds for bringing an action as plaintiff—the committee may be protecting unassisted defendants as well as the public purse.

7. The Legal Aid Scheme—A Critique

The legal aid scheme is kept under constant review by two bodies charged with that responsibility—The Law Society, as the administrators of the scheme, and the Lord Chancellor's Advisory Committee on Legal Aid.[51] The Law Society reports annually on the operation and finance of the scheme and their report is commented on by the Advisory Committee who can also add observations of their own about the provision of legal services generally. The two documents are published as the Legal Aid Annual Reports and ensure that attention is focused upon any alleged defects in the scheme and its administration.

The Royal Commission on Legal Services also gave extensive consideration to the working of the scheme and, having heard a great deal of evidence, made a number of recommendations which have been largely rejected by the Government.[52]

There is wide agreement that the *financial conditions of eligibility* for legal aid are too restrictive. A careful study of the decline in numbers eligible for legal aid showed that between 1950 and 1976 the proportion of the population eligible had been progressively reduced from 80 per cent. to 40 per cent. by the failure of the eligibility limits to keep pace with the rise in household incomes.[53] Substantial rises in the limits in April 1979[54] brought the scheme back to the position it had enjoyed in 1950 and the normal uprating in November 1979 kept pace with inflation. There was no increase in 1980 or 1981, but three upratings between April, 1982 and November, 1983 may have enabled the limits to remain realistic.[55] In particular, the alignment of the capital limits with the Supplementary Benefit capital levels[56] may provide a regular comparator for uprating in the future. However, annual uprating is still a matter to be determined by the Government and eligibility levels may begin to fall again. The Law Society lamented that the benefits of the legal aid could be steadily eroded,[57] but the Benson Commission took a much more fundamental view in their recommendation that the financial limits should be abolished

---

[51] Appointed by the Lord Chancellor and consisting of practitioners, academics and others with a special interest and experience in the field.

[52] R.C.L.S. Vol. 1, chaps. 12 and 13. See also, *The Government Response to the Report of the Royal Commission on Legal Services*, Cmnd. 9077 (1983).

[53] *26th Legal Aid Annual Reports* [1975–76] pp. 78–86.

[54] Disposable income upper limit from £2,600 to £3,600; capital from £1,700 to £2,500. Disposable income free limit from £815 to £1,500; capital from £365 to £1,200. The position was assisted further by the reduction in contribution from one-third to one-quarter of income in excess of the free limit in July 1979.

[55] For the current figures see above, p. 390.

[56] This was in response to recommendations from the Lord Chancellor's Advisory Committee and will presumably result in uprating in November each year when benefit levels are reviewed. See *33rd Legal Aid Annual Reports* [1982–83] p. 145.

[57] *31st Legal Aid Annual Reports* [1980–81] p. 12.

altogether.[58] If that recommendation were to be adopted the adjustmen would be made by fixing the contribution at an appropriate level.

The financial conditions, then, attract criticism not only because of their levels but because of their existence. The Benson Committee thought that an upper limit was arbitrary and might operate unfairly. A person just above the line would receive no assistance, a person just below might have to make a substantial contribution but would have the security of knowing that the contribution represented a maximum liability regardless of the cost or outcome of the case. In recommending the abolition of eligibility limits both for income and capital, the Commission professed itself satisfied that, " . . . as long as eligibility limits exist, the effect will, in some cases, be to create unfairness and to expose some individuals to a choice between abandoning their legal rights and accepting the risk of suffering an undue financial burden."[59] Supplementing this recommendation were further ones in support of a regular updating of whatever financial provisions applied to the scheme;[60] for a substantial uplift in the levels of disposable income and capital below which legal aid would be free[61]; and for a reduction in the contribution to one-fifth of the sum in excess of the "free" limits.[62]

The *exclusion of certain proceedings* from the scope of the scheme is also criticised, although there has been continued disagreement about the introduction of legal aid for tribunal representation. The arguments for the extension of legal aid to cover tribunal proceedings are based upon the increasing significance of the tribunal; the original intention of the 1949 Act; the inconsistency of the scheme in allowing aid for minor civil actions in the county court but not major actions in, say, an Industrial Tribunal; and the objective of securing proper legal assistance for all those who need it. Set against those arguments is a distrust of the effect lawyers would have on informality and flexibility of tribunal procedure; an unwillingness to commit the large sums of money which would be required; and an assertion that the availability of legal advice and possible extensions of "assistance by way of representation" will deal with the problem.[63]

It is not just an extension to tribunals that has been suggested. The Benson Commission recommended that legal aid should be permitted for defamation, relator actions, all civil proceedings in magistrates' courts and certain other matters.[64]

Administrative improvements in the scheme have been advocated at various times and The Law Society and the Advisory Committee have both drawn attention to the desirability of simplifying the assessment of resources and reducing the delay in granting legal aid. Other suggested reforms are also directed towards the problems of delay and include devising a scheme to release those in receipt of supplementary benefit from the need for a detailed assessment as well as fixing a standard contribution in personal injury claims.[65] A restructuring of the area and local

[58] R.C.L.S., Vol. 1, paras. 12.29–12.32.
[59] *Ibid.* para. 12.32.
[60] *Ibid.* para. 12.24.
[61] *Ibid.* paras. 12.40, 12.43.
[62] *Ibid.* paras. 12.46, 12.52.
[63] See further, p. 571 below.
[64] R.C.L.S., Vol. 1, Paras. 13.70–13.72.
[65] All contained in *31st Legal Aid Annual Reports* [1980–81] pp. 7, 88–89.

committees has already been undertaken.[66] The outcome of a review of the scheme recently undertaken by the Lord Chancellor's Advisory Committee is expected in Autumn 1984. This review is of the principles underlying the eligibility limits and the non-financial criteria for the grant of legal aid.

There remains an overriding criticism that the legal aid scheme does not really deal with the problem of *access* to lawyers for those who could not otherwise afford them.[67] This goes back to the problems we have discussed in Chapters 8 and 9 about the identification of legal issues and the encouragement that needs to be given to get certain people to go to lawyers at all. It may be argued that this is not a primary function of legal aid, that legal advice will almost always be a preliminary to an application for legal aid and problems of access need to be dealt with through the legal advice scheme and in other ways. However, the question that is raised relates to the division of resources between legal aid and legal advice services. If the overall object of the legal aid and advice schemes is to ensure equality of access to legal services is it right to spend a net sum in excess of £68 million on legal aid and less than £39 million on legal advice?[68]

B. THE COUNTY COURT

Before commencing an action in the county court the potential plaintiff must consider whether his claim is within the jurisdiction of the court and whether there are factors which might induce him to use the High Court instead. The jurisdiction of the respective courts is set out in Chapter 2[69] and it will have been observed that there is an overlap between the two courts. However, in cases where it would be possible for the plaintiff to use either court he, or his adviser, must consider the following factors.

There is a penalty in costs for the successful plaintiff who sues in the High Court when he could properly have sued in the county court.[70] If he recovers a sum[71] of less than £600 in the High Court he will be awarded no costs at all, and if it is less than £3,000 he will only be awarded costs on the county court scale. There is some discretion for the judge where it appears that there was reasonable ground for supposing that the amount recoverable on the plaintiff's claim would be in excess of the amount recoverable in the county court,[72] but the provision is obviously intended to "encourage" the use of the lower court. In addition, there is the obvious informal costs sanction associated with the system of fixing costs and the generally higher costs in the High Court. There are also further formal provisions which may assist the parties by providing for the county court to

[66] See above, p. 389.

[67] R.H. Grimes and R.I. Martin [1981] J.S.W.L. 283.

[68] Figures for 1982–83 taken from *33rd Legal Aid Annual Reports*, Appendix 4A, pp. 92–3. The net figures have been arrived at by deducting receipts attributable to legal aid and legal advice from the gross cost. No allowance has been made for the cost of administering the schemes which, together with the criminal legal aid scheme, stood at £14,484,596 in 1982–83.

[69] See pp. 59–64, 69–76.

[70] County Courts Act 1984, s.20. The current figures in the text are to be found in the County Courts Act 1984, s.20(9).

[71] "The sum recovered" includes interest on damages, so that if damages and interest combined exceed the stipulated figures the plaintiff will be entitled to the appropriate level of costs: *Matarazzo* v. *Kent Area Health Authority* (1981) 125 S.J. 862.

[72] County Courts Act 1984, s.19(2).

take jurisdiction in excess of the normal limit where the parties agree, and
by permitting the transfer of actions from one court to the other during
proceedings.[73]

Apart from costs, there are procedural factors to take into account. The
procedure of the county court is meant to be simpler and quicker and
although there are some difficult areas to deal with, can more easily be
handled by an unrepresented litigant. Special procedures have been
devised to deal with small claims[74] but even where the amount is in excess
of £500 (the small claims limit) there are procedural advantages in the
county court. It is likely to provide a quicker hearing and one which is
more convenient to the parties than a High Court hearing.[75]

A plaintiff may consider that a High Court writ is going to have a greater
threatening effect on a recalcitrant defendant than a county court summons
inducing him to settle the claim and he may also be attracted by the
generally higher damages awarded, higher fixed costs and better enforcement procedures, but the advantage may rebound if the defendant avails
himself of High Court pre-trial procedures which can be very protracted.
Those actions which are begun in the county court are still largely
concerned with small sums of money and would not, in any event, be at all
appropriate for the High Court. In 1982, of 2,048,568 actions entered in
the county court for the recovery of sums of money or value, 1,538,601
were for sums up to £500.[76] This figure may suggest that the problems of
selection of court occur in a relatively small number of cases, but also
points up the importance of the special procedure for small claims in the
county court described later in the chapter.

If a plaintiff decides to commence his action in the county court he must
then identify the court(s) having jurisdiction over his claim. There are over
300 county courts but the action must be commenced in the court for the
district in which:

(i) the defendant (or a defendant) resides; *or*
(ii) carries on business; *or*
(iii) the cause of action wholly or in part arose.[77]

This may present some problems for the plaintiff in locating the defendant
and his local court or in identifying the place in which the cause of action
arose.[78] In either case the appropriate court may be some distance from his
own home.[79] There is a procedure for the transfer of actions between

[73] *Ibid.* ss.75A, 75B, 75C as substituted by the Supreme Court Act 1981, s.149 and
Schedule 3.

[74] See below, p. 409.

[75] This is not always the case, if the county court action has to be begun in a district remote
from the plaintiff's home. See the following paragraphs in this part of the chapter relating to
choice of venue.

[76] *Judicial Statistics 1982*, (Cmnd. 9065) Table 7.3, p. 78.

[77] The County Court Rules 1981 (S.I. 1981 No. 1687) Order 4, Rule 2(1). Hereafter
references will be: C.C.R., Ord. 4, r. 2(1).

[78] The place in which the cause of action arose is easily identified in personal injury claims,
motor accidents etc., but can be awkward in cases involving a sale of goods, or breach of
contract generally. In cases where a contract is concluded by letter the cause of action arises
where the acceptance is posted.

[79] For example, a Mancunian may be on holiday in Torquay when his car is flattened by a
juggernaut driven by a Londoner employed by a firm carrying on business in Brighton. He
could sue the driver and his firm in London, Torquay or Brighton—but not Manchester.

county courts where the judge is satisfied that the proceedings could be tried more conveniently or fairly in another court[80] but the plaintiff is normally the one to travel!

1. COMMENCING AN ACTION

A county court action will be classified as a fixed date action or a default action depending upon the nature of the claim. A claim for any relief other than the payment of money must be brought as a fixed date action—any claim for money is a default action.[81] The procedure for the two actions though initially similar is different, so it is important to observe the distinction.

The plaintiff must file at the court office a formal document, the praecipe,[82] containing certain specified information, and the particulars of claim. There are different forms of request available from the county court depending upon the nature of the action and requiring information on which to base the jurisdiction of the court[83] but there is no specific form for the particulars of claim and the plaintiff must supply them himself. A lawyer is likely to rely on the precedents which are published,[84] the litigant in person may just concoct a statement, but the object of the particulars of claim is to inform the defendant with sufficient particularity of the claim against him.[85] A request for a summons against a defendant in a default action and the basic particulars of claim in the (imaginary) case of *Wilkinson* v. *Walkertronic Super Hi-Fi-Vid* are set out below.

Once the praecipe and the particulars of claim[86] have been filed and the appropriate fee paid[87] the registrar must enter a plaint in the court record and, for a fixed date action, fix a return day on which the pre-trial review is to take place or the action is to be heard.[88] He must also prepare and issue a summons together with the particulars of claim and this is normally served by a court officer on the defendant. Service of the summons does not necessarily have to be effected in person, postal service is likely to be sufficient and there are special rules for violent or threatening defendants![89]

Together with the summons the defendant will receive a form of admission, defence and counterclaim[90] which he must return to the court

---

[80] C.C.R., Ord. 16, r. 1(1).

[81] C.C.R., Ord. 3, r. 2.

[82] "Praecipe" simply means a request to the registrar of the court to issue a summons to commence the action.

[83] *i.e.* whether jurisdiction is based on the defendant's residence or place of business, or the action arising in the court district.

[84] *Atkin's Encyclopaedia of Court Forms in Civil Proceedings,* (2nd ed. 1975).

[85] Not least to prevent the delaying tactic of requesting further and better particulars of the claim.

[86] Reproduced below.

[87] On a scale in proportion to the amount of damages claimed. Where the claim is relatively small it will be advantageous to place a limit on the amount of general damages claimed so as to minimise the court fee.

[88] Pre-trial review, see below, p. 405. The date must be notified to the defendant along with the summons, but if it is inconvenient an application may be made for adjournment.

[89] C.C.R., Ord. 7, r. 5.

[90] Although he does not necessarily have to use the form in making a defence.

IN THE   NOTTINGHAM   **COUNTY COURT**

CASE No.

THIS SECTION TO BE COMPLETED BY THE COURT

Summons in form: **N.1 Fixed Amount** ☐   **N.2 Unliquidated** ☐

Service by: Bailiff ☐   Plaintiff('s solicitors) ☐   Post (Certificate overleaf) ☐   Post (At defendant company's R.O.) ☐   Date issued ☐

Statement of Parties	Please use block capitals
1. PLAINTIFF'S names in full, and residence or place of business.	CYRIL JACK WILKINSON,
2. If suing in a representative capacity, state in what capacity.	24 ACACIA AVENUE, NADDLEBOROUGH,
3. If a minor required to sue by a next friend, state that fact, and names in full, residence or place of business, and occupation of next friend.	NOTTINGHAM.
4. If an assignee, state that fact, and name, address and occupation of assignor.	--
5. If co-partners suing in the name of their firm, add "(A Firm)".	--
6. If a company registered under the Companies Act, 1948, state the address of registered office and describe it as such.	--

Plaintiff's solicitors name and address for service

POPP, LEES AND STONE,

23 HALTERGATE, NOTTINGHAM

Solicitor's reference

SP 123

7. DEFENDANT'S surname, and (where known) his or her initials or fore-names in full; defendant's residence or place of business (if a proprietor of the business).	WALKERTRONIC SUPER HI-FI-VID LTD.
8. Whether male or female.	--
9. Whether a minor (where known).	--
10. Occupation (where known).	--
11. If sued in a representative capacity, state in what capacity.	--
12. If co-partners are sued in the name of their firm, add "(A Firm)" or if a person carrying on business in a name other than his own name is sued in such name, add "(A trading name)".	--
13. If a company registered under the Companies Act, 1948 is sued the address given must be the registered office of the company, and must be so described.	37 GRINLING STREET, NOTTINGHAM (Registered Office)

WHAT THE CLAIM IS FOR

AMOUNT CLAIMED	£875	
ISSUE FEE	£ 38	
SOLICITOR'S COSTS	£ 75	
TOTAL	£988	

[Strike out if inappropriate:- I apply for this action, if defended to be referred to arbitration].

NOTES:

1. Two copies of the plaintiff's particulars of claim are required before a summons can be issued, and if there are two or more defendants to be served, an additional copy for each additional defendant.

2. Any claim for £500 or less which is defended will be referred to arbitration automatically, but the reference may be rescinded on application.

3. When a defended claim is arbitrated the right of appeal against the arbitrator's award is very limited.

4. If the defendant's address is outside the district of the court you must complete Section A overleaf.

5. The certificate in Section B overleaf should be completed and signed if service by post is required.

N.201 Request for default summons (single case) Order 3 Rule 3(1)

SECTION A

This section must be completed by the plaintiff to show that the court has jurisdiction under Order 4 Rule 2 of the County Court Rules, 1981.

NOTES:—

(i) Where the claim is for the amount of any instalment or instalments due and unpaid under a hire-purchase agreement Question 3 must be answered.

(ii) Where the claim is founded on a contract for the sale or hire of goods Question 2 must be answered and if the answer is "No" Question 3 must be answered.

(iii) Where the claim is founded on contract but neither of the foregoing descriptions applies such of Questions 1, 4 and 5 as are applicable should be answered, or, if none of these are applicable Question 6 must be answered.

(iv) Where the claim is not founded on contract, Question 6 only, is applicable and must be answered.

1.	Was the contract made in the district of the court, and, if so where? (If the address given is within the district of the court no further questions need be answered)	YES 37 GRINLING STREET, NOTTINGHAM
2.	Was the purchase price or rental payable in one sum?	
3.	Did the defendant reside or carry on business in the district of the court at the time when the contract was made and, if so, where?	
4.	Where, and how, was the order for the goods [or given by the defendant to the plaintiff [or assignor]?	
5.	Where was payment to be made by the defendant under the contract?	

6. What are the facts upon which the plaintiff relies as showing that the cause of action arose wholly, or in part, in the district of the court?

SIGNED .... C. J. WILKINSON .... PLAINTIFF DATED .... 1.5.84 ....

NOTE:— If the action is wrongly issued in this court because this section has been wrongly answered the court may transfer the action or order it to be struck out, and may order the plaintiff to pay the defendant's costs.

SECTION B

(1) State surname and where known initial(s) or fore names.

I request that the defendant(s) (1) WALKERTRONIC SUPER HI-FI-VID LTD

be served with the summons by post. I certify that I have reason to believe that the summons, if sent to the defendant(s) at the address(es) stated overleaf will come to his/their knowledge in time for him/them to comply with the requirements of it.

I/The plaintiff understand(s) that if judgment is obtained as a result of postal service and is afterwards set aside on the ground that the service did not give the defendant(s) adequate notice of the proceedings, I/the plaintiff may be ordered to pay the cost of setting aside the judgment.

DATED 1.5.84

Signed POPP, LEES AND STONE
Plaintiff('s solicitor)

Certificate for postal service Order 7 Rule 10(2)

Dd 8328007 250M S&K 4 83

IN THE NOTTINGHAM COUNTY COURT

CASE NO.

Between

CYRIL JACK WILKINSON   *Plaintiff*
and
WALKERTRONIC SUPER HI-FI-VID LTD *Defendant*

PARTICULARS OF CLAIM

1. The Plaintiff purchased for the sum of £75.00 from the Defendant on February 1st 1984 at the Defendant's place of business, a Magivid electronic football game for use in conjunction with a television owned by the Plaintiff.
2. At all material times the Defendant was an electrical retailer and the said game was sold in the course of the Defendant's business.
3. It was an implied term of the agreement that the goods supplied to the Plaintiff would be of merchantable quality.
4. Further, or alternatively, the Defendant was aware of the Plaintiff's purpose in purchasing the said game, namely for use in conjunction with the Plaintiff's television and it was an implied term of the said agreement that the said game would be fit for such purpose.
5. The Plaintiff used the said game on three occasions, but whilst in use on February 5th 1984 it exploded causing damage to the Plaintiff's television and setting fire to a pair of curtains. Decorations in the same room were damaged by smoke and scorching.
6. The said explosion was caused by the Defendant's breach of contract.
7. In breaching the said contract the good supplied to the Plaintiff was not of merchantable quality and/or was not fit for its purpose.

PARTICULARS

(When operated the said game malfunctioned causing it to explode.)

8. By reason of matters aforesaid the Plaintiff has suffered loss and damage.

PARTICULARS OF SPECIAL DAMAGE

1.	refund of price paid	£75.00
2.	value of the television	£250.00
3.	replacement of curtains	£60.00
4.	redecoration	£390.00
5.	costs	

Dated this . . . . . . day of 1984

To the Registrar of the
Nottingham County Court and
to the Defendant

Popp, Lees and Stone,
Solicitors,
Haltergate,
Nottingham
where they will accept service of
proceedings on behalf of the
Plaintiff

CASE No.

IN THE   NOTTINGHAM   **COUNTY COURT**

CYRIL JACK WILKINSON
24 ACACIA AVENUE
NADDLEBOROUGH   **PLAINTIFF**
NOTTINGHAM

(SEAL)

WALKERTRONIC SUPER HI-FI-VID LTD

37 GRINLING STREET,

NOTTINGHAM   **DEFENDANT**

TO THE DEFENDANT

THE PLAINTIFF CLAIMS

		£	p
(see particulars attached)		875	00
Court Fee		38	00
Solicitor's costs		75	00
TOTAL		968	00
This summons was issued on	3.5.84		

JUDGMENT MAY BE OBTAINED AGAINST YOU and enforced without further notice

UNLESS within 14 days after the service of this summons, you:

Pay the total amount of the claim and costs into court

or

Send to the Court an admission, defence or counterclaim using the attached form.

Address all communications to the Chief Clerk AND QUOTE THE ABOVE CASE NUMBER

THE COURT OFFICE AT

is open from 10 am to 4 pm Monday to Friday

N.1 Default Summons
(Fixed Amount)
Order 3 Rule 3(2)(b)
      IMPORTANT – FOR INSTRUCTIONS TURN OVER

GENERAL INFORMATION

(a) If you intend to defend this claim and the court issuing this summons is not your local county court, you may write to the Registrar of the issuing court requesting that the action be transferred to your local county court. You should note, however that if the action is transferred and you subsequently lose the case the costs against you may be increased.

(b) You can obtain help in completing the attached form at any county court office or citizens' advice bureau.

(c) If you dispute the claim, you may be entitled to legal aid. Information about the Legal Aid Scheme may be obtained from any county court office, citizens' advice bureau, legal advice centre and from most firms of solicitors.

(d) If this summons results in a judgment being entered against you, then if £10 or more remains outstanding one month after the date of judgment, your name and address will be entered in the Register of County Court Judgments. Registration may affect your ability to obtain credit although you may apply to the court for the registration to be cancelled when the judgment has been fully satisfied.

INSTRUCTIONS – WITHIN 14 DAYS AFTER THE DATE OF SERVICE, YOU MUST:

1. IF YOU ADMIT OWING ALL THE CLAIM EITHER, pay that amount into court together with the costs shown overleaf OR complete and return to the court the attached form of admission stating your proposals for paying the claim.

   If your offer of payment is accepted you will be sent an order from the court explaining how payments should be made.

   If your offer of payment is not accepted, you will be sent a notice telling you when the court will decide how payment must be made. You may if you wish attend that hearing.

2. IF YOU DISPUTE ALL OR PART OF THE CLAIM, complete and return to the court the attached form of defence stating clearly how much of the claim you dispute and your reasons for doing so.

   If you dispute only part of the claim you should also complete the admission part of the form stating how much you owe and either send that amount with the form or state how you propose to pay.

   If you have paid the amount of the claim since the date of issue of the summons, complete and return to the court the attached form of defence stating the date of payment and pay the costs into court.

   If you enter a defence you may have to attend court. The court will send you notice of hearing.

3. IF YOU HAVE A CLAIM AGAINST THE PLAINTIFF, complete and return to the court the attached form of counterclaim giving details of your claim. If your counterclaim exceeds the claim you may have to pay a fee. The court will notify you of this. Unless the plaintiff admits your counterclaim you will have to attend court to prove it.

4. UNLESS payment of the claim and costs in full is made into court within 14 days after the date of service of this summons you may be liable for additional costs.

METHOD OF PAYMENT

By calling at the Court Office Payment may be made in cash or by BANKER'S DRAFT, GIROBANK DRAFT (if a Girobank account holder) or by CHEQUE SUPPORTED BY A CHEQUE CARD SUBJECT TO THE CURRENT CONDITIONS FOR ITS USE. Drafts and Cheques must be made payable to H.M. paymaster general and crossed.

PAYMENT OTHERWISE THAN AT THE COURT OFFICE COUNTER DURING OFFICE OPENING HOURS IS AT THE PAYER'S OWN RISK. Remittances to the court by post must be by POSTAL ORDER, BANKER'S DRAFT or GIROBANK DRAFT (if a Girobank account holder) only, made payable to H.M. PAYMASTER GENERAL and crossed. Cheques, giro cheques and stamps are not accepted. Payment cannot be received by bank or giro credit transfer.

This form should be enclosed and postage must be prepaid. A stamped addressed envelope must be enclosed to enable this form, with a receipt, to be returned to you.

CASE No.

I certify that the summons of which this is a true copy was served by me on (date)

Service was effected

(a) By leaving it at (posting it to) the address stated on the summons (to be the registered office of the Company).

(b) At the address stated in the summons (or at

by delivering it to the defendant personally (or to

apparently not less than 16 years old, who promised to give it to the defendant on the same day or on   ).

(c) By posting it to the defendant on   , at the address stated on the summons in accordance with the certificate of the plaintiff or his solicitor.

(d) By posting it to the defendant on   , pursuant to the certificate at

(1) below.

(e) By inserting it, enclosed in an envelope addressed to the defendant, in the letter box at the address stated on the summons for the reasons at (1).

                    Bailiff / Officer of the Court

(1) I have reason to believe the summons will reach the defendant in sufficient time, because:

                    Bailiff / Officer of the Court

Or I certify that this summons has not been served for the following reasons:

                    Bailiff

N.12 Certificate of Service Order 7 Rule 6(1) (a) and (2)

S5688 (25369) Dd.8322708 250m 11/83 G.W.B.Ltd. Gp.870

within 14 days of service. In a *default* claim, failure to submit a defence will permit the plaintiff, on submission of the appropriate form, *to have judgment entered against the defendant immediately.* Therein lies the advantage of the default action. If a defendant in a default action does submit a defence in the prescribed time, the registrar will fix a date for a pre-trial review and the action will proceed in just the same way as a fixed date action. The defendant in a fixed date action is permitted to submit a defence at any point before the return day, but if it is outside the 14 day period he may have to meet any costs incurred as a result of his delay.[91]

2. THE DEFENCE

A defendant may wish to dispute all or part of the liability asserted by the plaintiff, or may disagree with the amount claimed whilst admitting liability, or may wish to dispute the claim and make a counterclaim against the plaintiff. The form served on him permits all these possibilities although it has been criticised as being too complicated. It is not necessary actually to use the form to make a defence, the defendant only needs to submit some document indicating that he disputes the claim.[92]

The registrar must send a copy of the defence to the plaintiff and the case will then proceed to pre-trial review. As already mentioned, the defendant may still submit a defence up to the return day and even at the pre-trial review if he is prepared to risk costs being awarded against him. However, if a defendant delays submitting his defence unduly the court has power to order him to deliver a defence or risk being debarred from defending the action at all.[93]

The defendant may request further and better particulars of the claim within eight days of the service of the summons and the court has power to require the plaintiff to supply them on pain of having the action dismissed.[94]

In our imaginary case, Walkertronic needs no further information and indicates an intention to defend in the following terms. The case will now proceed to pre-trial review.

3. THE PRE-TRIAL REVIEW

This stage of county court procedure was introduced in 1972 and was a part of the response to criticism that the county court did not cater adequately for the resolution of small claims.[95] The review can be used either to give judgment for the plaintiff (where the defendant fails to appear or has no real defence in law) or to give instructions for the future conduct of the action, being similar, in this respect, to the High Court summons for directions.[96] The instruction to the registrar is couched in similar language to the High Court. He must, " . . . give all such directions as appear to him

[91] C.C.R., Ord. 9, r. 9.
[92] C.C.R., Ord. 9, r. 2(1).
[93] C.C.R., Ord. 9, r. 11.
[94] C.C.R., Ord. 6, r. 7.
[95] The criticisms were most cogently expressed in *"Justice Out of Reach"*—a Consumer Council Study (HMSO, 1970) and T.G. Ison, "Small Claims" (1972) 35 M.L.R. 18.
[96] For the powers of the registrar on the pre-trial review see C.C.R., Ord. 17.

IN THE   NOTTINGHAM   **COUNTY COURT**

.... **v** ....

ADMISSION   CASE No.

Read the instructions on the back of the summons carefully before completing this form. Please use black ink. Immediately after you have filled in this form send it by post or take it to the Court Office as stated on the summons.

---

1.   Do you admit the plaintiff's claim in full?   YES/NO

2.   Do you admit **part** of the plaintiff's claim?   YES/NO

    If so, how much do you admit?   £.........
    (Put your reasons for disputing the balance overleaf)

3.   If you wish the court to consider whether to make an instalment order you should answer the following questions:—

    PAY AND MEANS

      (a)   What is your occupation? ....

      (b)   What is the name and address of your employer? ....
             ....
             ....

      (c)   What is your pay before deductions? ....   £......... per week/month

      (d)   What overtime, bonuses, fees, allowances or commission
          do you receive? ....   £.........

      (e)   What is your usual take-home pay? ....   £......... per week/month

      (f)   Do you receive a pension or any other income?   YES/NO
          Please give details:—

      (g)   What contributions, if any, are made by any member of your household?

    LIABILITIES

      (a)   What persons, if any, are financially dependent on you? Please give details
          including the ages of any dependent children:—

      (b)   What rent or mortgage instalments do you have to pay?   £......... per week/month

      (c)   What rates, if any do you have to pay?   £......... per week/month

      (d)   Do you have to pay under any Court Orders? Please give details including name of court
          and case number.

      (e)   What other regular payments do you have to make?

      (f)   Have you any other liabilities which you would like the Court to take into account?
          Please give details:—

WHAT OFFER OF PAYMENT DO YOU MAKE?

Payment in full on the   day of   19   OR   by instalments of £................ per month

Address to which notices { ....   SIGN HERE ....
about this case should be { ....
sent to you { ....   DATE ....

N.9   Form of Admission, Defence and Counterclaim to
accompany Forms N 1, 2, 3 and 4. Order 3 Rule 3(2)(c)

IN THE NOTTINGHAM COUNTY COURT

................WILKINSON........................v....WALKERTRONIC. SUPER .HI-FI-VID .LTD.........

CASE No.

DEFENCE

1. Do you dispute the plaintiff's claim or any part of it? YES/NO

2. If so, how much do you dispute and what are your reasons?

· See attached defence

COUNTERCLAIM

1. Do you wish to make a claim against the plaintiff? YES/NO

2. If so, for how much? £..................

3. What is the nature of the claim?

[To be completed where the sum claimed or amount involved exceeds £500

If you dispute the plaintiff's claim or wish to make a claim against him do you want the proceedings referred to arbitration? YES/NO]

NOTES:
1. Any claim for £500 or less which is defended will be referred to arbitration automatically, but the reference may be rescinded on application.
2. When a defended claim is arbitrated the right of appeal against the arbitrator's award is very limited.
3. If your claim against the plaintiff is bigger than his claim against you, you may have to pay a fee before it can be dealt with. You can find out whether a fee is payable by enquiring at any county court office.

Address to which notices about this case should be sent to you

.......37. GRINLING. STREET,.......

.......NOTTINGHAM................

SIGN HERE.........J. WALKER..............

DATE...... 10.5.84.................

N.9 Form of Admission, Defence and Counterclaim to accompany Forms N 1, 2, 3 and 4. Order 3 Rule 3(2)(c)

S5241 (24701) Dd.8309525 400m 5/82 GWB. Ltd. Gp.870

TO THE NOTTINGHAM COUNTY COURT

Dear Sirs,

I do not owe Mr Wilkinson anything and he has been pestering me for three months.

1. I did not sell the game to him (it was his son).

2. The game was in perfectly good condition when I sold it because I tested it in the shop.

3. I think that somebody probably wired it up wrong which was not my fault. Whoever did it probably couldn't understand the instructions.

4. I do not think that there is any proper claim against me.

Yours faithfully,

Jimbo Walker

necessary or desirable for securing the just, expeditious and economical disposal of the action."[97] He should also, " . . . endeavour to secure that the parties make all such admissions and agreements as ought reasonably to be made."[98]

The role of the registrar at this stage of the proceedings is clearly crucial, although whatever approach he may adopt towards the parties at least the review gives them the opportunity to meet and survey the relative strength of their cases. In another context[99] it has been found that, " . . . where the system of pre-trial review has been applied to matrimonial causes . . . under the registrar's guidance the parties are often able to compose their differences or to drop unsubstantial charges and defences, and to concentrate on the main issues in dispute."[1] However, the same Practice Direction concludes, "To avoid possible adjournments and delay it is especially important that the parties are represented on a pre-trial review hearing by their legal advisers who are fully conversant with the facts of the case." This perhaps lends support to the conclusions of Applebey[2] that, whilst useful to lawyers, the pre-trial review in the county court civil action has not been of enormous assistance to the ordinary person trying to conduct his own case.

The plaintiff, or defendant may, at the pre-trial review, ask for any necessary interlocutory order or any other direction or may request arbitration rather than trial.[3]

---

[97] C.C.R., Ord. 17, r. 1.

[98] *Ibid.* Ord. 17, r. 2.

[99] In relation to defended matrimonial causes and the operation of the Matrimonial Causes Rules, which gave a limited power to require a pre-trial review.

[1] *Practice Direction* [1979] 1 W.L.R. 2, issued by the Senior Registrar of the Family Division.

[2] George Applebey, *Small Claims in England and Wales*, Institute of Judicial Administration, (Birmingham University, 1978).

[3] Except in cases where a sum not exceeding £500 is involved (see below) the case cannot be referred to arbitration unless both parties agree.

A standard form for orders on pre-trial review exists as a guide for the registrar and the parties.

At the pre-trial review a date for trial may be fixed, or it may be left to the parties to notify the court when they are ready.

4. SPECIAL PROCEDURES FOR SMALL CLAIMS

1982
Total number of County Court : 2,301,364
proceedings commenced
Total number of "money plaints" : 2,048,568
Money plaints claiming less than : 1,538,601[4]
£500

Over 75 per cent. of money claims in the county court in 1982 were for less than £500. It is hardly surprising that special procedures have been devised to make provision for claims of this size, and that the way in which the county court handles such claims is the subject of close scrutiny and criticism. In arguments which we shall consider later it is said that the county court is not an adequate forum for the resolution of small claims. If that argument can be substantiated it is a very serious criticism. Are more than 1,500,000 claims being processed inadequately?

It is interesting to note that the county court owes its establishment to the cost and complexity of civil procedure, for those were the reasons which persuaded the government of the day to pass the County Courts Act 1846 against much opposition from parts of the legal profession.[5] With an original jurisdiction of £20, the court was intended to provide a cheap, accessible and simple forum for the recovery of small debts and demands.[6] It was the criticisms of cost and complexity in small claims put most convincingly by the Consumer Council in *Justice Out of Reach*[7] which led to the procedural reforms of the early 1970s and further published evidence[8] and public pressure has provoked more changes in recent years.

The procedural changes in the early 1970s were modifications of existing procedure and did not represent a major shift in emphasis. The pre-trial review (see above) was introduced with the object of assisting, *inter alios*, the litigant in person[9]; arbitration rather than trial could be used to resolve

[4] *Judicial Statistics 1982*, Cmnd. 9065, Tables 7.1 and 7.3, pp. 76, 78.

[5] The Bar were particularly strongly opposed, mainly on the grounds that it was proposed to give solicitors the right of audience in the new court. The history of initial and continuing opposition to the county court is chronicled in B. Abel-Smith and R. Stevens, *Lawyers and the Courts* (1967) and in W. Holdsworth, *History of English Law*, Vol. 1, pp. 187 ff.

[6] The Act was entitled, "An Act for the more easy Recovery of Small Debts and Demands in England."

[7] A pamphlet published in 1970 before the demise of the Consumer Council. The newer National Consumer Council has been no less critical of the alleged shortcomings of the county court.

[8] *e.g.* Appelbey, *op. cit.* (n. 2 above); National Consumer Council/Welsh Consumer Council, *Simple Justice*, (1979).

[9] "The pre-trial review was designed primarily to help small claimants and their opposite numbers, the defendants to small claims, and particularly litigants in person whether plaintiffs or defendants," from a speech by Lord Hailsham, L.C., made on March 2, 1973 at the opening of the Wandsworth County Court. See J. Neville Turner, "Small Claims and the County Court in England—a contrast to the Australian approach" (1980) 9 Anglo-Am.L.R. 150, at pp. 160–162. The pre-trial review procedure was introduced in March 1972.

the dispute at the request of one of the parties[10]; solicitors' costs would not be awarded to the successful party where the claim was for less than £100.[11] These modest reforms were intended to make the procedure more attractive and less expensive than before.

The latest changes, which came into effect in April 1981,[12] make arbitration the normal method of settling disputes where the amount of the claim is less than £500.

The plaintiff must follow the initial procedure outlined earlier in this chapter, but if his claim is for less than £500 the registrar of the county court will automatically refer the matter to arbitration and direct the parties to attend a preliminary hearing at a specified date and time.[13] There are a standard set of terms for the conduct of the arbitration which the registrar may vary if he thinks it necessary, and he may appoint himself to be the adjudicator or he may appoint some other suitable person.[14] Legal aid is not available for an arbitration hearing although the plaintiff and defendant may obtain legal advice if they meet the eligibility conditions.[15] It is expected that the parties will appear in person, but legal representation is not prohibited. No solicitor's costs will be allowed in an arbitration except for those stated on the summons, those incurred in enforcing the award, and those incurred through the unreasonable conduct of the opposing party.[16] (If the case goes for trial rather than arbitration solicitor's costs *will* be allowed subject to the normal rules).

Why arbitration? The object of providing for arbitration rather than trial in small claims is to allow litigants to represent themselves at a hearing where their ignorance of procedure and adversarial techniques will not be a handicap. It is intended that the hearing should be informal, and this is indicated by the following standard terms of reference.

The strict rules of evidence will not apply. Any method of procedure may be adopted by the arbitrator. The arbitrator may, with the consent of the parties, get in an expert witness or procure a report. These terms of reference indicate that the arbitrator may be expected to become the inquisitor and take it upon himself to ensure that all aspects of the case are put and that both sides have an opportunity to put forward all relevant considerations. It is anticipated that this type of hearing will be much more appropriate for small claims and will prove to be fairer, simpler and cheaper.

In one party *objects* to the arbitration he may ask the registrar to rescind the automatic reference to arbitration on one (or more) of a number of specified grounds.[17] The registrar can order a full trial instead of an arbitration, if he is satisfied that a difficult question of law or exceptionally

---

[10] Arbitration had always been available in the county court but was very rarely used. In September 1973, the Lord Chancellor issued a Practice Direction encouraging registrars to make use of the procedure: [1973] 1 W.L.R. 1178.

[11] The rule was introduced in 1973. For an analysis of the objectives of the rule see *Hobbs* v. *Marlowe* [1978] A.C. 16, and Applebey (*op. cit.*) at pp. 35–38.

[12] County Court (Amendment No. 3) Rules (S.I. 1980 No. 1807) now consolidated in The County Court Rules 1981 (S.I. 1981 No. 1687).

[13] C.C.R., Ord. 19, r. 3.

[14] C.C.R., Ord. 19, r. 5.

[15] See above pp. 339–342.

[16] C.C.R., Ord. 19, r. 1(11).

[17] C.C.R., Ord. 19, r. 2(4).

THE COUNTY COURT   **411**

IN THE   **COUNTY COURT**

                                          CASE No.

BETWEEN...PLAINTIFF

                                                                    SEAL

AND...DEFENDANT

TAKE NOTICE that these proceedings have been referred to arbitration by the Registrar of this Court on the following terms:-

1. There will be a preliminary hearing before the Registrar at

    on
    at   o'clock to consider how best to resolve the matters in dispute. He will give such directions as he considers necessary for the future conduct of the case. If you do not attend such order will be made as the Court thinks just. In the absence of the plaintiff the proceedings may be struck out and in the absence of the defendant judgment may be entered against him.

2. With the consent of the parties the arbitrator may decide the case on the statements and documents submitted to him, otherwise he should fix a date for the dispute to be heard.

3. The hearing shall be informal and the strict rules of evidence shall not apply.

4. At the hearing the arbitrator may adopt any method of procedure which he may consider to be convenient and to afford a fair and equal opportunity to each party to present his case.

5. If any party does not appear at the arbitration, the arbitrator may make an award on hearing any other party to the proceedings who may be present.

6. Where an award has been given in the absence of a party, the arbitrator may, on that party's application, set aside the award and order a fresh hearing.

7. With the consent of the parties and at any time before giving his decision and either before or after the hearing, the arbitrator may consult any expert or call for an expert report on any matter in dispute or invite an expert to attend the hearing as an assessor.

8. The costs of the action up to and including the entry of judgment shall be in the discretion of the arbitrator, but no solicitor's costs shall be allowed except for the costs stated on the summons, the costs of enforcing the award and such costs as are certified by the arbitrator to have been incurred through the unreasonable conduct of the opposite party in relation to the case.

    If you object to the reference to arbitration, or to any of the terms, you may apply to the Court in writing for the reference to be rescinded or for the terms to be varied, stating in either case the grounds of your application.

                                          DATED

Address all communications to the Chief Clerk AND QUOTE THE ABOVE CASE NUMBER

THE COURT OFFICE AT

is open from 10 a.m. to 4 p.m. on Monday to Friday.

N.18 Notice of reference to arbitration. Order 19 Rule 2(3).

                                          S5277 (24572) Dd.8309679 200m 4/82 G.W.B.Ltd. Gp.870

difficult questions of fact are involved; that fraud is alleged; that both parties agree to trial; or that it would be unreasonable to order arbitration in the particular case having regard to the subject-matter, the circumstances of the parties, or the interests of other persons affected by the claim. *Pepper* v. *Healey*[18] illustrates that arbitration may not always be the ideal solution in small claims and provides an example of an arbitration being rescinded.

In that case, Mrs Pepper alleged that Mrs Healey had driven into her car causing damage amounting to £133. Mrs Healey denied that there had been any collision and proposed to call expert evidence to prove that any damage to the plaintiff's car could not have been done by her car. Mrs Healey, comprehensively insured, would have had her legal expenses met by her insurance company. Mrs Pepper, insured only against third-party claims, would not. The registrar rescinded the automatic reference to arbitration on the grounds that the plaintiff needed legal representation in order to present her case properly and the costs burden on her in an arbitration would therefore be unfair. Because the insurance company were paying the defendant's costs, the contest would be unequal. The Court of Appeal upheld this view. (It may seem nicely ironic that the initial question of whether the case should go to arbitration or trial involved three hearings—two in the county court and one in the Court of Appeal).

The success of the county court arbitration procedure in making things easier for litigants will be judged in due course when the scheme has been in operation for a reasonable time. Initial reactions are not over-enthusiastic, with some reservations expressed about the ability of registrars, when acting as arbitrators, to throw off the habit of adversarial procedure and adapt themselves to the inquisitorial nature of the arbitration.[19] In 1982, 32,575 judgments were entered after an arbitration which represented a 49 per cent. increase over 1981. This compares with a figure of 27,637 judgments entered after trial in 1982.[20] As a method of resolving disputed cases arbitration is already more common than trial.

5. Do we need a new Small Claims Court?

This question has been the subject of debate since the Consumer Council published *Justice Out of Reach* in 1970, making a strong case for the establishment of informal courts for small claims as a branch of the county court. What were to become familiar arguments were rehearsed in this important publication and the questions of cost, legal representation, the *locus standi* of companies, the nature of the adjudication, and the physical arrangements for the hearing were considered. The Council had conducted research and had drawn on the experiences of American small claims,[21] as well as arbitrations by the Motor Agents Association in this country. A Small Claims Courts Bill, based largely on the Council's proposals, was

---

[18] [1982] R.T.R. 411. See also, R. Irving, "Avoiding County Court Arbitration" (1982) 79 L.S. Gaz. 607.

[19] R. Thomas, "A Code of Procedure for Small Claims" (1982) 1 C.J.Q. 52.

[20] *Judicial Statistics 1982*, Table 7.4.

[21] *e.g.* those in New York City, Washington D.C. and Philadephia. Another style of American procedure was on view on Channel 4 in the programme "People's Court."

introduced into Parliament in February 1971[22] under the ten-minute rule. It foundered.

The *issue* remained live, however, and there were developments in the course of the decade in four distinct areas: the response of the government to public pressure reflected in procedural changes in the county court; two voluntary initiatives in the establishment of working small claims courts; two major research publications; and a steady flow of academic and other articles on the deficiencies of the procedures.

The government indicated very clearly that it was not prepared to contemplate the creation of a new court.[23] Responses were made through the procedural reforms outlined in the last section, and it was thought those would be sufficient. The piecemeal and grudging nature of the reforms may well have stimulated action.

Two small claims courts were set up through individual initiative in Manchester and Westminister and provided a model which has been very valuable in formulating proposals for the future adaptation of the county court arbitration procedure.[24] The Manchester scheme was established in 1971 with a grant from the Nuffield Foundation and was latterly funded by the local authority. Funding is obviously crucial to any voluntary small claims scheme because to impose the costs of running the scheme on the users would be to create the cost problems for them which the scheme is trying to alleviate. The London scheme began in 1973, also assisted by the Nuffield Foundation, but ran into financial difficulties which forced its closure. The Manchester scheme is now also defunct.

The rules of the schemes differed in detail[25] but both placed restrictions on legal representation, the eligibility of the parties, costs and expenses, and on the maximum amount of the claim. The role of the administrator was crucial involving responsibility for ensuring that evidence was available, that the procedure was understood by the parties, and that the case was adequately prepared for adjudication. The adjudicator could be a lawyer or some other appropriate expert. The distinctive feature of both schemes was their *voluntary* nature. There was no obligation on the defendant to submit to the jurisdiction of the scheme. Some rough statistics indicate that the refusal to submit to jurisdiction was as high at 50 per cent. in Westminster and 20 per cent. in Manchester.[26] In an analysis by the National Consumer Council, the strengths of the schemes were said to be the active involvement of the administrator; the simplicity and informality; and the demonstration that schemes can work without legal representation.[27]

The two research publications,[28] *Small Claims in England and Wales,* (Appelbey) and *Simple Justice* (National Consumer Council) appeared in 1978 and 1979 respectively. The former contains much material on the

[22] By Mr. Michael Meacher, M.P. See (1971) 121 N.L.J. 95.

[23] See (1973) 123 N.L.J. 143, 215.

[24] For an account of the operation of these two courts, see K. Foster, "The Manchester Arbitration Scheme" (1972) 116 S.J. 502; K. Foster, "Problems with small claims" (1975) 2 B.J.L.S. 75; (1973) 123 N.L.J. 383; R. Egerton, "The Westminster Small Claims Court" (1974) 71 L.S. Gaz. 427.

[25] A comparison is to be found in *Simple Justice,* pp. 83–90.

[26] *Ibid.* p. 86.

[27] *Ibid.* p. 89.

[28] See n. 8 above.

operation of the "reformed" procedure after 1973, and the latter makes extensive recommendations for procedural change based on the creation of a new "small claims division" within the existing county court.

Academic contributions to the debate have included proposals for the abolition of certain types of small claim, notably those for debt and personal injury,[29] as well as suggestions for procedural models and analyses of how the deficiencies in the small claims structure affects the perception of law and justice of a sizeable proportion of the population.[30]

The conclusions of the National Consumer Council, contained in the final chapter of *Simple Justice,* were based on the creation of a "small claims division" within the existing county court structure. Such a division should be clearly recognisable and labelled as a distinct part of the county court with its own procedure. This, it is said, would alleviate the problems of those who experience confusion in the present system where *all* claims follow the same initial procedure, and might encourage claimants who would otherwise be deterred by the fear of the formalism of the county court. " . . . As the cornerstone of the proposed separate division, there should be a self-contained code of procedure to govern all small claims determined by arbitration."[31] These two recommendations would, it was argued, change the image of the county court, combining the authority, fairness and impartiality it currently represents with the simplicity and informality required in small claims.

A model code of procedure was subsequently produced[32] containing the essential features which the report said were necessary. Emphasis is placed on better forms for litigants with more guidance; a more active role is envisaged for the registrar assisted by a requirement of early disclosure of evidence; there would be a presumption that only one hearing would be necessary; legal representation would be prohibited in most cases; the adjudicator would determine the procedure to be followed in any particular case.[33] The model code of procedure seeks to attain the objectives set in the report, that any small claims procedure should be accessible, simple, informal, cheap, quick and just. These are fine objectives, but difficult to achieve!

At the moment, the argument seems to have turned away from the need for a completely new court and attention is directed towards devising a distinctive system within the county court. The case is likely to succeed or fail as a result of the success or failure of the latest round of county court reforms. If these fail to meet the problem, a more radical solution may ultimately be adopted.

[29] T. Ison, "Small Claims" (1972) 35 M.L.R. 18.

[30] See, *e.g.* J.N. Turner, "Small Claims in England—some recent developments" (1974) 48 A.L.J. 345; J.N. Turner, "Small Claims and the County Court in England—a contrast to the Australian approach" 9 Anglo-Am.L.R.150; G.W. Adams, "The Small Claims Court and the Adversary Process" (1973) 51 Can. Bar Rev. 583; K. Economides, "Small Claims and Procedural Justice" (1980) 7 B.J.L.S. 111.

[31] *Simple Justice, op. cit.* p. 93.

[32] The County Court Rules Committee made a response to *Simple Justice* in which it rejected both the major proposals for a small claims division and a model code of procedure. The latter was described as undesirable and unnecessary. Responding to that response, the National Consumer Council then published, *Model Code of Procedure for Small Claims Divisions of County Courts,* (May 1980).

[33] The provisions of the model code are explained and considered in, R. Thomas, "A Code of Procedure for Small Claims" (1982) 1 C.L.Q. 52.

C. THE HIGH COURT

The process of settlement or compromise referred to in Chapter 10 can continue throughout a civil action in the High Court, so that the procedural steps necessary to bring an action to trial may be taken in the knowledge that a hearing may yet be averted. Indeed, some parts of pre-trial High Court procedure have the effect of increasing the possibilities for compromise at the same time as preparing the issue for hearing by a judge.[34] We have chosen to consider as an example the action commenced by writ of summons in the Queen's Bench Division. This is but one of the types of action available in the High Court[35] but it is the one which accounts for the majority of common law actions. We shall assume that the action proceeds in a normal fashion up to the point immediately before trial.

1. COMMENCING AN ACTION

The plaintiff begins his action by way of a writ of summons, which is a formal document containing details of the parties, the plaintiff's claim, an instruction to the defendant to acknowledge the writ within a specified time and a warning to the defendant that he must acknowledge and indicate an intention to contest the case or risk the plaintiff proceeding directly to a judgment.[36]

On the back of the writ the plaintiff must set out ("indorse") the nature of his claim against the defendant either in a brief, general statement (a "general indorsement")[37] or in a full statement (a "special indorsement").[38] If the writ contains only a general indorsement and the defendant wishes to contest the case, a full statement of claim will become a necessary part of the pleadings which will follow in due course.[39]

It is the obligation of the plaintiff (or his solicitor) to draw up the writ, and he must then ensure that it is "issued" and "served." The "issue" of the writ is the process by which it is made a formal document with the authority of the court and is achieved by the presentation of sufficient copies of the writ to allow one to be filed at the Writ Department of the Central Office of the High Court[40] and one to be served on each

---

[34] In particular, properly drawn pleadings can have this effect by disclosing more clearly the precise areas of disagreement between the parties and the procedure whereby the defendant can make a payment into court may greatly increase the pressure on the plaintiff if the amount of the payment is shrewdly calculated. See p. 385, above.

[35] Actions may also be begun by originating summons, originating motion or petition; R.S.C. Ord. 5, r. 1. For a precise statement of the form appropriate to particular proceedings, see *The Supreme Court Practice 1982* (the "White Book"), Vol. 1, pp. 32–4.

[36] Before a new style of writ was introduced in June 1980, the writ included a command by the Queen to the defendant to "enter an appearance" at the suit of the plaintiff. The new rules governing the style of writ, its issue, service and acknowledgment by the defendant are contained in The Rules of the Supreme Court (Writ and Appearance) 1979 (S.I. 1979 No. 1716).

[37] See *Hacker* v. *Reliable Nag Supply Stables,* below.

[38] See *Maserati* v. *Lagonda,* below. Special indorsement would normally only be used where the claim is for a liquidated sum, or the plaintiff is very anxious to hurry the matter along.

[39] See below, p. 428.

[40] Or at a convenient District Registry.

defendant. Acknowledgments of Service for each defendant must also be handed in and the court officer then stamps the writs and assigns a year, letter and number to the action.[41]

Service of the writ is now normally effected by sending it by first-class post to the usual address of the defendant or to his solicitor who will accept service on his behalf.[42] Personal service, where the plaintiff or his agent actually gives to or leaves with the defendant a copy of the writ, is still possible under the new procedure, but postal service is obviously less onerous.[43]

The following are two examples of a writ of summons. The first, in the case of *Hacker* v. *Reliable Nag Supply Stables* (*a firm*), is a claim for damages for breach of contract, the writ being generally indorsed. The second, in the case of *Maserati* v. *Lagonda,* is a claim for the price of goods sold and delivered, the writ being specially indorsed.

2. THE ACKNOWLEDGMENT OF SERVICE—AND THE CONSEQUENCES OF FAILURE

We have already noted that a plaintiff is required to serve on the defendant, as well as a writ, a form on which he can acknowledge the service of the writ. Normally, an acknowledgment is required within 14 days and the acknowledgment must indicate whether the defendant intends to contest the claim.[44] If he does wish to contest the claim and the writ has been specially endorsed, he must serve a defence on the plaintiff within 14 days after the time for acknowledging service.[45] If the writ is generally indorsed, a defence need not be served until after a full statement of claim has been served by the plaintiff.

The defendant may not wish to contest the claim and the form makes provision for that response. If the defendant simply fails to indicate that he intends to contest the action (by not acknowledging service at all) the plaintiff is entitled to enter *final* judgment for the amount claimed, interest and costs, if his claim is for a liquidated amount[46] and interlocutory judgment if his claim is for an unliquidated amount.[47] In the latter case, the defendant would still be able to appear and dispute the amount of damages when they fell to be assessed by a master prior to final judgment being entered for the plaintiff. In both cases the judgment in favour of the plaintiff can, by order of the court, be set aside[48] if the defendant had a reasonable excuse for his default and also has some merit in his case.[49] If a

---

[41] *e.g.* 1982—A—No. 789, where A is the initial letter of the plaintiff's surname.

[42] This represented a fundamental change when it was introduced in June 1980—" . . . a landmark in the procedure and practice of the Chancery and Queen's Bench Divisions of the High Court": *Supreme Court Practice*, 1982, para. 10/1/2A, p. 84.

[43] There is now little scope for the athletic and ingenious defendant to avoid the service of a writ. Previously, the servers of writs might have been forced to adopt extreme tactics to ensure personal service on a determined defendant with a fast car!

[44] See example in the text, question 2 on the Acknowledgment of Service.

[45] *Ibid.* Directions for Acknowledgment of Service.

[46] R.S.C., Ord. 13, r. 1. A "liquidated" amount is, in effect a fixed amount in the nature of a debt due and payable under a contract—either ascertained or capable of being ascertained. See further, *Supreme Court Practice 1982*, Vol. 1, pp. 41, 43.

[47] R.S.C., Ord. 13, r. 2.

[48] R.S.C., Ord. 13, r. 9.

[49] This is not the only ground for setting aside the judgment, there may have been formal irregularities.

**Writ indorsed
with Statement
of Claim
[Unliquidated
Demand]
(O.6,r.1)**

IN THE HIGH COURT OF JUSTICE   1982.$\underline{H}$.—No.179

Queen's Bench Division

[NOTTINGHAM   **District Registry]**

Between

     PETER GEORGE MARTIN HACKER   Plaintiff

AND

    RELIABLE NAG SUPPLY STABLES (SUED AS A FIRM)
                                               Defendant

(1) Insert name.   **To the Defendant (¹)** RELIABLE NAG SUPPLY STABLES

(2) Insert address.   **of (²)** THE WIDE PADDOCKS, LEAK AVENUE, GROATHAM, NOTTINGHAMSHIRE

This Writ of Summons has been issued against you by the above-named
Plaintiff in respect of the claim set out on the back.

Within 14 days after the service of this Writ on you, counting the day of service, you
must either satisfy the claim or return to the Court Office mentioned below the
accompanying **Acknowledgment of Service** stating therein whether you intend
to contest these proceedings.

If you fail to satisfy the claim, or to return the Acknowledgment within the time stated,
or if you return the Acknowledgment without stating therein an intention to contest
the proceedings the Plaintiff   may proceed with the action and judgment may be
entered against you forthwith and without further notice.

(3) Complete
and delete as
necessary.

Issued from the (³) [Central Office] [NOTTINGHAM   District Registry]
of the High Court this   FIRST   day of   DECEMBER   1982

NOTE:—This Writ may not be served later than 12 calendar months beginning with that date unless
renewed by order of the Court.

IMPORTANT

Directions for Acknowledgment of Service are given with the accompanying form.

Statement of Claim

The Plaintiffs claim is for

Damages for breach of an implied term in the contract for sale of a piebald gelding by the Defendant to the Plaintiff on the 25th day of June 1982

(Signed)   George Washington

(1) If this Writ was issued out of a District Registry, this indorsement as to place where the cause of action arose should be completed.

(2) Delete as necessary.

(3) Insert name of place.

(4) For phraseology of this indorsement where the Plaintiff sues in person, see *Supreme Court Practice*, Vol. 2, para. 3.

(¹) [(²) [The cause] [one of the causes] of action in respect of which the Plaintiff claim   relief in this action arose wholly or in part at(³)   Groatham in the district of the District Registry named overleaf.]

(⁴)**This Writ was issued by** Popp, Lees and Stone

of   23, Haltergate, Nottingham

[Agent   for

of   ]

Solicitor   for the said Plaintiff   whose address   (²) [is] [are]

19 Long Road, Pegworth, Nottinghamshire

COURT FEES ONLY

Writ indorsed with
Statement of Claim
[Liquidated
Demand]
(O.6, r. 1)

IN THE HIGH COURT OF JUSTICE 19 82 .— M .—No. 792

QUEEN'S BENCH **Division**

[Group]

[*NOTTINGHAM* **District Registry]**

Between

ALFONSO FREDERICO MASERATI   Plaintiff

AND

WILLIAM DANIEL HENRY LAGONDA

(1) Insert name. **To the Defendant(¹)** *WILLIAM DANIEL HENRY LAGONDA*   **Defendant**

(2) Insert
address. of(²) *423, TALBOT GARDENS, MORGAN-CUM-MIDGET, NOTTINGHAMSHIRE*

This Writ of Summons has been issued against you by the above-named Plaintiff in respect of the claim set out overleaf.

Within 14 days after the service of this Writ on you, counting the day of service, you must either satisfy the claim or return to the Court Office mentioned below the accompanying **Acknowledgment of Service** stating therein whether you intend to contest these proceedings.

If you fail to satisfy the claim or to return the Acknowledgment within the time stated, or if you return the Acknowledgment without stating therein an intention to contest the proceedings the Plaintiff may proceed with the action and judgment may be entered against you forthwith without further notice.

(3) Complete
and delete as
necessary. Issued from the(³) [Central Office] [*NOTTINGHAM* District Registry] of the High Court this *FIRST* day of *DECEMBER* 19 82

NOTE:—This Writ may not be served later than 12 calendar months beginning with that date unless renewed by order of the Court.

IMPORTANT

Directions for Acknowledgment of Service are given with the accompanying form.

Statement of Claim

The Plaintiff's claim is for

*the sum of £3990 being the price of goods sold and delivered
to the Defendant*

Particulars

*A motorcar, registered number ABC 123, sold to the defendant
under contract contained in letters dated the 29th day of
June 1982 and delivered to the defendant at his house
by the plaintiff on the 30th day of June 1982*   *£3990*

(Signed)   *George Washington*

If, within the time for returning the Acknowledgment of Service, the Defendant
pay the amount claimed and *£300*   for costs and, if the Plaintiff   obtain an
order for substituted service, the additional sum of *£10.00*   , further proceedings
will be stayed. The money must be paid to the Plaintiff   ,   *his* Solicitor or Agent

(¹) [(²) [The cause] [One of the causes] of action in respect of which the Plaintiff
claims relief in this action arose wholly or in part at(³) *MORGAN-CUM-MIDGET*
in the district of the District Registry named overleaf.]

(⁴) **This Writ** was issued by   *POPP, LEES AND STONE*

of   *23, HALTERGATE, NOTTINGHAM*

[Agent for

of   ]

Solicitor for the said Plaintiff   whose address   (²) [is] [are]

423, TALBOT GARDENS, MORGAN-CUM-MIDGET

NOTTINGHAMSHIRE

(1) If this Writ was issued out of a District Registry, this indorsement as to place where the cause of action arose should be completed.

(2) Delete as necessary.

(3) Insert name of place.

(4) For phraseology of this indorsement where the Plantiff sues in person, see *Supreme Court Practice*, Vol 2, para 3.

judgment is set aside in this way, the defendant is likely to bear some penalty in costs.

Acknowledgments of service to the two writs are set out below. The stables wish to dispute the claim. Mr. Lagonda does not.

3. SUMMARY JUDGMENT

It would obviously be an unacceptable delaying tactic for a defendant to indicate an intention to defend in circumstances where there was no real defence, thus gaining time in which to pay debts or damages which could not seriously be disputed.[50] The procedure by which a plaintiff is permitted to request the court to enter judgment for him summarily is clearly very important, but it is equally important to ensure that a power given to a judge or master to award a case to the plaintiff who can show that there is no real answer to his claim should not be exercised lightly. The provisions of Order 14 of the Rules of the Supreme Court seek to achieve a balance.[51]

A plaintiff may apply to the court to enter judgment on his behalf for the whole or part of his claim if he can support the application with an affidavit swearing the truth of the facts of the case and stating that the plaintiff believes there to be no defence to the claim.[52] The defendant may, if he wishes, by affidavit or otherwise[53] seek to refute the plaintiff's contention and demonstrate, at least, that there is an issue to be tried. He is not obliged to prove a defence—merely that there is an issue to be tried.[54]

At the hearing, the master will have the task of balancing the rights of plaintiff and defendant but he must allow the defendant to go on if he believes the issue triable, even though he may think that the defendant's chances of success are slender. However, there are a number of options open to the master and he is entitled to attach conditions to the leave to defend[55] which may have the effect of discouraging the defendant, or at least making him consider carefully the strength of his case. Of course, the master may give judgment for the plaintiff and greatly speed up the process of litigation.

4. THE PLEADINGS

Since the adversarial system depends upon the two parties selecting the issues for resolution and acquiring the evidence to support them, it is necessary that the parties should communicate to each other the elements of their case. The system of pleadings amounts to a formal exchange of allegations and can offer an opportunity to narrow down the issue between the parties. The way in which the pleadings are conducted is, however,

---

[50] The origin of the summary judgment powers lies in the Summary Procedure on Bills of Exchange Act 1855—a measure passed to protect bankers and others from the delay and cost of the trial required if a defendant made a defence, however unmeritorious, to a claim in debt.

[51] The summary judgment procedure is commonly referred to as "Order 14 procedure."

[52] R.S.C., Ord. 14, r. 2.

[53] It is, however, unusual to allow oral examination of the parties at an Order 14 hearing.

[54] R.S.C., Ord. 14, r. 3.

[55] The order most favourable to the defendant is obviously an order for unconditional leave to defend, but the master may require money to be paid in by the defendant, or only give leave to defend as a "short cause" (a special list to cater for actions which can be tried in a short time—up to 4 hours).

Acknowledgment
of Service
of Writ
of Summons
(O. 12, r. 3)

Directions of Acknowledgment of Service

1. The accompanying form of **ACKNOWLEDGMENT OF SERVICE** should be detached and completed by a Solicitor acting on behalf of the Defendant or by the Defendant if acting in person. After completion it must be delivered or sent by post to the Central Office, Royal Courts of Justice, Strand, London WC2A 2LL.

2. A Defendant who states in his Acknowledgment of Service that he intends to contest the proceedings **MUST ALSO SERVE A DEFENCE** on the Solicitor for the Plaintiff (or on the Plaintiff if acting in person).

If a Statement of Claim is indorsed on the Writ (i.e. the words "Statement of Claim" appear at the top of the back of the first page), the Defence must be served within 14 days after the time for acknowledging service of the Writ, unless in the meantime a summons for judgment is served on the Defendant.

If a Statement of Claim is not indorsed on the Writ, the Defence need not be served until 14 days after a Statement of Claim has been served on the Defendant. If the Defendant fails to serve his defence within the appropriate time, the Plaintiff may enter judgment against him without further notice.

3. **A STAY OF EXECUTION** against the Defendant's goods may be applied for where the Defendant is unable to pay the money for which any judgment is entered. If a Defendant to an action for a debt or liquidated demand (i.e. a fixed sum) who does not intend to contest the proceedings states, in answer to Question 3 in the Acknowledgment of Service, that he intends to apply for a stay, execution will be stayed for 14 days after his Acknowledgment, but he must, within that time, **ISSUE A SUMMONS** for a stay of execution, supported by an affidavit of his means. The affidavit should state any offer which the Defendant desires to make for payment of the money by instalments or otherwise.

4. **IF THE WRIT IS ISSUED OUT OF A DISTRICT REGISTRY** but the Defendant does not reside or carry on business within the district of the registry and the writ is not indorsed with a statement that the Plaintiff's cause of action arose in that district, the Defendant may, in answer to Question 4 in the Acknowledgment of Service, apply for the transfer of the action to some other District Registry or to the Royal Courts of Justice.

See over for Notes for Guidance

Notes for Guidance

1. Each Defendant (if there are more than one) is required to complete an Acknowledgment of Service and return it to the appropriate Court Office.

2. For the purpose of calculating the period of 14 days for acknowledging service, a writ served on the Defendant personally is treated as having been served on the day it was delivered to him and a writ served by post or by insertion through the Defendant's letter box is treated as having been served on the seventh day after the date of posting or insertion.

3. Where the Defendant is sued in a name different from his own, the form must be completed by him with the addition in paragraph 1 of the words "sued as (*the name stated on the Writ of Summons*)".

4. Where the Defendant is a **FIRM** and a Solicitor is not instructed, the form must be completed by a **PARTNER** by name, with the addition in paragraph 1 of the description "partner in the firm of (..)" after his name.

5. Where the Defendant is sued as an individual **TRADING IN A NAME OTHER THAN HIS OWN**, the form must be completed by him with the addition in paragraph 1 of the description "trading as (..)" after his name.

6. Where the Defendant is a **LIMITED COMPANY** the form must be completed by a Solicitor or by someone authorised to act on behalf of the Company, but the Company can take no further step in the proceedings without a Solicitor acting on its behalf.

7. Where the Defendant is a **MINOR** or a **MENTAL** Patient, the form must be completed by a Solicitor acting for a guardian *ad litem*.

8. A Defendant acting in person may obtain help in completing the form either at the Central Office of the Royal Courts of Justice or at any District Registry of the High Court or at any Citizens' Advice Bureau.

9. A Defendant who is NOT a Limited Company or a Corporation may be entitled to Legal Aid. Information about the Legal Aid Scheme may be obtained from any Citizens' Advice Bureau and from most firms of Solicitors.

10. These notes deal only with the more usual cases. In case of difficulty a Defendant in person should refer to paragraphs 8 and 9 above.

Acknowledgment
of Service of
Writ of
Summons
IN THE HIGH COURT OF JUSTICE

*The adjacent
heading should
be completed by
the Plaintiff*
QUEEN'S BENCH **Division**

19 82 .—   .—**No.** *179*

H

[Group   ]

Between

PETER GEORGE MARTIN HACKER   Plaintiff

AND

RELIABLE NAG SUPPLY STABLES
(sued as a firm)
Defendant

**If you intend to instruct a Solicitor to act for you, give him this form
IMMEDIATELY. Please complete in black ink.**

IMPORTANT. Read the accompanying directions and notes for guidance carefully before
completing this form. If any information required is omitted or given wrongly, THIS FORM MAY
HAVE TO BE RETURNED. Delay may result in judgment being entered against a Defendant
whereby he or his solicitor may have to pay the costs of applying to set it aside.

*See Notes 1, 3, 4
and 5*
1 State the full name of the Defendant by whom or on whose behalf the service
of the Writ is being acknowledged. *ALICE MARY ARKLE, partner in the
firm of RELIABLE NAG SUPPLY STABLES.*

2 State whether the Defendant intends to contest the proceedings (*tick
appropriate box*) ☑ yes   ☐ no

See Direction 3
3 If the claim against the Defendant is for a debt or liquidated demand, AND
he does not intend to contest the proceedings, state if the Defendant intends
to apply for a stay of execution against any judgment entered by the Plaintiff
(*tick box*)   ☐ yes

See Direction 4
4 If the Writ of Summons was issued out of a District Registry and
   (*a*) the Defendant's residence, place of business or registered office (if a
limited company) is NOT within the district of that District Registry
AND
   (*b*) there is no indorsement on the Writ that the Plaintiff's cause of action
arose wholly or in part within that district,
state if the Defendant applies for the transfer of the action (*tick box*) ☐ yes

**State which
Registry*
If YES, state—   ☐ to the Royal Courts of Justice, London:
(*tick appropriate box*)   OR
                                  ☐ to the*   District Registry

Service of the Writ is acknowledged accordingly

(*Signed*) *Alice Mary Arkle*

*†Where words
appear between
square brackets
delete if
inapplicable.
Insert "Defendant
in Person" if
appropriate*
†[~~Solicitor~~] [~~Agent for~~   *Defendant in Person*   ]
Address for service *(See notes overleaf)*
   *The Wide Paddock,
   Leak Avenue, Groatham,
   Nottinghamshire*

Please complete overleaf

Indorsement by plaintiff's solicitor (or by plaintiff if suing in person) of his name address and reference, if any, in the box below.

> POPP, LEES AND STONE,
> 23 HALTERGATE,
> NOTTINGHAM

Notes as to Address for Service

Solicitor. Where the Defendant is represented by a Solicitor, state the Solicitor's place of business in England or Wales. If the Solicitor is the Agent of another Solicitor, state the name and the place of business of the Solicitor for whom he is acting.

Defendant in person. Where the Defendant is acting in person, he must give his residence OR, if he does not reside in England or Wales, he must give an address in England or Wales where communications for him should be sent. In the case of a limited company, "residence" means its registered or principal office.

Indorsement by defendant's solicitor (or by defendant if suing in person) of his name address and reference, if any, in the box below.

> ALICE MARY ARKLE,
> THE WIDE PADDOCK,
> LEAK AVENUE,
> GROATHAM,
> NOTTINGHAMSHIRE

Oyez Publishing Limited, Norwich House, 11/13 Norwich Street, London EC4A 1AB, a subsidiary of The Solicitors' Law Stationery Society, Limited.
F376—4-80
★ ★ ★ ★

High Court E22 (PR)

IN THE HIGH COURT OF JUSTICE

*The adjacent
heading should
be completed by
the Plaintiff*

QUEEN'S BENCH **Division**

[Group   ]

19 82.—*M* .—**No.** 792

Between

ALFONSO FREDERICO MASERATI   Plaintiff

AND

WILLIAM DANIEL HENRY LAGONDA

Defendant

**If you intend to instruct a Solicitor to act for you, give him this form
IMMEDIATELY. Please complete in black ink.**

IMPORTANT. Read the accompanying directions and notes for guidance carefully before
completing this form. If any information required is omitted or given wrongly, THIS FORM MAY
HAVE TO BE RETURNED. Delay may result in judgment being entered against a Defendant
whereby he or his solicitor may have to pay the costs of applying to set it aside.

*See Notes 1, 3, 4
and 5*

1 State the full name of the Defendant by whom or on whose behalf the service
of the Writ is being acknowledged.   WILLIAM DANIEL HENRY LAGONDA

2 State whether the Defendant intends to contest the proceedings *(tick
appropriate box)* ☐ yes   ✓ no

See Direction 3

3 If the claim against the Defendant is for a debt or liquidated demand, AND
he does not intend to contest the proceedings, state if the Defendant intends
to apply for a stay of execution against any judgment entered by the Plaintiff
(tick box)   ☐ yes

See Direction 4

4 If the Writ of Summons was issued out of a District Registry and

    (*a*) the Defendant's residence, place of business or registered office (if a
limited company) is NOT within the district of that District Registry
AND

    (*b*) there is no indorsement on the Writ that the Plaintiff's cause of action
arose wholly or in part within that district,

state if the Defendant applies for the transfer of the action *(tick box)* ☐ yes

**State which
Registry*

If YES, state—   ☐ to the Royal Courts of Justice, London:
(tick appropriate box)   OR
                           ☐ to the*   District Registry

Service of the Writ is acknowledged accordingly

(*Signed*)   Furlong and Co.

*†Where words
appear between
square brackets
delete if
inapplicable.
Insert "Defendant
in Person" if
appropriate*

†[Solicitor] [Agent for   ]

Address for service *(See notes overleaf)*

    43, BRIDLE LANE, NOTTINGHAM

Please complete overleaf

Indorsement by plaintiff's solicitor (or by plaintiff if suing in person) of his name address and reference, if any, in the box below.

```
POPP, LEES AND STONE,
23 HALTERGATE,
NOTTINGHAM.
```

Notes as to Address for Service

Solicitor. Where the Defendant is represented by a Solicitor, state the Solicitor's place of business in England or Wales. If the Solicitor is the Agent of another Solicitor, state the name and the place of business of the Solicitor for whom he is acting.

Defendant in person. Where the Defendant is acting in person, he must give his residence OR, if he does not reside in England or Wales, he must give an address in England or Wales where communications for him should be sent. In the case of a limited company, "residence" means its registered or principal office.

Indorsement by defendant's solicitor (or by defendant if suing in person) of his name address and reference, if any, in the box below.

```
FURLONG AND CO.,
43 BRIDLE LANE,
NOTTINGHAM.
```

Oyez Publishing Limited, Norwich House, 11/13 Norwich Street, London EC4A 1AB, a subsidiary of The Solicitors' Law Stationery Society, Limited.
F376—4-80
High Court E22 (PR)
★ ★ ★ ★

entirely a matter for the parties[56] and it is perfectly possible to leave the issue as wide and ill-defined as at the outset.

If the plaintiff has served a generally indorsed writ on the defendant, the first document to be prepared and served is the statement of claim in which he must set out his claim, the facts he will rely on to support it, the injury/loss he has suffered and the remedy which he is seeking.[57] The statement needs to be sufficiently full to allow the defendant to ascertain the case against him and to prepare a defence.

The basic rule governing all pleadings is contained in R.S.C. Ord. 18 r. 7(1):

> "Every pleading must contain, and contain only, a statement in a summary form of the material facts on which the party pleading relies for his claim or defence, as the case may be, but not the evidence by which those facts are to be proved, and the statement must be as brief as the nature of the case admits."

In the statement of claim, the plaintiff will probably wish to keep open all possible lines of attack and will draft the statement widely for that purpose. In *Hacker* v. *Reliable Nag Supply Stables*[58] the statement of claim could be set out as follows.

IN THE HIGH COURT OF JUSTICE   1982 H. No. 179
QUEEN'S BENCH DIVISION
NOTTINGHAM DISTRICT REGISTRY.
WRIT ISSUED THE 1st DAY OF DECEMBER 1982

Between

PETER GEORGE MARTIN HACKER   *Plaintiff*
and
RELIABLE NAG SUPPLY STABLES   *Defendants*
(SUED AS A FIRM)

STATEMENT OF CLAIM

1. The Plaintiff and the Defendants entered into an oral contract on June 25th 1982 at the Defendants' place of business for the sale of a piebald gelding, known as Skipper, by the Defendants to the Plaintiff for the price of £6500 which was paid by the Plaintiff to the Defendants on that day.
2. At all material times the Defendants were horse traders and the said horse was sold in the course of the Defendants' business.
3. The Plaintiff took delivery of the said horse from the Defendant on June 26th 1982.
4. There was an implied term in the said contract that the said horse was sound and in good health.
5. Further or alternatively the Plaintiff made known to the Defendants before and at the time of the said sale that he

---

[56] Subject, of course, to the Rules of the Supreme Court concerning pleadings which are contained in Order 18.

[57] R.S.C., Ord. 18, r. 15.

[58] The imaginary case which we began by writ of summons at p. 417 above.

required the horse for general hacking and for jumping at the local gymkhanas and accordingly it was an implied term of the said contract that it would be fit for such purposes.

6. In breach of the said contract the good supplied by the Defendants to the Plaintiff was not of merchantable quality and/or was not fit for its purpose.

Particulars

The said horse was found to be suffering from Bastard Strangles and in consequence thereof was entirely useless and worthless to the Plaintiff.

7. By reason of the matters aforesaid the plaintiff has suffered loss and damage.

Particulars of Special Damage

Cost price of horse	£6500
Fees paid to Sutton Riding Enterprises for the care of alternative horse from 1st July to 20th August	£290
AND the Plaintiff claims damages totalling	£6790

Served this 12th day of January 1983
by Popp, Lees and Stone, 23 Haltergate, Nottingham.
Solicitors for the Plaintiff.

The defendant may consider that the information given in the statement of claim is defective, or insufficient to allow him to prepare a defence to the claim. He is entitled, if he wishes, to request from the plaintiff any further information he requires and he does this by way of a request for "further and better particulars."[59] This procedure again illustrates the differing ways in which the parties may use the pleadings—it may be a genuine request for information so that the defendant may better understand the case, or it may be another delaying tactic designed to increase the pressure on the plaintiff who is anxious to get his damages. In the case of *Hacker*, the defendant wishes to know more . . . .

IN THE HIGH COURT OF JUSTICE   1982 H. No. 179
QUEEN'S BENCH DIVISION
NOTTINGHAM DISTRICT REGISTRY

Between

PETER GEORGE MARTIN HACKER   *Plaintiff*
and
RELIABLE NAG SUPPLY STABLES   *Defendants*
(SUED AS A FIRM)

REQUEST BY THE DEFENDANTS FOR FURTHER AND BETTER PARTICULARS OF THE STATEMENT OF CLAIM

Under paragraph 1

Give full particulars of all facts and matters relied on in support of the allegation that an oral contract was made between the Plaintiff and the Defendants on June 25th 1982.

[59] R.S.C., Ord. 18, r. 12.

Under paragraph 5

Give full particulars of all facts and matters relied upon in support of the allegation that the Plaintiff made known to the Defendants that he required the horse for general hacking and jumping at local gymkhanas, and of the allegation that there was an implied term that the horse would be fit for such purpose.

Under paragraph 6

State at what time it is alleged that the said horse was discovered to be suffering from Bastard Strangles and for how long it is alleged that the condition had existed.

Under paragraph 7

Give full particulars of the stabling provided for the alternative horse at Sutton Riding Enterprises and a detailed analysis of the fees charged.

Martin Martinson

SERVED this 18th day of February 1983,
By Furlong and Co., 43 Bridle Lane, Nottingham
Solicitors for the Defendants.

In due course the defendant must serve a defence on the plaintiff.[60] There are specified time limits for the conduct of pleadings,[61] but these are often dispensed with by the consent of the parties or by order of the court.[62] Having been given the necessary information about the plaintiff's claim, the defendant must settle on his tactics. In his defence he may choose to refute the whole of the plaintiff's claim and the facts on which it is based[63]; or he may admit the whole case whilst pleading an explanation which allows him to avoid liability[64]; or he may admit the whole case but object that it discloses no cause of action[65]; or he may adopt a combination of these approaches; or he may adopt them all as alternatives.[66] Naturally, the wider the defence, the wider the issues that remain for resolution at the trial and the greater must be the plaintiff's preparations. If the defendant is not prepared to admit any of the facts pleaded by the plaintiff they may all have to be proved in court with a consequent increase in the length and

[60] R.S.C., Ord. 18, r. 2.
[61] Contained in the provisions of Order 18.
[62] R.S.C., Ord. 3, r. 5. The advantage of obtaining the consent of the other party to an extension of time limits is that it saves the cost of an application to the court.
[63] Known as a "traverse."
[64] Known as a "confession and avoidance."
[65] Known as "objection in point of law."
[66] Pleadings in the alternative can sometimes appear extremely confusing. Hence, "(1) The Defendant denies that he was present at the time alleged and that he hit the plaintiff (traverse) (2) If, which is not admitted, the defendant was present and did hit the plaintiff, he did so in self-defence (confession and avoidance); (3) If, which is not admitted, the defendant was present and hit the plaintiff and did not act in self-defence, the statement of claim discloses no cause of action."

cost of the case (although either party may serve notice under Order 27 requiring the admission of facts with a penalty in costs for refusal.) If the defendant does make substantial admissions, the defence will have the effect of disclosing and narrowing the issue between the parties so that they are both aware of precisely what remains in dispute. In order that the pleadings should disclose clearly what remains in dispute, any issue of fact in a pleading must be specifically denied or it will be deemed to have been admitted.[67]

So far we have omitted consideration of one important possibility. The defendant may wish to make a claim against the plaintiff in addition to defending the plaintiff's claim. It is not necessary that he should begin a separate action, he is permitted simply to add a *counterclaim*[68] to his defence. Set out below is the defence and counterclaim of the Reliable Nag Supply Stables.

IN THE HIGH COURT OF JUSTICE   1982 H. No. 179
QUEEN'S BENCH DIVISION
NOTTINGHAM DISTRICT REGISTRY

Between

PETER GEORGE MARTIN HACKER   *Plaintiff*
and
RELIABLE NAG SUPPLY STABLES   *Defendants*
(SUED AS A FIRM)

DEFENCE AND COUNTERCLAIM

DEFENCE

1. It is admitted that by a contract made on June 25th 1982, the Defendants sold to the Plaintiff a piebald gelding for the price of £6500, which price was paid by the Plaintiff. Save as aforesaid the first paragraph of the Statement of Claim is denied.

2. Paragraphs 2 and 3 of the Statement of Claim are admitted.

3. It is admitted that the said horse was found to be suffering from Bastard Strangles after it had been delivered to the Plaintiff. Save as aforesaid, the implied terms and each and every fact and matter alleged in the fourth, fifth, sixth and seventh paragraphs of the Statement of Claim are denied, and it is denied that the Defendants were in breach of contract as alleged or at all.

4. Further or alternatively, it was an express term of the said agreement that the Defendant would exchange the said horse for another if the same should within 14 days prove unsuitable to the Plaintiff.

5. By a further agreement made at or about the beginning of July 1982 between the Defendants and the Plaintiff, pursuant to the express term referred to in paragraph 4 hereof, the Plaintiff

---

[67] R.S.C. Ord. 18, r. 13.
[68] *Ibid.* Ord. 18, r. 18.

     agreed to exchange the said horse for another and to take delivery of a suitable bay mare owned by the Defendants pending his decision to retain the said piebald gelding or the said bay mare.

6.   In breach of contract, the Plaintiff failed to make any decision as to which of the said horses he would retain, and, on or about August 21st 1982 returned the said bay mare to the Defendants thereby repudiating the said agreement.

7.   If and to the extent, if at all, which is not admitted, that the Defendants are liable to the Plaintiff they will seek to set off the damages and sums counterclaimed herein to extinguish or diminish such liability.

COUNTERCLAIM

8.   The Defendants repeat paragraphs 1 to 6 of their defence herein.

9.   It was an implied term of the agreement pursuant whereto the Defendants delivered the said bay mare to the Plaintiff that the Plaintiff would take reasonable care of the said bay mare whilst in his custody.

10.   In breach of the said implied term the Plaintiff failed to take reasonable care of the said bay mare.

PARTICULARS

When the Plaintiff returned the said bay mare to the Defendants its ribs were protruding, its hooves were broken, its coat was dull and ungroomed, 3 shoes were missing and it was in poor health.

11.   By reason of the said breaches and each of them, the Defendants suffered loss and damage.

PARTICULARS OF DAMAGE

(1)	Loss of profit on the sale of a horse	300.00
(2)	Transport costs on delivery and collection	50.00
(3)	Veterinary costs for said bay mare	120.00
(4)	Farrier's fees for said bay mare	90.00
(5)	Loss of value of said bay mare	400.00
		960.00

AND the Defendants counterclaim damages under paragraph 11 hereof.

William Naseby

Dated this 28th day of March 1983

Where a defence raises new facts the plaintiff may wish to enter a reply[69] and where a counterclaim has been made it is usual for the plaintiff to enter a defence. These can conveniently be combined and will usually be the final document in the pleadings. The defendant is, however, permitted to seek leave of the court[70] to enter a *Rejoinder;* the plaintiff, a *Surrejoinder;* the defendant, a *Rebutter;* the plaintiff, a *Surrebutter.* Despite these delightful names, the White Book comments, "None of these names for pleadings occurs in the former or present Rules. All except Rejoinder are rare to the point of extinction; and even Rejoinder is seldom seen."[71]

Below we set out a reply and defence to counterclaim in *Hacker's case:*

IN THE HIGH COURT OF JUSTICE   1982 H. No. 179
QUEEN'S BENCH DIVISION
NOTTINGHAM DISTRICT REGISTRY

Between

PETER GEORGE MARTIN HACKER   *Plaintiff*
and
RELIABLE NAG SUPPLY STABLES   *Defendants*
(SUED AS A FIRM)

REPLY AND DEFENCE TO COUNTERCLAIM

REPLY

1. The Plaintiff joins issue save insofar as paragraphs 1 to 3 of the Defence and Counterclaim are concerned.

DEFENCE TO COUNTERCLAIM

2. It is admitted that the further agreement referred to in paragraph 4 of the Defence and Counterclaim was made, but it is denied that the Defendants offered a suitable horse in exchange.

3. The Plaintiff paid employees of Sutton Riding Enterprises to attend to the said substitute horse and informed the Defendants at all times of the poor condition of the said horse.

4. The Plaintiff denies that the said horse was in the condition described in paragraph 10 of the Defence Counterclaim.

5. Whereas the Plaintiff had been informed and believed that the said horse was ill when returned to the Defendants the said illness was a direct result of the poor condition of the said horse at the time of its delivery to the Plaintiff by the Defendants.

6. Each and every claim for damages in paragraph 11 of the Defence and Counterclaim is denied by the Plaintiff.

George Washington

Dated this 25th day of April 1983

[69] *Ibid.* Ord. 18, r. 3.
[70] *Ibid.* Ord. 18, r. 4.
[71] *Supreme Court Practice* 1982, Vol. 1, p. 297.

"It has become fashionable in these days to attach decreasing importance to pleadings, and it is beyond doubt that there have been times when an insistence on complete compliance with their technicalities put justice at risk. . . . But pleadings continue to play an essential part in civil action . . . the primary purpose of pleading remains and it can still prove of vital importance. That purpose is to define the issues and thereby to inform the parties in advance of the case they have to meet and so enable them to take steps to deal with it.'[72]

5. THE SUMMONS FOR DIRECTIONS

Within one month of the close of pleadings, the plaintiff must take out a "summons for directions."[73] This procedure is designed to bring the action before a master who may then give directions to resolve any outstanding matters between the parties which should be dealt with by an interlocutory application and will also give directions about the future course of the action designed to "secure the just, expeditious and economical disposal thereof."[74]

The summons can, therefore, operate as a time-saving and cost-saving device in that its object is to ensure that the action is fully prepared for trial. It may also provide an opportunity for the parties to indicate to the master and to each other that points formerly in issue will not be pursued at trial. In that way, like the pre-trial review in the county court, it may serve to assist the process of settlement and compromise.

A standard form summons is used[75] which directs the parties to particular issues which might be relevant. The form refers to consolidation of actions; transfer of action; amendments to writ or pleadings; requests for further and better particulars; discovery of documents; inspection of property and the arrangements for the trial of the action. The master will strike out inapplicable directions and add any others as appropriate in the particular case.

Two changes have been made recently in the procedure in an attempt to save time and money for the parties. First, discovery of documents is now automatic in actions tried with pleadings[76] and the time limits associated with the summons for directions are such as to allow the parties to make discovery and consider the results. Secondly, automatic directions are given in personal injury cases in the Queen's Bench Division without the parties having to apply.[77] Two inquiries[78] found that directions were standard in almost all personal injury cases and the directions set out in

---

[72] *Per* Lord Edmund Davies in *Farrell* v. *Sec. of State for Defence* [1980] 1 W.L.R. 172, at p. 179. See also observations on the importance of pleadings by Scarman L.J. in *Fulham* v. *Newcastle Chronicle* [1977] 1 W.L.R. 651 at p. 659c, and Megaw L.J. in *Commission for Racial Equality* v. *Ealing London Borough Council* [1978] 1 W.L.R. 112, at pp. 117–8.

[73] R.S.C., Ord. 25, r. 1. If the plaintiff fails to take out the summons, the defendant may do so or apply to have the action dismissed.

[74] R.S.C., Ord. 25, r. 1(1)(*b*).

[75] See below.

[76] A rule introduced in 1962, now R.S.C., Ord. 24, r. 2.

[77] R.S.C., Ord. 25, r.8 (introduced in 1980) which specifies the directions. The rule excludes cases of medical negligence. For a comment on the purpose and likely effect of the new rule, see *Supreme Court Practice 1982*, Vol. 1, p. 485–486.

[78] The (Winn) *Committee on Personal Injuries Litigation*, (Cmnd. 3691, 1968); The (Cantley) *Working Party on Personal Injuries Litigation Procedure* (Cmnd. 7476, 1979).

R.S.C. Ord. 25, r. 8 now come into effect automatically on the close of pleadings. This does not prevent the parties making application for any special directions which are required,[79] but it does have the effect of expediting the action.

6. DISCOVERY OF DOCUMENTS

So that each party may be aware of documents relating to issues in the case, rules requiring "discovery" of those documents place an obligation on the litigants to disclose their existence and, possibly, to disclose their content.[80] As mentioned earlier, discovery is now automatic in actions with pleadings with the possibility of using the summons for directions to require additional information.

Each party must produce a list of documents " . . . which are or have been in his possession, custody or power relating to any matter in question . . . in the action."[81] The list must be in a prescribed form[82] and the documents are divided into three categories—those which the plaintiff or defendant has in his possession, custody or power and is willing to produce; those which he has, but is not willing to produce; and those which he has had, but has no longer. Objections to the production of documents for inspection will be based on one or more of the privileges[83] to which a litigant is entitled.

A list of documents in *Hacker* v. *Reliable Nag Supply Stables* is set out below.

The objects of discovery are further assisted by a power in the court to administer interrogatories to a party to the action at the request of the other party with a view to eliciting information which is relevant to matters in issue.[84] This is, in effect, a discovery of facts which are not contained in known documents. There are established rules about what sort of questions will be permitted[85] and they are always subject to the discretion of the master through whom application must be made. Ideally, interrogatories should be of assistance in assessing the relative strength of the case and thus assisting in a possible settlement or in presenting the case at trial.

A new power was given to the courts in 1970 to assist a party who wished to discover whether or not he had a case by acquiring information from the potential defendant. Now contained in the Supreme Court Act 1981, s.33(2), this provision permits a person who appears to be likely to be a party to a personal injuries claim to request the court to order discovery of any documents relevant to the issue held by another potential party. This provision is consistent with the increasing emphasis on assisting personal injury actions noted in connection with the summons for directions.

---

[79] R.S.C., Ord. 25, r. 8(3).

[80] R.S.C., Ord. 24.

[81] R.S.C., Ord. 24, r.2(1).

[82] See below.

[83] There are certain recognised privileges—legal professional privilege; the privilege against self-incrimination; "without prejudice" documents; Crown privilege.

[84] R.S.C., Ord. 26.

[85] *e.g.* "no fishing"—the question must relate to some definite issue and cannot merely be hoping to discover something of general use. Also, the questions must be relevant and are usually directed towards establishing the evidence by which the interrogator will seek to prove his own case.

List of
Documents
(O.24 r.5)

IN THE HIGH COURT OF JUSTICE   1982 .H .—No. 179

QUEEN'S BENCH **Division**

NOTTINGHAM DISTRICT REGISTRY

Between

PETER GEORGE MARTIN HACKER

Plaintiff

AND

RELIABLE NAG SUPPLY STABLES (SUED AS A FIRM)

Defendant

LIST OF DOCUMENTS

The following is a list of the documents relating to the matters in question in this action which are or have been in the possession, custody or power of the above-named (¹) plaintiff PETER GEORGE MARTIN HACKER

(1) Plaintiffs (or Defendant(s)) A.B.

and which is served in compliance with Order 24, rule 2 [or the order herein dated the   day of   , 19   ].

1. The (²) plaintiff   has in his possession, custody or power the documents relating to the matters in question in this action enumerated in Schedule 1 hereto.

(2) Plaintiff(s) or Defendant(s).

2. The (²) plaintiff   object s to produce the documents enumerated in Part 2 of the said Schedule 1 on the ground that (³) they are privileged documents as between solicitor and client.

(3) State ground of objection.

3. The (²) plaintiff   has had, but ha s not now, in his possession, custody or power the documents relating to the matters in question in this action enumerated in Schedule 2 hereto.

4. Of the documents in the said Schedule 2, those numbered   1 and 2   in that Schedule were last in the (⁴)plaintiffspossession, custody or power on (⁵) 19th May 1981   and the remainder on (⁶)

(⁶) They are now in the possession of the defendant's solicitors

(4) Plaintiff's or Defendant's.

(5) State when.

(6) Here state what has become of the said documents and in whose possession they now are.

5. Neither the (²)plaintiff nor h is Solicitor nor any other person on his behalf, ha s now, or ever had, in his possession, custody or power any document of any description whatever relating to any matter in question in this action, other than the documents enumerated in Schedules 1 and 2 hereto.

SCHEDULE 1.—Part 1.

(Here enumerate in a convenient order the documents (or bundles of documents, if of the same nature, such as invoices) in the (possession, custody or power of the party in question which he does not object to produce, with a short description of each document or bundle sufficient to identify it.)

Description of Document	Date
1. Copy letters between Plaintiff's solicitors and Defendant's solicitors	Various
2. Receipts for £100 signed by Alice Arkle	25th June 1982
3. Account of Sutton Riding Enterprises	22nd August 1982
4. Letter from Plaintiff to Defendants	20th August 1982
5. Letter from Defendants to Plaintiff	21st August 1982
6. Copy letter from Plaintiff to Defendants	3rd September 1982

SCHEDULE 1.—Part 2.

(Here enumerate as aforesaid the documents in the possession, custody or power of the party in question which he objects to produce.)

Description of Document	Date
Correspondence between Plaintiff's solicitor and Plaintiff	
Notes and documents related solely to the preparation of the Plaintiff's case	

SCHEDULE 2.

(Here enumerate as aforesaid the documents which have been, but at the date of service of the list are not, in the possession, custody or power of the party in question.)

1. Copy letters to Defendant's solicitors		
2. Copy letters from Plaintiff to Defendants	20th August 1982

Dated the 20th **day of** May , 19 82 .

NOTICE TO INSPECT

Take notice that the documents in the above list, other than those listed in Part 2 of Schedule 1 [and Schedule 2], may be inspected at [the office of the Solicitor of the above-named (⁷) POPP, LEES AND STONE, 23 HALTERGATE, NOTTINGHAM]

(⁷) Plaintiff(s) or Defendant(s) (insert address) or as may be.

on the 20th day of June , 19 82 , between the hours of 9.30 a.m. and 5.00 p.m.

(⁸) Defendant(s) (or Plaintiff(s)) C.D.

To the (⁸) Defendant

Served the 20th day of May 19 82,
by POPP, LEES AND STONE
of 23 HALTERGATE, NOTTINGHAM

and his Solicitor . Solicitor for the Plaintiff

7. Payment into Court

At any stage of the action after the issue of a writ, a defendant may pay money to the court in attempted satisfaction of the plaintiff's claim against him. The plaintiff may then choose whether to accept the amount paid in and discontinue the action, or carry on the action in the hope of obtaining a greater sum at trial. The penalty for the plaintiff is that he will normally bear all the costs of the action from the date of the payment in unless he is awarded a sum in excess of the amount the defendant has paid in.[86]

This is a very useful procedure for a defendant who may use it either to protect himself from a zealous plaintiff who wants to have his "day in court" or to put pressure on him to accept a sum in settlement rather than risk a heavy bill in costs. It is important to stress two points. First, that the plaintiff must "take it or leave it"—he cannot accept the sum as part settlement and carry on the action. Second, that the judge (jury) is not told of the payment in until the question of liability and damages have been settled.[87]

In the case of a claim for a liquidated sum, the plaintiff's decision is not likely to be difficult. Where the sum is unliquidated the inherent uncertainties of the value of the claim, the difficulties of proof, the desirability of money in hand will all combine to make the choice much harder.

---

[86] The matter of costs is within the discretion of the court, see above, p. 362, but the plaintiff normally suffers.

[87] R.S.C., Ord. 22, r. 7. If the judge is told inadvertently he must decide whether to continue the case or order a retrial.

CHAPTER 12

TRIBUNALS

IN the preceding chapter we used the actions in the county court and the Queen's Bench Division as examples of civil procedure. For this chapter there is no standard model. Generalisation about tribunal procedure is almost impossible in the face of widely divergent practice in different tribunals[1] and there is no accepted pattern. However, there are certain common principles and objectives in tribunal adjudication and there are common procedural problems to be solved. This chapter sets out to examine these objectives and the way in which they influence procedure prior to a tribunal hearing; the common problems which procedural rules must attempt to solve; the amount of legal advice or help which is available; and finally, the pre-hearing procedure adopted in two particular tribunals as illustrative of the various solutions designed to meet the needs of individual claimants and individual tribunals.

A. THE COMMON OBJECTIVES

The starting point of any discussion must be the Franks Report[2] and its assertion that tribunals should display three common characteristics: openness, fairness and impartiality.[3] It is clear that the attainment of each of these objectives will have implications for the procedural rules adopted.

In requiring that tribunals should be open, the Committee intended that the proceedings should be given sufficient publicity so that they were known to those who might need to make use of them. In addition, it was stated that the essential reasoning underlying decisions should be made known to the parties.[4]

Openness means more than the adoption of a rule of procedure that, save where the personal interests of the claimant would be prejudiced, tribunal hearings should be conducted in public. It signifies rather a notion of availability or accessibility—that tribunal adjudication is open to all those who might have a problem lying within the jurisdiction of a particular tribunal. In order that a tribunal is *accessible* to the public, each citizen needs to be aware of his right to use the tribunal where appropriate[5]; the information given in official publications and forms must be comprehensible; tribunal hearings need to be conveniently located; advice and assistance needs to be available either through the legal advice scheme or through other agencies; and the procedure to be followed both prior to and

---

[1] The various types of tribunal and their jurisdiction are discussed above, p. 31.
[2] Report of the Committee on Administrative Tribunals and Enquiries (Cmnd. 218, 1957).
[3] *Ibid.* In particular, paras. 23–25, 41–42.
[4] *Ibid.* para. 98.
[5] This goes back to the question of ensuring that problems are recognised and identified accurately, see p. 314 above.

during the hearing should be sufficiently clear that the claimant can follow it and understand the implications of seeking a tribunal hearing. Establishing the right procedural rules is but one aspect of making tribunals accessible to the public.

The objectives of fairness and impartiality are closely linked, and are especially important to a system which does not have the weight and authority enjoyed by the courts in the public esteem. Naturally, the claimant must be assured that the adjudication is even-handed or he will dismiss the whole proceedings as unfair, but the procedure to be followed is also crucial. Every claimant will judge the fairness of the tribunal (and hence assess its credibility and reputation) by reference to the way in which the case has progressed and the extent to which he has been able to put his own side of the argument in the knowledge of the case he has to meet. Procedural fairness—the feeling induced in the claimant that he has had "a fair crack of the whip"—is absolutely essential and, according to the Franks Committee, depends upon, " . . . the adoption of a clear procedure which enables parties to know their rights, to present their case fully and to know the case which they have to meet."[6]

As well as displaying these three characteristics, tribunals are also expected to offer informal, cheap and quick adjudication providing a contrast to the procedures of the High Court.[7] The problem lies in achieving an acceptable standard of decision-making based on adequate information and argument, without rendering tribunals as formal, expensive and slow as the civil courts.

Before a tribunal case reaches a hearing it must be prepared for adjudication and the parties must be in a position to participate fully at the hearing. There are, broadly, three stages in pre-hearing procedure which might be termed, "knowing your rights," "knowing the ropes," and "knowing the case."

B. "KNOWING YOUR RIGHTS"—IDENTIFYING THE TRIBUNAL

Courts do not have to advertise. There is a general awareness that civil courts are the venue for settling disputes, (although there may be some difficulty for individuals in perceiving that they have a problem capable of legal settlement) and as to criminal courts, defendants have little choice about whether they wish to avail themselves of the court's jurisdiction! In respect of tribunals, the first difficulty for the parties may lie in realising that there is a body with jurisdiction over their grievance whose assistance might be invoked. The various tribunals need to be sufficiently well publicised so as to alert people to their existence and powers.

In general, individuals may take their case to a tribunal as a result of a decision of a Government department which affects them (a citizen/State dispute), or as a result of experiencing an event or series of events which the law places within the jurisdiction of a particular tribunal, (normally a citizen/citizen dispute). Into the former category would fall appeals to

[6] Franks Report, *op. cit.* para. 42.
[7] For a comparison between courts and tribunals, see R.E. Wraith and P.G. Hutchesson, *Administrative Tribunals* (1973) Chap. 10. *Cf.* above, pp. 34–36.

Social Security Appeal Tribunals[8]; to the General Commissioners of Income Tax[9]; to Vaccine Damage Tribunals[10]; to the Immigration Appeal Tribunal[11] and many others. Into the latter category would fall applications to an Industrial Tribunal[12]; to a Family Practitioner Committee[13]; to a Rent Assessment Committee.[14] This division is significant because in a citizen/state dispute the individual concerned may be notified of the existence of the tribunal and of his right of appeal at the time that the decision is notified to him. Thus, the claimant knows of the right of appeal and, usually, how to make application. He may not know what are the implications of an appeal or precisely how to go about preparing his case, but he is given a start.

In respect of citizen/citizen disputes it is for the applicant to realise that if he is unfairly dismissed, or his rent is too high, or his doctor maltreats him, that he has an opportunity to pursue his grievance in a tribunal. Some tribunals must, therefore, give special consideration to how they can make the public aware of their jurisdiction.

1. THE AVAILABILITY OF LEGAL ADVICE

With very limited exceptions, legal aid is not available for *representation* at tribunal hearings.[15] The legal advice scheme, however, was intended to provide a source of advice for the public on matters relating to tribunals and how to use them.[16] The legal advice scheme has already been considered in detail,[17] but you will recall that a solicitor is permitted to give advice under the scheme to any suitably qualified applicant, "on the application of English law to any particular circumstances which have arisen in relation to the person seeking the advice and as to any steps which that person might appropriately take . . . ."[18]

It has been a source of regret to the Lord Chancellor's Advisory Committee on Legal Aid that the green form scheme is not used more

[8] Where the original decision is made by an adjudication officer at the Department of Health and Social Security, and the appeal will be to a Social Security Appeal Tribunal, a local tribunal constituted under the Social Security Act 1975 as amended by the Health and Social Services and Social Security Adjudications Act 1983, or a medical board. See above, pp. 55–58.

[9] Against an income tax assessment, the tribunal being arranged in accordance with the Taxes Management Act 1970.

[10] Against the decision of an adjudication officer that the claim of a person under the Vaccine Damage Payments Act 1979 is disallowed.

[11] Either against the decision of an immigration adjudicator or, in certain cases, directly against decisions of an immigration officer under the Immigration Act 1971.

[12] See above, pp. 52–54.

[13] Where complaints may be made about services provided by a general practitioner to his patients.

[14] Rent Assessment Committees exercise jurisdiction uner the Rent Act 1977 in the determination of the correctness of the decision of a rent officer as to a fair rent for a regulated tenancy. They also exercise the jurisdiction formerly exercised by rent tribunals, Housing Act 1980, s.72.

[15] See above, p. 389.

[16] In 1969, The Law Society asserted that the introduction of a legal advice scheme would encourage solicitors to operate in areas of unmet legal need and ensure that adequate legal services would be provided. See also, above, pp. 349–350.

[17] In chap. 9, above, pp. 339–351.

[18] Legal Aid Act 1974, s.2(1)(a) and (b).

extensively for advice on tribunal matters,[19] but that is part of the wider problem of encouraging those who could benefit from the green form scheme to get along to a solicitor's office.[20] There is some recent evidence that claims for payment by solicitors who have undertaken work on the green form scheme have been refused by officials in some legal aid area offices, particularly where the work relates to welfare benefit advice.[21] This would seem to be directly contrary to the objectives of the green form scheme and damaging to the system of tribunal adjudication. An applicant ought to be able to get advice from a solicitor on the jurisdiction and powers of the various tribunals as well as on the procedural steps necessary to pursue a claim.

It is difficult to quantify precisely the number of tribunal cases dealt with by solicitors under the green form scheme. There is no separate statistical category in the Legal Aid Annual Reports which could provide a figure. In 1982–1983, less than 10 per cent. of the 649,496 bills paid out of the Legal Aid Fund for green form advice related to the subjects of landlord and tenant, housing, employment, welfare benefits tribunals, and immigration and nationality.[22] Amongst that 10 per cent. will be some tribunal work. It seems that the legal advice scheme is not contributing substantially to the accessibility of tribunal adjudication.

2. OTHER SOURCES OF ADVICE

The agencies discussed in Chapter 9 (CABx, independent advice centres, neighbourhood law centres, Trade Unions, etc.) are available to offer help to individuals, but their work has been supplemented by the growth of specialist groups. Some of these are attached to large, generalist agencies, some exist independently.[23]

Although Citizens Advice Bureaux have been prominent in developing tribunal assistance and representation, no standard pattern of organisation has emerged. Instead, individual schemes have grown up according to the particular circumstances in different parts of the country. Inevitably, the availability of resources has had a great influence on the type of provision made and its effectiveness. In the West Midlands, a specially funded scheme set up an individual tribunal unit independent of the bureaux in the area, but offering training and support to them and their clients.[24] In Newcastle-upon-Tyne, a smaller unit was situated within the bureau dealing specifically with cases referred on to it through the bureau. In Chapeltown, Leeds, a Tribunal Assistance Unit offered a service to claimants through the local bureau.[25] In other areas, salaried welfare rights

[19] See, *e.g. 26th Legal Aid Annual Reports* [1975–76] p. 58, para. 7.
[20] See above, pp. 349–351.
[21] *LAG Bulletin*, July 1983, pp. 1, 5.
[22] *33rd Legal Aid Annual Reports* [1982–83] Appendix 1F, p. 57. Just over 70 per cent. of the bills paid in the same period relate to family or criminal matters.
[23] A survey of some of these specialist groups is contained in, R. Lawrence, *Tribunal Representation, The Role of Advice and Advocacy Services* (1980).
[24] The project was jointly funded by the National Association of Citizens Advice Bureaux and the EEC Action Against Poverty Programme. The report on the project and its significance for tribunal advice and advocacy services generally is R. Lawrence, *Tribunal Representation, op. cit.*
[25] *Tribunal Assistance, the Chapeltown Experience* (NACAB Occasional Paper No. 14, 1982), describes the scheme and evaluates its success.

workers have been appointed to provide expertise for a group of bureaux. The universal experience has been that contact with any form of expertise, however provided, has raised the general level of advice-giving in respect of tribunal matters by the ordinary volunteer in the bureau.[26] This, together with the greatly increased demand for assistance with social security and employment problems, has enhanced the value of the CAB service to the general public.

The London Free Representation Unit is an independent group based on the College of Law and offering an advocacy service in cases referred to it by other advice agencies. In fact, this Unit may not be involved at the pre-hearing stage and relies heavily on the referring agency for the initial advice to the claimant and preparation of the case.

Other independent groups[27] have based themselves in advice centres offering a service to clients of that centre and those referred by other statutory or voluntary agencies.

The advice available is, therefore, dependent partly upon local initiatives and there is certainly no national coverage. Whether the Government will choose to do anything about the recommendation of the Royal Commission on Legal Services[28] that funds should be made available to assist in the training of staff in approved lay agencies for tribunal advice and representation remains to be seen.[29] If money was made available, the lay agencies would have to decide on an appropriate scheme for the provision of advice and representation. That might not be easy!

C. "KNOWING THE ROPES"—MAKING APPLICATION TO A TRIBUNAL

Rules of procedure begin to take effect when an applicant decides that he will invoke the jurisdiction of the tribunal by making application for a hearing. Prior to that he may have tried to effect a settlement of his grievance in the same way as he would have done in a civil matter, but because a significant proportion of tribunal matters concern the correctness of a decision made by a Government department the scope of settlement is fairly limited.[30] The means of expressing disagreement with such a decision is not to complain about it to the individual responsible but to commence

---

[26] See Lawrence, *op. cit.* at p. 75. *Chapeltown Citizens' Advice Bureau, Leeds, Tribunal Assistance Unit, Progress Report—First Two years* (NACAB Occasional Paper No. 6. 1979) at pp. 7–8.

[27] *e.g.* Birmingham Tribunal Representation Unit; Walsall Advice and Representation Project; South Wales Anti-Poverty Action Centre.

[28] R.C.L.S., Vol. 1, Chap. 15.

[29] There is no indication currently that money will be available, although the whole question of tribunal advice and advocacy is under active consideration by the Lord Chancellor's Advisory Committee on Legal Aid: *33rd Legal Aid Annual Reports* [1982–83] pp. 194–209. See further, p. 563 below.

[30] This is dependent upon the procedures of the Department concerned. In social security matters an application to a tribunal ensures an initial review of the decision by an adjudication officer, and there is some evidence to suggest that the intervention of an advice agency can get "mistakes" straightened out without recourse to a tribunal. Chapeltown Tribunal Assistance Unit, *Progress Report—First Two Years* (see above, n. 26) at pp. 11, 12.

an appeal to the appropriate tribunal. In other cases, particularly where an application to an Industrial Tribunal may be in prospect, there are pre-hearing procedures designed to secure a mutually acceptable resolution of the problem.[31]

In relation to the making of an application there are three procedural aspects to be considered. What form should the application take? What information should it contain? Within what time limit, if any, should it be made? These are questions which have been considered and answered in the civil courts, and they are obviously questions which are common to all tribunals. It would be tempting to assume that a Code of Procedure could be devised to encompass all tribunals and make specific provision for these and other points. The Franks Committee[32] moved towards this position with a recommendation that a Council on Tribunals should formulate the procedural rules for each tribunal, based on principles common to all tribunals but tailored to suit the needs of the particular tribunal.[33] In the event, the Tribunals and Inquiries Act 1958 merely provided that the Council on Tribunals (established by the Act) should be consulted when procedural rules were made in respect of certain specified tribunals.[34] We shall return to the role of the Council on Tribunals in procedural matters later in the chapter.

What form should an application to a tribunal take? Many tribunals require the completion of a printed form—a method of application which can either assist or hinder the applicant. He may be deterred from pursuing his case by the complexity or unintelligibility of the questions, but he will at least be shown the information required and sometimes directed towards a source of help and advice.[35] Again, the nature of the dispute may have an effect on procedure in that in citizen/state disputes the jurisdiction is likely to be automatic and the applicant will not have to show the grounds which bring the matters within the tribunal's jurisdiction. In citizen/citizen disputes the applicant's first job will be to establish that his case falls within the tribunal's jurisdiction and a printed form with appropriate questions will be helpful both to tribunal and applicant.

The different procedural approaches of social security tribunals and Industrial Tribunals are illustrated later in the chapter,[36] and from those examples it can be seen that the amount of information required from the applicant differs, as does the form of application. In many cases the applicant has the opportunity of including matters for the consideration of the tribunal in his application, or in a subsequent statement. Ultimately, he

---

[31] In the Industrial Tribunal procedure, some emphasis is placed upon conciliation and the mediating role of the Advisory Conciliation and Arbitration Service, although this usually occurs after the application has been made.

[32] Report of the Committee on Administrative Tribunals and Enquiries (Cmnd. 218, 1957).

[33] *Ibid*. paras. 63–64.

[34] Now Tribunals and Inquiries Act 1971, s.10. Procedural rules are normally contained in a statutory instrument made by the Minister whose Department is responsible for the particular tribunal.

[35] *e.g.* the form of originating application to an Industrial Tribunal includes the words, "A Citizens' Advice Bureau or Trade Union may be able to help you complete the form or advise you as to whether you have a complaint which an Industrial Tribunal could consider."

[36] See below, pp. 448–475.

may make representations at the hearing (if one is held)[37] and it is likely to be the style and conduct of the hearing which determines how much advance information is required by the tribunal.

All tribunals find it necessary to impose time limits within which an application must be submitted, and some impose limits on later stages of the procedure.[38] The balance has to be struck between allowing a tribunal to make a speedy determination in a dispute (based on evidence which is not too far distant in time) and ensuring that an applicant is not unduly prejudiced by the limit. The Council on Tribunals have taken a particular interest in this matter and have welcomed the extension of time limits in some tribunals.[39] In addition it is desirable that there should be a procedural rule allowing for applications to be made out of time where there is good cause.[40]

D. "KNOWING THE CASE"—THE PRE-HEARING EXCHANGE OF INFORMATION

" . . . citizens should know in good time the case which they will have to meet, whether the issue to be heard by the tribunal is one between citizen and administration or citizen and citizen . . . We do not suggest that the procedure should be formalised to the extent of requiring documents in the nature of legal pleadings. What is needed is that the citizen should receive in good time beforehand a document setting out the main points of the opposing case. It should not be necessary . . . to require the parties to adhere rigidly at the hearing to the case as previously set out, provided always that the interests of another party are not prejudiced by such flexibility."[41]

The amount of pre-hearing activity and the precision with which the parties are required to formulate and disclose their respective cases varies very considerably from tribunal to tribunal. The applicant receives the greatest assistance (and is given the greatest latitude) in social security tribunals. He is not required to produce any specific grounds of appeal or indicate what his argument might be, but he will receive from the adjudication officer a full statement of facts, submissions, statutory authorities and Commissioner's decisions.[42] This document will also be

---

[37] Not all tribunals will hold an oral hearing. The Social Security Commissioner may determine an appeal without a hearing, as may a rent assessment committee. Needless to say, where there is to be no hearing the written submissions have to be much fuller.

[38] An application to a Social Security Appeal Tribunal must be made within 28 days of the decision appealed against; an application to an Industrial Tribunal in respect of unfair dismissal within three months of dismissal. Unfortunately there are no time limits on the hearings and the Council on Tribunals have recently expressed disquiet at the long backlog of cases awaiting hearing by the Social Security Commissioners: 2,352 on January 1, 1980; 2,042 on January 1, 1981; 2,258 on July 1, 1981; 1,679 on July 29, 1982. (Annual Reports of the Council on Tribunals, 1979/80, 1980/81, 1981/82).

[39] The Annual Report of the Council on Tribunals 1980/81, at p. 23.

[40] e.g. it is normally good cause for making application to an Industrial Tribunal in respect of unfair dismissal after three months have elapsed, that the applicant has been making use of internal grievance procedures or a domestic appeal process: Crown Agents v. Lawal [1979] I.C.R. 103, but see also Bodhu v. Hampshire Area Health Authority [1982] I.C.R. 200.

[41] Report of the Committee on Administrative Tribunals and Enquiries (Cmnd. 218, 1957) at pp. 17–18.

[42] See below, p. 450, where an example is reproduced.

sent to members of the tribunal and is likely to form the basis of the hearing. An applicant must make a tactical decision about the extent to which he indicates his particular grievance on his application. He may say little or nothing, in which case there will be virtually no possibility of reconsideration of his case before the hearing and he will have unlimited possibilities at the hearing. He may make a full statement which indicates the precise line of attack. This will not prevent him raising other issues at the hearing, but he may be asked why he has not made reference to them before.

Disclosure in social security tribunals certainly ensures that the applicant knows the case he is going to have to meet, but can leave the adjudication officer entirely in the dark.

By way of contrast, the parties before a rent assessment committee are likely to have had a full opportunity of finding out about the case.[43] In issue will be the determination of a fair rent and before the matter can come before a rent assessment committee, application must be made to a rent officer. This application can be made by either landlord or tenant or both jointly, but if the application is not joint, the other party is invited to take part in consultations with the rent officer and the applicant to consider what rent should be registered.[44] Only if one party is dissatisfied with the rent which is registered can he appeal to the rent assessment committee, who then invite both parties to make written or oral representations. By the time of the hearing, both parties will have had the opportunity to familiarise themselves with all the circumstances and the representations made by each of them.

A third approach is adopted in the Industrial Tribunal. The forms by which an applicant makes his application and the respondent indicates an intention to defend the case, require a certain minimum amount of information. In particular, the applicant is required to state the grounds of his application and particulars thereof.[45] This ensures at the outset that both sides will have some idea of the case to be met. Thereafter there are opportunities for both formal and informal exchange of information.[46]

Formal procedures exist whereby the tribunal may, at the request of one of the parties or of its own volition, require either side to provide further particulars of its case or risk losing the case.[47] These formal procedures reinforce informal requests for information which either party may make of the other. In addition, the tribunal has the power to order discovery of documents.[48] A new procedure was introduced in 1980 which has the effect of disclosing information to the parties. The pre-hearing assessment is an attempt to reduce the number of cases going to a hearing by bringing the

---

[43] See D. Yates and A.J. Hawkins, *Landlord and Tenant Law* (1981) pp. 313–315.

[44] Rent Act 1977, Sched. 11, para. 3, as amended.

[45] Strictly speaking, there is no requirement that the printed forms be used so long as the required information is given in another form, *e.g.* a letter. However, it is crucial that the grounds and particulars are given, so the form is usually regarded as helpful.

[46] For procedure in Industrial Tribunals generally see, I.T. Smith and J.C. Wood, *Industrial Law* (2nd ed., 1983) Chap. 6, pp. 191–205; M.J. Goodman, *Industrial Tribunals' Procedure* (2nd ed., 1979); B. Egan, *The Industrial Tribunals Handbook* (1978).

[47] Industrial Tribunal (Rules of Procedure) Regulations 1980 (S.I. 1980 No. 884), r. 4(1)(*b*)(i).

[48] *Ibid.* r. 4(1)(*b*)(ii).

parties together, without witnesses, to undergo a review of the application. This obviously operates to expose the case to both sides and although there is no power to strike out an unworthy case there is a possible penalty on costs at the hearing if the tribunal indicates, at the pre-hearing assessment, that there is no reasonable prospect of a successful application or defence.[49] These procedures owe more to the High Court and county court than to other tribunals, but they are operated speedily and flexibly.

Informally, there may be an exchange of information because of the involvement of conciliation officers. All applications and subsequent documents are sent to ACAS[50] and a conciliation officer is under an obligation to attempt a conciliation either at the request of one of the parties, or of his own volition.[51] This conciliation may be rejected by the parties but it is likely to lead to some informal exchange of information unless the conciliation officer never even gets his foot in the door. Could this process usefully be adapted to assist settlements in the High Court?

These examples of pre-hearing procedure, necessarily selective, are intended to illustrate three different approaches to the objective set out by the Franks Committee. Full obligatory disclosure by one side; opportunity to disclose by both sides, but no obligation and no penalty for non-disclosure; limited obligatory disclosure by both sides, with opportunities for further disclosure supported by sanctions. Each tribunal would say that it had developed a procedure suited to its own needs.

E. PRE-HEARING PROCEDURE IN TWO TRIBUNALS

We have already contrasted some of the procedural aspects of social security tribunals and industrial tribunals in making general points about procedure. Below we set out two cases which illustrate the progress of a case towards a hearing in a Social Security Appeal Tribunal and an Industrial Tribunal. It was noted at the outset that it is difficult to produce "typical" tribunals for consideration, and it is no easier to produce "typical" cases from a single tribunal. One of the alleged virtues of the tribunal system is its flexibility in dealing with differing circumstances. These examples at least demonstrate the documentation involved and indicate the normal procedure.

1. A SOCIAL SECURITY APPEAL TRIBUNAL[52]

Facts: Mr. Glum had for some time been receiving Invalidity Benefit. He received extra benefit in respect of his wife. In April 1982, Mrs. Glum was

---

[49] *Ibid*. r. 6.

[50] The Advisory Conciliation and Arbitration Service.

[51] Employment Protection (Consolidation) Act 1978, ss.133, 134.

[52] The Social Security Appeal Tribunal came into being on April 23, 1984 as a result of the merger of the National Insurance Local Tribunal with the Supplementary Benefit Appeal Tribunal under the provisions of the Health and Social Services and Social Security Adjudications Act 1983, s.25 and Sched. 8. The actual case which provides the example cited in the following text was heard by a N.I.L.T. under the old system, but the forms and procedure will remain substantially the same. Some other effects of the merger are dealt with below, at p. 544. D.H.S.S. officers who were formerly known as insurance officers are now given the title of adjudication officers.

notified by the DHSS that she would become entitled to retirement pension when she reached the age of 60 and was invited to make application for it. She did so. In August 1982, Mr. Glum made an annual claim for the extra benefit in respect of his wife and declared that she was not receiving any benefit or pension. In September 1982, Mrs. Glum began to receive retirement pension following her 60th birthday. In November 1983, when making the annual claim Mr. Glum declared the pension received by his wife.

Social security rules require that a retirement pension received by a wife should be offset against the amount of extra benefit payable with Invalidity Benefit, and only the balance remaining should be paid to the husband. An overpayment had therefore been made between September 1982 and November 1983. The DHSS wrote to Mr. Glum on January 30, 1984 requiring him to repay the £903.91 he should not have received.

He consulted the local citizens advice bureau.

There is a prescribed form on which an appeal may be made, but Mr. Glum chose to write a letter to the Clerk to the Tribunal. He sent it on February 8, 1984, well inside the 28–day time limit

1 Rotten Road,
Gumby,
Notts.

Dear Sir,

In reply to your letter of January 30, 1984, I wish to appeal against the decision of the officer on the grounds that our position was made clear to a member of your staff when the pension papers were received.

It was some time in April 1982 that my wife received papers to complete in order to claim a retirement pension. Thinking that she was not entitled to a pension until I reached the age of 65 she called at the Gumby Office and said this. She was told "If they think you are entitled to a pension you must be." The papers were completed.

It is therefore a great shock to learn now that this information was not correct but I cannot think that you hold me to blame for this and I hope that you will be able to cancel any claim for overpayment as this was done without any knowledge or intent on my part.

Yours faithfully,
G. Glum

You will observe that this statement reflects Mr. Glum's view of the case and, in the light of the law applicable to these circumstances, is not actually directed to the relevant matters. This illustrates the need for a document to tell Mr. Glum what case he will have to meet. In due course he received notification of a hearing date and the following set of papers.

SOCIAL SECURITY APPEAL TRIBUNAL

For hearing on	27.4.84	
Appeal Register Number		
Sheet	30	Line 4

IN CONFIDENCE   Appeal or Reference to Appeal Tribunal

Benefit ...... INVALIDITY PENSION .... Tribunal .... GUMBY ....

FULL NAMES OF PERSONS CONCERNED		National Insurance Number				
(Surname)	(Other names)	AA	00	00	01	A
GLUM	GEORGE					
		Benefit reference number				
		17456				

1

*Reference dated .... for **decision** whether

*Appeal received on .... 8.2.84 ....against the following decision of the Adjudication

Officer (Code no(s) .... 123 ....) which was issued on ..... 30.1.84 ....

Adjudication Officer's Decision

I have reviewed the decisions of the insurance officer awarding an increase
of invalidity benefit for Mrs J Glum from 5.9.82 to 14.11.82 (both dates
included) because there has been a relevant change of circumstances since
the decisions were given and from 15.11.82 to 14.11.83 (both dates included)
because I am satisfied that the decision was given in ignorance of a material
fact. (Social Security Act 1975 sec 104) and my revised decision is as follows:

Increase of invalidity benefit is payable at the reduced weekly rate of £3.63
from 5.9.82 to 21.11.82 and £4.01 from 22.11.82 to 14.11.83 (all dates
included) for Mrs J Glum because retirement pension is payable to Mrs J Glum
at the weekly rate of £13.37 raised to £14.84 from 22.11.82, and full payment
of both is not allowed (Social Security (Overlapping Benefits) Regulations
reg 10).

As a result, an overpayment of an increase of invalidity benefit amounting to
£903.91 has occurred, as detailed below (+). Repayment of this sum is required
because it has not been shown that the claimant has throughout used due care
and diligence to avoid overpayment. (Social Security Act 1975 sec 119(1)
and (2)).

(+) DETAILS OF OVERPAYMENT

5.9.82 to 21.11.82 - 11 weeks at £13.37 - £147.07
22.11.82 to 14.11.83 - 51 weeks at £14.84 - £756.84
                                              ―――――――――
                                               £903.91

---

2   Relevant provisions in Acts and Regulations

Social Security (Overlapping Benefits) Regulations 1979 Reg 10(2)(b)
Brown Book page 2918-2919
Social Security Act 1975 sec 119(10) and (2). Brown Book page 103
Social Security Act 1975 sec 104(1)(a). Brown Book page 92

---

3   Relevant reported decisions of the Commissioner

R(U)7/75 : R(G)5/51

Note: Copies of the Brown and Yellow Books (which contain the Acts and Regulations as amended), Neligan's Digest of
Commissioners Decisions and reported decisions of the Commissioners can be seen at the local office of the Department
of Health and Social Security. Copies of the Acts, Regulations, Neligan's Digest and reported decisions can be purchased
from Her Majesty's Stationery Office by phoning 01-622 3316 or writing to HMSO, PO Box 276, Publication Centre,
LONDON, SW8 5DT but it would be advisable first to ask the local office for details of any amending legislation, and for
full titles and reference numbers for ordering purposes.

Form AT 2   *Delete as necessary   OVER

Person(s) concerned ...GLUM, G, ...

4	**Claimant's grounds of appeal dated** 8.2.84

(Appeal cases only)

In reply to your letter of 30 January 1984 I wish to appeal against the decision of the officer on the grounds that our position was made clear to a member of your staff when the pension papers were received.

It was some time in April 1982 that my wife received papers to complete in order to claim a retirement pension. Thinking that she was not entitled to a pension until I reached the age of 65 she called at the Gumby office and said this. She was told "If they think that you are entitled to a pension then you must be." The papers were completed.

It is therefore a great shock to learn now that this information was not correct but I cannot think that you hold me to blame for this and I hope that you will be able to cancel any claim for overpayment as this was done without any knowledge or intent on my part.

Signed : G.Glum

5.SUMMARY OF FACTS

1) The claimant has been in receipt of invalidity benefit including an increase for his dependent wife since 14.11.80. On 2.8.82 the claimant completed form BF225 (claim form for an increase of benefit doc 1A). On 5.9.82 the claimant's wife completed the tear-off portion of form BR2100 and collected her retirement pension orderbook from the Post Office. Forms BF85A and BF228 (docs 4A and 5A) were sent to the claimant who completed form BF85A stating that there were no other matters which he thought might affect his title to benefit.

2) A further form BF225 (doc 2A) was issued on 14.11.83 and in reply to question 7 on that form the claimant reported his wife's retirement pension details. The form was dated 16.11.83.

6. INSURANCE OFFICER'S SUBMISSION

1) I submit that the award of retirement pension to the claimant's wife was a relevant change of circumstances which permitted the insurance officer to review the decision awarding an increase of invalidity benefit to the claimant from 5.9.82 to 14.11.82 (Social Security Act 1975 section 104(1)(b)). I further submit that the decisions awarding an increase of invalidity benefit from 15.11.82 to 14.11.83 were rightly reviewed in accordance with section 104(1)(a) of the Social Security Act 1975 because they were given in ignorance of the fact that the claimant's wife was in receipt of retirement pension.

2) Under Regulation 10 of the Social Security (Overlapping Benefits) Regulations any dependency benefit under the Act shall be adjusted by a personal benefit under Chapter I or II of Part II of the Act payable for the same period so that it does not exceed the difference between the weekly rate of the personal benefit and that of the unadjusted dependency benefit. Increase of invalidity benefit is a dependency benefit under the Act and retirement pension is a personal benefit under Chapter I of Part II of the Act.

3) I submit, therefore, that an increase of invalidity benefit is payable for the claimant's wife at the reduced weekly rate of £3.63 from 5.9.8.2 to 21.11.82 (both dates included) and £4.01 from 22.11.82 to 14.11.81 (both dates included) i.e. the difference between the unadjusted dependency benefit (£17.00 per week raised to £18.85 per week from 22.11.82) and the rate of retirement pension (£13.37 per week raised to £14.84 from 22.11.82). An overpayment has therefore been incurred for the period 5.9.82 to 14.11.83 (both dates included) amounting to £903.91.

(continue on separate sheet if necessary)

Originals of any documents which are copied in whole or in part will be available at the hearing.

Printed in the UK for HMSO Dd 8826212 3/84 (29004)

INSURANCE OFFICER'S SUBMISSION (CONT'D):

4) The effect of section 119(1) and (2) of the Social Security Act 1975 is that where as a result of a decision given on review benefit has been overpaid, repayment of that benefit must be required, unless it is shown to the satisfaction of the determining authorities that in the obtaining and receipt of the benefit the claimant throughout used due care and diligence to avoid overpayment, see for example R(U)7/75 and R(G)5/51.

5) In his statement dated 19.12.83 the claimant said that he did not realise that he should have notified the Department of his wife's pension as soon as she received it. At the foot of the form BF225 there is a note in the following terms "You must let the office dealing with your claim know if at any time there is any change in the facts given on this form." In addition, the form BF228 which is issued with each form BF225, explains on page 4 that if any of the benefits listed become payable the claimant should let the local office know. (Doc 5A). I submit that these two facts should have alerted the claimant to the need to notify the local office of his wife's pension award.

6) In his appeal the claimant states that in April 1982 when his wife received her pension forms they called at the office in Gumby to question the wife's entitlement to a retirement pension. I submit that the information given and received at that time as reported by the claimant related solely to the retirement pension aspect.

7) The claimant failed to notify the Department of Helath and Social Security of the award and payment of a retirement pension to his wife until 16.11.83 some 14 months after it became payable and I submit therefore that he failed to act with due care and diligence to avoid overpayment and that accordingly repayment of the amount overpaid must be required.

DEPARTMENT OF HEALTH AND SOCIAL SECURITY

Invalidity Pension, Non-contributory Invalidity Pension, Retirement Pension or Unemployability Supplement.

Increase for Wife

This form is to enable you to claim an increase of invalidity pension, non-contributory invalidity pension, retirement pension or unemployability supplement for your wife.

The conditions for payment of an increase of invalidity pension are explained in leaflet NI 16A and, for an increase of retirement pension in leaflet NP 32. If you are claiming an increase of either of these benefits a copy of the appropriate leaflet is enclosed. The conditions for payment of an increase of non-contributory invalidity pension are broadly the same as for an increase of invalidity pension, although the rate of the increase is lower. If you want to know more about the conditions for an increase of non-contributory invalidity pension or about the conditions for an increase of unemployability supplement please let the Social Security Office know.

You should read the leaflet before completing the claim form. If you require any advice or help in filling up this form your local Social Security Office will be pleased to assist you.

Please return the completed form as soon as possible using the addressed label or envelope enclosed. Delay in claiming may lead to loss of benefit.

---

1. Your full name (BLOCK CAPITALS)
    (Surname last)

NI No	AA	00	00	01	A
Claim Number					

    GEORGE GLUM

    Your full address (BLOCK CAPITALS) 1 ROTTEN ROAD,
    (including postcode) GUMBY NOTTS. NO1 3GU

    Your wife's Christian or other names (BLOCK CAPITALS)

Her NI No					

    JANE

    Her date of birth 5th (day) SEPT. (month) 1922 (year)

    The date of your marriage 22 (day) JULY (month) 1950 (year)

    Please send your wife's birth and marriage certificate(s) with this form. The certificate(s) will be returned as soon as possible. If you do not have her birth or marriage certificate do not buy one specially and do not delay sending in this form.

    Are you enclosing with this form:-

    Your wife's birth certificate *(YES or NO)* YES

    marriage certificate *(YES or NO)* YES

Form BF 225

continued on next page

2. Is your wife living with you at your present address? *(YES or NO)*......**YES**......
    If NO, please answer the following questions:-
    (a) Do you and your wife normally live at the same address? *(YES or NO)*.........
        If yes, please give details

    ....

    (b) What is her address? (It may be necessary to write to her about your claim)
        (including postcode)

    ....
    ....
    ....

    (c) How much do you send her each week?   £..............................

3. Has your wife an employer? *(YES or NO)*......**NO**......
    If YES please state
        Her employer's name and address..
        (including postcode)

    ....

    Her clock or check number (if she has one)..
    Her gross weekly earnings including earnings or fees as a director before
    deduction of income tax — holiday pay, bonus payments and regular tips
    should be included £..........................
    Whether her earnings vary from week to week *(YES or NO)*..........................
    Whether you are enclosing your wife's latest pay slip
    (You should do so if she has it)   *(YES or NO)*..........................
    Details of meal vouchers or anything else provided by the employer

    ....

    You may claim expenses such as your wife's National Insurance contribu-
    tion, her fares, the cost of meals, overalls, etc, and the cost of having a
    member of the household looked after because your wife is at work. Any
    expenses you wish to be considered should be listed below:—

    ....
    ....
    ....

    If your wife is absent from work,
        When did the absence start?..(date)

        What pay including maternity pay, if any, will she receive while she is
        away? £........................

4. Is your wife in business on her own account as owner or partner?*(YES or NO)*.........
If YES, please give the name and address of the business
(including postcode)

....

....

and her profit, gain or emoluments as adjusted and agreed
for income tax purposes for the last business year ending........................... (date)

£ ....

5. Does your wife have boarders or lodgers?*(YES or NO)*....................
If YES, please say how many, and how much each of them pays

....

....

6. If you are self-employed, has your wife
earnings from the business? *(YES or NO)*....................
(If you pay her a wage or if a charge is made in respect of
your wife's services against the profits from your business
for income tax purposes, you should write "YES")
If YES, what are her (weekly) earnings?   £ ....
Whether or not she has earnings from it,
does your wife help in your business?*(YES or NO)*.......................

7. Is your wife in hospital? *(YES or NO)* ......**No**.................
If YES, please give the name and address of the hospital

....

....

....

the date of her admission ....

Was your wife living with you up to the
date of going into hospital? *(YES or NO)*.......................

continued on next page

8. The benefit for your wife may be affected by other payments to or for her by this or any other government department or the Manpower Services Commission by way of

- any contributory, industrial injuries or non-contributory social security benefit, pension or allowance
- any supplementary allowance or supplementary pension
- any war pension
- any training allowance or training grant

Is any such payment being made
to or for your wife? *(YES or NO)* .... **NO**

If YES. please give the weekly amount £ ....

the kind of payment ....

the name and address of the
office making the payment ....

....

the number on the order book
or any other reference number ....

DECLARATION
(WARNING: TO GIVE FALSE INFORMATION MAY RESULT IN PROSECUTION)
I DECLARE

that to the best of my knowledge and belief, the information given is true and complete. I claim benefit accordingly.

Signature .... *G.Glnn* ....

If you are too ill to sign the declaration yourself it may be signed on your behalf by someone else who should state that he/she has done so.

Date .... **2/8/1982** ....

Note:—You must let the office dealing with your claim know if at any time there is any change in the facts given on this form.

52-3009 Dd 8212706 8/80 GBR LTD

DEPARTMENT OF HEALTH AND SOCIAL SECURITY

Invalidity Pension, Non-contributory
Invalidity Pension, Retirement Pension
or Unemployability Supplement.

Increase for Wife

This form is to enable you to claim an increase of invalidity pension, non-contributory invalidity pension, retirement pension or unemployability supplement for your wife.

The conditions for payment of an increase of invalidity pension are explained in leaflet NI 16A and, for an increase of retirement pension in leaflet NP 32. If you are claiming an increase of either of these benefits a copy of the appropriate leaflet is enclosed. The conditions for payment of an increase of non-contributory invalidity pension are broadly the same as for an increase of invalidity pension, although the rate of the increase is lower. If you want to know more about the conditions for an increase of non-contributory invalidity pension or about the conditions for an increase of unemployability supplement please let the Social Security Office know.

You should read the leaflet before completing the claim form. If you require any advice or help in filling up this form your local Social Security Office will be pleased to assist you.

Please return the completed form as soon as possible using the addressed label or envelope enclosed. Delay in claiming may lead to loss of benefit.

1. Your full name (BLOCK CAPITALS) *(Surname last)*	NI No _____
	Claim Number _____

GEORGE GLUM

Your full address (BLOCK CAPITALS) ... *1 ROTTEN ROAD,*
(including postcode)
GUMBY, NOTTS.

NO1 3GU

Your wife's Christian or other names (BLOCK CAPITALS)	Her NI No _____

JANE

Her date of birth ... *5th* (day) ... *SEP.* (month) ... *1922* (year)
The date of your marriage ... *2nd* (day) ... *JULY* (month) ... *1950* (year)

Please send your wife's birth and marriage certificate(s) with this form. The certificate(s) will be returned as soon as possible. If you do not have her birth or marriage certificate do not buy one specially and do not delay sending in this form.

Are you enclosing with this form:-

Your wife's birth certificate *(YES or NO)* .... /

marriage certificate *(YES or NO)* .... /

Form BF 225   *continued on next page*

2.   Is your wife living with you at your present address? *(YES or NO)*......**YES**............
     If NO, please answer the following questions:-
         (a) Do you and your wife normally live at the same address? *(YES or NO)*..........
             If yes, please give details

         ....

         (b) What is her address? (It may be necessary to write to her about your claim)
             (including postcode)

         ....

         ....

         ....

         (c) How much do you send her each week?   £................................

---

3.   Has your wife an employer? *(YES or NO)*............**NO**...........
     If YES please state
             Her employer's name and address...
             (including postcode)

             ....

             Her clock or check number (if she has one)...

             Her gross weekly earnings including earnings or fees as a director before
             deduction of income tax — holiday pay, bonus payments and regular tips
             should be included £.........................

             Whether her earnings vary from week to week *(YES or NO)*..........................

             Whether you are enclosing your wife's latest pay slip
             (You should do so if she has it)   *(YES or NO)*..........................

             Details of meal vouchers or anything else provided by the employer

             ....

             You may claim expenses such as your wife's National Insurance contribu-
             tion, her fares, the cost of meals, overalls, etc, and the cost of having a
             member of the household looked after because your wife is at work. Any
             expenses you wish to be considered should be listed below:—

             ....

             ....

             ....

             If your wife is absent from work,
             When did the absence start?..(date)
             What pay including maternity pay, if any, will she receive while she is
             away? £.........................

4. Is your wife in business on her own account as owner or partner?*(YES or NO)*.........
   If YES, please give the name and address of the business
   (including postcode)

   ....

   ....

   and her profit, gain or emoluments as adjusted and agreed
   for income tax purposes for the last business year ending........................... (date)

   £ ....

5. Does your wife have boarders or lodgers?*(YES or NO)*....................
   If YES, please say how many, and how much each of them pays

   ....

   ....

6. If you are self-employed, has your wife
   earnings from the business? *(YES or NO)*.....................

   (If you pay her a wage or if a charge is made in respect of
   your wife's services against the profits from your business
   for income tax purposes, you should write "YES")

   If YES, what are her (weekly) earnings?   £ ....

   Whether or not she has earnings from it,
   does your wife help in your business?*(YES or NO)*.......................

7. Is your wife in hospital? *(YES or NO)* .... **No**
   If YES, please give the name and address of the hospital

   ....

   ....

   ....

   the date of her admission ....

   Was your wife living with you up to the
   date of going into hospital? *(YES or NO)*.......................

continued on next page

8. The benefit for your wife may be affected by other payments to or for her by this or any other government department or the Manpower Services Commission by way of

- any contributory, industrial injuries or non-contributory social security benefit, pension or allowance
- any supplementary allowance or supplementary pension
- any war pension
- any training allowance or training grant

Is any such payment being made
to or for your wife? *(YES or NO)* .... YES .... RETIREMENT PENSION

If YES. please give the weekly amount £. 14.84 ....

the kind of payment ....

the name and address of the
office making the payment .... DHSS   GUMBY ....

....

the number on the order book
or any other reference number .... 2290090 FLC ....

DECLARATION
(WARNING: TO GIVE FALSE INFORMATION MAY RESULT IN PROSECUTION)
I DECLARE

that to the best of my knowledge and belief, the information given is true and complete. I claim benefit accordingly.

Signature .... G. Glun ....

If you are too ill to sign the declaration yourself it may be signed on your behalf by someone else who should state that he/she has done so.

Date .... 16|11|83 ....

Note:—You must let the office dealing with your claim know if at any time there is any change in the facts given on this form.

52-3009 Dd 8212706 8/80 GBR LTD

DEPARTMENT OF HEALTH AND SOCIAL SECURITY

16th June 19 83

Mr. G. Glum
1 Rotten Road,
Gumby.
Notts.
No1 3Gu

Dear Sir or Madam

As it is some time since you gave us information about your claim, please complete the statement overleaf, after reading the enclosed notes on Invalidity Benefit/~~Sickness Benefit/Non-contributory Invalidity Pension~~. The notes explain the changes that must be reported to the Department while you are getting benefit.

You should also complete any accompanying claim form relating to a dependant.

Please use the enclosed addressed envelope to return the completed form(s) to me.

Yours faithfully

Manager

Form BF 85A
(Env EW 18)

CLAIMANT'S STATEMENT

Are you claiming or receiving any other National Insurance benefit, an unemployability supplement of any kind or a training allowance? (YES or NO) .... **No** ....

If YES, please give details..

....

....

....

Are there any other matters which you think may affect your title to benefit? (YES or NO) .... **No** ....

If YES, what are they?...

....

....

....

....

....

....

I have read the notes on Invalidity Benefit/Sickness Benefit/Non-contributory Invalidity Pension and understand the conditions for receipt of benefit.

DECLARATION

I declare that to the best of my knowledge and belief the information given is true and complete.

Signature .... G.G.lun. .... Date **20/6/83**

Dd 8404885 680M S&K 4/83

DEPARTMENT OF HEALTH AND SOCIAL SECURITY
NOTES ON INVALIDITY BENEFIT

HAVE YOU CLAIMED ALL YOU ARE ENTITLED TO?

BENEFIT FOR DEPENDANTS

Your notice of entitlement to invalidity benefit (forms BS 49 and BS 50 series) shows whether or not you have been awarded benefit for dependants. Additional invalidity pension may be payable for—

● your wife, husband or a woman caring for your child(ren).

● a child.

The detailed conditions for additional benefit for dependants are explained in leaflet NI 16A. If you do not have a copy, your local Social Security office can supply one on request.

You should tell your local Social Security office if—

● you have not claimed for dependants and now wish to do so

● you become responsible for a dependant while you are sick

● you want further information about dependants.

YOU SHOULD SPECIALLY NOTE THAT—

● Additional benefit can only be paid for a child for whom someone is entitled to child benefit

● a married woman residing with her husband can only receive an addition for her child(ren) if her husband has no significant earnings (see leaflet NI 16A).

● you should not refrain from claiming an addition for your wife if she resides with you (or is temporarily away), even if she is in employment. If her earnings, after admissible expenses, are over £45 a week, the addition for her may not, however, be payable at the full rate. (See leaflet NI 16A for details).

● delay in claiming may result in loss of benefit for a past period.

Form BF 228

page 1

PAYMENT

For periods which are not complete weeks, one sixth of the weekly rate is payable for each weekday in the period, the payment being rounded to the nearest penny. Payment is not made for Sundays.

Payment will be made either by order book, which contains instructions about encashment, or by Girocheques which can be paid into a bank account or, unless crossed, cashed at any Post Office. If neither of these methods of cashing Girocheques is convenient, please get in touch with your local office of this Department who will consider whether payment can be made in some other way.

If you go to the Post Office to cash a Girocheque you should always take with you some evidence of your identity as the payee. Payment may be refused if you cannot produce it. Documents which will be accepted as evidence of identity are listed in the Notes on the back of the Girocheque. An item such as an addressed envelope is not acceptable. If you have difficulty in going to the Post Office and would like someone else to cash the Girocheque instead, you will find instructions on the back of it about how to authorise someone else to cash it for you. The person you have named must take the Girocheque to the Post Office with some evidence relating to your identity as "payee" (see the Notes on the back of the Girocheque) and must sign the Girocheque in the space marked "Signature of agent".

If a Girocheque cannot be cashed because the person named on it (the "payee") is too ill to sign it someone else should tell the local office of this Department so that other arrangements can be made.

The amount of benefit shown on any Girocheque you receive is paid on the understanding that you have been incapable of work during the period it covers and that you have reported any change or the receipt of any other payment which may affect your benefit as described in these Notes. *If at any time you receive a Girocheque which includes payment for days on which you have done any work of any kind* or you have any doubt about your right to the amount of benefit shown on the Girocheque, do not cash it but return it to the office from which it was issued, saying why.

WHAT YOU MUST DO WHILE YOU ARE CLAIMING BENEFIT

SEND IN DOCTOR'S STATEMENTS

If you are incapable of work for more than 6 days (not counting Sundays) see your doctor. If necessary he will give you a doctor's statement to enable you to continue your claim.

Unless you have already notified the local office of the last day you were unfit to work, before you resume work ask your doctor for a statement showing the day he expects you to be fit to go back to work. *If you start work BEFORE the day shown on the claim form or the doctor's statement you must let your local office know without delay.*

You should get each statement at the right time, complete it and send it in promptly; otherwise you may lose benefit or your payments may be delayed.

REPORT ANY WORK YOU DO

You must notify the local office if you do, or intend to do, *any* work of any kind while claiming benefit. If you are self-employed you must report any duties, however small in extent, which you undertake in connection with your work.

REPORT ANY CHANGES

You must tell your local office if any of the following changes occur while you are receiving benefit:—

IF YOU—

(1) change your address.

(2) leave this country. (You should consult your local office as soon as possible so that they can advise you whether benefit is likely to be affected during or after the absence from this country.)

(3) are admitted to hospital.

(4) marry.

(5) start to receive any payment listed in the paragraph headed "OTHER BENEFITS, PENSIONS OR ALLOWANCES" on the next page.

(6) are imprisoned or detained in legal custody.

If you are also claiming additions for dependants you must tell your local office if:—

(1) YOUR WIFE OR OTHER ADULT DEPENDANT

    (a) becomes employed or her earnings change; this applies whether she works for an employer, works on her own account or helps in your business. If you claim additional benefit for a wife or other adult dependant you are sent a separate notice which sets out the changes in your dependant's earnings which you must report.

    (b) ceases to reside with you.

(2) A CHILD—
    (a) leaves school.
    (b) goes away from home.

(3) ANY DEPENDANT FOR WHOM YOU ARE GETTING BENEFIT

    (a) leaves this country. (You should consult your local office as soon as possible so that they can advise you whether benefit is likely to be affected during or after the absence from this country.)

    (b) is admitted to hospital. (You need not report if a child is in hospital for less than 4 weeks.)

    (c) marries.

    (d) starts to receive any payment listed in the paragraph headed "OTHER BENEFITS, PENSIONS OR ALLOWANCES" on the next page.

(4) ANY OF THE FOLLOWING CHANGES OCCUR—

    (a) If for any reason the payments you have been told by your local office you must make while you are receiving benefit for a dependant (adult or child), who does not live with you, are reduced, interrupted or stop. You may no longer be entitled to any part of the addition(s) you are receiving.

page 3

(b) You cease to maintain any other dependant for whom you are receiving benefit.

(c) There is a change in the amount of child benefit paid for your child(ren).

(d) Another person becomes entitled to child benefit for your child(ren).

(e) A child is born.

(f) Any of the changes affecting the child benefit for a child for whom you are claiming additional benefit. The changes which must be reported are listed in the coloured instruction pages of the child benefit order book.

OTHER BENEFITS, PENSIONS OR ALLOWANCES

Your benefit and that for your dependants may be affected by other benefits, pensions or allowances payable out of public funds. Not all such payments affect your benefit but, if you have not already done so, please let your local office have details of any of the following which are being paid to you or to any of your dependants by or on behalf of this or any other government department or the Manpower Services Commission—

● any contributory or non-contributory social security benefit, pension or allowance

● any supplementary allowance or supplementary pension

● any war widow's pension

● any unemployability supplement

● any training allowance or training grant (including a Youth Training Scheme Allowance)

● any Job Release Allowance

● any Enterprise Allowance

AND give details of such payment being made to anyone else for you or your dependants.

ADDITIONAL COMPONENT

Additional component may be payable as part of your invalidity benefit depending on the amount of contributions you have paid since 6 April 1978; details of the way in which entitlement is calculated is given in leaflet NI 16A obtainable from your local office. No separate claim is needed for additional component.

WIDOWS AND WIDOWERS

Special invalidity benefit provisions apply to certain widows and widowers – details are given in leaflet NI 16A.

OTHER CONDITIONS FOR RECEIPT OF BENEFIT

Your benefit may be affected if you do anything which would delay your recovery, or if you leave your residence without leaving word where you may be found. You may be required, as a condition for receiving benefit, to attend for medical examination by a doctor in the Regional Medical Service.

please turn to page 5

FURTHER FINANCIAL ASSISTANCE

People aged 16 or over who require financial help during an illness may claim a Supplementary allowance. Leaflet SB1 can be obtained from any Post Office or from any local office of the Department of Health and Social Security.

NATIONAL INSURANCE CONTRIBUTIONS

Generally contributions need not be paid for weeks of incapacity for work. However there will be liability for Class 1 contributions in the normal way if your employer continues to pay you whilst you are sick.

NATIONAL INSURANCE NUMBER

Please quote your National Insurance number whenever you write to your local office.

YOU SHOULD KEEP THESE NOTES BY YOU AS LONG AS YOU ARE RECEIVING BENEFIT

WARNING

TO GIVE FALSE INFORMATION MAY RESULT IN PROSECUTION

Printed in the UK for HMSO. 8810178.9.83.36787

DEPARTMENT OF HEALTH AND SOCIAL SECURITY

STATEMENT

Notes

1. If you are not making the statement on your own behalf, but on behalf of your firm or organisation, please give its address and your rank or status in it.

2. If you are making the statement on behalf of a claimant or insured person please give his address as well as your own and state your connection or relationship with the person.

3. Please initial any amendments and draw a line through any space remaining between the statement and the declaration.

I, ... George Ghm ....
(Full name)

of .... 1 Rotten Road, Grimsby, Notts. ....

....
(Address)

state that

I UNDERSTAND THAT I HAVE BEEN PAID TOO MUCH MONEY (£903.91) BECAUSE OF MY WIFE'S PENSION. I DID NOT KNOW THAT I SHOULD HAVE TOLD THE DEPARTMENT ABOUT THE MONEY MY WIFE WAS GETTING FOR RETIREMENT, AS SOON AS SHE RECEIVED IT.

(continue overleaf if necessary)

*The above has been read over to me and I agree that it is a true and complete record of what I have said. I declare that to the best of my knowledge and belief the information given is true and correct.

Signature .... G.Ghm. .... Date .... 19. 12.83 ....

Witnessed by .... L.S. Woodmuk ....
(Signature)

*Delete if inappropriate

Before the hearing, on the advice of the Citizens Advice Bureau, Mr. Glum consulted a local solicitor under the Legal Advice and Assistance Scheme.[53] *This does not permit representation,*[54] *but the solicitor gave Mr. Glum a letter to hand in to the Chairman of the tribunal.*

Dear Sir,

Our Client—Mr. George Glum

Claim for Invalidity Benefit

Hearing at Gumby on 27.4.84

We write to advise you that we have been consulted by Mr. George Glum and we have been advising him under the auspices of the Law Society's Legal Advice and Assistance scheme.

Under the Scheme we cannot represent Mr. Glum at the Tribunal and in these circumstances we are writing this letter in order to put Mr. Glum's case and explain the reason for his appeal.

In fact we understand that our client may after all have the benefit of the representation, through the helpful assistance of the local citizens advice bureau.

It seems to us that Mr. Glum effectively stands accused of not making a full disclosure as to his wife's income and our instructions are that if this has happened, and it is not admitted, this was totally inadvertent and not intentional. In our respectful submission it is grossly inappropriate for your Insurance Officer to state blandly at number 7 in his submissions that "he failed to act with due care and diligence to avoid overpayment." The tribunal will form their own opinion of Mr. Glum and with great respect to him in the circumstances exception is taken to the remarks of the Insurance Officer. The precise circumstances of his applying for benefit in the first place and the information which he had to give will no doubt be explained to the Tribunal by Mr. Glum assisted by his representative.

The main purpose of this letter is to put it to the Tribunal that the Department was acting in an unduly harsh fashion and indeed acted precipitately in deducting £10.00 per week without any warning from the benefit due to our client in order to claw back the alleged overpayment.

If the Tribunal decides that there has indeed been an overpayment then in our respectful submission the claw back should be in a minimal weekly sum. As explained above it cannot be said that our client acted negligently. He simply did not know what was required of him and we would therefore say that a penalty of £10.00 per week by way of deduction from his benefit is unreasonable. The Department will already have full details of Mr. and Mrs. Glum's income and will know that he can barely afford any deduction whatsoever let alone £10.00 per week. We trust therefore that the Tribunal will if the overpayment is proved order a minimal weekly deduction in order to avoid hardship to our clients.

Yours faithfully,

Popple, Stone and Lees

---

[53] See above, p. 339.
[54] See above, p. 340.

This is not an outrageously difficult case,[55] and the documentation provided by the DHSS certainly gives Mr. Glum the fullest possible notice of the case. However, the material is laid out in such a way and in such detail that it might be very difficult for the average person to comprehend without the help of a knowledgable adviser. The problem of setting out the case clearly is compounded in social security matters by the complexity of the law. The insurance officer has to rehearse the case fully and substantiate every point although the real issue for Mr. Glum (indeed, the only issue) was whether he could establish that he had used "all due care and diligence" to prevent the overpayment. Would he have understood that from the documents? Is the objective of the Franks Committee impossible, except where the point is very simple or the claimant very intelligent?

2. An Industrial Tribunal[56]

Facts: Mr. Seamer had been employed by Convoy Carriers as a lorry driver for nearly 10 years. One day in May 1983 he was called into the office of the Managing Director where there were four bottles of gin on the table. The Managing Director said that they had been found in Mr. Seamer's car and accused him of stealing them. In the presence of Mr. Seamer he telephoned the Police and reported the alleged theft. An argument ensued in which Mr. Seamer protested his innocence. Both men lost their temper and abused each other. Eventually, the Managing Director told Mr. Seamer that he was sacked, with immediate effect, and that he could collect a week's wages from the Accounts Department.

Mr. Seamer subsequently went to the Department of Employment where he obtained an application form to send to the Industrial Tribunal. He filled in the form and sent it off, having been told by a friend that his Union might help him.

Mr. Seamer submitted the form to the central office of the Industrial Tribunals. To help him he was given an explanatory leaflet and a small booklet, "Industrial Tribunals Procedure."[57]

On receipt of an application the Central Office attempt to ensure that it discloses a cause of action within the jurisdiction of the tribunal.[58] Given that the information on the form can be very sparse this is not always an easy job. If it appears that there is no jurisdiction, the application is returned to the applicant[59] otherwise it is sent to the respondent with the form reproduced below. In this case the company wishes to dispute the application. It gives "notice of appearance."

---

[55] Although it always seems difficult for laymen to grasp the "due care and diligence" test.

[56] The jurisdiction of the tribunal is set out above, p. 52. The rules of procedure governing the tribunal are to be found in the Industrial Tribunals (Rules of Procedure) Regulations 1980 (S.I. 1980 No. 884).

[57] Published by the Department of Employment and available free.

[58] This is done by a vetting section at the Central Office.

[59] With a letter pointing out why it appears that the application is outside the jurisdiction. This does not prevent the applicant making a further application and, if it is accepted, the original defective application is not disclosed to the respondent.

ORIGINATING APPLICATION TO AN INDUSTRIAL TRIBUNAL

	For Official Use Only
Case Number	

IMPORTANT: DO NOT FILL IN THIS FORM UNTIL YOU
HAVE READ THE NOTES FOR GUIDANCE.
THEN COMPLETE ITEMS 1, 2, 4 AND 12
AND ALL OTHER ITEMS RELEVANT TO YOUR CASE,
AND SEND THE FORM TO THE FOLLOWING ADDRESS

To: THE SECRETARY OF THE TRIBUNALS
CENTRAL OFFICE OF THE INDUSTRIAL TRIBUNALS (ENGLAND AND WALES)
93 EBURY BRIDGE ROAD, LONDON SW1W 8RE   Telephone: 01 730 9161

1   I hereby apply for a decision of a Tribunal on the following question.   **(STATE HERE THE QUESTION TO BE DECIDED BY A TRIBUNAL. EXPLAIN THE GROUNDS OVERLEAF.**
BECAUSE I WAS SACKED WITHOUT REASON

2   My name is (Mr/~~Mrs/Miss~~ Surname in block capitals first):—
SEAMER   BARRY
My address is ...... 23 WOOD LANE
DARBYVILLE
NOTTS .... Telephone No. .... —
My date of birth is 23.9.50

3   If a representative has agreed to act for you in this case please give his or her name and address below and note that further communications will be sent to your representative and not to you *(See Note 4)*
Name of Representative:— NOT YET, BUT I AM GOING TO THE UNION
Address:— ....
.... Telephone No. ....

4   (a) Name of respondent(s) (in block capitals) ie the employer, person or body against whom a decision is sought
(See Note 3)
CONVOY CARRIERS PLC
Address(es) ...... 23 LONDON ROAD, DARBYVILLE, NOTTS
.... Telephone No. DARBYVILLE 1249

5   Place of employment to which this application relates, or place where act complained about took place.
LONDON ROAD DEPOT, DARBYVILLE

6   My occupation or position held/applied for, or other relationship to the respondent named above (eg user of a service supplied in relation to employment).
DRIVER (HGV)

7   My employment began on 1 FEBRUARY 1974 .... and *(if appropriate)* ended on 1 MAY 1983

8   (a) Basic wages/salary £150 per week
    (b) Average take home pay £190 per week

9   Other remuneration or benefits Free overalls

10 Normal basic weekly hours of work 45

11 (In an application under the Sex Discrimination Act or the Race Relations Act)
Date on which action complained of took place or first came to my knowledge ....

Please continue overleaf

IT I (Revised September 1981)

12 You are required to set out the grounds for your application below, giving full particulars of them.

My boss (Mr Hacker) told me that some bottles of gin that were missing from the depot had been found on the back seat of my car. The car was at the depot. He told me not to come back to work and gave me a week's wages. He called me a thief. I told him that I hadn't pinched the gin and that I had been fitted up, but he didn't believe me. I did not pinch the gin. I have been interviewed by the Police, but they have not told me whether they will prosecute me.

13 If you wish to state what in your opinion was the reason for your dismissal, please do so here.

14 If the Tribunal decides that you were unfairly dismissed, what remedy would you prefer? (Before answering this question please consult the leaflet "Unfairly dismissed?" for the remedies available and then write one of the following in answer to this question: reinstatement, re-engagement or compensation)

Reinstatement, because I am innocent

Signature _Barry Sumer_ Date 1 June 1983

	Received at COIT	Code	ROIT	Inits
FOR OFFICIAL USE ONLY				

(g) (To be completed only when the application relates to Maternity Rights)

When the applicant's absence began were you employing more than 5 persons?

*YES/NO

(h) (To be completed in other applications)

(i) When the applicant's employment ended were you employing more than 20 persons? *YES/NO

(ii) If NO, had you at anytime during the applicant's employment with you employed more than 20 persons? *YES/NO

5. If the claim is resisted, you should give below sufficient particulars to show the grounds on which you intend to resist the application.

(Continue on a separate sheet if there is insufficient space below).

(a) The applicant was fairly and properly dismissed on May 1 1983 for stealing goods belonging to a client of the company.

(b) The goods in question were found by a security officer in the back of the applicant's car.

(c) When questioned the applicant failed to give a satisfactory answer to the Managing Director, Mr P J R Hacker.

(d) Honesty is of the utmost importance amongst our staff.

(e) The matter is in the hands of the Police.

Signature ...... *P. J. R. Hacker* ...... Date 20 June 1983

IT3 (Revised August 1981)

**Delete inappropriate items*

INDUSTRIAL TRIBUNALS

NOTICE OF APPEARANCE BY RESPONDENT

To the Assistant Secretary of the Tribunals

Case Number

FOR OFFICIAL USE	
Date of receipt	Initials

1. I*do/do-not intend to resist the claim made by   MR B SEAMER

2. *My/Our name is *Mr/Mrs/Miss/Title (if a company or organisation):-

Name: CONVOY CARRIERS PLC

Address: 23 LONDON ROAD

DARBYVILLE

NOTTS

Telephone Number   1249

3. If a representative is acting for you, please give his/her name and address and note that all further communications will be sent to him/her, not to you:

Name: POPPLE, LEES AND STONE

Address: 83 MAIN STREET

GUMBY

NOTTS

Telephone Number

4. (a) Was the applicant dismissed?   *YES/NO

(b) If YES, what was the reason for dismissal? HE STOLE GOODS BELONGING TO A CLIENT OF THE COMPANY *YES/NO

(c) Are the dates given by the applicant as to the period of employment correct?

(d) If NO, give dates of commencement _____ and termination _____

(e) Are details of remuneration stated by the applicant correct? *YES/NO

(f) If NO, or if the applicant has not stated such details, please give the correct details:-

Basic Wages/Salary:

Average take home pay

Other remuneration or benefits

Please continue overleaf

**Delete inappropriate items*

At the same time as the originating application is sent to the respondent it is also sent to a conciliation officer.[60] *He receives a copy of the notice of appearance in due course. He is obliged to assist the parties in reaching a conciliation if he is requested to do so, or if he thinks there is a reasonable prospect of success.*[61] *In this case he sees both parties individually. Mr. Seamer wants his job back. Convoy Carriers will not give it to him. Mr. Seamer has sought the assistance of his Union and they ask the company for more information. The company refuses but is ordered to give further particulars after an application to the Tribunal by the applicant. A standard form direction would be:*

Regional Office of the Industrial Tribunals
(address)
To: Convoy Carriers PLC,
          23 London Road,
          Darbyville,
          Notts.
Case No. 12345/83 Seamer *v.* Convoy Carrier PLC

1. An application has been received from the Applicant for further and better particulars of the grounds on which you rely. This application has been referred to the Chairman of Tribunals who by virtue of the powers conferred upon him under rule 4(1)(*a*) of the Rules of Procedure has granted an order as follows.

2. The particulars requested in the letter dated September 4, 1983 (copy enclosed) should be furnished to Mr. D. York, National Union of Lorrymen, York Row, Darbyville by October 30, 1983 and a copy sent to this office.

3. Your attention is drawn to the fact that rule 4(5) provides that if an order under rule 4(1)(*a*) is not complied with, a tribunal, before or at the hearing, may, where the order relates to an originating application, dismiss the application, or where the order relates to a notice of appearance strike out the whole or part of the notice of appearance and, where appropriate, direct that a respondent shall be debarred from defending altogether.

                                              A. Bowler
Dated 1, October 1983   Assistant Secretary of the Industrial
                                                 Tribunals

Mr. York (Mr. Seamer's Union representative) had asked for further particulars of the company's normal security procedures; a list of other employees dismissed on the grounds of dishonesty in the preceding 5 years; and reasons why the company considered it reasonable to dismiss Mr. Seamer immediately without awaiting the outcome of police investigations. The necessary information was supplied. No pre-hearing assessment was

---

[60] An employee of ACAS.

[61] The evidence points to a considerable number of cases settled without a tribunal hearing. The conciliation officer is in a position to assist in negotiations leading to any result—compensation, reinstatment or the withdrawal of the application.

held[62] *and the case was listed for hearing on December 10, 1983. Mr. Seamer lost.*

This example demonstrates a relatively straightforward case where the issue between the parties is clear and unlikely to be resolved in advance of the hearing. Much more documentation can be generated, but this is essentially under the control of the parties and is dependent upon the amount of information that is requested. This is in contrast with the National Insurance Local Tribunal where the appellant receives the full documentation whether he wants it or not. Again, even in this simple case, the advisability of securing skilled assistance can be appreciated.

F. THE ROLE AND INFLUENCE OF THE COUNCIL ON TRIBUNALS[63]

"Our most important contribution over the years has, we believe, been our constant effort to translate the general ideals of the Franks Committee into workable codes of principles and practice, accepted and followed by all those who are responsible for setting up administrative tribunals, devising their manner of operation and, indeed, serving upon them as chairmen and members."[64]

The Franks Committee proposed a significant role for the Council on Tribunals in controlling and overseeing all aspects of tribunal operation[65] but, in the event, the Council was given only limited powers by the Tribunals and Inquiries Act 1958.[66] It emerged as an advisory body with the primary function of keeping under review the constitution and working of certain tribunals specified in a Schedule to the Act.[67] This function is assisted by a requirement that the Council should be consulted before any procedural rules or regulations are made in respect of the specified tribunals,[68] but there is no corresponding requirement of consultation on primary legislation affecting tribunals. Nor is there a requirement that the views expressed by the Council on consultation should be made known when the appropriate legislation is laid before Parliament.

In a review of the functions of the Council[69] other limitations were exposed. The terms of reference do not permit the Council to operate as a general advisory body on all matters pertaining to tribunals, including their overall pattern and organisation. The Council is hampered in dealing with complaints by the lack of any statutory power of investigation. Members of

---

[62] The assessment is only held where it is requested by one of the parties or where the Tribunal itself considers that the application or response is lacking in merit. In this case, both sides would appear to have a chance and the issue is primarily one of fact to be determined by the tribunal.

[63] See also above, p. 33.

[64] *The Functions of the Council on Tribunals*. Special Report by the Council (Cmnd. 7805, 1980), para. 6.3.

[65] Franks Report, *op. cit.* paras. 43, 49, 57, 63–64, 131–134.

[66] Now the Tribunals and Inquiries Act 1971.

[67] Tribunals and Inquiries Act 1971, s.1(1)(*a*) and Sched. 1. The tribunals currently under the supervision of the Councils are listed in each Annual Report. For the latest list see, The Annual Report of the Council on Tribunals for 1982–1983, Appendix C.

[68] Tribunals and Inquiries Act 1971, s.10.

[69] *The Functions of the Council on Tribunals*, see above, n. 64. The particular frustrations of the Council are expressed in Chaps. 5, 7 and 8.

the Council should be specifically empowered to be present at private hearings of tribunals and remain present during the deliberations of the tribunal. Despite these hindrances to the work that the Council would wish to do, there is no doubt that it has exerted a considerable influence in procedural and other matters.

There are a number of examples of procedural changes being effected as a result of the advice of the Council.[70] This advice is based not only on the expertise of the individual members, but also on the experience of other tribunals and other countries. The framing of procedural rules is still the obligation of the Ministry which is responsible for the tribunal and it is not easy for the civil servants in that Ministry to be aware of the procedural pitfalls discovered in other tribunals.[71]

On a more general level, research studies initiated and encouraged by the Council have revealed weaknesses in tribunal operation which have subsequently been eliminated. The research projects on National Insurance and Supplementary Benefit Appeal Tribunals undertaken by Professor Kathleen Bell[72] prompted the reforms in procedure which were contained in the Social Security Act 1979. The Council would like to have more research studies on particular tribunals, but also on problems that are common to all tribunals such as cost and the quality of decision-making.[73]

The Council is making some (slow) progress towards an extension of its powers.[74] Whatever its limitations, it remains the only body charged with the responsibility of considering the fairness of the tribunal system. As such it is a highly important part of the administration of justice.[75]

[70] They are discussed in the Annual Reports which also contain lists of the procedural regulations considered by the Council each year. See, *e.g.* references to the Civil Aviation Authority Regulations 1972 in the 1981/82 Annual Report, p. 13.

[71] This is particularly true where new tribunals are established. See the reference to the rules of procedure for the Vaccine Damage Tribunal in, *The Functions of the Councils on Tribunals, op. cit.* at pp. 20–21.

[72] *Report of a Research Study on SBATs* (H.M.S.O. 1975).

[73] *The Functions of the Council on Tribunals, op. cit.* Chap. 8.

[74] It has now agreed a code of practice on the process of consultation between the Council and Government Departments in respect of primary and secondary legislation. The code has been sent to the relevant Ministers by the Lord Chancellor and has been commended to them. (Annual Report for 1981–82 para. 2.1 and Appendix C.).

[75] If only because of the number of cases heard by tribunals. In the year 1982, Industrial Tribunals disposed of 37,597 cases; Local Valuation Courts, 36,598; Rent Assessment Committees, 16,185; National Insurance Local Tribunals, 29,500; Supplementary Benefit Appeal Tribunals, 57,650. In the same year, the House of Lords disposed of 53 cases. (Sources; Annual Report of the Council on Tribunals 1982/83, Appendix C: *Judicial Statistics 1982*, Cmnd. 9065.

CHAPTER 13

CRIMINAL COURTS

BEFORE a criminal trial can take place there must, inevitably, be a process of investigation and discovery which will establish the evidence to be presented against a defendant at trial. The responsibility for the investigation of criminal offences lies largely with the police and the way in which that responsibility is discharged is subject to legal constraints as well as public scrutiny. Pre-trial procedure in criminal cases could be taken to include the investigative process but we have chosen to begin our survey at the point at which the evidence gathered is considered with a view to instituting a prosecution. The earlier procedures of the questioning of suspects, arrest, search and seizure of evidence are all extensively covered in other works.[1]

A. THE RESPONSIBILITY FOR INSTITUTING PROSECUTIONS[2]

The historical development of the English prosecution process placed emphasis upon the role of the private individual as prosecutor. As the police forces grew so they began to assume the responsibility for bringing prosecutions (but only exercising individual rather than statutory rights); and practice diverged from that in Scotland where a public prosecutor (the procurator fiscal) became established and the right of private prosecution diminished.[3] In fact, the theory of the private prosecution in England and Wales no longer matches the reality of the situation not only because of the powers of the Director of Public Prosecutions,[4] but also because of restrictions placed by statute upon private prosecutions for many offences.[5] In practice, the majority of prosecutions are brought by the police and almost all the balance by other public agencies. Truly private prosecutions are highly unusual.[6]

1. POLICE PROSECUTIONS

There is no specific obligation on the police to institute prosecutions, other than in discharging their general duty to enforce the law, but the Royal

[1] L.H. Leigh, *Police Powers in England and Wales* (1979); S.H. Bailey, D.J. Harris, B.L. Jones, *Civil Liberties, Cases and Materials* (1980), Chap. 2.

[2] See generally, J. Sigler, "Public Prosecution in England and Wales" [1974] Crim. L.R. 642; *The Royal Commission on Criminal Procedure* (Cmnd. 8092, 1980); Justice, *The Prosecution Process in England and Wales* (1970); P. Devlin, *The Criminal Prosecution in England* (1960).

[3] Private prosecutions are not impossible in Scotland, but an individual who is aggrieved by a decision of the procurator fiscal not to prosecute must obtain authority to prosecute from the High Court (by petitioning by Bill for Criminal Letters). This procedure was recently successfully adopted, see p. 523 below.

[4] See below, p. 479.

[5] By requiring the consent of the D.P.P., the Attorney-General, a High Court judge or some other authority, to the proposed prosecution. See below, p. 480.

[6] *Prosecutions by Private Individuals and Non-Police Agencies*, Royal Commission on Criminal Procedure, Research Study No. 10 (HMSO, 1980) particularly the tables at Appendix A.

Commission on the Police listed the responsibility of deciding whether or not to prosecute suspects and the conduct of prosecutions for less serious offences as two of the main functions of the police.[7]

The procedure adopted will vary according to the practice of the force concerned but the initial steps are normally taken in the name of the officer who has decided on the prosecution.[8] If there is any legal difficulty, for example in deciding the appropriate charge or assessing the weight of the evidence on a particular charge, the police are able to take advice either from a specially established prosecuting solicitors' department or from a private firm employed for that purpose. The growth of prosecuting solicitors' departments has had a significant effect on police prosecutions, but that effect has been haphazard since the constitution, size and operation of such departments is entirely a matter for local decision and varies from force to force.

There are currently 31 of the 43 police forces in England and Wales which are able to draw on the expertise of their own prosecuting solicitors' department for legal advice and for representation in court.[9] The growth of such departments owes much to the recommendations of the Royal Commission on the Police,[10] but has lacked any statutory basis or central model for development. It is, at least, clear that a prosecuting solicitor acts on instructions from the police and is merely an adviser in a solicitor/client relationship, but the line of authority, the budgetary controls, the amount of advocacy undertaken and the degree of "independence" enjoyed vary greatly from force to force.[11] The existence of a prosecuting solicitors' department does not prevent the force making use of private practitioners where necessary and the exact use to which a department is put is very much a matter for the individual Chief Constable.

Despite these disparities the system of prosecuting solicitors' departments could, it is argued, be developed into the sort of public prosecutions system existing in Scotland, by establishing it on a statutory basis and prescribing precisely its functions. This was the approach advocated by the Royal Commission on Criminal Procedure[12] to be discussed in detail later in the chapter.[13]

The factors which may influence the decision made by the police whether or not to prosecute in a particular case are many and varied and the advice of the prosecuting solicitor may be only one consideration. A good deal has now been written about the exercise of this discretion to prosecute and it has been the subject of judicial scrutiny. We consider the issue in the next

[7] Final Report (1962) Cmnd. 1782, para. 59.

[8] This is sometimes in the name of the Chief Constable, more often in the name of the head of the appropriate division or subdivision. The fact that the case is in the name of an individual has little practical effect since the Divisional Court held that the Chief Constable or the force can be regarded as the prosecutor: *Hawkins* v. *Bepey* [1980] 1 W.L.R. 419.

[9] The Metropolitan Police and the City of London force have their own special arrangements, leaving ten forces to rely on private practitioners to provide the necessary service. See *Royal Commission on Criminal Procedure, The Investigation and Prosecution of Criminal Offences in England and Wales: The Law and Procedure* (hereafter R.C.C.P.I) (Cmnd. 8092–1, 1980) Appendix 22.

[10] Cmnd. 1782, para. 380.

[11] An analysis of the current system is to be found in, *The Prosecution System, Survey of Prosecuting Solicitors, Departments*, R.C.C.P. Research Study No. 11 (HMSO, 1980).

[12] R.C.C.P. Report, Cmnd. 8092, Chap. 7.

[13] See below, p. 517.

part of the chapter. If the police *do* decide on a prosecution it is quite possible for a police officer to present the case in the magistrates' court. The Royal Commission on the Police suggested that it was undesirable for police officers to act as prosecutors save in minor cases.[14] In practice, the police cannot conduct cases in the Crown Court and only prosecute in the magistrates' court in straightforward cases.[15] In some areas, *all* prosecutions are undertaken by prosecuting solicitors.

2. THE DIRECTOR OF PUBLIC PROSECUTIONS AND THE LAW OFFICERS

The office of Director of Public Prosecutions (D.P.P.) goes back to 1879 and the Prosecution of Offences Act of that year. After much consideration of a system of public prosecutors which had been advocated throughout the mid-nineteenth century,[16] the Disraeli government opted for a system of supervision rather than supplanting the existing prosecution procedure. The duties of the newly-created Director were defined in broad terms, " . . . to institute, undertake, or carry on such criminal proceedings . . . and to give such advice and assistance to chief officers of police, clerks to justices and other persons . . . as may be for the time being prescribed by regulations under this Act, or may be directed in a special case by the Attorney-General."[17]

The reference to regulations is significant since the detailed provisions were contained therein and always have been. The legislation is now consolidated into the Prosecution of Offences Act 1979 and the Prosecution of Offences Regulations 1978.[18]

The D.P.P. (currently Sir Thomas Hetherington) is appointed by the Home Secretary[19] and in outline his basic functions are to undertake prosecutions of particular importance or difficulty and to advise the chief officers of police. It is Regulation 6[20] which details the cases to be referred to the D.P.P. dividing them into two categories. In the first category are specified offences which must be reported by the chief officer of police when it appears to him that a prima facie case for proceedings exists.[21] The D.P.P. will normally take over the prosecution of these offences if satisfied that the suspect ought to be prosecuted. Included in this category are all offences which must be prosecuted by, or with the consent of, the D.P.P., Attorney-General or Solicitor-General; which are punishable with death; which involve homicide; abortion; and any other offences where it appears that the advice or assistance of the D.P.P. is desirable.[22] In the second category are offences specified from time to time by the D.P.P. as

[14] Cmnd. 1782, para. 381.

[15] R.C.C.P. I, paras. 144–145.

[16] For an account of the evolution and modern development of the office of Director of Public Prosecutions, see J.Ll.J Edwards, *The Law Officers of the Crown* (1964), Chaps. 16 and 17, and B. Dickens, "The Prosecuting Roles of the Attorney-General and Director of Public Prosecutions" [1974] P.L. 50.

[17] Prosecution of Offences Act 1879, s.2.

[18] S.I. 1978, No. 1357, as amended by S.I. 1978 No. 1846, deleting the requirement to report obscene exhibitions and publications.

[19] Prosecution of Offences Act 1979, s.1.

[20] Of the 1978 regulations.

[21] Regulation 7 prescribes the form and content of the report.

[22] Reg. 6(1).

appearing to him to be of importance or difficulty or requiring his intervention. Currently in this category are perjury; rape; kidnapping; robbery by use of firearms where injury is caused; criminal libel and a number of other serious offences.[23]

These regulations would, in themselves, give the D.P.P. an important co-ordinating function in prosecutions particularly in the light of his power to require specified offences to be referred to him. He will be able to introduce some measure of consistency and certainty into the prosecuting policies of the different police forces, so long as cases are referred to him. However, there are two additional provisions which further strengthen his control.

First, many statutes provide that prosecutions may only be brought in respect of certain offences with the consent of the D.P.P.[24] This has become a popular provision where the offence is controversial, or the statutory provision slightly ambiguous, or public policy considerations are involved, or mitigating factors might be present or where vexatious or trivial private prosecutions might be brought.[25] At the time that the D.P.P. gave evidence to the Royal Commission on Criminal Procedure there were 62 statutes creating offences requiring his consent to prosecution.[26]

Secondly, there is a general power vested in the D.P.P. by sections 2 and 4 of the 1979 Act[27] to take over criminal proceedings and then to deal with them as he wishes, including the offering of no evidence if he chooses. This power is equally applicable to private prosecutions and has been used to discontinue a private prosecution brought against a person to whom the D.P.P. had given a promise of immunity from proceedings in return for giving evidence for the prosecution at another trial.[28] In that case it was held that the court has no power to interfere with the Director's exercise of discretion in how he conducts proceedings taken over by him.

All these powers taken together give the D.P.P. a significant amount of control over prosecution policy in relation to serious criminal offences. Numerically, in 1979 15,507 applications were made to the D.P.P. as a result of which proceedings were concluded against 2,015 persons in 1,090 cases.[29] In respect of the other cases advice was given to the appropriate chief officer of police.

The Attorney-General and Solicitor-General both have some powers in connection with the prosecution process, although those of the Solicitor-General are effectively exercised as deputy to the Attorney-General if that

[23] Reg. 6(2).

[24] Not necessarily *all* the offences in a particular statute.

[25] See the evidence of the D.P.P. to the R.C.C.P., part of which is reproduced at R.C.C.P.I, para 159.

[26] D.P.P.'s evidence to the R.C.C.P., Appendix 12.

[27] "It shall be the duty of the Director . . . to institute, undertake or carry on such criminal proceedings . . . as may be prescribed" (s.2); "Nothing in this Act shall preclude any person from instituting or carrying on any criminal proceedings; but the Director may undertake, at any stage, the conduct of those proceedings, if he thinks fit." (s.4).

[28] *Turner* v. *D.P.P.* (1978) 68 Cr. App. R.70. See also statements about the circumstances in which it is proper to grant such immunity in *R.* v. *Turner* (1975) 61 Cr. App. R.67 (no relation). The matter has been further considered in *Raymond* v. *Att.-Gen.* [1982] 2 W.L.R. 849, where the Court of Appeal confirmed that the power to "conduct" proceedings included the power to discontinue them, pointing out that control was exercised over the D.P.P. by the Attorney-General who was, in turn, accountable to Parliament.

[29] *Criminal Statistics England and Wales 1979*, Cmnd. 8098, Table 16 pp. 468–469.

office is vacant, or the holder is unable to act.[30] The two important provisions relating to the Attorney-General are his power to enter a *nolle prosequi* in proceedings on indictment[31] and the requirement of his consent to the prosecution of certain offences.[32]

The grant of a *nolle prosequi* by the Attorney-General stops proceedings on indictment immediately and is entered on the court record. It does not actually amount to an acquittal so that accused might be indicted again on the same charge[33] but another *nolle prosequi* might then be granted! A request for such a grant may be made by any person and the exercise of the power is equivalent to the D.P.P. taking over proceedings and offering no evidence or a prosecutor offering no evidence, except that in both the latter cases the effect would formally be an acquittal.

The requirement of consent by the Attorney-General to prosecution is to be found in 39[34] statutes and included in that category are offences under the Public Order Act 1936,[35] the Hijacking Act 1971 and the Suppression of Terrorism Act 1978. These indicate that the primary responsibility of the Attorney-General in deciding whether to give consent will be to weigh factors of national and public significance, conscious that he is the Minister answerable in Parliament for all matters connected with the conduct of criminal proceedings. However, it is clearly established that the Attorney-General's decision should be made on quasi-judicial and not on political grounds.[36]

3. OTHER AGENCIES

There are a considerable number of other bodies who institute prosecutions who should not be left out of account. Government departments, local authorities, nationalised industries and other public bodies may all have cause to institute prosecutions within their particular field. A survey was undertaken on behalf of the Royal Commission on Criminal Procedure[37] which concentrated on particular courts and identified the Post Office, the British Transport Police, the Department of the Environment and local authorities as contributing almost 70 per cent. of the non-police prosecutions in those courts.[38]

4. PRIVATE PROSECUTIONS

"This historical right which goes right back to the earliest days of our legal system, though rarely exercised in relation to indictable offences, and

[30] Law Officers Act 1944, s.1.

[31] This is a common law power not subject to any control by the courts, *R.* v. *Comptroller of Patents* [1899] 1 Q.B. 909.

[32] *cf.* the powers of the D.P.P. referred to earlier.

[33] Archbold, *Criminal Pleading, Evidence and Practice* (41st ed.) para. 1–122, relying on *Goddard* v. *Smith* (1704) 3 Salk. 245.

[34] D.P.P.'s evidence to the R.C.C.P., Appendix 11.

[35] Including that created by the Race Relations Act 1976, of incitement to racial hatred, now s.5A of the 1936 Act.

[36] Statement by the Prime Minister to the House of Commons, February 16, 1959 (H.C. Deb., Vol. 600, col. 31), part of which is cited in R.C.C.P. I, para. 164.

[37] *Prosecutions by Private Individuals and Non-Police Agencies*, R.C.C.P. Research Study No. 10 (HMSO, 1980).

[38] *Ibid.* Table 2.3. at p. 15.

though ultimately liable to be controlled by the Attorney-General (by taking over the prosecution and, if he thinks fit, entering a *nolle prosequi*) remains a valuable constitutional safeguard against inertia or partiality on the part of authority."[39] Lord Wilberforce thus stated the traditional view of the private prosecution.

In fact, the growing practice of requiring the consent of the D.P.P. or Attorney-General to prosecution and the considerable cost of mounting a private prosecution now combine to minimise the significance of this historical right. We have already noted the requirement of consent,[40] but cost is an even more discouraging factor. Legal aid is not available to a private prosecutor who must meet the cost of investigation, preparation and representation out of his own pocket. A court may award costs to a successful private prosecutor[41] but he also runs the risk of having them awarded against him if he is not successful. In addition, if the prosecution was vindictive, the prosecutor risks the possibility of an action in malicious prosecution.[42]

There have, of course, been some notable private prosecutions,[43] but they are now generally confined to offences of shoplifting and common assault.[44] In some areas supermarkets and other large concerns are encouraged by the police to conduct their own prosecutions and it is the particular provisions of section 42 of the Offences Against the Person Act 1861 which dictate a private prosecution in the majority of cases where common assault occurs.[45]

B. THE EXERCISE OF DISCRETION IN PROSECUTIONS

Not every criminal offence is prosecuted. The courts could not possibly cope with the workload and, in any event, prosecution may not always be the most effective means of dealing with a violation of the criminal law. If some offenders are to be "let off" whilst others are brought before the courts it is important to know when such a decision may be made, by whom and on what principles. The exercise of this particular discretion has attracted increasing attention.[46]

[39] *Gouriet* v. *Union of Post Office Workers* [1978] A.C. 435 at p. 477.

[40] At p. 480 above.

[41] Costs in Criminal Cases Act 1973, s.1(1) (Magistrates' Court) and s.3(1) (Crown Court). The considerations are set out in *Practice Direction* [1977] 1 W.L.R. 181 in respect of the Crown Court.

[42] See *Winfield and Jolowicz on Tort* (11th ed.) pp. 512–520.

[43] Two cases brought by Mrs. Mary Whitehouse aroused interest—*R.* v. *Lemon* [1979] A.C. 617, where the accused was convicted of blasphemous libel and the Crown subsequently took over the case on appeal; and *Whitehouse* v. *Bogdanov*, where the accused was acquitted on a charge of procuring an act of gross indecency between males contrary to section 13 of the Sexual Offences Act 1956 which resulted from his producing a play (*The Romans in Britain*), containing a scene of intercourse between males (one non-consenting). The prosecution was discontinued after the judge had ruled that there was a case to answer and the Attorney-General eventually entered a *nolle prosequi*. See [1982] P.L. 165.

[44] R.C.C.P. Research Study No. 10 (see above, n. 37), Chap. 5.

[45] The section specifies that in cases of common assault the prosecution should be brought "by or on behalf of the party aggrieved."

[46] The literature is expanding. See A.F. Wilcox, *The Decision to Prosecute* (1972); N. Osborough, "Police Discretion not to prosecute Juveniles" (1965) 28 M.L.R. 179; *R.C.C.P. Report and Research Papers*, (Cmnd. 8092, 1980); D. Steer, *Police Cautions—A Study in the Exercise of Police Discretion* (1970); D.G.T. Williams, "Prosecution, discretion and the accountability of the police" (in R. Hood (ed.) *Crime, Criminology and Public Policy* (1974)).

A choice exists as soon as a police officer discovers that a criminal offence may have been committed. Should an investigation be started if the situation is unclear? Should action be taken to ensure that the offence is formally considered for prosecution if the facts are already clear? This problem is faced by every policeman present at an incident and it must be resolved on individual initiative and/or in accordance with instructions received from a superior officer. Although it may be the policeman's inclination to warn a motorist driving without lights not to repeat the offence, the Chief Constable may have decided, as a matter of policy, to prosecute all such offenders and issued instructions accordingly. The discretion exercised in this way by the policeman concerned is otherwise generally uncontrolled, except where his failure to take action may itself amount to a criminal offence or neglect of duty.[47]

Two cases have explored the exercise of discretion at a senior level which would affect the way that the man on the spot carries out his duties. In *R.* v. *Metropolitan Police Commissioner, ex p. Blackburn (No. 1)*,[48] Mr. Raymond Blackburn made application for an order of mandamus directed to the Commissioner requiring him to enforce the provisions of the Betting, Gaming and Lotteries Act 1963 in London gaming clubs. It appeared that the Commissioner had sanctioned a force order which effectively stopped observation in gaming clubs by the police and prevented any attempt to enforce the Act.[49] The Court of Appeal held that, whilst the police had a discretion not to prosecute, it was not proper to take a policy decision that certain offences would *never* be prosecuted since that was to negate the exercise of discretion and would amount to a failure in their duty to enforce the law. However, the courts will not interfere in cases where it is alleged that the police are not paying *enough* attention to particular offences or prosecuting in sufficient numbers. Mr. Blackburn again sought an order of mandamus in *R.* v. *Metropolitan Police Commissioner, ex parte Blackburn (No. 3)*,[50] this time in respect of the Obscene Publications Act 1959, but the court would not grant it. Whereas in the first case the police had deliberately decided not to prosecute, in this case they were hampered by lack of resources and the uncertainty of the law. "It is no part of the duty of this court to presume to tell the (Commissioner) how to conduct the affairs of the Metropolitan Police, nor how to deploy his all too limited resources . . . ."[51]

Given that an individual officer may be under instructions about how to deal with particular offences and will also have received training for his task, what considerations are likely to be taken into account by him in his exercise of discretion? Naturally, the gravity of the offence is likely to be uppermost but he may also think about the evidence likely to be available

---

[47] By virtue of the Police (Discipline) Regulations 1977, (S.I. 1977 No. 580), Sched. 2, para. 4.

[48] [1968] 2 Q.B. 118.

[49] The terms of the relevant instructions are set out in the judgment of Lord Denning M.R. at pp. 134–135. In the event, the instructions in question were withdrawn before the appellate hearing and the Commissioner, through counsel, gave an undertaking to that effect.

[50] [1973] Q.B. 241. For a further instalment in the drama see *R.* v. *Metropolitan Police Commissioner, ex parte Blackburn*, (1980) *The Times*, March 6, 1980. Mr. Blackburn referred to the Master of Rolls in the course of that case as, "the greatest living Englishman"—Lord Denning is reported to have replied, "Tell that to the House of Lords."

[51] *Per* Roskill L.J. at p. 262.

in a prosecution; the degree of certainty that the offence has been committed; the attitude of the victims; the personal circumstances of the offender and the efficacy of a prosecution compared with other ways of dealing with the problem. These are, on a local level, not dissimilar to the considerations appropriate to the decisions of the D.P.P. or the Attorney-General on whether to proceed to a prosecution.[52] In this case, however, the decision will need to be taken quickly and often without the help and advice of colleagues. If the officer decides not to arrest or report for prosecution he might issue his own warning to the offender; attempt a conciliation between offender and victim; or even take the offender into preventive arrest.[53] The traditional alternative of the "clip on the ear" may even return as a side-effect of the current vogue for "community policing."

Assuming that an officer has arrested an offender or reported him for prosecution the decision will pass to a senior officer.[54] At this stage the police may decide to prosecute, not to prosecute or to caution, and they may have the benefit of advice from a prosecuting solicitor or the Director of Public Prosecutions. If the decision is to prosecute, there is also an exercise of discretion in selecting the particular charge.

The caution, a formal warning issued by the police in circumstances where they are satisfied that the offence is capable of proof but do not intend to prosecute, has only twice received statutory mention[55] and its use has developed by practice rather than by law. An offender may only be cautioned if he admits the offence.[56] In 1982, nearly 161,000 offenders were cautioned in respect of all offences other than motoring offences, and of that figure 112,700 offenders were aged under 17.[57] The percentage of offenders cautioned out of the numbers of adults over 17 found guilty or cautioned has remained fairly constant at around 4 per cent. for the last 20 years.[58] Motoring offences are dealt with differently by the administration of a written caution which is not dependent upon an admission by the offender and may not be referred to in subsequent proceedings for another offence.[59]

It may be argued that a decision whether or not to institute proceedings should depend solely upon whether or not a prima facie case exists. To require a standard higher than a prima facie case or to take into account other factors would be to usurp the functions of the court in deciding on liability and in attaching appropriate weight to mitigating factors. However, it is clear that the police do not adopt a blanket policy of prosecution and do take other factors into account. There is little formal evidence of what those factors might be although Wilcox, a former Chief Constable, writes extensively[60] about various matters, drawing on his own experience. In traffic matters there is an attempt to achieve consistency

[52] See below, p. 485.

[53] Discussed by Wilcox, *op. cit.* at p. 106.

[54] Normally of the rank of chief inspector or above, although especially difficult or sensitive decisions may be taken by the Chief Constable himself.

[55] The Street Offences Act 1959, s.2; The Children and Young Persons Act 1969, s.5(2) (not in force).

[56] R.C.C.P. I, paras. 150–154 deal with the topic of cautions.

[57] *Criminal Statistics England and Wales 1982*, Cmnd. 9048, Chapter 5.

[58] *Ibid.*

[59] R.C.C.P. I, para. 153.

[60] *The Decision to Prosecute* (1972).

through agreement at regional conferences of the Association of Chief Police Officers.[61]

A succinct analysis of the principles upon which discretion may be exercised is contained in the evidence submitted by the D.P.P. to the Royal Commission on Criminal Procedure.[62] It may be supposed that the factors which weigh with him are likely to be the ones which are also taken into account by police officers in the decisions they take on less serious offences.

The initial decision for the D.P.P./police officer will be about the strength of the evidence against the suspect. In normal circumstances the test adopted is whether or not there is a reasonable prospect of conviction, although a higher standard is required if a conviction would produce unfortunate consequences, or the trial would be abnormally long and expensive on a relatively minor matter.[63] In weighing the evidence against the accused, the credibility, motives, character and reliability of the witnesses are evaluated as are the extent of any conflicts in evidence and the likely reaction of a jury to be accused and the witnesses.[64] If this evaluation leads to a conclusion that the evidence is sufficient to justify proceedings the prosecutor should go on to consider whether the facts and surrounding circumstances are such that a prosecution is "in the public interest."[65]

The D.P.P. stated that his, " . . . overall aim is to try not only to be fair to the victim of a crime and to the offender himself, but to try to satisfy responsible public opinion that the criminal law is being administered impartially in the interests of the whole community."[66] He then identified the most common factors having a bearing on his decisions as, staleness (a long lapse of time between the offence and trial); the youth of the offender; old age and infirmity; mental illness and stress; the relationship and age of offender and "victim," in sexual offences and the presence/absence of an element of corruption; the likelihood that a court will only impose a nominal penalty; the attitude and wishes of the "victim" of the crime.[67] In addition to these factors specified by the D.P.P. it is also reasonable to suppose that the obsolete, archaic, controversial or unpopular nature of the offence in question could be taken into account.[68]

The controls that exist over the exercise of this discretion by various officers are not substantial. The courts will only intervene in the most

[61] Wilcox, op. cit. p. 117–118; R.C.C.P. I, para. 147.
[62] A useful extract from the evidence submitted is to be found at R.C.C.P. I Appendix 25.
[63] D.P.P.'s evidence, paras. 89–94.
[64] Ibid. para. 97.
[65] The D.P.P. relies upon and associates himself with a statement made by a former Attorney-General, Lord Shawcross, in the course of a House of Commons debate. "It has never been the rule in this country—I hope it never will be—that suspected criminal offences must automatically be the subject of prosecution. Indeed, the very first Regulations under which the Director of Public Prosecutions worked provided that he should . . . prosecute . . . 'wherever it appears that the offence or the circumstances of its commission is or are of such a character that a prosecution in respect thereof is required in the public interest.' That is still the dominant consideration." H.C. Deb. Vol. 483, col. 681 (January 29, 1951).
[66] D.P.P.'s evidence, para. 102.
[67] Ibid. paras. 105–126.
[68] R.C.C.P. I, para. 148.

extreme cases[69]; Parliament has had little to say on the subject[70]; the D.P.P. has some influence but only in the more serious cases[71]; chief police officers have taken some limited initiatives[72]; judges take the opportunity to comment upon cases that ought not to have been brought.[73] The control system appears as haphazard as the prosecution decisions it relates to, yet the evidence is that both systems work reasonably well!

C. THE CLASSIFICATION OF OFFENCES

If a decision is taken to prosecute an offender, the police (with advice from the prosecuting solicitors' department where necessary) must decide on the appropriate charge. The selection of the charge is important because it may determine the court in which the case will be tried and, hence, the mode of trial. We have already recorded that both the magistrates' court and the Crown Court have original criminal jurisdiction and the work is divided between them according to the seriousness of the charge. In the Crown Court, the trial is "on indictment" with a judge and jury, and in the magistrates' court the trial is summary and conducted by the magistrates. Criminal offences are classified according to the way in which they are to be tried and the number of categories was reduced to three by the Criminal Law Act 1977[74] which was based upon the report of the James Committee on the Distribution of Criminal Business between the Crown Court and the magistrates' courts.[75]

Section 14 of the 1977 Act provided that there should be offences triable only on indictment; offences triable only summarily and offences triable either way.[76]

1. OFFENCES TRIABLE ONLY ON INDICTMENT

All offences at common law were triable on indictment. The other two categories are the creatures of statute and, therefore, in the absence of any specific provision an offence will be triable on indictment. In practice, this

[69] R. v. Metropolitan Police Commissioner, ex p. Blackburn (No. 1) [1968] 2 Q.B. 114, see above, p. 483.

[70] Save by the device of requiring the consent of the D.P.P. or Attorney General's consent to prosecution and being able to hold the Attorney-General responsible and accountable to Parliament for the conduct of prosecutions. Questions can be asked in the House and, on one celebrated occasion, led to the downfall of a Government, see Lyman, The first Labour Government 1924 (1957); Patrick Hastings, Autobiography (1948); J. Ll.J. Edwards, The Law Officers of the Crown (1964) Chap. 11; F.H. Newark, (1969) 20 N.I.L.Q. 19; N.D. Siederer, (1974) 9 Journal of Contemporary History 143.

[71] See above, p. 480.

[72] Wilcox op. cit. pp. 117–118.

[73] See for example the comments of the House of Lords in Smedleys Ltd. v. Breed [1974] A.C. 839 at pp. 855–6, 861; the Lord Chief Justice in R. v. Preston Justices, ex p. Lyons [1982] R.T.R. 173, 175 (cf. [1982] Crim. L.R. 620); and the Deputy Chairman of the Middlesex Sessions quoted in Wilcox, op. cit. p. 67.

[74] The pertinent parts of this Act have been re-enacted in the Magistrates' Courts Act 1980.

[75] (Cmnd. 6323, 1975). The Committee was chaired by Lord Justice James.

[76] Section 14 was repealed by the Magistrates' Courts Act 1980 and not re-enacted but it is a convenient statement of the three categories. The procedures hereafter stated apply to adults. In the case of juveniles summary trial is almost always the mode of trial (see Magistrates' Courts Act 1980, s.24, as amended by the Criminal Attempts Act 1981).

category is reserved for the most serious offences including murder, manslaughter, rape, robbery, causing grievous bodily harm with intent and blackmail. Some offences were "downgraded" by the Criminal Law Act 1977, Schedule 2[77] so as to be triable either way in recognition of the fact that, *inter alia*, appearing to be the keeper of a bawdy house[78]; not providing apprentices or servants with food[79]; assaulting a clergyman at a place of worship[80] and bigamy[81] are no longer regarded as the gravest of offences.

2. OFFENCES TRIABLE ONLY SUMMARILY

Magistrates actually deal with the vast majority of trials in this country and they have exclusive jurisdiction in summary trial. Summary offences must be created by statute and the designation of an offence as summary prevents a jury trial. It was the proposed reclassification of certain offences as triable only summarily which caused much heated criticism of the James Report.[82] The Criminal Law Act 1977 subsequently made provision for the "downgrading" of certain offences which might previously have come before a jury, and no strenuous objection was taken to allocating a number of road traffic offences (including driving with a blood-alcohol concentration above the prescribed limit[83]) assaulting a police constable,[84] threatening behaviour in public places[85] and other offences to the magistrates alone. The controversy was caused by a proposal about theft.

"We think that small thefts should not be triable on indictment . . . society has to choose between two conflicting aims. On the one hand is the existing right of the citizen to be tried by a judge and jury on any charge of theft or criminal damage, however small the amount involved. On the other is the right, especially important to anyone defending a serious charge, to be tried as soon as possible . . . At present, defendants on serious charges are suffering the injustice of long-delayed trial, while the time of the Crown Court is partly occupied with minor cases of low monetary value."[86] The Committee went on to recommend that where a person is charged with theft or a related offence where the value of the property involved did not exceed £20, that offence should be triable only summarily.[87] That was included in the Criminal Law Bill.

This raised squarely the question of what sorts of offence should entitle a defendant to trial by jury and the reactions to the proposal were

---

[77] Now to be found in Magistrates' Courts Act 1980, Sched. 1, and the crucial date is the date of the trial. If the defendant is over 17 at the date of trial he has the right to elect jury trial: *R. v. Islington Juvenile Court, ex p. Daley* [1982] 3 W.L.R. 344.

[78] Disorderly Houses Act 1751, s.8.

[79] Offences Against the Person Act 1861, s.26.

[80] *Ibid.* s.36.

[81] *Ibid.* s.57.

[82] The Distribution of Criminal Business between the Crown Court and Magistrates Courts. (Cmnd. 6323, 1975).

[83] Road Traffic Act 1972, s.6, as substituted by Transport Act 1981, Sched. 8.

[84] Police Act 1964, s.51(1).

[85] Public Order Act 1936, s.5 as substituted by Race Relations Act 1965, s.7.

[86] James Committee Report (see n. 82 above) para. 87.

[87] *Ibid.* para. 100.

emotional.[88] The Bill was introduced into the House of Lords and by the time it reached the House of Commons the clause which would have enacted the proposal had been withdrawn by the Government. It is interesting to note that a similar proposal relating to criminal damage where the value of the property damaged is less than £200 was accepted and such an offence is now triable only summarily.[89] The crucial difference was said to be the element of dishonesty inherent in the offence of theft, " . . . people lose a lifetime's reputation for probity by a single action of dishonesty of a material triviality . . . [small thefts] remain offences which are serious in the eyes of all honest men."[90]

3. OFFENCES TRIABLE EITHER WAY

This category is now comprised of those offences specifically mentioned in the First Schedule to the Magistrates' Courts Act 1980 and all other offences which were formerly triable either on indictment or summarily which have not been redesignated.[91] Amongst the important offences triable either way are all indictable offences under the Theft Act 1968 (save for robbery, blackmail, assault with intent to rob and some burglaries); most of the offences under the Criminal Damage Act 1971, including arson; certain offences under the Perjury Act 1911, the Forgery Act 1913 and the Sexual Offences Act 1956.

In respect of offences triable either way it was, of course, necessary to provide a procedure for determining the mode of trial. Save where the prosecution is being carried on by the D.P.P., the Attorney-General or the Solicitor-General and trial on indictment is required by him,[92] the accused effectively has the right to opt for summary trial or trial on indictment. The court may impose a trial on indictment, but may not insist on summary trial if the defendant objects. The procedure to be followed by the magistrates is as follows[93]:

(i) the charge is written down and read to the accused;
(ii) the court listens to representations from the prosecutor and the accused about the most suitable mode of trial;
(iii) the court proceeds to decide on the more suitable mode of trial, taking into account the nature of the case, whether the circumstances make the offence one of serious character, whether the limited powers of punishment of a magistrates' court would be adequate, and any other appropriate factors;
(iv) if the court considers summary trial more appropriate, that should be explained to the accused, and that he need not consent to summary trial but can opt for trial by jury, and that after a summary

---

[88] See the speeches of members of the House of Lords during the debate on the second reading of the Criminal Law Bill. H.L. Deb. Vol. 378, cols. 801–873, December 14, 1976.
[89] Magistrates' Courts Act 1980, s.22 and Sched. 2.
[90] Per Lord Edmund-Davies in the debate referred to in n. 88, above.
[91] Magistrates' Courts Act 1980, s.17.
[92] Ibid. 19(4).
[93] Ibid. ss.19–21.

trial the magistrates have power to send him to the Crown Court for sentence;

(v) if the accused consents to summary trial, the case proceeds;

(vi) if the accused opts for trial on indictment, the magistrates shall proceed with committal proceedings[94];

(vii) if the court considers that trial on indictment is more appropriate it will proceed with committal proceedings and the accused effectively has no choice in the matter.

Finally, it is important to stress that the magistrates must give proper consideration to all the factors and should not be persuaded by the accused (or prosecutor) to allow a summary trial where the offences ought really to be tried on indictment. There are a number of examples of magistrates' courts being severely criticised for allowing serious cases to be tried summarily.[95] The justices are aided somewhat by a provision that they may, during a trial, decide to change the mode of trial to indictment if the prosecution case reveals the offence to be more serious than might at first have appeared.[96] The reverse change is possible, from committal proceedings to summary trial subject, in this case, to the consent of the accused.[97]

D. GETTING THE ACCUSED INTO COURT

When charged with a criminal offence an accused must actually be brought before a court to have the charge tried or to have it determined how and when the trial process should begin. The appearance of a defendant may be secured by the issue of a summons; or by the issue of a warrant for his arrest; or by an arrest without warrant. The first two procedures depend upon the decision of a magistrate after the laying of information by any person, the latter upon rules of law which permit the arrest of suspected offenders without warrant and charging at the police station.

An information is merely a statement of the suspected offence and offender, either written or verbal, in terms specified by the Magistrates Courts Rules 1981,[98] which is placed before a magistrate or the justices' clerk[99] so that a summons or warrant may be issued. If a warrant is required the information must be in writing and on oath,[1] so requiring the attention of a magistrate since a clerk may not act where the information is on oath.[2] A typical information would be set out as follows:

---

[94] For committal proceedings, see below, p. 500.

[95] See *R. v. Coe* [1968] 1 W.L.R. 1950, and the statements of principle about the circumstances in which the justices can commit for sentence to the Crown Court after a summary trial in *R. v. Lymm Justices ex p. Brown* [1973] 1 W.L.R. 1039; *R. v. Harlow Justices ex p. Galway* [1975] Crim. L.R. 288. In general, unless new factors emerge during the trial or afterwards the justices should not consider the evidence which they heard before deciding how to proceed, on the question of whether to commit for sentence.

[96] Magistrates' Courts Act 1980, s.25(2).

[97] *Ibid.* s.25(3), (4).

[98] S.I. 1981 No. 552, and the accompanying Magistrates' Courts Forms Rules 1981, (S.I. 1981 No. 553).

[99] Justices of the Peace Act 1979, s.28(1).

[1] Magistrates' Courts Act 1980, s.1(3).

[2] Justices' Clerks Rules 1970 (S.I. 1970 No. 321). r. 3.

NOTTINGHAM MAGISTRATES COURT

DATE:	March 1st 1984
ACCUSED:	Henry Frederick Smailey
ADDRESS:	32 Woodland Hall Grove, Cripston, Nottingham.
ALLEGED OFFENCE:	Henry Smailey on February 27th 1984, at the Department of Law, University Park, Nottingham, dishonestly stole £5, the property of N. P. Gravells, Esq., contrary to section 1 of the Theft Act 1968.
THE INFORMATION OF:	Gavin Edmunds, Police Constable 1234
ADDRESS:	Cripston Police Station, Jug Road, Cripston, Nottingham.
TELEPHONE:	257699

WHO UPON OATH STATES THAT THE ACCUSED COMMIT-
TED THE OFFENCE OF WHICH PARTICULARS ARE GIVEN
ABOVE.

TAKEN AND SWORN BEFORE ME

Cordelia Lear
JUSTICE OF THE PEACE

JUSTICES' CLERK[3]

The information procedure does not seem to be used very often to procure a warrant[4] (the conditions for the grant of which are, in any event, carefully prescribed[5]) and on the grant of a summons the magistrate, or his clerk, should satisfy himself that the offence is known to the law; that it is not out of time; that the court has jurisdiction and that the informant has the requisite authority to prosecute.[6] A warrant should only be issued if it appears that a summons will be ineffective.[7] The summons, if issued, will not look very different from the information.[8]

---

[3] Magistrates' Courts Forms 1981, No. 1.
[4] R.C.C.P. I, para. 179.
[5] By the Magistrates' Courts Act 1980, ss.1(4), 13(2). Broadly speaking, the alleged offence must be indictable or punishable with imprisonment or the accused must have failed to respond to a summons, or his address is not sufficiently known for a summons to be served.
[6] R. v. Metropolitan Stipendiary Magistrate, ex p. Klahn [1979] 1 W.L.R. 933.
[7] O'Brien v. Brabner (1885) 49 J.P.N. 227.
[8] Magistrates' Courts Forms 1981, Form 2.

NOTTINGHAM MAGISTRATES COURT

DATE: March 1st 1983
TO THE ACCUSED: Henry Frederick Smailey
OF: 32 Woodland Hall Grove, Cripston, Nottingham

YOU ARE HEREBY SUMMONED TO APPEAR ON May 18th 1984, AT 10.30 a.m. BEFORE THE MAGISTRATES' COURT at the Guildhall, Nottingham to ANSWER TO THE FOLLOWING INFORMATION

ALLEGED OFFENCE: You on February 27th 1984 at the Department of Law, University Park, Nottingham dishonestly stole £5, the property of N. P. Gravells, Esq., contrary to section 1 of the Theft Act 1968.

PROSECUTOR: Trevor Gunn, Chief Inspector of Police
ADDRESS: Cripston Police Station, Jug Road, Cripston, Nottingham.

Cordelia Lear
JUSTICE OF THE PEACE

The accused should then respond to the summons and his attendance at court on a specified day has been secured. The process can be continued on that day. If he fails to respond, a warrant may then be appropriate.

If the accused has been arrested by warrant or without warrant it is the duty of the police then to procure his attendance at court. He will have been given bail by the police or by the warrant to appear on an appointed day or will have been brought to court in custody. If the accused is in custody after arrest without a warrant he must be brought before a magistrates' court as soon as practicable.[9] The police may, of course, request the magistrate to remand the accused in custody but they must normally put the accused in court within 48 hours of arrest.[10]

Technically, when an accused is arrested without warrant and charged at the police station an information is laid when the charge sheet is remitted by the police to the justices' clerk for inclusion on the court list,[11] but this is in reality a fiction and offenders who are brought to court in this way may never have the facts initially scrutinised by a magistrate.

(The Royal Commission concluded that the summons and warrant procedure was a virtual dead letter since the consideration given to the decision to prosecute by the justices' clerk or magistrate is minimal. It was

[9] Magistrates' Courts Act 1980, s.43(4). For bail procedures, see the following Section.
[10] R. v. Holmes, ex p. Sherman [1981] 2 All E.R. 612, approving R. v. Houghton (1978) 68 Cr. App. R. and R. v. Hudson (1980) 72 Cr. App. R. 163. See also, C. Munro, "Detention after arrest," [1981] Crim. L.R. 302. It has, however, been noted that "48 hours" is not mentioned in the section (R. v. Malcherek, R. v. Steel (1981) 73 Cr. App. R. 173, per Lord Lane C.J. at p. 187) and that there is no rigid rule that, after the lapse of 48 hours there would necessarily be a breach of s.43(4). (R. v. Nycander, The Times, December 9, 1982).
[11] The process is described and commented on in R.C.C.P. I. para. 182.

proposed that there should, in future, be a single procedure for getting an accused to court, the making of a formal "accusation" by the police fixing the date and time of the first court appearance.[12])

Where an accused is arrested it will immediately become relevant to ask at what stage, if at all, he should be given his liberty before trial.[13]

E. BAIL OR CUSTODY?

To deprive an accused[14] of his liberty pending trial may be to keep in custody an innocent man or one who, though convicted, ultimately receives a non-custodial sentence. To allow an accused his liberty pending trial may be to permit him to disappear, commit further offences, or interfere with witnesses and obstruct the course of justice. It is a difficult decision. The issue is raised as soon as a person is taken into custody and remains live until trial and, indeed, between conviction and appeal. The procedure by which the accused is permitted his liberty subject to a requirement to surrender to custody again at a specified time and place is termed the granting of bail. Bail may be granted by the police,[15] the magistrates' court,[16] the Crown Court,[17] the High Court[18] and the Court of Appeal[19] under a variety of statutory and common law provisions, but the granting of bail in all criminal proceedings must be in accordance with the principles set out in the Bail Act 1976.

This Act, which came into force in the Spring of 1978 was a response to the widespread disquiet about the operation of the system of bail and resulted from the Report of a Home Office Working Party[20] which had been established in 1971 "to review practice and procedure in magistrates' courts relating to the grant or refusal of bail and to make recommendations."[21] Before considering the general principles it is helpful to define two important terms.

A *surety* is a person who is willing to undertake to secure the surrender of the accused to custody. The grant of bail may be made conditional upon the accused finding suitable surety or sureties.[22] Whoever is willing to be a surety must enter into a *recognizance*, which is a formal acknowledgment that he will owe the Crown a specified sum of money if the accused fails to surrender to custody. No money is payable by the surety unless the accused

---

[12] R.C.C.P. Report, para. B.4.

[13] See generally, M. King, *Bail or Custody*, Cobden Trust (1971); A.K. Bottomley, *Decisions in the Penal Process* (1973) pp. 93–105, and "The Granting of Bail: Principles and Practice" (1968) 31 M.L.R. 40; M. Zander, "Bail: A Reappraisal" [1967] Crim. L.R. 25, 100, 128.

[14] We use the term "accused" throughout this section to include those arrested, those on trial, and those convicted.

[15] See below, p. 497.

[16] See below, p. 498.

[17] See below, p. 498.

[18] See below, p. 499.

[19] See below, p. 498.

[20] *Bail Procedures in Magistrates' Courts*, Report of the Home Office Working Party (1974).

[21] Although the terms of reference of the Working Party referred specifically to magistrates' courts the provisions of the Bail Act 1976 actually go somewhat wider.

[22] Bail Act 1976, s.3(4).

actually absconds.[23] The amount of the recognizance is a matter for the police officer or court granting bail.

Statutory criteria are now fixed for determining the suitability of persons who may offer to be sureties where the grant of bail is conditional upon finding sureties.[24] In considering the suitability of a proposed surety, regard may be had, *inter alia*, to his financial resources, his character and any previous convictions, and his "proximity" to the accused.[25] If a court or police officer considers a proposed surety to be unsuitable there is provision for appeal.[26]

Prior to the Bail Act it was quite common for the accused to be required to enter into a personal recognizance but this has now been abolished[27] and the only circumstances in which the accused may be required to provide security is if it appears likely that he will leave Great Britain.[28]

1. General Principles Relating to the Grant of Bail

The Bail Act introduced a general right to bail for accused persons and certain others subject to exceptions specified in a Schedule to the Act. In fact, the exceptions are substantial and this has led commentators to speak rather of a "presumption in favour of bail" rather than a "right to bail." In addition the Act focused attention upon the need for information about the accused to be available to the court so that the bail decision could be an informed one, and required reasons to be given to the accused where bail was not granted so that he might more effectively conduct an appeal against the decision.

Section 4 of the Bail Act 1976 creates the *right to bail*:

"(1) A person to whom this section applies shall be granted bail except as provided in Schedule 1 to this Act.
(2) This section applies to a person who is accused of an offence when—
  (*a*) he appears or is brought before a magistrates' court or the Crown Court in the course of or in connection with proceedings for the offence, or
  (*b*) he applies to a court for bail in connection with the proceedings."

[23] The recognizance may not be forfeited if the surety has made every effort to secure the appearance of the accused and acted with all due diligence, but the obligation is upon the surety to satisfy the court that all or part of the sum should not be forfeited. Only in exceptional cases will the court order that the recognizance should not be forfeited: Magistrates' Courts Act 1980, s.120; *R.* v. *Southampton Justices, ex p. Green* [1976] Q.B. 11; *R.* v. *Waltham Forest Justices, ex p. Parfrey* [1980] Crim. L.R. 571; *R.* v. *Knightsbridge Crown Court, ex p. Newton* [1980] Crim. L.R. 715; *R.* v. *Ipswich Crown Court, ex p. Reddington* [1981] Crim. L.R. 618; *R.* v. *Uxbridge Justices, ex p. Heward-Mills* [1983] 1 W.L.R. 56.
[24] Bail Act 1976, s.8(2).
[25] "Proximity" to the accused includes consideration of kinship, place of residence or other matters.
[26] Bail Act 1976, s.8(5).
[27] *Ibid.* s.3(2).
[28] *Ibid.* s.3(5).

There are additional categories brought within the entitlement and some which are excepted.[29] It is important to note that this section applies to the grant of bail by courts only. The grant of bail by the police, considered below, is not subject to this provision.

Schedule 1 of the Act creates the *exceptions to the right to bail*, and distinguishes between defendants accused or convicted of offences punishable with imprisonment[30] and those not punishable with imprisonment.[31] In respect of the imprisonable offences the accused need not be granted bail if the court is satisfied that there are substantial grounds for believing that the accused would, if released on bail:

(a) fail to surrender to custody, or
(b) commit an offence while on bail, or
(c) interfere with witnesses or otherwise obstruct the course of justice.[32]

The accused need not be granted bail where the court is satisfied that it has not been practicable to obtain sufficient information since the proceedings were instituted to make a proper decision on bail.[33]

This latter point emphasises that the court must have access to information about the defendant because it is required to have regard to specified matters (as far as they appear relevant) including:

(a) the nature and seriousness of the offence (and the probable method of dealing with it);
(b) the character, antecedents, associations and community ties of the defendant;
(c) the defendant's record in respect of any previous grants of bail;
(d) the strength of the evidence against him.[34]

In respect of non-imprisonable offences the defendant may only be denied bail if it appears to the court that he has previously failed to surrender to bail and that the court believes that, if released, he would again fail to surrender to custody.[35]

The court, if it is to refuse bail, must be "satisfied that there are substantial grounds for believing" that one of the specified situations exists. This formulation of the standard of proof is a compromise reached after much debate both in the House of Commons and the House of Lords. The original draft was "satisfied that it is probable"; an amendment in the Lords substituted, "satisfied that there is an unacceptable risk"[36]; and the

[29] Within the entitlement—a person remanded for reports after conviction (Bail Act 1976, s.4(4)); a person brought before the court for breach of a probation or community service order (s.4(3)). Excluded from entitlement—a person convicted of the offence charged (unless remanded for reports) (s.4(2)); a fugitive offender (s.4(2)); a person in respect of whom the court is satisfied that he should be kept in custody for his own protection or (if a child or young person) his own welfare (Sched. 1, Part I, para. 3; Part II, para. 3); a person charged with treason (s.4(7)); a person arrested for absconding or breach of bail granted (Sched. 1, Part I, para. 6; Part II, para. 5).
[30] Sched. 1, Part I.
[31] Sched. 1, Part II.
[32] Sched. 1, Part I, para. 2.
[33] *Ibid.* para. 5.
[34] *Ibid.* para. 9.
[35] Sched. 1, Part II, para. 2.
[36] See the speech of Lord Hailsham, H.L. Deb., Vol. 369, col. 1544 *et seq.*

eventual compromise was thought to pitch the standard of proof somewhere between the two.[37]

If bail is refused by the court or conditions are imposed on the grant of bail in respect of anyone to whom section 4 of the Act applies, the court must give reasons for withholding bail or imposing the conditions with a view to enabling the accused to make application to another court.[38] This is a logical provision, given that the courts are now directed towards specific considerations in the refusal of bail. The accused is entitled to know in what respect he is considered unsuitable for bail.

The imposition of conditions on the grant of bail can be a very serious matter. It is not uncommon for the magistrates to require the accused to report regularly to a police station as a condition of bail, or to observe a curfew, or to reside in or keep away from particular places. In serious matters the accused may be required to surrender his passport. It is arguable that the conditions attached ought to relate primarily to securing the attendance of the accused in court but they can also be used to curtail potentially criminal activities pending the trial of the alleged offence.[39]

2. APPLICATION OF THE PRINCIPLES

The Bail Act has now been in operation for six years and there are suggestions that it has not made a substantial difference to the practice of the courts. It is true that there have been two significant reductions in the number of prisoners on remand in the last ten years,[40] but such research as there is shows little general change.[41]

An issue which initially concerned the courts was the procedure to be adopted on successive applications for bail. The magistrates' court is given power, prior to the commencement of the hearing, to remand an accused person in custody for a period not exceeding 8 clear days[42] and this may be appropriate where the prosecution are not yet ready to proceed with the case. In complex cases this meant a court appearance every 8 days for a considerable length of time.[43] At every appearance the accused was entitled to request bail and he would normally appear before differently constituted courts each time.[44] In Nottingham, the City justices adopted a

[37] H.C. Deb., Vol. 918, col. 1323–4, Mr. Brynmor John, then Minister of State, Home Office.

[38] Bail Act 1976, s.5(3).

[39] During the recent dispute between the NCB and the NUM, pickets charged with criminal offences were granted bail on condition that they did not go on or near NCB property. This caused considerable controversy.

[40] One after the Home Office Circular (HOC 155/1975) which urged the courts to take a more liberal view on bail, and the other after the Bail Act 1976.

[41] M. Zander, "The Operation of the Bail Act in London Magistrates' Courts" (1979) 129 N.L.J. 108. A substantial extract is included in M. Zander, Cases and Materials on the English Legal System (3rd ed. 1980) at pp. 181–187. See also, R. Vogler, "The Changing Nature of Bail", LAG Bulletin, February 1983, 11; R. East and M. Doherty, "The Practical Operation of Bail", LAG Bulletin, March 1984, 12.

[42] Magistrates' Courts Act 1980, s.128(6).

[43] This can clearly be oppressive since the accused is being held in custody without trial, but it is well established than an unreasonable delay on the part of the prosecution will be a good reason for granting bail. R. v. Nottingham Justices, ex p. Davies [1981] Q.B. 38 at p. 44.

[44] At the time of Davies' application (see note above) the Nottingham bench consisted of 320 justices, with up to 25 courts sitting each day. The chance of getting the same justices two weeks running is negligible.

policy under which after a second application[45] for bail they would not consider on subsequent applications matters previously before the court unless there had been a change in circumstances.[46] In effect, remand in custody became automatic. A group of Nottingham solicitors organised an application for mandamus by one Clive Edgar Davies, charged with various offences of criminal damage and rape, directing the justices to hear the full facts supporting an application for bail made on April 10, 1980[47] and determine it accordingly. In *R* v. *Nottingham Justices, ex p. Davies*[48] the Divisional Court refused the application.

It was argued on behalf of Davies that he had a right to bail which was only defeasible on the specified grounds; that the court has a duty to consider the grant of bail on every occasion on which the accused appears; and that the fact of a previous remand could not, of itself, satisfy the justices that one of the specified grounds still existed. The court did not accede to the argument and Donaldson L.J. based his judgment primarily upon a notion of *res judicata*.[49] The finding of the original court that Schedule 1 circumstances existed, " . . . is to be treated like every other finding of the court. It is res judicata or analogous thereto . . . It follows that on the next occasion when bail is considered the court should treat, as an essential fact, that at the time when the matter of bail was last considered, Schedule 1 circumstances did indeed exist. Strictly speaking, they can and should only investigate whether that situation has changed since then."[50] The court also indicated that the position of the accused is safeguarded by the provision for an application to a High Court judge for bail.[51]

This decision excited both favourable[52] and unfavourable[53] comment, but the position has been affected to some extent by the provisions of section 59 and Schedule 9 of the Criminal Justice Act 1982. It is now possible to remand an accused in his absence for up to three successive remand hearings provided that he consents and is legally represented. This alleviates the problem of constant weekly journeys for the accused who does not wish to contest his remand, but *Davies'* case will still apply to prevent the non-consenting accused from seeking bail on every remand appearance.[54]

[45] After the *second* application, because the first is usually made by a duty solicitor (see above, p. 343) who may not be fully briefed so as to make a proper application. On the second application the accused will normally be legally aided and represented by his own solicitor who should then be in a position to place all relevant matters before the court.

[46] A policy apparently inspired by certain remarks made by Ackner J. to a meeting of justices' clerks and reported in (1980) 36 *The Magistrate* 34, 97. The actual wording of the Nottingham policy is contained in the report of *Davies*, [1981] Q.B. 38 at p. 41.

[47] The date was significant because that was Davies' third application for bail.

[48] [1981] Q.B. 38.

[49] A final judgment already decided by a competent court on the same question.

[50] [1981] Q.B. 38 at p. 44. See also, *R.* v. *Slough Justices, ex p. Duncan and Embling* (1982) 75 Cr.App.R. 384.

[51] See below, p. 499.

[52] Anon. "Bail Applications" (1980) 144 J.P.N. 319; Editorials in (1980) 36 *The Magistrate* 97, 135; K. Polak, "Applications for Bail" (1980) 144 J.P.N. 525.

[53] M. Hayes, "Where Now the Right to Bail" [1981] Crim. L.R. 20. See also a letter to *The Times*, July 19, 1980, from Mr. Jeremy Allen, Secretary to the Nottinghamshire Law Society. In "Bail—a Suitable Case for Treatment" (1982) 132 N.L.J. 409, J. Burrow analyses other less predictable effects of the decision.

[54] See also *R.* v. *Reading Crown Court, ex p. Malik* [1981] Q.B. 451.

The only reported case on the application of the relevant considerations when refusal of bail is contemplated is *R.* v. *Vernege*[55] where the Court of Appeal regretted that the grant of bail on committal on a charge of murder had prevented the examination of the accused by a prison doctor and, consequently, the early submission of psychiatric evidence. On a charge of murder, the obtaining of such reports is a "relevant matter" in relation to bail and it will usually be in the accused's interests to be remanded in custody, at least until the examinations have been carried out.

3. POLICE BAIL

Where an accused has been arrested without warrant, a police officer not below the rank of inspector, or the officer in charge of the police station to which the person is brought:

(a) *may* inquire into the case; or
(b) *must* inquire into the case if it will not be practicable to bring the accused before a magistrates' court within 24 hours;

and *shall* grant the offender bail subject to the Bail Act 1976 to appear before a magistrates' court at a specified time and place unless it appears to him that the offence is a serious one.[56]

If the officer considers that the inquiry into the case cannot be completed forthwith then he may, alternatively, grant the offender bail subject to the Bail Act 1976, with or without sureties to appear back at the police station at a specified time and place.[57] As we have already noted, where the officer considers the offence to be a serious one and the offender is retained in custody, he must be brought before a magistrates' court as soon as practicable.[58]

If the accused is in police custody as the result of a warrant issued by a magistrate or the Crown Court, then the warrant itself will dictate the granting of bail and the previous provisions will not apply. Either the warrant will be "endorsed for bail"[59] in terms which must be observed by the police, or it will require the police to bring the accused before the court immediately.[60] In this case, of course, the grant of bail is, strictly speaking, made by the court and not the police.

The use of police bail is substantial. In 1982, 670,000 persons were arrested and charged of whom 546,000 (81.5 per cent.) were bailed and the remainder, 124,000 (18.5 per cent.) held in custody. In general, the more serious the offence, the higher the proportion of those arrested who are held in custody. The highest proportion is in respect of robbery (56 per cent.); and burglary (26 per cent.), sexual offences (27 per cent.), and violence against the person (19 per cent.) all exceed the average.[61]

---

[55] [1982] 1 W.L.R. 293.
[56] Magistrates' Courts Act 1980, s.43(1).
[57] *Ibid.* s.43(3).
[58] *Ibid.* s.43(4). See p. 491 and n. 10 above.
[59] *Ibid.* s.117. The magistrate issuing the warrant will state on the warrant that the person arrested is to be released subject to a duty to appear at a specified court and time.
[60] See the form of warrant set out as Form 4, the Magistrates' Courts, Forms Rules 1981 (S.I. 1981 No. 553).
[61] *Criminal Statistics England and Wales 1982*, Chap. 8.

4. BAIL FROM THE MAGISTRATES' COURT

If the accused has been arrested without warrant, and has not been bailed by the police, or if he has been arrested with a warrant which is not endorsed for bail, he must be brought before a magistrates' court and will then have an opportunity to request bail. Indeed, the court is under an obligation to consider the question of bail even if no application is made.[62] The court must, in these cases, *remand* the accused, which simply means a direction that he should be held in custody for a period not exceeding 8 days,[63] or that he should be released on bail with an obligation to appear again before the court on a specified date.[64]

The court must also exercise the power of remand where the committal proceedings before a trial on indictment have begun or when they are deciding on the mode of trial for an offence triable either way and the accused has previously been remanded at some stage in the proceedings.[65]

In deciding whether to remand on bail or in custody the magistrates must have regard to the provisions of the Bail Act but may take advantage of the *Davies*[66] case to lessen the burden of continuing applications. The position is further eased by the provision for automatic remand in custody under Criminal Justice Act 1982, s.59, where the accused consents to the remand and is legally represented (see above).

The magistrates' court also has power to grant bail where a hearing before it is adjourned.[67] This may be on the date specified for the commencement of a summary trial or during the hearing; before or during the proceedings for determining the mode of trial of an offence triable either way; before or during committal proceedings. On an adjournment the magistrates may direct that the accused be kept in custody or may grant bail, with or without sureties, directing the accused to appear at the end of the remand period, or at every time and place to which during the course of the proceedings the hearing may from time to time be adjourned.[68]

5. BAIL FROM THE CROWN COURT

The Crown Court may grant bail to an accused who is in custody pending a hearing in the Crown Court (after committal for trial or sentence); or pending an appeal against conviction or sentence by the magistrates; or pending the completion of the hearing in the Crown Court; or pending the statement of a case for the High Court or the outcome of an application to have proceedings removed from the Crown Court to the High Court; or pending an appeal to the Court of Appeal where the Crown Court has given a certificate under the Criminal Appeal Act 1968.[69]

---

[62] Because of the provision in the Bail Act 1976, s.4(1) that a person to whom the Act applies *shall* be given bail except where Schedule 1 applies.

[63] Magistrates' Courts Act 1980, s.128(6).

[64] *Ibid.* s.128(4).

[65] *Ibid.* s.18(4).

[66] *R. v. Nottingham Justices, ex p. Davies* ['1981] Q.B. 38, see above, p. 496.

[67] Magistrates' Courts Act 1980, ss.5(1), 10(1) and 18(4).

[68] *Ibid.* s.128(4).

[69] Supreme Court Act 1981, s.81, as amended by Criminal Justice Act 1982, s.29. See also, *Practice Direction* [1983] 1 W.L.R. 1292.

If, in any of those cases, the accused is actually before the court then application is made orally to the judge, otherwise the application is in writing in a specified form and the accused is not entitled to be present at the hearing.[70] The jurisdiction of the court is quite separate from that of the justices and the High Court, and prior applications to either of those courts will not diminish the obligation of the Crown Court judge to consider the application on its merits and exercise discretion.[71] However, the accused may not make repeated applications to the Crown Court unless there is a change in his circumstances.[72]

An important recent addition to the powers of the Crown Court is the power to grant bail on an application by a person who has been refused bail by a magistrates' court.[73] The application may only be made where the magistrates have heard full argument before refusal[74] and legal aid will now be available for the application.[75] This reform is a response to criticism that there was no effective appeal against refusal of bail by the magistrates other than an expensive and difficult application to the High Court.

6. BAIL FROM THE HIGH COURT

A judge of the High Court may exercise both the inherent jurisdiction to grant bail and the statutory powers vested in the High Court by the Criminal Justice Act 1967.[76] The application for a writ of habeas corpus has now largely been superseded by a bail application. The ability of the accused to make application to the High Court was specifically mentioned in the *Davies* case[77] as a check on the accuracy of magistrates' decisions, and an additional safeguard is now provided by the application to the Crown Court set out above. Application to the High Court was always a difficult operation because legal aid was rarely granted, forcing applicants to rely on the Official Solicitor.[78]

The accused must apply to a judge in chambers either through his own solicitor by summons and affidavit, or by giving written notice to the judge that he wants bail.[79] In the latter case, the judge will then appoint the

---

[70] Crown Court Rules 1982, r.17.

[71] *R. v. Reading Crown Court, ex p. Malik* [1981] 1 Q.B. 451.

[72] There is no specific provision in the Crown Court Rules to this effect, but the Divisional Court in *Malik* (above) indicated that simultaneous or immediately consecutive applications to more than one Crown Court judge will not be permitted.

[73] Criminal Justice Act 1982, s.60, amending the Supreme Court Act 1981, s.81. See also, *Practice Direction* (1983) 77 Cr. App. R. 69.

[74] For the certification procedure to be adopted see Criminal Justice Act 1982, s.60(3), inserting new subsections 5(6A), (6B), (6C) in the Bail Act 1976.

[75] Criminal Justice Act 1982, s.60(4), amending the Legal Aid Act 1974, s.30.

[76] s.22, as amended by the Bail Act 1976.

[77] *R. v. Nottingham Justices, ex p. Davies* [1980] 3 W.L.R. 15, see above, p. 496.

[78] It is civil legal aid which is appropriate for these applications and the evidence suggests that it has generally been refused on the basis that applicants can rely on the assistance of the Official Solicitor in presenting a case. This is not, apparently, a procedure that is followed willingly by The Law Society, for it made strong criticisms of the Official Solicitor procedure in a paper, *Report on Legal Aid for Bail Applications*, (January 1972). See comment in *LAG Bulletin* January 1980, p. 28.

[79] R.S.C., Ord. 79, r.9(4), (5).

Official Solicitor to act on his behalf. The Official Solicitor will not actually represent the applicant at a hearing in chambers (as his own lawyer would) but merely prepares a set of papers for the judge to consider, along with the police submissions. This is widely regarded as an unsatisfactory form of procedure and research demonstrates that the success rate in bail applications made by the Official Solicitor is much lower than in applications made by a lawyer instructed by the applicant.[80] The legally-aided right of appeal referred to above ought to obviate this problem.

7. BREACH OF BAIL

The Bail Act 1976 replaced the defendant's personal recognizance with a new criminal offence of failing to surrender to custody without reasonable cause.[81] If a defendant has reasonable cause for failure to surrender to custody at the appointed time and place, he must surrender as soon as reasonably practicable thereafter, or be guilty of an offence.[82] The accused may be fined or imprisoned on summary conviction, or by the Crown Court where the offence is treated as a criminal contempt of court. Powers of arrest are attached to the offence.

In the event of failure to surrender, any personal security given by the accused under the limited powers in the Act[83] may be forfeited, as may the sums of money promised by the sureties. Normally those sums would be forfeited in full, but the court must exercise a proper discretion as to whether any part of the sum should be remitted on account of the sureties' behaviour, responsibility or means.[84]

F. COMMITTAL PROCEEDINGS

Before an accused can be tried on indictment there must normally be a preliminary inquiry into his case conducted in the magistrates' court in order to establish whether there is a prima facie case against him. The magistrates, referred to in this context as "examining justices," will be required to decide whether to commit the accused for trial at the Crown Court, or whether to call a halt to the proceedings at that point if there is not "such evidence that, if it be uncontradicted at the trial, a reasonably minded jury may convict on it."[85] However, if the accused is discharged by the magistrates at the end of the committal proceedings this is not the equivalent of an acquittal at trial. He may be charged again with the same offence and be required to undergo committal proceedings again, whereas an acquittal at trial effectively prevents any further proceedings for the

---

[80] N. Bases and M. Smith, "A study of bail applications through the Official Solicitor to the judge in chambers" [1976] Crim. L.R. 541.

[81] Bail Act 1976, s.6(1).

[82] *Ibid.* s.6(2).

[83] *i.e.* any security taken where it appears likely that the accused will leave Great Britain, Bail Act 1976, s.3(5).

[84] See above, p. 493.

[85] R. v. *Governor of Brixton Prison, ex p. Bidwell* [1937] 1 K.B. 374.

same offence.[86] This distinction has an important influence on the conduct of committal proceedings and the defendant's attitude towards them.

Committal proceedings have evolved from the special role of the magistracy as policemen and prosecutors prior to the establishment of police forces,[87] but their object is still said to be the elimination of ill-founded prosecutions for serious offences. The only alternative to committal is for the prosecution to seek a voluntary bill of indictment which permits the case to be taken straight to the Crown Court. This procedure is discussed further later in this section.

1. The Form of Proceedings

The Magistrates' Courts Act 1980, s.6(1) states clearly the obligations of the magistrates' court:

"Subject to the provisions of this and any other Act relating to the summary trial of indictable offences, if a magistrates' court inquiring into an offence as examining justices is of opinion, on consideration of the evidence and of any statement of the accused, that there is sufficient evidence to put the accused on trial by jury for any indictable offence, the court shall commit him for trial; and, if it is not of that opinion, it shall, if he is in custody for no other cause than the offence under inquiry, discharge him."

Until 1968 there was only one form of committal proceedings. This procedure is still available and is normally termed a "full" or "old-style" committal to contrast it with the alternative form introduced by section 1 of the Criminal Justice Act 1967 now termed a "new-style," "paper," or most commonly, "Section 1" committal.

The "old-style" committal proceedings consist of the oral presentation of evidence for the consideration of the court. The prosecution must call sufficient of its witnesses to establish a prima facie case against the defendant (although there is no obligation to call every potential prosecution witness) and they will be subject to cross-examination and re-examination with the whole of their evidence written down, read back to them and authenticated.[88] The defence must, at the close of the prosecution case, select its tactics. A submission may be made that the evidence given discloses no prima facie case. If the court accedes to the submission it will discharge the defendant; if it does not, the charge will be written down and read to the defendant. The defence will then choose whether to offer any evidence. If it does, the witnesses called and their evidence will be treated in exactly the same way as for the prosecution, and

---

[86] If re-tried in respect of an offence for which he has been acquitted, the accused is entitled to the plea of *autrefois acquit* (see below, p. 588). If he is discharged after committal proceedings this plea is not available because he has not been tried for the offence. The prosecutor will have to choose whether to abandon the prosecution, or seek further evidence with a view to beginning proceedings again, or invoke the voluntary bill procedure discussed at p. 507 below.

[87] See above, p. 132.

[88] These are referred to as depositions, and, of course, form the basis of the evidence to be given at trial.

the court must make its decision on the evidence. If it does not, the magistrates will commit for trial immediately.

The full oral procedure has been varied somewhat by provisions which permit the court to accept written evidence subject to specified conditions.[89] This can lead to a marginally shorter hearing, but the old-style committals tend to take a long time and may be rendered fairly ineffective if the defendant decides that he will "accept" committal by not contesting the evidence offered by the prosecution. Criticism can also be made of the expense and waste of resources involved. It was, therefore, a welcome relief when the Criminal Justice Act 1967 provided an alternative procedure.

The "Section 1" committal permits the magistrates to commit a case for trial at the Crown Court without giving any consideration to the prosecution (or defence) evidence provided that certain conditions are fulfilled. So long as all the evidence is in the form of written statements tendered to the court in accordance with section 102 of the Magistrates' Courts Act 1980, the court may commit for trial without considering the contents of the statements unless the accused is not legally represented or the defence submits that the statements disclose insufficient evidence.[90] In effect, if the prosecution request a committal under this procedure, the defendant may simply choose to be committed for trial without further ado.

The obligation will be on the prosecution to select the procedure—the defendant may object to a "Section 1" committal but he cannot demand one. Statistics do not reveal the number of cases which proceed under the "old-style" committal, but the evidence suggests that there are very few indeed.[91] What factors might induce the prosecution or defence to opt for a full hearing?[92] The prosecution, in a complex case, would have to assemble the evidence and arguments which will be pertinent at the trial and would also have an opportunity to observe the behaviour and composure of their witnesses under examination and cross-examination. Additional information may be obtained from the witness which does not appear on the original statements. The defence, if it chooses to put its case at all, will enjoy both those advantages and in addition will be given the opportunity of probing the prosecution evidence ahead of trial. The case to be met by the defendant is likely to emerge more clearly from an oral hearing and will give him an opportunity to make realistic judgments about the strength of the evidence against him. Evidence established in careful cross-examination may require investigation for which there would be little

[89] Criminal Justice Act 1967, s.2. Now Magistrates' Courts Act 1980, s.102. The conditions are that the statement is signed; that it contains a declaration that it is true to the best of the maker's knowledge; that a copy is given to the other party; that no party objects.

[90] Now contained in Magistrates' Courts Act 1980, s.6(2), as amended by the Criminal Justice Act 1982, s.59. However, as old habits, especially lawyers' habits die hard, it will no doubt be some time before the procedure is referred to as a "Section 6 committal." Section 6(2) of the 1980 Act has been amended by the Criminal Justice Act 1982, s.61, to the effect that "legally represented" now means merely that the accused has a solicitor acting for him, not that his solicitor or counsel must be present in court.

[91] R.C.C.P. I, para. 193.

[92] These are considered more fully in D. Napley, *A Guide to Law and Practice under the Criminal Justice Act 1967* (1967), Chap. 1.

opportunity if the facts had emerged for the first time at trial.[93] It may even be that press reports of committal proceedings (see below) produce witnesses who have their memories jogged by reading about an incident. Finally, the accused may want to demonstrate at as early a stage as possible that he rejects the charges laid against him. Even though a discharge after committal proceedings will not prevent further charges, an accused may prefer not to be tried at all than to be tried and found not guilty.

Only the final consideration, the desire to establish innocence/avoid committal, is not related to tactics at trial and this puts committal proceedings in their true context. Their objective may be to filter out trivial and ill-founded cases which should not go to trial, but that objective is very difficult to achieve where the vast majority of committals are unconsidered by the magistrates and the few that are considered are not necessarily strongly contested on the issue of whether or not to commit.

The *Confait* case illustrates the inadequacy of committal proceedings in their present form. After a fire at 27 Doggett Road, Catford, in April 1972 the body of Maxwell Confait was discovered in a first floor room. Following confessions which they were said to have made, an 18-year-old boy and a 15-year-old boy were charged with the murder of Confait and, jointly with a 14-year-old boy, with setting fire to 27 Doggett Road. They were convicted of murder and manslaughter (diminished responsibility) respectively and all three were convicted of arson. They were refused leave to appeal in July 1973, but after representations by an M.P. the Home Secretary referred the case to the Court of Appeal in June 1975. That court quashed the two homicide convictions because of discrepancies in the evidence so serious that the convictions were unsafe and unsatisfactory. Why had these discrepancies not been revealed at the committal?

A subsequent Inquiry by Sir Henry Fisher[94] revealed that an "old style" committal had been held, but the magistrates received written statements in lieu of oral testimony.[95] The solicitor for the prosecution had not noticed the discrepancies and could not draw them to the attention of the magistrates. The defence were handicapped by the absence of early statements of key witnesses[96] and, presumably, by the general tactic at committal to discover prosecution evidence and then not offer much by way of defence. "There is obviously scope for using committal proceedings to a greater extent to test the prosecution's case. But this will not happen unless there is either a defence submission or the person appearing for the prosecution himself draws the attention of the magistrates to a point of difficulty in the prosecution's case. And this will not happen unless there is a careful and dispassionate survey and review of the evidence . . .

[93] Little is seen in English courts of the Perry Mason style of investigative advocacy where crucial facts emerge in the course of cross-examination, are investigated by Della Street in the luncheon adjournment and the results communicated to the intrepid advocate in time to secure another forensic triumph before the credits roll. (For younger readers, "Perry Mason" was an American TV courtroom drama series starring Raymond Burr who re-emerged later as "A Man Called Ironside").

[94] A former High Court judge. *Report of an Inquiry by the Hon. Sir Henry Fisher into the circumstances leading to the trial of three persons on charges arising out of the death of Maxwell Confait and the fire at 27 Doggett Road, London, SE6* (HMSO, 1977).

[95] *Ibid.* Chap. 27.

[96] *Ibid.* para. 27.2.

Committal proceedings cannot therefore act as a safeguard against a failure to perform this duty . . . the magistrates do not take the initiative."[97]

Sir Henry Fisher concluded, on this point, that if there is a serious case for an independent review of every serious case before trial, a *viva voce* hearing is necessary and committal proceedings cannot be relied upon at present unless a full old-style committal with oral testimony is used.[98]

2. THE TASK OF THE MAGISTRATES ON COMMITTAL

On committing an accused for trial the magistrates must select the place and time of trial, the appropriate charge and decide whether to grant bail. All these decisions are guided by established rules and the scope for discretion is, in fact, limited.

The magistrates will commit on the offence charged if there is a section 1 committal because they have no opportunity to review the evidence, but on a full committal they may substitute a new charge if the evidence fails to support the original one but does indicate another offence.[99]

The place of the trial is determined mainly by the nature of the charge on which the accused is committed. Criminal offences triable on indictment are divided into four classes according to their seriousness[1] and the classes are distinguished by stipulations about the seniority of the judge required to try the case. Class 1 offences (including treason, murder and genocide) must be tried by a High Court judge. Class 2 offences (including manslaughter, rape and mutiny) must be tried by a High Court judge unless a particular case is released by or on the authority of the presiding judge of the circuit.[2] Class 3 is the residual class consisting of offences triable only on indictment and not specified in classes 1, 2 and 4 and those offences may be listed for trial by High Court judge, circuit judge or recorder. Class 4 offences (including all offences triable either way, causing grievous bodily harm and robbery) may be tried by High Court judge, circuit judge or recorder, but will normally be listed for trial by a circuit judge or recorder.

This classification will normally determine the place of trial since it is provided that magistrates shall specify, in respect of classes 1, 2 and 3, the most convenient location of the Crown Court where a High Court judge regularly sits and in respect of Class 4, the most convenient location of the Crown Court.[3] There is some discretion, in that the magistrates may make specific recommendation that a class 4 offence should be tried by a High Court judge if it involves death or serious risk to life; serious violence; dishonesty in respect of a substantial sum of money; an accused in a public position or owing a professional duty to the public; a novel or difficult issue of law or is giving rise to widespread public concern.[4] Once the justices

---

[97] *Ibid*. para. 27.7.

[98] *Ibid*. para. 27.8.

[99] That will then form the basis of the indictment drafted for the trial at the Crown Court. The magistrates should not reduce the charge unrealistically so as to bring the offence within their summary jurisdiction; *R.* v. *Coe* [1968] 1 W.L.R. 1950.

[1] *Practice Direction* (*Crime: Crown Court Business*) [1971] 1 W.L.R. 1535, as amended by [1978] 1 W.L.R. 926: Supreme Court Act 1981, s.75. See p. 66, above.

[2] See above, p. 68 for the role and functions of the presiding judge.

[3] [1971] 1 W.L.R. 1535, para. 2(i).

[4] *Ibid*. para. 2(ii).

have committed for trial the placement of the case is the responsibility of the circuit listing officer acting in consultation with the presiding judge.[5]

An accused or the prosecutor may make application to a High Court judge to vary the specified place of trial[6] and such applications are usually made in cases where it is feared that local prejudice and hostility will endanger the prospects of a fair trial.[7]

The committal by the magistrates for trial should ensure that the trial does not begin before the expiration of 14 days or after the expiration of eight weeks from committal.[8]

Finally, the magistrates must decide the question of bail in accordance with the principles discussed above, and should give the accused a warning about the notice required of evidence to be adduced at trial in support of an alibi.[9] If the accused is intending to rely on such a defence he must notify the prosecution of the particulars of his alibi not later than seven days after the end of the committal proceedings. If he fails to give the requisite notice he can only rely on the alibi defence at trial with the special permission of the court.[10]

3. THE REPORTING OF COMMITTAL PROCEEDINGS

The form of committal proceedings prior to 1968, with full oral testimony, was a great boon to local newspapers in search of material for their columns. The hearing was held in public and there were no restrictions on reporting.[11] This led to certain difficulties for the defendant and, it was said, could prejudice his chances of a fair trial if he was committed, by influencing readers who might ultimately be members of the jury in the particular case.

Often the defence would not offer any evidence so that only the prosecution case would be reported, thus distorting the overall impression. The prosecution might call witnesses who were not ultimately called at trial. Reference might be made in the prosecution evidence to matters which were not the subject of charges, or charges on which the accused was committed might not be proceeded with at trial. The result of extensive publicity of the committal might therefore be to influence potential jurors with a one-sided review of the evidence or to provide them with information about matters or charges which would form no part of the eventual trial. The difficulties were exposed by Devlin J. at the trial of Dr. Bodkin Adams in 1957. Dr. Adams was charged with murder and, in the course of the committal proceedings, reference was made to the death of

---

[5] *Ibid.* para. 12.

[6] Supreme Court Act 1981, s.76.

[7] For example, the trial of Brady and Hindley, the Moors Murderers, was held in Chester rather than the more likely location in Manchester, and the trial of the "Birmingham bombers" was held in Lancaster. Prejudice is not the only ground for altering the venue, see *Halsbury's Laws of England* (4th ed.) Vol. 11, para. 221.

[8] Supreme Court Act 1981, s.77; Crown Court Rules 1982, r.19.

[9] Magistrates' Courts Rules 1981, r.6(4), 7(9).

[10] Criminal Justice Act 1967, s.11.

[11] Other than the general constraints on newspapers which prevent them from publishing proceedings in certain circumstances.

two other patients, whose demise was not the subject of the charge. The trial judge expressed a view that the committal would have been better conducted in private when publicity could not have been given to these potentially prejudicial facts. In the event, Dr. Adams was acquitted.

The Tucker committee[12] subsequently considered the problem and although it could not produce firm evidence of cases where the accused had actually been prejudiced, formed the view that the reporting of committal proceedings should be restricted. Amid great controversy and anguished protests about attacks on the freedom of the press, the Criminal Justice Act 1967 placed a ban on the full reporting of proceedings where the accused is committed for trial, unless a defendant requests that restrictions should be lifted.[13] On committal, all that may be reported are matters of formal record.[14]

A defendant may require reporting restrictions to be lifted by order of the court[15] and there are certainly occasions on which a report of a full committal may prove advantageous to him. If the case is particularly controversial or sensational, more damage may be done by the circulation of gossip and rumour prior to the trial than by the report of the factual statements given in support of the prosecution case at committal.[16] It is possible that additional witnesses may emerge prompted by recognition of the case.[17] The immediate public protestation of innocence may be important to the accused. The desire of one of a number of co-defendants being tried together to have the restrictions lifted caused a problem where the other defendant(s) was not in agreement.[18] A recent statutory amendment has stipulated that where one of two or more accused objects to the court making an order lifting restrictions at the request of a co-accused the court shall only make the order if, after hearing representations, it is satisfied that it is in the interests of justice to do so.[19]

---

[12] The chairman was Lord Tucker, a Lord of Appeal. *Proceedings before Examining Magistrates*, (Cmnd. 479, 1958). See M. Jones, *Justice and Journalism* (1974), Chap. 7.

[13] Now contained in Magistrates' Courts Act 1980, s.8.

[14] *Ibid*. s.8(4).

[15] *Ibid*. s.8(2). It will be possible for magistrates to lift reporting restrictions but forbid the publication of particular matters under s.4(2) of the Contempt of Court Act 1981: *R. v. Horsham JJ. ex p. Farquharson* [1982] Q.B. 762.

[16] This is argued by Napley, *op. cit.* p. 26. This was certainly the case in respect of the Moors Murderers, Brady and Hindley, from the authors' own experience. Ironically, however, the publication of details of the committal proceedings, gruesome as they were, did not scotch the even more horrific rumours. Local people still chose to believe the rumours on the basis that the truth was too dreadful even to reveal in court.

[17] This is not likely to happen often, but a recent example was provided at the trial of P.C. Kneale on charges arising out of a demonstration in Liverpool. A witness who had been present only realised that his evidence could be significant on reading press reports of the trial. As a result of his coming forward to give evidence the defendant was acquitted. See *The Times*, May 9–12, 1984.

[18] The courts had ruled that the desire of one co-defendant to have the restriction lifted was enough, *R. v. Russell, ex p. Beaverbrook Newspapers* [1969] 1 Q.B. 342, but the matter was given wide exposure in the Jeremy Thorpe case where the committal proceedings were given publicity against the wishes of three of the defendants.

[19] Criminal Justice (Amendment) Act 1981, s.1, amending the Magistrates' Courts Act 1980, s.8(2). The magistrates must weigh the balance of interest between defendants who disagree over the reporting of the proceedings: *R. v. Leeds Justices, ex p. Sykes* (1983) 76 Cr. App. R. 129.

4. THE VOLUNTARY BILL PROCEDURE

It is convenient, if somewhat anomalous, to deal with the voluntary bill procedure at this point since it is a way of getting an indictable offence tried *without* committal by the magistrates. At the trial, a bill of indictment must be preferred against a defendant as a preliminary to the trial. A bill may only be preferred if the defendant has been committed for trial, or as directed by the Court of Appeal, or a High Court judge, or pursuant to an order under the Perjury Act 1911.[20]

Any person may make a written application to a High Court judge for consent to the preferring of a bill of indictment and must state reasons for the application. If committal proceedings have been taken, the application must be accompanied by depositions and certain statements of belief about the truth of the case.[21]

This procedure allows an accused to be put on trial at the discretion of a High Court judge and is rarely used, but can be effective in circumventing committal proceedings where unusual problems arise. Recently, two controversial cases have proceeded by voluntary bill. Three prison officers were put on trial for murder in this way after a stipendiary magistrate discharged them after committal proceedings, and 15 youths charged variously with murder, affray and riotous assembly were put on trial by voluntary bill after committal proceedings had been in progress for nearly three weeks with no sign of finishing.[22] Both cases excited considerable comment.

G. DISCLOSURE OF EVIDENCE

In a civil case, the pre-trial procedure can be operated so as to allow each party to discover the essentials of the case he has to meet and to discover the basic issues in dispute between the parties. In a criminal matter, the two sides have much less scope for selecting the ground on which they wish to fight and all issues are likely to be left in dispute until the trial.[23] However, it can be a considerable advantage to prosecution, defence and court if by the time of the trial the two sides have some indication of the evidence to be given and the arguments to be raised. At the very least, this will obviate the necessity for an adjournment of the trial if new matters which require investigation are raised for the first time. What do the two sides currently have to disclose?

---

[20] See *Halsbury's Laws of England*, (4th ed.) Vol. 11, para. 199 and see p. 582 below.

[21] The Indictments (Procedure) Rules 1971, (S.I. 1971 No. 2084), govern the procedure.

[22] The three men were charged with the murder of Mr. Barry Prosser, a prisoner, in Winson Green prison, Birmingham. One of the accused had been the subject of *two* unsuccessful committal proceedings on the same charge. This case provides another example of change of venue, the trial being transferred to Leicester Crown Court because of all the publicity that had been generated. The charges against the youths arose out of the death of Terence May, a motor cyclist, in Thornton Heath, South London.

[23] Although there is a procedure whereby formal admissions can be made under Criminal Justice Act 1967, s.10, thus eliminating the necessity for undisputed evidence to be given orally at trial.

1. Disclosure by the Prosecution

At the committal proceedings the defendant is likely to get sight of a substantial part, if not all, of the prosecution evidence. Whether the committal is "old-style" or "section 1" the prosecution is required to supply the defence with copies of the depositions or written statements, as the case may be.[24] Additionally, the prosecution normally gives notice to the defence of any further evidence which is to be called at trial and a copy of the evidence.[25] As a result, the defence will know the total extent of the prosecution evidence and, if an old-style committal has taken place, will have had the opportunity of testing prosecution witnesses in cross-examination.

What was less clear was the obligation of the prosecution to tell the defence of any additional material of which they were aware, but which was not actually to be used as part of the prosecution case. Much was left to the discretion of prosecuting counsel and a good deal of information would be communicated on a confidential "counsel to counsel" basis. Some requirements had to be observed by the prosecution including that of notifying the defence of, at least, the name and address of a witness who could give material evidence but would not be called by the prosecution[26]; making expert and technical evidence available; giving the defence a copy of any statements made by a prosecution witness which conflict with the evidence given at trial[27]; making known any convictions affecting the credibility of prosecution witnesses.[28] In addition, there is a Practice Direction which sets out the additional material which must be made available to the defence, with exceptions for especially prejudicial or sensitive information.[29]

This information will be of use to the defence in formulating their case and there is nothing to stop them asking for any other information which may be of assistance. The prosecution, however, is under no obligation to supply it and even the extent of the propositions listed above is somewhat uncertain. Prosecuting counsel are often asked to consider, and advise on, the extent of the material which should be disclosed.

All the foregoing relates to trial on indictment. In respect of summary trial there is effectively no obligation to make disclosure. The rule about notification of witnesses with material evidence applies,[30] and in certain cases a statement of facts is given to the accused in advance,[31] but apart

[24] Magistrates' Courts Act 1980, s.102.

[25] Archbold, *Criminal Pleading, Evidence and Practice* (41st ed.), para. 4–185. There is very little authority for this proposition, but it is clearly accepted practice.

[26] There was disagreement between Lord Denning M.R. and Diplock L.J. in *Dallison* v. *Caffery* [1965] 1 Q.B. 348 on the extent of the obligation. The Master of the Rolls was of the opinion that prosecuting counsel should make the witness' statements available to the defence. Diplock L.J. thought it was enough to make the witness available by notifying a name and address.

[27] *R.* v. *Howes*, March 27, 1950, C.C.A. (unreported) cited in Archbold, *op. cit.* para. 4–179.

[28] *R.* v. *Collister and Warhurst* (1955) 39 Cr. App. R. 100.

[29] [1982] 1 All E.R. 734, issued by the Attorney-General.

[30] Failure to notify the defence, if it is a gross failure, can lead to the decision of the court being quashed: *R.* v. *Leyland JJ. ex p. Hawthorn* [1979] Q.B. 283.

[31] These are cases in which the procedure under the Magistrates' Courts Act 1980, s.12, has been followed, and the accused may plead guilty by post if he wishes: see p. 577 below.

from those limited provisions the defence can go into a trial in the magistrates' court with no idea at all of the particulars of the prosecution case. Not surprisingly, this results in adjournments where the defence are caught unprepared. Section 48 of the Criminal Law Act 1977 makes provision for the adoption of rules of court to provide for disclosure in summary trial, but the section has not yet been brought into force despite a Home Office working party convened to study the problem and the establishment of two trial projects. The latest information indicates an intention to implement the section 48 procedure, but there are problems over the evaluation of the results of the two projects and over the allocation of costs between central and local government.[31a]

2. DISCLOSURE BY THE DEFENCE

The defence is entitled, very largely, to reserve the whole of the defence for the trial and say nothing about their case until then. The only exceptions to this principle are the requirements to disclose an alibi defence on a trial on indictment[32] and to give notice of certain specific defences in minor regulatory offences.

This appears to leave the disclosure requirements very unbalanced as between prosecution and defence and, at various times and in various circumstances, proposals have been made to impose a general requirement of disclosure on the defence after the conclusion of committal proceedings in a trial on indictment, or rather more specific requirement in respect of particular defences.[33] The object of such proposals is to prevent the "springing" of a defence at trial when the prosecution may face the choice of asking for a costly adjournment or meeting the defence unprepared.

3. A PRE-TRIAL REVIEW

A relatively recent development in criminal procedure has been the provision of a hearing between committal and trial designed to fulfil the same objects as the pre-trial review in civil proceedings. The rules for such a hearing were promulgated by the Central Criminal Court[34] and apply to cases to be heard in that court where application is made by either party. The rules provide for a hearing at which both defence and prosecution make stipulated disclosures to the court and the judge may make such orders as may be necessary to secure the proper and efficient trial of the case.

Among the matters of which counsel will be expected to inform the court are the pleas to be tendered by the accused; prosecution evidence; points of law arising; agreed exhibits and schedules and other evidentiary matters.

[31a] Evidence given by the Home Office to the Home Affairs Committee of the House of Commons, April 4, 1984: *The Times*, May 16, 1984.

[32] Criminal Justice Act 1967, s.10. See above, p. 505.

[33] *The (Butler) Committee on Mentally Abnormal Offenders* (Cmnd. 6244, 1975), recommended that notice should be given if the defence is to put in issue the mental state of the accused. The Law Commission made a similar proposal in respect of duress (1977, Law Com. No. 83).

[34] They are reproduced in Appendix 27 of R.C.C.P. I, together with the rules adopted on the North Eastern Circuit.

The object of disclosure is to indicate as clearly as possible the likely issues in the case and so save time and money at and before the trial. The costs of such a review can, therefore, only be justified in the more complex cases where the savings in time and money will exceed the amount expended on the review itself. A number of the circuits have adopted the procedure and varied it according to their own needs.

In the magistrates' court the same problem occurs before summary trial, but the number of cases in which a formal pre-trial review is beneficial may be more limited. Reference has already been made to section 48 of the Criminal Law Act 1977 and its non-implementation, but the Nottingham justices' clerks have already instituted a scheme on their own initiative which is alleged to save money as well as reducing delay and frustration caused by the repeated adjournment of trials where the defence have been caught unprepared by the prosecution.[35] In approximately 20 cases each week, prosecution and defence meet at an appointed time for "an informal but candid discussion" without a magistrate present. The benefits of such a scheme are said to include a saving of court time by inducing "realistic" pleas; early notification of points of law that may arise; a reduction in the length of contested cases; confirmation of readiness for trial and a general tidying-up to ensure that the case can go ahead when listed. Apparently, several courts are introducing similar schemes.

The Home Office Working Party referred to above is considering the detail of pre-trial review schemes and is expected to produce a standard model which can be implemented by regulations. Some disquiet has been expressed by practitioners about the extent to which defence disclosure may be required.[36]

H. OBTAINING LEGAL ADVICE AND REPRESENTATION

We stressed the importance of legal aid and advice in civil proceedings by dealing with it at the beginning of the civil procedure chapter. Its availability may determine whether the case goes ahead at all. In criminal proceedings it is not relevant to that issue, but must be made available as a way of ensuring that the accused has what specialist help he needs in the presentation of his defence. Different criteria are obviously required for the grant and administration of criminal legal aid.[37]

Legal advice and professional assistance may be required by the accused at two quite different stages. He will initially have to deal with the police and face interrogation by them, the results of which are likely to have a considerable influence on his case at trial. He may wish to be advised how to conduct himself to the best advantage at this stage of the procedure. Then, if charged, he will want assistance in the preparation and presentation of his case at and before the trial. The extent to which lawyers are involved in these two distinct situations is markedly different. Almost

---

[35] The scheme is glowingly described and commended in A. Debruslais, "Pre-Trial Disclosure in Magistrates' Courts: Why Wait?" (1982) 146 J.P.N. 384.

[36] "Pre-Trial Reviews in the Magistrates' Court: Guidance for Defence Solicitors," (1983) 80 L.S.Gaz. 2330.

[37] It is only recently that both schemes have been put under the aegis of the same Government department. Formerly, criminal legal aid was the responsibility of the Home Office.

all those charged with serious offences are represented at trial, hardly any are "represented" during interrogation at the police station.

1. LEGAL ADVICE AT THE POLICE STATION

The Judges' Rules[38] are unambiguous on this point:

" . . . every person at any stage of an investigation should be able to communicate and to consult privately with a solicitor. This is so even if he is in custody provided that in such case no unreasonable delay or hindrance is caused to the processes of investigation or the administration of justice by his doing so."[39]

The provision is amplified by the Administrative Directions appended to the Judges' Rules.

"(a) A person in custody should be supplied on request with writing materials. Provided that no hindrance is reasonably likely to be caused to the processes of investigation or the administration of justice:
  (i) he should be allowed to speak on the telephone to his solicitor or to his friends;
  (ii) his letters should be sent by post or otherwise with the least possible delay;
  (iii) telegrams should be sent at once, at his own expense.
(b) Persons in custody should not only be informed orally of the rights and facilities available to them, but in addition notices describing them should be displayed at convenient and conspicuous places at police stations and the attention of persons in custody should be drawn to these notices."[40]

The Criminal Law Act 1977 contains a provision granting a person arrested and held in custody in a police station a specific entitlement to have notice of his arrest and current location sent to one person named by him without unreasonable delay.[41] An accused might wish to take that opportunity of alerting his solicitor.

The legal advice scheme can be used for the purpose of securing the services of a solicitor at the police station[42] and the eligibility of the accused and the extent of any financial contribution are calculated according to the figures set out earlier in our discussion of the scheme.[43] In theory, the accused has the opportunity, the means and the motive to ensure that he is properly advised on the most advantageous way to conduct himself at the police station. In practice, very few accused persons receive that advice.

From a study conducted by Professor Zander[44] through the interviewing

---

[38] The Judges' Rules have a long history which is reviewed in R.C.C.P. I, Appendix 13. They were last revised in 1978 and issued as Home Office Circular 89/1978.

[39] Introduction to the Judges' Rules, para. c.

[40] Administrative Directions, para. 7.

[41] s.62.

[42] If the accused can actually contact a solicitor!

[43] See above, p. 341.

[44] "Access to a solicitor in the police station" [1972] Crim. L.R. 342.

of appellants to the Court of Appeal, Criminal Division, it emerged that only 11 per cent. of those interviewed (15 out of 134) had contacted a solicitor when first taken to the police station. A further 32 per cent. (42) said that they had asked to speak to a solicitor and had been refused. A study by Baldwin and McConville[45] produced similar results, with 31 per cent. (109) of a sample of 352 defendants at Crown Court having asked to see a solicitor and over three-quarters (84) of that group having been refused. The most recent study by Softley for the Royal Commission on Criminal Procedure[46] produced lower figures of 12 per cent. (19) of a sample of 168 suspects being interrogated in a police station, with only one-third (6) refusals. In addition, Softley records that the police asked 8 suspects whether they wished to speak to a solicitor and all but two declined.

That part of the Administrative Directions which requires that persons in custody should be informed orally of the rights and facilities available to them does not seem to be widely observed,[47] and it has been suggested that this is the main reason for the failure to seek legal advice. The police have also been criticised for simple obstruction of those who have got as far as asking to be allowed to contact a solicitor. This is a serious criticism and the Royal Commission on Criminal Procedure took note of it in their final recommendations.[48] The proposition that more information about the availability of advice leads to greater take-up was treated more circumspectly in the light of American experience after the *Miranda* v. *Arizona*[49] decision required every suspect to be told of his right to consult a lawyer and have him present during interrogation. Studies carried out in the United States still revealed surprisingly small numbers of suspects getting legal advice.[50]

2. ADVICE AND REPRESENTATION AFTER CHARGE

Both the legal advice scheme and the criminal legal aid provisions are applicable in enabling an accused to seek advice and representation at all stages of the proceedings.

We have already mentioned the use of legal advice at the police station, but the green form scheme[51] is also used to deal with defendants in the initial stages in the magistrates' court. The Legal Advice and Assistance Act 1972 first introduced a provision whereby a magistrates' court could request a solicitor in the precincts of the court to give advice to and represent a person appearing before them.[52] This provision paved the way

---

[45] "Police interrogation and the right to see a solicitor" [1979] Crim. L.R. 145.

[46] *Police interrogation: An Observational Study in Four Police Stations* R.C.C.P. Research Study No. 4, (HMSO, 1980).

[47] *Ibid.* p. 65.

[48] R.C.C.P. Report, para. 4.87.

[49] 348 US 436 (1966).

[50] See, for example, M. Wald *et al.* "Interrogation in New Haven: the Impact of Miranda" (1967) 76 Yale Law Journal 1519.

[51] See above, p. 339.

[52] Now, Legal Aid Act 1974, s.2(4).

for duty solicitor schemes[53] and enabled assistance to be given for applications for bail or legal aid.[54] It is important to emphasise that this help is given under the green form schemes and is subject to the normal conditions controlling eligibility and the amount of advice that can be given.[55]

The principles upon which legal aid is granted, and the obligations of the recipient, are established by the Legal Aid Act 1974 and the Legal Aid Act 1982, together with regulations made thereunder.[56] It has been argued that fundamental questions relating to criminal legal aid remain unanswered,[56a] but the present system attempts to ensure that every person charged with a serious offence, or an offence which may have particularly serious consequences for him, is provided with sufficient professional assistance to allow his case to be properly prepared and presented, subject to a contribution towards the cost according to his means.

An application for criminal legal aid is normally made to the magistrates' court, although the Crown Court also has the power to grant legal aid,[57] and even the appellate courts in appropriate circumstances.[58] There is also a role for the area and general committees which administer the civil legal aid scheme, since they constitute the criminal legal aid committee required by the 1982 Act.

Legal aid is only *mandatory* in cases of murder; where the prosecutor is seeking to appeal to the House of Lords; where the accused is brought before a magistrates' court in custody, is liable to be remanded in custody, and wishes to be represented; and where the accused is kept in custody after conviction for medical or other reports.[58a] In all other cases, the court may make an order for legal aid for a defendant, " . . . where it appears desirable to do so in the interests of justice . . . and it appears to the court that his disposable income and disposable capital are such that he requires assistance in meeting the costs which he may incur."[59]

A single legal aid order may now be made by a magistrates' court to cover the committal proceedings, the trial on indictment (if committed),

---

[53] It is interesting to note that the Widgery Committee (*Legal Aid in Criminal Proceedings* (1966) Cmnd. 2934) thought that it would not be practicable to introduce such a scheme, not least because it would be unnecessarily wasteful of public funds. The Legal Aid Act 1982, s.1 makes provision for these schemes to be put on a statutory basis under Legal Aid Act 1974, s.15. The Council of the Law Society is charged with the responsibility of drawing up the scheme and will administer it. See pp. 343–349, above.

[54] Assistance is not restricted to these applications—they are merely the most common form of help.

[55] See above, p. 341 and n. 53 above. When the new scheme is drawn up it will be quite distinct from the green form scheme.

[56] Legal Aid in Criminal Proceedings (General) Regulations 1968 (S.I. 1968 No. 1231), as amended by Legal Aid in Criminal Proceedings (General) (Amendment) Regulations 1983 (S.I. 1983 No. 1863). See generally, A. Samuels, "Criminal Legal Aid: The Issues of Principle" [1983] Crim.L.R. 223, especially the materials noted on p. 223; H. Levenson, "Contributions and the new criminal legal aid" [1984] *Legal Action* 37, and "Appeals and reviews in criminal legal aid" [1984] *Legal Action* 49.

[56a] See Samuels, *op. cit.* n. 56 above.

[57] Legal Aid Act 1974, s.28(5), (7).

[58] *Ibid*. s.28(8), (9).

[58a] *Ibid*. s.29(1), as amended by the Bail Act 1976, s.11(4).

[59] *Ibid*. s.29(1), (2) as amended by the Legal Aid Act 1982, s.10.

and advice and assistance on appeal (if convicted).[60] There is little disagreement about legal aid for trials in the Crown Court and the statistics show a remarkable degree of consistency. In each of the years 1972–1982, 99 per cent. of applications for legal aid for trial at the Crown Court were granted and the proportion of legally aided defendants in the Crown Court rose slightly from 93 per cent. (in 1972) to 97 per cent. (in 1982).[60a] The statutory condition that legal aid should be granted where it is in the interest of justice has been amplified by the "Widgery criteria."[61] If a case exhibits one or more of the following factors, there are grounds for thinking that representation is desirable:

> "(a) That the charge is a grave one in the sense that the accused is in real jeopardy of losing his liberty or suffering serious damage to his reputation;
> (b) that the charge raises a substantial question of law;
> (c) that the accused is unable to follow the proceedings and state his own case because of his inadequate knowledge of English, mental illness or other mental or physical disability;
> (d) that the nature of the defence involves the tracing and interviewing of witnesses or expert cross-examination of a witness for the prosecution;
> (e) that legal representation is desirable in the interest of someone other than the accused as, for example, in the case of sexual offences against young children where it is undesirable that the accused should cross-examine the witness in person."[62]

There is rarely any difficulty in establishing that an offence to be tried on indictment can be fitted into one or other of the categories.

The problems in the criminal legal aid scheme have related to the application of these principles in magistrates' courts when a defendant seeks legal aid in respect of a summary offence or an either-way offence to be tried summarily. An application for legal aid in magistrates' court proceedings may be made orally to the court (who may then refer it to the justices' clerk to be dealt with) or in writing direct to the justices' clerk. The clerk must make an order, *or* refer the application to the court for decision, *or* refuse an order if the application is one to which the provisions permitting review by the criminal legal aid committee apply.[62a] The role of the clerk in administering legal aid led to some disquiet about the rate of refusal in certain courts, particularly where it appeared that the clerks were acting vigorously to implement undisclosed policies or Government directives on cost-saving.[63] The review procedure instituted by the Legal

---

[60] Legal Aid Act 1982, s.2. Previously, legal aid for the whole criminal procedure had to be the subject of separate applications.

[60a] *Criminal Statistics England and Wales 1982*, Cmnd. 9048, Chap. 9.

[61] Contained in *Legal Aid in Criminal Proceedings* (Cmnd. 2934, 1966) the report of a Departmental Committee chaired by Widgery J., as he then was.

[62] *Ibid.* para. 180. These criteria have received some judicial recognition and are incorporated, in the form of questions, into the application form for criminal legal aid which is prescribed by S.I. 1983 No. 1863.

[62a] S.I. 1968 No. 1231, as amended, reg. 1.

[63] L.C.D. Circular 81(3), reproduced in (1981) 131 N.L.J. 359, and see H. Levenson, (1978) 128 N.L.J. 52; (1979) 129 N.L.J. 375; *LAG Bulletin*, January 1980, April 1980, May 1981. Especial attention was paid to Waltham Forest, "What a difference a clerk makes," *LAG Bulletin*, March 1982.

Aid Act 1982 is an attempt to meet some of those criticisms in relation to committal proceedings and the trial of either-way offences. The cases in which legal aid must be granted in the magistrates' court are very few and it is clear from the statistics that very few defendants charged with summary offences receive legal aid, whereas a significant number of defendants tried on either-way offences receive aid.[64] The magistrates' court, however, does not have an easy task. It is alleged that the Widgery criteria do not work well because they are complex, imprecise and open to a wide range of interpretation.[64a] Inevitably, this leads to substantial variation in the grant of legal aid, and the refusal figures are further distorted by the unwillingness of solicitors even to apply for aid to courts where they know that the application is likely to be unsuccessful. Financial pressures are added to the uncertainties of interpretation. A circular from the Lord Chancellor's Department to justices' clerks in March 1981 expressed concern that, ". . . legal aid in criminal proceedings should secure value for money . . . every effort must be made to avoid waste . . . legally-aided defendants should be asked to contribute . . . realistic down payments should be required in all suitable cases."[65]

The defendant is meant to be given the benefit of the doubt, in that section 29(6) of the Legal Aid Act 1974 provides that, "Where a doubt arises as to whether a legal aid order should be made for the giving of aid to any peson, the doubt shall be resolved in the person's favour," but the 1981 circular reminds justices' clerks that applicants are not entitled to the benefit of those doubts, " . . . on the strength of vague applications . . . a simple statement that the applicant is in danger of losing his liberty or livelihood or, as the case may be, that the charge raises a point of law does not suffice."

What matters to a defendant is the refusal to grant aid and the possibility of having such a decision reviewed depends upon the type of offence with which he is charged. In the case of a *summary* offence, he may make a further application, for the court has power to grant aid at any stage of the proceedings,[66] or he may seek judicial review in the High Court.[66a] Neither course of action is likely to be successful in the majority of cases. In the case of an *either-way* offence which is to be tried summarily, he may seek a review by the criminal legal aid committee[67] so long as the application for review is made after the first refusal of legal aid, *and* the refusal was based on lack of merits, *and* the application for legal aid had been made at least 21 days before the date fixed for the trial of the offence.[68] On a review, the criminal legal aid committee may make an order subject to the contribu-

---

[64] Two per cent. of defendants in summary trials receive legal aid; 69 per cent. of defendants in the trial of either-way offences in the magistrates' court receive legal aid: *Criminal Statistics 1982, op. cit.* Chap. 9, Table 9.4.

[64a] The Royal Commission on Legal Services described the evidence to this effect as "compelling": R.C.L.S., Vol. 1, para. 14.7.

[65] L.C.D. Circular 81(3); see n. 63 above.

[66] S.I. 1968 No. 1231, reg. 5.

[66a] See p. 742, below.

[67] The criminal legal aid committees required by the Act have been constituted by designating the area and general committees functioning under the civil legal aid scheme for this additional purpose: (1984) 81 L.S.Gaz. 322.

[68] S.I. 1968 No. 1231, as amended, reg. 6E(2).

tion conditions that will already have been fixed by the court.[68a] As an alternative to the review, the defendant may renew his application for legal aid or seek judicial review as above. In the case of a refusal of legal aid for *committal proceedings*, the defendant has the same remedies as in respect of either-way offences. When the magistrates refuse legal aid for a *trial on indictment* the simplest course will be to make a fresh application to the Crown Court.[69] .

Legal aid in criminal cases may be made subject to a contribution from the defendant. In recent years the amount of contributions actually collected has not been significant when set against the overall cost of criminal legal aid,[70] but the contribution system has been restyled by the Legal Aid Act 1982[70a] and defendants may, in future, pay more towards the cost of their defence.

The effect of this new provision is to require a means test which leads to a fixed contribution. The court appears to have no discretion over whether to order a contribution or over the amount.[71] In applying the means test, the regulations provide for a calculation closely linked to that made in the grant of civil legal aid[72] which results in the assessment of disposable income and disposable capital. In respect of disposable income the defendant must contribute a weekly amount (determined by reference to the Third Schedule of the regulations)[72a] for a period of six months,[73] and in respect of disposable capital, the whole of the amount in excess of £3000.[74] In any event, the contribution shall not exceed the actual costs of the defence and any excess will be refunded.[74a] In addition, the court has a discretion to remit the contribution where a defendant is acquitted or his appeal against conviction is allowed.[75]

This new system only came into operation very recently[76] and it will be some time before the full effects can be assessed. It is certainly very different from that proposed by the Royal Commission on Legal Services which would have involved a statutory right to legal aid save for summary offences[77] and the abolition of contribution orders in magistrates' court proceedings.[78]

[68a] As the court has no discretion to vary the stipulated contribution, neither does the committee.

[69] Legal Aid Act 1974, s.28(7).

[70] In 1982, the total amount spent on criminal legal aid was £108,000,000. Contributions amounted to £1,540,000, collected from 24,000 out of 478,000 defendants who were granted aid: *Criminal Statistics 1982, op. cit.*, Chap. 9, Table 9.5.

[70a] See H. Levenson, "Contributions and the new criminal legal aid" [1984] *Legal Action* 37.

[71] Legal Aid Act 1982, s.7(1)(2).

[72] S.I. 1968 No. 1231, as amended, reg. 19(1) and Sched. 2.

[72a] Average weekly disposable income, £42.01–£48, contribution £1; £48.01–£52, contribution £2; £52.01–£56, contribution £3; £56.01–£60, contribution £4; £60.01–£64, contribution £5; thereafter at the rate of £1 for every £4 or part of £4 in excess of £64. Thus, the income contribution from a man with an average weekly disposable income of £59, would be £104, and for a man with a disposable income of £100 would be £364.

[73] The "contribution period": S.I. 1968 No. 1231, as amended, reg. 15.

[74] *Ibid*. reg. 19(3).

[74a] *Ibid*. reg. 26A.

[75] Legal Aid Act 1982, s.8(5).

[76] March 1, 1984.

[77] R.C.L.S., Vol. 1, para. 14.9.

[78] *Ibid*. paras. 14.30–31.

I. EVALUATIONS

So far in this chapter we have described rather than commented. However, criminal procedure is a subject which excites considerable discussion, primarily because views differ about the "right" balance to be achieved between the public interest in the apprehension and conviction of offenders and the necessary preservation of adequate safeguards for those suspected or accused of offences. It should not be assumed that the rules of procedure designed to balance interests can remain unchanged. As circumstances change, so the rules may need to change and the latest review of two major areas of criminal procedure was undertaken by a Royal Commission appointed in 1978. Its Report has considerable bearing on the questions we have selected for consideration from amongst the many that are relevant and contentious.

The Royal Commission on Criminal Procedure,[79] under the chairmanship of Sir Cyril Philips, was instructed to examine whether changes are needed in England and Wales, in:

> "(i) the powers and duties of the police in respect of the investigation of criminal offences and the rights and duties of suspects and accused persons, including the means by which these are secured;
>
> (ii) the process of and responsibility for the prosecution of criminal offences; and
>
> (iii) such other features of criminal procedure and evidence as relate to the above."[80]

In the course of its work the Commission took evidence from all interested parties and also commissioned a series of Research Studies[81] which contain much valuable material. In addition to its Report, the Commission also produced an account of the relevant law and procedure covered by the terms of reference[82] so as to allow the main Report to concentrate on the strengths and weaknesses of current procedure and develop proposals for reform. Although the Report was presented to Parliament in January 1981,[83] progress on the recommendations has been slow.

1. Do we need a System of Independent Public Prosecutors?

The system of police prosecution described earlier[84] was subjected to close scrutiny by the Royal Commission and comparisons were made with prosecution arrangements in other countries. Our present system has been the subject of growing criticism which has only been slightly tempered by the increasing role of the prosecuting solicitors' departments attached to county police forces. The most cogent criticism appeared in a JUSTICE

---

[79] *Report*, (Cmnd. 8092, 1981) *The Investigation and Prosecution of Criminal Offences in England and Wales: The Law and Procedure*, (Cmnd. 8092-1, 1981).

[80] R.C.C.P. Rep. p. iv.

[81] Twelve in all, published in 9 pamphlets listed in Annex D of the Report.

[82] See n. 79 above.

[83] Debated in the House of Commons in November 1981.

[84] At p. 477 above.

report in 1970,[85] where it was argued that the responsibility for prosecutions in all but trivial cases should be taken out of the hands of the police and given to a national prosecuting authority. In support of this recommendation it was said that:

(a) a police officer may convince himself of the guilt of a suspect and become psychologically committed to a prosecution;

(b) public policy and the circumstances of the individual are relevant considerations in the decision to prosecute;

(c) the English system is unique in Europe in allowing the whole process from interrogation to prosecution to be effectively under the control of the police in the majority of cases;

(d) investigators find it difficult to achieve the necessary detachment in taking what is essentially a "judicial-type" decision whether or not to prosecute;

(e) police involvement may influence the conduct of the prosecution in deciding appropriate charges or otherwise "bargaining" with a suspect, or in putting pressure on counsel at trial to take a particular line;

(f) police officers are not trained as lawyers or advocates and those tasks involving the expertise of lawyers or advocates should not be undertaken by the police.

The Royal Commission took account of these and similar arguments, and also the fact that, "The present arrangements have grown gradually and piecemeal, adapting themselves to changing conditions, over the 150 years since an organised modern police service was first created. Since the late 1870s, there has been no major legislative attempt to alter them and until recently little manifestation of public concern about them. It might be concluded, therefore that by and large the arrangements work and have worked satisfactorily; the functions they are supposed to fulfil are fulfilled, as nearly as is possible with any man-made and administered procedures."[86] The Commission then chose to analyse and establish the standards for judging the adequacy of a prosecution system; to measure the present system by those standards; and then to recommend any changes necessary to achieve the standards. Put briefly, the Commission decided that the system should be judged on fairness, openness and accountability, and efficiency.

"Is the system fair; first in the sense that it brings to trial only those against whom there is an adequate and properly prepared case and who it is in the public interest should be prosecuted (that is, tried by a court) rather than dealt with in another way (by cautioning, for example), and secondly in that it does not display arbitrary and inexplicable differences in the way that individual cases or classes of case are treated locally or nationally? Is it open and accountable in the

---

[85] *The Prosecution Process in England and Wales*, (1970). The gist of the 1970 Report is reproduced in *Pre-Trial Criminal Procedure* (1979), the evidence submitted by JUSTICE to the Royal Commission. See also, J. Sigler, "Public Prosecution in England and Wales," [1974] Crim. L.R. 642; A.S. Bowley, "Prosecution—A Matter for the Police," [1975] Crim. L.R. 442.

[86] R.C.C.P. Rep. , para. 6.6.

sense that those who make the decisions to prosecute or not can be called publicly to explain and justify their policies and actions as far as that is consistent with protecting the interests of suspects and accused? Is it efficient in the sense that it achieves the objectives that are set for it with the minimum use of resources and the minimum delay? Each of these standards makes its own contribution to what we see as being the single overriding test of a successful system. Is it of a kind to have and does it in fact have the confidence of the public it serves?"[87]

In considering the question of *fairness* in present arrangements the Commission concentrated on the issues of whether the "right" people are brought to trial in a way which demonstrates "consistency" in policy and practice in the various police forces. On the former issue, the Commission discussed the extent to which it is possible/desirable to separate the role of the investigator from that of lawyer in the prosecution process. In an analysis of the respective functions of the United States District Attorney, the Scottish Procurator Fiscal and the Canadian Crown Counsel, the Commission considered that the two roles had not been entirely separated.[88] The District Attorney uses his staff in an investigative capacity both to improve the quality of cases presented by the police and to deal with major fraud, corruption and "white-collar" crime.[89] The Procurator Fiscal is directly involved in the investigation of violent deaths and also in the most serious cases will see and take statements from police and witnesses before deciding whether to prosecute.[90] In the provinces of British Columbia and Ontario, Crown Counsel are responsible entirely for the conduct of prosecutions *once the police have decided to bring a person to trial*. Crown Counsel have no investigative function, but the police retain a part of the lawyer's function in the initial decision to prosecute.[91] The Commission concluded that if any of these systems are more effective in putting the "right" people on trial it is not because they have succeeded in separating the functions of investigator and prosecutor. On the same issue the Commission considered the evidence of acquittal statistics compiled by Baldwin and McConville,[92] the Prosecuting Solicitor's Department of Greater Manchester and the Association of Chief Police Officers[93] which indicated that a high proportion of acquittals ordered and directed by the judge at the Crown Court are the result of insufficient prosecution evidence. The failure of prosecution witnesses at trial accounts for many of these cases, but there are clearly some cases where it should have been foreseen that the evidence would be inadequate. The lack of fairness

---

[87] *Ibid*. para. 6.8.

[88] *Ibid*. paras. 6.30–6.39.

[89] See further, J. Sigler, *An Introduction to the Legal System* (1968), p. 79 *et seq.*; H. Mueller, "The Position of the Criminal Defendant in the U.S.A.," in *The Accused* (Ed. A. Coutts) (1966), at p. 102–104.

[90] The role and powers of the Procurator Fiscal are described in *Criminal Procedure in Scotland and France*, (HMSO Edinburgh, 1975), and by Lord Kilbrandon, "Scotland: Pre-Trial Procedure," in *The Accused, op cit.*

[91] In British Columbia the system has only been introduced in the last few years and is likely to prove the most instructive example for further study.

[92] Recently published in M. McConville and J. Baldwin, *Courts, Prosecution and Conviction* (1981).

[93] Referred to in R.C.C.P. Rep. , para. 6.19.

demonstrated by such cases is only mitigated by their relative infrequency.[94]

Statistics contained in the Report show that there is, indeed, a degree of inconsistency in prosecution policy and practice,[95] and there is no effective machinery for achieving conformity.[96] Although this creates unfairness the Commission concluded that it was not the main focus of public concern and that the solution, the strengthening of central control or a national prosecution service, could find better justification on the ground of openness and accountability than on the ground of improved fairness.

The question of *accountability* is complicated because of the implications for the defendant of any public scrutiny of the exercise of the discretion to prosecute. Questioning the decision of the prosecutor after an acquittal might amount to a "retrial" if the prosecutor attempted to defend his decision. If he was required to defend a decision not to institute proceedings he might cast unwarranted doubts on the suspect without giving him the opportunity of defending himself. However, the Commission considered that those problems could be overcome by generalising the issue involved and that accountability in the "explanatory and cooperative mode"[97] to a local supervisory authority was desirable. Additionally, a prosecution agency would clearly be accountable to the body providing it with funds for its economic efficiency and organisation. At present, there is an obligation on the Attorney-General to answer in Parliament questions on the exercise of discretion and the courts have some limited degree of control, but there is no real local supervision.[98]

The *efficiency* of a prosecuting system is not to be judged solely in economic terms. Delays in preparation causing adjournment and inadequate preparation causing the collapse of cases certainly cost money, but they can also cause injustice, inconvenience and frustration to all those concerned in the process from the defendant to the usher. Yet given that the problems exist, what should be the objectives? The Commission do not really identify objectives in efficiency, but prefer to advocate uniformity in prosecution procedures.[99] At least if there is a uniform national procedure it will be easy to see where it is not being followed. This is not necessarily a very helpful analysis, but it is true to say that it is easier to identify waste in individual cases than it is to define a standard by which that waste can be measured.

[94] The R.C.C.P. Report suggests that one-fifth of directed acquittals may fall into this category. However, directed acquittals only form 7 per cent. of all cases disposed of by the Crown Court and the Crown Court only deals with approximately 15 per cent. of all indictable offences. See R.C.C.P. Rep. , para. 6.22.

[95] *Ibid*. para. 6.40. Inconsistency is primarily evident in the statistics relating to the use of the caution for both adults and juveniles.

[96] See above, p. 485.

[97] The Commission adopted terminology coined by G. Marshall, "Police Accountability Revisited," in *Policy and Politics* (Ed. Butler and Halsey) (1978). The "explanatory and cooperative mode" is described as a type of accountability in which the supervisory authority has no power to bind or to reverse executive decisions, but where a means is provided for challenge, for the requirement of reasoned explanation and the communication of advice and recommendation. R.C.C.P. Rep. , para. 6.50.

[98] See p. 486 above for the current controls. It would appear that police authorities could look into the exercise of prosecution discretion by the Chief Constable, but very few do so.

[99] R.C.C.P. Rep. , para. 6.64.

Concluding the chapter in the Report dealing with the present arrangements and the standards by which they should be judged the Commission said, " . . . there is a case for some change. Indeed, not a single witness who has addressed this part of our terms of reference in detail has argued that there should be absolutely no change made. The areas of debate are on the direction and extent of change."[1]

Different proposals for change had been made by JUSTICE, the Metropolitan Police Commissioner and the D.P.P., and the Home Office evidence consisted of a summary of the various possibilities.[2] The evidence of JUSTICE recommended an adoption of its 1970 proposal, that of the Metropolitan Police Commissioner and the D.P.P. advocated much less drastic changes with ultimate control of prosecutions remaining with the police.

Obviously impressed with the Canadian experience the Commission recommended that the police should retain sole responsibility for the investigation of offences and the initial decision whether to prosecute, and that thereafter the prosecutor should take over the conduct of the case and decide whether to proceed as charged, or modify or withdraw the charges.[3] The major advantage of this proposal appears to be that it indicates a reasonably clear demarcation of function, but it will also serve to maintain the primary responsibility of the police for investigation whilst enhancing the independent status of the prosecutor. The Commission proposes that the prosecutor should be designated "Crown prosecutor" and that the organisation should be locally based drawing heavily upon the existing prosecuting solicitors' departments. Obviously, every police force would need to have such a department (which would then also offer an advice service to the police) and, consistent with the Commission's declared standards, a local supervisory authority would need to be designated for the purposes of accountability. After examining various possibilties,[4] a majority of the Commission favoured the development of existing police authorities into police and prosecutions authorities with additional powers to supervise the functioning of the prosecution service.

Central involvement in the prosecution process should, it is recommended, continue in the form of the D.P.P. who would have a significant part to play in the development of any new system. The extent to which he would be required to intervene in prosecutions were a uniform system to be established is debatable and the Commission recommend that his functions would need to be reviewed after the new system had been in operation for five years.[5] Ministerial responsibility for the new prosecution service should rest either with the Home Secretary or the Attorney-General, and the Minister should be empowered to set national standards for staffing and performance.[6]

These proposals have had a mixed reception. Predictably the criticisms

---

[1] *Ibid.* para. 6.65.

[2] A summary of the evidence on this point is to be found in M. Zander, *Cases and Materials on the English Legal System* (3rd. ed., 1980) pp. 167–170.

[3] R.C.C.P. Rep. , paras. 7.5 *et seq.*

[4] *Ibid.* paras. 7.21 *et seq.*

[5] *Ibid.* para. 7.57.

[6] *Ibid.* para. 7.60.

range from the "too little"[7] to the "too much"[8] although there is a common view that the choice of a supervisory authority for any new service is of considerable significance. The initial reaction of the Government to the proposals was given by the Home Secretary in reply to a Parliamentary Question in July 1982.[9] The Home Secretary expressed misgivings about whether the proposal for a locally-based service is workable and whether the establishment of local accountability would compromise the independence of the prosecutor. Equally, there were doubts about the wisdom of setting up a central structure, which led the Government to think that it would be unwise to dismiss altogether the concept of a prosecution system organised on a local basis. Consequently, the Government reappointed the working party on prosecution arrangements. "Given that the Government do not find the Royal Commission's proposals acceptable as they stand, the working party's task now will be to advise ministers on what would be the best model for the organisation of an independent prosecution service on some other basis."

After the further deliberations of the working party, the Government published a White Paper in 1983[10] containing the report and the Government proposals for implementation. The Government have finally opted for a national prosecution service headed by the Director of Public Prosecutions and under the superintendence of the Attorney-General. Local prosecutors will be appointed as officers of the independent national service, but accountability will be on a national, rather than a local, level.

2. SHOULD THE RIGHT TO BRING PRIVATE PROSECUTIONS BE ABOLISHED?

We have already noted that the limitations placed on the right of an individual to bring a private prosecution and the cost involved have effectively reduced private prosecutions to an insignificant level. Traditionally this right is represented as an important safeguard against "official" inertia and regarded as fundamental, but the Royal Commission could see little justification for that view.[11]

In considering the rights of an individual in the criminal process, we are forced to consider the function and purpose of the criminal law and ask whether there are certain "personal offences" which it is proper to allow a private individual to pursue,[12] or whether the criminal law ought only to be used for the vindication of "public" rights at the instigation of a prosecutor

---

[7] A. Samuels, (1981) 78 L.S. Gaz. 885; D. Woodcock, (1981) 78 L.S. Gaz. 457.

[8] R. Lawrence, (1981) 78 L.S. Gaz. 323. For a general view, see A.F. Wilcox, "The Proposed Prosecution Process" [1981] Crim. L.R. 482.

[9] The reply is reproduced in (1982) 126 S.J. 528.

[10] *An Independent Prosecution Service for England and Wales*, Cmnd. 9074. See also, the Home Office news release noted in (1984) 81 L.S. Gaz. 1093.

[11] R.C.C.P. Rep., para. 7.47. The Commission was greatly assisted by its Research Study No. 10: *Prosecutions by Private Individuals and Non-Police Agencies*, Lidstone, Hogg and Sutcliffe in collaboration with Bottoms and Walker, (HMSO 1981). This study contains not only an interesting analysis and comparison of the right of private prosecution in other jurisdictions, but also of prosecutions by other agencies.

[12] For example, in West Germany, these would include trespass to domestic premises, inflicting minor bodily injury, insult and patent and copyright violation. It will be noted that these are not necessarily crimes in England but would give rise to a civil action. This represents a possible alternative approach of leaving an aggrieved citizen to vindicate his rights through the civil courts.

acting in the public interest. Some European jurisdictions permit private prosecution in very limited circumstances[13]; Scotland permits an application, by petition to the High Court by Bill for Criminal Letters, for authority to prosecute which is only granted in very exceptional circumstances.[14] The difficulty is to reconcile the view that public rights should be vindicated only by public prosecutors with the need to provide some form of challenge to act as a control on potential inaction or abuse.

The Commission recommended that a private citizen wishing to initiate a prosecution should be required to apply first to the Crown prosecutor. If the prosecutor refused to proceed with the case, then the citizen should be permitted to seek leave to commence proceedings from a magistrates' court. If leave is granted the cost of the case should be met from public funds, thus removing a major obstacle to the private prosecutor.[15] However, the Government has indicated that the right of private prosecution will be retained,[16] despite the Commission's view and the problems that may arise in the difficult areas of obscenity and public morality.[17]

3. SHOULD PARLIAMENT CONTROL THE EXERCISE OF THE DISCRETION TO PROSECUTE?

The Royal Commission considered the criteria adopted by the police, prosecuting solicitors and the D.P.P. in deciding whether to prosecute suspected offenders and concluded that whilst it would be difficult to produce a comprehensive list of matters to be taken into account, it was nonetheless unfortunate that there were differences amongst prosecutors about the amount of evidence necessary to justify a prosecution and about the factors to be considered.[18] We have dealt at some length with the current considerations earlier in the chapter.[19]

In any strengthened prosecution service with uniform standards and organisation it would obviously be easier to establish a consistent policy and gain agreement about relevant factors, whilst still allowing for the degree of local flexibility which is needed. The present rather haphazard arrangements would be improved. Even without any marked development in the prosecution service it would be possible for an initiative to be taken

[13] West Germany and France: see R.C.C.P. Research Study No. 10, *op. cit.* at p. 197 and pp. 231–236.

[14] The continuance of this right was examined recently and although it has fallen into disuse it was recommended that it should not be abolished: Criminal Procedure in Scotland (Second Report) (Cmnd. 6218, 1975), paras. 31.02, 31.03 (The Thomson Committee). An application by Patrick Meehan in 1974 for authority to bring a private prosecution for perjury was refused (1974 S.L.T. (notes) 61) but a Bill for Criminal Letters was granted to Mrs. X in April 1982, to begin a private prosecution for rape and assault. This was the first successful application since 1909 (*The Times*, April 2, 1982).

[15] R.C.C.P. Rep., paras. 7.50 and 7.51.

[16] *An Independent Prosecution Service for England and Wales*, (Cmnd. 9074, 1983), p. 9.

[17] There are already limitations imposed by way of the requirement of consent by the D.P.P. or Attorney-General in some sensitive areas (see above, p. 480) but the Williams Committee on Obscenity and Film Censorship referred specifically to this issue—"We doubt if it is in the public interest for people . . . to be able to use the courts for the purpose of pursuing their own unrepresentative view of offensiveness" (Cmnd. 7772, 1979) para. 9.49).

[18] R.C.C.P. Rep., paras. 8.6–8.11.

[19] See above, p. 485.

to co-ordinate policy and the Commission recommended that, " . . . an attempt must be made under the auspices of the Director of Public Prosecutions to develop and promulgate throughout the police and prosecution services criteria for the exercise of the discretion to prosecute."[20] The Government has recently announced that, as an interim measure, the Attorney-General proposes to give all who prosecute on behalf of the public some guidance on the criteria for prosecution which will be closely in accordance with the spirit of the Royal Commission's recommendations. The Home Office will bring this guidance to the attention of chief officers of police.[21]

That this is said to be an interim measure will give some encouragement to those who would argue that statutory guidelines ought to be formulated after full debate in Parliament. The burden of this argument[22] is that such guidelines would render prosecutors more accountable for their decisions by providing a yardstick to judge them by, and that Parliament could ensure that once a criminal offence had been created its effect was not nullified by want of prosecution. This would appear to be an attractive argument but it seems to be implicit that the guidelines could be used to comment on individual cases, a development which could be highly prejudicial to an acquitted defendant or a suspect who is not actually prosecuted. The exercise of discretion is always a difficult matter to challenge and it is doubtful whether statutory guidelines would be of any greater assistance than Attorney-General's guidelines, even if it is accepted that it is proper to allow a challenge to the discretion of the prosecutor once it has been shown that he has actually considered the merits of the particular case.[23]

4. Do Committal Proceedings Serve Their Purpose?

There is a marked contrast between the expressed objective of committal proceedings and their practical utility:

> " . . . I think that it is clear that the function of committal proceedings is to ensure that no one shall stand his trial unless a *prima facie* case has been made out."

(Lord Widgery C.J., *R.* v. *Epping and Harlow Justices, ex p. Massaro* [1973] 1 Q.B. 433, at p. 435).

> "Having regard to . . . evidence, to the views of practitioners experienced in the criminal work of the courts and to our own experience, we are satisfied that the section 1 committal procedure can result in cases being committed for trial which ought not to be committed . . . "

(*Report of the James Committee on the Distribution of Criminal Business between the Crown Court and Magistrates' Courts*, 1975, para. 232).

---

[20] R.C.C.P. Rep. , para. 8.10.

[21] Contained in the Home Secretary's reply to a Parliamentary Question, reproduced in (1982) 126 S.J. 528.

[22] F. Bennion, "Who should lay down prosecution guidelines?" (1981) S.J. 534.

[23] That is the point at which the courts have currently drawn the line, *R.* v. *Metropolitan Police Commissioner, ex p. Blackburn* [1968] 2 Q.B. 118, and see above, p. 483.

"Committal proceedings date from a time when the magistrates were the check upon unfounded cases coming to court. That function has gradually fallen into disuse."

(*R.C.C.P. Report* 1981, para. 8.26).

"It might be expected . . . that committal proceedings would provide an effective screening mechanism that would at least prevent the Crown Court from being clogged up by hopelessly weak cases. It is now clear, however, that adequate review of the prosecution evidence is, save in a small minority of cases, little more than legal fiction."

(McConville and Baldwin, *Courts, Prosecution and Conviction* (1981), p. 78).

We have already mentioned the *Confait* case[24] and the observations of Sir Henry Fisher on the efficacy of the committal proceedings in that case, but there is now some statistical evidence to support the critical views expressed above. Cases which ought not to have been committed for trial become exposed when the trial judge in the Crown Court orders or directs an acquittal on the grounds of the insufficiency of the prosecution evidence. The need to treat the evidence of directed acquittals carefully has already been stressed[25] and it is clear that the insufficiency of prosecution evidence may be due to factors which were not foreseeable.[26] However, research undertaken by McConville and Baldwin shows that a proportion of directed acquittals occur in cases which ought not to have been allowed to proceed beyond the committal stage.[27] They record the considerable anguish and serious consequences for some of the defendants involving loss of job, loss of business, loss of reputation and, in one case, loss of custody of a child.[28] We are not dealing with legal technicalities but with the very real hardships caused by unjustified prosecution in the Crown Court.

Are the proceedings themselves ineffective, or is it the way in which they are operated? The old-style committal ought to give a clear opportunity to weigh the evidence and make an effective decision. Two problems have been identified. Very few cases now proceed through an old-style committal. In the survey by McConville and Baldwin, out of 2,406 cases sent for trial at Birmingham Crown Court during the period of the research only 4 had an old-style committal, and 18 had had some oral evidence given.[29] It is not known how many full committals had taken place where the accused was discharged, but the figures reveal that in 2,384 cases the magistrates had given no consideration to the evidence in following the section 1 procedure. The second problem is the alleged unwillingness of

---

[24] At p. 503 above.

[25] In connection with the standards adopted by prosecutors: see above, p. 519.

[26] For example, prosecution witnesses may fail to appear at the trial; may not "come up to proof"; may antagonise the jury. Another possibility is that the defence have decided not to object to a weak case at the committal stage in order to secure the advantage of an acquittal rather than a discharge, see above, p. 500.

[27] *Courts, Prosecution and Conviction* (1981), particularly chaps. 3 and 4.

[28] *Ibid.* pp. 48–50.

[29] *Ibid.* p. 81.

magistrates to discharge an accused in any event.[30] It may be easier for the examining justices to dodge the responsibility by ordering committal and letting the jury decide. Even so, the old-style committal could fulfil the stated objective, as Sir Henry Fisher observed of the *Confait* case, but at an enormous cost in time and money.[31]

The section 1 committal procedure has effectively shifted the burden of deciding whether there should be a trial from the magistrates to the lawyers involved.[32] If there is any doubt, it is always possible for the defence to object to a section 1 committal and demand an old-style committal. The Royal Commission, relying on evidence provided by McConville and Baldwin, concluded that the reason for the failure to weed out the weak cases which are allowed to go through to the Crown Court under the section 1 procedure is the, " . . . lack of effective scrutiny of the case by prosecution and defence (who may often only receive the papers on the day of the hearing)."[33] This echoes the general observation of Sir Henry Fisher on the use of committal proceedings to test the prosecution case, " . . . this will not happen unless there is a careful and dispassionate survey and review of the evidence by the counsel, solicitor or police officer responsible for presenting the case . . . Committal proceedings cannot therefore act as a safeguard against a failure to perform this duty."[34] The James Committee had speculated on the reasons why a defence solicitor may not be able to scrutinise the prosecution case fully before agreeing to committal, identifying lack of time and resources as particular problems.[35]

Recognising that the prevalence of section 1 committals places the responsibility for weeding out weak cases firmly on the shoulders of the prosecutor and the defence lawyer, the James Committee and the Royal Commission came up with different solutions to the problem. The James Committee recommended the retention of the section 1 procedure with the additional requirement that both the prosecution and defence signed a certificate to the effect that they had examined the witness statements and were satisfied that the case was suitable for committal for trial. The imposition of sanctions for abuse of this procedure was to be left to the legal profession.[36] The Royal Commission recommended the abolition of committal proceedings subject to the provision of a right to make a submission of no case to answer to a magistrates' court if the delay before trial of the offence would exceed a specified period. This procedure would be termed "application for discharge" and would depend partly upon improved provisions for disclosure of prosecution evidence to the defence.

---

[30] See the views expressed by B.F. Harrison, "Advocacy at Petty Sessions" [1955] Crim. L.R. 153; C. Allen, "The Report of the Departmental Committee on Proceedings Before Examining Justices" [1958] Crim. L.R. 647; E. Goldrein, "Proposals to Expedite Criminal Trials: Some Comments" [1959] Crim. L.R. 273.

[31] The time and expense involved in the old-style committal were major and well-founded criticisms. There is no suggestion that this system should be reintroduced as the standard procedure.

[32] By relieving the magistrates of the obligation even to consider the evidence.

[33] R.C.C.P. Rep. para. 8.26.

[34] *Report of an Inquiry by Sir Henry Fisher* . . . (1977), paras. 27.6–27.7 (see n. 84 above).

[35] *The Distribution of Criminal Business between the Crown Court and the Magistrates' Courts*, (Cmnd. 6323, 1975) para. 233.

[36] *Ibid.* paras. 235–239.

The responsibility thus placed upon the Crown prosecutor was recognised by the Commission and accepted as appropriate.[37]

The Royal Commission proposal is clearly more radical than that of the James Committee since it would allow defendants to be put on trial in the Crown Court at the instance of the Crown prosecutor, without an opportunity to challenge the decision, so long as the trial began within a specified period (the Commission suggested 8 weeks). In the light of the personal evidence gathered by McConville and Baldwin this may seem to be a proposal which requires the closest scrutiny and the Government have not yet indicated a view.

[37] R.C.C.P. Rep., paras. 8.27–8.31.

PART IV

THE HEARING

CHAPTER 14

THE CIVIL TRIAL

It is the criminal trial that captures the attention both of the public and of law students, and there is less to say about the trial process in civil proceedings. From the variety of different civil proceedings we take the action in the Queen's Bench Division as our example, as we did in the chapter on pre-trial civil procedure.[1] However, we shall also make reference to the county court and the resolution of issues in that court by the arbitration process.[2]

A. ADVERSARIAL PROCEDURE

"You have two adversaries in every civil dispute—someone asserting a right, someone denying it. Someone contending for one thing, someone contending against it."[3]

The trial procedure reflects this view of the conduct of civil cases, as well as the principles of judicial neutrality and unpreparedness. It is the function of the parties, normally through counsel, to bring the evidence and argue the law which will win the case.[4]

At the beginning of trial, the *opening speech* is made on behalf of the plaintiff. As in the criminal trial, the object of the opening speech is to outline the case with reference to the evidence that is to be called. The opening may be briefer in a civil trial since counsel will not normally have a jury and, one hopes, he will not have to explain to the judge the standard and burden of proof. However, counsel cannot assume that the judge has any familiarity with the papers in the case and his job has been summarised thus: " . . . to explain the whole case to the judge: to read the pleadings, the letters and other documents . . . to summarise what all the witnesses he is calling will say, and how his client views the issue."[5] It is also normal in the opening speech to put in any agreed reports or other documentary evidence.[6] If the judge has had the opportunity to read the pleadings and other documents in the case he may indicate to counsel that there is no need to cover all the points in the opening speech. This illustrates the advantage of trial by judge alone—the judge can move counsel on where matters are understood or undisputed without the constraint of ensuring that the jury have grasped the issue. At the conclusion of the opening speech for the plaintiff, the first witnesses are called.

[1] See Chap. 11.
[2] For county court small claims procedure prior to the arbitration see above, pp. 399–412.
[3] Sir Jack I.H. Jacob, "The Adversary System in Civil Litigation," City of London Law Review, [1983] Pt. 2, 17 at p. 18.
[4] This view is reflected right from the stage of pleadings (see above, p. 421) to trial.
[5] *Going to Law* (1974), a report by JUSTICE, at para. 16.
[6] *e.g.* medical reports or the reports of other experts. Barnard notes the value of a clear letter before action which can set out concisely the plaintiff's case, so giving the judge a succinct statement of the issues, which can be included with the documentary evidence: *The Civil Court in Action* (1977), p. 161.

It is no accident that there are witnesses *for* the plaintiff and witnesses *for* the defendant. Each party is free to choose the people who can give evidence to support his contentions and the witnesses line up behind the "litigant gladiators,"[7] clearly identified with one side or the other.

Counsel for the plaintiff will call each of his witnesses in turn and will question them to extract testimony which he expects will be favourable to the plaintiff. The plaintiff's solicitor will have prepared in advance a statement of the evidence already given by the witness and counsel will use this "proof of evidence" as the basis of his questions. The questioning of a witness by his "own" counsel is termed *examination in chief*. Counsel must observe two rules during the examination. He must not ask leading questions[8] and he must not try to contradict the evidence of his witness given in court by reference to a conflicting statement in the proof of evidence.[9] Because the "coaching" of witnesses by counsel is forbidden by the Code of Conduct[10] it is quite possible that there may be variations in testimony when the witness is under examination.

At the conclusion of the examination in chief of each witness for the plaintiff, counsel for the defendant is given the opportunity to *cross-examine* in an attempt to shake the testimony of the witness or to extract information useful to the defendant's case. In cross-examination counsel is at liberty to exploit contradictory statements made by the witness but he will not, of course, have available to him the witness' proof of evidence which is the property of the other side.

The case for the defendant is put in exactly the same way with an opening speech and the examination of witnesses.[11] After the defence evidence has been heard, counsel for the defendant may make a closing speech summarising his view of the evidence and the law, to which counsel for the plaintiff may reply. Again, the judge has a discretion to indicate to counsel that he does not wish to hear argument on a particular point which he may already have decided or which he considers to be irrelevant. At any point in the proceedings the judge may decide to look at the place in which the events in issue took place.[12] He would normally be accompanied at a "view" by the parties and their legal representatives.

[7] A phrase taken from Jacob, "The Adversary System in Civil Litigation," see n. 3, above.

[8] A leading question is one which suggests to the witness the answer which counsel expects. "What time did the accident occur?" is a proper question: "The accident occurred at 7.30 p.m., did it not?" is a leading question and, therefore, prohibited. It is commonly agreed between counsel that a witness may be "led" on non-contentious issues to save time.

[9] It is, of course, open to counsel to ask a witness to think again about an answer, but he may not suggest the discrepancy between the answer and the earlier statement. In an extreme case, counsel might seek to have the earlier statement put in as evidence at the end of the examination in chief: Civil Evidence Act 1968, s.2(2).

[10] *Code of Conduct for the Bar of England and Wales*, para. 142.

[11] Defence counsel is only permitted an opening speech if he is actually calling witnesses: R.S.C., Ord. 35, r. 7(4). In the county court, defence counsel must normally choose between an opening and a closing speech.

[12] R.S.C., Ord. 35, r. 8. The viewing is not necessarily restricted to places, although that is most common. The rule provides for an inspection of "any place or thing with respect to which any question arises." The Hertford Lent Assizes 1862 were enlivened by the presence in court of an allegedly vicious dog whose disposition was in issue. Serjeant Ballantine proposed that the dog should be brought into court in charge of his keeper. His opponent, Chambers, objected "as the experiment would be useless, while the dog was under the control of his keeper, and perilous, if he were not so." The dog was produced; the jury decided it was not vicious. *Line* v. *Taylor* (1862) 3 F. & F. 731.

Ultimately, the judge is required to give a reasoned judgment in which he will state his conclusions on the factual issues in dispute and the legal implications of those findings of fact.

B. WITNESSES AND EXPERT EVIDENCE

In criminal trials, the witnesses may be under pressure in giving evidence.[13] In many civil trials part of the evidence is likely to be given by witnesses who are under no such pressure and who have had much time to reflect on their testimony. Expert witnesses are those asked to give evidence on technical matters, so that the court may form a proper view on matters of which it will have no other knowledge. Expert evidence is, in one sense, opinion evidence,[14] but it is treated as factual since it is based on the training and professional expertise of the witness. There are any number of matters on which expert evidence may be relevant—the extent and effect of personal injuries; the operation of machines; the implementation of proper safety procedures; handwriting; questions of the interpretation of foreign law and many other matters.

The right of the parties to adduce expert evidence is somewhat restricted by the Civil Evidence Act 1972[15] and the Rules of the Supreme Court[16] and provision is made for pre-trial disclosure of such evidence in most cases. The object of such disclosure is to save expense, where possible, by discovering whether there is a real dispute between the parties and to avoid either party being taken by surprise on a technical matter and being forced to seek an adjournment. A party will not normally be allowed to call expert evidence at trial unless the disclosure procedure has been followed or unless the other party agrees.[17] It is, therefore, possible for the parties to make explicit agreement that each side may call what expert evidence it wishes at trial, thus getting round the disclosure provisions, but the prospect of savings in time and money both before and at trial might be a powerful inducement to disclose.

The expert witness may be different from an "ordinary" witness in that he is giving evidence on matters within his field of knowledge, often after a prolonged examination, but he is examined and cross-examined in just the same way. More importantly, he is just as much the "property" of one party. There is a temptation for parties to indulge in a battle of experts in court, sometimes hoping to win the point by the sheer volume of evidence or by the eminence of their witness(es). Some have argued[18] that it is unedifying to see leading members of the same profession being forced to disagree under skilful cross-examination; that such disagreement may serve to confuse rather than clarify the issues for the court; and that additional costs are unnecessarily incurred by taking evidence from two or more people on the same point. However, this is an almost inevitable

---

[13] For example, the incident may have happened extremely quickly, or there may be other perils involved in giving evidence against particular defendants.

[14] Which would not normally be admissible as evidence.

[15] s.2.

[16] Ord. 38, Part IV.

[17] Ord. 38, r. 36.

[18] See, e.g. A. Kenny, "The Expert in Court" (1983) 99 L.Q.R. 197.

consequence of the adversarial system of procedure and the power of the parties to adduce what relevant evidence they wish.

There is a power in the court to alleviate some of these problems by appointing an independent expert in any matter which is to be tried by judge alone.[19] This may seem to present an ideal solution to the problem of the battle of experts but it is subject to a serious limitation. The court may only make such an order on the application of a party to the action. The *Supreme Court Practice* notes that such applications have been very few in number.[20] Perhaps the court should be given the power to appoint an independent expert on its own authority even though that begins to erode the adversary system.

An additional power, which is useful in this context, is contained in the Supreme Court Act 1981, s.70 which allows the appointment of assessors or scientific advisers to assist in the hearing and disposal of the action. These are people who sit with the judge at the trial of the action and their role is considered more fully later in the chapter.

C. THE USE OF THE JURY IN CIVIL CASES

Until 1883 trial by jury was the normal method of trial in civil cases in the common law courts. In 1983 it is wholly exceptional and confined to a handful of cases. What happened in between?

New Rules were made in 1883[21] for the Supreme Court which had been created by the Judicature Acts 1873–1875.[22] These rules appear to have changed the emphasis in respect of the availability of civil trial by judge alone. They provided that a plaintiff might have trial by jury as of *right* in six specific causes of action[23] by giving notice to the court, whereas in all other matters application had to be made and could, in certain circumstances, be refused.[24] The first breach in the principle of jury trial had been made by the Common Law Procedure Act 1854 but the statistics seem to indicate that 1883 marked the beginning of the decline.[25]

Temporary restrictions on jury trial necessitated by the lack of eligible jurors during the First World War were continued until 1925 before being

---

[19] R.S.C., Ord. 40, r. 1.

[20] *The Supreme Court Practice* 1982, para. 40/1–6/2, p. 697. There has been some judicial encouragement for the appointment of a court expert but this has obviously not had any significant effect: *Re Saxton* [1962] 1 W.L.R. 968, *per* Lord Denning M.R., at p. 973.

[21] The 1883 Rules of the Supreme Court were made under the authority of the Judicature Acts 1873–1875 and represented a substantial redrafting of preceding rules of practice. The relevant rule was Order XXXVI.

[22] See above, p. 29.

[23] Namely, libel, slander, malicious prosecution, false imprisonment, seduction and breach of promise of marriage. These provisions formed the basis of the statutory reform in 1933.

[24] The most significant ground of refusal was that the matter required " . . . prolonged examination of documents or accounts or any scientific or local investigation which could not in the opinion of the Court conveniently be made with a jury." Order XXXVI, 1883 Rules.

[25] An analysis of statistics then available is contained in R.M. Jackson, "The Incidence of Jury Trial during the Past Century" (1937) 1 M.L.R. 132. That analysis does not appear to advance the view that the 1883 Rules were significant in reducing the number of jury trials, but the figures would seem to support this contention. See also, M.G. Buckley, "Civil Trial by Jury" (1966) 19 C.L.P. 63. A good chronological account is provided by Bankes L.J., in *Ford v. Blurton* (1922) 38 T.L.R. 801, at pp. 802–803.

removed,[26] but the reprieve was short-lived. Legislation in 1933[27] established the current position and the relevant provisions are now to be found in the Supreme Court Act 1981. There is a qualified right to jury trial in certain cases and a discretion in the court to order jury trial in other cases. Section 69 of the Act provides:

"(1) Where, on the application of any party to an action to be tried in the Queen's Bench Division, the court is satisfied that there is in issue—
(a) a charge of fraud against that party; or
(b) a claim in respect of libel, slander, malicious prosecution or false imprisonment; or
(c) any question or issue of a kind prescribed for the purposes of this paragraph,
the action shall be tried with a jury unless the court is of the opinion that the trial requires any prolonged examination of documents or accounts or any scientific or local examination which cannot conveniently be made with a jury . . .
(3) An action to be tried in the Queen's Bench Division which does not by virtue of subsection (1) fall to be tried with a jury shall be tried without a jury unless the court in its discretion orders it to be tried with a jury."

1. THE RIGHT TO JURY TRIAL

It is in defamation actions that the right to trial by jury is most frequently exercised, but even in these cases the court *may* order trial by judge alone. Recent decisions have demonstrated the conflict between the desire to grant trial by jury in cases where the reputation of the parties in issue, and the need to take a realistic view about what a jury can be expected to cope with. In *Rothermere* v. *Times Newspapers*,[28] the decision of the trial judge that the extent and complexity of the documentary evidence made trial by judge alone desirable was reversed by the Court of Appeal. Although it would be difficult for a jury to deal with the documentary evidence—the plaintiff's list of documents alone ran to 77 pages with 2033 items—the national importance of the issues involved rendered jury trial appropriate.[29]

The hardships which may be inflicted on a jury in a complex civil matter were illustrated in *Orme* v. *Associated Newspapers Group*,[30] a case involving the alleged defamation of the director of The Holy Spirit

[26] The Juries Act 1918 provided for trial by judge alone unless the court ordered otherwise, subject to the right to jury trial in a category of cases slightly wider than that in the 1883 Rules. This provision was continued by the Administration of Justice Act 1920, but repealed by the Administration of Justice Act 1925. The number of jury trials declined sharply after 1933.

[27] The Administration of Justice (Miscellaneous Provisions) Act 1933, s.6.

[28] [1973] 1 W.L.R. 448. The case concerned an article written by Bernard Levin in *The Times*, March 19, 1971, entitled "Profit and dishonour in Fleet Street."

[29] The court was not unanimous but the fact that the defence of fair comment would be in issue and its particular significance to the newspaper industry weighed heavily with the majority.

[30] March 31, 1981 (unreported) (Q.B.D.); December 20, 1982 (unreported) (C.A.)

Association for the Unification of World Christianity.[31] The trial began in October 1980 and lasted until the end of March 1981. 117 witnesses were called. Very many documents had to be considered. The closing speeches lasted several days. The original estimate of the length of the trial was six to seven weeks.[32]

Allegations of fraud bear on the reputation of a party to litigation in the same way as alleged defamatory statements so that it is unsurprising to find fraud included in this category.[33] Actions for malicious prosecution and false imprisonment raise somewhat different issues and will often present the means of redress for a citizen who alleges ill-treatment at the hands of the police. In these circumstances the presence of a jury may reassure the plaintiff that the decision will be totally impartial and avert any suggestion that a judge may too readily accept the evidence of the police.[34]

The need to maintain the right to trial by jury, even in this limited category of cases, is still actively in question. As a result of the *Orme* case an amendment was proposed to the Supreme Court Bill (1981) which would have added a further restriction—that trial by jury could be denied where the length of the trial would make it inconvenient for a jury to try the action. After the same sort of impassioned rhetoric which was produced when the Criminal Law Bill 1977 was under consideration, the Government reluctantly accepted the rejection of the proposal by the House of Commons.[35] Lawyers have since been urged to take great care in estimating the length of trials so as to avoid hardship for potential jurors.[36]

2. THE DISCRETION TO GRANT JURY TRIAL

Either party to an action may ask the court to exercise its discretion to order a jury trial in cases not falling within section 69(1), but it is very rare for the court to grant the application. It has been on such applications that the courts have had the opportunity of considering the advantages and particular merits of jury trial and weighing them against the obvious difficulties that such trials occasion.

In *Ward* v. *James*[37] the plaintiff in a personal injuries action made application for trial by jury. On appeal, a full Court of Appeal declined to interfere with the judge's order that the case should go for trial by jury but

---

[31] Better known as the "Moonies." The Daily Mail had published a feature about the organisation which made a number of damaging allegations. The action in defamation was ultimately unsuccessful.

[32] It is ironic that the judge at trial was Comyn J., who as Comyn Q.C. had unsuccessfully opposed trial by jury in the *Times* case in 1973 (see n. 28, above). He lists the problems of the case in a judgment dated January 28, 1981 (unreported) which was concerned with the defence submission that the trial should have been stopped after the plaintiff's case had finished. By that time there had already been three appeals to the Court of Appeal, three months of trial and the provision of £215,000 security for costs by the plaintiff.

[33] The meaning of fraud in this context was considered by Sir Robert Megarry V.-C. in *Stafford Winfield Cook* v. *Winfield* [1981] 1 W.L.R. 459.

[34] This factor is fully considered in W.R. Cornish, *The Jury* (1968), Chap. 8.

[35] The annotations to the Supreme Court Act 1981, s.69, in *Current Law Statutes Annotated* are very helpful on this point.

[36] *Practice Direction* (*Juries: Length of Trial*) [1981] 1 W.L.R. 1129. This direction makes it clear that those jurors who will suffer inconvenience or hardship by having to serve for the estimated length of the trial should be excused.

[37] [1966] 1 Q.B. 273.

made some general observations on the exercise of a judge's discretion to make such an order. In particular, Lord Denning M.R. placed emphasis on the need for uniformity in the award of damages in personal injury cases and referred to the jury's ignorance of the conventional figure in comparable cases.[38] He concluded that trial by jury ought not to be ordered save in exceptional circumstances.[39] It appears that the severity[40] or unusual nature[41] of the injuries are not to be taken as exceptional circumstances, but if the injuries are unique, or nearly so,[42] a jury may be appropriate.

There have been suggestions that the possibility of a strong conflict of evidence or dishonesty,[43] or deliberate lying, or the fact that honour and integrity may be at stake[44] are reasons for ordering jury trial, but these views must be doubted after the most recent House of Lords decision. The plaintiff in *Williams* v. *Beasley*[45] bought an action for damages against his solicitor alleging professional negligence. An order by the trial judge rejecting the plaintiff's application for trial by jury was reversed by the Court of Appeal. That court gave two reasons for overriding the discretion of the trial judge, namely that the case involved issues of credibility, integrity and honour, and that the plaintiff was especially anxious to have trial by jury because of his deeply-held belief that judges as a class are prejudiced in favour of lawyers.

The short judgment of the House of Lords restored the judge's original order and reversed the judgment of the Court of Appeal. The two grounds on which the Court of Appeal had proceeded were specifically rejected. As to the first point, Lord Diplock said that the great majority of personal injury cases involved issues of credibility and that alone is not sufficient reason to depart from the "usual rule" that cases, other than those in which a prima facie right to trial by jury is conferred by statute, should be tried by judge alone.[46] Honour and integrity may be weighty considerations for the judge in deciding whether to exercise his discretion, but only where it is the honour and integrity of the party applying for jury trial that is being impugned.[47] As to the second point, Lord Diplock observed:

> "If, as in the instant case, all rational considerations point to the conclusion that trial by judge alone would involve a shorter and less expensive hearing and would be more likely to achieve a just result than trial by jury, it would be the height of injustice to the defendant to deprive him of his right to have his case tried by the appropriate

---

[38] *Ibid*. at pp. 296–300, 303.

[39] *Ibid*. p. 303. In the event, *Ward* v. *James* was sent for trial by jury but the court was influenced by other factors peculiar to that case.

[40] *Sims* v. *William Howard and Son Ltd.* [1964] 2 Q.B. 409.

[41] *Watts* v. *Manning* [1964] 1 W.L.R. 623.

[42] *Hodges* v. *Harland and Wolff Ltd.* [1965] 1 W.L.R. 523. In this highly unusual case the plaintiff was injured whilst using a diesel driven air compressor. The spindle of the machine caught in his trousers and avulsed his penis and scrotal skin. Trial by jury was ordered. The observations of Davies L.J. at pp. 1087–1088 are helpful in setting out the difficulties of jury trial.

[43] *Sims* v. *William Howard and Son Ltd.* [1964] 2 Q.B. 409, *per* Pearson L.J. at p. 419.

[44] *Ward* v. *James* [1966] 1 Q.B. 273, *per* Lord Denning M.R., at p. 295.

[45] [1973] 1 W.L.R. 1295.

[46] *Ibid*. pp. 1298–1299.

[47] *Ibid*. p. 1298H.

method merely because of the mistaken belief of the plaintiff that judges as a class are likely to be biased against him or in favour of his opponent. To allow the court's decision as to the mode of trial to be swayed by the existence of such a belief by one of the parties, however sincerely it might be held, would be to acknowledge that there was some substance in it and that our system of justice lacks the firm foundation of an impartial judiciary."[48]

It will remain, therefore, very difficult to persuade a judge to exercise his discretion to order trial by jury.

3. SHOULD THE JURY BE RETAINED IN CIVIL CASES?

If the debates on the Supreme Court Bill (1981) are any guide then this is, indeed, an academic question. The House of Commons showed itself unwilling to countenance any further restriction on the right to jury trial, let alone its abolition.[49] However, all the disadvantages associated with jury trial were brought together so effectively by *Orme* v. *Associated Newspapers Ltd.*[50] that it is still pertinent to question the real value of the jury in our system of civil procedure.

On the debit side of the account, one would normally place the additional time, and consequent additional expense, of a jury trial; the variability of jury verdicts; the potential hardship and inconvenience suffered by individual jurors in lengthy cases; the unrealistic expectation that laymen should listen to and comprehend complex and extensive evidence; the unpredictability of jury verdicts and the reluctance of the Court of Appeal to interfere with jury awards; the additional burden which may be placed on counsel and judge where complex questions of law are in issue.[51] All these are very sound reasons in support of the propositions that jury trial is not the best mode of trial in all civil actions and that trial by judge alone will normally be preferable. But are any of them sufficiently strong to support the view that trial by jury should not be permissible?

The Faulks Committee on Defamation[52] gave detailed consideration to the role of juries in defamation actions and recommended restrictions on their use whilst rejecting arguments for their total abolition. The conclusion of the Faulks Committee was that in defamation cases the court should be given just the same discretion to order trial by jury as in all other civil cases and that the function of the jury should be limited to deciding

---

[48] *Ibid.* p. 1299H.

[49] Lord Hailsham, L.C., described the opponents of the proposal that the length of a trial should be a factor in determining whether trial by jury was convenient, as " . . . troglodytes, reactionaries and pterodactyls, and other strange creatures in the undergrowth who oppose law reform . . . ."

[50] See above, n. 30.

[51] These defects of the jury as a mode of trial are culled from various sources including M.G. Buckley, "Civil Trial by Jury" (1966) 19 C.L.P. 63; W.R. Cornish, *The Jury* (1968), Chap. 8; P. Devlin, *Trial by Jury* (1956), pp. 130–135; *Hodges* v. *Harland and Wolff Ltd* [1965] 1 W.L.R. 523; *Ward* v. *James* [1966] 1 Q.B. 273; and the *Report of the Committee on Defamation* (Cmnd. 5909, 1975) (The Faulks Committee).

[52] *Report of the Committee on Defamation* (Cmnd. 5909, 1975). Chap. 17 gives a very good account of the role of the jury in defamation actions.

issues of liability, leaving the assessment of damages to the judge.[53] This conclusion was based on a substantial amount of evidence and was very carefully argued. If one paragraph of this chapter of the Report may be used to summarise the view of the Faulks Committee it might be the following:

> "We believe that much of the support for jury trials is emotional, and derives from the undoubted value of juries in serious *criminal* cases, where they stand between the prosecuting authority and the citizen. But the true function of the civil jury is to weigh facts impersonally and recompense the claimant for an injury that he may have sustained—tasks for which the judge is trained by many years of experience and for which jurors have no training at all."[54]

That there is emotional support for the jury is undoubted. Various distinguished judges have declared the constitutional importance of the right to jury trial. Atkin L.J., in *Ford* v. *Blurton*, said that trial by jury is an essential principle of law which, " . . . has been the bulwark of liberty, the shield of the poor from the rich and the powerful. Anyone who knows the history of our law knows that many of the liberties of the subject were originally established and are maintained by the verdicts of juries in civil cases."[55] Bankes L.J., in the same case, expressed himself equally convinced of the value of the jury in civil matters. Lord Denning M.R., in a dictum which has been much quoted, said:

> "Let it not be supposed that this court is in any way opposed to trial by jury. It has been the bulwark of our liberties for too long for any of us to seek to alter it. Whenever a man is on trial for serious crime, or when in a civil case a man's honour or integrity is at stake, or when one or other party must be deliberately lying, then trial by jury has no equal."[56]

Mr. Frank Dobson put the point in more colourful terms in the House of Commons debate on the Supreme Court Bill: "Jury service is more important to the preservation of individual liberty and the preservation of our judicial system than all the scurvy race of lawyers put together."

On a less emotional level we encounter the arguments that it is desirable to involve as many people as possible in the administration of justice[57] and that the jury stands between the judges and the man in the street to ensure that ordinary standards are applied in the doing of justice.

In the end it is difficult to avoid the view that the law is currently broadly acceptable, although there may be criticism of the distinction between the four specified causes of action (and fraud) and other civil cases. Trial by jury is unlikely to be abolished in civil matters but responsibility lies with the judges for ensuring that the worst features of jury trial are not often evident.

---

[53] *Ibid*. paras. 455–457.
[54] *Ibid*. para. 496.
[55] (1922) 38 T.L.R. 801 at p. 805.
[56] *Ward* v. *James* [1966] 1 Q.B. 273, at p. 295.
[57] See, for example, the evidence of Sir Peter Rawlinson Q.C., and Lord Dilhorne given to the Faulks Committee. *Report, op cit.* at para. 477.

4. The Operation of the Jury

The operation of the jury in civil proceedings, as in criminal, is controlled by the provisions of the Juries Act 1974. The qualification for service of jurors, the procedure for summoning, the compilation of panels and the ballot and swearing of jurors are all exactly the same for civil and criminal trials.[58] Majority verdicts may be accepted in civil cases, although there is greater flexibility than in criminal matters since the parties to the action may proceed by agreement with an incomplete jury.[59] The right to challenge is available in civil matters, but there is no right of peremptory challenge.[60] The discretion to excuse a juror from service which may be exercised by the appropriate officer or by the court[61] is likely to be exercised more freely in civil matters where there may be considerable hardship or inconvenience caused by a long trial.[62]

D. THE ROLE OF THE JUDGE

In civil matters the judge normally sits alone to determine the outcome of the action. The incidence of jury trial has already been explained, but there are a number of situations in which the judge may have the assistance of others sitting with him. The composition of the Employment Appeal Tribunal and the Restrictive Practices Court with lay members and High Court judges[63] exemplifies the formal introduction of lay expertise into the judicial process, but there is a general power vested in the High Court to call in the aid of one or more assessors or scientific advisers in particular cases.[64]

Assessors are used especially in admiralty proceedings in the Queen's Bench Division,[65] but there is nothing to prevent a judge using an assessor in other cases. It may cause expense and inconvenience to the parties if the hearing has to be adjourned so that the judge may find and appoint an appropriate expert, but there is strong support for that course of action.[66] It is less satisfactory for the judge to obtain assistance from an expert after the hearing has concluded and before he gives judgment.[67]

Scientific advisers may be appointed in an action for the infringement of a patent and will render similar assistance to the judge.[68] The role of both assessor and scientific adviser is to listen to the evidence and give the judge such assistance as he may require in the formulation of his judgment and if he gives an opinion on the outcome, then that opinion and the reasons for

[58] See below, pp. 608–613.
[59] Juries Act 1974, s.17.
[60] *Creed* v. *Fisher* (1854) 9 Exch. 472.
[61] Juries Act 1974, s.9(2),(4). The "appropriate officer" is the person who is designated by the Lord Chancellor for this purpose.
[62] *Practice Direction (Juries: Length of Trial)* [1981] 1 W.L.R. 1129.
[63] See pp. 54, 77, above for the composition of the respective courts.
[64] Supreme Court Act 1981, s.70.
[65] Where the assessor is normally one or more of the Elder Brethren of Trinity House.
[66] From Devlin J., in *Esso Petroleum Co. Ltd* v. *Southport Corporation* [1956] A.C. 218 at pp. 222–223. His view was supported by the House of Lords, in the same case.
[67] *Ibid.* at p. 223.
[68] Supreme Court Act 1981, s.70. See also *Supreme Court Practice* 1982, para. 33/6/1, p. 601.

it may be taken into account by the Court of Appeal in the event of an appeal.[69]

In the criminal trial, with a jury, it is of great importance that the judge should display objectivity and neutrality.[70] In a civil action it may prove difficult for him to refrain from intervening with questions and observations. The procedure is slightly more flexible than in a criminal trial and the absence of a jury (in most cases) enables the judge to take a more positive line over matters which he may consider to be irrelevant or uncontentious. However, he must not take such an active part in the case that he appears to deprive counsel of the conduct of the action. In the statement of the judge's role to be found in *Jones* v. *National Coal Board*,[71] Denning L.J. put it thus:

> "The judge's part . . . is to hearken to the evidence, only himself asking questions of witnesses when it is necessary to clear up any point that has been overlooked or left obscure; to see that the advocates behave themselves seemly and keep to the rules laid down by law; to exclude irrelevancies and discourage repetition; to make sure by wise intervention that he follows the points that the advocates are making and can assess their work; and at the end to make up his mind where the truth lies."[72]

If he is sitting alone, a judge may take time to make up his mind where the truth lies and give a reserved judgment at a later date, or he may give an *extempore* judgment at the conclusion of the hearing. If sitting with a jury, the judge must sum up the evidence and direct on the law as he would do in a trial on indictment.[73] Ultimately, judgment will be given.

E. THE JUDGMENT

A judgment is a reasoned decision in which the judge will normally set out the facts of the case, as he has decided them, and give his conclusions on the law applicable to those facts. He may rehearse some of the arguments put by counsel so as to set his decision in context,[74] and he is likely to give an opinion on all matters relating to the action which might be relevant if the losing party were to appeal from his judgment. In particular, there may be findings of fact which are not crucial to the judgment given at first instance but which might become relevant if the Court of Appeal take a different view of the law. The trial judge will be attempting to avoid the expense and difficulty of a new trial if the appellate court change a part of his judgment.[75]

---

[69] *Hattersley and Sons* v. *G. Hodgson Ltd.* (1905) 21 T.L.R. 178.

[70] Below pp. 598–606.

[71] [1957] 2 Q.B. 55.

[72] *Ibid.* at p. 64.

[73] See below pp. 602–606.

[74] Because it is the responsibility of the parties to advance argument on the issues which they wish to be decided it is always important to know whether a particular line of argument has been canvassed or not when assessing a judgment. In respect of appellate decisions reported in the Law Reports series, the major arguments of counsel are normally set out as part of the report.

[75] *e.g.* although a judge may find against a plaintiff on the question of the defendant's liability in negligence, he will nonetheless determine the quantum of damages lest he is reversed on the liability point by the Court of Appeal. If no finding had been made on quantum the issue would have to be the subject of another trial.

At the end of the judgment, counsel for the successful party must ask formally for judgment to be entered for his client in the terms which the judge has probably indicated. Counsel may ask for "judgment for the plaintiff for £45,000," or "judgment for the defendant and that the plaintiff's claim be dismissed." At this stage the question of any interest payable on a money judgment will be raised by counsel and he will also ask for costs. The principles applicable to the award of interest and costs have been discussed earlier.[76] Traditionally, money judgments were expressed in sterling but since 1975 it has been possible for a court to give judgment in a foreign currency.[77]

The final responsibility rests with the solicitor who must draw up the terms of the judgment on a special form and then have the form and the original writ in the action sealed in the Judgment Office.[78] Having obtained judgment, the successful party must then go on to enforce it. Contrary, perhaps, to his expectations, his troubles may only just be beginning![79]

F. ARBITRATION IN THE COUNTY COURT

The significance of the arbitration procedure in small claims in the county court is growing rapidly. In 1982, there were 31,575 judgments entered after arbitration (an increase of 49 per cent. over the figure for 1981); there were 27,637 judgments entered after trial.[80] 1982 was the first year in which the number of arbitrations exceeded the number of trials.

The situations in which a small claim will reach arbitration in the county court and the standard terms of reference for the arbitration have been set out in Chapter 11.[81] We only need to remind ourselves at this point of the particular features of the arbitration which distinguish it from the trial procedure we have been considering in this chapter.

This strict rules of evidence will not apply to the hearing[82] and it is intended to be informal. In order to afford a fair and equal opportunity to each party to present his case, the arbitrator is free to adopt whatever form of procedure he thinks appropriate. This clearly marks a substantial deviation from the adversarial procedure of trial, although quite how flexibly the procedures are operated will depend upon the registrar of the court who is likely to be the arbitrator.

In one respect the rules for the arbitration seem to be narrower than the rules in the High Court. There is a power given to the arbitrator to consult

---

[76] At p. 384 and pp. 362–365 respectively.

[77] *Miliangos* v. *George Frank (Textiles) Ltd.* [1976] A.C. 443 not following the previous authority, *Re United Railways of Havana and Regla Warehouses Ltd.* [1961] A.C. 1007. On the precedent implications of this decision see above pp. 290, 297.

[78] R.S.C., Ord. 42, r. 5.

[79] One of the considerations which a plaintiff must have in mind at the commencement of his action is whether the defendant will be able to satisfy any judgment that may be given against him. The enforcement of judgments is by no means a straightforward process where the defendant is determined to avoid payment. See generally, Walker and Walker, *The English Legal System* (5th ed., 1980), Chap. 20B; Sir Jack I.H. Jacob, "The Enforcement of Judgement Debts," in *The Reform of Civil Procedural Law* (1982); and below, p. 659.

[80] *Judicial Statistics, Annual Report* 1982, Cmnd. 9065, Table 7.4 at p. 79.

[81] See above, pp. 410–412.

[82] Unless the court on making the reference to arbitration should determine otherwise, C.C.R. 1981, Ord. 19, r. 5.

an expert, or call for an expert report, or invite an expert to attend the hearing as an assessor, *but only with the consent of the parties.*[83] As against the power of the High Court to appoint an assessor of its own volition[84] this is a surprising limitation, and although the arbitrator may use his own initiative in suggesting expert evidence (in the High Court it must be on the application of a party[85]), either party may frustrate his objective. It is presumably to prevent additional cost being forced on the parties that the arbitrator does not have the power to call evidence of his own motion, but that problem might be circumvented by a requirement that the arbitrator gain the agreement of the parties to a reasonable fee for the evidence, rather than to the obtaining of the evidence.

However, this restriction does not seem to be affecting the growth of arbitration in the county court and it will be interesting to see whether the apparent popularity of the procedure has any effect on the adversarial procedure adopted in other courts.

---

[83] This power may be exercised at any time before the decision of the arbitrator is given, and either before or after the hearing. C.C.R. 1981, Ord. 19. r. 5.

[84] Supreme Court Act 1981, s.70; see p. 540, above.

[85] R.S.C., Ord. 40, r. 6.

CHAPTER 15

THE TRIBUNAL HEARING

At the hearing, the chairman of the tribunal has the difficult task of ensuring that a sufficient level of informality is achieved so that the parties do not feel inhibited in putting their respective cases, whilst maintaining some procedural and evidentiary safeguards so that the rights of the parties are not prejudiced in an unacceptable way.

We made the point in the previous chapter on tribunals that it is scarcely possible to choose a "typical" tribunal and the observations hereafter draw on a variety of sources. However, just as there are common problems to be solved in devising an appropriate pre-hearing procedure, so there are common problems in the conduct of hearings. What procedural rules, if any, should be followed? What evidence will be admitted? What role should the chairman play and what responsibilities does he have? What sort of representation, if any, should be permitted/encouraged, and how should it be funded?

A. PROCEDURE

Differing approaches to the achievements of procedural fairness may be observed, but in most tribunals much is left to the chairman in determining the form of the hearing. Three illustrations may demonstrate that the amount of guidance given by the appropriate rules is often minimal.

1. THE SOCIAL SECURITY APPEAL TRIBUNAL

The Social Security Appeal Tribunal came into being in April 1984, as a result of the merger of National Insurance Local Tribunals and Supplementary Benefit Appeal Tribunals. New procedural rules have been made but they do not differ substantially from those previously applicable and it is still instructive to consider the alleged defects of the former tribunals, to expose the difficulties which the new tribunal must try to avoid. The new regulations still contain the following general provision:

> "Subject to the provisions of the Act and of these regulations— . . . in the case of a local tribunal the procedure shall be such as the chairman of the tribunal shall determine."[1]

This general power is qualified in certain respects by other provisions. Representation is permitted[2]; witnesses may be called[3]; every person who has the right to be heard shall be given an opportunity of putting questions directly to any witnesses called at the hearing and of addressing the

---

[1] Social Security (Adjudication) Regulations 1984, (S.I. 1984, No. 451) reg.2(1).
[2] *Ibid.* reg.2(1)(*b*).
[3] *Ibid.* reg.4(8).

tribunal[4]; the hearing shall be in public unless the chairman directs otherwise on the grounds that intimate personal or financial circumstances may be disclosed or that public security is involved[5]; the person making the appeal, the claimant, the adjudication officer, the Secretary of State and any person who, in the opinion of the chairman, is a person interested in the decision, are all entitled to be heard.[6]

It is the chairman who decides how these requirements should be fulfilled and it is to be expected that there will be variations in procedure from chairman to chairman. The Social Security Commissioners[7] may correct procedural irregularities on appeal, but it will be apparent that the provisions are so widely drafted that such an irregularity will have to be very serious before it will be regarded as material.[8]

It is somewhat difficult to forecast, at the time of writing, what style of procedure will be adopted in the new tribunal. The order of events differed in the two former tribunals, but it would now be surprising if the chairman adopted a different order of proceedings depending on whether the claim was for supplementary benefit or for some other social security benefit. The requirement that the chairman should be a qualified lawyer[9] might mean that the procedure normally followed by the N.I.L.T.s. will become standard.[10] In that tribunal, it was usual for the claimant (or his representative) to state the case and call witnesses[11]; the claimant and his witnesses might then be questioned by the chairman, and/or the members, and/or the presenting officer[12]; the presenting officer would then make his submission and be subject to questioning; the claimant would be asked for

---

[4] *Ibid.* reg.4(8).

[5] *Ibid.* reg.4(4).

[6] *Ibid.* reg.4(5). The adjudication officer is an officer of the DHSS whose job is to make the original decision on entitlement to benefit.

[7] See above, p. 58. The Commissioners constitute an appeal body from the decisions of Social Security Appeal Tribunals.

[8] It is rare for decisions to be upset on the grounds of procedural irregularity. See A. Ogus and E. Barendt, *The Law of Social Security* (2nd ed., 1982) p. 590, and the Commissioners' Decisions cited therein. Failure to explain new grounds of disqualification from benefit, first raised at the hearing, has been criticised by the Commissioner (R(U)2/71) as has the admittance of a witness to the hearing before the claimant is admitted (R(U)44/52). The latter decision contains some observations by the Commissioner about the procedural obligations of the local tribunal.

[9] See below, p. 561.

[10] On the basis that the great majority of chairmen of N.I.L.T.s were lawyers, so that it is logical to expect "lawyerly procedure" to prevail. The procedure outlined is recorded as standard in Ogus and Barendt, *op. cit.* at p. 590. However, it is not just the order of events which is significant but the attitude and appearance of the tribunal members. One of the authors, representing a nervous claimant at a N.I.L.T. had been at pains to explain in advance the informality of the procedure and distinguish it from court procedure as seen in "Crown Court" on television. The opening remarks of the chairman of the tribunal were, "Good afternoon, I must warn you, Mrs. X, that you must tell the truth in these proceedings—we are just like a court." If the claimant had been unrepresented, the niceties of procedure would have mattered little after that!

[11] This assumes that the claimant attends or is represented. The tribunal will proceed with the hearing in the absence of the claimant unless there are good grounds for an adjournment: Adjudication Regulations (above, n. 1) reg.4(3).

[12] The presenting officer is an officer of the D.H.S.S. specifically assigned to present cases before tribunals. Some presenting officers, therefore, become very experienced "advocates" and well known to their local tribunal. This job may not, however, occupy all the time of an officer, in which case he may also carry out the duties of an adjudication officer.

any final observations. Thereafter, the members of the tribunal would consider their decision in private.[13]

There was no substantial criticism of procedure in N.I.L.T.s although the ancillary arrangements were said to deter claimants from making an appeal,[14] or to give an impression that the tribunal was part of the departmental machinery rather than an independent review body.[15] It was certainly the case that attendance at the hearing improved, and representation greatly improved, the chances of success for the claimant.[16]

In the S.B.A.T., the presenting officer was normally allowed to go first and the wide variations in procedure which were observed raised serious doubts about the quality of the decision-making.[17]

In any case, whatever the order of events, there are some specific procedural requirements (see above) and the claimant must be informed, in writing, of the decision as soon as may be practicable after the case has been decided.[18] The written decision must include a statement of the grounds of the decision, a record of the material facts found and, where the decision is not unanimous, that one of the members dissented and the grounds for that dissent.[19]

The role of the presenting officer in the procedure of the S.S.A.T. is interesting in that he is expected to put forward the view of the officer who made the decision against which the claimant is appealing, but is also expected to exercise individual judgment and assist the tribunal in reaching a proper resolution of the case.[20] This may require him to advance arguments on behalf of the appellant if he thinks that they should be brought to the attention of the tribunal, although there have been differing views expressed about the enthusiasm with which presenting officers fulfil that function.[21] The tribunal and the claimant may be assisted insofar as it is unlikely that a presenting officer will find himself defending at a hearing his own decision on an original claim and objectivity may be easier to display in those circumstances. The unusual practice of allowing adjudication officers to defend their own decisions as presenting officers is likely to

[13] This is just the same under the new regulations which permit the clerk to the tribunal to remain with the members during their deliberations: Adjudication Regulations, (above, n. 1) reg.2(2).

[14] The apparent complexity of the pre-hearing procedure; fears about the hearing; the inaccessibility of some tribunal venues; see K. Bell *et al* "National Insurance Local Tribunals: A Research Study" (1975) 4 *Journal of Social Policy* 1, at pp. 5–6.

[15] The independence of N.I.L.T.s was always difficult to establish. The Department of Health and Social Security did all the administration and the hearing was often held in a "government" building. The chairman often stressed at the hearing that the tribunal was independent but the claimant might find it hard to believe!

[16] Bell, *op. cit.* at pp. 11–21.

[17] M. Herman, *Administrative Justice and Supplementary Benefits* (1972); J. Fulbrook *Administrative Justice and the Unemployed* (1978); M. Adler, E. Burns and R. Johnson, "The Conduct of Tribunal Hearings," in M. Adler and A. Bradley, *Justice, Discretion and Poverty* (1976); K. Bell, *Research Study on Supplementary Benefit Appeal Tribunals, Review of Main Findings: Conclusions: Recommendations*, DHSS (1975).

[18] Adjudication Regulations, (above, n. 1) reg.19(3).

[19] *Ibid.* reg.19(2).

[20] For a lawyer's analysis of his function, see Diplock L.J. in *R.* v. *Deputy Industrial Injuries Commissioner, ex p. Moore* [1965] 1 Q.B. 456 at p. 486. A claimant would not necessarily take the same view, even if he knew what was meant by *lis inter partes* and *amicus curiae*!

[21] Herman, *op.cit.* and Bell, *op.cit.* above, n.17.

emphasise the adversarial nature of the proceedings at the expense of the inquisitorial.[22]

It is legitimate to ask to what extent an inquisitorial mode is adopted in the hearing. It is true that the tribunal members are more involved in the direct questioning of both sides than a judge would be, and the informal structure of the proceedings allows particular points, once raised to be followed through to a conclusion immediately if that appears convenient.[23] However, apart from the obligations of the presenting officer to give a balanced view, the essential nature of the proceedings still appears to be adversarial with the responsibility resting on the two "sides" to raise the arguments and provide the evidence that will ultimately decide the case.[24]

2. The Industrial Tribunal

The rules of procedure for a hearing at an Industrial Tribunal are, in some respects, more explicit. The objectives to be attained at the hearing are included as part of the rules. In respect of the S.S.A.T., we noted that the normal provision is simply for the chairman to determine the procedure; for the Industrial Tribunal, the rules specify that:

> "The tribunal shall conduct the hearing in such manner as it considers most suitable to the clarification of the issues before it and generally to the just handling of the proceedings; it shall so far as appears to it appropriate seek to avoid formality in its proceedings. . . . "[25]

Although those may be the implicit objectives of other tribunals, it is interesting that they should be explicit for the Industrial Tribunal, and consequently ironic that the Industrial Tribunal is generally reckoned to be one of the more formal and legalistic of the tribunals.

The hearing takes place in public unless the tribunal is of the opinion that a private hearing is appropriate on the grounds of national security or other specified grounds[26]; any person entitled to appear at the hearing is entitled to give evidence, call witnesses, question any witness and address the tribunal.[27] If a party has failed to attend the hearing, any documents that he has submitted may be treated as written representations, but subject to that provision the hearing may proceed or may be adjourned at the discretion of the tribunal.[28]

The order of events at a hearing is likely to differ with the nature of the

---

[22] Apparently this practice is increasing in some parts of the country, as a result of DHSS staff shortages.

[23] One of the authors experienced a N.I.L.T in which he was interrupted in the midst of representations by comments from the claimant's husband who was attending the hearing as a "member of the public" and was sitting at the back of the room. The chairman encouraged him to speak up and proceeded to deal with the point he raised by questioning both the claimant and the insurance officer. Having dealt with it to his satisfaction the chairman asked if the husband had any further observations . . .

[24] But see pp. 551–554 on the burden of proof in social security tribunals.

[25] The Industrial Tribunals (Rules of Procedure) Regulations 1980 (S.I. 1980 No. 884) reg. 8(1).

[26] Ibid. reg. 7(1).

[27] Ibid. reg. 8(2).

[28] Ibid. regs. 7(3), 8(3).

claim.[29] In the ordinary unfair dismissal case the burden of proof lies with the employer to show that the dismissal was not unfair and he will normally be called on first. If the employee alleges constructive dismissal, or the employer otherwise disputes the fact of dismissal, then it will be for the employee to begin and make out his case. Whoever has the first word, the procedure thereafter is, in form, similar to court procedure with the calling, examination and cross-examination of witnesses leading to final statements on both sides. The chairman and members of the tribunal may ask more questions and become more involved in the proceedings than a judge would, and the rules about the correct form of examination and cross-examination are relaxed along with the rules of evidence,[30] but an observer at a hearing would receive a strong impression of adversarial procedure and formality.

3. RENT ASSESSMENT COMMITTEES

The Rent Assessment Committee exercises jurisdiction of two kinds. It receives and determines objections against the fixing and registration (or confirmation) of a fair rent by a rent officer[31] and, when exercising the powers of a rent tribunal, it controls rent and security of tenure in respect of "restricted contracts."[32] Some potential confusion has been created by the Housing Act 1980 in the abolition of the rent tribunal and the reallocation of its functions to a Rent Assessment Committee[33] but we shall attempt to distinguish the two by reference to R.A.C. and R.A.C. (R.T.).

The R.A.C. and R.A.C. (R.T.) share a feature which distinguish them from the other tribunals we have so far considered, in that they do not need to hold a hearing. The obligation lies on the landlord and the tenant to request the opportunity to make oral representations and there are provisions for the disposal of the matter on written representations in the

---

[29] For Industrial Tribunal procedure generally, see S. Anderman, *The Law of Unfair Dismissal* (1978), Appendix IV; I.T. Smith and J.C. Wood, *Industrial Law* (2nd ed. 1983), pp. 197–206; B.A. Hepple and P. O'Higgins, *Encyclopaedia of Labour Relations Law*, paras. 1–1541, 1–5000 and Part 4A.

[30] S.I. 1980, No. 884, reg. 8(1) (see n.25 above), and see pp. 549–559 below for further discussion.

[31] Under the provisions of the Rent Act 1977 Part IV. See J.T. Farrand and A. Arden, *Rent Acts and Regulations* (2nd ed., 1981); D. Yates and A.J. Hawkins, *Landlord and Tenant Law* (1981), Chap. 11

[32] As defined in Rent Act 1977, ss. 19–21. See Farrand and Arden, *op.cit.*; Yates and Hawkins, *op.cit.* Chap. 14.

[33] s.72. The provisions of the section are, at first sight, so startling that they may properly be set out in full:

  "(1) Rent tribunals, as constituted for the purposes of the 1977 Act, are hereby abolished and section 76 of the 1977 Act (Constitution, etc. of rent tribunals) is hereby repealed.

  (2) As from the commencement of this section the functions which, under the 1977 Act, are conferred on rent tribunals shall be carried out by rent assessment committees.

  (3) A rent assessment committee shall, when constituted to carry out functions so conferred, be known as a rent tribunal."

The object appears to be to achieve a uniformity of appointment for the two bodies, without diminishing their functions. See Farrand and Arden, *op.cit.* at pp. 104–105.

absence of an application for a hearing.[34] It should be emphasised that the absence of a hearing does not relieve the tribunal of considering the matter, indeed it points up the inquisitorial role because the committee then have an obligation to make such inquiry as they think fit and consider any information supplied or representation made by the parties.[35] This demonstrates the necessity for procedural safeguards throughout the determination of an issue—they are not confined to a hearing.

If the landlord or tenant requests the opportunity to make oral representations then the R.A.C. or the R.A.C. (R.T.), as appropriate, will arrange a hearing. For the hearing, the procedural rules are slightly different in respect of the R.A.C. and R.A.C. (R.T.) but is is unlikely that the formal differences are reflected in the actual procedure adopted by the chairman.

The R.A.C. rules provide that, " . . . the parties shall be heard in such order, and . . . the procedure shall be such as the committee shall determine: a party may call witnesses, give evidence on his own behalf and cross-examine any witnesses called by the other party." No reference is made to a right to representation, and the rules specify that the hearing shall be in public unless the committee decide otherwise "for special reasons."[36]

In respect of the R.A.C. (R.T.), "the procedure at a hearing shall be such as the rent tribunal may determine" and a party may appear in person or be represented by anyone he wishes. However, the hearing will be in private unless the tribunal, on their own initiative or the application of a party, determine otherwise. There is no specific provision for the calling of witnesses, giving of evidence, or cross-examination.[37]

These formal differences may not actually affect the *style* of the hearing but it is odd that there should be discrepancies in the procedural rules, particularly where the same members are involved in each type of hearing. The R.A.C. (R.T.) rules are the later and there are echoes in them of the rules which have been developed in social security tribunals, yet the allocation of the functions of the rent tribunal to the R.A.C. in 1980 ought to have provided an opportunity for standardisation. If there can be no accepted procedural criteria in this case, what hope is there for establishing uniform procedure across the wide range of tribunals?

B. EVIDENCE

In civil and criminal trials there are clear rules about the sort of evidence which may be given; the location of the burden of proof; and the standard of proof. Such clear rules are not to be found in tribunal adjudication. In the adversarial procedure of the civil or criminal trial the burden of proof is readily identified, but in the inquisitorial atmosphere of most tribunals it is

[34] Rent Act 1977, Sched. 11, paras. 6, 7(1)(*b*); Rent Assessment Committee (England and Wales) Regulations 1971 (S.I. 1971 No. 1065) reg. 6 and Rent Act 1977 Sched. 1 para. 9(1) (R.A.C.s): Rent Assessment Committees (England and Wales) (Rent Tribunal) Regulations 1980 (S.I. 1980 No. 1700) reg. 4 and Rent Act 1977, s.78(1), (2) (R.A.C. (RT)).

[35] S.I. 1971 No. 1065, (n.34 above) paras. 7(1)(*a*), 9(1). (R.A.C.s): Rent Act 1977, s.78(2) (R.A.C. (RT)).

[36] S.I. 1971 No. 1065, regs. 3(1), 4.

[37] S.I. 1980 No. 1700, regs. 6, 7.

more difficult to locate. Some of the rules which render relevant evidence inadmissible at a trial rely heavily for their justification on the inability of a jury to decide the proper weight to be given to potentially prejudicial evidence.[38] An experienced tribunal chairman, it is said, ought to be able to attribute the correct amount of weight to almost every piece of relevant information. Further, it is always argued that the absence of "strict" rules of evidence enhances the informality of tribunal procedure and makes it more comprehensible to the layman.

However, a balance needs to be maintained between the requirements of informality and the interests of the parties to the tribunal. It may be assumed that some rules of evidence are specifically designed to prevent a conclusion being reached on unreliable information,[39] so that it would not be acceptable to abandon the principles of evidence altogether in tribunal adjudication. We shall hope to illustrate how tribunals cope with the problems of onus and standard of proof, relevance and admissibility.

1. GENERAL PRINCIPLES[40]

There is an important difference between courts and tribunals in that many tribunals rely on the expertise of the chairmen and members in determining questions of fact.[41] It is interesting to note that the jury, at its inception, was intended to rely upon the collective knowledge of its members, although such knowledge could now constitute a reason for excusal or challenge.[42] The justification for tribunal adjudication rests partly on the expertise of the adjudicators in the appropriate field, and there is ample authority for the proposition that they may rely on their own specialist knowledge to interpret evidence given to them by the parties or to fill in gaps where evidence has not been given.[43] Were this not the case there would be no possibility of an appeal succeeding in a social security matter where the appellant chose not to appear, was unrepresented and made no written representations. The chances of success for such an appellant are slender but they do exist![44]

Those tribunals which are not merely administrative bodies but exercise

---

[38] A detailed consideration of rules of evidence is outside the scope of this book, but an example of the exclusionary rules referred to is that which prevents the admission of evidence of previous convictions in a criminal trial. Though highly relevant, that particular evidence needs to be weighed carefully in arriving at a conclusion about whether the accused has committed a crime on *this* occasion.

[39] The exclusion of hearsay evidence is based mainly on its unreliability, and such evidence is treated with considerable caution in tribunal proceedings although it is admissible, see p. 556, below.

[40] There is little available material about the use of evidence in tribunals, but see Carolyn Yates, "Supplementary Benefit Appeals and the Rules of Evidence" [1981] J.S.W.L. 173; J. Fulbrook, *Administrative Justice and the Unemployed* (1978), pp. 268–276; R.E. Wraith and P.G. Hutchesson, *Administrative Tribunals* (1973), pp. 265–273.

[41] Indeed, expertise is a criterion for the appointment of members in many tribunals, see above, p. 151.

[42] See below, pp. 607, 611.

[43] J.A. Smillie, "The Problem of 'Official Notice'—Reliance by Administrative Tribunals on the Personal Knowledge of their Members" [1975] P.L. 64.

[44] There are reported instances in K. Bell *et al*, "National Insurance Local Tribunals: A Research Study" (1975) 4 *Journal of Social Policy* 1.

a judicial function are bound to apply the rules of natural justice.[45] The way in which a tribunal deals with evidence must accord with those rules which require, broadly, that the proceedings must be fair in all the circumstances. In respect of the giving of evidence it seems that every party to a hearing must be given an opportunity to put his case and to call relevant evidence in support.[46] That right is supported by the rules of procedure of some tribunals[47] and although there was a discretion on the part of the chairman of Supplementary Benefit Appeal Tribunals to exclude evidence which is clearly irrelevant or immaterial, that discretion had to be exercised with care and with a due regard to the necessity of allowing justice to be seen to be done.[48] In the Industrial Tribunal there is, apparently, no discretion to exclude evidence which would be admissible in civil proceedings by virtue of the Civil Evidence Act, but there is discretion to include evidence which would be inadmissible.[49] Such a discretion is often referred to as a discretion to disregard the "strict" rules of evidence.[50]

2. THE STANDARD OF PROOF AND THE BURDEN OF PROOF

Proof beyond reasonable doubt is the standard adopted in the trial of criminal matters, and in civil cases the party bearing the burden of proof must establish the case on a balance of probabilities.[51] It is the latter standard that is adopted in tribunal proceedings, although some writers suggest that in particular tribunals the chairman and members may not always identify the standard as clearly as that.[52] The standard of proof is closely linked in reported decisions of tribunals with the question of the burden of proof and who bears it. In an early decision of a National Insurance Commissioner the formulation of Lord Birkenhead L.C. in *Lancaster* v. *Blackwell Colliery Co.*[53] was adopted:

> "If the facts which are proved gave rise to conflicting inferences of
> equal degrees of probability, so that the choice between them is a
> mere matter of conjecture, then of course the applicant fails to prove

[45] See H.W.R. Wade, *Administrative Law*, (1982), 5th ed., Chap. 15. All the tribunals we have so far considered have a judicial function.

[46] *R.* v. *Hull Prison Board of Visitors, ex p. St. Germain (No. 2)* [1979] 1 W.L.R. 1401.

[47] See above, pp. 544, 547, 549.

[48] Although this proposition is taken from R(SB) 6/82 and related to Supplementary Benefit Appeal Tribunals, it is likely to have wider application as an expression of one of the requirements of natural justice. The dilemma for a tribunal chairman is that he may not be able to take a view about the relevance of evidence until he has heard it. Presumably, the same principle will be applied in respect of the new Social Security Appeal Tribunals.

[49] *Rosedale Mouldings Ltd.* v. *Sibley* [1980] I.R.L.R. 387.

[50] This is a significant phrase because it embodies the notion that some basic rules of evidence must still apply, even in tribunals. The phrase is also to be found in the standard terms of reference to arbitration under the small claims procedure in the county court, see above, p. 411.

[51] For a full consideration of the standard of proof in civil and criminal matters, see, *Cross on Evidence* (1979), 5th ed., Chap. 5.

[52] There was particular doubt about S.B.A.T.s.: J. Fulbrook, *Administrative Justice and the Unemployed* (1978) p. 272. There are isolated examples where a higher standard of proof has been required, *e.g. Judd* v. *Minister of Pensions and National Insurance* [1966] 2 Q.B. 580, where the Divisional Court held that the Minister must establish his case beyond reasonable doubt in certain matters before the Pensions Appeal Tribunal.

[53] (1919) 12 B.W.C.C. 400 at p. 406, cited in C.I. 401/50.

his case, because it is plain in these matters the onus is on the
applicant. But where the known facts are not equally balancing
probabilities as to their respective value, and where a reasonable man
might hold that the more probable conclusion is that for which the
applicant contends, then the arbitrator is justified in drawing an
inference in his favour."

The question of which party, if any, bears the burden of proof in tribunal
proceedings really needs to be examined in respect of each individual
tribunal,[54] starting from the assumption that it will normally be the party
making the assertion who must prove it. That assumption, which derives
from the position in the civil or criminal trial,[55] may not be appropriate
where the proceedings are conducted on a truly inquisitorial basis with the
tribunal reaching an evaluation of the information presented, yet it
exercises a powerful influence.

It may not, of course, be necessary to rely on an assumption. Provision
may have been made by statute,[56] or by procedural rules,[57] or in the
decisions of particular tribunals,[58] stipulating where the burden of proof
will lie. Where the jurisdiction of the tribunal is original, rather than
appellate, it will also usually be clear where the burden lies, even if it may
shift during the hearing. In the Industrial Tribunal, for example, when the
applicant alleges that he has been unfairly dismissed it will be for the
employer to prove that the dismissal was not unfair. If the employer
disputes that there has been a dismissal the onus lies with the *employee* to
prove that there has.[59]

In respect of some tribunals, no importance attaches to the question of
burden of proof because the tribunal is arriving at a valuation rather than
establishing a right or claim. The Rent Assessment Committee provides an
example in that it is the obligation of the committee to arrive at its own
judgment of a fair rent in the light of any representations made by the
landlord and/or tenant.[60] Neither has the burden of proof—the committee
must make its own decision which may not reflect the contentions of either
party.

---

[54] We have already made the point that it is impossible to generalise about tribunals. The
examples which follow are from tribunals which we have described elsewhere.

[55] See *Cross on Evidence* (1979) 5th ed. at pp. 94–98.

[56] *e.g.* Redundancy Payments Act 1965, s.9(1), (2) providing that on a reference to a
tribunal a persons's employment during any period shall be deemed to have been continuous
unless the contrary is proved, and that a dismissal shall be presumed to have been on account
of redundancy, unless the contrary is proved. *Cf. Secretary of State for Employment* v. *Globe
Elastic Thread Co. Ltd.* [1980] A.C. 506. See also, Social Security Act 1975, s.19(1) excusing
from disqualification for unemployment benefit those who can prove that they were not
participating in or directly interested in the relevant trade dispute.

[57] *e.g.* The Immigration Appeals (Procedure) Rules 1972 (S.I. 1972 No. 1684), r.31, which
deals specifically with the burden of proof and locates it on the appellant or the Secretary of
State depending on the fact in issue.

[58] *e.g.* The decision of the National Insurance Commissioner that the burden of proof on
the allegation of cohabitation should lie with the insurance officer, R(G) 1/53. This decision
has been consistently followed. Where the insurance officer alleges that a claimant is
disqualified from unemployment benefit for leaving employment voluntarily without just
cause, the onus is initially with him but switches to the claimant to establish just cause, R(U)
20/64.

[59] See above, n.29.

[60] See above, p. 549.

The new Social Security Appeal Tribunal presents difficulties in that it is not easy to decide who is making the assertion. In respect of supplementary benefit and national insurance benefits the claimant will be appealing against the refusal of a claim, in whole or in part, by the Department. On the face of it one might expect that the claimant would therefore bear the burden of proof at the hearing either because he is the appellant, or because he is asserting entitlement. Alternatively, one might argue that it should be for the Department to show why it has refused to allow the claim, proving the lack of entitlement of the claimant.[61] The position may become clearer as the new tribunal develops a practice, but it may not gain too much help from the practice of two former tribunals of which it is composed.

In Supplementary Benefit Appeal Tribunals,[62] it was the duty of the tribunal to determine, subject to the law, what was fair and just in the circumstances of any particular case—establishing the facts of the case to its satisfaction and determining any contested issues.[63] This has been described as an inquisitorial function, although a Tribunal of Social Security Commissioners[64] recently declared that the claimant was under the primary duty to make out his case and that he should not expect to rely on the tribunal's own expertise.[65] This appeared to cast an evidential burden on the claimant, although it was conceded that there would be an obligation on a tribunal to canvass a particular factual point (unprompted by either party) where it was obvious and self-evident.[66] With some allegations—the discontinuance of benefit on the ground of cohabitation is one[67]—the onus of proof was clearly placed on the benefit officer, but the more general point had been left vague.[68] Where the appeal was against the refusal of a single payment, the claimant had to, " . . . bring himself within the provisions of [the regulations]."[69]

---

[61] J. Fulbrook, *Administrative Justice and the Unemployed* (1978) pp. 272–273.

[62] Carolyn Yates, "Supplementary Benefit Appeals and the Rules of Evidence" [1981] J.S.W.L. 273.

[63] This is a paraphrase from *Supplementary Benefit Appeal Tribunals—Guide to Procedure* (D.H.S.S.).

[64] Normally appeals are heard by one Commissioner, but a tribunal of three is convened where there are important points for decision. Their decision carries greater weight than that of a single Commissioner.

[65] R(SB)2/83. It was contended on behalf of the claimant that the local tribunal should, of their own motion, investigate the origin and nature of funds in a personal account in a building society, in order to determine whether they truly represented business assets and not personal monies. That contention was rejected.

[66] However, "We would be slow to convict a tribunal of failure to identify an uncanvassed factual point in favour of the claimant in the absence of the most obvious and clear-cut circumstances." R(SB) 2/83, para. 11.

[67] The same principles both in relation to the burden of proof and the appropriate criteria are applied to supplementary benefit as to insurance benefits, R(SB) 17/81; *Crake* v. *Supplementary Benefits Commission* [1982] 1 All E.R. 498; *cf.* above, n.58.

[68] This vagueness is illustrated by an example postulated by Carolyn Yates, *op. cit.* at p. 276. On a claim for a single payment for clothing the evidence of the Investigating Officer and the claimant concerning need is in conflict. The claimant writes to the tribunal but does not attend; the Investigating Officer's view will be put through the presenting officer. No-one with any personal knowledge is present at the tribunal. In the absence of a clear guide as to who bears the onus of proof what is the tribunal to do?

[69] R (SB) 15/81. If this phrase is read literally it appears to place an onus on the claimant who would, therefore, lose the appeal in the example considered in the preceding footnote.

In National Insurance Local Tribunals the position was only slightly clearer. There was a good deal more guidance from the Commissioners as to the onus of proof on specific matters,[70] but the general position still exhibited confusion. In dealing with a case which came out of a claim for industrial disablement benefit, Buckley L.J. had this to say:

> "As regards the burden of proof, as Lord Denning M.R. has pointed out, these are not adversary proceedings: they are inquisitorial proceedings; and in such proceedings questions of burden of proof do not arise in the same way in which they would in proceedings between parties in a law suit. It is for the medical board or the medical appeal tribunal, as the case may be, to investigate the case inquisitorially and to decide whether the claimant is entitled to benefit under the Act. But, of course, the fact remains that the medical board or the medical appeal tribunal, as the case may be, must be satisfied that the claimant is entitled to benefit: and so, in a sense, and subject to such statutory assumptions as are prescribed by the Act itself, it does rest with the claimant in the end to make out his claim."[71]

Again, where there were specific assertions by the insurance officer he bore the onus of proof. In a case of disqualification from unemployment benefit it was for the insurance officer to prove that the claimant lost his job through misconduct,[72] or that there was a stoppage of work due to a trade dispute,[73] or that one of the other grounds provided for in the regulations existed.[74] It was for the claimant to establish the basic conditions of entitlement.[75]

The considerable uncertainties reflected in the practice of the two former tribunals need to be resolved by the S.S.A.T. Indeed, it might be regarded as one of the primary responsibilities of the new tribunal to clarify this difficult question. It can hardly be appropriate to adopt differing rules according to the nature of the claim and a code of procedure might be advantageous, so that claimants and their representatives could be certain about their obligation to adduce evidence and establish the relevant facts.

3. RELEVANCE AND ADMISSIBILITY

Detailed exclusionary rules have been developed in civil and criminal matters which render certain evidence inadmissible on the grounds that it would be unduly prejudicial or unreliable. Inevitably, the operation of such rules can lead to the exclusion of evidence which is highly relevant to the facts in issue. In tribunal proceedings the test of *relevance* is given

---

[70] The collected decisions can be found in D. Neligan, *Social Security Case Law. Digest of Commissioners' Decisions, Vols. 1 & 2* (1979 and updated).

[71] *R. v. National Insurance Commissioner, ex p. Viscusi* [1974] 1 W.L.R. 646 at p. 654.

[72] R (U) 2/60.

[73] By inference from s.19(1) Social Security Act 1975.

[74] The onus may shift to the claimant if the insurance officer establishes the basic grounds for disqualification, see above, n. 58; *n.b.* the insurance officer is now referred to as the adjudication officer: Health and Social Services and Social Security Adjudications Act 1983, s.25 and Sched. 8.

[75] R(I) 32/61 supports this proposition, at least with regard to industrial injury claims and it may also be supported by the dictum of Buckley L.J. cited in the text.

priority with the consequence that very little evidence is likely to be excluded altogether from consideration. It may be that particular sorts of evidence are treated with some circumspection by the chairman and members, but it is expected that they will be able to assess the value and reliability of the evidence given and accord it appropriate weight in their deliberations. Many of the strict exclusionary rules of evidence result from a fear that the jury will be unable to judge satisfactorily how much significance to attach to inherently unreliable or prejudicial evidence,[76] and that fear should not be present when it is tribunal members who are adjudicating. Consequently, the strict rules of evidence are normally disregarded in favour of a much wider test of admissibility:

> " . . . technical rules of evidence, however, form no part of the rules of natural justice. The requirement that a person exercising quasi-judicial functions must base his decision on evidence means no more than it must be based upon material which tends logically to show the existence or non-existence of facts relevant to the issue to be determined, or to show the likelihood or unlikelihood of the occurrence of some future event the occurrence of which would be relevant. It means that he must not spin a coin or consult an astrologer, but he may take into account any material which, as a matter of reason, has some probative value in the sense mentioned above. If it is capable of having any probative value, the weight to be attached to it is a matter for the person to whom Parliament has entrusted the task of deciding the issue."[77]

This statement of Diplock L.J. has been cited with approval on a number of occasions and applied to different adjudications. The judge was actually dealing with the decision of a deputy Industrial Injuries Commissioner on a claim for industrial injury benefit, but his words have also been held to apply to an appeal to the Minister under the Town and Country Planning Act 1962[78]; an adjudication by a prison Board of Visitors under the Prison Rules 1964[79]; and a formal investigation of a complaint of unlawful discrimination under the Race Relations Act 1976.[80] This general rule, that evidence is admissible in tribunal proceedings if it is of some "probative value", even though it would be inadmissible in court, has been embodied in procedural rules[81] and adopted in tribunal decisions.[82] It would appear that probative means relevant.

This rule of admissibility has been formulated in the context of the principles of natural justice and it is still the case that there is an obligation to ensure that each party has a full and fair hearing. In the Industrial Tribunal the general rule has been expressed in a slightly modified way to permit the exclusion of evidence where its admission, " . . . could in some

---

[76] That is why the rules are stricter in criminal cases, but have been relaxed in civil cases where it is now highly unusual to have a jury, see p. 534, above.

[77] *R.* v. *Deputy Industrial Injuries Commissioner, ex p. Moore* [1965] 1 Q.B. 456 at p. 488.

[78] *T.A. Miller Ltd.* v. *Minister of Housing and Local Government* [1968] 1 W.L.R. 992.

[79] *R.* v. *Hull Prison Board of Visitors, ex p. St. Germain (No. 2)* [1979] 1 W.L.R. 1401.

[80] *R.* v. *Commission for Racial Equality, ex p. Cottrell* [1980] 1 W.L.R. 1580.

[81] The Immigration Appeals (Procedure) Rules 1972 (S.I. 1972 No. 1684).

[82] See below, n. 85.

way adversely affect the reaching of a proper decision in the case."[83] In *R.* v. *Hull Prison Board of Visitors, ex p. St. Germain (No. 2)*,[84] Geoffrey Lane L.J. held that there may be circumstances in which a prison Board of Visitors should not admit hearsay evidence unless the prisoner accused was given the opportunity to cross-examine the maker of the statement. The powers of the tribunal to dispense with the strict rules of evidence must always be subject to the overriding obligation to provide a fair hearing. In social security tribunals the general rule was followed and many reported decisions expressed the power of the tribunals to admit any relevant evidence.[85]

The weight that is to be attached to relevant evidence is a matter for the tribunal and it is instructive to consider the approach of various tribunals in respect of hearsay evidence—the sort of evidence which tribunals have most often been invited to exclude.

4. HEARSAY

A hearsay statement is one which is made, orally or in writing, by a person other than the witness testifying and which is offered to prove a fact asserted in the statement.[86] An adjudication officer, investigating the question of whether a person in receipt of unemployment benefit is actually working, states that he has interviewed the claimant's next door neighbours who have told him that they saw the claimant leave his house every morning with a bag of tools, and that the claimant has admitted to them that he is "making a bit on the side." The statement of the adjudication officer, when put to the tribunal by the presenting officer at the hearing of the claimant's appeal against disqualification from benefit, would constitute hearsay.

The rules restricting the admissibility of hearsay evidence in civil courts are less stringent than they were,[87] but the rules in criminal matters remain strict and their justification is said to be that hearsay evidence may not be relevant; cannot be tested in court because of the absence of the maker of the statement; and depends upon the potentially inaccurate repetition of the statement by the witness.[88] Set against those difficulties is the undeniable fact, recognised by tribunals, that, "If tribunals were obliged to reject hearsay evidence . . . many claimants would find it quite impossible to establish their claims."[89]

The solution adopted by tribunals in most circumstances is to admit the evidence whilst expressing caution as to the weight to be attached to it, and

---

[83] *Coral Squash Clubs Ltd.* v. *Matthews* [1979] I.R.L.R. 390 at p. 392. The Employment Appeal Tribunal in that case held that it was, " . . . clear that an Industrial Tribunal is not bound by the strict rules of evidence but should exercise its good sense in weighing matters which come before it."

[84] [1979] 3 All E.R. 545.

[85] *e.g.* R(I) 36/61, R(I) 13/74, R(U) 12/56, R(U) 5/77.

[86] This is a very abbreviated definition. Interested students should consult *Cross on Evidence* (5th ed., 1979), Chap. 17.

[87] Reforms were effected by the Civil Evidence Act 1968. See Cross, *op. cit.* Chap. 18.

[88] See Law Reform Committee, 13th Report, *Hearsay Evidence in Civil Proceedings* (Cmnd. 2964, 1966); Criminal Law Revision Committee, 11th Report, *Evidence (General)* (Cmnd. 4991, 1972) pp. 132–154.

[89] R(U) 12/56.

stressing the desirability of having other evidence available as well. Hearsay evidence may well be unreliable and some consideration has recently been given to safeguards that may be appropriate. It is useful first to look at the particular case and then to consider the extent to which it may influence other tribunals in their treatment of hearsay.

R. v. *Hull Prison Board of Visitors, ex p. St. Germain (No. 2)*[90] dealt with the propriety of disciplinary proceedings conducted by the Board of Visitors of Hull Prison in the aftermath of a serious riot at the prison in 1976. The proceedings were conducted under the Prison Rules 1964[91] and it was later alleged, in the course of an application to the Divisional Court for an order of certiorari,[92] that the board had admitted and acted on hearsay evidence in that it had heard evidence from the governor of the prison about the contents of reports made by prison officers who did not give evidence to the board in person. It was argued before the Divisional Court that the admission of such evidence constituted a breach of the rules of natural justice. In dealing with this argument, Geoffrey Lane L.J. referred to the statement of Diplock L.J. in *Moore's* case which is set out above.[93] He reaffirmed the general rule that hearsay evidence is admissible but stated that it should be subject to the overriding obligation to provide a fair hearing.[94]

The provision of a fair hearing may oblige the board, depending upon the circumstances of the case and the nature of the evidence, not only to give the accused an opportunity to know of and comment on the evidence, but also to cross-examine the maker of the original statement. The court recognised the enormous burden which might be placed on the board by a requirement that the witness be made available for cross-examination, but also noted that hearsay evidence would not be resorted to in the total absence of direct evidence and therefore directed that where the problem of producing the witness is insuperable the hearsay evidence should not be admitted or, if admitted already, should be dismissed from consideration. The court found support for this view in a Home Office report on Adjudication Procedure in Prisons.[95]

This may fairly be regarded as an unusual case and, perhaps, of limited application. The proceedings involved were akin to criminal proceedings; the procedural irregularities were clear[96]; the Home Office report had also concluded that unsupported hearsay should not be admitted. However, it may provide a basis on which other tribunals can decide a clearer policy about the circumstances in which hearsay will be admitted. The crucial disadvantage in the admission of hearsay is the denial of the opportunity of cross-examination with its twin objectives of eliciting information, and testing the memory, veracity and credibility of a witness.[97]

In the Industrial Tribunal the policy merely seems to be to require the

[90] [1979] 1 W.L.R. 1401.
[91] (S.I. 1964 No. 388).
[92] See below, p. 747.
[93] R. v. *Deputy Industrial Injuries Commissioners, ex p. Moore* [1965] 1 Q.B. 456. See above, p. 555.
[94] [1979] 1 W.L.R. 1410 at p. 1409D.
[95] *Ibid.* at p. 1410.
[96] The board of visitors had also refused to call certain witnesses requested by the accused.
[97] See Cross, *op. cit.* at pp. 256–257.

members of the tribunal to consider carefully what *weight* to attach to admitted hearsay evidence. In *Coral Squash Clubs Ltd.* v. *Matthews*,[98] the Industrial Tribunal had refused to admit hearsay evidence about alleged licensing offences by the manager of a squash club, on the grounds that where the allegation was of a criminal offence and where the witnesses could have been located and produced the strict rule of exclusion should be applied. Their decision was reversed by the Employment Appeal Tribunal who ruled the evidence to be admissible, holding that the question of criminality was not in issue before the tribunal and that the failure to produce witnesses merely went to the weight of the evidence. The E.A.T. stated that a tribunal should, " . . . exercise its good sense in weighing the matters that come before it."[99]

Social Security tribunals have taken much the same view. In an early decision, a Commissioner warned that the value of evidence which would be inadmissible in a court of law must be carefully considered and may be of very little weight,[1] and that phrasing has been adopted in subsequent decisions.[2] A particular type of hearsay which social security tribunals have been unwilling to accept is the statements of claimants' representatives. The Commissioner has said that such statements are not evidence and that where questions of fact are in issue on which a claimant or other qualified witness can speak they should be called to give evidence.[3]

What is lacking is a clear policy on the criteria to be applied in determining the admissibility and reliability of hearsay evidence.[4] Our tribunals have contented themselves so far with the broadest of exhortations to weigh such evidence carefully, and the *Hull Prison* case is likely to be regarded as of specific, rather than general, application. Even where the matter has been considered and included in procedural rules, the tribunal is given no guidance.[5]

5. THE EXCLUSION OF WITNESSES

The requirement of natural justice that a party should be given a fair hearing is normally taken to comprehend the right to put his own case and correct or contradict statements that have been made by the other party.[6] This is likely to be achieved by the calling of witnesses. The right to call witnesses is set out in the procedural rules for the tribunals we have so far considered in detail.[7] However, the right appears to be subject to the

---

[98] [1979] I.R.L.R. 390.

[99] *Ibid.* at p. 392.

[1] C.I. 97/49.

[2] R(G) 1/51; R(U) 12/56; R(U) 5/77.

[3] R(I) 36/61.

[4] An Australian commentator put it thus:" . . . English administrative case law has taken the question very little further than merely saying that hearsay can be admitted. It is therefore to the U.S. experience that we must turn . . . ." G.A. Flick, "The Opportunity to Controvert Adverse Testimony in Administrative Proceedings: A Search for Criteria" (1978) 28 U. Toronto L.J. 1.

[5] The Immigration Appeals (Procedure) Rules 1972, (S.I. 1972 No. 1684) r.29(1): "An appellate authority may receive oral, documentary or other evidence of any fact which appears to the authority to be relevant to the appeal, notwithstanding that such evidence would be inadmissible in a court of law."

[6] See generally H.W.R. Wade, *Administrative Law* (5th ed., 1982), Chap. 15.

[7] See above, pp. 544, 547.

discretion of the chairman. His obligation is to ensure a fair hearing, but he is not required to hear every witness that one of the parties might wish to call.

In the *Hull Prison*[8] case, where this point was also in issue, Geoffrey Lane L.J. held that it was not inconsistent with the principles of natural justice that the chairman of the board of visitors should have a discretion to refuse to allow evidence to be given.

> "However, that discretion has to be exercised reasonably, in good faith, and on proper grounds . . . . A more serious question was raised whether the discretion could be validly exercised where it was based on considerable administrative inconvenience being caused if the request to call a witness or witnesses was permitted . . . mere administrative difficulties, simpliciter, are not in our view good enough. Convenience and justice are often not on speaking terms."[9]

The Divisional Court concluded that the exclusion of witnesses because the chairman considered there to be ample evidence against the accused, or because he misunderstood the nature of the prisoners' defence would clearly be wrong, but that it may be justifiable where the accused is merely trying to render the hearing impracticable or where it would be unnecessary to call so many witnesses to establish the point at issue.[10]

Again, as with the hearsay point, the decision of the Divisional Court may be rather narrower than the current practice in other tribunals and may be restricted to its own facts if its principles were to be argued in general. The position in Social Security tribunals was stated recently by a Commissioner in R(SB)6/82. The decision related to a S.B.A.T., but the principles will presumably be equally applicable to the new S.S.A.T. In that decision, the chairman of a S.B.A.T. had refused to hear a witness whom the claimant wished to call. On the facts, the Commissioner concluded that there had been an error of law since the witness appeared to have relevant and material evidence to give, and the case was remitted for re-hearing. On the general point the Commissioner said:

> "Tribunals are not bound to hear evidence which is clearly irrelevant or immaterial, whether it be from a witness actually giving evidence before the tribunal or from a proposed witness. The discretion to stop or curtail such evidence should, however, always be exercised with care, and in its exercise due regard should in my view always be paid to the necessity of allowing justice to be seen to be done."[11]

Industrial Tribunals will, no doubt, adopted similar criteria. The Employment Appeal Tribunal has stated specifically that an Industrial Tribunal has no discretion to exclude evidence that is admissible at law,[12] and an attempt by any tribunal to exclude such evidence is likely to constitute an infringement of the principles of natural justice.[13]

[8] [1979] 1 W.L.R. 1401, see above, p. 557.
[9] *Ibid.* at p. 1406.
[10] *Ibid.* at p. 1406.
[11] R (SB) 6/82, para. 5, a decision of Mr. J.S. Watson.
[12] *Rosedale Mouldings Ltd.* v. *Sibley* [1980] I.R.L.R. 387.
[13] Evidence which is admissible at common law must, by definition, be relevant and the discretion to exclude such evidence must be very limited indeed. Presumably there are *some* situations in which it may be excluded, *cf. Hull Prison* case (n. 78 above), but very few.

C. THE ROLE OF THE CHAIRMAN

The references to the chairman in the last two sections of this chapter will already have demonstrated the significance of his role. The task of any chairman, whatever the nature of the tribunal, is to ensure that:

> " . . . the proceedings are conducted with scrupulous fairness to all parties and that the proper balance is struck between formality and informality. In particular, he must make sure at the outset that the parties fully understand the issue, especially when they are not legally represented; and he must ensure that they have an opportunity to present their cases adequately."[14]

Different chairmen may quite properly take different views about how to conduct tribunal hearings whilst pursuing the objectives referred to in the preceding paragraph, and the chairman's discretion is substantial. Since so much depends on the chairman it is important briefly to examine three issues—the appointment and qualification of chairmen; training provision; the adequacy of judicial and other safeguards intended to ensure procedural fairness. The first and last of these issues also fall to be considered elsewhere in the book but it is important to review them here in the context of the tribunal hearing.

1. APPOINTMENT AND QUALIFICATION

The formal position on appointment and qualification is set out in Chapter 4.[15] The involvement of the Lord Chancellor in the appointment of the majority of tribunal chairmen is intended to demonstrate, and preserve, their independence of the relevant government department. As to qualification, the controversy is over the desirability of requiring that a chairman should be legally qualified.

The inherent difficulty in tribunal adjudication will by now have become apparent. It is desirable to achieve a high standard of decision-making coupled with demonstrable procedural fairness, whilst retaining the informality, cheapness and speed which are meant to be the hallmarks of the tribunal. Lawyer–chairmen seem to have less difficulty in achieving the former than the latter. Two examples will suffice.

When the Industrial Tribunal was created, the procedural rules specifically required the chairman, in setting the procedure, to seek to avoid formality so far as it was appropriate to do so.[16] All chairmen of Industrial Tribunals are barristers or solicitors of not less than seven years' standing[17] and the appellate body is presided over by a High Court judge.[18] The Industrial Tribunal has become formal, with predictable procedure

---

[14] *Report of the Council on Tribunals 1959*, p. 6.

[15] Above, pp. 149–152.

[16] Now contained in the Industrial Tribunals (Rules of Procedure) Regulations 1980 (S.I. 1980 No. 884) reg. 8(1).

[17] Industrial Tribunals (England and Wales) Regulations 1965 (S.I. 1965 No. 1101) reg. 5.

[18] For the composition of the Employment Appeal Tribunal, see above, p. 54.

and a growing body of case-law.[19] That can hardly be a coincidence.

The Supplementary Benefit Appeal Tribunal was accustomed to non-lawyer chairmen. There was no prohibition on the appointment of lawyers but by 1980, after 14 years of existence,[20] only one chairman in four was legally qualified.[21] Kathleen Bell's research,[22] published in 1975, was not especially complimentary to the existing chairmen: " . . . generally speaking, they did not fully comprehend the complexities of the work . . . too often proceedings were unsystematic, inconsistent and over-influenced by sympathy or otherwise. Separate deliberations were frequently non-existent when the appellant was absent, and in other instances were quite often somewhat rambling and of rather poor quality. We examined a large number of official Reports of Proceedings, the majority of which did not adequately record a reasoned decision."[23] This view was supported by other commentators.[24] Following the Bell Report there was a determined effort to appoint more lawyers as S.B.A.T. chairmen and the arguments have now been sharpened following the merging of S.B.A.T.s and N.I.L.T.s into Social Security Appeal Tribunals by the Health and Social Services and Social Security Adjudications Act 1983.[25] The chairmen of the S.S.A.T.s will all be lawyers of at least seven years' standing,[26] and a regional and national structure of full-time chairmen has been created.[27]

The new tribunal is obviously more closely modelled on the N.I.L.T. than the S.B.A.T., and will be expected to achieve the standards set by the N.I.L.T. The N.I.L.T. certainly achieved a reputation as one of the best models of an informal tribunal with a qualified chairman.[28] In the view of Professor Lewis, who had some harsh criticism of S.B.A.T.s, N.I.L.T.s [were] " . . . usually a model of balancing informal expertise with order and legality."[29]

The debate over the desirability of lawer–chairmen involves many of the same arguments that are deployed in respect of legal representation at

---

[19] It has begun to attract both judicial and academic criticism on that account. The criticism reflects a particular view of the functions of an I.T. See the observations of Lord Denning M.R. in *Walls Meat Co. Ltd.* v. *Khan* [1979] I.C.R. 52 at p. 56; Lawton L.J. in *Clay Cross (Quarry Services) Ltd.* v. *Fletcher* [1979] I.C.R. 1 at p. 8; Ormrod L.J. in *National Vulcan Engineering Insurance Group Ltd.* v. *Wade* [1978] I.C.R. 800 at p. 808; Dunn L.J. in *Methven* v. *Cow Industrial Ltd.* [1980] I.C.R. 463 at p. 470.

[20] S.B.A.T.s were created by the Ministry of Social Security Act 1966 as the successor to national assistance appeal tribunals.

[21] N. Harris, "The Appointment of Legally Qualified Chairmen for S.B.A.T.s" (1982) 132 N.L.J. 495.

[22] *Research Study on Supplementary Benefit Appeal Tribunals, Review of Main Findings: Conclusions: Recommendations* (1975) H.M.S.O.

[23] *Ibid.* at p. 6.

[24] A. Frost and C. Howard, *Representation and Administrative Tribunals* (1977); M. Herman, *Administrative Justice and Supplementary Benefits* (1972); N. Lewis, "Supplementary Benefits Appeal Tribunals" [1973] P.L. 257.

[25] s.25. and Sched. 8. These arrangements came into effect in April 1984 and there are transitional provisions which will eventually eliminate all non-lawyer chairmen.

[26] *Ibid.*

[27] There is a President of Social Security tribunals and a number of Regional Chairmen with supervisory and training responsibilities.

[28] There appears to have been no specific requirement that chairmen of N.I.L.T.s should be qualified lawyers, but it was an almost unbroken rule of practice.

[29] N. Lewis, "Supplementary Benefit Appeal Tribunals" [1973] P.L. 275.

tribunals.[30] The skills of the lawyer are thought to lie in order, objectivity and procedure rather than speed, informality and expertise. The Franks Committee were early advocates of the legally-qualified chairman. "Objectivity in the treatment of cases and the proper sifting of facts are most often best secured by having a legally qualified chairman."[31] The Committee also noted that there had been substantial agreement on this matter among witnesses. Later writers have advanced further arguments[32]: the ability of lawyers to uphold basic legal principles in the field of administrative adjudications[33]; the maintenance of firm control over tribunals bred out of confidence and expertise[34]; the natural inclination of lawyers to control bias and prejudice in the presentation of cases; and the grasp of legal questions which is relevant in most areas of tribunal work.[35]

These views have not gone unopposed,[36] and even the advocates of lawyer–chairmen have not usually gone so far as to suggest that chairmanship should be the exclusive province of lawyers,[37] yet the recent developments have been along that line.[38] It is unfortunate that the adoption of a convenient definition of "legally-qualified" as meaning solicitor or barrister will exclude other very suitable people from chairmanship. It seems that there has been a move away from defining the necessary qualities of chairmanship and seeking appropriate candidates, to defining the profession which alone possesses those qualities.

2. TRAINING

The training of tribunal chairmen has so far been notable for its absence. The systematic training of new and experienced magistrates[39] has not been extended into the tribunal system and the initiatives that have been taken, have largely been at the instance and under the organisation of the chairmen themselves. Regional and national conferences of chairmen of particular tribunals have taken place, and some schemes operated for the instruction of chairmen of S.B.A.T.s. These latter involved instructors from outside the appropriate government department and the S.B.A.T. system and attempted to provide a broad view of the chairman's role and responsibilities. The Bell Report recommended an organised training

---

[30] See below, p. 569.

[31] Report of the Committee on Administrative Tribunals and Enquiries (Cmnd. 218, 1957) para. 55.

[32] They are collected and analysed by J. Fulbrook, *Administrative Justice and the Unemployed* (1978), pp. 215–219.

[33] H.W.R. Wade, *Towards Administrative Justice* (1963), p. 43.

[34] H.L. Elcock, *Administrative Justice* (1969), pp. 50–53.

[35] Especially in the Industrial Tribunals, and in the determination of claims for industrial injuries.

[36] R.M. Titmuss, "Welfare 'Rights', Law and Discretion" *Political Quarterly* (1971) 42, pp. 113–132.

[37] The Franks Committee (above, n. 31) recommended that, " . . . the appointment of persons without legal qualification should not be ruled out when they are particularly suitable." (para. 55).

[38] *i.e.* the stipulations contained in H.A.S.S.A.S.S.A.A. 1983 (above, n. 25) that the chairmen of the Social Security Appeal Tribunals shall be barristers or solicitors of seven years' standing. See J. Mesher, "The Merging of Social Security Tribunals" (1983) 10 *Journal of Law and Society* 135.

[39] Introduced in 1966, see above, p. 140.

programme for chairmen *and* members[40] but there is little sign of full implementation. Why not?

3. CORRECTION OF PROCEDURAL IRREGULARITIES

In the major tribunals we have so far considered there is a provision for a right of appeal to an appellate body who have the power to correct procedural irregularities.[41] Where there is no appellate body[42] or where the appeal does not properly deal with the defect alleged the remedy of certiorari may be sought. That remedy is considered fully, in Chapter 19.[43] Both the existence of the appellate body and the ultimate oversight of the courts provide the safeguard against the wrongful exercise of chairman's considerable discretion.

D. THE ROLE OF THE "WINGMEN"

It is a distinctive feature of the tribunal system that it gives considerable scope for lay participation in adjudication. Some of the alleged disadvantages of lawyer–chairmen may be moderated by the presence of laymen as members of the tribunal.

The appointment of the lay members has already been described,[44] and there is little in the way of research work into how the laymen approach their task and the nature of their relationship with the chairman.[45] At least in relation to social security tribunals there is doubt about the extent of their participation in the hearing and the adjudication, although it is recognised that a lack of participation may result from the absence of training and guidance.

E. REPRESENTATION BEFORE TRIBUNALS

" . . . it is desirable that every applicant before any tribunal should be able to present his case in person or to obtain representation."[46]

In order to achieve this objective, the Royal Commission on Legal Services asserted that tribunal procedure would need to be simplified wherever possible; the existing schemes for representation by lay persons would need to be developed and funded; and legal aid would need to be made available for certain cases.[47] These findings were based on a significant amount of evidence received by the Commission[48] which was in

---

[40] *Op. cit.* (see above, n. 22), pp. 7, 20–21.

[41] The Employment Appeal Tribunal for Industrial Tribunals, and the Social Security Commissioners for S.S.A.T.s.

[42] *e.g.* there is no appeal from the Rent Assessment Committee (see above, p. 548).

[43] pp. 742–749.

[44] Above, p. 151.

[45] See J. Fulbrook, *Administrative Justice and the Unemployed* (1978) pp. 226–229.

[46] R.C.L.S. Vol. 1 para. 15.11, p. 169.

[47] *Ibid.*

[48] The Commission received evidence from both lawyers and non-lawyers active in the tribunal representation field. Its own research is contained in Vol. 2, Section 4, pp. 91–101.

addition to the published research already available.[49] The whole question
of tribunal representation is one which attracts much attention, especially
because of the large numbers of cases currently being determined by
tribunals.[50]

In this section we consider six related issues, the first three relating to the
present position and the second three to possible future provision of
representation. What are the rules about representation? Who are the
representatives? What do they do? Should lawyers be involved in
representation less often, more often, or not at all? Should legal
involvement be funded under the Legal Aid Scheme? In what way, if at all,
should schemes of representation by lay persons be developed?

1. THE RULES

Whether or not there is an absolute right to legal representation protected
by the principles of natural justice,[51] it is rare for such a right to be
specifically denied by tribunal rules.[52] However, a right to legal representation is only useful if the applicant has sufficient funds to pay a lawyer[53]; can
find one who is competent in the field; and if the case is one in which the
skills of a lawyer will be significant. As we shall see, representation by
lawyers in tribunals is not generally common.

Some tribunals place restrictions on representation by persons other
than lawyers,[54] but the usual provision is for an unfettered right to
representation.[55] The ability of the applicant to select an appropriate
representative has resulted in the appearance before tribunals of a wide
variety of representatives.

2. WHO ARE THE REPRESENTATIVES?

Some distinctions must be made between the different tribunals in that
they attract different representatives. The Industrial Tribunals attract a

---

[49] Notably the studies carried out by Professor Kathleen Bell, *Research Study on
Supplementary Benefit Appeal Tribunals. Review of Main Findings: Conclusions: Recom-
mendations* (D.H.S.S. 1975); "National Insurance Local Tribunals," *Journal of Social Policy*,
Vols. 3, 4 and 4.1 (1974/5). More recently published studies include R. Lawrence, *Tribunal
Representation* (1980); E. Kessler *et al*, *Combatting Poverty: CABx, Claimants and Tribunals*
(NACAB Occasional Paper No. 11, 1980); R. Lawrence, "Solicitors and Tribunals" [1980]
J.S.W.L. 13; *Tribunal Assistance, the Chapeltown experience* (NACAB Occasional Paper,
No. 14, 1982).

[50] The numbers of cases disposed of in 1982 by the tribunals under the general supervision
of the Council on Tribunals are to be found in Appendix C of its *Annual Report* for 1982–83,
pp. 34–45. S.B.A.T.s disposed of 57,650; N.I.L.T.s, 29,500; Industrial Tribunals, 37,597;
Rent Assessment Committees, 16,185. (All those figures apply to England and Wales only).
The House of Lords heard 53 appeals in 1981, and the Court of Appeal (Civil Division), 966.
(*Judicial Statistics 1982*, Cmnd. 9065.)

[51] See H.W.R. Wade, *Administrative Law* (5th ed., 1982) at pp. 485, 810.

[52] The only exception seems to be the service committee to the Family Practitioner
Committee, which hears complaints against general practitioners made by their patients.
Before that Tribunal paid representation by a lawyer is not permitted, he may only appear as
a "friend": National Health Service (Service Committees and Tribunal) Regulations 1974
(S.I. 1974 No. 455), reg. 7, (substituted by S.I. 1974 No. 907).

[53] Save in exceptional circumstances, see p. 566, below.

[54] For example, representation by non-lawyers is only permitted at the discretion of the
Performing Rights Tribunal, The Lands Tribunal and the Commons Commissioners, see
R.C.L.S. Vol. 1, para. 15.3.

[55] See the procedural rules of the tribunals considered at pp. 544–549, above.

high number of lawyer-representatives; the former National Insurance Local Tribunals, the highest number of trade union or employers' representatives; and the former Supplementary Benefit Appeals Tribunals, the highest number of friends, relatives or "other" representatives.[56]

Although there will always be some who defy categorisation, it is possible to discern five groupings from amongst those people who undertake representation.

First, there are those who represent at tribunals as a result of a *professional interest in their members or clients*. Lest that definition would appear to include lawyers we would stress that we are referring here principally to trade union representatives, employers' organisation representatives and social workers who go to a tribunal with a client. Representation has been a significant feature of the legal services supplied by trade unions to their members,[57] and this is particularly marked in the field of national insurance, industrial injuries and employment issues. This has resulted in the trade unions taking a cautious view over the future development of lay or legal representation. They are not anxious to have competitors providing alternative services to their members![58] Social workers have been particularly prominent in S.B.A.T.s. This group of representatives will normally offer effective representation as a result of skill and experience acquired in particular tribunals. In addition, they may perform the important task of "filtering out" cases which are obviously unmeritorious and assisting in the settlement of other cases before they reach a hearing.[59]

The second group consists of representatives provided by *voluntary organisations* for the benefit of their members. The Benson Commission noted the work done by the Royal British Legion in Pensions Appeal Tribunals,[60] and the Claimants' Unions have specialised in the area of social security tribunals.[61]

The third group consists of representatives provided by *generalist or specialist advice agencies* for the benefit of anyone who wishes to consult the agency and accept an offer of help. The Citizens Advice Bureaux have provided such a service to the public,[62] and there are other examples of advice agencies becoming involved in representation as an incidental part

---

[56] R.C.L.S. Vol. 2, Section 4, Tables 4.7; Bell, *Research on S.B.A.T.s*, at pp. 15–16 (see n. 49, above). Presumably the new Social Security Appeal Tribunal will attract the same variety of representatives.

[57] G. Latta and R. Lewis, "Trade Union Legal Services" (1974) *XII British Journal of Industrial Relations* 561; R. Lewis and G. Latta, "Union Legal Services" (1973) 123 N.L.J. 386.

[58] See G. Bindman, "Trade Unions and Legal Services" *LAG Bulletin*, March 1979, 56.

[59] This is a neglected aspect of the functions of representatives but it has some significance. The figures on the relative success rate of appeals in tribunals which are conducted by representatives may well be affected by the fact that the representative may only advise appeal where there is a chance of success.

[60] R.C.L.S., Vol. 1, para. 15.16.

[61] On the role of the Claimants' Unions, see H. Rose, "Who Can De-Label the Claimant," in M. Adler and A. Bradley, *Justice, Discretion and Poverty* (1976).

[62] Although it is fair to point out that much has depended on the ability and willingness of volunteers in a particular bureau to undertake the task of representation. The coverage has consequently been patchy.

of their general service. Specialist agencies, like the Child Poverty Action Group, provide representation in their own field and there are many local examples of advice agencies which offer representation as part of their services.[63] The United Kingdom Immigration Advisory Service (U.K.I.A.S.) provides an interesting example of a specialist agency set up with public funds to deal with enquiries on a particular topic. It was described by the Benson Commission as, " . . . a unique counselling and advocacy service dealing with one field of tribunal work and manned by a full time salaried staff."[64]

The fourth group consists of representatives provided by various specific *tribunal representation projects*, of which a number have been established in the last few years. The C.A.B. service is associated with major schemes in Birmingham, Leeds, Sheffield, Newcastle and Wolverhampton and has also provided the stimulus for other local initiatives.[65] The Free Representation Unit provides representation before tribunals in London and is staffed by young barristers and bar students. The various tribunal representation schemes have come under close scrutiny, since they may provide a model for the development of lay representation. They are all organised on a different basis and attract funds from different sources but this variety may prove fruitful in the evaluation of alternative models. We consider their organisation further, at a later point in this chapter.

The fifth group consists of *lawyers*. We have already noted that lawyers do provide some representation in tribunals, but this is normally at the expense of the client. Very few tribunals have rules as to costs which would allow the recovery of legal expenses.[66] Some representation is funded publicly but it is exceptional. Legal aid is available for representation before the Lands Tribunal, the Commons Commissioners and the Employment Appeal Tribunal, and the legal advice scheme is available for representation at Mental Health Review Tribunals—assuming that the applicant can satisfy the general criteria of eligibility.[67] The legal advice scheme may be used to fund preparatory work for tribunal hearings and to pay for a solicitor to "assist" a client at the hearing.[68] Assistance short of representation can no doubt prove very irritating for the tribunal and it appears that solicitors may have been remunerated for assistance which has spilled over into representation.

There must inevitably be a composite group of "everybody else." Particularly in S.B.A.T.s, the category of friends and relatives as representatives was significant. As we shall shortly demonstrate, the role of a "representative" can be very restricted, and it may be sufficient that his attendance has ensured the attendance of the applicant. That job can be done as well (possibly better) by a friend as by an advocate.

---

[63] *e.g.* in Hull, welfare rights advice was dispensed from a market stall every Friday. Representation was also offered in appropriate cases.

[64] R.C.L.S. Vol. 1 para. 15.17. For the role of U.K.I.A.S. see p. 368 above.

[65] See above n. 49, for the literature relating to Birmingham, Leeds and Wolverhampton.

[66] See above, p. 367.

[67] For legal aid, see pp. 388–393 above; for advice by way of representation see pp. 342–343 above.

[68] The legal advice scheme covers everything short of actual representation: Legal Aid Act 1974, s.2(3).

3. WHAT DO REPRESENTATIVES DO?

This may seem to be an odd question. However, we use it to demonstrate that the assistance offered by a representative may range more widely than simply putting the applicant's case at a hearing.

From the outset, the representative is likely to be involved in an advice-giving role whether he is an expert in the field or not.[69] It is obvious that those experienced representatives who have gained a thorough knowledge of their subject are able to evaluate the merits, and likely success, of the applicant's case and can act accordingly. This advisory role is significant because it may operate to exclude the weak and unmeritorious cases at an early stage. If the effect of this screening is to allow the representative only to pursue those cases he believes to be worthwhile, he gains an enhanced reputation with the tribunal in respect of the cases he does pursue through to a hearing.

There are some reservations expressed about the validity of this advisory role, not least because the adviser may be constituting *himself* as the adjudicator rather than the tribunal, and he imposes himself between the applicant and the tribunal. It is argued that applicants should be given the confidence and expertise to use the system themselves rather than experience the "interference" of another expert who would come to some tidy arrangement with the tribunal leaving the claimant as isolated as ever.[70] This is a minority view, however, and most of the representation schemes that have been established place emphasis on the provision of advice by an "expert" at an early stage.[71]

A second function of a representative may be to act as a negotiator on behalf of the applicant with a view to effecting a settlement of the problem. We noted the importance of settlements in the civil process in Chapter 10[72]—they also have their place in the tribunal process. The intervention of a third party on behalf of an applicant may produce a change in the decision which satisfies the claimant. This might be called anti-representation since it has the effect of preventing a tribunal hearing, but it benefits both the applicant and the tribunal.[73]

A third function of representation may be simply to ensure the attendance of the applicant. This is sometimes referred to as a "hand-holding exercise."[74] The published figures demonstrate that an applicant has a higher chance of success at a tribunal if he attends, whether or not

---

[69] Even the next-door neighbour might be asked whether or not to appeal!

[70] The Claimants' Union recognises a "right" to be represented whatever the merits of the case might appear to be. See generally, R. Lawrence, *Tribunal Representation* (1980), p. 18; H. Rose, "Who Can de-label the Claimant?" in M. Adler and A. Bradley, *op. cit.*

[71] Some of the tribunal representation schemes operate on a "consultancy" basis whereby volunteer lay representatives themselves receive help and guidance at the early stages of a possible appeal (see, for example, the West Midlands project—*Combatting Poverty*, n. 49, above). Others give a direct service to the claimant but rely heavily on the expertise of the representatives.

[72] Above, pp. 379–386.

[73] One of the arguments advanced in favour of the extension of representation is its effect in diminishing the caseload of tribunals.

[74] Particularly by the Citizens Advice Bureau. See the NACAB Administrative Circular (1974) cited in R. Lawrence, *Tribunal Representation* (1980), p. 59. This circular is no longer current, but the function remains the same!

represented, than if he does not attend.[75] Many supplementary benefit claimants who receive an unfavourable decision on their claim immediately give notice of appeal without giving thought to how to pursue the appeal.[76] On receipt of the appeal papers they decide not to go along to the hearing because the case is not arguable, or they are frightened, or ignorant of the process, or no longer interested. If they seek advice at all, they may simply need the reassurance that someone will attend the tribunal with them and help them through the procedure—not necessarily as an advocate but as a friend. Once at the hearing, with the presence of a supporter they are able to respond sufficiently to the tribunal to allow the case fully to be considered.

This may seem quite a late stage to be arriving at the representative's job of representing. At the hearing, the function of the representative is to put forward the applicant's case without placing himself completely between the applicant and the tribunal. He should not forget that the tribunal will be interested to hear from the applicant directly.[77] The need to marshal the arguments for the benefit of the tribunal will be dictated partly by the complexity of the subject matter and partly by the procedure adopted.[78] The skills required are not necessarily those of the advocate—but it helps the tribunal if the representative can present a logical, orderly, relevant analysis of the issues and the evidence. Statistics show that the represented claimant is better off at a tribunal.[79]

Finally, the expertise gained by the representative and his familiarity with the system may be used for the benefit of others in the exchange of infomation and pressure for reform. In the informal world of tribunals the shared experience is invaluable. This sharing may be formal, through publications,[80] or informal, through word of mouth but it is undoubtedly a factor in the increasing success of lay representatives.

Much of this section has been directed towards the less formal tribunals and the experience of the Industrial Tribunal is somewhat different. There, the actual representation at the hearing takes on the major significance and the other functions are consequently diminished.[81] It is not surprising that with considerable lawyer representation the emphasis has been placed upon advocacy.

Some fears have been expressed about the extent to which an involvement with representation will inevitably result in a commitment to reform of the system, an over-identification with the position of the

---

[75] K. Bell, *op. cit.* (above, n. 49); this is not a surprising finding. Attendance at least allows the tribunal the possibility of questioning the claimant.

[76] This almost automatic reaction to the receipt of an unfavourable decision is assisted by the notification of the right of appeal which is contained with the decision.

[77] The Social Security Commissioner has, on occasion, criticised a representative who appears to have dominated the hearing to the exclusion of the applicant. (See, R(I) 36/61).

[78] In the Industrial Tribunal, for example, the representative has his job defined by the adoption of a fairly standard, adversarial procedure. See pp. 547–548 above.

[79] Although there are some reservations about the interpretation of the evidence: R. Lawrence, *Tribunal Representation* (1980), pp. 19–20.

[80] The Chapeltown CAB Tribunal Assistance Unit produced guides to S.B.A.T.s and N.I.L.T.s which concentrate on the practical experience gained, and infomation is also disseminated through N.A.C.A.B. and C.P.A.G. literature and other periodicals.

[81] The negotiation function is, to some extent, undertaken by the conciliation officers of A.C.A.S., see above, p. 474.

applicants, or an engagement in political activity.[82] How objective/ disinterested can a representative remain? This anxiety has been examined and answered effectively by David Bull whose analysis of the range of advocacy and its implications for the representatives is very convincing.[83]

4. SHOULD LAWYERS BE INVOLVED MORE? LESS? AT ALL?

The answer to this particular question depends upon the skills which lawyers bring to tribunal representation and the effect that the deployment of those skills is likely to have on the style and procedure of tribunals. It further depends upon the objectives which a system of tribunals seeks to achieve, and upon the complexity of the law which is being administered. It further depends upon the nature of the particular tribunal under consideration, for the answer may not always be the same in every tribunal. It further depends upon the nature of the particular case under consideration, for there may be especial circumstances which warrant the attention of a lawyer.

Given all these variables it is difficult to formulate a single answer. Perhaps the convenient starting-point is to ask whether lawyers have a place in tribunal representation at all. Against the proposition that a citizen should have a right to legal representation in all forms of judicial or quasi-judicial proceedings[84] may be put the assertion that lawyers "spoil" tribunal adjudication by detracting from those qualities which tribunals are alleged to display, namely speed, informality, cheapness and expertise.[85] In particular, it has been argued, that in respect of areas in which discretion is an important element, the introduction of "legalism" is likely to hinder the operation of discretion to the disadvantage of the claimant.[86] These arguments have not prevailed and there is, apparently, only one example of a tribunal which positively prohibits legal representation.[87] It would certainly be difficult now to make a case for a blanket prohibition on legal representation, and it is generally accepted that lawyers have *some* part to play.

The more difficult question is the *extent* to which lawyer-representation is desirable. In practice, this question is closely linked with the possibility of providing public funds for such representation, for without funding the likelihood that an applicant will be able to pay for the services of a lawyer is

---

[82] This has been a particular fear of N.A.C.A.B. who are very sensitive about allegations of political involvement and campaigning.

[83] D. Bull, "The Anti-Discretion Movement in Britain: Fact or Phantom?" [1980] J.S.W.L. 65.

[84] See above, p. 564.

[85] For the virtues (alleged) of tribunal adjudication, see above, pp. 35–36. It is interesting to note that in the County Court small claims procedure (see above, p. 409) legal representation is not prohibited but it is discouraged because of the no-costs rule. Some commentators would have argued for a complete ban on lawyers, see p. 414.

[86] R.M. Titmuss, "Welfare 'Rights', Law and Discretion," *Political Quarterly* (1971) 42, pp. 113–132. The subject is discussed fully in J. Fulbrook, *Administrative Justice and the Unemployed* (1978), pp. 276–293.

[87] The service committees of the Family Practitioner Committee, see p. 442 and n. 52, above.

slim.[88] However, until a positive case has been made for legal representation, funds will not be made available. What is the strength of the case?

There is little evidence at present of the extent to which lawyers are
involved in tribunal work nor, incidentally, of their likely response if
money were to be made available to allow them to undertake more.[89]
Statistics from the research studies that have been done demonstrate the
very low proportion of cases in social security tribunals which have lawyer
representatives[90] and although the proportion is much higher in Industrial
Tribunals[91] there is little to indicate whether a few firms provide
representation as a specialist service or whether most firms will undertake
this type of work.[92] If the Industrial Tribunal is any guide the presence of
lawyer-representatives is likely to formalise procedure and reinforce the
adversarial style of the proceedings. This fear has been expressed also in
respect of social security tribunals, not least because the criticisms levelled
at such tribunals by lawyers tend to focus on the failure to follow a
consistent and clear judicial process in adjudication.[93] The lawyers'
response to such a failure is normally to formulate procedural rules and
safeguards to be operated by lawyers.

The research conducted by Professor Bell indicated that there was no
great enthusiasm amongst appellants for professional advocates rather they
were anxious to see the tribunal play a more *enabling* role thereby
improving the opportunity for appellants to put their own case.[94]

Despite fears that lawyerly skills may frustrate some of the objectives of
tribunal adjudication, the prevailing view is that legal representation is
desirable in particular circumstances. This view is based mainly upon the
combined arguments of legal complexity in certain fields and the
importance of the issues to the individual claimant. The Royal Commission
on Legal Services was content merely to state, " . . . there are cases when
a denial of legal aid for representation by a lawyer will put the applicant at
a disadvantage. We have in mind, for example, cases before Supplementary Benefit Appeal Tribunals which involve allegations of cohabitation or dishonesty, and some of the claims before Industrial Tribunals
which involve difficult problems of law and fact."[95]

The Benson Commission had considered much evidence on the
provision of legal representation in tribunals and concluded that there are
some cases before *all* tribunals in which it was necessary. The identification
of those cases is problematic, but some indication of the factors which
might necessitate legal representation is given by the tests formulated to
govern the granting of legal aid. The assumption seems to have been made

---

[88] This is especially the case in social security tribunals where there is likely to be only a
relatively small amount of money at stake. Costs are not normally awarded by tribunals, see
p. 367, above.
[89] R. Lawrence, "Solicitors and Tribunals" [1980] J.S.W.L. 13. N. Harris, "Solicitors and
Supplementary Benefit Cases" (1983) 34 N.I.L.Q. 144.
[90] K. Bell, *op. cit.* below, n. 93; R.C.L.S. Vol. 2, Section 4.
[91] R.C.L.S. Vol. 2, Section 4, Tables 4.7, 4.8.
[92] R. Lawrence, *op. cit.* n. 49 above, inclines to the former view.
[93] K. Bell, *Research Study on Supplementary Benefit Appeal Tribunals. Review of Main
Findings: Conclusions: Recommendations.* (DHSS, 1975) at pp. 19–20.
[94] *Ibid.* p. 18.
[95] R.C.L.S. Vol. 1 para. 15.24.

that legal representation will only really be available when legal aid is available[96] and we discuss in the next section the criteria which might be adopted in determining eligibility.

5. WHEN SHOULD LEGAL AID BE AVAILABLE FOR TRIBUNALS?

There is no serious dispute that it would be inadvisable for legal aid to be made immediately available for all cases in all tribunals. Different reasons would be given by different people. The expense[97]; the inappropriateness; the difficulty of applying the "merits" test[98]; the availability of skilled lay representation; the possible lack of interest amongst the solicitors' profession[99] would all be reasons used to reject the extension of legal aid to all cases. There is an equal measure of agreement about the need to extend legal aid to *some* tribunal cases, but two difficulties arise. First, it is difficult to agree the criteria which would establish eligibility; second, the advocates of the development of lay representation would not wish the extension of legal aid to be viewed as an alternative to funding better organised and more comprehensive schemes of lay representation.

The Council on Tribunals has consistently advocated the extension of legal aid,[1] and its view has been supported by the Lord Chancellor's Advisory Committee,[2] by the President of Industrial Tribunals[3] and by other groups and individuals. It was the formulation of the test of eligibility submitted by the Council on Tribunals which won the approval of the Benson Commission, subject to some additions. The Council proposed in their evidence to the Commission that an applicant for legal aid should show, " . . . that in the particular circumstances of his case he reasonably requires the services of a lawyer, and the certifying committee shall in this respect have regard to the suitability and availability of any other forms of

---

[96] This is why the two issues of whether lawyers should be involved, and whether they should be paid out of the Legal Aid Fund are extremely difficult to disentangle. When they are needed, they should be paid for . . . See the evidence of The Law Society in *R.C.L.S. Memorandum No. 3* (1978). Evidence to the same effect was received from the Council on Tribunals, the President of Industrial Tribunals and other individuals. This view is supported by the Lord Chancellor's Advisory Committee on Legal Aid: *33rd Legal Aid Annual Reports* [1982–83], pp. 194–209, contains a full discussion of the whole question of representation.

[97] The Lord Chancellor's Department would faint dead away at the additional cost involved—the current signs are that they are trying to restrict expenditure on the advice scheme, not increase it on legal aid, see *LAG Bulletin*, July 1983.

[98] This is the standard test for legal aid—"Would a solicitor advise a private client to pursue or defend the action?"—see above, p. 390. The test is almost unworkable in relation to many tribunals because of the lack of correlation between the amount at stake and the cost of legal representation.

[99] See R. Lawrence, "Solicitors and Tribunals" [1980] J.S.W.L. 13, at pp. 19–25.

[1] *e.g. Annual Report*, 1976–77, p. 6. The Franks Committee had made such a recommendation in 1958: *Report*, para. 89.

[2] This subject is first considered at length in the *24th Report of the Law Society on Legal Aid and Advice*, 1973/74, pp. 47–55. Thereafter it recurs in the *27th Report* (1976/77) p. 116; the *28th Report* (1977/78), pp. 91–92; and is fully discussed in the *33rd Report* (see n. 96 above).

[3] In his evidence to the Royal Commission on Legal Services, referred to in R.C.L.S. Vol. 1, at para. 15.28.

assistance." The Council instanced several situations where representation by a lawyer might be regarded as appropriate—

"(i)   where a significant point of law arises,
 (ii) where evidence is likely to be so complex or specialised that the average layman could reasonably wish for expert help in assembling and evaluating the evidence and in its testing or interpretation,
 (iii) where a test case arises,
 (iv) where deprivation of liberty or the ability of an individual to follow his occupation is at stake."[4]

To these situations the Commission added three others: where the amount at stake is significant *to the claimant*; where suitable lay representation is unavailable; where the special circumstances of the individual make legal representation desirable.[5]

These criteria, it is suggested, would be applied by the appropriate legal aid committee[6] and used to determine whether the "merits" tests for legal aid had been satisfied. An alternative view, that legal aid should be granted or recommended by the chairman of the appropriate tribunal,[7] was not supported by the Benson Commission.

It is evident that these criteria have been formulated upon the assumption that there will be an adequate lay representation service available, and the supporters of such a service fear that these may be regarded as alternative, rather than complementary, developments. This dilemma confronts the reformer who wishes to advance the cause of tribunal representation but takes the view that the more important use of public funds is in the training and organisation of lay representatives. To oppose the extension of legal aid may appear to be siding with the forces of darkness; to support it, with limited funds available, may be reducing the possibility of more general improvement.[8]

The Government may have helped in the solution of this dilemma. In the recent response to the Benson Commission,[9] it was pointed out that all those involved in tribunal proceedings are already eligible, subject to means, for legal advice and assistance[10] and that assistance by way of representation is available for proceedings in mental health review tribunals.[11] There are no grounds for optimism based on the bleak statement that, "Extension of assistance by way of representation and legal

---

[4] *Ibid.* para. 15.28.
[5] *Ibid.* The Commission's formulation has been criticised and rejected by the Lord Chancellor's Advisory Committee on Legal Aid: *33rd Legal Aid Annual Reports* [1982–83] at p. 205.
[6] Now the legal aid general committee, see p. 389, above.
[7] See, for example, R. Micklethwait, *The National Insurance Commissioners* (1976) at p. 56.
[8] The Annual General Meeting of N.A.C.A.B. passed a resolution in 1983, advocating the immediate extension of legal aid to Industrial Tribunals, against the recommendation of N.A.C.A.B's own advisory Welfare Rights Group which wants to see the development of lay representation as the stated priority of the Association.
[9] *The Government Response to the Report of The Royal Commission on Legal Services*, (Cmnd. 9077, 1983).
[10] See above, p. 339.
[11] Introduced in December 1982, see above, p. 342.

aid are made where it is shown to be necessary and resources allow."[12] The future development of representation may indeed lie with the laymen.

6. HOW SHOULD LAY REPRESENTATION BE DEVELOPED?

"If agencies which provide advice and representation before tribunals are to give an adequate service, they should have enough money to provide training for staff, an up-to-date information service and proper administrative support . . . we recommend that public funds should be made available to approved agencies to assist in the training of tribunal representatives."[13]

"[The recommendation is] accepted in principle subject to further consideration being given to timing and the availability of resources."[14]

If the Government seriously envisages that resources will, in due course, be made available to implement the Benson Commission recommendation, then consideration must be given to the most effective method of organising schemes of lay representation. The role of the lay representative has obviously been accepted and there are a variety of schemes already in existence, which might provide a guide for national development.

Lawrence[15] distinguishes three types of scheme which can be observed amongst the 16 or so existing tribunal units. He characterises these types as *referral agencies*, *advice bureau based* and *support units*.[16]

The *referral agencies* accept tribunal cases at the hearing stage from another agency which has done all the preparatory work and got the case ready for the tribunal. The representatives attached to such agencies operate purely as advocates and will send the applicant back to the original agency if there is any follow-up work to be done after the hearing has taken place. Typical of this kind of organisation of specialist advocates is the Free Representation Unit which draws its members from amongst Bar students and young barristers. Such a unit relies heavily on the initial competence of some other agency[17] to prepare the case in such a way that it is ready for a hearing.

Advice bureau based units operate from or alongside established agencies, often C.A.Bx., with particular responsibility for taking on the tribunal representation work of that agency. This is, in some ways, the easiest unit to develop since it can emerge from the expertise of workers in

---

[12] *Response*, above n. 9, p. 18. Considering that since the beginning of the legal aid scheme in 1959, and advice by way of representation in 1979, the only extensions have been legal aid for the Lands Tribunal (1970); the Commons Commissioners (1972); and the Employment Appeal Tribunal (1976); and advice by way of representation for the mental health review tribunal (1982), the portents are not good. It would appear that advice by way of representation is more likely to be extended to particular civil proceedings currently outside the legal aid scheme, see p. 342, above.

[13] R.C.L.S. Vol. 1, paras. 15.20, 15.21.

[14] *Response*, above n. 9, at p. 18.

[15] R. Lawrence, *Tribunal Representation* (1980).

[16] *Ibid.* at p. 84.

[17] This is an unsatisfactory feature of such a scheme. The particularly fruitful parts of the other two types of scheme depend on the contact between representative and adviser and the building up of the general level of advice-giving.

the bureau in response to a perceived need for the work.[18] The Newcastle Tribunal Assistance Unit[19] exemplifies that process, and the Chapeltown unit in Leeds is similarly bureau-based.[20] These units have a wider role because of the close connection with a bureau and find themselves involved in formal and informal training of bureau workers as well as advice and representation. The value of having a unit attached in this way is the effect it has of raising the general level of advice-giving in the host agency. It is clear that the tendency at first is for the agency to push *all* problems in the subject area of the unit onto the unit, including perfectly routine enquiries. After an initial period, however, the general competence to handle such enquiries increases and the work of the agency is consequently strengthened.[21]

Support units are those which are not intended directly to offer representation, but rather to train, inform, advise and assist other representatives in the area which is served by the unit. The NACAB/EEC Tribunal Project in the West Midlands[22] operated in this way from the outset although the staff found the need to deal with some casework in order to retain their own expertise in representation. Of course, such units depend on their ability to stimulate interest in representation amongst agencies in the area and it can be difficult to break down reluctance on the part of volunteers.[23] The task is less easy for support units than for bureau-based services with their constant contact with both workers and clients.

This categorisation does not take account of all the units presently in operation[24] but it may offer some guidance for future development. The organisations involved in the provision of tribunal representation will be preparing a case for funds, but it is not easy to see precisely what proposals can be made. The Citizens Advice Bureaux network would seem to provide a good basis for bureau-based units, but the bureaux are autonomous and may not welcome such a development. Geographical coverage is still incomplete and it might prove hopelessly expensive to provide bureau-based units in rural areas where there is relatively less work to do. Support units are not directly effective and seem to take longer to stimulate a reliable service. In the longer term, however, they have a much broader effect on the area they serve.

Any progress depends upon resources being made available, but lay representation does underpin the recommendations for the extension of legal aid and it is difficult to see how an effective service could do without extensive lay participation.

---

[18] The drawback of this type of unit is that it relies heavily on the skills of few people. Holidays, illness, pressure of work can then disrupt the representation service quite significantly.

[19] Established in 1974 with the support of the Newcastle CAB. It has experienced a rapid rise in workload and now attracts work from a wide area.

[20] See *Chapeltown CAB, Leeds, Tribunal Assistance Unit Progress Report—First Two Years Aug. 1976—Aug. 1978* (NACAB Occasional Paper No. 6, 1979); *Tribunal Assistance, The Chapeltown experience* (NACAB Occasional Paper No. 14, 1982).

[21] R. Lawrence, *op. cit.* esp. Chap. 5; *Tribunal Assistance* (above, n.20) pp. 56–58.

[22] *Combatting Poverty: CABx, Claimants and Tribunals* (NACAB Occasional Paper No. 11, 1980).

[23] *Ibid.* pp. 47–56.

[24] R. Lawrence, *op. cit.* at p. 85.

The Lord Chancellor's Advisory Committee advocate the development of a strong voluntary lay representation service, possibly based on the CABx, utilising the skills of "resource lawyers." This scheme would complement legal representation funded by legal aid in difficult cases and would be closest to the *support units* of the models we have discussed.[25]

7. Procedural Reform

The preceding sections have all made one important assumption: that the tribunal system will continue in much the same way, becoming, if anything, rather more legalistic. The need for improved representation is based on that assumption.

The Benson Commission recommended a review of the procedures of tribunals in order to ensure that applicants in person are able to conduct their own cases whenever possible.[26] Such a review might have more effect on the need for representation than all the other proposals put together, but it will raise again the fundamental principles of tribunal adjudication. In the end, the question, "What kind of representation do we need?" is linked inextricably with the question, "What kind of tribunals do we want?"

[25] *33rd Annual Legal Aid Reports* [1982–83] pp. 194–209.
[26] R.C.L.S., Vol. 1., paras. 15.12, 15.13.

CHAPTER 16

THE CRIMINAL TRIAL[1]

It is the criminal trial that attracts a great deal of attention from writers, researchers and students because it is when a citizen's liberty is at stake that the fairness and impartiality of trial procedure assumes a paramount importance. That is not to say that the procedures of the civil courts and tribunals can be unfair—merely, that public attention and concern is primarily directed towards the methods by which we determine the liability of a person accused of crime. Within the criminal process, the closest scrutiny is reserved for the Crown Court and jury trial although the magistrates deal with well in excess of 90 per cent. of all criminal charges which proceed to trial.[2] In this chapter we shall reflect the balance which concentrates attention upon the Crown Court and its procedures, but we begin with a brief consideration of the trial in the magistrates' court and conclude with an examination of plea bargaining—a process which can lead to the by-passing of the trial through the entering of a guilty plea by the accused.

A. SUMMARY TRIAL

Trial by the magistrates of summary offences or offences triable either way[3] is not a subject which has given rise to a great deal of literature.[4] In some respects this is understandable since the bulk of the magistrates' work concerns minor offences, their powers of sentencing are limited, and they are primarily judges of fact, yet it remains true that they deal with the vast majority of criminal matters and are the tribunal most likely to be encountered by the "ordinary" man. By that criterion their job, and the manner in which they perform it, is of considerable significance.

We have already considered the ways in which the appearance of a person accused of a summary offence (or an offence triable either way) can be secured.[5] We have also explained the procedure adopted by the court in selecting the mode of trial of an offence triable either way.[6] If summary trial is the appropriate way of determining liability for the offence charged,

---

[1] See generally, Archbold, *Criminal Pleading, Evidence and Practice* (41st ed., 1982); C. Hampton, *Criminal Procedure* (3rd ed., 1982); A.P. Carr, *Criminal Procedure in Magistrates' Courts* (1983); C.J. Emmins, *A practical approach to Criminal Procedure* (1982); D. Barnard, *The Criminal Court in Action* (2nd ed., 1979).

[2] Magistrates also, of course, conduct committal proceedings for trials on indictment. See p. 500, above.

[3] For the classification of offences, see p. 486, above.

[4] J. Vennard, *Contested Trials in Magistrates' Courts* (1980) R.C.C.P., Research Study No. 6, (HMSO); J. Vennard, *Contested Trials in Magistrates' Courts,* Home Office Research Study No. 71 (1981), (HMSO); A.E. Bottoms and J.D. McLean, *Defendants in the Criminal Process* (1976); E. Burney, *J.P. Magistrate, Court and Community* (1979); J. Gregory, *Crown Court or Magistrates' Court?* (1976) Office of Population Censuses and Surveys (HMSO).

[5] See p. 489, above.

[6] See p. 488, above.

the first formal step is for the magistrates' clerk to read the information to the accused and secure a plea.

1. The Information

The information is the formal document containing the allegation(s) against the accused.[7] Unlike an indictment it does not contain a separate statement of the alleged offence and then the particulars which are alleged to constitute the offence,[8] it merely contains a statement which combines the essential facts with the alleged offence. So long as the accused is given reasonable notice of the charge he is to meet and the way in which he is alleged to have committed the offence that will be sufficient.[9] The use of plain, non-technical language is intended to simplify matters for the accused. Specimen informations[10] relating to criminal damage, theft and carrying an offensive weapon follow:—

   (i) Henry Frederick Smailey on the 1st day of March 1984 did without lawful excuse damage a motor vehicle, namely a Ford Escort number ABC 123, belonging to John Smith intending to damage the property or being reckless as to whether that property would be damaged; contrary to section 1(1) of the Criminal Damage Act 1971.

  (ii) Henry Frederick Smailey on the 1st day of March 1984 stole £15 belonging to John Smith; contrary to sections 1 and 7 of the Theft Act 1968.

 (iii) Henry Frederick Smailey on the 1st day of March 1984 without lawful authority or reasonable excuse had with him in a public place, namely the Victoria Shopping Centre, Nottingham, an offensive weapon namely a bayonet; contrary to section 1(1) of the Prevention of Crime Act 1953.

2. The Plea

At a trial on indictment, the accused must be in court to make his plea and would normally be present through the whole trial.[11] Summary trial is different in that provision is made for the accused to plead guilty by post[12] and, where the accused fails to appear at the appointed time and place, for trial in the absence of the accused.[13] Both these procedures are designed to

[7] For the full form of an information, see p. 490, above.

[8] Specimen indictments are set out at p. 583, below.

[9] The rules relating to the drafting of an information are contained in the Magistrates' Courts Rules 1981. The most informal style permitted is to be found in rule 100.

[10] The prescribed full form of information is to be found in the Magistrates' Courts (Forms) Rules 1981, Form 1.

[11] See p. 587, below.

[12] Magistrates Courts Act 1980, s.12 allows a plea of guilty by post where the offence does not carry a sentence of more than 3 months imprisonment, and the summons is before the magistrates' court, and the accused has been served a notice explaining the procedure and containing the prosecution allegations. The guilty plea may then be made by post together with any mitigation. The procedure is most commonly used for traffic offences.

[13] Magistrates Courts Act 1980, s.11. A plea of not guilty is entered on behalf of the accused and the prosecution evidence is heard. Service of the summons must be proved and the accused is permitted to show, within 21 days after he found out about the proceedings, that he did not know of the summons or proceedings until after their commencement.

spare the time and expense of the participants where there is no real intention to defend the charge, but they are hedged with certain safeguards to ensure that injustice does not result.

In a summary trial where the accused is present, the information is read out to the accused by the magistrates' clerk and he is asked if he pleads guilty or not guilty. His plea must be freely made and unambiguous, and should normally be made personally.[14] Special pleas may be made, but they are highly unusual.[15] The defendant's response then determines the remainder of the procedure.

3. THE GUILTY PLEA

If the accused enters a guilty plea, the court can proceed to hear the facts of the case from the prosecution, including any further offences which the accused wishes to have taken into consideration and the antecedents and any previous convictions of the accused. These facts are not usually elicited from witnesses unless there is some substantial disagreement,[16] but are presented by the prosecutor or police officer concerned.

In addition to the offence(s) with which he is charged the accused may wish to admit to other crimes and have them "taken into consideration" when sentence is passed. The magistrates have a discretion whether to take such admitted offences into consideration[17] and may decline to do so, especially where the offences are more serious than those with which the accused has actually been charged. If the offences are taken into consideration on sentence it is technically still possible for the accused to be prosecuted for them at a later date[18] but in practice this is not done and the procedure operates as a useful means of clearing up outstanding crimes.[19]

In certain circumstances social inquiry reports are required[20] and it would be normal for a case to be adjourned if such a report is necessary or desirable.[21] The probation service is responsible for compiling a report and this would be available to the bench at the adjourned hearing.[22] With or without a report, the bench will listen to anything that may be said by the accused or his representative by way of mitigation of sentence.

---

[14] R. v. Wakefield Justices, ex p. Butterworth [1970] 1 All E.R. 1181; R. v. Gowerton Justices, ex p. Davies [1974] Crim.L.R. 253.

[15] These are the same as the special pleas in response to an indictment: see p. 588, below, although technically the pleas of autrefois acquit and autrefois convict only apply to indictments. The same effect is achieved in the magistrates' court.

[16] Magistrates Courts Act 1980, s.9(3).

[17] R. v. Collins [1947] K.B. 560. Magistrates should not take into consideration any indictable offences.

[18] R. v. Nicholson [1947] 2 All E.R. 535.

[19] The benefit for the accused is that the admissions of other offences wipe the slate clean so as to prevent future prosecution without very substantially increasing sentence in respect of the offence(s) charged.

[20] Before a community service order can be imposed: Powers of Criminal Courts Act 1973, s.14(2)(b). It is also recommended that a report should be obtained before certain other sentences are passed, see Carr, op.cit., p. 94.

[21] The defendant or his representative is entitled to request a social inquiry report either to investigate the personal circumstances of the accused, or his suitability for a particular kind of sentence.

[22] When the defence would have the opportunity of seeing and commenting upon it.

4. The Not Guilty Plea

A plea of not guilty normally results in an immediate adjournment to an agreed date so that the prosecution and defence can assemble their witnesses and court time can be allocated. One of the arguments in favour of the requirement of a far greater degree of disclosure of evidence by the prosecution is the avoidance of unnecessary adjournments.[23] The not guilty plea may be entered merely because the defence has little idea of the strength of the prosecution case and will not discover it until the hearing. This is in marked contrast to the position before the trial on indictment where the defence have the evidence of all the prosecution witnesses presented at the committal proceedings.[24] The moves towards greater pre-trial disclosure in the magistrates' court are discussed in Chapter 13.[25]

At the adjourned hearing the procedure will follow the normal adversarial lines. The prosecution is entitled to an opening speech and will then lead evidence through witnesses who will be subject to examination in chief, cross-examination and, perhaps, re-examination. If the case is not especially difficult, the prosecution will often start straight away with witnesses, since, with an experienced bench, there is not the need to stress general points which might have to be made to a jury at a trial on indictment.[26]

On the close of the prosecution case, the defence may submit that there is no case to answer and request the magistrates to end the hearing at that point. This submission does not, if rejected, prejudice the right of the defence to call witnesses and build a defence.[27] It is a submission which invites the magistrates to find that no reasonable tribunal could safely convict on the prosecution evidence, either because an essential element of the offence has not been proved or because the evidence has been discredited on cross-examination.[28] It is important to note that the magistrates do not indicate whether *they* would convict on the evidence so far presented, merely whether a reasonable bench *could* convict. If the submission is accepted, the accused is discharged. If rejected, the defence is then entitled to call witnesses.

At the close of the defence case, the defendant or his representative is entitled to make a closing speech to the bench. Exceptionally, the prosecution may be permitted to speak again and, if so, the defence will be given a second opportunity.[29] The defence is entitled to the last word.

---

[23] Criminal Law Act 1977, s.48 has not yet been brought into force. See further pp. 507–510, above.

[24] See pp. 500–504, above.

[25] At pp. 507–510.

[26] *e.g.* the burden and standard of proof, the need to listen carefully to the evidence, etc., etc. See p. 594, below.

[27] Apparently it is possible for a bench to mistake a submission of no case for a closing speech with the defence having elected to call no evidence. The bench, or the representative, should establish the nature of the speech, lest the bench mistakenly announce a premature conviction. See Carr, *op.cit.* p. 114.

[28] The criteria are contained in a *Practice Note* [1962] 1 All E.R. 448. Justices are warned against forming a view without hearing the whole of the evidence save in the two cases mentioned in the text.

[29] Magistrates Courts Rules 1981, r. 13.

5. THE VERDICT

The magistrates will normally retire to consider their decision. A majority[30] must be satisfied beyond reasonable doubt that the charge is proved before they can convict and they are the sole judges of fact. On matters of law relating to the charge they will have the benefit of advice from their clerk[31] who will also be able to offer advice on sentencing. As with the relationship of judge and jury in a trial on indictment, matters of fact are for the layman and matters of law for the lawyer. However, there is a particular difficulty for the clerk in giving legal advice to the magistrates since he must not appear to be influencing their decision on the facts.

The appellate courts have been quick to establish that justice must be seen to be done in magistrates' courts and it is clearly improper for a third party to be with the magistrates in the retiring room whilst they consider their verdict. Even the briefest of interventions by an outsider may raise doubts about what has transpired between him and the magistrates, and is strictly forbidden.[32] A similar rule is imposed to preserve the inviolability of the deliberations of a jury.[33] There is though, a difference between the position of a jury engaged on fact-finding and the position of magistrates. The jury have already received instruction on the law from the judge in his summing-up. The magistrates will only receive instruction if they ask for it from the clerk, and they are likely to receive it in the course of their deliberations.

The extent to which magistrates may be influenced by their clerk is a matter of conjecture, and speculation that the clerk may have played too substantial a role in the verdict can be fuelled by his presence in the retiring room for a substantial period. The embargo on outsiders does not apply to the clerk[34] but he must be careful not to give the impression that he has done more than offer advice on the legal aspects of the case. Carr, himself a deputy clerk, offers fellow clerks two principles as guidance:

    (i) only advise on the law;

    (ii) give advice in open court,

whilst acknowledging that this guidance is often impossible to follow.[35] Strictly speaking, the clerk may only enter the retiring room when requested to do so, and Carr offers the view that he should remain only as long as strictly necessary, informing the defence and prosecution on his return of any advice on points of law which he may have given to the magistrates.[36] It is said that this will allow the advocate to check the accuracy of the advice given and to know the legal basis on which the magistrates have arrived at their decision. It should also ensure that the clerk has to account for the length of time he has been absent from the court.

On returning to court the magistrates will give their verdict of guilty or

[30] Which is the reason why three magistrates normally sit, see p. 46, above. The chairman has no casting vote so that if a two-man court is divided the case must be retried.

[31] For a fuller consideration of the status and role of the clerk, see p. 143, above.

[32] R. v. Stratford upon Avon Justices, ex p. Edmonds [1973] R.T.R. 356.

[33] See p. 614, below.

[34] Practice Direction [1981] 1 W.L.R. 1163, para. 4.

[35] A.P. Carr, Criminal Procedure in Magistrates' Courts (1983) at pp. 9–10.

[36] Ibid. p. 10.

not guilty without giving any reason.[37] If the verdict is guilty the procedure will follow the same course as after a plea of guilty. If not guilty, the accused will be discharged.

6. Do Magistrates Reach the Right Result?

The answer to this question is almost always an impressionistic one. The difficulty of assessing objectively what is the "right" result in a contested trial applies similarly to magistrates as it does to juries, and there has been far less research into the quality of magisterial decision-making. It is certainly true that on a simple comparison of acquittal rates between the magistrates' court and the Crown Court, it would appear that magistrates convict a far higher proportion of defendants than juries. However, this simple analysis may be misleading. It seems, for example, that in respect of offences triable either way defendants believe that they have more chance of acquittal before a jury.[38] The consequence of this belief is that many more "winnable" cases go to the Crown Court and boost the acquittal statistics. Alternatively, this belief may be taken to indicate the lack of confidence of the criminal fraternity in magisterial decision-making. Is that because magistrates get decisions wrong, or because they get them right?

The work of Vennard in studying contested trials in the magistrates' court[39] gives some support to the view that magistrates weigh evidence carefully and reach a verdict which is broadly in line with identifiable features of the evidence heard. The criticism that is most frequently made of magistrates is that they place too much credibility on the evidence of police officers and are generally too "prosecution-minded."[40] This criticism emanates not only from the defendants who opt for trial by jury because it is "fairer," or because magistrates are amateurs who cannot be expected to get it right, or because they estimate that there is a better chance of acquittal,[41] but also from amongst those individuals and organisations who gave evidence to the James Committee.[42] The research study undertaken by Vennard had as its aims[43]:

(i) to appraise and itemise for contested cases the substance of the evidence presented by the prosecution and the defence, and attempt to quantify weaknesses and strengths in that evidence—such as whether or not the credibility of witnesses was impugned; and

---

[37] Juries are similarly excused from explaining the basis of their decisions: see p. 614, below. However, magistrates may be required to record their findings of fact and the principles of law upon which they reached their decision, if required by the convicted defendant to state a case for consideration by the Divisional Court: see pp. 703–704, below.

[38] A.E. Bottoms, and J.D. McLean, *Defendants in the Criminal Process* (1976), includes information on choice of venue.

[39] J. Vennard, *Contested Trials in Magistrates' Courts* (1980) R.C.C.P. Research Study No. 6 (HMSO); *Contested Trials in Magistrates' Courts* (1981) Home Office Research Study No. 71 (HMSO).

[40] See, for example, evidence to the James Committee, *The Distribution of Criminal Business Between the Crown Court and the Magistrates Court* (1975), Cmnd. 6323; B. Wootton, *Crime and Penal Policy* (1978).

[41] J. Gregory, *Crown Court or Magistrates' Court?* (1976) Office of Population Censuses and Surveys (HMSO).

[42] See n. 40, above.

[43] Vennard, Home Office Research Study No. 71 (n. 39 above), p. 4.

    (ii) to attempt to explain trial outcome in contested cases in relation to the type of evidence presented by both parties and to criteria pertaining to witness credibility.

On somewhat limited evidence Vennard concludes that her findings indicate that, " . . . magistrates' decisions whether to convict or acquit are strongly associated with a few quantifiable indices of the evidence adduced by the parties and the credibility of witnesses."[44] Strong associations were detected between direct evidence implicating the defendant given by prosecution witnesses whose credibility was not impugned and conviction. Conversely, there was a strong association between acquittal, the prosecution witnesses' lack of credibility, and the lack of direct evidence. These findings are not startling but they may reassure critics that magistrates are generally operating along rational lines.

For an alternative view which relies partly on different work by Vennard on acquittal rates,[45] one may look at King's response[46] to proposals by the Justices' Clerks Society[47] that more trials should be diverted into the magistrates' court. He is dismissive of claims that magistrates offer a better quality of justice than juries and argues vigorously against proposals to reduce the right to jury trial.[48]

Until more extensive work is carried out on magisterial decision-making the arguments about its quality are likely to remain as impenetrable as the decisions themselves.

B. TRIAL ON INDICTMENT

If the prosecution has secured the committal of the accused for trial following committal proceedings[49] or has obtained a voluntary bill,[50] then proceedings in the Crown Court are commenced by the preferment of a bill of indictment. This procedure simply involves the delivery of the bill of indictment to the appropriate officer of the court for his signature.[51] Once the bill is signed, the accused may be brought before the court and asked to plead to the indictment in a process known as arraignment.

The indictment is the formal statement of the charge(s) against the accused and should contain the description of the offence and a brief statement of the essential facts which constitute the offence. The

---

[44] *Ibid.* p. 20.

[45] J. Vennard, *Acquittal Rates in Magistrates' Courts*, Home Office Research Unit, Bulletin 11.

[46] M. King, "Against Summary Trial" *LAG Bulletin*, April 1982, p. 14.

[47] "A Case for Summary Trial—Proposals for a Redistribution of Criminal Business," published by the Justices' Clerks Society.

[48] It was certainly the experience of the James Committee (see n. 40 above) that their proposals to remove the right to trial by jury for minor thefts brought an outraged response, not least in the House of Commons. The proposal, originally incorporated in the Criminal Law Bill 1977, disappeared in the Bill's progress through Parliament. The opposition was, it is true, based more upon a commitment to jury trial than an antipathy to magisterial justice. See p. 487, above.

[49] See pp. 500–506, above.

[50] See p. 507, above.

[51] The officer may, in fact, draft the indictment himself on the basis of the depositions which have come from the magistrates on committal. In such a case the indictment is preferred as soon as he has completed the draft and signed it.

description of the offence should be precise, using either the recognisable common law name,[52] or the statutory name and derivation,[53] or sufficient details of a statutory offence.[54] The indictment must also contain, " . . . such particulars as may be necessary for giving reasonable information as to the nature of the charge,"[55] so that the accused knows the details of the charge and so that the prosecution may not shift its ground during the trial. Three specimen indictments follow: a common law offence, a precise statutory offence and a statutory offence for which there is no short description. They are taken from decided cases and reflect particular difficulties of those cases. Simpler cases will produce simpler indictments.

(i) *Shaw* v. *D.P.P.*[56]

STATEMENT OF OFFENCE

Conspiracy to corrupt public morals

PARTICULARS OF OFFENCE

Frederick Charles Shaw on divers days between the 1st day of October 1959 and the 23rd day of July 1960 within the jurisdiction of the Central Criminal Court, conspired with certain persons who inserted advertisements in issues of a magazine entitled 'Ladies' Directory' numbered 7, 7 revised, 8, 9, 10 and a supplement thereto, and with certain other persons whose names are unknown, by means of the said magazine and the said advertisements to induce readers thereof to resort to the said advertisers for the purposes of fornication and of taking part in or witnessing other disgusting and immoral acts and exhibitions, with intent thereby to debauch and corrupt the morals as well of youth as of divers other liege subjects of Our Lady the Queen and to raise and create in their minds inordinate and lustful desires.

(ii) *R.* v. *Miller* [57]

STATEMENT OF OFFENCE

Arson, contrary to section 1(1) and (3) of Criminal Damage Act 1971

PARTICULARS OF OFFENCE

James Miller on a date unknown between August 13 and 16, 1980, without lawful excuse, damaged by fire a house known as No. 9, Grantham Road, Sparkbrook, intending to do damage to such property or reckless as to whether such property would be damaged.

[52] *e.g.* murder; manslaughter; blasphemy; conspiracy to corrupt public morals.
[53] *e.g.* theft, contrary to s.1 of the Theft Act 1968; robbery, contrary to s.8(1) of the Theft Act 1968; arson, contrary to s.1(1) and (3) of the Criminal Damage Act 1971.
[54] *e.g.* removing an article from a place open to the public, contrary to s.11(1) of the Theft Act 1968; sexual intercourse with a girl under 13, contrary to s.5 of the Sexual Offences Act 1956; conniving at a corporation fraudulently inducing the investment of money, contrary to ss.13(1)(*b*) and 19 of the Prevention of Fraud (Investments) Act 1958.
[55] Indictment Rules 1971 (S.I. 1971 No. 1253), r. 5(1).
[56] [1962] A.C. 220.
[57] [1983] 2 A.C. 161.

(iii) *R.* v. *Markus*[58]

STATEMENT OF OFFENCE

Conniving at a corporation fraudulently inducing the investment of money contrary to sections 13(1)(*b*) and 19 of the Prevention of Fraud (Investments) Act 1958

PARTICULARS OF OFFENCE

Edward Jules Markus between August 25, 1970, and January 15, 1971, within the jurisdiction of the Central Criminal Court being a director of Agricultural Investment Corporation S.A. of the First National Investment Corporation S.A. and of Agri-International S.A. and of Agri-International (U.K.) Ltd. connived at the fraudulent inducement of Agricultural Investment Corporation S.A., through its agents First National Investment Corporation S.A. and Agri-International S.A. and Agri-International (U.K.) Ltd. of Dr. Hermann Schlick and Mrs. Theodoline Schlick to take part in an arrangement to invest $1038.32 in Agri-Fund (the said investment being an arrangement with respect of property other than securities, the purpose or pretended purpose of which was to enable the said Dr. Hermann Schlick and the said Mrs. Theodoline Schlick to participate in the profits alleged to be likely to arise from the holding of Agri-Fund) by representations that Agricultural Investment Corporation S.A. was genuinely carrying on an honest business and that moneys invested in Agri-Fund were immediately redeemable at the option of the investor which representations both he and the said corporation knew to be misleading false and deceptive.

From a perusal of these indictments it will be apparent that the details must include the time and place of the offence[59]; a description of any property involved[60]; the identity of any "victim"[61]; any factual circumstances necessary to the offence[62]; any special intent required by the offence which is not inherent in the statement of offence.[63]

Indictments may contain more than one offence but the charges must be separated and are then known as "counts." There are many technical rules about the drafting of indictments which are to be found in the works on criminal procedure.[64]

---

[58] [1976] A.C. 35.

[59] As precisely as possible: *Shaw's* indictment covers a period of 10 months, but the two dates may be quite a long way apart so long as the accused is able to know which acts of his are alleged to constitute the offence.

[60] In *Miller's* case, No. 9 Grantham Road, Sparkbrook.

[61] In *Markus'* case, Dr. Herman Schlick and Mrs. Theodoline Schlick.

[62] For example, in an indictment for theft, the particulars must state that the property in question belonged to another.

[63] For example, the particulars on an indictment for an offence under section 18 of the Offences Against the Person Act 1861 should allege an intent to do grievous bodily harm to the victim.

[64] Archbold, *Criminal Pleading, Evidence and Practice* (41st ed., 1982); C. Hampton, *Criminal Procedure* (3rd ed., 1982); C. J. Emmins, *A Practical Approach to Criminal Procedure* (1982).

1. The Order of Proceedings

We shall consider the proceedings at trial in some detail in this chapter but we shall see them from the point of view of the various parties to the trial: the accused, the judge, the jury, counsel and witnesses. At the outset, therefore, it is useful to set out the chronology of the trial from the first appearance of the accused until he leaves the court.[65] The sequence is as follows:

(a) The arraignment

The accused is brought to the bar of the court, the indictment is read out to him and he is asked to enter a plea in respect of each count.

(b) The empanelling and swearing of the jury

After a plea of not guilty a jury of twelve will be empanelled and, after an opportunity for challenges, sworn. The indictment will be read over to the jury who will be told of their obligation to listen to the evidence and to determine guilt or innocence.

(c) The opening speech

Counsel for the prosecution addresses the jury.

(d) The prosecution case

Witnesses called by the prosecution give their evidence in turn (examination in chief) and may be subjected to questioning by the defence (cross-examination). Counsel for the prosecution may have the final word with each witness (re-examination) but must confine himself to matters raised in the course of cross-examination.

(e) Defence submissions

Matters of law requiring a ruling from the judge may be raised at any stage of the trial, but the close of the prosecution case allows the defence to ask the trial judge to direct the jury to acquit the accused because there is no case to answer.

(f) Defence opening speech

Defence counsel is only entitled to make an opening speech to the jury if he is calling at least one witness (other than the defendant) as to the *facts* of the case. Otherwise, he must simply start to call evidence.

(g) The defence case

Witnesses called by the defence are examined, and may be cross-examined and re-examined.

(h) Closing speeches

Both counsel may address the jury at the close of the evidence. The prosecution goes first and the defence has the last word.

---

[65] See also D. Barnard, *The Criminal Court in Action* (2nd ed., 1979).

(i) The summing-up

The trial judge must sum up the evidence to the jury, directing them as to the law and explaining their function.

(j) The verdict

The jury retire to consider their verdict. A unanimous verdict is the first objective, but a majority verdict may eventually be acceptable. The verdict of the jury is announced by the foreman in open court.

(k) Plea in mitigation

After conviction, defence counsel (or the defendant) is given an opportunity to address the judge on any matters relevant to the sentence.

(l) Sentence

The judge passes sentence on the defendant in accordance with the principles discussed in Chapter 18.

2. THE ACCUSED

Historically, the accused has laboured under a considerable disadvantage in the criminal trial. When the Criminal Law Revision Committee considered the rules of evidence in criminal cases[66] it noted these disadvantages and referred to them as significant factors in the formulation of rules of evidence which were designed to protect the interests of the accused. Whether, after the removal of these disadvantages one by one, the balance has now been weighted too heavily in favour of the accused is a question which gives rise to spirited debate. The C.L.R.C. identified the following difficulties which formerly hindered the accused.[67]

The "indecent haste" with which trials were conducted could greatly prejudice the chances of a fair trial. Mr. Justice Hawkins wrote of an Old Bailey trial in the 1840s which lasted 2 minutes 53 seconds and which he described as "a high example of expedition," but he went on to say that trials after dinner lasted on average four minutes.[68] Representation, legal aid and judicial unwillingness to curtail trials now ensure that there are few complaints of brevity. Indeed, the criticism currently appears to be that trials go on too long!

Legal representation was severely restricted before 1836,[69] and representation has only extended to all serious cases with the coming of legal aid. In the absence of skilled legal assistance the accused was expected to do what he could for himself.

The accused was not permitted to give evidence on oath until the reforms introduced by the Criminal Evidence Act 1898.[70] The accused had

---

[66] Criminal Law Revision Committee, *Eleventh Report, Evidence (General)* Cmnd. 4991 (1972).

[67] *Ibid.* pp. 10–12.

[68] Hawkins, *Memoirs*, cited in the C.L.R.C. Report (n. 66, above) at p. 11.

[69] Prior to the Trials for Felony Act 1836, the defending counsel in felony trials was limited to argument on points of law and giving advice to the defendant on how he should conduct his case.

[70] This Act gave the accused this right in all cases. There were a few examples of specific cases before 1898 in which this right had been granted.

previously been able to make an unsworn statement from the dock which could not be tested by cross-examination, so that it lacked credibility with the jury.[71]

The right of appeal against conviction was rarely available until the Criminal Appeal Act 1907 established the Court of Criminal Appeal and provided wide grounds for challenging a conviction.[72] Up to that point the accused had been limited to an appeal on narrow legal grounds. The existence of an authoritative appellate body is not only significant in doing justice in individual cases but also in setting proper standards for trial courts to observe.

All these obstacles to a fair trial have now been removed and, in addition, the C.L.R.C. asserted that the improved quality of juries and magistrates together with the increasing sophistication of certain criminals had put the accused in a very strong position in the criminal trial.[73] A contrary view is to be found in the writings of Doreen McBarnet.[74].

The first procedural question relating to the accused concerns his appearance in court. If the accused is in custody he is brought to court from prison; if on bail, he is informed of the time and date of the trial and told to appear. He *must* appear in court, because he must answer in person when the indictment is put to him. He cannot be arraigned in his absence and no other person is entitled to enter a plea on his behalf.[75] The requirement that the accused be present at the arraignment does not extend to the whole trial, but it is only in exceptional cases that a trial will proceed in the absence of the accused.[76] If he is violent or disorderly[77]; seriously ill[78]; likely to intimidate a witness[79]; or absconds from the trial,[80] proceedings may go on in his absence.

The second procedural question concerning the accused relates to his response on arraignment after the indictment has been read to him. He is required to answer to every count on the indictment and his plea will be

---

[71] See M. Cohen, "The Unsworn Statement from the Dock" [1981] Crim.L.R. 224.

[72] The widest being that the verdict of the jury should be set aside on the ground that under all the circumstances of the case it was unreasonable. This provision is now contained in Criminal Appeal Act 1968, s.2(1)(a): see below, pp. 709–712.

[73] C.L.R.C. Eleventh Report (see n. 66, above) at pp. 10–12.

[74] D. McBarnet, *Conviction, Law, the State and the Construction of Justice* (1981).

[75] In some circumstances, the failure of the accused to plead personally to the indictment results in a mistrial: *R.* v. *Boyle* [1954] 2 Q.B. 292, *R.* v. *Ellis* (1973) 57 Cr.App.R. 571. However, if the trial had proceeded as though a "not guilty" plea had been recorded no material irregularity had necessarily occurred: *R.* v. *Williams* [1978] Q.B. 373.

[76] "There must be very exceptional circumstances to justify proceeding with the trial in the absence of the accused. The reason why the accused should be present at the trial is that he may hear the case made against him and have the opportunity . . . of answering it": *per* Lord Reading C.J. in *R.* v. *Lee Kun* (1916) 11 Cr.App.R. 293, 300. See generally, G. Zellick, "The Criminal Trial and the Disruptive Defendant" (1980) 43 M.L.R. 121, 284.

[77] *R.* v. *Berry* (1897) 104 L.T. Journ. 110, where the accused anticipated current fashion by performing an impromptu striptease act on the clerk's table. This may be the earliest reported example of courtroom exhibitionism. See also, *Gohoho* v. *Lintas Export Advertising Services Ltd., The Times,* January 21, 1964, for a modern example of in-court divestment. *R.* v. *Streek* (1826) 2 C. & P. 413, unfortunately deals with another aspect of the absence of a defendant (through illness) but is entitled to be noted in this context.

[78] *R.* v. *Orton* (1873), cited in Archbold, *op.cit.* para. 3–47.

[79] *R.* v. *Smellie* (1919) 14 Cr.App.R. 128.

[80] *R.* v. *Jones (No. 2)* [1972] 1 W.L.R. 887.

recorded. In the great majority of cases the plea will be "guilty" or "not guilty" although there are several other possibilities open to the accused.

(a) The plea of guilty

This acknowledgment of guilt must be made freely by the accused himself,[81] without any pressure from counsel or the court. It is quite proper for defending counsel to advise the accused, perhaps in very forceful terms, that a plea of guilty could be advantageous in securing a lesser sentence and/or that the evidence seems to point strongly to the guilt of the accused, but he must also stress that a plea of guilty should only be entered if the accused has actually committed the alleged offence.[82] The importance that is attached to the accused's freedom to enter the plea he wishes is reflected in the cases relating to "plea bargaining" in which it was suspected that unfair pressure might have been placed on the accused.[83] The topic of plea bargaining is dealt with fully in the last section of this chapter.[84]

A plea of guilty may be offered to an offence less than that charged on the indictment, and it will be a matter for the judge whether he accepts such a plea.[85] For example, on a charge of murder, the accused may wish to plead guilty to manslaughter. Usually, this offer will be made by defending counsel to the prosecution before the trial gets under way and the prosecution may accept the offer and commend it to the judge. Where the prosecution agrees to the plea, the judge must decide whether the evidence merits the acceptance of the plea.[86] If the plea is not accepted by the judge, it is a nullity and it is not open to the judge to sentence on the basis of the plea if the jury acquit the accused after trial.[87]

The prosecution have to make a considered and responsible decision about whether to accept an offered plea of guilty to a lesser offence, weighing up the public interest in securing a certain conviction with that of ensuring that the accused is ultimately punished for what he has done.

(b) The plea of not guilty

This plea occasions little difficulty. It constitutes a denial of the prosecution's allegations and requires them to prove all the elements of their case. The plea must be entered by the defendant himself.

(c) Autrefois acquit and autrefois convict

These pleas (properly referred to as "special pleas in bar"[88]) may be made by an accused who claims that he has already been acquitted (or convicted) for the same offence, or substantially the same offence. The

---

[81] If the plea is not made by the accused himself but the trial proceeds upon the basis that a "not guilty" plea has been entered, this is not likely to constitute a material irregularity, *R.* v. *Williams* [1978] Q.B. 373; it is a material irregularity if the accused has a guilty plea entered by someone else, *R.* v. *Boyle* [1954] 2 Q.B. 292.

[82] See below, p. 596 on the obligations of defence counsel.

[83] The particular pressure that gives rise to concern is where it appears to the accused that the judge has indicated to counsel that an unsuccessful plea of not guilty will attract a heavier sentence: *R.* v. *Turner* [1970] 2 Q.B. 321.

[84] At pp. 625–631.

[85] The judge may only accept the plea if it is to an offence of which the jury could properly convict the accused at trial.

[86] *i.e.* the judge has the same obligations as the prosecution (see pp. 592–593, below) to decide whether the public interest is served by accepting the plea.

[87] *R.* v. *Hazeltine* [1967] 2 Q.B. 857.

[88] The third special plea in bar is pardon: see below, p. 590.

appropriate plea is normally made in writing before the beginning of the trial, although it may be made at any stage. After such a plea, a jury will be empanelled to try the issue and it will be for the defence to show, on a balance of probabilities, that the plea is well founded. However, difficult questions of law are likely to be involved and it appears to be acceptable for the judge to give a very clear direction to the jury as to the result that they should reach.[89]

The circumstances in which either plea will be available were explored at length in *Connelly* v. *D.P.P.*[90] and they give rise to difficulties which are quite out of proportion to the practical significance of the pleas.[91] The basic proposition that an accused should not be tried for an offence which in law, and on the facts, is identical to one of which he has previously been acquitted or convicted is indisputable, but the pleas are actually available more widely.[92] The power of a jury to convict the accused of a lesser offence on an indictment charging a greater offence[93] leads to the conclusion that where the accused is acquitted, he is also being acquitted of any lesser offence of which he could have been convicted by the jury on that indictment. Consequently, the plea of *autrefois acquit* extends to cover any offence of which the accused could have been convicted on the previous indictment.[94] It may also be that the accused has previously been acquitted of an offence which, as a matter of fact, is essential to establish guilt on the offence charged. An earlier acquittal of theft should preclude a later conviction, on the same facts, of robbery since theft is an essential element of the offence of robbery.[95] Hence, the plea of *autrefois acquit* is made available where the offence charged is, in substance, the same as the previous one. The limits of this latter proposition are uncertain[96] and the courts have had problems in deciding whether the previous offence charged involves an element necessary to the proof of the present charge.

The plea of *autrefois convict* will not operate to prevent a person being tried on a charge which is more serious than the one of which he was originally convicted. A person convicted of causing grievous bodily harm with intent may later be charged with murder if the victim dies within a year and a day.[97]

Two other matters have a bearing on the operation of these pleas. There has been some suggestion that "issue etoppel" may operate in criminal

[89] *R.* v. *Coughlan and Young* (1976) 63 Cr.App.R. 33. This represents an example of the judge's ability to influence substantially a jury decision, see p. 606, below.

[90] [1964] A.C. 1254. See especially, the speech of Lord Morris.

[91] There is a body of case law on the subject of *autrefois acquit,* but it is mainly concerned with whether the current charge involves, "the same offence" as the previous charge. See C. Hampton, *Criminal Procedure* (3rd ed., 1982) pp. 190–1.

[92] *Connelly* v. *D.P.P.* [1964] A.C. 1254, pp. 1305–6.

[93] Criminal Law Act 1967, s.6(1)(*b*). For example, on a charge of murder, a jury may convict of manslaughter; on a charge of robbery—theft; on a charge of rape—indecent assault.

[94] Therefore, a person previously acquitted of robbery may not later be tried on a charge of theft arising from the same circumstances.

[95] "A person is guilty of robbery if he steals, and immediately before or at the time of doing so, and in order to do so, he uses force . . . ." Theft Act 1968, s.8(1).

[96] In *Connelly*'s case (n. 92, *supra*) Lord Devlin doubted the validity of the proposition and would have confined the plea to the first two situations noted.

[97] *R.* v. *Dyson* [1908] 2 K.B. 454. The year and a day rule is discussed in J.C. Smith and B. Hogan, *Criminal Law* (5th ed., 1983), p. 276.

proceedings to prevent the prosecution from raising again any issue of fact which has already been decided in a previous case.[98] The difficulty of establishing issue estoppel in a criminal matter lies in proving that any particular fact has been decided in a previous case since it will rarely be clear what facts have actually been determined by the jury in arriving at a verdict. In *D.P.P.* v. *Humphrys*[99] the House of Lords rejected an argument based on issue etoppel and held that it was not applicable in criminal proceedings. Finally, it would seem that the judges have an inherent power to prevent oppression of an accused by halting a prosecution in circumstances where it is considered to be an abuse of the court.[1] This may turn out to be the most effective way of ensuring that an accused is not placed in jeopardy of two convictions on the same facts.

(d) Pardon, demurrer, jurisdiction

These three pleas are real rarities. The accused may plead that he has already received a *pardon* in respect of the offence, or he may *demur* by objecting to the wording of the indictment,[2] or he may claim that the court has no *jurisdiction*[3] to try the offence.

(e) Standing mute

The accused may make no reply, or no intelligible reply, when the charge is put to him. He is then said to be "standing mute" and a jury must be empanelled[4] in order to determine whether he is "mute of malice" or "mute by visitation of God." This issue is tried like any other jury matter by the bringing of evidence, examination, summing-up and verdict. If the accused is found to be mute of malice (the prosecution having proved it beyond reasonable doubt) then a plea of not guilty is formally entered on his behalf. If the accused is found to be mute by visitation of God then the question will arise as to whether he is fit to plead to the charge at all. If he is found to be fit to plead, in accordance with the principles discussed below, then a not guilty plea will be entered.

(f) Fitness to plead

The question of whether the accused if fit to plead to the charge at all may arise for consideration either because he has remained silent on arraignment and been found mute by visitation of God or because there is a defence submission of unfitness. The question is determined by a jury[5]

---

[98] Three members of the House of Lords in *Connelly*'s case seemed prepared to entertain the application of issue estoppel in criminal proceedings but see D.J. Lanham, "Issue Estoppel in the English Criminal Law" [1970] Crim.L.R. 428.

[99] [1976] 2 W.L.R. 857; P. Mirfield, "Shedding a tear for issue estoppel" [1980] Crim.L.R. 336.

[1] This view was advanced in the House of Lords both in *Connelly* and in *Humphrys*.

[2] This plea is now almost obsolete because the normal procedure would be to seek to quash the indictment as a preliminary matter before the arraignment. Even a motion to quash the. indictment is unusual because of the substantial powers of the court to amend any defects in drafting, see D. Barnard, *The Criminal Court in Action* (2nd ed., 1979), pp. 97–8.

[3] Normally on the basis that the alleged offence occurred outside the territorial jurisdiction of the court. However, this may also be dealt with by a motion to quash the indictment: see Archbold, *Criminal Pleading, Evidence and Practice* (41st ed., 1982), para. 4–63.

[4] In the normal way, see pp. 609–613, below.

[5] If a jury has found the accused mute by visitation of God the same jury may be resworn to try the issue of fitness, or a new jury may be used.

who consider evidence and reach a verdict in the normal way. The consequence of a verdict of unfitness to plead is that the court must direct that the accused be detained in a mental hospital without limitation of time,[6] only being released with the consent of the Home Secretary.[7] This consequence seriously inhibits the number of submissions of unfitness to plead.

If the matter goes to the jury, they will have to determine whether the accused can understand the charge, the significance of his plea, and sufficient of the procedure properly to instruct counsel and follow the evidence.[8] Fitness to plead should not be equated with insanity, for a person who can establish a defence of insanity at trial may nonetheless be quite able to understand the trial and give proper instructions for the conduct of his defence.[9] Because it is desirable that a person charged with a criminal offence should stand trial if possible, and should have the opportunity of showing that the prosecution case is inadequate, the question of fitness to plead may be deferred until the opening of the case for the defence at the discretion of the trial judge.[10] The onus of proving the question of unfitness lies with the party raising it. If it is raised by the defence it must be proved by them on a balance of probabilities; if it is raised by the prosecution (or the judge) it must be proved beyond reasonable doubt.[11]

The whole issue of fitness to plead was considered by the Butler committee[12] which made interesting recommendations for reform. In particular, Butler recommended that there should always be a trial of the facts in the case at an appropriate time; that the issue of fitness should normally be decided by the trial judge; and that two doctors should always give evidence on the question. Finally, it was suggested that the phrase, "under disability in relation to the trial" should be substituted for "fitness to plead."[13] There is no indication as to when, if at all, these recommendations will be put into effect.

There are other procedural matters which concern the accused as well as his appearance and the arraignment, particularly the extent to which his character and his antecedents can be referred to, and the extent to which he can attack the credibility of prosecution witnesses, but these matters can be dealt with in discussing the roles of other participants in the trial.

3. REPRESENTATION AND THE OBLIGATIONS OF COUNSEL

The availability of legal aid[14] now ensures that it is very unusual to find an unrepresented defendant in the Crown Court. Those who are unrepre-

---

[6] Criminal Procedure (Insanity) Act 1964, s.5(1)(c).

[7] Mental Health Act 1959, ss.47 and 65 as amended.

[8] *R. v. Robertson* [1968] 1 W.L.R. 1767. See generally, J.C. Smith and B. Hogan, *Criminal Law* (5th ed., 1983) pp. 164–8.

[9] Royal Commission on Capital Punishment, *Report* Cmnd. 8932 (1953) p. 78.

[10] Criminal Procedure (Insanity) Act 1964, s.4.

[11] The question of the onus and standard of proof is considered in *R. v. Podola* [1960] 1 Q.B. 325, which is of general interest on the question of fitness to plead.

[12] *Report of the Committee on Mentally Abnormal Offenders,* Cmnd. 6244 (1975).

[13] *Ibid.* Chapter 10. See also N. Walker, "*Butler v. C.L.R.C.* and others" [1981] Crim.L.R. 596, and A.R. Poole, "Standing Mute and Fitness to Plead" [1968] Crim.L.R. 6.

[14] See p. 512, above.

sented have normally chosen to conduct their own defence. Both prosecution and defence counsel are under obligations to behave in a particular manner in the course of the trial and we shall examine some specific circumstances. However, in any discussion one must remember that counsel should always be acting in accordance with the rules and etiquette of the Bar[15] and must never knowingly mislead or deceive the court as to facts or law.[16] This latter principle is of the utmost importance and impinges upon the task of counsel at several points in the trial.

(a) Prosecuting counsel

The Code of Conduct for the Bar of England and Wales asserts that:

> "It is not the duty of prosecuting counsel to obtain a conviction by all means at his command but rather to lay before the jury fairly and impartially the whole of the facts which comprise the case for the prosecution and to see that the jury are properly instructed in the law applicable to those facts."[17]

This view has found judicial expression at various times and prosecuting counsel have even been described as "ministers of justice assisting in the administration of justice."[18] A distinguished Old Bailey judge who had been Senior Prosecuting Counsel at that court, warned a prosecutor against feeling pride or satisfaction in the mere fact of success, or boasting of the percentage of convictions secured over a period of time. It is, he said, " . . . no rebuff to his prestige if he fails to convince the tribunal of the prisoner's guilt."[19]

These are all very proper sentiments and, no doubt, a correct statement of the position of counsel, but it must prove difficult for the prosecution to be totally dispassionate. What is required is an element of objectivity in approaching the tasks of prosecuting counsel in the conduct of the trial process. Three broad areas may be identified which will all necessitate careful consideration and the exercise of judgment by counsel: the desirability and propriety of a plea arrangement; the nature and presentation of the prosecution case at trial; the amount of assistance which needs to be given to the defence or the judge.

(i) The plea arrangement

Where there are a number of counts on the indictment, or where one count contains alternative charges; or where the jury might convict of a lesser charge, it is not uncommon for the defence to offer a plea of guilty to a lesser charge in return for an agreement from the prosecution to offer no evidence on the more serious charge. This is a form of plea bargaining which is considered fully later in the chapter,[20] and it has the effect of

---

[15] *Code of Conduct for the Bar of England and Wales* (2nd ed., 1983).
[16] *Ibid.* para. 130.
[17] *Ibid.* para. 159.
[18] *R. v. Puddick* (1865) 4 F. & F. 497; *R. v. Banks* [1916] 2 K.B. 621.
[19] C. Humphreys, "The Duties and Responsibilities of Prosecuting Counsel" [1955] Crim.L.R. 739.
[20] At pp. 625–631, below.

creating a certain amount of pressure on the defendant. In this context, however, we are more interested in the problems it may create for prosecuting counsel and what his approach should be in deciding when it is proper to accept a plea of guilty to less than the full indictment.[21]

The advantages for the prosecution of a guilty plea are obvious: there is a saving of time and money; witnesses are spared the experience of testifying; the inevitable uncertainty of the trial is exchanged for the certainty of a plea. Yet it is the responsibility of prosecuting counsel to ensure that if the evidence in the depositions appears to support the offence charged in the indictment, then the indictment is presented and no reduction in plea is accepted. The primary consideration appears to be the strength of the evidence and other factors might, therefore, be regarded as secondary. This view is supported by *R.* v. *Soanes,*[22] which also illustrates the role of the judge in determining the propriety of the course of action adopted by prosecuting counsel.[23] In that case the accused had been charged with the murder of her child (which was less than one month old) and had indicated her wish to plead guilty to the offence of infanticide, a plea which prosecuting counsel was willing to accept. The trial judge refused to accept the plea and directed that the trial should proceed on the charge of murder. The accused was convicted of infanticide and on her appeal the Court of Criminal Appeal commented upon the judge's refusal to accept the lesser plea. Lord Chief Justice Goddard said that it was impossible to lay down a hard-and-fast rule on when a plea for a lesser offence should be accepted by prosecuting counsel, but indicated that the strength of the evidence was the major factor. If there is nothing in the depositions which can reduce the charge to a lesser offence, the indictment should be proceeded with.[24]

If this principle is observed rigidly then it would seem to offer far less scope for plea arrangement than might be imagined, unless it is the practice to include in the indictment counts which are not entirely supported by the evidence.[25] In the event, the likely performance of prosecution witnesses; any indication which may have been given of the defence case; the range of sentence available on difference charges, may all be significant considerations for prosecuting counsel. He must balance brevity and certainty against the need to ensure that the charges reflect the weight of the evidence. As a "minister of justice" and as a representative of the public interest he must seek the correct balance carefully and dispassionately.[26]

---

[21] There is very little written about the difficulties experienced by the prosecution in these circumstances, partly because there is always the recourse to having the full indictment tried and leaving the jury to determine the appropriate convictions.

[22] (1958) 32 Cr.App.R. 136.

[23] The judge will always have discretion to refuse to accept the guilty plea if he is of the opinion that it has been given improperly or accepted improperly by the prosecution. See above, p. 588.

[24] In the *Soanes* case the jury ultimately convicted of the lesser offence (to the obvious disapproval of the appellate court) and the prosecutor's view was vindicated. In the recent Yorkshire Ripper case, the judge's refusal to accept a plea of manslaughter led to a conviction of murder.

[25] The practice of "overcharging" by the prosecution. See p. 628, below.

[26] The prosecutor's discretion in the United States is considered in B. Grosman, *The Prosecutor: An Inquiry into the Exercise of Discretion* (1969).

(ii) *The presentation of the prosecution case*

Apart from planning the general strategy of the prosecution case, counsel will have four specific tasks in its presentation. He will make opening and closing speeches, he will examine the prosecution witnesses and cross-examine the defence witnesses. In each of these tasks he must observe rules of conduct as well as rules of procedure and evidence.

The *opening speech* to the jury is of the utmost importance. There is little need to remind undergraduates that the greatest level of concentration and understanding is likely to be exhibited at the beginning and end of any particular formal instruction, whether it be a lecture or a trial. Jurors, especially, are likely to be taking their duties very seriously at the outset of the trial and the opening speech is bound to have considerable impact. The function of the opening is to explain to the jury the basic elements of the prosecution case, the evidence that is to be called, and the burden and standard of proof. Even allowing for the fact that any mistakes may ultimately be corrected by the judge in his summing-up, it is vital that prosecuting counsel does not claim in his opening more than the depositions will prove for it may eventually be difficult for the jury to remember whether allegations made in the opening speech were actually substantiated in the evidence.[27] Equally he must not open any evidence which is inadmissible,[28] or which defending counsel has indicated that he will challenge as inadmissible. It is highly undesirable that prosecuting counsel should open the case with unnecessarily emotive language, and where the offences charged are likely to excite particular sympathy for the victim or prejudice against the accused counsel should warn the jury not to be influenced by such emotions in weighing the evidence.[29]

In *examining prosecution witnesses* counsel should not use leading questions[30] (except on uncontentious matters and with the agreement of the defence) and there are certain other constraints on the line of questioning that may be adopted.[31]

In *cross-examination* of defence witnesses, prosecuting counsel is entitled to test their evidence fully and fairly subject to the normal constraints on the line of questioning,[32] save that when questioning the accused, prosecuting counsel cannot put questions designed to discredit him (*e.g.* to show previous convictions) unless the accused has himself set up evidence of good character or cast imputations on prosecution witnesses.[33]

---

[27] A particular example of the dangers of the over-optimistic opening speech is to be found in the trial of James Hanratty, where a vital piece of evidence was referred to in the opening but never proved in evidence, see L. Blom-Cooper, *The A6 Murder*. In any event, it may be tactically more sensible to pitch the opening on a relatively low key lest the jury should later be disappointed with the prosecution witnesses!

[28] The opening of such evidence will not automatically lead to the questioning of a subsequent conviction: *R.* v. *Jackson* (1953) 37 Cr.App.R. 43. The normal course would be for the judge to discharge the jury and recommence the trial if the defendant has been seriously prejudiced.

[29] Archbold, *Criminal Pleading, Evidence and Practice* (41st ed., 1982), para. 4–177.

[30] *i.e.* a question which by its form suggests the desired answer. "You saw the defendant take the jewellery and put it in his pocket, didn't you?"

[31] *e.g.* questions about previous inconsistent statements may not be put, nor questions impugning the witness' credit.

[32] That it should be relevant and directed to a material issue.

[33] The question of what amounts to claiming good character, or discrediting prosecution witnesses is very difficult and causes problems for defence counsel. See further below, p. 598.

In the *closing speech* prosecuting counsel may review the evidence and point up alleged strengths in his case and weaknesses in the defence. He is likely to remind the jury once again of the burden and standard of proof.

(iii) Assisting the other participants—the defence and the judge

Prosecuting counsel has an obligation to assist the defence by the disclosure of certain evidence. The disclosure provisions are considered more fully elsewhere,[34] but in brief the prosecution must inform the defence of the name and address of any person who has made a statement related to the prosecution but is not to be called as a witness; of the existence of statements made previously by a prosecution witness which are inconsistent with evidence given at trial by the witness; and of the previous convictions, if any, of prosecution witnesses which are known to the prosecution. These disclosures may materially assist the defence case, and further assistance requested by the defence may be rendered by the prosecution at their discretion.[35]

Assisting the judge is a slightly more difficult problem, although the obligation is made clear in the Code of Conduct. As well as assisting by argument on points of law or procedure that may arise during the trial, "it is the duty of prosecuting counsel to assist the Court at the conclusion of the summing-up by drawing attention to any apparent errors or omissions of fact or law which, in his opinion, ought to be corrected."[36] Needless to say, this duty will have to be discharged with considerable tact.

Influencing the court with regard to sentence is no part of the duties of prosecuting counsel.[37]

(b) Defending counsel

It is perhaps for counsel defending a client in a criminal case that there is the greatest potential conflict between his duty to the court and his duty to his client. Laymen frequently ask how counsel can act as advocate for someone who is "obviously guilty," or how he can put forward a defence or a mitigation which appears to be based on the slenderest of evidence. The answer given by the Bar is that, consistent with counsel's duty not knowingly to deceive or mislead the court,[38] every accused person has a right to have the prosecution case tested and his own case put.[39] In a statement following the case of *R.* v. *McFadden*,[40] in which the trial judge had criticised counsel for wasting time,[41] the Chairman of the Bar said:

---

[34] See p. 508, above.

[35] For examples of assistance, see C. Humphreys, "The Duties and Responsibilities of Prosecuting Counsel" [1955] Crim.L.R. 739.

[36] *Code of Conduct, op. cit.* para. 162.

[37] *Ibid.* para. 163, and see G. Zellick, "The Role of Prosecuting Counsel in Sentencing" [1979] Crim.L.R. 493, and M. King. "The Role of Prosecuting Counsel in Sentencing—What About Magistrates' Courts?" [1979] Crim.L.R. 775.

[38] *Code of Conduct, op.cit.* para. 130.

[39] This is one of the fundamental principles of the Bar: see pp. 119–121, above.

[40] (1976) 62 Cr.App.R. 187.

[41] Melford Stevenson J. had taken a very dim view of the length of the trial in which the evidence had occupied over 30 days, and the closing speeches for the defence 6½ days. There were seven defendants, but the judge thought that counsel had behaved improperly and took the unusual course of inviting the taxing master to look carefully at the fees allowed to counsel on legal aid taxation.

"It is the duty of counsel when defending an accused on a criminal charge to present to the court, fearlessly and without regard to his personal interests, the defence of that accused. It is not his function to determine the truth or falsity of that defence, nor should he permit his personal opinion of that defence to influence his conduct of it . . . Counsel also has a duty to the court and to the public. This duty includes the clear presentation of the issues and the avoidance of waste of time, repetition and prolixity. In the conduct of every case counsel must be mindful of this public responsibility."[42]

The "cab-rank" principle is intended to ensure that every defendant will be able to engage an advocate,[43] and that advocate must, " . . . endeavour to protect his client from being convicted except by a competent tribunal and upon legal evidence sufficient to support a conviction for the offence with which his client is charged."[44] Counsel's opinion of the weight of evidence and the credibility of any defence being suggested by the client will obviously be factors in the advice which defending counsel will give to his client.

(i) Advising on plea and the defendant's confession

Counsel's duty is to advise his client generally about plea, whilst making it clear that the client has freedom of choice and is responsible for his plea.[45] Given the advantages that accrue to a defendant who pleads guilty,[46] counsel may have to achieve a difficult balance in telling the client of those advantages and giving his opinion of the case, whilst not placing undue pressure on him which will rob him of freedom of choice.[47] Counsel's advice to the client may be in "strong terms,"[48] but there has been criticism of the improper pressure which may be exerted by defending counsel.[49]

In the course of advising the client on plea and weighing the prosecution evidence counsel may be told by his client that he is, in fact, guilty of the offence charged. This may emerge in clear terms or as a result of inconsistent statements made by the client, or accidentally. This creates a conflict between the duty to the client (on the assumption that he still wishes to plead not guilty) and the duty to the court, which is difficult for counsel to resolve. It should be emphasised that we are referring to "confessions" of guilt by the accused and not to counsel's suspicions or speculations about guilt on the basis of the evidence.

The rules of professional conduct give precise guidance. If the confession is made before the trial, counsel is required to withdraw from the case or to make it clear that he can only proceed with a not guilty plea within very

---

[42] (1976) 62 Cr.App.R. 193. The complaints against defending counsel were investigated by the Professional Conduct Committee of the Bar, and rejected.

[43] See p. 120, above.

[44] Code of Conduct, op.cit. para. 146.

[45] Ibid. para. 150(a).

[46] Primarily, a lesser sentence: see pp. 626–627 below.

[47] Giving rise to the concern expressed about plea-bargaining.

[48] R. v. Turner [1970] 2 Q.B. 321.

[49] J. Baldwin and M. McConville, Negotiated Justice (1977), especially Chap. 3, and see p. 630, below.

strict limitations.[50] On such a plea he is only permitted to take objection to the competence of the court, the form of the indictment, the admissibility of evidence and sufficiency of the prosecution case.[51] He may not put forward an affirmative case which would involve calling evidence he knows to be false,[52] nor may he suggest that the crime has been committed by someone else. In cross-examination of prosecution witnesses he is entitled to test the strength of their evidence, but not to suggest an affirmative defence. Similarly, if the confession is made during the trial, when counsel could not withdraw without compromising his client, the defending counsel must observe these limitations.[53]

(ii) Correcting defects

The potential conflict of duty is also apparent in counsel's obligations in respect of procedural error, or factual or legal errors made by the court, which are noticed by him but not necessarily by the prosecution.[54] The orthodox view, proceeding partly from the conception of the trial as a game in which the underdog (defendant) is entitled to the benefit of any errors, is that defending counsel is under no obligation to correct the judge, if the judge has erred in matters of fact or law, but he should inform the court as soon as practicable if a procedural irregularity has occurred.[55] Naturally, defending counsel has a discretion to draw attention to factual and legal errors and he will presumably do so if it is to the advantage of his client.

In *R. v. Cocks*[56] the judge had conducted a discussion on a point of law with both counsel after the jury had retired. The judge had, in fact, failed to direct them on an element which was vital to the offence. The Court of Appeal, in quashing the conviction, criticised the practice of hearing argument at that stage of the trial, but also sympathised with defending counsel who was caused embarrassment by being forced to consider a point which might operate to the disadvantage of his client. It was not his duty to correct the judge. However, a later decision[57] has cast some doubt on the correctness of this proposition, at least in relation to fundamental errors in the summing-up.

(iii) The conduct of the defence

The formal procedure for the defence case will be the same as for the prosecution, with an opening speech, witnesses and a closing speech, but it is the tactical conduct of the case which gives rise to greater difficulties. The major problem will often be the extent to which prosecution witnesses can be attacked without allowing the prosecution to place in evidence

---

[50] *Code of Conduct, op.cit.* para. 149(a).

[51] *Ibid.* Annex B.

[52] For example, evidence of alibi.

[53] *Code of Conduct, op.cit.* para. 149(b). In either case, the solicitor and client should both be fully advised of counsel's position.

[54] If they are noticed by the prosecution, they should be raised with the judge: see p. 595, above.

[55] *Code of Conduct, op.cit.* para. 154.

[56] (1976) 63 Cr.App.R. 79.

[57] *R. v. Edwards* (1983) 77 Cr.App.R. 5. See also R. Munday, "The Duties of Defence Counsel" [1983] Crim.L.R. 703, for a full review of the two decisions.

details of the (bad) character of the accused, including any previous convictions.

The normal rules of evidence prevent evidence being given by prosecution witnesses about the defendant's character, and also forbid cross-examination of the accused on that subject.[58] However, those rules cease to operate where the defendant or his counsel has sought to establish his good character or cast imputations upon the character of the prosecutor or prosecution witnesses.[59] It is this latter rule which creates the problem, for the dividing line between an emphatic denial of innocence and an allegation of lies or misconduct by prosecution witnesses (particularly policemen) may be a very narrow one.[60] Counsel, if instructed by the accused to allege that the whole of the prosecution case is a "put-up job," will have to advise on the consequences of running that particular defence. To assist counsel, the trial judge will usually warn him when he is adopting a line of cross-examination or examination which may expose the accused to cross-examination on his character.[61]

(iv) After the verdict

Defending counsel, after a plea or verdict of guilty, will usually make a plea in mitigation of sentence on behalf of his client. He will attempt to put as favourable a view as possible of his client's circumstances and may suggest why particular sentences would, or would not, be appropriate. He must be careful in referring to third parties during his plea for they will have no opportunity to contest assertions made then, and he must not make any allegation which is " . . . merely scandalous, or calculated to vilify or insult any person."[62]

It is the duty of defence counsel to see his client after conviction and sentence, or at least to ensure that the instructing solicitor does so.[63] This can hardly be a popular duty but it may be of significance in giving initial advice on appeal, or the existence of grounds of appeal.

4. THE ROLE OF THE JUDGE[64]

The characterisation of the judge as the umpire or referee in our adversarial system of procedure is not entirely appropriate in the context of

---

[58] See generally, *Cross on Evidence* (5th ed., 1979), pp. 417–440.

[59] Criminal Evidence Act 1898, s.1(*f*).

[60] See *R.* v. *Tanner* (1977) 66 Cr.App.R. 56, and the discussion in Archbold, *Criminal Pleading, Evidence and Practice* (41st ed., 1982), para. 4–357. The most helpful dictum is that of Lord Hewart C.J. in *R.* v. *Jones* (1924) 17 Cr.App. 117, 120: It is " . . . one thing to deny that he had made the confession, but it is another thing to say that the whole thing was a deliberate and elaborate concoction on the part of the inspector: that seems to be an attack on the character of the witness." General guidance is to be found in a decision of the House of Lords, *Selvey* v. *D.P.P.* [1970] A.C. 304, and recent examples include *R.* v. *McGee and Cassidy* (1980) 70 Cr.App.R. 247, and *R.* v. *Britzmann* [1983] 1 W.L.R. 350.

[61] *Selvey* v. *D.P.P.* [1970] A.C. 304, at p. 342A; *R.* v. *Cook* [1959] 2 Q.B. 340, 348.

[62] *Code of Conduct, op.cit.* para. 157.

[63] *Ibid.* para. 158.

[64] *Jones* v. *National Coal Board* [1957] 2 Q.B. 55, and see p. 541, above. This case is discussed by Lord Denning in *The Due Process of Law* (1980) pp. 58–62. On the criminal trial, see in particular R. Pattenden, *The Judge, Discretion and the Criminal Trial* (1982), A. Samuels, "Judicial Misconduct and the Criminal Trial" [1982] Crim.L.R. 221.

the trial on indictment. It is true that he should apply the rules, that he should allow counsel to present the case without undue hindrance, that he should not intervene unduly and that ultimately the decision on matters of fact belongs to the jury. However, it is equally true that the judge exercises a very considerable discretion in respect of many aspects of the trial and it is reasonably clear that the way in which he chooses to exercise that discretion may have a significant bearing on the outcome. Indeed, in certain circumstances, the judge's ruling will determine the case. In considering the extent of the judge's discretion and the possible effects of its exercise we should bear in mind the relationship between judge and jury. We shall note, later in this chapter, the criticism that the jury is uncontrollable, unpredictable, amateur, and given to the rendering of "perverse" verdicts which are contrary to the evidence. Take note, however, in this section of the circumstances which may permit the judge to influence, even control, the jury's verdict.

In procedural matters, issues of substantive law arising in the trial, issues of fact, verdict and sentence, the judge has a part to play and we shall look at these situations in turn.

(a) Procedural matters

From the outset the judge has control over the progress of the trial and the administrative and procedural problems that may arise. He must decide questions relating to the form of the indictment[65] and any necessary amendment to it[66]; the taking of the plea from the defendant and its acceptability[67]; the determination of preliminary points raised by counsel[68]; the desirability of separate trials.[69] Whilst these may be classed as procedural questions, their importance should not be underestimated. In some cases the determination of the procedural point may settle the whole issue.

The empanelling and swearing of the jury is subject to judicial control. He will settle any question over challenges,[70] and has the right to direct that the jury panel should include a coloured man.[71] Once sworn, with the case proceeding, the jury may be discharged by the judge for a variety of

[65] For example, a motion to quash the indictment is taken before the defendant is required to plead and deals with whether the indictment discloses any offence. Defects can now often be met by amendment. See Archbold, *Criminal Pleading, Evidence and Practice* (41st ed., 1982), paras. 1–110 to 1–114.

[66] Indictments Act 1915, s.5 permits the judge to allow amendment to the indictment at any stage of a trial so long as there will be no injustice in all the circumstances. See *R.* v. *Nelson* (1977) 65 Cr.App.R. 119, which is also instructive on the obligations of defending counsel to draw irregularities to the notice of the court, *cf.* p. 597, above.

[67] For the significance of the judge's discretion to refuse a plea in relation to prosecuting counsel's obligations on the arrangement of pleas, see p. 593, above, and p. 628, below. In *R.* v. *Winterflood* (1978) 68 Cr.App.R. 291, the trial judge appears to have taken the initiative in suggesting the addition of a charge to the indictment to which the accused might plead guilty.

[68] For example, in relation to the hearing of the case *in camera* or the restriction of publicity in certain circumstances.

[69] Not only separate trials of co-accused, but also separate trials for the accused on separate charges. The practice is to join several charges together on one indictment where they are founded on the same facts or form part of a series of offences of the same or similar character. Indictment Rules 1971, r. 9. See C. Yates, "How Many Counts to an Indictment?" [1976] Crim.L.R. 428.

[70] See p. 612, below.

[71] See p. 612, below.

reasons.[72] We have noted the power to discharge where inadmissible evidence is opened by the prosecution,[73] but this is merely an example of a wider power which may be exercised where the judge perceives it to be necessary, or where death or illness of a juror occurs, or where there is jury misconduct. The power ought not to be exercised lightly and the overall question is really whether there is a danger of the jury being prejudiced against the defendant.[74] The effect of discharging the jury is not to acquit the defendant—he may be remanded for a second trial.[75]

It is also the judge's responsibility to maintain order in court and he is given powers of punishment for contempt where there is misbehaviour.[76]

Although counsel for the prosecution and the defence must conduct their respective cases in accordance with the rules of etiquette for the Bar, the judge has a significant role in controlling the questioning of witnesses by counsel[77] and in restraining counsel from improper practices. The control should be discreet and the judge must resist the temptation to take over the questioning himself[78] or to criticise counsel's conduct to such an extent that the jury might thereby be prejudiced.[79]

(b) Matters of law

The division between matters of law and matters of fact is not one that is always easy to discern in the criminal trial. The traditional view is that matters of law are for the judge to determine and matters of fact should be left to the jury, but that is dependent upon knowing what *are* matters of law, and the statement also ignores the judge's control over certain factual issues.

(i) Evidence and its admissibility

The situation is further complicated because it is necessary to acknowledge the extent of the judge's discretion in dealing with the admissibility of evidence, a question which is clearly characterised as a matter of law.

---

[72] See generally, Archbold, *op. cit.* paras 4–167 to 4–173. *R.* v. *Binns* [1982] Crim.L.R. 522.

[73] See p. 594, above.

[74] The trial of some women from the Greenham Common peace camp was halted and the jury discharged because of the risk of prejudice resulting from an article about the camp in the Daily Express which appeared before the end of the trial. *Daily Express,* April 11, 1984.

[75] *R.* v. *Randall* [1960] Crim.L.R. 435. In this case the jury was discharged after returning verdicts of not guilty, which were then stated to be majority verdicts. (Majority verdicts were not at that time acceptable.) The plea of *autrefois acquit* at the second trial was rejected.

[76] There is a summary power to punish contempts "in the face of the court" which is given to maintain the dignity and authority of the judge and to ensure a fair trial. See *Balogh* v. *Crown Court at St Albans* [1975] 1 Q.B. 73, discussed in Lord Denning, *The Due Process of Law* (1980) at pp. 12–18. The accused was apprehended before he had livened up court proceedings by introducing "laughing gas" into the ventilating system at St Albans Crown Court. See also, *Morris* v. *Crown Office* [1970] 2 Q.B. 114 (group of students breaking up a libel trial); *R.* v. *Aquarius* [1974] Crim.L.R. 373, (disruptive behaviour of defendant); *R.* v. *Logan* [1974] Crim.L.R. 609 (outburst by defendant after sentence); *Lecointe* v. *Courts Administrator of the Central Criminal Court* (1973, unreported) (distribution of leaflets at the Old Bailey inciting people to picket the court).

[77] The line of questioning must be relevant and material and witnesses should be treated courteously.

[78] See n. 64, above.

[79] *R.* v. *McFadden* (1976) 62 Cr.App.R. 187, and see A. Samuels, "Judicial Misconduct in the Criminal Trial" [1982] Crim.L.R. 221, 223.

Whether a piece of evidence will, or will not, be admitted will be determined by the application of established principle after legal argument from both counsel in the absence of the jury,[80] but even the principles allow the judge such a degree of discretion that it is not always possible to talk about rules. The following consideration of the judge's role in deciding on the admissibility of evidence is set in that context.

Evidence which is likely to have an unfair prejudicial effect on the jury outweighing its probative value may be excluded by the trial judge.[81] This proposition is founded on a number of judicial decisions which have transformed a cautiously expressed view about the ability of a trial judge to suggest to counsel that certain evidence be not led, into a clear principle of exclusion at the discretion of the judge.[82] It would appear that this balancing of probative value against prejudicial effect allows the judge to come to an impressionistic view with little fear of being corrected by the Court of Appeal.[83] Pattenden identifies some of the situations in which the exercise of this discretion may be relevant: similar fact evidence; hearsay evidence; statements made in the presence of the accused, and certain voluntary confessions.[84]

Evidence which is apparently admissible to show the bad character of the accused after he, or his counsel, has made imputations about the character of prosecution witnesses, may also be excluded at the discretion of the trial judge if it would be unfair to allow it in.[85] The discretion to exclude the evidence in these circumstances has been evolved in line with the general discretion to exclude prejudicial evidence described in the preceding paragraph. Fairness will be the major factor in deciding whether to exclude and the court may place particular weight on the way in which the imputations have been made,[86] the relative probative value of evidence of the accused's character and whether the imputations were genuinely part of the accused's defence rather than a specific attack on prosecution witnesses.[87]

The exclusion of illegally obtained evidence is less a matter for discretion than for the application of a fairly clear rule of law. Provided evidence is relevant, it will be admissible even though it has been obtained by unfair or

[80] The "trial within a trial." The likely sequence of events in the event of a possible dispute over evidence is for defending counsel to give notice of his objection to the prosecution who should then omit reference to it in the opening. Immediately before the evidence is to be called the prosecution (or the defence) will tell the judge that a question of law has arisen and the jury will be sent out. Defending counsel will address the judge, call evidence if necessary and argue his case. Prosecuting counsel has similar rights.

[81] *Noor Mohamed* v. *R.* [1949] A.C. 182; *Harris* v. *D.P.P.* [1952] A.C. 694.

[82] The development is traced in R. Pattenden, *The Judge, Discretion and the Criminal Trial* (1982), pp. 64–66.

[83] *R.* v. *Morris* (1969) 54 Cr.App.R. 69.

[84] Pattenden, *op. cit.* pp. 70–75.

[85] The circumstances in which the prosecution may take advantage of the Criminal Evidence Act 1898, s.1(*f*) have been noted at p. 598, above. Even where the Act applies it appears that there is a discretion to exclude.

[86] For example, if they have been made accidentally, inadvertently or in response to questions from the judge, it may be unfair to allow in evidence of the accused's character.

[87] The existence of the discretion eases the difficulty for defending counsel referred to at p. 598, above. If there is genuine doubt about whether the imputations have been made deliberately or as part of a defence, that may be a reason for exclusion: *R.* v. *Cook* [1959] 2 Q.B. 340; *R.* v. *Flynn* [1963] 1 Q.B. 729.

illegal means.[88] The discretion noted in the last two paragraphs to exclude prejudicial evidence of negligible probative value, may also be exercised in respect of illegally obtained evidence, but there are very few examples.[89] The emphasis is certainly placed upon the admissibility of the evidence and the judge's role is limited.

The particular form of evidence which is often alleged to have been improperly obtained is the confession. The admissibility of such evidence may be hotly contested by the defence because it is so damning. The exclusion of confessions has nothing to do with their minimal probative value—they are obviously highly probative—but rather with their unfairness and unreliability if obtained in dubious circumstances. In respect of confession evidence there is a rule to be applied together with an additional element of discretion. The rule is that evidence of a confession is only admissible if the confession has been made voluntarily, in that it had not been obtained by means of threats or inducements by a person in authority.[90] Where the voluntariness of the confession is contested by the defence, the judge will hear argument in the absence of the jury and must then give a ruling. Compliance with the Judges' Rules will be a significant factor for the judge to take into account, but there is authority to suggest that a breach of the Rules is only to be considered in deciding whether the confession was voluntary rather than as a reason for excluding the evidence automatically.[91] It is also suggested that where there is no breach of the Rules and the confession appears voluntary, there is still a discretion to exclude the evidence if its admission would be unjust and unfair to an accused.[92] In sum, the judge's role is to decide on the voluntariness of the confession, taking into account all the factors and ultimately to decide whether there is any reason why a voluntary confession should be excluded.

(ii) The summing-up

The other major matters of law which are the responsibility of the judge are those which must be explained to the jury so that they can reach a proper decision. He will deal with these matters in the summing up, telling the jury that they must accept his direction on issues of law.

First, he should tell the jury again about the burden and standard of proof. Prosecuting counsel may have done this in his opening speech and it may have been referred to during the trial, but the judge will tell the jury that the burden of proof is on the prosecution[93] and that the standard they must satisfy is proof beyond reasonable doubt.[94] If there are any variations

---

[88] *Kuruma* v. *R.* [1955] A.C. 197; and see *Cross on Evidence* (5th ed., 1979), pp. 324–6. *R.* v. *Sang and Mangan* [1979] 3 W.L.R. 263.

[89] *Callis* v. *Gunn* [1964] 1 Q.B. 495; *Jeffrey* v. *Black* [1978] Q.B. 490.

[90] *Ibrahim* v. *R.* [1914] A.C. 599; and see Cross, *op. cit.* pp. 534–546.

[91] *R.* v. *Prager* [1972] 1 W.L.R. 260; *Conway* v. *Hotten* [1976] 2 All E.R. 213; *R.* v. *Lemsatef* [1977] 1 W.L.R. 812.

[92] See Cross, *op. cit.* p. 548.

[93] As it is in most circumstances in the criminal trial. It is otherwise in respect of the defence of insanity.

[94] The actual formulation of the direction to the jury has varied. "Satisfied so that you feel sure" has its supporters: *Walters* v. *The Queen* [1960] 2 A.C. 26; *R.* v. *Summers* (1952) 36 Cr.App.R. 14. So does, "satisfied beyond all/any/a reasonable doubt": *D.P.P.* v. *Woolmington* [1935] A.C. 462; *R.* v. *Lawrence* [1982] A.C. 510. For the judge who wishes to be doubly safe, the direction, " . . . satisfied beyond reasonable doubt so that you feel sure of the defendant's guilt" has also been approved: *Ferguson* v. *The Queen* [1979] 1 W.L.R. 94.

in the burden and standard[95] the judge must direct the jury accordingly and he is also likely to deal with the effect of the accused raising a particular defence.[96]

Secondly, he must explain to the jury the legal requirements of the offence charged and the facts of which the jury must be convinced before they can convict. This may not be easy! In a case of theft, for example, he should say that the property stolen must have belonged to someone else and must have been appropriated by the accused, who must have been dishonest and intending to deprive the other person permanently of the property.[97] Yet there are already difficulties. What is an appropriation? What amounts to dishonesty? What if the property has been "borrowed," to be returned at some (distant) future date?

It is clear that the judge must explain the law in the context of the evidence in the case. It may be that there has obviously been a theft, but the accused says that it is a case of mistaken identity. If the only issue is whether the person who took the goods was indeed the accused, a sophisticated analysis of the meaning of "an appropriation" would be out of place. Where the evidence does not limit the issues then the judge must try to instruct the jury in terms that they will understand.

The example of theft raises another problem which we referred to in the introductory chapter, namely the distinction between issues of fact and issues of law.[98] The judge must direct the jury on issues of law—what then does he tell them about "dishonesty"? When the jury have come to a view about the defendant's actions and his state of mind do they have to try and match this to some legal definition recited to them by the judge, or do they simply ask themselves, "Is this sort of conduct dishonest by our standards?" The difference in approach is significant, and the recent tendency had been for judges to leave such matters to the jury as questions of fact.[99] However, the latest cases have re-established that the meaning of dishonesty is a matter of law[1] and that the accused will be dishonest if the jury decides: (i) that what he did was dishonest by the standards of ordinary, decent people; and (ii) that he must have realised that what he was doing was by those standards dishonest.[2] Whether the appellate courts will seek to re-assert control over the jury in other areas remains to be seen, but the measure of freedom granted to juries by the classification of issues as fact rather than law is an important part of the argument about the effectiveness of the jury. The greater the number of issues of law upon

---

[95] The defendant will occasionally bear the burden, *e.g.* on a defence of insanity, or in certain statutory offences, and when he does the standard is satisfied by proof on a balance of probabilities, see Archbold, *op. cit.* para. 4–425.

[96] For example, he would probably tell the jury that if the defendant says, "I wasn't there" or "I hit him in self-defence," it is not for the defendant to prove that, but for the prosecution to prove beyond reasonable doubt that he was there, or was not acting in self-defence.

[97] Theft Act 1968, s.1.

[98] At pp. 6–11, above.

[99] See *R.* v. *Feely* (1973) 57 Cr.App.R. 312: "We can see no reason why . . . [the jury] . . . should require the help of a judge to tell them what amounts to dishonesty": *per* Lawton L.J. at p. 317.

[1] In particular, *R.* v. *Ghosh* [1982] 2 Q.B. 1053.

[2] *Ibid.* p. 1064. See commentary in [1982] Crim.L.R. 608, and D.W. Elliott, "Dishonesty in Theft: A Dispensable Concept" [1982] Crim.L.R. 395.

which the judge gives direction, the fewer the opportunities for the legitimate[3] exercise of discretion/common sense by the jury.

Thirdly, the judge may have to give the jury directions about the evidence which they have heard. Although questions of fact are to be decided by the jury they may have to be warned of the legal requirements on the corroboration of evidence,[4] or on evidence of identity.[5]

(c) Matters of fact

The issues of law with which the judge deals in his summing-up are obviously important to the outcome of the case, and it is equally clear that matters of fact are normally determined by the jury. However, the summing-up is vital in presenting the case to the jury, and thus the judge has a role to play in the resolution of the factual issues in the case. A recent pronouncement by the Lord Chancellor emphasises the judge's obligations in leaving the case to the jury:

"The purpose of a direction to a jury is not best achieved by a disquisition on jurisprudence or philosophy or a universally applicable circular tour round the area of law affected by the case . . . A direction to a jury should be custom-built to make the jury understand their task in relation to a particular case. Of course, it must include references to the burden of proof and the respective role of jury and judge. But it should also include a succinct but accurate summary of the issues of fact as to which a decision is required, a correct but concise summary of the evidence and arguments on both sides and a correct statement of the inferences which the jury are entitled to draw from their particular conclusions about the primary facts."[6]

The object of the summing-up, then, is to put the case before the jury, and in a complex case a substantial amount of the evidence will be rehearsed for the jury.[7] The judge is likely to stress in his direction that on matters of fact the jury are the sole arbiters and should not be influenced by any opinions that he may express about the evidence.[8] Although this direction may be given, it would be naive to think that the views of the judge, if expressed, have no bearing on the jury's decision.[9] Consequently, it becomes important to establish the extent to which a judge may legitimately comment upon the evidence, the witnesses and the arguments.

---

[3] See D.W. Elliott, "Law and Fact in Theft Act Cases" [1976] Crim.L.R. 707; G. Williams, "Law and Facts" [1976] Crim.L.R. 472, 537; E. Griew, *Dishonesty and the Jury* (1974).

[4] See Archbold, *op. cit.* Chap. 16.

[5] *R.* v. *Turnbull* [1977] 2 Q.B. 224.

[6] *R.* v. *Lawrence* [1982] A.C. 510.

[7] The judge keeps a note of the evidence—a process which has a significant effect on the speed of the criminal trial—and he will remind the jury of it in the summing up. He must also be careful to put the defence case fully and properly. For a particularly abbreviated summing-up consisting almost entirely of a low, prolonged whistle, see *Pie-powder*, by a circuit tramp (1911), p. 70, cited in A. Samuels, "Judicial Misconduct in the Criminal Trial" [1982] Crim.L.R. 221.

[8] *R.* v. *Bradbury* (1920) 15 Cr.App.R. 76; *R.* v. *Mason* (1924) 18 Cr.App.R. 131.

[9] At its lowest, the position of the summing-up at the end of the trial must give it significance. Add to that the respect accorded to a professional's view by laymen and their natural tendency to rely on the judge's analysis and the judge's influence is clear.

In general, the judge is entitled to comment on matters arising out of the evidence,[10] including the strength of the respective cases, the demeanour and quality of the witnesses,[11] the credibility of evidence, and even the verdict that he considers appropriate.[12] This comment may be in strong terms provided that, overall, the comment is not unfair[13] and the jury is reminded clearly and forcefully that they have the ultimate responsibility for deciding issues of fact.[14] The judge's comments may be other than verbal: gesture, tone of voice and facial expression can all speak volumes in indicating the judge's view of the merits, and they have the added merit of not appearing on the transcript.[15] The Court of Appeal appears to be unwilling to interfere with a conviction on the ground that the judge has overstepped the permissible limits of comment unless the summing-up is very defective.[16] An informal constraint on the extent of judicial comment is the possibility that the jury will react against a very strong direction to convict and, out of perversity or sympathy for the accused, bring in a verdict of acquittal.

In appropriate cases, where the evidence warrants it, a judge may tell a jury that they must convict.[17]

There are two particular circumstances in which a judge must be careful in what he says to the jury, namely when the defendant has made no answer to the police and/or has not disclosed his defence until trial, and when he has not exercised his right to give evidence at trial. Both these are examples of the so-called "right to silence" based upon the propositions that the accused should not be required to provide any evidence which might incriminate him and that he is entitled to make the prosecution prove the case against him without answering questions before or at his trial.[18] The question has arisen as to the extent to which the jury are able or obliged to draw prejudicial inferences from the silence of the accused.

It will be safest for the judge to make no comment on the defendant's failure to disclose a defence until trial or to answer questions before trial.[19] He must certainly avoid inviting the jury to draw inferences adverse to the defendant[20] and it will be difficult to find an appropriate comment which

---

[10] For an interesting account of the summing up in the *Oz* case, see T. Palmer *The Trials of Oz* (1971). There was a great deal of comment contained in that summing-up which was later the subject of appeal: *R.* v. *Anderson* [1972] 1 Q.B. 304.

[11] "I thought he was a jolly good witness. He wasn't prepared to whitewash all of *Oz* like some of the other so-called experts and I can't say fairer than that": *per* Judge Argyle, quoted in Palmer, *op. cit.* p. 252.

[12] *D.P.P.* v. *Stonehouse* [1978] A.C. 55.

[13] *R.* v. *Middlesex Justices, ex parte D.P.P.* [1952] 2 Q.B. 758.

[14] *e.g.* ". . . if I now express an opinion and you agree, well, that's alright. If not, you can disagree. You do not have to do what I tell you. What I think is irrelevant. *You* have to decide": per Judge Argyle, Palmer *op.cit.* p. 239.

[15] Winks and grimaces defeat even the shorthand writer.

[16] *Cf. R.* v. *Anderson* [1972] 1 Q.B. 304.

[17] *R.* v. *Ferguson* (1970) 54 Cr.App.R. 410, although these cases are likely to be very unusual.

[18] See Criminal Law Revision Committee, *Eleventh Report Evidence* (*General*) Cmnd. 4991 (1972); R.C.C.P. Cmd. 8092 (1981), pp. 80–91.

[19] *R.* v. *Tune* (1944) 29 Cr.App.R. 162. ". . . observations of different sorts by judges have from time to time been made the subject of appeals to this court. If nothing is said by way of comment, no point can be raised."

[20] *R.* v. *Sullivan* (1967) 51 Cr.App.R. 102.

does not have that effect. On the failure of the accused to testify at trial the judge may comment, so long as he points out to the jury that the accused has a right to remain silent and that they should not equate his silence with guilt.[21] Again, a comment which avoids inviting the jury to draw an adverse inference may be difficult to frame.

(d) Verdict and sentence

In the summing-up the judge will have asked the jury to reach a unanimous verdict if possible. He may thereafter give a direction about, and ultimately accept, a majority verdict if there is no unanimity.[22] In the event of ambiguous or inconsistent verdicts it will be the obligation of the judge to clarify them. Should the jury fail to reach a verdict at all the judge must either send them back to the jury room to consider the matter further, or discharge them.[23]

Sentencing is dealt with in Chapter 18, below.

(e) The judge's influence

From the foregoing it can be seen that the judge has a very considerable influence over the outcome of the trial, not only in matters of procedure and law but also in the influence and control that he exercises over the jury. One further matter should now be mentioned that does not fit happily into the preceding categories, namely the judge's power to direct an acquittal on a submission by defence counsel that there is no case to answer, or on his own initiative. This power gives him a direct control over the decision and, although the principle is presented as one of law, in reality the judge is making an assessment of the evidence presented up to that point by the prosecution.

In *R.* v. *Galbraith*[24] the Court of Appeal examined the principles upon which the judge should proceed. Where there is no evidence that the defendant committed the crime alleged the judge should stop the case and direct an acquittal. Where there is some evidence of a tenuous character against the accused the judge may stop the case if, in his opinion, no reasonable jury properly directed could convict on it even if it were accepted. If the question is merely as to the credibility of the evidence the case should go on.[25] Since there is no provision for an appeal by the prosecution against an acquittal, the judge's powers of directed acquittal are highly significant. We shall return to them in the next section in relation to the functions of the jury.[26]

5. THE JURY[27]

The jury has received much attention from writers and, latterly, researchers. The secrecy in which its deliberations are shrouded and the

---

[21] *R.* v. *Bathurst* [1968] 2 Q.B. 99; *R.* v. *Sparrow* (1973) 57 Cr.App.R. 352.
[22] See p. 615, below.
[23] See above. p. 600.
[24] (1981) 73 Cr.App.R. 124.
[25] *Ibid.* p. 127.
[26] See below, p. 620.
[27] Much material is available. That to which we shall particularly be referring in this section includes: W.R. Cornish, *The Jury* (1971); Lord Devlin, *Trial by Jury* (1956); N. Walker (ed.), *The British Jury System* (1975); J. Baldwin and M. McConville, *Jury Trials* (1979); M. McConville and J. Baldwin, *Courts, Prosecution and Conviction* (1981); M.D.A. Freeman, "The Jury on Trial" (1981) 34 C.L.P. 65.

inscrutability of its decisions have together ensured that the majority of the opinions about the quality of its decisions and the desirability of its existence are based on speculation, sentiment and personal values. We shall attempt to reflect the varying views on the jury, whilst describing the research which has been undertaken and the procedural context in which the jury operates. In the beginning was trial by ordeal.[28]

(a) Historical background[29]

The decision of the Fourth Lateran Council in 1215[30] to withdraw the support of the Church from the process of trial by ordeal is generally recognised as the factor which prompted the adoption of the jury system for the determination of criminal cases. That the jury was in existence before 1215 is undisputed, since it would have been almost the only means of collecting information on administrative as well as judicial matters.[31] As well as determining issues which were relevant to the king, juries came to be used for determining issues of interest to private individuals and were available to replace trial by battle.[32] When trespass was alleged, including the allegation of a breach of the king's peace, a writ of *venire facias* went to the sheriff who summoned a group of twelve[33] men to meet and give a verdict on the allegation. On the demise of trial by ordeal the jury was used to determine the guilt of alleged criminals.[34]

In the beginning, the role of the jury was unclear.[35] Were the twelve individuals to deliberate and deliver a verdict to the judge, or was the judge to treat them as witnesses, examine them and come to his own decision about the case? The resolution of this question shaped the future of the jury and the future of criminal procedure.[36] In the event, the collective deliberative role of the jury prevailed and the transition from knowledge to ignorance as the primary characteristic of a juror began. The landmarks are well known. By 1367 it had become established that the verdict had to be unanimous.[37] Witnesses began to give evidence and the jury were prevented from talking to any outsider until they had reached a verdict.[37] In *Bushell's* case it was established that the jury had the right to give a verdict according to their conscience.[38] By the eighteenth century it was finally established that a juror should not take part in a case of which he had personal knowledge. Now a juror is excused if he is closely

---

[28] See above, p. 6.

[29] Pollock and Maitland, *History of English Law* (2nd ed., 1898), Vol. II, pp. 618–50; W.S. Holdsworth, *History of English Law* (3rd ed., 1922) Vol. I, pp. 312–50; J.H. Baker, *An Introduction to English Legal History* (2nd ed., 1979), Chap. 5.

[30] Inspired by Pope Innocent III—what an appropriate name for the Pontiff who caused the institution which has received so much modern criticism over acquittal rates.

[31] The practice of getting a group together and putting them under oath to tell the truth had been highly effective for the Normans.

[32] Under Henry II. Two assizes existed: the grand assize and the petty assize. It was the petty assize which evolved into the jury.

[33] Why twelve? The answer is unknown.

[34] C. Wells, "Instructions given by Henry III to Itinerant Justices 1219" (1914) 30 L.Q.R. 97.

[35] Pollock and Maitland, *op.cit.* p. 622ff.

[36] Guiding procedure into the adverserial system and away from the inquisitorial system with its emphasis on judicial involvement.

[37] J.H. Baker, *op.cit.* p. 66.

[38] *R.* v. *Sheriffs of London, ex p. Bushell* (1670) Vaughn 135.

connected with a party to the proceedings or with a prospective witness, or personally concerned in the facts of the case.[39]

The jury's role is now indicated in the oath taken by each juror at the beginning of a trial on indictment:

> "I swear by Almighty God that I will faithfully try the several issues joined between our Sovereign Lady the Queen and the prisoner(s) at the bar and give a true verdict according to the evidence."[40]

(b) Qualification for jury service and selection

To qualify for selection as a juror a person must be aged between 18 and 65, registered as a parliamentary or local government elector, and have been ordinarily resident in the United Kingdom[41] for any period of at least five years since the age of 13.[42] In addition, a person must not fall into the categories of people disqualified or rendered ineligible by Schedule 1 of the Juries Act 1974.[43]

Those persons *disqualified* are those who have at any time been sentenced in the United Kingdom to five years or more imprisonment or youth custody, or to be detained at Her Majesty's pleasure, *and* those persons who at any time in the last ten years have been sentenced in the United Kingdom to three months or more imprisonment, detention or youth custody or have been detained in a youth custody centre.[44]

The lists of those persons *ineligible* for jury service also appear in Schedule 1 and are divided into four groups headed, "The Judiciary," "Others concerned with the administration of justice," "The Clergy, etc." and "The mentally ill."

The objective of disqualification and ineligibility is to exclude from participation those who are, or have been, intimately connected with the administration of justice (from one standpoint or another)[45] or those who are demonstrably incompetent. Inevitably, a number of people are excluded who might make very good jurors.

The qualifications for jury service were revised in 1972[46] when the requirement that a juror should be an occupier of a house with a prescribed rateable value was abolished, and the electoral register adopted as the basis of qualification. There had been growing criticism of the composition of the jury before 1972, and its unrepresentative nature.[47] Since the

---

[39] *Practice Direction* (1973) 57 Cr.App.R. 345.

[40] *Practice Note* [1957] 1 W.L.R. 355. An alternative form is provided for jurors who wish to affirm.

[41] Or the Channel Islands or the Isle of Man.

[42] Juries Act 1974, s.1.

[43] As amended by the Criminal Justice Act 1982, Sched. 14, para. 35, to add youth custody into the disqualification provisions.

[44] Juries Act 1974, Sched. 1, Part II as amended.

[45] Legislation is imminent to increase the numbers of those disqualified by widening the criteria.

[46] By the Criminal Justice Act 1972, which implemented some of the recommendations of the Morris Committee, *Jury Service*, Cmnd. 2627 (1965).

[47] In Lord Devlin's oft-quoted phrase, the property qualification produced a jury which was, " . . . predominantly male, middle-aged, middle-minded and middle-class": *Trial by Jury*, p. 20. It is reported that when Bernard Rothman and others were tried at Derby Assizes in 1932 on charges relating to a mass trespass on private land near Kinder Scout in the Peak District, the jury consisted of two brigadier-generals, three colonels, two majors, three captains and two aldermen: *The Guardian*, January 18, 1982.

adoption of the new qualification, research has demonstrated[48] that, as expected, the composition of juries has changed profoundly. Juries are less middle class[49] and much younger than before,[50] but there still appears to be an under-representation of women and members of ethnic minorities. These latter deficiencies may be partly explicable on the grounds of selection policy[51] and excusal of women jurors, but it does appear that a totally representative jury has not yet been achieved.[52]

Selection of jurors from the electoral register has previously been a matter for individual summoning officers, but experiments are presently been conducted to facilitate selection by computer.[53] A number having been allotted to all those on the electoral register, random number selection by computer can be utilised. Depending on the results of the experiment and the computerisation of electoral lists this could become the standard system.

(c) Summons, empanelling and vetting

Those persons selected by whatever process is used by the summoning officer receive a summons requiring them to attend at the Crown Court at a specified time. Accompanying the summons is a form which is intended to identify those ineligible or disqualified, and a set of notes which explain something of the procedure of jury service and the functions of the juror.[54] A failure to attend the Crown Court can result in a fine, as can unfitness for service through drink or drugs after attendance![55]

Those summoned for service constitute the jury panel and from the panel the jury for individual cases will be selected.[56] The panel may be divided into parts relating to different days or sittings.[57] It was formerly the case that the jury list would contain the names, addresses and occupations of the panel but the occupation was deleted in 1973 when the Lord Chancellor exercised his powers to determine the information included on the list.[58] Knowledge of the occupation of the juror was, of course, of assistance to counsel in deciding whether to challenge any of the jurors.[59]

[48] *Jury Trials*, pp. 94–99.

[49] *Ibid.* Table 10, p. 95.

[50] *Ibid.* Table 11, p. 96. 27 per cent. of jurors empanelled in Birmingham in 1975 and 1976 were under 30.

[51] A policy of summoning twice the number of male jurors than females has now been abandoned in Birmingham but would have influenced the figures.

[52] Language problems may also serve to excuse some jurors, but the problem has surfaced in another way when defendants have objected to the lack of coloured jurors on a panel. There is a discretion in the trial judge to discharge the whole panel to achieve a more representative selection: see p. 612, below.

[53] R. Tarling, "The Random Selection of Jurors," Home Office Research Bulletin No. 13 (1982). Some officers proceed by alphabetical selection, or selection from a particular street or ward.

[54] The notes assist the juror in his task by dealing with the swearing-in and challenges, trial procedure, the verdict, secrecy, taking notes, etc.

[55] Juries Act 1974, s.20(1).

[56] See p. 611, below.

[57] Juries Act 1974, s.5.

[58] See, H. Harman and J. Griffith, *Justice Deserted, the Subversion of the Jury* (1979). The power was exercised under what is now Juries Act 1974, s.5, then the Courts Act, 1971, s.32.

[59] See below, p. 612.

The subject of jury vetting has been under consideration in the last few years accompanied by the allegation that the practice of vetting undermines the basis on which the jury is established as a random selection of fellow citizens assembled for the purpose of determining guilt.[60] Vetting involves the investigation of members of the jury panel with the object of revealing previous convictions which may disqualify a juror, political beliefs which are so biased that they might interfere with a juror's fair assessment of the facts in security or terrorist cases, or dangers that a juror might make improper use of evidence heard *in camera* in a security trial. Information gleaned from such vetting may then be made available to counsel for the prosecution so as to allow him to exercise the right of stand by[61] and exclude particular people from the jury.

The procedure surfaced in 1978 as a result of the trial of a soldier and two journalists (Aubrey, Berry and Campbell) at the Old Bailey on charges under the Official Secrets Act 1911. It became apparent during the trial that the jury panel had been investigated[62] and in the ensuing public debate, the Attorney-General published the guidelines under which the vetting had been carried out.[63] The guidelines reaffirm three basic principles relating to jury selection, namely:

(i)   members of juries should be selected at random from the panel;
(ii) no-one other than those specified in the Juries Act 1974 should be treated as disqualified or ineligible;
(iii) the correct way of excluding a member of the panel is for prosecuting counsel to exercise the right to stand by or challenge for cause.[64]

However, they go on to specify situations in which vetting is permissible with the results being passed on to the prosecution. The type of cases involved are identified as those involving national security or terrorist acts. Special Branch records may be used and checks will be made on security and political beliefs. Certain safeguards are incorporated.

Annexed to the guidelines was a statement of the practice of the police in carrying out checks on the previous convictions of the jury panel to ensure that disqualified persons do not sit on a jury.[65]

The legality of the guidelines was contested in *R.* v. *Sheffield Crown Court, ex p. Brownlow*[66] where a majority of the Court of Appeal (Civil Division) said *obiter* that they were unconstitutional.[67] The point was not strictly in issue since the court decided, in any event, that it had no

---

[60] See H. Harman and J. Griffith, *op. cit.*; A. Nicol, "Official Secrets and Jury Vetting" [1979] Crim.L.R. 284; M. Zander, *Cases and Materials on the English Legal System* (3rd ed., 1980), pp. 299–305.

[61] See p. 612, below, and J. F. McEldowney, "Stand By for the Crown: an Historical Analysis" [1979] Crim.L.R. 272.

[62] In the first trial, defence counsel made an application to have the jury discharged. One of the defendants said so on television with the result that the first trial was stopped and the jury discharged. This gave the opportunity for the matter to be raised directly at the beginning of the second trial. The guidelines were actually published in the middle of the second trial on October 11, 1978.

[63] The full text is to be found at (1981) 72 Cr.App.R. 14.

[64] See p. 612, below.

[65] (1981) 72 Cr.App.R. 16.

[66] [1980] Q.B. 530.

[67] Lord Denning M.R. and Shaw L.J. Brandon L.J. expressed serious doubts about the practice.

jurisdiction to review an order made by the Crown Court judge, but the condemnation of the practice was clear. In the Criminal Division of the Court of Appeal the point was argued in *R. v. Mason*[68] and the court had no hesitation in upholding the legality of vetting although the judgment is specifically restricted to the use of vetting for the purpose of ascertaining convictions. The wider point remains to be argued.

In sum, *Mason* confirms the propriety of vetting the panel for convictions; passing the information to the prosecution; using it to exercise the right to stand by; and passing the information to defence counsel if it would be fair to do so. The court in *Mason* did not comment upon the guidelines which are presumably still in use.[69]

(d) Excusal, ballot, challenges and swearing-in

Any member of a jury panel may be excused service on the basis of previous service,[70] or on showing entitlement to be excused,[71] or at the discretion of the judge,[72] or may be discharged if there is doubt about his capacity to act as a juror.[73] The first two provisions are straightforward but the discretion to excuse from service is not one which is widely known. The notes which accompany the jury summons make no mention of excusal. The grounds upon which the discretion might be exercised are set out in a *Practice Direction*[74]:

> "A jury consists of twelve individuals chosen at random from the appropriate panel. A juror should be excused if he is personally concerned in the facts of the particular case or closely connected with a party to the proceedings or with a prospective witness. He may also be excused at the discretion of the judge on the grounds of personal hardship or conscientious objection to jury service. It is contrary to established practice for jurors to be excused on more general grounds such as race, religion, political beliefs or occupation."

This direction followed a case in which, agreeing to a suggestion by the defence, the judge asked members of the panel to exclude themselves if they held certain beliefs or belonged to certain organisations.[75] This practice was disapproved. Excusal is possible, but the importance of jury service as a public obligation is strongly emphasised to those who are summoned.

From the jury panel, the jury for the particular case is selected by ballot in open court.[76] The clerk of the court will have the names of all the jurors

---

[68] (1980) 71 Cr.App.R. 157.

[69] No doubt the jury in the trial of Michael Bettaney, on charges under the Official Secrets Act 1911, was vetted since much of the trial was held *in camera*. Only a short prosecution opening speech was given in public.

[70] Juries Act 1974, s.8. If a person summoned has served on a jury in the preceding two years or been excused jury service for a period which has not finished, he is entitled to be excused.

[71] *Ibid.* s.9(1) and Sched. I, Part III. Those entitled to be excused include peers, M.P.s, members of the armed forces and medical and allied practitioners.

[72] *Ibid.* s.9(2).

[73] *Ibid.* s.10. This section is used to discharge the obviously unfit, whether the disability is physical, mental, linguistic or whatever. The power must be exercised by the judge.

[74] [1973] 1 W.L.R. 134.

[75] See M. Zander, *Cases and Materials, op. cit.* at pp. 298–9.

[76] Juries Act 1974, s.11.

on the appropriate panel and will call out their names at random. This is normally achieved by putting the names on cards and shuffling them. Hence, a random selection should be achieved from a randomly-selected panel.

As each juror enters the jury box to be sworn he may be challenged by the prosecution or the defence. The challenge may be *peremptory* or *for cause*. Each defendant is permitted a maximum of three peremptory challenges[77] which will permit him to exclude up to three members of the jury. No reason need be given for exercising the right to challenge and it is normally used in order to achieve a more sympathetic jury, as far as it is possible to tell from appearances.[78] The jurors' occupations are no longer known to counsel.[79] Counsel for the Crown is permitted to require a juror to stand by (which is the equivalent of a peremptory challenge) until there are only enough jurors left on the panel to fill the jury box.[80] After that he will have to show cause for a challenge. The defendant may also challenge any number of times for cause.[81] However, the grounds upon which the challenge for cause can be made must already be known to the defendant for it is not permitted to examine jurors to attempt to establish the grounds.[82] Challenge for cause is fairly unusual.

One of the problems which has been met by contrived use of the challenge is the under-representation of ethnic minority groups on the jury panel.[83] The desire of coloured defendants to have at least some coloured members of the jury has been expressed in a few reported cases and the judicial approach has varied. In *R.* v. *Broderick*[84] on an application for an all-coloured jury, the judge merely ascertained whether there was a coloured juror on the panel. The Court of Appeal said that he had gone, " . . . quite as far as law or consideration required." In *R.* v. *Binns*[85] the judge and the prosecution agreed that it was desirable to have coloured people on the jury and facilitated matters by bringing the whole of the panel into court. As it happened a balanced jury was achieved without the use of challenges, but the judge took the view that he would have been entitled to discharge the whole panel if a balanced jury could not otherwise

---

[77] The number used to be seven. It was reduced to three by the Criminal Law Act 1977, s.43, amending the Juries Act 1974, s.12(1)(*a*).

[78] Theories exist about the "type" of people who are challenged. It is said to be advantageous to wear a smart suit, regimental tie and carry a copy of the Financial Times if you are desirous of avoiding jury service.

[79] See p. 609, above.

[80] Technically, the Crown is exercising a challenge for cause but the trial of the cause is postponed until the panel is exhausted: *R.* v. *Parry* (1837) 7 C. & P. 836; *R.* v. *Casement* [1917] 1 K.B. 98. See also, J. F. McEldowney, "Stand By For the Crown: an Historical Analysis" [1979] Crim.L.R. 272.

[81] The cause is likely to be alleged prejudice, or disqualification. See Archbold, *op.cit.* para. 4–159ff.

[82] The situation is different in the United States where potential jurors may be questioned to ascertain whether they might be prejudiced. In one case it took four months to question 1035 people before a jury could be sworn. See, H. Harman and J. Griffiths, *op.cit.* pp. 26–27.

[83] J. Baldwin and M. McConville, *Jury Trials*, pp. 97–98.

[84] [1970] Crim.L.R. 155, and see A. Dashwood, "Juries in a Multi-racial Society" [1972] Crim.L.R. 85, commenting on the case of *R.* v. *Inniss* (1971), the "Mangrove Restaurant" case.

[85] [1982] Crim.L.R. 522. A decision of Stocker J. at Bristol Crown Court, in the trial of offences arising out of the St. Paul's disturbances which took place in Bristol in April 1980.

have been achieved. In *R.* v. *Danvers*[86] the judge rejected a challenge to the array (*i.e.* the whole panel) on the ground that it was unrepresentative, holding that there was no requirement in law that there should be a coloured member of a jury or a jury panel. Perhaps this is a matter to which the Lord Chancellor should give his attention in directing how jury panels should be selected under the Juries Act 1974, s.5.[87]

A juror, having entered the jury box and remained unchallenged, is then sworn in.[88] When twelve have been sworn the defendant may be "given in charge" to the jury and the trial can begin.[89]

(e) The trial, the summing-up and the deliberations

During the course of the trial the jury will sit together in the jury box and listen to the evidence and the speeches of counsel. Jurors are entitled to take notes if they wish[90] as the case proceeds, but any notes taken are subject to the same restrictions of secrecy as the jurors' deliberations. At an early stage of the trial, probably at the first adjournment, the jury will be warned not to discuss the case with anyone else except amongst themselves, and then only in the jury room. This instruction is designed to prevent outside influences on jurors[91] and may be reinforced by a reminder not to come to a view about the case until all the evidence and arguments have been heard.[92]

A long trial can place a considerable strain on the jury and there are provisions which allow the discharge of individual jurors in the course of a trial in the event of illness or other good reason.[93] So long as the jury does not fall below nine members, the trial can proceed.[94]

The contents of the summing-up have been noted in the preceding section, as well as the significant place it has in the chronology of the trial. The initial direction on verdict will be that unanimity should be achieved, and although the jury will know from the notes provided that a majority verdict is possible, the object of the deliberations should be unanimity. At the end of the summing-up the jury will retire to the jury room to consider

---

[86] [1982] Crim.L.R. 680. A decision of Mr. Recorder Cowley Q.C. at Nottingham Crown Court.

[87] A suggestion contained in the commentary on *Danvers,* by G.W. Hoon at [1982] Crim.L.R. 681.

[88] Using the oath set out at p. 608, above.

[89] This is not an essential part of trial procedure. At the end of the swearing-in, the clerk may read the indictment to the jury and tell them that it is their "charge" to say whether the accused is guilty or not.

[90] This is a dubious advantage unless the juror happens to be reasonably skilled at note-taking. See Cornish, *op.cit.* pp. 50–51.

[91] Not necessarily sinister influences: the juror must give his verdict according to the evidence adduced in court and not on any other basis.

[92] This instruction may not always be heeded. The anonymous juror in the Thorpe case, (see n. 3, below) revealed that the jury had decided on an acquittal on the first day of the trial.

[93] The decision to discharge should be exercised generously. Trial by jury depends upon the willing co-operation of the public and, in any event, an aggrieved and inconvenienced juror is not likely to be a good one: *R.* v. *Hambery* [1977] Q.B. 924. The (apocryphal) story is told of the juror who asked to be discharged in the course of a trial, " . . . because his wife was conceiving." The judge replied that he assumed the juror meant giving birth, " . . . but in either event he ought to be present."

[94] Juries Act 1974, s.16(1). The number required for a majority verdict is adjusted accordingly: see p. 615 below.

their verdict and are kept together privately until a verdict is reached or they are discharged.[95] The jury bailiff must ensure that no one comes into contact with the jury except by leave of the court.[96] In particularly difficult cases it may be necessary to provide overnight hotel accommodation for the jury which is again done under the close supervision of the court. If the jury requires further information from the judge to explain a point in the summing-up, or if guidance is required, the normal practice is to communicate by note which is read out in open court, or to bring the jury back into court for the foreman to make the request.[97]

The jury will select a foreman to speak for them on all matters and, ultimately, to deliver the verdict. The role of the foreman is important because he will act as chairman in the deliberations and will have the possibility of influencing the decision thereby.[98] The method of selection is a matter for the jury.[99]

The deliberations of the jury are kept secret. Jurors are told that what is said in the jury room should not be disclosed to anyone even after the trial is over.[1] There have been examples of this instruction being ignored and some of what is known about the jury and the way in which it approaches its task emanates from the published experiences of individual jurors.[2] Following a case in which proceedings for contempt of court were brought against a journal which published an interview with one of the jurors in the Thorpe trial,[3] it appeared that such disclosure would only be contempt in certain circumstances.[4] However, the position is now regulated by statute which makes it a contempt to obtain, disclose or solicit any particulars of statements made, opinions expressed, arguments advanced or votes cast by members of a jury in the course of their deliberations in any legal proceedings.[5] Proceedings for contempt arising out of this provision may only be brought by, or with the permission of, the Attorney-General, or on the motion of a competent court.[6]

The secrecy of the jury room is said to be the basis on which trial by jury continues to exist. The implication is that if the public knew how juries

[95] Circumstances are now somewhat less primitive than when juries were locked up without refreshment to encourage them to concentrate.

[96] This rule is enforced very strictly and any breach of it is likely to lead to the discharge of the jury or the later quashing of any conviction: *R.* v. *Prime* (1973) 57 Cr.App.R. 632; *R.* v. *Goodson* [1975] 1 W.L.R. 549; *R.* v. *Davis* (1960) 44 Cr.App.R. 235.

[97] *R.* v. *Lamb* (1974) 59 Cr.App.R. 196.

[98] J. Baldwin and M. McConville, "Juries, Foremen and Verdicts" (1980) 20 Brit. J. Criminol. 35.

[99] The question often put is, "Has anybody been on a jury before?". If a juror admits to experience he often becomes foreman.

[1] As they are informed in the notes accompanying the jury summons.

[2] E. Devons, "Serving as a Juryman in Britain" (1965) 28 M.L.R. 561; D. Barber and G. Gordon (eds.), *Members of the Jury* (1976).

[3] In which Jeremy Thorpe was indicted, with others, for conspiracy to murder. The New Statesman later published an article, "Thorpe's trial: how the jury saw it" (July 27, 1979) based on an interview with an anonymous juror.

[4] *Attorney-General* v. *New Statesman and Nation Publishing Co.* [1981] Q.B. 1. Widgery L.C.J. was of the opinion that a contempt would only be committed if the breach of secrecy tended to imperil the finality of the jury verdict or affect adversely the attitude of future jurors.

[5] Contempt of Court Act 1981, s.8(1).

[6] *Ibid.* s.8(3). A competent court for this purpose is one which has jurisdiction to deal with the alleged contempt.

reached decisions, then the jury would lose its place in the public esteem. The process is only acceptable so long as we do not know how it works. The effect of secrecy is certainly to place considerable difficulty in the way of researchers who are unable to analyse the decision-making process of "real" juries.[7]

(f) Majority verdicts[8]

The requirement that a verdict be unanimous, which had stood since the thirteenth century, was abandoned in 1967. Fears of jury "nobbling" had been expressed and it was argued that the unanimity rule made it too easy for professional criminals to threaten or intimidate one member of a jury into holding out for a not guilty verdict. In the event of a jury failing to reach a unanimous verdict they were discharged and the defendant might or might not be retried at the discretion of the prosecution.

The Criminal Justice Act 1967 introduced the majority verdict and the governing provisions are now contained in the Juries Act 1974, s.17:

"(1) . . . the verdict of a jury in proceedings in the Crown Court or the High Court need not be unanimous if—

(a) in a case where there are not less than eleven jurors, ten of them agree on a verdict; and

(b) in a case where there are ten jurors, nine of them agree on a verdict.

(3) The Crown Court shall not accept a verdict of guilty by virtue of subsection (1) above unless the foreman of the jury has stated in open court the number of jurors who respectively agreed to and dissented from the verdict.

(4) No court shall accept a verdict by virtue of subsection (1) . . . unless it appears to the court that the jury have had such period of time for deliberation as the court thinks reasonable having regard to the nature and complexity of the case; and the Crown Court shall in any event not accept such a verdict unless it appears to the court that the jury have had at least two hours for deliberation."

At the outset the jury are directed to reach a unanimous verdict[9] and no mention should normally be made of the majority verdict procedure.[10] It is reasonable to suppose that at least some of the jurors will know of the procedure and the majority verdict is also referred to in the notes accompanying the jury summons.

A *Practice Direction*[11] sets out the procedure which should be followed to ensure that the safeguards contained in the Act (a minimum period of

[7] See below, p. 620.

[8] See generally, Archbold, *op.cit.* paras. 4–444ff; Emmins, *op.cit.* pp. 108–9.

[9] See p. 606, above.

[10] *R. v. Thomas* [1983] Crim.L.R. 745. The fact that the judge told the jury in the summing-up that he was entitled to take a majority verdict after at least two hours was held not to be such a significant irregularity that there was the risk of a miscarriage of justice. The fear is of "inviting" the jury to disagree from the start: see also *R. v. Modeste* [1983] Crim.L.R. 746.

[11] [1967] 1 W.L.R. 1198, as clarified by *Practice Direction* [1970] 1 W.L.R. 916.

deliberation[12] and a statement in open court of the majority[13]) are observed. The stages are as follows:

1. If the jury returns[14] within two hours, only a unanimous verdict is acceptable. If there is no unanimity the jury are sent back for further deliberation.

2. If the jury returns after two hours and ten minutes[15] have elapsed they are asked if a verdict has been reached. If it is not unanimous and the judge considers that the jury have had a reasonable time for deliberation having regard to the nature and complexity of the case[16] the judge will direct them that a majority verdict is acceptable, although they should still try to reach unanimity.

3. When the jury finally return, a precise set of questions is asked of them:

   (i) Have at least ten (or nine as the case may be) of you agreed upon your verdict? If "Yes,"

   (ii) What is your verdict? Please answer only "Guilty" or "Not Guilty."

   (iii) (a) If "Not Guilty"—accept the verdict without more ado.

       (b) If "Guilty"—is that the verdict of you all or by a majority?

   (iv) If "Guilty" by a majority, how many of you agreed to the verdict and how many dissented?

The requirement that the foreman state in open court the number of jurors who agreed to and dissented from the verdict is mandatory before the judge can properly accept a guilty verdict, but there is no requirement that the clerk use the precise words of the Practice Direction so long as it is clear to the ordinary person how the jury divided.[17] The formulation of the questions in the practice direction is intended to prevent anyone (other than the jurors) knowing whether or not a not guilty verdict was by a majority.[18] The statutory requirement that not less than two hours should be allowed for the initial deliberation is mandatory.[19]

6. DO JURIES REACH THE "RIGHT" VERDICTS?

Ultimately, the answer to this particular question depends very much upon a personal view as to the principles upon which the correctness of a jury verdict can be assessed, and the application of that principle to any particular set of circumstances. The secrecy of the jury room[20] makes it

---

[12] Juries Act 1974, s.17(4).

[13] *Ibid.* s.17(3).

[14] "Returns" in the context of the Practice Direction includes being sent for by the judge who may be wondering how the deliberations are progressing.

[15] *Practice Direction* [1970] 1 W.L.R. 916. The period that has elapsed since the last member of the jury left the jury box must be stated in open court before the jury are asked for their verdict.

[16] The length of time in which the jury should be trying to reach a unanimous verdict is entirely a matter of discretion for the trial judge.

[17] *R.* v. *Pigg* [1983] 1 W.L.R. 6.

[18] Thus avoiding a sort of second-class acquittal.

[19] *R.* v. *Barry* [1975] 1 W.L.R. 1190.

[20] See p. 614, above.

impossible to ascertain the precise reasoning of the jury or the particular features of the case which some or all of the jurors found significant. That fact alone makes research into, or assertions about, the quality and correctness of jury verdicts a hazardous business. However, before we can consider the evidence and isolate the particular standpoint from which we might evaluate it, it is necessary to set out the differing tests which might be advanced as the determinant of what amounts to a "right" decision.

(a) What is a "right" verdict?

According to personal conviction about the role of the jury in our system of criminal justice, it may be asserted that a verdict is right if:

   (i) it accords with the absolute objective fact of the guilt or innocence of the accused of the crime charged as known to some omniscient observer, e.g. God;

  (ii) it is reached by the jury after an honest, careful and reasonable attempt to apply the law (as explained by the judge in the summing-up)[21] to the facts as they find them, taking no other circumstances into account;

 (iii) it is a verdict of acquittal which, after a consideration of the evidence has indicated guilt or without any consideration of the evidence at all, results from a reasonable exercise of discretion in favour of the accused[22] reflecting the jury's sympathy, clemency or disapproval of the prosecution;

 (iv) it is the verdict of the jury lawfully given and accepted by the judge, however it may have been reached and on whatever grounds.

Of these possibilities we ought to dismiss (i) and (iv) as inappropriate principles upon which to assess whether or not a jury verdict is "right." Apart from the fact that principle (i) requires contact with an omniscient being to test the correctness of the verdict,[23] it does not reflect the constraints under which the jury work. They only have available the evidence that has been given in court and one can hardly criticise the jury for failing to know about matters which have not been put in evidence. Principle (iv) is equally inappropriate for it posits that *all* verdicts are "right" providing that the formalities are complied with.[24] The end result of adopting (iv) would be that the jury could decide each case on any basis without regard to the law or the evidence and claim to have reached the "right" result.

That leaves us with principles (ii) and (iii) as the different criteria on which the quality of jury verdicts might be judged. These two approaches might conveniently be termed the "narrow" and the "broad." The validity of criticisms of jury decisions will depend on whether you think that the

---

[21] See p. 602, above.

[22] This formulation is meant to indicate that it can never be right to exercise discretion *against* an accused, *i.e.* to convict him in circumstances where the evidence does not warrant it. The possibility of this occurring should be extremely limited because of the judge's power to direct an acquittal on a submission of no case: see p. 606, above.

[23] This may have been the basis of trial by ordeal, but direct intervention by the Almighty has not been a feature of English justice since 1215: see p. 607, above.

[24] It is true to say that all such verdicts are presently lawful for they may properly be delivered even if an improper verdict of guilty may be challenged on appeal, but it would hardly be correct to call them right.

narrow or the broad approach is the one which it is legitimate for juries to adopt.

The *narrow approach* is favoured by those who want to limit the influence of the jury, control its work and achieve the greatest consistency of jury verdict that is possible.[25] It is not a complete negation of the discretion of the jury for they must still take a (reasonable) view about the weight and credibility of the evidence and they will have to determine any questions of fact which are left to them by the judge. Very often, this narrow approach will reflect a professional concern with the desire to impose professional standards and values upon the jury. Any deviation from the application of the law to the facts found will be characterised as "perversity," although it will normally be impossible to determine the basis on which a jury has arrived at a particular verdict.[26] It is further argued that in so far as "perverse" verdicts may reflect the desire of the jury to ensure that the accused is not punished for a crime that the jury does not consider serious, that is an improper use of the power since the matter of sentence ought to be determined by the judge. Find the facts, apply them to the law as directed, return the consequent verdict and leave any other matters to the judge would be the instruction to the jury based on the narrow approach. The similarity of those instructions to the directions currently given in a summing-up[27] indicates that the law, in theory, requires the jury to adopt the narrow approach.

The *broad approach* admits of a degree of discretion in the jury, to be exercised in favour of the defendant, to give expression to their feelings of justice and fairness. The discretion to acquit might be exercised because the jury considers the charge, though proved in law, to be inappropriate; the prosecution to have been unnecessary; the defendant to be deserving of sympathy; the defence to have practical, if not legal, merit; the victim/prosecutor to be unsympathetic. We do not include within this approach where the jury's view of the witnesses (including the defendant) is coloured by their personal characteristics—that is a matter which is properly taken into account in weighing the evidence and considering the standard of proof according to the more narrow approach. Advocates of the broad approach acknowledge that the discretion need only be exercised where the jury is otherwise convinced of guilt, or where they have not thought about the evidence at all. In its favour is argued the moderating influence of the jury on the inflexibility and rigour of the law, and the opportunity to exercise clemency.

Whichever approach commends itself to your sense of justice and your estimation of the jury's role, there will be occasions on which you think that the jury has not reached the right result, either because they have acted on the wrong principle or because they have, on a matter of judgment, erred. When considering the evidence of jury deviation from the right result it is important to acknowledge *why* you think the decision to be wrong.

---

[25] See generally, Lord Devlin, *The Judge* (1979), Chap. 5; E. Griew, *Dishonesty and the Jury* (1974); G. Williams, *The Proof of Guilt* (1963), Chap. 10.

[26] The alternative bases on which the jury *might* have proceeded are discussed at p. 618, below.

[27] See pp. 602–605, above.

(b) Jury deviation

When a jury returns a verdict which is considered to be incorrect by some or all of the other participants in the case, the discrepancy may have occurred in one of three ways:

(i) the jury may have considered the evidence diligently and carefully and, despite the conclusion to which the evidence led, returned a verdict inconsistent with the evidence for reasons of their own[28]; or

(ii) the jury may have considered the evidence diligently and carefully and returned the verdict which they, in their judgment, consider is consistent with the evidence; or

(iii) the jury may have been careless or incompetent in their considera- tion of the evidence and returned a slipshod decision.

There may be blurrings of the distinction between these approaches in individual cases but they are likely to reflect, overall, the bases on which the jury might have decided the case.

Criticism which has been made of the number of cases in which the jury deviates from the "right" verdict ought to distinguish between these alternatives, for it is obviously quite different to criticise juries for deliberate "perversity," for honest differences of judgment or opinion, and for carelessness and incompetence. Before we look at the research which has been published on jury deviation we should briefly examine the factors which may cause an honest difference of opinion between the jury and the professional participants over the verdict.

In finding the facts of a particular case and then applying the relevant law to reach a verdict, the members of the jury must follow a difficult process. Primarily they will have to exercise judgment about the credibility of witnesses and then reach a common view about "what happened" based on conflicting testimony or on the correct inferences to be drawn from circumstantial evidence. This task is often difficult enough for an experienced judge[29]; the members of the jury must carry it out in unfamiliar surroundings, with strangers, subject to the advocacy of counsel and with a possible ignorance or incomprehension of the issues involved. The difficulties of testimony are well documented, and there is the additional problem of the mistakes that may be made in the perception and recollection of the evidence of witnesses. A jury will be exercising collective judgment about the facts and the implications thereof and it is hardly surprising, in the circumstances outlined, that their judgment will, on occasions, be different from the professionals. Indeed, two juries may well reach different conclusions from the same evidence, and it would be impossible to characterise either decision as wrong unless it was so far removed from a reasonable standard that it was one which *no* reasonable jury could possibly have reached.[30] In so far as a verdict is founded on an honest exercise of judgment on the part of a jury it can hardly be criticised, save on the basis that the members of the jury are not equipped to perform

[28] Thus following the "broad approach" discussed above. Whether this verdict is acceptable depends upon your view of the jury's role, although most people would accept that a verdict of guilty in these circumstances is not acceptable.

[29] The difficulties are disguised for law students who are told, or read, that, "The facts of the case were as follows. . . . " The facts become the starting point for a discussion of the law. In practice, the difficult part of most cases is determining the facts.

[30] This would be the basis on which the Court of Appeal might overturn a conviction: see p. 709, below.

the task allotted to them—the institution is at fault, not the individuals. We return to that argument later.

(c) The research

Because of the limitations imposed upon researchers, the methods employed to analyse and explain the decision-making process and the verdicts reached in particular cases have necessarily been indirect. One approach has been to compare the verdict of the jury in selected cases with the "verdict" of the professional participants in the trial; the other has been to arrange for a 'mock' or 'shadow' jury to listen to a case and then observe their deliberations when required to give a verdict. Both methods have their drawbacks but they are illustrative of different features of jury decisions.

Two major studies have been conducted which take account of the views of the professionals.[31] The first, by McCabe and Purves,[32] dealt with 475 defendants tried on indictment over a two-year period, concentrating solely on the 115 who were acquitted by the jury. The second, by Baldwin and McConville,[33] dealt with the 2406 defendants who appeared in the Birmingham Crown Court over an eighteen month period, concentrating on the 500 defendants who contested their cases. The latter study is, therefore, of wider significance since it looks at all jury verdicts and not solely acquittals. There were some differences of methodology but both studies sought to explain the relevant verdicts by reference to the views of counsel,[34] solicitors, the judge, and police officers.[35]

The first study attempted to categorise the 115 acquittals[36] according to the views of the professionals. Using the somewhat simplified version for jury verdicts discussed above, it would appear that only 15 of the 115 acquittals were based on a deliberate decision to go counter to the evidence. All the others were explicable on the grounds of weaknesses in the prosecution case, the failure of prosecution witnesses or the credibility of the defendant's explanation. Many of the acquittals were regarded as correct by the professionals and the proportion of perverse verdicts was established as low in relation to acquittals[37] and very low in relation to all contested cases.[38]

The second study was less reassuring. Baldwin and McConville concluded that it was not possible to determine an overall pattern in the cases where the outcome was regarded as questionable. Those cases included convictions as well as acquittals and that fact raises doubts about the conventional wisdom that the defendant gets the benefit of the doubt from the jury. A similar proportion of wayward verdicts occurred in this study[39] and the authors agree that it is a tiny fraction of all cases that pass

---

[31] Reference should also be made to M. Zander, "Are Too Many Professional Criminals Avoiding Conviction?—A Study of Britain's Two Busiest Courts" (1974) 37 M.L.R. 28.

[32] S. McCabe and R. Purves, *The Jury at Work* (1972).

[33] J. Baldwin and M. McConville, *Jury Trials* (1977).

[34] The bar did not co-operate in the Birmingham survey.

[35] The police did not participate in the Oxford survey.

[36] In the Oxford study there were a further 58 cases in which the defendant was acquitted on the direction of the judge.

[37] One verdict in eight amongst the jury acquittals, and one verdict in eleven amongst all acquittals.

[38] One verdict in thirty-two amongst the defendants dealt with in the period of the study.

[39] *Jury Trials, op.cit.* Chaps. 4 and 5.

through the criminal courts, yet they point to the serious nature of the cases tried by jury and conclude that trial by jury is, " . . . an arbitrary and unpredictable business."[40] The authors recognise that the significance of their research is limited to an assessment of the accuracy of verdicts and that the political and constitutional issues involved are also very important. They believe, however, that the political and constitutional debate should be informed by as much knowledge as possible about the veracity of jury verdicts.

In sum, the English evidence[41] demonstrates that there is an identifiable, if relatively small, number of cases in which juries reach perverse verdicts, although views differ on whether these deviations can be explained on any particular basis.

In the course of the Oxford study,[42] McCabe and Purves also utilised the "shadow" jury technique. In thirty cases, a second "jury" was installed in the court to listen to the proceedings and then to deliberate and reach a verdict. This method has the drawback that the degree of pressure which exists when a jury is dealing with the fate of a defendant is lacking in mock deliberations, but the main conclusions pointed to the care and determination of the jurors to go about their task methodically, discount their prejudices and look for evidence on which to base their verdict.[43] This would suggest that in real cases the jury are likely to display the same, or an even greater, degree of conscientiousness and application.

(d) The value of the jury

Baldwin and McConville have few illusions about the effect which research may have on a discussion about the value of the jury in our system of criminal justice: " . . . we fully recognise that the whole question of trial by jury is one that raises strong emotions and that views about the value of the jury are unlikely to be much affected one way or the other by the evidence of empirical research."[44] This brings us back to the original point that an estimation of the value of the jury is essentially personal.

The protagonists of jury trial[45] have often used the most colourful language to express the significance and importance of the jury as a constitutional safeguard for the subject.[46] Its proved independence from

[40] *Ibid.* p. 132.

[41] There has been more extensive research in America, starting from H. Kalven and H. Zeisel, *The American Jury* (1966) (The Chicago Jury Project). In England, Zander's conclusions are broadly in line with the other studies (see n. 31, above).

[42] S. McCabe and R. Purves, *"The Shadow Jury at Work"* (1974). See also, A.P. Sealy "What Can be Learned from the Analysis of Simulated Juries," in N. Walker (ed.), *The British Jury System* (1975).

[43] *Ibid.* p. 61.

[44] *Jury Trials, op. cit.* p. 125.

[45] The judges have always been in the forefront. Whether this indicates an unwillingness on their part to shoulder the responsibility of determining guilt is uncertain! See G. Williams, *The Proof of Guilt* (1955): "Most of the great pronouncements on constitutional liberty from the eighteenth century onwards have been the work of judges . . . ." (at p. 197).

[46] *e.g.* "Trial by jury, ever has been, and I trust ever will be, looked upon as the glory of the English law. . . . The liberties of England cannot but subsist so long as this palladium remains sacred and inviolate": Blackstone, *Commentaries*, iii–379, iv–350; " . . . trial by jury is more than an instrument of justice and more than one wheel of the constitution: it is the lamp that shows that freedom lives": Lord Devlin, *Trial by Jury* (1956), p. 164; "Trial by jury . . . has been the bulwark of our liberties for too long for any of us to seek to alter it. Whenever a man is on trial for serious crime . . . trial by jury has no equal": *per* Lord Denning M.R. in *Ward v. James* [1966] 1 Q.B. 273, 295.

the judiciary and the executive and the secrecy and inviolability of its decisions combine, it is argued, to offer protection to the subject which could not be achieved by the judiciary alone.[47]

Linked to, and strengthening, the independence of the jury is its composition from virtually all members of society. The random selection of the jury and almost universal eligibility[48] is intended to provide a fact-finding tribunal of demonstrable impartiality and of a broadly representative nature. The -idea that a defendant should receive "the judgment of his peers"[49] does, in fact, comprehend several possible objectives[50] but the phrase is strongly rooted in the public consciousness and is understood to indicate impartiality. Public confidence in the jury is said to be based, at least in part, on its composition.

On a more practical level it would be argued that the involvement of laymen in the administration of criminal justice both emphasises the community responsibility for determining liability for punishment and also keeps the law and procedure comprehensible and responsive to the average man.[51] The continued presence of members of the public as the trial jury requires lawyers to ensure that, through their jury experience, citizens retain confidence in and respect for the criminal law.

The presence of laymen further permits the introduction of general standards of behaviour and morality into decision-making. Apart from situations in which the law specifically requires that the attitude of the reasonable man be taken into account,[52] it is also clear that the combined judgment and expertise of juries is put to good use in the evaluation of evidence and in judging the credibility of witnesses.[53]

Advocates of jury trial may differ over the desirability of allowing the jury their undoubted flexibility to take into account matters which are not strictly relevant, in law, to the verdict. This difference between the narrow approach and the broad approach[54] is unlikely to be resolved, particularly if we continue the current practice of defending the right of the jury to reach a "perverse" verdict without ever telling them that they may do so and, indeed, specifically directing them that the verdict must be according to the evidence.[55]

These various propositions in support of the jury all tend to emphasise its political and constitutional significance, deflecting attention from the ability of randomly-selected members of the public to undertake the specific fact-finding task allotted to them in the criminal trial. If the

[47] On the assumption that the alternative to trial by jury is trial by judge alone, see below, p. 624.

[48] See pp. 608–611, above.

[49] The phrase derives from Magna Carta, see W.S. Holdsworth, *History of English Law* (3rd ed., 1922) Vol. 2, p. 214.

[50] They are considered by G. Marshall, "The judgment of one's Peers: some Aims and Ideals of Jury Trial," in N. Walker (ed.), *The British Jury System* (1975).

[51] Through the necessity that the jurors should be able to follow the trial and understand the law when the judge explains it to them in the summing-up.

[52] *e.g.* in determining the question of dishonesty for the purposes of the Theft Act 1968: *R.* v. *Ghosh* [1982] Q.B. 1053; see p. 603, above.

[53] This is one of the conclusions reached in S. McCabe and R. Purves, *The Shadow Jury at Work* (1974).

[54] See above, p. 618.

[55] No judge would invite the jury to acquit despite the evidence, although the summing-up might indicate his view of the propriety of the prosecution.

advocates of the jury are forced to consider the point, the English affection for the amateur and the alleged virtues of common sense are offered as justification.

Conversely, the opponents of jury trial attack the incompetence of the jury and the capricious, arbitrary nature of its decisions. Some of the language employed is just as vigorous as that used in praise of the jury and the claims are just as extreme. At the most basic level it is the unfitness of jurors for their appointed task which excites condemnation. Oppenheimer[56] makes most of the points shortly and emphatically in this way:

"We commonly strive to assemble 12 persons colossally ignorant of all practical matters, fill their vacuous heads with law which they cannot comprehend, obfuscate their seldom intellects with testimony which they are incompetent to analyse or unable to remember, permit partisan lawyers to bewilder them with their meaningless sophistry, then lock them up until the most obstinate of their number coerce the others into submission or drive them into open revolt."[57]

Apart from doubting the ability of jurors, critics also deny some of the alleged advantages of the jury[58] and argue that the jury's power to ignore the law is harmful rather than beneficial.[59] In addition, the lay nature of the jury renders its members vulnerable to attempts to threaten or influence by criminals intent on securing jury disagreement.[60]

Inevitably, critics of jury trial find much ammunition in the longer and more complicated criminal trials. Especially where there are large numbers of defendants or where commercial fraud is involved, the presence of a jury is alleged to be an inhibiting factor. The evidence may be very difficult to understand; the length of the trial makes it very hard for the untrained person to remember the evidence; the length of the trial is, in any event, increased by the need to explain everything to the jury very carefully; costs increase as the length of the trial increases.

It is not easy to gauge the current standing of the jury in public and professional opinion. It has been argued that the jury is under attack[61] and that the introduction of majority verdicts,[62] the restriction of the right of challenge,[63] the transfer of jurisdiction to magistrates' courts,[64] the acceptance of vetting,[65] and the removal of jurors' occupations from the

[56] B.S. Oppenheimer, "Trial by Jury" (1937) 11 Univ. of Cincinn. L.R. 141, cited in *Jury Trials, op. cit.* p. 2.

[57] The situation has changed slightly in England with the introduction of majority verdicts but the sentiments are largely the same!

[58] In particular, its alleged representative nature. This advantage is denied in respect of juries who try cases involving members of ethnic minorities, since it is alleged that the jury panel is likely to be unrepresentative of those communities. See above, p. 609.

[59] *i.e.* the narrow approach taken to its logical conclusion.

[60] The tactic of jury "nobbling." The intimidation of juries in Northern Ireland was a major factor in the introduction of trial without jury for terrorist offences, the so-called "Diplock courts."

[61] See, in particular, H. Harman and J.A. Griffith, *Justice Deserted* (1979); M.D.A. Freeman, *"The Jury on Trial"* (1981) 34 C.L.P. 65.

[62] See above, p. 615.

[63] See above, p. 612.

[64] As a result of the James Committee and the Criminal Law Act 1977: see above, p. 487.

[65] See above, p. 610.

jury list[66] have all indicated the growing pressure for conviction and a diminution of the historic freedom of the jury. On the other hand, the increased eligibility for service[67] and the much better information given to jurors about their task[68] strengthen the jury. The preservation of secrecy in the Contempt of Court Act 1981[69] is also, paradoxically, intended to strengthen the jury, for as one former juryman observed, " . . . if the jury is to remain part of the English legal system, it is as well that its proceedings should remain secret."[70] Public opinion may have been most accurately reflected in the debates on the Criminal Law Bill in 1977, as a result of which the proposal to remove the right to jury trial in respect of some thefts was defeated.[71]

Two major factors protect the position of the jury and will, probably, continue to do so. It retains the confidence of the public and there is no clearly acceptable alternative.

(e) Alternatives to the jury[72]

Is there anything better? There would appear to be only three possible alternatives to the jury as finders of fact in criminal matters.[73] The issue might be left to a single judge, a bench of judges, or a composite tribunal of laymen and judge(s). Each of these forms of tribunal finds a place in our legal system at the present time.

(i) The single judge

Most civil trials are conducted by a judge alone[74] who decides both fact and law and, in criminal matters, the stipendiary magistrate[75] has the same function. The role of the stipendiary is somewhat restricted because of the lesser degree of seriousness of the offences which he is trying and also because the appeal against his decision is by way of rehearing, so that there would be significant differences in merely translating him to the Crown Court. In addition, there are well-grounded fears that a single judge may become hardened or prosecution-minded and there would be little protection against eccentricity.[76] The determination of guilt in serious cases by one man alone might prove to be too great a burden for him to bear, as well as being unacceptable to the public. Trial by single judge in Northern Ireland, although it has been in existence since 1973,[77] is still regarded as a temporary and unsatisfactory measure.

---

[66] See above, p. 609.
[67] See above, p. 608.
[68] See above, p. 609.
[69] See above, p. 614.
[70] E. Devons, "Serving as a Juryman in Britain" (1965) 28 M.L.R. 561, 570.
[71] See above, p. 487.
[72] See in particular W.R. Cornish, The Jury (1968), Chap. 10.
[73] Assuming that we are considering alternative types of tribunal rather than adjustments to the jury, such as the reduction of the number of jurors to six.
[74] See p. 534, above, for the insignificance of the jury in the civil trial.
[75] See p. 148, above.
[76] "Eccentricity" is used charitably to include all mental and physical states which prejudice fair and impartial decision-making.
[77] The provisions are now contained in the Northern Ireland (Emergency Provisions) Act 1978.

(ii) *The bench of judges*

Whilst three, or five, judges might avoid some of the problems of a single judge, the expense would be enormous and the recruitment difficult. Such a reform would certainly transform the nature of the judiciary[78] and have considerable implications for the profession.[79] Apart from the practical problems there remains the question of the desirability of entrusting the decision on criminal liability to professionals. The willingness of a bench of judges in the Court of Appeal to permit convictions to stand where new evidence has emerged after the trial which might cause a jury to entertain reasonable doubt,[80] will not have done anything to enhance public confidence in professional decision-making.

(iii) *The composite tribunal*

In the Crown Court a judge may sit with lay justices on appeals and committals for sentence from the magistrates' court[81] and in certain other matters originally dealt with by the magistrates.[82] Lay justices may sit with a judge at a trial on indictment[83] but this is unusual and they will take no part in the decision.

Some European jurisdictions[84] rely upon the composite tribunal of laymen and judge and one observer, at least, has professed himself to be impressed by the system.[85] The judge will play a leading role in the decision-making, guiding the laymen through the law and the evidence, but because they can outvote him he must convince them of his view and explain his reasoning. There is the possibility of a direct exchange of lay and legal views with their tempering effects on each other.

Would the judge have things too much his own way? Should the laymen be justices, or trained in any way, or merely selected at random as at present? Would such a system retain the fact and appearance of independence and impartiality essential to the maintenance of public confidence?

In this, as in other matters, the force of inertia and the fear of change may turn out to be the most important factors.

C. PLEA BARGAINING

"Plea bargaining . . . describes the practice whereby the defendant enters a plea of guilty in return for which he will be given some consideration that results in a sentence concession."[86]

---

[78] It is argued that a considerable increase in numbers would weaken the bench both by dilution of quality and diminishing the social pressure of a small group.

[79] It might, for example, lead to a career judiciary.

[80] A development initiated by the decision of the House of Lords in *Stafford* v. *D.P.P.* [1974] A.C. 878. It is heavily criticised in Lord Devlin, *The Judge* (1979), pp. 148–176.

[81] See p. 147, above.

[82] For example, on licensing and gaming appeals and some juvenile and family matters.

[83] Supreme Court Act 1981, s.8(1), and p. 147, above. See *R.* v. *Orpin* [1975] Q.B. 283.

[84] Described in Cornish, *op. cit.*

[85] Cornish was particularly complimentary about the operation of composite tribunals in Scandinavia: *op. cit.* Chap. 10.

[86] J. Baldwin and M. McConville, *Negotiated Justice* (1977), p. 19. This research study is a prerequisite for any detailed study of the subject. See also, P. Thomas, "Plea Bargaining and the Turner Case" [1970] Crim.L.R. 559; A. Davis, "Sentences for Sale: A New Look at Plea Bargaining in England and America" [1970] Crim.L.R.150, 218; R. Purves, "That

The value of a plea of guilty in the criminal process is that it reduces the time and money spent on achieving convictions; it obviates the need for a trial and the inherent difficulties of proof; it spares the witnesses an experience which can be both unpleasant and distressing[87]; and it is alleged to demonstrate an attitude of contrition and remorse on the part of the accused. In order to secure the certainty and economy of a guilty plea it may be worthwhile to offer concessions or inducements to the accused which will persuade him to plead guilty in order to take the benefit of the concessions. The extent of the concessions will vary in each case and the prosecution must always have in mind the public interest in ensuring that offenders are convicted of offences which properly represent the seriousness of their behaviour.[88] For the truly guilty defendant and the prosecution this represents a mutually beneficial compromise. A guilty plea is obtained and a sentence concession is obtained.

However, the concessions made to defendants also operate (intentionally) as inducements and must create pressure on the defendant. How severe are these pressures on the innocent defendant, or on the defendant against whom the prosecution have a less than cast-iron case? The controversy surrounding the question of plea bargaining centres on this question: to what extent, if at all, is it legitimate to serve the interests of the prosecution and the guilty defendant by establishing principles and procedures which will inevitably place some pressure to plead guilty upon defendants who would, or might, be acquitted after trial?

We shall look first at the concessions currently on offer and then at their effect and legitimacy.

1. THE SENTENCING DISCOUNT

A plea of guilty attracts a lighter sentence.[89] The practice of discounting a sentence to take account of a guilty plea is universally accepted,[90] even though the Court of Appeal has forbidden trial judges to indicate that a more severe sentence would be imposed if the accused is found guilty after trial than if he pleads guilty.[91] The amount of discount which is allowed is

---

Plea-Bargaining Business" [1971] Crim.L.R. 470; S. McCabe and R. Purves, *By-Passing the Jury* (1972); A.E. Bottoms and J.D. McLean, *Defendants in the Criminal Process* (1976); J. Baldwin and M. McConville, "Plea Bargaining: legal carve-up and legal cover-up" (1978) 5 Brit. J. Law & Society, 228; "Plea Bargaining and the Court of Appeal" (1979) 6 Brit. J. Law & Society, 200; "The Influence of the Sentencing Discount in Inducing Guilty Pleas" in *Criminal Justice: Selected Readings* (eds. J. Baldwin and A.K. Bottomley, 1978); "Preserving the Good Face of Justice: Some Recent Plea Bargain Cases" (1978) 128 N.L.J. 872; *Courts, Prosecution and Conviction* (1981); S. Moody and J. Tombs, "Plea Negotiations and Scotland" [1983] Crim.L.R. 297; *Prosecution in the Public Interest* (1982).

[87] This may be a particularly significant factor where the charges include sexual offences: *R. v. Grice* (1977) 66 Cr.App.R. 167.

[88] See above, p. 592, for the obligations of prosecuting counsel.

[89] See below, p. 688.

[90] It is " . . . trite to say that a plea of guilty would generally attract a somewhat lighter sentence than a plea of not guilty after a full dress contest on the issue. Everybody knew that it was so, and there was no doubt about it. An accused person who did not know about it should know it." *R. v. Cain* [1976] Q.B. 496.

[91] *R. v. Turner* [1970] 2 Q.B. 321; *Practice Direction* [1976] Crim.L.R. 561.

not quantified[92] but research findings show that it can be substantial.[93] In some cases the discount will operate not only to reduce the severity of a particular form of sentence but also to alter the type of sentence from, for example, custodial to non-custodial.

The justification for the sentence discount is said to be the contrition exhibited by the accused,[94] but this has a hollow ring to it. Saving time and money is much more significant. It is not proper to increase sentence merely because the accused has pleaded not guilty,[95] so that references to a discount are intended to indicate that the sentence will be less than "normal," but this is all fairly theoretical. Provided that the trial judge does not exceed the tariff maximum, and is not sufficiently unwise to admit that he has increased the sentence because of the accused's plea of not guilty he can quite easily penalise the accused for his plea.

The form of words is of little significance to the accused, the fact remains that he will receive a greater punishment having been found guilty than having pleaded guilty.

2. DEALS BETWEEN THE PROSECUTION AND DEFENCE

A less direct form of sentence reduction occurs where the prosecution agrees to accept a plea of not guilty to one or more counts on the indictment, in return for a plea of guilty to others. In a sense, there is a double sentence discount in these circumstances. Assume that the accused is charged on one indictment containing two separate counts of rape, two counts of attempted rape and a count of indecent assault. If, in return for an agreement to accept not guilty pleas to the counts of rape, the accused agrees to plead guilty to the other counts he will render himself liable to a less severe sentence on the lesser charges and also receive credit for a guilty plea.

The arrangement of pleas in this way is achieved by negotiation between counsel. The obligations of counsel have been considered earlier in the chapter,[96] but in this context, counsel for the prosecution must balance the public interest in achieving economy and conviction of the guilty, with the interest in ensuring that the accused is convicted of offences which reflect the evidence against him. Defence counsel will merely be negotiating for an "offer" which he can put to his client, whilst reminding the client that he must only enter a plea of guilty if he is actually guilty of the offence. The vigour with which defence counsel commends the arrangement which he has negotiated may be related to factors other than the strength of the evidence and the story of the client.[97]

The arrangement of pleas is a common feature of the trial on indictment and it is alleged that it can be facilitated by "overcharging" the accused at

---

[92] The case of *R. v. Davis*, (unreported, cited in Baldwin and McConville, "Plea Bargaining and the Court of Appeal" (1979) 6 Brit. J. Law & Society, 200, 204, 213) in which the trial judge told counsel that for a guilty plea he supposed there would be an allowance of 20 to 30 per cent., is described as "exceptional" by those authors.

[93] See the cases cited by Baldwin and McConville, *op.cit.* (n. 92, *supra*), pp. 213–4.

[94] *R. v. Turner* [1970] 2 Q.B. 321, 326E; *R. v. De Haan* [1968] 2 Q.B. 108.

[95] *R. v. Jamieson* [1975] Crim.L.R. 248; *R. v. Harper* [1968] 2 Q.B. 108.

[96] See p. 592, above.

[97] See p. 621, below.

the outset. If more serious charges are included on the indictment when the evidence is, at best, equivocal then prosecuting counsel has more to bargain with. This touches both on the discretion of the police in selecting appropriate charges[98] and the inadequacy of committal proceedings for eliminating dubious charges at an early stage.[99]

Two constraints should be noted. Prosecuting counsel exercises no significant influence over sentence.[1] He is not therefore able to bargain directly about the length of sentence on particular charges, he may only bargain about the charges that are to be proceeded with. This distinguishes the process of plea bargaining in this country from that in America where, in many states, the prosecutor may make direct recommendations about sentence.[2] The second constraint is that the judge must consent to the arrangement agreed between counsel. We have already noted that the judge's consent is required where the prosecution wishes to accept a plea of guilty to a lesser offence of which the accused could be convicted on the indictment, but it is also required where the prosecution offer no evidence in response to a plea of not guilty.[3] This judicial involvement should ensure that the arrangement is proper: if too much has been conceded by the prosecution (thus placing considerable pressure on the accused) the judge may intervene to ensure that the matter is tried. This offers an indirect protection to the accused but also provides a check on the propriety of the agreement.

3. Advice from Defence Counsel

The two preceding inducements will create direct pressure on the accused and it appears that the pressure may be increased by forceful advice from defence counsel. Counsel cannot leave his client unaware of the concessions to be gained from sentence discount or plea arrangement, but the code of conduct requires him to make clear to the accused that he has complete freedom of choice in his plea and complete responsibility for it.[4] In practice the advice and attitude of defence counsel can be crucial as the study of Baldwin and McConville[5] demonstrates. It is a difficult task to undertake, offering advice which will inevitably carry great weight whilst leaving the accused free to make his mind up.

What information can counsel give? He may give his own assessment of the strength of the prosecution case and the likelihood of acquittal; the details of any plea arrangement which has been, or might be, negotiated;

---

[98] See pp. 482–486, above.

[99] See pp. 500–506, above.

[1] Prosecuting counsel is limited, in effect, to rehearsing the facts about the previous record of the defendant. See, G. Zellick, "The Role of Prosecuting Counsel in Sentencing" [1979] Crim.L.R. 493, and M. King, "The Role of Prosecuting Counsel in Sentencing—What about Magistrates' Courts?" [1979] Crim.L.R. 775.

[2] Sentencing structures also differ: see Baldwin & McConville, Negotiated Justice (1977), pp. 18–24.

[3] The agreement of the judge is by no means automatic. The judge in the recent Yorkshire Ripper trial refused to accept a guilty plea to manslaughter where the charge on the indictment was murder. As a result Peter Sutcliffe was convicted of murder. See also, R. v. Broad (1978) 68 Cr.App.R. 281; R. v. Coward (1980) 70 Cr.App.R. 70.

[4] Code of Conduct for the Bar of England and Wales, (2nd ed., 1983), para. 150(a).

[5] Negotiated Justice (1977), Chap. 4.

the possible range of sentence and the discount for a guilty plea; the credibility of any defence which may be advanced; the dangers of attempting to discredit prosecution witnesses, especially the police. Added to this information is the attitude and demeanour of counsel. If he gives the accused the impression that he has no hope or confidence of an acquittal or appears indifferent to the accused's protestations of innocence, then the pressure on the accused will be further increased.

The Court of Appeal has stated the obligations of defence counsel to advise his client and said that, if need be, the advice may be in strong terms, but that counsel should emphasise that the accused should only plead guilty if he *is* guilty.[6] If the defence counsel gives advice in such terms as to deprive the accused of his freedom of plea, a plea of guilty would be a nullity.[7] However, such cases are rare and the advice would need to be couched in extreme terms. If a client tells counsel that he is innocent but intends to plead guilty nonetheless, unless he can be persuaded to change his plea then counsel must continue to represent him on the basis that he is guilty and any plea in mitigation will assume guilt.[8]

4. THE ROLE OF THE JUDGE

It is inevitable that the judge will have some place in the plea bargaining process because his sanction will often be required in plea arrangements. Difficulties have arisen, however, over the extent to which it is proper for the judge to indicate the nature of the sentence discount which may be appropriate in a particular case if the accused enters a guilty plea. Whilst the benefit to the accused is tangible when the prosecution offers an arrangement, it is not precisely quantifiable. When the judge indicates a view about sentence, the inducement is precise and the pressure greatly increased.

The Court of Appeal considered the matters of principle involved in judicial intervention in the case of *R. v. Turner*.[9] The defendant, Turner, had pleaded not guilty on a charge of theft, but during an adjournment he was advised by counsel to change his plea. Turner knew that counsel had seen the judge and thought that counsel was relaying the views of the judge when he said that a guilty plea was likely to result in a non-custodial sentence, whereas a finding of guilt would bring a custodial sentence. Turner was repeatedly told that the choice of plea was his. He changed his plea to guilty and later appealed on the ground that he did not have a free choice in retracting his original plea.

The appeal was allowed on the basis that the defendant may have felt that the views expressed were those of the trial judge and might, therefore, have been deprived of his freedom of plea.[10] On the general issue Lord Parker C.J. made four observations[11]:

---

[6] *R. v. Turner* [1970] 2 Q.B. 321, 326, and see p. 630, below.

[7] *R. v. Peace* [1976] Crim.L.R. 119; *R. v. Inns* (1975) 60 Cr.App.R. 231.

[8] *Code of Conduct for the Bar* (n. 4 above), para. 150(b).

[9] [1970] 2 Q.B. 321.

[10] This is the basic question which the court will consider in all cases of this kind—"Has the plea been made freely and voluntarily?" *cf. R. v. Inns; R. v. Peace* (n. 7 above).

[11] [1970] 2 Q.B. 321, at p. 326-7.

(i) Counsel must give the best advice he can, in strong terms if need be, including the advice that a plea of guilty is a mitigating factor which may allow the court to pass a lesser sentence. The accused must be told not to plead guilty unless he has committed the offence charged.

(ii) The accused must have freedom of choice of plea.

(iii) There must be freedom of access between counsel and judge in order that matters which cannot be mentioned in open court may be communicated. Counsel for the defence and the prosecution should both be present as well as the defence solicitor, if he so wishes. Any such meetings should only take place when really necessary and the judge should only treat them as private where necessary.

(iv) A judge should never indicate the sentence he is minded to impose, save that he may tell counsel that whatever the plea, he is minded to impose a particular type of sentence, *e.g.* probation, or a fine, or a custodial sentence. A judge should never say that on a finding of guilt a more severe sentence would be passed, nor should he indicate that on a guilty plea he would pass a particular sentence, lest it be thought that a more severe sentence would result after a finding of guilt. Any discussion on sentence should be communicated by his counsel to the accused.

Those observations appeared to have limited the judicial role substantially and established a clear code of procedure, but they contain at least one major difficulty. The judge is told never to indicate that a sentence passed after a conviction would be more severe than a sentence passed after a guilty plea. Given the generally acknowledged rule that guilty pleas lead to sentence discounts,[12] how can this principle be observed? The judge is not permitted to say what everyone knows. A later Court of Appeal in *R.* v. *Cain*[13] acknowledged this difficulty, but the authority of *Turner* was strengthened by a subsequent Practice Direction[14] which reaffirmed the procedure set out by Lord Parker.

To sum up, the judicial role should be limited to the considerations of arrangements negotiated between counsel and to the indication of particular type of sentence whether that sentence follows a guilty plea or a conviction after a not guilty plea. Once the judge becomes involved in indicating alternative sentences any accused is likely to find himself under the same pressure as Turner, and, " . . . once he felt that this was an intimation emanating from the judge, it is really idle in the opinion of this court to think that he really had a free choice in the matter."[15]

5. WHAT IS THE PROPER BALANCE TO BE ACHIEVED?

The inducements to plead guilty, if they are regarded as legitimate at all, should not be such that they create a substantial danger of the innocent pleading guilty in order to avert the risks of unmerited conviction. The pressures exerted by defence counsel giving his advice to the accused "in strong terms" were identified by Baldwin and McConville in a research study which concentrated on 121 Crown Court defendants who made late

---

[12] See p. 626, above.
[13] (1975) 61 Cr.App.R. 186; [1976] Q.B. 496.
[14] [1976] Crim.L.R. 561.
[15] [1970] 2 Q.B. 321, 326B, *per* Lord Parker C.J.

changes of plea from not guilty to guilty.[16] The criticisms made of the attitude and performance of counsel caused the publication of the research to be surrounded with controversy, but the conclusions of the study are that the sentencing discount and the rules governing the interrogation of suspects by the police are primarily responsible for any deficiencies exposed, rather than the conduct of the participants in the criminal process.[17]

Although lip-service is paid to the notion that the discount is based on the expression of remorse, the primary justification for the inducements to plead guilty is administrative expediency. In a system which places so much emphasis upon the assumed innocence of the accused and his right to require the prosecution to prove their case, the existence of strong pressures to plead guilty may appear quite contradictory. The evidence currently available allows no complacency and suggests that more attention needs to be focused on those who plead their guilt and, as a result, do not participate in the elaborate procedures described in the rest of this chapter.[18]

[16] *Negotiated Justice* (1977). The research technique involved detailed interviews with defendants accused of serious crimes. The interviews were conducted soon after the trial had finished and it is inevitable that the particular sample might be inclined to protest innocence and exaggerate the pressures involved. Nonetheless, it would appear that the number of people wrongly convicted after a guilty plea may be underestimated.

[17] *Op. cit.* Chapter. 6.

[18] See further, S. Dell, *Silent in Court* (1971); S. McCabe and R. Purves, *By-Passing the Jury* (1972); A.E. Bottoms and J.D. McLean, *Defendants in the Criminal Process* (1976).

PART V

POST-TRIAL

CHAPTER 17

REMEDIES

A. INTRODUCTION

IN developed legal systems the civil law has two major functions: these may be characterised as preceptive (or prescriptive) and remedial. The two functions not surprisingly overlap in their operation and interact considerably. In contrast, the criminal law is primarily preceptive: it lays down rules of behaviour to be followed by its subjects, and prosecutions and consequent trials are the means of enabling breaches of those rules to be sanctioned. Of course, the granting by the civil law of remedies to a person who complains of a breach of its substantive rules will, at least in theory, have something of the same kind of sanctioning. In English law, however, at least in current times, the civil law carries much less moral force than the criminal with most of the population and by and large the sanctions are normally less severe and less deterrent.[1] This division between criminal and civil has been heightened by the law itself in its steady diminution of the availability of penal damages.[2] Only where the order of a court is flagrantly flouted and thus a contempt of court involved will there be anything like the sanction afforded directly by the criminal law.

The remedial function of the civil law is calculated to provide settlements to disputes between citizens or, often with special rules and processes, between citizens and public authorities. The history of English civil law, in common with its Roman counterpart, was for centuries one of introduction, elaboration and development of remedies with little or no reference to any real substantive law and with a gradual outdating and ignoring of the original simple and primitive precepts of the pre-existing customary law.[3] Eventually, however, a combination of three major, interacting factors resuscitated the preceptive function.[4] First, in the capitalist world that emerged out of the feudal era commercial men progressively needed to know not just what might happen if they behaved in a particular way that could give rise to an action against them but also how the law expected them to conduct their business generally. Secondly, the growing use of documents to bring about results allowed by the law required formulation of rules of substance beyond the technicalities of the bringing and defending of lawsuits. Lastly, theory and analysis were beginning slowly to infiltrate lawyers' thinking and by the late eighteenth century lawyers were beginning eagerly to discourse and write in terms of rights and duties and other abstract concepts rather than of the lying of actions and defences, or even of simple precepts of "thou shalt" and "thou shalt not."

[1] See, *e.g.* the law of squatting where up-to-date criminal sanctions had to be introduced by the Criminal Law Act 1977, Part II, mainly because of the disregard for the civil law rights of the property owners involved.

[2] See below, p. 654.

[3] See, *e.g.* F.W. Maitland, *The Forms of Action at Common Law* (2nd ed., 1936).

[4] The transition is traditionally described by reference to the change about of the maxim *ubi remedium, ibi jus* (where there is a remedy, there is a right) to *ubi jus, ibi remedium.*

These developments have meant that both students' and practitioners' textbooks are now couched mainly in terms of general rules with remedies occupying normally a portion of the work near the end—important still, but no longer dominant. Vital practitioners' works[5] on remedies do still exist and are much used, but primacy in education and in legal development is given to substantive rules stated analytically. This can hold dangers for the beginner. The fact that a civil action may theoretically lie will prompt the formulation of a substantive rule, but that formulation may cloak a reality that shows the rule often to be an empty one. This realism rests on the limits of the remedies involved and is thus distinct from the caution which every lawyer soon learns in the face of difficulties of proving facts or of inducing judges to operate a discretion or to apply a standard such as reasonableness. Examples may illustrate the distinction.

The tort of nuisance is a markedly imprecise wrong in much of its coverage.[6] The plaintiff must not only prove a sufficiently great infringement of the enjoyment of his land or a sufficient number of lesser, but still substantial infringements but must also satisfy the court that the infringement is unreasonable, or at least beyond what neighbours can expect "to give and to take." Anyone who has suffered the persistent annoyance of a neighbour whose principal hobby is bonfires will recognise the limitations of the law. To obtain the really effective remedy of injunction or even to achieve the satisfaction of damages the hurdles of proof and of application of standards are formidable. In contrast, the tort of trespass to land seems precise and remarkably inflexible: he who walks but once unbidden on the land commits trespass and is open to action. Yet not only is the plaintiff faced with a difficulty reminiscent of nuisance if he seeks an injunction to prohibit repetition, he knows that the nominal, perhaps even contemptuous, damages which alone sanction the wrong at common law will make any action not just profitless, but very probably a source of loss in legal costs as well as time and strain. The substantive rule has the narrowest of lives in the law court on the direct issue. The law of trespass to land has its true life in the extra-judicial remedy of self-help and in the differential rules the laws of crime and tort apply to trespassers as distinct from other entrants on land.[7]

Again, it is at the heart of the law of simple contract that even a totally executory contract[8] is enforceable at law. Yet, if the bargain is and remains an even one, then unless specific performance is available as a remedy[9] one promisor can disappoint his promisee with virtual impunity: the damages are awarded only for loss and if the price and the value are the same and there is no consequential loss bringing an action would be senseless. Thus

---

[5] e.g. H. McGregor, Damages (14th ed. 1980); E. Fry, Specific Performance (6th ed., 1921).

[6] See, e.g. Winfield and Jolowicz, The Law of Tort (11th ed., 1979), pp. 352–97.

[7] e.g. as an ingredient of the criminal offence of burglary; in the rule that a trespassing police officer may not lawfully require a person to submit to a breath test: Morris v. Beardmore [1981] A.C. 446 (cf. Transport Act 1981, s.25 and Sched. 8, which have the effect in some situations of reversing Morris v. Beardmore and creating a statutory power of entry for specified purposes); and in the rule that occupiers of land only owe a duty of care to lawful visitors: trespassers are only owed a lesser duty, commonly termed one of "humanity": British Railways Board v. Herrington [1972] A.C. 877. On self-help, see below, pp. 639–641.

[8] Viz. a promise for a promise.

[9] See below, p. 656.

the sale of land, for which specific performance is normally available, prima facie commands a sanction which the sale of even a more expensive chattel will normally not.

Even if the student grasps this lesson on the frequent shortfall of a remedy's effectiveness he has also to learn that in trying to work out the ratio of a case[10] he may find it essential to identify the remedy that is being accorded or refused. A classic example is *Denny* v. *Hancock*[11] where the refusal of specific performance to the vendor was consistent with (i) leaving the vendor with any remedy he might have in damages, (ii) the contract's being void *ab initio*, (iii) the contract's having been avoided by the purchaser, (iv) the contract's being valid on the terms understood by the purchaser.

A parallel danger arises from misunderstanding the operation of a remedy. In *Cooper* v. *Phibbs*[12] the remedy granted was the equitable one of cancellation of documents. The court order effecting such a remedy is that the document be "set aside and cancelled": it is available just as much where the transaction incorporated in the document was void *ab initio* as where it has been avoided by an act of rescission or discharge by a party. In either case the existence of a seemingly effective instrument will usually be an embarrassment if not also a danger. It is arguable that the highly questionable modern doctrine that a court has power to rescind at its discretion for unilateral mistake[13] is based on the false premise that in *Cooper* v. *Phibbs* it was the contract and not the document that was set aside.

It seems therefore that even the student of the substantive law cannot afford to ignore the contribution that the various remedies make to the breadth, direction and limitations of that law. Happily, there is today a masterly conspectus of legal remedies by Lawson[14] and all students should regard it as a "must" for understanding the law.

B. CONCEPTS AND CLASSIFICATIONS

A remedy is the means which the law provides or permits so as to enable a claimant to be in the position in which he should have been if the substantive law had been or were being duly observed. By their very nature and the facts of the real world remedies will often fall far short of fulfilling this aim even when they are pursued totally successfully. Rescinding a contract, whether or not there is hope of compensation as well, is a poor substitute in most cases for a full performance, whilst few would argue that any amount of damages can make up for a death or loss of a limb.

The major classification of remedies is into extra-judicial and judicial. With the extra-judicial the operation of the remedy concludes the process unless it is frustrated: the claimant who resorts to self-help achieves his end in applying the remedy. On the other hand, most judicial remedies involve

---

[10] See above, p. 280.

[11] (1870) L.R. 6 Ch. 1: *cf.* J.C. Smith and J.A.C. Thomas, *A Casebook on Contract* (7th ed. 1982) pp. 89–91.

[12] (1867) L.R. 2 H.L. 149.

[13] See, *e.g. Bell* v. *Lever Bros. Ltd.* [1932] A.C. 161; *Solle* v. *Butcher* [1950] 1 K.B. 671; G. Treitel, *The Law of Contract* (6th ed., 1983), p. 211.

[14] *Remedies of English Law* (2nd ed., 1980).

an order with which a defendant is bound to comply: if he does not, the plaintiff proceeds to execution of the judgment that made the order. Execution may almost be considered the secondary remedy for the unsatisfied remedy, a further stage towards the achievement of the ultimate goal of rectifying the wrong done the plaintiff.

At one time the major practical difference between the operation of the common law and of equity was that under the former execution was always *in rem*, while in equity it was *in personam*. The *in rem* signified satisfaction of the judgment by action against the property of the defendant, *e.g.* to effect restitution or to force payment of damages by seizing and either withholding or eventually selling goods or other property. Execution *in personam* involved action against the body of the defendant, in effect imprisoning him for contempt of court in not complying with an order. Since 1875 the fusion of law and equity (or at least of their administration)[15] has meant that both forms of execution, as well as new statutory forms such as attachment of earnings,[16] are available as seems appropriate, regardless now whether the judgment to be satisfied is to be characterised as legal or equitable.[17]

The terminology *in rem* and *in personam* is a source of confusion. In the sphere of execution it is acceptably apt, but it has traditionally also been used to classify common law remedies themselves[18] according as whether the judgment sought would achieve specific recovery of the property or merely damages. When the common law was in its initial stages in the twelfth and thirteenth centuries only freehold land was specifically recoverable by court action and so it alone became characterised as *real* property or realty: all other property, including copyhold and leasehold land, was not so recoverable and its loss could be compensated for only by damages, so that all species of such property came to be called *personal* property or personalty.[19] Over the centuries all land of whatever tenure became specifically recoverable through the invention and adaption of new remedies,[20] and even though chattels retain the general rule that defendants may satisfy judgment either by returning them or by paying their value in damages the courts do nowadays[21] have the power to order specific recovery in suitable circumstances, particularly where the chattel is irreplaceable or has no ready market value.

The word "remedy" naturally imports the notion of a wrong to be set right (or, in other words, a right to be vindicated). This, of course, will normally be the case. However, by a natural extension of language the term can fairly be extended to cover cases of actions undertaken by a

---

[15] See, *per* Lord Diplock in *United Scientific Holdings Ltd.* v. *Burnley B.C.* [1978] A.C. 904 at p. 925.

[16] See, Attachment of Earnings Act 1971; Lawson, *op. cit.* p. 8.

[17] See Lawson, *op. cit.* pp. 7–10, and also pp. 10–12 for the vital factor of possibility of insolvency rendering an order of court, or even an execution, virtually valueless where damages are involved.

[18] Based on a medieval misappreciation of the original Roman Law significances: *cf.* Maitland, *op. cit.* pp. 73–78.

[19] See *e.g.* R.E. Megarry and H.W.R. Wade, *The Law of Real Property* (4th ed., 1975) pp. 10–12, 1167–74.

[20] *Loc. cit.*

[21] Since the Common Law Procedure Act 1854, s.78: *cf.* Lawson, *op. cit.* pp. 204–205.

claimant that can scarcely be called attempts to redress a wrong in whole or in part. Thus, in the extra-judicial sphere, an owner of land (at least in the days before town and country planning legislation interfered) could erect a hoarding on his land to prevent a neighbour from acquiring a right of light by 20 years enjoyment under the Prescription Act 1832,[22] the neighbour of course having committed no wrong and infringed no right, indeed having done nothing at all beyond build on his own land with a window facing the owner's property. Nowadays statute[23] has actually provided an alternative, less expensive and drastic "remedy" by allowing the owner to register a local land charge which, with considerable sophistication, operates as a notional hoarding of dimensions specified in the charge.

In the judicial sphere the action for a declaration,[24] used especially in the public law sphere, is a means of establishing a right without the seeking of an order enforceable by execution against the defendant. In theory, the declaration can be ignored with impunity,[25] but in reality it will virtually always be effectively observed by defendants who either wish to avoid the opprobrium of lawlessness or are afraid of the costs that will inevitably accrue if the plaintiff has to sue out a "full" remedy. In substance, it is as entitled to the caption of "remedy" as a friendly action for a "true" remedy is, for instance where neighbours not in disharmony have traditionally used a symbolic act of trespass to ground an action to test uncertain ownership.[26]

One stage further from the strictest sense of "remedy" is the process whereby a litigant approaches a court for advice or direction on how to perform a legal function or asks for endorsement or indemnification in respect of a performed or contemplated act. The classic example is the proceeding in Chancery by way of originating summons brought by a trustee or other fiduciary to take advantage of the equitable jurisdiction to give assistance in such circumstances.[27]

Whatever the position may be in strict conceptual terms, the use of the word "remedy" to denominate any form of judicial proceeding ending in a judgment or order may surely be regarded as not only legitimate, but sensible.

C. EXTRA-JUDICIAL REMEDIES

1. SELF-HELP

Traditionally the two most usual examples of self-help are recaption (*viz.* the retaking) of land or chattels by an owner and abatement of nuisance. Both are clearly alternatives to recourse to the courts. It has also been traditional to contrast this type of self-help with forms of self-defence, including defence of one's property. Yet the distinction is scarcely

---

[22] s.3: See Megarry and Wade, *op. cit.* pp. 861–864.
[23] Rights of Light Act 1959, s.2: *cf.* Megarry and Wade, *op. cit.* pp. 854–855.
[24] See below, p. 658.
[25] As was done by Southwark L.B.C.: *cf. Webster* v. *Southwark L.B.C.* [1983] Q.B. 698.
[26] See, *e.g.* Lawson, *op. cit.* p. 237.
[27] Under R.S.C., Ord. 85, r. 2: see P.H. Pettit, *Equity and the Law of Trusts* (4th ed., 1979) pp. 371–372.

clear-cut. If one thinks of the legal consequences of each type of act rather than tries to analyse the motive of the act the same considerations apply: the user of self-help and the self-defender both have defences to actions brought against them for trespass, whether to the person or to the property involved; and accordingly neither is a wrongdoer or suffers the disabilities of a trespasser in respect of any duty of care owed him by an occupier of land.[28]

Lawson[29] carries this logic to the point of questioning whether ejection of a trespasser on one's land is an act of self-help or of self-defence: once one has re-entered one's own land one is lawfully there and one can then use self-defence to protect one's possession. In effect, of course, one has achieved what a court order for possession would have given one.

Both self-help and self-defence are hedged around by restrictions in modern law. In most instances the person acting on such a claim must behave reasonably, using no more force than is reasonably necessary to achieve his permitted aim (and perhaps also using no force at all if the damage or loss inflicted by it would be disproportionate to the benefit intended[30]). In fact, the standard of reasonableness may have two important consequences in this context. First, it allows the acts permitted by the law to be tailored to the particular circumstances of the case. Secondly, it engenders a measure of uncertainty of prediction that is likely to deter recourse to self-help (and even self-defence) except where there exists the strongest moral case for its use. Besides any particular restrictions this operates strongly to narrow the scope for self-help, and even self-defence, and this accords well with the overall policy of the modern law, namely not completely to outlaw use of self-help where public opinion might still feel it to be a justifiable liberty, but at the same time to establish use of judicial procedures as always the prime remedy. Even so, the concertina of reasonableness can occasionally be extended a remarkably long way, as where an occupier of a furnished room was held not guilty of a crime when discharging a firearm against persons attempting to evict him unlawfully.[31] Perhaps it is in this type of case that a distinction between self-help and self-defence is most readily seen—the self-defender is likely to be accorded more latitude than the self-helper. However, again it must be recognised that the self-helper who finds himself resisted, especially where resistance was unexpected, will rapidly become a self-defender entitled to escalate the force he uses in proportion to the force unlawfully used against him.[32]

Recaption of goods shows how particular restrictions may apply. An owner may repossess his property where he finds it on public premises, or perhaps even where it is on the wrongdoer's land, but he will normally have no right of entry on to the premises of any third party who has been in no way involved in the loss of the chattel.[33] Still less will he have a right to enter for recaption where it is his own fault that the chattel has found its way on to another's land: that other may not handle the chattel, but he can

[28] See, Winfield & Jolowicz, op. cit. pp. 211–217.
[29] Op. cit., p. 27.
[30] This may, of course, be regarded as one special factor in reasonableness.
[31] See Hussey (1924) 18 Cr.App.Rep. 160; A.M. Prichard, Squatting (1981) pp. 146–150.
[32] See Prichard, op. cit. p. 145.
[33] See Winfield & Jolowicz, op. cit. pp. 465–468.

let it lie where it falls and refuse to let the owner come in to collect it (which, at least, may prove some form of deterrent to the games-player who lets his ball travel on to his neighbour's land). The animated chattel that wanders on to another's land gave rise to a special form of self-help, distress damage feasant.[34] Where trespassing cattle damaged the land the owner of that land might impound or "distrain" the cattle until the cattle-owner paid compensation for the damage. This ancient, very specialised remedy was the one form of distress that did not arise as an attribute of a pre-existing legal relationship between the parties.

Repossessing one's land has for long proved an area of controversy and legal difficulty. Using force to evict a possessor of land was first made criminal in the middle ages by various Statutes of Forcible Entry and is now governed by the Criminal Law Act 1977, s.6., and, in the case of residential tenants, by the Protection from Eviction Act 1977. However, although the act may attract criminal sanctions it may not necessarily endow the dispossessed with full civil remedies. No doubt he may sue for assault and battery in respect of any force applied to his person, but the eviction itself appears to be effective in civil law, certainly under the old, pre-1977 law,[35] and probably even today.[36] After all, how can a court properly put someone back into a possession to which he has no entitlement or award damages for loss of such a possession? Once again, this is an example of the point that whether a remedy is available may be more significant than the conceptual wrongness of the act complained of.

These classic examples of self-help have tended to be treated most fully in textbooks on torts, whether under the headings of defences or remedies.[37] Often they will involve the sort of physical act by the self-helper that might be expected to evoke resentment, and even resistance, from all but the most reasonable or pacific of wrongdoers. Accordingly, the law has tended to be jealous of the extent of the right for fear of breaches of the peace. In other spheres of law, particularly contract and property, an aggrieved person may have powers and options open to him to rectify or ameliorate his position without the need to go to court and without any great danger of a breach of the peace ensuing. In such instances the term "self-help" has rarely been used and the law has not shown either hostility or doubt, but has rather evinced considerable enthusiasm for their use.

2. Contract and Property Powers

Such powers can be divided into two groups: those the law confers directly (whether or not it allows parties to oust or to qualify them by agreement) and those which parties create for themselves. A good example is rescission of contract.

Rescission is in fact a highly ambiguous expression.[38] In particular there

---

[34] See Winfield & Jolowicz, *op. cit.* pp. 440–441. The Animals Act 1971, s.7, now covers much the same ground.

[35] See *Hemmings* v. *Stoke Poges Golf Club* [1920] 1 K.B. 720.

[36] See Prichard, *op. cit.* pp. 152–155.

[37] See *e.g.* Winfield & Jolowicz, *op. cit.* p. 626 (re abatement of nuisance).

[38] See A. Bate, (1955) 19 Conv. N.S. 116–120; J.T. Farrand, *Contract and Conveyance* (4th ed., 1983) pp. 209–211.

is a vital distinction between rescission *ab initio* and rescission for breach, to use the time-honoured but very dangerous[39] terminology lawyers have evolved. In the former the result of the rescinding is that the contract disappears altogether, normally leaving the parties in the position they were in before their agreement: to achieve a return to that position as fully as possible the law makes available additional remedies such as (i) damages at common law for quasi-contract, (ii) the close counterpart in equity of such damages, a right to indemnity, (iii) return of any deposit, (iv) specific restitution (where ownership in property has been passed) and (v) specific recovery (where possession only has passed). Rescission for breach were better termed repudiation (itself, however, not unambiguously used) or discharge for breach, but it is too late to hope for a uniform abandonment of the phraseology. It arises where one party has committed a sufficiently serious breach of contract[40] to justify the other in refusing to carry on with performance of that contract. In this case the rescinding party still has the contract to sue upon and can claim to be put into the position he would have been if the contract had been properly performed, *i.e.* his remedy will be in contract (not quasi-contract) for damages for loss of any bargain (as distinct from *restitutio in integrum* to his position before contract). Between these two poles there is alleged to be a shadowy and controversial *judicial* remedy of rescission available whereby the Courts may in equity avoid the contract on application, but impose terms to achieve a fair result[41]: this would mean that a party wanting to rescind could not do it on his own, but would have to sue to do so and, before doing so, have to consider what terms might be imposed.

The form of rescission *ab initio* conferred by law on a party may be for any of several reasons, such as misrepresentation by the other party, undue influence, infancy, insanity, drunkenness,[42] although expressions such as avoiding and repudiating are more common in the cases other than for misrepresentation. All the rescinder has to do is unequivocally notify the other party that the contract is rescinded, provided, of course, all the requirements for rescission on the ground claimed are satisfied. Whether or not the rescinder sues out any additional remedy the law allows him will often depend most on the likely solvency of the debtor and the degree of indignation or determination in the rescinder.

All the forms of rescission so far discussed are clearly remedies in the full sense. The power to rescind which is often conferred by the agreement itself on one or both of the parties is, of course, closely analogous, but less patently a remedy. A regular example is the right conferred on vendors of land under most formal contracts of sale to rescind if the purchaser persists in pressing a requisition on title which the vendor cannot satisfy.[43] No one would suggest that such a purchaser is in any way in the wrong—he is

---

[39] See, *e.g. Horsler* v. *Zorro* [1975] Ch. 302, where even Homer, in the form of Megarry J., nodded.

[40] Traditionally called a breach of condition as distinct from one of mere warranty—terminology again too established to change despite the need to qualify by such expressions as fundamental and innominate terms. Probably no other area of law has achieved such chaos in terminology.

[41] See Treitel, *op. cit.* pp. 239–243; and above, p. 637, nn. 12 and 13.

[42] See Treitel, *op. cit.* pp. 282–299; 312–318; 416–434; 434–436; 436 respectively.

[43] See Farrand, *op. cit.* pp. 122–125.

indeed pursuing a right: it is just that vendors' bargaining positions have over the years established the propriety of their having this escape route from liability. Any contract can provide for its own premature termination at the option of a party[44] just as the parties themselves can subsequently undo their agreement completely and this is another common instance where the term "rescission" is used.[45] Statute has even interfered to establish rights of rescission, not so as to remedy specific wrongdoings or other causes, but to rule out all possibility of unfairness or undue pressure: an example is the "cooling off" period allowed with respect to certain consumer credit contracts signed in the home.[46]

Rescission is essentially a negative remedy: the rescinder decides to terminate the operation of legal obligations. The fact that a party may rescind obviously can be a deterrent to breach by the other party, often all the more so if there is the possibility of an action for damages as well. But for the rescinder the principal advantage is the facility to cut losses and to escape from obligations that appear unlikely to produce compensating rewards. Other extra-judicial remedies can be more positive while at the same time having no less deterrent effect.

3. DEPOSITS

Vendors and other suppliers often require as part of their contracts payment of a deposit. In sales of land, deposits, usually of 10 per cent. of the price, are almost invariably required from purchasers. The deposit will count as a part payment when the sale is completed, but its most important role is to induce performance of the contract because on breach by the purchaser the vendor will be entitled to retain the deposit without having to prove that the measure of any loss he may have suffered is as great as that deposit. As such the deposit is a powerful deterrent to breach of the contract and, for the vendor, a wonderful complementary weapon to rescission. Even where a vendor clearly suffers substantial loss it is still a great benefit to him not to have to itemise and prove that loss in litigation.

Forfeiture of a deposit is conceptually a clear anomaly: it seems to evade completely both the legal distinction between penalties and liquidated damages[47] and the equitable jurisdiction of relieving against penalties.[48] In sales of land there is a statutory jurisdiction under section 49(2) of the Law of Property Act 1925 to order return of a deposit in the court's discretion, but there is too little clear case law to gauge how liberally that discretion will be exercised and, in consequence, to allow an aggrieved purchaser to estimate his chances of success in any challenge.[49] Whether or not the theory of equity that land is uniquely valuable and so is the natural candidate for the award of specific performance[50] affects the latitude granted to vendors by the law is a matter for speculation.

---

[44] "Break clauses" in leases are a classic example.
[45] See Treitel, *op. cit.* pp. 79–80.
[46] See Consumer Credit Act 1974, ss.67–68; Treitel, *op. cit.* pp. 319–320.
[47] See Farrand, *op. cit.* pp. 203–205.
[48] See Farrand, *loc. cit.*; Snell, *Equity* (28th ed., 1982), pp. 527–530.
[49] See Farrand, *op. cit.* pp. 205–206; Emmet on *Title* (18th ed., 1983), pp. 259–261.
[50] See below, p. 656.

4. Other Forfeitures

A sum of money is the easiest subject for forfeiture, but the idea goes far beyond the retention of deposits. Here, however, equity is much more likely to intervene. The earliest and still most important example is the mortgage. The idea is that the creditor should have the ownership or some other interest in the property as security for the payment of the debt or the performance of another obligation: if the debtor defaults the creditor retains or recovers the property and so avoids both the need to sue for the debt and the risk of losing part or all of that debt if the debtor becomes bankrupt. Equity interferes to prevent the simple appropriation of the property by the creditor on a mere delay in performance by the debtor: the debtor's right to have the property back free of the security—his "right to redeem"—is safeguarded in that it can be lost only by a court order of foreclosure, which will be awarded only as a last resort to the creditor. As a result the mortgage has become over the centuries a much more sophisticated concept engendering for the creditor a whole range of remedies, judicial and extra-judicial, including (a) sale of the property with division of the proceeds with the debtor receiving any surplus of funds after the creditor's claims are satisfied, (b) appointment of a receiver to collect rents and profits from the property, and (c) the taking of possession and enjoyment by the creditor as well as (d) foreclosure. This battery of options for the creditor is a strong stimulus to an ordinary debtor to honour his obligations, but the unevenness of bargaining power and the risk of disaster for the debtor where he becomes unable to pay everything due with little or no fault on his part has led to increased intervention not only by equity but by statute as well, especially where the debtor's dwelling is involved.[51] Accordingly what originally was an extra-judicial remedy will often now be precluded without an application to a court for an order.[52]

Mortgages and charges[53] are capable of applying to all sorts of property, but are especially relevant to land. With chattels the original security is also the simplest: the pledge. It confers the right to withhold possession and enjoyment of the property till performance of the obligation secured together with the vital extra weapon of sale after elapse of the stipulated period.[54]

The remedial attractions of these extra-judicial remedies are recognized by the law itself as well as by creditors. Accordingly, both law and equity have created powers of withholding property to stimulate payment, more and more often coupled with powers to sell in due course: these are liens.[55] An aspect of the same policy of the law is the immemorial power of a landlord to distrain for rent owed him: the landlord seizes chattels on the land let belonging to the tenant so as to induce payment, and here too a right to sell has been added as final sanction. Once again, both the law and statute have ensured that this is a highly technical and complicated area of law in an attempt to limit exploitation by unscrupulous landlords.[56]

---

[51] See, *e.g.* the Administration of Justice Acts 1970 (s.36) and 1973 (s.8).

[52] See generally Megarry and Wade, *op. cit.* pp. 904–925; Snell, *op. cit.* pp. 385–446.

[53] Charges are forms of security over property which do not confer any actual ownership or property interest but do accord much the same remedies in whole or part.

[54] See Snell, *op. cit.* pp. 447–449.

[55] See Snell, *op. cit.* pp. 450–462.

[56] See Megarry and Wade, *op. cit.* pp. 691–694.

One further example from a whole host of instances of such extra-judicial remedies may be given. This is the right to forfeit a lease or other estate or interest in land for failure to perform an obligation or other breach of condition: often called alternatively a right of re-entry (*viz.* to go back into possession and thereby to destroy the interest of the ousted holder: this must be distinguished from the right of entry, which confers a right to enter or even to take possession but without any effect on any interest in the property). Again, equity and statute have intervened radically to restrict this right being effected without court order, or at least without the right in the tenant to seek relief from a court where the forfeiture would be harsh and the landlord would not be seriously prejudiced by the relief.[57]

5. SET-OFF AND RETAINERS

In any transaction or even continuing legal relationship a debt owed by one party to another may obviously not be just a simple pre-calculated sum, but will often involve additions and subtractions on either side for expenses and other incidental factors. The deductions may be fairly regarded as integral to the debt itself. Where, however, there are clearly separate (even though perhaps related) debts owed in each direction the ability of the creditor in the lesser sum to pay merely the difference between the two sums can be both convenient and valuable both in and out of court. Where the law allows this process it is know as set-off. There are important restrictions on this right. Thus, normally only a liquidated (*i.e.* presently quantified or at least immediately quantifiable) sum may be set off[58]: usually an unliquidated sum can be achieved only by court action, whether by an initiated action or by a counterclaim. Obviously, where it is available set-off is not only attractive in its avoidance of litigation, it can also be of great value where the other party is insolvent.

Not entirely dissimilar is the right of retainer occasionally accorded by the law. The classic example is the right of a personal representative to deduct a debt owed by a legatee to the deceased's estate from the legacy given him by the will.[59]

D. JUDICIAL REMEDIES

The law provides a vast variety of proceedings before courts and other tribunals aimed at affording to claimants some form of redress. The complexities of modern life have greatly multiplied this traditional variety. Thus, security of tenure provided by statute in modern landlord and tenant law may in effect be broadly comparable across the major species of leasehold, but the variation in type of action involved to ground that security is bewilderingly diverse. In respect of residential tenancies[60] the

---

[57] See generally, Megarry and Wade, *op. cit.* pp. 654–667.

[58] See Lawson, *op. cit.* pp. 38–39.

[59] See Lawson, *op. cit.* pp. 39–40.

[60] Under the Rent Acts for the private sector (and the Housing Act 1980 for local authority and other "public sector" lettings): see Megarry and Wade, *op. cit.* pp. 1124–1148 (somewhat out of date now).

tenant is protected by being irremovable in law until the landlord sues in
the county court for possession on one of the statutorily provided grounds.
With business tenancies[61] the tenant may sit tight until the landlord serves
a set form of notice, but when the landlord does do so it is the tenant who
has to initiate court proceedings by applying for a new lease to be granted.
For the agricultural tenant[62] the régime is that security subsists until the
landlord establishes before a special body, the Agricultural Land Tribunal,
grounds for it to consent to the giving of an effective notice to quit.

A restrictive covenant is a means whereby one piece of land can have its
use and exploitation restricted for the benefit of a neighbouring piece. An
owner of apparently restricted land was traditionally faced with a dilemma:
either to go ahead in breach of the covenant and risk being held liable in an
expensive action by a neighbouring owner or himself to go to court to try
for a declaration[63] against the neighbour. The Law of Property Act 1925,
s.84, affords two extra options. First, under section 84(2), a much more
attractive declaration is specially available: one that is effective not just in
establishing the non-existence or limited operation of the covenant so that
it cannot thereafter be challenged, but also in being binding on all the
world, including even possible claimants who through ignorance of their
existence have not been served with any notice of the action. Secondly, the
rest of section 84[64] set up an entirely new procedure whereby an applicant
could seek from the Lands Tribunal an order discharging or modifying a
covenant of even admitted validity. Again, any order obtained will be good
against all the world.

A final example from a totally different area of law will have to suffice to
complete the illustration of the number and diversity of modern legal
remedies involving adjudication. At common law an employee has always
been able to sue, normally for damages, rarely if ever for specific
performance or injunction (or even declaration) when he has been sacked
in breach of contract. The nature of that contract is such that it will so often
be vulnerable to termination by short notice that damages for *wrongful*
dismissal will rarely produce substantial compensation. Statute has stepped
in to allow industrial tribunals to award what will usually be much larger
sums (though not always[65]) for *unfair* dismissal.[66]

1. Criminal Prosecutions

Ever since the middle ages English law has maintained a remarkable
exclusivity of the civil from the criminal law. Even if originally both
misdemeanours[67] and torts had a common origin in the medieval

---

[61] Under the Landlord and Tenant Act 1954, Part II; see Megarry and Wade, *op. cit.* pp.
1109–17.

[62] Under the Agricultural Holdings Act 1948: See Megarry and Wade, *op. cit.* pp.
1117–1124.

[63] See below, p. 658.

[64] As amended by Law of Property Act 1969, s.28; see C.H.S. Preston and G.H. Newsom,
Restrictive Covenants (7th ed., 1982) pp. 189–302, 202–323.

[65] *e.g.* where the contract specifies tenure of post for a substantial period or until retirement
age.

[66] Employment Protection (Consolidation) Act 1978, Part V.

[67] *Viz.* indictable offences less heinous than felonies and treasons.

trespass,[68] differences in procedure, and perhaps particularly in the burden of proof, have produced the sharpest of divisions. A private individual may, it is true, bring a private prosecution[69] or induce the police to proceed to prosecute or to take other cautionary action, and this can have both a deterrent effect and even remove the delinquent from his position of being able to harm the complainant. What, however, in general the complainant cannot do is to combine the criminal sanction with a suit for compensation in one and the same action. However, since the Forfeiture Act 1870 the practice has been growing of Parliament's conferring on criminal courts powers to order compensation for a large range of crimes when the defendant has been convicted.[70] Moreover, police action may result in recovery of stolen property. Quite often, the criminal law may be speedier, more effective and cheaper in attaining redress than seeking damages, an injunction or specific recovery.[71]

Where a complainant has been injured, but the wrongdoer is not worth suing or untraceable, recourse may be had to the Criminal Injuries Compensation Board. The awards are not only discretionary,[72] but are in fact made entirely *ex gratia*. Even so, the function is exercised judicially and it may be regarded as a very welcome remedy.[73]

2. CIVIL PROCEEDINGS

(a) Classification

Naturally it is the remedies afforded by orders of the civil courts that are regarded as the primary and central forms of legal redress and so receive the greatest prominence in legal textbooks, even though litigation is a fearful last resort for most citizens and extra-judicial remedies are always the most readily attractive. On the other hand, the existence and the fear of this last resort provide the greatest stimulus for out of court settlements and compromises: the mere presence of a rule of law on its own is rarely enough as the concept of unenforceability shows. Under a number of statutes[74] a rule of substantive law may subsist but the action which enforces it is denied. Thus, in conveyancing a contract for the sale of land may be binding in law, but in the absence of written evidence of it or of an act of part performance referable to the contract a defendant can with impunity refuse to perform his legal duty[75]: the profession readily equates this unenforceability with substantive voidness so far as advising clients in normal circumstances is concerned.

The initial classification of English law was into real and personal remedies[76] depending on whether specific recovery of property would be

---

[68] *cf.* S.F.C. Milsom, *Historical Foundations of the Common Law* (2nd ed., 1981), pp. 287, 404–405.

[69] Subject to the power of the Attorney-General to intervene and end the action by entering a *nolle prosequi*: see above, pp. 481–482.

[70] See Powers of Criminal Courts Act 1973 in particular.

[71] See, generally, Lawson, *op. cit.* pp. 16, 260–263.

[72] Like those of the criminal courts under the 1973 Act, above.

[73] See Lawson, *op. cit.* p. 168.

[74] *e.g.* the Limitation Acts where, however, only a right of action is barred rather than a substantive right is destroyed by lapse of time.

[75] Under the Law of Property Act 1925, s.40: see Megarry and Wade, *op. cit.* pp. 545–572.

[76] See above, p. 638.

ordered or merely damages for the loss involved. Subsequently, the distinction between legal and equitable remedies became increasingly important. Later, particularly through the operation of statute, a wholly distinct class of remedies has emerged. These may usefully be called "constitutive" actions.[77] These are extremely various and extend across many areas of law. Examples in the civil law are: adoption and legitimation orders, award of custody and guardianship, divorces, appointment of trustees, dissolution of partnerships, liquidation of companies, adjudication in bankruptcy. Sometimes the order merely records a fact, an example being the declaration that a seeming marriage was in fact always null and void as distinct from an order that actually annuls a hitherto valid, but voidable marriage.[78] In a way the equitable remedies of rectification and cancellation of documents are special examples of constitutive remedies.[79] Sometimes the remedies are "as of right" where the specified grounds are proved, sometimes—as with equitable remedies—dependent also on the discretion to be exercised by the court.

(b) Recovery and restitution

By what laymen must regard as lawyer's perversity of language the word "recover" is used as the technical expression to signify "obtain" in respect of damages and other money awards: "Can he recover?" is synonymous with "Will he obtain damages?" Rather similarly, but less paradoxically, the word restitution is frequently used to denote a payment of money to rectify a loss or to effect a return to a previous position: the Latin phrase "*restitutio in integrum*" is commonly employed by lawyers to signify such a restoration in full to conditions prior to the event or act complained of. The return of property to an owner or to someone else entitled to it is accordingly more explicitly referred to as "specific recovery" or "specific restitution."

The distinction between these two terms is scarcely uniformly observed or even recognised. Purists might insist that specific recovery involves merely the restoration of possession or enjoyment of property to the owner, while specific restitution involves a retransferring of the actual ownership to the previous owner.[80] If, for instance,[81] on an exchange of land one transferor has been substantially misled by a misrepresentation by the other and elects to rescind the contract of exchange[82] after there has been a formal conveyance of each piece of land, the ownership would have to be passed back and a court order to achieve this might be best termed "restitution." However, it is arguable whether the terminology needs to be so precise: if the plaintiff gets back control and enjoyment he can happily leave it to the substantive law to analyse the event and can be content with an order that "he do recover the land."

Nowadays all land, freehold and leasehold, is specifically recoverable as of right by the owner, but in the most frequent instances, recovery by

[77] See Lawson, *op. cit.* Chap. 17.
[78] See Lawson, *op. cit.* pp. 241–243: see also above, pp. 640–642 re rescission of contracts.
[79] See Snell, *op. cit.* pp. 610–619 and 608–609 respectively.
[80] See Lawson, *op. cit.* Chaps. 12 and 13 (and 14 for the shadowy and controversial specific substitution).
[81] Admittedly what must be an extremely rare instance.
[82] *e.g.* for fraud.

landlords and mortgagees, there are formidable barriers erected by statute against the common law rights of recovery. In addition, even against wrongdoers, the remedy can be infuriatingly slow and expensive. In the aftermath of the squatting phenomenon of the late 1960s and early 1970s speed and simplicity have been achieved by the invention of an expedited procedure against certain types of dispossessor.[83]

In an action for recovery of land it is normal form to add a claim for "mesne profits," that is compensation for the loss of enjoyment of the land during the wrongful dispossession. The normal measure of damages will be the rent that could reasonably be expected to have been payable during that period.

Specific recovery of chattels as distinct from land is nowadays in the discretion of the court.[84] The plaintiff can insist upon an order for damages to cover his loss, but if he seeks to obtain redelivery of the chattel the defendant has the option to retain the chattel and pay its value instead unless the court decides it is an appropriate case to order the redelivery (e.g. if it has a unique or perhaps sentimental value). In any case the plaintiff may claim and be awarded also damages for any consequential loss.[85]

(c) Damages

Except for specific recovery (originally only of freehold land) an award of damages is the only major common law remedy and it covers a vast range of wrongs and indebtednesses. It is the common law term for any order requiring payment of money. In fact, in modern English law orders to pay money, even only orders of courts (let alone tribunals[86]), extend over a vast range of areas of law, statutory and non-statutory, beyond the traditional common law species of contract, quasi-contract and tort. In particular, while it is normally treated as axiomatic that equity provides discretionary remedies of a specific kind in cases where damages are deemed inadequate redress, equity quite often affords bases for money awards. Thus, if rescission is allowed in equity,[87] full *restitutio in integrum* may require the payment of a sum of money as well as return of property and release of obligation. Since 1875 the fact and the form of the order are more important than the historical source and little turns on whether it be termed indemnity or damages. Again, where a trustee commits a breach of trust,[88] the beneficiary may sue not just for property and money in the trustee's hands but also for compensation for consequential loss inflicted on the beneficiary (or for interest on sums withheld): in many ways this liability for loss is so proximate to common law damages as to warrant considering breach of trust as a species of tort (just as the tort of "passing

---

[83] See Prichard, *op. cit.* Part II: R.S.C., Ord. 113 and C.C.R., Ord. 26.

[84] See above, p. 638.

[85] See, generally, Torts (Interference with Goods) Act 1977, especially ss.3 and 6 under which an honest defendant may be allowed compensation for any improvements effected on the goods, in contrast with the probable position in respect of improvements to land: see Snell, *op. cit.* pp. 460–461.

[86] *e.g.* for unfair dismissal: see above, p. 646, n. 66.

[87] *e.g.* for innocent misrepresentation, p. 642 above.

[88] See Snell, *op. cit.* pp. 282–295, generally.

off"[89] is a contribution of equity to the list of established torts). For various reasons, perhaps principally lawyers' conservatism, that reclassification has not yet been adopted. It may be as well: adaptation of common law doctrines of remoteness of damage and measure of damages may not be so readily applicable—for instance, whether reasonable foreseeability restricts liability and, if so, what is the moment for the exercise of the foresight, both questions to be settled in an area where the wrong is much more often an omission than an act, in contrast with the law of negligence.[90]

The basic traditional division of damages is into liquidated and unliquidated: liquidated where the plaintiff specifies a set sum of money as owed to him at law in his original claim; unliquidated where, in default of agreement or compromise between the parties, the court must calculate the sum to be paid if liability is established. The distinction has important practical consequences, for instance in the law of set-off, where normally only liquidated sums can be set-off against other sums without the need to go to court.[91] The law also allows more readily the assignment of liquidated debts, whereas it is much more cautious about trafficking in the fruits of litigation.[92]

This distinction is sometimes identified with that between debt and compensation.[93] In a way this impedes an appreciation of the essential purpose of damages—to satisfy the entitlement of the plaintiff. What that entitlement is will vary from branch to branch of the law. If one takes the simplest case of debt, the obligation to repay a loan, the entitlement is such as to restore the claimant's financial position to what it was in that respect before the obligation was incurred. As such it is equatable with compensation. Except that the sum is liquidated it is closely comparable with the entitlement that a lender of a chattel has to have its value paid to him if the borrower fails to return it[94] (although the choice of date to estimate that value is one of the trickiest and most capricious that the law has to make).[95]

However, if one turns to another ancient and almost as simple species of debt the entitlement is radically different, although whether the medieval mind fully appreciated the difference may be questioned. Where goods are sold—whether delivered or not—from early times the common law has provided that the goods may be sued for by the buyer and the price by the seller.[96] The better the bargain either way, the greater the discrepancy between the price recovered by action and the sum that would have been needed to restore the vendor to his pre-contractual financial position in

---

[89] See Snell, op. cit. p. 657.

[90] See Lawson, op. cit. pp. 72–90.

[91] See above, p. 645.

[92] See Snell, op. cit. pp. 76, 85.

[93] See, e.g. Lawson, op. cit., p. 49.

[94] Originally, the formula of words (except, of course, for the specified sum or chattel) was the same in the writ—debt or detinue—which was used to claim repayment of the loan or restoration of the chattel.

[95] See Lawson, op. cit. pp. 125–126.

[96] In the case where there has been no delivery this availability of remedies had the startling conceptual consequence of passing property in the goods merely by the reaching of agreement without any other act, let alone passage of possession.

respect of the chattel. Each party is put into the position promised to him by the other, not restored to his initial condition: it is much more a case of the damages being awarded to enforce the obligation, not directly to compensate for its breach. Of course, if the agreement were for a reasonable or "market" price (whether expressly or by implication of the law) the discrepancy would evaporate. However, the theory would remain: if there were an agreement, the law would be giving the vendor his price, not compensation; if there were no agreement by reason of fundamental mistake or otherwise, there could be no "price" (which is a *promised* sum), so the damages could only be the value and thus compensation. Similarly where the "price" is a wage or fee for work done. In each case not only the sum awarded, but the Latin name the law uses (*quantum valebant* for goods, *quantum meruit* for work) are the same, but still the theory differentiates.

From such simple beginnings the law has developed a basic theory of damages for contract on the one side and for the tort and quasi-contract on the other: the former accords a sum that will, financially at least, fulfil the claimant's expectation under the promise made him; the other returns the claimant, so far as money can, to the pre-existing position before the wrong was done or the obligation to recompense arose. The classic example of this has traditionally been the difference in effect between a misstatement in a term of a contract and a misrepresentation inducing a party to enter into a contract.

Supposing P agrees to buy from V property for £30,000. The market value, however, is only £28,000. P agreed to pay the higher price in reliance on an untrue statement by V. Had the statement been accurate, the property would have been worth £34,000. If P does not rescind the contract, he can claim £2,000 damages if V's statement was not a part of the contract, but £6,000 if it was.

The reason for this difference is that in English law a false statement, unless it is a term of a contract, is a tort only—fraud if there is the necessary mental element,[97] negligence[98] or a statutory tort[99] if not. However, the division between the two approaches is not clear-cut, and modern law appears to be taking a much more pragmatic attitude.

First, breach of contract may involve not only loss of a bargain, but also substantial consequential loss. An example is *Andrews* v. *Hopkinson*,[1] where a misstatement as to a car sold to the plaintiff not only reduced the value of the vehicle from the "expected" level, but also led to the plaintiff's being injured in an accident. He was awarded damages for the injury as well as for the bargain element. This type of case has led to a distinction being drawn between "expectation" and "reliance" damages even within contract law.[2] The distinction may be useful, but perhaps not too much should be made of it. After all, in *Andrews* v. *Hopkinson* if the car had come up to expectation no accident would have occurred, so the damages

[97] See *Derry* v. *Peek* (1889) 14 App.Cas. 337.
[98] See *Hedley Byrne & Co. Ltd.* v. *Heller & Partners Ltd.* [1964] A.C. 465.
[99] Misrepresentation Act 1967, s.2(1): but *cf. Watts* v. *Spence* [1976] Ch.165, where the Court seems to have awarded "expectation" damages under s.2(1). Many American jurisdictions award "contractual" damages for fraud.
[1] [1957] 1 Q.B. 229.
[2] See Lawson, *op. cit.* pp. 128–131.

for the injury and for the loss of bargain would together have been putting him where he would have been if the contract had been properly performed.

Secondly, it may not be possible to predict with any hope of accuracy what the bargain would have been worth. In such circumstances the court must just do its best to assess the extent of loss. In *Chaplin* v. *Hicks*[3] the plaintiff was, in breach of contract, deprived of a chance of a stage career when she had entered a beauty contest. At the time such cases were still triable by a jury[4] and the jury there awarded the then fairly substantial sum of £100 for the loss of her "chance." The Court of Appeal refused to upset the verdict of damages—the plaintiff was entitled to compensation for breach and £100 could not be shown to be an unreasonable sum in the circumstances. The case is normally cited as authority for the proposition that a court cannot decline to award damages, whether in contract or in tort, because it is too difficult to assess them. However, it is also a good example of a "bargain" award—the plaintiff was certainly not being put back to her position before either contract or its breach.

Thirdly, tort damages can sometimes appear to be very close to contractual ones. Thus in *Ross* v. *Caunters*[5] a solicitor's negligence allowed a testator to execute a will with a principal beneficiary's spouse as one of the witnesses. As a result, while the rest of the will was valid, the gift to the beneficiary was void.[6] The solicitor's contract was, of course, solely with the testator and his damages would have been relatively slight—probably nothing for annoyance, just return of the fee and the cost and trouble of making a fresh will or codicil. Once he was dead any damages for breach of the contract would be most problematical: after all only his estate could sue now and the estate was by reason of the breach already *richer* by the extent of the avoided legacy. The beneficiary could sue only in tort. How could she be put *back* into the position she was before the tort was committed. Till the will was executed she had nothing. Had it been executed properly she would have had a good hope of the legacy, but the will could be revoked any time up until the testator died. If one dissects the solicitor's conduct one can argue that the correct drafting of the legacy gave the beneficiary a "property chance" which the witnessing error snatched away—so the negligence destroyed her chance.[7] She was awarded the whole amount of the legacy by way of damages—perhaps a sensible enough decision on the facts, with the will so unlikely to be revoked, but the damages do seem to be very much "expectation" ones. She was certainly put into the position she would have been in if the contract with the testator had been properly performed and if the tort towards her had not been perpetrated: she was scarcely restored to the position she was in before the breach of the duty to her. The negligence had deprived the testator of the knowledge and the opportunity of making an effective fresh legacy to her. The moral certainty that he would have made such a fresh legacy presumably justifies the award of the full sum.

---

[3] [1911] 2 K.B. 786.
[4] See above, p. 534.
[5] [1980] Ch. 297.
[6] By reason of the Wills Act 1837, s.15.
[7] But what if the negligence had been in the *drafting* of the legacy, so there would have been nothing to snatch away?

The only lesson that seems to be deducible is that bargain and compensation/expectation and reliance principles are scarcely hard-and-fast rules. Instead, they indicate lines of approach that seek and usually achieve a basic fairness. Moreover, damages are not limited to these two major principles. In certain rather ill-defined areas[8] defendants have been held liable to pay over not just compensation for injury or damage or loss of profit but even profits made by them which the claimants could not have made themselves.[9] In such cases the effect is as if the defendant had been retrospectively converted into an agent or trustee so far at least as the profit is concerned. (In equity especially the process can be taken further because the profit made or other money owed can be traced or followed through bank accounts, investments and other property acquired with it.)[10]

It is in these areas of law where entitlement to profit is claimed that plaintiffs often find a supplementary equitable remedy invaluable. This is the taking of an account under the order of the court.[11] Wherever there is intricate bookkeeping involved a claimant is unlikely to know how much he may be owed: "account" solves this problem for him. The original common law courts were without the machinery to keep and check sophisticated accounts, so their own writ of account was primitive and gave way over the years to applications to Chancery to carry out an account. Chancery's experience in overseeing trusts and the administration of deceaseds' estates built up the necessary expertise.

In contract and tort the existence and extent of liability will frequently rest respectively on whether the loss or damage is too remote a consequence from the wrong and on whether, if there is some liability, a particular head of loss or damage falls within it. These questions on the borderline between substantive law and remedies are traditionally and sensibly dealt with in the substantive treatises,[12] especially as the rules vary considerably within as well as between contract and tort. The distinction between remoteness of damage going to the existence or not of liability of any sort and measure of damages identifying what heads will and will not be compensated is not at all easy[13] and even seems scarcely justifiable. One practical, even if anomalous difference does follow: occasionally, but rarely very predictably, a court will award an extra amount of damages to cover a head of loss which would not apparently be actionable on its own: this practice has attracted the name of "parasitic damages" and usually denotes an area where the courts are hesitant about extending a general policy but have sympathy for the particular plaintiff and no great concern for the defendant. Contained in this way, perhaps parasitic damages can be regarded as a welcome relaxant of often rigid and unedifying principles without constituting such a major growth in liability as to affect appreciably the predictive factors upon which insurance cover can be assessed and

[8] See Lawson, *op. cit.* pp. 139–146.

[9] See *Reading* v. *Att.-Gen.* [1951] A.C. 507.

[10] These very difficult rules are normally taught and discussed in books and courses on equity and trusts: *cf.* Snell, *op. cit.* pp. 295–303 for the rules, and Lawson, *op. cit.* pp. 147–160 for the problems in theory.

[11] See Lawson, *op. cit.* pp. 142–143.

[12] But Lawson, *op. cit.* Chap. 4, especially, pp. 72–90, discusses the overall picture in depth.

[13] See Lawson, *loc. cit.*

premiums calculated (so much of modern tort of course being underlaid by that insurance factor).[14]

In tort there is an important distinction between torts actionable *per se* (*viz.* without proof of any damage) and those actionable only on proof of special damage, trespass and libel being prime examples of the first category, negligence the predominant one of the second. In the first category damages are often said to be "at large," that is they are awarded in one lump without any attempt to itemise calculation and often without any pretence of exactness[15]: loss of reputation in libel is a classic example. An example in contract has already been given—the beauty contest case, *Chaplin* v. *Hicks*.[16]

Where damages are at large—in tort, though probably not in contract[17]—those damages can be readily augmented where the manner of infliction of the wrong has been wanton, distressing or humiliating. Such damages are usually characterised as "aggravated." Such damages could clearly have some deterrent force for defendants, but they are in theory supposed to be compensatory only, not punitive. Until recent years both the common law and statute have not been afraid to allow damages to act as a punishment, thus regulating behaviour beyond merely according compensation. Such damages are classified as "penal," "punitive" or "exemplary," and are perhaps most vividly exemplified by the old practice of allowing a plaintiff to recover multiple damages (*e.g.* twice or more times the sum owed or the amount of compensation) where a particular social policy was thought to be best so served. Examples are double the rental element where a tenant of land holds over illegally after his lease expires[18] and the formerly obtainable triple damages for the idiosyncratic tort of pound breach.[19] Not altogether dissimilarly, Parliament in the past not infrequently allowed common informers and other private citizens to sue civilly for a stated fixed penalty[20] as an alternative to using the machinery of the criminal laws. In the last generation the House of Lords has dramatically and controversially cut back the scope of penal damages,[21] in a somewhat puritanical crusade to ensure that punishment shall be almost exclusively the function of the criminal law (which in turn safeguards the interests of the defendant by requiring a higher burden of proof than the civil one of just the balance of probabilities). Where penal

---

[14] See H. McGregor, *Damages* (14th ed., 1980), pp. 116–125. *e.g.* while damages may not normally be awarded for interference with a view, they may be claimed where the interference results from a wrongful obstruction of the highway: *Campbell* v. *Paddington Corporation* [1911] 1 K.B. 869. In *Spartan Steel and Alloys* v. *Martin and Co.* [1973] Q.B. 27 the Court of Appeal declined to permit the plaintiff to recover damages for purely economic loss on a "parasitic" basis. Lord Denning M.R. expressed his dislike for the doctrine at p. 35: " 'A parasite' is one who is a useless hanger-on sucking the substance out of others. 'Parasitic' is the adjective derived from it. It is a term of abuse. It is an opprobrious epithet."

[15] See Lawson, *op. cit.* pp. 55–60.

[16] [1911] 2 K.B. 786: see above, p. 652.

[17] See Lawson, *op. cit.* p. 137.

[18] Landlord and Tenant Act 1730, s.1, and Distress for Rent Act 1737, s.18.

[19] Distress for Rent Act 1689, s.3.

[20] Now abolished by the Common Informers Act 1951, s.1, and the House of Commons Disqualification Act 1957.

[21] *Rookes* v. *Barnard* [1964] A.C. 1129; *Cassell & Co. Ltd.* v. *Broome* [1972] A.C. 1027: see Lawson, pp. 133–138, for a discussion of this development and the difference in attitude in common law jurisdictions overseas.

damages are still allowed (*e.g.* where there has been a flagrant wrong with the defendant calculating his profit as likely to exceed any compensatory damages[22]), it is not always easy to differentiate in practice the aggravated from the penal element. Similarly, the law can scarcely be regarded as satisfyingly consistent where "sentimental" damages are concerned. It compensates for pain and suffering where personal injuries are involved and for inconvenience and discomfort, even where they emanate from a breach of contract.[23] In recent years the latter head of damages has been extended to cover even distress and disappointment where a contract for a holiday has been broken,[24] and in both cases the feelings of the non-contracting family of the plaintiff have been included in this basis of assessment. On the other hand English law has until recently never allowed compensation for the bereaved on a wrongful death (the *solatium* of Scottish law).[25]

Where damages are at large and there is no question of calculable injury or loss, damages can be insubstantial: either nominal or contemptuous. Nominal damages are a token sum merely to indicate there has been a wrong committed. Traditionally it has operated to establish the plaintiff's right for future reference, and it might be the result of what were essentially friendly proceedings to clarify disputed or unclear boundaries or other property rights.[26] The evolution of the remedy of declaration[27] seems gradually to be eliminating actions for such damages. Contemptuous damages occur where the court (in old days, the jury) wishes to stress the unmeritorious nature of the plaintiff's claim. It is usually the smallest coin in circulation (for many centuries the farthing whereas the shilling was a typical nominal sum). Apart from the contempt in the sum itself, the "successful" plaintiff is likely to be further penalised in costs. The award will obviously be less than any sum which may have been paid into court so that he would, under normal rules, be liable for the defendant's costs from the time of payment in.[28] Alternatively, the award of contemptuous damages is often accompanied by no order for costs in favour of the plaintiff[29] or, exceptionally, an order that he should pay the costs of the unsuccessful defendant.[30]

In practice, High Court judges are most commonly called upon to assess damages in cases where the defendant has negligently inflicted personal

---

[22] Especially in libel. Viewed in another way, such damages could be a special example where damages are apt to give the plaintiff a share in profits illegally obtained: see above, p. 653.

[23] *Hobbs* v. *L.S.W.R. Co.* (1875) L.R. 10 Q.B.111.

[24] *Jarvis* v. *Swan's Tours Ltd.* [1973] 1 Q.B. 233; *Jackson* v. *Horizon Holidays Ltd.* [1975] 1 W.L.R. 1468.

[25] The Administration of Justice Act 1982, s.3 introduced a new right to claim damages for bereavement in an action under the Fatal Accidents Act 1976. The claim may only be for the benefit of the spouse of the deceased or the parents of a deceased unmarried minor (the mother only if the deceased was illegitimate) and there is an upper limit of £3,500. Apart from the 1982 Act, if D negligently causes P distress, P may not sue in tort; however, he may sue where D wrongfully causes him some form of psychiatric illness (termed "nervous shock" by lawyers) : see *McLoughlin* v. *O'Brian* [1983] 1 A.C. 410.

[26] See Lawson, *op. cit.* p. 132.

[27] See below, p. 658.

[28] *e.g. Dering* v. *Uris* [1964] 2 Q.B. 669 at pp. 672–3.

[29] *Ibid.*

[30] *e.g. London Welsh Estates Ltd.* v. *Phillip* (1931) 100 L.J.K.B. 449.

injuries upon the plaintiff.[31] Damages are awarded in a lump sum and, as the action lies in tort, are designed to compensate the plaintiff for his losses. There are normally two basic aspects of an award: (i) compensation for non-pecuniary losses, and (ii) compensation for pecuniary or economic losses. Under the first head there may be damages for pain and suffering and loss of amenity[32] or, where the part of the body injured has no apparent function, for the injury itself.[33] Under the second head fall damages for such items as lost earnings[34] and medical expenses. Damages for loss of amenity are awarded roughly in accordance with a tariff dependent on the seriousness of the injury or injuries.[35]

For example, in *Lim Poh Choo* v. *Camden and Islington Area Health Authority*[36] the plaintiff, an N.H.S. registrar, suffered severe brain damage after a minor operation. She was ultimately awarded £229,298.64. This included £20,000 for pain and suffering and loss of amenities; £3,956 for expenses to the date of trial; £16,500 for the cost of her care in Malaysia; £1,923 travelling expenses; £4,226.64 for the cost of care in the United Kingdom to date; £14,213 for loss of earnings to the date of trial; £76,800 for the cost of future care and £92,000 for the loss of future earnings including pension rights.

(d) Equitable remedies

Equitable remedies may be divided into the supplementary and the determinative on the basis whether they would contemplate the need for a further court order if the losing party did not give way or they finally settled all issues. Thus rectification[37] and cancellation[38] of documents each in theory leaves open the question of enforcement or not of the underlying agreement, although in practice achievement of such an order will most frequently settle matters. Similarly, as already seen,[39] with account: once the indebtedness is clarified, the need to sue further will be rare. Often, of course, the suit for such remedies will seek determinative orders as well.

The major equitable remedies seem to have achieved such overwhelming integration into the substantive law that they call for little treatment here. Examples are actions for breach of trust[40] and their counterpart in the law of administration of deceased's estates, the *devastavit*.[41] Similarly, specific performance is central to much of land law and conveyancing and contract law and injunction to tort, contract and property law.

Specific performance is essentially a positive order and confined to contractual obligations. Most often it sanctions a promise to transfer

---

[31] See Winfield and Jolowicz, *The Law of Tort* (11th ed., 1979), pp. 599–621.

[32] *e.g.* damages for the loss of a leg, which may be increased where P. was a keen sportsman whose enjoyment of life is thus more substantially impaired.

[33] *e.g.* a spleen: *Forster* v. *Pugh* [1955] C.L.Y. 741.

[34] In the most serious cases there will be the difficult task of estimating the loss of earnings in the future.

[35] Details of damages awards in personal injury cases are given in *Kemp and Kemp on the Quantum of Damages* (Revised ed., 1982).

[36] [1980] A.C. 174.

[37] See Snell, *op. cit.* pp. 6, 10–9.

[38] See Snell, *op. cit.* pp. 608–609 and above, p. 637.

[39] See above, p. 653.

[40] See Snell, *op. cit.* Chap. 9; and see above, pp. 649–650.

[41] See Snell, *op. cit.* pp. 351–353 and 354.

property, particularly interests in land, but it can be used to enforce duties to carry out promised operations, such as building works in appropriate cases.[42] It will not be awarded where its execution could not practically be supervised by the court through its officers or where it would seek to make an unwilling employer or employee co-operate in working.

Injunction is essentially negative. The prime form, the prohibitory, is just that: forcing a defendant to desist from wrongful conduct or even forbidding him to do so when he has not even started to do wrong; but this latter type, the *quia timet* injunction,[43] will be granted normally only where the danger is both great and imminent. The mandatory injunction is admittedly positive in requiring the doing of some act, but it is essentially negative in that it enforces a negative obligation by forcing a wrongdoer to *undo* his wrong, as where the infringer of a right of light is obliged to pull down an offending obstruction. Usually the courts are much less ready to grant a mandatory injunction than they would have been to award a prohibitory one before any act was done, especially when the defendant has not acted wittingly or irresponsibly and the cost of the works would be substantial. This is all the more the case when the plaintiff is seeking a *quia timet* mandatory injunction (*e.g.* to require preventive measures to sustain a positive obligation of support for land or buildings).[44]

A special form of the injunction is the interlocutory or interim one. This is an order (rarely, if ever, mandatory, it would seem) to protect a plaintiff from suffering harm by having to wait for redress till a full hearing of his case is possible. Examples are the temporary prevention or interruption of allegedly wrongful building work and the restraining of publication in alleged breach of defamation or copyright laws. The court's decision is obviously a delicate balancing of the interests of two as yet undefeated antagonists, but a former tendency to lean more heavily against the plaintiff in this balancing has been abandoned in recent years.[45] The fact that an ultimately unsuccessful plaintiff will have to indemnify the defendant helps not only to preserve the balance but also to deter irresponsible applications.

There are two forms of interim injunction of recent development but considerable practical importance. First, the so-called *Mareva* injunction[46] may be granted to prevent a debtor from disposing of his assets or transferring them out of the jurisdiction before judgment can be given against him.[47] This power is exercisable whether or not the defendant is domiciled, resident or present within the jurisdiction of the High Court.[48]

Secondly, the court may grant an *Anton Piller*[49] order to prevent the defendant from destroying evidence in his possession before the action

---

[42] See Lawson, *op. cit.* pp. 216–219.

[43] See Snell, *op. cit.* pp. 630–631.

[44] See *Redland Bricks Ltd.* v. *Morris* [1970] A.C. 652; Lawson, *op. cit.* pp. 199–202.

[45] *American Cyanamid Co.* v. *Ethicon Ltd.* [1975] A.C. 396; Lawson, *op. cit.* pp. 187–188.

[46] From *Mareva Compania Naviera S.A.* v. *International Bulk Carriers S.A.* [1975] 2 Lloyd's Rep. 509; [1980] 1 All. E. R. 213.

[47] See D.B. Casson and I.H. Dennis, *Modern Developments in the Law of Civil Procedure* (1982), pp. 42–47; D.G. Powles, [1978] J.B.L. 11, [1981] J.B.L. 415 and [1982] J.B.L. 383, 489.

[48] Supreme Court Act 1981, s.37(3).

[49] From *Anton Piller K.G.* v. *Manufacturing Processes Ltd.* [1976] Ch. 55.

against him reaches the stage of discovery or trial. The order may include a direction to the defendant that he permit the plaintiff to enter his premises, to search for goods or documents belonging to the plaintiff or which are relevant to his claim and to remove, inspect, photograph or make copies of such material according to the circumstances of the case. The defendant may be compelled to disclose the names and addresses of his suppliers or customers.[50] Such orders are commonly used in actions concerning industrial and intellectual property, for example, patents, copyright, passing-off, trade secrets and abuse of confidential information.

Equitable remedies are always said to be discretionary. Traditionally the expression "leaving a plaintiff to his remedy at law" was a major example of this discretion in the days when the Chancery Court was separate from the common law ones.[51] In theory this remains the position, but it is likely that nowadays the equitable principles that will preclude award of specific performance especially will be strong enough to be extended to destroy the obligation itself: thus, in contract, refusal of the equitable remedy will most often be supplemented, if need be, by a right in the defendant to rescind. On the other hand, since 1858[52] statute has intervened to permit the courts to award damages in lieu of an equitable remedy (even a *quia timet* injunction, quite boldly[53]) where that would produce a fairer result on the balance of each side's interests.

However, it is wrong to stress too greatly the element of discretion. Usually it is really only the factors of clearly unconscionable conduct on the part of the plaintiff or an inability to make the order effective that will preclude the award of a remedy. Indeed, equity itself has built much of its substantive rules on the predictability of the award of specific performance and injunction when it applies its maxim of "looking on as done that which ought to be done." Thus the laws of equitable leases[54] and of licences[55] depend on the theory that the remedy will be awarded unless an exceptional circumstance obtains. On the other hand, the discretionary element is most valuable and important in allowing the courts to suspend the operation of the order or to attach terms to its award. Such terms may be built into the order or depend on undertakings given by the parties' lawyers. An interesting example is *Christie* v. *Davey*[56] where the plaintiff obtained an injunction against noise maliciously generated by his neighbour, but only on the basis of restrictions on the noise he himself might make.

(e) Declarations

The origins of the English action for a declaration are unclear.[57] The remedy may well have had forerunners in the Chancery process whereby application might be made by originating summons to settle some issue of

[50] See Casson and Dennis. *op. cit.* pp. 48–52; A. Staines (1983) 46 M.L.R. 274.
[51] *Viz.* before the 1875 legislation fusing the administration of law and equity.
[52] Chancery Amendment Act 1858 (Lord Cairns' Act). *Cf.* also Misrepresentation Act 1967, s.2(2), where damages may be awarded in lieu of the primarily extra-judicial remedy of rescission.
[53] *Leeds Industrial Co-operative Society* v. *Slack* [1924] A.C. 851.
[54] *Walsh* v. *Lonsdale* (1882) 21 Ch.D. 9.
[55] *Hurst* v. *Picture Theatres Ltd.* [1915] 1 K.B. 1.
[56] [1893] 1 Ch. 316.
[57] See Lawson. *op. cit.* pp. 232–233, and 231–238 generally.

entitlement or construction. However, the modern action has a clear statutory basis in rules of court.[58] Even so, it is specifically made discretionary and so has many of the features of equitable remedies. It cannot be used to settle purely hypothetical legal questions: there must be a clear, current, disputable issue between the particular parties to the action. The declaration is expected to be observed, so it is conceivable that it might be refused when specific performance or an injunction would be refused and damages only be awardable (e.g. where a declaration of duty to perform a contract is sought, but damages would be regarded as the sole appropriate sanction). It is often sought—and granted—along with other, coercive remedies. Whether, when it is awarded on its own, it can be ignored with legal impunity is uncertain, but disobedience, for various reasons, is almost unheard of.[59] It is particularly valuable in public law actions and is normally the only remedy pursuable against the Crown.

E. EXECUTION

Successful litigation will produce an order of the court. In some cases, that order will be declaratory or constitutive[60] and nothing more will be needed to be done. Thus a plaintiff (or counter-claiming defendant) may achieve a declaration that he has lawfully rescinded a contract and forfeited a deposit paid him under it; or an order dissolving a marriage, or declaring it null, or effecting an adoption may be given; or an order vesting land and so becoming a link in the chain of titles to that land. In other cases, the court itself may put its order into effect through its own officers, as where a document is rectified or stamped as cancelled.[61] In most instances, however, the order will require the performance of some further act or acts or the abstention from acts.

The law appears to lean heavily in favour of inducement rather than direct compulsion. The form of the court order will frequently demonstrate this: thus the normal order in an action for damages requires the defendant to pay the plaintiff the specified figure.[62] Again in the ordinary procedure for recovering possession of land the modern formula is that the defendant "do give" possession to the plaintiff[63]; while in the expedited procedure[64] the formula is a throwback to the original wording of orders for possession—that the plaintiff "do recover" possession: the distinction reflects the ease and speed with which a plaintiff under the expedited procedure can activate repossession by bailiffs in contrast with the position under the normal procedure.

Of course, however many defendants obey court orders out of ordinary law-abiding motives, many others will be influenced more by the appreciation that practical procedures exist to secure performance or obedience. These procedures designed to "execute" judgments are variously derived from common law, equity and statute. They are primarily aimed at specific forms of judgment, but they are capable of being used for

[58] R.S.C., Ord. 15, r. 6.
[59] See above, p. 639.
[60] See above, p. 648.
[61] See above, p. 637.
[62] Cf. R.S.C., Appendix A, Forms Nos. 39–51.
[63] Cf. R.S.C., Forms 42, 44, 45 and C.C. Form 134.
[64] Under R.S.C. Ord. 113 and C.C. Ord. 26: cf. R.S.C. Form 66A and C.C. Form 400.

any type of judgment for which they can be effective in particular circumstances. Thus sequestration and committal are both drastic sanctions suitable for flagrant breaches of orders such as injunctions, but in extreme circumstances they can be used to enforce other types of judgment where, in effect, there has been a civil contempt of court.

1. MONEY ORDERS

(a) Fieri facias

This writ of execution is traditionally pronounced "fiery fayshus" or, most often, simply "fie fay." The writ is issued to the sheriff of the county where the defendant's goods are located and his officers enforce the writ by seizing goods sufficient to cover in value the amount owed under the judgment and relevant costs and expenses. In county court proceedings, the court bailiff carries out the order. Seizure of more goods than are reasonably necessary to cover the moneys owed can constitute excessive execution, rendering the officer liable in effect to an action for trespass to goods.

Once seized, the goods are held with a view to sale, usually by auction, although the debtor or others acting on his behalf may satisfy the debt and thus forestall the sale. The whole procedure is subject to many technical rules and is notoriously technical, but has been simplified in various particulars over the years.

(b) Garnishee proceedings

This is a procedure whereby the judgment creditor may obtain the judgment debt by "attachment" of a debt owed to the judgment debtor by a third party (known as the "garnishee," the creditor being the "garnishor").[65] The garnishor applies in the first place for an order nisi, which is served on the garnishee. That "freezes" the debt until an order absolute is made requiring the garnishee to pay the debt to the garnishor. This procedure is at the discretion of the court.

(c) Attachment of earnings

Earnings constitute a debt for which a garnishee order is not available. However, the Attachment of Earnings Act 1971 for the first time empowered the courts to enforce employers to make deductions from the earnings of employees to be paid into court to satisfy the employees' debts. The jurisdiction is primarily in the county court, the High Court having power only to attach for payment of maintenance orders.[66] As befits a power that was regarded as revolutionary when it was introduced at long last, it is much hedged round by safeguards and technicalities.

(d) Charging orders

Just as garnishee orders and attachment of earnings are means of securing payment of a judgment debt where *fi. fa.* is likely to produce little or nothing to satisfy it, so also there are now statutory ways of creating charges on property: the judgment creditor becomes in effect an equitable

---

[65] *Cf.* R.S.C. Ord. 49.
[66] s.1.

chargee with rights to recoup his debt from income of the property or from its sale in due course. The principal property so chargeable is land or any interest in land, and the charge is registrable under the Land Charges Act 1972, so that purchasers may receive notice of it. Under the Order[67] of the Rules of the Supreme Court, government and company stocks and dividends and interest on such stock, and moneys in court, may also be subjected to a charging order.

(e) Receivership

The appointment of a receiver by a creditor is an ancient equitable remedy,[68] often used as one of the sanctions which a mortgagee stipulates for his loan. It is also a means of execution where none of the other forms is likely to be effective and, as such, it is comparatively rarely used. Under it, a receiver is appointed to take income due to the judgment debtor and apply it towards the debt. Once again, the power to appoint a receiver is in the discretion of the court.[69] A recent example is where a landlord of a block of flats failed to carry out his obligations under the leases and a receiver was appointed to collect rents and to use them towards the proper management of the block.[70]

2. POSSESSION ORDERS

(a) Land

Formerly, when a judgment for possession of land was given, the courts exercised a considerable discretion in postponing or suspending the operation of the order, but statute[71] has now greatly restricted that discretion, except where a specific protective jurisdiction applies.[72] In theory, a plaintiff could peaceably occupy the land without any further order of the court,[73] but this is a notoriously dangerous process and it is normal to apply for a writ of possession in the High Court[74] or a warrant for possession in the County Court.[75] The bailiffs acting under the writ or warrant clear the premises of everyone they find upon them whether they were parties to the action or not (even though any such person should have been notified at the earlier stage when the writ or warrant was applied for). If an evicted person re-enters the land unlawfully, a writ (or warrant in the County Court) of restitution is readily and simply obtainable to recover possession.[76] Against trespassory occupiers an expedited procedure is available and the writs (and warrants) of possession can be more easily and quickly obtained.[77]

---

[67] R.S.C. Ord. 50.

[68] See above, p. 644.

[69] R.S.C. Ord. 51.

[70] *Hart* v. *Emelkirk Ltd.* [1983] 1 W.L.R. 1289.

[71] Housing Act 1980, s.89(1).

[72] *e.g.* under the Rent Acts, or with respect to forfeiture or mortgage proceedings: *cf.* s.89(2).

[73] *Cf. Aglionby* v. *Cohen* [1955] 1 Q.B. 558: *cf.* A.M. Prichard, *Squatting* (1981), pp. 18–20.

[74] R.S.C. Ord. 45(3): special rules under Ord. 88 apply to a mortgage action.

[75] C.C.R. Ord. 25.

[76] R.S.C. Ord. 46(3).

[77] *Cf.* R.S.C. Ord. 113; C.C.R. Ord. 26; *cf.* Prichard, *op. cit.* pp. 38–39.

In any case, the writ or warrant may have a *fi. fa.* attached to it for covering costs. In the expedited procedure, it is not possible to join further claims beyond possession, so there is no question of an additional *fi. fa.* to secure damages as may happen in the ordinary procedure.

(b) Goods

Judgments for delivery of goods may or may not contain an option in the defendant to pay the value instead of giving up the goods.[78] Where there is no such option the execution is by way of a writ of "specific delivery" which instructs the sheriff to cause the goods to be delivered to the plaintiff. Where there is an option, the writ is one of "delivery," instructing the sheriff to deliver the goods or, if not, to proceed in effect to a *fi. fa.* Whereas with specific delivery there is no need to assess the value of the goods, the more general writ requires such an assessment so that the sheriff's officers may know how much to take in execution by way of *fi. fa.* In exceptional circumstances, the court has power to issue a writ of specific delivery even where the option was granted to the defendant in the judgment (*e.g.* where there are no other goods within the jurisdiction).

3. MANDATORY AND PROHIBITING ORDERS

(a) Specific performance

While the general sanctions of committal and sequestration are applicable, a failure by a vendor to execute an instrument in response to a judgment for specific performance can be specially overcome: the court has power to appoint someone else (usually a Chancery master or a registrar) to execute it in the vendor's stead. The order of the court plus the conveyance will constitute a safe link in the plaintiff's title thereafter.[79] If a purchaser does not obey an order for specific performance, the general sanctions are in theory available, but the usual reason is the purchaser's impecuniosity, in which case the vendor is best advised to apply for revocation of the order and rescission of the contract instead, with a view to re-sale and any possible recoupment of shortfall in price by damages.

(b) Injunction

Originally, equity acted *in personam*, which meant that performance or observance of an order was on pain (*sub poena*) of imprisonment for contempt. Committal to prison is still a possible sanction, but it is felt nowadays to be too drastic for all but the most flagrant frustrations of court orders. In 1970,[80] its use against defaulters on money judgments (except orders of maintenance) was abolished after a long history of imprisonment for debt.

The power of committal is in the discretion of the court and the safeguards built into the procedure (*e.g.* the requirement that any application must normally be made in open court[81]) are formidable. The

---

[78] See above, p. 649.
[79] *Cf.* Law of Property Act 1925, s.204.
[80] *Cf.* Administration of Justice Act 1970, s.11: the County Court has power to imprison also for certain tax defaults. By s.12, magistrates' courts have retained very restricted powers of committal.
[81] *Cf.* R.S.C. Ord. 52, r.6.

sentence must be for a specific term, but the defendant can apply for release before expiry, *e.g.* if he is ready to purge his contempt. The tipstaff is the officer of the court who arrests and transports the defendant to gaol. Committal serves both as a punishment for disobedience and as an inducement for performance. The two aims sometimes seem to conflict and a court may well be reluctant to keep imprisoning even a persistently contumacious defendant is he has once served a sentence proportionate to the offence committed.

The process of sequestration is almost as drastic. It authorises the seizure of all or any property of the defendant within the jurisdiction. It too is subjected to many safeguards. However, it has recently become a most effective weapon, allied with the power to fine for contempt, to achieve compliance with court orders, as witness a series of proceedings against trade unions. Against any defendant with substantial assets it is likely to be an "ultimate weapon" of peculiar force, not constituting that defendant as much a "martyr" as a committal might well do.

CHAPTER 18

SENTENCING[1]

Once a person has been convicted of a criminal offence the question arises of how to deal with him. In the case of a few offences there will be no choice—the appropriate penalty will be fixed by law.[2] For the most part, however, there will be a choice of measures open to the court. The purpose of this chapter is to consider the range of available measures and the basis on which a court is likely to make its selection of the measure or measures it considers most appropriate.

A. THE ROLE OF THE SENTENCER

The English sentencing system proceeds on the basis that the individual judge or bench of magistrates is to be allowed a degree of discretion in choosing from the ever-increasing number of possible methods of disposing of offenders. Such limitations as there are upon total freedom of choice are imposed either by Parliament, which frequently creates conditions precedent to the use of sentencing powers, or by the decisions of appellate courts concerning the proper use of such powers.

The Court of Appeal (Criminal Division), which hears appeals against sentences passed by Crown Court judges after trials on indictment, has formulated a considerable body of principles aimed at achieving a degree of uniformity among sentencers, but often these principles are sufficiently flexible to allow two sentencers dealing with substantially the same type of case to select different measures, or, in the case of custodial penalties, to impose sentences of different lengths.[3]

The first lesson for the student then, and it is recognised that it may come as a surprise, is that like will not necessarily be treated as like. If more uniformity were to be achieved, a number of fundamental changes would have to be made in the present system. First, the rôle of the sentencer would have to be more clearly defined than it is at present. There is no statutory code or fundamental principle of the common law which instructs him always to consider a particular aim as paramount, such as, for

---

[1] See generally D.A. Thomas, *Principles of Sentencing* (2nd ed., 1979); *Current Sentencing Practice* (1982); Sir Rupert Cross and A. Ashworth, *The English Sentencing System* (3rd ed., 1981) V.G. Hines, *Judicial Discretion in Sentencing by Judges and Magistrates* (1982); A. Ashworth, *Sentencing and Penal Policy* (1983).

[2] The most obvious example being murder, for which the trial judge is obliged to pass a sentence of life imprisonment: Murder (Abolition of Death Penalty) Act 1965, s.1(1). See also, *e.g.* Genocide Act 1969, s.1(2) (mandatory life sentence); Treason Act 1814, s.1 (mandatory sentence of death).

[3] See Thomas, *Principles of Sentencing* (1979) pp. 3–6. The Court of Appeal (Criminal Division) will reduce a sentence which is "excessive" according to its principles, but will not interfere with a sentence simply because the members of the Court would themselves have imposed a lower sentence: *R.* v. *Gumbs* (1926) 19 Cr.App.R. 74.

example, the rehabilitation of the offender, the need to reflect society's disapproval of his crime, or the need to deter others from emulating his behaviour. In *R. v. Sergeant*,[4] Lawton L.J. advised sentencers always to bear in mind the "classical principles" of retribution, deterrence, prevention and rehabilitation. Such aims may obviously be in conflict in particular cases, and the outcome at present depends largely on the individual sentencer's scale of priorities.

Secondly, uniformity could only be achieved if a judge who "under-sentences" could be corrected on appeal as well as the judge who has exceeded the appropriate penalty. At present the prosecutor has no right of appeal against a sentence passed after trial in the Crown Court[5] on the basis that it was unduly lenient, though such a right exists in some Commonwealth jurisdictions.[6] Nor does the Court of Appeal have power on its own initiative to increase sentence.[7] Cogent arguments have been advanced for changing both rules,[8] but as the law at present stands the judge who keeps a low profile by sentencing consistently below the norm can safely experiment with his own penal theories without fear of correction.[9] Of course he might attract some bad publicity. In 1982 there was public consternation over a case in which a trial judge imposed a fine rather than a prison sentence on a convicted rapist because of the "contributory negligence" of the victim in accepting a lift in the defendant's car.[10] Shortly afterwards, the Court of Appeal established guidelines for sentencing in rape cases in which the first principle was said to be that "other than in wholly exceptional circumstances [rape] calls for an immediate custodial sentence."[11]

One solution to the problem of under-sentencing would be to make greater use of fixed penalties, or at least to make a prison sentence mandatory for certain crimes. In relation to rape, however, the Government resisted a move towards such developments, one of the reasons being that in exceptional cases non-custodial measures could be justified.[12] A better solution would appear to be to subject the trial judge to appellate

---

[4] (1974) 60 Cr.App.R. 74. The sentencer is helped in some cases by appellate advice to give priority to one of these aims in dealing with a particular type of offence or offender.

[5] Though either the prosecutor or the defendant may appeal from the Court of Appeal (Criminal Division) to the House of Lords: Criminal Appeal Act 1968 s.33. Appeals to the House of Lords are rare in sentencing matters; effective control lies in the hands of the Court of Appeal.

[6] See D.A. Thomas, "Increasing Sentences on Appeal—a Re-examination" [1972] Crim. L.R. 288 at p. 300.

[7] Criminal Appeal Act 1968, s.11(3). A power to increase sentence was conferred on the Court of Criminal Appeal upon its creation in 1907. The power was removed in 1966. The Crown Court may increase sentence when hearing appeals from magistrates, up to the maximum which the magistrates could have imposed: Supreme Court Act 1981, s.48(4).

[8] D.A. Thomas, *op.cit.* n. 6, above.

[9] In his book *The Judge* (1979) Ch. 2, Lord Devlin, who regards himself as having been an orthodox sentencer, provides an interesting insight into the judicial role and concedes that lack of appellate correction could be due as much to a trial judge's leniency as to his correctness of approach.

[10] *The Times*, January 6 and 7, 1982.

[11] *R. v. Roberts and Roberts* [1982] 1 W.L.R. 133, decided on January 15, 1982.

[12] Less than six months later a 25 year-old man was placed on probation by the Scottish High Court for raping his estranged wife after she admitted having provoked him and a social inquiry report suggested there was hope of a reconciliation. (*The Times*, June 3, 1982).

control in the selection of such cases,[13] or to lay down more specific "guidelines" for sentencers of the kind which are imposed in other jurisdictions.[14] The guidelines could be statutory or devised by the judges themselves, and a sentencer wishing to depart from them could be obliged to give reasons for doing so.

In magistrates' courts it is arguable that sentencing gives less scope for creativity under the present system. One reason for this theory is that sentencing is undertaken "by committee" where lay magistrates are concerned, so that compromise tends to produce results closer to a "norm."[15] On the other hand, some studies have revealed quite frightening variations in the penal philosophies and policies of different benches,[16] and whereas it may be just as important to preserve a degree of discretion in magistrates' courts as in the Crown Court it is arguable that the controls are at present inadequate. However, there is a limited right of appeal against sentence by the prosecutor in summary trials,[17] and some guidance is provided by the Magistrates' Association's publication of suggestions for sentences for particular types of offence which are frequently applied.[18]

Having dispensed with the notion that there is, at least at present, a "correct" sentence for every offence, let us now proceed to consider what happens in practice. We will first need to know something of the procedure for passing sentence, in particular the amount of information made available to the sentencer about the offender and his crime which may help him to reach his decision.

[13] If this were thought to be unfair to the convicted defendant whose sentence might be increased on appeal, a procedure could be adopted similar to that under section 36 of the Criminal Justice Act 1972 by which, following an acquittal, points of law may be argued at the instance of the Attorney-General before the Court of Appeal (Criminal Division), but their decison does not affect the outcome of the trial, providing a precedent for future cases only.

[14] e.g. in some parts of America. See L.T. Wilkins, "Sentencing Guidelines to Reduce Disparity" [1980] Crim. L.R. 201; D.A. Thomas, "The Control of Discretion in the Administration of Criminal Justice" in R.G. Hood (ed.) Crime, Criminology and Public Policy (1974); D.J. Galligan, "Guidelines and Just Desserts," [1981] Crim. L.R. 297. The various methods of controlling judicial discretion are discussed by A. Ashworth, Sentencing and Penal Policy (1983) pp. 68 et seq. To an extent the judgments of the Court of Appeal (Criminal Division) may be regarded as guidelines, but that Court is handicapped by the need to wait until a suitable case comes before it before expressing an opinion.

[15] Another obvious reason is that the powers of magistrates to fine and imprison are more limited. See below pp. 676, 686.

[16] The most famous studies are both by R. Hood, Sentencing in Magistrates' Courts (1962), and Sentencing the Motoring Offender (1972). On a less scientific level see E. Burney, J.P.-Magistrate Court and Community (1979).

[17] An appeal lies to the Divisional Court by case stated on the ground that the sentence is wrong in law or in excess of jurisdiction: Magistrates' Courts Act 1980, s.111. In R. v. St Albans Crown Court, ex p. Cinnamond [1981] Q.B. 480 the view was expressed that this procedure could be used where it was claimed by the defendant that a sentence was so harsh that no reasonable court could have imposed it. (Cf. the view of the Divisional Court in R. v. Battle Justices, ex p. Shepherd and Another [1983] Crim. L.R. 550 disapproving of the use of certiorari before statutory appeals procedures had been exhausted). In other cases the defendant alone has the right of appeal to the Crown Court: Magistrates' Courts Act 1980, s.108. After such an appeal either party may apply to that court to state a case for the opinion of the Divisional Court: Supreme Court Act 1981, s.28. Ultimately, an appeal lies to the House of Lords from the Divisional Court: Administration of Justice Act 1960, s.1.

[18] Occasionally one reads of the reluctance of magistrates to be guided in this fashion. See, e.g. Burney, op. cit. n. 16 above, Chap. 8.

B. SENTENCING PROCEDURE[19]

This is substantially the same whether it takes place in the Crown Court or before magistrates. The procedure is similar to the production of evidence in the trial proper in that both prosecutor and defence may in turn attempt to throw light on the issues. In other respects, however, it is quite different. The most noticeable difference is the comparatively informal way in which information is presented to the court: the normal rules of evidence are relaxed once the factual basis for sentence has been determined,[20] while the prosecutor plays an even more "neutral" role in the sentencing process than in the trial proper,[21] and generally confines himself to supplying information without suggesting the adoption by the sentencer of a particular course.[22] Whether the sentence is to be passed by a judge or by magistrates, the procedure may well vary according to whether there has been a trial of the issue of guilt. Where such a trial has taken place, the sentencer will know something of the circumstances in which the offence was committed and may indeed already have come to some provisional conclusions about the appropriate sentence. Where the convicted person has pleaded guilty it will be necessary for the sentencer to glean information about the nature of the offence before proceeding further.[23] If there are gaps in his knowledge of the circumstances, the sentencer must begin by establishing a "factual basis" for his sentence.

1. ESTABLISHING THE FACTS

Where further information about the nature of the offence is required, the prosecutor commences by outlining to the court the way in which he contends the offence was committed. The mere fact that the convicted person has pleaded guilty does not necessarily mean that he accepts the prosecution case in its entirety, and it may be that the defence in its turn will wish to challenge some aspects of the account. For example, where the defendant has been convicted after pleading guilty to a charge of unlawful wounding the prosecutor may claim that the defendant's attack on his victim was premeditated and unprovoked, whereas the defendant may admit the attack but claim it occurred on the spur of the moment and under the gravest provocation. These matters would not affect his guilt of the

---

[19] For a detailed description, see D.A. Thomas, *Principles of Sentencing* (2nd ed., 1979) pp. 365–402.

[20] See "Establishing the facts," below. Where the sentencer is seeking to resolve doubt as to facts on which his sentence is to be based, he should apply the same rules of evidence as in the trial proper. *Cf.* Ashworth, *Sentencing and Penal Policy*, p. 94.

[21] Above, p. 595.

[22] It has been said that such suggestions might be useful; G. Zellick, "The Rôle of Prosecuting Counsel in Sentencing" [1979] Crim. L.R. 493; A. Ashworth, "Prosecution and Procedure in Criminal Justice" [1979] Crim. L.R. 480; M. King, "the Role of Prosecuting Counsel in Sentencing—What About Magistrates' Courts?" [1979] Crim. L.R. 775.

[23] The same need may arise where the offender is committed for sentence to a court other than the convicting court, or where sentence is determined by a differently constituted court, *e.g.* after an adjournment for reports. See below, p. 672.

crime charged[24] but would naturally have some bearing on the appropriate sentence.[25]

A formula for the resolution of such issues has eluded the courts until recently. It now appears to be settled that, where the defendant in a trial on indictment[26] contests the version of the facts alleged by the prosecution, the judge should either hear evidence and decide whether the prosecution have proved their version, or he should accept the version put forward by the defence.[27]

Where the defendant has been convicted of murder, the penalty is fixed by law,[28] so that the sentencer knows what sentence he must pass. Nevertheless, the revelation of the facts of the case may still serve a useful function in that the general public has an opportunity, which might otherwise have been denied them,[29] to understand the grounds on which the sentence was imposed. Thus the ritual should be observed, even in such cases.

2. THE ANTECEDENTS

The prosecutor then moves on to call evidence of the convicted person's previous convictions and background, known collectively as the "antecedents."[30] These are likely to be elicited by calling as a witness a police officer who has dealt with the case. If the convicted person has a criminal record by far the most important part of the officer's testimony will consist of his being taken through a prepared list[31] of previous convictions—or as much of it as the sentencer wishes to hear—by the prosecutor. In the unlikely event that the convicted person wishes to challenge any of the information contained in this document the prosecutor will have to supply proof.[32]

The remainder of the information given as part of the antecedents will relate to such matters as the convicted person's education, employment

---

[24] Provocation is only a defence to a charge of murder, reducing the crime to manslaughter.

[25] Note that the same difficulty can arise in trials on indictment after conviction following a plea of not guilty: the jury's verdict will not necessarily tell the judge all he needs to know. Indeed the jury may not even have discussed all the issues of fact bearing upon sentence, as they are not required to be in agreement on matters going beyond the basis of a verdict of guilty. Magistrates who have determined guilt are in a better position in this respect to pass sentence. See generally D.A. Thomas, "Establishing a Factual Basis for Sentencing" [1970] Crim. L.R. 80.

[26] The rule should in principle be the same in summary trials.

[27] See, e.g. R. v. Newton [1983] Crim. L.R. 199 and commentary. The judge is discouraged from asking juries to indicate the basis on which their verdict was reached: R. v. Stosiek [1982] Crim. L.R. 615; R. v. Ekwuyasi [1981] Crim.L.R. 575.

[28] Murder (Abolition of Death Penalty) Act 1965, s.1.

[29] Particularly since the introduction of committal proceedings in which the evidence is not examined in detail. See Practice Direction [1968] 1 W.L.R. 529.

[30] Practice Direction [1968] 1 W.L.R. 529.

[31] Copies of which will have been given in advance to the defence and to the court. Under the Rehabilitation of Offenders Act 1974 certain convictions become "spent" after a period of time. Such convictions are marked as spent on the document, usually by an asterisk: Practice Direction [1975] 1 W.L.R. 1065, para. 5.

[32] By producing the certificate and identifying the defendant as the convicted person (Prevention of Crimes Act 1871, s.18). Cf. Criminal Justice Act 1948, s.39 (identification by fingerprints). The Police and Criminal Evidence Bill 1983–4 will make further provision for the proof of convictions.

record, home circumstances and resources. Again, the defence may challenge the accuracy of the account, and the prosecutor be made to prove it.[33]

3. REPORTS

Further information about the offender may be contained in a *social inquiry report*,[34] prepared by a probation officer or sometimes a local authority social worker. Such a report may contain much helpful information about the offender's circumstances (particularly his domestic background) his personality and his prospects. Obviously the main source of such information is likely to be the offender himself, so it is perhaps surprising to find that, at least so far as the Crown Court is concerned, most such reports are prepared *before* the trial, even if the subject of the report proposes to plead not guilty. In such cases important areas for discussion cannot be aired in interview with the compiler of the report. This is particularly true of the accused's attitude to his offence, which may include such matters as his contrition and his intention to make reparation. This disadvantage was thought to be outweighed in most cases by the need for sentence to follow immediately upon conviction,[35] and it is possible that the impact of sentences on the public consciousness would be impaired if too long a period elapsed after the finding of guilt.[36] The question then becomes whether the preparation of social inquiry reports is a matter in which the public interest in an immediate result ought to prevail over the needs of the offender where the two appear to be in conflict. Whatever the answer, it seems that a number of convicted defendants may suffer as a result of the present practice.

In addition to considering the factors which may have led an offender into crime, the report may also contain suggestions about his likely response to particular measures.[37] If the report has been carefully prepared[38] such a recommendation is likely to carry great weight, and it

---

[33] The rule is that if there is a dispute the prosecutor must prove his account by calling admissible evidence: *R. v. Sargeant* (1975) 60 Cr.App.R. 74. Where the prosecutor is aware that facts are disputed he should not allow the police officer to allude to them unless proof is available.

[34] The present position has come about largely through the recommendations of the Streatfeild Committee (Report of the Committee on the Business of the Criminal Courts) (Cmnd. 1289 (1961)).

[35] Streatfeild Report, above, n. 34, para. 310. Magistrates often have to adjourn to allow reports to be prepared or completed in any event. See Home Office Circular 118/1977, in which the difficulties in preparing pre-conviction reports are acknowledged.

[36] It could also be argued that the wait between the commission of a notorious crime and the trial of the offender is so long that a wait of a few weeks for sentence is unlikely to make much of a difference.

[37] Not just to probation. See as to preparation Home Office Circulars 28, 29 and 30/1971, 195/1974, 118/1977. See also B. Harris, "Recommendations in Social Inquiry Reports" [1979] Crim. L.R. 73, Home Office Research Study no. 48, "Social Inquiry Reports—A Survey" (1978).

[38] Criticism has from time to time been voiced that suggestions in reports are unsuitable bearing in mind the nature of the offence (see *e.g. R. v. Smith and Woolard* (1978) 67 Cr.App.R. 211) or that inadequate consideration is given to the availability of the measure suggested, *e.g.* when places in a particular hostel are limited.

appears that in up to three-quarters of cases in which a recommendation is made the court will act upon it.[39]

There is no general statutory compulsion upon courts to consider a social inquiry report when sentencing an adult offender,[40] and the practice varies slightly from one area to another.[41] However, it is likely to be the case that a report will be available in most Crown Court cases and in serious cases in magistrates' courts.[42]

The report can in theory be challenged in the sense that the defence may insist that the probation officer responsible for the report should give evidence and be open to questioning about it. However, the criticism has been voiced that in practice the officer is unlikely to be in court and an adjournment in order to call him may not be practicable, so that challenge becomes difficult.[43]

Other reports to which a sentencer may in appropriate cases refer include medical and psychiatric reports, and reports from persons in charge of institutions in which the offender may have spent some time, on remand or otherwise, which may assist in calculating the effect of a particular sentence.

4. MITIGATION

When any reports available to the court have been considered, the defence has an opportunity to acquaint the court with any factors which may act in mitigation of sentence on behalf of the offender. Normally, the presentation of mitigating circumstances is considered a matter for an advocate, and courts are discouraged from sentencing some unrepresented defendants[44] who might be unaware of the mitigation which could be put

---

[39] In a study by K. Pease and J. Thorpe ((1976) British Journal of Criminology 393) of a sample of adult offenders in Kent and Nottingham it was found that in 83 per cent. of the sample recommendations were made, of which 78 per cent. were taken by the court. The figure is high by comparison to some other studies.

[40] Though there are several specific statutory requirements including one recent provision dealing with young offenders in the Criminal Justice Act 1982, s.2 (report before passing custodial sentence on offender under 21) and s.62 (report before first prison sentence). See also, e.g. Powers of Criminal Courts Act 1973, s.14 (as amended by Criminal Justice Act 1982, Sched. 12) (report before making community service order), and s.2(3) (report before including residence requirement in a probation order).

[41] The Home Secretary has power under section 45 of the Powers of Criminal Courts Act 1973 to make rules requiring reports in certain cases, but so far no such rules have been made. The gentle cajoling of Home Office circulars seems to be preferred.

[42] The reader may be forgiven for thinking that reports should be available in all cases, but this is not desirable. Many cases are obviously too trivial, or too straightforward, to require reports. It has also been suggested that such reports are of little use in the case of offenders with several previous convictions who know precisely what answers to give to the compiler of the report!

[43] See D. Barnard, The Criminal Court in Action (2nd ed., 1979) at 164. Under s.14(2) of the Powers of Criminal Courts Act 1973, substituted by Criminal Justice Act 1982, Sched. 12, the court may, if it thinks it necessary, hear a probation officer or social worker before making a community service order, in addition to its obligation to consider a report. (See n. 40, above).

[44] Powers of Criminal Courts Act 1973, s.21, as amended: a court should not pass a first sentence of imprisonment on an unrepresented defendant unless either he does not qualify for criminal legal aid and has chosen to be unrepresented, or has been told of his right to apply for aid and has failed to avail himself of it. See to the same effect in respect of young offenders Criminal Justice Act 1982, s.3.

forward on their behalf. Not that there is any great magic about mitigating, but the circumstances of the offence may reveal that it was not a bad example of its type—an argument likely to be best put by an advocate. There is also a special rule that nothing can be urged in mitigation which would have amounted to a defence to the crime charged. Apart from that the advocate can only stress the parts of the information about his client's circumstances which show him in a good, or at least a hopeful, light.[45]

5. TAKING OFFENCES INTO CONSIDERATION

By a long-established practice,[46] a convicted person may ask the court to take into account when sentencing him the commission of admitted offences other than those of which he has been convicted. From the offender's point of view this rather unlikely request has two advantages. It "clears up" other offences, prosecution for which might otherwise follow at a later date,[47] and furthermore his honesty is likely to be rewarded by substantial discounts in sentencing.[48] Such an inducement, though it may sound a little improper, helps to expedite proceedings in the courts and is generally regarded as valuable. Lest the offender should be tempted, for whatever reason, to admit to offences he has not committed, the procedure for taking offences into consideration is accompanied by a degree of formality, both in the preparation of an agreed list of offences and in the manner in which the court endeavours to ensure that the offender fully understands the implications of what he is doing.[49]

In addition, the court may only take into account offences in respect of which it is able to impose a suitable penalty, bearing in mind that it cannot in any event exceed the maximum penalty for the offence in respect of which there has been a conviction.[50] Even where its powers of disposal are adequate the court may consider that the offences should be dealt with separately, for instance where they are totally different in kind.

Where offences have been taken into consideration there is no conviction in respect of them, and the offender technically remains open to prosecution.[51] This is only likely to happen, however, when the original conviction is disturbed on appeal.[52]

---

[45] The fact that the offender has never sought to deny his guilt and has pleaded guilty may here be urged in his favour. As to the effect of a guilty plea on a custodial sentence, see below, p. 688.

[46] Acknowledged by the House of Lords in *R. v. Anderson* [1978] A.C. 964 and see *R. v. Batchelor* (1952) 36 Cr.App.R. 64 at p. 67.

[47] Particularly distressing if he has just been released from prison after serving a sentence imposed for the earlier crimes. See Cross and Ashworth, *The English Sentencing System* (3rd ed., 1981) p. 87.

[48] S. White, M. Newark and A. Samuels, "Taking Offences into Consideration" [1970] Crim. L.R. 311.

[49] *Cf. R. v. Anderson*, above, n. 46.

[50] *R. v. Hobson* (1942) 29 Cr.App.R. 30.

[51] *i.e.* the plea of *autrefois convict* would not be open to him. *R. v. Nicholson* (1947) 32 Cr.App.R. 127.

[52] *R. v. Neal* [1949] 2 K.B. 590 at 600; *R. v. Brandon* (1969) 53 Cr.App.R. 466. White, Newark and Samuels (*op.cit.* n. 47, above) suggest that an offence once taken into account should be treated as though there had been a conviction in respect of it.

6. PASSING SENTENCE

As already noted,[53] sentence should follow immediately upon conviction. There are, however, a number of exceptions to the general rule.

(a) Adjournments

The Crown Court and magistrates' courts have power to adjourn before passing sentence on a convicted person. The Crown Court's powers are derived from the common law and extend in theory to delaying the imposition of the whole or part of a sentence which has been passed[54] but in practice this power is generally only exercised to obtain reports or to await the outcome of the separate trial of accomplices.[55] The power of magistrates to adjourn is statutory, and there are limits on the length of adjournments for pre-sentence inquiries.[56]

(b) Committal for sentence

A number of statutory provisions allow courts to commit offenders to the Crown Court for sentence. The most important[57] are committals under sections 37 and 38 of the Magistrates' Courts Act 1980.

Under section 38 magistrates may commit an offender who has attained the age of 17 years and who has been summarily convicted of an offence triable either way[58] if on obtaining information about his "character and antecedents"[59] they conclude that they have insufficient power to punish him. The Crown Court may then dispose of him as though he had just been convicted on indictment.[60] It is of course likely that the Crown Court will inflict a punishment which goes beyond anything the magistrates would have had power to impose, but it is not bound to do so if it take a different view of the case.

Under section 37 certain juvenile offenders may be committed to the Crown Court for sentence where the magistrates at the trial consider that a sentence of youth custody longer than that which they have power to

---

[53] Above, p. 669.

[54] Cf. R. v. Annesley (1975) 62 Cr.App.R. 113, R. v. Ingle (1974) Cr.App.R. 306.

[55] Perhaps because it is usually more convenient to defer sentence under the Powers of Criminal Courts Act 1973, s.1, than to delay the imposition of a sentence already passed. See below, p. 673.

[56] Magistrates' Courts Act 1980, s.10. Magistrates may adjourn for up to four weeks (3 if the offender is in custody) to enable such inquiries to be made: Magistrates' Courts Act 1980, s.10(3). Note also the provisions of s.30 in respect of defendants whose mental condition indicates the need for special reports.

[57] Other powers exist where the offender is in breach of various orders imposed by the Crown Court with which magistrates cannot deal, for example a probation order or a suspended sentence of imprisonment. See also the Criminal Justice Act 1967, s.56.

[58] Excluding offences of damage to property tried summarily under s.22(2), Magistrates' Courts Act 1980.

[59] Thus, s.38 is not a way of re-thinking the decision which the magistrates will have made initially to permit summary trial. Rather it allows them to take account of factors they could not have known about at that stage, particularly the previous criminal record of the offender.

[60] Powers of Criminal Courts Act 1973, s.42, as amended. In 1982, over half of the offenders committed under s.38 were given sentences which the magistrates could have given. (Criminal Statistics 1982 p. 169).

impose is merited.[61] This replaces the system of committal for borstal training which was available until the borstal training sentence was abolished by the Criminal Justice Act 1982. As with section 38, the Crown Court is not bound to act on the magistrates' recommendation.

(c) Deferment of sentence[62]

The Crown Court and magistrates' courts may defer passing sentence on an offender for not more than six months in order that regard may be had, when passing sentence, to the conduct of the offender after conviction (including, where appropriate, the making of reparation for his offence) or to any change in his circumstances. The power is limited by a requirement that the court should be satisfied that deferment is in the interests of justice.[63] The sort of case where sentence might be deferred is where the court believes that there is a realistic possibility that the offender might be about to change his ways; maybe he has found a steady job, or decided to give up drinking where that has been an apparent cause of his criminal behaviour, or to settle down and get married.[64] The court can wait to assess the effect of these changes, and may hope that the prospect of a return to court will increase the likelihood of improvement. When he returns he should if possible be sentenced by the same judge or bench of magistrates who deferred sentence,[65] and of course the penalty imposed should reflect any improvement in his behaviour.[66]

7. Reasons for Sentence

A judge or bench of magistrates is not generally obliged to give reasons for its decision,[67] though many sentencers do so. The absence of any such

---

[61] Magistrates' Courts Act 1980 s.37, as amended by the Criminal Justice Act 1982, Sched. 14. Offenders eligible for committal are those of not less than 15 or more than 16 years of age who have been convicted of offences which, on indictment, are punishable with more than six months imprisonment. The Crown Court then has power to sentence the offender to a term of youth custody not exceeding the maximum term of imprisonment available on conviction on indictment, or to deal with him in any manner open to the magistrates: Powers of Criminal Courts Act 1973, s.42(2), added by Criminal Justice Act 1982, Sched. 14. Note, however, the restrictions on youth custody sentences for 15 and 16 years-olds: Criminal Justice Act 1982, s.7(8) to which the new s.42 is subject.

[62] Powers of Criminal Courts Act 1973, s.1, as amended by Criminal Justice Act 1982, s.63. See J. Corden and D. Nott, "The Power to Defer Sentence" (1980) *British Journal of Criminology*, 358.

[63] Furthermore the convicted person must consent to the deferment: 1973 Act, s.1(3).

[64] It is not a method of enabling the court to avoid making up its mind: Thomas, *Principles of Sentencing* at p. 381, nor does the fact of deferment bind the court which eventually has to decide how to deal with the offender to use or refrain from using a particular measure. In particular the power of magistrates to commit *after* deferment is unaffected: 1973 Act, s.1(8), substituted by Criminal Justice Act 1982, s.63. According to Corden and Nott, power to defer is sometimes used where the court is reluctant to accept the recommendations in a social inquiry report.

[65] *R. v. Gurney* [1974] Crim. L.R. 472—where this is not possible, the court should be told of the reasons for deferment and the circumstances of the case.

[66] If he is convicted of another offence during the period for which sentence was deferred he may be dealt with before the end of the period of deferment: Powers of Criminal Courts Act 1973, s.1(4).

[67] In some cases reasons must be given for various decisions. See, *e.g.* the special provisions relating to custodial sentences passed on young offenders under the Criminal Justice Act 1982, below p. 695.

obligation has been severely criticised,[68] and it has been said that the position is not excused by the modern trend towards volunteering reasons:

> "To recite the fact that most judges in the Crown Court now do give reasons as an argument against imposing the obligation to do so in all cases is surely inadequate: if the practice has merit, then it ought to be universal."[69]

C. POWERS OF SENTENCING

The modern sentencer, unlike his nineteenth century predecessor,[70] has a bewildering number of options open to him in dealing with offenders. His sense of bewilderment is likely to be compounded by the complexity of the various conditions attaching to each option, the different aims these options may be designed to achieve, and the need to consider their suitability in a particular order.[71] In the pages which follow, we will examine these options, and discover as we do so something of the sentencer's difficulties.

1. CLASSIFICATION OF MEASURES

Some measures are intended to punish, others to rehabilitate. Some are intended to do both.[72] Some involve a measure of restraint on the liberty of the offender, others do not. Some apply only to young offenders,[73] others only to adults. Yet others can be used to deal with offenders of all ages. Any of these distinctions could be employed as a means of classification, but it is proposed to consider the various measures according to whether they are custodial in nature. This is because the courts regard depriving an offender of his liberty as something of a last resort after other possible means of disposal have been considered and rejected: so also shall we. But it should not be forgotten that the other distinctions referred to above may cut across our classification and require some explanation as we proceed.

---

[68] Notably by D.A. Thomas, "Sentencing—The Case for Reasoned Decisions" [1963] Crim. L.R. 243. Some judges enjoy indulging in a little homily for the benefit of the offender. Some amusing examples are among those collected by Spreutels, "Giving Reasons for Sentence in the Crown Court" [1980] Crim. L.R. 486, and see S. White, "Homilies in Sentencing" [1971] Crim. L.R. 690.

[69] Cross and Ashworth, *The English Sentencing System* (3rd ed., 1981) at p. 107.

[70] A full account of the historical development of sentencing is given in Part I of the Report of the Advisory Council on the Penal System, "Sentences of Imprisonment: A Review of Maximum Penalties" (1978).

[71] A small handbook for sentencers, *The Sentence of the Court*, is produced regularly by the Home Office and is of great interest also to the student of sentencing.

[72] It would be a mistake to assume that all custodial measures are intended to punish. Some perform no such function (e.g. hospital orders under the Mental Health Act 1983, s.37, below p. 697). Others couple a degree of punishment with a therapeutic régime, e.g. youth custody, below, p. 696.

[73] The age of criminal responsibility is ten, though children between the ages of 10 and 14 may only be convicted on proof of "mischievous discretion" which involves awareness of wrong-doing: J.C. Smith and B. Hogan, *Criminal Law* (5th ed., 1983) p. 162 Offenders between the ages of 14 and 17 are referred to as "young persons," though juvenile is a handy expression to denote a person under the age of 17. Between 17 and 21, the offender is a "young adult."

By way of exception, and simply for ease of reference, special powers relating to mentally disordered offenders are considered separately, at the end of the chapter.

2. NON-CUSTODIAL MEASURES

The Crown Court and magistrates' courts[74] have power to fine offenders, to discharge them absolutely or conditionally, to bind them over to keep the peace or to be of good behaviour,[75] to place them on probation[76] or to make a community service order in respect of them. In addition, young offenders may be required to attend an attendance centre, and juveniles may be subjected to a supervision order or taken into care.

The power to pass a suspended sentence of imprisonment which is essentially non-custodial unless activated by the offender's continued misconduct, is difficult to separate from its custodial counterpart and is therefore considered in detail in the next section.[77]

(a) Fines

The fine is by far the most popular penalty, particularly in magistrates' courts. "In 1982, magistrates courts imposed a fine on over a half of all offenders sentenced for indictable offences, on 98 per cent. of those sentenced for summary motoring offences and on 89 per cent. of those sentenced for other summary offences."[78] It has maintained this popularity despite the proliferation of new methods of disposal,[79] and has the advantage of simplicity and of cheapness, if only initially, for unpaid fines create a great deal of business for the magistrates courts, through which they are collected.[80]

The Crown Court has the power to fine for any offence except treason or murder,[81] and there is no statutory restriction on the amount of the fine which may be imposed.[82] It is not, however, a penalty which is considered appropriate, used alone, for many serious offences, particularly offences of

---

[74] In most cases offenders under the age of 17 will be dealt with in juvenile courts rather than in adult magistrates courts or in the Crown Court (see above, p. 46). In the following pages the powers attributed to magistrates' courts apply also to juvenile courts unless otherwise stated. The powers of an adult magistrates' court in sentencing juveniles are limited by the Children and Young Persons Act 1969, s.7(8).

[75] Though only the Crown Court may bind over to come up for judgment: below, p. 680.

[76] Not available in respect of juveniles: below, p. 680.

[77] The position is further complicated by the power to pass a partially suspended sentence contained in section 47 of the Criminal Law Act 1977 which was brought into force in 1982 and almost immediately revised by the Criminal Justice Act 1982, s.30 and Sched. 14, and by the fact that a suspended sentence supervision order may accompany a suspended prison sentence, the order being akin to a probation order. See below, pp. 693–695.

[78] Criminal Statistics 1982, p. 138. In relation to indictable offences dealt with in the Crown Court, where the most popular sentence is immediate imprisonment, the fine was used in 10 per cent. of cases in 1982.

[79] Though there are some indications from the Criminal Statistics that it has been slipping a little in popularity in recent years, possibly because of higher unemployment resulting in inability to pay: Criminal Statistics 1982, p. 140.

[80] See R. Morgan and R. Bowles, "Fines: Where Does Sentencing End and Enforcement Begin?" [1983] Crim. L.R. 78.

[81] Powers of Criminal Courts Act 1973, s.30.

[82] See Criminal Law Act 1977, s.32(1).

violence. Reference has already been made to the view expressed by the Court of Appeal that the crime of rape almost invariably calls for a custodial sentence.[83] On the other hand, a fine may be coupled with a sentence of imprisonment for a serious offence where, for example, the offender has made a considerable profit out of his criminal enterprise which he might otherwise be able to enjoy on his release.[84]

Magistrates' courts may also fine for any offence: indeed a fine is the only punishment laid down in many statutes creating summary offences.[85] The maximum fine which may be imposed is, however, limited by statute,[86] with the resultant difficulty that rising inflation rapidly eats away at the real value of the penalty.[87] Section 143 of the Magistrates' Courts Act 1980 therefore empowers the Secretary of State to vary maximum fines on summary conviction of offences triable either way in order to reflect any changes in the value of money, and, for the same reason, Part III of the Criminal Justice Act 1982 makes provision for a standard scale of fines for summary offences so that levels of fines may more easily be kept under review.[88] Existing offences are assimilated to a level on the scale, and the maximum appropriate to that level can be varied by order.[89] Later statutes will be able to refer directly to a level of the scale rather than to a fixed amount.[90]

Where the circumstances of an offence are such that the sentencer considers that either fine or imprisonment might be appropriate, it is a nice question whether the means of the offender to pay a fine may be taken into account.[91] It seems clear that a wealthy offender should not be able to "buy himself out" of a prison sentence[92] which is clearly appropriate, nor should a man be sent to prison when a fine is appropriate simply because he

---

[83] Above, p. 665. A fine is a very unusual penalty for rape even in the "exceptional case" where prison is not appropriate. For the normal approach to sentencing in rape cases see D.A. Thomas, *Principles of Sentencing* (1979) pp. 112–117, *Current Sentencing Practice*, para. B4–1.

[84] See, *e.g.* R. v. *Savundranayagan* [1968] 3 All E.R. 439.

[85] This does not, however, preclude the use of probation or discharge where appropriate.

[86] In the case of summary offences, by the statute creating the offence. If no express provision is made, the limit is £400. In respect of offences triable either way, many are at present subject to a maximum fine of £2,000 by virtue of section 32(9) of the Magistrates Courts Act 1980 and Schedule 1 to that Act, and recently raised by Order. Offences not contained in that Schedule may be subject to higher (or, if contained in statutes enacted after 1977, lower) maxima: see s.32(2). There are special statutory restrictions on the fining of juveniles by juvenile and adult magistrates' courts—Magistrates' Courts Act 1980, s.24(3) and (4), s.36. The present limits are £100 (child) and £400 (young person). In some cases the parent may be ordered to pay: Children and Young Persons Act 1933, s.55.

[87] Or, as it is succinctly put by C. Emmins, *A Guide to the Criminal Justice Act 1982* (1982). "Criminals must be one of the few groups in society to have benefited from inflation," p. 28.

[88] Criminal Justice Act 1982, s.37. The Act also provides for an increase in fines for many summary offences, ss.38–48 and see also Scheds. 2 and 3. In particular s.38 makes provision for the increase of many existing fines to the next point on the new scale.

[89] s.48.

[90] See article in (1983) 147 J.P. 134.

[91] The means of the offender *should* be taken into account, once a fine has been decided on, in fixing the *amount* to be paid: D.A. Thomas, *Current Sentencing Practice*, para. J1, 2(c).

[92] R. v. *Markwick* (1953) 37 Cr.App.R. 125, decided when the Court of Appeal had the power to increase sentence. A £500 fine had been imposed on a wealthy man convicted of petty theft from a golf club's changing rooms, in circumstances in which suspicion was cast on the staff of the club. On appeal the Court of Appeal substituted a two months prison sentence.

appears unable to pay,[93] but where either measure is appropriate the means of the offender is likely to be a deciding factor, however inequitable this may appear to be.

Less inequitable, perhaps, are the recent moves towards making it easier for courts to fine parents for the misdeeds of their children. Until the Criminal Justice Act 1982 came into force there was a *power* to order neglectful parents or guardians to pay a fine[94] imposed on a young person, and (in theory) a *duty* to make such an order where a child was fined, though some difficulty surrounded the proper interpretation of this provision.[95] The 1982 Act creates a duty[96] to order payment by a parent or guardian of a fine imposed on a child or young person unless it would be unreasonable to make such an order in all the circumstances.[97]

(b) Compensation[98]

Any court[99] may order an offender to pay compensation for any "personal injury, loss or damage"[1] resulting from his offence. Until 1982 a compensation order could only be made in addition to dealing with the offender in some other way. Now it may be employed on its own.[2] Where it is so used, it may have the appearance of being a species of fine, yet it would be incorrect so to regard it.[3] Its primary function is to save the victim of the offence the time and trouble of pursuing civil remedies.

Compensation should only be ordered where liability for the damage, etc., is clear or uncontested.[4] If there is any doubt a civil court is the proper forum in which to try the issue. The amount of compensation awarded must take into account the means of the offender.[5] Any discrepancy between the loss suffered and the amount to be paid by way of compensation would again have to be recouped in a civil action.[6]

(c) Ancillary financial orders

The true cost of a criminal conviction may not, as far as the offender is concerned, be reflected in the main penalty imposed on him by the court.

---

[93] *R. v. Reeves* (1972) 56 Cr.App.R. 366.

[94] Or costs or compensation.

[95] Children and Young Persons Act 1933, s.55. See also Children and Young Persons Act 1969, s.3(6) (compensation in care proceedings).

[96] s.27, substituting a new s.55. S.28 amends s.3(6) of the 1969 Act (above, n. 95).

[97] Nor need the court make an order if the parent or guardian cannot be found: substituted s.55(1)(b)(i). A parent or guardian has the right to be heard when an order is being contemplated (s.55(2)) and may appeal against the order (s.55(3), (4)).

[98] Powers of Criminal Courts Act 1973, s.35.

[99] Magistrates cannot order more than £2,000 compensation in respect of any one offence: Magistrates' Courts Act 1980, s.40. (Increased in 1984).

[1] There are some limitations on the types of loss for which compensation can be awarded by a criminal court: s.35(3).

[2] Criminal Justice Act 1982, s.67, amending Powers of Criminal Courts Act 1973, s.35.

[3] Interestingly the 1982 Act also provides that a court should make a compensation order in preference to fining an offender where it appears he lacks the means to pay both.

[4] *R. v. Vivian* [1979] 1 All E.R. 48, though see the new subs. (1A) added by the 1982 Act, the practical effect of which is uncertain.

[5] Powers of Criminal Courts Act 1973, s.35(4), and see *R. v. Webb and Davies* (1979) 1 Cr.App.R. (S.) 16).

[6] In which case the amount regained as compensation will be deducted from any damages awarded: Powers of Criminal Courts Act 1973, s.38.

In some cases he may also have to meet an order for costs,[7] for restitution[8] or forfeiture[9] of certain property, or may be subjected to a criminal bankruptcy order.[10] Such orders are frequently of more consequence to the offender than the main penalty, particularly where the latter consists of a small fine, though they are seldom referred to in press reports of proceedings. Such omissions have occasionally contributed to the public feeling that fines often do not reflect the gravity of offences, particularly of crimes against the person and against property.[11]

(d) Absolute/conditional discharges

Statute provides that a court may make an order discharging a convicted person, absolutely or conditionally, if it considers that it is "inexpedient" to inflict punishment upon him, and that putting him on probation would not be an appropriate step.[12] Here, then, is one example of a statute obliging a court to consider other options before using a particular measure.

An absolute discharge allows the convicted person to leave the court without a stain on his character, and is the clearest indication that the court, whilst appreciating that he has broken the law, can find no fault in him. Not surprisingly it is a rare occurrence. It may be used to reflect dissatisfaction with the state of the law, or with the decision to prosecute. In *R.* v. *Preston Justices, ex p. Lyons*,[13] a learner driver was instructed to perform an emergency stop without looking in his rear-view mirror. He did as he was told and was struck by another vehicle travelling close behind. He was convicted of careless driving,[14] but the magistrates ordered an absolute discharge, perhaps because they felt that the fault really lay with the careless instructor.[15] It is worth noting that despite the order, the driver was sufficiently aggrieved to appeal against conviction to the Divisional Court, where, incidentally, he met with no success.[16]

A conditional discharge, on the other hand, while not in itself a punishment, has the potential to become one. If the offender commits a further offence within a period stipulated by the court[17] he becomes liable

---

[7] Costs in Criminal Cases Act 1973.

[8] Theft Act 1968, s.28.

[9] Powers of Criminal Courts Act 1973, s.43.

[10] *Ibid.* s.39.

[11] *Cf.* Sir Thomas Skyrme, *The Changing Image of the Magistracy* (1979) at p. 130, where the point is made in regard to the failure of the press to mention compensation orders in press reports.

[12] Powers of Criminal Courts Act 1973, s.7(1). S.13 provides that a conviction in respect of which an order for absolute or conditional discharge is made is deemed not to count as a conviction at all, except for certain limited purposes, amongst which is now numbered an appeal against sentence: Criminal Justice Act 1982, s.66, Scheds. 14, 16.

[13] [1982] Crim. L.R. 451.

[14] Road Traffic Act 1972, s.3.

[15] The instructor was also convicted of aiding and abetting the offence. See the correspondence at [1982] Crim. L.R. 620.

[16] It appears to have been accepted that the standard of care to be expected of the learner driver in performing such a stop is the same as that of the reasonably prudent qualified driver who, it seems, always checks his rear-view mirror first! This has been criticised: M. Wasik, "A Learner's Careless Driving," [1982] Crim. L.R. 411, and commentary on the case at p. 451.

[17] Which must not exceed three years from the date of the order: Powers of Criminal Courts Act 1973, s.7(1). The period may be varied by order of the Home Secretary: s.7(3), added by Criminal Law Act 1977, s.57(2).

upon conviction to be sentenced for the original offence as well. He will not know in advance of reconviction what penalty, if any, is likely to be imposed,[18] so the effect is supposed to be to "keep him on his toes" for a while.[19] The power is quite widely used, particularly in dealing with juveniles.[20]

Because these orders can only be used where punishment for the offence is "inexpedient," they cannot be coupled with any order which is of the nature of a punishment, such as a fine, for the same offence.[21] An order to pay costs or compensation, however, would not be an inappropriate accompaniment.

(e) Binding over

Since at least 1361 there has been a power to bind over offenders to keep the peace and be of good behaviour.[22] The person bound over enters into a recognisance, which is an undertaking, breach of which is likely to be punished by forfeiture of a sum of money fixed at the time of the bind-over.[23] An undertaking to keep the peace and be of good behaviour may obviously be broken by conduct falling short of an offence, so the power is distinguishable from the conditional discharge of offenders.[24]

In one sense the bind-over is voluntary—the convicted person must agree to enter into the recognisance—but as the sanction for failure to agree is imprisonment[25] he is unlikely to refuse.[26]

Binding over may be used on it own or in conjunction with other measures, as it is not imposed in lieu of punishment. There must, however, be reason to suppose that the offender is a person likely to cause a breach of the peace.[27]

[18] Unlike the suspended sentence (below, p. 693) where the penalty is fixed at the outset.

[19] The Court is required to explain to the offender in ordinary language what will be the consequences of breach of the order: Powers of Criminal Courts Act 1973, s.7(3).

[20] In 1982, 33 per cent. of males under the age of 14 convicted of indictable offences were dealt with in this way: *Criminal Statistics* 1982, p. 140. The figure in respect of all male offenders convicted of indictable offences is around 12½ per cent. (*ibid.* p. 138). The rate of breach of the order for all offenders is around 10 per cent.

[21] Though it may be convenient when dealing with a number of offences at the same time to impose a penalty in respect of one and conditionally discharge the offender in respect of the others.

[22] The power to bind a person over to be of good behaviour is referred to in the Justices of the Peace Act of that year. The power to bind a person over to keep the peace derives from the common law. See also Magistrates Courts Act 1980, s.115; Justices of the Peace Act 1968, s.1(7) (Crown Court).

[23] The court may also ask for "sureties": guarantors who may also forfeit a fixed sum if the offender breaks his undertaking.

[24] Furthermore the maximum sanction for breach of the bind-over is fixed at the outset. There is a separate statutory power to bind over parents or guardians of juveniles. (Children and Young Persons Act 1969, ss.1(3); 7(7)).

[25] Magistrates may commit for up to six months: Magistrates' Court Act 1980, s.11(3). There seems to be no limit on the power of the Crown Court to commit: Justices of the Peace Act 1968, s.1(7).

[26] Though problems may arise in relation to offenders who are too young to be sent to prison in the event of their refusal to consent: *Veater* v. *G. and Others* [1981] Crim. L.R. 563. It has recently been suggested that other sanctions may apply in the case of young offenders. but this seems unlikely: see (1984) 148 J.P.N. 23, 275.

[27] *R.* v. *Aubrey-Fletcher, ex p. Thompson* (1969) 53 Cr.App.R. 380.

In addition the Crown Court enjoys a common law power[28] to bind over an offender to "come up for judgment": a power very similar[29] to conditionally discharging offenders and seldom used because the latter is much simpler to do.

(f) Probation

Probation is a substitute for sentencing an offender.[30] It is available in respect of those who have attained the age of 17 years[31] at the time of conviction, and consists of an order placing the offender under the supervision of a probation officer for a specified period of not less than six months or more than three years, and requiring him to comply with such conditions as the court considers necessary "for securing the good conduct of the offender or for preventing a repetition by him of the same offence or the commission of other offences."[32] Probation has the advantage over binding over that the offender receives a degree of support to help him overcome difficulties which may have led him into trouble. The probation officer's function is to "advise, assist and befriend"[33] the offender, and the success of his task turns on "the ability of the individual probation officer first to gain the offender's confidence, and then to work with him to overcome some of the problems which may have given rise to the offence."[34] Although the offender must consent to the order,[35] this is a far cry from an indication of his desire that it should succeed in its purpose.[36] The probation order is regarded by some offenders as a "let-off," and courts in the last decade have seemed sceptical of its usefulness. However, the most recent indications are of a greater willingness to make use of

[28] Preserved by Supreme Court Act 1981, s.79(2)(b). Such an order cannot be made in cases of murder, where the penalty is fixed by law.

[29] But wider in that conditions can be attached so that the offender needs to do more than simply avoid reconviction. The order is most frequently accompanied by undertakings to keep the peace and be of good behaviour.

[30] Powers of Criminal Courts Act 1973, s.2. The court must be of opinion that it is "expedient" to make the order instead of passing sentence. Once the order is made the conviction is deemed not to be a conviction for any purpose other than proceedings giving rise to it or arising out of it: *ibid.* s.13(1). The right of appeal against sentence is no longer prejudiced by this provision: Criminal Justice Act 1982, s.66, Sched. 14.

[31] A similar effect can be achieved in respect of younger offenders by using a supervision order: below, p. 681.

[32] Powers of Criminal Courts Act 1973, s.2(3). Conditions frequently imposed include keeping the peace and being of good behaviour. In addition, s.4(A), added by the Criminal Justice Act 1982, Sched. 11, allows a condition to be imposed requiring attendance at a day centre. These centres had been in existence for some time prior to the 1982 Act but there was no statutory power to compel attendance: *Cullen* v. *Rogers* [1982] 1 W.L.R. 729. Day *training* centres which a probationer *could* be required to attend under s.4 of the 1973 Act, were few in number and provisions relating to them were repealed by the 1982 Act. Section 3 of the Powers of Criminal Courts Act 1973 permits a requirement to be attached that the offender submit to treatment for a mental condition.

[33] Powers of Criminal Courts Act 1973, Sched. 3.

[34] *The Sentence of the Court* (1978) at p. 17.

[35] Powers of Criminal Courts Act 1973, s.2(6). The subsection also contains a requirement for the court to explain the effect of the order and the sanctions for its breach.

[36] Chances of success may be increased if the offender is considered suitable for a place in a probation hostel, and such a place can be found for him. See s.2(5) of the Act; Home Office Research Study No. 52, "Hostels for Offenders" (1979).

probation,[37] perhaps as a reaction to the ever-increasing number of offenders and the overcrowding of custodial institutions. Like absolute and conditional discharge probation should not be coupled with a punitive measure, though it may be accompanied by, for example, an order to pay compensation.[38]

Breach of probation may be dealt with in various ways.[39] In some circumstances the order may be revoked altogether and the offender will then become liable to be punished for the original offence.[40] In other cases he may be fined.[41]

(g) Supervision orders

In the case of juveniles a similar effect to probation may be achieved by making a supervision order.[42] A supervisor, who may be a probation officer or a local authority social worker, undertakes to "advise assist and befriend"[43] the supervised person, and this may well include befriending the family to which he belongs.[44] As with a probation order conditions may be attached aimed at encouraging the juvenile to improve his behaviour.[45] The order may last for up to three years, and there is a special power to require that for a number of days, not exceeding 90, the juvenile should submit to "intermediate treatment," that is, falling between the normal conditions of a supervision order and the stricter conditions which would apply if he were placed under a care order.[46] In addition, there is a recently-added power for the court to make a "night restriction order."[47]

[37] Figures for 1982 show that 7 per cent. of all offenders convicted of indictable offences received probation compared with 5 per cent. in 1977–78 and 8 per cent. at the beginning of the decade.

[38] Cf. R. v. Parry [1950] 1 K.B. 590. Powers of Criminal Courts Act 1973, s.35. The Advisory Council on the Penal System Report on Non-Custodial and Semi-Custodial Penalties (1970) considered that it ought to be possible in some cases to combine probation with a fine (paras. 173–192), and the combination is possible for separate offences: R. v. Bainbridge (1979) 1 Cr.App.R. (S).36. Note also that a court may not impose probation for one offence and a suspended sentence of imprisonment for another (Powers of Criminal Courts Act 1973, s.22(3). See instead the provisions relating to suspended sentence supervision orders, below, p. 695.

[39] Powers of Criminal Courts Act 1973, ss.6, 8. The breach may consist of the commission of a further offence or the breaking of a requirement attached to the order. In some cases an attendance centre order may be an appropriate sanction: Criminal Justice Act 1982, s.27(1)(b).

[40] Powers of Criminal Courts Act 1973, ss.6(3)(d), (6)(c), 8(7).

[41] Compare with the provisions on breach of a suspended sentence supervision order, below, p. 695.

[42] Children and Young Persons Act 1969, s.7(7)(b). As with probation, the order cannot be used in the cases of murder.

[43] Ibid. s.14.

[44] For a detailed description of the supervisor's work, see The Sentence of the Court (1978) at p. 61.

[45] Children and Young Persons Act 1969, s.12, see also s.18(2), (visits to supervisor).

[46] Children and Young Persons Act 1969, s.12, as amended by Criminal Justice Act 1982, s.20. The power to decide whether conditions were imposed on the juvenile subject to the intermediate treatment was, under the 1969 Act, vested in the supervisor. The 1982 Act allows, as an alternative, the courts to stipulate that certain conditions be fulfilled, as well as giving a new power to make some conditions, negative in nature, which could not previously have been made. (1969 Act, s.12(3C)), added by the 1982 Act, s.20. The supervisor must be consulted before such conditions are added: s.12(3F).

[47] s.12(3C)(b), added by the 1982 Act, s.20. A night restriction may not be imposed in respect of more than 30 days in all: s.12(3L).

under which a curfew is imposed on the supervised person to prevent him venturing out unaccompanied in the evenings. Some doubts have been expressed about the enforcement of such conditions: will it be possible to keep track of all the young people who are subject to such orders in order to discover whether they abide by the curfew? It may be that the recent street disturbances of 1981, in which some very young children were involved, have provoked an over-reaction on the part of the legislature.

The procedure for dealing with breach of a supervision order[48] is similar to the procedure in respect of probation. One important difference is that the consent of the juvenile is not a prerequisite of a supervision order, although some conditions may only be imposed with consent.[49]

(h) Care orders

Care orders may be made in dealing with juvenile offenders found guilty of offences other than murder, and have the effect of committing the juvenile to the care of the local authority for the area in which he resides.[50] The local authority, by virtue of the order, acquires all the rights and duties of the juvenile's parent until either the order is revoked or the juvenile reaches the age of 18.[51] Care orders, as their name suggests, are not really punitive, but since a juvenile may well regard the possibility of being sent away from home as a punishment, the court making the order must be satisfied that it is appropriate to do so having regard to the seriousness of the offence, and that the offender is in need of care or control which he is unlikely to receive unless the order is made.[52]

Until recently the court making the order had no say in the type of accommodation provided for the juvenile. A care order does not necessarily involve the removal of the juvenile from his home, and some disquiet was expressed by magistrates when juveniles they had placed in care were allowed to remain at home and subsequently re-offended, often leaving them with no choice but to make another care order. The Criminal Justice Act 1982 now allows a court, upon finding such a juvenile guilty of an offence punishable with imprisonment, to attach a residential condition, in effect requiring his removal from home for up to six months, or a condition requiring residence with a specified parent, guardian, relative or friend.[53] The court must be satisfied that no other method of dealing with

[48] Children and Young Persons Act 1969, s.15 as amended by Criminal Law Act 1977, s.37(2). The order is more flexible than a probation order. In some circumstances it can be replaced with a care order, or an attendance centre order.

[49] The offender (or, if he is under 14, his parents) must consent to the imposition by the Court of the intermediate treatment requirements described above, any negative requirements (above n. 46) and a night restriction order: s.12(3F) added by the 1982 Act, s.20. Any other person whose co-operation is required must also consent s.12(3G)(a).

[50] Children and Young Persons Act 1969, s.7(7)(a). Care orders may also be made in respect of juveniles who have not offended but who are in need of care or control for other reasons, such as parental neglect.

[51] 19 if he is 16 or over when the order is made.

[52] Criminal Justice Act 1982, s.23, amending the Children and Young Persons Act 1969, s.7. The 1982 Act also requires that the offender be represented, or if not, that he has been refused legal aid or declined to apply for it: s.24, adding s.7A to the 1969 Act.

[53] s.22, adding s.20A to the Children and Young Persons Act 1969, on the recommendation of the White Paper on Young Offenders, Cmnd. 8045 (1980). If the juvenile is found guilty of an offence punishable with imprisonment within the six months period he may be subjected to a similar condition for a further period of six months: Children and Young Persons Act 1969, s.20A(2).

the offender is appropriate and that the seriousness of his offence merits the attachment of the condition. The court cannot reject other methods of disposal without obtaining and considering information about "the circumstances," *i.e.* normally a social inquiry report.[54]

(i) Community service orders[55]

This has been the most enthusiastically received of the "new breed" of non-custodial and semi-custodial penalties. It is open to any court, in respect of offenders who have attained the age of 16[56] years and who have been convicted of offences punishable with imprisonment.[57] The offender must consent to the order being made.[58]

The order compels the offender to perform unpaid work in the community for a specified period of between 40 and 240 hours.[59] The work is supervised by a probation officer or equivalent and is expected to be completed within 12 months.[60]

The order is not suitable for all types of offender,[61] and the court should consider a social inquiry report before making an order.[62] Another obvious consideration is that there must be a place available on a local scheme, and many sentencers have found their intentions frustrated by the lack of availability of places.[63]

All sorts of work has been done under the scheme, from outdoor conservation and painting and decorating to swimming coaching for the disabled and gardening for the elderly.

The scheme has a number of advantages:

"The offender is penalised by being deprived of his leisure time, but for a constructive and outward-looking purpose; he has an opportunity to make reparation to the community against which he has offended by working for its benefit; and in some cases he will be

---

[54] s.20A(3). He must also have the opportunity of legal representation: s.20A(3).

[55] Powers of Criminal Courts Act 1973, ss.14–17, as amended by Criminal Justice Act 1982, s.68 and Sched. 12.

[56] Reduced from 17 by Criminal Justice Act 1982, Sched. 12.

[57] It is technically incorrect to speak of a person under 17 as having been "convicted," where he is tried by magistrates in an adult magistrates' or juvenile court. What happens is that a "finding of guilt" is made in respect of him: Children and Young Persons Act 1933, s.59. Similarly, offences are not "punishable by imprisonment" where the offender is under 21: Criminal Justice Act 1982, s.1(1). The expressions will, however be used in the text to avoid the inconvenience of adopting different terminology according to the age of the offender.

[58] Powers of Criminal Courts Act 1973, s.14(2).

[59] In the case of an offender aged 16 years, 120 hours is the maximum: s.14(1A), inserted by Criminal Justice Act 1982, Sched. 12. The hours to be served can be varied by order of the Secretary of State: s.14(7)

[60] The work should not interfere with the offender's education, paid employment or religious practices: s.15(3).

[61] See generally, W.A. Young, *Community Service Orders* (1979), Home Office Research Study No. 29, *Community Service Orders* (1975).

[62] s.14(2), substituted by the 1982 Act, provides that in addition the court may, if it thinks it necessary, hear a probation officer or social worker: Criminal Justice Act 1982, Sched. 12.

[63] There is a possibility that the scheme will not be available immediately for 16-year-olds—Criminal Justice Act 1982, s.14(2A)(*b*). (Courts not to make orders for 16-year olds until informed by the Secretary of State that local facilities are available.)

brought into direct contact with members of the community who most need help and support."[64]

It has been suggested as being of particular use in the case of "those who have consistently under-achieved, under-functioned and for those with a poor self-image."[65] It is also said to help the offender to shed his sense of guilt.[66] With so many advantages it ought to be as widely available as possible, but it has sometimes been interpreted by the courts as available only when a prison sentence would have been appropriate but for the power to order community service.[67] Nevertheless the criminal statistics seem to show that the popularity of community service is increasing partly at the expense of the fine,[68] particularly in respect of offenders in the 17–21 age group.

Community service orders are imposed instead of dealing with the offender in any other way, and so cannot be combined with punitive orders though they may be accompanied by an order for costs or compensation.[69]

Failure to comply with the order, or the commission of other offences while serving it, may result in its revocation or in some cases the imposition of a fine.[70] Where the order is revoked the court may deal with the offender for the original offence. All of this should be explained to the offender when the order is imposed.[71]

(j) Attendance centres

The Crown Court and magistrates' courts may make attendance centre orders in respect of certain offenders under the age of 21.[72] The power to make such an order depends on a number of conditions. First, the offence must be one which, in the case of an adult, is punishable with imprisonment. Secondly, the court must have been notified that a suitable centre is available, and thirdly it must be of the opinion that it is reasonable to expect the offender to travel to it. One of the major criticisms of the present system is that there are not enough centres.[73]

---

[64] *The Sentence of the Court*, at p. 21.

[65] H. Prins, "Whither Community Service?" (1976) *British Journal of Criminology* 73.

[66] Although any penalty seeking to achieve this end is hampered by the long delay between apprehension and trial which is likely to dampen enthusiasm for deserved punishment.

[67] *R.* v. *Mulcahy* (unrep.) discussed in Cross and Ashworth, *The English Sentencing System* (3rd ed.) p. 31. Although this is consistent with the intentions of the Home Office and the proposals of the Advisory Council on the Penal System it appears not to represent the practice of most courts: see K. Pease, "Community Service and the Tariff" [1978] Crim. L.R. 269. Recent studies have concluded that the length of service ordered reflects "individualised" rather than "tariff" principles: E. Jardine, G. Moore & K. Pease, "Community Service Orders, Employment and the Tariff" [1983] Crim.L.R. 17.

[68] *Criminal Statistics* 1982, p. 140, accounting for six per cent. of all offenders sentenced for indictable offences in 1982, compared with 3 per cent. in 1978.

[69] Powers of Criminal Courts Act 1973, s.14(8). In *R.* v. *Starie* (1979) 69 Cr.App.R. 239 it was said to be bad sentencing practice to combine a community service order for one offence with a suspended sentence of imprisonment for another.

[70] Powers of Criminal Courts Act 1973, ss.16–17.

[71] *Ibid.* s.14(5).

[72] Criminal Justice Act 1982, ss.16–19. The Crown Court was given a general power to make such orders by the Criminal Justice Act 1982, s.17. Magistrates have enjoyed the power since 1948.

[73] There were no attendance centres for girls till 1979, and few exist for male offenders between the ages of 17 and 21. At the time of writing there are plans to introduce more centres.

The offender "serves" a fixed sentence of between 12 and 36 hours[74] at the centre, usually in units of two hours. Centres are often located in schools or youth clubs, and are supervised by volunteer staff.[75] Not uncommonly offenders spend Saturday afternoons at the centre, where the accent is on discipline and making constructive use of leisure time. Success is only likely to be achieved[76] in the rehabilitation of young people who could not be described as "hardened" criminals, and for this reason there are statutory restrictions on its use in respect of offenders who have served custodial sentences.[77]

(k) Miscellaneous

The remaining non-custodial options open to a court in dealing with offenders are beyond the scope of this work.[78] It should, however, be noted that the power of the courts when dealing with motorists to disqualify them from driving is of great importance, particularly in magistrates' courts. A full description of such powers may be found in works dealing with road traffic offences.[79]

3. Custodial Sentences

Imprisonment is the only custodial penalty available to the courts in dealing with sane offenders[80] over the age of 21 years. Under that age the main custodial measures are youth custody and detention in a detention centre.[81] As these two measures may only be resorted to where the court would have power to imprison an adult offender, let us begin by considering the extent of that power.

(a) Imprisonment

Not all offences are punishable by imprisonment. Where an offence is proscribed by statute, as most modern crimes are, reference should be made to the enactment creating the offence to see whether provision is

---

[74] Except in the case of a child for whom 12 hours might be excessive: Criminal Justice Act 1982, s.17(4). Twelve hours is the normal sentence unless the court is of the opinion that this period would be inadequate, in which case the limit is 24 hours if the offender is under 17 and 36 hours if he is over 17 and under 21: s.17(5).

[75] Often, according to *The Sentence of the Court*, police officers who have given up their spare time.

[76] Breach of the order may ultimately lead to its revocation, with the result that the offender may be dealt with for the original offence. The order can also be used to deal with young fine defaulters: Criminal Justice Act 1982, s.17(1).

[77] Criminal Justice Act 1982, s.17(3).

[78] Powers include the making of recommendations for the deportation of offenders who are not British citizens: Immigration Act 1971, s.3(6), as amended by the British Nationality Act 1981, Sched. 4.

[79] P. Halnan and J. Spencer, *Wilkinson's Road Traffic Offences* (11th ed., 1982) contains a comprehensive guide.

[80] For the powers relating to the disposal of mentally disordered offenders see below, p. 697.

[81] Criminal Justice Act 1982, ss.1–10. These provisions replace the system of imprisonment or borstal training for young offenders, abolition of which was recommended in the White Paper on Young Offenders, Cmnd. 8045 (1980). See also the Report of the Advisory Council on the Penal System on Young Adult Offenders (1974) and the Green Paper on Youth Custody and Supervision Cmnd. 7406 (1978).

made for the imprisonment of offenders. In the case of the few common law crimes still in existence, punishment may include imprisonment at the discretion of the court, so that, in theory anyway, life imprisonment could be imposed.[82] Where provision is made for imprisonment it is likely that a maximum term will be prescribed, leaving the court a measure of discretion in the matter of length of sentence. The Crown Court judge will usually have more freedom of choice than magistrates where length of sentence is concerned, as summary offences tend to be accompanied by lower maxima, and it is not uncommon in the case of offences triable either way to find that a lower maximum penalty is provided if the offence is tried summarily. Even where this is not the case magistrates may not by reason of a general statutory limitation impose a sentence of more than six months imprisonment in respect of one offence,[83] or 12 months where consecutive sentences are imposed for offences triable either way.[84]

Where trials on indictment are concerned, it may come as a shock to the lay reader to discover the lack of uniformity among the maxima available for different offences which might be thought very similar in terms of their gravity.[85] The most frequently quoted example is the provision of a maximum penalty of 10 years imprisonment for indecent assault on a man or boy,[86] compared with two years for indecent assault on a woman.[87] Readers who are horrified not only by the disparity but also by the apparently sexist overtones may be comforted to know that the sex of the assailant is irrelevant in both offences.

Often the reason why some maxima seem to be out of line is that the attitude of society towards a particular offence has changed while the penalty remains the same. This is particularly true of some offences last reviewed in the nineteenth century; bigamy, punishable with a maximum of seven years imprisonment,[88] being an example. Though penalties are kept under review, by the law reform bodies in particular, changes tend to be piecemeal, and even comprehensive reforms such as those contained in the Theft Act 1968[89] often serve only to heighten the oddity of penalties for other crimes by comparison. A comprehensive review of all maxima would seem to be called for, but the disappointing conclusion of the Advisory

---

[82] Even in the case of common law crimes penalties may be limited by statute. So an attempt at common law was punishable by the same maximum penalty as the completed offence: Powers of Criminal Courts Act 1973, s.18(2). See now the Criminal Attempts Act 1981, creating a statutory crime of attempt, section 4 of which makes provision for penalties.

[83] Magistrates' Courts Act 1980, s.31. The restriction may be expressly excluded: s.31(2).

[84] Ibid. s.133(2). Consecutive sentences for summary offences may not exceed six months in aggregate: s.133(1).

[85] Readers anxious to try the exercise should procure a copy of the Advisory Council on the Penal System's Report *A Review of Maximum Penalties* (H.M.S.O., 1978) and peruse Appendix A, Table I, p. 147.

[86] Sexual Offences Act 1956, s.15.

[87] Five years if the victim is a girl under 13: Sexual Offences Act 1956, s.14, as amended by Indecency with Children Act 1960. The anomaly will be rectified if a proposal of the Criminal Law Revision Committee is enacted. There would then be one offence, punishable with a maximum of 10 years (Fifteenth Report, Cmnd. 9213 (1984)).

[88] Offences against the Person Act 1861, s.57.

[89] The 8th Report of the Criminal Law Revision Committee on Theft and Related Offences, Cmnd. 2977 (1966) contains some interesting insights into the views taken of the comparative seriousness of the offences under review.

Council on the Penal System in their Report on Maximum Penalties[90] was that this was too daunting a task as there was likely to be considerable disagreement over such matters as the comparative seriousness of offences. Instead they suggested some degree of rationalisation based on current sentencing practice, leaving the rectification of the greater anomalies to piecemeal reform. Not surprisingly, nothing has resulted from this proposal.

The function of a statutory maximum penalty at present, particularly a modern one, is to suggest to the sentencer what is considered by Parliament to be an appropriate sentence for the worst possible example of the offence.[91] It enables him to "scale down" his sentence accordingly. Where the maximum penalty provided is unrealistic judges are likely to have developed their own ideas of the penalty appropriate to the most serious cases that have come before them.[92]

(i) Sending offenders to prison

D.A. Thomas, in his book *Principles of Sentencing*,[93] identifies the "primary decision" of the sentencer as being a choice between a measure designed primarily to reflect the culpability of the offender and one designed to help him by seeking to influence his future behaviour. In many, if not most, cases one of these aims will have to be sacrificed to the other, for the punishment which fits the crime may well not be best suited to the interests of the individual offender.[94]

(1) *The Tariff.* In most cases a decision to send an offender to prison will reflect a preference for the first aim, in which case the length of sentence to be served will be determined according to the principles of the "tariff" appropriate to the offence. The tariff is not, as its name may suggest, a concise table of appropriate penalties, but rather a body of judicial (and sometimes academic)[95] opinion that can only be discovered by consulting the decisions of appellate courts, becoming acquainted with the practice of fellow sentencers, keeping up to date with the literature on sentencing and,

---

[90] Above, n. 85.

[91] *R.* v. *Harrison* (1909) 2 Cr.App.R. 94. Sentencers are therefore required to bear in mind the worst example of the offence when fixing sentence. So in *R.* v. *Smith* [1975] Crim. L.R. 468 the Court of Appeal reduced a three year maximum sentence for taking a conveyance without the owner's consent because it was possible to imagine worse cases as taking an emergency service vehicle to the danger of the public. However it has also been stressed that sentencers should not conjure up fanciful and unlikely "worst cases": *R.* v. *Ambler and Hargreaves* [1976] Crim. L.R. 266. It might fairly be asked whether the example envisaged in *R.* v. *Smith* was of this kind.

[92] The Advisory Council on the Penal System's Report (above, n. 85) recommends that, where an offence other than homicide carries a maximum penalty of life imprisonment and no sentence of life imprisonment has been passed for a period of 10 years the power to imprison for life for that offence should lapse: para. 233.

[93] (2nd ed., 1979) p. 8. For a thought-provoking examination of this part of the process see A. Ashworth, *Sentencing and Penal Policy* (1983) p. 42.

[94] Where young offenders are concerned the punishment best suited to the offender is normally preferred as a matter of policy. Lord Elton, introducing the provisions of the Criminal Justice Bill dealing with custodial sentences for the young, (now the 1982 Act) indulged in Gilbertian parody to produce the sentiment " 'Our object less subliminal' is 'to make the punishment fit the criminal' ": See H.L. Deb. Vol. 431, cols. 4–72.

[95] Chiefly that of D.A. Thomas, contained in *Principles of Sentencing* (n. 92 above) *Current Sentencing Practice*, and his monthly commentaries on recent cases in the Criminal Law Review.

in the case of magistrates' courts, making reference to any published guidelines. Its object, very broadly speaking, is to achieve a measure of uniformity whilst making allowance for the infinite variety of possible mitigating or aggravating circumstances which may be present in individual cases.

The key principle of the tariff is one of proportionality. The length of sentence is first provisionally determined by the gravity of the offence compared to others of the same type: a process Thomas refers to as "fixing the ceiling." When this has been done, mitigating factors may be taken into account to reduce the term. Thus, aggravating factors which do not relate to the offence itself, such as the offender's previous bad record, cannot in theory serve to increase the sentence beyond the "ceiling" already fixed,[96] though they may operate to deny the offender the benefit of any mitigation to which he would otherwise have been entitled.[97] This is the reason why a plea of not guilty cannot be said to increase the sentence, though a plea of guilty, which may be taken into account in mitigation, may decrease it. To the offender the simple proposition is that he can expect a higher sentence if he pleads not guilty; to a lawyer this sentence is not "higher" at all because it merely conforms to the norm. It may be questioned whether any discounting should be done on the basis of guilty pleas, particularly as the effect on a defendant who is dithering over his plea may be to offer an inducement to plead guilty whether he wishes to or not. On the other hand, it must be conceded that the practice allows the court to recognise the element of contrition that may be involved in a plea of guilty, or the reluctance of the defendant to waste the court's time by running hopelessly unlikely defences.

(2) *Prison as an individualised measure.* Where the court opts for an individualised measure, it is likely to have non-custodial possibilities in mind, but it by no means follows that imprisonment cannot be used to tailor a sentence to fit the offender. Life sentences in particular are frequently so used where the paramount need is to reflect the dangerousness of the offender rather than the gravity of his offence. Where imprisonment is used for this purpose the guidelines of the tariff are inapplicable.[98] Where a substantial sentence of imprisonment is passed as an individualised measure the offender may well find himself worse off

[96] Though Mr. Thomas himself concedes that in some cases the 'ceiling' appears to be exceeded, *e.g.* in the case of dangerous offenders: see *e.g. R.* v. *Chadbund* [1983] Crim. L.R. 48 and commentary.

[97] In cases where the offender's record is very bad he may qualify for an extended sentence under the Powers of Criminal Courts Act 1973, s.28. The Crown Court, dealing with an offender who persistently commits serious offences, may, *inter alia,* sentence him to a term exceeding the statutory maximum for the offence. The provisions of s.28 are complicated and so seldom used that the section is not considered in detail. See D.A. Thomas, *Principles of Sentencing* (1979) Chap. 8. Abolition of the power was recommended by the Advisory Council on the Penal System, *op. cit.* n. 85 above, para. 115.

[98] D.A. Thomas, *Principles of Sentencing* (1979) p. 10 discussing *R.* v. *Rose* [1974] Crim. L.R. 266. The Court of Appeal will be handicapped by the lack of any power to increase sentence where it considered that an individualised life sentence would have been preferable to the tariff sentence awarded. Furthermore where the trial judge has used the tariff in such a case the Court of Appeal is bound to reduce the sentence if it does not conform with tariff principles, even though a life sentence would have been correct!

than under the tariff,[99] and appeal in the hope that the Court of Appeal finds the "primary decision" unsatisfactory.[1]

(3) *The move towards shorter sentences.* Where a court decides that a tariff prison sentence is inevitable, the modern trend is towards keeping the length of the term as short as possible. It cannot be denied that the thinking behind the new trend has been much influenced by the problem of overcrowding in prisons,[2] but at the same time it is claimed that such sentences are equally as effective as longer terms because the prisoner is most encouraged to mend his ways by the "clang of the prison gates" and the consequent shock of losing his liberty which he feels in the early stages of confinement. It is even suggested that this shock wears off after a while, which may make shorter sentences positively advantageous. These propositions are difficult to prove, as are most penological theories, but if they may reasonably be well founded they are clearly worth pursuing.

The "short sharp sentence" theory passed into current sentencing practice in the judgment of the Court of Appeal (Criminal Division) in the case of *R. v. Bibi.*[3] In that case the defendant had been convicted on two counts of being concerned in the fraudulent importation of the drug cannabis. At the time of her conviction she was aged 49, a widow with a dependant grandchild, and she lived with her son-in-law who arranged for the drug to be posted from Kenya to the house which they shared. Her part in the crime was limited to unpacking parcels of the drug as they arrived. Sentences of three years' imprisonment on each count, the terms to run concurrently, were reduced on appeal to six months' concurrent on each count. The Lord Chief Justice, Lord Lane, took the opportunity to give general guidance on the use of shorter sentences for offences the nature of which made prison unavoidable. He said:

"This case opens up wider horizons because it is no secret that our prisons at the moment are dangerously overcrowded. So much so that sentencing courts must be particularly careful to examine each case to ensure, if an immediate custodial sentence is necessary, that the sentence is as short as possible, consistent only with the duty to protect the interests of the public and to punish and deter the criminal.

Many offenders can be dealt with equally justly and effectively by a sentence of six or nine months' imprisonment as by one of 18 months or three years. We have in mind not only the obvious case of the first

---

[99] A number of serious offences normally attract tariff sentences, but this does not preclude the use of an individualised *custodial* sentence in a proper case. Life sentences which are not fixed by law are likely *only* to be used as individualised measures. Offences in respect of which an individualised life sentence may be passed include robbery, assault with intent to rob, aggravated burglary, rape, manslaughter, wounding with intent and arson. For a complete list see the Report of the Advisory Council on the Penal System, *Sentences of Imprisonment, A Review of Maximum Penalties* (1978) p. 214.

[1] For an interesting example of a case in which the Court of Appeal felt that a case "cried out for a life sentence" which could not have been imposed because of a plea of guilty to simple burglary (maximum 14 years) had been accepted on an indictment charging aggravated burglary (maximum life) see *R. v. McCauliffe* [1982] Crim. L.R. 316.

[2] The prison population at present being around 44,000 and in dire need of reduction. One justification for the shift towards shorter sentences is that an overcrowded prison imposes extra hardships on the inmates.

[3] (1980) 71 Cr.App.R. 360; [1980] Crim. L.R. 732.

offender for whom any prison sentence however short may well be an adequate punishment and deterrent, but other types of cases as well.

The less serious types of factory or shopbreaking; the minor cases of sexual indecency; the more petty frauds where small amounts of money are involved; the fringe participant in more serious crime: all these are examples of cases where the shorter sentence would be appropriate.

There are, on the other hand, some offences for which, generally speaking, only the medium or longer sentences will be appropriate. For example, most robberies; most offences involving serious violence; use of a weapon to wound; burglary of private dwelling-houses; planned crime for wholesale profit; active large-scale trafficking in dangerous drugs. These are only examples. It would be impossible to set out a catalogue of those offences which do and those which do not merit more severe treatment. So much will, obviously, depend on the circumstances of each individual offender and each individual offence.

What the Court can and should do is to ask itself whether there is any compelling reason why a short sentence should not be passed. We are not aiming at uniformity of sentence; that would be impossible. We are aiming at uniformity of approach."[4]

In this and in other similar judgments[5] the Court of Appeal has set a new pattern for sentencing offenders convicted of certain types of offence, and there is every indication that the guidance is being followed.[6] This change may be timely for it has seemed for some time that the alternative to a measure of judicial self-discipline in restricting the use of prison sentences would be legislative interference aimed at reducing the prison population by more direct (and perhaps more dubious) means. The initiative taken by the Court of Appeal, together with the introduction of partly suspended sentences[7] and some of the measures in the Criminal Justice Act 1982[8] may eliminate the need for anything more drastic. It remains the fact that more people are imprisoned in this country than in most civilised nations, and it may well prove to be the case that the fault lies not in the tendency to sentence more people to imprisonment, but rather in the habitual imposition of longer sentences. The change effected by the Court of Appeal (Criminal Division) in sentencing policy in cases such as *R.* v. *Bibi* could well turn out to be the most important move of the decade.

(4) *Consecutive and concurrent sentences.* Sentencers enjoy a discretion to order that terms of imprisonment should be served consecutively rather than concurrently.[9] Where a number of offences have arisen out of a single event, however, it is considered wrong in principle to impose consecutive

---

[4] (1980) 71 Cr.App.R. at pp. 361–362.

[5] *e.g. R.* v. *Upton* (1980) 71 Cr.App.R. 102; [1980] Crim. L.R. 508.

[6] For early indications see *Criminal Statistics* 1982, p. 152 *et seq.* However, it seems more people are being sent to prison, so the effect on total prison population may be negligible.

[7] Criminal Law Act 1977, s.47, brought into force on March 29, 1982 and swiftly amended by the Criminal Justice Act 1982, s.30.

[8] For example, the power to grant early release in emergencies (below, p. 692) or to vary the periods applicable to the granting of parole (below, p. 691).

[9] Subject to the statutory limitation in the case of magistrates noted above, p. 686.

sentences.[10] It has also been held that a sentencer imposing consecutive sentences should keep the total length under review in case it is out of keeping with the gravity of the offences, even if the individual sentences imposed are correct in principle,[11] a doctrine which owes more to clemency than to logic. It is not uncommon for a substantial sentence to be imposed in respect of the most serious offence and for other sentences to be made to run concurrently.

(5) *Restrictions on imprisonment.* In addition to the sentencing system's built-in tendency to regard prison as a last resort, there is a statutory restriction on sending offenders to prison for the first time.[12] An offender on whom a sentence of imprisonment has not previously been passed[13] may only be sentenced to imprisonment if the court, after considering information about his circumstances, considers that no other method of dealing with him is appropriate.[14] A social inquiry report must be obtained unless the court is of the opinion that it is unnecessary,[15] and the offender must have at least the opportunity of being legally represented before he is sentenced.[16]

(ii) *Release from prison*

An offender may at present serve as little as one third of a fixed-term sentence of imprisonment if he obtains the full benefit of both remission and parole.

(1) *Remission.* Under Rules made under the Prison Act 1952 a prisoner serving a fixed sentence of more than one month may qualify for remission of one third of the term if he is of good behaviour. Remission, or more precisely the prospect of losing it, helps to maintain discipline within the prison system.

(2) *Parole.* Under the Criminal Justice Act 1967, s.60(1) the Home Secretary may release on licence a prisoner who has served at least a third of his sentence or 12 months,[17] whichever is the greater. Parole is, thus, only available where the original sentence is one of more than 18 months. In granting licences the Home Secretary acts on the recommendation of

---

[10] D.A. Thomas, *Principles of Sentencing* (1979) pp. 52–61, and see, *e.g. R.* v. *Taylor* [1983] Crim. L.R. 121. On the other hand some situations call for consecutive sentences as a general rule, such as offences committed while the offender is on probation or in breach of a suspended sentence or conditional discharge.

[11] *e.g. R.* v. *Smith* [1972] Crim. L.R. 124.

[12] Powers of Criminal Courts Act 1973, s.20.

[13] Which includes a suspended or partly suspended sentence, but not a suspended sentence which has never been brought into operation: Powers of Criminal Courts Act 1973, s.20(3); Criminal Law Act 1977, s.47(2B) added by Criminal Justice Act 1982, s.30.

[14] Powers of Criminal Courts Act, s.20(1). The provision is inapplicable where the sentence for the offence is fixed by law: s.20(4). Magistrates must give reasons for their opinion that no other method is appropriate: s.20(2).

[15] *Ibid.* s.20A, inserted by Criminal Justice Act 1982, s.62.

[16] *Ibid.* s.21.

[17] Criminal Justice Act 1982, s.33, confers power on the Home Secretary to reduce the twelve-month period by order. Prisoners serving extended sentences (above p. 688, n. 97) are subject to special conditions concerning release on licence: 1967 Act, s.60(3)(*a*); (5A)(*a*). For a stern criticism of the present system see N. Morgan, "The Shaping of Parole in England and Wales" [1983] Crim. L.R. 137.

the Parole Board,[18] which in turn considers reports from local review committees attached to each prison.[19]

Every year the cases of all prisoners eligible for parole are considered by the local committees.[20] The rules of "natural justice" do not apply, and the prisoner who is refused parole is not entitled to be given reasons.[21] While this may be capable of being justified on technical grounds,[21a] it has been objected that it contributes to the sense of frustration felt by prisoners whose sentences are rendered indeterminate by the annual prospect of parole.

Release on licence involves allowing the prisoner to return to the community under supervision subject to revocation of the licence and recall to prison for misconduct until such time as he would have qualified for remission. There have been a number of proposals relating to the earlier release of prisoners or automatic remission or parole in order to relieve the overcrowding of the prison population. Section 32 of the Criminal Justice Act 1982 gives the Home Secretary the power to order the release of certain classes of offenders[22] up to six months earlier than would otherwise have been possible if he considers it necessary to do so in order to make better use of the places available for detention.

(3) *Life sentences.* Prisoners serving life sentences do not qualify for remission but may be released on licence at any time by the Home Secretary on the recommendation of the Parole Board and after consultation with the Lord Chief Justice and the trial judge, if he is available.[23] The licence endures for the life of the offender and he can be recalled to prison at any time.[24]

(iii) *Suspended and partially suspended sentences*

Where a court has decided that an offender merits a prison sentence, it does not necessarily have to order that the whole of the term should be served immediately. Special powers exist whereby a prison sentence may be suspended, in whole or in part, in such a way that the offender may not

---

[18] An independent body whose members generally include psychiatrists, penologists, judges, members of the probation service and some lay members.

[19] In some cases the Home Secretary can act on the direct recommendation of the local committees under the power conferred by the Criminal Justice Act 1972, s.35.

[20] Whose members include the prison governor, a member of the Board of Visitors and a probation officer. They consider not only the offender's conduct while in prison but also, more importantly, the likelihood of his becoming a law-abiding citizen when released. See *The Sentence of the Court* (1978) p. 38.

[21] *Payne* v. *Lord Harris of Greenwich* [1981] 2 All E.R. 842.

[21a] Parole is said to be a privilege rather than a right. However, the recent decision of the Home Secretary to all but withdraw parole from offenders serving sentences of five years or more provoke some prisoners to take legal action. No final conclusion has been reached at time of writing. See *R.* v. *The Secretary of State for the Home Department, ex parte Findlay and Others, The Times,* May 23, 1984.

[22] Those serving life sentences or sentences for "excluded offences" cannot benefit. All serious crimes of violence are excluded. Criminal Justice Act 1982, Sched. 1.

[23] Criminal Justice Act 1967, s.61. The Home Secretary's deliberations will in any event take account of any minimum period of imprisonment recommended by the trial judge when passing sentence on a convicted murderer under the Murder (Abolition of Death Penalty) Act 1965, s.1(2).

[24] Similar provisions apply to prisoners serving extended sentences: Criminal Justice Act 1967, s.60(3).

go to prison at all, or may serve only part of his term, if he avoids conviction for further offences within a fixed period, known as the "operational" period, of the suspension.

The effect of suspension has understandably been likened to a "Sword of Damocles" hanging over the offender's head: he knows at the time sentence is passed what the effect of future misconduct is likely to be. In theory the power to suspend sentences ought to be a useful weapon in the armoury of sentencers. In practice its efficacy is hampered by a complicated statutory framework for its use.

(1) *Suspended sentences.*[25] Any court has power, when imposing a sentence of imprisonment of not more than two years' duration, to order its suspension for not less than one or more than two years. If the offender is convicted[26] of a further offence punishable with imprisonment during the operational period of the suspension a court having power to deal with him[27] for this breach *must* bring the suspended sentence into effect unless, having regard to the circumstances,[28] it considers that it would be unjust to do so.[29] The Court which passes the suspended sentence is under a statutory duty to make clear to the offender the consequences of committing further offences during the operational period.[30]

When the power to suspend was first introduced it found some favour with sentencers who, it appears, were happy to impose suspended sentences in cases where, in the absence of any power to suspend, an immediate sentence of imprisonment would never have been contemplated. So it was used in cases which might otherwise have been dealt with by fine, or conditional discharge. Section 22(2) of the Powers of Criminal Courts Act 1973 in theory puts paid to this option by providing that the case must be one where a sentence of imprisonment would have been called for had there been no power to suspend. Some sentencers, however, continue to advocate the use of what may be colloquially termed a "cheat" suspended sentence, and their theory might have met with more support if the pressures of the prison system had not been so great. In the present climate, however, the danger of the "cheat" suspended sentence is that the offender who commits further offences will almost inevitably be added to the prison population, a fate which would not necessarily have befallen him had, say a fine been imposed in respect of the original offence.

Another temptation which the sentencer must avoid is to compensate for the clemency of the suspension by increasing the term which may have to be served, with the result that if the term is brought into operation the

---

[25] Powers of Criminal Courts Act 1973, s.22(1).

[26] Which does not include being absolutely or conditionally discharged, or put on probation, by virtue of s.13 of the Powers of Criminal Courts Act 1973, above, p. 678, n. 12.

[27] Under the Powers of Criminal Courts Act 1973, s.24 sentences suspended by the Crown Court may not be activated by magistrates' courts, although magistrates may commit an offender to the Crown Court, or that court may take it upon itself to deal with him.

[28] Until 1983 the Court was limited to a consideration of circumstances arising since the sentence was passed. This limitation was removed by the Criminal Justice Act 1982, s.31.

[29] If the court does so consider it may bring the sentence into effect for a shorter term, extend the operational period for a limited term, or make no order. If the sentence is not activated in full the court must state its reasons: Powers of Criminal Courts Act 1973, s.23.

[30] *Ibid.* s.22(4).

offender spends longer in prison than his original offence merits.[31] A considerable number of offenders commit further offences during the operational period, so that the failure of sentencers to resist this temptation has also been identified as a factor contributing to prison overcrowding. All in all it may be said that the suspended sentence has not so far lived up to expectations despite its appeal to sentencers:

> "Indeed it has acquired perhaps a special psychological attraction to sentencers in that they can feel they are being punitive and passing a severe sentence, while at the same time allowing themselves the warmth of recognising the humanity of their leniency."[32]

(2) *Partly suspended sentences.* Section 47 of the Criminal Law Act 1977 made provision for partial suspension of sentences, but it was only in 1982 that the section was brought into force. It provides[33] that where a sentence of not less than three months or more than two years is imposed the court may order that part only be served and the remainder held in suspension.[34] The philosophy underlying the provision is the same as that expressed in cases such as *R.* v. *Bibi,*[35] to the effect that the first few weeks of prison are the most salutary part of the experience of losing one's liberty. The danger, as with the suspended sentence, is that sentencers may feel tempted to give a "taste of prison"[36] to those who would not otherwise be in any danger of hearing the clang of the prison gates. The power should only be exercised where the court has considered passing a wholly suspended sentence and decided that that course would be inappropriate.[37] It remains to see whether the "pecking order" thus established between sentences of

[31] The term suspended should be of the same length as the period of imprisonment otherwise appropriate: *R.* v. *Trowbridge* [1975] Crim. L.R. 295. Normally an activated suspended sentence should run consecutively to any sentence imposed by the court for the subsequent offence or offences: *R.* v. *Ithell* [1969] 2 All E.R. 449 (though there is power to order that it be made concurrent: Powers of Criminal Courts Act 1973, s.23(2)). The point is that the offender should not feel that he has committed two crimes "for the price of one."

[32] A.E. Bottoms. "The Suspended Sentence in England" (1981) British Journal of Criminology 2.

[33] As amended by Criminal Justice Act 1982, s.30. The original minimum period which could be split in this way was six months. The significance of the reduction is that magistrates' courts may now make use of this option.

[34] The part to be served must be not less than 28 days, and the part held in suspense must be not less than one quarter of the whole term: Powers of Criminal Courts Act 1973, s.47(2), as amended by Criminal Justice Act 1982, s.30(5). The Secretary of State has power to vary the minimum term of imprisonment which can be suspended as well as the minimum term to be served: Criminal Justice Act 1982, s.30(8).

[35] Above, p. 689. Some doubts have been expressed as to the relationship between these two new developments: see *e.g.* commentary by D.A. Thomas on *R.* v. *Morton* [1983] Crim. L.R. 49.

[36] In the House of Lords debates on the 1982 Act, several members of the House expressed concern about this. Lord Wigoder admitted that he might have been tempted so to use the power when he was a recorder (H.L. Deb. Vol. 431, cols. 4–72). In 1982, it appears that the new power was used in preference to a non-custodial sentence in some cases: *Criminal Statistics* 1982, p. 160.

[37] s.47(1A), added by the Criminal Justice Act 1982. See also *R.* v. *Clarke* [1982] Crim. L.R. 464, in which guidance was given by the Court of Appeal on the use of the new power as it existed before the 1982 Act came into force. The mental gymnastics a sentencer is supposed to perform before imposing a partly suspended sentence are, if not impossible, unrealistic.

immediate imprisonment and sentences wholly or partly suspended will be adhered to.[38]

(3) *Suspended sentence supervision orders.*[39] Where an offender has been sentenced in respect of one offence to a suspended sentence of more than six months'[40] duration he may be made the subject of a suspended sentence supervision order. The effect is similar to probation, which, it will be remembered, cannot be coupled with a prison sentence, immediate or suspended. The order may run throughout the operational period of the suspended sentence.[41] One important difference between such an order and probation is that the subject of a suspended sentence supervision order has the prospect of a fixed prison term hanging over his head if he is tempted to re-offend.[42]

(b) Young offenders

Offenders under the age of 21 may not be sent to prison.[43] Where young people have to be punished by custodial measures, they are kept separate from adult offenders wherever possible.

We have seen that the courts regard imprisonment as very much the last resort in sentencing adults. Where young offenders are concerned this attitude is reinforced by section 1(4) of the Criminal Justice Act 1982, which provides that a court must first consider the suitability of non-custodial penalties and may not resort to a custodial sentence unless:

> "It is of the opinion that no other method of dealing with [the offender] is appropriate because it appears to the court that he is unable or unwilling to respond to non-custodial penalties or because a custodial sentence is necessary for the protection of the public or because the offence was so serious that a non-custodial sentence cannot be justified."[44]

In addition, it will in most cases be a statutory requirement that a social inquiry report be considered before a young offender is deprived of his liberty. The 1982 Act also imposes an obligation on the court in most cases to give reasons for passing a custodial sentence.[45]

Thus, a fairly rigid framework for decision-making is imposed on the sentencer of the young offender, but it must be acknowledged that for the

---

[38] Note that the "pecking order" operates without prejudice to the restrictions on imprisonment generally, laid down in Powers of Criminal Courts Act 1973, s.20, (above, p. 691).

[39] Powers of Criminal Courts Act 1973, s.26. See also the Report of the Advisory Council on the Penal System on Non-Custodial and Semi-Custodial Penalties (1970).

[40] This effectively limits the order to the Crown Court, as magistrates cannot pass a sentence of more than six months duration for one offence (above, p. 686).

[41] It may be discharged before then, and will cease to have effect if the suspended sentence is activated: Powers of Criminal Courts Act 1973, s.26(8)(a).

[42] As with probation there are penalties for breach of the requirements of the order.

[43] Criminal Justice Act 1982, s.1(1).

[44] s.1(4) restricts the availability of the custodial alternatives of youth custody, detention in a detention centre, and custody for life. S.1(5) applies a similar restriction to the use of detention under s.9 of the Act (committal in default or for contempt).

[45] ss.2(4) and 6(1)(b). Oddly, the Crown Court need not give reasons for considering non-custodial measures inappropriate when passing a sentence of detention in a detention centre, though it must do so when passing a sentence of youth custody.

most part the new statutory rules echo the approach of decision-makers before the Act came into force.

Where there is no alternative to a custodial sentence the 1982 Act aims to provide a flexible structure of custodial penalties for offenders under the age of 21 years consisting in most cases[46] of determinate sentences either of youth custody or of detention in a detention centre. Youth custody sentences are normally of four months or longer,[47] and are likely to be served in what used to be Borstal training centres, or in the young person's wing of an adult prison, or a Young Prisoner's centre. Young offenders serving terms of 18 months or less will be guaranteed some form of training during their sentences, and it is hoped that training facilities will also be provided for those serving longer sentences.

Release dates are affected by remission and parole in a fashion similar to that applicable to older offenders, and release is followed by a period of supervision.[48]

Detention centres, which were in existence before the 1982 Act, continue to cater for offenders serving short custodial sentences. In these centres the accent is on intensive discipline, often referred to as the "short sharp shock" treatment. Before the Act there had been some experimenting with "sharper" shocks—centres with a more rigorous régime than is customary— and the Act[49] makes provision for "shorter" shocks by reducing the minimum period of detention from three months to just three weeks. This adjustment reflects the new thinking in relation to custodial sentences generally that the initial impact of loss of liberty is crucial and the effect may be weakened by lengthy captivity.

Some serious doubts about the detention centre régime have been expressed. It is obviously most suited to healthy youngsters who might benefit from army-type discipline, and some of the criticism has focussed on cases where unsuitable offenders were placed in the centres. The vigorous régime may also be unsatisfying to the staff who have to impose it; a state of affairs conducive to relaxation of discipline. It will be interesting to see how the "sharper shock" centres work.

---

[46] Other provisions may apply if serious offences are committed. A person found guilty of murder who was under eighteen when the crime was committed must be sentenced to be detained "during Her Majesty's Pleasure": i.e. until the Home Secretary orders his release: Children and Young Persons Act 1933, s.53(1). Sentences of detention may also be passed by the Crown Court on juveniles convicted of offences punishable in the case of adults with 14 years imprisonment or more: ibid. s.53(2). Detainees may be kept in special homes, hospitals or such other institutions as the Home Secretary thinks fit. A sentence of custody for life must be passed on a person under twenty-one convicted of murder or any other offence punishable with a fixed term of life imprisonment unless he is liable to detention under s.53(1) of the 1933 Act: Criminal Justice Act 1982, s.8(1).

[47] In some cases sentences of custody for life may be passed: 1982 Act, s.8(2). The sentence cannot exceed the maximum period of imprisonment available in the case of an offender over the age of 21: s.7(1). An upper limit of 12 months applies to offenders who are aged less than 17 years: s.7(8). Magistrates' powers to sentence to youth custody are limited in a way similar to their powers to imprison: 1982 Act Sched. 14, amending Magistrates' Courts Act 1980.

[48] 1982 Act, s.15. Despite these similarities there is no power to suspend sentences on young offenders, which is a strange omission from the sentencer's armoury.

[49] There was a recommendation to do away with the detention centre régime in favour of one sentence of youth custody, but the Government, besides being committed to the idea of the disciplined activities, considered there was no point of instituting a training programme for offenders serving such short sentences.

The choice between youth custody and detention in a detention centre is, under the 1982 Act, largely determined by the length of sentence the court considers appropriate. Sentences of less than four months will normally be served in a detention centre unless this would be inappropriate having regard to the physical or mental condition of the offender, or his past record.[50]

4. MENTALLY DISORDERED OFFENDERS[51]

A description of the sentencer's powers would be incomplete without some reference to the special measures which he may employ in dealing with mentally disordered offenders. It should be stressed at the outset, however, that these powers are supplementary to those already discussed, so that the fact that an offender is suffering from some form of mental disorder will not necessarily result in his being dealt with differently from an offender who is under no such disability.

Where the mental condition of an offender requires (and may be susceptible to) treatment, but it would not be appropriate to detain him in hospital, a court which elects to place him on probation may attach a condition requiring him to submit to psychiatric treatment[52] during the whole or part of his probation. This course may be taken even if the offender's conduct has had serious consequences, for example, has placed lives in jeopardy,[53] but any risk to the public of leaving him at large is obviously a factor which is likely to persuade a sentencer that such a solution would be inappropriate.[54]

Further control over the liberty and freedom of choice of the mentally disordered offender may be achieved by making a guardianship or hospital order under the Mental Health Act 1983.[55] Such drastic steps may only be taken where the court is satisfied that the making of the order is the most suitable method of disposing of the case.[56]

A guardianship order can be made in the case of an offender who is aged 16 or over and who has committed an offence[57] punishable with imprisonment,[58] provided he is suffering from one of the kinds of mental

---

[50] Criminal Justice Act 1982, s.4(5). In such cases a short term of youth custody may be appropriate: ss.6(2), 7(6). Similar provisions relate to female offenders who have attained the age of 17: s.7(6), 6(4).

[51] See generally the Report of the Committee on Mentally Abnormal Offenders (the Butler Committee) Cmnd. 6244, B. Hoggett, *Mental Health* (1976); L.O. Gostin, *A Human Condition*, vol. 2, (1977).

[52] Powers of Criminal Courts Act 1973, s.3. The court must be satisfied on the evidence of a duly qualified medical practitioner that the conditions for making the requirement are fulfilled. The court may not specify the nature of the treatment, though it does stipulate, *e.g.* whether the offender is to be an in-patient or out-patient, *ibid.* s.3(2).

[53] *R.* v. *Hoof* (1980) 2 Cr.App.R. (S) 299 (arson).

[54] D.A. Thomas, *Current Sentencing Practice*, para. F1.2(b).

[55] s.57.

[56] Having regard to all the circumstances including the character and antecedents of the offender, and other available methods of disposal: 1983 Act, s.37(2)(*b*). In some cases an offender can be remanded in hospital for reports on his mental condition: s.35. S.35 is not in force at time of writing, but is expected to be implemented shortly.

[57] Other than murder.

[58] s.37(1).

disorder specified in the Act[59] and the nature or degree of that disorder warrants his reception into guardianship.[60] The guardian[61] acquires certain powers[62] including the power to direct where the offender is to reside and attend for treatment, and to supervise his education or training.

Alternatively, if the court considers a hospital order to be appropriate, an offender of any age who has committed an offence punishable with imprisonment[63] may be committed for treatment to a specified hospital.[64] As with a guardianship order the offender must be shown to be suffering from one of the types of disorder specified in the Act, and in some cases his condition must be treatable.[65] Once in hospital the offender is in much the same position as a patient who has not committed any offence. His case will be reviewed periodically and he will be released when he is considered to be fit to return to the community.

In some serious cases the Crown Court may add a restriction order when making a hospital order.[66] This is done where, in order to protect the public from serious harm[67] it is necessary to prevent the release of the offender through normal channels.[68] Until recently a patient subject to a restricted order could be released only with the consent of the Home Secretary,[69] but a recent decision of the European Court of Human Rights[70] has necessitated the addition of a power of release by a Mental Health Review Tribunal.[71]

D. CONCLUSIONS

The natural reaction of a student bringing a fresh mind to bear on the law relating to sentencing might well be one of shock, both at the number of methods of disposal and at the complexity attaching to the exercise of some of them. An understandable reaction would be to wonder whether the sentencing system had got out of hand. It may be that the time has come for some simplification. Over the last few decades there has been a sharp increase in new methods of disposal which now exist side by side with the "old favourites." Yet there is little real evidence of the efficacy of the different measures.[72] Perhaps interest has been concentrated on the wrong

---

[59] Mental impairment, severe mental impairment, psychopathic disorder and mental illness: s.2(2), the first three are defined by the Act.

[60] s.37(2)(a)(ii).

[61] Who is normally the local social services authority or a relative.

[62] Under previous legislation the guardian acquired the powers normally enjoyed by a parent of a child. The decision to specify particular powers is welcome.

[63] Other than murder.

[64] 1983 Act, s.37(4). The court must be satisfied that arrangements have been made for the offender's admission.

[65] In the case of psychopathic disorder or mental impairment: s.37(2)(a)(i).

[66] s.41.

[67] s.41(1).

[68] The order can be made with or without limit of time; only in exceptional circumstances should a time limit be imposed: R. v. Gardiner (1967) 51 Cr.App.R. 187.

[69] See Mental Health Act 1959, s.65.

[70] X. v. United Kingdom, November 5, 1981 and see L.O. Gostin, "Human Rights, Judicial Review and the Mentally Disordered Offender" [1982] Crim. L.R. 779.

[71] s.70.

[72] For an interesting study which includes a review of the difficulties of methodology see S.R. Brody, "The Effectiveness of Sentencing," Home Office Research Study no. 35 (1976).

priorities, and experimentation has taken place without knowing enough about the real nature of the problems which need to be solved. In the early nineteenth century it was said:

"Penal legislation hitherto has resembled what the science of physic must have been when physicians did not know the properties and effects of the medicines they administered."[73]

In many ways we have not advanced far enough since those words were written to have cause for self-congratulation. Some recent trends, such as the move towards shorter prison sentences, are prompted more by the needs of the system than of the offender; in that case, the need to relieve prison overcrowding. Maybe we have done the right thing for the wrong reasons.[74] It is high time we understood more of the right reasons, and substituted a basis of understanding of the "effects of the medicines" which are administered for the sometimes unfounded hopes which may accompany the introduction of change at present.

---

[73] Romilly, quoted by the writers of the Advisory Council on the Penal System's Report on Maximum Penalties of Imprisonment (1978). The Advisory Council itself has ceased to function; its resurrection would be a step in the right direction.

[74] By the same token sometimes the wrong thing is done for the right reasons. The need for research before charge is stressed by A. Ashworth, *Sentencing and Penal Policy* (1983).

CHAPTER 19

APPEALS AND JUDICIAL REVIEW

A. INTRODUCTION

In this chapter we consider the various mechanisms for correcting errors in, and otherwise reviewing, the decisions of courts and tribunals. There are two basic kinds of legal procedure that are available for these purposes. An *appeal* may be provided by statute: indeed it will only be available if a statute has so provided, as the common law does not recognise any rights of appeal as such. The common law has provided only for the *review* of decisions either on the ground that the body which made the decision had no jurisdiction in the matter, or on the ground that the formal record of proceedings revealed that there had been some error of law. Where the body was an inferior body of limited jurisdiction, the appropriate remedy was a writ of certiorari to remove the proceedings into the Court of King's Bench: if the decision was shown to be defective it would be quashed. If such a body was proposing to act outside the jurisdiction in the future, a writ of prohibition would lie to prevent it from so acting; if it failed to perform a duty, the appropriate remedy was a writ of mandamus. These "prerogative" remedies would be available to challenge, for example, the decisions of justices of the peace in summary criminal proceedings or in civil cases. Where, however, the decision was that of one of the superior courts, or followed a criminal trial on indictment at the assizes or quarter sessions, the remedy was a writ of error, closely analogous to certiorari.[1] There were also informal devices whereby matters could be adjourned so that the views of other judges could be obtained[2] and special procedures for the review of decisions in the Court of Chancery.[3]

In the nineteenth and early twentieth centuries, writs of error were replaced by statutory appeals. The prerogative writs continued to be available in respect of the courts of summary jurisdiction, but now in parallel to statutory appeals. They were also increasingly used to correct the decisions of local authorities, government departments and statutory tribunals. In 1938 they became prerogative "orders" rather than writs,[4] and in 1978 they came to be exclusively available on a new procedure termed an "application for judicial review."[5]

Apart from these basic options there are various other avenues for the redress of grievances, some of which are enshrined in statute (*e.g.* references by the Home Secretary to the Court of Appeal (Criminal Division)), some dependent on an exercise of the royal prerogative (*e.g.* the prerogative of mercy) and some informal.

---

[1] See above, p. 7.
[2] See above, p. 7.
[3] See above, p. 4.
[4] Administration of Justice (Miscellaneous Provisions) Act 1938, s.7.
[5] See below, pp. 742–749.

There are two basic functions fulfilled by mechanisms for appeal or review. The first is that of the correction of errors of fact, substantive law or procedure made by the court or tribunal below. The second is that of the harmonious development of the law. Appellate courts commonly comprise a number of judges whereas trial courts and tribunals normally have a single judge or legally qualified chairman, sitting alone or with a jury or lay members. Appellate judges tend to be of greater experience and seniority than trial judges and their case load tends to be smaller, giving greater time for consideration; these factors become more pronounced the higher one moves up the courts hierarchy. In limited circumstances fresh evidence may be admitted before the reviewing court. Appellate courts may also correct divergences of approach among different courts of first instance.[6]

B. VARIABLE FACTORS IN APPEAL AND REVIEW MECHANISMS

There are a number of factors which must be taken into account when considering any legal procedure for redressing a grievance:
   (1) Who can institute an appeal?[7]
   (2) Can the appeal be brought as of right or only by the leave of a court or other body?
   (3) What are the permissible grounds for an appeal?
   (4) What is the time limit within which an appeal must be brought?
   (5) To which court or tribunal does the appeal lie?
   (6) What material may the appellate body consider?
   (7) Who may appear as parties on the appeal?
   (8) What are the powers of the appellate court?

C. APPEALS

In this section we consider appeals from courts and tribunals.[8] We concentrate on appeals in basic civil and criminal cases: in addition a vast number of rights of appeal have been created in special cases which cannot be covered in detail.[9] The appeals are presented in four groups:
   (1) Summary criminal proceedings and civil proceedings originating in magistrates' courts;
   (2) Criminal proceedings on indictment;
   (3) Civil cases originating in a county court or the High Court;
   (4) Appeals in administrative law matters.
   The basic principles governing rights of appeal from a court seem to be that: (1) there should be one chance to appeal on the facts or merits and a series of opportunities to take points of law up the hierarchy of the courts; (2) there should be one chance to appeal as of right, with further appeals being dependent upon obtaining leave; and (3) that an acquittal by a jury in a criminal case should be regarded as final. Appeals from tribunals or public authorities tend to be limited to points of law.

---

[6] *e.g.* the Court of Appeal in *Froom* v. *Butcher* [1976] Q.B.286 settled the difference between judges who held that failure to wear a seat belt in a car would normally constitute contributory negligence and those who did not: the former approach was approved.

[7] For convenience this is to be taken here to include "seek review."

[8] As to the constitution and functions of appellate courts, see Chap. 2.

[9] A full list may be found in D. Price, *Appeals* (1982).

1. APPEALS FROM MAGISTRATES' COURTS

A person aggrieved by a decision of a magistrates' court in a criminal case, or in certain civil cases, has the option of (1) appealing on fact or law to the Crown Court or (2) appealing on a point of law alone direct to the High Court, by way of "case stated." If the first option is chosen, an appeal lies thereafter to the High Court as in (2). In domestic cases, the appeal lies only to the High Court.

Once a case reaches the High Court, further appeals in criminal cases lie only to the House of Lords, and further appeals in civil cases lie on the same basis as in other civil cases determined by the High Court. In a criminal case, where the magistrates commit a convicted person to the Crown Court for sentence, the appeal thereafter lies to the Court of Appeal (Criminal Division).[10]

(a) Appeals from magistrates' courts to the Crown Court

The defendant in a criminal case may appeal to the Crown Court, as of right, (a) if he pleaded guilty,[11] against his sentence; or (b) if he did not plead guilty, against the conviction or sentence.[12] "Sentence" includes any order made on conviction other than an order for costs and certain other orders.[13] Similarly, a person may appeal against an order for contempt of a magistrates' court[14] or an order binding him over to keep the peace or to be of good behaviour.[15] The prosecutor or complainant may not appeal against an acquittal or a refusal to make an order.[16]

Notice of appeal must be given within 21 days after the day on which the decision or sentence appealed against was given.[17] The notice must state the grounds for appeal. The Crown Court may extend the time for giving notice of appeal either before or after it expires.[18]

The appeal is treated as a complete rehearing,[19] and the procedure is exactly the same as at a summary trial in the magistrates' court. For

---

[10] Criminal Appeal Act 1968, s.10 : see below, p. 715.

[11] If the plea of guilty was "equivocal" the defendant may appeal to the Crown Court to set aside the conviction and remit the case to the magistrates with a direction to enter a plea of "not guilty" and try the case summarily. A plea is equivocal where something emerges during the trial which throws doubt on it, e.g. "guilty, but I took it by mistake." See R. v. Durham Quarter Sessions, ex p. Virgo [1952] 2 Q.B. 1. The Crown Court should seek affidavit evidence from the chairman of the bench or the clerk before sending it back: R. v. Rochdale JJ., ex p. Allwork [1981] 3 All E.R.433. The Crown Court may also remit a case where it subsequently transpires that a plea of guilty was made under duress : R. v. Huntingdon Crown Court, ex p. Jordan [1981] Q.B. 857.

[12] Magistrates' Courts Act 1980, s.108(1).

[13] Ibid. s.108(3). Probation orders and orders for conditional discharge were formerly excluded : see now the Criminal Justice Act 1982, s.66(2).

[14] Contempt of Court Act 1981, s.12(5).

[15] Magistrates' Courts (Appeals from Binding Over Orders) Act 1956, s.1.

[16] Such a right may be expressly conferred, e.g. the Customs and Excise Management Act 1979, s.147 : offences under the Customs and Excise Acts.

[17] Crown Court Rules 1982 (S.I. 1982 No. 1109), r.7.

[18] Ibid.

[19] See Drover v. Rugman [1951] 1 K.B. 380; Northern Ireland Trailers v. Preston Corporation [1972] 1 W.L.R. 203 : these cases show that the court must, however, consider the state of affairs existing at the time the order was appealed against. Appeals against binding-over orders are to be conducted as a rehearing: Shaw v. Hamilton [1982] 1 W.L.R. 1308.

example, the relevant witnesses will attend the court and give evidence as at the original trial. The parties are not, however, confined to the evidence placed before the magistrates. Where the appeal is against sentence only, it is usual for the prosecution merely to put forward facts which had been admitted or found by the magistrates, although there is no technical reason why sworn evidence should not be given.[20]

The powers of the Crown Court are as follows.[21] It may correct any error or mistake in the order or judgment against which the appeal is brought, and at the end of the hearing may:

(a) confirm, reverse or vary the decision appealed against;
(b) remit the matter with its opinion thereon to the authority whose decision is appealed against; or
(c) make any order in the matter as it thinks just and exercise any power which that authority might have exercised.

These powers are subject to any limit or restriction imposed by any other enactment. A punishment in a criminal case may be more or less severe than that awarded by the magistrates' court, provided that it could have been imposed by that court.

In civil matters, appeals lie to the Crown Court in respect of the making or refusal of an affiliation order,[22] care orders[23] and a variety of licensing matters.[24]

(b) Appeals from magistrates' courts to the High Court by "case stated"

Any person who was party[25] to any proceedings before a magistrates' court or who is "aggrieved"[26] by its decision may question the decision on the ground that it is wrong in law or in excess of jurisdiction by applying to the justices for them to state a case for the opinion of the High Court.[27] An application may not be made following committal proceedings,[28] or where there is otherwise a right of appeal to the High Court or where the decision is said by an enactment to be "final."[29] The application must be made within 21 days, and any right to appeal to the Crown Court is lost when this is done.[30] The justices may refuse to state a case if they are of opinion that

---

[20] *Paprika Ltd.* v. *Board of Trade* [1944] K.B.327; *Shaw* v. *Hamilton* [1982] 1 W.L.R. 1308.

[21] Supreme Court Act 1981, s.48.

[22] Affiliation Proceedings Act 1957, s.8.

[23] See the Children and Young Persons Act 1969, ss.2(12), 3(8), 16(8), 21(4). Under s.2(12) an appeal to the Crown Court can be made by the infant's parents : *B.* v. *Gloucestershire County Council* [1980] 2 All E.R. 746; and this is so even where the child has been independently represented in the magistrates' court: *Southwark L.B.C.* v. *C. (A minor)* [1982] 1 W.L.R. 826.

[24] See, *e.g.* Licensing Act 1964, ss.21, 50, 81B, 146, 154.

[25] *e.g.* defendant *or prosecutor* in a criminal case : *R.* v. *Newport (Salop) JJ. ex p. Wright* [1929] 2 K.B. 416.

[26] This covers a person who is not a party but whose legal rights are affected by the decision: *Drapers Company* v. *Hodder* (1892) 57 J.P. 200, *e.g.* the owner of stolen goods who seeks a restitution order.

[27] Magistrates' Courts Act 1980, s.111(1).

[28] *Atkinson* v. *United States Government* [1971] A.C. 197.

[29] 1980 Act, s.111(1).

[30] *Ibid.* s.111(4). An appeal by case stated against conviction will not debar an appeal to the Crown Court against sentence, and vice versa: an appeal by case stated on both matters debars the appeal to Crown Court completely: *R.* v. *Winchester Crown Court, ex p. Lewington* [1982] 1 W.L.R. 1277.

the application is "frivolous,"[31] but may not do so where the application is made by or under the direction of the Attorney-General. If they do exercise their power to refuse, the applicant may seek an order of mandamus from the High Court to compel them to state a case, and the High Court has a discretion whether to make an order.

The procedure for stating a case is regulated by the Magistrates' Courts Rules 1981.[32] The application is made to the clerk to the justices. Unless the application is refused, a draft case must be sent to the parties, and it may be amended by the justices in the light of any representations received. The case must state the facts found and the questions of law or jurisdiction on which guidance is sought. It must specify any finding of fact which is claimed to be unsupported by evidence, but it may not otherwise contain a statement of evidence. In practice it is normally prepared by the clerk.

In criminal cases the appeal is heard by a Divisional Court of the Queen's Bench Division; otherwise, it is normally heard by a single judge. Where the appeal relates to affiliation or care proceedings, or the enforcement of a maintenance order, the appeal lies to the Family Division.[33] The appellant must lodge the case in the Crown Office or the Principal Registry of the Family Division within 10 days of receiving it, and must serve a copy on the respondent within four days of so lodging it. The High Court may return the case for amendment.[34]

On an appeal, the High Court may reverse, affirm or amend the decision or remit it to the justices for their reconsideration in the light of the court's opinion, or make such other order as the court thinks fit.[35] Apart from the obvious power to correct errors of law, such as the misinterpretation of a statute, the court will treat any decision unsupported by the evidence, or otherwise one which no reasonable magistrates could reach, as erroneous in law.[36] The court may take the view that in the light of its ruling on the law the defendant is clearly guilty or clearly innocent, in which event it will direct the magistrates to convict or acquit as the case may be. Otherwise the matter will be left to the magistrates.

(c) Appeals from magistrates' courts to the High Court in domestic cases

In certain domestic matters an appeal lies to a Divisional Court of the Family Division. These include the making or refusal of orders under the Domestic Proceedings and Magistrates' Courts Act 1978,[37] guardianship orders, adoption orders and variations of maintenance orders. The appeal can raise matters of fact or law and is not by case stated. A notice of appeal must be served and the appeal entered within six weeks of the decision challenged.[38] The court may receive further evidence, draw its own

---

[31] This term includes cases where the argument on the point of law cannot succeed, e.g. where the law has been authoritatively stated in a superior court.

[32] S.I. 1981 No. 552, as amended, rr. 76–81.

[33] R.S.C., Ord. 56, rr.4A, 5. An appeal is normally heard by a single judge unless the court directs that it should be heard by a Divisional Court.

[34] Summary Jurisdiction Act 1857, s.7.

[35] Ibid. s.6, as amended.

[36] Bracegirdle v. Oxley [1947] 1 K.B. 349. This is significantly narrower than the appeal on the merits to the Crown Court: see section (a) above.

[37] Other than interim maintenance orders, against which no appeal lies. Appeals as to the enforcement of maintenance orders lie by case stated : see section (b), above.

[38] R.S.C., Ord. 55, r.4(2) applied by Ord. 90, r.16 (2) and Ord. 109.

inferences of fact and may make any order that the magistrates might have made and any other order that the case might require, or may remit the matter with its opinion for rehearing by the magistrates.[39]

(d) Appeals from the Crown Court to the High Court

Where there has been an appeal from a magistrates' court to the Crown Court, any party to the proceedings[40] may appeal by case stated on a point of law or jurisdiction to the High Court.[41] The procedure is similar to that for such appeals from the magistrates' court direct to the High Court.[42] The same right of appeal is available in respect of any other decision of the Crown Court[43] except one relating to trial on indictment and in certain licensing matters.[44]

(e) Appeals from the High Court to the House of Lords

In civil cases which have reached the High Court on appeal, further appeals lie on the same bases as in other civil matters determined by the High Court.[45] Until 1960 there was, however, no further right of appeal in a criminal case, and the Divisional Court of the Queen's Bench Division was the final authority on many matters concerning summary offences.[46] Under the Administration of Justice Act 1960[47] either the prosecutor or the defendant may appeal to the House of Lords on a point of law of public general importance. Leave must be obtained from either the Divisional Court or the House of Lords: the Divisional Court must certify that a point of law of general public importance is involved,[48] and it must appear either to that court or to the House of Lords[49] that the point ought to be considered by the House. On the appeal, the House may exercise any of the powers of the Divisional Court or may remit the case to it.

2. APPEALS FOLLOWING TRIAL ON INDICTMENT

(a) Appeals from the Crown Court to the Court of Appeal (Criminal Division)

An acquittal by a jury in a criminal case is regarded as sacrosanct: the prosecutor has no right of appeal however perverse the verdict of the

[39] R.S.C., Ord. 55, r.7.

[40] *i.e.* in a criminal case, either prosecutor or defendant.

[41] Supreme Court Act 1981, s.28.

[42] Crown Court Rules 1982, (S.I. 1982 No. 1109), r.26, and *cf.* above pp. 703–704.

[43] *e.g.* matters such as firearms licensing where an appeal lies direct to the Crown Court : see P.J. Clarke and J.W. Ellis, *The Law Relating to Firearms* (1981) pp. 104–111; *Kavanagh* v. *Chief Constable of Devon and Cornwall* [1974] Q.B. 624.

[44] Supreme Court Act 1981, s.28(2). As to appeals in relation to trials on indictment, see below, pp. 705–719, and on the relationship between appeals by case stated and applications for judicial review, see below, pp. 748–749.

[45] See below, pp. 723–734.

[46] For example, there was no right to appeal against the unsatisfactory decisions in *Thomas* v. *Sawkins* [1935] 2 K.B. 249 and *Duncan* v. *Jones* [1936] K.B. 218: see S.H. Bailey, D.J. Harris and B.L. Jones, *Civil Liberties : Cases and Materials* (1980) pp. 64–68, 172–175.

[47] ss.1–9.

[48] There is no right to appeal against the refusal of a certificate : *Gelberg* v. *Miller* [1961] 1 All E.R. 618n, H.L.

[49] The application for leave is made first to the Divisional Court and only if that court refuses to the House of Lords.

jury.[50] However, persons convicted[51] of an offence on indictment may appeal to the Court of Appeal (Criminal Division).[52]

(i) *Appeals against conviction*

(1) *Grounds and procedure.* The person convicted may appeal as of right on any ground which involves a question of law alone.[53] Where a ground is one of fact alone or of mixed law and fact he may only appeal if he obtains either (a) a certificate from the trial judge that the case is fit for appeal or (b) leave of the Court of Appeal (Criminal Division). In addition, the Court of Appeal may grant leave "on any other ground which appears . . . to be a sufficient ground of appeal."[54]

Where a point of law alone is involved the appellant or his legal advisers must serve a notice of appeal on the Registrar of Criminal Appeals within 28 days of the conviction.[55] The notice must contain the grounds of appeal.[56] If it appears to the registrar that it does not show any substantial ground he may refer the appeal to the court for summary determination, and the court, if it considers the appeal to be frivolous[57] or vexatious may dismiss the appeal summarily.[58]

In other cases, the appellant must either serve the trial judge's certificate on the registrar with his notice of appeal, or serve notice of application for leave to appeal. The notice must be served within 28 days of conviction and the grounds of the appeal or application stated. The grounds of an appeal or application may be varied or amplified within such time as the court may allow.[59] The appellant may apply for bail,[60] and be present at the hearing.[61]

The defendant at the trial should be seen by his solicitor and counsel in the event of conviction or sentence and advised on whether there appear to be reasonable grounds for an appeal.[62]

---

[50] The Attorney-General may refer cases where there has been an acquittal to the Court of Appeal (Criminal Division), but not so as to affect the defendant : see below, p. 717. It is proposed that a prosecutor should be given the right to appeal against sentence.

[51] This includes a person who pleaded guilty; *R.* v. *Lee* (*Bruce*) [1984] 1 W.L.R. 578.

[52] See above, p. 78; Criminal Appeal Act 1968; Criminal Appeal Rules 1968 (S.I. 1968 No. 1262) (hereafter "C.A.R."); *Guide to Proceedings in the Court of Appeal Criminal Division* [1983] Crim.L.R. 415; (1983) 77 Cr.App.R.138.

[53] 1968 Act, s.1(2)(*a*). See A.W. Barsby [1982] Crim.L.R.642.

[54] *Ibid.* s.1(2)(*b*).

[55] *Ibid.* s.18(1). The time limit may be extended by the court: *ibid.* s.18(2).

[56] C.A.R. 1968, r.2(*a*).

[57] *e.g.* the ground of appeal could not possibily succeed on argument: *R.* v. *Taylor* [1979] Crim. L.R. 649.

[58] Criminal Appeal Act 1968, s.20.

[59] C.A.R. 1968 r.2(2)(*c*). This may be after the 28–day period.

[60] Bail may be granted by the Crown Court (Supreme Court Act 1981, s.81(1)(*f*) and (1A) to (1G), inserted by the Criminal Justice Act 1982, s.29(1)) or the Court of Appeal (Criminal Division) (Criminal Appeal Act 1968, s.19, as substituted by the 1982 Act, s.29(2)(*b*)).

[61] *Ibid.* s.22. He is entitled to be present except in four cases where the leave of the court is necessary : (1) the appeal is on a point of law alone; (2) for an application for leave to appeal; (3) for an ancillary application; (4) where he is in custody after a verdict of not guilty by reason of insanity or of a finding of disability.

[62] This, and work in preparing an application for leave or a notice of appeal, are covered by a trial legal aid order : Legal Aid Act 1974, s.30(7). In 1972, Michael Zander published research which showed, *inter alia,* that in at least 10 per cent. of the cases surveyed the lawyers had failed to comply with their statutory duty to advise; that in at least a quarter of the cases where they had advised an appeal, they had failed to draft the grounds of appeal; and that in a

Applications for leave to appeal are normally dealt with by a single judge who examines the papers and may grant leave, refuse it, or refer the case to the court. If he refuses leave an application may be renewed to the court within 14 days. The court will hold a hearing, which may be combined with the hearing of the appeal on the merits. Legal aid may be granted for further advice and assistance and for representation before the single judge or the court.[63] The single judge and the court have power, when refusing an application for leave to appeal, to direct that part of the time during which a person has been in custody after lodging his application should not count towards sentence.[64] In both 1970 and 1980 the then Lord Chief Justice issued a reminder of the existence of this power in view of the delay caused to the hearing of meritorious appeals by the lodging of huge numbers of hopeless applications.[65] In the two years after 1970 the number of applications for leave to appeal was cut by a half, although the problem subsequently recurred. In the 1980 Direction, it was stated a direction for loss of time "will normally be made unless the grounds are not only settled and signed by counsel, but also supported by the written opinion of counsel." Counsel should only so act where he considers that the proposed appeal is properly arguable. Moreover, a direction will also normally be made where an application is renewed to the court after the single judge has refused it as wholly devoid of merit: here, whether or not the grounds have been settled and signed by counsel.

The administrative tasks in relation to appeals are performed by the Criminal Appeal Office, headed by the Registrar of Criminal Appeals. The documents in the case, including, if appropriate, a transcript, are assembled by the office.[66] If leave is granted, a lawyer on the staff of the office then prepares a descriptive "summary" of the facts and grounds of appeal to assist the full court.

(2) *Evidence.* The court, under section 23(1) and (3) of the Criminal Appeal Act 1968, *may* "if they think it necessary or expedient in the interests of justice":(1) order the production of any document, exhibit or other thing connected with the proceedings; (2) order the examination of any witness who would have been a compellable witness at the trial, whether or not he was called; and (3) hear evidence from a non-compellable witness.

Without prejudice to these powers, the court by virtue of section 23(2) of the 1968 Act, *must* receive any evidence if:

"(*a*) it appears to them that the evidence is likely to be credible[67] and

---

majority of cases they had not seen the client immediately after conviction: [1972] Crim.L.R. 132. The procedures were accordingly clarified and improved: *Practice Note* [1974] 2 All E.R. 805; see M. Zander [1975] Crim. L.R. 364. See now the *Guide to Proceedings in the Court of Appeal Criminal Division* [1983] Crim.L.R. 415, (1983) 77 Cr.App. R. 138.

[63] Legal Aid Act, 1974 ss.28(3), 30(8).

[64] Criminal Appeal Act 1968, s.29(1).

[65] Lord Parker C.J.: (1970) 54 Cr. App. R. 280; Lord Widgery C.J.: (1980) 70 Cr. App. R. 186.

[66] Criminal Appeal Act 1968, s.32; C.A.R., rr.18–20. The Registrar may determine that only a "short transcript" is necessary, covering charges, pleas, summing-up and evidence after verdict. The appellant here may obtain a full transcript at his own expense. In practice, a transcript of evidence is rarely needed: *R.* v. *Campbell, The Times,* July 21, 1981.

[67] This has been interpreted to mean "evidence well capable of belief": *per* Edmund Davies L.J. in *R.* v. *Stafford and Luvaglio* (1968) 53 Cr.App.R. 1, 3.

would have been admissible in the proceedings from which the appeal lies on an issue which is the subject of the appeal[68]; and

(b) they are satisfied that it was not adduced at the trial but there is a reasonable explanation of the failure to adduce it."[69]

The court can only refuse to receive such evidence if it is satisfied that it would not afford any ground for allowing the appeal. This *duty* to receive evidence in the circumstances stated was first introduced by the Criminal Appeal Act 1966: the conditions stated are similar to those on which the *discretion* to receive fresh evidence, which dates back to the Criminal Appeal Act 1907, was exercised in pre-1966 cases.[70] The discretion under section 23(1) must now logically be available in a wider range of circumstances than those specified in section 23(2). However in *Stafford and Luvaglio* Edmund Davies L.J. stated that notwithstanding this development:

> "Public mischief would ensue and legal process could become indefinitely prolonged were it the case that evidence produced at any time will generally be admitted by this Court when verdicts are being reviewed. There must be some curbs, the section specifies them. . . . "[71]

Subsequently, the Court of Appeal (Criminal Division) emphasised in *R.* v. *Lattimore and others*[72] that this did not mean that the conditions limiting the duty of section 23(2) were to be read as limiting the discretion under section 23(1).[73] This case arose out of the killing of Maxwell Confait, which was shortly followed by a fire at the house where he lived. Two youths were convicted of killing him (one for murder, one manslaughter) and those two and another were convicted of arson, solely on the basis of their own confessions. Three years later the Home Secretary referred the cases to the Court of Appeal (Criminal Division).[74] The court, acting under section 23(1), received the evidence of three expert witnesses who had given evidence at the trial (two fire experts and a pathologist) and two further medical witnesses who gave evidence as to the time of death. However, they refused to admit evidence of persons who sought to throw light on the killer's identity, as they doubted its credibility and admissibility and in any event did not need to rely upon it. In addition the Crown was permitted to call a fire expert and a forensic pathologist who had given evidence at the trial. The court held that this evidence showed that the

---

[68] *i.e.* the issue must have been raised first at the trial : *R.* v. *Melville* [1976] 1 W.L.R. 181.

[69] *Ibid.* s.23(2). Under (b) the test is whether evidence could with "reasonable diligence" have been obtained for use at the trial: *R.* v. *Beresford* (1971) 56 Cr. App. R. 143: B had failed to mention his presence at the "Poco a Poco Club" until he sought leave to introduce an alibi witness on the appeal. The court held that he had not used reasonable diligence and in any event disbelieved the witness.

[70] *R.* v. *Parks* [1961] 1 W.L.R. 1484. The pre–1964 position was narrower than s.23(2) in that evidence available at the date of trial but not introduced was not normally admitted on an appeal, even where there was a reasonable explanation. There was some relaxation between 1964 and 1966: see M. Knight, *Criminal Appeals* (1970) pp. 93–96, 115–118.

[71] (1968) 53 Cr. App. R. 1, 3. The court declined to hear evidence from any additional witnesses.

[72] (1975) 62 Cr. App. R. 53.

[73] *Ibid.* p. 56.

[74] See below, p. 716.

lapse of time between the killing and the fire was much greater than had originally been thought and it threw sufficient doubt on the confessions for the homicide and arson convictions to be quashed. Scarman L.J. stated that the medical evidence was presented to the Court of Appeal "in a much sharper focus than it was at the trial."[75] In other cases fresh evidence has been admitted where another person confesses to the crime for which the appellant was convicted,[76] where prosecution witnesses subsequently make statements inconsistent with their testimony[77] and where it is claimed that there was an irregularity at the trial.[78] Exceptionally, fresh evidence may be admitted following an unequivocal plea of guilty.[78a]

(3) *Disposition.* There are a number of ways in which the Court of Appeal may dispose of an appeal. The key section is section 2 of the Criminal Appeal Act 1968:

"2(1) Except as provided by this Act, the Court of Appeal shall allow an appeal against conviction if they think—
(a) that the verdict of the jury should be set aside on the ground that under the circumstances of the case it is unsafe or unsatisfactory; or
(b) that the judgment of the court of trial should be set aside on the ground of a wrong decision of any question of law; or
(c) that there was a material irregularity in the course of the trial,
and in any other case shall dismiss the appeal:

Provided that the Court may, notwithstanding that they are of the opinion that the point raised in the appeal might be decided in favour of the appellant, dismiss the appeal if they consider that no miscarriage of justice has actually occurred.

(2) In the case of an appeal against conviction the Court shall, if they allow the appeal, quash the conviction."

These grounds for intervention are somewhat wider than those that were open to the Court of Criminal Appeal under the Criminal Appeal Act 1907.[79]

Verdicts have been set aside as unsafe and unsatisfactory where, for example, there has been a misdirection as to the ingredients of the offence charged or the burden of proof, the judge has improperly withdrawn an issue from the jury or failed to put a line of defence to them, or evidence was wrongfully admitted or excluded. Decisions on some of these points

---

[75] *Ibid.* p. 60. The events were subsequently the subject of an Inquiry by Sir Henry Fisher : 1977–78 H.C. 90, which concluded that "on a balance of probabilities" all three were involved in the arson and that two (excluding one of the two originally convicted for it) were involved in the killing. The report made a number of recommendations concerning the interrogation process and other aspects of the case. See further above, p. 503.

[76] *R.* v. *Ditch* (1969) 53 Cr. App. R. 627.

[77] *R.* v. *Conway* (1979) 70 Cr. App. R. 4.

[78] *R.* v. *Leggett and others* (1969) 53 Cr. App.51: interruptions by the Chairman of Quarter Sessions (*e.g.* when it appeared that an address by counsel to the jury would be protracted "he observed in a loud voice, 'Oh, God,' and then laid his head across his arm and made groaning noises" : p. 56). Appeal dismissed.

[78a] *R.* v. *Lee* (*Bruce*) [1984] 1 W.L.R. 578; *R.* v. *Foster, The Times*, March 31, 1984.

[79] The court could allow an appeal if they thought that the verdict was unreasonable, or could not be supported by the evidence or otherwise there was an error of law or a miscarriage of justice. The wider grounds were first enacted in the Criminal Appeal Act 1966.

may also amount to a wrong decision on a point of law under section
2(1)(*b*). The "material irregularity" ground in section 2(1)(*c*) was designed
to cover procedural irregularities,[80] although other defects are sometimes
so described. Under this head the Court of Appeal may interfere with an
exercise of discretion[81] by the judge where he has "erred in principle or
there is no material on which he could properly have arrived at his
decision."[82]

The approach to section 2(1)(*a*) was described as follows by Widgery
L.J. in *R*. v. *Cooper*:[83]

> "[I]n cases of this kind the court must in the end ask itself a subjective
> question, whether we are content to let the matter stand as it is, or
> whether there is not some lurking doubt in our minds which makes us
> wonder whether an injustice has been done. This is a reaction which
> may not be based strictly on the evidence as such; it is a reaction which
> can be produced by the general feel of the case as the court
> experiences it."

Indeed, a conviction may be quashed as unsafe and unsatisfactory where
the specific grounds of appeal are rejected.[84]

Where fresh evidence is admitted, the question for the court is still
whether, in the light of the evidence overall, the verdict is unsafe and
unsatisfactory.[85] This point was made by the House of Lords in *Stafford* v.
D.P.P.[86] After referring to the concept of the "lurking doubt" mentioned
in *R*. v. *Cooper*[87] Viscount Dilhorne continued, "That this is the effect of
section 2(1)(*a*) is not to be doubted,"[88] although he also emphasised that
the Court of Appeal should not place any fetter or restriction on its power
under section 2. The court was not bound to ask in a case where new
evidence was admitted whether that evidence "might . . . have led to the
jury returning a verdict of not guilty?": if *it* was satisfied that there was no
reasonable doubt about the guilt of the accused the conviction should not
be quashed even though the jury might have come to a different view.

This approach to "fresh evidence" cases has been roundly criticised by
Lord Devlin[89] on the basis that it is wrong in principle for judges rather
than juries to determine whether the appellant is guilty: the proper course
of action where the fresh evidence *could* have made a difference to the
verdict[90] would be for the court to order a new trial.[91] The first verdict

[80] *Per* Lord Salmon in *D.P.P.* v. *Shannon* [1975] A.C. 717, 773.
[81] *e.g.* to sever counts in an indictment, to permit cross-examination of a defendant on his
previous convictions or to discharge a jury.
[82] Devlin J. in *R*. v. *Cook* (1959) 43 Cr.App. R. 138, 147.
[83] [1969] 1 Q.B. 267, 271. The case was one of alleged mistaken identification and another
man of similar appearance had admitted to a witness that he had committed the crime: even
though all the evidence had been before the jury, the conviction was quashed. For another
example of a "lurking doubt" see *R*. v. *Pattinson* (1973) 58 Cr.App.R. 417.
[84] *R*. v. *Bracewell* (1978) 68 Cr. App. R. 44.
[85] The fresh evidence will not reveal an error of law or constitute a "material irregularity"
under s.2(1)(*b*) and (*c*) of the Criminal Appeal Act 1968.
[86] [1974] A.C. 878.
[87] Above
[88] *Ibid.* p. 892
[89] *The Judge* (1979) pp. 133–135, 148–176.
[90] This is in effect the same test as that for applying the proviso: see below, p. 712.
[91] See below, p. 712. Indeed, the court can *only* order a new trial in fresh evidence cases.

should be regarded as unsatisfactory simply on the ground that it was not given upon the whole of the evidence.[92] Given that the appeal in *Stafford* v. *D.P.P.* was dismissed, the appellants were thereafter imprisoned on the basis of the verdict of the judges.

Given that the matter is to be tested by reference to the views of the appeal court judges rather than the views of a hypothetical jury, a further question arises whether that is so in all fresh evidence cases. In particular, should the judges determine issues as to whether the oral testimony of a new or re-examined witness is credible?[93] In a number of cases the court has ordered a new trial,[94] but in *R.* v. *Cooper and McMahon*[95] the court determined such a question itself. The case is one of the most publicised examples of a miscarriage of justice, and came before the Court of Appeal on no less than five occasions. Three men, Cooper, McMahon and Murphy, were convicted of the murder of a Luton subpostmaster during an unsuccessful robbery. They were identified by a professional criminal, Mathews, who admitted taking part in the robbery but denied involvement in the murder. He turned Queen's evidence and the men were convicted solely on his testimony. They appealed without success to the Court of Appeal. Mathews subsequently received part of the reward offered by the Post Office. In 1973 Murphy's conviction was quashed by the Court of Appeal following the discovery of a fresh alibi witness. This naturally threw doubt on Mathews' identification of Cooper and McMahon and the Home Secretary referred the case to the Court of Appeal on three further occasions. On the first of these in 1975, the court refused to permit Mathews to be recalled for further cross-examination, indicated that the jury "could" have acquitted Murphy and convicted the others, and dismissed the appeal. The court refused leave to appeal to the House of Lords, reaffirming that in the light of *Stafford* v. *D.P.P.*[96] it was "not a necessary function of this Court, when considering fresh evidence, to evaluate the effect which it would have on the jury at the trial."[97] On the second, in 1976, Mathews was recalled and cross-examined: the judges concluded from their observations that he was telling the truth on the "vital part of his story" although other parts were discredited (a "cock and bull story"). This self-evidently surprising result does not inspire confidence in trial (or at least partial trial) by judges alone. The final reference by the Home Secretary (of the case of McMahon alone) was unsuccessful on the ground that the fresh alibi evidence sought to be tendered was not likely to be credible, and even if believed would be insufficient to afford a ground for allowing the appeal.[98] In 1980, following the publication of a book on the case edited by Ludovic Kennedy (*Wicked Beyond Belief*), the Home Secretary, William Whitelaw, ordered the release of Cooper and McMahon[99]: the case was "wholly exceptional" and there was a "widely

---

[92] See counsel's argument in *Stafford* v. *D.P.P.* [1974] A.C. 878, 884C.

[93] The test for admissibility is merely whether the fresh evidence is *capable* of belief : see above, p. 707.

[94] See Devlin (1979), pp. 165–166.

[95] See Devlin (1979), pp. 166–173; L. Kennedy (ed.) *Wicked Beyond Belief* (1980).

[96] [1974] A.C. 878.

[97] (1975) 61 Cr. App. R. 215.

[98] *R.* v. *McMahon* (1978) 68 Cr. App. R. 18 : criticised in Kennedy *op. cit.* (1980) pp. 132–135.

[99] 988 H.C. Deb., July 18, 1980, written answers cols. 719–720.

felt sense of unease about it" which he shared. He was not to be taken as criticising his predecessors, who had "acted with scrupulous regard to the constitutional conventions in referring each piece of alleged new evidence to the Court of Appeal and in acting in accordance with the court's judgment. Any general departure from that rule would clearly be disastrous." His action was not to be taken as a precedent.

It is commonly the case that an appeal is dismissed under the proviso at the end of section 2(1). The test for applying the proviso was stated as follows by Viscount Simon L.C. in *Stirland* v. *D.P.P.*[1]:

> "When the transcript is examined, it is evident that no reasonable jury, after a proper summing-up, could have failed to convict the appellant on the rest of the evidence to which no objection could be taken. There was, therefore, no miscarriage of justice. . . . [The proviso] assumes a situation where a reasonable jury, after being properly directed, would, on the evidence properly admissible, without doubt convict."

Other possibilities that may be open to the Court of Appeal are the substitution of a conviction for an alternative offence, where the jury would have found him guilty of that offence and it appears to the court that the jury must have been satisfied of facts which proved him guilty of it,[2] and the substitution of a finding of insanity or of unfitness to plead.[3]

(4) *New Trials.* Where the Court of Appeal allows an appeal against conviction solely on the basis of fresh evidence received under section 23,[4] it may order that the appellant be retried where it appears that this is required by the interests of justice.[5] The appellant may only be retried for the offence in respect of which the appeal was allowed, an offence of which he could have been convicted at the original trial on an indictment for that offence or an offence charged in an alternative count of the indictment at the trial on which the jury were discharged from giving a verdict.[6] This is the only circumstance in which a new trial can be ordered.[7]

The fact that the power to order a new trial is so limited has been cogently criticised.[8] In a number of cases where (1) the appellant appears to have a good argument in law but little or none on the merits, but (2) the case is not suitable for an application of the proviso,[9] the Court of Appeal or House of Lords has succumbed to the temptation to "bend" the law to enable the appeal to be dismissed. Justice has appeared to be done in the case itself but at the expense of the development of the law in a consistent, coherent and principled way. This problem could be cured by giving the Court of Appeal power to amend an indictment, power to order a retrial

---

[1] (1944) 30 Cr. App. R. 40, 46–47.

[2] Criminal Appeal Act 1968, s.3. The sentence may not be higher than that originally passed.

[3] *Ibid.* s.6, Sched. 1.

[4] See above, p. 707.

[5] 1968 Act, s.7(1). For the procedure on retrial see s.8 and Sched. 1. Any sentence passed after a retrial may not be longer than the original one.

[6] *Ibid.* s.7(2).

[7] For the analogous power to award a *venire de novo*, see below, p. 718. This can only be done where the original trial is a nullity.

[8] J.R. Spencer, "Criminal Law and Criminal Appeals" [1982] Crim. L.R. 260.

[9] See above, p. 712.

where a conviction has to be quashed for a technicality which cannot fairly be cured by such amendment after the event, and a wider power to substitute an alternative conviction.

Other arguments in favour of a wider power to order a new trial have been regularly put forward for over a century.[10] In 1954, however, the Departmental Committee on New Trials in Criminal Cases[11] recommended by a majority of five to three that there should only be such a power in fresh evidence cases. The arguments against a second trial in other circumstances were as follows:

(a) This would make an inroad on the principle that justice should be swift and final.

(b) It was "repugnant to public opinion that a man should be put in peril twice for the same offence,"[12] contrary to the rule against "double jeopardy."

On the other hand, both these arguments were used in the nineteenth century against the creation of proper appeal procedures following trials on indictment.[13] "Finality is a good thing, but justice is better."[14] Moreover, the "double jeopardy" rule is not really in point as the power to order a new trial would be restricted to counts where there was a conviction: it has not been seriously argued that there should be a power to order a new trial following an *acquittal* by a jury. It is already possible to hold a new trial where the jury at the first trial disagree, or the first trial is a nullity,[15] and it is difficult to see why the position should be different here.

(c) The prolongation of proceedings might often be unfair and oppressive to the appellant, especially as he would almost certainly not be responsible for the irregularity in the first trial.

As against that, "it would occasionally be in the public interest that an accused person should have to undergo two trials before a verdict is properly reached, rather than that a guilty man, whose guilt or innocence has never been properly ascertained, should go free."[16]

(d) There must necessarily be a doubt whether the second trial can be a fair one. However, this has not been perceived to be sufficient to exclude "second trials" in the cases mentioned above, and in any event seems to exaggerate both the likelihood of publicity concerning the first trial and the dangers of juries being unable to ignore any such publicity and the circumstances surrounding the previous proceedings in the case.

(e) There would be a danger that the power to order new trials would be exercised with increasing frequency. In practice, however, judges who

[10] See, *e.g.* the Report of the Departmental Committee on New Trials in Criminal Cases (Cmd. 9150, 1954); A.L. Goodhart, (1954) 70 L.Q.R. 514 (a critical commentary on the Report); the Justice Report on *Criminal Appeals* (1968) pp. 28–38; M.L. Friedland, *Double Jeopardy* (1969) pp. 221–263; M. Knight, *Criminal Appeals* (1970) Chap. 7.

[11] Cmd. 9150, Chairman : Lord Tucker.

[12] *Ibid.* p. 15.

[13] See M. Friedland (1969) pp. 231–232.

[14] *Per* Lord Atkin in *Ras Behari Lal* v. *The King-Emperor* (1933) L.R. 60 I.A. 354, 361, cited by Friedland (1969) p. 226.

[15] In the former situation the first trial does not end in a verdict of guilty or not guilty : in the second, the first "trial" technically has no legal status, and the second trial in time is the first occasion in which the defendant is "put on trial." However, in each situation it looks like "two trials" from the defendant's point of view.

[16] Tucker Committee minority, Cmd. 9150, p. 17.

handle criminal appeals, and who commonly favour the extension of their power to order a new trial, claim that the power would be used sparingly.[17] There could also be a limit of one new trial on any one indictment.

Further arguments in favour of an extended power, apart from that advanced by Spencer,[18] are that it would ensure that an obviously guilty man would not go free, with the effect which, in the words of the Justice Committee,[19] that has:

> "(a) on the public, (b) on honest witnesses who gave truthful evidence, (c) on the jury who have given the true verdict, (d) on the victim whose neighbours, knowing that the man has "got off," sometimes conclude that the victim must have been lying after all, and (e) sometimes on the man's next victim in a crime which he could not have committed if his conviction had not been quashed."

The Committee noted that it was unusual for the Court of Appeal to apply the proviso where an obviously guilty man was convicted on overwhelming evidence but appealed on the ground of misdirection or misrepresentation of evidence.

It is noteworthy that a wider power to order a new trial exists in almost every common law jurisdiction outside England and Wales and Northern Ireland, and without apparently proving controversial.[20] The arguments in favour of such a power seem compelling.

(ii) *Appeals against sentence*

A person who has been convicted of an offence on indictment may appeal to the Court of Appeal (Criminal Division) against any sentence[21] passed on him for the offence, except where the sentence is fixed by law.[22] Leave to appeal must be obtained from the Court of Appeal, or the judge who passed the sentence must certify that the case is fit for appeal,[23] and the procedure is essentially the same as in appeals against conviction. The

---

[17] The Justice Committee on *Criminal Appeals* (1968) estimated that no more than 45 to 50 new trials would be ordered in a year, and possibly less. Commonwealth experience showed, however, that the power might be used more frequently.

[18] See above, p. 712, n. 8.

[19] *Op. cit.*, at p. 37.

[20] See Cmd. 9150, pp. 10–11, Appendices V and VI; Friedland (1969) pp. 228–231; L.H. Leigh [1977] Crim. L.R. 525. In the United States a second trial following a successful appeal is not regarded as infringing the provision in the Fifth Amendment of the Constitution that no person shall be "subject for the same offence to be twice put in jeopardy of life and limb:" *U.S.* v. *Ball*, 163 U.S. 662 (1896). On the position in the Republic of Ireland see M. Knight, *Criminal Appeals* (1970) Chap. 6.

[21] This includes any order made by the court when dealing with an offender including a hospital order under the Mental Health Act 1983, a recommendation for deportation, a probation order or an absolute or conditional discharge : Criminal Appeal Act 1968, s.50, amended by the Criminal Justice Act 1982, s.66(1). Apart from the orders expressly mentioned in s.50, the section covers such matters as driving disqualifications, costs orders, compensation orders : see *R.* v. *Hayden* [1975] 1 W.L.R. 852. It also includes binding-over orders contingent on a conviction: *R.* v. *Williams (Carl)* [1982] 1 W.L.R. 1398, but not a recommendation as to the minimum period that a person convicted of murder should serve (Murder (Abolition of Death Penalty) Act 1965, s.1(2)): *R.* v. *Aitken* [1966] 1 W.L.R. 1076; *R.* v. *Bowden and Begley* (1983) 77 Cr.App.R. 66; or an order to contribute toward legal aid costs: *R.* v. *Hayden* [1975] 1 W.L.R. 852; *R.* v. *Raeburn* (1981) 74 Cr.App.R.21.

[22] Criminal Appeal Act 1968, s.9.

[23] 1968 Act, s.11 as amended by the Criminal Justice Act 1982, s.29(2)(*a*).

court, if it considers that the appellant should be sentenced differently, may quash any sentence or order which is the subject of the appeal and substitute any other sentence or order that it thinks appropriate, provided that it would have been within the jurisdiction of the court below. The appellant may not, however, be dealt with more severely than by the court below,[24] except that the court may bring a suspended sentence into effect.[25]

The court will interfere with an exercise of discretion as to sentence where the sentence is not justified by law, where matters are improperly taken into account or improperly ignored, where fresh matters are to be taken into account, or where the sentence is manifestly excessive or wrong in principle. One of the accepted functions of the Court of Appeal is that of laying down guidelines for sentencing.[26]

The court has the same powers to deal with sentences imposed in cases where a person convicted after summary trial is committed to the Crown Court for sentence,[27] or where a person previously made the subject of a probation order, conditional discharge, attendance centre order or suspended sentence is further dealt with by the Crown Court for his offence.[28] However, an appeal in such a case only lies if the sentence of imprisonment or youth custody is for six months or more,[29] or the sentence is outside the power of the court which convicted him, or the court recommends deportation, orders disqualification from driving, or activates a suspended sentence.[30]

(iii) *Appeals against findings of insanity*

A person in whose case a verdict of not guilty by reasons of insanity[31] is returned may appeal to the Court of Appeal on the same grounds as against a conviction.[32] The powers of the court are similar. However it may dismiss the appeal if none of the grounds for allowing it relates to the question of the appellant's insanity under the *M'Naghten* rules and, but for that insanity, the proper verdict would have been that he was guilty of some other offence.[33] In appropriate cases, the court may substitute a conviction for an offence, or a verdict of acquittal[34]: in the former case it has power to pass an appropriate sentence or make a hospital order, in the latter it may order that the appellant be admitted to hospital for assessment.[35]

[24] *Ibid.* A hospital order with an indefinite restriction order was held not to be more severe than a sentence of three years' imprisonment in *R.* v. *Bennett* [1968] 1 W.L.R. 980. The court may add a recommendation for deportation.

[25] 1968 Act, s.11(4).

[26] See generally, *R.* v. *Newsome and Browne* [1970] 2 Q.B. 711, and above, p. 664.

[27] Not in cases where the defendant *appeals* to the Crown Court.

[28] 1968 Act, s.10, as amended by the Criminal Justice Act 1982, Sched. 14, para. 23.

[29] Two sentences are treated as a single sentence if they are passed on the same day, or expressed by the court to be a single sentence, or are consecutive sentences.

[30] 1968 Act, s.10(3).

[31] "Insanity" here means insanity under the *M'Naghten* rules, which do not cover all cases of mental disorder and do cover some situations where there is no mental disorder : see generally J.C. Smith and B. Hogan, *Criminal Law* (5th ed., 1983) pp. 168–182.

[32] 1968 Act, s.12 : see above, p. 706.

[33] *Ibid.* s.13(3).

[34] *Ibid.* s.23(4).

[35] *Ibid.* s.24 and Sched. 1 as amended by the Mental Health (Amendment) Act 1982, Sched. 3, Part I, para.38.

Similar provisions govern appeals against a finding that a person is under a disability and is accordingly unfit to be tried[36]: if the appeal is successful other than by the entry of an acquittal the defendant is returned to the court below for trial. A hospital order may be continued.

(iv) *Appeals against conviction on special verdict*

If the Court of Appeal consider that the trial judge has drawn an incorrect conclusion from a special verdict entered by a jury, they may substitute the correct conclusion, and pass any sentence that may be authorised by law.[37]

(v) *References by the Home Secretary*

Where a person has been (1) convicted on indictment or (2) tried on indictment and found not guilty by reason of insanity or (3) found by a jury to be under a disability, the Home Secretary may refer the case to the Court of Appeal.[38] Two kinds of reference are possible. The first is a reference of the whole case, in which event the reference is treated as an appeal.[39] The court is not limited to the grounds mentioned in the Home Secretary's letter of reference.[40] A further appeal may then lie to the House of Lords. The other possibility is that a particular point may be referred for the opinion of the court.[41] The court gives what is essentially only an advisory opinion, with any further action to be taken by the Home Secretary.[42] This form of reference is uncommon.[43]

The Home Secretary prefers to refer a case to the Court of Appeal rather than to recommend the exercise of the prerogative to grant a pardon or remit a sentence[44]: it is thought that persistent use of the power to recommend a pardon would undermine the distinction between the functions of the executive and of the judiciary.[45] Indeed it was, in part, dissatisfaction with the review by the Home Office of criminal convictions that led to the establishment of the Court of Criminal Appeal. The Home Secretary's approach was summarised in a memorandum to the Home Affairs Committee[46]:

"In considering convictions on indictment, the Home Secretary . . .

---

[36] *Ibid.* ss.15, 16; *cf.* above, p. 590.

[37] 1968 Act, s.5.

[38] 1968 Act, s.17.

[39] *Ibid.* s.17(1)(*a*). The powers of the court are the same whether a case comes before it as an appeal or a reference of this kind : *Stafford* v. *D.P.P.* [1974] A.C. 878, although the criteria for permitting fresh evidence to be adduced may be applied less strictly than on ordinary appeals so that the court can consider the matters mentioned in the letter of reference: *R.* v. *Swabey* [1972] 1 W.L.R. 925.

[40] *R.* v. *Chard* [1984] 1 A.C. 279.

[41] 1968 Act, s.17(1)(*b*).

[42] See *Thomas (Arthur)* v. *The Queen* [1980] A.C. 125, where the Privy Council held that advice given to the Governor-General under an identically worded provision was not binding on him, and could not be the subject of an appeal to the Privy Council.

[43] See, *e.g. R.* v. *O'Neill* (1948) 33 Cr. App. R. 19; *R.* v. *McCartan* (1958) 42 Cr. App. R. 262; *R.* v. *McMahon* (1978) 68 Cr. App. R. 18.

[44] See below, pp. 757–759.

[45] 1981–82 H.C. 421, 6th Report on *Miscarriages of Justice*, p. 2.

[46] *Ibid.*

(a) will not normally intervene where normal avenues of appeal to the Court of Appeal have not been exhausted;
(b) will, where the normal avenues are not available and intervention seems justified, consider using his power of reference to enable the Court to hear the case;
(c) will consider recommending the exercise of the Royal Prerogative where intervention seems justified but for some reason (*e.g.* lapse of time, inadmissibility as evidence of salient new facts) a resort to the judicial appeal process would not be appropriate."

However, the Home Secretary will not intervene on the basis of evidence already considered by the courts. A case will only be referred where there is fresh evidence that might lead to the view being taken that the conviction was unsafe and unsatisfactory.[47] Moreover, if a case is referred to the Court of Appeal and the conviction is upheld, the Home Secretary will only intervene thereafter if the case is wholly exceptional.[48]

(vi) *Attorney-General's References*[49]

Section 36 of the Criminal Justice Act 1972 introduced a new procedure whereby the Attorney-General may refer a point of law to the Court of Appeal where the defendant in a trial on indictment has been acquitted. The point must actually have arisen in the case. The court gives its opinion and may thereafter refer the point to the House of Lords. The Attorney-General may appear in person or be represented by counsel: the acquitted person may be represented by counsel, or with leave may appear in person.[50]

The reference has no effect on the trial or the acquittal. No mention must be made in the reference of the proper name of any person or place which is likely to lead to the identification of the acquitted person.[51] His identity must not be disclosed during the proceedings except with his consent.

The aim of this procedure is to ensure that an erroneous direction by a trial judge on the law is corrected at the earliest opportunity and without the need for legislation. Whereas the defendant may appeal where such a direction leads to an erroneous conviction, the prosecution has no right to appeal against an erroneous acquittal in a trial on indictment. The sanctity of an acquittal by a jury is maintained by the provisions designed to secure that the reference procedure cannot operate to the detriment of the person acquitted.

---

[47] *Ibid.*

[48] *e.g. R.* v. *Cooper and McMahon*, above, p. 711. The previous Home Secretaries had firmly taken the view that they should not override the court's decision : see L. Kennedy, (ed.) *Wicked Beyond Belief* (1980) pp. 130, 159–160, 169.

[49] See J. Jaconelli, [1981] Crim. L.R. 543.

[50] In practice, however, the defendant is normally not represented and counsel for the Attorney-General is opposed by counsel appearing as *amicus curiae*, instructed by the Treasury Solicitor. In *Attorney-General's Reference* (*Nos.* 1 *and* 2 *of* 1979) [1980] Q.B. 180, the Law Commission, who had instigated the references in order to secure clarification of the law concerning conditional intention to steal, submitted a memorandum for the assistance of the court.

[51] Criminal Appeal (Reference of Points of Law) Rules 1973, (S.I. 1973 No. 1114) r.3.

In general, judges have resisted the introduction of procedures whereby matters may be referred to them for an advisory opinion.[52] One of the grounds for refusing in the exercise of their discretion to grant a declaration on a disputed matter of law is that the dispute is hypothetical rather than real.[53] However, the opinions under the reference procedure relate to a real case, and, moreover, one in which an opinion has already been expressed by the trial judge. The exact status of the opinions as precedent is, however, uncertain: as they have no actual effect on the outcome of the case as far as the defendant is concerned, it is arguable that they are not binding, either on trial judges or on the Court of Appeal itself; however, they are obviously of strong persuasive force.

The reference procedure has been characterised as "problematic"[54] in view of the doubts as to precedental status and the fact that the defendant often has little interest in contesting the case.[55] Nevertheless, the procedure has been of value in providing authoritative guidance in a number of areas of criminal law, most notably that of conditional intention to steal, where the Court of Appeal's decision on a reference put an end to a line of argument that had led to a large number of undeserved acquittals.[56]

(vii) *Venire de novo*

Where there has been a "mistrial," in the sense either that the trial has never been validly commenced or the jury has not validly returned a verdict, the Court of Appeal may order the issue of a writ of *venire de novo* for a "new" trial: the first "trial" is treated as a nullity.[57] This may be done, for example,[58] where proceedings have not been properly instituted,[59] where the court is not properly constituted,[60] where the defendants although separately indicted are tried together,[61] where there is an equivocal plea of guilty which should not have been accepted as such,[62]

---

[52] There was weighty judicial opposition to clause 4 of the Rating and Valuation Bill 1928, which would have enabled the Minister of Health to seek advisory opinions from the High Court on questions of rating law: the clause was dropped: see Lord Hewart, *The New Despotism* (1929) Chap. 7; E.C.S. Wade, (1930) 46 L.Q.R. 169, and (1931) 47 L.Q.R. 58; C.K. Allen, (1931) 47 L.Q.R. 43, 60.

[53] *e.g. Blackburn* v. *Att.-Gen.* [1971] 1 W.L.R. 1037, where the court declined to make a declaration on the hypothetical question whether by signing the Treaty of Rome, Her Majesty's Government would irreversibly surrender in part the sovereignty of Parliament.

[54] J. Jaconelli, *op. cit.*

[55] The Supreme Court of the United States refuses to consider "moot" points even where they arise out of real and not hypothetical situations.

[56] *Attorney-General's References* (*Nos.* 1 *and* 2 *of* 1979) [1980] Q.B. 180. See *R.* v. *Bayley and Easterbrook* [1980] Crim L.R. 503, J.C. Smith and B. Hogan, *Criminal Law* (5th ed., 1983) pp. 258–259, 499–500.

[57] This jurisdiction, formerly exercised by the Court for Crown Cases Reserved, was preserved for the Court of Criminal Appeal (*Crane* v. *D.P.P.* [1921] 2 A.C. 299) and is now exercised by the Court of Appeal under the Supreme Court Act 1981, s.53(2).

[58] See R.B. Cooke, (1955) 71 L.Q.R. 100; M. Knight, *Criminal Appeals* (1970) pp. 216–219.

[59] *R.* v. *Angel* (1968) 52 Cr. App.R. 280: the consent of the D.P.P. was necessary but had not been obtained.

[60] *R.* v. *Cronin* (1940) 27 Cr. App. R. 179: trial presided over by a person unqualified to act as a deputy recorder.

[61] *Crane* v. *D.P.P., supra.*

[62] See above, p. 702, n. 11; see, *e.g. R.* v. *Baker* (1912) 7 Cr. App. R. 217, 252.

where the jury is not properly constituted,[63] where the jury is improperly discharged before giving a verdict,[64] or the verdict is ambiguous. It is open to the Court of Appeal simply to quash a conviction without ordering a retrial.[65] Moreover, there may be a rule that the court may not order a *venire de novo* where the "mistrial" led to an acquittal.[66]

In *R.* v. *Rose*[67] the House of Lords emphasised that the power to order a *venire de novo* was not available where there was an irregularity in the course of the trial occurring between the time that it had been validly commenced and the discharge of the jury after returning a verdict. Here, the judge had applied improper pressure on the jury to reach a verdict by imposing a time limit: the House held that the Court of Appeal had no alternative but to quash the conviction under section 2 of the Criminal Appeal Act 1968, and had no jurisdiction to order a *venire de novo*.

The court of trial may direct a *venire de novo* where the jury is discharged before giving a verdict, for example where they fail to agree or there is an irregularity in the conduct of proceedings.[68]

(b) Appeals from the Court of Appeal (Criminal Division) to the House of Lords

An appeal lies from the Court of Appeal (Criminal Division) to the House of Lords at the instance of either the defendant or the prosecutor.[69] The Court of Appeal must certify that a point of law of general public importance is involved. In addition, leave must be obtained from either the Court of Appeal or the House of Lords and this can only be granted where it appears that the point is "one which ought to be considered by the House."[70] If leave is granted, the House may in its discretion allow a point to be argued that is not connected with the point certified.[71]

An application for leave to appeal is normally made immediately after the Court of Appeal's decision, but may be made in writing within 14

---

[63] *e.g.* where a juror was personated by his bailiff, who was neither on the jury panel nor qualified to be so : *R.* v. *Wakefield* (1918) 13 Cr. App. R. 56, or where the defendant is denied his right of challenge : *R.* v. *Williams* (1925) 19 Cr. App. R. 67; *R.* v. *Gash* (1967) 51 Cr. App. R. 37.

[64] *R.* v. *Hancock* (1931) 100 L.J.K.B. 419 : the defendant changed his pleas from not guilty to guilty, but the jury did not formally return a guilty verdict.

[65] See, *e.g. R.* v. *Golathan* (1915) 11 Cr. App. R. 79. It is not clear whether it is open to the prosecution to recommence proceedings : if the court is simply regarded as holding the decision of the "first" trial to be a nullity, it seems that there could be such proceedings; if, however, the conviction is quashed under the Criminal Appeal Act 1968, s.2, the position is as if there had been a judgment and verdict of acquittal and fresh proceedings could be met by a plea of *autrefois acquit*.

[66] *R.* v. *Middlesex Quarter Sessions, ex p. D.P.P.* [1952] 2 Q.B. 758. An alternative ground for the decision was that the irregularity was not such as to cause a mistrial. There may be exceptions to the supposed rule where the defendant is party to the irregularity or is tried by a court with no jurisdiction over charges of the kind in question : R.B. Cooke (1955) 71 L.Q.R.100, 116.

[67] [1982] A.C. 822.

[68] See R.B. Cooke, *op. cit.* pp. 120–125; Juries Act 1974, s.21(4).

[69] Criminal Appeal Act 1968, s.33(1). Where a point of law is referred to the Court of Appeal by the Attorney-General under the Criminal Justice Act 1972, s.36 (see above, p. 717) the court may thereafter refer the point to the House of Lords.

[70] 1968 Act, s.33(2).

[71] *Att.-Gen. for Northern Ireland* v. *Gallagher* [1963] A.C.349. Where, however, the certificate relates to conviction only the House will not deal with matters of sentence : *Jones* v. *D.P.P.* [1962] A.C. 635.

days.[72] The point is normally formulated by counsel for the applicant, sometimes with the assistance of counsel for the other side. If a certificate is refused the matter may not be taken any further: the refusal is not itself a decision that may be subject to appeal.[73] Reasons are not normally given for refusing a certificate.[74] Where a certificate is granted, the application for leave should be made first to the Court of Appeal, and only then if leave is refused by that court, to the House of Lords, within 14 days.[75] The Court of Appeal may grant bail[76] and legal aid.[77]

Where the prosecutor is granted leave to appeal or gives notice that he intends to apply for leave, and but for the decision of the Court of Appeal the defendant would be liable to be detained, the Court of Appeal may make an order for his detention or direct that he is not to be released except on bail so long as the appeal is pending.[78] An order under the Mental Health Act 1983 may be continued.[79] A defendant who is detained may apply to the Court of Appeal or House of Lords to be present at the hearing of the appeal of preliminary or incidental matters.[80] If no order for continued detention is made, or the defendant is released or discharged before the appeal is disposed of, the defendant cannot be detained again as the result of the decision of the House of Lords on the appeal.[81]

The rules governing petitions to the House of Lords for leave to appeal and petitions of appeal are prescribed by the House of Lords Directions as to Procedure 1979.[82] The former are heard by an Appeal Committee, the latter by the House itself or an Appellate Committee.[83] If leave is granted by the Court of Appeal there is no statutory time limit for lodging the petition of appeal although it is recommended that this is done within three months: if leave is granted by an Appeal Committee, the committee may set a time limit.[84] The appellant must lodge 12 copies of a record of the proceedings, but no "printed cases"[85] are normally required. If any of the parties intend to invite the House to depart from one of its own previous decisions, this intention must be clearly stated.

The House in disposing of an appeal may exercise any of the powers of the Court of Appeal or remit the case to that court.[86] Any sentence

---

[72] Criminal Appeal Act 1968, s.34. The time limit may be extended : *ibid.*

[73] *Cf.* in relation to appeals to the House of Lords from the Divisional Court, *Gelberg* v. *Miller* [1961] 1 W.L.R. 459, above, p. 705, n. 48.

[74] *R.* v. *Jones* (1975) 61 Cr. App. R. 120; *R.* v. *Cooper, R.* v. *McMahon* (1975) 61 Cr. App. R. 215.

[75] Criminal Appeal Act 1968, s.34. The time limit may be extended.

[76] *Ibid.* s.36.

[77] Legal Aid Act 1974, s.28(10) : legal aid may be granted by the Registrar or the single judge, but not the House of Lords. If the prosecutor appeals or applies for leave to appeal legal aid must be granted if the defendant's means warrant it : *ibid.* s.29(1)(*b*), (2).

[78] Criminal Appeal Act 1968, s.37(2). The order ceases to have effect if leave is refused, or the application for leave is not made within the due time, or the appeal is determined, or the liability for detention otherwise ceases, as the case may be : *ibid.* ss.34(3), 37(3).

[79] *Ibid.* s.37(4)(4A).

[80] *Ibid.* s.38.

[81] *Ibid.* s.37(5). See *D.P.P.* v. *Merriman* [1973] A.C. 584, 606.

[82] See the *Supreme Court Practice 1982*, paras. 2575ff.

[83] See above, p. 82.

[84] House of Lords Directions as to Procedure 1979, Dir. 14.

[85] See above, p. 83.

[86] Criminal Appeal Act 1968, s.35(3).

substituted by the House of Lords runs from the time when the other sentence would have begun to run, unless the House otherwise directs.[87] Any time spent on bail pending hearing of the appeal does not count towards the sentence.[88]

Until 1960, an appeal could only be taken from the Court of Criminal Appeal to the House of Lords if the Attorney-General granted a *fiat* or certificate that a point of law of exceptional public importance was involved and that it was in the public interest that a further appeal be brought.[89] Between 1907 and 1960 there were 23 successful applications for a *fiat*. The exercise of the Attorney-General's discretion to grant or refuse a *fiat* was in certain instances highly controversial. The Administration of Justice Act 1960[90] introduced the present arrangements which, *inter alia*, brought an end to the involvement of the Attorney-General. The number of criminal appeals to the House of Lords has, accordingly, increased. However, it has been debated whether, on balance, the increased involvement of the House in criminal law matters has proved beneficial. In his commentary on *R.* v. *Caldwell*,[91] Professor J.C. Smith noted that the "House of Lords has a dismal record in criminal cases. All too often their Lordships' decisions have to be reversed by legislation."[92] His criticisms were echoed by Professor Glanville Williams,[93] who remarked that the average age of Law Lords is higher than that of members of the Court of Appeal, and that "old men" are "often fixed in their opinions" and "tend to ignore the opinions of others." He noted that a further drawback was the breadth of the House's jurisdiction:

"It is particularly inapt that a Chancery judge should have the casting vote in the House of Lords in a criminal case, as Lord Cross did in *Hyam*."[94]

3. APPEALS IN CIVIL CASES

In this section we consider appeals in civil cases originating in the county court or the High Court. Appeals in civil cases originating in the magistrates' court or Crown Court have already been discussed.[95]

(a) Appeals from the county court to the Court of Appeal (Civil Division)

In general, a person dissatisfied with a decision of a county court may appeal to the Court of Appeal.[96] In certain cases, however, the appeal is expressly excluded[97]:

---

[87] *Ibid.* s.43(2).
[88] *Ibid.* s.43(1).
[89] See "Appeals to the House of Lords" [1957] Crim. L.R. 566.
[90] See D.G.T. Williams, [1961] Crim. L.R.87.
[91] [1982] A.C. 341.
[92] [1981] Crim. L.R. 393.
[93] *Ibid.* pp. 581–582.
[94] [1975] A.C. 55.
[95] See above, pp. 704–705.
[96] County Courts Act 1984, s.77(1). Until 1934 the appeal lay first to a Divisional Court and thereafter to the Court of Appeal. In bankruptcy cases the appeal lies to a Divisional Court of the Chancery Division; an appeal lies from that court to the Court of Appeal with the leave of either, and the decision of the Court of Appeal is final : Bankruptcy Act 1914, s.108.
[97] County Courts Act 1984, s.77(6); Supreme Court Act 1981, s.18(1)(*b*)(*c*)(*d*); 1984 Act, s.79(1).

—questions of fact arising in certain actions by a landlord for possession of the premises;

—an order extending the time for appealing;

—an order expressed by statute to be final[98];

—a decree absolute of divorce or nullity of marriage, by a party who, having had time and opportunity to appeal from the decree nisi, has not done so;

—where the parties have agreed in writing that the judge's decision shall be final.

An appeal only lies with the leave of the county court judge from any order made with the consent of the parties or relating only to costs which are by law left to the discretion of the court.[99]

In certain cases an appeal may only be brought with the leave of the county court judge or the Court of Appeal: the classes prescribed[1] include those where the claim (or counter-claim if larger) is for an amount not exceeding one-half of the relevant county court limit for contract and tort, equity, probate and miscellaneous matters,[2] and where the decision of the county court judge is made in an appellate capacity. However, no leave is required where the court's determination includes or preserves an injunction or is related to the custody of, or access to, a child.[3]

In other cases, an appeal lies as of right.

Appeals may be based on questions of fact, discretion or law. The procedure for appealing and the powers of the Court of Appeal are discussed in the section on appeals from the High Court.[4]

Appeals lie from decisions of a county court registrar to the county court judge.[5] In interlocutory matters, the judge considers the issue de novo, and may substitute his view for that of the registrar. Where the appeal is from a judgment or final order, the role of the county court judge is analogous to that of the Court of Appeal on appeals from decisions of the judge.[6] Accordingly, he may only order a new trial in the same circumstances as the Court of Appeal,[7] and may only interfere with a discretionary decision if no reasonable registrar could have so decided.[8]

---

[98] It is not open to the Court of Appeal to entertain an appeal in such a case on the ground of lack of jurisdiction : *In Re Racal Communications Ltd.* [1981] A.C. 374 (otherwise entitled *In Re A Company*) disapproving *Pearlman* v. *Keepers and Governors of Harrow School* [1979] Q.B. 56. A final order may be set aside if procured by fraud : *cf. Lazarus Estates Ltd.* v. *Beasley* [1956] 1 Q.B. 702, and in matrimonial cases, a final order may be set aside if there is fraud, mistake or material non-disclosure : *Robinson* v. *Robinson* (*practice note*) [1982] 1 W.L.R. 786.

[99] Supreme Court Act 1981, s.18(1)(f)

[1] By the Lord Chancellor under the County Courts Act 1984, s.77(2)–(4): the County Court Appeals Order 1981 (S.I. 1981 No. 1749). See also the restrictions on appealing from interlocutory orders or judgments imposed by the Supreme Court Act 1981, s.18(1)(h): below, p. 723.

[2] See above, pp. 60–62.

[3] S.I. 1981, No. 1749, art. 3.

[4] See below, pp. 723–734.

[5] County Court Rules 1981, Ord. 13r. 1(10) (interlocutory matters) and Ord. 37, r. 6 (final orders or judgments).

[6] See below, pp. 729–732.

[7] *Devenish* v. *P.D.I. Homes (Hythe) Ltd.* [1959] 1 W.L.R. 1188.

[8] *Woodspring District Council* v. *Taylor, The Times* May 15, 1982.

(b) Appeals from the High Court to the Court of Appeal (Civil Division)

(i) *When does an appeal lie?*

Appeals normally lie from the High Court to the Court of Appeal (Civil Division).[9] In some circumstances, the appeal may be direct to the House of Lords.[10] Generally, there is a right to appeal. In respect of some matters, however, the appeal is expressly excluded by statute:

—any criminal cause or matter[11];
—any order allowing an extension of time for appealing[12];
—any decision expressed by statute to be final[13];
—a decree absolute of divorce or nullity of marriage, by a party who, having had time and opportunity to appeal from the decree nisi, has not done so[14];
—any decision of the High Court on an appeal under section 1 of the Arbitration Act 1979 on a question of law arising out of an arbitration award, or under section 2 of the Act on a question of law arising in the course of a reference, other than as provided by the 1979 Act[15];
—a judgment or order of the High Court sitting as a Prize Court[16];
—an order refusing leave to a vexatious litigant to institute or continue legal proceedings.[17]

In other cases an appeal only lies if leave is obtained:

(1) The leave of the High Court is necessary for appeals in relation to orders made with the consent of the parties or relating only to costs which are by law left to the discretion of the court.[18]

(2) The leave of the Divisional Court or the Court of Appeal is necessary for appeals from the determination by a Divisional Court of any appeal to the High Court.[19]

(3) The leave of the High Court or the Court of Appeal is necessary for appeals from an interlocutory order or judgment,[20] except:

—where the liberty of the subject or the custody, education[21] or welfare of a minor is concerned;

[9] Supreme Court Act 1981, s.16(1).
[10] See below, pp. 734–735.
[11] Supreme Court Act 1981, s.18(1)(*a*). Here, the appeal lies to the House of Lords under the Administration of Justice Act 1960: see above, p. 705.
[12] 1981 Act, s.18(1)(*b*).
[13] *Ibid.* s.18(1)(*c*). See above p. 722, n.98.
[14] *Ibid.* s.18(1)(*d*).
[15] *Ibid.* s.18(1)(*g*).
[16] *Ibid.* s.16(2). An appeal lies to the Privy Council.
[17] *Ibid.* s.42(4).
[18] *Ibid.* s.18(1)(*f*).
[19] *Ibid.* s.18(1)(*e*), *i.e.* in civil cases : *cf.* above, p. 704.
[20] There is much case law on the distinction between interlocutory and final orders: "The question . . . is so uncertain that the only thing for the practitioner to do is look up the practice books and see what has been decided on the point. Most orders have now been the subject of decision. If a new case should arise, we must do the best we can with it" *per* Lord Denning M.R. in *Salter Rex & Co.* v. *Ghosh* [1971] 2 Q.B. 597, 601. An order refusing unconditional leave to defend an action is not to be treated as an interlocutory order : 1981 Act, s.18(2)(*a*).
[21] "Education" includes training and religious instruction : *ibid.* s.18(2)(*b*).

—where an applicant for access to a minor is refused all access to the minor;

—where an injunction or the appointment of a receiver is granted or refused;

—in the case of a decision determining the claim of any creditor, or the liability of any contributory or of any director or other officer, under company law;

—in the case of a decree nisi in a matrimonial cause, or a judgment or order in an admiralty action determining liability;

—in such other cases as may be prescribed.[22]

In situations (2) and (3) the application for leave must be made first to the court below, unless there are special circumstances which make that impossible or inappropriate,[23] and if leave is refused, then to the Court of Appeal. In the latter event the application may be determined by a single judge of the Court of Appeal[24]: he may, if he thinks fit, refer the application to a full court; if he refuses leave, a fresh application for leave may be made within 10 days to the full court.[25]

Even where leave to appeal is not necessary, the Court of Appeal may decline to entertain an appeal where, for example, the issue is or has become hypothetical,[26] or the parties have agreed not to appeal.[27]

(ii) *Who may appeal?*

Where in principle an appeal lies, any party to proceedings in the court below and any person on whom notice of the order or judgment is served[28] may appeal. In addition, any person who *could* have been made a party to the action may appeal, provided he obtains leave from the Court of Appeal.[29]

(iii) *Procedure for appealing*

The appellant must serve a "notice of appeal" on all parties to the proceedings in the court below who are directly affected by the proceedings,[30] and any other person directed by the Court of Appeal, the single judge or the Registrar of Civil Appeals.[31] The notice may be given in respect of the whole or a specified part of the judgment or order of the court below. For example in a personal injuries case there might be an appeal against the quantum of damages only. The notice must specify the grounds of the appeal and the precise form of the order which the appellant proposes to ask the Court of Appeal to make: the appellant will need leave

---

[22] *Ibid.* s.18(1)(*h*).

[23] R.S.C. Ord. 59, r. 14(4).

[24] 1981 Act, s.54(6).

[25] R.S.C. Ord. 59, r. 14(10)(12).

[26] *e.g. Sutch* v. *Burns* [1944] K.B. 406; *Sun Life Assurance Co. of Canada* v. *Jervis* [1944] A.C. 111.

[27] *Jones* v. *Victoria Graving Dock Co.* [1877] 2 Q.B.D. 314.

[28] R.S.C. Ord. 44, r. 3.

[29] *per* Jessel M.R. in *Crawcour* v. *Salter* (1882) 30 W.R. 329; *Re B (an infant)* [1958] 1 Q.B. 12.

[30] R.S.C. Ord. 59, r. 3(5).

[31] *Ibid.* r. 8.

to rely on any ground or apply for any relief at the hearing not specified in the notice of appeal.[32]

The notice must normally be served within four weeks from the date on which the judgment or order of the court below was signed, entered or otherwise perfected.[33] The exceptions are (1) where a certificate is granted for an appeal direct to the House of Lords, but the House refuses leave, where the four week period runs from the date of refusal,[34] and (2) social security appeals, where there is a six week time limit.[35] The time limit may be extended or abridged by the court below, provided that the application for extension or abridgment is made within the specified period,[36] or by the Registrar of Civil Appeals, the single judge, or the Court of Appeal.[37] Where, however, the time limit for appealing has expired, an extension will only be granted in exceptional cases[38]: a more liberal exercise of this discretion would be unfair to the other party or parties.

A respondent who is served with a notice of appeal may, within 21 days, serve a "respondent's notice" on the appellant and all parties to the proceedings in the court below directly affected. This must be done where the respondent wishes to contend that the decision of the court below, in respect of the cause of action related to the notice of appeal,

   (a) should be varied; or

   (b) should be affirmed on grounds other than those relied upon by that court; or

   (c) was wrong in whole or in part.

The notice must specify the grounds of the respondent's contention, and, in cases (a) and (c), the precise form of the order which he proposes to ask the court to make: the respondent will need leave to apply for any relief not specified in the notice or to rely upon any ground which is either not specified in the notice or relied upon by the court below.[39]

Where the respondent is dissatisfied with the decision of the court on a *separate* cause of action from that raised in the notice of appeal, his proper course is to serve a separate notice of appeal.[40]

The notice of appeal or respondent's notice may be amended without leave before the date on which the appeal appears in the List of Forthcoming Appeals, and, thereafter, with the leave of the Court of Appeal, the single judge or the registrar.[41]

The purpose of the notice of appeal is to:

"define and confine the area of controversy on the hearing of the appeal, thus saving both time and expense to the parties. It is intended

[32] *Ibid.* r. 3(2)(3).

[33] R.S.C. Ord. 59, r. 4(1).

[34] R.S.C. Ord. 59, r. 4(2): see below, p. 735.

[35] R.S.C. Ord. 59, r. 21.

[36] R.S.C. Ord. 59, r. 15.

[37] R.S.C. Ord. 3, r. 5.

[38] *Practice Note* (*Court of Appeal : New Procedure*) [1982] 1 W.L.R. 1312 (Sir John Donaldson, M.R.)

[39] R.S.C. Ord. 59, r. 6.

[40] *National Society for the Distribution of Electricity by Secondary Generators* v. *Gibbs* [1900] 2 Ch. 280.

[41] R.S.C. Ord. 59, r. 7. Applications for leave are made first to the registrar, who will require good reasons why the amendment was not made earlier and to be satisfied that the application is made at the earliest possible moment : *Practice Note* (*Court of Appeal : New Procedure*) [1982] 1 W.L.R. 1312, 1313–14.

that wherever possible the members of the court will have read the notice of appeal and any respondent's notice and the reasons for the judgment under appeal before the appeal is called on, and a properly drawn notice of appeal will enable counsel to come at once to the central issues without any prolonged opening."[42]

The same principles apply to a respondent's notice.[43] The grounds should be stated shortly and simply: these notices are not designed to be as elaborate as pleadings.[44]

Within seven days of service of the notice of appeal, or within such further time as may be allowed by the Registrar of Civil Appeals, the appellant must leave certain specified documents, including two copies of the notice of appeal, with the registrar. The registrar thereupon causes the appeal to be set down in the appropriate list of appeals[45]: there is a series of lists depending on the court or tribunal from which the appeal is taken.[46]

The next stage is the appearance of the appeal in the "List of Forthcoming Appeals." The appellant then has 14 days to lodge copies of a series of specified documents, including the notice of appeal, any respondent's notice, the judgment or order of the court below, the pleadings, a record of the judge's reasons, relevant parts of the transcript or judge's note of evidence and relevant affidavits and exhibits.

At any time after an appeal has been set down in the appropriate list of appeals the registrar may give:

" . . . such directions in relation to the documents to be produced at the appeal, and the manner in which they are to be presented, and as to other matters incidental to the conduct of the appeal, as appear best adapted to secure the just, expeditious and economical disposal of the appeal."[47]

This has been described as "perhaps the most important single change in the rules."[48] As experience of the new system builds up, it is hoped that the rate of disposal of appeals can be increased without detriment to, and even with an improvement in, the quality of the justice which is administered.[49] Possible time-saving devices include "perfected grounds of appeal," which refer to the key authorities and the relevant portions of the summing up and evidence or the provision of a skeleton outline of the argument annotated by reference to the documents and authorities.[50] Notice has also been given that time limits will be strictly enforced unless there are good grounds for granting an extension.[51] Doubts have, however, been expressed:

"[T]here prevails at present an emphasis on efficiency, time saving and expedition, which tends to undermine the English system of appeal

[42] *Ibid.* p.1312.
[43] *Ibid.* pp. 1313–14.
[44] *Sansom* v. *Sansom* (*Practice Note*) [1956] 1 W.L.R. 945.
[45] R.S.C. Ord. 59, r. 5.
[46] *Practice Note* (*Court of Appeal : New Procedure*) [1982] 1 W.L.R. 1312, 1313.
[47] R.S.C. Ord. 59, r. 9.
[48] *Practice Note* (*Court of Appeal : New Procedure*) [1982] 1 W.L.R. 1312, 1315.
[49] *Ibid.*
[50] See *Practice Note* (*Court of Appeal : Skeleton Arguments*) [1983] 1 W.L.R. 1055.
[51] *Practice Note* (*Appeal: Documents*) [1983] 2 All E.R. 416.

(which is predicated upon the advocate's right to conduct the appeal in the way most beneficial to his client's interests) and to assimilate it to American and continental procedure. For all practical purposes this has dispensed with oral presentation and leaves the conduct of a very short hearing to the court rather than Counsel, while in England tradition entitles Counsel to be to a large extent 'in possession of the court.' "[52]

Eventually, appeals which are ready for hearing and have been given fixed dates and other appeals of an urgent character appear in a "warned list."

(iv) *Interlocutory applications*

Interlocutory applications, for example for a stay of execution,[53] for leave to adduce fresh evidence,[54] or for security for the costs of appeal, are heard by a single judge or the registrar: only the judge, however, may deal with matters concerning an injunction or a stay of execution.[55] The Court of Appeal has all the powers and duties as to amendment and otherwise of the High Court.[56] An appeal lies respectively from the registrar to the single judge and from the single judge to the Court of Appeal, by means of a fresh application brought within 10 days.

However, an appeal does not lie to the Court of Appeal without leave of that court in respect of a determination of the registrar which has been reviewed by the single judge.[57]

(v) *Evidence in the Court of Appeal (Civil Division)*

An appeal to the Court of Appeal is expressed to be "by way of rehearing."[58] This is not a rehearing in the same sense as appeals from magistrates' courts to the Crown Court[59] but a rehearing "on the documents." The court has power:

—"to draw inferences of fact and to give any judgment and make any order which ought to have been given or made, and to make such further or other order as the case may require;"[60]

and

—"to make any order, on such terms as the Court thinks just, to ensure the determination on the merits of the real question in controversy between the parties."[61]

---

[52] F.A. Mann, (1983) 2 C.J.Q. 320, 322–325, at p. 325.

[53] R.S.C. Ord. 59, r. 13: an appeal does not operate as a stay of execution unless directed by the court below, a single judge of the Court of Appeal or the court itself.

[54] See below, p. 728.

[55] R.S.C. Ord. 59, r. 10(9).

[56] R.S.C. Ord. 59, r. 10(1).

[57] R.S.C. Ord. 59, r. 14(11) and (12). The judge must consider the matter afresh and use his own discretion : *C.M. Van Stillevoldt BV* v. *E.L. Carriers Ltd.* [1983] 1 W.L.R. 207.

[58] R.S.C. Ord. 59, r. 3(1).

[59] See above, pp. 702–703.

[60] R.S.C. Ord. 59, r. 10(3). This power may be exercised notwithstanding that the relevant point is not covered by a notice of appeal or respondent's notice : r. 10(4).

[61] R.S.C. Ord. 59, r. 10(4).

The court should take account of any new authorities and of any relevant, retrospective, legislation. For example, in *Attorney-General* v. *Vernazza*,[62] Mr. Vernazza was declared to be a vexatious litigant and prohibited by the High Court from *instituting* legal proceedings without leave. By the time his appeal was heard by the Court of Appeal, the High Court had been given a new statutory power to prohibit vexatious litigants from *continuing existing* proceedings without leave. The House of Lords held that the new legislation, as it affected procedural and not substantive rights, was retrospective, should have been applied to Mr. Vernazza by the Court of Appeal, and should be applied to him now. Where there are new authorities or legislative provisions which are relevant to a decision of the High Court, leave to appeal out of time will be granted if it is just to do so.[63]

Similarly, the court should take account of any material changes in the facts since the trial. For example, in *Murphy* v. *Stone-Wallwork (Charlton) Ltd.*[64] an action was brought by an employee against his employers for breach of statutory duty. The judge and the Court of Appeal assessed the damages on the assumption that the plaintiff would continue to be employed by the defendants on lighter work. A fortnight after the decision in the Court of Appeal, the plaintiff was dismissed because of his incapacity. The House of Lords[65] held that even though it did not appear that the employers had acted in bad faith or oppressively, evidence of the change of circumstances was admissible, as the basis on which the case had been conducted on both sides had been suddenly and materially falsified. It should, however, be noted that the change occurred within the time limit for appealing: it is unlikely that a leave to appeal out of time would be granted in such circumstances, in view of the need for finality in litigation, unless, perhaps, there was bad faith or oppression.

Where a party to an appeal seeks to adduce fresh evidence concerning matters other than events that have occurred since the trial, a more restrictive approach is adopted. Where judgment has been given after trial or hearing of the cause or matter on the merits,[66] such fresh evidence is only admitted on "special grounds."[67] Three conditions were laid down by Denning L.J. in *Ladd* v. *Marshall*[68]:

(1) It must be shown that the evidence could not have been obtained with reasonable diligence for use at the trial.

(2) The evidence must be such that, if given, it would probably have an important influence on the result of the case, although it need not be decisive.

---

[62] [1960] A.C. 965.

[63] *In Re Earl of Berkeley, Borrer* v. *Berkeley* [1945] Ch. 1; *Anns* v. *Walcroft Property Co. Ltd.* [1976] Q.B. 882; *Property and Reversionary Investment Corporation Ltd.* v. *Templar* [1977] 1 W.L.R. 1223.

[64] [1969] 1 W.L.R. 1023. See also *Mulholland* v. *Mitchell* [1971] A.C. 666.

[65] The same principle would have applied by the Court of Appeal if the change had occurred after the trial.

[66] This includes summary judgment under R.S.C. Ords. 14 or 86 : *Langdale* v. *Danby* [1982] 1 W.L.R. 1123.

[67] R.S.C. Ord. 59, r. 10(2).

[68] [1954] 1 W.L.R. 1489, 1491 : approved by the House of Lords in *Skone* v. *Skone* [1971] 1 W.L.R. 812 and *Langdale* v. *Danby*, *supra*.

(3) The evidence must be such as is presumably to be believed, or, in other words, must be apparently credible, though it need not be incontrovertible.[69]

The Court of Appeal similarly adopts a restrictive approach to points not taken at the trial and presented for the first time in the Court of Appeal. The court will not decide in favour of an appellant on a new point unless it is satisfied beyond doubt (1) that it has before it all the facts bearing upon the new contention as completely as if it had been raised at the trial, and (2) that no evidence could have been adduced at the trial which by any possibility could prevent the point from succeeding.[70] Accordingly it may permit a new question to be raised on the construction and application of a regulation where the facts are not disputed.[71]

(vi) *Decision-making in the Court of Appeal*

The approach of the Court of Appeal varies according to whether the appeal concerns (1) questions of fact; (2) awards of damages; (3) exercises of judicial discretion; and (4) questions of law.

(1) *Questions of fact.* In the vast majority of cases, the trial will have been conducted by a judge sitting without a jury. His findings of fact will be set out in his judgment. On an appeal, a distinction will be drawn by the Court of Appeal between findings of "primary fact" and inferences of fact drawn from those primary facts (sometimes termed "secondary facts").[72] The Court of Appeal is most reluctant to disturb findings of primary fact where they are based on the testimony of witnesses who have been seen by the judge, and who, in accordance with the practice of the Court of Appeal, will not be seen in person on the appeal.[73] The judge's finding will normally have been based, at least in part, on his observations of manner and demeanour, and this advantage is denied to the Court of Appeal. In exceptional cases, the court may find that the trial judge has "failed to use or has palpably misused his advantage."[74] The judge's impression of the witnesses' demeanour "should be carefully checked by a critical examination of the whole of the evidence."[75] A judgment:

" . . . may be demonstrated . . . to be affected by material inconsistencies and inaccuracies or [the trial judge] may be shown to have failed to appreciate the weight or bearing of circumstances admitted or proved or otherwise to have gone plainly wrong."[76]

The court is a little less reluctant to interfere with findings based upon expert evidence.[77]

---

[69] See, *e.g. Roe* v. *Robert McGregor & Sons* [1968] 1 W.L.R. 925.

[70] See Lord Herschell in *The Tasmania* (1890) 15 App. Cas. at p. 225 and Jessell M.R. in *Ex p. Firth, re Cowburn* (1882) 19 Ch. D. 419, 429.

[71] *Donaghey* v. *P. O'Brien & Co.* [1966] 1 W.L.R. 1170, 1180; on appeal : *Donaghey* v. *Boulton & Paul Ltd.* [1968] A.C. 1, 14, 23, 31.

[72] See above, p. 8.

[73] *SS. Hontestroom (Owners)* v. *SS. Sagaporack (Owners)* [1927] A.C. 37; *Powell* v. *Streatham Manor Nursing Home* [1935] A.C. 243; *Watt or Thomas* v. *Thomas* [1947] A.C. 484.

[74] *Per* Lord Sumner in *SS. Hontestroom* v. *SS. Sagaporack, supra,* at p. 47.

[75] *Per* Lord Greene M.R. in *Yuill* v. *Yuill* [1945] P. 15, 22.

[76] *Per* Lord Macmillan in *Watt or Thomas* v. *Thomas* [1947] A.C. 484 at p. 491.

[77] *Joyce* v. *Yeomans* [1981] 1 W.L.R. 549. (Medical witnesses).

On the other hand, the Court of Appeal is much more willing to draw inferences from the primary facts different from those drawn by the trial judge: it is generally in as good a position as the judge to draw such inferences.[78]

The role of the Court of Appeal in appeals on questions of fact was considered in *Whitehouse* v. *Jordan*.[79] The trial judge held a senior hospital registrar to have been negligent in the course of delivering a baby by pulling too hard and too long on obstetric forceps, causing brain damage. This finding was based on a combination of expert evidence, a report by the consultant professor who was the registrar's head of department, and the testimony of the mother. This finding was reversed by the Court of Appeal (Lord Denning M.R. and Lawton L.J., Donaldson L.J. dissenting). The majority held that the expert evidence against the registrar was defective in certain respects, and could not stand up against the expert evidence in his favour; that the judge had acted incorrectly in interpreting a crucial word in the report in its dictionary sense rather than in that now stated by the professor to be the sense intended; and that as the judge had disbelieved most of the mother's evidence, he ought not to have relied upon any of it. The mother had testified that force had been applied to the extent that her hips had been lifted off the table. The judge accepted that this could not literally have been true, but held that it showed that she "could" have been pulled towards the bottom of the delivery bed. On this last point, Lawton L.J. said that this was one of the rare cases where the appeal court was entitled to disregard the trial judge's assessment of the reliability of a witness. He had "palpably misused his advantage" in seeing the witness by turning her account of what had happened, which physically could not have taken place, into one which could. The House of Lords unanimously endorsed the conclusion of the majority of the Court of Appeal. They stressed the point that apart from the mother's testimony, the issues concerned inferences from the primary facts in the sense of the evaluation of testimony accepted to have been honestly given.[80] As to the mother's testimony, the House agreed unanimously that the judge's "reconstruction" of it should be disregarded.

Where the trial is conducted with a jury, the powers of the Court of Appeal are more limited. A verdict will be set aside if the evidence was such that no jury properly directed could reasonably have returned it.[81]

(2) *Awards of damages.* The Court of Appeal will not vary an award of damages merely because the judges sitting on the appeal would have awarded a different figure. It will only do so:

" . . . if satisfied that the judge has acted on a wrong principle of law or has misapprehended the facts, or has, for those or other reasons, made a wholly erroneous estimate of the damage suffered."[82]

In practice, the Court of Appeal is much more likely to interfere with an award of damages than a finding of fact, especially where, as with large personal injuries awards, complex calculations are necessary.

---

[78] *Benmax* v. *Austin Motor Co. Ltd.* [1955] A.C. 370.
[79] [1981] 1 W.L.R. 246.
[80] See Lord Wilberforce, *ibid.* pp. 249–250; Lord Fraser of Tullybelton, *ibid.* p. 263.
[81] See below, p. 733.
[82] *Per* Morris L.J. in *Scott* v. *Musial* [1959] 2 Q.B. 429, 437.

Where damages were assessed by a jury, the Court of Appeal was only prepared to interfere with an award where it was "so excessive or so inadequate that no twelve reasonable jurors could reasonably have awarded it."[83] The consequence of this cautious approach was that awards of significantly different amounts in similar cases were permitted to stand. This was one of the factors in the move away from trial by jury in civil cases.[84] In *Ward* v. *James*,[85] Lord Denning M.R. said[86]:

> "In future this court will not feel the same hesitation as it formerly did in upsetting an award of damages by a jury. If it is 'out of all proportion to the circumstances of the case' (that is, if it is far too high or far too low), this court will set it aside."

This approach brings the position closer to that applied to awards by judges, but has not been tested in practice.

The Court of Appeal may substitute an award of damages for that made by a judge. If the award was made by a jury the Court of Appeal may only vary an award with the consent of the parties[87]: otherwise it must order a new trial, which may be by judge alone.

(3) *Exercises of discretion.* On many matters, a decision may be left to an exercise of the judge's discretion. This is commonly so in interlocutory matters such as pleading, discovery, venue and mode of trial. Here, the matter will normally have been considered first by a master or registrar, and then, by way of a fresh application to the judge. At this stage the judge will consider the matter afresh and may substitute his discretion for that of the master. However, if the matter is then taken to the Court of Appeal, that court will only interfere with the judge's exercise of discretion if he has erred in law, applied an incorrect principle, misapprehended the facts, taken irrelevant matters into consideration or ignored relevant considerations, or if the court is satisfied that his decision was wrong.[88] This is not regarded as enabling the Court of Appeal to interfere merely because the judges sitting on the appeal would have exercised the discretion differently.[89] An example is *Charles Osenton & Co.* v. *Johnston*,[90] where the House of Lords reversed an order for trial by an official referee on the ground that the judge had not given sufficient weight to the point that the professional reputation of surveyors was at stake.

In addition, modern statutes commonly leave decisions on substantive as distinct from procedural matters to the discretion of judges. Examples include awards under the Inheritance (Provision for Family and Dependants) Act 1975, financial provision after divorce and decisions concerning custody of and access to children. The same principles have been applied to

---

[83] *Ibid.* pp. 437–8.

[84] See above, p. 534.

[85] [1966] 1 Q.B. 273.

[86] *Ibid.* p. 301.

[87] R.S.C. Ord. 59, r. 11.(4). Where a head of damages has been erroneously included or excluded the only consent required is that of the person entitled to receive or the person liable to pay the damages, as the case may be: *ibid.*

[88] *Evans* v. *Bartlam* [1937] A.C. 473. This is regarded as broader than the tests applied by the court in reviewing exercises of administrative discretion under the principles stated in the *Wednesbury* case (see below, p. 744, n. 98) : *Tsai* v. *Woodworth, The Times,* November 30, 1983.

[89] *Per* Viscount Simon L.C. in *Charles Osenton & Co.* v. *Johnston* [1942] A.C. 130, 138.

[90] *Ibid.*

the role of the Court of Appeal here,[91] and it has been stressed that the court should be particularly unwilling to interfere where the exercise of discretion is based on the impression made by a person in the witness box.[92]

However, in custody cases there appears to be a difference between: (1) those who take the view that the appellate court should only interfere where the judge has erred in law, taken some irrelevant matter into account or failed to take some relevant matter into account, or where his decision is "plainly wrong" in the sense that no reasonable judge could have so decided[93]; and (2) those who take the view that, in addition, the appellate court may interfere on the ground that the judge's decision is "plainly wrong" as a consequence of erring in the course of balancing the relevant factors.[94] The House of Lords in *B. v. W. (Wardship: Appeal)*[95] seemed to endorse the second school of thought, but did not so indicate expressly.[96] In turn, *B. v. W.* was not cited in *D. v. M. (Minor: Custody Appeal)*,[97] the most recent pronouncement of the Court of Appeal on the topic and which clearly endorses the second school of thought. The adherents of both schools are agreed that the Court of Appeal may not interfere merely because the members of that court would have exercised the discretion differently.[97a]

If an appellate court wishes to vary a discretionary order, it may either substitute an appropriate order, remit the case to the judge (or to another judge) or, in exceptional cases, hear evidence in order to resolve any doubts.[98]

(4) *Questions of law.* Here, the Court of Appeal may simply substitute its opinion for that of the court below.

(vii) *Applications for a new trial*

Section 17 of the Supreme Court Act 1981 provides that applications for a new trial must normally be directed to the Court of Appeal. However, rules of court may prescribe cases or classes of cases where applications are to be made to the High Court: such cases can only be those where trial was by a judge alone and no error of the court at the trial is alleged.[99] The procedure for applications to the Court of Appeal for a new trial is virtually the same as for an appeal.[1]

---

[91] See, *e.g. In re Thornley, Decd.* [1969] 1 W.L.R. 1037; *Preston* v. *Preston* [1982] Fam. 17.

[92] *B.* v. *W. (Wardship : Appeal)* [1979] 1 W.L.R. 1041.

[93] Stamp L.J. dissenting, in *Re F (A Minor) (Wardship : Appeal)* [1976] Fam. 238, 249–255; Sir John Arnold P. in *Clode* v. *Clode* (1982) 3 F.L.R. 360, 363.

[94] *Re O (Infants) (Wardship : Appeal)* [1971] Ch. 748; Browne and Bridge L.JJ. in *Re F (A Minor) (Wardship: Appeal)* [1976] Fam. 238; *D.* v. *M. (Minor : Custody Appeal)* [1983] Fam. 33.

[95] [1979] 1 W.L.R. 1041.

[96] *Re F (A Minor), supra,* was mentioned, but not Stamp L.J.'s dissent.

[97] [1983] Fam. 33. See generally, S. Maidment, (1983) 133 N.L.J. 1032.

[97a] *Re F (A Minor), supra,* at pp. 250 (Stamp L.J.); 257–258 (Browne L.J.); *Clarke-Hunt* v. *Newcombe* (1983) 4 F.L.R. 482, 486–487 (Cumming-Bruce L.J.). In *Re F (A Minor), supra,* Browne L.J. did not think that the word "plainly" added anything to the test ([1976] Fam. at p. 258), but the term "plainly wrong" was used by Lord Scarman in *B.* v. *W.* [1979] 1 W.L.R. 1041 at p. 1054, and has been used since: *e.g. Clarke-Hunt* v. *Newcombe, supra.*

[98] *Per* Lord Scarman in *B.* v. *W., supra,* at p. 1055, in relation to custody orders.

[99] *e.g.* where judgment has been obtained in the absence of a party : Ord. 35, r. 2(1) (see *Re Edwards' Will Trusts, Edwards* v. *Edwards* [1982] Ch. 30).

[1] R.S.C. Ord. 59, r. 2.

Where a case is tried by judge alone, the proper course for a dissatisfied party is normally[2] to appeal. On an appeal, the Court of Appeal may, as we have noted, correct any error of fact or law and may vary the judgment. However, in some cases it may be appropriate for the Court of Appeal to order a new trial.[3] This may be so where, for example, the essence of the complaint is that there has not been a fair trial. For example, a party may be "taken by surprise" where a case is called on for hearing unexpectedly, or develops in a wholly unexpected manner. Similarly, a new trial may be ordered where fresh evidence is discovered,[4] or a witness confesses that his evidence was false,[5] or in cases of misconduct by the judge[6] or counsel.

Where a case is tried by a judge sitting with a jury, the proper course for a party dissatisfied is to apply for a new trial. The grounds for such applications mentioned above in relation to trial by judge alone will also be relevant here. In addition, there are a number of grounds related particularly to jury trial, including misdirection of the jury, the improper admission or rejection of evidence, and claims that there was no evidence to go to the jury, that the verdict was against the weight of evidence or that the damages are excessive or inadequate.[7] However, the court is not bound to grant a new trial on the ground of misdirection, or the improper admission or rejection of evidence, or because the verdict of the jury was not taken upon a question which the judge at the trial was not asked to leave to them, unless the Court of Appeal is of the opinion that this caused some "substantial wrong or miscarriage."[8] In other words, there will be no new trial in these circumstances if the court is satisfied that the jury, if rightly directed, would still have returned the same verdict.[9]

A verdict supported by no evidence is regarded as erroneous in law: if it is claimed, however, that a verdict is against the weight of evidence, it will only be set aside if it was one that no reasonable jury could have found.[10]

A new trial may be ordered on one particular aspect of a case, without affecting the other aspects.[11] For example, there may be a new trial on a question of damages without prejudice to a finding of liability.

(viii) *Appeals from masters, registrars and referees*

Generally speaking, an appeal lies from the decision of a High Court master or registrar or a District Registrar, to a judge of the appropriate division sitting in chambers.[12] The judge will rehear the matter and is not

---

[2] *i.e.* unless an application must be made to the High Court : n. 99, *supra.*

[3] Jurisdiction to do so is conferred by R.S.C. Ord. 59, r. 11(1).

[4] See above, p. 728 : *Meek* v. *Fleming* [1961] 2 Q.B. 366. (Court misled by concealment of material evidence).

[5] *Piotrowska* v. *Piotrowski* [1958] 1 W.L.R. 798.

[6] *Jones* v. *National Coal Board* [1957] 2 Q.B. 55, above, p. 541.

[7] See above, p. 731.

[8] R.S.C. Ord. 59, r. 11(5).

[9] *Rowell* v. *Pratt* [1938] A.C. 101, 116.

[10] *Metropolitan Ry. Co.* v. *Wright* (1886) 11 App.Cas. 152; *Mechanical Inventions Co. Ltd.* v. *Austin* [1935] A.C. 346. If it is obvious that no verdict for the plaintiff on all the available evidence could be supported, the court may save the waste of time in ordering a new trial by ordering judgment to be entered for the defendant: *Mechanical Inventions Co. Ltd.* v. *Austin, ibid.*

[11] R.S.C. Ord. 59, r. 11(3).

[12] R.S.C. Ord. 58, rr. 1(1), 3.

fettered by the decision of the master or registrar.[13] An appeal lies from a decision of a judge in chambers, whether or not the matter has previously been before a master or registrar, to the Court of Appeal, subject to the restrictions applicable generally to appeals to that court.[14]

In certain cases, an appeal lies direct from a master of the Queen's Bench or Chancery Divisions to the Court of Appeal.[15] These are cases where a matter has been tried by him or referred to him for a final decision, and decisions on an assessment of damages.[16]

An appeal lies from a decision of a special referee to the Court of Appeal.[17] However, no decision of an official referee[18] may be called in question by appeal or otherwise, except:

(1) on a point of law; or

(2) on a question only of costs;

(3) on a question of fact relating to a charge of fraud or breach of professional duty; or

(4) where he has made or refused to make an order of committal for contempt of court.[19]

(c) Appeals from the High Court to the House of Lords

In certain circumstances an appeal in a civil case may be taken directly from the High Court (whether a single judge or a Divisional Court) to the House of Lords, "leap-frogging" the Court of Appeal. The conditions are prescribed by Part II of the Administration of Justice Act 1969.[20]

Any of the parties to civil proceedings[21] in the High Court may apply to the trial judge[22] for a certificate to the effect that he is satisfied:

(1) that the "relevant conditions" are fulfilled in relation to his decision in the proceedings;

(2) that a sufficient case for a "leap-frog" appeal has been made out to justify an application for leave to appeal; and

(3) that all the parties consent to the grant of a certificate.[23]

Where apart from the provisions of Part II of the 1969 Act no appeal would lie to the Court of Appeal without the leave of the trial judge or the Court of Appeal, the judge is not to grant a certificate unless it appears to the judge that apart from those provisions "it would be a proper case for granting leave."[24]

The "relevant conditions" are:

---

[13] *Evans* v. *Bartlam* [1937] A.C. 473, 478.

[14] See above, p. 723; and see also R.S.C. Ord. 58, r. 6.

[15] R.S.C. Ord. 58, r. 2.

[16] Under, respectively, R.S.C. Ord. 36, r. 11 and Ord. 37.

[17] R.S.C. Ord. 58, r. 5.

[18] See above.

[19] R.S.C. Ord. 58, r. 4; Administration of Justice 1960, s.13(2)(*b*).

[20] This possibility was recommended by the Evershed Committee on Supreme Court Practice and Procedure, Final Report (Cmd. 8878, 1953) paras. 483–503. The Law Lords at the time were not in favour of the proposal, but attitudes had changed by the late 1960s. See L. Blom-Cooper and G. Drewry, *Final Appeal* (1972) pp. 149–151.

[21] *i.e.* "proceedings other than proceedings in a criminal cause or matter": Administration of Justice Act 1969, s.12(8).

[22] Or Divisional Court, as the case may be : *ibid.*

[23] 1969 Act, s.12(1).

[24] *Ibid.* s.15(3).

(1) that a point of law of general public importance is involved in the decision; and

(2) that the point of law either—

"(a) relates wholly or mainly to the construction of an enactment or of a statutory instrument, and has been fully argued in the proceedings and fully considered in the judgment of the judge in the proceedings, or

(b) is one in respect of which the judge is bound by a decision of the Court of Appeal or of the House of Lords in previous proceedings, and was fully considered in the judgments given by the Court of Appeal or the House of Lords (as the case may be) in those previous proceedings."[25]

No certificate can be granted if by virtue of any enactment no appeal would lie from the High Court to the Court of Appeal or from the Court of Appeal to the House of Lords, or if the decision or order of the judge was made in the exercise of jurisdiction to punish for contempt of court.[26]

Otherwise, the judge has a discretion whether to grant a certificate,[27] and no appeal lies from a refusal.[28] The application for a certificate should normally be made at the hearing but may be made within 14 days.[29]

If a certificate is granted any party may apply within one month to the House of Lords for leave to appeal directly.[30] No hearing is held. The House may grant leave "if . . . it appears . . . to be expedient to do so," whereupon no appeal will lie to the Court of Appeal.[31] Moreover, no appeal will lie to the Court of Appeal once a certificate is granted until either the time for an application for leave has expired or, where an application is made, until it has been determined by the House.[32]

The "leap-frog" procedure is used in comparatively few cases,[33] although it does enable there to be a significant saving in time and expense if a case is destined for the House of Lords. One of the problems is that it may be difficult for a trial judge to perceive that a case is so destined; it may only become so in the light of the decision in the Court of Appeal.[34]

(d) Appeals from the Court of Appeal to the House of Lords

An appeal lies from any judgment or order of the Court of Appeal to the House of Lords, provided that leave is obtained from either court.[35] No

---

[25] *Ibid.* s.12(3).

[26] *Ibid.* s.15(1)(2)(4).

[27] *I.R.C.* v. *Church Commissioners for England* [1975] 1 W.L.R. 1383.

[28] 1969 Act s.12(5).

[29] *Ibid.* s.12(4).

[30] The House may grant an extension of time : *ibid.* s.13(1).

[31] *Ibid.* s.13(2).

[32] *Ibid.* s.13(5).

[33] The early practice is reviewed by G. Drewry in "Leapfrogging - And a Lord Justices' Eye View of the Final Appeal" (1973) 89 L.Q.R. 260. Between 1970 and the end of 1972 certificates were granted in five cases.

[34] *e.g.* as in *Cassell & Co. Ltd.* v. *Broome* [1972] A.C. 1027 : see above, p. 286. The Lord Chancellor suggested that in view of the doubts raised about the direction in *Rookes* v. *Barnard* [1964] A.C. 1129, the proper course would have been to wait for a case in which the point was directly raised and suggest that the parties take *that* case directly to the House of Lords: *ibid.* p. 1053.

[35] Appellate Jurisdiction Act 1876, s.3; Administration of Justice (Appeals) Act 1934, s.1.

appeal lies from a decision of the Court of Appeal to refuse leave for an appeal to itself; such a refusal does not constitute a "judgment or order."[36] An application for leave is made first to the Court of Appeal, normally immediately after judgment. It is only if leave is refused that a petition for leave may be made to the House.

Among grounds commonly given by the Court of Appeal for refusing leave to appeal are that the point concerns an interlocutory matter, the point is one of fact rather than law, the subject matter is trivial, the matter has become of academic interest only to one or both of the parties and that the Court of Appeal was unanimous and not divided. On the other hand, leave is normally granted in revenue cases.[37]

Petitions to the House of Lords for leave are heard by an Appeal Committee of three Law Lords,[38] and must be lodged within one month from the date of the order of which complaint is made.[39] The parties may appear in person or may be represented by solicitors (known as "agents" on appeals to the House) or counsel. The committee sits in public except for considering application for leave to appeal direct from the High Court. No reasons are normally given for refusing leave. Conditions may be attached to a grant of leave: this is commonly done on appeals by the Inland Revenue in tax cases, where leave is only granted if the Revenue undertake to pay the costs of the appeal for the respondent in any event. If a condition is imposed by the Court of Appeal, the applicant may treat this as a refusal and apply for leave to the House of Lords. Petitions for leave which appear to be incompetent are considered without a hearing by three Law Lords and may be certified as such by them. If one or more has any doubts, the petition is referred to the Appeal Committee.[40]

Where an application for leave to appeal has been refused, it is nevertheless possible, in exceptional cases, for a fresh application to be made and granted.[41]

An appeal must be lodged in the House of Lords within three months of the date of the order appealed from, unless the House otherwise orders,[42] or a different period is fixed by statute. Leave to appeal out of time may be obtained. Unless legal aid has been granted, or the respondent agrees to waive the requirement, the appellant must give security for costs in the sum of £4,000.[43]

---

[36] *Lane* v. *Esdaile* [1891] A.C. 210; *Whitehouse* v. *The Board of Control* [1960] 1 W.L.R. 1093.

[37] See L. Blom-Cooper and G. Drewry, *Final Appeal* (1972) pp. 146–149.

[38] See above, p. 82 and L. Blom-Cooper and G. Drewry, *Final Appeal* (1972) Chap. VII.

[39] House of Lords Appeals, Directions as to Procedure, Dir. 1 : *Supreme Court Practice 1982*, para. 2473.

[40] *Practice Direction (House of Lords : Petitions)* [1970] 1 W.L.R. 1218; Directions as to Procedure, Dir. 6.

[41] See *Buttes Gas* v. *Hammer* [1982] A.C. 888 (leave to appeal from [1975] Q.B. 557 in the light of related proceedings : but note the criticisms of F.A. Mann, (1983) 2 C.J.Q. 320, 325–326); *R.* v. *Home Secretary, ex p. Khera* [1983] 2 W.L.R. 321, (the House of Lords invited the appellant to re-apply for leave following their Lordships' decision to review *R.* v. *Home Secretary, ex p. Zamir* [1980] A.C. 930).

[42] Directions as to Procedure, Dir. 12.

[43] Directions as to Procedure, Dir. 20; *Practice Direction (House of Lords : Costs : Security)* [1981] 1 W.L.R. 1213.

The appeal is normally considered by an Appellate Committee of five Law Lords.[44] The parties may appear in person or be represented by counsel. The parties must each lodge a printed "Case," "being a succinct statement of their argument in the Appeal, settled by counsel" and stating "what are, in their view, the issues arising in the Appeal."[45] All members of the Appellate Committee will have read the Case and the judgments in the court below in advance of the hearing. The House has noted and deprecated a tendency to expand the written cases to incorporate and develop in them detailed written arguments, supported by lengthy citations and references to numerous authorities:

" . . . much on the same lines as the written "briefs" submitted by the parties in appeals to appellate courts in the United States, which have resulted in oral argument playing a relatively insignificant role in the decision-making process adopted by appellate courts in that country."[46]

The pre-reading was, it was emphasised, not intended to reduce the process played by oral argument in the decision-making process. Cases should include the *heads* of argument on each issue, and only *key* authorities should be mentioned. It has, however, been doubted whether all members of the Committee do always read all the papers in advance, and whether all the members always come to a hearing without at least a provisional conclusion in mind.[47] It would obviously be undesirable for preconceived opinions to be based on limited information. Indeed, it has been suggested that changes in the practice of both the Court of Appeal[48] and the House of Lords may inevitably transform the nature of oral argument:

" . . . which is bound to lose its force where it is no longer a dialogue in the traditional sense, but an attempt to dislodge or fortify an existing impression, however provisional it may be said to be . . . .
[T]he introduction of radical changes under the heading of practice and procedure is outside the province of judges."[49]

The respective approaches of the House to question of fact, discretion and law are similar to that taken by the Court of Appeal.[50] The House "may determine what of right, and according to the law and custom of this realm, ought to be done" in relation to the appeal. Where the House reverses or varies an order of the court below, or orders anything to be done by the court below, the order of the House of Lords must be made an order of the High Court[51]: the House itself has no machinery for enforcement.

---

[44] See above, p. 82.
[45] See above, p. 83. Directions as to Procedure, Dir. 22.
[46] *M.V. Yorke Motors* v. *Edwards* [1982] 1 W.L.R. 444, 446–448.
[47] F.A. Mann, (1983) 2 C.J.Q. 320, 327–328, 334–335.
[48] See above, pp. 724–727.
[49] F.A. Mann, *supra,* pp. 334, 335.
[50] See above, pp. 729–732.
[51] See R.S.C. Ord. 32, r. 10.

4. APPEALS IN ADMINISTRATIVE LAW MATTERS

(a) Introduction

No neat classification is possible of the vast range of functions performed by administrative authorities. Neither is it possible to discern any clear pattern in the availability of rights of appeal from administrative decisions.[52]

The Franks Committee[53] noted that:

" . . . over most of the field of public administration no formal procedure is provided for objecting or deciding on objections. . . . Of course the aggrieved individual can always complain to the appropriate administrative authority, to his Member of Parliament, to a representative organisation or to the press. But there is no formal procedure on which he can insist. . . . It may be thought that in these cases the individual is less protected against unfair or wrong decisions [than where there is provision for a formal procedure involving a tribunal or inquiry]."[54]

Such decisions were outside the committee's terms of reference, although it did express "much sympathy" with the proposal by Professor W.A. Robson that there should be a general administrative appeal tribunal, with jurisdiction to hear not only appeals from tribunals and from ministers after a public inquiry, "but also appeals against harsh or unfair administrative decisions in that considerable field of administration in which no special tribunal or enquiry procedure is provided."[55] The committee, however, felt that it had to consider the proposal in relation to its limited terms of reference, and that, viewed from that standpoint, the proposal was to be rejected.

Since then, the problem noted by the Franks Committee has been partly met by the establishment of "Ombudsmen" of various kinds. The Parliamentary Commissioner for Administration and Local Commissioners have power to investigate complaints that there has been injustice consequent on "maladministration" in central and local government.[56] The concept of "maladministration" covers such matters as corruption, bias, unfair discrimination, giving misleading advice, failure to explain the reasons for a decision, losing correspondence and unreasonable delay. The relevant defects are mostly procedural, although where a decision is "thoroughly bad in quality" maladministration may be inferred, and in certain circumstances authorities may be required to reconsider a rule that has caused hardship. The commissioners may not, however, question the merits of a discretionary decision taken without maladministration,[57] and may not entertain a complaint in respect of which there is a right of appeal

---

[52] See S.A. de Smith, *Constitutional and Administrative Law* (4th ed.) pp. 530–531.

[53] See above, p. 32.

[54] Cmnd. 218, pp. 2–3.

[55] Cmnd. 218, p. 28.

[56] See generally, S.A. de Smith, *Constitutional and Administrative Law*, (4th ed., 1981) Chap. 31; H.W.R. Wade, *Administrative Law* (5th ed., 1982) pp. 73–93, 123–127; P.P. Craig, *Administrative Law* (1983) pp. 239–252. There is also an office of National Health Service Commissioner (held by the P.C.A.) and there are two Commissioners in Northern Ireland.

[57] Parliamentary Commissioner Act 1967, s.12(3); Local Government Act 1974, s.34(3).

to a tribunal or a remedy by way of proceedings in a court of law, unless it is not reasonable to expect the complainant to utilise those possibilities.[58]

As to the availability of statutory appeals against administrative decisions, the late Professor de Smith noted[59] that there is in general no appeal against discretionary decisions of central government involving questions of national policy or the allocation of scarce resources, against decisions of public corporations or against most discretionary decisions of local authorities on the allocation of limited resources.

However, in certain other areas of public administration, particularly where no sensitive issue of policy is involved, where questions of law may loom large or where a decision has a significant impact on individual rights of liberty or property there may be provision for an appeal.

(b) Particular areas

(i) *Regulatory functions*

Many activities are subjected to state regulation for such purposes as the protection of public health and welfare. Certain activities are prohibited by law. Others are permitted provided that those who participate in them register with a public authority.[60] Yet others require a specific permission or licence from a public authority: the ease with which a licence may be obtained, and the grounds upon which a licence may be refused are almost infinitely variable.

Control may also be exerted by procedures for inspection. For example, health and safety inspectors may inspect factory premises, offer advice on safety matters, issue notices requiring the cessation of dangerous activities, and, in the last resort, bring criminal proceedings for breaches of the law.

Decisions made in the course of regulatory procedures of this kind are commonly subject to a statutory right of appeal to a tribunal,[61] the Crown Court,[62] a county court[63] or, most commonly, a magistrates' court.[64]

In a small number of cases, such as decisions of the Director-General of Fair Trading concerning consumer credit licensing and the supervision of estate agency work, an appeal lies to a minister, in these examples the Secretary of State for Trade.

It is normal for it to be possible on such appeals to challenge a decision on the merits as well as on any point of law. This may be so even where it is expressly stated that the decision is "at the discretion" of the authority in

---

[58] *Ibid.* ss.5(2) and 26(6) respectively.

[59] *Constitutional and Administrative Law* (4th ed., 1981) pp. 530–1.

[60] Registration requirements may also be imposed to raise revenue.

[61] *e.g.* appeals to an industrial tribunal against an improvement or prohibition notice served by a health and safety inspector.

[62] *e.g.* decisions of a chief officer of police in relation to firearms certificates and the registration of firearms; refusal of a permit for the commercial provision of amusements with prizes and many decisions of justices of the peace in administrative matters: see D. Price, *Appeals* (1982) pp. 37–40.

[63] *e.g.* a person aggrieved by a notice requiring him to carry out works of repair, by a demand for the recovery of expenses where the authority has acted in default or by a demolition or closing order: Housing Act 1957, ss.9, 11 and 20: Price, *op. cit.* (1982), pp. 46–49.

[64] *e.g.* revocation of a pilot's or slaughterman's licence; refusal of a pet shop or knacker's yard licence; refusal of registration of a nursery, child minder, or nursing home: Price, *op. cit.* (1982) pp. 53–60.

question. For example, a grant of a permit for amusements with prizes[65] is "at the discretion of the local authority."[66] An appeal lies to the Crown Court. In *Sagnata Ltd.* v. *Norwich Corporation*,[67] the Court of Appeal held that the recorder at quarter sessions (now the Crown Court) had been correct to go into the merits of a refusal of a permit afresh on appeal, although this did not mean that he "ought not to pay great attention to the fact that the duly constituted and elected local authority have come to an opinion on the matter, and ought not lightly to reverse their opinion."[68]

(ii) *Welfare benefits*

Another important sphere of state activity is that of the provision of many kinds of welfare benefits. Here, it is common for rights of appeal to be granted to a tribunal[69] or, in a few cases,[70] a minister.

(iii) *Tribunals*

Where a decision-making function has been entrusted to a tribunal, it is normal for there to be a further appeal on points of law, either to a special appellate tribunal such as the Social Security Commissioners or the Employment Appeal Tribunal,[71] to the High Court or to the Court of Appeal.[72] For example, the Tribunals and Inquiries Act 1971 provides[73] for a right of appeal on a point of law to the High Court from the decisions of over 10 tribunals,[74] and there are several others for which similar provision is made by specific statutes. Appeals from tribunals to the High Court on points of law may be required to be made by means of a case stated procedure. Most lie to the Queen's Bench Division, but some, such as those against decisions of the Commons Commissioners and the Special and General Commissioners of Income Tax, lie to the Chancery Division. Appeals are generally heard by a single judge, unless the High Court's decision will be final, in which case the appeal will normally be heard by a Divisional Court.[75]

(iv) *Land use*

Given the traditional concern of the law for the protection of property rights it is perhaps not surprising that statutory rights to appeal figure prominently in respect of governmental decisions that infringe or affect property rights. Two kinds of procedure require special mention here.

---

[65] *e.g.* fruit machines.

[66] Lotteries and Amusements Act 1976, Sched. 3. para. 7(1)(*a*).

[67] [1971] 2 Q.B. 614.

[68] *Per* Lord Goddard C.J. in *Stepney Borough Council* v. *Joffe* [1949] 1 K.B. 599, 603, endorsed by Edmund Davies L.J. in *Sagnata, supra*, at p. 637.

[69] See above, pp. 55–58.

[70] *e.g.* on questions whether contribution conditions for national insurance conditions have been satisfied: Social Security Act 1975, s.93(1)(*b*).

[71] See above, pp. 54, 58.

[72] *e.g.* from the Lands Tribunal and the Foreign Compensation Commission.

[73] s.13.

[74] *e.g.* industrial tribunals (for certain matters), rent assessment committees and pension appeal tribunals.

[75] The procedure on ordinary appeals is regulated by R.S.C. Ord. 55 and on appeals by case stated by Ord. 56. R.S.C. Ord. 57 makes further provision for appeals to Divisional Courts.

First, planning permission is generally necessary for "the carrying out of building, engineering, mining or other operations in, on, over or under land" or "the making of any material change in the use" of buildings or land.[76] Applications for permission are made to the local planning authority and an appeal on merits, fact or law lies against a refusal to the Secretary of State for the Environment. An appeal may involve a hearing by way of a public local inquiry conducted by an inspector appointed by the Secretary of State, unless the appellant wishes simply to make written representations. The inspector may make the decision himself, except in the thirty per cent. or so of larger scale applications, where the decision is taken by the Secretary of State. An appeal thereafter lies on a point of law to the Queen's Bench Division.

Secondly, there are many powers which authorise the compulsory acquisition of land. The typical procedure provides for a compulsory purchase order to be made by a local authority, subject to confirmation by a minister. If there are objections, a hearing before an inspector must be held on behalf of the minister. If he confirms the order, the typical provision[77] governing further appeals enables a person aggrieved by the order to apply within six weeks to the High Court for the order to be quashed on the ground either:

(1) that it is "not within the powers of the Act"; or

(2) that the applicant has been substantially prejudiced by failure to comply with a requirement of the Act.

The order may not otherwise be challenged: thus the person aggrieved may not, for example, seek to challenge an order by applying for judicial review[78] whether within the six week period or not.[79]

The first limb of the grounds of challenge purports to approximate to judicial review under the *ultra vires* doctrine,[80] although it has been given a wider interpretation by the courts. The correct approach was stated as follows by Lord Denning M.R. in *Ashbridge Investments Ltd.* v. *Minister of Housing and Local Government*[81]:

> "The court can only interfere on the ground that the Minister has gone outside the powers of the Act or that any requirement of the Act has not been complied with. Under this section it seems to me that the court can interfere with the Minister's decision if he has acted on no evidence; or if he has come to a conclusion to which on the evidence he could not reasonably come; or if he has given a wrong interpretation to the words of the statute; or if he has taken into consideration matters which he ought not to have taken into account, or vice versa; or has otherwise gone wrong in law. It is identical with the position when the court has power to interfere with the decision of a lower tribunal which has erred in point of law."

[76] Town and Country Planning Act 1971, s.22.

[77] *e.g.* Acquisition of Land Act 1981, ss.23–25; Housing Act 1957, Sched. 4, paras. 2, 3; Town and Country Planning Act 1971, ss.244, 245.

[78] See below, pp. 742–749.

[79] See *Smith* v. *East Elloe R.D.C.* [1956] A.C. 736; *R.* v. *Secretary of State for the Environment, ex p. Ostler* [1977] Q.B. 122.

[80] See below, pp. 743–745.

[81] [1965] 1 W.L.R. 1320, 1326. Applied by the Court of Appeal in *Coleen Properties Ltd.* v. *Minister of Housing and Local Government* [1971] 1 W.L.R. 433, and subsequent cases.

This would appear to extend the grounds of challenge to include errors of law not of a kind to cause the authority to act *ultra vires*.

(v) *Appeals from ministers*

In a small number of situations where ministers have to determine questions which may have a significant legal content, there is a further right of appeal on a point of law (or analogous grounds) to the High Court. These include the procedures mentioned in the previous section, decisions of the Secretary of State for Trade on appeals from the Director-General of Fair Trading, decisions of the Secretary of State for Social Services on national insurance contribution conditions and deportation decisions.[82]

(vi) *Immigration*

The impact on individual liberty of decisions to refuse entry to or to deport persons who have no legal right to enter or remain in the United Kingdom is such that a special appellate structure has been established.[83] The decisions of immigration officers or the Home Secretary, whether discretionary or not, may normally be the subject of an appeal to an Immigration Adjudicator, and then to the Immigration Appeal Tribunal.[84] The decision of the tribunal is final, but may be the subject of judicial review.[85] Where a deportation order is made on the ground that it is conducive to the public good "as being in the interests of national security or of the relations between the United Kingdom and any other country or for other reasons of a political nature," there is no appeal, but representations may be made to "three advisors," who may advise the Home Secretary but may not make a binding decision.[86]

D. APPLICATIONS FOR JUDICIAL REVIEW

An appeal will only lie if expressly provided by statute. Apart from, but parallel to, any appellate structure is the control exercised by the High Court over the decisions of any statutory authority[87] with a limited jurisdiction or area of power. This "judicial" control is exercised on the basis of two doctrines. By far the more significant is the *ultra vires* doctrine. The other is the power of the High Court to quash any decision within the reach of the prerogative order of certiorari if an error of law is apparent on the face of the decision-making body's record of proceedings: for this purpose it is immaterial whether the error of law is such as to cause the body to act *ultra vires*.[88] There is not the space here to give more than a very brief account of the *ultra vires* doctrine, and the procedures for seeking judicial review.[89]

[82] See below.

[83] Immigration Act 1971, Part II.

[84] In certain cases, the appeal lies directly to the I.A.T.

[85] See below.

[86] Immigration Act 1971, s.15(3). See *R. v. Secretary of State for the Home Department, ex p. Hosenball* [1977] 1 W.L.R. 766.

[87] Or bodies established under the royal prerogative: *R. v. Criminal Injuries Compensation Board, ex p. Lain* [1967] 2 Q.B. 864.

[88] *R. v. Northumberland Compensation Appeal Tribunal, ex p. Shaw* [1952] 1 K.B. 338.

[89] The leading works include de Smith's, *Judicial Review of Administrative Action* (4th ed. 1980); H.W.R. Wade, *Administrative Law* (5th ed., 1982); P.P. Craig, *Administrative Law* (1983). For a briefer account see S.A. de Smith, *Constitutional and Administrative Law* (4th ed., 1981) Chaps. 28, 29.

1. The Ultra Vires Doctrine

Public authorities are normally given a circumscribed area of authority by Parliament. The function of the courts is to ensure that such authorities, whether inferior courts, tribunals, ministers or local authorities, do not exceed any of the limits expressly set by Parliament, and that they perform any statutory duties. If that were all to be done, the *ultra vires* doctrine would simply be an exercise in statutory interpretation, and more or less straightforward as the case might be. However, the courts have in addition read certain implied limitations into governmental powers aimed at ensuring that those powers are not abused, and that decision-making processes are fair procedurally. It is assumed that these limitations are to be observed unless Parliament expressly provides otherwise.

If express or implied limits are exceeded, the body in question is said to have acted "*ultra vires*" *i.e.* beyond its powers: if they are not, the body has acted "*intra vires*." Where a decision is judicial rather than administrative[90] the term "jurisdiction" is used rather than "power," but the difference is one of terminology rather than substance. For convenience of exposition a number of different *ultra vires* situations are commonly distinguished.

(a) Straightforward situations

In some cases a question may arise whether a particular activity falls within the scope of existing statutory authority. For example, in *Attorney-General* v. *Fulham Corporation*[91] the establishment of a municipal laundry was held not to be within the corporation's statutory powers to provide wash-houses. The courts, however, accept that authority may be "reasonably implied" from the express provisions of a statute,[92] and, furthermore, that matters "reasonably incidental" to activities expressly or impliedly authorised will also be held to be *intra vires*.[93]

(b) Jurisdiction over fact and law

In many situations, a body may only act where it is first established that a given state of affairs exists. For example, a court or tribunal may only have jurisdiction over a certain geographical area; a rent tribunal may only have jurisdiction in respect of "leases" of "furnished" premises; there may be a monetary limit to jurisdiction. In these examples, the "preliminary," "collateral" or "threshold" question is clearly distinguishable from the "main" question the court or tribunal has to determine. Moreover, the former is determinable at the commencement of that body's hearing. The superior courts have taken the view that inferior courts and tribunals may not extend their jurisdiction by erroneous determinations of these "preliminary," "collateral" or "jurisdictional" issues, whether or not the error is one of fact or law.[94] If challenged, decisions on these points will be redetermined by the High Court on an application for judicial review.

---

[90] These categories represent each end of a spectrum rather than two discrete categories.
[91] [1921] 1 Ch. 440.
[92] *Baroness Wenlock* v. *River Dee Co.* (1885) 10 App. Cas. 354, 362.
[93] *Att.-Gen.* v. *Great Eastern Railway Co.* (1880) 5 App. Cas. 473, 478.
[94] See, *e.g. R.* v. *City of London, etc. Rent Tribunal, ex p. Honig* [1951] 1 K.B. 641.

In other cases, however, the distinction between "preliminary" and "main" questions is less easy to draw. This is particularly so where it is alleged that a tribunal with jurisdiction at the commencement of an inquiry has "wandered outside its designated territory" by misconstruing the statute which gives it power to act. This area of administrative law has been the subject of much sophisticated analysis: it has, however, been doubted whether there is any clear cut or convincing test to distinguish "jurisdictional" questions from others. It may be that in the last resort the classification applied by a reviewing court turns more on whether that court wishes to intervene than on the application of any clear principle.

The decision of the House of Lords in *Anisminic Ltd.* v. *Foreign Compensation Commission*[95] was widely regarded as broadening significantly the range of errors of law that would be regarded as causing a tribunal to exceed its jurisdiction.

In *Pearlman* v. *Keepers and Governors of Harrow School*[96] Lord Denning M.R. said that the traditional distinction between jurisdictional and non-jurisdictional errors should be discarded and replaced by a rule that all errors of law, as distinct from errors of fact, should be regarded as jurisdictional. This view has been broadly endorsed by certain members of the House of Lords, but only in respect of tribunals other than courts of law.[97]

(c) Discretion

The courts under the *ultra vires* doctrine ensure that bodies entrusted with a discretion do not fetter it unlawfully by developing rigid rules which preclude a genuine consideration of each case on its merits or by entering contracts or other agreements incompatible with a proper exercise of discretion. Similarly, a body may not be estopped from exercising a statutory discretion and may not delegate the exercise of a discretion without express or implied statutory authority.

Furthermore, an administrative body may not "abuse" its discretion by exercising powers in bad faith or for an improper purpose, by taking account of irrelevant considerations or ignoring relevant considerations, or by making a decision that is so unreasonable, no reasonable authority could make it.[98]

(d) Natural Justice

There are two basic principles of natural justice. The first, the *nemo judex in sua causa* rule, provides that no man should be a judge in his own cause, and is applied to judicial or quasi-judicial decisions. The rule is breached where the adjudicator has a direct financial interest[99] or has acted

---

[95] [1969] 2 A.C. 147.

[96] [1979] Q.B. 56.

[97] *In Re Racal Communications Ltd.* [1981] A.C. 374 *per* Lord Diplock and Lord Keith. It remains to be seen whether this view will become established.

[98] These principles were expounded by Lord Greene M.R. in *Associated Provincial Picture Houses Ltd.* v. *Wednesbury Corporation* [1948] 1 K.B. 223.

[99] *e.g. Dimes* v. *Grand Junction Canal Proprietors* (1852) 3 H.L. Cas. 759 (decision of Lord Cottenham L.C. set aside by the House of Lords on the ground that he held shares in the plaintiff company).

both as prosecutor and judge, or where there is a reasonable suspicion or real likelihood of bias.[1]

The other, the *audi alteram partem* rule, applies to a wider range of decision-making functions and requires prior notice to be given of a decision adverse to individual interests together with an opportunity to make representations. The detailed content of this rule varies from the rigorous procedural standards expected of courts to the minimal standards of "fairness" required in respect of purely administrative decisions: the content in any given case will depend on the court's appraisal of what is appropriate in the circumstances.[2]

(e) Procedural Ultra Vires

The procedure to be adopted for a particular decision-making process may be expressly prescribed by statute or statutory instrument. However, the consequences of failure to observe a particular step are not commonly spelled out. The courts draw a distinction between *mandatory* and *directory* requirements: failure to observe a mandatory step renders the ultimate decision *ultra vires*; failure to observe a directory step does not have this effect, although in some cases "substantial compliance" may be necessary. Important safeguards such as an obligation to consult[3] or to inform a person of rights of appeal[4] are normally held to be mandatory: trivial typographical errors which do not mislead[5] are normally regarded as directory matters, although the distinction is not always easy to draw.

2. THE METHODS OF OBTAINING JUDICIAL REVIEW

(a) Introduction

Judicial review of judicial and administrative decisions and delegated legislation may be sought "directly" or "collaterally." A direct challenge may be made either:

(1) by an "application for judicial review" in the Queen's Bench Division, where the court may award one or more of a number of remedies: namely, certiorari, mandamus, prohibition, an injunction, a declaration and damages; or

(2) in an ordinary action in the Queen's Bench or Chancery Divisions for an injunction, a declaration, or damages.

A challenge is made collaterally where the argument that an act or decision, such as a bye-law, is *ultra vires* is raised as a defence to enforcement proceedings or prosecution.[6]

The new, unified, procedure for an application for judicial review was introduced in 1978. In 1982, the House of Lords held that as a general rule

---

[1] The test currently favoured was expounded by Lord Denning M.R. in *Metropolitan Properties Co.* v. *Lannon* [1969] 1 Q.B. 577, 599: whether "right-minded persons would think that, in the circumstances, there was a real likelihood of bias."

[2] See, *e.g. Ridge* v. *Baldwin* [1964] A.C. 40 (dismissal of a chief constable without prior notice and a proper hearing held to be void); *R.* v. *Commission for Racial Equality, ex p. Cottrell & Rothon* [1980] 1 W.L.R. 1580, 1586–7 (emphasising the variable content of the *audi alteram partem* rule and the duty to act fairly).

[3] *Agricultural etc. Training Board* v. *Aylesbury Mushrooms Ltd.* [1972] 1 W.L.R. 190.

[4] *London & Clydeside Ltd.* v. *Aberdeen District Council* [1980] 1 W.L.R. 182.

[5] *e.g. R.* v. *Dacorum Gaming Licensing Committee* [1971] 3 All E.R. 666.

[6] See, *e.g. Kruse* v. *Johnson* [1898] 2 Q.B. 91.

it will be contrary to public policy and an abuse of the process of the court for a plaintiff complaining of a public authority's infringement of his "public law rights" to seek redress by an ordinary action rather than an application for judicial review.[7] Private law claims against public authorities, such as actions for damages, may still be brought by ordinary proceedings.[8] The distinction between public law and private law matters is, however, a novel one, and may prove in some, if not many, cases difficult to draw.

(b) Procedure on applications for judicial review

The procedure on applications for judicial review is prescribed by section 31 of the Supreme Court Act 1981 and R.S.C. Order 53. An application for mandamus, prohibition or certiorari, or for an injunction restraining a person from acting in an office in which he is not entitled to act, *must* be brought under Order 53. An application for a declaration or injunction (other than of the kind just mentioned) *may* be brought under Order 53,[9] and such a remedy may be granted where the court considers it just and convenient so to do, having regard to the nature of the matters in respect of which, and the persons and bodies against whom, mandamus, prohibition or certiorari may be granted, and all the circumstances of the case.

On an application for judicial review, the applicant may claim any one or more of the remedies listed above, and may be awarded damages if there is a good cause of action. The procedure is in two stages. The applicant must first obtain leave from a High Court judge of the Queen's Bench Division. Where the application for leave is refused, the applicant may renew it by applying, in a criminal case, to a Divisional Court, and in a civil case, to a judge sitting in open court. The applicant must specify the relief sought and the grounds for his claim and file an affidavit verifying the facts relied on. He may be allowed to amend his claim on such terms, if any, as the court thinks fit.

The court may not grant leave unless it considers that the applicant has a "sufficient interest" in the matter (*locus standi*): it is not necessary, however, for him to show that his legal rights are affected.[10]

Once leave is granted, the application is made to a judge sitting in open court, unless the court directs that it be made to a judge in chambers or a Divisional Court: criminal cases are, however, always heard by a Divisional Court. The court may entertain interlocutory applications for orders such as those for discovery, interrogatories and cross-examination on affidavits. Evidence is given in affidavit form,[11] and leave to cross-examine is in practice rarely granted.

An application must be made promptly, and in any event within three months from the date when grounds for the application first arose, unless the court considers there are good grounds for extending the period.

---

[7] *O'Reilly* v. *Mackman* [1983] 2 A.C. 237.

[8] *Davy* v. *Spelthorne Borough Council* [1983] 3 W.L.R. 743.

[9] Subject to the principle expressed in *O'Reilly* v. *Mackman, supra.*

[10] *Inland Revenue Commissioners* v. *National Federation of Small Businesses* [1982] A.C. 617.

[11] As to the principles governing the admission of fresh evidence, see *R.* v. *Secretary of State for the Environment, ex p. Powis* [1982] 1 All E.R. 788, 797–8.

All the remedies are discretionary, and may be refused, for example, where the applicant is actuated by improper motives or on the ground of undue delay.

(c) A comparison with ordinary actions

It should be noted that in ordinary actions for a declaration or injunction there is no requirement of leave, the limitation period is normally six years, although a remedy may still be refused on the ground of undue delay, and the applicant is not required to swear an affidavit in support of his factual allegations. Moreover, it is the more useful procedure where it is necessary for a witness to give evidence orally. However, a person will only have *locus standi* to be granted a declaration or injunction in an ordinary action if his legal rights are affected or he has suffered special damage.[12] Otherwise, that person must either apply for judicial review under Order 53, where the test for *locus standi* is less strict, or seek the consent of the Attorney-General for "relator proceedings." Here, the Attorney-General is the nominal plaintiff, although the proceedings are taken at the expense of the applicant (or "relator").[13] The Attorney-General's decision to grant or refuse consent may not be challenged.[14]

(d) The remedies

(i) *Mandamus*

The prerogative[15] order of mandamus[16] lies to compel performance of a public (not necessarily statutory) duty. For example, it may be granted where a tribunal wrongfully declines to hear a matter that does in fact lie within its jurisdiction, or, where there has been an *ultra vires* abuse of discretion, to ensure that the matter is reconsidered according to law.[17]

(ii) *Prohibition and Certiorari*

The prerogative orders of prohibition and certiorari[18] are similar in scope. Prohibition lies to restrain a tribunal or other authority where it is about to act *ultra vires* or to complete an *ultra vires* act already begun. Certiorari lies to quash[19] a decision already made where:

(1) it is *ultra vires*; or
(2) it has been obtained by fraud;[20] or
(3) there is an error of law apparent on the face of the record of proceedings.

These orders were formerly confined to decisions in respect of which there was a duty to act judicially, but they may now be sought in respect of any judicial or administrative (but not legislative) act.

---

[12] *Boyce* v. *Paddington Corporation* [1903] 1 Ch. 109; *Gouriet* v. *Union of Post Office Workers* [1978] A.C. 435.

[13] See, *e.g. Att.-Gen ex rel. McWhirter* v. *Independent Broadcasting Authority* [1973] Q.B. 629.

[14] *Gouriet* v. *Union of Post Office Workers, supra.*

[15] So called because the writ replaced by the modern order was thought to be especially associated with the Crown.

[16] Normally pronounced "mandaymus."

[17] *e.g. Padfield* v. *Minister of Agriculture* [1968] A.C. 997.

[18] Normally pronounced "sersheeorair'eye."

[19] Not "squash," "quosh" or "gnash" (*cf. R.* v. *Pressick* [1978] Crim. L.R. 377).

[20] See *R.* v. *Wolverhampton Crown Court, ex p. Crofts* [1983] 1 W.L.R. 204.

(iii) *Declarations and Injunctions*

A person may obtain a declaration on a disputed matter of law, or an injunction, whereby a party to an action is required to do or refrain from doing a particular thing.[21] These were in origin private law remedies but are today frequently sought in respect of the decisions of public authorities.

(iv) *Habeas Corpus*[22]

The prerogative writ of *habeas corpus ad subjiciendum* lies to secure a person's release from wrongful imprisonment. An *ex parte* application for a writ must be made to a Divisional Court of the Queen's Bench Division or, if no such court is sitting, to a single judge of any Division of the High Court, and takes precedence over other business. In an emergency, an application may be made to a judge out of court, for example at home at night. If prima facie grounds are shown by an affidavit by or on behalf of the prisoner the matter is normally adjourned to a Divisional Court for a full hearing. In exceptional cases the writ may be issued forthwith to the custodian, requiring him to produce the prisoner to the court at the time specified for the full hearing. In either event, the burden of justifying the detention lies on the custodian: if he fails, the prisoner's release is ordered.

The grounds for granting a writ of habeas corpus are essentially the same as for an application for judicial review. An appeal lies in civil cases as of right to the Court of Appeal and then with leave to the House of Lords. In criminal cases, no appeal can lie from an order made by a single judge,[23] but an appeal does lie from the Divisional Court to the House of Lords, with the leave of either.[24] An appeal may be taken from a refusal to discharge the prisoner or an order of release: in the latter event the person's right to remain at large cannot be affected by the outcome of the appeal.[25] After a refusal to grant habeas corpus no further application may be made on the same grounds and evidence.[26]

An application for habeas corpus is the standard method of challenging extradition decisions.

(e) Relationship between applications for judicial review and appeals

The remedies available on an application for judicial review are discretionary, and will not be awarded if there is some equally convenient and beneficial remedy such as a right of appeal. However, an appeal to a minister against a planning condition will not, for example, be regarded as convenient as certiorari where the issue is purely one of law.[27] Indeed, it has sometimes been stated that an application for judicial review must be

---

[21] See further above, p. 658.

[22] See R.J. Sharpe, *The Law of Habeas Corpus* (1976); *de Smith's Judicial Review of Administrative Action* (4th ed., 1981) appendix 2; R.S.C. Order 54.

[23] Administration of Justice Act 1960, s.15(2): a single judge may only grant an application: the matter must otherwise be referred to a Divisional Court: *ibid.* s.14(1).

[24] *Ibid.* ss.1, 15(3).

[25] *Ibid.* s.15(1)(4). In criminal cases an order may be made providing for the continued detention of the defendant or directing that he shall not be released except on bail: *ibid.* s.5.

[26] *Ibid.* s.14(2).

[27] R. v. *Hillingdon London Borough Council, ex p. Royco Homes Ltd.* [1974] Q.B. 720.

made where a challenge is based on the *ultra vires* doctrine, rather than exercising a right to appeal on a point of law.[28]

Conversely, an application for judicial review will be less appropriate than an appeal by case stated where complicated findings of fact are involved,[29] and will not be entertained in respect of points arising in the course of trials or committal proceedings[30]: such proceedings must be concluded before any challenge can take place, whether by appeal or application for judicial review.

Statutory provisions may purport to exclude or restrict judicial review. For example, the Crown Court is made amenable to the supervisory jurisdiction of the High Court in respect of matters other than those relating to trial on indictment.[31]

An application for judicial review may be made to challenge a sentence or order on the ground that it is harsh or oppressive.[32]

E. REFERENCES TO THE EUROPEAN COURT OF JUSTICE[33]

One of the major functions of the Court of Justice of the European Communities[34] is that of ensuring consistency in the decision making of national courts in community law matters. The governing provision in the EEC Treaty is Article 177[35]:

"(1) The Court of Justice shall have jurisdiction to give preliminary rulings concerning:
    (a) the interpretation of this Treaty;
    (b) the validity and interpretation of acts of the institutions of the Community;
    (c) the interpretation of the statutes of bodies established by an act of the Council, where those statutes so provide.

(2) Where such a question is raised before any court or tribunal of a Member State, that court or tribunal may, if it considers that a decision on the question is necessary to enable it to give judgment, request the Court of Justice to give a ruling thereon.

---

[28] *Metropolitan Properties Co.* v. *Lannon* [1968] 1 W.L.R. 815; *Chapman* v. *Earl* [1968] 1 W.L.R. 1315; *Henry Moss Ltd.* v. *Customs and Excise Commissioners* [1981] 2 All E.R. 86, 90 (*per* Lord Denning M.R.), criticised by A.W. Bradley [1981] P.L. 476; *contra, Elliott* v. *Brighton Borough Council* (1980) 79 L.G.R. 506.

[29] *R.* v. *Crown Court at Ipswich, ex p. Baldwin* [1981] 1 All E.R. 596.

[30] *R.* v. *Wells Street Stipendiary Magistrate, ex p. Seillon* [1978] 1 W.L.R. 1002 (committal proceedings); *R.* v. *Rochford JJ. ex p. Buck* (1978) 68 Cr. App. R. 114. (summary trial).

[31] Supreme Court Act 1981, s.29(3); *R.* v. *Sheffield Crown Court, ex p. Brownlow* [1980] Q.B. 530: jury vetting order held to relate to trial on indictment. See also above, p. 610.

[32] *R.* v. *St. Albans Crown Court, ex p. Cinnamond* [1981] Q.B. 480; *R.* v. *Tottenham JJ., ex p. Joshi* [1982] 1 W.L.R. 631; the court may, however, refuse in the exercise of its discretion to entertain an application for judicial review if a right to appeal against sentence has not been exercised: *R.* v. *Battle Magistrates' Court, ex p. Shepherd* (1983) 5 Cr.App.R. (S.) 124.

[33] F.G. Jacobs and A. Durand, *References to the European Court* (1975); L. Collins, *European Community Law in the United Kingdom* (2nd ed., 1980) Chap. 3; T.C. Hartley, *The Foundations of European Community Law* (1981) Chap. 9; L.N. Brown and F.G. Jacobs, *The Court of Justice of the European Communities* (2nd ed., 1983) Chap. 9.

[34] See above, pp. 85–89.

[35] The equivalent provision in the Euratom Treaty (Art. 150) is virtually identical.

(3) Where any such question is raised in a case pending before a court or tribunal of a Member State, against whose decisions there is no judicial remedy under national law, that court or tribunal shall bring the matter before the Court of Justice."

The equivalent provision in the European Coal and Steel Community Treaty (Art. 41) is more narrowly drawn:

"The Court shall have sole jurisdiction to give preliminary rulings on the validity of acts of the High Authority and of the Council where such validity is in issue in proceedings brought before a national court or tribunal."

Thus only questions of *validity* can be referred. It should be noted, however, that within these narrower limits the jurisdiction of the court is exclusive: the label "preliminary" ruling is in this context misleading.

It should be noted that the reference procedure is not strictly an appeal: the decision to refer is taken by the national court and not a party and the court will only rule on the point of Community Law raised and remit the case to the national court to apply the law to the facts of the case. The remainder of this discussion will relate to the EEC and Euratom. We now examine the elements of Article 177 in more detail.

1. THE MATTERS THAT MAY BE REFERRED

The court may give rulings concerning (1) the interpretation of Treaty provisions; and (2) the interpretation and validity of acts of the Community institutions (certainly the Council and Commission and probably the Parliament and the Court itself). Where, however, the act of the Council in question is the "statute" regulating the operation of an institution or body established by the Council, the court may only give a ruling if the statute so provides,[36] and the ruling may only concern interpretation, not validity.[37] The task of "interpretation" is taken to include that of determining whether a provision is directly effective.[38]

2. "ANY COURT OR TRIBUNAL"

Article 177(2) of the EEC Treaty provides that "any court or tribunal" may refer a question if the conditions stated are applicable. In the United Kingdom, procedural rules have been made governing references from the High Court and the Court of Appeal (Civil Division),[39] the Court of Appeal (Criminal Division),[40] the Crown Court[41] and county courts.[42] However, it is clear that magistrates' courts[43] and statutory tribunals[44]

---

[36] Under Art. 150/Euratom, rulings concerning "statutes" may be given "save where those statutes provide otherwise."

[37] Art. 177(1)(c)/EEC.

[38] See above, pp. 219–222.

[39] R.S.C. Ord. 114.

[40] Criminal Appeal (References to the European Court) Rules 1972, (S.I. 1972 No. 1786).

[41] Crown Court Rules 1982 (S.I. 1982 No. 1109) r. 29.

[42] County Court Rules 1981, Ord. 19, r. 11.

[43] See, *e.g. R.* v. *Plymouth JJ., ex p. Rogers* [1982] Q.B. 863.

[44] By 1984 references had been made by the Employment Appeal Tribunal, a National Insurance Commissioner and Special Income Tax Commissioners.

have power to refer matters to the European Court even though no procedural rules have been made. The meaning of the expression "court or tribunal" will in the last resort be determined by the European Court, and the title of an institution and its status in national law is not decisive.[45] It seems that any institution which exercises judicial or quasi-judicial functions and which has at least "a measure of official recognition"[46] will be included, and not, therefore, bodies whose functions are advisory,[47] investigatory, conciliatory, legislative or executive,[48] and not arbitrators[49] or (probably) domestic tribunals which exercise jurisdiction solely by virtue of a contractual arrangement between the parties.[50]

3. THE POWER TO REFER

Where any "question" within the scope of the preliminary rulings procedure is "raised before" any national court or tribunal that body may, "if it considers that a decision on the question is necessary to enable it to give judgment," refer the question to the European Court.

(a) "Question . . . raised before"

The question can be raised by a party or by the court itself.[51] Moreover, it is immaterial that the parties take the same position on the point of Community law.[52] The question for reference will be formulated by the national court, although the European Court will confine itself to ruling on matters of *interpretation* and *validity:* it will not rule on the *application* of Community law to the facts or the compatibility of national law with Community law even if requested to do so. The Court will reformulate questions put too widely, and may even formulate the question for itself if the national court fails to do so.[53]

(b) "A decision on the question is necessary to enable it to give judgment"

This wording makes it clear that the material issue is whether a *decision* on the point of Community law is necessary and not whether a *reference* is necessary. The European Court will not normally review the decision of the national court that a reference is "necessary,"[54] although in exceptional circumstances it may decline to accept a reference on the ground that the matter has not arisen in real, genuine, litigation: it is not willing to render

[45] See W. Alexander and E. Grabandt, (1982) 19 C.M.L.R. 413. Case 61/65 *Vaassen* [1966] E.C.R. 261; Case 36/73 *Nederlandse Spoorwegen* [1973] E.C.R. 1299; Case 138/80 *Borker* [1980] E.C.R. 1975; Case 246/80 *Broekmevlen* [1981] E.C.R. 2311; Case 102/81 *Nordsee* [1982] E.C.R. 1095.

[46] *e.g.* supervision or regulation by a minister: *Vaassen* and *Broekmeulen, supra.*

[47] The fact that functions are technically advisory will not prevent the institution from being regarded as a "court or tribunal" if in reality it operates as a judicial body; accordingly, the Dutch *Raad van State* (Council of State), in practice the supreme administrative court, has been held to be within Article 177: *Nederlandse Spoorwegen, supra.*

[48] *e.g.* the professional association of the Paris Bar: *Borker, supra.*

[49] *Nordsee, supra.*

[50] Hartley *op. cit.* (1980) pp. 255–258.

[51] See, *e.g.* R.S.C. Ord. 114, r. 2(1).

[52] Advocate General Slynn in Case 244/80 *Foglia* v. *Novello (No 2)* [1981] E.C.R. 3045, 3071–3072.

[53] This was done in Case 6/64 *Costa* v. *E.N.E.L* [1964] E.C.R. 585.

[54] *Ibid.*

advisory opinions, of academic interest only, on "general or hypothetical questions."[55] Accordingly, the Court has now said that the national court should state in its order for reference the reasons for which it considers it necessary to obtain a preliminary ruling, unless these can be clearly deduced from the file on the case.[56]

Essentially, however, the decision to refer is for the national court or tribunal. However, in the *Rheinmuhlen* cases the European Court held that: (1) "a rule of national law whereby a court is bound on points of law by the rulings of a superior court cannot deprive the inferior courts of their power to refer . . . questions" to the Court,[57] but that (2) Article 177 does not preclude a decision of an inferior court to refer a question "from remaining subject to the remedies normally available under national law."[58] This suggests that any attempt to fetter the discretion of a court under Article 177(2) will be contrary to Community law. Nevertheless, in *Bulmer* v. *Bollinger*[59] Lord Denning M.R. laid down certain "guidelines," which have been relied upon in a number of cases since, but which have also, in some respects, been the subject of widespread criticism, not least on the basis that they may constitute "fetters" which are contrary to Community law.[60] His Lordship set out the guidelines in two groups: (1) guidelines as to whether a decision is "necessary"; and (2) guidelines as to the exercise of the "discretion" to refer. He regarded the question of "necessity" as a condition precedent to the exercise of the discretion and, presumably, as raising matters of law or jurisdiction rather than discretion.[61] However, it seems that his Lordship erroneously thought that it was the *reference* that had to be "necessary," whereas Article 177(2) makes it clear that the significant point is whether a *decision* by the national court on the point is "necessary."[62] Accordingly, two of the matters mentioned by Lord Denning M.R. in relation to "necessity" should have been placed with the other group: the presentation here has been revised accordingly.

---

[55] Case 104/79 *Foglia* v. *Novello* (*No. 1*) [1980] E.C.R. 745; Case 244/80 *Foglia* v. *Novello* (*No. 2*) [1981] E.C.R. 3045: see A. Barav, (1980) 5 E.L. Rev. 443, G. Bebr, (1980) 17 C.M.L.R. 525 (*Foglia No. 1*); D. Wyatt, (1981) 6 E.L. Rev. 449, G. Bebr, (1982) 19 C.M.L.R. 421 (*Foglia No. 2*). It should be noted that this litigation was between private parties in Italy but was in reality directed at the alleged incompatability of a French law with Community law.

[56] *Foglia* v. *Novello* (*No. 2*), *supra*, at p. 3062.

[57] Case 166/73 *Rheinmühlen-Düsseldorf* v. *EVSt* (*No. 1*) [1974] E.C.R. 33: the lower court was, under German law, bound on points of law by decisions of a superior court; the European Court held that this could not take away the lower court's power to refer under Art. 177(2). See also Case 106/77 *Italian Minister for Finance* v. *Simmenthal* (*No. 2*) [1978] E.C.R. 629.

[58] Case 166/73 *Ibid.* (*No. 2*) [1974] E.C.R. 139. The court rejected the suggestion by A.G. Warner that the existence of a right to appeal against an order referring a question to the European Court was contrary to Community law: see [1974] E.C.R. 33, 43–44.

[59] [1974] Ch. 401, 422–425.

[60] See, *e.g.* F.G. Jacobs (1974) 90 L.Q.R. 486; J.D.B. Mitchell (1974) 11 C.M.L.R. 351; E. Freeman [1975] C.L.P. 176; Collins *op.cit.* (1980) pp. 112–116. In *Bulmer* v. *Bollinger*, Stephenson L.J. (with whom Stamp L.J. agreed) stated that judges should "bear in mind" the considerations set out by Lord Denning M.R. ([1974] Ch. 401, 430) but was also conscious of the requirement that the discretion must not be fettered (*ibid.* p. 431).

[61] Collins, *op.cit.* (1980) p. 115.

[62] *Ibid.* pp. 113, 114.

(i) *Jurisdiction to refer: is a decision "necessary?"*

(1) *"The point must be conclusive"* and (2) *"find the facts first."* According to Lord Denning M.R. the point must be conclusive in the sense that a decision one way must lead to judgment for one party and a decision the other way to judgment for the other. Where the point would only be conclusive if decided one way, and the trial would have to go its full course in respect of the contested issues of fact or of English law if decided the other, then, according to Lord Denning M.R., a reference might be "desirable" or "convenient" but could not be "necessary." Moreover, "[a]s a rule you cannot tell whether it is necessary to decide a point until all the facts are ascertained. So in general it is best to decide the facts first."[63]

It seems to be generally agreed that this is too narrow, and that the correct view is that it may be appropriate to refer a point where there are still matters outstanding which will have to be determined should the European Court's decision go one way rather than another.[64] This broader view has been adopted by Ormrod L.J. in the Court of Appeal,[65] by the Divisional Court[66] and by Bingham J. in the High Court.[67] These cases suggest, however, that while there is jurisdiction to refer at an early stage, the facts should normally be found first.[68] A difficulty here is that it may not be clear which facts are relevant for the purposes of Community law until after the reference has been made. On the other hand, it has also been stressed by English courts that it may be impossible to formulate the questions to be referred until after a case has been argued.[69]

A further point is that it is not necessary that the whole of a case be affected by Community law for a decision to be necessary: it is sufficient if a particular aspect, such as the measure of damages or the terms of a court order should be so affected.

The move away from Lord Denning's M.R. attempt to formulate a narrow, clear-cut rule in this context means that the matter is so much one for the appreciation of the court itself that it would be artificial to seek to perpetuate the supposed distinction between "necessity" and "discretion": the approach of an appellate court is in practice likely to be similar in each case.

(ii) *Exercise of the discretion to refer*

(1) *Previous ruling.* In *Da Costa* v. *Nederlandse Belastringadministratie*[70] the European Court stated that where it has given a ruling on a particular question of interpretation, and the same question arises in a subsequent case before a national court of last resort, the earlier ruling may "deprive

---

[63] [1974] Ch. 401 at p. 422, 423.

[64] R.S.C. Ord. 114, r. 2(1) provides that an order for reference may be made at any stage.

[65] *Polydor Ltd.* v. *Harlequin Record Shops Ltd.* [1980] 2 C.M.L.R. 413, 428: "necessary" to mean "reasonably necessary" and not "unavoidable."

[66] *R.* v. *Plymouth JJ., ex p. Rogers* [1982] Q.B. 863, 867–870.

[67] *Customs and Excise Commissioners* v. *ApSSamex* [1983] 1 All E.R. 1042, 1054.

[68] Templeman L.J. in *Polydor, supra,* at p. 426; Lord Lane C.J. in *R.* v. *Plymouth JJ., supra,* at p. 182; Bingham J. in *Samex, supra,* at p. 1056c. See also Lord Diplock in *R.* v. *Henn and Darby* [1981] A.C. 850, 904. In *R.* v. *Plymouth JJ.* and *Samex* the matters outstanding were not significant in extent.

[69] *Church of Scientology* v. *Customs and Excise Commissioners* [1981] 1 All E.R. 1035, 1039 (Brightman L.J.); *Lord Bethell* v. *S.A.B.E.N.A.* [1983] 3 C.M.L.R. 1 (Parker J.).

[70] Cases 28, 29 and 30/62 [1963] E.C.R. 31.

the obligation [under Art. 177(3)] of its purpose and thus empty it of its substance."[71] There would thus be no *obligation* to refer, although the Court also stressed that a national court still had a *discretion* to refer the question. In *Bulmer* v. *Bollinger*[72] Lord Denning M.R. noted that the European Court was not bound by its own previous decisions and said that an English court should only refer a case in such circumstances if it thinks the earlier ruling to be wrong or if there are new factors which ought to be brought to the notice of the European Court.

(2) *Acte clair.* It has been a matter of much controversy whether a national court, whether a court of last resort or not, may decline to refer a question to the European Court on the ground that, notwithstanding the absence of any prior ruling on the point by the European Court, the point is clear and so no "question" arises. Commentators, both academic and judicial, have argued against the *acte clair* doctrine on the basis that there is a real risk that the national courts of different countries may each regard a question as "clear" but in fact decide it differently.[73] Conversely, national courts in several member states have endorsed and relied upon the doctrine. In *Bulmer* v. *Bollinger*[74] Lord Denning M.R. stated that there was no need to refer a question if the point is considered to be "reasonably clear and free from doubt."[75] Rather to everyone's suprise, in *C.I.L.F.I.T.* v. *Ministry of Health*[76] the European Court approved the doctrine, although not in nearly so broad a formulation as Lord Denning's: thus, there is no *obligation* to refer if:

" . . . the correct application of Community law is so obvious as to leave no scope for possible doubt. The existence of such a possibility must be assessed in the light of the specific characteristics of Community law, the particular difficulties to which its interpretation gives rise and the risk of divergences in judicial decisions within the Community."

In practice in United Kingdom courts the *acte clair* issue has arisen in courts other than of last resort, which accordingly have a discretion to refer. There appears to have been a variation in approach depending on the context. Thus, the unwillingess of judges to refer possible defences arising under European law to actions for breach of intellectual property rights has been contrasted with an apparent willingess to refer questions concerning equal pay and sex discrimination in employment law.[77] Points regarded by judges as clear turn out on closer examination by commenta-

---

[71] *Ibid.* p. 38. The same effect may be produced where previous decisions of the court have already dealt with the point of law in question "irrespective of the nature of the proceedings which led to those decisions, even though the questions at issue are not strictly identical": Case 283/81, *C.I.L.F.I.T.* v. *Ministry of Health* [1982] E.C.R. 3415, 3429.

[72] [1974] Ch 401, 422.

[73] See, *e.g.* Judge Pescatore in M.E. Bathhurst *et al.,* (eds.) *Legal Problems of an Enlarged European Community* (1972) pp. 27–46; A.G. Capotorti in Case 283/81 *C.I.L.F.I.T.* v. *Ministry of Health* [1982] E.C.R. 3415; G. Bebr (1981) 18 C.M.L.R. 475, 484–489.

[74] [1974] Ch. 401. See also the decision of the Conseil d'Etat in *Cohn-Bendit* [1980] 1 C.M.L.R. 543; G. Bebr (1983) 20 C.M.L.R. 439.

[75] *Ibid.* p. 423.

[76] [1982] E.C.R. 3415. See D. Wyatt (1983) 8 E.L. Rev. 179; N.P. Gravells, (1983) 99 L.Q.R. 518.

[77] See A.M. Arnull, "Article 177 and the Retreat from Van Duyn" (1983) 8 E.L. Rev. 365.

tors to be at least arguable. The dangers of a reluctance to refer questions have been stressed by the House of Lords in *R.* v. *Henn and Darby*,[78] where Lord Diplock noted the different approaches to statutory interpretation adopted respectively by the European Court and English courts[79] and the point that each of the six texts of Community law is of equal authority. His Lordship said that English judges should not be "too ready to hold that because the meaning of the English text . . . seems plain to them no question of interpretation can be involved."[80] However, where the point was one "to which an established body of case law plainly applies" an English court might properly take the view that no real question of interpretation was involved.[81]

(3) *Other points.* Other factors identified by Lord Denning M.R. in *Bulmer* v. *Bollinger*[82] as relevant to the exercise of a court's discretion included: (1) the time to get a ruling; (2) the need not to overload the European Court; (3) the need to formulate the question clearly, which was another reason for finding the facts first; (4) "Unless the point is really difficult and important, it would seem better for the English judge to decide it himself;" (5) expense and (6) the wishes of the parties:

"If both parties want the point to be referred to the European Court, the English court should have regard to their wishes, but it should not give them undue weight. The English court should hesitate before making a reference against the wishes of one of the parties, seeing the expense and delay which it involves."

The tenor of Lord Denning's judgment was obviously restrictive: references should only be made in exceptional cases, and (possibly) only by the House of Lords. The possibility that the guidelines may, to an extent, conflict with Community law has already been noted.[83] However, the breadth of the discretion to refer has also been noted:

"The matters referred to by Lord Denning are specifically stated only to be guidelines and, as Lord Denning himself said, when referring to the guidelines laid down by the House of Lords in *The Nema*,[84] with reference to applications for leave to appeal in matters of arbitration, 'guidelines may be stepped over, and are flexible.' I take it that he would apply the same standard to his own guidelines. At all events, it is perfectly clear that, where a discretion is conferred upon the court, that discretion cannot be fettered."[85]

---

[78] [1981] A.C. 850.

[79] See above, p. 270.

[80] [1981] A.C. 850 at p. 906. See also Lord Diplock's speech in *Garland* v. *British Rail Engineering Ltd.* [1983] 2 A.C. 751; cf. Bingham J. in *Customs and Excise Commissioners* v. *Ap S Samex* [1983] 1 All E.R. 1042: on three of four points the judge held clear views, but accepted that each was not so clear as to be *acte clair*.

[81] [1981] A.C. 850, 906. Lord Diplock thought that the interpretation of Art. 30 was clear in this sense, but as the Court of Appeal had taken a different view, the point was referred to the European Court.

[82] [1974] Ch. 401, 423–425.

[83] See above, p. 752.

[84] [1980] 2 Lloyd's Rep. 83.

[85] *Per* Parker J. in *Lord Bethell* v. *S.A.B.E.N.A.* (1983) 38 C.M.L.R. 1, 4.

One point not stressed expressly in *Bulmer* v. *Bollinger*[86] is whether references should normally only be made by appellate courts. It has since been suggested that references should only exceptionally be made by trial judges in the Crown Court[87] and by magistrates' courts.[88] It is, however, often argued that an early reference may save time and expense.

4. THE OBLIGATION TO REFER

Article 177(3) of the EEC Treaty provides that where a decision on a question of Community law is necessary to enable a court or tribunal to give judgment in a pending case, and that court or tribunal is one "against whose decisions there is no judicial remedy under national law," an *obligation* to refer arises. The points discussed above concerning "necessity," previous rulings and the *acte clair* doctrine are equally applicable here: indeed the decision in *C.I.L.F.I.T.* v. *Ministry of Health*[89] arose in respect of Article 177(3).

In addition, there is the question as to which courts are covered by Article 177(3). The wording of the paragraph suggests that it applies only to courts from which an appeal never lies.[90] The view more widely favoured, however, is that it applies to any court from which an appeal or other "judicial remedy" does not lie in the case in question.[91] One difficulty that has not been settled is whether the remedy has to be available as of right. In *Hagen* v. *Fratelli D. & G. Moretti S.N.C.*[92] Buckley L.J. stated that the "ultimate court of appeal" in this country "is either [the Court of Appeal] if leave to appeal to the House of Lords is not obtainable, or the House of Lords."[93] It is not clear whether "obtainable" means "obtainable ever" or "obtainable in the particular case" but the latter interpretation seems more likely. It is equally uncertain whether the availability of the remedy of certiorari, which may only be sought if leave to apply is obtained, counts as a "judicial remedy."[94]

The fact that an interlocutory order may not be the subject of an appeal does not render it final for the purposes of Article 177(3) provided that the decision is subject to review in the main or subsequent proceedings from which a reference may be made.[95]

---

[86] [1974] Ch. 401.

[87] *R.* v. *Henn and Darby* [1981] A.C. 850, 906: Lord Diplock regarded this as equivalent to referring before the facts are found.

[88] *R.* v. *Plymouth JJ., ex p. Rogers* [1982] Q.B. 863, 870–871.

[89] Above, p. 754.

[90] This view was stated to be the correct view by Lord Denning M.R. *obiter* in *Bulmer* v. *Bollinger* [1974] Ch. 401: the other members of the Court of Appeal expressed no view on the matter.

[91] See the European Court, *obiter,* in Case 6/64, *Costa* v. *E.N.E.L.* [1964] E.C.R. 585, 592.

[92] [1980] 3 C.M.L.R. 253.

[93] *Ibid.* p. 255.

[94] It was so held by Mr. J.G. Monroe in *Re a Holiday in Italy* [1975] 1 C.M.L.R. 184 (decision of a National Insurance Commisssioner) but see F.G. Jacobs, (1977) 2 E.L. Rev. 119.

[95] Case 107/76 *Hoffman-La Roche* v. *Centrafarm* [1977] E.C.R. 957: see F.G. Jacobs, (1977) 2 E.L. Rev 354; Cases 35 and 36/82 *Morson* v. *Netherlands; Jhanjan* v. *Netherlands* [1982] E.C.R. 3723: see N.P. Gravells (1983) 8 E.L. Rev. 250.

5. PROCEDURE

As mentioned above, procedural rules have been made for county courts, the Crown Court, the High Court and the Court of Appeal.[96] All references from these courts must be channelled through the Senior Master of the Queen's Bench Division.

An appeal lies against a decision or refusal to refer in the ordinary way. An order for reference by the High Court is deemed to be a final order and so an appeal lies without leave. Notice of appeal must be served within 14 days and the order is not transmitted until this time limit has expired, and, if an appeal is lodged, until after it has been disposed of.[97] Leave is necessary to appeal against refusal of an order for reference.[98]

F. THE ROYAL PREROGATIVE OF MERCY

The Crown has retained certain of its prerogative powers as "fountain of justice" in the field of the administration of justice. One such area is the prerogative of mercy exercised by the Crown on the advice of the Home Secretary. This may take one of three forms:[99]

"(i) *A Free Pardon*, the effect of which is that a conviction is to be disregarded, so that, so far as is possible, the person is relieved of all penalties and other consequences of the conviction; or

(ii) *A Conditional Pardon*, which excuses or varies the consequences of the conviction subject to conditions—this power has been used primarily to commute a sentence of death to one of life imprisonment, a purpose which it still serves in respect of sentences in the Isle of Man and Jersey; or

(iii) *Remission* of all or part of the penalty imposed by the Court."

The power to recommend special remission is normally used for reasons unconnected with the merits of the conviction, for example, to reward assistance to the prison authorities or to release a dying prisoner. Occasionally it may be used where new information casts doubt on the rightness of a conviction but the case is not suitable for reference to the Court of Appeal.[1] A free pardon[2] is "normally only recommended when

---

[96] See above, p. 750.

[97] R.S.C. Ord. 114, rr. 4, 5, 6.

[98] *Bulmer* v. *Bollinger* [1974] Ch. 401, 420–421, 430–431.

[99] *Sixth Report from the Home Affairs Committee of the House of Commons* (1981–82, H.C. 421), Home Office Memorandum, p. 1. The Home Secretary may refer cases to the Court of Appeal (Criminal Division): see above, p. 716. The following summary is based on this Memorandum. See also the comprehensive survey by A.T.H.Smith, [1983] P.L. 398, and the works cited therein; C.H. Rolph, *The Queen's Pardon* (1978); C.H.W. Gane, 1980 J.R. 18.

[1] *Home Office Memorandum*, pp. 2–3.

[2] There is much confusion over the exact implications of a "free pardon": see A.T.H. Smith, *op.cit.*, pp. 417–422. It seems to depend on the exact terms of the pardon in question. The terminology is clearly inappropriate where a person has been pronounced to be innocent. In New Zealand it has been held to be technically no more than an indication that the person concerned was wrongly convicted: *Re Royal Commission on Thomas* [1980] 1 N.Z.L.R. 602, and in *R.* v. *Foster*, *The Times*, March 31st, 1984, the Court of Appeal (Criminal Division) held that the effect of a free pardon was to remove from the subject of the pardon all pain, penalties and punishments ensuing from the conviction but not to eliminate the conviction. (The court proceeded to quash the conviction.) Compare the current Home Office view, above.

there are not merely doubts about the defendant's guilt but convincing grounds for thinking that he was innocent"; and this means "morally as well as technically innocent. This 'clean hands' doctrine implies that the Home Secretary must be satisfied . . . that in the incident in question the defendant had no intention of committing an offence and did not in fact commit one."[3] In practice the prerogative is more freely used in respect of cases tried summarily than tried on indictment.

A person who is acquitted on a criminal charge or whose conviction is quashed on appeal normally has no legal right to compensation.[4] However, it is the normal practice of the Home Secretary to offer *ex gratia* compensation where a person is granted a free pardon, or, following the emergence of new evidence, has had his conviction quashed on appeal out of time or after the Home Secretary has referred the case to the Court of Appeal. A payment may also be made where there has been misconduct or default by the police or some other agency of the criminal justice system and in other, exceptional, cases. Payments are not, however, made simply because there has been an acquittal or a quashed conviction. The amount of compensation is fixed on the recommendation of an independent assessor (in practice the chairman of the Criminal Injuries Compensation Board) whose advice is always accepted.[5] The assessor takes account of pecuniary losses, damage to character or reputation and physical hardship. The offer is made without admission of liability, and while the claimant is free to accept or refuse, if he accepts he must waive any legal claim.[6]

Cases for the exercise of the prerogative of mercy and requests for compensation are considered by the Home Office's Criminal Department.[7] The relevant papers are scrutinised, and, if it is thought to be necessary, further inquiries are commissioned.

The working of the system has been considered in recent reports by the Home Affairs Committee and Justice.[8] The Home Affairs Committee thought that cases should continue to be processed by the Home Office, but noted that decisions were often presented in such a way as to seem arbitrary: delays should be explained and reasons given for a refusal to take action normally given. However, there should be an independent review body to advise the Home Secretary on the exercise of the prerogative of mercy. This body should be able to take into account a

---

[3] *Ibid.* p. 3.

[4] It is difficult to establish a cause of action for malicious prosecution: it is necessary to prove, *inter alia,* that the prosecution lacked reasonable and probable cause and that the defendant acted maliciously: *Winfield and Jolowicz on Tort,* (11th ed., 1979) pp. 512–520.

[5] The procedure was set out in H.C. Deb, 29 July 1976, written answers, cols. 328–330.

[6] Between 1972 and 1981 there were 47 *ex gratia* payments: 16 of £10,000 or more and 3 of £20,000 or more: *Home Office Memorandum,* Appendix A(4). In 1983, £77,000 was paid to a man convicted of murder in 1973 on the basis of evidence of a Home Office scientist subsequently discredited. In 1984 Patrick Meehan accepted an offer of £50,500 after 7 years in prison: he had previously rejected an offer of £7,500 and the amount was reassessed by an Edinburgh advocate: *Daily Telegraph,* February 2, 1984.

[7] See the Devlin Report on *Evidence of Identification in Criminal Cases,* 1975–76 H.C. 338, pp. 55–56, 142–145; *Home Office Memorandum,* pp. 4–5.

[8] 1981–82, H.C. 421; JUSTICE Report, *Compensation for Wrongful Imprisonment* (1982). See also the JUSTICE Report, *Home Office Reviews of Criminal Convictions* (1968), and, on the compensation issue, G.H.L. Fridman, (1963) 26 M.L.R. 481; C. Shelbourn [1978] Crim. L.R. 22.

wider range of matters than those currently considered by the Home Office, including evidence which was known to counsel or the police but not put before the jury, for example for tactical reasons that turn out to have been misguided. It should also be able to advise the exercise of the royal prerogative where its investigation has shown the verdict to be unsafe and unsatisfactory: it should not be necessary for the convicted person to prove his innocence. The committee were impressed by Sir David Napley's statement that he was unable from his own experience to recall "a single case where the Home Office has, as a result of its own investigations, felt able to recommend a pardon or any other recognition that a conviction was necessarily wrongful." On the other hand, officials had expressed disquiet about certain cases where the courts had refused to interfere with a verdict.[9]

The government rejected most of the Committee's proposals, apart from those concerning matters of presentation.[10] The Home Secretary indicated that he would in future be prepared to exercise his power of reference more readily and the Lord Chief Justice that there was scope for the Court of Appeal to be more ready to exercise its powers to receive evidence or order a retrial. The Home Office would also examine the possibility of legislation to allow the Home Secretary to refer doubtful summary convictions back to the courts.

The Justice Committee considered the issue of compensation. It thought that persons given a free pardon and those whose convictions are quashed after a reference by the Home Secretary should have a *right* to compensation. Other persons whose convictions are quashed on appeal should be entitled to apply for compensation although that compensation could be refused or reduced in the light of the claimant's conduct or if the conviction was quashed on a technicality. In certain circumstances compensation should be paid to persons committed for trial in custody and acquitted or discharged, and persons who have had part of their sentence remitted. Claims should be dealt with by an Imprisonment Compensation Board established on the lines of the Criminal Injuries Compensation Board.

---

[9] 1981–82 H.C. 421, p. x.
[10] *Government Reply to the Sixth Report from the Home Affairs Committee Session 1981–82 H.C. 421*, (Cmnd. 8856, 1983).

INDEX

761